RHONE
RENAISSANCE

RHONE
RENAISSANCE

REMINGTON NORMAN

WITH A FOREWORD BY
HUGH JOHNSON

PHOTOGRAPHS BY
GERALDINE NORMAN

WINE APPRECIATION GUILD
San Francisco

CONTENTS

Caption for page 1
Dry stone wall terraces dating back to Roman times
are a feature of the Northern Rhône.

Caption for page 2
Vineyards and abandoned terraces below the
ruined tower at Condrieu.

Caption for page 8
The château of Condrieu with the Rhône beyond.

REMINGTON NORMAN
RHONE RENAISSANCE
Published in North America by
The Wine Apprceiation Guild Ltd,
155 Connecticut Street
San Francisco, CA 94107
(415) 864-1202

First published in Great Britain in 1995
by Mitchell Beazley,
an imprint of Reed Consumer Books Limited,
Michelin House, 81 Fulham Road
London SW3 6RB

A CIP catalogue record for this book is available from the
British Library

Edited and designed by SIENA ARTWORKS, London

Designer *Nigel O'Gorman*
Typesetting and page makeup *MacGuru*

Colour reproduction by Colourscan, Singapore

Printed in Italy by L.E.G.O. (Vicenza)
Library of Congress Catalog No. 95-061878
ISBN: 0-932664-95-4

CONTENTS

MEASURES & CONVERSIONS

MEASURES OF CAPACITY

In continental Europe, the litre is the unit of liquid measure; in the UK and USA the gallon is used, as well as fluid ounces (for bottle sizes). However the UK and US gallons and fluid ounces differ (see below).

0.75 litres = 75 centilitres = 1 standard bottle
1.50 litres = 150 centilitres = 1 magnum
3.00 litres = 300 centilitres = 1 double-magnum
9.00 litres = 12 standard bottles = 1 case
100 litres = 1 hectolitre = 133 standard (75 cl) bottles = 11 cases of 12 bottles + 1 bottle = 26.42 US gallons
1 UK gallon = 4.55 litres
1 US gallon = 3.78 litres
1 UK fluid ounce = 28.4ml
1 US fluid ounce = 29.6ml
1 standard bottle (75cl) contains 25.36 UK fluid ounces

CASKS

1 barrique = 1 pièce = 225 litres (Bordeaux) or 228 litres (Burgundy) Standard cask size.
1 feuillette = 1/2 cask
1 quarteau = 1/4 cask
1 demi-muid = 600 litres (however, demi-muid is often used to refer to casks of larger size)
Vat capacity is usually expressed in hectolitres or gallons, according to country convention.

MEASURES OF YIELD

Yields are expressed in hectolitres per hectare (Europe), tonnes per acre (US and Australia) or tonnes per hectare (South Africa). These are metric tonnes (=1,000 kilos =2,204 pounds).
1 tonne per acre = 14 hectolitres per hectare
1 hl/ha = 100 litres/hectare = 133.3 bottles/hectare = 11.1 cases/hectare
1 hl/ha = 53.9 bottles per acre = 4.5 cases per acre
40 hl/ha = 5,332 bottles per hectare = 444 cases per hectare
40 hl/ha = 2,158 bottles per acre = 180 cases per acre
At a planting density of 10,000 vines per hectare, a yield of 40hl/ha equates to about half a bottle of wine per vine. At 40hl/ha, 1 hectare will yield 17.8 standard cask-fulls (ie 17.8 x 225 litres = 444 cases)
A plant density of 11,000 vines per hectare and 8 bunches per vine is approximately equivalent to a yield of 55hl/ha. It takes approx 130 kilograms of grapes to produce 1hl of wine.

MEASURES OF DISTANCE (LINEAR) AND AREA (SQUARE):

Metric systems work in kilometres, metres, centimetres and millimetres; others in miles, yards, feet and inches.
1 kilometre = 1,000 metres = 0.621 miles
1 metre = 100 mentimetres = 1,000 millimetres = 1.094 yards = 3.281 feet
1 mile = 1,760 yards = 1.609 kilometres
1 hectare = 100 ares = 10,000 square metres = 2.471 acres
1 are = 100 square metres
1 square kilometre = 100 hectares = 0.386 square miles
1 acre = 4,840 square yards = 0.405 hectares
1 square yard = 9 square feet
1 square mile = 640 acres

MEASURES OF TEMPERATURE

The centigrade scale is not linear, so one centigrade degree is not equivalent to one degree centigrade. To convert Centigrade to Fahrenheit, multiply by 9/5 then add 32. To convert Fahrenheit to Centigrade, subtract 32 then muliply by 5/9.

Fahrenheit	Centigrade
12.0	-11.1
32.0	0.0
41.0	5.0
50.0	10.0
59.0	15.0
68.0	20.0
77.0	25.0
86.0	30.0
95.0	35.0
100.0	37.8

MEASURES OF ALCOHOL

Alcohol content of wine is normally expressed as the percentage by volume. The French (Gay-Lussac) system carries out this measurement at 15°C; the OIML[1] (Organisation Internationale de Metrologie Legale) system at 20°C, giving marginal differences which consumers can safely ignore.

BIBLIOGRAPHY

GENERAL

Coombe, B G and Dry, P R (Eds) *Viticulture* Vol 1 Resources, Vol 2 Practices, Winetitles, Adelaide, 1988 & 1992 (ISBN 1 875 130 02 2)
INAO, *L'Appellaton D'Origine Contrôlée*, INAO, France
Johnson, Hugh, *The Story of Wine*, Mitchell Beazley, London 1989 (ISBN 0 85333 696X)
Johnson, Hugh, *The World Atlas of Wine* (Fourth Edition), Mitchell Beazley, London 1994 (ISBN 1 85732 268 1)
Robinson, J, *Vines Grapes and Wines*, Mitchell Beazley, London 1986 (ISBN 0 85533 581 5)

AUSTRALIA

Aeuckens, Annely & Bishop, Geoffrey, *Vineyard of The Empire, Early Barossa Vignerons 1842-1939*, Australian Industrial Publishers Pty Ltd, Adelaide 1988 (ISBN 1 875130 04 7)
Dunstan, David, *Wines and Winemakers of the Pyrenees*, Pyrenees Vignerons

Association (ISBN 0 646 12349 1)
Evans, Len, *Complete Australian Book of Wine*, Paul Hamlyn Pty Limited, New South Wales, 1978 (ISBN 0 7271 0331 8)
Halliday, James, *Coonawarra, The History, the Vignerons and the Wines*, Yenisey Pty Ltd, Sydney, 1983 (ISBN 0 9592306 0 2)
Halliday, James, *Wine Atlas of Australia and New Zealand*, Harper-Collins, London, 1991 (ISBN 0 207 16476 2)
Moodie Heddle, Enid & Doherty, Frank, *Chateau Tahbilk, Story of a Vineyard 1860-1985*, Lothian Publishing Company Pty Ltd (ISBN 0 85091 236 9)
Norrie, Dr Philip, *Lindeman, Australia's Classic Winemaker*, Apollo Books, Sydney, 1993 (ISBN 0 947068 24 4)
Zekulik, Mike, *Wines and Wineries of the West*, St George Books, Perth, 1990 (ISBN 0 86778 041 X)

CALIFORNIA:

Halliday, James, *Wine Atlas of California*, Viking 1993

THE RHONE AND SOUTHERN FRANCE

Berry, Liz, *The Wines of Languedoc-Roussillon*, Ebury Press, London 1992 (ISBN 0 09 175361 9)
Charnay, Pierre, *Vignobles et Vins des Côtes du Rhône*, Aubanel, 1985 (ISBN 2 7006 0110 6)
Livingstone-Learmonth, John, *The Wines of the Rhône* (Third Edition) Faber, London 1992 (ISBN 0 571 15111 6)
Mayberry, Robert W, *Wines of the Rhône Valley, A guide to Origins*, Rowman & Littlefield, New Jersey, USA 1987 (ISBN 0 8476 7430 4)
Portes, Jean-Claude, *Châteauneuf-du-Pape Memoire d'un village*, Editions Barthelemy, Avignon 1993 (ISBN 2 87923 031 4)

SOUTH AFRICA

Fridjhon, Michael, *The Penguin Book of South African Wine*, Penguin Books, London 1992 (ISBN 0 140 17075 8)
Hughes, Dave, Hands, Phyllis and Kench, John, *South African Wine*, Struik (Pty) Ltd, Capetown, 1992 (ISBN 1 86825 270 1)
Platter, John, *New South African Wine*

FOREWORD

How is it that every generation of wine-lovers comes to the Rhône with the feeling it has they have stumbled on a secret cache of treasure? Simply, I believe, because in the past the supply of fine Rhône wines was infinitesimal beside the deep wells of Burgundy, let alone the great gusher of Bordeaux.

It is not that its qualities were ever in doubt. Here is Cyrus Redding, writing in the 1830s, on white Hermitage: "This is the best white wine France produces... It keeps much longer than the red, even to the extent of a century".

There was never, I believe, a time when Hermitage and Côte-Rôtie were not bottled by the leading London wine merchants as part of the essential well-stocked cellar. But even taking into account Châteauneuf-du-Pape from the remote south (northern Rhône growers looked on it as *vin ordinaire*) there was not enough Rhône wine of any quality for its flavours to be familiar to more than a few — except, perhaps, as the muscle in Côte d'Or wines of fashionable but improbable darkness and strength.

Nor was there any plantable land of the same quality on which the great Rhône vineyards could be expanded.

Wine-growing in the Rhône valley is probably the oldest-established in France. It is the direct descendant of the Greek colonisation of the Rhône delta six hundred years before the Romans — and maybe more. The Romans established the vineyards of Bordeaux and the west, and the eastern Gallic vineyards of Burgundy and Champagne. In the west they installed the Cabernet family or its ancestors; in the east the sub-alpine strain of grapes that became the Pinots.

The Rhône vineyards were already based on Mediterranean varieties that adapted perfectly to its warmer ripening conditions; above all the Syrah. Its territory could only expand, though, by improving the produce of less than ideal vineyards. In France this meant "ameliorating" the low-grade wines of the Côtes du Rhône in the south, and the *vins ordinaires* of the Midi, with a proportion of the noble Syrah.

Almost unknown to the French, however, the same Syrah had found a new home, and a new name, in Australia. There just have been far more Shiraz vines planted in Australia early in this century than were ever planted in the Rhône valley. Its wines, whether sold as "burgundy", "port", or even sometimes claret, were for generations the solid backbone of the Australian wine industry, with scarcely a backward glance at its origins.

Then, in the late 1950s, came the vision of Max Schubert of Penfolds: Grange Hermitage. The New World had its first First Growth. It was time for California, South Africa... all those countries with a Mediterranean climate, to realise that most of their vineyards come closer in conditions to the Rhône valley than Bordeaux, let alone Burgundy. For them the range of Rhône varieties, starting with Syrah, are the logical choice — and the current interest in their wines the logical outcome.

Remington Norman first made his name as merchant of very fine wines. He made a second reputation, as an author, with his detailed and profound review of the best estates of Burgundy. With this book, exploring the Rhône valley and its worldwide zone of influence, he launches a new genre of wine-book, aimed at consumers whose palates react as much to vine variety as to *terroir*, and whose interest in wine is ready for a dip below the surface into some tough technical territory.

On the talking point of the day, the relative importance of variety and *terroir*, grape and ground, he is dispassionate and shrewd. He has heard every shade of opinion, and presents a fair picture of the scores of winemakers he has visited in making his unique personal survey of the Rhône around the world. There is no question that this book will fan the flames of enthusiasm already making the Syrah/Shiraz and its allies a major force in wine for the new millennium.

A book that guides you to new tastes, and sets out their *raisons d'être* clearly, is the best companion a wine-lover can have. He will not be disappointed in this one.

Hugh Johnson

INTRODUCTION

Twenty-five years ago, I tasted a truly memorable wine. Though by no means from the greatest of vintages, this magnificent Hermitage (it was Chave's 1967) left an indelible impression – not the more familiar taste of claret or burgundy, but something with an intriguingly different character. I was fascinated and wanted to find out more.

The research which followed inspired not only an enduring passion for Rhône wines, but also a love of the Rhône Valley itself. Being a London wine merchant gave me an excuse for regular visits, and through these I came to know many of the Rhône's greatest *vignerons*, which added immeasurably to the experience. Inevitably, this interest widened to encompass the many excellent wines made from Rhône grape varieties in other countries, and thus ultimately provided the inspiration for this book. The intervening years have diminished neither the fascination nor the passion for wines which I regard as among the world's noblest and finest.

It thus became something of a mission to bring the best of the Rhône to wider notice. Where people were prepared to taste open-mindedly, there was little difficulty – the wines spoke for themselves more eloquently than any ambassador. However, among entrenched claret and burgundy drinkers there was then, and still is, a reluctance to stray from the safe, marked paths. Excellent as those wines undoubedly are, such inflexibility has always seemed to me narrow-minded – a mark of snobbery, even, rather than of a genuine love of fine wine. Because Rhône wines were then relatively unknown, and absurdly cheap, many also seemed convinced that they were somehow buying second-best.

Now the scene has shifted dramatically. The finest Rhônes today command the international respect of top clarets and burgundies, and the rarest often surpass them in price. Some have become "collectables", with cachet values to match. This market acceptability has stimulated a deepening interest not only in the Rhône but also in wines made from Rhône varieties elsewhere, both among growers who see an opportunity and consumers who like what they taste. A nucleus of high-quality winemakers – unquenchable Rhône fanatics – in the Midi, Australia, California and South Africa has risen to the challenge and demonstrated the excellence achievable with Rhône grapes, especially Syrah, Grenache, Mourvèdre and Viognier, given fine raw materials and skilful vinification. It is only in recent years that their considerable potential has begun to be realised.

Surprisingly, beyond a couple of books on the Rhône, this growing interest has not been reflected by writers. At a time when France no longer dominates the popular international market for wine, it seemed appropriate to broaden the scope of this book to include southern France and the New World. This turned a relatively simple project into a massive undertaking, spanning 18 months, with visits to over 300 estates in four countries around the world.

This book charts the progress of Rhône and Rhône-variety wines, and describes the regions and estates which excel at them. Although the final choice of the best remains my responsibility, selection was far from easy. It involved considerable consultation and tasting before each itinerary was planned, especially in the areas I knew least well – the Midi and South Africa. The vastness of the territory to be covered made the ideal of completeness unattainable, but as my aim is to give a feel for the styles of Rhône-variety wine produced in each country and region, rather than a comprehensive listing (which would have been much easier), any omissions should not diminish the overall picture.

To make the profiles as accurate and thorough as possible, each estate visit was designed to last half a day or longer, to allow time for detailed discussion and in-depth tasting. While specific help is acknowledged elsewhere, I would like to record here my gratitude to all the owners, viticulturalists and winemakers who made me so welcome and gave so generously of their time and wisdom. It is they who make the wines which I and others who are not winemakers, then dissect and evaluate: in such circumstances, their patience and courtesy is admirable.

The months spent outside the Rhône – in southern France, South Africa, Australia and California – were especially revelatory. I found wonderful, world-ranking wines not just at well-known estates, but at ones which, despite a good prior working knowledge, I had scarcely heard of: some of the finest wines do not, as yet, leave their homeland. Tasting old-vine Shiraz at Wendouree, in Australia's Clare Valley, Nico van der Merwe's remarkable Syrah at Saxenburg (South Africa), Laurent Vaille's first vinification (in Aniane, France), or Sean Thackrey's splendid wines in Bolinas (California), none of which is currently exported, further convinced me of the need for an international perspective, rather than yet another single-region exposé.

The village of Gigondas and behind it the striking backdrop of the Dentelles de Montmirail.

In planning and writing this, I have tried to keep a "target" reader constantly in mind: someone interested in wine, perhaps even in the Rhône; willing to explore the unfamiliar, yet needing information beyond that offered by pocket guides and magazines – and, above all, someone who still thrills at discovery. To give this book lasting value – beyond the usual deathless litany of unadorned tasting notes – involved digging beneath the surface to a level of detail with which some may be unfamiliar. To extract fully the character of each estate and its wines, a certain amount of technical explanation is inevitable. This has been kept to a minimum, but to have avoided it altogether would have meant eschewing those very elements which differentiate one region, estate or style from another. Unfamiliar terms requiring further definition are explained in the glossary (page 333). These profiles also reflect my firm belief that knowing something about the background and making of a wine adds enormously to one's appreciation of it.

Tasting, of course, plays a role but alone will only get you so far. The idea that someone who tastes 100 wines is,

ipso facto, more knowledgeable than someone who only tastes 10, ignores the fact that the value of tasting depends as much upon what you bring to it as to what it offers you. Searching for yet another "valid descriptor" to differentiate one wine from the next is, by itself, just superficial play. Those who taste themselves witless in the belief that this is the swifest route to connoisseurship lose much of the real enjoyment of great wine that comes from a single bottle, intelligently shared.

As well as introducing the majestic Rhône and Rhône-style wines to those who may not know them, this book is designed to assist (and inspire!) further exploration. Those setting out to discover more should be encouraged by the fact that, apart from a few luxurious special bottlings, most of the wines described here are modestly priced, and even the rarest have affordable alternatives in the same style. However, although price bears no simple relationship to pleasure, the wide price-range makes direct comparisons invidious – it is unreasonable to expect the same from a South African Shiraz at 20 Rand (at time of writing, c £3.50,

US$6, Aus$8) as a 150-franc Côte-Rôtie (£20, US$32, Aus$45).

The book is arranged by country and region, with profiles of selected estates. These give a picture of the moving spirits behind each property and their philosophy, and describe how they operate and what a consumer can expect in style and quality from a bottle of their wine. Introductions extend this perspective to countries and regions, and discuss the factors which make one wine fine and another ordinary. Greater attention has been accorded to the Rhône itself, as the focus of·interest not only for consumers, but also for many winemakers outside France.

Tasting notes on individual wines are in a special section at the back of the book. These are intended to complement the individual profiles, not to supplant them. I should reiterate that opinions expressed both in tasting notes and elsewhere are, as normal with any such critique, purely personal.

Lack of space unfortunately precludes discussion of either sparkling or fortified wines made from Rhône varieties. It is a great regret, in particular, to exclude the many delicious *vins de dessert* made from Syrah, Mourvèdre, Grenache and Muscat – from the sumptuous *vins doux naturels* of southern France, to the "ports" of the Crimea, California, Australia and South Africa and the unique Australian "liqueur Muscats" and "Madeiras".

Some purists may cavil at the inclusion of Carignan and Petite Sirah – by no means mainstream Rhône varieties; however, both are capable of nobility and have a more than tangential importance in Rhône-style wines. They also deserve better treatment than they currently receive.

I felt it essential to include accurate maps of those major Rhône appellations – Côte-Rôtie, Condrieu, Cornas, Hermitage and Châteauneuf-du-Pape – where individual vineyard sites play a particularly important role in determining quality. As far as I am aware, these have not been published in such detail before. Apart from their value in providing a deeper insight into each *vignoble*, these maps also reflect the increasing trend towards vineyard-designated wines.

The rest of this Introduction provides background to some of the important issues being discussed in wine-producing circles. Far from being sterile debates over technicalities, these arguments are likely to have a profound influence on future directions, in the Old World as much as in the New.

TERROIR

This French term encapsulates various factors which play a role in differentiating one vineyard or site from another, including climate, altitude, aspect and, in particular, the physical and chemical aspects of soil. Although well understood in France, where its role in reflecting the uniqueness of a wine's origins provides the basis for *appellation contrôlée*, terroir is less widely accepted as a useful, or even valid, concept in the New World. There, until recently, the character of the grape has been considered more influential than its environment. In the USA and Australia, the tradition of trucking grapes large distances to a processing cellar diminished the importance of origin in determining wine quality and, moreover, cut the link between grape grower and winemaker. This is the antithesis of European ideology, which binds a wine's typicity to grape origin. Now, however, the worldwide trend towards regional and estate wines has brought the idea of *terroir* back into debate. As understanding of the subtle influence of site, soil and local climatic variations upon grape composition deepens, site selection is becoming infinitely more refined, and the notion of *terroir* more respected.

APPELLATION CONTRÔLÉE

The French *appellation contrôlée* system relies not only the notion of *terroir* but ties vine variety to site. In other words, the inherent nobility of a particular grape-variety is essentially related to a specific growing environment. For example, Syrah planted on the hill of Corton can never become *Grand Cru* burgundy, however fine the resulting wine, since by definition red Corton must be made entirely from Pinot Noir.

In parts of France, especially the Midi, such conventions are seen by many as unduly restrictive, especially where well-entrenched appellations (usually those of mediocre quality potential) allow only a limited selection of grapes, and then only within pre-ordained percentages. With greater feel for different varieties and more sophisticated viticulture and vinification techniques, growers are finding that they can improve significantly on the "loyal, local and constant" usage which encapsulates "*la tradition*". Many of the more experimentally-minded growers express open frustration at an official inflexiblity which denies wines *appellation contrôlée* status, and forces them to be sold as *vin de pays*, or even *vin de table*, because they don't conform to regulations which producers regard as outmoded. Opponents of change would prefer to keep the appellations intact, but adapt the rules to reflect modern resources. However, beyond some cosmetic tinkering, the reality is that French stubbornness makes radical change improbable until the younger generation is fully in control. Meanwhile,

AC evolution continues at a snail's pace, while the more adventurous simply opt out and sell their wine under a lesser designation.

France's cumbersome AC apparatus, designed in the 1920s, was principally intended to prevent the sale of an inferior wine as something superior. It was not long before people realised that a wine may be genuine, but still of poor quality; so the idea came of adding quality, and the third plank of AC, typicity, to the original guarantee of authenticity. This system was just about capable of working provided there was general consensus on what, for example, Châteauneuf-du-Pape should typically taste like, and the political will to police it properly. Now, with a wide range of styles even within a single appellation, it has become unviable. Many ACs set minimum acceptable standards at the lowest common denominator, effectively caving in to the vested interests of volume producers at the margins of quality. This has resulted in much disgracefully poor wine, often bearing the "guarantee" and high price-tag of exalted appellations: the product of high yields, sloppy vinification, poor hygiene and rapacity. Until France manages to exercise some credible semblance of quality control, especially at the lower levels, producers elsewhere will continue to gnaw away at its fragile market share.

There are lessons here for parts of the New World, where moves towards an equivalent of the AC system are being considered, or have even been implemented – eg America's AVAs or Australia's Geographical Indications. Anyone contemplating such a regime, especially in countries with evolving wine industries, large tracts of land still to be developed, and with little accumulated wisdom on *terroir* selection, should take careful account of the European experience. In particular, they should note that it took France several centuries to establish the best combinations of site and grape variety – a sphere in which the French of the Middle Ages were remarkably prescient. They should also weigh carefully the advantages and disadvantages of the restrictiveness which inevitably accompanies any such system, and which can do more harm than good – however logical the ground-rules.

For example, one South African winemaker complained bitterly of assessment panels made up largely of officials with little experience of anything other than local wines – "they could even be accountants!" – who automatically reject anything which does not conform to their blinkered norms. This prospect might well hamper other forward-looking producers elsewhere, if faced with inflexible rules

Early morning in the Cape.

and limits based on too narrow a perception of "typicity" or "tradition". The freedom, enjoyed by most winemakers of the New World, to experiment with new techniques and to develop new blends, is an inestimable advantage which they should cherish and preserve.

As well as being logical, the sanctions built into any AC-type scheme should also be practicable. Experience suggests that, rather than trying to force conformity at the production stage, controls are more effective once a wine is in bottle. At present, the low credibility of the European system means that this task has effectively passed to the market-place, where buyers now trust their palates more than they do the label. An independently-judged classification system, based entirely on finished wine, would engender much greater consumer confidence than weaker, largely unenforceable guarantees provided by pre-emptive controls on grape varieties or wine styles.

WINE STYLES

Wine writers often see "style" as the basis for differentiating one estate or region from another. As far as Rhône varieties are concerned, one can draw the deeper distinction between the idea of *vin de cépage*, where varietal characteristics are pre-eminent, and that of *vin de terroir*, where the grape variety is regarded as secondary – the means through which the *terroir* is best able to express itself. Such a contrast provides many winemakers with food for thought in choosing their own particular direction. Those who do not consider grape variety an essential part of origin, argue that the same *terroir* can express itself perfectly well through many grapes as, for example, in Alsace, where a single *Grand Cru* may be home to several varieties, or Coonawarra (qv) where a unique *terra rossa* soil imprints its individuality on Cabernet Sauvignon, Shiraz, Rhine Riesling and Chardonnay. Others argue for a tighter, altogether less flexible, concept which entrenches grape-variety as an integral part of *terroir*. This is the case in the northern Rhône, where most wines are effectively made from one variety – *mono-cépage*.

In much of the southern Rhône and the Midi, wines are seen differently – as *vins d'assemblage*, a blend of grape varieties, each of which adds something to the whole. This notion evolved from experience in hotter, Mediterranean climates, where traditionally-cultivated grapes had low acidities and high sugars (ie high potential alcohol) which meant that single varieties rarely yielded balanced or durable wine. Growers found that using Mourvèdre and Syrah, for example, to complement the loose-knit Grenache, contributed essential structure and complexity and gave wines interest and longevity. The greatest expression of this philosophy is in Châteauneuf-du-Pape, where any (or all) of 13 permitted varieties are used.

For consumers, most of whom remain blissfully unaware of such niceties, wine styles are more closely identified with grape variety than anything else. Unfortunately nearly two decades of skilful marketing, particularly in the USA, have inculcated an almost unshakeable faith in the single varietal, and a belief that "blending" is somehow disreputable. Although this flies in the face of the fact that virtually all great clarets, and many of the greatest champagnes, are the products of the blender's art, so ingrained is the "quality equals varietal" message that rehabilitating blends will take another determined bout of persuasive marketing – probably by those who sold the varietal message in the first place.

The concepts of *vin de cépage* and *vin d'assemblage* are not implacable opponents. Bordeaux uses several *cépages* in its red wines – although in practice Cabernet Sauvignon or Merlot predominate – realising that small additions of other grapes undoubtedly add quality. This experience seems to have made little impact in parts of the New World, where many estates soldier doggedly on with 100% varietals although local rules allow a percentage of other grapes in blends without sacrificing varietal labelling. Winemakers (or perhaps marketing departments) are shamefully unadventurous in developing new mixes. Why not a touch of Viognier to finesse a Chardonnay, or a spoonful of Marsanne or Viognier to lighten a tough Shiraz?

CLIMATE

A thoroughly dangerous belief, prevalent among many producers, is that wines produced in "cool" or "marginal" climates are inherently superior to those from hotter regions. In France, this carries the equally insidious implication that grapes indigenous to these climates (Pinot Noir, Chardonnay, Riesling, Cabernet and, the odd man out because of its supposedly southern origins, Syrah) somehow have greater natural nobility. Proponents cite as examples such "marginal" regions as Burgundy, Bordeaux, Australia's Clare Valley and the northern Rhône, and point to the heavier, less elegant, blended wines of Mediterranean climates. The standard argument is that cooler regions benefit from a longer, more even, growing season which produces a complexity of fruit and wine not found in less temperate places. It is true that both white and red wine made from over-ripe grapes grown in hotter climates tend to lack varietal character, are (not surprisingly) naturally high in alcohol, and mature unevenly – but this does not prove the point. In France, the indigenous varieties were those which ripened well and provided high yields – the qualities needed to supply the volume market over the past 100 years. Coincidentally these also tended to be varieties, such as Grenache, which were prone to oxidation and so matured quickly. But it is wrong to conclude either that all hotter-region wines must inevitably share these failings or that cool-climate wines are invariably superior. Better grape varieties with modern canopy management now enable growers in hotter regions to create a "cooler" vine environment, which dramatically alters the quality of the fruit they harvest. Technical advances in the cellar (eg temperature control) allow winemakers to control extraction and increase finesse. These are skills known to the younger generation taking over in southern France, who are now making some excellent, well-defined varietal wines, without recourse to *assemblage* to correct deficiencies. If the "cool" camp relied more on quality potential than on global generalisations, they might just have a tenable case.

TYPICITY

The French concern with typicity has boxed many growers into a corner demanding skilful escapology to extricate themselves. For the concept of appellation to have any value for the consumer, wines sharing an AC must have something in common – and that is typicity, derived from common origins and grapes. However, as enlightened winemakers are finding that they can make better, more interesting (if often atypical) wines from other grapes and sites outside appellation boundaries, tension between typicity and absolute quality is mounting. This is bringing the value of AC into question, especially in France's blend-dominated Midi, where a new wave of younger *vignerons*, forced by the high prices of AC land to plant in new areas, are making fine wines from non-traditional varieties and causing much controversy among die-hard traditionalists.

OAK

While the length of time that a wine spends in bulk before bottling is generally being shortened to preserve fruit and aroma, the value of traditional wood as against stainless steel (or some other inert maturation medium) is now being openly re-assessed. In particular, winemakers are questioning the hitherto widespread assumption that wine aged in new wood (or in the case of whites, vinified in it) is superior to wine aged in old. New oak, so the argument runs, adds elements of subtlety and finesse and rounds out structure and flavour in a way that other ageing materials cannot. In the New World, where many wines have been flagrantly over-oaked, consumers are now looking for greater finesse, rather than for the sledgehammer style of high-alcohol, high-impact wine, tasting of little other than over-ripe fruit and oak chips.

As winemakers seek to increase expression of varietal character and *terroir*, the use of new wood is being more finely tuned. Not necessarily suited to every variety and style, oak is now coming to be regarded as subtle seasoning, rather than as the main dish.

Poppy field near Vacqueras in the Southern Rhone.

THE SHOW CIRCUIT

In Australia, and to a lesser extent in other parts of the New World, success on the show circuit is seen as an indication of an estate's quality. So powerful is this influence that one suspects that winemaking is often compromised to accomodate the need to win. To the extent that they give minnows a chance to compete on equal terms with giants, shows are beneficial. However, their custom of very early judging (when any really great wine would barely be fit for tasting, let alone drinking) casts doubt on their real value – particularly for very young reds. The need, for sales purposes, to have a wine judged when it is barely out of cask, has defeated the far saner idea of assessment after a few years in bottle. It has also led to a culture of specially-crafted "show" wines, which gives the whole proceeding a distinct artificiality. Although several top estates participate in shows, many others refuse to become involved.

IMITATION

The spread of Rhône varieties around the world has given winemakers the skills and resources to imitate Rhône styles. Given the near-fanatical enthusiasm of many for the Rhône, generally intensified by distance, it is understandable that some have tried to make a Chave Hermitage, Vernay Condrieu, Guigal Côte-Rôtie or Reynaud Grenache. Since even next-door neighbours of these luminaries regularly fail to emulate them, it is hardly surprising that these attempts, often in totally dissimilar conditions, usually founder. The desire to copy the Rhône has led at times to an exaggerated search for cool-climate sites – although the northern Rhône is not itself particularly cool – and to vinifications designed to emphasise those aroma and flavour qualities which are seen (often wrongly) as essentially Rhône. Such mimicry rarely produces anything whose origins might be mistaken for the Rhône, and all too often achieves the desired qualities – eg "pepperiness" – at the costly expense of others – fruit and balance. The majority of outside winemakers who love the Rhône and admire its wines strive not to imitate, but to tap into the accumulated wisdom of its finest producers to refine the cultivation and vinification of their own Rhône-variety grapes. As most realise, insights gained must be treated with caution – what applies in one region does not necessarily hold good elsewhere.

ELSEWHERE...

I am aware, before anyone writes to point it out, that there is significant production of wines, made wholly or in part from Rhône varieties, in Spain, Argentina and Brazil. Unfortunately, most of this wine is of ordinary quality, and tastings have so far revealed nothing worthy of inclusion here from any of these countries. However, the new-wave Spanish Carignans and Grenaches, especially those from the arid Monstant mountain range of the Priorato region of Catalonia, show distinct promise and are worth trying should they come your way (eg the Tinto from Clos Mogador - 60% Garnacha, 20% Cabernet Sauvignon, plus Syrah, Carignan and Pinot Noir). I have not managed to track down the Greek Viognier from Roxani Matsa's Château Matsa in Attica, where there is an experimental planting: one of the more exotic outposts of that noble variety.

One discovery is the excellent Syrah from Didier Joris's estate at Chamoson, between Martigny and Sion, in the Swiss sector of the Rhône Valley. Here, half a hectare of Syrah vines, from a *sélection massale*, are planted at 11,100 plants per hectare on steep, mountainous terrain. Soils are principally of glacial origin and mainly schist and limestone, often rich in pyrite. The climate is hot and dry, with only 200mm of rain between May and August; strong, drying winds, from the south-west, exacerbate the effects of low rainfall, and a covering of gravelly topsoil intensifies the heat. Vinification is relatively straightforward: 15 days or so of fermentation with four pump-overs daily and temperatures peaking at 28°C. Only early pressings are incorporated back, before maturation for 10–14 months in small Vosges and Nevers casks (half new, half second-fill). The wine is neither fined nor filtered. The 1992, labelled Ophiuchus, had a good, deep colour, an elegant, peppery nose and flavour, with plenty of ripe fruit to fill the mouth, good length and persistence, and some power. A shade one-dimensional perhaps, but otherwise most attractive.

THE FUTURE

As the emotional and physical links between the Rhône and the rest of the wine world strengthen, quality improves at every level. As well as spawning a great deal of excellent drinking for a fast-growing band of international admirers, this cross-fertilisation has stimulated a worthwhile debate on ways and means of handling Rhône varieties and helped focus the development of individual and regional styles. I hope that this book encourages those unfamiliar with these wines to an unprejudiced trial, and the already converted to deeper exploration. With little doubt that the "Rhône Renaissance" is gathering pace, for producers and consumers alike the new millenium promises great excitement.

THE RHONE

From the famous vineyards of the Rhône Valley come some of the world's most impressive wines. Ranked the equal of any in France a century ago, these are now being "rediscovered" by wine-lovers world-wide and are becoming the most sought-after of all. Although the very best are rare and expensive, there are affordable treasures to be mined from top growers in less starry appellations.

The valley of the Southern Rhône – vines beginning to change colour in late September.

THE RHONE

Despite the considerable critical attention of recent years, the wines of the Rhône Valley continue to present an enigma. To some they are incomparable, among the greatest on earth, while others cannot understand all the fuss; for them they are just run-of-the-mill wines of marginal interest.

This apparent blind spot – Rhône's disciples would undoubtedly say "prejudice" or "ignorance" – means that many knowledgeable palates, tuned to the minutest nuance of Bordeaux and Burgundy, would probably be hard put to name the Rhône's top appellations or producers, let alone its most important grapes. In common with most drinkers, who rarely venture beyond the baseline Côtes du Rhône, they deprive themselves of the diversity and excitement this region has to offer.

In contrast, among those who love the area and its wines, its great winemakers are revered and discussed with the same intensity of passion accorded to the superstars of the Côte d'Or or the Bordelais. Given the individuality and quality of the Rhône's finest wines, it is high time that its (often eminently affordable) vinous riches are brought to the attention of a wider public.

Although the river itself runs for 808km, from its glacier source in Switzerland to its mighty delta west of Marseilles, the vineyards stretch only 200kms – from Vienne, south of Lyons, to just beyond Avignon. In a valley pitted by factories, hydro-electric plants and nuclear power-stations, industry competes with viticulture, offering a more secure and congenial alternative for many potential vineyard and cellar workers. Despite this, wine retains supremacy, giving the region a feeling of quality that it would otherwise lack.

Principally because of its historic role as a navigable waterway, the Rhône has attracted visitors since pre-Roman times. Vines are believed to have arrived with the Phocaean invaders in the 6th century BC, and archaeological finds indicate both Greek and Roman viticultural activity. A favourable climate, and the Rhône's importance as a trade route, ensured the continuity of a healthy wine trade over subsequent centuries.

Nowadays the region churns out a vast volume of wine, much of which is simple, staple drinking from the warm, prolific southern sector. But the real focus of interest lies in a dozen or so appellations, mainly in the north, where wines of international top quality are produced by a caucus of exceptional growers.

The Rhône divides neatly into two separate areas: the northern "Septentrionale" region, between Condrieu and St-Péray, is dominated by the red Syrah grape and produces deep, long-lived reds: Hermitage, Côte-Rôtie, Crozes-Hermitage, St-Joseph and Cornas. There are also fine whites – from the delicate, yet rich, Viognier of Condrieu and Château Grillet, to the more muscular Hermitages, Crozes-Hermitages, St-Josephs and St-Pérays made from Marsanne and Roussanne grapes. The southern, "Meridionale", sector, where the Grenache Noir grape holds sway, stretches from Donzère down to Avignon and includes Châteauneuf-du-Pape, Gigondas and Vacqueyras as its main quality appellations, as well as the sweet Muscat de Beaumes de Venise, the unusual fortified Rasteau, and sparkling Clairette de Die. Separating the two is some 54km of viticultural no-man's-land, with little but the sticky nougat of Montélimar to detain the traveller.

Young vine in springtime.

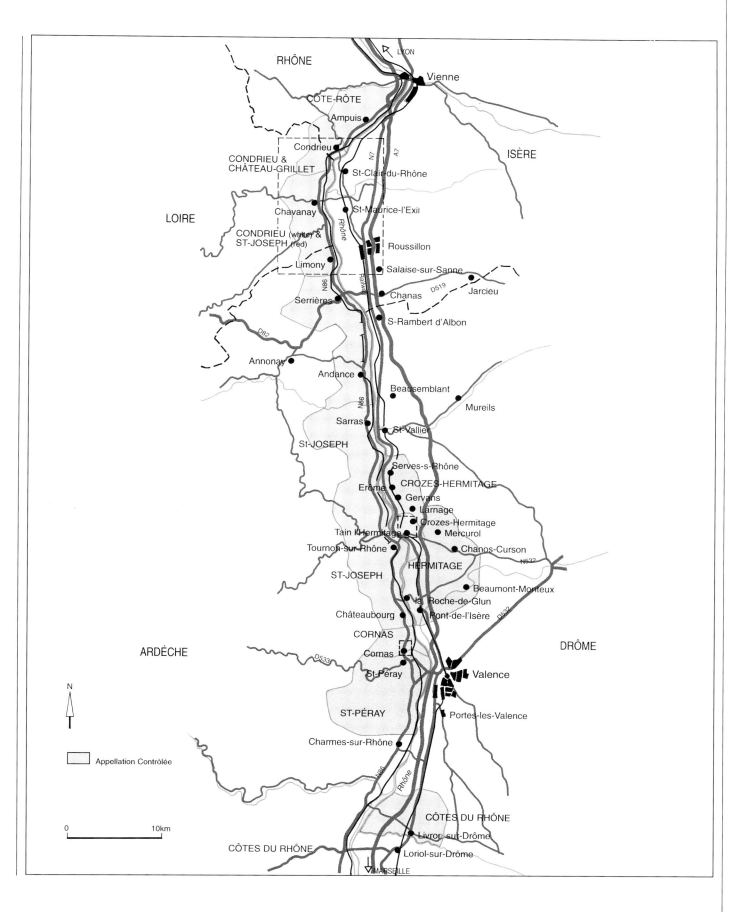

Their topography differs strikingly. The Septentrionale vineyards are chiefly concentrated on steep valley sides, with vines planted on vertiginous, narrow terraces at Côte-Rôtie, Condrieu and certain parts of St-Joseph, and on well-exposed hillsides at Hermitage, Crozes-Hermitage and St-Péray.

In contrast, the Meridionale landscape is flat, or gently undulating, delta land with broad expanses of open vineyard, exposed to the Mistral and often scented strongly with aromas of pine and wild herbs. This is picture-book Provence, dotted with tall, pointed cypresses and with fields of sunflowers and purple lavender. Here the houses have terracotta roofs and thick stone walls as insulation against the hot, dry summers – a climate inviting indolent repose against a background of ceaselessly clicking cicadas. The wines of the south are mouth-filling, heady and abundantly satisfying, but generally lack the finesse and complexity of their Septentrionale cousins.

PRODUCTION

In both sectors, the finest estates are generally small, family-run affairs; only in Châteauneuf, and patchily elsewhere, are large vineyard-owning enterprises to be found – and few of these produce serious quality wine. On small estates every stage of production from vine to bottle can be closely controlled: an advantage, provided those involved are competent in all departments, which is not always the case. In the north, some top-class estates – Guigal, Jaboulet, Chapoutier and Delas, for example – have developed into respected *négociants* that buy grapes (in preference to wine) from appellations throughout the Rhône, in order to offer a wider range than their own vineyards permit. In the south, *négociants* abound, but they buy mainly wine to blend and bottle for a volume market, and quality is rarely other than mediocre.

The north has two principal cooperatives, at Tain l'Hermitage and St-Désirat-Champagne, producing a sound range of Septentrionale appellations. In the south, hundreds of co-ops exist – 64 for the Côtes du Rhône alone – to support the thousands of small growers who have neither motivation nor equipment for making wine. Quality here, although improving, is generally uninspiring compared with similar-priced wine from the New World.

CLIMATE

The northern and southern Rhône also have different climates, which determine the choice of vine variety and thereby the style of wine. The Septentrionale sector is firmly continental. The annual averages show around 2,100 hours of sunshine, 7-900mm of rainfall, and a mean annual temperature of between 11.3°C (Lyon) and 12.5° (Tain l'Hermitage, which averages 3°C in January and 22°C in July). At Valence, the Septentrionale's southerly limit, annual rainfall is less than 900mm; this increases as one goes south (Montélimar averages 970mm) before falling back to 819mm at Lapalud, on the Drôme/Vaucluse border.

Beyond Montélimar, the pattern progressively changes to a Mediterranean climate, with significantly higher temperatures and more sunshine (Montélimar averages 12.8°C and 2,550 hours, Orange/Châteauneuf-du-Pape 13.5°C and 2,700 hours) and lower rainfall (Orange, 700mm and Avignon, 660mm). The lower Septrentionale heat forces a choice of early-maturing varieties, in particular Syrah; while the greater warmth of the Meridionale favours the later-ripening Grenache.

Then there are the winds. The south wind (*vent du sud*) generally brings cloud and rain, though the infrequent, southerly Sirocco imports Saharan sand and searing heat. The northerly Bise (Mistral), blows south of Valence – with ever-increasing strength as the valley funnels it southwards. While Montélimar's annual average of Mistral wind-speeds over 16 metres/second is 112 days, records at Châteauneuf show a figure of 122 days. Strong winds also buffet the north, but with less frequency. Physically, such wind-power breaks branches from traditionally trellised vines, so a special training system involving a wigwam of chestnut supports (*taille Côte-Rôtie*) has been developed to combat the problem. In the south, the Grenache vines are simply bush-trained (*en gobelet*) to avoid damage.

Unpleasant as it is for inhabitants and visitors, the Mistral brings benefits: drying the vines, ridding them of pests and fungal diseases and providing an element of protection against spring frosts. It also helps create the renowned clear Provençale light beloved of photographers and painters. Towards harvest, a strong Mistral concentrates extract and juice in the grapes by evaporation, and is capable of increasing sugar levels by one degree of potential alcohol per day.

Interesting recent research in Châteauneuf-du-Pape reveals that four decisive climatic parameters coincide with great vintages. First, the incidence of winter temperatures below 10°C, which determines the length of the following

The terraced hillside of Côte-Rôtie in early summer.

year's vegetative cycle: the longer this cycle, the better the wine; second, the number of rain-days between July 1 and August 15 – the more, in general, the better; third, the number of days between August 16-31 when humidity exceeds 80% (the Mistral plays a helpful role in limiting these); and, fourth, the rainfall between September 1-15 – the less the better for maturity, fruit intensity and balance.

Surprisingly, summer temperature appears to be of secondary importance; in the south (but not always in the north), there is enough sunshine and heat to ripen the grapes. In general, water is a limiting factor in the Rhône, where irrigation is outlawed (with the exception of a small section of Châteauneuf-du-Pape); deep roots are necessary to survive the stress of severe drought, which gives old, well-established vines a distinct advantage in dry seasons. However, these are broad correlations and not necessarily indicative of causes.

While the south is effectively a two-season climate, the north has less defined transitions between its four seasons. The climate here is less reliable, bringing more significant vintage variations, with heat, sunshine and rainfall the critical variables. It is this marginality that brings finesse to the wines – but at the expense of depth in less ripe vintages.

VITICULTURE

A wide range of viticultural considerations affect final quality. Yield and vine age, in particular, have a dramatic impact on a wine's structure and concentration. Yield is greatly influenced by the choice of clone and how each vine is trained, pruned and handled throughout the growing season. The majority of the 20 Grenache clones now available to vignerons were developed in the Vaucluse in the 1970s. Local experts are convinced that a clonal mix is better all round than using a single clone, as different clones are selected for different attributes – health and disease resistance, taste, yield, quality etc. For rootstocks (the lower, phylloxera-resistant, part of the vine) it is important to adapt to soil and site, especially considering tolerance to drought and wind. To really extract the typicity of any individual *terroir*, vines also need roots which delve deep into the subsoil.

As always, low yields are critical for quality, particularly with naturally high-cropping varieties such as Syrah and Grenache. Severe pruning and debudding are essential, as well as limiting the use of fertilisers – especially those based on nitrogen which simply proliferate vegetation. An innovative, but important, quality procedure is green-pruning (*vendange verte*): the removal of bunches a month or so before harvest. Although this is controversial among growers, many of whom regard it as akin to chopping cash off their vines, there are few top-class producers who doubt its efficacy. They are supported by increasing research evidence that crop-thinning, if carefully performed and precisely timed (at *véraison*), increases bunch weight and sugar levels and advances the date of maturity, particularly with younger vines. Syrah, Carignan and Cinsaut respond well, though the results with Grenache are less reliable.

The way the vegetation is spaced out also matters. Each grape variety has a natural canopy which needs individual training. Rhône growers will tell you that the Bordeaux *Guyot* training "*pisse le vin*", so *gobelet* or *cordon de Royat* are used for better aeration and lower yields. Syrah is notoriously vigorous and floppy, so generally needs an upright post or wire trellis, while other varieties, especially Grenache, perform better bush-trained. Too dense a canopy, however, can shade out valuable sunlight, so in some places the more spread-out vegetation of *cordon de Royat* is preferred. Vigour can also be controlled by increasing plant density; for example, Syrah at Hermitage is planted at much greater density (8,000 vines per hectare) than Grenache at Châteauneuf (2,500-4,000).

The commercial aspects of viticulture cannot be ignored. Jean-Louis Grippat has calculated that, excluding the cost of the land, it takes around 300,000 francs to clear and plant a hectare of terraced vineyard and to see it through to its third summer. Given also that one worker can cope with only one hectare of terraced vines compared with seven hectares on the flatter, mechanisable land, the terraces of Côte-Rôtie and Condrieu add their own significant costs to each bottle.

GRAPES

Septentrionale appellations generally allow only one grape (*mono-cépage*), whilst Meridionales permit a selection from which growers can choose and blend, within stipulated limits. In the south, Grenache is the bedrock, providing warmth, alcohol and quality for Châteauneuf, Gigondas, Côtes du Rhône and the rest. However, for balance, it needs keeping in proportion, so the recent raising of maximum Grenache content in Gigondas from 65% to 80% is considered by many a retrograde step. In general, growers have been given, and accepted, encouragement to increase plantings of other quality varieties – Syrah and Mourvèdre in particular – to add finesse and structure to their blends, and to decrease plantings of Cinsaut (and of Carignan in Côtes du Rhône) which gives poor alcoholic degree, over-produces and is difficult to ripen properly. Mourvèdre is gaining ground, because, unlike Grenache which oxidises easily, it has high natural resistance to oxidation. However, it requires careful siting in humid locations with a southerly exposure and clay-based soils – which makes it impractical for Gigondas and for much of Châteauneuf.

In the north, the only noteworthy trend has been an increase in popularity of Roussanne in white Hermitage, Crozes-Hermitage and St-Péray. Widely regarded as a difficult grape, because of its tendency to oxidation, it is valued as contributing both richness and freshness to blends. Roussanne and Marsanne have also become highly fashionable as "improvers" among iconoclastic Côtes du Rhône producers, as has the Viognier which is seen as adding individuality. Its notorious capriciousness provides a tough, but interesting, challenge for growers and wine-makers who are weary of the dull Clairette and Grenache Blanc staples.

While the AC rules at Cornas, for example, permits only Syrah, Châteauneuf's laws offer growers 13 different grape varieties from which to make their "cocktail" and Côtes du Rhône a choice from 23. The reason is partly that Grenache is seen as a "*vin d'assemblage*" – producing wine with low acidity, soft tannins and high alcohol and thus lacking the natural structure to stand alone. Also, in the south, ease of cultivation and the diversity of *terroirs* have not developed the tradition of specific adaptation of grape to site, as it has in the north where wines are justifiably regarded as *vins de terroir* rather than *vins de cépage* or *vins d'assemblage* (cf Introduction, page 14). Historically, Meridionale growers were able to produce large volumes to satisfy a French thirst which absorbed 130 litres per head per year; now consumption is nearer 90 litres quality, not quantity or alcoholic strength, is becoming increasingly important. In contrast, Septentrionale topography is not adapted to volume – Châteauneuf alone produces around 50% more than all the northern appellations put together – so the north wisely concentrated on quality.

Many southern estates found themselves replanting in the 1970s and 1980s, when vines planted just after World War II, often from poor-quality material, became unproductive and riddled with disease. Faced with a choice, many owners opted for high yielding clones and varieties, which contributed to an overall decline in quality.

VINIFICATION

While "tradition" appears to be clinging on by its fingernails, a younger, better-trained, generation is taking over and bringing improvements and innovations into their cellars throughout the Rhône Valley. Aware that the quality of raw material is critical, winemakers are taking much greater care in their vineyards, refining grape growing so that yields are lower and overall fruit quality more consistent.

Tradition, for both red and white wines, often meant a long period in old wood before bottling – which usually happened when an order arrived to justify the cost of bottles, corks and capsules. Now, with a greater realisation of the benefits of earlier bottling to preserve fruit flavours and aromas, the needs of the wine are given much more weight.

White wines have improved dramatically since the heavy, flabby, oxidative styles of the pre-1980s. The technical means now exist to control fermentation temperatures, to suppress acid-reducing malolactic fermentation and to control potential microbial spoilage – a problem "traditionally" solved by the heavy use of antiseptic sulphur to ensure the wine didn't re-ferment. Both southern and northern whites are now fresher and cleaner, smelling and tasting of grapes rather than of desiccating old wood and cardboardy sulphur. Stainless steel abounds, and new wood is being used in winemaking to great effect. Fermentation in clean oak (even of part of the crop) gives an even development and an harmonious balance, as well as adding elements of richness and structure. Low acidities are a constant problem, particularly for Grenache Blanc and Marsanne, exacerbated in hotter vintages which produce more natural sugar (and thus higher alcohol) at the expense of acidity. Adding acid to rectify an imbalance needs care; fortunately, Clairette, Roussanne and Bourboulenc retain more natural acidity which improves matters in the south, while in the north, where the problem is less acute, Roussanne is being used more widely, where allowed. A better acid balance means less need for harsh filtration, which takes body and finesse from a wine.

Progress has been equally striking for the reds. There is now a strong tendency to destem bunches before fermentation – a return to the 18th century, when destemming was considered indispensable to making great wine. Now growers weigh the advantages and disadvantages in a more informed manner, realising that with ripe, not green, stems the decision has less importance. In years of dilution, vats are more likely to be "bled" (*saignée de cuve*) to increase concentration and balance solids and liquids, and

A candle bearer at a L'Echansonnerie des Papes banquet. Guilds and their festivities are an important part of most winegrowers' lives.

much more attention is paid to how fermentation is conducted to maximise extraction of colour, tannins, aromas and flavours. In particular, winemakers are more skilled at fine-tuning the period of vatting (*cuvaison*) – when juice and solids remain in contact – and adapting it to the natural power and character of the wine involved.

The greatest improvements have come from more sophisticated use of oak, both new and old, in maturing red wines. It has long been recognised that Grenache oxidises and develops too rapidly in small (225-litre) casks, and so is now generally kept in bigger volumes where it evolves more slowly (often 600-litre *demi-muids* or larger *foudres*); Syrah and Mourvèdre, however, evolve best in small wood. "Tradition" left wine for two years or longer in wood before bottling, irrespective of the character of the vintage. This practice – which invariably dried out all but the richest of wines – often destroying them completely if the barrels weren't clean or regularly topped up, has now largely disappeared in favour of earlier bottling. Nonetheless, some good wine is still left too long in wood in the erroneous belief that this, by some undefined alchemy, somehow improves it. While poor vintages will rarely support more than 12 months' wood ageing, even the best vintages only merit 6–12 months longer. After two years in wood, wine gains nothing and starts to lose nuance and flesh. Equally reprehensible is the habit of waiting too long before transferring wine from vat to cask – a practice usually dictated by the availability of cask space. The optimal time is just after malolactic, not a year after harvest.

New wood is creeping in – even at the most traditional of domaines. Used sparingly, and prudently, it not only adds structure to a wine, but also evens out its development and softens rough edges. There is passionate debate about how much new oak is appropriate and how long wine should spend in it. Some staunch conservatives argue that new wood stifles fruit and varietal character and destroys typicity, standardising tastes and masking origins. This view depends on the false belief that appellations are incapable of either improvement or refinement and fails to recognise that a single wine designation is entirely compatible with a variety of styles. Traditionalists generally overstate their case, as most informed opinion now recognises the benefits of judicious use of new oak.

The worst sin, of which many southern estates are guilty, is having several bottlings of a "single" wine. The reasons are entirely commercial – to minimise delays between incurring labour and material costs and selling the wine – but the effect is to create as many different wines as bottlings. Bottling too early stunts development and too late can lead to volatility and premature oxidation. Either is unfair to the buyer, often unaware of the practice.

APPELLATION CONTRÔLÉE

(see also General Introduction, pages 12–14). The founding fathers of Appellation Contrôlée, including the influential Baron Pierre le Roy of Châteauneuf-du-Pape, intended the rules and controls to protect growers from others passing off inferior wines as something superior, and to guarantee the consumer authenticity and typicity. In the Rhône, the system patently isn't working: it neither protects anyone against counterfeiters nor ensures a minimum standard of quality for the consumer. Virtually all wines declared, from good and bad vintages alike, are passed fit for AC, irrespective of their intrinsic quality. In fact, according to a now-retired inspector from the Répression des Fraudes, the service responsible for policing appellations, in one vintage the Côtes du Rhône AC was given to more wine

(80,000hl – nearly a million cases) than was actually produced. This highlights the absurdity of trying to police more than 2.5 million hectolitres of Côtes du Rhône alone, with a handful of "fonctionnaires".

Such bizarre consequences reflect the service's haphazard methods of working. Vat samples are rarely taken from more than one AC, even if the grower being tested has half a dozen in his cellar, leaving ample scope for cheating. Moreover, the system permits a sample from a single vat or cask to represent a much larger, unsampled, batch. So, naturally, samples tend to be drawn from the best lots – growers aren't fools – allowing any sub-standard wine to gain the AC if this limited sample passes the requisite analytical and tasting tests. The effect is demonstrated by an actual case: a batch of unacceptably volatile Châteauneuf with perfectly correct accompanying documentation. How does this protect either the appellation or the consumer?

Equally unconvincing are the mandatory blind-tasting tests (*agréments*) before any wine is certified for AC. These are conducted by panels in which producers are always in the majority. Fearful of rejecting their own wine, the tendency is to accept virtually everything – nonsensical for any system seriously claiming to protect minimum quality standards. Attempts by the authorities to intervene against a sub-standard producer are met by protective action from the powerful growers' Syndicat of the appellation involved.

The "Fraudes" is often up against wily, un-cooperative producers, to whom an extra vat or two of wine is worth several thousand Francs, and is bogged down with a hopeless work overload. The AC administration is drowning in paper, with one inspector claiming that he spent only four days each month visiting estates, the rest dealing with the mounting demands of local and European bureaucracy. With 300 annual harvest declarations in Châteauneuf-du-Pape alone, and only six inspectors to cover 15 départements, it is hardly surprising that the system is failing. Those subjected to it regard it with undisguised derision: the cheats mock its pathetic controls and continue to profit handsomely, while top-class growers despair at what they see as an ineffectual waste of resources.

The proof (if proof is needed) that the system is toothless, is that there has been no prosecution against a wine producer, and no significant declassification of wine (if any at all), in the entire Rhône Valley over the last 35 years. In other words, we are invited to believe that every drop of AC wine produced has been fault-free, authentic and of acceptable typicity!

The AC apparatus is now little more than a sham – providing politicians, who lack the will to really grasp the nettle, with the comforting illusion that the industry is under control. Its only useful purpose is to ensure that the state collects all the wine tax due, in which role it is peculiarly effective. Part of the problem is that when the system was set up, it was principally designed to police the *négociants*, then seen as the most likely villains, and was not given the means to intervene effectively at the production level. Worse still, the inflexibility of this cumbersome dinosaur is blocking innovation; eg rosé cannot be produced in Châteauneuf, and elsewhere in southern France producers are restricted by out-dated grape selections. As in Tuscany, this forces many better wines out of the AC system, declassified into *vin de pays* or *vin de table*, where there is more flexibility.

A few improvements would transform the AC system into a respected, worthwhile instrument. Tastings should be conducted by oenologists and brokers armed with clearly defined and credible quality standards, and the Répression des Fraudes should be staffed by trained experts rather than by seconded civil servants who know little about wine. With diminishing bulk sales, there is a strong case for restricting AC eligibility to bottled wines. At present raw, unfinished, vat samples (*prélèvements*) are submitted for analysis and tasting around December, just three or four months after the harvest. In some cases three years will elapse between a wine's acceptance for the appellation and its bottling, with no further mandatory controls – plenty of time for all sorts of mishandling and destructive incompetence, let alone imaginative cheating.

At the production level, there should be a specific register of approved low-vigour rootstocks and low-yielding clones. Denying the AC to growers currently producing 100hl/ha from prolific Syrah clones – a level not remotely compatible with quality – would, of itself, do much to raise standards. Thereafter, yields should be strictly policed, with immediate declassification of an entire batch for any overproduction; the present system of only declassifying the excess makes no sense at all. At harvest, grapes not reaching an acceptable level of ripeness should automatically be disqualified from producing AC wine. The use of sugar or concentrate (to remedy a natural deficiency (chaptalization) should be rigorously monitored. In a region as hot as the Rhône Meridionale, it is difficult to make a case for permitting any chaptalization whatsoever. Miscreants who both water their vines and chaptalize should be especially firmly dealt with.

Beyond tightening up existing controls, the rules themselves need revision to promote quality. It is absurd to tell a winemaker producing a fabulous pure Syrah in the Côtes du Rhône that archaic rules mean that it is disqualified from the appellation and must be declassified into *vin de pays*.

In reality, it is unlikely that the political will exists to face the battles from obstinate growers and powerful vested interests that any such changes would inevitably bring. The only possible mechanism of change is the market-place, where fierce international competition for market-share is slowly making the French realise that, whatever the appellation, value for money is what ultimately counts. And at present, indifferent quality is driving prices downwards, as consumers turn to the New World and Eastern Europe for better value.

At the top level, minimum quality standards and AC restrictions make no difference to those producers who already consider them too lenient. Their principal concerns centre round the undoubted damage done by the appearance on foreign shelves and tables of expensive, yet inferior, wine bearing the stamp of superior appellations. This diminishes what they are striving to achieve at their own domaines, and undermines their collective efforts to enhance the Rhône's international reputation. A consumer unimpressed by a badly made 10-franc bottle of Côtes du Rhône is perhaps no great disaster; a disappointment with a 100-franc Châteauneuf-du-Pape is far more serious. With proper controls, there should be neither.

Despite these manifest failings, which mainly affect the lower quality levels and bulk production, the picture is far from one of unremitting misery. The Rhône has much to offer, particularly from its greatest appellations. Here one finds true magnificence in compelling wines which both inspire and delight.

The pages which follow introduce the Rhône Valley's principal appellations and finest growers. Unfortunately, lack of space precludes inclusion of either fortified or sparkling wine. However, for the first time in recent print, there are specially-commissioned, detailed maps of Côte-Rôtie, Condrieu, Hermitage, Cornas and Châteauneuf-du-Pape which should help those interested to understand more of the subtleties of these great appellations.

COTE-ROTIE

Côte-Rôtie is the most northerly of the Rhône Valley's appellations. Centred round the small town of Ampuis – which also markets the region's excellent fruit and vegetables – the *vignoble* spans three communes: St-Cyr-sur-Rhône, Ampuis and Tupin-Semons, stretching some 8km from the Ruisseau de Vézérance beyond St-Cyr to the Ruisseau de Bassenon just south of Semons.

Since the 1980s, when the world seemed to rediscover Côte-Rôtie, an air of subdued prosperity has pervaded Ampuis. Shabby restaurants, hitherto patronised by commercial travellers or tourists who happened to be passing through, have smartened themselves up, shops have blossomed to a limited extent opposite the church and, most noticeable and welcome of all, signposts have appeared directing visitors to wine domaines. Ampuis, though still not a candidate for a throbbing night out, is definitely taking notice of its increasingly international clientele.

HISTORY

The wine of Ampuis is of ancient lineage. It was among those of the Roman Viennois cited by Pliny the Younger, Plutarch and Martial in the first century AD. For the wealthy of thriving first and second century Vienne, Ampuis was their countryside and its "*vinum picatum*" (wine stabilised with pitch to protect it on long voyages) their finest wine.

The Pilat region, which covers most of the Côte-Rôtie *vignoble*, is know to have been continuously occupied since the Neolithic age. Archaeological remains demonstrate a strengthening north-south trade route during Roman times, with St-Romain-en-Gal as the main entrepôt between France (Gaul) and Italy.

Throughout the middle ages, Ampuis remained under the Archdiocese of Vienne. The renown of its wine spread so widely that, by the French Revolution, it was exported to most of the great courts of Europe. By 1890, the fame of Côte-Rôtie was at its apogee, with every patch and terrace cultivated.

Then decline set it. At the end of the 19th century, mildew, *oïdium* and phylloxera wreaked successive devastations which, together with a co-incident fall in demand following two world wars and the economic problems these entrained, lured growers off the vineyards into the more profitable and secure occupation of fruit and vegetable growing – *maraichage* – for which the Ardèche was (and still is)

Côte-Rôtie's steep, narrow, unmechanisable vignoble.

renowned. By 1945 a kilo of apricots fetched one franc, a kilo of Côte-Rôtie grapes 45 centimes.

Increasing industrialisation of the Rhône Valley fuelled the exodus by providing attractive, secure jobs that tempted a younger generation away from the uncertain rewards and certain hard toil of the land. Neither the Ampuis wine-market, inaugurated in 1928 to stimulate demand, nor the Syndicat des Vignerons, founded by Jean Vidal-Fleury in 1953, helped to reverse growers' fortunes. Côte-Rôtie reached its nadir in 1956, with a mere 48.41ha in production.

By 1975, cautious replanting had added 10ha, and growers, encouraged by rising sales and *négociant* interest, were increasingly bottling their own wine, although few managed to live wholly from the vine.

By 1980, with 108ha in production, there were distinct signs of rejuvenation. In particular the international interest sparked by the wines of Maison Guigal brought buyers and media to the region in unprecedented numbers. Recent years have seen these trends accelerate: in particular, planting fever took hold, and by 1995 200ha of a theoretical maximum of 500 were under vine.

Most encouraging of all, and a powerful sign of progress, was the willingness of younger men to take on the challenge of Côte-Rôtie's steep, arduous terraces: in 1975 the average age of Côte-Rôtie growers was

more than 55; by 1992 it had fallen to 35.

The renaissance was not without problems. In the late 1970s, the erstwhile Mayor of Ampuis, French Senator and leading grower Alfred Gerin, seeing the increase in demand, joined with a group of American investors and started to plant vines on the plateaus above Ampuis and Verenay. Although technically within the appellation, this land was unsuitable for quality – and the resulting high-profile marketing of relatively large volumes of undistinguished wine did little for Côte-Rôtie's fragile international confidence. The enterprise has now been disbanded.

VINEYARDS & LIEUX-DITS

A first-time visitor can hardly fail to be impressed by the sight of the vineyards which greets him as he crosses the Rhône. Shelf upon shelf of precipitous, narrow terraces – some just a vine or two wide – reach down into the villages on the river's west bank. Even for seasoned visitors, the place retains an indelible aura of magic and authority: majestic, impressive slopes, back-breaking to the *vigneron*, fascinating to the wine-lover.

These Roman terraces (*chaillées*) are held in place by dry-stone walls (*cheys*) which appear to be anchored to nothing whatever – somehow just balanced on the hillsides. These, and the stony soils, store up heat which is reflected back onto the vine – an indispensable aid to ripening the heat-thirsty Syrah grape. They also help retain valuable topsoil which is easily dislodged and washed away by rain. When this happens, the unfortunate *vigneron* has to collect it and return it to the vineyard – on his back. Now, special drainage channels are constructed to try and prevent damage in the first place.

Until around 1940, Côte-Rôtie officially extended only to the area referred to as the Côtes Brune and Blonde – around 300ha to the immediate north and south of Ampuis respectively. The names derive from an ancient legend relating the two daughters of the Seigneur de Maugiron (one brunette, the other blonde) to the two hillsides, characterised by darker and lighter soils.

In 1956 and 1966, the appellation was extended to incorporate parcels which had been "forgotten" in the original delimitation – settling its northern and southern boundaries in their present places. Then a further study in 1969 again extended the *vignoble*, a mistake which was rectified by a significant downward revision in 1993.

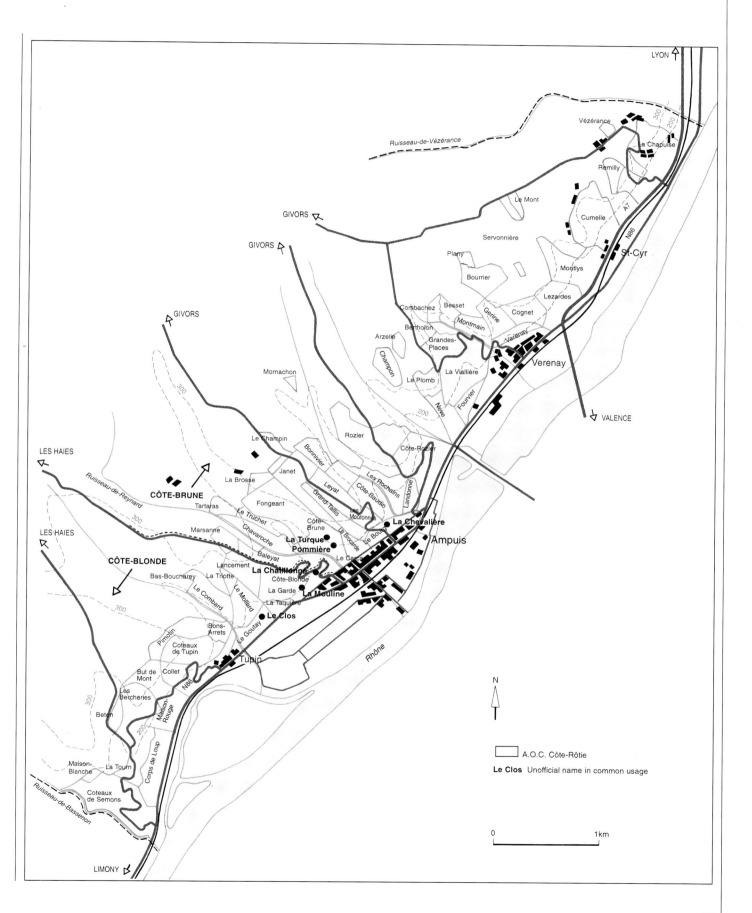

LYON

Ruisseau-de-Vézérance

Vézérance

La Chapulse

Remilly

Le Mont

Cumelle

GIVORS

St-Cyr

GIVORS

Servonnière

Plany

Montlys

Bourrier

Lezardes

GIVORS

Combachez

Besset

Gerine

Cognet

Bertholon

Montmain

Arzelle

Grandes-Places

Verenay

Verenay

Mornachon

Champon

Le Plomb

La Viallière

Fournier

VALENCE

Le Champin

Rozier

Bonnivier

Côte-Rozier

Janet

Leyat

Les Rochains

Côte-Baudin

LES HAIES

Ruisseau-de-Reynard

CÔTE-BRUNE

La Brosse

Fongeant

Grand-Taillis

Landonne

Tartaras

Le Truchet

Côte-Brune

Les Moutonnes

La Chevalière

LES HAIES

Marsanne

Chavaroche

La Brocarde

Le Bout

Ampuis

CÔTE-BLONDE

Baleyat

La Turque
Pommière

Le Car

Lancement

La Triotte

Le Mollard

La Chatillonne

Côte-Blonde

Bas-Boucharey

Le Combard

La Garde

La Mouline

La Taquière

Pimolin

Bons-Arrets

Le Goutay

Le Clos

Coteaux
de Tupin

But de Mont

Collet

Tupin

N86

Rhône

Lès
Bercheries

Maison-
Rouge

N

Beton

Corps de Loup

Maison-
Blanche

La Tourn

Ruisseau-de-Bassenon

Coteaux
de Semons

LIMONY

A.O.C. Côte-Rôtie

Le Clos Unofficial name in common usage

0   1km

While most Côte-Rôties are generally a blend from both Brune and Blonde sectors (the old names have stuck) recent years have seen many more wines being vineyard-designated – a cachet for which the producers exact a premium price. Unfortunately, the naming of individual vineyard sites (*lieux-dits*) has given rise to confusion. People tend to think simply of Côte Brune as the entire northerly sector and Côte Brune as its more "feminine" southerly sibling. As the accompanying map shows, the reality is more complex. There are indeed two distinct sectors – divided by the Chemin de la Côte Blonde which separates the *climats* Baleyat and Lancement – to which Brune and Blonde soil types broadly correspond. However, "Côte Brune" and "Côte Blonde" are also named *lieux-dits* within their respective sectors. European and local legislation only permits growers to use vineyard names which are marked on the official appellation map (*cadastre*); so for example, La Mouline and La Turque, which designated individual sites in times past, may not now be used on labels to designate specific vineyards. Marcel Guigal legitimises his own use of them by registering both as trade marks, thus circumventing the European Union laws.

CLIMATE & SOILS

Viewed from Ampuis, it is difficult to imagine the *vignoble* extending to 200ha. What one sees is a small (and the steepest) part of Côte-Rôtie, which extends several kilometres into the hinterland and ranges in elevation from 152 metres (in the village) to 325 metres.

What makes this such a special site? Apart from soil, which plays a significant role, the main quality factors are:

☐ **aspect:** these slopes face south or south-east, giving maximum sun exposure and excellent ripening

☐ **slope:** steepness up to 60% in places (to verify this, drive a kilometre up the Chemin de la Côte Brune and walk to the top of the vineyard and then peer over the edge of La Turque), ensuring minimal shading

☐ **rainfall:** equivalent to that on the Ile de France, which tends to arrive in short, violent downpours

☐ **wind:** the vines are eposed to the dry, burning southerly wind but suffer little from the Bise (north wind).

As with all the great French appellations, soil is a major determinant of taste. Geologically, the slopes of Côte-Rôtie derive from the ferruginous mica-schists of the Massif du Pilat. Although in the northern sector – especially at Verenay – these tend to be masked by scree, they are readily

visible elsewhere. (For example, continue to walk downwards from the top of La Turque, if your nerve can stand it, and you will start to slide on these small, thinnish slates.) In general form these are finely leaved, allowing deep penetration of the vine's roots and providing excellent drainage.

There is more iron in the Côte Brune sector, and in some places clay, which gives these wines a denser, more substantial and structured character compared with the Côte Blonde, whose lighter, sandier, topsoil produces finer, more elegant wine. Chemically, these hard, stony Côte-Rôtie soils are strongly acidic.

As one travels south, the terrain becomes more complex, with a higher proportion of limestone, gneiss and "granulite". Towards Semons, the soil's granite content increases – and it is this which forms the basis for the subsoil of the adjoining appellation, Condrieu.

GRAPES AND VITICULTURE

Syrah (locally known as Serine) is the sole permitted red variety in Côte-Rôtie, and 95% of the appellation is planted with it. Here, by tradition, it is trained *Guyot simple* on a curious wigwam made up of two long and two short stakes of chestnut, as protection from wind damage. The fruiting cane (*baguette*) is bent into a curve and tied (*fichage*) to the shorter stake, leaving a residual spur (*courson*) with two "eyes". Some growers have modified their pruning, training the vines either *en cordon de Royat* or *en gobelet* to take account of the higher natural productivity of newer clones; where the land is flat enough, one sees vines trained along wires – which is far less work.

The AC rules allow up to 20% of the white Viognier grape in Côte-Rôtie. This long-established custom evolved because its proximity to Condrieu meant that 19th century nurserymen probably delivered a mixture of the two varieties, science not being then too precise; and also because growers found that a dab of Viognier lightened the rather brutal young Syrah.

Viognier is poorly adapted to the iron-rich soils of the Côte Brune and, in consequence, is rarely found there (although Marius Gentaz had some very old vines on his plot); however, it performs tolerably in the Côte Blonde and many growers still retain around 5% or so complanted among their Syrah vines. Nonetheless, Viognier presents a problem for growers. It matures earlier than Syrah, but cannot be picked separately as the rules stipulate that it be added at fermentation, not blended in as wine later. So, by the time the Syrah is ripe, the Viognier is overripe. Thus 5% of

Viognier in the vineyard ends up as 0.5% by volume in the final wine.

On the terraces mechanisation is impossible, and everything has to be done' by hand – energy-sapping work during the heat of the summer, which is when the vines need de-budding and clipping. This ensures adequate aeration and exposure of the bunches to minimise rot and increase ripeness. The advent of helicopter treatments in the last decade has spared growers many hours climbing around with massive spray-canisters on their backs. The pilots' precision and skill is marvellous to behold as they duck and weave their dragonfly-like machines a few metres above the vines – dangerously close, especially in the narrow *combes* between the slopes. Some growers refuse to participate in this group effort, maintaining that the results are only superficial and that the underside of the foliage and the bunches are not treated properly.

The harvest (manual, of course) usually starts around the beginning of October, when the weather is most liable to dramatic change. The convoluted topography means that much of the crop has to be carried on pickers' backs to the nearest road for transport to the cellars.

PRODUCERS & STYLES

The Syndicat des Vignerons list shows 44 producers (excluding non-vine-owning *négociants*). Recorded production varies widely with the vintage, but rarely reaches the permitted 40hl/ha *rendement de base*. Figures for a few selected vintages are as follows:

VINTAGE	VINES (ha)	PRODUCTION (cases)	YIELD (hl/ha)
1959	49	20,416	37.89
1969	62	8,657	12.59
1976	70	23,452	32.86
1978	92	33,847	33.44
1988	135	44,000	29.63
1989	135	54,824	36.91
1990	145	66,517	41.70
1991	156	70,895	41.31
1992	165	67,925	37.42
1993	180	77,407	39.09

Growers fall broadly into three groups. First, the older traditionalists who are largely impervious to modern techniques and use little or no new wood. Among these are some of Côte-Rôtie's finest winemakers – in particular, Emile Champet, Marius Gentaz, Albert Dervieux (before he retired), Louis de Vallouit, and Robert Jasmin. Then come those who use a significant amount of new wood – considered by many as the anathema in classic Côte-Rôtie vinification. King of these is Marcel

Guigal; other important practitioners are René Rostaing and Jean-Michel Gerin. Finally, there are the "young turks" – growers of a younger generation who are more flexible and experimental in their vinifications – the Jamets, Gilles Barge and Clusel-Roch are in the forefront here.

Styles vary from the huge, heavily-extracted, tannic wines, needing years to soften out, to lighter, supple, less structured examples which give pleasure within a few years of bottling. For anyone contemplating laying down Côte-Rôtie, it is advisable to stick to the firmer, more traditional styles; what matters most is the overall balance of constituents – tannin, fruit, alcohol and acids.

As usual, the willingness to sacrifice yield for quality distinguishes the great from the merely good. Top growers prune severely, de-bud rigorously and take trouble to ensure that only as many bunches as the vine is capable of nourishing properly come to fruition. In years where flowering is disrupted by wind or rain, resulting in uneven set (*coulure*) which naturally reduces potential crop size, a reduced harvest is the pay-off. Minimum spray treatments and eschewing chemicals wherever possible are essential long-term policies.

The extent to which bunches are destemmed, the range of fermentation temperature and the length of vatting before the new wine is run off its solids, all contribute to individual style. The amount of new wood used, and how long the wine spends in cask – new or old – before bottling, also vary from *vigneron* to *vigneron* and are critical elements in the complex equation of style and quality.

Between vintage variation and growers' house styles, fine Côte-Rôtie encompasses a wide spectrum. However, there are common threads which make this wine so seductive and fascinating. While great Côte-Rôtie is eminently drinkable after two or three years in bottle, (and most of it is, in local restaurants), it is only with time that it takes on its real character, and shows the true magnificence of which this *vignoble* is capable.

Youthful aromatic finesse and a delicacy of flavour help distinguish Côte-Rôtie from Hermitage, though the dividing-line is often less clear-cut than some would have us believe. In maturity the two appellations tend to coalesce – exuding complex and utterly seductive secondary aromas of violets, *sous-bois* and tar.

Uncorking a great vintage before the wine has a decade of ageing under its belt is a criminal waste. Wait, then find some well-hung meat – winged game works wonderfully – and enjoy one of the world's greatest red wines.

Wetting straw used for tying up vines to make it pliable.

THE FUTURE

The clamour for Guigal's (qv) single-vineyard wines, and the international interest that they have aroused, has done much to increase Côte-Rôtie's standing and growers' prosperity. There is a buzz and a confidence about the place that was not there 15 years ago.

There is also a welcome stability, underpinned by a younger generation of skilled, enthusiastic winemakers. Too many Rhône enthusiasts – even seasoned hands – stick doggedly to Guigal, Jaboulet and Chapoutier. Reliable as these are, there is much for the mildly adventurous to discover from other growers.

Côte-Rôtie is now widely exported, especially the higher-priced *cuvées*. However, international markets are fickle and a falling Yen, D-Mark or Dollar can easily tip the supply/demand scales against the growers. The more sensible, mindful of the competition from Australia and California in particular, try to keep prices to levels which markets will bear and have little problem selling their wine. Others, who refuse to tailor their prices to reflect vintage variations in quality, suffer for their inflexibility.

The difficulty for most seems to come in second-rank vintages (1992 for example) when international buyers justifiably demand a substantial price-drop. With high fixed costs of production, this squeezes margins; and many growers (or their wives, who usually keep the books) faced with minimal returns are reluctant to comply. Local restaurants and passing trade – who are perhaps less price conscious – sometimes step in to mop up any balance, but with excellent Syrahs available from southern France, even these outlets are becoming less secure. Provided they manage to contain price-folly, Côte-Rôtie seems set for a fine future.

OTHER PRODUCERS

Besides those growers profiled here, there are excellent wines to be had from Delas (qv), Jaboulet (qv) who market their *cuvée* under the "Les Jumelles" label but own no vines here, and Chapoutier (qv), who do own vines and offer both a regular *cuvée* and the excellent La Mordorée, from parcels mainly sited in the Côte Brune, on its border with the Côte Blonde.

VINTAGES

It is wrong to assume that vintages are equivalent in quality across the entire Northern Rhône; Tain l'Hermitage is 46km from Ampuis and does not automatically have the same weather during any given growing season. For instance, 1961 was a five-star Hermitage vintage – but only good to upper-middle for Côte-Rôtie. In contrast, 1985 was top-notch for Côte-Rôtie but less starry for Hermitage.
1978: A spectacularly fine year, marked by a hot September which added an element of super-ripeness to the wines. Wines from the top growers started out black, with masses of ripe tannin, huge extract, and a

vast concentration of fruit. Inherently fine balance has kept them beautifully poised throughout their development. For those who have them, they still provide magnificent drinking – complex aromatically, well structured, long, complete and thoroughly seductive. Quintessential Côte-Rôtie.

1979: Excellent wines, by and large; but without the extract and concentration of the 1978s. The best have developed into stylish, mid-weight wines, and have held up well. There is no point in further keeping: drink now.

1980: Soft, attractive wines: sound but now beginning to fade. Guigal's Mouline and Landonne will still develop but, again, there is no real benefit to be had from waiting longer.

1981: A notably wet harvest resulted in many dilute wines which were not structured for longevity. This imbalance led to uneven development and apart from Guigal's top *cuvées*, what remains must be something of a gamble.

1982: Almost the converse of 1981. A very hot dry summer continued into an early September harvest. Thick skins and hot grapes compounded the problems, making vinification difficult for most who had no cooling equipment. Overheated fermentations imparted a cooked, jammy aspect to many wines which has never entirely deserted them, and naturally low acidities compounded the problem by removing freshness. Guigal's Mouline and Landonne are still magnificent – opulent, fat, concentrated, and beginning to open out. These will keep, but most of the rest need drinking sooner rather than later.

1983: For some this was a magnificent year, resulting in wines which were characterised by firm tannins and ripe, concentrated fruit. For others, the tannins were just too much, irremediably unbalancing the wine. A period of intense heat during the vintage replicated many of the problems of 1982 – although an even growing season meant that the wines were by and large in better balance. Some are distinctly cooked, but the best, although reaching maturity, will continue to develop, if not improve, over the next few years.

1984: Although the weather turned fine for a late vintage (early October), rain had swelled the berries to the point where dilution was inevitable. The wines show this – especially from those who like to crop as near to the permitted 40hl/ha yield as possible. Unripe grapes and stems in the vats also contributed a green, astringent element which has not disappeared. Drink now – or cook with it!

1985: A fine vintage – from a long, warm, summer. As in Bordeaux and Burgundy, the wines started out with a seductive, fleshy character that made them delicious

from infancy. For the most part they lack the sheer depth of extract and concentration of the 1978s, but have lasted well and are beginning to drink beautifully. 1985 marked the debut of Guigal's La Turque – an extraordinary wine from very young vines – with the usual opulent majesty in the Mouline and Landonne. Wines from the top growers were highly successful and will continue to improve over the next few years. Those with well-cellared bottles should seize the opportunity and not overstretch their luck.

1986: A distinctly patchy vintage, mainly spoiled by rain which diluted the crop and spread rot. Those who picked carefully made sound wines, but many are tainted. Even the better *cuvées* seem to have retained a disagreeable element of greenness which is unlikely to go. A few – notably Marcel Guigal, Bernard Burgaud, Robert Jasmin and Marius Gentaz – bucked the trend, producing delicious wines for the medium term.

1987: Mediocre. Not really enough sun and heat to ripen the grapes properly. Result: rather thin wines, generally lacking in stuffing; some tainted with rot. For the best, call them "elegant" if you will, and feel the finesse as you drink them; but these are far from what great Côte-Rôtie should be.

1988: Altogether different. A very fine, but small, crop of confident, tightly-structured wines. Some are too tannic for top quality, but most are evolving well – if somewhat slowly. Where there is enough fruit to balance the tannins (Gentaz, Guigal, Jasmin, Barge, for example) the wines are excellent and have a good future. Others who mis-calculated the balance – Dervieux is one – made wines which will certainly last, but which are likely to remain scarred by their aggressively harsh tannins.

1989: A good to very good vintage, in which heat and drought combined to ripen the grapes for one of the earliest harvests growers can remember (most started picking during the third week of September). Some wines are marked by heat (Burgaud, Duclaux and Bonnefond in particular), others by high acidity (Jamet, Barge and de Boisseyt stand out). Where the balance is right, the wines are fleshy and tannic; some tending to burliness. Christophe and Patrick Bonnefond, Clusel-Roch (both the standard *cuvée* and Les Grandes Places), Jasmin, Drevon and of course Guigal were notable successes.

1990: A good to very good vintage. A hot growing season meant that ripening was slow and sometimes incomplete, with less than adequate rainfall to keep photosynthesis going. Apart from Guigal's Turque, Mouline and Landonne, which are massive, brooding wines, many of the best

show surprising elegance and are beginning to make attractive drinking. Overall, the wines are well balanced, with plenty of ripe, sweet fruit – rather than the pepper-and-spice one expects from young Côte-Rôtie – good depth and long, satisfying flavours. Most need several years more to show their real qualities. Clusel Roch, Gerin and Jamet also excelled (cf tasting notes starting on page 299).

1991: Another fine vintage. The largest crop to date (only surpassed by the 1993). The wines are more variable in overall quality than the 1990, with rather more in the middle to upper-middle bracket than in the top league. While some first-division growers disappointed (in particular, Burgaud and Jamet) there were successes from unexpected sources: François Gerard, Louis Drevon and Bernard Chambeyron. (cf tasting notes).

1992: A moderate-sized crop which, but for *coulure*, would have been much larger. The wines have turned out patchily: some good with reasonable colour, sound fruit and good balance; others poor and astringent. Rain marred the latter part of the harvest – although much of the crop was in by then. Attractive, medium-weight wines from the usual sources; otherwise a vintage to avoid and certainly not a keeper.

1993: Every prospect of a respectable vintage – until two weeks of heavy rains arrived on 25 September. A cool summer had presaged a late harvest, so the grapes were still on the vine. Rot spread rapidly, especially in sites where too much fruit had been left on the vine, giving thin, relatively fragile skins. The result was a big crop – but with many wines lacking in real depth and balance. Growers who were diligent in excluding substandard fruit, and who didn't try to compensate for natural ripeness and lack of extract by unduly long vatting, generally produced attractive *cuvées*. Not a vintage for prolonged cellaring.

1994: The growing season was marked by a very hot and dry summer, punctuated by some rainfall at the start of September. Despite the reappearance of rain at the start of harvest, a healthy crop was gathered. The quality is likely to be above average, but not exceptional.

AC COTE-ROTIE

Created	18 October 1940 (revised 1993)
Area (max)	500ha
Area under vine 1994	200ha
Base yield	40hl/ha
Minimum alcohol	10% (14% maximum)

DOMAINE GILLES BARGE

From his cellars, home and office, just up the route de Boucharey, the wiry, chain-smoking, gravel-voiced Gilles Barge runs both the Côte-Rôtie growers' Syndicat and his own 6.1ha domaine.

The former role combines the functions of diplomat, conciliator and organiser. Keeping the peace between growers is no sinecure, whether dealing with a complaint that the helicopter has or hasn't sprayed someone's vines, or simply collecting samples from 25 of his members for visiting journalists.

Gilles' vineyards consist of vines ceded by his father, who produced under his own label until retiring in 1993, plus various rentals and plantings made since joining him in 1979. In particular, there is a fine half-hectare of 50-year-old vines rented from Joseph Duplessis in 1978 which contributes to a special 3,000 bottle offering – the Cuvée Goutillonage – which is only released after *goutillonnage* (approval) from a tasting panel from the wine university at Suze-la-Rousse.

The Barge wines are good, sometimes excellent, often showing less than well in youth, but coming through with depth and elegance after a decade or so. Gilles professes himself more concerned with finesse than size, but compromises this by putting all the stems into his *cuves*: "I have no intention of de-stemming – why have expensive equipment which you only use once every ten years?" In marginally ripe vintages, such as 1992 and 1993, this imparts a distinctly raw edge to his young wines.

A helicopter spraying near Ampuis.

To set them off on the right rails, the Barge reds are kept in *pièces* and *foudres* for two to three years – some four to five months longer for the Goutillonage. Gilles is not an aficionado of new oak – "it's not in my idea of the reflection of *terroir*" – so there are only enough new casks to maintain a reasonably youthful cask population.

He considers that his wines evolve more harmoniously with a longish *élevage* than they would with earlier bottling. The special *cuvée* apart, there are several separate bottlings of each vintage. The Condrieu and tiny production of white St-Joseph are plate-filtered; the reds neither filtered nor fined.

The Gilles Barge wines are not for early drinking. However, if the older vintages are any indication, this is a domaine worth following.

APPELLATION	VINEYARD	DETAILS	AREA
COTE-ROTIE	COTE BRUNE	½ 40–50; ¼ planted 1970; ¼ 1979	2.00
COTE-ROTIE	COTE BLONDE & BALEYAT	Duplessis vines; planted 1946	0.50
COTE-ROTIE	COMBARD	0.15 planted 1950s; 0.25 pl 1985; 0.40 pl 1972	0.80
COTE-ROTIE	COTE BLONDE	Planted early 1960s; behind house; fermage	0.20
COTE-ROTIE	BOUCHAREY	Planted early 1960s; fermage	1.00
COTE-ROTIE	LANCEMENT	Steep slopes, planted 1987; "tres belle"	0.60
CONDRIEU		30 yr old average	0.20
CONDRIEU		First crop 1994	0.25
ST-JOSEPH	CHAVANAY	Syrah planted 1990	0.80
ST-JOSEPH	CHAVANAY	Marsanne planted 1993	0.20
ST-JOSEPH	CHAVANAY	Syrah planted 1993	0.20
		TOTAL (hectares):	6.75

DOMAINE BERNARD BURGAUD

This is a stylish, small (4ha) domaine run by the likeable, loquacious Bernard Burgaud. Like many of his *confrères*, he started with little enough – just 2ha from his father Roger, who died suddenly in 1980, pitching him in at the deep end.

Fortunately, a Beaune education and years of working with his father enabled him to continue producing wine and selling it: "we had the luck that our wine was remunerative and that we could live from it". Encouraged, he bought, cleared and planted land, often in places abandoned since phylloxera; hard work on these inimical, scrubby terraces – in one place it took 1,000 man-hours to re-establish just 3,000 square metres.

For all his engaging manner, Bernard is a thoughtful and serious *vigneron*. He considers the fragmentation of his vineyards over three distinct micro-climates provide a natural palette: terraces, exposed south-southwest, protected from the north wind; tops of hillsides getting some north winds at the heads of the combes; and plateau vines which get more cooling north wind and thus ripen later – their wine has more acidity. The upper slopes generally give the finest wine, the plateaux the most mediocre. "I'm lucky to have this palette at Côte-Rôtie; it helps me to fall on my feet every year".

In the Burgaud cellars, at Le Champin, a tiny hamlet in the hills above Ampuis, each vintage's colours are fashioned into a picture, driven by a rigorous logic as to ends and means. Bernard prefers big, confidently-structured wines and

APPELLATION	VINEYARD	DETAILS	AREA
COTE-ROTIE	LE CHAMPIN	Plateau vines; ½ planted 1983; ½ c 1963	1.00
COTE-ROTIE	LEYAT	Terrasses; ⅓ planted 1983; ⅔ c 1963	1.00
COTE-ROTIE	LES MOUTONNES	Mixture of 50 and 10 yr old vines	0.60
COTE-ROTIE	COTE BLONDE	Planted 1981/2	0.30
COTE-ROTIE	FONJEAN	(= Fongent) 40+ yr old vines	0.40
COTE-ROTIE	LA BROSSE	Têtes de coteaux; 40+ yr old vines	0.40
COTE-ROTIE		Various lieux-dits	0.30
		TOTAL (hectares):	4.00

discounts as transitory the current lighter trend. For him a fine Côte-Rôtie must have concentration, deep colour, substance and noble tannins.

This means extracting as much of the good without the bad; in practical terms, this entails de-stemming to remove the risk of hard stem tannins which never soften out; a *saignée de cuve* when necessary, bleeding off excess juice to restore a workable liquid: solid balance; *pigeage* by hand up to eight times a day during the height of fermentation, and allowing the temperature in the *cuve* to rise to 34°C. The new wine is run off as soon as fermentation has finished – by then there's nothing worth extracting left – and the press-wine added back.

Sooner rather than later, Bernard tastes each lot to identify those which least

please him – perhaps a vat higher in acidity or less coloured – for the 20% of each year's crop which will be sold in bulk: "this wine isn't lamentable, just less acceptable". After malolactic, which takes place in *foudres*, the wine is racked into *pièces* for a year or so's maturation.

There is only 20% of new (Allier) oak annually. Bernard is clear about its role: "Our wines have character, definitely not *boise*, which may not please everyone. You can make wine with 100% new wood anywhere – easy...delicious… they all taste the same. This is not the way to go.

"To make good wine, you must put it into wood – but the wood doesn't make the wine, so I'm not obsessed with its origin. I'm in the middle – some *vignerons* have 100% new wood; older *vignerons*

use none, as they think it changes the character of their wine too much".

After bulk sales, enough wine remains for some 10–13,000 bottles. The *pièces* are blended together in January of the second year and then returned to a warmish cellar, since Bernard has discovered that wine bottled cold inexplicably develops a small amount of carbon dioxide gas after some months in bottle, whereas the same wine bottled at 16–17°C does not. There is neither fining nor filtration.

Bernard Burgaud's wines are good and dependable: satisfying Côte-Rôties of substance and character, which reflect their *terroirs* and reward cellaring. Regularly among the top echelon.

DOMAINE CHAMPET

Emile Champet is one of Ampuis' most engaging *vignerons* – a short, ebullient, lively character with grey-green beady eyes, a piercing stare and an irrepressible, galvanic manner which suggests that he has somehow become overcharged with electricity and is busy shedding the surplus. He combines an infectious sense of humour with a profound knowledge of Côte-Rôtie.

After some fifty vintages Emile, now in his seventies, has handed over to his son Joel all the family vineyards, save 0.4ha of very old vines in the unlisted *climat* of Molin, in the Côte Blonde "next to Vidal Fleury – as old as me", Emile confides. This constitutes the state's liberal allowance for a retirement income, although there isn't much evidence that Emile has any intention of retiring as he comes bounding in from an afternoon's *attachage* under a hot sun, bursting with vitality and good humour.

From about 1985, Joel progressively took over the main vinifications – although wines continued to appear under separate "father" and "son" labels. Now, according to Emile, all the wine is assembled and put out under the same label, except for a quantity reflecting his 0.4ha, which appears as "Emile Champet".

Meanwhile, the 40-year-old Joel has left the quiet family home next to the river in Le Port sector of Ampuis and moved with his wife and two children to a new house and cellars at Verenay, near to most of his two hectares of vines.

Emile's vinification is thoroughgoing traditional – no de-stemming, 24–30 months' *élevage* in old wooden *foudres*

The exuberant Emile Champet in his cellar after a hard day's work in the vineyards.

or *pièces* (from Denis Mortet in Gevrey-Chambertin) with cask-by-cask hand-bottling to order: there was still some 1990 in cask in June 1994!

Joel prefers 20–30% of new oak and has filled all his 8–10,000 bottles by 18 months after the vintage, although he does agree that – up to a point – the wine evolves more evenly in cask than it does in bottle.

The Champet wines have been variable – sometimes (for instance, 1978) truly excellent with fine depth of fruit and structured for ageing, at others (for example, 1985) disappointing – probably reflecting the variation in *élevage*. Since Joel Champet's arrival, consistency has noticeably improved. If the trend continues, all the ingredients are in place for a top-flight domaine.

APPELLATION	VINEYARD	DETAILS	AREA
COTE-ROTIE	LA VIALLIERE	(Joel Champet); 20+ yr old vines	2.00
COTE-ROTIE	MOLIN	(Emile Champet); 60+ yr old vines	0.40
		TOTAL (hectares):	2.40

DOMAINE CLUSEL ROCH

Here is a young enterprise by northern Rhône standards, started in 1980 with one hectare each of Côte-Rôtie, vegetables and fruit trees. Now, following the retirement of Gilbert Clusel's father, and with some replanting, the estate has grown to 3.5ha – 3ha in Côte-Rôtie and a precious 0.5 in Condrieu. The estate operates from an unpretentious base at Verenay, in the northern sector of the appellation where a new cellar has just been built, cut into the hillside behind the Clusels' house.

Initially Gilbert and his wife Brigitte (Roch) lived off her salary as a teacher. Now they work together full-time on their wines, jointly taking any major decisions. He works principally in the vineyards and she in the cellars. "I am the work-force", the stalwart Brigitte confides. The production is modest – some 10,000 bottles of Côte-Rôtie in a normal year, and a mere 900 of Condrieu – but what there is, is first-rate. Theirs is a rising star in the region.

The Condrieu, from half a hectare of young vines on the Coteau de Chery, is a yardstick example – elegantly perfumed yet with depth and power. The grapes are left overnight, without crushing – a sort of maceration – which adds a touch of richness to that derived from expressly low yields. Fermentation in cask at around 18–20°C lasts 1–3 weeks. The malolactic follows at its own pace – often slowly as in 1992 when it didn't finish till July. Bottling, on a small filler shared with Gaillard, Barges and other friends, follows shortly after, with a light polishing filtration "just for the look of it".

The Côte-Rôties are well-extracted and elegant wines, made with plenty of *pigeage* at the start of fermentation and careful temperature control – a peak of

Brigitte Roch and the rocky terrain which needed blasting to plant vines.

30°C to avoid a distasteful cooked character which appears beyond this. "We tried de-stemming in 1991 and 1992", admits Brigitte, "but didn't like the results; we prefer to leave all the stems and have a shorter *cuvaison*". So, some 12 days later the free-run wine is decanted and the pulp pressed. Press-wine is kept apart until after malolactic and then assembled back: "we have to put it all in – nothing is sold to the *négoce*, so we can't afford

not to get it right", is the honest explanation.

Since 1988, there have been two Côte-Rôties: a "classic" blend and the superior, single-vineyard "Les Grandes Places" bottling from the 0.7ha of 60-year-old vines. Quantities are less than generous – from three casks in 1988 to nine, the maximum, in 1990 and none in 1992. As one might expect, this wine has greater overall depth and structure than the standard issue, and is less flattering when young – qualities derived in part from the soil's high iron content in this sector of the appellation.

It also spends somewhat longer in cask: nearer 24 months than the 18 for the standard wine. For Les Grandes Places, half the casks are new Allier oak (plus a touch of Vosges) and half casks which have been broken in with one wine. The "classique" sees only 10–15% of new oak. Since 1990 this enterprising team have been buying their own wood and having it dried at their *tonnellier* in Burgundy – "it's a bit more expensive in the end, but we see our casks.and the others which all arrive on the same lorry. Ours are better". The reds are bottled with an egg-white fining and no filtration, and the bottles kept for at least six months before despatch.

This may be a fledgling domaine, and cash may be tight, but what has been achieved is of five-star quality. As it and its wines mature, expect great things.

APPELLATION	VINEYARD	DETAILS	AREA
COTE-ROTIE	LES GRANDES PLACES	60 yr old vines	0.70
COTE-ROTIE	LA VIALLIERE	Mainly 5–14 yr old vines	1.50
COTE-ROTIE	LE CHAMPON	En fermage	0.80
CONDRIEU	COTEAU DE CHERY	Planted 1984	0.50
		TOTAL (hectares):	3.5ha

MAISON GEORGES DUBOEUF

Duboeuf, best known as major producers of Beaujolais, have recently developed a two-pronged Rhône programme. This is based round the 10-ha Côte-Rôtie Domaine de la Bonserine (which they acquired, with the help of starred chef George Blanc, from Alfred Gerin and his US associates in 1988), and the 150ha of contracted Ardèche Viognier from which they buy must, but own no vines.

The Ardèche connection began in 1989/90 with Gamay Nouveau, and extended to Viognier, whose aromatic

qualities and "touch of mystery" attracted Franc Duboeuf and his father, Georges. They have persuaded growers to plant on carefully chosen sites – limestone soils, good exposition with low frost risk and low humidity. Yields are around 35-40hl/ha, though the ideal is less than 30hl/ha at 13–13.5° potential alcohol. Since the first vintage in 1993, crops have been regularly good. Grapes are harvested late, almost over-ripe, and taken to Villeneuve-de-Berg near Alba for vinification. Experiments are under way

to find the most suitable treatment: at present, the regime comprises skin-contact, cool fermentation in new wood to enhance aromas and only part of the crop undergoing malolactic, since Viognier is notoriously low in acidity. Finding "the best expression of Viognier" is clearly going to take time; meanwhile Duboeuf's long-term confidence in the variety will do much to enhance its reputation.

As for Côte-Rôtie, much progress has been made since they arrived in 1988 to find the 1985 still in wood. "What struck us here was that a long sojourn in *foudre* produced volatility". A *chef de culture* was installed to oversee the necessary reconstruction of this highly fragmented *vignoble* and a *chef de cave* appointed to superintend vinification.

"We are looking for a Duboeuf style", is how Franc sees the evolution of the Domaine de la Rousse, as they have renamed it. There are two blends: one from wines matured for 18 months in *foudre* and *cuve*, another from wines from *foudres* and *tonneaux*, with a touch of new wood.

Each blend contains some 5% of Viognier. Bottling of both is contemporaneous – but the latter blend remains in the cellars for further ageing, while the former is sold "as soon as possible". Franc Duboeuf dismisses any possible confusion: "there will be no difference for the consumer". Really?

VARIETY/APPELLATION	VINEYARD	DETAILS	AREA
SYRAH (COTE-ROTIE)	LEYAT	27 yrs average vine age	1.30
SYRAH (COTE-ROTIE)	BONNIVIERES	25 yrs average vine age	2.45
SYRAH (COTE-ROTIE)	LE CHAMPIN	30 yrs average vine age	2.00
SYRAH (COTE-ROTIE)	COTE BRUNE	15 yrs average vine age	0.65
SYRAH (COTE-ROTIE)	LES MOUTONNES	13 yrs average vine age	0.42
SYRAH (COTE-ROTIE)	FONGENT	20 yrs average vine age	1.50
SYRAH (COTE-ROTIE)	MARSANNE	5 yrs average vine age	1.00
SYRAH (COTE-ROTIE)	COTE BLONDE	16 yrs average vine age	0.14
		TOTAL COTE-ROTIE (hectares):	9.46
VIOGNIER	PLATEAU DE L'ARDECHE	Vineyards under contract (1995)	150.00

Many will look askance at such a radical diversification from the usual Duboeuf territory. However, first results are promising. Techniques will obviously develop with experience and the wines gain in depth with time. Much effort and investment have gone into the project; it deserves to succeed.

DOMAINE HENRI GALLET

The Gallets work a mixed farm – cereals, cattle and wine – in Boucharey, a quiet little hamlet in the hills four kilometres behind Ampuis. Up to 1983 they only bottled a quarter of their production; now it is three-quarters.

The vines are good and old here, averaging 40 years; some are septuagenarians. Vinification is solidly traditional: no de-stemming, 15–21 days' *cuvaison* and an *élevage* of 18–24 months, depending on bottling date, in 600-litre *demi-muids* and *pièces*. In principle, says Madame Gallet, the wines are not filtered, although part was in 1989 and 1990. There was no filtration at all in 1991 and 1992 – curious this, for these were more problematic vinifications than the earlier

two vintages – and this policy is to continue. There are three bottlings, at 18, 20 and 24 months, which more or less follow demand.

The 1989 and 1990 tasted blind, along with a range of others from each vintage, had rather aggressive hard edges, while later vintages were far better balanced with greater finesse and complexity.

After some delving the answer appeared – Henri Gallet had decided to entirely renew his casks in 1989, so the cask fraction of this vintage was entirely matured in new wood.

Now things seem to have settled down *chez* Gallet, the wines are steadily improving. There are good things here – an impressive 1991, an attractive, elegant 1992 for the medium term and a lightish, succulent 1993.

It is better to wait for the later bottlings, which have longer wood maturation and are in consequence rounder and more harmonious.

A domaine to watch.

APPELLATION	VINEYARD	DETAILS	AREA
COTE-ROTIE	LANCEMENT	Part plateau, rest Coteaux; average age 40, some 70+.	2.55
COTE-ROTIE	LE COMBARD		0.45
		TOTAL (hectares):	3.00

DOMAINE GENTAZ-DERVIEUX

In the rush for the undoubtedly fine named *cuvées* from Guigal and Chapoutier, people seem to forget – if they ever knew – that there are other sources of remarkably fine Côte-Rôtie to be had, at a fraction of the price of those from the international super-stars. For anyone who cares to search, the northern Rhône is peppered with growers of experience and proven quality – Marius Gentaz-Dervieux is one.

For all the excellence of his wine, you won't find luxury in this attractive corner house in a side-street towards the river; just a bright-eyed man and his petite wife of fifty years, comfortably retired and enjoying the peace that years of hard work have brought. The dynamism may perhaps have diminished, but the feel for

grapes, and the art of turning them into something fine and special, remains.

Since 1952 Marius has worked 1.2ha of vines in Côte Brune ("within 50 metres of La Turque") and La Landonne, at first with his father, from 1965 on his own. Now, in their early seventies, they are as old as him. In 1993, with only daughters who weren't interested in vineyards, he rented out to his nephew René Rostaing all but the 42 ares which the state allows him and his wife in retirement. Sadly, there is less Côte-Rôtie Marius Gentaz for his faithful customers, but splendid memories remain of the great wines which his skills have wrought.

Perhaps the only great regret of this kindly old *vigneron* might be that he refused the offer of the La Turque vineyard in 1980 from Monsieur Battier of Vidal-Fleury, who turned up one day in the vineyards with a sale proposal. Marius felt that wine was not selling as well as his vegetables, and that he had enough on his plate without additional responsibility.

Marius knows every centimetre of his vines and their ways. Climb the Chemin de la Côte Brune nearly to the top and walk down into the vineyard. Apart from appreciating its slope, one of the steepest of any in Côte-Rôtie, one can see clearly the heavy scree of broken flat rock which litters the surface. This is *terre forte*: soil which contributes power and depth to wine. The Syrah vines here are not those of Mauves (a variety well-recognised locally) but rather a variant which gives thicker-skinned berries and looser clusters, so better aeration and less tendency to rot.

The older vines are pruned *en guyot*, with one cane of four to seven eyes, depending on the vine, the weather and the growth pattern, with a two-eyed spur left for the following year. Pruning is a skilled amalgam of craft and judgement – it is the last few eyes at the end of each cane which are most fruitful, so too severe a pruning in years where the grape set is poor means reduced yields, whereas too generous an allowance means possible dilution if you don't remove excess bunches later on. The amount of fruit per vine is the important measure – one plant can only properly ripen so much; if you try to coax it further, you lose fruit concentration.

When the time comes, Marius invariably harvests his Côte Brune fruit in the morning, so it is cool when it arrives at the cellar – an inconspicuous breeze-block shed attached to the back of the house. Probably originally designed for cool storage of fruit and vegetables, it has an uneven earth floor on which are ranged several rows of very old casks. Their wood has long since lost its hue and, like Marius, given up any pretence of youth and turned gently grey with age.

Even after a lifetime's experience, Marius naïvely refuses to recognise that some people seem quite incapable of making decent wine: "if you have ripe, healthy grapes, you have to do something special to make poor wine". Once in a cement *cuve*, his own fruit is crushed

with boots. "Before, we didn't have boots and people would put a knife in the *cuve* as a 'joke' so we cut our feet". Albert Dervieux, with whom Marius used to harvest, was apparently tougher and always used bare feet. The first night there is a pumping-over without aeration – to mix up the crush – another the following day with aeration to make sure fermentation is as even as possible. Because both *cuverie* and crop are cold, there are some 48 hours' maceration before the yeasts (bought ones, surprisingly for this traditionalist) get to work which, in Marius' view, gives excellent extraction.

This, and an 18–20 day slow *cuvaison*, contribute significantly to the fleshy richness and complexity of Marius' wine. Also, since the press-wine (added back immediately) contains sugar, the alcoholic fermentation is further prolonged into cask; sometimes it even dribbles on into November.

There is no new wood: "this has only been fashionable since the young went to oenological school in Beaune; Burgundy and Bordeaux are all new casks – it's an illness!", Marius avers, adding "what good is it to change what is good?"

After a first racking in February/March,

work on the wines parallels that in the vineyards: racking again at flowering and once more at *veraison*. In September, Marius allows himself a little holiday, in the mountains near Briançon, but returns, with his wife, every eight days to top up the casks. These are then left until March of the second year when they are adjusted for sulphur dioxide, fined as analysis dictates with fresh egg whites ("I've never used powdered egg-white") and bottled, cask by cask, by hand.

It takes Marius three and a half hours to bottle a 228-litre cask, so he fills 18 bottles at a time then bungs the cask up, rests, and starts again. Incidentally, the egg yolks are not wasted – his wife turns them into vanilla ice-cream for their grandson.

Less vines to work and wine to make mean a little more time for relaxation: a coach-trip to Venice, perhaps...but never too far from the cellar.

As he contemplates half a century of marriage – he still gets the date wrong, which provokes his wife into a show of indignation and then both of them to laughter – Marius Gentaz should take quiet pride in the great pleasure that he has given thousands of wine-lovers for over 40 vintages.

APPELLATION	VINEYARD	DETAILS	AREA
COTE-ROTIE	COTE BRUNE	60+ yr old vines	0.42

DOMAINE JEAN-MICHEL GERIN

The Gerin family is well known in Côte-Rôtie circles. Alfred, Jean-Michel's father, erstwhile mayor of Ampuis and French Senator, was responsible for some less than fine wine from plateau plantings made with a consortium of American investors during the 1970s and 1980s. These did little to enhance the reputation of the appellation, of which he was then a leading figure.

Jean-Michel broke away from his father in 1990 and founded his own domaine from a mixture of his own plantings, family vines, rented land and purchases, mainly around grandiose new cellars at Verenay, but also with an important 2ha of Condrieu and some plateau Côtes du Rhône. Jean-Luc Colombo is consultant oenologist.

A didactic and indeed high-handed manner notwithstanding, Jean-Michel is turning out good, often excellent, Côte-Rôtie. It comes in two *cuvées*: Le Champin Seigneur, *élevé* in one-quarter each of new, first-, second- and third-year

casks; and some 5,000 bottles of the single-vineyard Les Grandes Places, which has 100% new wood. This vineyard, sloping steeply away from Verenay, imparts structure and depth from its thin, mica-schistous soil, helped by patches of 80-year-old vines.

There is no doubt in Jean-Michel's mind on the proper contribution of oak to the overall result: "there is much nonsense talked about wood – so many factors intervene, between cutting the oak and making the barrel; people think you should dry wood for three years in the open, but consider that every year the climate is different – more or less rain, heat, sunshine; you get a much more regular drying by heating in kilns." What matters to him is the taste the cask imparts, and for this the best is a strong charring.

In wet harvests such as 1993, it is essential to discard any rotten grapes before vatting. Many growers use a moving belt along which grapes pass before a team of sorters; Jean-Michel is

scathing: "sorting belts are unfeasible and don't work"; the only way of achieving this is to sort in the vineyard, as the grapes are picked. Many growers who use belts successfully would disagree, arguing that, however carefully performed, vineyard sorting is bound to be crude and incomplete.

Colombo's lines of vinification are designed to maximise polyphenolic extraction – basically tannins and pigments. This signals a month of *cuvaison* at high temperatures ("up to 35°C – no problem") as much *pigeage* as is possible with narrow-topped *inox cuves*, a *saignée de cuve* in dilute vintages to restore a more favourable liquid:solid ratio, minimum sulphur dioxide throughout and malolactic in cask rather than in *cuve*. After 14–20 months, depending on the character of the vintage, the wines are bottled. Early bottlings are likely to be filtered; the norm is no filtering.

The wines are individual in style, hallmarked by sweet, plummy fruit with soft, round tannins. They show none of the hard, aggressive tannin so often found in young Côte-Rôtie in the 1970s and 1980s – usually the product of under-ripe stems, over-extraction and too long a stay in old wood, irrespective of the vintage. The Grandes Places tends to start out dominated by new wood and to have a much slower evolution than the fleshier, more easy-drinking Le Champin Seigneur. The wines tend to show well in blind tastings, although for purists they might seem rather too *tendre* and accessible. A good source, if you like this style.

APPELLATION	VINEYARD	DETAILS	AREA
COTE-ROTIE	LES GRANDES PLACES	Verenay; part 80+ part 8 yr old vines	1.50
COTE-ROTIE		Several lieu-dits, vines 2–80.	3.50
CONDRIEU		Part south of Coteau de Chery; part near Verin; vines 6–9 yrs old. Sold as "Coteau de la Loye"	2.00
COTES DU RHONE	LA BROSSE	Plateau vines, above Ampuis, opposite village of Boucharey	1.00
		TOTAL (hectares):	8.00

ETABLISSEMENTS GUIGAL

The story of this remarkable house began when Etienne Guigal left Vidal-Fleury in 1946, having worked his way up since 1927 from cellar-hand to cellar-master, to found his own wine business in Ampuis, a mere few hundred yards away. This prospered, quietly but undramatically, until Etienne was joined by his son Marcel in 1961. In the early 1980s, it simply took off.

Etienne, who died in 1988, was a charming, warm-hearted man, who would welcome the increasing tide of visitors to his cellars with old-fashioned courtesy, invariably dressed as a French version of the English country squire, with a dissonant *casquette* apparently glued to his head. He took immense, quiet pride in the achievements of Marcel and his wife Bernadette. Now his grandson, fresh from studies in Bordeaux, has joined his father; so there is once again an Etienne Guigal in Ampuis.

Marcel Guigal's phenomenal success is due to an amalgam of hard work, single-minded purpose, enormous wine-making talent and an unquestionable flair for the market. On a wider level, his success is responsible for the renaissance of Côte-Rôtie.

He attributes his skills to his father – "my best teacher" – whom he regarded as a genius with red wine. Although the reds remain the flagship of the house, the whites have improved dramatically in recent years, headed by an invariably thrilling Condrieu.

In 1986, the business expanded significantly with the acquisition – after hot competition – of Etienne's old employer, Maison Vidal-Fleury, from Joseph Vidal-Fleury's widow. This not only increased Marcel's market profile, but added valuable vineyards to the portfolio, in particular Côte-Rôtie's La Turque and La Chatillone. Etienne Guigal was now owner, not employee, at Vidal-Fleury.

In 1995, the Guigals bought the crumbling Château d'Ampuis, opposite

Marcel Guigal beside the specially carved cask of his father, Etienne.

René Rostaing's house, down by the river, which they plan to restore over the next few years.

Although the two houses continue to operate independently, there is a strong measure of integration and one suspects, though nothing is vouchsafed, common sourcing. Where there is overlap, the *négociant* wines have a marked similarity and are of good to excellent quality.

Although he vinifies one-third of each appellation, Guigal owns only 12ha of Côte-Rôtie (out of a planted total of 200ha) and 2ha of "good vines" at Condrieu (out of 100ha), bought in 1994. To make the Condrieu and Côte-Rôtie Brune et Blonde *cuvées*, grapes – never juice or wine – are bought from 104 small growers.

Apart from an excellent Côtes du Rhône Blanc, the white Rhône

appellations are represented by Condrieu and Hermitage – this last entirely from purchased grapes. There are some 70,000 bottles of the former – by far the largest output in the appellation – rather less of the latter.

Their vinification reflects their style: the Condrieu – because in Marcel's view it lacks inherent structure – is vinified one-third in new oak. He has also been using cryo-extraction recently, with spectacular results. This process decreases the volume of juice by 20%, by removing water, not flavour, and thus markedly increases concentration.

The Hermitage Blanc (95% Marsanne, 5% Roussanne) with its naturally firm, almost red-wine constitution, needs no such strengthening; so it gets no new oak but spends eight months, following malolactic, in last year's Condrieu casks.

It is bottled after 18 months' *élevage*, in contrast to the Condrieu which is bottled early, in May or June following the vintage, to preserve its powerful fruit aromas and flavours.

It is one of the top wines of the appellation – packed with concentrated, exuberant fruit – and best drunk within a few years of release. As Marcel Guigal puts it: "the best bottle of Condrieu is the first, the best of Côte-Rôtie the last".

Côte-Rôtie apart, northern reds are represented by a Hermitage, mainly from the Diognières *climat*, with additions from Beaumes, Méal, Peléat and Bessards – all vinified separately and assembled much later. "I would like most of it to be from Bessards", Marcel admits, "but it isn't!" While carefully made from excellent raw material, the bottled wine often seems to suffer from too long in wood, showing signs of premature drying out. Earlier bottling would make a noticeable difference.

Guigal's battle-engine is an exemplary Côtes du Rhône, which far transcends its appellation. Although produced in large volume it is accorded all the care of a Côte-Rôtie, including a period in small wood. The secret lies in low yields and in the blend: limiting Grenache to around half, and using a quarter each of Syrah and Mourvèdre. This gives a depth and structure which allow the wine to age well over a decade in vintages such as 1990. For Marcel, the wine is also a bargaining chip with wine buyers – your allocation of the three prized Côte-Rôtie *crus* depends as much as anything on how much Côtes du Rhône you absorb.

As for the southern red appellations – Gigondas and Châteauneuf – these are matured in larger wooden *foudres* for three years (up to four for the Châteauneuf), since their high Grenache content evolves too rapidly in smaller casks. The Châteauneuf is usually a reliable example, with 85% of 50-plus-year-old vine Grenache, with a touch of Syrah and Mourvèdre, and dabs of Cinsaut, etc.

These are good, sometimes excellent, wines but such long wood-ageing often gives a grainy, desiccated feel, as with the 1990 Gigondas and Châteauneuf, both of which had irredeemably hard edges. Again, earlier bottling would preserve the fruit with which the wines clearly started.

However, it is with his three single-vineyard Côte-Rôties, La Mouline, La Landonne and La Turque, that Marcel has made his reputation and incidentally taught an international market, blinkered by Bordeaux, to appreciate great Côte-Rôtie. These are intense, massively extracted, powerful and yet supremely

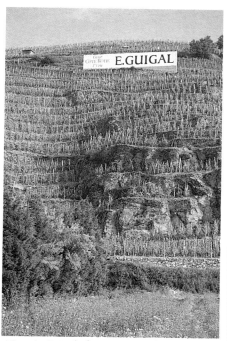

Vines in Guigal's famous La Mouline vineyard.

elegant wines, matured for 42 months – irrespective of the vintage – in 100% new Allier and Nevers casks – a proceeding which a "traditionalist" café society of Ampuis stigmatises as the antithesis of Côte-Rôtie. However, visit others growers and it is precisely these bottles that you find tucked away in a corner of their cellars awaiting a special occasion.

Each *cuvée* reflects an individual *terroir* and is vinified to extract this typicity. La Mouline, from 1ha in the Côte Blonde acquired in 1965, first appeared under the Guigal label in 1966. It is not a *lieu-dit* on the *cadastre*, rather a single parcel of vines within the larger *lieu-dit* "Côte Blonde". Marcel Guigal estimates that the vines average 60 years of age – most were planted just after the phylloxera and few have been uprooted since. When one dies or becomes diseased, it is simply replaced – *repiqueage*.

About 11% of Viognier is complanted in the vineyard, contributing, with the lighter soils of the Côte Blonde, to the wine's considerable elegance. There is no punching down of the grape mass during fermentation: this would extract too much tannin; rather, a regular pumping over of juice in order to keep the cap moist and extract finesse.

La Turque is the most recent of the three, made from a hectare on the Côte Brune, planted by Pierre Gaillard from cleared land in 1982 when he was at Vidal-Fleury. It contains 5% of Viognier. Once again, the name is not recognised

as a *lieu-dit*, although known as such in the past, as the terraces were unplanted when the *cadastre* was delimited in 1957. Rather it is legally a *marque déposée* – a brand name. However, the wine comes only from this single plot – on a superb slope, with south exposure, at the point which divides the Côte Brune from the Côte Blonde.

This vineyard was offered to Marius Gentaz by Monsieur Battier of Vidal-Fleury in 1980, but he turned it down since his vegetables and fruit were at the time better business than wine. So Vidal-Fleury bought it in 1981. When the first *cuvée* was made in 1984, those who tasted it – including Marcel Guigal – judged it the best of all the Vidal-Fleury wines, even though the vines were then only three years old and still a year away from their fourth flowering and thus entitlement to the appellation.

As these are still relatively young vines, Marcel ferments in a closed *cuve* with an automatic *pigeage* to extract fat and softness, rather than an open fermenter which would impart harsher tannins and thereby destroy the wine's balance. The first La Turque appeared, to universal acclaim, in 1985 – a masterly amalgam of depth and finesse, remarkable for its equilibrium and extract from such youthful vines.

La Landonne is perhaps the most magisterial of this spectacular trio. In contrast to La Turque, for which the Rhône-loving public had been well prepared, and to La Mouline, which was already a seasoned campaigner, it appeared without great trumpeting in the five-star 1978 vintage.

Its provenance – 2ha on the Côte Brune, replanted mostly in 1974 (also 1986 and 1990) – presented a problem of nomenclature, since the *cadastre* had unfortunately divided the *lieu-dit* in two – only 0.3ha of Guigal's original holding were properly in La Landonne, the rest being in the adjoining *climat*. A dispensation was eventually granted to use the name La Landonne for the entire *cuvée*.

With the acquisition of Vidal-Fleury came a further slice of the Landonne vineyard – La Petite Landonne. This concave, south-facing slope gives even better quality than the rest, according to Marcel, adding further depth to an already remarkable wine. Vinification is in a special, closed vat which operates a continuous *remontage* to obtain maximum extraction from the fruit.

The absence of Viognier in this vineyard and the stronger, ferruginous soil gives the wine a youthful austerity which needs more time than the others to evolve. However, when it finally decides to sing – what music!

These three *cuvées* are among the world's most compelling wines. Although made for longevity (the 15-year vintage port rule would not see the greatest Landonnes properly mature) they are so finely crafted as to be approachable after relatively few years in bottle. They are also as rare as Romanée-Conti: La Mouline and La Turque each produce around 5,000 bottles in a reasonable vintage; La Landonne 8–8,500 rising to 9,000 as Marcel managed to acquire a patch more land in 1994.

Now that the early dissent and thinly disguised jealousy of Guigal's success have died down, the Ampuis wine community realises the extent to which Côte-Rôtie's very survival and the present strength of its fortunes is due to the talent and marketing flair of Marcel Guigal and his late father. While a few growers still resent the continuing media attention to Guigal, and lament the fact that people won't explore other Côte-Rôties, there is widespread respect and admiration for their achievements.

Their success is undoubted. While Marcel may grumble to visitors about the 12% increase his carton supplier is demanding, or the price of corks, one only has to look around to see that things are going well. The Guigal street frontage, blackened by a constant stream of heavy traffic double-de-clutching on the corner opposite the church, may be dreary and functional, probably designed by someone whose favourite shape was square, but descend through the old bottling and despatch hall to the cellars beneath, and you enter a palace of design and prosperity. A distinct air of Monsieur Hulot pervades the place, with gadgets everywhere: great transparent doors whizz upwards when you approach

them, a splendidly space-aged panel monitors a battery of 45 stainless steel *cuves*, and a computer console controls what Marcel describes as the best fermentation technology in France – if you ask for 33% you get 33, not 32.5 or 34. Beware – technology is servant not master here and will never take over Marcel's supreme feel for grapes and how best to vinify them.

The *pièce de resistance* is an innocuous tunnel which was cut in the late 1980s to link the main cellar with the old Vidal-Fleury cellars across the road. Above, a mere 1.5 metres separates the precious barrels from one of the region's busiest (and noisiest) roads, carrying freight juggernauts and tourists south. Constructed at enormous expense by the Channel Tunnel engineers (nothing but the best), it is intended to remain vibration-free, but there are rumours of cracks....!

While *vignerons* of lesser fibre would be weakened by such a gratifying tidal wave of cash into taking long, exotic holidays, Marcel and Bernadette Guigal stray little from Ampuis – the best chefs invariably stay at their ovens. Visit (if you are allowed) and you will probably find a couple of groups being shown round, while someone else waits in the small

office to talk to Marcel. At times their cramped house-cum-office appears close to mayhem – people everywhere, bells ringing, a couple of phones going, and Bernadette lifting another to put it down immediately without bothering to identify the caller on the other end. But, once admitted, the reception is warm and genuine – clients are the most important part of the business and are well looked after.

The reception facilities now boast a helicopter pad on the far side of the vast garden, which backs down to the railway line – "we have several requests each week for landing facilities", Marcel adds, in case you should question the need. Here, money has been poured into a splendid, beautifully crafted neo-Roman extravaganza – columns, pediments and an illuminated swimming pool, backed on its southern side by the new cellar building. Opulent, but highly stylish. Perhaps, when the cash-box is next unlocked, Marcel might spare a thought for his long-suffering and supremely diplomatic Bernadette (now the châtelaine of Ampuis) and arrange for an assistant to help with the filing and letter-writing, and to cope with the human visitor-flood. "But you see", he explains, "we try to remain a family business".

APPELLATION	VINEYARD	DETAILS		AREA
COTE-ROTIE	COTE BLONDE – "LA MOULINE"	60+ yr old vines; trade-mark, not a lieu-dit; (lieu-dit is "Cote Blonde"); first release 1966; c 11% Viognier		1.00
COTE-ROTIE	COTE BRUNE – "LA TURQUE"	Vines planted 1981; first release 1985; 4–5% Viognier; lieu-dit is "Cote Brune"		1.00
COTE-ROTIE	LA LANDONNE	Planted 1974, first release 1978. No Viognier; lieu-dit is "La Landonne"		2.00
COTE-ROTIE	Various			8.00
CONDRIEU				2.00
		TOTAL (hectares):		14.00

DOMAINE JAMET

This domaine evolved, as did many in the northern Rhône, from a polyculture which included grapes grown for sale to the larger *négociants* – Jaboulet, Chapoutier and Delas – into a wine monoculture which today sells all its produce in bottle.

Joseph Jamet, now in his late 60s and theoretically retired, ceded charge to his sons Jean-Luc and Jean-Paul (both in their 30s), in the mid-1980s.

They planted 4ha during that decade to bring the total holding to 6ha, spread over 19 separate plots varying in size from 15 ares to just over a hectare.

They see adapting graft and root-stock to each soil-type as an essential pre-requisite to growing properly ripe, balanced, grapes. Some of their vines are at 300 metres altitude, others at the base of hillsides; so *terroirs* differ greatly and it clearly doesn't make sense just to buy any grafts and plant them out. What matters is even ripening with sensible yields and loose clusters to ensure good bunch aeration and thus minimal rot. Short-pruning and hours of careful debudding, foliage removal and where necessary, crop thinning ultimately improve the quality of fruit delivered to

Jean-Paul to vinify.

The first Jean-Paul and Jean-Luc wine appeared in 1986. Joseph has kept 40 ares of vines for his retirement income, and this wine continues to be sold under his personal label; otherwise, there is just a single Côte-Rôtie bottling.

The style seems to have settled down into wine with, characteristically, plenty of flesh and fruit, well-judged oak (15-20% new Allier) and moderate structure. Nothing of the old, heavy, rustic mould, but wines which drink well after 3–4 years in bottle and have the depth and structure to carry on for many more. Even in awkward vintages – 1987, for example – the Jamets manage to turn out something with clean lines and attractive complexity. There is a brand-new cellar now, prominent behind the family house at Le Vallin, in the hinterland well away from Ampuis' bustle and traffic, and there should be a new press soon, to replace the long-serving wooden vertical screw.

In the cellar below, rows of *demi-muids* and *pièces* receive the young wine, preferably before its malolactic ("the harmony is better if the malo takes place in wood") and mature it for 18–24 months – deliberately nearer 18 months now there is more small wood. The wines are bottled unfiltered, using an ancient filler, in one go – a relatively rare occurrence for Côte-Rôtie.

The only point of doubt is whether the Jamets' inflexible policy of not de-stemming makes sense in naturally less ripe years. They are aware of the risks they run of extracting herbaceous, green, bitter flavours and take care to avoid

APPELLATION	VINEYARD	DETAILS	AREA
COTE-ROTIE	LANCEMENT	Planted 1988; top of Coteaux, but not plateau	0.75
COTE-ROTIE	CHAVAROCHE	0.75 planted 1980–83; 0.35 planted 1991	1.10
COTE-ROTIE	LE TRUCHET	Planted 1973	0.70
COTE-ROTIE	FONJEAN	Planted 1991	0.60
COTE-ROTIE	COTE BRUNE	½: 50 yrs+; ½ 5–11 yrs	0.40
COTE-ROTIE	BONNIVIER	Top of Coteaux; 25+	0.60
COTE-ROTIE	MORNACHON	300 metres altitude; planted 1988; surrounded by trees; thin schistous soils onto friable rock	0.90
COTE-ROTIE	LES MOUTONNES	Foot of Coteaux; ¾ planted 1980; ¼ 1940	0.50
COTE-ROTIE	LA LANDONNE	Planted 1986/7	0.40
COTE-ROTIE	VERENAY	Planted 1992	0.15
		TOTAL (hectares):	6.05

them. Tasting a range of 1993s from both stemmed and de-stemmed lots suggests that this isn't doing any noticeable harm. If there were to be any stemminess, it would certainly show in a rainy vintage such as this. Overall, the results are excellent: mid-weight Côte-Rôties of considerable charm.

DOMAINE JASMIN

It all started with Robert Jasmin's great-grandfather, who arrived from Champagne to be cook at the Château d'Ampuis. He purchased a hectare of vines, which his son took over; this grew to 1.5ha when in turn his son, Robert's father, took over in 1935. In 1960 Robert joined in, building up the estate to its present 4ha. Since 1984 Robert and Josette Jasmin's son, Patrick, has worked with his father. Robert is a large, friendly man, with a lamentable sense of time, dubbed by friends variously "the Jean Gabin of Côte-Rôtie" – a comment on his appearance – and "the fugitive", because he is never at home when you call!

This is a good example of how a small domaine operates, having evolved from a mixed culture of vines and fruit. There is no question of expensive, high-tech equipment, nor of grand cellars full of new casks, rather of using what you have intelligently and following, with growing confidence, the methods that have worked well for a couple of generations.

You certainly won't find an oenologist sticking his analytical nose in the Jasmin vats and casks: "I do things just as grandfather did them; some years I lack a bit of colour" Robert admits candidly – probably a consequence of an inflexible policy of leaving stems, which absorb colour, in the vats. Since the Jasmins have no de-stemmer, there is no choice. The vinification is a touch idiosyncratic, in that there are just four *remontages*, two before and two after fermentation. This, with a submerged cap, leads to rather less extraction than would more frequent

Robert Jasmin.

pumping over. Nor is there any means of cooling the must, should temperatures climb; when the solid cement *cuves* get near to 30°C, they just draw off and recycle the juice, in the hope that this will cool it.

The Jasmins sell only one Côte-Rôtie , an *assemblage* of two separately vinified parts – one from old vines in the Côtes Baudin and Blonde, the other a mixture of younger and middle-aged vines in Baleyat and the Coteau de Tupin. The Coteau de Turpin regularly has one degree of potential alcohol less at harvest than the Baleyat, but one degree more acidity, which explains the good fresh feel of the final wine.

Robert feels strongly that new wood is "standardising all the wines of France", so uses no more than 10% a year, to keep the cask population to a manageable average age. According to what is available, *élevage is* roughly half in cask and half in 600-litre *demi-muids*. There are three rackings in the first year, and *assemblage* is carried out at the second, which takes place in May.

The wine is bottled by Jean-Luc Colombo's team in two main lots, one after 15 months in wood, the other after 24 months. "We used not to sell before three years; then it was two; now we have to bottle at 15 months – for the export market".

A pity, since the extra cask age undoubtedly improves the wine. His US importer manages wisely to delay the bottling until September, and has persuaded Robert and Patrick to suppress the customary plate-filtration.

Robert and Patrick have been unjustly criticised, notably by one American writer, for allegedly selling two different *cuvées* – one for their long-standing UK importer, another for the rest. This has never been the case, although Robert has always kept back two *pièces of* the best Côte Blonde and Côte Baudin for himself, of which a case or so have been allocated as a personal privilege to both his US and his UK importers – a different matter altogether.

Further confusion was caused by Robert's use of the Chevalier d'Ampuis attribution on his labels, giving rise to the impression that this was something special. In fact, 0.37ha of Jasmin vines originally belonged to the Château

APPELLATION	VINEYARD	DETAILS	AREA
COTE-ROTIE	LA CHEVALIERE	35 yr.old vines	0.37
COTE-ROTIE	LES MOUTONNES & COTE BAUDIN	60+ yr old vines	0.30
COTE-ROTIE		2 parcelles in between Moutonnes in Baudin; 25–30 yr old vines	0.40
COTE-ROTIE	LE BALEYAT	Defriche 1960; planted 1960–61	1.00
COTE-ROTIE	COTE BLONDE	La Garde ; 25 yr old vines	0.80
COTE-ROTIE	COTEAUX DE TUPIN	12 yr old vines	0.70
COTE-ROTIE	BALEYAT	15 yr old vines	0.30
COTE-ROTIE	BAUDIN	2 yr old vines	0.12
		TOTAL (hectares):	3.99

d'Ampuis and are in the no longer officially recognised *lieu-dit*, La Chevalière. The use of the designation was disallowed from 1984 as the entire *cuvée* does not come from this particular plot. Robert could register the name as a trade-mark and continue to use it, but doesn't seem attracted by the idea.

Despite these misunderstandings, the Jasmin Côte-Rôtie is a supremely well-crafted wine, always at the elegant end of the appellation's wide spectrum. An apparent lack of colour in some vintages does not imply a lack of fruit, although yields turn around the 38–39hl/ha mark. The mix of firmer Côte Brune wine from these stronger soils, with a more elegant fraction from the higher clay soils of the southerly part of the Côte Blonde,

produces wine which has finesse from the start, yet in the best vintages, ages well, deepening with time. Memories of sublime 1971s, 1976s and 1978s drunk during the late 1980s testify to their lasting quality.

The lasting impression of visits *chez* Jasmin, in their modest house by the level crossing in Ampuis is, perhaps more than the fine wine, the *joie-de-vivre* and friendliness of Robert and his wife Josette.

This is a close-knit family; son Patrick and his wife are next door, with their new daughter, Caroline (with whom Robert is clearly besotted), and his sister, Geneviève, proprietor of a successful flower shop in Condrieu's main square. Robert and Josette enjoy life, the contacts and the pleasure their wine entrains.

DOMAINE MICHEL OGIER

Michel Ogier, a smiling, friendly middle-aged man, runs a fine small *exploitation* from a newish house on the edge of Ampuis below the railway line. Not a high-profile estate by any means, but a source of intelligently-crafted wines including a remarkably good *vin de pays*, La Rosine, made from 0.6ha of Syrah planted on what ought to be AOC Côte-Rôtie soil.

With his wife's vineyards, Michel has 2.57ha, with enough old vines to add depth and complexity to the final *cuvée*. In 1980, after years of selling the crop to Chapoutier and Guigal, he decided to concentrate on the vineyards rather than the apricot and cherry trees, and set about equipping himself for life as a *vigneron*.

In times past most growers had fruit trees and vegetables as well as vines – you only needed a horse for ploughing. Now, if you intend making and bottle your own wine, you need *cuves*, a press, vats and somewhere to store everything. So the decision to change tack took courage – and cash.

While the younger vines are pruned *en gobelet*, Michel reckons that his oldest vines are "le vrai Syrah de Mauves", which must be pruned *en guyot* if they are to fruit at all. Pruning is short – better this than to cull bunches later on. When harvest comes round, he reaps the benefit of being small-scale by harvesting in three days – 25 friends turn up to help – so that he can pick quickly if rain is forecast, as in 1993.

From the *grandes lignes* of vinification, one would expect massively structured wines with enough muscle to bend a railway track. What you find are supremely soft tannins and silky elegance – the Volnays of the appellation perhaps;

a striking contrast to the muscle-bound, heavily extracted, body builders of some other growers.

However, there is no stinting on either *cuvaison* (15 days in square *inox cuves* with a system of chains to hold down the cap, and temperatures which rise to 35°C) or on *élevage*: 18 months or so entirely in *pièces* – even for the *vin de pays* – of which 20% are new Tronçais oak. The three principal lots are assembled just before bottling, fined and lightly earth-filtered.

Michel's wine sells out rapidly – especially "my Rosine" to an appreciative and obviously faithful clientele. There are still a few cherry trees to fill in the time, but the heart of this domaine is firmly in the cellars below, rather than in the branches above.

APPELLATION	VINEYARD	DETAILS	AREA
COTE-ROTIE	ROZIER	40+ yr old vines	0.32
COTE-ROTIE	LANCEMENT	20% 60+yrs; 80% 16 yrs.	1.30
COTE-ROTIE	LE CHAMPIN	Young vines	0.35
VIN DE PAYS, COLLINES RHODANIENNES	LA ROSINE	Syrah, 7 yrs old	0.60
		TOTAL (hectares):	2.57

DOMAINE RENE ROSTAING

Whatever else most wine-makers may be, they are rarely talented businessmen. René Rostaing is an exception. Although he professes his heart to be in his grand new cellar, complete with six new state-of-the-art auto-vinificators, he will also admit that this was financed not from wine, but from his property management company, 4km away in Condrieu. Here, flats are let and buildings managed to sustain his 6.4ha of Côte-Rôtie and 0.2ha of Condrieu.

This is not to imply that the domaine is not self-supporting; rather, that the lean, aggressively enterprising Rostaing believes that small wine holdings need outside sources of capital for growth and stability. However, for him, unsolicited fortune has played a significant hand since he started with 0.22ha on the Côte Blonde and 0.25ha in La Landonne in 1971.

In 1990, just before the vintage, his father-in-law, Albert Dervieux-Thaize, for 33 years Président of the Côte-Rôtie growers' association, retired, 'ceding to René *en fermage* a fine trio of vineyards. These 3.5ha are superbly sited in Fongent, La Garde and La Viallière and contain a good proportion – especially Viallière – of ancient vines.

When in 1993 his uncle Marius Gentaz-Dervieux conveniently followed suit, a further 1.2ha of very old vines arrived on the same arrangement. No amount of hard work could possibly bring such good fortune – a fact which René tends to overlook when disparaging the efforts of other *vignerons*, equally hard-working, but distinctly less favoured.

Rostaing's wines are made with care and thought. It is one of wine's universal, yet fascinating, conundrums that, of two growers both making fine wine, one will set forth a cogent justification for his way of working, while his neighbour will argue equally plausibly for doing more or less the opposite.

Rostaing argues forcibly for his *cuves auto-pigeantes* – a species of vinous food-processor comprising a closed vat, rotatable to facilitate extraction and avoid the inconvenience of managing a cap of grape solids – maintaining that he gets more complete extraction over the three weeks of *cuvaison* than with normal *pigeage*. Others would argue that the grape and *terroir* typicity are blurred by this process, and that the final tannin balance is less than ideal.

It must be said that this long *cuvaison*, including three to four days at 34–37°C to extract maximum anthocyanins (colour pigments), with 100% de-stemming for the Côte-Rôtie "generique" and 50% for the La Landonne, produces deeply coloured wines – but no more so than those of (for example) Guigal, Clusel-Roch or Gerin. There are plenty of well-developed, ripe, soft-fruit flavours, but the wines sometimes lack the structure and concentration one seeks in top Côte-Rôtie. Perhaps a mix of part auto-*pigeante* and part open-vat fermentation would strike a better equilibrium.

The La Landonne *cuvée*, from parcels of vines in La Landonne and La Rozier, is the pick of this cellar. There may be some argument as to whether a wine from a named *lieu-dit* should get half its fruit from another vineyard, albeit one adjoining and with similar soils, but for the moment that's how it is.

There are also *cuvées* labelled "Côte Blonde" and "Viallière" – this last from Albert Dervieux's vines. In 1992, all the Landonne and Viallière fruit went into the generic Côte-Rôtie, which undoubtedly benefited from this extra support.

There are two bottlings of this *cuvée*, and one of the others. None is filtered: "I tried filtration once, in 1988 – and all the journalists wrote that Rostaing filters his wine". There is much plausibility in the view that filtering is pointless if analysis shows that there are no active bacteria left; why process a wine unnecessarily?

This is a sound, if individual, source of Côte-Rôtie – and also of a respectable young-vine Condrieu.

APPELLATION	VINEYARD	DETAILS	AREA
CONDRIEU			0.20
COTE-ROTIE	COTE BLONDE	65 yr old vines	0.23
COTE-ROTIE	COTE BRUNE	Planted 1970; ex-Albert Dervieux-Thaize	0.23
COTE-ROTIE	COTE BLONDE	2 parcels – 0.08 is 100% Viognier	0.22
COTE-ROTIE	COTE BRUNE	30 yr old vines	0.20
COTE-ROTIE	COTE BRUNE	Planted by RR – young vines	0.20
COTE-ROTIE	FONJEAN	Also spelt Fongent; Albert D-T's vines – 23 yrs old	1.00
COTE-ROTIE	COTE BRUNE	Marius Gentaz-Dervieux's vines; 70+ ; same sector as La Turque	0.35
COTE-ROTIE	LA LANDONNE	50+ yr old vines	0.45
COTE-ROTIE	LA LANDONNE	Planted by RR	0.30
COTE-ROTIE	LA LANDONNE	Marius G-D's vines; 60+	0.28
COTE-ROTIE	LA VIALLIERE	Albert D-T's vines; 80+;	0.40
COTE-ROTIE	LA VIALLIERE	Planted by RR; next to Champet vines; 10 yrs old	0.55
COTE-ROTIE	LE PLOMB	Plateau vines 40+	0.40
COTE-ROTIE	LEYAT	Marius G-D's vines; 35+	0.50
COTE-ROTIE	LEYAT	Albert D-T's vines; 70+	0.10
COTE-ROTIE		Plateau, secteur Boucharey; 30+	1.00
		TOTAL (hectares):	6.61

DOMAINE L DE VALLOUIT

This is an underrated estate, quietly turning out a competent quiver of northern Rhônes, spiced by more than occasional flashes of brilliance. The present head of the firm, Louis de Vallouit, is an ex-French athlete and Monte Carlo rally driver. He runs his operation from old-fashioned cellars, fronted by an incongruous little shop, near the municipal swimming-pool in the pedestrian town of St-Vallier, 15km north of Tain on the Rhône's east bank, where he was born in 1936. His undimmed passion for cars – his first act on leaving the army was to buy a sports car – is now indulged by karting which his wife, who also works in the firm, refuses to watch, apparently content to let him spend the weekend rocketing round race-tracks at 100 miles per hour.

His wines, however, appear at a more moderate rate of speed, from 30 well-sited hectares spread between Côte-Rôtie and Montpellier as well as from some *négociant* activity. His father had bought wine from Albert Dervieux since 1925 and it was Dervieux who helped him buy the first plot of Côte Blonde, opposite Guigal's cellars, in 1961. Gradually more terraces were acquired, bringing the total holding to 10ha.

In 1990, Louis bought the 11th-century Château de Châteaubourg, a magnificent, exaggerated edifice, perched on a rock between Mauves and St-Péray. This is now de Vallouit's flagship sales outlet, capturing visitors who trundle up and down the Rhône on the RN86.

Louis is also the firm's winemaker. Trained at Beaune and Dijon, "where I learned about short *cuvaisons*", he brooks little compromise on tradition: "I started with traditional methods, and haven't changed much". For him, what matters above all, is structure, which is what enables a wine to stay in balance and age gracefully. To demonstrate his point, he has kept a cask of Hermitage from the light 1974 vintage, which is offered for tasting blind. The wine, though faded and rather leathery, is still sound, retaining enough fruit to make it pleasurably drinkable.

Working with the naturally tannic Syrah and *terroirs* which tend to enhance tannins, Louis' main concern is establishing and keeping a tannin balance. A late harvest to ensure maximum berry and stem ripeness, fermentation in wooden vats, to increase fat and 15–20 days' *cuvaison* to extract substance and fix colour all play their part. The first pressing, and possibly the second, is blended back before maturation in *foudres, pièces* and *demi-muids*, with 5-15% of new wood.

Since the early 1980s, there has been a range of *cuvées spéciales*, all red: a Crozes Hermitage, from the Château de Larnage vineyards, St-Joseph, Cornas, a pair of Côte-Rôties, and a Hermitage from 90-year-old vines in the Clos des Greffières – which is apparently the oldest plot of vines on the hill.

These have 30–40 months in wood, 12–16 months longer than the standard *cuvées*. Louis de Vallouit argues that low yields and a vinification designed to impart body and balance can support such lengthy maturation. However, the bottled wines have a desiccated, woody flavour which suggests that, on the contrary, the promise and fruit evident early on is being destroyed by so long in cask. Bottling after 18 months or so would make a considerable difference.

The whites, headed by an excellent Condrieu, are subject to a long, light pressing, which amounts to a *macération pelliculaire*, before fermentation in wood or *cuve*. No stainless steel is used, since Louis de Vallouit believes that this is less neutral than people think.

Experiments have showed that the same wine clarified twice as quickly in wood than *inox* or fibre vat, a fact that Louis explains by static electricity and temperature differences between one part of the vat and another, which keep the lees in constant suspension; in wood, temperature differentials are much more attenuated. A novel theory, which should provoke some interesting reappraisal of stainless steel.

All de Vallouit whites spend six to eight months in two- to three-year-old-casks, with a touch of new wood (20%) for the Hermitage and Condrieu, and four to six weeks' *bâtonnage*. Low natural acidities means that these wines are sensitive to oxidation and maderization, hence the early bottling. Low yields (35–40hl/ha) help balance natural constituents and thus give the wines ageing potential in most vintages.

The regular *cuvées* are generally of sound quality and worth considering. However, it is the Condrieu and the *cuvées spéciales* – the majority of which are made from old vines – which really merit attention.

In cask, these show a sure touch – wines of excellent, sometimes stunning, quality. However, 30–40 months in wood compromises this youthful promise. They need much earlier bottling to conserve their richness and balance.

Vineyards: Louis de Vallouit was not prepared to provide details.

DOMAINE VIDAL FLEURY

As the street facade of its wedge-shaped headquarters at the northern end of Ampuis proclaims, this house was founded in 1781. Then, six years after the death of the last Vidal-Fleury, Joseph, in 1979, the firm was sold to Etienne and Marcel Guigal. Etienne had been trained by Joseph, who took him on in the 1920s, and the purchase fulfilled a long-cherished ambition.

The house is now under the direction of Jean-Pierre Rochias, an urbane, skilled winemaker. Despite vigorous denials, there remains the distinct feeling that communality of ownership means pooling of resources and that Vidal-Fleury is just another arm of Etablissements Guigal.

Indeed, both share the same vineyard team, and all the wines are vinified in the magnificent new Guigal facility. However, it is Rochias who makes the Vidal wines and Marcel Guigal his.

What is less credible is that there is no deliberate sharing of grape sources, especially for the distant appellations of the Southern Rhône, where doubling up would seem to be pointless; or that, should Marcel have a spare vat of this or that, it would not be offered to Jean-Pierre. What is beyond doubt is that the two marketing and distribution chains are entirely separate – different personnel, different importers, different labels and the rest.

After transferring La Turque to Guigal, Vidal-Fleury has 10ha of vines, all in Côte-Rôtie, including La Chatillonne – a 0.8ha plot of vines over 50 years old in the *lieu-dit* Côte Blonde, which is vinified and sold as a separate *cuvée*. Its *encépagement* comprises some 15% of field-mixed Viognier, which gives the wine an attractive elegance. The remaining 8ha produce around 40,000 bottles of Côte-Rôtie, matured in *pièces* and *foudres for* up to 30 months. The wine is good, without the sheer elegance and panache of Guigal's version.

Vidal-Fleury offer a comprehensive range of Rhônes, including excellent red and white Côtes du Rhône. The latter is from 50% Bourboulenc, 30% Viognier, 10% Clairette and 10% other varieties; the unusually high proportion of Viognier gives the wine aromatic elegance, while the Bourboulenc provides a crisp freshness, so often lacking in white Côtes du Rhône. The red blend is 50% Grenache, 30% Syrah plus 10% each of Mourvèdre and others. The house also produces a worthy Condrieu and one of the best (and most expensive) Muscat de Beaumes de Venise, now vintage-dated.

This is an upper-middle producer of Côte-Rôtie, and a dependably respectable source of other Rhône appellations.

APPELLATION	VINEYARD	DETAILS	AREA
COTE-ROTIE	LA CHATILLONNE	50+ yr old vines in lieu-dit Côte Blonde;	
		includes 15% Viognier	0.80
COTE-ROTIE		Several locations	9.20
		TOTAL (hectares):	10.00

CONDRIEU & CHATEAU GRILLET

Condrieu is one of the rarest, both in quality and quantity, of all France's great white wines. This has as much to do with the capricious Viognier grape from which it is made as with the smallness of the appellation (80ha in 1995), or the skill required to vinify it successfully. At its best, this remarkable wine combines at once a strikingly strong, yet elegant perfume with a powerfully individual flavour.

Taking its name from a corruption of "coin du ruisseau" (corner of the stream), and shoe-horned onto a small flat of land between the steep hillsides of the right bank and the Rhône itself, Condrieu sits on a great bend in the river as Ampuis' southern, and larger, neighbour. Although administratively a town, its compactness and community spirit give it the atmosphere of a village. Here the visitor finds, crunched into a maze of absurdly narrow streets, modest essential shopping, a sprinkling of restaurants and the Rhône's best wine-merchant – Christian Denoues' La Bouteillière – whose shelves stock most of the great Rhône producers (when

he can get stock to sell), plus some fine champagnes and clarets. The commune has recently splashed out on a new visitor centre, which opened in June 1994.

VIGNOBLE

When the appellation was created in 1940, Condrieu covered just three adjoining communes – Condrieu, St-Michel and Chavanay. Now, the *aire* stretches over 22km, encompassing seven communes, which are in three départements. From north to south the communes are: Condrieu (Rhône), Verin, St-Michel-sur-Rhône, Chavanay, St-Pierre de Boeuf, Malleval (all Loire) and Limony (Ardèche). Of 300 designated hectares, only 100 are currently in production. This represents a meteoric increase on the 8ha of 1965, however – which by 1986 had struggled to 20. As with Côte-Rôtie, Condrieu had flourished at the end of the 19th century; but the two great wars felled demand and forced disillusioned growers to look elsewhere for employment.

Things were bleak until the 1970s and 1980s, when increasing international interest persuaded a younger generation to take over and work these difficult vineyards, and tempted a new breed of commercially-minded entrepreneur to clear and replant disused terraces. Fear of an indiscriminate explosion of planting led the INAO to a complete revision of the appellation during the 1980s, principally designed to restrict production to suitable land – ie hillsides with *arzelle* soils – and to withdraw the appellation from sites with heavier clay soils on plateaus or on the valley floor.

While they were at it, they were misguidedly persuaded to increase the base yield from 30 to 37hl/ha – a level top growers would regard as incompatible with quality. In 1991 the local Syndicat, headed by Georges Vernay, reduced this to 35hl/ha and voluntarily suppressed the PLC – a derogation which extends this yield by 10% in abundant years. The possibility of allowing a yield of up to 40hl/ha where the vintage merits it, but

Late afternoon above Condrieu. Note the cherry tree – fruit growing supplements many a vigneron's income.

with a commensurate retrospective reduction in permitted yield for the previous vintage, is now under discussion.

ECONOMICS

The economic crises of the late 1980s and early 1990s took their toll on the growers. Younger enterprises, which started and indeed flourished during the 1980s, helped by a run of sound vintages ('83, '85, '88, '89) and world affluence which sky-rocketed prices, have particularly suffered. Many, encouraged by banks to borrow to buy land and capital equipment, are now having difficulty paying the interest, let alone the principal. Some have closed down – an example is Patrice Porte, a promising young grower who gave up an unequal struggle and sold his hectare of vines to Marcel Guigal in 1993 – while others teeter on the razor's edge. For the rest, prices have fallen to meet the market, a trend exacerbated by lower demand and the weak vintages of 1992 and 1993. The lesson is clear: high prices must be justified by quality.

A study of 18 *vignerons* in Côte-Rôtie and Condrieu in 1993 showed the base production cost of a bottle from these appellations to be between 47 and 83 francs – the precise figure being determined by number of employees, quality of cork used, etc. In Condrieu the 1994 ex-cellars price varied between 50 and 100-plus francs. Clearly, this margin leaves little latitude for negotiation in a depressed and competitive world market.

Although the Condrieu's 40 listed growers produce an average of 22,000 cases annually, a high proportion of this comes from three principal sources – Georges Vernay, Marcel Guigal and Delas Frères. The rest is the produce of small *superficies,* often as part of a family polyculture, including fruit and vegetables. For these growers, the *négociant* houses of Guigal, Delas, Chapoutier and Jaboulet have performed an important role in keeping them and the appellation alive: economically, by buying grapes, and in prestige from their high marketing profile.

VITICULTURE

A strong contributor to Condrieu's decline was the difficulty of working the steep, narrow, granitic terraces, often one or two vines wide, which rise sharply from the valley floor. Most are superbly exposed to the south and south-east where the morning sun quickly burns off any early humidity and where the strong evening sun cannot grill the vines. These terraces make uncomfortable offices – baking in the summer heat and freezing in icy winter winds.

Except for a few upper plateaus, only hand cultivation is possible. Despite sturdy, dry-stone retaining walls the fine sandy topsoil, *arzelle,* which is a seminal contributor to the wine's bouquet and character, is prone to erosion by heavy rain. The *vigneron* has then to collect it, carry it back up the hill and redistribute it. This, together with a grape which is infamously temperamental, susceptible to disease, and unpredictable in its yield has, not surprisingly, driven many would-be *viticulteurs* to choose the financial and physical comfort of an indoor job. Other growers prefer neglect: a walk through the vineyards finds many vines in a sorry state.

An unforeseen difficulty has been the appearance of a mutant strain of Viognier with entirely different visual and taste characteristics. While most is planted in the southern Côtes du Rhône, this heavy-cropping impostor has found its way to Condrieu. Georges Vernay identifies it by its unusual leaves and berries and has even counted a few plants in his own vineyards which he has top-grafted back to the true variety. The surreptitious export of cuttings since the war mean that there may also be substantial plantings of the alien outside France.

TASTE

Even if you manage to coax your Viognier vines into a reasonable harvest, the difficulty of turning it into decent wine is a test which many fail. An essential part of the grape's charm is its distinctive aroma. This courts a wide variety of descriptions – everything from "a mixture of Vouvray and Moselle with an element of Alpine flowers", through honeysuckle and peaches to "an impression of slightly unripe pears or of eating fruit near the pear skin", or "citrus expressed as candied peel". In essence, classic Viognier is marked by a strong element of dried fruit or apricot on the nose, a powerful dry flavour and a characteristic richness.

Balancing this precarious equation is a delicate business in which finely-judged harvesting and supremely careful vinification are paramount. It is all too easy to strive to preserve the marvellous Viognier aromas only to find that the palate is thin and fleshless, or to extract plenty of richness which usually leaves the wine lumpen and stripped of aroma. The aroma/flavour balance is critical, and it rests on a knife edge. While Chardonnay will respond uncomplainingly to a variety of winemaking incompetence, Viognier requires an intimate knowledge of ways and means and a fine feel for subtleties. Thus it is that many Condrieus lack the balance and finesse that make for real palatability.

HARVEST

This is especially important. Too early and you have thin, unbalanced wine, too late and you lose perfume and varietal flavour. If you are greedy or lazy and over-crop, then the wine loses all typicity and grip. Yields are decisive: up to 30hl/ha is compatible with top quality – even 35hl/ha in a great vintage. In Georges Vernay's words: "you must have 13 [% alcohol] natural". He also recommends only picking Viognier in the morning: this helps clarification.

Many growers will tell you that it was tradition to harvest late – often at All Saints in early November – and to make sweet wine. Indeed, but such late harvests only happened when maturity was poor. In marvellous vintages such as 1947 and 1949, picking would be over by September 20. In the 19th century, when Condrieu was little known outside the region, they might leave grapes on the vine and harvest *a l'assiette* – a plate under the bunch which was shaken to dislodge the super-ripe berries, but this was unusual.

VINIFICATION

Although, in the past, growers made both sweet and sparkling wines (though not together as an entity), most modern Condrieu is dry. The basics of vinification vary little from one producer to another: direct pressing, in a horizontal or pneumatic press, followed by 3-24 hours *débourbage* to settle out gross impurities. Some prefer to cool the juice at this stage, rather than to use anti-oxidant sulphur. Fermentation at 15-18°C (too hot and you lose aroma) may or may not be followed by malolactic fermentation, which reduces taste-acidity; some growers encourage malolactic, others suppress it, while many prefer to adapt to the character of the vintage. Acidities tend to be low in Condrieu (around 2.9g/litre). No-one seems to mind very much although the prevailing trend is to encourage malolactic in less ripe years to reduce green acidity and avoid it when natural acidity is at a premium.

Many growers are now experimenting with *macération pelliculaire,* giving the juice a few hours' skin contact before fermentation to extract extra aroma and richness into the wine. This used to happen naturally, in the harvest baskets, with juice liberated by sheer weight of fruit. Now the process is better understood and more carefully controlled. However, some believe that this can unbalance the wine with excess aroma, and also that the resulting pulp is more compact and difficult to press. Others prefer to press out the

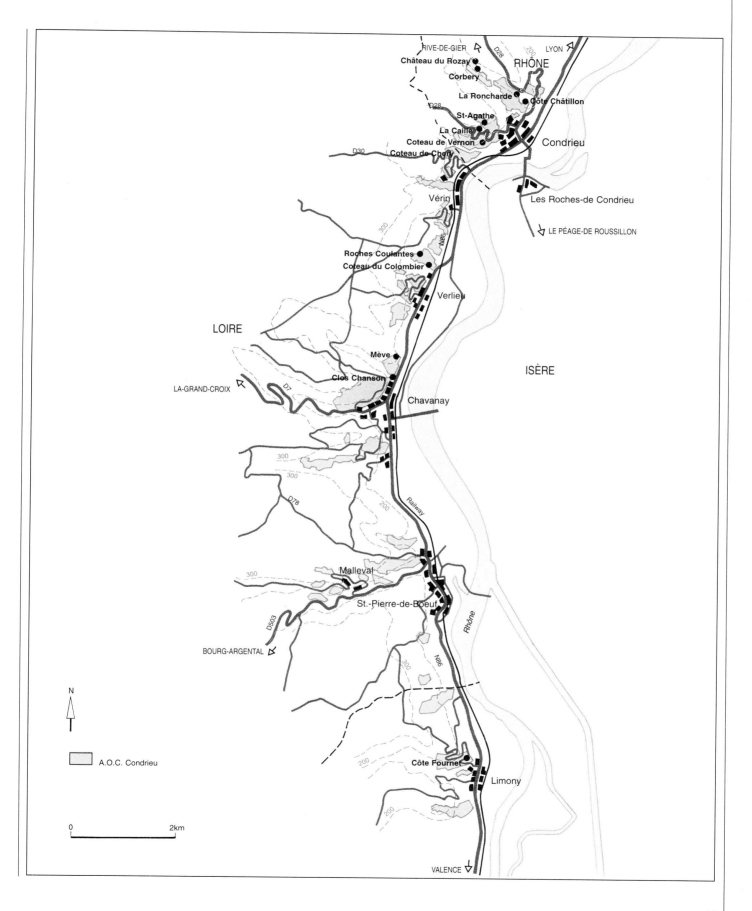

juice immediately and to rely on lees-stirring rather than *maceration* to add fat. A few compromise, blending macerated and non-macerated wine to achieve a balance.

There are also significant differences between growers as to the vessel used for fermentation and maturation. For the former, some have veered away from the more usual stainox, cement or enamelled vats or tanks, to part fermenting in new wood. Guigal and Perret both ferment one-third of their crop in new wood, considering that this adds important structure to the wine without destroying its integral finesse. Some, less talented, operators misjudge the impact of wood, old or new, and leave the wine too long in cask: this can lead to either premature oxidation – usually detectable through excessive browning – or dessicated, skeletal wines. Fortunately, these faults are relatively rare. For maturation, the choice is between *foudres, pièces* or tanks. Some believe that large old wood imparts roundness and evens out a wine's development; others prefer small casks, often for much the same reasons. Most permutations are to be found, if you look long enough.

A difficulty for many conscientious growers is that Viognier vines only really give of their best when they are over 20 years old. For established houses, such as Vernay or Perret, declassifying the produce of their young vines into Côtes du Rhône involves no serious financial hardship, whereas fledgling domaines would find the price differential crippling. So there are many rather lean Condrieus – a situation that will improve as vines mature.

WINE STYLES

Most Condrieu is dry and should be drunk young. This covers a broad division between those whose wine improves with a year or two in bottle, and those whose wine is best consumed almost direct from the cask. Those with only young vines often refer to an "elegant" or "primeur" style: sales-speak for a leaner, less generous wine from vines whose fruit lacks the natural richness of older plants. Even so, among these are several stylish, entirely typical Condrieus, delicious after a few months in bottle to settle down.

Condrieu – indeed most Viognier – does not age well: cellaring it for more than 3–5 years is generally a waste of space, cash and patience. This is not to say that the odd bottle, especially of the likes of Vernay's Coteaux de Vernon, Cuilleron's Les Chaillets, Niero's Coteau de Chery or Dumazet's Clos Fournet will not make interesting old bones, but rather that the variety itself does not age gracefully. If you keep Chardonnay for 20 years you have old Chardonnay, if you keep Viognier for half that time, you have something else altogether, which bears no resemblance to the original and is little more than a vinous necrophiliacs' curiosity.

Another interesting enigma is that if you cellar a case of Condrieu, each bottle seems to age differently; so when you uncork a bottle for the table, you don't know quite what to expect – an unpredictability which perhaps adds to the fun for some, but can prove expensive if you have to open half a dozen carefully cellared wines to find one that is "correct".

Though the sparkling version has disappeared – the AC decree does not mention it – there are still a few growers making small amounts of sweet Condrieu: notably Philippe Faury and Yves Cuilleron at Chavanay, Georges Vernay in Condrieu, and the Pichons at Verlieu. These now account for around 10% of the production.

Sweet wines can be made either by blocking the fermentation of normally harvested grapes, or with normal vinification of over-ripe or botrytised grapes which are naturally higher in sugar. The results are not equivalent. Practically, these methods present different problems: in one case you must stop fermentation leaving the wine either *demi-sec* or *moelleux*; in the other, you must wait for sufficient natural grape-sugar to be able to attain the minimum AC alcohol of 11% and yet leave enough residual sugar for the wine to be sweet. Late harvest, where bunches are left to concentrate naturally on the vine (*passerillage*), or selection of especially ripe grapes (as in Sauternes) achieve the latter – while a good dose of sulphur is the usual route to the former. A very late harvest enables growers like Yves Cuilleron to have sugar concentrations which allow him simply to cool the vats when the wine has reached 15-16% alcohol, and then to sterile-filter before bottling. Some growers argue that stopped fermentations are the antithesis of Condrieu, since it is during the final stages of fermentation that much of the characteristic aromatics of the Viognier are released. Block these and you remove them.

A generation ago, growers would make a barrel or so of *moelleux* for family use; often referred to as *Vin de Noël*, the wine was destined by virtue of its inherent instability and low acidity to be finished by Christmas. None the less, it is good to see the tradition being refined and kept alive; many of the villagers still seek out some sweet wine for special occasions; "it's our little champagne", one local lady remarked.

CONDRIEU AND FOOD

At a gastronomic level, Condrieu presents similar difficulties to the great German *Spätlesen*. In truth, apart from the richer special *cuvées*, Condrieu is probably at its best solo – *en apéritif*. The problem is that the Viognier's aromas, though opulent, are easily stifled by competing flavours. This is specially true of the more "elegant" styles, which don't have the flavour structure to support much rivalry. Richer Condrieus – often wood-fermented or -matured – will happily march into battle with food, provided the flavours are not overplayed. In general, as with so many fine wines, the simpler the fare, the better. Georges Vernay vehemently abjures fish as an accompaniment, while others talk approvingly of *quenelles de brochet*, guinea fowl, *queues d'ecrevisses* and *foie gras de canard*. An excellent companion is the mildly acidic, chalky local goat's cheese, *Rigotte de Condrieu* – warm on a piece of toast or a leaf-salad dressed with good walnut oil.

Condrieu seems to be slowly shrugging off the difficulties created by the 1980s planting euphoria and the economic crises which followed. The best wines are indisputably *Grand Vin* and indeed, among the most individual and remarkable in the world. The cult of the Viognier has just begun.

GROWERS

Apart from the estates profiled here, good Condrieu is made by Delas, Louis Cheze, Jean-Michel Gerin, Alain Paret, Jaboulet, Clusel Roch, Guigal and Chapoutier (all profiled elsewhere in this book); there is also a remarkable Viognier made by the Chaves from the late Lord Gray's vineyard at Hermitage.

VINTAGES

Condrieu is best drunk young. Good wines were made in 1990, '91, '92 and '93; however, '92 suffered from rain during the harvest and 1993 was hailed on, and was less structured than the earlier two years. These are still showing well from growers who vinify in the *vin de garde* style. Château Grillet follows Condrieu.

AC CONDRIEU

Created	27 April 1940 (revised 1989)
Area (max)	300ha
Area under vine 1994	100ha
Base yield	37hl/ha (35hl/ha actual)
Minimum alcohol	11% (12% maximum)
Growers	40

AC CHATEAU GRILLET

Created	8 December 1938 (revised 1986)
Area (max)	3.08ha
Area under vine 1994	3.08ha
Base yield	37hl/ha
Minimum alcohol	11% (14% maximum)
Growers	1

DOMAINE YVES CUILLERON

Antoine Cuilleron made good, but not great, Condrieu. Since taking over, his nephew Yves, a slim, close-bearded man in his thirties, has transformed the estate into one of the appellation's finest.

The domaine nearly vanished altogether in the 1980s, when lack of obvious succession led the family to contemplate selling their vineyards. Yves, with a passion for gastronomy, a taste for wine and driven by a strong desire to excel, persuaded his relatives to give him a chance.

After a year with Maurice Courbis in Châteaubourg and an intensive course at Mâcon, he took charge in 1986.

Realising that the European bureaucrats intended clamping down on the EU's wine production to limit an excess, Yves bought, rented and planted furiously in the years that followed, increasing the estate from 4ha to 17. Now an EU ban is indeed in force, he still has 3ha of Condrieu land which he is forbidden to plant.

While there is a sound Côte-Rôtie (mostly from young vines), and three thoroughly respectable *cuvées* of St-Joseph (a regular, a particularly good Prestige red, and a white), this is at heart a Condrieu domaine. It is here that Yves is at his most animated and eloquent – the passion shines through.

He offers three Condrieus from his 6.5ha: a generic wine, a *cuvée* Les Chaillets (from 1.5ha of 50-plus-year-old vines) and an extraordinary Récolte Tardive from grapes picked around the end of October or later. This sweet wine seems to have become something of a yardstick for other *vignerons*, who often refer to it.

To obtain quality raw material, Yves and his team of five work hard during the growing season. Apart from two separate

passages to tie up the shooting vegetation (there are 10,000 vines per hectare and each requires 3–4 separate straw ties); the critical operation is a green-pruning in late summer to limit production and ensure an even charge on each vine.

Together with a late parcel-by-parcel harvest when the vintage permits (which it didn't in 1992 or 1993), and a double *trie* to eliminate sub-standard grapes, these exigencies provide ripe, clean, balanced, and above all, sugar-rich, fruit. Yves surprises his harvesters by asking them to pick slowly – "we're not in the Beaujolais here".

In contrast, this precious fruit is pressed rapidly, yet gently, settled for 12 hours then, with only its fine lees, left to start fermentation in bulk. When there is no further risk of the temperature running above 20°C, 30% goes into casks (10–15% new each year) the rest remaining in *inox* to conserve youthful fruit aromas and freshness. For the Vieilles Vignes Cuvée Les Chaillets (terraces), 80% is matured in cask to give structure, since this is intended as a *vin de garde*.

Yves has been studying the benefits of *macération pelliculaire* and would have put part of the crop through this, were it not for heavy rain at harvest in 1992 and 1993 which required the quickest possible extraction of juice. Instead, the casks are *bâtonnées* regularly, which adds richness

and provides a measure of protection against premature oxidation. After 6–8 months the cask and *inox* fractions, malolactic completed, are re-assembled, polish-filtered and bottled with an apparatus shared by ten growers.

The generic *cuvée* is designed to emphasise the fruitier, fresher side of Condrieu, while Les Chaillets is fuller and more structured, needing a few years to show its form. The Récolte Tardive (officialdom blocked the use of "Vendange Tardive" to prevent confusion with Alsace), harvested in late October or early November, is altogether remarkable.

The inspiration for a late-harvest wine came from Yves' grandfather who told him that years ago Condrieu was generally harvested around All Saints (1st November) and picked *à l'assiette*. This procedure consisted of holding a plate under each bunch while it was shaken to dislodge the over-ripe berries – the principle of the modern mechanical harvester, but slower and more labour-intensive! The resulting wines were invariably sweet.

Nowadays, 90% of Condrieu is vinified dry from grapes harvested in September or October; and most of what is sweet – according to Yves – is just the stopped fermentation of a regular harvest to retain sugar, rather than the product of a selective late harvest of naturally over-ripe and (where possible) botrytized fruit. Yves Cuilleron, for one, is determined to revert to the "old way".

APPELLATION	VARIETY	DETAILS	AREA
ST-JOSEPH	MARSANNE	Hauts de coteaux at Verlieu; ½ 30 yrs plus, ½ 10 yrs	1.50
ST-JOSEPH	SYRAH	Mainly coteaux; 1.2 ha 30–50 yrs, 0.5 ha 6–20 yrs	7.00
CONDRIEU	VIOGNIER	5 ha 4–20 yrs; 1.5 ha 50 yrs	6.50
CONDRIEU		Unplanted	3.00
COTE-ROTIE	SYRAH	Bassenon (ie south end of AC) – new plantings	1.10
COTE-ROTIE	SYRAH	Viaillière; new planting and some 30 yr old vines	0.40
		TOTAL (hectares):	19.50

LUCIEN DEZORMEAUX

Lucien Dezormeaux is an tall dark moustachioed man in his forties. In manner phlegmatic and laid-back, to the point of seeming disinterested, he is in fact perfectly capable of making decent wine, which he does, albeit in minuscule quantity.

He and his father, André, work a single hectare of old vines on the Coteau du Colombier at St-Michel-sur-Rhône, south of Château Grillet, on terraces that were originally cleared and planted by his grandfather after the 1914–18 war.

They also own some fruit trees, but these, conveniently, are harvested before the vines.

Until the 1970s the wine was vinified almost 100% semi-sweet, and sold without a vintage date. Gradually, as tastes changed, the wine became dry and vintaged. "Then, we attached less importance to the vintage", says Lucien, but nowadays, as he is well aware, the customer realises that vintages vary enormously in quality and expects the price to reflect this.

Soils on the Coteau de Colombier are more or less deep *arzelle*; the bedrock however is not uniform: in one place impenetrable granite, a metre away more easily worked, friable, rock. There are vivid stories of topsoil being washed down by heavy rain in the 1930s and 1940s and André recalls carting 100 cubic metres back up the hillside. Now, specially constructed water-channels minimise soil erosion, and the widespread use of herbicides for weeds has compacted the soil, further reducing rain damage.

Lucien sells most of his grapes at harvest – to Marcel Guigal among others

– leaving himself enough for 1,500 bottles or so, and much less trouble with bottling and sales.

The wine used to spend time in cask – no longer.Since 1993, everything is vinified in epoxy vats in the neat cellar up a narrow hillside track by the level crossing at St-Michel. No *macération pelliculaire*, no malolactic, and a tight, but not sterile, filtration. A single June *mise* has replaced several smaller bottlings.

Though many would disagree with him, Lucien is adamant that the AC's base yield of 37hl/ha is entirely compatible with top quality providing that the charge is equally distributed between the 10,000 vines per hectare and that these are healthy. He considers it essential to supplement helicopter sprays with hand treatments for *oïdium,* rot etc. Helicopters can't get underneath the foliage or treat the bunches. In his view, growers rely too much on them to save themselves time and effort.

Lucien's wine is not intended for keeping, but is an excellent example of the *primeur* style one often finds in Condrieu. It is invariably well made and fresh, and none the worse for being better consumed young.

PIERRE DUMAZET

At 1.2ha this is hardly a grand estate, but size is no predictor of quality. Pierre Dumazet, a loquacious, silver-haired man in his fifties, took over from his father Marc in 1978. Until 1990 he continued to live in Lyon, working as director of a transport company, returning to the cellars at weekends. Now the vines have his full attention and the quality is excellent.

From this small vineyard emerge four grades of Viognier: a *vin de pays* from 12-year-old vines planted in 1982; a Côtes du Rhône from vines of similar age; a Condrieu from two parcels *en coteaux* at Limony and, in good vintages, a Condrieu Côte Fournet from vines planted by André's grandfather in 1930. These are well-made, interesting wines, invariably good, sometimes superb. In addition, Pierre has set up as a *négociant-éleveur* dealing in Côte-Rôtie, St-Joseph and Cornas. All this is run from the domaine's headquarters, a pleasant, unpretentious house on the main road at Limony, at the southern extremity of the Condrieu *vignoble*.

Low yields are at the heart of Pierre's philosophy. "When you get past 40hl/ha with Viognier, the aroma disappears". So even his *vin de pays* comes in at below this level, while for the Côte Fournet, yields average 20–25hl/ha. He learned to vinify from his father who taught him to follow his own instincts when it comes to detail. Fermentation is started in bulk and then finished in cask (20% new) for 60% of each *cuvée*, the rest remaining in *inox* or glass-lined vats with regular *bâtonnage* to add *gras* and complexity. Pre-fermentive maceration is eschewed: "Viognier has plenty of aroma already; if you add more, people will say that you have too much". The malolactic is encouraged and left to happen naturally, whether before or after *assemblage* of the wood and non-wood *cuvées*. The lesser Viogniers have 8–10 months' *élevage*, the Côte Fournet (which is vinified 100% in cask) has 16–18 months before fining, gravity plate-filtration and bottling.

Although the Côte Fournet *cuvée* first appeared in 1989, Pierre Dumazet points out that earlier vintages were in fact, though not labelled as such, mostly from these old vines, since the rest of the plantings were relatively young. Production ranges from 1,000–1,400 bottles and so far only 1989, 1990 and 1991 have been made.

Soils at Limony differ from those 22km north at Condrieu in that they are less schistous and more obviously granitic. On the Côte Fournet, acidic granitic scree imparts power to the wine, while larger, less acidic, quaternary loess contributes more floral elements.

Pierre is firm on the question of new wood: "Condrieu doesn't need all the artifice of new oak to be *Grand Vin*. However, for Côtes du Rhône and *vin de pays*, new wood can be interesting". Hence only 20% new casks in the mix – principally to ensure that no cask is more than five years old.

His three sons help when they can. Two have unrelated jobs, the third has just finished a *stage* with Marcel and Etienne Guigal – a star apprenticeship! Pierre's charming wife admits to avoiding the office work: "if I stick my nose in there… Pierre says I never help him, but I shop, cook, wash up and look after the house". No riposte from Pierre!

APPELLATION	VINEYARD	DETAILS	AREA
CONDRIEU	COTE FOURNET	Vines planted 1930	0.40
CONDRIEU		2 parcels, en coteaux, Limony, vines planted 1977-1981	0.40
COTES DU RHONE		Viognier. Bas de coteaux, Limony, more granitic soils, less clay; vines planted 1982	0.20
VDP COLLINES RHODANIENNES		Viognier. Bas de coteaux, Limony, more granitic soils, less clay; vines planted 1982	0.20
		TOTAL (hectares):	1.2ha

PIERRE GAILLARD

High above the Rhône, beyond Malleval, is the domaine of Pierre Gaillard. The drive, up a sinuous, narrow road, sprinkled with vertiginous, unprotected drop-offs, is worth it for the views, especially in late spring when the road-sides are covered in wild poppies and everything is deep, fresh green.

Pierre is a bluff, articulate, thick-set man, whose career started as *chef de culture* for Vidal-Fleury in Ampuis. He stayed on when Etienne Guigal bought the firm and helped with vinification (but not, as has been reported, as cellar-master of either establishment) buying and planting land on his own account, in St-Joseph and Condrieu, all the while.

His first vintage was a 1987 St-Joseph, from vines in the Clos de Cuminaille planted in 1981. Subsequent additions have brought the domaine up to its present 13ha. As with many northern Rhône estates, the vines are relatively young, which limits potential at present. As the plants mature, the wine will undoubtedly improve.

However, there are good things *chez* Pierre, especially his whites. From a single hectare of five-year-old vines, he is turning out a splendid Condrieu; if this is too expensive, then there is also a good Côtes du Rhône Viognier from 12-year-old vines in the Clos, or an excellent white

St-Joseph from a hectare of Roussanne.

Vinification is well thought-out – the Condrieu is fermented in Allier and Nevers casks (20% new), following 16 hours – "one long night" – of maceration, with temperature peaking at 18°C and plenty of *bâtonnage* to add richness to the young-vine fruit. A rapid malolactic is encouraged reflecting Pierre's belief that a slow malolactic without sulphur results in loss of perfume. To conserve the fruity aspect of the wine, bottling is relatively early, in March or April.

The criticism that new oak is not traditional for Condrieu doesn't deter Pierre, who believes that wood breathes, providing the wine with a steady tannic and aromatic evolution; but old wood he dislikes, hence a five year cask rotation programme. "In any case," Pierre adds, "there is an 18th-century letter in Pierre Barge's cellar at Ampuis stating that then Condrieu was sent to Paris in a new barrel". Not quite the same thing, but some justification for his policy. The soils at Malleval tend to give a lighter, more elegant, Viognier, so the *bâtonnage* and

APPELLATION/VINEYARD	DETAILS	AREA
ST-JOSEPH, LE CLOS DE CUMINAIILLE	Syrah, planted 1982	3.00
CDR VIOGNIER, LE CLOS DE CUMINAILLE	Viognier, planted 1982	0.30
COTE-ROTIE	Viaillière, Cote Rozier, Brune Blonde; planted 1984	2.50
CONDRIEU	Viognier, planted 1989	1.00
ST-JOSEPH (blanc)	Roussanne, planted 1989	1.00
ST-JOSEPH (rouge)	Syrah, planted 1979	2.00
VIN DE PAYS	Planted 1974	2.00
	Young vines	2.00
	TOTAL (hectares):	13 ha

new wood add useful fat and structure.

Pierre's reds are less uniformly good than his whites. Both St-Joseph vineyards are of respectable age – 12 in the Clos and 15 for the rest; the Côte-Rôtie is only 10, so this needs a few more years before it will produce its best. The natural lack of concentration from these youngish vines is not helped by keeping all the stems in the vats. In justification, Pierre reasons that the Syrah stem usually ripens with the berry, so that green, bitter tannins are unlikely to result from including them

– and, furthermore, that a cap of skins without stems is much harder to work and thus gives much less extraction than with stems added. This may be, but except in very ripe vintages such as 1991 and 1990, Pierre's reds have an irremediable streak of green which is unlikely to integrate. So a measure of de-stemming would be desirable. This appears to be under discussion.

This is a domaine where it pays to taste carefully, but the flashes of brilliance suggest that it is certainly one to follow.

CHATEAU GRILLET

A kilometre or so south of Condrieu itself, in the village of St-Michel-sur-Rhône, is Château Grillet. Although within the geographical area of Condrieu, it has its own Appellation Contrôlée; not, as many believe, the smallest appellation in France – that title falls to La Romanée in Burgundy – but at 3.08ha definitely the smallest in the Rhône.

The site is magnificent: a fine natural amphitheatre facing south and south-east, rising in narrow terraces some 80 vertical metres from valley to summit. At its eastern end is the curious, yet attractive, little Château – grey stone surmounted with red Provençale roofing and a pair of round turrets – which from a distance gives the appearance of two outsized, rotund, Chinese coolies out for a walk.

History records this site as special even in the early 19th century. Jullien, Tovey and others classed its wine among the finest in France, and thus, *a fortiori*, the world – excellent but different. As at Condrieu, the sole permitted grape is the Viognier, so one might well ask what sets Grillet apart from the appellation which surrounds it and why it merits its own. The answers lie in the soil which, for reasons for which no-one seems to have a credible explanation, is particularly rich in decomposed mica. The soils are broadly similar to those of Condrieu, which however tend to be less fine and

André Canet on the terrace at Château Grillet.

more mixed. The subsoil is a friable beige granite, useless for quarrying.

The estate has attracted controversy. The château has been criticised as a "hotch-potch" of architectural styles – with several accretions to the earliest, central part which dates from the 13–14th centuries. Here, metre-thick walls attest to quality building and wooden bars at the windows to ancient security precautions. Later additions had to deal with a difficult hillside site, incorporate a cellar and

above all avoid taking valuable vineyard land from this tiny appellation. The building may be somewhat unusual, but time seems to have mellowed these old stones into an harmonious entity.

Condrieu is no stranger to conflict. During the wars of religion, Protestants from the Ardèche made repeated sorties against the Catholics of Condrieu – and Grillet was in direct line of fire. The last attack was in 1580, when Condrieu was occupied for six months. The front

Château Grillet surrounded by its vines.

facade, being only 50cm thick, suggests a reconstruction – probably by the noted architect Desargues, who owned the property in the early 17th century.

Since 1840, Grillet has been in the hands of the Neyret-Gachet family. The present owner, André Canet, married Hélène Neyret-Gachet, the youngest of three sisters, in 1943, having been invited to dine at the château and having fallen in love there and then. On the sudden death in 1961 of Monsieur Maillet, who was married to André Canet's sister-in-law, André took over as manager. Between 1965 and 1970, the Canets bought out the rest of the family.

André Canet, now well into his seventies, is a man of powerful character and courteous charm. Infirmity may keep him in a wheel-chair for much of the day, but he oversees the domaine with the help of his dark, vivacious youngest daughter, Isabelle Baratin.

Vinification is in the overall care of Max Leglise, one of the finest of Burgundian oenologists, who is passionately fond of Grillet and, although now retired, helps out "for the pleasure". André went to Max's laboratory to shadow his work, and admits to having learned much from that experience.

Since the mid 1980s, there has been persistent criticism of Grillet's wine.

Repeated refrains are that it is dilute, not what it used to be, inferior to many Condrieus and that the vineyard is over-cropped. Even the use of perfectly effective, if not particularly beautiful, plastic corks by André's brother-in-law after the 1939–45 war, when real cork was unobtainable, has been resurrected by critics as further evidence of slipping standards. "They even criticised me for being an engineer", André Canet laments. "What's the crime in that?"

The force of the charges is not that Grillet produces poor wine, but rather that it is too often inferior to many Condrieus at half the price and – in the opinion of those who had tasted older vintages – fails to deliver the quality of which the estate is capable. The inspiration of post-war wines – in particular a memorable 1969 and 1971 Cuvée Renaissance – is said to be no longer there; and moreover, that at Grillet's price level people expect something special and are not getting it.

These criticisms are not without justification – although, as so often, the hand has been somewhat overplayed. Although Grillet's yield per hectare is invariably higher than that of Condrieu, this is not an adequate foundation for such vehemence. Such crop-levels are not incompatible with top quality; Georges

Vernay reckons that Viognier will take up to 35hl/ha in a first-class vintage, 25–30 in less propitious ones.

However, the expansion in Grillet's *vignoble* since 1965, from 1.75 to 3.08ha, has meant a significant proportion of young-vine fruit in the final wine which, as the property doesn't produce a second wine, is bound to diminish quality. As the vineyard matures, the wine should improve in power and structure naturally, other things being equal.

Another factor is the harvest which is now earlier rather than later – "at full ripeness, rather than over-ripeness; we think it better" – but certainly not, as one US critic has suggested, three weeks in advance of Condrieu. Within two hours of picking, the fruit is in the château's pneumatic press: "this crushes fewer pips and stalks", André Canet explains. The juice is clean, so there is rarely the need for a further settling of lees, before fermentation in 20hl metal *cuves*. The indigenous yeasts are used, and the temperature is kept to 20–21°C.

After primary fermentation, the *cuves* are filled up and left until the malolactics have finished in the spring. The new wine then passes to a splendid row of ancient casks in an adjoining earth-floored cellar for six months, before a light filtration and château-bottling. On the matter of wood – new or old – André Canet is dryly cynical: "new casks – I don't think these are good; old casks – they don't contribute much". Recently, the *élevage* has been nearer 50% in cask with the rest in *cuve*.

There is little doubt that many recent offerings have been disappointing – attractive and elegant wines, often with depth, but with none of the staying power, concentration or complexity of older vintages. Why?

This is probably the result of an amalgam of factors, rather than a cataclysmic shift in direction. A few seminal changes are needed to put the wine back on top: first, a later harvest would increase natural richness and develop aromatic intensity. Even at these latitudes, Viognier will pick up a couple of degrees of potential alcohol and valuable aromatics, given a few extra days of autumn sunshine. Secondly, some

new wood would add both structure and depth (in any case, the present population of old casks badly needs replacing). Thirdly, an earlier bottling would preserve the intensity of fruit both on the nose and on the palate – an area of notable deficiency in some recent vintages.

Finally, and most importantly, a reduction in yield to 25–30hl/ha, and a separate vinification of young-vine fruit with a view to deciding later whether it should be incorporated into the *Grand Vin*, would greatly increase concentration. After all, it used to happen: Grillet's *cuvée* Renaissance was a *tête de cuvée* – a selection of the best casks. André Canet claims that such progress has been made that differences have been eradicated,

eliminating the need for selection. This smacks of casuistry.

However, ideals must be balanced by credible economics. An annual production of 10,000 bottles selling at an average of 150 francs per bottle produces 1,500,000 francs. With five full-time employees, plus the costs of vinification, laboratory analyses, vineyard and cellar materials, there won't be much over at the year-end. In addition, this ignores any capital expenses and the fact that many vintages don't produce 10,000 bottles. The profit-and-loss must indeed be marginal. It takes courage to make fundamental changes, but these must happen if André Canet and his family hope to see the noble reputation of Château Grillet convincingly restored.

APPELLATION	VARIETY	AREA
CHATEAU GRILLET	VIOGNIER	3.08

DOMAINE NIERO-PINCHON

The handsome, muscular Robert Niero, now in his thirties, married the late Jean Pinchon's daughter, and thereby inherited the mantle of one of Condrieu's more illustrious sons.

Robert had worked for 13 years in a bank, a training which he fully admits was not ideal for the *métier* of *vigneron*. A "professional conversion" course followed, then learning "on the hoof". Judging by the results, this far from conventional background seems, against the odds, to have produced a skilled and conscientious *vigneron*.

The Pinchon domaine was not by any means extensive – 40 ares of Condrieu, 20 ares of Côtes du Rhône Viognier and 25 ares of Côtes du Rhône Syrah. Robert set about enlarging the holdings and by 1995 there were 4.71ha – the original 2.4 in Condrieu, including 0.7ha of old vines in the *quartiers* Roncharde and Châtillon (plus 90 ares of young vines) and 80 ares – equally old and young vines – in the Coteau de Chery. To these, 1.06ha of vines in the Rozay *quartier* have recently been added. So now his Condrieu is 50% young vines, planted in 1985 and 1987, and 50% 30- to 60-year-old vines.

The Condrieu vinification is cautiously traditional – a quarter of the crop being fermented and matured in older wood, the remainder being consigned to *inox*. Bottling, following a light fining and a "nearly sterile" filtration – surprisingly since he encourages malolactic – is either before or after the heat of summer, in May or September.

Robert Niero.

From the 1994 vintage, Robert has decided to vinify separately the produce of the Coteau de Chery and La Roncharde in the *quartier* Châtillon, to the north of Condrieu. Curiously, part of the Chery vines are administratively in the Coteaux

de Vernon – but this doesn't seem to worry Robert who insists (despite his role as secretary of the Syndicat des Vignerons) that the official map – the *cadastre* – is nonsense.

He is trying to follow Jean Pinchon's precepts as far as possible, for wines with "fat, unctuousness and power". This memorial does not extend to reproducing Jean's single cask of "liquoreux", which was made by stopping the fermentation with a huge dose of sulphur while there was still sugar in the juice. This works, but produces an unstable wine best drunk in the few months before Christmas. Instead, Robert would like to try his hand at a *vendange tardive* – picking late for a greater concentration of sugar; "I missed the opportunity in 1991", he admits, smiling. No doubt there will be others.

Tasting a splendid 1990, with 14% alcohol, confirmed the quality of Robert Niero's wines: a fine example of mature Condrieu – an ample, seductive, secure woman rather than a giggly, nervous adolescent – to be savoured with a *viande blanche* or a *tarte au saumon*, not sipped carelessly as an aperitif!

APPELLATION	VINEYARD	DETAILS	AREA
CONDRIEU	RONCHARDE/CHATILLON	0.9 planted 1985-7; 0.7 30-50 yr old vines.	1.60
CONDRIEU	COTEAU DE CHERY	0.5 planted 1985-7; 0.5 30-50 yr old vines.	1.00
CONDRIEU	ROZAY		1.06
COTE-ROTIE		Planted 1986	0.60
COTES DU RHONE	SYRAH		0.25
COTES DU RHONE	VIOGNIER		0.20
		TOTAL (hectares):	4.71

ANDRE PERRET

André Perret would have been a Burgundian if his great-uncle had not sold the Clos de Maltroie in Chassagne-Montrachet in 1942. However here he is, jovial and contented, turning out exceptionally fine Condrieu and top-quality St-Joseph. An easy-going, smiling man, he took over his father's 0.5ha domaine in 1982. Then, the principal activity was fruit-growing; now Perret *père* minds the fruit, leaving André in charge of the wine department.

Expansion was rapid: renting and planting increased the original half-hectare to eight, divided equally between Condrieu and St-Joseph. An early addition was 0.7ha of Condrieu which Jean Pinchon was farming for the Jurie des Camiers estate. There is also the one-hectare Clos Chanson at Chavanay, surrounded by a fine stone wall, just by the village petrol-station.

The soils differ between the two *lieux-dits*. At Chery the vines sit in a deep layer of *arzelle* – decomposed sandy particles of mica, granite and schist. This soil is very strong, imparting power and ageing potential to the wine. In contrast, the Clos Chanson has a greater proportion of clay and rock, which tends to accentuate the aromatic side of the Viognier, especially when the wine is young.

The domaine's HQ is split between cellars in Chavanay and a *cuverie* at Verlieu; this latter, at the home of André's grandparents, is squeezed uncomfortably between the bustling RN86 and the main freight railway line. What were disused stables have been transformed into a good working cellar.

Here amid the casks, André fashions his wine. No secrets, just plenty of lees

contact and a regime of 50/50 old wood and *inox* for both fermentation and *élevage*. There is an irregular *bâtonnage*, and the wood-matured fraction is exchanged with the *inox* fraction for one to two months, to de-gas the former and add a touch of *rondeur* to the latter. Otherwise, a bentonite fining and a polishing filtration: "Condrieu is very sensitive to filtration – you mustn't manipulate the wine too much" precede a deliberately late bottling between September and November of the year following the vintage. This, in André's view, integrates the two fractions more fully and endows the final blend with better keeping potential. He swims against the prevailing tide in believing that "a well-structured Condrieu needs at least two years in bottle before drinking".

André's training as a biologist seems to have left him with an experimental turn of mind. In 1990 he decided to leave some bunches on the vine, to make a *vendange tardive*. Picked on October 15th, the grapes were fermented to dryness to avoid problems with residual sugar and the need for an excoriating sterile filtration.

He had another go at *vendange tardive* in 1992 and both wines are superb – full, rich yet still retaining finesse and acidity; not perhaps

quintessential Viognier, but fine wine none the less.

Part of the extract one finds in André's wines undoubtedly comes from his practice of fermenting at 20°C – higher than most other *vignerons*. However, to ensure that this maximum is not exceeded, he has cobbled together a small heat exchanger in the form of a bent stainless-steel tube through which water circulates, expressly designed to fit 225-litre casks.

At a time when falling sales and lower prices have driving many Condrieu growers to the financial margin, André's sales seem to be robust. The short 1993 Condrieu crop, caused not by a poor *sortie* but later, when bunches failed to develop properly, left him with yields of only 14hl/ha and demand for wine from twice that. An even allocation between export, restaurants, French distributors and private clients seems to have struck a viable balance. Many growers who acceded too readily to export demands in the 1980s now find that they lack the local clientele which is sustaining many of their less greedy colleagues. On a foundation of fine Condrieus and excellent St-Josephs, André has built a reliable, high-quality, domaine.

APPELLATION	VINEYARD	DETAILS	AREA
CONDRIEU	COTEAU DE CHERY	50 yr old + 10 yr plantings	3.00
CONDRIEU	CHAVANAY – CLOS CHANSON	25–30 yr old vines	1.00
ST-JOSEPH		Syrah. Young + older vines	3.50
ST-JOSEPH		Marsanne. Young and older vines	0.50
		TOTAL (hectares):	8.00

PHILIPPE & CHRISTOPHE PICHON

In an end-of-terrace house, down a pot-holed earth track beside the railway line just north of Chavanay, live the Pichons. Philippe and his son Christophe have 1.10ha of St-Joseph and – more importantly – 3.85ha of Condrieu. The latter is split between Les Roches Coulantes, where a deep *arzelle* soil with a touch of clay imparts elements of *fruits secs* and *fruits confits* to the wine, and the Mève hillside above Chavanay, which contains considerably more clay, giving both floral aromas and a marked hardness on the palate.

Sadly, uneconomic yields forced them to grub up a 1922 Viognier plot in 1993.

The hillsides here face south or south-east – as in most of Condrieu – which protects them from the Mistral, that ferocious north wind known here as the Bise. However, they don't escape the *vent du Midi* which blows from south to north wreaking damage on any untied canes, especially during late spring when the vegetation has started to shoot.

The Pichons are good winemakers. They do all the right things in their immaculate cellars a hundred yards from the family house: indigenous yeasts, malolactic, and careful *élevage*, one-fifth in older casks. Bottling – which they perform themselves – now happens

between September and November, rather than May/June as before, since they found this gave more roundness and a generally better evolution.

Despite an attractive femininity, the wines seem to emphasise elegance at the expense of concentration – a problem that the Pichons appear to recognise. This is surprising, since their yields – the usual source of dilution – are by no means excessive: their stated average is 32hl/ha, although in 1991, '92 and '93 the actual figures were respectively. 22, 32 and 27hl/ha (Most informed opinion would put the break point at which Viognier starts losing grip at around 30-35hl/ha.)

The fact that the vines' average age is 16 years perhaps contributes, but cannot account for a persistent sense of dilution. Reducing yields still further would undoubtedly help tighten up the wine.

The 1990 Condrieu was, as Philippe frankly admitted, exhausted and losing *tonus*. The 1991 was a bit more in touch, but its undoubted elegance was not sustained by fruit, and the underlying power was driven more by alcohol than *terroir*. A clean and attractive 1992 was the most harmonious wine of the recent vintages.

Philippe and Christophe are among the few remaining *vignerons* to make a sweet Condrieu which, in the years when

APPELLATION	VINEYARD	DETAILS	AREA
CONDRIEU	LES ROCHES COULANTES	0.90 Fermage from Dezormeaux; 15 yr old vines	2.90
CONDRIEU	MEVE (CHAVANAY)	15 yr old vines	1.00
ST-JOSEPH	CHAVANAY		1.10
		TOTAL (hectares):	5.00

it appears, accounts for some 10% by volume of their Condrieu production. In fact this is *demi-sec* rather than the *moelleux* advertised on the neck label.

The method is to leave a plot of old vines to bunch-ripen for two to three weeks longer than normal, and then to stop fermentation with sulphur just before Christmas. A short period in old casks

and sterile filtration precede a March bottling. The 1991 *moelleux*, tasted in late May 1994, was quite attractive, but with a rather short finish and a distinct touch of *rancio*, which Philippe admitted disliking.

This is a charming, hard-working family who should be in the first division, but who have some fine-tuning to do before they get there.

CHATEAU DU ROZAY

There have been Multiers at Château du Rozay since 1898, when Claude, great-grandfather of the current incumbent, Jean-Yves, sold his textile business to indulge a passion for Condrieu and bought the property. His son, Paul, tried a variety of enterprises – chickens, eggs, fruit, sheep and cereal – before settling on wine as his principal activity.

Since being pitched in, on Paul's death in 1984, as *chef d'exploitation*, Jean-Yves Multier has produced two *cuvées* of Condrieu from his 3.2ha. The simpler version, from vines planted mainly in the *quartier* Corbery in 1981, is a clear, fresh, green-tinged wine, with typicity and youthful attraction. The flagship, Château du Rozay, comes from 90 ares planted between 1931 and 1970, of a total 1.5ha in the Coteau du Chery, some 7km further south. Here, site and vine age combine to produce a much more structured and complex wine, at its peak between three and eight years of age.

Yields are low – 13-25hl/ha for the old Chery vines, up to 37hl/ha for the younger parcels. In 1993 both areas were hailed on in May which greatly diminished the crop; a few kilometres south at Chavanay there was no hail and they harvested normal quantities. In that same year, rains washed down the deep *arzelle* topsoil taking with it solid dry-stone walls. These have now been repaired – but with cement, as an insurance against future floods.

Vinification leans towards the traditional, with an *élevage* mix of *inox* and old *foudres*. Since 1988, when Jean-Yves enlisted the services of Jean-Luc Colombo as consulting oenologue, small but important changes have been implemented, notably the addition of sulphur in the press and the use of lactic

Jean-Yves Multier, straw gripped pirate fashion in his mouth, ties young vines to traditional Condrieu stakes.

acid bacteria to ensure a regular malolactic (Jean-Yves recalls years in his father's day when the malolactic didn't finish until the summer.) Otherwise, the regime is ten days of fermentation at 17–18°C ("too low a temperature gives too neutral aromas"), *assemblage* of the wood and *inox* fractions immediately after malolactic, and June bottling.

Jean-Yves is lively and articulate; less of a tear-away now that he is married with a small daughter, Perrine, to consider. His beloved BMW motor-bike ("I used to ride in formation with friends – I stayed at the back – much more fun on the bends", he recollects, somewhat wistfully) was transformed into a lustrous

engagement ring for Fabienne, so he now spends any spare time he has crewing catamarans for friends. Also gone are his wilder theatrical days, when his solo act seemed much in demand: "playing the clown in front of a few friends in a room is fine – but standing up on stage in front of people you don't know – whew!, that's something else".

Now his energies are concentrated in restoring his partly 17th century pink-washed château. From its terrace, beyond the domaine's Côtes du Rhône Syrah vines, one looks south and west towards the distant prospect of the Ardèche hills, while the Condrieu-Côtes du Rhône boundary passes through the vegetable patch below the parapet. This is the French facade; the front is in the Italian style and the younger west facade comes complete with two asymmetrical towers of German design.

This is potentially a very fine domaine and Jean-Yves is perfectly capable of making top-class wine. However, he seemed to have lost interest at one point and many have noticed a dip in quality over the last decade; there have also been mutterings about poor vineyard

APPELLATION	VINEYARD	DETAILS	AREA
CONDRIEU	CORBERY	Mainly younger vines, planted 1981	1.70
CONDRIEU	COTEAU DE CHERY	0.9 old vines, 0.6 younger vines	1.50
COTES DU RHONE	CORBERY	Syrah	0.40
		TOTAL (hectares):	3.60

maintenance. Recent vintages, though, have shown a marked improvement, and the domaine seems now to be returning to its old form.

Perhaps *la petite Perrine* has given Jean-Yves the impetus to take a firmer grip on the reins. Not to do so would be a great waste of past achievements.

DOMAINE GEORGES & LUC VERNAY

The name Vernay is inseparable both from Viognier and from Condrieu. Since Georges Vernay, now in his sixties, started in 1952 with a single hectare of vines in the Coteau de Vernon he has become the undisputed authority on both appellation and grape. He has guided younger *vignerons* in Condrieu and supplied advice and cuttings to scores of Viognier growers world-wide. Square and avuncular, Vernay is no sterile technician, but someone who has worked his vines assiduously for nearly half a century and knows how to handle the temperamental Viognier. His Condrieus are among the finest to be found, particularly his Coteau de Vernon, made from 2ha of 50- to 60-year-old vines which Vernay farms for his father, yielding a miserly 13–25hl/ha.

For the rest, Georges and his younger son Luc have a further hectare of 25-year-old vines on the Coteau de Vernon, plus 4ha scattered over the commune of Condrieu, 2ha of Côte-Rôtie, 1ha of St-Joseph and 4ha of *vin de pays* – both red Syrah and white Viognier. This last is planted on Condrieu *arzelle* soil, but was re-classified as *vin de pays* in 1986 when a revision of the appellation limited Condrieu to below 300 metres altitude – the Vernay Viognier is just higher, beneath the plateau.

These are yardstick Condrieus, treading with deft skill the troublesome Scylla and Charybdis between finesse and the power which the Viognier exacts from those who work with it. Much depends on the harvest; the older Vernon vines usually ripen and are picked first, followed by the best from the older vines elsewhere; finally the younger Viogniers come in. "We harvest as late as possible", Luc explains; "even though this reduces acidity, it gives far more of the peach and apricot Viognier aromas". To ensure a cool start to fermentation, Viognier is only harvested in the mornings, afternoons being devoted to Syrah. Within two hours the grapes are sorted and pressed, and

the cool juice is then left to settle in tank for 12–18 hours. Enzymes are added to help clarification and the juice yeasted to give a long, slow, fermentation.

The Coteau de Vernon is generally vinified in 225-litre casks, the only new wood being whatever is needed by way of replacements. As the harvest arrives, it fills up whatever *pièces* remain, then the 2,000-litre *foudres* and finally the younger-vine juice and the Viognier *vin de pays* goes to *inox*. Luc uses a heat exchanger, even for the casks, to ensure that fermentation starts off cool and rises gradually to peak at 17–18°C, coming back to finish at about 14°C. "You must have a peak of temperature – this acts on fine lees which are important for wood maturation – these lees are rich and aromatic". Malolactic fermentation normally follows, since the Vernays reckon it enhances both aroma and wine stability.

Since 1993, the Coteau de Vernon spends one year in cask, with periodic *bâtonnage*, before being racked to *inox* and ultimately cold stabilised, bentonite fined ("we have a lot of problems with proteins"), and polish-filtered. This is intended as much to release casks for the new crop as to benefit the wine, but allows a further period of slower maturation before bottling.

For this *cuvée*, bottling is late – in May 1994, the 1992 Vernon was still not bottled and the 1991 had just 4–5 months' bottle-age. There is always an early bottling of the generic Condrieu, both for the market, which likes a fresh, more

directly fruity wine, and for the cash register – which by then needs an injection.

To fill the space between the generic Condrieu *cuvée*, by far the largest part of the range, and the Coteau de Vernon (some 450 cases in a good year), the Vernays introduced an intermediate offering in 1992. This – Les Chaillées de l'Enfer ("the terraces of hell") – comes in a tall dark brown fluted bottle and is a selection of most propitious Coteaux. Vinification and maturation mirror Vernon and, although in quality somewhere between this and the generic Condrieu, its character leans more to the former than to the latter. The Chaillées de l'Enfer will help reduce pressure on the sought-after, but expensive, Vernon and provide a more affordable *vin sérieux* for the private-sales market which absorbs 60% of Vernay output.

Since 1986, the Vernays have employed the services of consulting oenologue Jean-Luc Colombo (qv). His main impact has been on the domaine's reds – in particular the Côte-Rôtie, where a significant increase in de-stemming and length of *cuvaison* has added finesse and eliminated the rather rustic tinge of past vintages. "We felt that we were too introspective and needed an outside opinion", Luc explains. This does not apply to their Viogniers where, as acknowledged experts, they hardly need refinement. Having taken over the vinification from his father, Luc has made a good start. A top-class domaine – as reliable as the fickle mistress Viognier ever allows her master to be!

APPELLATION	VINEYARD	DETAILS	AREA
CONDRIEU	COTEAU DE VERNON	Includes 1 ha 25 yr old vines, 2 of 50–60 yr old	3.00
CONDRIEU		Various climats	4.00
COTE-ROTIE	COTE BLONDE	Adjoins Condrieu	2.00
ST-JOSEPH			1.00
VIN DE PAYS		Viognier & Syrah	4.00
		TOTAL (hectares):	14.00

CROZES HERMITAGE

Until the early 1980s Crozes-Hermitage presented merchants and growers, with a few notable exceptions, with a tailor-made excuse to trade dull, often badly-made red and white wine – thin, flabby or soupy, depending upon your supplier – on the back of its more illustrious neighbour. Now, a caucus of younger growers and revitalised domaines are setting quality standards which were unthinkable a decade earlier. Here one finds clean, interesting whites, and intense, firm reds bursting with Syrah; many with a depth and complexity more than meriting their public image as junior Hermitages.

The AC started in 1937 with the single commune of Crozes, a dozy village within the north-eastern lee of the great Hermitage hill. Now, since a 1952 revision upgrading land then classified as Côtes du Rhône, it is dispersed over 11 communes around, and including, Tain l'Hermitage itself. To the north Gervans, Larnage, Erôme, Serves and Crozes-Hermitage; to the east, Mercurol and Chanos-Curson and to the south, Beaumont-Monteux, Roche-de-Glun and Pont-de-l'Isère. 4,200ha are officially designated AC, with 1,020ha actually planted, giving a vineyard seven times the size of Hermitage.

Apart from the understandable eagerness of growers to ally their wine to the great Hermitage – if only by association – this re-classification provided *négociant* houses with wines of standing, in reasonable volume, to offer as an alternative to the highly-priced and limited Hermitage: satisfaction for producers' egos and the market all at once.

While Syrah is King for red Crozes, the rules permit 15% of white grapes to be included at fermentation, both because older plantings were a mix of red and white varieties which would be impossible to disentangle and also because a dab of white juice would take the edge off the raw Syrah. Nowadays, white grapes are rarely found in the red *cuves*, though the dispensation remains in force.

As with Hermitage, it would be a mistake to think of the *vignoble* as a single expanse producing a uniform quality of wine. In fact, the area divides into five distinct sectors, differentiated mainly by soil.

To the north, Gervans shares broadly similar topography with parts of Les Bessards at Hermitage – south- and southwest-facing hillsides composed largely of decomposed granitic soils; *terroir* which gives firm, tight, tannic red wines needing time to evolve. Further south, around Larnage, the soil becomes heavier, with more

Colourful old cement fermenting vat.

clay. This, known locally as "paste de Larnage", imparts breadth and depth to both red and white wines which, in the latter, sometimes shows as a rather overblown, flabby character.

Away from the Rhône, on the higher slopes round Larnage and Mercurol in particular, soils are stonier and sandier, with a significant proportion of clay and limestone. This is white wine country, especially at Mercurol where exposition and soils combine to bring out something special in the Marsanne and Roussanne grapes planted there.

Mercurol extends over several different types of *terroir*. To the south, near the Carolans quarry, where the hills fall away, the soils are pure white, on a very deep bed of inert gravel. This well-drained land suffers badly in years of drought but, when conditions are favourable, produces wines more elegant than substantial.

It is generally considered, though the growers of Gervans would probably argue the point fiercely, that the finest reds come from the plateau around Les Chassis and Les Sept Chemins, which straddles the busy N7 to the south of Tain. Here, the land is covered with *cailloux roulés*, great drift boulders resembling those of Châteauneuf. These store up heat and moisture, giving the vine an unique microclimate and evening out ripening. Here is Jaboulet's magnificent Domaine de Thalabert and some of Alain Graillot's best land. Wine from top producers in this sector tends to combine *ampleur*, strength and finesse, a combination.

On the plateau, the machine harvester

has made its appearance. The old guard, who staunchly defend hand-picking, look askance at these mechanical monsters and grumble to themselves discontentedly. However, there is as yet no evidence that quality suffers in the long term and, given their cost-effectiveness, these machines are more than likely to become a permanent feature of the autumn landscape.

More contentious, however, are irrigation systems, which have been spotted dripping or fizzing away in times of great heat. Growers understandably dislike seeing vines (and income) wilt for lack of a few litres of water. While none will admit to transgression, one important *négociant*-grower reported being unable to find anywhere to drive a coachload of visiting winemakers because there were illicit sprinklers hard at work in every direction.

VINIFICATION

Vinifications vary from grower to grower along all the usual parameters. However, in broad outline they mirror Hermitage. Syrah, Marsanne and Roussanne are treated here very much as they would be there: the same considerations and difficulties apply. Styles, however, exhibit a broader spectrum – encompassing everything from the almost *primeur* fruitiness to satisfy the impatient (and restaurants), to the mightier, meatier, more robust offerings, architected with plenty of tannin and concentration, for those prepared to wait. The best have the balance to be drinkable after three or four years and, in fine vintages, the constitution to develop over another decade.

Older growers – *la tradition* – tend to mature wines in old wood, often for too long, which dries them out. The younger fraternity, concerned to preserve fruit and balance structure, use new wood, sparingly and tailor *élevage* to the style of the vintage. Some simply go for fruit, pure and unalloyed, using large wood or stainless steel and early bottling for freshness. Styles thus reflect individual tastes, but the overall quality is steadily improving.

TASTE

Crozes-Hermitage, whether white or red, is fairly considered as a scaled-down version of its grander neighbour. The best whites will start out with plenty of sappy, floral fruit – delicious drinking young, but capable of interesting development over 5-10 years. Unlike great white Hermitage, Crozes seems not to suffer from mid-life reticence, but changes in an even transition from fruit and flowers to acacia, nuts and peach kernels, as it deepens in colour.

Red Crozes of the keeping variety – Jaboulet's Domaine de Thalabert or Graillot's La Guiraude are the pick of the bunch – develops in much the same way as a great Hermitage, but at an accelerated pace. Young, they exude delicious ripe fruit, which ensures most bottles a short life. Those who do wait, for 10-15 years in the finest vintages, find something subtle, complex and gamey. Jaboulet's 1978 Thalabert is at its peak now, while the 1983 is only just starting to put its head above the parapet. Perhaps because Crozes represents some of the finest value in the entire Rhône Valley, the impatient have less to reproach themselves for than the wealthy

visitors who swig back great bottles of young Hermitage and Côte-Rôtie in the three-star restaurants of the Lyonnais.

PRODUCERS

The evolution in quality since the mid-1980s has been truly remarkable. While a few of the older generation are hanging on, more or less, the momentum now comes from a band of younger Turks who are committed to excellence and taste widely enough to know what they are competing against. Several of the top estates are discussed in detail. These apart, Chapoutier (qv), Etienne Pochon, Charles Tardy, Bernard Ange and Louis de Vallouit (qv) all produce excellent Crozes. Unfortunately, the AC still suffers

from a great deal of poor "Crozes-Hermitage" which finds its way onto international markets. The provenance of much of this disgraceful fluid can only be surmised, but it is disheartening to see the efforts of many conscientious growers being undermined.

VINTAGES

These broadly follow Hermitage.

AC CROZES HERMITAGE

Created	4 March 1937
Area (max)	4,200ha
Area under vine 1994	1,020ha
Base yield	45hl/ha
Minimum alcohol	10% (13% maximum)
Growers	35

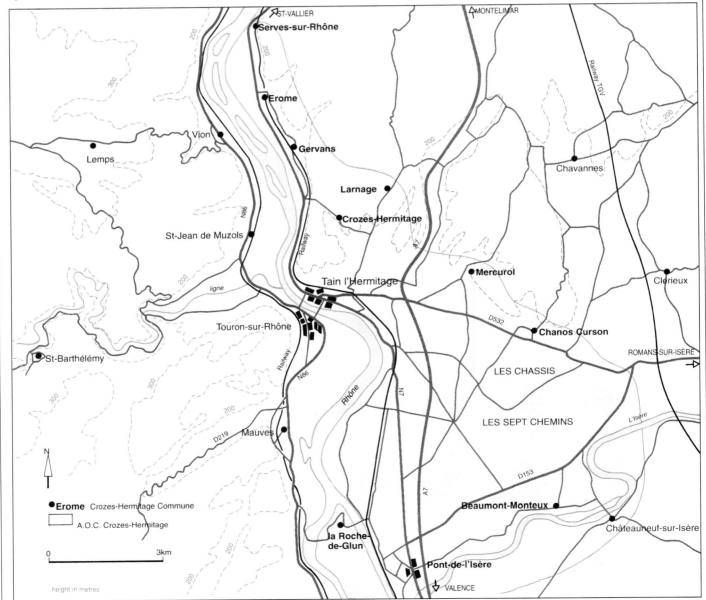

Erome ● Crozes-Hermitage Commune
▢ A.O.C. Crozes-Hermitage
0 — 3km
height in metres

DOMAINE ALBERT BELLE

Albert Belle and his son have made great strides since breaking away from the Tain growers' cooperative in 1990 to make, bottle and market the wine from their nineteen hectares.

There's a red Hermitage from Les Diognières and a white Hermitage from Les Murets, but it is the three *cuvées* of Crozes-Hermitage – a standard red, Les Pierrelles; the superior, old-vine Louis Belle; and a white – which form the spine of this production.

Albert's passion for wine is evident; a lean man, rather reserved in manner, he waited to start out on his own until his son was old enough to help him. Although everything – including 200 virgin casks – is brand new, the thought processes are thoroughly traditional.

The domaine's physical manifestation consists of a great new breeze-block warehouse-type *cuverie* and cellars, behind the cemetery at Larnage. The place has a somewhat clinical air – reflecting perhaps the hygiene necessary for the produce of their 19ha of fruit-trees, which complement the vines.

The vineyards are mostly on hillsides at Larnage, with a little on flatter land round Pont de l'Isère and Les Chassis. The soils are mainly clay-limestone, with a high granitic gravel content (the Carolans quarry is in the commune), and particularly adapted to white grapes.

The style of wine here is still evolving, helped by the advice of Jean-Luc Colombo, who also does the bottling. Red vinification is aimed at *vins de garde* with no de-stemming, three weeks' *cuvaison* and maturation for 12 months (Crozes) to 18 months (Hermitage) in cask, with 18–25% new Allier oak for Les Pierrelles, 25–35% for Louis Belle and 50% for the red Hermitage. The wines are lightly fined, but unfiltered.

Although not yet top-class, the results are good. Some movement in Albert's presently inflexible stance on de-stemming – "we've never asked the question of why not de-stem; there's no need to break my head, it has no interest" – would significantly improve the balance and character of his reds, which tend to show unattractive youthful stalkiness both on nose and palate. Partial de-stemming need not compromise ageing potential; on the contrary, it would enhance it.

Both Crozes and Hermitage whites contain a good dollop of Roussanne (15% and 25% respectively), which adds florality and finesse to complement the Marsanne's structure. Yielding nearer 15 than 30hl/ha, Roussanne also adds concentration.

Vinification is presently all in *inox*, although Albert wants to use some new wood "when we have some to spare" – but cash considerations and the "need to monitor these carefully" delayed the experiment until 1995. Without doubt, a seasoning of oak would add structure and richness to what are already delicious whites.

The Belles are still finding their feet. The wines are well made but need a distinct touch of lushness for real excellence.

A domaine to watch.

APPELLATION	VARIETY	DETAILS	AREA
CROZES HERMITAGE (PONT DE L'ISERE)	SYRAH	22 yrs old; goes into Les Pierrelles; flat, gravelly soils; 500 metres from Graillot	10.00
CROZES HERMITAGE	SYRAH (COTEAUX DE LARNAGE)	Raw material for Cuvée Louis Belle; 50+ yr old vines	6.00
CROZES HERMITAGE	MARSANNE (85%) + ROUSSANNE (15%) (COTEAUX DE LARNAGE)	50+ yr old vines	1.50
HERMITAGE (LES MURETS)	SYRAH	20+ yr old vines	1.00
HERMITAGE (LES DIOGNIERES)	MARSANNE (75%) + ROUSSANNE (25%)	25+ yr old vines	0.50
		TOTAL (hectares):	19.00

BERNARD CHAVE

Bernard Chave is an interesting individual, making some of the best red and white Crozes there is. Since his translation from agricultural worker to *vigneron* in 1970 – he always wanted to make wine – he has created something of a self-sufficient enterprise, with which he is completely content.

An open, friendly almost schoolboyish manner hides a thoroughgoing distaste for towns and travel, hence the desire to be self-contained. Fruit trees and 8ha of vines, near the family home which lies next to the busy A6 motorway, provide the income. Chickens, a vegetable garden and a swimming pool (for his daughter, he never uses it), are the resources which allow Bernard to stay at home and avoid

Bernard Chave.

travel. The acquisition of a pig, for properly reared pork, is under discussion, although his wife does not seem entirely convinced of the practicalities.

He entertains a deep-rooted distrust of bureaucracy – especially the EU – and, closer to home, is a severe critic of those who by over-cropping devalue "a good appellation", as well as the integrity and hard work of others.

On offer here are a red and white Crozes and a red Hermitage. The white comes mostly from 1.5ha of hillside vineyards in the commune of Larnage and 0.3ha of very old vines behind the vegetable patch – a mix of Roussanne and Marsanne. The red comes from 6ha in Mercurol. These contain a variety of planting configurations – from 2x1.5 metres to 2x1 – with soils which vary from the sandy loams of Larnage (excellent for whites) to the Mercurol limestones and the stony *galets* of Les Chassis – which are ideal for Syrah.

Bernard and his son Yann prefer to work the land rather than using weed-killers, and are no lovers of machines. Hence the reds are hand-harvested and not de-stemmed; this latter has caused a family rift, since his wife and son consider that partial de-stemming would make a difference and want him to buy an *erafloir*. Bernard, on the other hand, counters that "each time you take something out of the grape you take something out of the wine".

Madame Chave doesn't just look after the office; in 1993 she persuaded her husband to green-prune their Hermitage vines, against considerable resistance: "one kilo is worth 50 francs", groans Bernard.

The main vinification idiosyncrasy involves putting a layer of straw at the bottom of each *cuve* to act as a filter. Otherwise, things proceed uncontroversially – three weeks' vatting with a *pigeage* every other day and *remontage* twice daily, which is the sole means of cooling if the temperature

should rise above 30°C. The Crozes spends six months in *pièces, foudres* and *demi-muids*, the Hermitage one year. Ideally, the Crozes would have longer maturation but demand dictates otherwise. Second-hand wood is preferred, but Bernard had to buy four new *demi-muids* in 1994 as there were no used ones available.

There appear to be two separate *cuvées* of red Crozes – one for the USA, unfiltered; the other, for everyone else, plate-filtered at the instigation of a UK importer.

According to Bernard, most people harvest their white grapes when they are still green, to preserve fruit flavours; he

waits until the bees arrive to feast off the super-ripe grapes. The Marsanne and Roussanne for the Crozes are vinified together, entirely in *cuve* – fermented at 18-20°C because above that Bernard considers that "the fruit disappears". In 1993 a new Allier cask appeared in the cellar, as an experiment.

Bottling, preceded by a bentonite fining, is normally in early summer following the vintage "unless demand really gets heavy".

Despite their wrangles – invariably amicable – the Chaves are a delightfully close-knit family, whose excellent wines deserve greater recognition.

APPELLATION	VINEYARD	DETAILS	AREA
CROZES-HERMITAGE	LARNAGE	Marsanne & Roussanne en coteau.	1.50
CROZES-HERMITAGE	MERCUROL	Marsanne & Roussanne; very old vines – age unspecified; behind house.	0.30
CROZES-HERMITAGE	MERCUROL	Syrah; 5–20 yrs. old;	6.00
		TOTAL (hectares):	7.80

DARD & RIBO

In 1984 Jean-René Dard and François Ribo teamed up to make wine. Today they work 5.35ha of vines, spread over three appellations – Crozes, St-Joseph and Hermitage – producing mainly reds, with a touch of white from Crozes and St-Joseph.

The operation is run from a set of dilapidated outbuildings adjoining Château Blanche-Laine, below the village of Mercurol. Inside, behind a hessian curtain, casks and implements litter the jumbled cellar. However, as so often, appearances are deceptive. The disorder reflects their stronger interest in the vineyards, where they seem to spend most of their time. This effort pays off, with yields averaging 25–30hl/ha for both colours, and it shows in the wines, which are well constituted.

The whites are vinified from very ripe fruit: "there are grapes in our wine", explains the ginger-bearded Dard, unnecessarily. Fermentation starts in stainless steel and finishes in old *pièces*; there is minimum chaptalization, fining but no filtration and bottling a year or so later. Their eventual goal is to work without sulphur – at present some is added to the must – but they are not there yet.

The range starts with two red Crozes: a fresh, fruity, *vin nouveau* bottled in May for picnic drinking, and a normal *cuvée* bottled unfined and unfiltered after a year

Jean-René Dard with his fine old press.

in cask. There are two white Crozes: one from 0.6ha of 10-year-old Roussanne and Marsanne vines, the other, two casks only, from 40-year-old Marsanne.

Then come a trio of St-Josephs: a pure Roussanne white and two reds – one from St-Jean-de-Muzols, the other, a mere 2–3 casks, from the more classic granitic "*terroir de Tournon*"; this wine is characterised by firm ripe almost Cornas-like tannins supporting plenty of dark fruit from 40- to 50-year-old vines. There is also a red Hermitage. All the reds are matured in cask and *demi-muid* – but none new: "we tried it".

This is a fine, if somewhat eccentric, domaine. A sign on the approach road proclaims that the cellar is open on Saturday mornings for sales and tasting. If you don't mind the disorder, it's well worth the visit.

APPELLATION	VINEYARD	DETAILS	AREA
ST-JOSEPH	TOURNON & ST-JEAN-DE-MUZOLS	40–50 yr old vines, en coteaux; Tournon is granitic soil. Includes patch of Roussanne	2.00
CROZES-HERMITAGE	LARNAGE & MERCUROL	10–50 yr old vines; 60% en coteaux	2.30
CROZES-HERMITAGE	LARNAGE	⅘ Roussanne, ⅕ Marsanne	0.70
HERMITAGE (VAROGNES)		0.25 ha of 100+ yr old vines; 0.1 young vines	0.35
		TOTAL (hectares):	5.35

DOMAINE ALAIN GRAILLOT

Alain Graillot is Crozes-Hermitage's brightest new star, demonstrating that generations of "tradition" are not a pre-requisite of quality. He and his attractive wife arrived 15 days before their first harvest in 1985, exchanging an itinerant life in agro-chemicals (one of their sons was born in Guatemala, the other in Costa Rica) for that of *vigneron*. Discounting tradition and mystique, he believes that fine wine comes from the intelligent application of basic principles. A decade later he is one of the Crozes' top producers.

His domaine is on flat ground, near Roche de Glun, where the soil is composed of 10cm of red earth, overlaid with boulders, atop 30 metres of chemically inert sand. Such conditions can produce fruity wines with finesse but lacking structure and depth. Over-cropping on such land brings immediate sanction, making it essential to compensate by reducing the normally high yields. Low crop levels mattered less in the 1960s and 1970s when *vignerons* were more concerned with volume than with intensity, but for anyone serious about quality, yield is a key factor. "My objective for both red and white is 40hl/ha, 5hl/ha less than the permitted maximum" Alain explains; the white varies from 20–50hl/ha and the red from 35 in 1992 to 48 in 1991 and 1993.

Severe double cordon pruning, a green harvest and late picking all help. The aim is not over-ripeness, just picking when the grapes taste right and with an eye to "acids, tannins and the weather-forecast". In 1993, Alain was horrified to see people harvesting "tons and tons of fruit" on 15 September, at ridiculously poor maturity. He waited six days longer for his whites and 13 for the reds. "I am ready to take risks with the white – it's the sugars that matter; they support a touch of rot and will live well without much acidity".

Before 1992, Alain's 2.5ha of white grapes were fermented in *cuve*; now, half the crop is vinified in 2-8 year old casks, for *rondeur*, and half at lower temperatures (16–18°C) in *cuve*, for fruit. There is generally neither malolactic nor lees-stirring. "I've noticed that the tradition is to clarify both must and wine as soon as possible. Chave doesn't keep his wine on lees for long – his experience is good enough for me". Because protein levels are naturally high here, the whites are usually lightly bentonite-fined then sterile filtered. *Cuve* and cask wines are assembled just a few days before bottling.

Alain Graillot.

Alain's white Crozes is fat and stylish, gorgeous young, and well repays keeping. Even lesser vintages – eg 1993 – are most attractive. He is bullish about the potential of Crozes whites: "people think that they oxidize easily; in fact, white Rhônes are virtually unoxidizeable, provided they are carefully made".

The two red Crozes are also top-flight. The finer, La Guiraude, first appeared in 1985 (250 cases then) and consists of a blend of the *cuvées* which please Alain most – wines without imbalances or faults (eg an excess of wood or lack of substance), yet with finesse and harmony. There is no fixed proportion – La Guiraude simply represents "the Patron's taste", not necessarily the best lots, selected from a comprehensive tasting of all the casks in the cellar just before the final racking in October of the second year. The process is complex – the wine in each cask being assigned to a "style-family", depending on its flavour and evolution. Once the Guiraude has been isolated the remaining "families" are racked to cask and *cuve*, keeping the same percentages of each provenance.

These reds are vinified for three weeks and not de-stemmed – "the great debate" – with 20–30% of intact berries in each *cuve*, preceded by a cold maceration without sulphur. This is important – the carbon dioxide released extracts both fruit and colour-precursors, to which latter Alain attributes the fact that his wines tend to develop density with ageing. "People are rarely impressed by our wines in cask and rate them much better in bottle".

Only the fine lees find their way into cask, rackings eliminate the rest. Young, but not new, casks bought from top Burgundy producers Sauzet and Dujac are used to develop structure and roundness without overt oakiness. The standard Crozes has a proportion of wine matured in *cuve*, which varies from 50% in 1988 to 20% in 1992. Both Crozes *cuvées*, but not the Hermitage, are lightly filtered but not (since 1987) fined. Alain is vigorously dismissive of "certain journalists who think wine is better unfiltered".

In addition to the Crozes, there is a touch of St-Joseph and two casks of red Hermitage. "None of it's any good", Alain smiles, referring to the small volume of Hermitage, "but – all.the same!". The wine is as yet somewhat one-dimensional, but has plenty of style.

The estate has matured and expanded. Even though the old cold-room for peaches remains, a storage and office complex has now appeared, as well as an attractive house, light and airy, looking out over the vines.

Alain is modest and reflective – in outlook more Bordelais perhaps than Rhône. He selects and blends to make "his wine", the idea of "brand" or "house style" usurping that of *terroir*. What matters is that his wines please him. That they also please others appears to be a bonus rather than a motive.

APPELLATION	VINEYARD	DETAILS	AREA
CROZES-HERMITAGE	PONT DE L'ISERE	Syrah: 10 planted 1973; 3.50 in 1960; 3.50 1985/9	17.00
CROZES-HERMITAGE	PONT DE L'ISERE	White: planted 1980	2.50
HERMITAGE	LES GREFFIEUX	80 yr old vines, en fermage	0.12
HERMITAGE	LES GREFFIEUX	Planted 1994	0.12
ST-JOSEPH	TOURNON /ANDANCE	En fermage	1.60
		TOTAL (hectares):	21.34

DOMAINE DES GRIVES

The Combiers came to Roche du Glun in the 1950s, when the construction of the Canal du Rhône forced them to move. Income from 25ha of fruit kept things going, while *grandpère* planted some vines whose fruit went to the Tain co-op. The return of Maurice Combier's son Laurent, in 1986, from work experience gained at Vieux Lazaret in Châteauneuf, Ott in Bandol and Dubreuil-Fontaine in Pernand Vergelesses, led to some domaine-bottling.

Now, the original 4.5ha has grown to 11 – mostly red Crozes – sales have taken off, and the domaine's reputation strengthens year by year. The team has recently been strengthened by Laurent's wife, a policeman's daughter from Montelimar, and their newly-minted son, who has developed a usefully healthy appetite for fresh fruit.

Their land, on the Les Chassis plateau, is similar to Alain Graillot's – flat, with 1.5m of stony alluvium giving directly on to 30m of inert sand. Laurent works both vines and fruit *en culture biologique*, with no weed killers or toxic chemicals treatments. The Syrah vines are planted at 4–5,000 per hectare, trained *en cordon de Royat*, and spaced to allow machine harvesting, although the Combiers have no intention of doing so. Once the fruit crop is harvested, their experienced team of pickers can turn their attention to the vineyards.

When they went solo, the Combiers needed expert winemaking advice. The stark choice lay between the Chambre d'Agriculture in Valence, who offer help to *vignerons*, self-help, and Jean-Luc Colombo from Cornas. They chose Colombo.

His influence is evident – especially on the reds, where the aim is full, supple wines for relatively early drinking. So, rather than classical open-vat-with-stems vinification, the crop is de-stemmed and macerated for up to a month in thermo-regulated *inox* vats.

There are two red Crozes – a standard issue and the prestige brand Clos des Grives made largely (80%) from 40- to 50-year-old vines. Whereas only 5–15% of the standard *cuvée* sees wood, and then only for six months (the major part being *élevé* in *cuve* to conserve fruitiness), the Grives spends a year in cask – with 30% new oak. Interestingly, the Grives contains no press-wine, which is used to firm up the lesser *cuvée*. Any sub-standard wine is sold in bulk to *négociants*.

In the sopping wet, testing, 1993 vintage, the domaine made its first white Crozes, a worthy effort from Marsanne vines planted in 1990, fermented one third in new casks, two thirds in tank. These components were assembled "at the last moment" and the result bottled in February. The wine was stylish enough but lacked the finesse or length that Alain Graillot managed to extract in that year. A healthier, riper, crop would give Laurent the chance to show his mettle. Some Roussanne has recently been planted and will come on stream in the late 1990s. In dilute vintages, such as 1993, and to a lesser extent 1991 and 1992, the reds vats are *saignées* and the juice made into a fresh, peachy rosé.

The domaine has prospered, helped by flattering press comment and plaudits from fellow *vignerons*. The usual physical manifestation of success, a magnificent new stone *cuverie* and cellar – this one faced with *galets roulés* – stands proudly behind an imposing new entrance, strategically sited beside the busy Tain–Pont de l'Isère road.

Here, summer tourists stop to buy boxes of Combier apricots, peaches, plums and cherries – a market opportunity not lost on Laurent, who uses the fruit as a magnet to sell his wine. "Sales are not a problem for us", he remarks – their 3,500 cases split equally between France and export.

The standard red is soft, easy drinking, but nothing special. The serious wine here is the Clos des Grives – named after the abandoned petrol-station at the entrance to the property. This is generally a plump, structured wine, fit for ageing half a decade or more – a different style to neighbour Graillot, whom Laurent admires, but delicious nonetheless. In the end, it's a matter of preference.

APPELLATION	VINEYARD	DETAILS	AREA
CROZES-HERMITAGE	SYRAH	40–50 yr old vines, plus younger plantings	9.70
CROZES-HERMITAGE	MARSANNE	Planted 1990; first vintage 1993	0.80
ST-JOSEPH	SYRAH	Planted 1990; first vintage 1994	0.50
		TOTAL (hectares):	11.00

DOMAINE DU PAVILLON

As with many smaller appellation wine enterprises in the Northern Rhône, the Domaine du Pavillon grew out of fruit farming. *Grandpère* Cornu bought the estate, then planted it with pears and apricots in 1961. A decade later his son took over and planted vines which, until 1989, supplied Jaboulet and Delas with Crozes. In turn his son, Stephane, joined him and in 1990 they started bottling some red. A white *cuvée* followed in 1991 with an old-vine *cuvée* of red. Now some 70% of their 10ha is domaine-bottled.

Stephane is undoubtedly the driving force behind the excellent quality. Thin, wiry and definitely not "*passionné du vin*" he spent two terms at the Université du Vin at Suze la Rousse before taking sole charge of winemaking. Visit at the right time and you are just as likely to find father and son up ladders picking apricots for the market at Rungis as in the vineyards; fruit remains an important part of this enterprise.

The vineyards form a single block, round the family home in the hamlet of Sept Chemins at Les Chassis. The best wine comes from 5ha of older vines, on a steepish hillside topped off by a small stone pavillon, which gives both domaine and its prestige *cuvée* its name. Young vines, on flatter land, go into "Le Chai-Cornu" *cuvée*.

The aim is to produce wines with matter, which means systematic additions of tannin – "it gives more richness in the mouth" – long extraction and high fermentation temperatures. The reds are not de-stemmed: "nature gives stems and I don't want to go against nature" is Stephane's view of the matter. In the

APPELLATION	VARIETY/VINEYARD	DETAILS	AREA
CROZES-HERMITAGE	SYRAH, MERCUROL, SEPT CHEMINS	5 ha of 15–22 yr old vines; 4.5 ha of 3–7 yr old vines	9.50
CROZES-HERMITAGE	MARSANNE, SEPT CHEMINS	18 yr old vines, all en coteaux	0.50
		TOTAL (hectares):	10.00

opinion of many, stems are coat-hangers, and there is nothing *a priori* which dictates their presence in the vats. *Cuvaison* lasts three to four weeks and peaks at 36–37°C to "have the best colour and tannin extraction". The old-vine *cuvée* spends up to four months in cask (50% new) or, as in 1993, six months with no new wood. There are two bottlings of red Crozes, one in the spring and the other in the autumn, whenever practicable, without filtration.

The white Crozes in vinified in *inox* at 18-20°C and spends seven months on fine lees before bottling. The malolactic is blocked with sulphur dioxide, so the wine is sterile-filtered.

What has been produced so far has been well-received. Gold medals and guide accolades have encouraged Stephane who is rapidly gaining confidence. Cornu *père,* a jolly, short man with a thoroughly mischievous grin, is proud of what has been achieved. This domaine seems set to go from strength to strength.

Stephane Cornu drawing wine with a pipette.

DOMAINE RAYMOND ROURE

Raymond Roure used to make the finest Crozes-Hermitage bar none – the red especially. Sadly, since the late 1970s, the wines have been distinctly patchy and strong rumours have recently circulated that the 80-year-old Roure had lost interest in his domaine, for which illness may have been partly responsible.

His vines are some of the best in the appellation – 8ha of Syrah and 3ha of Marsanne, 50–80 years old, all on south-exposed coteaux, none on plains. "We are the only ones to make Crozes from coteaux", claims the welcoming and loquacious Madame Roure, adding, with evident pride and reasonable justification: "our Crozes is better than many Hermitages". The geology is indeed not dissimilar to parts of the great Hill – very fine top-soils giving onto granite – a composition which produces both finesse and perfume. Rain drains away quickly here, whereas the flat ground at the southerly extremity of Tain l'Hermitage, on which grow the Roure apricots, holds water for days.

Raymond is one of Crozes-Hermitage's *éminences grises.* He married his splendid, supportive wife in 1946 and started bottling wine two years later. During the years which followed they scrimped and saved, no holidays or frivolities, with any spare cash going to buy vineyard land. "We never went to the cinema when we were young", she

Madame Raymond Roure.

laments. These days, they have bought a seaside apartment at Port Camargue, to which they repair for a few days every month. In their absence, their son-in-law is drafted in to mind the shop.

The whites are fermented in glass-lined cement and then kept in *foudres* for

six to eight months, then in cask until bottling some two to two and a half years after the vintage.

Provided that they don't spend too long in wood, the wines are full, powerful, substantial mouthfuls, with depth and plenty of flesh. Later bottlings often have an oxidative, dry note, however, which detracts somewhat from their overall appeal.

The reds are partly de-stemmed – depending on the harvest – and fermented in cement for 8–10 days; the press-wine is kept apart while the free-run wine spends seven or eigh months in *cuve,* followed by 2–3 years in *tonneaux* and *demi-muids.* There are invariably several bottlings of each vintage.

Raymond Roure is capable of making stunning wine. His 1978 red, for example, has evolved into a fine example of mature Crozes. Aficionados must wish him a speedy recovery, so that he can once more devote his full attention to his fine estate.

APPELLATION	VINEYARD	DETAILS	AREA
CROZES-HERMITAGE	GERVANS	50–80 yr old vines; en coteaux	8.00
CROZES-HERMITAGE	GERVANS	50–80 yr old vines; en coteaux	3.00
		TOTAL (hectares):	11.00

HERMITAGE

Some seventy-five kilometres south of Lyons, the Rhône makes a dramatic turn eastwards. On the left bank is the busy little town of Tain l'Hermitage, home to some of the larger *négociants* and general trading centre for much of the region's wine. Opposite, separated by two bridges – one a modern road bridge, the other a rickety pedestrian crossing – is its twin town, Tournon. Above Tain towers a dramatic saddle of vine-clad hillside. This is Hermitage.

HISTORY

According to archaeologists – who have excavated enough artefacts to substantiate the claim – vines have been grown here since Roman times. Local lore, however, dates the start of viticulture at some 600 years earlier. A particularly cherished relic, the Taurobole, an altar dating from 180 AD, is still in the town's possession. The wines of Tain (then known as Tegna) were of sufficient repute to merit specific reference by both Pliny and Martial. Until the Middle Ages, when Tain came under the protection of the Seigneurie of the powerful Abbey of Tournon, the wines were part of the district of Vienne. It was not until the 16th century that "Hermitage" was used – a name that derived, according to legend, from the 13th-century Crusades. A wounded knight, Gaspard de Sterimberg, sought refuge on the hill, planted vines and lived there as a hermit. His sojourn is commemorated by the small, empty chapel of St. Christopher near the summit. It belongs to Paul Jaboulet, who illuminate it at night, and the worthy knight returns the compliment by appearing on the label of their white Hermitage, *cuvée* Chevalier de Sterimberg.

By the 17th century, following a visit from Louis XIII to Tain, Hermitage had established a firm reputation throughout Europe and was drunk by the nobility, including the French and Russian courts. A century later, it was openly – and proudly – being used by the Bordelais as an "improver" for their wines. The broker Nathaniel Johnston records in letters to his partner, Daniel Guestier (quoted by John Livingston-Learmonth, 1992) that he was "averse to using Roussillon on our best wines, unless it be a gallon or two", and that "if you could get a sufficient quantity of good Hermitage to put a couple of Cans of it, it would be better". He also confirms that "The Lafitte of 1795, which was made up with Hermitage, was the best-liked wine of any of that year". Contemporary

Jaboulet's chapel near the top of the Hermitage hill.

wine lists reinforce the message with Margaux or Lafite *Hermitagé* commanding a premium over the unblended wine.

This ascendancy lasted until after the phylloxera devastation – in fact, until after the First World War, when manpower was short and demand slack. As with many Northern Rhône appellations, the end of the Second World War signalled a nadir – consumers' interest evaporated and wine fetched around a franc a litre. In view of its proven quality (and absurdly low price) the virtual disappearance of Hermitage from international markets seems particularly curious. Perhaps it was simply easier for buyers to travel to Bordeaux, where the variety and quantity was greater and the market better established.

Somehow, growers managed to survive until the 1970s when interest began to return. It was probably the remarkable 1978 vintage, coinciding with the rise of the quality wine-merchant in the USA and Britain, which really kick-started Hermitage's (and the entire region's) modern renaissance. Those massively dense, concentrated wines brought a swarm of eager buyers prospecting round growers' cellars – and, in their wake, world-wide press interest.

The 1980s and 1990s have seen Hermitage become a cult wine – with Côte-Rôtie, the supreme expression of the Syrah grape. At the top level, Jaboulet's La Chapelle and Chave's red Hermitage have become collectables, with buyers scrambling for an allocation, retail rationing and rocketing prices. Media stardom for the growers, backed up by "in-depth" profiles and exhaustive vertical tastings, reinforce the stampede. In the salerooms, rarity has driven the price of older vintages skywards. Although many would argue that the quality/price ratio has at last reached a level comparable to Burgundy or Bordeaux, the boom shows no sign whatever of busting.

A novelty, at least to the modern consumer since the tradition died out and has only recently been revived, is Hermitage's sweet wine, *vin de paille*. It is made by late-harvesting bunches of white grapes – not just the berries – and leaving them to dry indoors. When they have become raisin-like, the tiny amounts of juice are pressed out and undergo a long, slow, fermentation. Gérard Chave resurrected the practice in 1984 and Chapoutier now also makes a *vin de paille*. Both wines are remarkable – highly concentrated yet with enough acidity to keep the flavours fresh – and in very short supply. While Chapoutier sell their *vin de paille*, the Chaves keep theirs to share with friends and visitors.

THE VINEYARD

Looking across from the terrace of the Château de Tournon (a superb viewpoint) at this spectacular hill, it is all too easy to think of it as a single, uniform, slab of land. This impression is false. Although only covering 130ha (less than twice the area of Château Lafite, for example), the Hermitage AC is made up of a multitude of *terroirs,* each of which imprints a distinct stamp on the wine. Although the mapped AC area extends to 146.8ha, this includes unplantable rocks and even the site of the dreadful low-cost housing-block at the foot of the slope.

It is generally supposed, and written, that the hill is entirely composed of granite. In fact only the western section – Les Bessards and part of Gros des Vignes – are granitic; the remaining *climats* being on soils derived from *loess* (notably l'Hermite, Maison Blanche and La Croix) or deposited material of varying depths and composition, from the receding Rhône (Méal, Beaume, Rocoule, Murets, Peléat, Diognières and Greffieux, in particular). To the observant eye of anyone walking through the vineyard – an energetic half-hour from the railway station to the summit, but worth it for the views – this soil diversity is obvious.

The rules allow up to 15% of the white grapes Marsanne and Roussanne to be co-fermented with the Syrah for red Hermitage, an expedient reflecting the mixed plantings of earlier times; this concession is largely unused. White wines must come entirely from Marsanne or Roussanne, or both. In practice, Marsanne dominates, though Roussanne has seen a revival.

The vines, both red and white, are trained *en gobelet*, against chestnut stakes where the vines are old or the slope steep, and on wires on flatter ground where some mechanisation is feasible.

Most of the finest *climats*, including the main spine, Les Bessards, face broadly south, giving maximum sunshine. The difference in elevation from top to bottom (323 to 122 metres) means that higher sites are cooler – thus later-ripening – and more exposed to the violent drying winds which funnel up and down the valley. The more important of the *climats* are as follows:

Les Beaumes, between Peléat and Le Méal, at moderate altitude, has a mixture of limestone and iron-bearing clay soils, covered in parts with pudding-stones and crystalline *galets*. These gives a fine, scented and complex-flavoured wine – typically evoking raspberries and red-currants, with lowish tannins; sometimes a touch more vegetal in character than elsewhere on the hill.

Les Bessards forms the dorsal spine at the western end of the hill, below the famous landmark chapel which crowns the summit. Its thoroughgoing granite-based soils provide the backbone of Hermitage. The soils are "gore" – decomposed, oxidised and strongly ferruginous. Its fruit produces deeply-coloured wine, high in tartaric acids (not tannins), with notable concentration and intensity: both spicy and powerful, sometimes coming across as "crème de cassis". Bessards grapes need de-stalking, otherwise their wine would be too hard.

Diognières, at the lower eastern end of the hill, has very light soils giving quality in a good vintage, but less useful in a poor year. Its wine tends to be dark, brooding, powerful and tannic, with good acidity and sometimes a vegetal note.

L'Hermite, above Le Méal and delimiting Hermitage from Crozes-Hermitage to the north, has been owned in its entirety by the Chaves since they bought the domaine from the British impresario Terence Gray in 1984. Jean-Louis Chave has restored its buildings, behind a row of cypress trees on the skyline above Tain, for his own use. A walk through this vineyard shows how dramatically soils vary: from friable *loess* to hard pudding-stone agglomerations, from yellow-brown sandy clay to deeper layers of pebbles. This comes through as a soft, supple wine, all finesse and fruit – redolent of roses, red fruits and cherries in particular.

Le Méal, bounded by Les Bessards, Les Greffieux and L'Hermite, is different again:

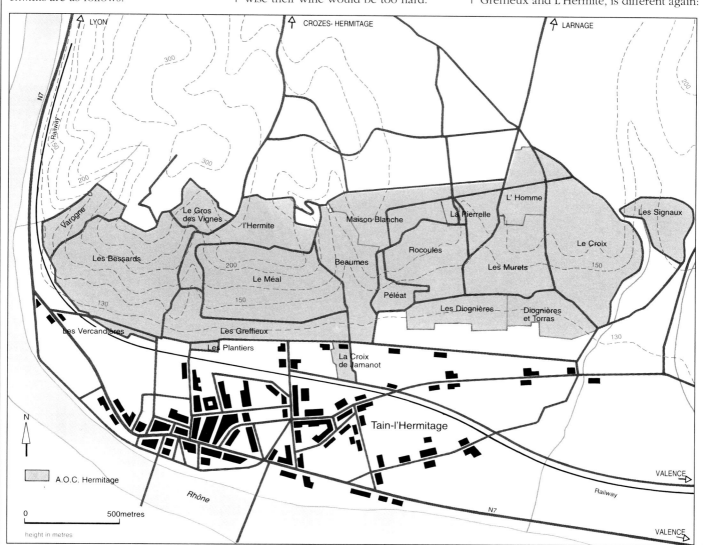

chalky soils, with a high content of small glacial stones. Typified by a finely perfumed, almost floral, elegant nose, and moderate tannins – suppleness and *rondeur* above all.

Peléat, below Le Méal, has stony sandy-clay soils that give deep, very fruity wine, often smelling of burnt toast or bitter chocolate – both supple yet tannic. Vigorous and racy in character, with highish acidity, yet fine and elegant. The Chaves are sole proprietors.

Les Rocoules, in the middle of the slope between Maison Blanche and Peléat, is quintessentially white-grape territory. Its soil is clay-limestone with some pudding-stones, which imparts a peachy, nutty character to white wines, and a strongly blackberry, liquorice and *fruits rouges* (sometimes even violet) scent to red wines. However, the red tends to coarseness and heavy tannins, which provide valuable support for development but are not sufficiently well-balanced to stand gracefully alone.

Les Greffieux, a long band of land crossing the base of the hill below Méal, is principally brown limestone, the top section mixed with sandy clays. This produces generous, quite supple, rich, fruity wines, needing the structure of Bessards or the tannin of next-door Diognières for completeness.

Most red Hermitages come from one or two *climats* – not necessarily those producing a complementary spectrum of qualities; so many wines start life lacking inherent balance. The best come from a blend of several *climats*, which, as few producers have that resource, means that the quantity of really fine Hermitage is small. In addition, growers who own vines on the hill are tempted to over-crop. A bottle of Hermitage will sell for several times the price of a bottle of St-Joseph; so many offerings, while perfectly respectable, are unacceptably dilute – a basic deficiency which no amount of cellaring will correct.

Hermitage's 130 planted hectares are owned by 40 proprietors, of whom 20 make and bottle wine. This includes the Tain l'Hermitage co-op, run, as it has been for many years, by the quality-oriented Michel Courtial. It vinifies both as a substantial proprietor and also for many of the remaining small proprietors, and its output accounts for some 35% of total volume. The wine is usually sound and carefully made, though less complex than the best.

TASTE

For the consumer, great Hermitage – red and white – is above all a matter of ageing, of having the patience to wait. As with

"Pudding stone" profile in the L'Hermite climat – one of many soil types on the Hermitage hill.

most fine wines, tasting Hermitage young will only give a feel for its overall composition and structure, with little hint of the glories to come. Those of both colours made with shorter vinifications (or, for whites, in stainless steel) start with an element of fruitiness which makes them appealing a few months after bottling. However these are not the bottles by which Hermitage is truly judged. The best whites – Grippat, Chave, Jaboulet (since 1988), Sorrel (Marc) and Chapoutier's *cuvée* l'Orée – begin life tightly budded, offering excellent drinking during their first few years. Then – a characteristic of white Hermitage – they seem to lose everything that seduced the taster in youth: florality, complexity, and even flavour disappear, and they shut down to a frustratingly dumb neutrality. When, often after many years, they emerge from hibernation, the wine is different; stronger, more confident in flavour, altogether fleshier and rounder – youthful fruit and flowers transformed into acacia, lime blossom, honey and hazelnut. These are individual wines – an acquired taste without the universal appeal of great white Burgundy – but fine, none the less. Properly stored the best will last half a century, evolving slowly along the same path – a gentle, oxidative, senescence.

Hermitage's mighty reds, however, should not be drunk young. While lighter vintages need 5–8 years to unravel, the greatest evolve at the imperceptible rate of a slow-growing plant and rarely reach maturity before a decade has passed. For vintages of the quality of 1978 and 1990,

the pace slows almost to a halt, as if the wine's supreme balance made it reluctant to change – the comfort and counterpoise of the Yogi's Lotus. Once unpacked, the natural power and depth of these wines become apparent. A fully mature Hermitage from a top grower and a fine vintage is a truly remarkable amalgam of aromatic and flavour complexity.

In character, old Syrah – particularly Hermitage – is often confused with old Bordeaux. Jaboulet's 1961 La Chapelle, perhaps the most celebrated of all postwar Hermitages, slipped into a range of 1961 First Growths was taken by experienced tasters for Château Margaux, an error to whose commission Gérard Jaboulet himself, who has undoubtedly tasted this wine more often than anyone, is not ashamed to admit.

With so little really top-class wine (Chave c 6,000 cases; La Chapelle c 10,000 cases), it is heart-breaking to watch four-year-old bottles being uncorked in the region's best restaurants – Pic, Pyramide, Chabran and the rest – so much pleasure forgone and promise squandered. For anyone who manages to buy some of these extraordinary wines the dilemma is to know when to start drinking them. If you get it wrong, the chance of replacing them and starting again is distinctly slender. No wonder these bottles are so cherished.

VINTAGES

1978: A very fine vintage indeed from a small, healthy crop. A late flowering (15 June), consequent on a cold and wet spring, produced significant *coulure*, which reduced crop size, but undoubtedly accounts for the great concentration of many wines. July, August and September were all fine, and the vintage took place in perfect weather in early- to mid-October. This was the first year in which a helicopter was used to spray Hermitage vines. The vintage shares common features with the remarkable 1961, to which it has often been compared; in particular an extraordinary concentration and an exemplary natural balance. These, supported by fine, round tannins have ensured the wines a long, frustratingly slow evolution. The top domaines all made excellent wine; in the case of Chave and Jaboulet these are still a long way from full maturity. They have great depth of extract and masses of tight, berryish fruit. The lesser Hermitages can be drunk now while the best need yet more time. The white 1978s also started out closed, and are just beginning to show their complexity and character.

1979: Another good vintage, although overshadowed by 1978. The reds are mostly well-constituted, more elegant than heavy-framed, with mature aromas and flavours. The crop was 56% higher than 1978 and this shows in the wines which are generally less concentrated. Apart from Chave and Jaboulet, there was a particularly fine red Hermitage from Henri Sorrel (Marc and Jean-Michel's late father). A vintage to enjoy now and over the next few years.

1980: Five per cent less crop than 1979. Rain during the vintage spoiled a promising harvest. The wines are of moderate quality and anything still left is unlikely to improve much. Drink soon.

1981: Another mediocre vintage, which was also affected by torrential rain during the harvest. The final crop was smaller than either 1979 or 1980, probably due to the need to eliminate damaged grapes. Even so, the wines have no great concentration and need drinking. Curiously, La Chapelle was only released in the USA, not in the UK and Europe.

1982: An under-rated vintage. As in Bordeaux, the summer was dry and hot, producing a large crop of super-ripe grapes. The top wines have developed well, with deep colours, open, seductive aromas and plenty of opulent, almost sweet fruit. Gérard Chave's red is wonderfully sensuous, completely different from either his

1978 or 1983, and eminently drinkable now; its impeccable balance will keep it alive for years. La Chapelle is in a similar vein, if somewhat more masculine. The whites have also developed well and are now fully mature.

1983: Another fine vintage, in theory at least. A good crop (marginally less than 1980) from fully ripe grapes. Excessive heat, however, and not quite enough rain gave the grapes tremendous levels of extract which show in the wines, which are dense and highly concentrated. Apart from a little rain in early September, fine, hot weather began in early June and lasted right through the harvest. Many reds still show little sign of real maturity and are still tightly-packed parcels with the fruit held firmly in place by a heavy layer of dryish tannins. Once again, this year, it was Chave and Jaboulet who made the best wines – Chave's white is particularly fine. Drink the whites over the next decade or more and the reds whenever you are brave enough to draw a cork.

1984: Generally poor to mediocre. Not an overly large crop, but one diluted by mid- and late-season rain. The wines (red and white) are ready to drink and will not – except perhaps for magnums of Chave – benefit from further keeping.

1985: Excellent vintage: well-constituted reds and whites that have developed well. The growing season was notable for a late cold snap at the end of spring and a lack of rain which reduced the crop size. Summer was very hot, punctuated by a little rain on 15 August. As a result, some of the whites lacked acidity which has affected their development; others, such as Chave's, are approaching maturity. The reds, including both La Chapelle and Chave, are surprisingly forward and characterised by plenty of ripe, open fruit which is deliciously supple and fragrant – rather like the 1985 red burgundies. Apart from Chave, Marc Sorrel's Le Greal and Bernard Faurie, all of whose wines have better balance and structure, these are not destined for exceptionally long ageing. Drink now and over the next few years.

1986: A very mixed vintage, spoiled by a combination of heat in July and August and rain at the start of the vintage in late September which spread rot throughout the vineyard. Some growers produced good, interesting wines which will do well over the medium term, while others, who did not sort their crop carefully, failed to produce anything of quality. In the former group, Chave, Jaboulet, Grippat, Faurie and Guigal were notable successes.

The westerly part of the Hermitage hill with the climat of Les Bessards on the left and the town of Tain l'Hermitage below.

Orientation table above Tournon overlooking the entire Hermitage hill.

1987: A distinctly mediocre vintage. The problem was not rain, but under-ripeness, which led to a rather austere, tannic bunch of wines. Some – from the usual top sources – have turned into quite attractive, lightish wines; many are fundamentally out of balance and without the fruit to match their structures. There was no La Chapelle released in this vintage. As in the Côte d'Or, the whites are superior to the reds – some fine wines which have good acidities and enough fat to give pleasure.

1988: A fine vintage of firm, dense, tannic wines – the product of a mild winter, a fine and hot spring, and a hottish and very dry summer. Some welcome rain fell in July, but August was torridly hot. The vintage started in mid-September and continued in perfect weather. The whites are more substantial and slow to develop than usual, but show considerable promise. This is the first vintage (since the 1970s) in which Jaboulet reverted to oak maturation, and the wine is excellent, showing something of the class of the magnificent old Sterimbergs. Chave also produced a fine white in this vintage. Some reds have too much tannin to make great Hermitage, but those with balance are long stayers, with a fine future. The best won't be properly mature, on either nose or palate, before the turn of the century; the wait should be worth it.

1989: The largest crop so far recorded (5,398hl). An ideal growing season, with exceptional heat and barely enough rainfall to produce a good balance of sugar, extract and tannin. Both whites and reds have abundant flesh and richness and almost decadent sensuousness. Nothing restrained about this vintage – pure enjoyment. The reds, although not as impressively dense as the 1990s, have the structure to age well and should make excellent drinking into the early years of the next century.

1990: A classic vintage and another record crop (6,047hl). The reds, in particular, have a depth and concentration which remind many of the 1978s and even of the 1961s. They also have the extract and balance of that vintage. Exuberant, super-ripe fruit brings the wine complex aromas and flavours and an almost sweet berry-like character. The sheer density of some *cuvées* (La Chapelle, Chapoutier, and Chave's standard and special Cathelin bottling in particular) is remarkable; also an excellent result from Marc Sorrel. The whites are also highly promising with both the power and structure for a long life. In short, true *vins de garde*.

1991: The severe frosts which hit most of viticultural France in April reduced crop size here also, although the loss was not catastrophic. A cold spring and early sum-

mer was followed by a spell of great heat which lasted until the vintage. The rain arrived after most of the white crop had been picked – these wines are generally well-constituted and fat – but some of the reds suffered. However, the top sources have made excellent wines in the classic mould, with firm structures and plenty of fruit. These seem to be evolving attractively. An upper-middle vintage.

1992: The season didn't start well: a poor spring and early summer with rain at flowering which led to *coulure*, severely reducing potential crop size for both red and white Hermitage (down to 3,775hl from 5,780ha in 1991). However, the vines recovered, and those who picked in advance of the rains which arrived during the first week of October had sound, reasonably concentrated fruit to vinify. The wines are mid-weight, with fair depth and correct constitutions, but overall this is no more than a fair vintage. Better than 1987, perhaps, but without the depth of 1988, 1989 and 1990.

1993: A fine spring and reasonable summer made for promising quality. The last week of September brought persistent, heavy rains. The grapes swelled and diluted, then rot spread. Those who were rigorous about discarding substandard fruit made small quantities of sound wine; but many *cuvées* are irremediably dilute. Where the fruit is sound, the reds have too much dry tannin ever to be very attractive. There are some promising whites, however – in particular the Chaves', whose wine has some attractive fat, although not the usual power. No La Chapelle was made in this vintage. Altogether, not much to get excited about.

1994: Rather better than the last two vintages. A dry, warm summer, then some helpful rain at the beginning of September fleshed out the fruit. The harvest was healthy, though small. Had the rain come in August, it would have had a far more beneficial impact. First reports suggest "correct" wines of above-average quality.

AC HERMITAGE

Created	4 March 1937
Area (max)	146.8ha
Area under vine 1994	130ha
Base yield	40hl/ha
Minimum alcohol (red)	10.5% (13.5% max)
Minimum alcohol (white)	11% (14% max)
Minimum alcohol (vin de paille)	14%
Growers	20

CHAPOUTIER

Chapoutier, founded in 1808 by Polydor Chapoutier and passed from father to son ever since, is one of the oldest firms in Tain l'Hermitage and, in common with many organisations of such age, has seen its fair share of upheavals. It is currently trying to come to terms with what is probably the most fundamental of these, a radical change in direction.

Until recently, the firm was directed by Max Chapoutier. A man of Napoleonic stature and turn of personality, he was not really interested in wine: he went through the motions of producing and selling it, but showed little appetite for immersing himself in the details. Until, and for a decade beyond, his retirement in 1977, the wines of both colours were generally hard and dry, lacking in charm and flesh, and more often than not, marked by prematurely oxidative aromas and flavours: the result of far too long spent in old wood.

Max's sons Michel and Marc took over and, for a time, things went on much as before. Then, in 1986, after several visits to Australia and California, the brothers found themselves together in America and, away from Tain, began discussing what they should do with the firm. They had a good working relationship and discovered broad agreement about future direction – an all-out effort for quality and a fundamental move from Max's non-vintage, "*Grande Cuvée*", style-driven wines to a philosophy which emphasised vintage differences and, above all, *terroir*.

They observed, in particular, that consumers were becoming increasingly exacting about the quality, for which they were prepared to pay the highest prices, and felt that top quality was the only viable route. An intensive technical course in Paris prepared Michel to implement the necessary changes in vinification, while Marc continued to concern himself more with their international sales effort.

The firm has an impressive 63.16ha of vines – including, it is claimed, more than a quarter of Hermitage's 140ha (although Marc Chapoutier was not himself prepared to supply details). In 1993 they acquired from the Montgolfier family a further 4ha of vineyard surrounding the tiny stone chapel at the top of the hill in the Bessards *climat*. Their southern Rhône flagship is the 27ha of 35- to 40-year-old vines at the Domaine de Bernadine in Châteauneuf-du-Pape.

Michel views the production of "*grand vin*" as a year in the vineyards and a month in the cellars. So a great deal of

Wooden boxes are lined with straw (paille) to dry grapes for Chapoutier's vin de paille.

effort, and expense, has apparently been poured into the vineyards. Soil is regarded as the main source of typicity – the top three metres ("bio-top") being critical. They stress the importance of low-yielding old vines and of using only indigenous yeasts in fermentation; selected yeast cultures tend to produce the same aromas every year, which is totally opposed to their wish to maximise the aroma difference.

The Chapoutiers also say that, in contrast to almost everyone else, their vineyards are entirely run on bio-dynamic lines. They boast that in wet vintages, such as 1993, their bio-dynamic vines have only 10% of the rot suffered by their neighbours – an assertion strongly disputed by other growers, however.

Finding, from their travels, that most consumers – especially in the USA – drank any wine they bought within two weeks of purchase, convinced the Chapoutiers that what was required were wines which are approachable young yet had the structure to age well. To achieve this required the development of a more precise scheme of vinification.

In essence, this specifies that grapes from Châteauneuf and the left bank – Crozes and Hermitage – are 100% de-stemmed, to avoid herbaceous flavours. Fermentation temperatures are kept down to 20–25°C for the first three days because they believe that below 5% alcohol, the must is particularly vulnerable to undesirable yeasts which

won't work beyond this level. These early days are critical to the extraction of structure; thereafter, the temperature is allowed to rise to 34–35°C. The use, as far as possible, of the small-grained "Petite" Syrah, is also important for its better pigment extraction.

Red grapes from the right bank – Côte-Rôtie, St-Joseph and Cornas – are not fully de-stemmed, since, it is said, the stems and berries ripen at the same time, lessening the impact of a proportion of stems in the *cuves*. The global aim is to maximise the aroma palette and to extract structure without undue heaviness. The overall vinification scheme recognises that tannins transform during fermentation in a predetermined sequence: *primeur* tannins leach out first; these are harsh and never totally absorbed into a wine (a classic example are the 1975 Bordeaux, most of which after 20 years are still irredeemably tannic). Thereafter, tannins polymerise (short-chain molecules combining into longer, softer-tasting ones), first soft, then fine, tannins.

The reds are vinified by soil-type rather than by *lieu-dit*; the La Bernadine vineyard, for example, has eight different soils. A deliberately long *cuvaison* is designed to ensure that unstable *primeur* tannins are removed from solution, to bring greater colour stability, and to maximise the development of fine tannins. *Pigeage à pied* in the firm's ancient 12,600-litre wooden vats adds further tannic support, but the press-wine is never added back to the free-run wine because it contains undesirable harsh tannins.

Instead of Max's 24 months or longer in wood, the Chapoutier reds now spend a maximum of 18 months in cask – with one quarter to one third new wood, 80% of which is Tronçais, the rest of different origins. After one year, the casks are given a quarter turn – *bande de côté* – and left, without further racking, in the old, *mycelium*-walled Calvet cellars up a side street in Tain. When the right moment arrives, the wines are bottled unfined and unfiltered; the Chapoutiers try to bottle each *cuvée* in one go – but this is not always possible for the larger volumes.

A cornerstone of Marc and Michel's plans involved the release of a number of *têtes de cuvées*: For Côte-Rôtie, there is La Mordorée, made from 100% de-stemmed grapes from 60-year-old vines on the Côte Brune; red Hermitage appears as Ermitage Le Pavillon, from 60- to 70-year-old vines at the base of Les Bessards; and white Hermitage as Cuvée l'Orée, from le Méal. St-Joseph comes as Deschants, both red and white, from their own vineyards on the steep granitic terraces behind Mauves, the traditional heart of this appellation. The top *cuvée* of Crozes, in both colours, is Les Meysonniers, made from vineyards at Les Chassis. Finally, since 1990 there has been an annual release of Hermitage Vin de Paille, from bunches left indoors to concentrate for two months in wooden boxes before being fermented and matured in cask for 16 months; this finishes up at 15% alcohol with a residual sugar of 105 grammes/litre.

For both red and white wines, Michel considers that the potential for ageing is based principally on the acid/alcohol balance. Before 1991, the whites were vinified at 17–18°C in enamelled *cuves*, but didn't have either the structure or the potential of the reds. Tasting a complete range of progressively older wines, Marc and Michel concluded that white vinification had to be adapted to make the wines more accessible young.

The solution they came up with was a tri-partite fermentation: part in *inox* at 14-15°C for freshness and attack; part in enamel at 18-19°C to flesh out the middle palate; and part in cask at 22-23°C to contribute structure and length, because at higher temperatures you gain these qualities but lose aromas. The elements are assembled after malolactic and the wines bottled when tasting suggests the moment is right. The sole exception is their Condrieu, which is fermented at 17–21°C. These changes came in 1988/9 for the red wines, two years later for the whites and have been received considerable international acclaim – especially for the *têtes de cuvées*.

Credit for the undoubted improvement in quality is not only due to Michel Chapoutier, who is usually identified as the firm's winemaker. Since the late 1980s, the influence of Jacques Grange, a talented winemaker trained by Jean-Luc Colombo and his colleague Alberic Mazoyer, has also been evident. Mazoyer now works full-time for the firm. From 1989 onwards, Colombo has been responsible for training the firm's vineyard and cellar staff and for routine wine analyses. He has also had a hand in shaping the broad brush-strokes of winemaking policy.

This renaissance has not been achieved without cost. The vineyard expansion and re-establishment have been expensive, as has the Chapoutiers' high-profile marketing campaign to bring their new wines to the attention of the world's wine media. Also, a couple of difficult vintages – 1992 and 1993 – have helped no one in the northern Rhône, least of all the larger houses with heavy purchasing contracts and consequently greater exposure to a world market depressed by economic difficulties.

Praise for the revitalised Maison Chapoutier has not been universal. There has been less well-publicised comment on the state of the vineyards, which some suggest are not receiving the fullest attention, and suggestions that the wines do not live up to the hype bestowed on them. Tasting the range leaves an impression of unevenness: some wines are very good, while others fall short of the quality one finds elsewhere.

Marc and Michel are working hard to revitalise and secure the foundations of their business, and they deserve to succeed. Meanwhile, a little less hype would do much to help their cause.

APPELLATION	VINEYARD	DETAILS	AREA
HERMITAGE	LES BESSARDS	Syrah; 4.86 ha provides fruit for Pavillon; includes Montgolfier vines.	13.87
HERMITAGE	GREFFIEUX	Syrah	3.05
HERMITAGE	CHAPELLE	White grapes	1.31
HERMITAGE	MEAL	White grapes; 3.02 ha provides fruit for L'Orée	3.29
HERMITAGE	MURET	White grapes	5.25
HERMITAGE	CHANTE-ALOUETTE	White grapes	3.29
COTE-ROTIE	VARIOUS CLIMATS	53% Côte Brune; 34% Côte Blonde; 13% Jury des Carniers; average vine age 60+	2.60
CROZES-HERMITAGE	LES CHASSIS	20% 15 yrs average age; 80% 50+ average age	4.72
CROZES-HERMITAGE	CHAVANASSIEU	25 yrs. average age	0.53
ST-JOSEPH	ST-JOSEPH	50+ average age	2.02
ST-JOSEPH	MONTAGNON	Mauves; 25+ average age	1.38
ST-JOSEPH	DESCHAMPS	50+ average age	2.02
CONDRIEU	UNDISCLOSED	Undisclosed	
CHATEAUNEUF-DU-PAPE	LA BERNADINE	Communes of Châteauneuf and Bedarrides; vnes planted pre-1960, now 35-40 yrs old.	27.00
		TOTAL (hectares):	70.33

GÉRARD & JEAN-LOUIS CHAVE

This is one the greatest wine estates of France, respected not only in the Rhône Valley, but by *vignerons* and wine-lovers throughout France and far beyond. Much may be learned from such supreme masters of their craft.

Gérard took over from his father in 1970, having made wine from his own vines since 1952, when he was only 17. Now his intelligent and conscientious son Jean-Louis has joined him, after a year's study at the University of California, Davis and an MBA from Hartford – thus continuing an extraordinary unbroken – succession from father to son through all the generations since 1481.

This is a modest, close-knit family of great quality. No flashy or gaudy manifestations of success, just hard work peppered with occasional holidays. Gérard enjoys fishing and shooting, is well-read on military strategy, and harbours a thoroughly sound dislike of over-paid, incompetent government and the European Community, and laments the general lack of education he finds around him. Travel takes him and his wife, Monique, to China, Japan, the USA and Ireland – and anywhere else that he thinks might interest them.

The domaine's headquarters is a pleasant, unpretentious house in Mauves, an unremarkable village on the right bank of the Rhône between Tournon and Cornas. The only advertisement is a barely legible dusty metal sign protruding from the architrave – battered, weathered and disfigured by the daily pollution of 9,000 cars and lorries which thundered past the front door until the ring-road came in 1994. This used to proclaim "J-L Chave, *viticulteur*" with a telephone

Gérard and Jean-Louis Chave.

number, but decay has worn out the latter and bad driving bent the rest. It will probably fall down one day, but until then, there it stays, a memorial perhaps to less prosperous times when they needed customers.

The demand from visitors ringing the bell, even – *sacre folle!* – during Sunday lunch, became too much for the family; so suppliants are now scrutinised through a video-entry device, which has reduced the tide to a manageable stream. Inside, a large courtyard gives onto the *cuverie* on one side, a small office on another and a comfortable family apartment above. Next to the *cuverie*, a green metal door guards the entrance to the cellars – an intricate network of chambers approached by a steep ramp. Here, the Chave reds and whites mature in a mixture of old Hungarian oak ovals and *pièces*, the casks used for red being mostly bought second-hand from Christian Serafin in Gevrey-Chambertin.

At the heart of this maze is a small cellar, whose walls and ceiling are covered in spongy, black *mycelium* – punctuated by the occasional calcified spider who has mistakenly tried to spin himself lodgings among the inhospitable fungus. Here repose mouldy bins of old vintages, their punts barely discernible in the dim half-light.

Gérard Chave's success derives from an infinite attention to detail, and from a rare feel for grapes and their treatment. There are no secrets, nor indeed the wizardry with which some have sought to cloak him – just hawk-eyed zeal to ensure that every operation, from attaching the growing shoots to their chestnut posts to meticulous cellar-management, is done properly. For him, the quality of the salt is just as important as the salmon you put it on.

To the fundamental that "every detail counts", Gérard Chave adds the skill of making the right choices: you may know about the importance of salt, but make the wrong selection. As with all great estates, little is systematic; there are no rules or formulae, but a willingness to treat each crop individually and tailor its upbringing to its personality.

The hill of Hermitage, far from being an unitary geological entity, conceals a diversity of soil-types and micro-climates – you only have to walk it to realise this. Each *climat* has its wine-character, which comes through year-on-year despite the common factors of grape, vintage and *vigneron*; a more convincing proof of the importance of *terroir* would be hard to imagine. The Chaves have vines in nine of the 18 *climats*, including a 2ha slab of Les Bessards, the granitic central spine, which acts similarly as a backbone for their red wine. This diversity enables Gérard and Jean-Louis to put together an *assemblage* which balances aromatic complexity with palate finesse and structure. Growers with a more restricted colour palette produce accordingly. Their 46 ares of La Vercandière, at the base of Bessards, rarely contribute to the final blend, but play a valuable role as a vegetable patch for Chave's workers.

The white Hermitage comes from roughly 85% Marsanne and 15% Roussanne harvested from mainly 60-plus-year-old vines from four *climats*: Les Roucoules, l'Hermite, Peléat and Maison Blanche, picked "at full maturity; we attach great importance to that". This doesn't mean waiting for over-ripeness, rather for the grape qualities which will give richness and *gras*. It entails low yields and exacting harvesting. As with the whites, so with the reds, Gérard tastes the berries and stalks to determine when to harvest and trains his experienced pickers to select only ripe, undamaged fruit; it takes training to recognise an acceptable Chave bunch of grapes. If it rains, they take off their shirts and cover the baskets – the grapes come first! In the sodden 1993 harvest, the picking team was increased from 40 to 60 to allow more time to discard rotten grapes. The results show in the wine.

The white grapes are bladder-pressed, then the juice settles for 24 hours or more, with cooling if necessary, before passing to casks and stainless steel (in a ratio around one third/two-third, depending on the vintage) for fermentation. It is essential not to remove yeasts and yeast-nutrients from the juice, so there is no fining at this stage. New wood is not part of the Chave philosophy, so it does not appear unless a cask needs replacing. Fermentation temperature is maintained at around 20°C to extract maximum glycerol; any lower would give more primary fruit aromas, which is not what is wanted. But there are no rules: "wine is like cooking – a good chef doesn't use the same cooking temperature for all meats – he adapts".

The wine remains on its fine lees until after malolactic when it is racked clear and lightly sulphured; thereafter, treatments are kept to the minimum necessary for stability and clarity. Some *climats* tend to produce an excess of protein and these lots may be fined with bentonite during late winter or early spring (not fish-fining which is to remove turbidity – "this is not for us"). Fining is kept to the absolute minimum since bentonite removes glycerol.

Elevage, in stainless-steel or casks, depending on frequent tasting, lasts around 18 months. Above all, the Chaves want to avoid any obvious taste of oak. "I don't like wood to be the first impression for the taster", Gérard comments, adding "even in difficult years such as 1993, our whites have enough natural richness". This is why such care is taken to refine the proportions of cask and *inox*. When the taste is right, the two parts are assembled, left for a few months to harmonise, then lightly plate-filtered (by gravity, not pumps), and bottled.

A Chave white Hermitage can be relied upon for richness and elegance, with a balance and structure finely-tuned for long ageing; even in lesser vintages, such care is taken with harvest and fruit selection, that these qualities are maintained. Gérard is not among those who consider acidity of supreme importance; for him its the overall balance of life-giving constituents which matter. He considers that his whites have fewer peaks and troughs than the reds because neither tannin or colour extraction are involved.

They are best drunk young – if you really can't wait – or left for a decade or more to develop complex aromas and flavours, typically honey, acacia, lime-blossom and hazelnut, supported by a finely-tuned combination of acidity, glycerol and alcohol. These wines have great longevity, as bottles from the 1920s and 30s tasted during the 1980s demonstrated. Far from falling apart, they had depth and complexity which transcended mere curiosity value. Lesser vintages, such as 1993, 1987 and 1982, develop earlier, and are worth seeking out for sheer value.

The reds may peak and trough, but year-in, year-out they are among the best Hermitages to be found. The high average Chave vine-age undoubtedly contributes depth, but even more, it is Gerard's skill in blending the distinctive characters of seven *climats* which gives such complexity and finely-tuned structure.

The mainstay of the blend is Bessards, which contributes sturdiness, depth of colour, finesse, intensity and spicy, powerful flavours; next, le Méal, for fine perfume and suppleness; then l'Hermite, whose 15% of complanted white grapes add elegance and softness. The clay-limestone soils of Rocoule – which is traditionally a white-wine *climat* – gives high tannins and an element of coarseness, which support development. From Beaume, adjoining Rocoule, comes relatively light wine with considerable aromatic finesse and full, complex flavours. Peléat, in Chave's sole ownership, produces wine that is simpler and more tannic; deeply coloured, often smelling of burnt bread and bitter chocolate: racy, vigorous and elegant –

Mouline rather than Landonne, perhaps.

Complicated as the fashioning of a Chave red Hermitage may be, it is not surprising to learn that everything starts in the vineyard. Minimal treatments, short pruning to moderate the Syrah's natural vigour, and meticulous harvesting are subject to the closest of scrutiny by Gérard and Jean-Louis who spend a great deal of time among their vines. They castigate those who spend their time in the cellars and rarely set foot in the vineyards: "you can't make great wine like that".

Once picked, the bunches are more or less de-stemmed, according to the state of the crop – 99% de-stemming for the unripe, dilute 1993, 50% for the near-perfect 1990. "If you don't de-stem, there is always astringency and you can't have a long *cuvaison*". Each *climat* (and where possible, its press-wine) is vinified separately – although, as with the whites, there may be some early mixing of fruit to fill the *cuves*, as in 1993.

Cuvaison generally lasts two to three weeks, with temperatures topping 30°C to maximise extraction, particularly at the end of the fermentation cycle. Part of the crop is vinified in large, ancient, open wooden vats, with *pigeage à pied*, part in cement *cuves* with regular *remontage*, and part in two stainless steel *cuves* equipped with compressed-air *pigeage* facilities. The character and size of the crop determine which fruit goes into which *cuve*.

What happens thereafter is largely dictated by tasting. After malolactic in *cuve* or in cask, depending mainly on the space available, the important decision is taken as to whether to add back the press-wine. If the wine is to go into new wood, Gérard considers it essential for it to have its malolactic there – not elsewhere; "in Bordeaux, it is the opposite – they wait until the malolactic has finished then put the wine into new wood", he explains, with a characteristically impish grin.

Gérard has given the subject of new wood careful consideration over his 44 vintages: "I am persuaded that there is a very strong bond between the origin of the wood and the grape variety". However he also considers that "Syrah is very easily marked by new wood", so it is used sparingly – perhaps two or three casks one year and none the next. In general, he prefers Serafin's used barrels. Nothing, of course, is systematic: "wine is far more complex than that".

Maturation lasts 15–18 months in either casks or old 1,300-litre Hungarian ovals. Gérard tends to favour cask *élevage* and the cask population has consequently

grown in recent years. There is now a splendid new back-lit cellar, complete with vaulted arches and dimmer-switches – "the dancing-girls come down those stairs in the corner", quips Gérard with another mischievous grin. Fortunately, Monique is not listening.

Tasting to determine whether casks need racking is only carried out when atmospheric pressure is lowered by a south wind: "If you taste in a north wind, all the wines taste fine". To rack, you must then wait until the high pressure of a north wind.

When the time is deemed right, the critical task of making up the blend gets under way. Each vintage is approached without preconception of its possible composition – just tasting, tasting and more tasting, before the final mix is decided. Gérard keeps no notes of past years which might influence him. Furthermore, there is no question of using everything at their disposal. The aim is simply to craft the best possible wine from what the vintage has provided. Anything over will probably sold in bulk as generic Hermitage.

In 1990, the artist Bernard Cathelin, a long-time family friend, whose paintings the Chaves admire, designed a label for them. This spurred a super-blend – "a *top-de-top*" – from that superb vintage. Only 2,500 bottles were produced. This sumptuously concentrated, yet superbly elegant wine represented a first selection, made before the main blend was put together, from wines vinified and *élevé* in exactly the same manner as everything else. Gérard professes to have forgotten what went into it – but its density and finesse would suggest a good dollop of old-vine Bessards, some Méal for perfume and *rondeur* and some Hermite for suppleness and elegance. We'll never know!

The Chaves' red Hermitages mirror their whites in richness, completeness and finesse. Even after a few years in bottle, a vein of seductively silky fruit starts to emerge, a quality retained in the stately progression through the various "ages of wine". The Chaves' style is not for massively extracted, heavily structured young wines which give the taster the impression of chewing scaffolding. Gérard also reproaches those who focus on acidity to give their wines life: "if a wine has enough tannins and extract, acidity isn't so important".

The keys are simple: low-yielding old vines for naturally balanced, concentrated fruit, harvested at optimum ripeness, with a vinification designed to maximise extraction of flavours and fine tannins; thereafter, an *élevage* to encourage the expression of each *terroir* through its fruit and then blending to produce a wine of balanced structure and complexity. Gérard is clear what he is doing: "the *vigneron* makes the wine for his own taste, not necessarily for that of this customers; if I produced a million bottles, I would have to pay much more attention to what the consumer wanted".

Jean-Louis' sojourn in California convinced him that there, far too much emphasis was put on sheer size – the more fruit, tannin and oak you managed to pack in the "better" the wine. "People don't talk of finesse, elegance any more, but size, richness and power. You find these big wines – and don't want a second glass", he grimaces, adding, "they don't age well and lack finesse". For both Gérard and Jean-Louis, the ultimate proof of a winemaker is in his mature wines, and here, the contest is a short one. After 5–15 years in bottle a Chave Hermitage really starts to outpace the field. There are magnificent aromas of *sous-bois*, truffle, game, mushrooms and violets – complex, long, still beautifully balanced whatever the richness of the vintage, and above all wonderfully stylish.

Gérard is a man who thinks things out carefully and likes to view problems from every conceivable angle before acting – whether it concerns the purchase of a fish for lunch, or changing his cork supplier, as he has recently done, to add one extra millimetre in diameter to his corks so that they fit more perfectly into the neck of the bottle. "Every detail counts", and he might as well have added, "leave as little as possible to chance".

In common with most great winemakers, Gérard and Jean-Louis taste widely – wines from around the world as well as other Hermitages. Beneath the family's bolt-hole – an attractive, simply furnished farmhouse in the hills above the valley, some half-hour's drive from Mauves – an eclectic collection of fine wine provides pleasure for them and their friends.

Sometimes with Monique, Jean-Louis, and their daughter Geraldine, a medical student, sometimes alone, Gérard escapes from the entire media and customer circus to reflect on what is going on elsewhere. "I'll try two or three different wines", he says, admitting to a particular, untypically French, love of Vintage Port, of which the cellar contains a fine collection. Wines exchanged with top estates in Bordeaux, Burgundy, Loire and Alsace attest to the wide esteem in which he and his wine are held.

Gérard is not impressed by the modern cult of the consulting oenologist, who seem to him to be standardising

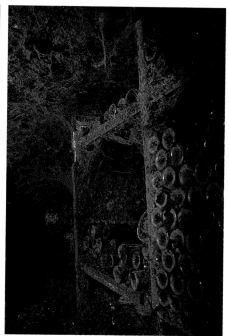

Old vintages maturing in the Chaves' personal cellar: the mould helps keep it pest-free.

wines. He draws an analogy with doctors, who are often consulted from habit rather than necessity. "Oenologists can't afford to take risks and so will sometimes prescribe two boxes of pills when one would do. It's all a matter of self-confidence – if you know how to make wine, you don't need the props of oenologists and publicity machines".

For Gérard – and now Jean-Louis – wine is something to enhance life, to give pleasure, and to accompany the food which Gérard cooks so well. You might hear him mutter, in a mischievous stage-whisper, that there is no real gastronomy left these days, although he clearly cherishes his many friendships among France's *maîtres cusiniers*.

For him, fine food consists of first-class ingredients, uncluttered by the ever more complex artifices of chefs trying to prove their flair and skill, cooked simply –

seasoned with the right salt – and shared with Monique, the family, or friends. Wine should be drunk and enjoyed, not intellectualised: "there seem to be more spitters than drinkers", he observes.

Gérard's energy leaves him time to experiment for amusement. Apart from 3,000 bottles of a succulent, fruity red St-Joseph which finds its way to local restaurants and, for some curious reason, to one American importer, there have been notable essays at Viognier, both medium-sweet and dry, from vines planted in l'Hermite. The 1984 was quintessential dry Viognier, perfumed, and most attractive, with a strongish *goût de terroir*.

The Chaves have also revived the traditional Hermitage "*vin de paille*", made by drying out whole bunches almost to raisins on straw mats, before expressing and fermenting their tiny amounts of juice. This gorgeous, super-concentrated wine is not generally sold commercially but dribbled out to favoured customers and friends, such as Guy Jullien's famous restaurant La Beaugravière.

Jean-Louis has clearly inherited his father's inquiring mind – there is now a patch of Zinfandel on the Hermitage hill. "It's not hot enough", appears to be the provisional verdict.

Winemakers could learn much from the Chaves' art and from their approach to wine. Gérard is a man whose personality fuses a serious, reflective streak with abundant *joie-de-vivre*; someone who abhors incompetence and dislikes cant. Above all, he makes magnificent Hermitage. The wine world, far beyond Mauves, is richer for his gifts.

APPELLATION	VINEYARD	DETAILS	AREA
HERMITAGE	BEAUMES	50+ yr old vines	0.31
HERMITAGE	LES BESSARDS	80 yr old vines	2.05
HERMITAGE	DIOGNIERES	40 yr old vines	0.58
HERMITAGE	L'HERMITE	2–6–10–50 yr old vines	3.45
HERMITAGE	MAISON BLANCHE	50–60 yr old vines	0.33
HERMITAGE	LE MEAL	50 yr old vines	1.02
HERMITAGE	PELEAT	50–80+ yr old vines; climat is Chave monopole.	1.51
HERMITAGE	LES ROCOULES	80 yr old vines	3.45
HERMITAGE	VERCANDIERE	30 yr old vines	0.46
ST-JOSEPH		Mauves	1.50
		TOTAL (hectares):	14.66

DELAS FRERES

This is one of those medium-sized, well-reputed firms which it is frustratingly difficult to evaluate. There are fine vineyards – nearly 10ha of well-sited Hermitage, four each of Côte-Rôtie and St-Joseph and 4.5ha of Condrieu. The range of wines is distinctly mixed, some attractive and interesting, others rather one-dimensional and pedestrian, none more than very good. However, there seem to be genuine efforts to improve on what has gone before, so perhaps one should delay any definitive assessment.

The present manager and wine-maker is Dominique Lallier, a plausible man in his thirties, who took charge in 1990, 13 years after his father André had bought the firm from the Delas family, in the name of Champagne Deutz, which they then owned. In 1993 Deutz itself was absorbed by Louis Roederer, but all of this seems to have impacted little on goings on at the Delas base at St-Jean-de-Muzols, where the wheels continue to turn much as ever.

No expense is spared on equipment. There are modern cellars and plant, with 100% oak *élevage* for all the red Hermitage – although none is new. The white range is attractive and stylish , topped off with a well-crafted white Hermitage, vinified in 100% new oak.

The reds are more uneven – a somewhat flat and coarse-grained Crozes-Hermitage (the 1990 definitely showing the heat of the vintage) a pleasant but rather insubstantial St-Joseph and a firm, mildly rustic, big, sunny Cornas. The St-Joseph comes from a mixture of young and older vines on the Côte St-Epine – one of the finest sites in the appellation. With more rigorous cask selection this could be top-class.

Delas' flagships are a trio of red Hermitages and a Côte-Rôtie. These are the wines by which Dominique Lallier's skills are best judged. The Côte-Rôtie Seigneur de Maugiron is a Brune and Blonde mix containing 5–6% of Viognier.

The Hermitages start with Les Grandes Chemins from vines at the base of Les Bessards, continue through the well-known Marquise de la Tourette, which is an *assemblage* from a number of different parcels, and culminate with 3,500 bottles of Les Bessards, which has so far only appeared in 1990 and 1991, from vines in the heart of that *climat*.

There is no doubt of the potential for quality here, but it isn't yet being achieved. The difficulties seem to be an amalgam of several peccadilloes: firstly, having just one manager to oversee both commerce and production of a business of this size inevitably results in a certain amount of neglect. Dominique Lallier is an oenologist by training – from Champagne – so perhaps he should be allowed to concentrate on winemaking, allocating sales responsibilities elsewhere. Secondly, the strong pressure for commercial results, especially at a time of considerable financial stringency throughout Champagne, may have led to over-production in the Rhône vineyards. If there is a single fault it is that the wines lack the concentration for *grand vin*.

As any great winemaker will confirm, it is essential for whoever makes a wine to spend as much time as possible in the vineyards, and to get a close feel for the fruit he has to vinify. With so many other pressures on him, it could be that Dominique Lallier does not have the time for what may seem to him a luxury. The wines could be better than they are, given Delas' excellent resources.

APPELLATION	VINEYARD	DETAILS	AREA
HERMITAGE	LES BESSARDS	Marsanne vines, 35 yrs old; at base of Bessards and Gros des Vignes	2.50
HERMITAGE	LES BESSARDS	Syrah, 35 yrs	3.50
HERMITAGE	GROS DES VIGNES	Syrah, 20 yrs	3.50
ST-JOSEPH	COTE ST-EPINE	St-Jean de Muzols; 2 ha 5 yr vines; 2 ha 30 yr old vines	4.00
COTE-ROTIE		En fermage from M Delas; 5–6% Viognier co-planted; 25–30 yr old vines	4.00
CONDRIEU	VERIN	Terrasses; 35–40 yr old vines; en fermage from M Delas	4.50
		TOTAL (hectares):	22.00

DOMAINE BERNARD FAURIE

Bernard Faurie is the fourth generation of Fauries in Tournon, exploiting a domaine of 3.4ha, split equally between Hermitage and St-Joseph. He has bought out two members of his family and still has a third to persuade.

This is a domaine where, despite strenuous efforts to do the right things, the wine never quite hits the heights. There is fine raw material: vines in Bessards, Méal and Greffieux, planted in 1914, are modestly cropped and are capable of adding depth to the Faurie wine.

There is also a raft of sensible practices in the cellars – long *cuvaison*, *saignée de cuve* if necessary, *pigeage à pied*, natural yeasts, keeping the press wine apart for blending back later, and minimum filtration. All this points to a finer result than Bernard Faurie sometimes seems to achieve.

More detailed scrutiny suggests reasons for the shortcomings. Crucially, there is no de-stemming; if you foot-crush stemmed grapes you are bound to extract harsh, green tannins along with the finer tannins which really matter. This is clearly the case here. The evidence is there in the wines, which invariably come hallmarked with a line of more or less green herbaceousness, sensible both on nose and palate.

This is combined with almost three weeks of maceration – excellent for de-stalked fruit, but not otherwise. The longer you leave crushed stems in a vat the more green, bitter tannins you leach into solution – irredeemable tannins which don't soften with time.

If you add to this 18–24 months in wood, then you have every chance of this hard, tannic vein marking the wine for life.

There are two *cuvées* of red Hermitage and one of white, plus a red and white St-Joseph. Until 1993 there was also a red Crozes from share-cropped vines, but Bernard decided he didn't want this additional financial exposure, so he let them go.

The Méal *cuvée* is distinctly the better of the Hermitage pair and the "standard" *cuvée* no more than that. Even in better vintages, it bears more than a touch of old-fashioned rusticity. The St-Joseph is a worthy example – firm and well-structured with the elements for a few years' ageing. The stalkiness is less noticeable in riper vintages, but in years like 1992 it stands out and unbalances the wine.

If Faurie could bring himself to destem – even by stages, if it would help psychologically – this would greatly enhance the quality of the wines.

The whites are attractive, with finesse and length, although they are not structured for great ageing. The 700 bottles of Hermitage Blanc comes from juice fermented in old casks and bottled with fining in preference to filtration, after 16 months' *élevage*. Bernard will probably shorten this, though he is concerned that he will only gain fugitive primary aromas.

When he took over from his father in 1980, he sought advice from qualified friends, such as François Ribo in Mercurol, and read all the relevant

APPELLATION	VINEYARD/LOCATION	DETAILS	AREA
HERMITAGE	LE MEAL	Planted 1914; Syrah	0.20
HERMITAGE	LES GREFFIEUX	Planted 1914; Syrah but includes 0.2 ha of Marsanne	1.50
ST-JOSEPH	TOURNON	30 yr old vines	0.35
ST-JOSEPH	TOURNON	Bought 1985; planted 1986/7/8	0.10
ST-JOSEPH	TOURNON	Recent purchase; vines under 10 yrs old. ST-JOSEPH vines include 0.16 Marsanne	1.25
		TOTAL (hectares):	3.40

books he could find. Bernard's clients also helped form his style. Perhaps, after 15 years of listening, it is now time for him to distance himself from this plethora of advice and to try and evaluate where his wines stand in the Hermitage spectrum.

A few adjustments here and there would undoubtedly result in much more attractive, even wines.

PAUL JABOULET AINE

Since recorded history began in 1834, there have been Jaboulets making wine at Tain l'Hermitage. The firm's founder, Antoine (1807–1864) had twin sons, Henri and Paul (both 1846–1892) who expanded the business, naming it after Paul, the elder (*Aîné*) by several minutes. Thereafter, management passed to successive Jaboulet sons: Louis (1887–1912), Henri (1879–1959), Louis (b.1912) and his brother Jean (b.1914).

The current head of the House is Louis' son Gérard (b.1942), a cultured and urbane ambassador not only for his own wines but for those of the entire region. Although he has a degree from Montpellier in business studies and viti-viniculture, you are unlikely to find him tending the vines or peering into the company's vats, since he spends much of the year travelling the world – occasionally fishing or shooting, more often conducting tastings and visiting customers. Day-to-day operations are in the hands of his cousin Philippe, who is responsible for their 80ha of vines and also for vinification which he took over from Gérard's brother Jacques in 1992, after a scuba-diving accident in 1992 left him severely disabled. Philippe's brother, Michel, oversees sales in France and northern Europe. Despite its size and high international profile, this remains essentially a family business.

From their modern cellars at Roche de Glun, just south of Tain, they market a complete array of Rhône reds and whites throughout the world. These range from a good, very Rhônish *vin de table* through an excellent Côtes du Rhône – Parallèle 45 – to a good cluster of southern Rhône appellations culminating in a fine Châteauneuf-du-Pape Les Cèdres and including a delicate, rose-petal and almondy Muscat de Beaumes de Venise.

Philippe Jaboulet among his Hermitage vines.

However, it is the Septentrionale sector that constitutes the heart and greatest strength of the Jaboulet range, where they own vineyards in Hermitage, Crozes-Hermitage, Cornas, St-Joseph and Condrieu. In particular, it is their red Hermitage La Chapelle which has introduced many to the greatness of Rhône Syrah.

Wines which are not from their own vines used to be made from purchased grapes. However, they now prefer to buy young wine, working through six local *courtiers*, considering that this allows them to select whatever pleases most, rather than buying grapes over whose production and harvesting they have had no direct control. It also relieves them of the responsibility of vinification, for which they presently lack space in their old cellars below Louis' house at Tain. Looking to the future, they have bought "a whole mountain" honeycombed with natural cool grottoes, to which all their vinification operations will be transferred in due course. However, with a couple of difficult recent vintages, world-wide economic problems and important vineyard acquisitions, this project is not top priority.

The cream of the Jaboulet cellars are the Hermitage La Chapelle, its white sister – the Hermitage Chevalier de Sterimberg – and the splendid red Crozes-Hermitage, Domaine de Thalabert. La Chapelle is often reported as coming from the vineyards round the small chapel, which Jaboulet own and maintain, on top of the Hermitage hill. In fact, these vines – which are not particularly well-sited, being more exposed to wind and therefore cooler – belong to Chapoutier. La Chapelle is effectively a brand, being a selection of the finest Jaboulet Hermitages, issuing generally from vines in Les Bessards and adjoining Le Méal. It does not appear systematically every year – there was none for example in 1992, 1987 and (except for a small quantity for the US market) in 1981. Since 1989, the "ordinary" red Hermitage *cuvée* has been labelled La Pied de la Côte.

Harvest is some days later than most of the other 20 *vignerons* on the hill – though earlier than Chapoutier who tend to pick very late; Hermitage is all hand-picked, as are all but the younger Crozes vines at Roche de Glun. Since 1988, the Hermitage and Crozes-Hermitage grapes are completely de-stemmed before vatting, but not crushed beyond what occurs naturally with the weight of grapes one on another. Philippe argues that stems, even if ripe, contribute only water – and thereby dilution – and undesirable hard tannins to the wine. However, without them, the cap is more compact and so there are two strong daily *remontages* during fermentation.

Each cement *cuve* contains the produce of a particular parcel of vines, so young and old vines and each *lieu-dit* can be kept apart until after malolactic, when tasting will determine which will become La Chapelle, Crozes-Thalabert, Pied de la Côte, Crozes Les Jalets and so on.

De-stemming allows Philippe to prolong *cuvaison* for 18–21 days after fermentation has ceased – now with anaerobic pumping-over to homogenise the wine. He finds that, after 18 days, extraction of fine tannins and colour pigments increases significantly, in both quality and quantity.

Vatting can even last 30 days for very ripe vintages such as 1990. "We refined this technique in 1990", Philippe confirms. The first three pressings are added back – *cuve* by *cuve* to retain each individual identity and then, at the end of the year, everything is tasted to determine its final designation. The lots for each *cuvée* – La Chapelle, La Pied de la Côte, Thalabert and Les Jalets, are unified and coarse Kieselguhr-filtered, before the wine goes to 228-litre casks (*cuves* for the Crozes Les Jalets) for 6–18 months.

There is no new wood for the Jaboulet reds – nor, as one writer reported, do they ever buy second-hand casks from

Securing burgeoning vegetation – an essential part of Northern Rhone viticulture.

Leflaive or Sauzet, or anyone in Burgundy. What new oak there is, is bought from François Frères in St-Romain and broken in with white Sterimberg. Red *élevage* lasts from 6-8 months for 1990 Thalabert to 18 months for 1990 La Chapelle, during which the wine is periodically racked and re-unified before returning to the same cask population.

Just before bottling, the sulphur dioxide is adjusted and the wine more finely Kieselguhr-filtered. A sample of every red is centrifuged to establish whether it needs further filtration; if not it is bottled unfiltered. There is a single *mise* for the 7,500 cases of La Chapelle, usually a couple for the 1,000 cases of Thalabert.

In 1988 there was an important change in the Sterimberg and white Crozes Mule Blanche vinification, bringing it back to the richer, longer-lived pre-1971 style. Between 1971 and 1988 the Jaboulet whites saw no wood and were bottled early to conserve the primary fruit aromas and flavours.

In contrast with earlier vintages – such as a fine 1969 and a truly remarkable 1967 white Hermitage which, from a magnum in 1993, resembled a fine old Meursault, full of acacia, hazelnuts, and honey – they aged poorly. Now, Philippe tries to harvest the grapes slightly over-ripe, and vinifies them with their fine lees, in glass-lined vats for 10–15 days at between 15–18°C.

Yeasts are added to ensure a complete and regular fermentation. There is neither

macération pelliculaire nor *bâtonnage*, as these may add aroma and fat but take the wine far from its *terroir*. Thereafter, the Crozes goes to 50hl *inox* tanks (a part may spend a short time in old casks), and the Sterimberg to casks – a quarter to a third of which are new – depending on the character of the vintage. The Sterimberg is bottled around July, the Mule Blanche somewhat earlier. If the malolactic has happened naturally, the wine is simply fined with casein and lightly filtered; the Crozes is generally sterile-filtered.

This change in vinification has added greatly to the depth and quality of the top Jaboulet whites. The wines are still lovely to drink young, with plenty of fruit and character; but now have an additional dimension and the potential for bottle-ageing which those of the 1970s and 1980s singularly lacked. The *volte-face* was largely brought about by a clientele who wanted a return to the older style and by a succession of ripe vintages which were well adapted to wood ageing. In the 1970s the proportion of Roussanne in the Sterimberg blend was increased from 10% to its present level of 30-35%, which has also added richness and structure.

Philippe Jaboulet has a monumental task in caring both for vines and vinification. He is excited about the firm's acquisitions at Cornas, St-Joseph and Condrieu, despite the fact that these will greatly increase the workload of his 18-strong vineyard team.

The Cornas Domaine St-Pierre vines are at some 380m altitude; there are terraces and scrub to be cleaned up, and vines to be replaced. At St-Joseph planting is slow, since they have to start from scratch and clear the terraces. One hectare has been replanted, there are six more to go. The Condrieu vineyards are a frustratingly slow prospect – they have 2.5ha and planting rights only for 0.7ha in 1994. EU bureaucrats in Brussels have indiscriminately frozen all French plantings to try and reduce community-wide over-production.

In the domaine's established vines, each plot is overseen by a particular member of the team, so they can establish a rapport with an individual parcel of vines. The Hermitage Syrah is trained *en gobelet* – Guyot is no good since it encourages the natural over-productive tendencies of this variety – or where possible (eg in the Thalabert vineyards), on either single or double *cordon de Royat*.

The vineyard work is hard, often starting early in the morning and not finishing until dusk. Philippe, like most conscientious *vignerons*, fully realises the importance of first-class, low-yield fruit. Whatever your *terroir*, this is fundamental for making *grand vin*.

The Jaboulets strive to produce the best. Their *négociant* range is generally dependable and often reaches great heights; for example, the 1990 Châteauneuf Les Cèdres is a top example from that fine vintage, and older vintages of this and Côte-Rôtie Les Jumelles are well worth seeking out. However, where competition for wine is greatest, the quality is sound, but rarely spectacular. In particular, recent vintages of Côte-Rôtie and Gigondas – appellations where many more growers are now bottling their own produce – have been somewhat disappointing, as have been early releases of Condrieu.

Jaboulet's Hermitage La Chapelle and Crozes-Hermitage Domaine de Thalabert are invariably among the finest in their respective appellations. Both are much sought-after and the Thalabert represents one of the best quality/price ratios in the Rhône Valley.

La Chapelle is one of the world's greatest wines, with the concentration and structure for long ageing in great vintages such as 1961, 1966, 1978, 1983 and 1990. Here, 20 years cellaring brings out riches which are barely discernible in the dense, tightly-knit, tannic young Syrah. For relatively less grand vintages such as 1971, 1972, 1979 and 1988, a

APPELLATION	VINEYARD/LOCATION	DETAILS	AREA
CROZE HERMITAGE	LES CHASSIS,	White cépages; 50:50 Marsanne planted c 1944	
	DOMAINE DE THALABERT	Roussanne. planted 1972.	6.70
CROZES-HERMITAGE	LES CHASSIS,	Syrah; 2 main blocks; 20 ha + 11 ha;	
	DOMAINE DE THALABERT	10–40 yrs old; 50% old vines	31.00
CROZES-HERMITAGE	LARNAGE & TAIN	Just in Hermitage AC, but not considered	
		good enough for Hermitage cuvées	3.80
CROZES-HERMITAGE	LES JALETS	Syrah: young vines on stony ground	
		around cellars at Roche de Glun.	6.00
HERMITAGE	MAISON BLANCHE;		
	ROCOULES; LA CROIX	30–35% Roussanne; 70–65% Marsanne	4.40
HERMITAGE	LES BESSARDS	Syrah on granite soils	2.50
HERMITAGE	LE MEAL	Syrah	7.00
HERMITAGE	DIOGNIERES	Syrah	2.50
HERMITAGE	LA CROIX	Syrah	2.30
HERMITAGE	ROCOULES	Syrah	1.70
HERMITAGE	SIGNAL	Syrah	0.70
ST-JOSEPH		Secteur Serrières; coteaux; Syrah;	
		only 1 ha planted 1994	6.00
CONDRIEU	LIMONY	0.7 planted 1994; rest to follow	2.50
CORNAS		Domaine St-Pierre; bought 1994; 10 yr old vines;	
		coteau	2.30
		TOTAL (hectares):	79.40

decade or so develops gorgeously seductive aromas of *sous-bois* and spice, and elegant, silky, flavours. Sadly, unlike Bordeaux, where a deep purse will secure almost any vintage one could wish for, older vintages of La Chapelle or, indeed other great Rhônes, are virtually unobtainable. The only

answer is to buy young and wait.

Gérard Jaboulet and his father, Louis, have done much to bring the riches of the Rhône Valley to the world. Credit for this achievement must be shared with Jacques, Michel and Philippe. Altogether an inspiring family business, and one of the Rhône's very finest.

DOMAINE JEAN-MICHEL SORREL

There have been Sorrels at Tain l'Hermitage for at least a century. Henri Sorrel was the local *notaire* and owned 4ha of Hermitage, which on his death in 1984 had to be shared between his four children. Marc (qv) took most, leaving Jean-Michel with the law practice, the splendid, if neglected, family home and one hectare of vines, these latter shared with his two brothers. However, relations between Marc and Jean-Michel became strained and it is only the fragile presence of Henri's aged widow which glues the family together. Madame Sorrel remains at home, with Jean-Michel stuck on one side and Marc on the other, both wings clinging tenuously to the fuselage.

For Marc, wine is his living; for Jean-Michel and his *juriste* wife, Michelle, it is a passionate hobby. Both sons, and Michelle, learnt much from Henri's *ouvrier* who had tended the vines and helped make the wine for 30 years; he retired in 1987. Now, Michelle makes the wine – with the occasional aid of

oenologist Jean-Luc Colombo from Cornas, while her husband supervises their half-time vineyard hand.

Whatever the mix of responsibilities, the wine here is excellent. A mere three or four casks of fullish, sappy white Hermitage come from very old vines at the bottom of Les Greffieux – land more ideally suited to red *cépages*. This is fermented in young, but not new, casks and matured for six months in polystyrene *cuves* then six months in cask before light filtration and bottling. In lesser vintages, like 1993, the wine tends to a slightly high acidity, probably a function of the less than propitious soil.

The red is de-stemmed – a new machine has now replaced the old wooden *erafloir* – then vatted for 21 days in a epoxy-resin tank, with *pigeage à pied* and pumping-over. Because of its occasionally high volatile acidity, the press wine remains separate until just before bottling, when it is either blended back or sold to the local

négoce, as in 1993. *Elevage* lasts some two years, with several aerated rackings "to avoid filtration".

Michelle is clear that they are making *vins de garde*, which are of necessity austere when young, and gently laments that the appreciation of fine Hermitage has been somewhat distorted by more easily drinkable wines vinified in new wood: "it's what people seem to want".

The Sorrels are more than the amateurs they would have you believe. Being driven by considerations other than financial – the domaine apparently just covers its costs – they are free to make wines to their own taste instead of vinifying at the behest of market fashion. However a single hectare means little spare cash for investment – so the *cuverie* is a bit *artisanale*, with disused farm utensils lying around among the winery equipment and a general air of stitch and patch. There is no bottling machine, so this is done, in one batch, by Colombo's team – in the case of the red, without filtration.

This red is an excellent, fleshy wine – no green stem-tannins and a real *fond* of old-vine fruit. Not a wine for drinking before its fifth birthday, but one with all the structural elements for evolving attractively over a decade or more in most vintages.

The Sorrels are friendly with the Graillots – a valuable source, one suspects, of informal advice and probably practical help. Michelle would like to put that relationship on a more formal footing

APPELLATION	VINEYARD	DETAILS	AREA
HERMITAGE	LES GREFFIEUX	80+ yr old Marsanne, lower part of climat	0.10
HERMITAGE	LES GREFFIEUX	80–100 yr old Syrah	0.70
HERMITAGE	LE MEAL	80–100 yr old Syrah	0.20
		TOTAL (hectares):	1.00

– perhaps a joint enterprise, sharing material and pooling marketing facilities; it would make eminent sense.

Meanwhile, they have managed to buy the Méal plot from the other brothers, and would like to acquire the rest when the conditions are right. This is a splendid small domaine. If you can find some of their 5,000 or so bottles, don't hesitate!

DOMAINE MARC SORREL

This is a fundamentally fine domaine, capable of making excellent wine. With almost two hectares of red Hermitage, split between four *lieux-dits*, and half a hectare in Les Roucoules (the heart of white Hermitage) with a good proportion of 50-year-old vines, all the necessary ingredients are there.

The dark, lean, olive-complexioned Marc Sorrel was pitched in on the death of his father, Henri, a local lawyer, in January 1984. Fortunately, he had returned from his job as a chemical engineer, at Henri's request, two years earlier – and worked closely with the estate's *vigneron* after taking charge until he felt confident to assume sole responsibility for vines and cellar. He has the air of a man who is fit and alert; outdoor work is clearly to his taste, and he enjoys skiing and wind surfing when time permits. He reads avidly – particularly wine literature.

His father left him 2ha of Hermitage – his three other brothers taking fewer vines and being otherwise compensated, as French law requires bequests to be divided equally between any surviving children. Further purchases in both Hermitage and Crozes, and rental of a half-hectare parcel of 50-year-old Marsanne at Larnage, increased the domaine to its present 4ha.

The Hermitages and the white Crozes are the pick of this cellar. Following Henri's practice, there are usually two red Hermitages: a "*classique*", from 25-year-old Syrah vines on flatter land in Les Plantiers, bordered by Les Greffieux and the Lyon-Valence railway line, and the superior "Le Gréal", a blend of older vines from Les Gréffieux and Le Méal. In 1992, Marc decided to make only Le Gréal, rather than demoting the Gréal into a better "*classique*". The Gréal fetches more, but this is something of a surprising decision, given the difficulty of the vintage.

Bluish-green Bordeaux mixture on Syrah vines.

In top vintages, such as 1989 and 1990, Le Gréal is among the best half dozen Hermitages; in lesser years it generally merits good plus. Henri had a spectacular success with his Gréal 1979 which Marc trumped with a magnificent Gréal 1985. However, creaming off the best cannot but diminish what remains. Even in great years, the *Classique* is rarely more than modest; in second-rank years, it is light and lacking in fruit depth.

Marc Sorrel's policy of not de-stemming – which was relaxed for 1993, when only Gréal was produced – doesn't help, adding a line of green stemminess. In Le Gréal, this is to some extent submerged by ripe tannins and a natural concentration of old-vine fruit, but there can be little doubt that the structure and overall balance of both Hermitages would be improved by partial or total de-stalking, especially in weaker vintages, such as 1992.

There are no such reservations over the whites. Both the Hermitage blanc – from 45-year-old vines (10% Roussanne and 90% Marsanne) and the Crozes Blanc from 50-year-old vines, which first appeared in 1991, are excellent examples of their respective appellations.

Four weeks of fermentation at 17–18°C in six- to seven-year old Burgundy *pièces*, working on a potential alcohol which generally turns around 13.5–14% for the Hermitage, are followed by a year's *élevage* in cask. The wines are fined, then bottled unfiltered in stages, over 6–12 months.

The Crozes is generally well developed on the nose and clean and fresh on the palate, with good acidity and plenty of sappy fruit to keep it going over three to five years, with sometimes a hint or two of the old-fashioned straw-and-nuts which one still finds in some cellars.

The Hermitage is markedly more powerful and complex, tighter in structure and altogether more complete, taking some time to integrate and open out. Even in vintages such as 1992 and 1993, the wine is well-crafted and worth following; the key is the high proportion of old vines which enables Marc to harvest relatively early after the *ban de vendanges* at good levels of maturity.

APPELLATION	VINEYARD	DETAILS	AREA
HERMITAGE	LES ROCOULES	90% Marsanne, 10% Roussanne; 45+ yr old vines	0.60
HERMITAGE	LES GREFFIEUX	Syrah, planted 1984	0.20
HERMITAGE	LE MEAL	Syrah, c 50 yrs old	1.00
HERMITAGE	LES BESSARDS	Syrah, planted 1984	0.15
HERMITAGE	LES PLANTIERS	Syrah, c 25 yr old	0.55
CROZES-HERMITAGE	LARNAGE	Marsanne, 50 yrs old, rented, first vintage 1991	0.50
CROZES-HERMITAGE		Syrah, planted 1989, first vintage 1993	1.00
		TOTAL (hectares):	4.00

ST-JOSEPH

St-Joseph is one of the Rhône's less easily fathomed appellations. Not only because it comes in a great variety of styles and qualities but also that, due to its extent, there is little by way of vineyard identity to bind quality with origin.

At its creation in 1956, the appellation covered some 90ha in six communes, from Vion, north of Tournon, southwards via Lemps, St-Jean-de-Muzols, Tournon and Mauves to Glun, north of Cornas – a total extent of 13km. The vineyards were mainly well-exposed terraces, which could yield significantly better wine than plain Côtes du Rhône. Then, in 1969, the appellation was extended to 26 communes from Chavanay, just south of Condrieu, to Guilherand, south of Valence – almost five times the length and a staggering 70 times the original permitted area. So St-Joseph now covers virtually all of the Rhône's west bank from Condrieu to Valence. In the north, ACs Condrieu and St-Joseph overlap: where there's Viognier, the wine becomes Condrieu, where Syrah, St-Joseph.

Of this revised 7,000ha, only 700 were actually planted. Unfortunately, much was on easily workable flat land with rich soils: excellent for vegetables; no good for grapes. In 1994, at the behest of the Syndicat des Vignerons themselves, came a further radical reassessment which cut the *vignoble* to 3,004ha. Of the excluded land 170ha were already planted (young vines mostly, planted in a hurry on poor sites as wind of a revision spread). These growers will have 30 years' derogation to continue producing St-Joseph, but any new plantings will be scrutinised to ensure they conform to site specifications.

The kernel of St-Joseph remains the six original communes. Outside these there are good wines; but site, vine-age and – as usual – grower, are critical. Styles vary from the exuberant fruit of Trollat and Chave (best drunk young, with simple, substantial food – if not lying directly beneath the cask), to the more structured wines of, for example, Pierre Coursodon, Clos de l'Arbelestrier and Alain Paret, which are designed for ageing and will improve over several years.

For some, red St-Joseph (Syrah with up to 10% Marsanne and Roussanne) is best drunk during in its first few years – leave longevity to Hermitage, Cornas and Côte-Rôtie. However, growers without vines in these appellations, who want to make a *vin sérieux*, strive to produce something approximating to them. Thus it is that recent years have seen the emergence of superior *cuvées*, for example: Louis Chèze's

Prestige de Caroline, Pierre Coursodon's l'Olivaie and Paradis St-Pierre, Bernard Gripa's Le Berceau, and Alain Paret's Larmes du Père. In good vintages these wines are richly constituted, heavily extracted mouthfuls, full of fruit and tannin. Lay them down for 5–10 years and you will find a wine of depth and complexity: not a little Hermitage or Cornas, but something individual and fine. In lesser vintages, though, the wines often lack the substance and power for balanced ageing and these are less successful. Whether you prefer your wine young, sparky and gutsy or more polished and reflective is a matter of personal taste. There is no "typical" St-Joseph.

The whites are an equally mixed bag. Made mainly from Marsanne, sometimes enriched with some Roussanne, the main variable seems to be freshness. The best have a lively vein of acidity – not green and aggressive, but clean and zingy. This gives balance and allows them to age without falling apart. Sadly, many growers still keep white wine for too long in wood that is too old, which results in dull, flabby

flavours lacking grip and definition. These wines often taste rather like one imagines straw would, if liquidised. Too many of these deplorably poor wines find their way past the AC tasting panels onto the market. Neither these, nor the all too common thin, stalky and woody reds, help promote this appellation.

The name "St-Joseph" is of relatively recent coinage. Its first known mention was in 1668, in a proclamation addressed by the *Intendant* of the Lyons province to Louis XIV's Seneschal at Valence. This preceded his visit to the Jesuit Fathers of the Collège du Cardinal at Tournon as part of a "vast enquiry" to establish the wealth of the universities. The document refers to the Collège's vegetable garden and to "a vineyard situated at Ryf de Leys, at Tournon, called St-Joseph, containing 25 *fessoirées*" (about 10ha). Why "St-Joseph"? Local speculation suggests that since Tournon was the seat of the Cardinal, it was appropriate that this, the finest property, should be named after the patron saint of educational establishments. Others

Vineyards south of Tournon – the heart of the St-Joseph appellation.

point out that St-Joseph was also the patron saint of cuckolded husbands, but what this has to do with wine is unclear.

The creation of these vineyards, however, pre-dates their modern naming by several centuries. The Carmelite monks of Tournon, major landowners here in the 13th century, encouraged viticulture. In 1292 Odon II, Lord of Tournon, issued a Charter of Immunity to inhabitants of the city and neighbouring parishes which, along with privileges governing everyday life, customs and dress, had several clauses on the quality and provenance of wine. Stocks had to be sampled by the Lord Mayor and given his seal of approval – a one-man Appellation Contrôlée!

Local historians record that "Vin de Tournon" was regularly served at the royal table; Henri II (1519-59) apparently "kept a personal reserve of several barrels" (Livingston-Learmonth, 1992); Victor Hugo refers to "le bon vin de Mauves" in *les Misérables*; St-Joseph in *la Légende des Siècles*.

The finest St-Joseph still comes from the original heartland between St-Jean de Muzols and Mauves, from predominantly granitic soils with patches of schist and limestone. The dry-stone walled terraces were built, by hand, to minimise erosion. As elsewhere on the west bank, heavy rainstorms wash away the friable topsoil, which has then to be replaced by hand.

There are some 50 growers. With small land holdings and a prevailing polyculture, much of the fruit is vinified by cooperatives, notably those at Sarras, Tain l'Hermitage, Le Péage-de-Roussillon and the excellent outfit at St-Désirat-Champagne. Among the larger of the producer-*négociant* houses, Jaboulet, Chapoutier and de Vallouit all produce excellent St-Josephs.

VINTAGES

Given the geographical spread of the appellation, the wines reflect the vintage in the local area from which they are produced. Thus a St-Joseph from Chavanay will show the factors which affect nearby Ampuis, in the Côte-Rôtie – whereas a St-Joseph from Mauves will reflect the influences prevailing at Tain l'Hermitage or Cornas. Thus in 1985, St-Joseph wines from the north of the *vignoble* were generally fuller and better-balanced than those from the south, while in 1983 the reverse was the case.

AC ST-JOSEPH

Created	15 June 1956 (revised 1969/1994)
Area (max)	3,004ha
Area under vine 1994	700ha
Base yield	40hl/ha
Minimum alcohol	10% (13% maximum)
Growers	50

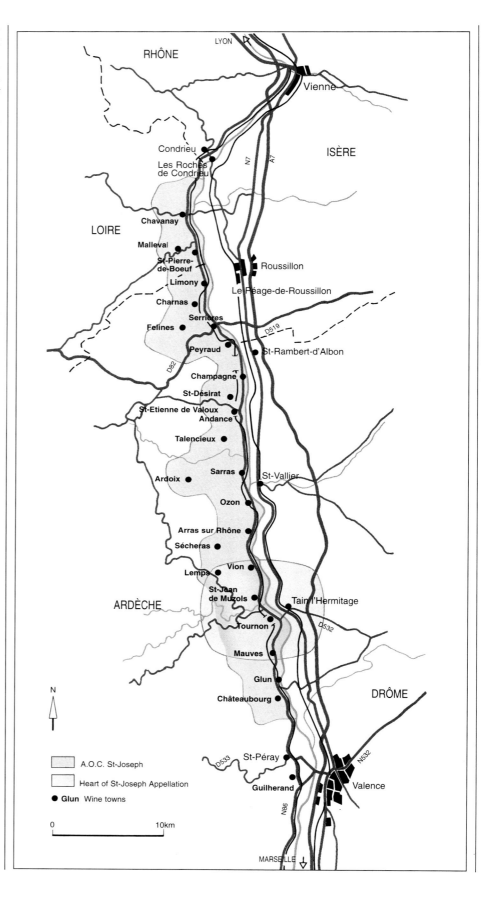

DOMAINE LOUIS CHEZE

Louis Chèze's friends took him for "a lunatic" when, in 1978, fresh from Burgundy and "*passioné du vin*", he took over his parents' polyculture farm in the hills behind Limony, and decided to start making wine. His father's practice had always been to sell the grapes to *négociants* or to the excellent St-Désirat cooperative, which Chèze *père* helped to found.

With guidance from Georges Vernay, whom he met by chance, and later from Jean-Luc Colombo in Cornas (his oenologist since 1984), Louis' winemaking skills have consolidated and now turn out some of the finest St-Josephs available.

Louis has not stood still. The original hectare of St-Joseph and two of *vin de table* have increased by eight of St-Joseph and two of Condrieu, to 13ha; and vinification under Colombo's aegis extended to include a proportion of new wood for maturation of the standard red St-Joseph – more for the Cuvée Prestige de Caroline.

This last, named after his daughter – a plump and energetic girl born in 1986 – is also something of a commemoration for another daughter who died, aged five, of a rare genetic disorder in 1993. Her loss knocked this close-knit family sideways, and Louis cannot talk of her without

obvious emotion. This special wine channels Louis' grief into an annual celebration of both.

There is a new *cuverie* and cask cellar next to the house. Here the reds are vinified in polyester vats, with some *pigeage* "by foot, if we can". A 15-day *cuvaison*, at up to 33-34°C for two days, extracts the maximum of colour, flavour compounds and fine tannin, before the wine passes to 50% *cuve* and 50% old casks for the St-Joseph *classique* and between 10% (1993) and 80% (1990) of new Allier wood for the 6–8,000 bottles of Caroline.

First and second press-wines are matured apart until just before bottling when they are tasted and then assembled or not with the main *cuvée*. After about 14 months' ageing, fining and a Kieselguhr filtration, the wines are bottled in one go.

Jean-Luc Colombo has changed old parental ways here; in particular, there is now total *égrappage*, higher fermentation temperatures, yeasting and more careful filtration. His work is complemented by Louis' determination to maximise fruit quality. In 1993, after losing 2ha of St-Joseph to hail, he spent a month defoliating his vines, especially the Marsanne, to ensure good aeration and thus less rot – "I simply couldn't afford to miss a vintage". The result is an excellent range of well-constituted wines, a contented *vigneron* and a healthier bank account.

The Condrieu is fair, but would benefit immeasurably from a touch of *macération pelliculaire* and fermentation at a temperature a degree or two higher than the 15–16°C it currently receives, to add depth and richness. However, it is the fine St-Josephs which are worth the winding drive, 4km up to Pangon in the hills between the Rhône and Mont Pilat, to search out.

APPELLATION	DETAILS	AREA
CONDRIEU	Pl. 1988–89; vinified in 30% new oak.	2.00
ST-JOSEPH (W)	Marsanne pl. 1979; vinified in 30% new oak.	1.00
ST-JOSEPH (R)	Syrah pl. 1979	6.00
ST-JOSEPH (R)	Syrah pl. circa 1963, source of Cuvée de Caroline	3.00
VIN DE TABLE (R)	Gamay	1.00
	TOTAL (hectares):	13.00

DOMAINE PIERRE COURSODON

Gustave Coursodon used to make good, if somewhat heavy-framed, St-Josephs. Since his son Pierre, a quiet, handsome forty-year-old, took the helm in 1982, styles have changed for the better. Unfortunately, his efforts risk being compromised by gruff old Gustave who has been put in charge of the passing trade, and wanders round the courtyard dispensing a distinctly brusque welcome which must frighten off many of those who have come to buy his son's wines.

There are two *cuvées* of white St-Joseph and three of red. The top wine in each colour is the Paradis St-Pierre, from one hectare of vines of 50 or more years old on steep granite terraces above Mauves – the heart of St-Joseph. "Paradis" is a Coursodon brand name: the white comes from the *lieu-dit* St-Joseph at Mauves and the red from another vineyard nearby. In addition to the standard *cuvées* of red and white, there is also l'Olivaie red, from a hectare of equally old vines on finer, more

fragmented soils at St-Jean-de-Muzols, just north of Tournon – the *lieu-dit* here is in fact "Olivet".

Pierre is a master of St-Joseph, and his whites match his reds for quality. The whites are attractive young, but develop well over 3–10 years depending on the vintage – invariably interesting expressions of Marsanne, part fermented in *cuve*, part in cask (*bâtonné*). After blocking the malolactic in 1992, Pierre decided that it added freshness; so from 1994, the whites have been a 50:50 mix of malolactic and non-malolactic wine. The white Paradis is exactly the same must as

the *classique*, but entirely matured in *barrique*.

The reds have also been improved, with the introduction of de-stemming in 1988 – apart from the Paradis which keeps its stems. Pierre follows the broad style of Gustave, who sought big, dense traditional wines "with character". This means plenty of foot treading, two to three weeks' *cuvaison* then 12–15 months in *demi-muids* and *foudres,* with the press-wine assembled or not, just before bottling. There is 15% of new or second-year casks for l'Olivaie, but none for the Paradis. This is a house where you can buy with complete confidence.

APPELLATION	VINEYARD	DETAILS	AREA
ST-JOSEPH	ST-JOSEPH (MAUVES)	Marsanne; 20 yr old vines	2.00
ST-JOSEPH		Syrah – 28 yrs old vines	8.00
ST-JOSEPH	ST-JEAN-DE-MUZOLS	50+ yr old ines	1.00
ST-JOSEPH	ST-JOSEPH (MAUVES)	50+ yr old vines	1.00
		TOTAL (hectares):	12.00

DOMAINE FLORENTIN

At a bend in the road at the southern end of Mauves is a long, low farm building. This houses one of the northern Rhône's most unusual domaines – the Clos de l'Arbelestrier. This, since 1956 the property of Dr Emile Florentin, a talented Paris physician, consists of a 3.5ha slab of more than 50-year-old vines enclosed by walls built in the 16th century, with a further 1.8ha outside.

Tradition abounds here: this friable, sandy, decomposed granite soil continues to be ploughed by horse – an ancient, sluggish, apparently nameless, wheezy creature with a mind of her own, driven by Monsieur Despesse, who has looked after the Clos since 1982.

Dr Florentin, now well into his eighties, has ceded control to his son Dr Dominique Florentin – a rather formal homoeopathic doctor with a successful practice in nearby Valence – and his daughters; one of whom,

Françoise, deals with the administration while the other, who lives in Paris, participates less.

Despite the aura of uncompromising tradition, there have been marked improvements here. Until the late 1980s, both red and white wines were made in a distinctly oxidative style. The whites tended to dark colours and strong straw and sherryish aromas and flavours, and the reds had an astringency attributable at least in part to well-crushed stems.

Now 100% de-stemming for the reds, and more careful *élevage* for both, has resulted in finer, fresher, more harmonious wines, without sacrificing any of the depth which these old vines are capable of contributing.

Apart from periodic passages of the recalcitrant quadruped, this flat, rich sandy-limestone soil is largely left to nature – using only copper-based treatments, without systemics. Short

gobelet pruning gives yields of some 28hl/ha, against a permissible base yield of 40hl/ha, which further adds to the concentration of the wines. If the horse breaks down, modernity, in the shape of a splendid museum-piece tractor, takes over.

In the old *cuverie* and cellars, housed in the long stables visible from the road, things proceed as they have for decades. Here, one feels, stainless steel is for kitchens and operating theatres, not for *cuveries*. No new wood, but *élevage* of up to five years for reds (there was still 1989 in wood in summer 1994) and a minimum of two years for the whites, in old *demi-muids* and sometimes larger cooperage.

No sulphur is used, either for red or white, except in the form of candles to sterilise the casks. This is riskier with the whites, but the Florentins feel that avoiding such additions increases the wines' purity and ensures a natural, balanced evolution.

For the family, there is also a small

Monsieur Despesses at work with the anonymous quadruped in the Clos de l'Arbelestrier.

quantity of pink sparkling wine produced from *saignée* material; it is delicious with a picnic on a hot day, this "Tisane de Mauves".

One gets an impression of almost feudal patronage, of jumping a century, where major decisions are taken by Dr Florentin with as much or as little advice as he chooses. No outside oenologist to make the wine here: it is Florentin wine, made by them, in their

APPELLATION	VINEYARD	DETAILS	AREA
ST-JOSEPH, MAUVES	CLOS DE L'ARBALESTRIER	Vines 50+; inc Marsanne for white	3.50
ST-JOSEPH, MAUVES		Younger plantings, outside Clos; inc	
		Roussanne which forms ⅔ of white blend.	1.80
		TOTAL (hectares):	5.30

own fashion. This is a fine source of St-Joseph – well-crafted, thoughtful wines. This said, it would be good to see

earlier bottling for both red and white, which would retain freshness and fruit which lesser years sometimes lack.

DOMAINE BERNARD GRIPA

It is difficult to write credibly about a domaine without accurate information. Madame Gripa, who stood in for her absent husband, seemed uncertain of anything other than the broadest detail. Fortunately their five wines are uniformly well thought out and finely crafted. This is a serious and under-appreciated domaine.

The St-Péray is one of the best from that often unexciting appellation, as are both red and white St-Josephs. The Berceau *cuvées*, so named because the St-Joseph hill, where Bernard Gripa has his vines, is the cradle (*berceau*) of the appellation, are especially good.

Bernard is the fourth successive generation at Mauves. His father handed over in 1968/9, at a time when the estate, like most others in those days, was a polyculture – mixing cereals and fruit trees with vines. Even now the vineyards are only 80% of the *exploitation*. He is a cousin of Jean-Louis Grippat, the different spelling being attributed by Madame Gripa to a clerical error at the Marie in Tournon, when his birth was registered.

There are 10ha in all – one of St-Péray, (90% Marsanne, 10% Roussanne) and the rest St-Joseph, spread between the communes of Mauves and Tournon, comprising 3ha of Marsanne and 6ha of Syrah. The red and white Berceau *cuvées* represent a selection from vines on the

On the unmechanisable terraces only manual – or helicopter – spraying is possible.

St-Joseph hill, mostly planted in the 1930s and with thereafter only individual vine

replacements. Yields turn around 25hl/ha. The white is part-fermented in new wood – Madame Gripa wasn't sure whether it was 10% or 20% – without *bâtonnage* or *macération pelliculaire*, and bottled with a plate filtration in the April following the vintage.

The red grapes are not de-stemmed – "never; people who de-stem find that the temperature rises quickly and they can't control it" from Madame. Instead a high proportion of whole bunches deliver a slow start to fermentation, with *pigeage* by foot in open *cuves* and 15 days' *cuvaison* to extract the maximum from the fruit. The details of chaptalization appear something of a mystery to Madame Gripa: "I don't know – it has no importance". The press wine is kept separate until bottling, which generally occurs after a year in a mixture of *demi-muids* and *pièces*, with a proportion (unknown) of new oak for the Berceau.

The white Berceau *cuvée* was first released in 1983, the red the following year. Despite Madame Gripa's apparent indifference to detail, her hsuband is clearly a master of his craft.

APPELLATION	VINEYARD	DETAILS	AREA
ST-PERAY		90% Marsanne; 10% Roussanne; 20 yr old vines	1.00
ST-JOSEPH	MAUVES	5–6 & 26 yr old vines	1.00
ST-JOSEPH	TOURNON	10–60 yr old vines	6.00
ST-JOSEPH	TOURNON & MAUVES	4 yr old vines	2.00
		TOTAL (hectares):	10.00

JEAN-LOUIS GRIPPAT

Although he has a touch of red and white Hermitage, Jean-Louis Grippat is best known for his St-Josephs, especially for his red Hospices *cuvée*, made from half a hectare of vertiginously steep vineyard which he tends on behalf of the Hospice de Tournon.

In 1950, Jean-Louis took over from his grandmother at the age of 16. Later, returning from viticultural school and military service, he found the cellars

badly neglected: "it was a thorough mess. Broken-down casks – everything needed putting right". Then, in 1968, the *négociants* who habitually bought his wine in bulk ended the contract. So, 15 days before the harvest he was driven to touring local merchants to find a buyer – without success. Jaboulet, however, while declining his wine, offered to lend him casks; so Jean-Louis started bottling for himself. He learned how to bottle-off a

cask, down to the lees, and the habit remained; thereafter, less and less in bulk, more and more in bottle.

Now in his fifties, he has been joined by his 24-year-old daughter, Sylvie. She has no formal qualifications, apart from a spell with a wine retailer in Tournon, but enjoys working in the vineyards and clearly has a feel for wine.

This is a St-Joseph domaine, above all. The Hermitages are mixed, often lacking the complexity of those blended from different *climats* on the hill. The white, from Marsanne vines of more than 70 years old, planted on sandy-clay soils in Les Murets, is usually quite stylish and fat, but leans to a rather old-fashioned dry-edged character. The 1991, while powerful, lacked grip and complexity and had a distinctly hollow centre. Perhaps 16 months' *élevage* is simply too long.

The red Hermitage suffers from similar problems, exacerbated by a dogged insistence on not de-stemming. As a result the wine appears rustic and one-dimensional, with an unattractive herbaceous nerve. The 1992 suffered from a further difficulty – a cask made in Spain from American oak. This apparently heavily-charred vessel contributed a burnt flavour, stifling the sound fruit underneath. With only 0.3ha of Syrah here, even a single cask can have a significant impact.

There are no such reservations about the St-Josephs, of which Jean-Louis is clearly master. Neither Marsanne and Syrah vines are particularly old, but benefit from their superb siting: the

majority are on the St-Joseph hill itself, which rises behind the Grippat HQ between Tournon and Mauves. Here, granitic soil produces firm, structured wines which need keeping. Both reds and whites are matured for 16–18 months, part in *cuve* and part in cask. The exception to this rule is the four casks of the Hospice *cuvée*, which remain entirely in *pièces* – of which one or two may be new.

The Grippats reckon that wine from de-stemmed fruit is better young, but doesn't age as well as that from stemmed grapes. So the stems remain, occasionally

to the detriment of the red wine – noticeably in years like 1992. However, the whites are long, fattish wines, often spicy and sometimes earthy, but none the worse for that.

The reds are sound, well-made wines, but are definitely not for drinking young. The undoubted pick of the cellar is the red Hospices *cuvée*, which has distinctive depth and class. This is a good source of St-Joseph, but one from which to select carefully.

APPELLATION	VINEYARD	DETAILS	AREA
ST-JOSEPH	ST-JOSEPH	Marsanne, 25 yr old vines	1.38
ST-JOSEPH	ST-JOSEPH	Syrah, 25 yr old vines; 0.5 ha belongs to Hospice de Tournon	3.00
HERMITAGE	LES MURETS	Marsanne; 70 yr old vines	1.20
HERMITAGE	LES MURETS	Syrah; 40 yr old vines	0.30
		TOTAL (hectares):	5.88

ALAIN PARET

Alain Paret started out in 1972, when his father died. He trained in accountancy, but it was his passion for machinery (especially tracked vehicles) combined with a childhood love of wine, which led him to viticulture. He bought steep, virtually unworkable, terraces which no-one wanted, and over 20 years cleared and planted some 36ha of land around the fine medieval village of Malleval, in the hills above St-Pierre-de-Boeuf.

Luck played its part. In the mid-1970s the actor Gérard Depardieu drank a bottle of Alain's wine at a restaurant and telephoned him. They became friends, and eventually partners. This connection is clearly important both in terms of prestige and of resource, enabling Alain to undertake projects which would otherwise be beyond him, such as late-harvesting his Viognier, or the creation of a specially moulded bottle.

Twenty years on, there is still a strong vein of evolution in all three of Alain's appellations – Côtes du Rhône, Condrieu and St-Joseph. The reds are carefully made, with attractive ripe fruit and good concentration, but often show an unattractive greenness which derives from leaving virtually all the stems in the vats. This *goût de rafle* is less noticeable in vintages such as 1990, when the wood is properly ripe, than in leaner years, such as 1992, when it is not. The sooner Alain starts de-stemming, the better; the tannin stems add nothing positive to the wine

and the resulting green edge won't integrate with time. This modification is apparently under active consideration.

Côtes du Rhône is sold as Valvigneyre, St-Joseph as Les Pierres Dendes and the superior *cuvée* as Les Larmes du Père. The Condrieu, released under the Ceps de Nebadon label, is very good. Although only planted in 1980, these vines are beginning to give an attractive depth and richness, helped by a late harvest, a long, slow fermentation over a month or even longer and a touch (8%) of new Tronçais oak – to add to that *élevé* in epoxy-resin *cuves*. Yields are low – around 20hl/ha "to keep the typicity of former days; my grandfather harvested 10–15hl/ha, not the high yields you find now". Even in the rainy 1992 vintage, Alain's Viognier came in at 14–15% potential alcohol.

There are currently two separate Condrieu bottlings, in May and August, each preceded by a fish fining, one or two Kieselguhr filtrations and a further cartridge filtration. These operations reflect security rather than necessity and could beneficially be reduced.

Apart from the regular Condrieu release, Alain is planning a *tête de cuvée* when conditions are right, under the

Château Volan label. His historical researches suggest that in the 19th century this property, on top of a hill overlooking Malleval, was known for the quality of its Viognier (then spelt Vionnier). Depardieu would like to buy the château to go with the fine original bottle which he found, rummaging around there one day, and which he intends to replicate.

Alain Paret has established a thriving domaine and is clearly ambitious. He admits to taking a great deal of informal advice from friends, professionals and anyone else qualified to give an opinion; not quite wine by committee, but more of a compromise than ideal. He should concentrate on ploughing his own furrow rather than listening to too many outside voices. Nonetheless, a good source of both Condrieu and St-Joseph.

APPELLATION	LOCATION	DETAILS	AREA
COTES DU RHONE	MALLEVAL	Planted 1973	10.00
CONDRIEU	MALLEVAL	Planted 1980, south facing coteaux	6.00
ST-JOSEPH	MALLEVAL, LIMONY, CHAVANAY, ST-PIERRE-DE-BOEUF	Planted 1973	20.00
		TOTAL (hectares):	36 ha.

RAYMOND TROLLAT

Raymond Trollat used to be on his own when he first built his house high above St-Jean-de-Muzols, just outside Tournon. Now others have followed suit, and the Quartier Aubert is thoroughly colonised. He and his wife still live up there, surrounded by wonderful views and their 2ha of vines, from which come some of the best red and white St-Joseph.

It takes only a glance round the grey old casks and *demi-muids* in the earth-floored cellar to realise that this is a traditional estate. Raymond learned his skills from his father, and is wryly cynical of technology and most things modern. His guiding principle: "you mustn't leave anything to chance; it's like a good cook, you must be fanatical".

How he manages to turn out such consistently good wine is something of a puzzle – even to him. "There is no secret – people think there is a mystery; there isn't". So deeply ingrained is his work that he seems genuinely surprised that anyone should seek to discover what it is that makes his wines stand above those of his colleagues.

His soils are almost all schist – no clay here. This well-drained land doesn't distinguish itself in drought years, but otherwise ripens its 7-8,000 vines per hectare respectably.

Raymond is one of the diminishing band of non-de-stemmers; however the fact that he only crushes the crop lightly and then foot-treads the cap in his old, open wood and cement vats, often leaving grapes intact when they arrive at the press, may explain why his wines rarely show any stemminess. Also, when he chaptalizes – which is practically every year ("those who tell you they don't – lie") he waits until the end of the cycle to add the sugar, which prolongs fermentation and is felt by many to add greatly to harmony and quality.

The press wine is often somewhat high in volatile acidity – a fact Raymond attributes to the low pH of his clayless soils – so he keeps it on one side to be either assembled with the rest later or sold to the local *négoce*.

As he wanders round the two chambers which constitute the cellar – drawing samples here and there from ancient casks with the odd chalk-mark or piece of faded cardboard stapled to them for identification – this rather laid-back, slightly crumpled but friendly man muses on matters vinous in general and "*la tradition*" in particular.

It all seems rather haphazard – is the first or last bottling the best? "I don't

Raymond Trollat.

really know". How many bottlings are there of any given vintage? "There are about 10,000 bottles so I do several *mises*, like Monsieur Clape". He deplores those who leave a cask half-empty after bottling: "the wine just becomes volatile and tastes of rotten wood". On clones Raymond is unequivocal. "Clones are a catastrophe – before we had small berries like little peas – now the bunches are as big as bottles.

"People won't keep their old vines because they always want greater yields; it's a mistake". He is also dismissive of *viticulteurs* who still keep a few fruit trees for income: "they should stick to their vines – it would be better if they spent more time in the vineyards and looked after them properly. People have cherries, peaches and apricots – so the casks don't get filled up; they haven't got time". Surprisingly, Raymond Trollat approves of red wines made with new wood: "if it's done well, I like it, but if there's too much, its just an oaky *infusion*". He is firmly disapproving of the new breed of winemaking technocrat. "I learnt here – with my father, on the land. People should come back to that. The young need three to four years' re-education after their training."

Despite being at some 280 metres above the valley floor, the Trollat vines are on plateau land, so Raymond treats by hand and doesn't participate in the helicopter spraying. It whirrs perilously close to the hillside before performing a half-pirouette, nose down. "There it goes, see... oh no, it won't touch my vines".

Raymond was at school with Gérard Chave in Tournon, years ago: "he was a serious pupil and studied hard". They have old vines in common: Raymond's were almost all planted in 1918, some in 1945 and 1956. His 89-year-old father still wanders round, poking his nose in everywhere in order to make sure that young Raymond is doing things as they were done 50 years ago.

Raymond is not at all in tune with those whose job it is to administer the rules. "We are controlled by people who know nothing", he complains, recalling with amusement an ex-senior *inspecteur* with the Répression des Fraudes who, as a junior, was given the unfortunate task of visiting the vineyard belonging to the wife of the then Minister of Agriculture. Finding some non-permitted vines, he filled out his report and started disciplinary action. Shortly after, he was transferred to Marseille to oversee grain shipments. However, the region's winemakers clamoured for his reinstatement, which duly happened.

Both whites and reds are excellent. The former, help by a firm chunk of Marsanne vines more than 80 years old, is invariably well structured, with flavours of greengage and quince, and often with a spicy note underneath – although Raymond believes in the quality of these less than of his reds. "My terrain is not for whites – they lack fat, the soil is too acid and needs more clay". Despite these misgivings, the wines are delicious and worth cellaring for a few years to bring out their hidden qualities.

The reds are characterised by ripe, almost sweet, fruit – firm in structure yet with rarely any trace of *goût de rafle*. Since there are several bottlings, and since the cooperage of any one *mise* may differ from another, expect some variation in qualities, but not in overall quality, from this fine domaine.

APPELLATION	VINEYARD	DETAILS	AREA
ST-JOSEPH	AUBERT	Marsanne, 40–80 yr old vines; south-east exposure	0.20
ST-JOSEPH	AUBERT	Syrah, 40–80 yr old vines; south-east exposure	1.80
		TOTAL (hectares):	2.00

CORNAS

Cornas is something of an enigma. Famed in the past for the density and opacity of its 100% Syrah wines, its quality rating among Rhône devotees has of late fallen into a curious no-man's-land, straddled between the heights of Hermitage and Côte-Rôtie and the lesser realms of St-Joseph and Crozes. No-one quite knows where to place it.

Part of the problem seems to be that while Cornas fulfils the two main criteria for excellence – longevity and complexity – when maturity arrives, in all but a few vintages from a handful of growers, the wines lack that extra-sensory dimension of excitement. This, however, is no less true of their more lauded northern neighbours. So where has Cornas failed?

Difficulties have certainly been compounded by the absence of any unified marketing strategy or of an international ambassador; these days, you need a media star or a high-profile eccentric to keep your flag flying: Côte-Rôtie has Marcel Guigal, Châteauneuf fields Jacques Reynaud and Hermitage Gérard Jaboulet. To anyone who knows Cornas, this deficiency is hardly surprising: the growers are strong individualists, with an inflexible streak of stubbornness. Here, the communal air is riven with internal politics of unfathomable complexity with factions getting up support for this, or against that, with the winemaking fraternity permanently at loggerheads about something or other. The surface may appear calm, but underneath everyone seems to be paddling furiously... in opposite directions.

The democratic mechanism itself is a chronic source of discontent, with complaints that the "one-vote-per-grower" arrangement operated by the Syndicat des Vignerons takes no account of the amount of land owned, and frequent references to Hermitage's "one-vote-per-hectare" system as a more equitable alternative. In these circumstances, small wonder that no-one feels qualified to speak for all.

The size of the AC, and the relatively low price of its wine, also contribute to the current state of affairs. A century ago, people came to Cornas as workers, married and started up on their own account. By 1945, this small appellation was dominated by a few large land-holdings: the Arnauds, the Jaboulet cousins with 10ha each, grandfather de Barjac with 8ha and the Ogiers from Mauves.

Over the last 50 years these enterprises have given way to smaller holdings that became uneconomic, forcing growers to take other jobs to make a decent living.

Not being devoted full time to either the vineyards or the appellation has bred disinterest and a strong disincentive to give time, still less cash, to fund marketing schemes. The situation is not improved by those *négociants* selling Cornas who tend to devote more publicity to their Hermitages and Côte-Rôties, which they regard as "grander" wines.

The arrival in the 1980s of the controversial oenologist and grower Jean-Luc Colombo (qv) in Cornas added yet another "cause" of divisiveness. Critical of much of what he found, he set about recruiting clients throughout the Rhône Valley who shared his vision of what fine wine was all about. Although his approach was moderately successful, his attitude caused continuing ripples from his laboratory and epicentre in the rue Pied-la-Vigne. Although his influence has waned recently, the strong animosities his views aroused locally still remain.

So, for a multitude of reasons, both self-inflicted and circumstantial, Cornas lacks a champion and finds itself semi-permanently on the margins. This is unfortunate; despite their uncompromising individuality the *vignerons* are hard-working and deserve better. The quality of their wines has never been higher, and the time for a more sympathetic international understanding of this great Rhône *vignoble* is long overdue.

THE PLACE

Cornas lies on the RN86, with Mauves and Châteaubourg to the north and St-Peray, which it adjoins, to the immediate south. Off the main road one finds a workaday village, dominated by a fine church with an exaggeratedly tall spire. Below it is the social hub of the village, from which narrow streets of old houses radiate in several directions, punctuated by the *boulangeries*, the cafes and the usual run of shops.

There is one restaurant, Ollier, on the RN86, presided over by the bustling Madame Ollier, where the fare is simple, nourishing and inexpensive; the *vin du patron* is young-vine Cornas from Auguste and Pierre-Marie Clape opposite, delicious even slightly chilled in the summer with the *hors d'oeuvres*. In the 1970s the population of Cornas numbered 150; now it is nearer 2,000. To house the overflow (mainly workers from Valence), functional modern houses have sprung up, particularly to the north of the village, around the *quartier* Pied-la-vigne.

THE VINEYARDS

These form an extended, concave bowl behind the village, rising steeply from some 100 to over 400 metres in height at Chaban, the appellation's westerly extremity. The terrain is scarred by ravines, giving a variety of expositions: the best sites face east and south-east, though some less favoured plots face north and north-east. On the higher ground, the sun exposure is critical if the grapes are to ripen fully. Unfortunately, when the appellation was mapped, in 1938, the experts involved did not foresee that people would want to plant on the more exposed higher ground, so less trouble was taken to determine the suitability of those sites. These higher plantings are not objectionable *per se*, but do represent a permanent risk to the grower: the higher you are the greater the likelihood of spring frost and the later the grape maturity. The delimited *vignoble* is large – 550ha – of which some 80 are currently planted (1994). The flatter land on both sides of the RN86 is zoned for the lesser appellation of Côtes du Rhône.

Understanding the *vignoble* is complicated by the widespread use of traditional site names, rather than those officially recognised on the *cadastre* (both are on the accompanying map). The common geological factor is a granitic soil – similar to parts of Les Bessards of Hermitage. Soils vary both from parcel to parcel, and within a single plot. Some give less concentrated wine, others less typicity – aspects of nature with which the grower must live.

Overall, the vineyard divides into three sectors: to the south and south-west of the village, bordering St-Péray, are Combe and Les Côtes; northeast-facing slopes here, and soils which have some limestone and clay admixed with the granite. Due west are the *quartiers* Sauman and Reynard, with St-Pierre beyond. Here, on the lower slopes, one finds many of the best sites – east- and southeast-facing vineyards with strongly granitic, stony soils, very well-drained and thereby prone to drought. To the north-west are the *quartiers* Chaillot, Pied-la-vigne, and Les Eygas whose soils contain varying proportions of limestone.

QUALITIES AND STYLES

The topography has a significant influence on making Cornas what it is, and is partly responsible for differentiating it from the other northern Rhône Crus. Surrounded by hills, which shelter the vines from all but the severest winds and concentrate summer

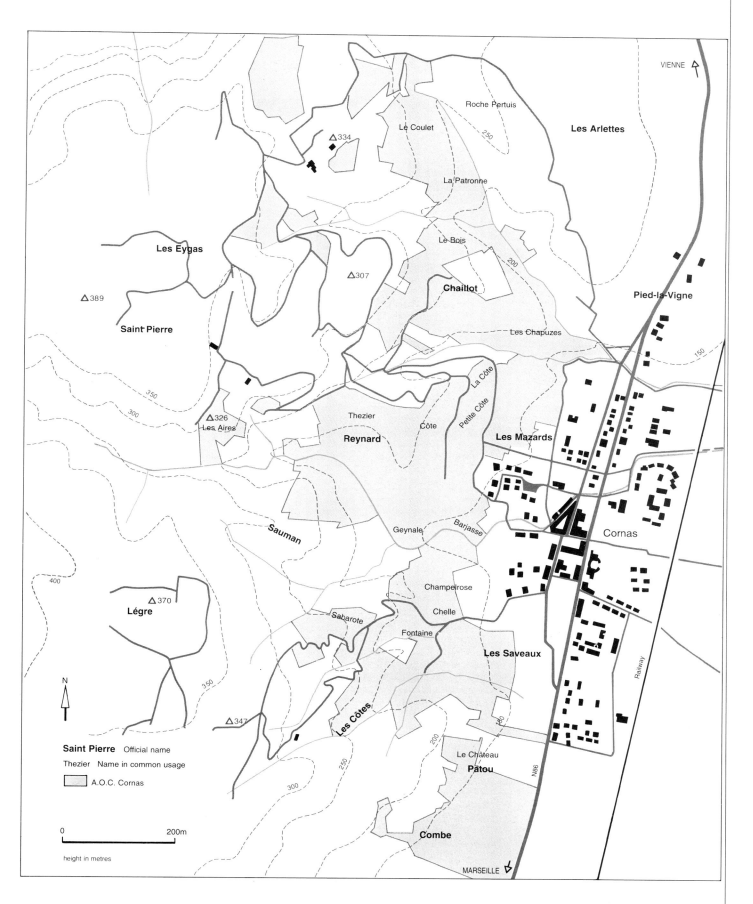

VIENNE

Roche Pertuis

Le Coulet

Les Arlettes

△334

La Patronne

Les Eygas

Le Bois

Pied-la-Vigne

△307

Chaillot

△389

Saint Pierre

Les Chapuzes

La Côte

Thezier

Petite Côte

Côte

Les Mazards

△326
Les Aires

Reynard

Geynale

Barjasse

Cornas

Sauman

△370

Légre

Champelrose

Chelle

Sabarote

Fontaine

Les Saveaux

△347

Les Côtes

Le Château

N86

Railway

Patou

Saint Pierre   Official name

Thezier   Name in common usage

A.O.C. Cornas

Combe

0 ——————— 200m

height in metres

MARSEILLE

heat to the extent that work is all but impossible at noon, Cornas tends broadly to a meaty earthiness. That is not to say that it lacks finesse, but rather that plain, honest speaking generally takes precedence over intellectual nuance. This down-to-earth rusticity is, however, slowly giving way to more subtlety.

Growers, now mainly bottling and selling for themselves and thus more market-aware, are offering different *cuvées* of Cornas. Vines on slopes, on half-slopes and at the foot of slopes produce decreasingly fine wine, so Coteaux, Mi-Coteaux and Pied-de-Coteaux are now regularly on Cornas labels. Some prefer to use vineyard sites to distinguish qualities, while others have latched onto Vieilles Vignes for their superior *cuvées*, but the principle is the same.

Although styles run the gamut, from the young-and-fruity to the firm, tannic *vins de garde*, growers know that markets are moving away from old-fashioned, whale-bone-corseted wines and looking for something approachable sooner. Guy de Barjac commented that "forty years ago, Cornas was almost undrinkably heavy" – a reputation which, despite a sea-change in styles, has proved annoyingly tenacious.

The raw material is first-class; the problem is largely a matter of controlling tannins, which were too often excessive in quantity and aggressive in quality. Shorter vatting, lower temperatures, less extraction, less time dessicating in old casks and earlier bottling to conserve fruit and flesh have largely corrected this, but the message has barely got through to buyers, let alone to consumers. Modern Cornas from a good source and vintage exudes ripe, firm fruit, with enough round tannins to live for a decade or two. Its robust earthy richness is marvellous with full-flavoured, even spicy, dishes – especially the great pies, stews and meat puddings of winter. After a decade or so, fine Cornas takes on a more elegant and complex character, marked by animal and undergrowth aromas, the scents of wild flowers, and warm, satisfying flavours: confident, compelling wines for a more refined cuisine. These are exciting Syrah wines from dedicated, professional growers; they deserve a reappraisal by a wider, unprejudiced audience.

VINTAGES:

1978: A magnificent vintage. A hot summer and autumn gave growers fully ripened grapes from which most made yardstick wines. The best (Clape in particular) are still superb, with plenty of extract and great complexity. On the palate, in particular, they show far greater finesse than one normally expects from Cornas. Jaboulet's version, which showed considerable youthful promise, seems stuck in perpetual adolescence.

1979: A reasonable year, whose mid-weight wines have developed well. Well-cellared wines from top growers should still be attractive and fully mature.

1980: A good vintage. Well-constituted wines have turned out attractively, with some complexity and plenty of finesse. The best, including an excellent Juge and Clape, should still be drinking well.

1981: Good. Some *cuvées* were rather green, and lacked depth and colour; the best, though, are sound wines with reasonable concentration and should still be in fine form: de Barjac in particular.

1982: All France had prolonged, intense heat, which fully ripened the grapes but made things difficult for growers with no means of cooling fermentation. Some wines are a touch jammy; others lack acidity. However, those that have stayed the course are perfumed and very attractive. Drink now or in the next few years.

1983: A good-plus vintage. Dry conditions and heat thickened grape skins and concentrated the juice. This left many wines with an overbalance in tannins that could not be corrected. These are still tough, and some believe they'll remain so. However, *cuvées* from Clape and de Barjac, tasted recently, had enough fruit to balance out the structure and showed a good aromatic development. Drink now – or wait.

1984: Not much of a year. Rain spoiled a harvest of barely ripe grapes. Most *cuvées* tasted were lean and angular, with little richness of fruit and too much acidity and green tannin (Noel Verset, Guy de Barjac were among the best). Drink now – if ever.

1985: A crop of rich, fleshy wines – as near to decadence or exuberance as Cornas is likely to come. Heat, and enough rain, produced ripe grapes, bursting with fruit flavour. These matured well and are drinking wonderfully. Clape, de Barjac, Voge, Verset and Jaboulet particularly fine.

1986: Mediocre. Wines which vary widely in quality – some (eg Jaboulet, de Barjac and Michel's Geynale) have the constitution to last and have developed well over the medium term (ie into the mid 1990s); others were weak-kneed with meagre flavours and green tannins. Those who left stalks in their vats added hardness.

1987: Better than 1986, but not that exciting. A good summer, but harvest rain diluted grapes. Growers who picked early made the best wines; others taste mean, dilute, out of balance. Guy de Barjac, in particular, made an attractive wine.

1988: A fine vintage. A hot, quite dry summer made North Rhône '88s big-framed and powerful, sometimes even burly, with strong tannins. Plenty of fruit, though, and this is starting to come through. Most top growers made fine wine, but these need more time to fully develop the finesse and interest that is undoubtedly there.

1989: Again mirrors the rest of the region. Substantial wines: rich, exuberant concentration of very ripe fruit. Far more flattering to the palate than the '88s – without the severity often found in young Cornas. Good from all top growers.

1990: As elsewhere, wines combine the opulence and fruit of '89 with the structure of '88. Terrific power and intensity, and inherent balance will make them drinkable early – which would be a pity, given their near-exemplary constitutions. Most have a fine depth of ripe tannins and good acidities to sustain a decade or so of maturity. With their great concentration of fruit, should be remarkable wines around 2005 – especially top *cuvées* like Juge's SC, Lionnet's Rochepertuis, Michel's Geynale and Voge's magisterial Vieilles Fontaines.

1991: Good to very good. Ripe grapes with ripeish tannins and good solid:liquid balance made for firm but concentrated wines. The best display fleshy, succulent fruit, good length and the constitution to develop over medium term. Fine results from Voge, Verset, Michel, Lionnet, Juge, Clape, Thierry Allemand and de Barjac.

1992: Some *coulure* at flowering; otherwise a good growing season, though spoilt by some harvest rain. The wines are a mix: some fine *cuvées* (Clape, Lionnet's Rochepertuis and Verset in particular), other rather lean and gawky. Select carefully and keep for the medium term.

1993: Lamentable harvest weather all but ruined a promising vintage. Some growers stopped picking to wait for better weather: it didn't come. Others left the bunches to rot – the cost of harvesting and sorting was greater than the likely price of the wine. Growers who rigorously weeded out rotten or damaged fruit made small amounts of reasonable wine, not heavily extracted or densely flavoured, but with enough to live for a few years. The best are Verset, Geynale, Rochepertuis, Reynard, Clape. Perhaps best forgotten.

1994: First reports indicated a reasonable to good vintage; some rain at harvest, but not enough to restore the balance in grapes suffering from intense summer heat and drought. Another 1988 in the making?

AC CORNAS

Created	5 August 1938 (revised 1971)
Area (max)	n/a
Area under vine 1994	550ha
Base yield	40hl/ha
Minimum alcohol	10.5% (13.5% maximum)
Growers	40

DOMAINE THIERRY ALLEMAND

In Cornas, where most of the great *vignerons* are as old as their appellation – and many as their vines – it is refreshing to encounter a spirit of more recent making. Thierry Allemand is the youthful *esprit* of Cornas, but junior in no other sense.

He grew up in the village where his father – a Valence factory worker – came to live. Besotted by wine, he worked full-time from 1981 to 1992 with Robert Michel, whose late father, Joseph, he regards as his mentor. In 1981 he bought some old, long-abandoned vines and some *friches*, which he cleared and planted at weekends. He still works half-time *chez* Robert, since his own production won't support him and his new wife, who works in the Cornas Post Office; "she knows nothing about wine, but is starting to learn about paperwork".

Thierry, a dark, hirsute 30-year-old, is indelibly smitten with wine – his own, but also the sweet wines of the middle Loire, if the contents of his private cellar are any indication. He seldom leaves Cornas – except to present his wines in Paris, where he enjoys notable success among the *cognoscenti* wine bars.

Without recognised qualifications, the financial support offered to young *vignerons* by the French system were not open to him. However, as the people of Cornas realised his commitment, help of a less formal kind appeared. A 17th-century house and magnificent, if small, cellars materialised at a "*prix favorable*", thanks to an old friend who saw Thierry's promise and instructed his wife to sell him the house, and some fine antique furniture, when he died. He renovated the house himself, put the cellars in order and tended his vines – all in his free time. His quiet, cool and spacious home exudes care and taste.

Fine old vines also came, notably from Noël and Louis Verset, who had confidence in his abilities. He now has 2ha of Cornas and 1.03 of St-Joseph – this latter all goes to the co-op. His first vintage (1982) produced 300 bottles; now, in a good year, there are 8,000.

Thierry is clear about where he is going and how best to get there. Cornas should not be hard and tannic, rather a round wine, which ages well. For this, low yields are essential – 20hl/ha in 1993, 28 in 1992 and 31 in 1991 – as is a vinification which concentrates on structure and flesh. The crop is not de-stemmed, but 10% is crushed by foot before vatting to liberate some juice so fermentation can start. Thereafter, *pigeage à pied*, which adds *gras*, with a gentle increase of temperature from 20 to 35°C. "The best wines are always those which have the slowest temperature curve". The press is a vertical basket press which Thierry bought in Burgundy, in 1992.

There have been two *cuvées* of Cornas since 1990: Les Chaillots, from younger vines here and in La Côte, which is *élevé* 40:60 in cask and *inox*, and Reynard, which has the reverse proportions. The wines are left for 12-15 months, without racking, cask bungs vertical; this is possible because Thierry only leaves one litre of fine lees in each cask, otherwise the wine risks acquiring a disagreeable *goût de lie*. In March or so of the second year the wines are racked by gravity, fined if necessary, and bottled unfiltered.

Thierry's style is for wines which evolve slowly – unlike, for example, the Clapes and Guy de Barjac whose Cornas are more *flatteur* and approachable from the start. This is a highly promising domaine.

APPELLATION	VINEYARD	DETAILS	AREA
CORNAS	LES CHAILLOTS & LA COTE	Young vines – under 20 yrs.	1.10
CORNAS	REYNARD	60-80 yr old vines – ex Noël Verset	0.90
ST-JOSEPH		Sold to co-op	1.03
		TOTAL (hectares):	3.03

DOMAINE GUY DE BARJAC

Guy de Barjac is one of Cornas' finest and most respected *vignerons*. A year or two ago it was mischievously (and widely) reported that he had sold up and retired. In fact, since his son – an army major – did not want to take over, Guy decided to rent his vines out *en fermage*, which gives him a third of the fruit without the hard vineyard work. So now Jean-Luc Colombo has 0.4ha of his younger vines, and Sylvain Bernard from St-Péray the finest 1.13ha of 1904 vines *en coteaux*, while Guy continues to make 4,000 bottles of his excellent product, rather than his previous 12,000.

De Barjacs have never been far from Cornas, where the Barjasse plot bearing their name has been exploited by them since 1460. They were in the Gard from 1060-1340, then in the Cévennes before finally turning up in Cornas in 1760 to build the family home, a quiet, pleasant accommodation in the Grande Rue, for them, their wine and their silk-worm business. Guy's grandfather ran the wine business while his father pursued a banking career in Lyon, where Guy was born. He rapidly grew to dislike city life and moved out to Cornas, vinifying his first vintage in 1949.

Guy is a neat, articulate and clear-sighted man – not tall, but with quietly impressive authority. He believes that the *vigneron's* role is to express Cornas' unique *terroir* through the Syrah grape. To this end, perfect raw material is essential – "no rot and very ripe grapes" – which demands meticulous care of the vine. However, the fruit has then to be vinified, and years of tasting bore in on him that "traditional" Cornas generally equated with a coarse rusticity.

Visits to Burgundy in the 1950s confirmed his impression that Cornas lacked the finesse he particularly appreciated in the Pinot Noir, and also that the structure for ageing and youthful suppleness were not incompatible. The problem was tannin – too much and poor quality. Rather, he reflected, like the girl who had underlying beauty but didn't know how to dress herself. In short, Cornas needed re-designing.

This necessitated two fundamental changes: de-stemming and shorter *cuvaisons*. De Barjac tradition fixed the latter at three weeks which Guy, by stages, reduced to 10-12 days. "If you accentuate the tannin with stalks and excess maceration, it becomes a fault in my view". Changing what many regarded as entrenched habits was not easy: "people criticised me and said I was castrating Cornas". De-stemming had to wait until 1985, when suitable equipment appeared: "as soon as I found a small enough *erafloir* I fell on it". Removing stalks improved the wine's early drinkability without compromising its character and typicity.

The material of the vinification vessel plays no role in Guy's view: "I attach no importance to the *cuve* – you can get a good fermentation in almost anything"; but using indigenous yeasts does matter, unless there is an over-riding reason to think that fermentation may not finish properly: "we've had good yeasts here for ten centuries".

Guy allows temperatures to reach 34-35°C, since this give more complex and complete aroma extraction, de-*cuves* and then gently presses out the pulp with an ancient vertical screw-press.

After adding back the press-wine, and following malolactic in *cuve*, the wine passes to a population of old *pièces* for 18 months. There is no new wood, it gives tannins which are alien to the wine's character, and interestingly, no racking during this period – racking aerates the wine which is "contradictory", since it then needs more sulphur dioxide. In any case, any *goût de reduit* passes when the wine is racked into tank before bottling. A generation ago, the barrels would be given a quarter-turn – *bande de côté* – so

there was no air beneath the bung; this gave superb aromas, but although Guy admits this would be preferable, he leaves his casks with their bungs upright.

A light fining precedes the single bottling, by Colombo's team, without filtration, "this takes out flavour, aroma, everything. I'm a cottage industry", Guy admits, "I couldn't do things this way with large volumes".

Guy's wines exemplify the finesse of which many believe the hot, granitic *terroir* of Cornas incapable. Denser or lighter according to the vintage, they exude suppleness and elegance. Even

after three or four years, most are starting to decompress their aromas and flavours. In the finest vintages they evolve beautifully over a decade or so, softening out on the palate and changing from fruit-based aromas to those of *sous-bois* and spice, often developing a quite gamey, *faisandé*, character on the way.

Cornas needs secure, thoughtful winemakers like Guy de Barjac. After all, it is the wines, not the people, which ultimately defend an appellation's reputation. Guy is one of the best.

APPELLATION	VINEYARD	DETAILS	AREA
CORNAS	LA BARJASSE	Planted 1904; coteaux; en metayage to Sylvain Bernard, St-Péray	1.13
CORNAS	CHAILLOT	Planted 1979 on SO4 roots; en metayage to Jean-Luc Colombo	0.40
		TOTAL (hectares):	1.53

DOMAINE AUGUSTE & PIERRE-MARIE CLAPE

While one can argue *ad infinitum* about typicity, there are few who would dispute that if you are looking for quintessential Cornas, this is the place. No signs; nothing to invite those who hurtle through the village to stop and taste; merely a door-bell marked "Clape" in a terrace of ordinary houses opposite Restaurant Ollier on the RN86.

Auguste, a distinguished, silver-haired man in his sixties, is long-time Mayor of Cornas and its most respected citizen. Both in this office and as a winemaker, he is held in high regard, even by his fellow *vignerons* in this unduly pugnacious appellation. With his son, Pierre-Marie, who returned from an engineering career in 1989 when he could see a future as a *viticulteur*, he exploits 5.7ha in Cornas and St-Péray. These are charming, abundantly friendly people who have a strong attachment to their land and a masterly feel for turning grapes into wine.

While Auguste can account for 150 years of Clapes in Cornas, and believes the double, he personally came into the *métier* when his future mother-in-law invited him to harvest in 1949.

He recalls vividly that his first job, pouring wine for the harvesters, nearly went wrong, when he simply provisioned the men, passing over the women – a prime error of judgement in a *milieu* where, even today, women share much of the outdoor work. His diplomatic skills obviously prevailed, however, since he married the daughter that December.

The single Clape Cornas – no *vieilles*

Pierre-Marie and Auguste Clape.

vignes or special *cuvées* here – is an ample, darkish wine, packed with plumptious, old-vine fruit, the whole cemented together by a firm, round tannins. The vines are old and include 2ha not replanted since the phylloxera; damaged vines are simply replaced with either a field-grafted scion or nowadays, with a clone; better for quality than grubbing up an entire parcel. They try to harvest late – "it's a sort of lottery" – which pays off in some vintages, though not in the disastrously wet 1993.

In the important matter of de-stemming, the Clapes are clear: young vines – yes, old vines no – because their wood is usually ripe. Max Leglise, who trained Auguste in Beaune, taught him to beware of de-stemming machines: "you can't help crushing the stems and often, unripe berries as well". However, leaving the stems keeps unripe berries intact until pressing liberates their bitter juice into the wine. The answer is a rigorous *trie de vendange*, to eliminate all unripe fruit. Another small but highly important

Leglise detail: no must-pumps to transfer the crushed, un-de-stemmed fruit to the *cuves* – these risk extracting bitter chlorophylls from the green stems.

Old vines and the ripest fruit are the essential ingredients of an otherwise straightforward vinification. The older the vine, the lower the yield, the riper the wood and the berries, the longer you can leave the pulp to steep in its new wine. Here, six or seven days of fermentation at up to 34°C ("perfect"), is followed by three to seven days of maceration to extract the maximum of fine tannin. Thereafter, malolactic in wood ("it's a mystery"), and 18 months *élevage* in old *demi-muids* and *pièces*. A barrel gently oxygenates the wine and has a less reductive effect than a sealed *cuve* – particularly on the Syrah, which is prone to developing reduced aromas. There is no new wood used, both because it would mark the wine with oak, and also because small casks have thinner staves which dry out more rapidly than their thicker-clad larger brethren.

Each *lieu-dit* gives its own wine character – some fruitier, others more floral or harder – so they are kept separate until just before bottling, when a blend is made to harmonise these different "colours". This, perhaps, is a key to the complexity of a Clape Cornas, even in relatively light vintages, such as 1980, 1984 and 1987. Surprisingly for such a quality-conscious family, there are three bottlings of each vintage – the first in May

of the second year, another in July/August and the final *tirage* in September, before the harvest. The fruity young-vine Cornas is not used in the main blend, but appears in a less exalted role – *en carafe chez* Ollier – quaffed chilled, to great effect, with a modest collation on a hot summer's day.

Down in the small, cool cellars, the young wines evolve in their ancient wooden containers alongside bins of assorted old vintages, maturing at a more stately pace in grimy nooks and crannies. Upstairs, a couple of simple rooms are devoted to the administration, both of the domaine and of the Syndicat des Vignerons, of which Pierre-Marie is currently *Président*.

A few years ago, precious space was sacrificed to a lift for hauling casks and bottles around and, in 1994, an impressive new *cuverie* materialised

across the road, improving things still further.

Clape's Cornas is of international repute – not through any conscious marketing, but just because it is widely regarded as the finest and most consistent in the appellation. domaine-bottling came in 1968, and by 1969 stock had crossed the Atlantic. They used to sell in bulk to Jean Jaboulet, Louis' brother – but no longer. Another, more controversial, destination for their wine was one of Beaune's most illustrious grower-*négociant* houses. That trade has also gone, but many an appreciative Corton drinker may have unwittingly modelled his perception of that fine appellation on something a little more southerly. An oblique compliment to an excellent Cornas domaine.

APPELLATION	VINEYARD	DETAILS	AREA
CORNAS	LA COTE		2.00
CORNAS	REYNARDS		1.50
CORNAS	LES MAZARDS		0.30
CORNAS	PIED-LA-VIGNE		0.20
ST. PERAY			0.20
COTES DU RHONE		Old vines in Pied-La-vigne sector of Cornas	1.00
VIN DE TABLE			0.50
		TOTAL (hectares):	5.70

Note: Cornas: 2 ha 50-70 yr old vines, not replanted since phylloxera.
1 ha 35 yr old vines; 1 ha 15-20-25 yr old vines.

JEAN-LUC COLOMBO

Jean-Luc Colombo and his wife Anne, both qualified oenologists, arrived in Cornas in the early 1980s to set up a winemaking consultancy and technical analysis laboratory. In 1987 they started making their own wines from vines in Cornas.

His forthrightly critical views have made Colombo a controversial figure far beyond Cornas. These stem from his observation that much of what he has tasted, from appellations throughout the Rhône, is inherently faulty – poorly vinified wines which don't develop well and tend to taste much the same after a decade or so. Growers may talk of *terroir* but their old-fashioned methods did little to allow it to express itself. In particular, his undisguised belief that tradition was flawed and could be improved upon did not readily endear him to the older generation of his fellow *vignerons* and engendered much suspicion. Nonetheless, growers began to listen and now, after more than a decade, the Centre

Oenologique des Côtes du Rhône has more than 100 client-estates, from Côte-Rôtie to Nîmes and beyond; an impressive list which includes Jerome Quiot of Châteauneuf, the current *président* of France's INAO, the AOCs' supreme govering body, Chapoutier (qv), Château Fortia (qv) and Vernay (qv). Despite this high-profile acceptance, Colombo's presence in Cornas still provokes strong feelings among the *vignerons*; some express open dislike, while others barely acknowledge his existence.

In fact, Jean-Luc Colombo's views are not unduly revolutionary. Like Guy Accad in Burgundy, he believes that balanced, ripe fruit is essential for making fine wine, and encourages as nearly organic viticulture as possible; but otherwise he works to no *a priori* formulae, bar an insistence on de-stemmed grapes and long maceration, to extract "the full potential exuberance" from the fruit. His critics, also

reflecting those of Accad, allege that all his wines taste the same – a patently false assertion to anyone who has tried them. Beneath the continuing ripples is a serious attempt to bring *terroir* to the forefront and to improve the general quality of winemaking in a region in which quality has been notoriously patchy.

His own estate covers 6.3ha – including 1.6 of vines more than 90 years old vines *en fermage* from Guy de Barjac in Les Ruchets, which gives its name to Colombo's top Cornas *cuvée*. This is generally a big, firmly structured wine designed for long ageing. Its more forward sibling, Les Terres Brulées, comes from eight separate plots scattered throughout the appellation. The estate range is completed with Les Collines de Laure (his daughter) – a Vin de Pays des Collines Rhodaniennes – and a Côtes du Rhône. A recently established negociant enterprise produces Cornas, St-Joseph, Côtes du Rhône and Côtes du Roussillon, all made from purchased grapes.

Plantings, at 8,000 vines per hectare, are denser than the norm; this, along with severe pruning and an August bunch thinning of vines up to 50 years old, reduces yields and increases concentration. Harvesting is late, when the berries stain to the touch, and Jean-Luc likes to keep solids and juice/wine in contact for 18–21 days. After primary fermentation, the Ruchets and Terres Brulées are matured in new oak casks for 15–20 months before egg-white fining and bottling, unfiltered. Jean-Luc's open admiration for the wines of Guigal, Chave and Jaboulet has practical application in his use of La Mouline, La Turque, Chave's Hermitage and Jaboulet's La Chapelle as comparators at blending time.

The results are big, plummy wine with plenty of concentration and personality. They show no signs of the rusticity which one still finds masquerading as "tradition", here and elsewhere in the northern Rhône, and they have the structure to age – though, in lesser vintages, not perhaps for the 30–40 years that Jean-Luc considers possible for his Ruchets.

If there is a criticism it is that they seem to lack the purity and focus of other Cornas, with flavour profiles blurred by the long *cuvaison* and 100% new wood – rather less of each would make an immeasurable improvement. They are also expensive – some 20–30% or more than elsewhere in Cornas - a fact which has attracted criticism as has the use of Bordelais bottles for the Ruchets. Jean-Luc would argue that presentation is part of the image – and that classy packaging and new wood have to be paid for.

His activities as oenologist require

Jean-Luc Colombo in vineyards above Cornas.

extensive travelling both in the Rhône and throughout the Midi. In the late 1980s, seeing a need (and also a publicity

benefit) to bring together those who share his outlook, Colombo formed "Rhônes Vignobles", a loose assocation of some of his clients who meet and travel to promote their wines and discuss matters of common interest.

The parallels between Colombo's progress and that of Guy Accad in Burgundy are inescapable – initial derision and distrust, creeping acceptance then modest success. In both cases an outspoken manner and an unwillingness to cover unpalatable views in diplomatic language have undoubtedly contributed. Nonetheless, Jean-Luc Colombo's influence has clearly been for the good, with many of his clients making consistently finer wine than before.

Time alone can provide the evidence to test the allegations of atypicity and standardisation, but the clear success of many of Colombo's clients' wines seem to have pre-empted that judgement. Should the weight of innuendo and personal criticism become too onerous, Jean-Luc could do worse than enlist the dispensing services of his wife – Mme Columbo runs the local pharmacy.

APPELLATION	VINEYARD	DETAILS	AREA
CORNAS	COTES + CHAILLOTS	1 plot, 90+ year-old vines; provides fruit for Les Ruchets	1.60
CORNAS	EYGATS + ST. PIERRE	8 plots; 30–50 yr old vines and some younger plantings; provides fruit for Les Terres Brulées	3.50
VIN DE PAYS DES COLLINES RHODANIENNES	VARIOUS PARTS OF CORNAS	2 plots of 3–6 yr old Syrah; provides fruit for Les Collines de Laure	1.00
		TOTAL (hectares):	6.30

DOMAINE MARCEL JUGE

At just over three hectares, this is one of Cornas' medium-sized domaines; it is also one of its finest. Marcel Juge is a somewhat phlegmatic man, politically well right of centre, with an attitude which seems to suggest that he has given up on the state, which he regards with considerable cynicism.

When he is not expounding family history or discoursing on the decline of the French nation, Marcel seems perfectly content tending his vines and looking after his wife's sizeable vegetable plot, which doubles as the front garden of their plain house in the Cornas *place du marché*.

Even this modest task evokes the comment that "it's far cheaper to buy the vegetables in our grocery across

Marcel Juge.

the square" – which it almost certainly is in this *primeur* corner of France.

He has a further unplanted hectare of Cornas up his woolly sleeve, but has no intention of planting it: "you simply

have more taxes to pay and then when you expire – the gun really goes off.

"In France, *viticulteurs* keep the pot of state boiling – in Switzerland they are a protected species".

Marcel is a fine winemaker – traditional, as he and everyone else claims – but here with good reason. No de-stemming and plenty of foot-treading; "mechanical *pigeage* destroys the crop", he reckons, adding that "with your feet you feel the *cuve* – its temperature and the cap, it's much more gentle". No yeasting – "I don't muck around with bought yeasts – you just end up with Bordeaux".

Cuvaison lasts 15 days, rising to 35°C – no low temperatures tolerated here. Marcel reckons his vinification to be the most natural and traditional in the world. With such attractive, fleshy and seductive wines, it hardly matters whether it is or not.

There are three cuvees of Cornas – Pied de Coteaux, Coteaux, and Sélection des Coteaux – this last appearing in 1989, 1990 and 1991. Officialdom will not allow the use of "Coteaux" and "Sélection" unless they are part of an appellation; so Marcel simply labels his wines "Pied de Coteaux" – which seems somehow to be legal – "C" and "SC".

He is considering stopping the top SC *cuvée* – a late-harvest selection of grapes, because "they all want SC – but there are only 2,000 bottles".

The largest *cuvée* is the 8,000 bottles of the Coteaux. This – as are the others – is bottled after some two to three years' *élevage* in *demi-muids*, in Marcel's cellar. It is fined, but unfiltered.

APPELLATION	VINEYARD	DETAILS	AREA
CORNAS		50 year old vines	2.70
ST. PERAY	Marsanne & Roussanne	60 year old vines	0.35
		TOTAL (hectares):	3.05

These are some of the most elegant and finely crafted of any Cornas wines. No grating, herbaceous edges, no clumsily extracted, rough-hewn tannins. Here you will find simply pure, uncluttered often blackcurrant fruit, concentrated and fleshy, with enough round tannins to ensure a gentle, slow, evolution.

Anyone in need of convincing that Cornas is not just a massive mouthful of brainless muscle, should try one of Marcel Juges' charming trio. You are unlikely to be disappointed.

DOMAINE SYLVIANE & JACQUES LEMENICIER

This is a small domaine, operated from a small house approached by way of a narrow, elongated courtyard, up a small flight of stone steps past a large, pot-bellied tub of geraniums. Cellars nowhere and everywhere, concealed behind anonymous doors in quiet, winding back streets, house casks and bottles of wine awaiting bottling and despatch. But, as we know, size is no barrier to quality.

The Lemeniciers have been turning out excellent wines since Jacques took over 0.8ha of vines for an old *vigneron* who was disabled by an accident. He didn't recover, so the arrangement became permanent.

Parcels were added and then in 1994 Jacques bought outright 2.15ha of the Domaine St-Pierre, next to Jaboulet's plot acquired at the same time.

Although avowedly not scholastic, Jacques studied at Beaune, before a year's *stage* chez Robert Michel; then he worked for Alain Voge during the week, squeezing in work on his 3.05ha at weekends. Now his attractive, lively companion Sylviane helps, especially in the vineyards, a facet of the business at which he admits himself least skilled. Jacques especially respects Guy de Barjac and Alain Voge, to whose counsel he readily resorts. Voge's cellars provide facilities for his vinifications, which require expensive de-stemming equipment. The Lemenicier Cornas *cuvée* is a blend of non-de-stemmed old vine fruit and de-stemmed younger material, fermented at as high a temperature as he dares during a 12-day *cuvaison*. Maturation lasting 18-24 months, 20% in *cuve* and 80% in old casks, precedes bottling without filtration.

There are also 1,500 bottles of St-Péray split between two *cuvées* – one oaked, fermented in 50:50 new and one-year-old

casks, the other unoaked, made in neutral *cuves*. The former is *bâtonné* to add richness, and both are bottled after 6-10 months. As both, especially the wood-fermented wine, are sell-outs, the Lemeniciers are looking to add to their present half-hectare.

In style the Cornas lies firmly in the de Barjac mould – supple fruit and fine, round tannins. It doesn't have the

concentration or finesse yet of Jacques' mentor's wine, but is evolving in that direction. Of the two St-Pérays, the *cuvée boisée* is by far the more interesting and none the worse for being the less typical of the pair of that rather neutral appellation.

Jacques and Sylviane Lemenicier are making great strides. Let's hope that they manage to maintain the momentum.

APPELLATION	VINEYARD	DETAILS	AREA
CORNAS	DOM. DE ST. PIERRE	Planted 1986/90; 4.90 ha in total only	
		2.15 currently planted; owned outright	2.15
CORNAS		Bas de Coteaux; planted 1903; en fermage	0.40
ST. PERAY		Planted 1933; 100% Marsanne; en fermage	0.50
		TOTAL (hectares):	3.05

Sylviane and Jacques Lemenicier.

DOMAINE JEAN LIONNET

In size, Jean Lionnet's 10 hectares makes him one of the Cornas' more important domaines. He is a sound, sometimes excellent source of this wine, as well as of St-Péray where he has 2.5ha.

The Cornas *vignoble* consists mostly of *gobelet*-trained vines 45- 80 and more year old, split between Les Chaillots, Arlettes and Pied-la-Vigne, where Jean lives and vinifies, helped by his daughter Véronique. Here a neat, newish pine-fitted reception area awaits the individual clients who account for half his business. The remaining half goes to export, with a flattering smattering of grand restaurants.

Jean Lionnet is tall, grey-haired, with plenty of charm. He took over from his father in 1978, since when bulk sales have given way too 100% domaine-bottling and, since 1986, traditional vinification has been replaced by methods advocated by his neighbour, Jean-Luc Colombo.

He admits to being criticised for wines that are considered too oaky but counters that in the past the only material available to *vignerons* for *cuves* and maturation was wood. The second prong of Jean's self-defence is that, in any case, typicity is indefinable; a line aimed at destroying the foundations of those who argue that new wood removes differences between appellations, which matter so much to these small communities. However, under pressure, he agrees that the difficulty of defining a typical Cornas, St-Péray, or Bresse chicken, doesn't preclude being clear about what is atypical.

Disregarding typicity, Jean's wines are excellent. The St-Péray, made from a thoroughly non-traditional blend of 50% new wood and 50% *cuve* fermentations at 18°C and 13°C respectively, is invariably ripe and stylish; supported, but not obviously marked, by oak, with plenty of fleshy fruit. The wood adds fat and structure to what would otherwise be rather neutral wine, as does a useful 20% of Roussanne in the mix – a grape which is an irregular yielder and distinctly more disease-prone than its Marsanne stable-mate. He was recently refused the *agrément* for a *cuvée* of St-Péray, not because the wine was faulty, but because it was considered to lack typicity. Jean is unruffled – the wine is fine and he can sell it.

There are two *cuvées* of Lionnet Cornas: a standard issue and the Domaine de Rochepertuis – a brand, named after a pierced rock in the vineyards – which is a crop selection of fruit from old, well-exposed, low-yielding vines. Since Colombo's advent, the bunches are totally de-stemmed and given four hours pre-fermentive cool maceration; after four to five days fermentation the wine is left to further macerate for 29 days in closed *cuves*,

protected by a carbon dioxide blanket. In Jean's mind, prolongued post-fermentive maceration extracts fine tannins and cask ageing replaces stem tannins, to restore the fruit-alcohol-acid-tannin balance. The press wine is kept apart for as long as possible from the *vin de goutte*, 20% of which is *élevé* in *cuve* and 80% in cask. One-fifth of the Rochepertuis has new wood, the rest (and the standard Cornas) one- to five-year-old barrels. After 18 months *élevage* – 12 in cask, 4 in *cuve* – the wines are fined and plate-filtered. Jean insists on a single bottling for everything: "several *mises*, several tastes".

The Rochepertuis *cuvée* first appeared in 1985 and now accounts for a third of Cornas production. At 25-30hl/ha, yields are well below those for the standard *cuvée* – 35-38hl/ha. Others can argue whether or not it is fine Cornas, but it certainly is fine wine. Typified by concentrated, almost sweet, ripe fruit, it needs a few years in bottle for the wood elements to dissolve and for its real character to emerge. The standard *cuvée* is built on less grand lines, showing attractive earlier finesse and development.

Jean and Véronique are honest, conscientious *vignerons*, producing interesting and carefully made wines. Whether or not you like them must be a matter of personal taste.

APPELLATION	DETAILS	AREA
CORNAS	Chaillots, Arlettes, Pied-la-Vigne; 95% granite soils; av. vine age 42+; oldest vines 80+	10.00
ST-PERAY	En metayage; vine-age 40+; 80% Marsanne, 20% Roussanne	2.50
COTES DU RHONE	Soils contain higher % of clay & limestone; 20+yr old vines	1.50
	TOTAL (hectares):	14.00

DOMAINE ROBERT MICHEL

The Michels are one of the oldest families in Cornas. Robert, a balding, gingery man, now in his fifties, is the ninth generation to make wine here. "I've never had the luck of buying or renting vines which were in a decent state", he bemoans, referring to the three hectares he has added to the four he took over in 1977. "People thought me mad to clear scrub then", when the wine didn't sell well, and there was always the flatter, though far less favourable, land round the village.

Robert produces three grades of Cornas: Pied de Coteaux and Coteaux are a selection of different soil-types; the former, from richer, more *limoneux* and scree soils on flatter ground where "the

vine eats and drinks as it wants"; the latter from sloping sandy-clayey soils where water and nutrients are less easily obtained. Finally, there is Le Geynale, from vines planted by "*le grandpère*" in three goes between 1910 and 1930, on gneiss and granite in the lower third of the Thezier sector.

This used to be a *lieu-dit*, on the pre-1956 *cadastre*, but is no longer. Robert asked the INAO what was required to put a defunct *lieu-dit* on the label and was told to register a trade-mark, which is what Le Geynale now is. It first appeared in 1984, because Robert felt that this top-quality raw material was being "drowned" in the Coteaux blend – by his father.

These vineyards are hard work –

especially those Robert has on slopes – 30% is the average, with "La Grande Pente, exposed south-west, behind Thezier – 40%, very steep and slippery, a *bête noire* for everyone". Somehow the rugged, florid, Robert manages it, although he notes that while it takes one man full-time to work 2-2.5ha of coteaux, on flatter, mechanizable land, he could handle ten. All this inevitably adds to the cost of a coteaux Cornas.

Unlike some of his competitors, Robert has lengthened his *cuvaison* from 12 days to three weeks; "after 12 days you had hard tannins; lengthening the maceration gives more elegant tannins, more completeness, and softens the product". The new wine remains on its fine lees all winter in closed *cuves*. Come spring, it is racked into 6- to 20-year-old Burgundy casks, bought from Christophe Roumier and Michel Juillot. There it spends a year on quarter bung – *bande de côté* – without racking; this because, says Robert, "I'm lazy – I do nothing". In reality, he believes that this imparts more elegance and roundness to the wine, but "you must have your cask in a perfect state for this".

The various lots of each *cuvée* are finally blended – "an *assemblage* of *parfums*" adds Robert, "each cask has its perfume" – fined then bottled, Geynale in one go, the other *cuvées* in two or three batches. In years where there are problems – such as 1992, when the Michel vines were "seriously hailed on" – there may be no Pied de Coteaux: only the Coteaux appears. In 1993, so rotten were the Pied vines, that Robert didn't even bother to harvest them: "I prefer not to chaptalize; in any case what was OK

was only 9% (potential alcohol)". A potter who works hard is guaranteed his vase, or whatever; no such luck for the wretched *vigneron*.

The Michel style is distinctly masculine – no gentle, youthful silkiness here, just uncompromising structure with good, concentrated fruit. A policy of no de-stemming – only broken in 1993 – means that the lesser *cuvées* may sometimes show an unattractive *goût de rafle* which may or may not be covered by the fruit.

This is a domaine capable of producing fine wine – not far off the top-level. It is difficult not to feel that even 50% de-stemming would make a significant improvement to all the wines, without compromising the structure which Robert Michel clearly wants. In 1993, he bought an *égrappoir* "in a hurry – within 24 hours of the harvest". Let's hope he continues to use it – every year.

APPELLATION	DETAILS		AREA
CORNAS	Coteaux vines, mostly in Thezier, 1.5 ha. c 10 yrs old; 3+ ha. 80-90 yrs old.		
	Av. age 45; soils: decomposed granite + gneiss + some flat stones		6.50
CORNAS	Flatter ground	0.50	
	TOTAL (hectares):		7.00

DOMAINE NOEL VERSET

Noël Verset, now in his late 70s, has made Cornas since 1942. Though nominally retired, having sold his old vines in Reynard to Thierry Allemand, he still works just over half a hectare of over 80-year-old vines in Les Chaillots, bought from his parents-in-law in 1931, and 1.20ha of 1903 vines in Les Sabarottes, bought in 1948, vinifying their concentrated fruit into magnificent, yardstick Cornas.

He is above all a modest, quiet man, living alone now in the house he built for his wife who died in 1985. Her picture adorns his desk and mantlepiece, along with that of his father who died in the same year, having just managed his century – a reminder of happier days with their children in the Drôme countryside.

Her memory is obviously evergreen. Piles of business letters lie scattered round the small sitting room in flower vases and boxes – a pine desk in one corner overflowing with paper, more on the sideboard; a burden which they no doubt shared, chatting together over the day's work and welcoming the visitors who still appear from all corners of the world. Noël's work is now for his daughters and grandchildren – but with the death of his wife he seems to have lost some of his inspiration and *raison d'être*.

These are steep, hard-labour vineyards for Noël, who limps after having a cartilege removed: "I can get up the hills, but find it more difficult to come down again", he adds giving a painful demonstration shuffle. Fortunately, "the son-in-law – he's in flowers in Thonon –

Noel Verset relaxing in his garden.

comes over to help me when he can"; otherwise it's a solo performance.

Up to 1994, Noël Verset made his own grafts to replace damaged vines. Now he buys in clones from the nurseryman – although one suspects that he doesn't like them one bit.

He doesn't seem to have ever stopped to consider what makes for top-quality wine – presumably he just took its yardstick for granted. Old vines, very low yields and super-ripe fruit have something to do with it. he muses; for the rest, much the same vinification as you find among "*la tradition*" in the village: no de-stemming, *pigeage à pied* in open cement *cuves* and 12-15 days' *cuvaison* at 30°C or so. The only modernisation is a short settling before the new wine goes into 600-litre *demi-muids* and *foudres* for 18 months' maturation before bottling unfiltered; "we didn't do this in the old times". Noël still uses an ancient vertical press – it works perfectly well and, in any case, a bright new one would be totally out of place in his tiny *cuverie*.

His lifetime has seen great changes, even in this small community. When he started out on his own, Noël remembers the vineyard terraces being virtually abandoned during the Second World war. Later on, the pines and scrub which rapidly replaced the vines had to be cleared once again for planting. Now, where there were once vines, there are homes for middle-class city workers – particularly on the westerly hillsides near to St-Péray and Valence.

After the war, many of the Cornas *vignerons* preferred to work the flatter land round the village, which produced high volumes of lighter wine for the local *négociants* and the bistros of

APPELLATION	VINEYARD	DETAILS	AREA
CORNAS	LES SABAROTTES	Planted 1903; v. fine soils	1.20
CORNAS	LES CHAILLOTS	80 yr old vines	0.56
CORNAS	CHAMPELROSES	Pied de coteaux	0.18
		TOTAL (hectares):	1.94

Lyon. A popular bistro might get through a cask a day then, patronised by a discerning clientele which knew who offered the best wine.

"The *coteaux* land is the real Cornas land", Noël adds, "it's like a sponge when it rains. My old vines are planted one metre square – 10,000 per hectare; nowadays its 1 x 2 metres – so half the density and more yield".

Wandering round his small cellars, climbing with difficulty up his ladder, pipette and glass in hand, to draw off samples from two great ovals with "CORNAS 1993" chalked boldly on each, one has the sense of a vanishing tradition alive in this kindly, smiling man. A generous friend had brought him some fresh *girolle* mushrooms, the preparation and cooking of which was much on his mind.... Tomorrow, another hard day's work on the hill, to finish *l'attachage* – the next important detail to be attended to in the cycle of yet another vintage of his splendid wines.

Even the local baker enters the spirit: a grape-decorated loaf in the window of a Tournon boulangerie.

DOMAINE ALAIN VOGE

In an appellation where three hectares is large, Alain Voge, with seven, is positively heavy industry. Understandably more sales-oriented than some of his colleagues, his bright signs direct customers to the cellars off the RN86, behind Ollier.

An ex "Valence Sportif" rugby player, Alain is now in middle-age. Dark-haired, tight-lipped, with a touch of egotism in his manner, yet friendly underneath, he recounts how he came to Cornas in 1958, aged 18, after trying his hand as a nurseryman and then as proprietor and operator of a travelling still. With Robert Michel, he was among the earliest domaine bottlers, starting in 1959.

His 7ha of Cornas albeit fragemented, include 4.5ha of *vieilles vignes*. This enables him to offer three wines – a standard blend, a Vieilles Vignes, which appears annually, and the Vieille Fontaine made from the finest old vines, many planted in the 1920s, and released only in exceptional vintages (so far 1985, 1988, 1990 and 1991). He attributes his high average vine-age to his being among the handful of *vignerons* to remain working when everyone else left, disillusioned, in the late 1950s.

As far as Cornas goes, he argues that it is "made to have fruit" so vinification is adapted to "retain the fruit at all costs". Young vines are not de-stemmed – unnecessary "if you've worked your vines properly"; the old vines, however, are,

because their low yields would over-balance the proportion of stems to berries. *Pigeage à pied* and 13-15 days' *cuvaison* for the young vines, longer for the rest, which has *remontage* but no *pigeage*. Alain stresses the importance of alcohol balance in a fine Cornas: "I don't want wines of more than 12.5°; some want 13-13.5° – these are very presentable immediately, but not typical".

The specially-picked small bunches destined for the 3,000 bottles of massive, silky Vieille Fontaine are de-stemmed and given 15-16 days' *cuvaison*, with *pigeage* only towards the end. Thereafter, 22-26 months in casks – a few new ones each year; then fining, filtration and bottling – "the Syrah has so much matter, you must filter", Alain explains.

There are also a couple of good still St-Pérays: a Cuvée Boisée, fermented half in new wood, half in second-year oak, with

occasional *bâtonnage* – "poof – no, not regularly, it's not Chardonnay". This popular wine comes out as heavily oaked, with whatever fruit there is struggling from underneath to make an appearance; attractive to some perhaps. If you don't appreciate this style, you could try the "non-*boisé*" version; this sees no wood and generally has pronounced flavours of quince and apple. Both wines undergo malolactic: "if you don't, you have to filter sterile and add lots of sulphur dioxide and the wines don't keep". Both wines are bottled after five to six months – "any longer and the colour oxidises".

Alain is responsible for a group which makes 50,000 litres of sparkling St-Péray. His own wine has zero *dosage* and, in his view, needs five years in bottle before drinking. The window is narrow – "don't keep it any longer – it maderizes"!

This is a fine estate. Excellent Cornas; fine, if individual St-Péray, and the remarkable Vieille Fontaine – if any comes your way, grab it!

APPELLATION	VINEYARD	DETAILS	AREA
CORNAS	LES COTES		0.70
CORNAS	REYNARD		1.00
CORNAS	LES MAZARDS		0.30
CORNAS	LES CHAILLOTS		1.50
CORNAS	PATOU		0.70
CORNAS	COMBE		1.00
CORNAS	LES SAVEAUX		0.15
CORNAS		Small plots – Pied-la-Vigne etc.	1.65
ST. PERAY			4.00
		TOTAL (hectares):	11.00

ST-PERAY

St-Péray marks the southern limit of the Rhône Septentrionale. Here, Syrah gives way to the white Marsanne and Roussanne, interspersed with patches of Roussette.

The commune clings doggedly to its independence, spared only by the Rhône from becoming a westerly dormitory for nearby Valence. As it is, creeping urban sprawl has seen the *vignoble* diminish as older growers, fed up with the struggle in vineyard and marketplace, succumbed to the blandishments of property developers.

From a late 19th-century heyday, when its sparkling wine often out-priced champagne, St-Péray has shrunk from a theoretically plantable 1,900ha to a stable rump of 65ha. A score of dedicated producers soldier manfully on – eight or so in the village, the rest mainly Cornas growers stimulated presumably by the challenge of making a white to complement their tannic red.

Modern St-Péray turns out some 30,000 cases annually – a mixture of still and *méthode champenoise* sparkling, both *demi-sec* and *brut*, most of which is sold locally. Styles vary from grower to grower – especially for the *tranquille*, where vine age, grape mix and the use of wood contribute significantly. Marsanne accounts for more than 90% of plantings, although recent years have seen a significant increase in Roussanne, as growers recognise its quality potential. Chaboud produces a pure Roussanne (the only house to do so), while Bernard, Gripa, Lionnet and the Clapes have recently increased their plantings of this variety. However, it is recognised as a "susceptible" grape, difficult to crop evenly, and capricious – which probably explains its unpopularity. Also, it yields less than the Marsanne, so planting percentages are a poor guide to its real contribution. Even its identity is not entirely secure as some aver that their Roussanne is distinct, both ampelographically and in taste character, from the Hermitage Roussanne.

The little-seen Roussette is also contentious: some say it is the Altesse of Savoie, source of the crisp, staple white of Tarentaise ski resorts, while others claim it as the local name for Roussanne – or vice versa. Either way, it gets no particular mention or special treatment from anyone.

Despite its small size, St-Péray has a variety of soils and exposures. To the north, in the Hongroie *quartier* bordering Cornas, mainly southeast- facing slopes of white clay and granite give richer, broader wines with some staying power. To the south-east lies Crussol, with its distinctive ruined château; here, more limestone produces lighter wines with more finesse and less muscle. The southern limit of the AC is Toulaud, where Jean-Louis Thiers is based and where Sylvain Bernard, Darona and Bernard Gripa from Mauves have vines; here notably more white clay gives supple wines with less acidity; growers compare this soil, especially in the *quartier* Thioulet, to the chalk of Champagne. The best vineyard in this sector, the Côte du Pin, rises to an altitude of 300 metres.

In general, fruit from the oldest vines from the most-favoured sites is usedfor *tranquille*, while that from lower slopes and younger plants goes into the sparkling *cuvées*, contributing useful acidity to base wines. The *mousseux* sells well in the locality and is worth keeping for a year or two. Some growers offer a zero-*dosage cuvée*, which can be somewhat more brutal than *brut*, while others stick to the 1.5–2.5g/bottle *dosage* softener to take the edge off acidity. There is no unanimity as to whether or not to vintage the sparkling wine. Those who don't, have the freedom of adding older reserve wine to deepen and broaden the final blend – which, as in champagne, is often the better for it. St-Péray *mousseux* tends to be full and earthy – perfectly acceptable and attractive *in situ* but no competitor on the international stage.

The best of the *tranquilles*, on the other hand, merit more attention than they usually get. As well as the wines from the estates profiled below, good bottles come from Jean Lionnet, the Clapes, Bernard Gripa, Jacques Lemenicier and Alain Voge (who also runs St-Péray's Cave des Vignerons, from cellars beneath the ex-Hotel des Bains). Some – notably Voge and Lionnet – produce an oaked St-Péray, which seems to have struck a local marketing note since they are generally the first to sell out.

St-Péray has never entirely got over the 100-bottle order which Richard Wagner placed with Maison Chapoutier in 1877, during the composition of Parsifal (a copy can be seen in their offices in Tain). Despite his notorious reluctance to pay for his provisions, the wine was duly despatched to Bayreuth. Whether his other request – for delayed payment – was also granted is not entirely clear.

It would be wrong to elevate St-Péray above its worth. Wines are well made, worth drinking and good value – generally better than white St-Joseph but without the depth of the best white Crozes.

Jean-François Chaboud. Larger bottle sizes to order!

JEAN-FRANCOIS CHABOUD

Jean-François Chaboud's ancestors arrived in St-Péray in 1750 – 80 years in advance of the commune's first sparkling wine, then called "Champagne – St-Péray". By their first vintage in 1778, much of the family harvest – and doubtless, everyone else's too – was bought by Champagne houses. Now, Jean-François and his wife are concerned to nurture and respect the tradition which his ancestors helped to create. He took over the house from his father in 1957, and their son, Stefan, fresh from studies in Champagne, joined him in turn in 1993. Madame Chaboud doubles as the family historian and archivist – a role which clearly gives her great pleasure.

The domaine's St-Péray head-quarters consist of a large complex of old buildings, part dating from 1736, fronting onto the rue Fernand Mallet, which is named after Jean-François' great-grand-father. Things do not appear to have changed visibly over the years except for a modern addition built over existing cellar beams. The office, with its dusty hand-written ledgers, insignia and memorabilia, seems somehow incomplete without a frock-coated, top-hatted clerk or two.

The wines, from 12.5ha in St-Péray (and one in the Champelrose *secteur* of Cornas) are among the most traditional in the appellation: 45,000 bottles of *mousseux* – a standard *cuvée* from 100% Marsanne, and since 1992, a limited bottling of a *cuvée prestige* – and rather less *tranquille*. Both *mousseux* remain for two to three years on lees before *dégorgement,* during which time Stefan is responsible for manual *remuage* – no grinding of mechanical riddling-machines here! The *liqueur de tirage* consists of yeasts, phosphates (to aid clarification) and tannins, which give a finer, more even bead. The Prestige base is a blend of 50% of the previous vintage's Marsanne and 50% of the current year's Roussanne – the one for depth, the other to keep a "regular quality". The result – only sold to "good restaurants and *clients particuliers* – is excellent: more complex than either of the drier standard *mousseux* , with a fizz which doesn't fill the mouth with froth and thus detract from the underlying flavour. The Roussanne contributes depth and richness, the Marsanne elegance. Altogether a harmonious wine, with interest and length; stamped, of course with a touch of St-Péray *goût de terroir.*

The still wines come from *coteaux* and old-vine fruit, yielding around 20–25hl/ha. After a short fermentation in *inox* – "no oak, we aren't in Burgundy here" – and fining and filtration, they are bottled in Feburary or March following the vintage. The pure Roussanne is kept away from air and given a good fining, to minimise the oxidation to which it is notoriously susceptible. In character it is quite malic, with flavours of straw and hay, fullish and reminiscent of unripe plums. In contrast, its Marsanne stable-mate is sappier and broader, with spicier, peely flavours redolent of apricots.

The Chabouds are fighting hard for St-Péray; this independently-minded enclave could wish for no finer champions!

PIERRE DARONA ET FILS

With nine hectares of St-Péray (90% Marsanne, 10% Roussanne) and one of Syrah, *vin de pays,* Pierre Darona and his son are the second-largest growers in the appellation and the third and fourth generations since Daronas started making *mousseux* here in the 1940s. Their vines are mostly round the family home, an unpretentious farmhouse with a western-style loggia, off the road to Toulaud, south-west of the village. 80% of production is made into *mousseux,* the rest is vinified *tranquille.*

This latter is a sound, attractive example of what the *terroir* gives – full, quite sappy and honeyed, rather old-fashioned and generally better for food. The *mousseux* comes without a vintage, as both *brut* and *demi-sec* – a big, firm wine with a distinct *goût de terroir* and an underlying hint of Roussanne oxidation.

JEAN ET JEAN-MARIE TEYSSEIRE

The third and fourth generations of Teysseires produce both Cornas and St-Péray from their St-Péray base. For the latter, there are 1.6ha of close-planted 75-year-old vines – mix unknown but thought by Jean-Marie, a lively short-cropped man in his early thirties, to be about 85% Marsanne. As all the vines are old, exposition is the only means of selection – *coteaux* fruit for *tranquille,* that from flatter ground for *mousseux.* The fruit is harvested cool, since even a few hours of heat after picking can result in premature oxidation, then rapidly pressed and fermented at 20–24°C, a level which gives "more differences from other wines". The whites are not bottled before 18 months here, and then, even though *malo fait,* are sterile-filtered to prevent refermentation. High soil pH and "something in the *terroir*" seems to encourage secondary fermentation, so these precautions are deemed necessary. The Teysseires only bottle 40% of their white and 20% of their red – the remainder is sold to the local *négoce.*

The sparkling St-Péray is the best of this cellar – that made largely from a 1990 base wine, including 5-10% of Roussanne, showed a fine mousse, hay and greengages on the nose and plenty of ripe, earthy flavours: good, sound stuff, albeit a bit frothy and evanescent. The whites lacked real depth and definition, as did the 1992 and 1990 Cornas, both of which would have been improved immeasurably by lower yields, de-stemming and earlier bottling.

JEAN-LOUIS THIERS

A relative newcomer to the St-Péray scene, Jean-Louis Thiers bottled his first vintage in 1980. Now, there are 20,000 bottles of *mousseux* from vines on largely granitic soil, 5,000 bottles of *tranquille* from mostly clay-limestone ground – both from 100% Marsanne – and 2,000 bottles of Cornas from 45- and 75-year-old vines; altogether 5.8ha in production. The still wine is from fruit from 40- to 50-year-old vines, vinified from direct-press juice, in enamelled *cuves.* The Cornas is made in open wood *cuves* with daily *pigeage* and then spends a year in small wood before bottling. Good results in recent vintages – in particular an attractive, floral and honeyed 1991 St-Péray *tranquille.* An excellent source – especially of St-Péray.

WINE AREAS OF THE SOUTHERN RHONE

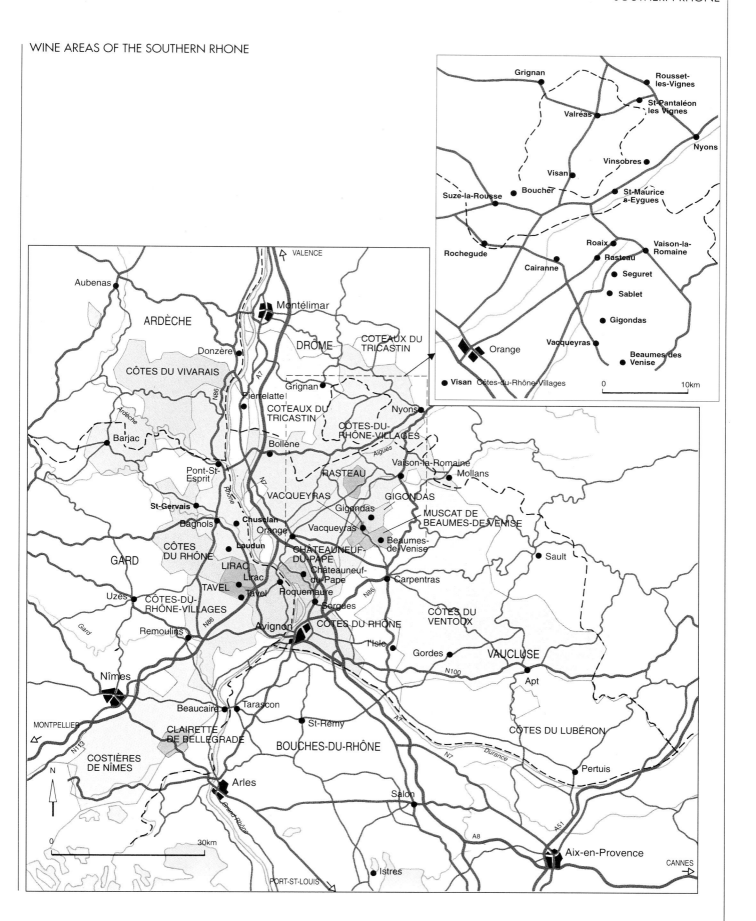

Grignan
Rousset-les-Vignes
Valréas
St-Pantaléon-les-Vignes
Nyons
Vinsobres
Visan
St-Maurice-s-Eygues
Suze-la-Rousse
Boucher
Rochegude
Roaix
Vaison-la-Romaine
Cairanne
Rasteau
Seguret
Sablet
Gigondas
Vacqueyras
Beaumes des Venise
Orange

● **Visan** Côtes-du-Rhône-Villages

0   10km

VALENCE

Aubenas

ARDÈCHE

Montélimar

DRÔME

COTEAUX DU TRICASTIN

Donzère

CÔTES DU VIVARAIS

Ardèche

Grignan

Pierrelatte

COTEAUX DU TRICASTIN

Nyons

Barjac

Bollène

CÔTES-DU-RHÔNE-VILLAGES

Aigues

Pont-St-Esprit

RASTEAU

Vaison-la-Romaine

Mollans

St-Gervais

VACQUEYRAS

GIGONDAS

Bagnols

Chusclan

Gigondas

MUSCAT DE BEAUMES-DE-VENISE

CÔTES DU RHÔNE

Orange

Vacqueyras

Laudun

CHÂTEAUNEUF-DU-PAPE

Beaumes-de-Venise

Sault

GARD

LIRAC

Lirac

Châteauneuf-du-Pape

TAVEL

Tavel

Roquemaure

Carpentras

Uzès

CÔTES-DU-RHÔNE-VILLAGES

Sorgues

CÔTES DU VENTOUX

Remoulins

Avignon

CÔTES DU RHÔNE

Gard

N86

l'Isle

Gordes

VAUCLUSE

Nîmes

N100

Apt

Beaucaire

Tarascon

CLAIRETTE DE BELLEGRADE

St-Rémy

CÔTES DU LUBÉRON

MONTPELLIER

N113

BOUCHES-DU-RHÔNE

N7

Durance

COSTIÈRES DE NÎMES

N

Pertuis

0   30km

Arles

Salon

A8

A51

Aix-en-Provence

Grand-Rhône

CANNES

Istres

PORT-ST-LOUIS

97

CHATEAUNEUF-DU-PAPE

Châteauneuf-du-Pape wears the undisputed crown among Southern Rhône appellations, known worldwide for its red wines and, to a much lesser extent, for its whites. It holds an unique place in the French wine industry as the cradle of the *appellation contrôlée* system, which began here and developed throughout viticultural France during the 1920s and early 1930s.

The little town, more an overgrown village, lies some 20km north-west of Avignon, in the Vaucluse, clustered round a prominent hillside dominated by its ruined château. Encircling it are 3,244ha of vineyard, split between some 225 estates who make and bottle their own wine, and a further 80 growers who sell their grapes to the cooperative at Courthézon.

The village, a maze of narrow, winding, streets, radiates out towards neighbouring conurbations. At its centre, a small *place*, a fountain, and a bench generally occupied by the *"papets"* – the older generation who while away spring and summer days watching the bustling ebb and flow of visitors, accompanied by the constant cabaret of frustrated drivers trying to negotiate the invariable traffic blockage.

In 1994 there was near uproar when it was proposed to remove the "Grand Fountain", which had stood there since 1635; after much heated debate, involving most of the village, a compromise was reached, and the grey-stone ornament re-sited nearby, outside the architecturally bold new Office de Tourisme.

Apart from a handful of restaurants, serving a stream of captive tourists, commercial activity is limited to a few shops and a plethora of cellars selling wine. A welcome improvement has appeared in the shape of a mass of dun-coloured signposts indicating the whereabouts of selected domaines. Unfortunately, diminutive lettering coupled with strategic siting at busy road junctions causes all but the sharpest-sighted motorist to brake violently to work out where he is going.

GRAPES

The principal grape, accounting for around 60% of plantings, is the Grenache Noir, which gives a well-coloured, alcoholic wine. However, solo it tends to lack structure, so to achieve balance, a further 12 varieties are permitted in the red blend: Mourvèdre, Syrah, Cinsaut, Vaccarèse, Counoise, Terret Noir, Muscardin and Picpoul Noir – all red varieties – together with five whites for freshness:

Mistral-blasted conifers in the Southern Rhone.

Clairette, Grenache Blanc, Roussanne, Picpoul Gris and Picardan. The rules allow these to be fermented together or separately. White Châteauneuf – which accounts for 3-8% of total production – comes from any or all of Grenache Blanc, Clairette, Roussanne, Bourboulenc, Terret Blanc and Picardan.

These curious grape cocktails have no particular logic, but represent what was most widely planted when the rules were codified, and Châteauneuf's AC decree finally settled, on May 15 1935. They also echo the 19th century, when mixed plantings were common, reflecting a limited supply of any one variety and the belief that co-planting gives better pollination and diminishes any loss from coulure, to which Grenache, in particular, is susceptible. The present AC rules leave the grape mix elective, entrenching neither limits nor guidance as to appropriate proportions. One famous Châteauneuf *vigneron*, Commandeur Joseph Ducos, proprietor of Concordet and of Château La Nerte in the early 1900s, published his personal dream formula: 20% of Grenache and Cinsaut for "warmth, liqueur-like sweetness and mellowness", 40% Mourvèdre, Syrah, Muscardin and Vaccarèse for "solidity, durability, colour... and a thirst-quenching flavour", 30% Counoise and Picpoul for "vinosity, charm, freshness and accentuation of bouquet" and 10% of white grapes, Clairette and Bourboulenc, for "finesse, fire and sparkle" (Livingstone-Learmonth, 1992). Nowadays, the more usual red mix

would be 50-70% Grenache, 20-30% Syrah, 10-20% Mourvèdre with splashes of the minor varieties.

The post-war decades have seen an increase in plantings of Syrah and Mourvèdre and, to a lesser extent, Cinsaut. Many of these vines are now mature, contributing usefully to overall structural balances. However, choice of site, especially for Mourvèdre, is critical: while Syrah seems to perform best in cooler, sandier places, mimicking to some extent its northern terroirs, Mourvèdre needs a fully south-facing, sheltered site to give of its best. Muscardin is also attracting fringe attention, with planting at La Gardine (qv) and serious contemplation from Jacques Reynaud at Château Rayas (qv). In general, the use of firmer, more structured varieties to complement Grenache should not be seen as providing support for an essentially weak grape which can then be overcropped. Grenache is perfectly capable of producing excellent stand-alone wine, but only if yields are very low – witness the magnificent wines of Château Rayas. What matters is that, even at lowish yields, the fusion of several varieties can provide extra complexity and an altogether more harmonious result.

This flexibility results in a wide diversity of Châteauneuf "recipes". At one extreme, Château Rayas is made from virtually 100% Grenache, while Château de Beaucastel uses all 13 permitted varieties. As both make consistently fine wine, this destroys any attempt at defining

Domains situated in village of Châteauneuf-du-Pape

Clos des Papes
Henri Bonneau
Dom de Beaurenard
Les Cailloux
Dom de Mont Olivet
Dom de Monpertuis
Dom du Pégau
Vieux Donjon
Dom des Relagnes
Clos l'Oratoire des Papes
Dom de Père Caboche
Dom de la Roquette
Comte de Lauze
Les Clefs d'Or
Dom Durieu
Chante Perdrix
Dom du Vieux Lazaret
Les Reflets
Chante Cigale
Dom de Saint Prefert

COMMUNE DE COURTHEZON

COMMUNE D'ORANGE

COMMUNE DE BÉDARRIDES

COMMUNE DE SORGES

ORANGE

ORANGE

COURTHÉZON

ROQUEMAURE

SORGUES

SORGUES

Ch de Beaucastel
Coudoulet
La Barnouine
La Janasse
Boilauzon
Chapouin
La Bertaude
Vieille Julienne
Dom de la Janasse
Palestor
La Gardiole
Ch Maucoil
Cabrières
Barratin
Le Plaine des Blancs
Maucoil
Les Bêdines
Le Mourre de Vidal
Dom de Mont Redon
Les Brusquières
Boidauphine
Pignan
Mont Redon
Ch Cabrières
Guigasse
Farguerol
Cabrières
Les Pielons
Pignan
Pied de Baud
Ch Rayas
Le Cristia
Les Pradel
Pignan
Valori
La Carrière
Combes d'Arnavel
La Roquette
Le Grès
L'Etang
St-Georges
Grandés Gualiguières
Le Pointu
Le Cristia
Beau Renard
Four à Chaux
Vaudieu
Grand Pierre
Combes Masques
Terres Blanches
Dom de Nalys
Le Mourre de Gaud
Le Mourre des Perdrix
Les Saintes Vierges
Ch la Gardine
Charbonnières
La Crau
Fontdu Loup
Les Saummades
Roumiguières
Castelas
Pelous
Colombis
Devés d'Estonard
Cuvée du Vatican
Bois Senescau
Les Blaguières
Duvet
Barbe d'Asne
Les Bourguignons
Dom de Marcoux
La Font du Pape
Montolivet
La Crau
Vieux Télégraphe
La Croze
Coste Froide
Jacquinotte
Châteauneuf-du-Pape
St-Joseph
La Cerise
Relagnes
Dom de la Solitude
La Crau
Pierre à Feu
Le Boucou
Monpertuis
Reveirores
Le Limas
D192
La Fortiasse
La Grenade
Mont de Vies
La Font du Loup
Font de Michelle
Moulin à Vent
Ch Fortia
Ch des Fines Roches
Bs de la Vieille
Les Marines
Ch la Nerthe
Pied Redon
Les Garrigues
Marron
Bois de Boursan
La Nerthe
Les Combes
Gr des Serres
Petite Bastide
Les Escondudes
Gr. Serres
Les Plagnes
La Bigote
Sauvinas
Pigeoulet
Plan du Rhône
Les Galimardes
Terre Ferme
Ras Cassa
Petites Serres
Cansaud
Les Revès
Les Coulets
Rhône
Les Serres
Franquizons
La Lionne
Le Grand Collet
Plan du Rhône
Châteune

height in metres

N

0   2 km

A.C. Châteauneuf-du-Pape

Lavender and vines – summer landscape near Domaine Gramenon.

Châteauneuf typicity. The current predominance of Grenache in part reflects the situation in the 1930s, when Châteauneuf wine was used as a blending component in Burgundy, providing a cheap, rich, warm and eminently market-acceptable filler – a practice which continued into the 1960s. This, together with an equally idiosyncratic range of vinifications, compounds the difficulties for buyers, who are often unaware of the complexities.

The whites, whose volume has increased since the 1930s, when Château Rayas was the only significant producer, comes from mainly Grenache Blanc and Clairette. The percentage of Roussanne (a grape which many perceive as oxidising easily and thus undesirable) and Bourboulenc have been increased at some estates, providing a welcome counter-balance to the dull Grenache. Regrettably, Marsanne – the mainstay grape of white Hermitage – which is attracting much interest in Southern France at present, is not a permitted variety.

HISTORY

The history of Châteauneuf dates back to Gallo-Roman times. The Roman winemaking tradition was continued by the Bishop of Avignon, Geoffroy, who planted and personally managed his own estate here in 1157, and thereafter by successive Popes, in particular Clement V, a Frenchman, installed in 1308 and John XXII, who con-

structed a "new castle" (Château Neuf) between 1318 and 1333 as a summer residence to escape the oppressive heat of Avignon. This impressive castle formed one link in a line of fortifications encircling Avignon, which included Bédarrides and Sorgues. The Popes remained at Avignon until 1378, although the rift with Rome was not finally healed until 1410. Despite various depredations, the castle remained substantially intact until August 1944, when retreating German forces, who had used it as an ammunition dump, blew it up. Today, this prominent ruin remains a focal point for Châteauneuf's growers; several rooms have been restored and are used by the Confrérie – l'Echannsonnerie des Papes – for inductions and grand dinners, the most important of which falls on St. Mark's day (April 25), the culmination of days of blind tasting to find the best wines from the previous and older vintages.

Until 1893, the village was known as "Châteauneuf-Calcernier" on account of the numerous lime-kilns spread over the locality and the wine as "Vin du Pape". Its increasing reputation brought moves to regulate and guarantee quality, resulting in a law of 1919, encapsulating a classification of the commune.

Baron Pierre le Roy de Boiseaumarie, lawyer and proprietor of Château Fortia, was responsible for developing this into the basis for the *appellation contrôlée* system by which French wine production has been governed since the 1930s.

The modern history of Châteauneuf has been chequered. While its wines are steadily exported and have a reputation for sound quality, they have never, with rare exceptions, been accorded the distinction of their Northern Rhône counterparts. This low esteem is, in part, self-inflicted, attributable to inconsistency and flagrant over-production of perfectly drinkable, but dull wines, and to the postwar practice, now thankfully in decline, of carbonic maceration as a means of vinifying for early drinking. This technique, originally developed by Flanzy for use in the Beaujolais, was pioneered in Châteauneuf by Pierre Lançon at the Domaine de la Solitude in the early 1960s. In essence, it involves fermenting whole bunches in a closed vat filled with carbon dioxide gas which slowly degrades the skins, extracting colour and fruit, but not tannin. Châteauneufs made by this means generally lack the extract and structure to develop and tend to taste somewhat similar. In naturally ripe, high-alcohol vintages, the results are liable to be particularly unsatisfactory, because the sugar is liberated so slowly from the berries that the requisite alcohol levels are not attained.

There is also the matter of official quality control. As so often the case in France, a theoretically workable system is ineffectively policed, blind eyes being turned in every direction. In consequence, too much indifferent wine comes onto the market, compromising the efforts of those who are dedicated to quality. Matters might be improved were the rules to sanction the production of Châteauneuf rosé, for which there is undoubtedly a demand.

This would provide a useful outlet for the 5% compulsory *triage* and encourage *vignerons* to *saignée* their vats, especially Grenache, in more abundant vintages.

THE VINEYARDS

Châteauneuf's vines extend in a rough oval, oriented north-west:south-east, 15km long and 8km wide. Bounded to the west by the river Rhône and to the east by the A7 Autoroute, they encompass parts of the contiguous communes of Châteauneuf, Orange, Sorgues, Bédarrides and Courthézon. The area is traditionally divided into named *quartiers* (sections of land) which, although not officially recognised (as there is only a single appellation) remain in common usage. The topography is gently undulating, at elevations up to 130m above sea level, interchanging plateaus (eg at Cabrières, Mont Redon and Vieux Télégraphe) with more sloping sites (as at at Fines Roches and towards Roquemaure to the west of the village).

The climate is dominated by long, hot summers (1,000 hours of sunshine: seven hours a day at around 25°C), and the Mistral which blows from the north-west, often violently, for up to 120 days a year – a beneficial influence, drying the vine, concentrating the juice and sanitising the atmosphere of pests and airborne diseases. Exacerbated by the Mistral, spring can be very cold, and rainy, with frost risk up to the end of March. The growing season is relatively wet and humid – rainfall averages 500-570mm – and punctuated with some 16 days of storms.

At 2,500-4,000 vines per hectare, planting density is one-third to a half that of Hermitage. Vines are bush-trained, *en gobelet*, except for the Syrah and some white varieties, where *Guyot* or *cordon de Royat* are authorised. Yields are restricted to 35hl/ha and, at present, only hand-harvesting is allowed. The rules also demand that a minimum of 5% of each year's crop is discarded – a rather crude measure to discourage the vinification of sub-standard fruit; this is generally made into *rapé – vin ordinaire* – for the estate workers. However, growers have been reported as slipping in Côtes du Rhône (if they make any) in place of *rapé*, thus giving themselves a bit more Châteauneuf to sell.

Unusually, irrigation is allowed, although the AC decree is delightfully contradictory on the subject: "spraying, in any form, is banned during the vegetative period; nonetheless, in case of persistent drought, spraying may be tolerated up to 15 August, but limited to twice per harvest and per parcel, in as much as it improves quality". Officially, the practice is intended for land with poor moisture retention – in particular the lower-lying gravels overlaid with *galets roulés* in the sector below the canal, south of La Nerthe and Fortia. In reality, according to some growers, (over) watering is common at many estates throughout Châteauneuf.

SOILS

Understanding Châteauneuf's geology is essential to understanding its wine. Baron le Roy originally stipulated that only soils upon which lavender and thyme would grow (ie organically the poorest), were suitable for Châteauneuf. However, this common factor hides a wide diversity of soil types, scattered throughout the appellation. Millions of years ago, in the Miocene epoch, a marine environment of inland seas receded, leaving a continental plain. During this process, the Alps wore away, tearing boulders from the sides of the valleys, which then rolled into the Bas-Rhône region, where the seas were shallower. The heaviest Alpine Quartzite "pebbles" escaped erosion, and it is these much-pictured drift-boulders (*galets roulés*) which constitute the higher terraces of Châteauneuf, especially round Beaucastel and Mont Redon. Apart from ruining farm machinery, these substantial terracotta-coloured stones absorb valuable moisture and store up daytime heat, which is then reflected back onto the vines at night. This extra warmth increases ripeness and reduces acidity. The plateaus cover five different levels, and it is on the higher of these that most of the choicest vineyards are to be found. Many believe that the finest wines come from land covered with *galets*; others disagree.

The areas not covered by boulders have other important soil types: to the south of the village, between Sorgues and the river, the land is predominantly gravelly, while much of the easterly sector, towards Courthézon and Bédarrides, has outcrops of finer, and sandier, soil. These *quartiers* are particularly dry, and vines have to root deep to survive. Elsewhere, it is land without water-retaining clay subsoils which suffer most from drought. To the north, towards Orange, a small escarpment of clay-limestone, with less depth of soil, favours the production of white wine.

Before the days of *appellation contrôlée*, *Grands Crus* existed (for the likes of Mont Redon and Rayas) as a superior designation, and there were various abortive attempts at an official classification of the vignoble. Although *Grands Crus* had long ceased to exist, Louis Reynaud continued to label his Château Rayas "*1er Grand Cru Classé*", until *les officiels* finally stopped him. Some still feel that, in such a large, diverse appellation, a classification would

The impressive ruins of the château at Châteauneuf-du-Pape.

have value; others (especially Paul Avril of Clos des Papes (qv), disagree, using this very diversity to argue that there is no sensible basis for classification. In their view, Châteauneuf derives an essential element of its character from being an *assemblage* of different grapes and *terroirs*. The problem could be resolved by an annual tasting for the award of *Grand Cru*. This would concentrate minds on quality without the inflexibility of an immutable classification.

PATTERNS OF PRODUCTION

In some respects, Châteauneuf is akin to Bordeaux. Although the majority of holdings are small, there are several grand estates, with Mont Redon, Vieux Télégraphe, La Nerthe and Beaucastel all having over 70ha under vine – the size of Château Lafite – and many with more than 30ha. As in Bordeaux, quality cuts right across the size spectrum; for example, in the top league, Château Rayas has 11ha and Château de Beaucastel 100. As the accompanying profiles show, many of the finest estates are relative minnows.

As well as a principal red Châteauneuf, many estates produce a second wine as an outlet for less good vintages and lots which don't merit the first label. At the other extreme, since the late 1980s – in particular, in the fine 1989 and 1990 vintages – there has been a fashion for superior *cuvées*, representing a selection of better lots or older vines. This has caused controversy among growers, many of whom argue that to cream off the best inevitably diminishes what remains. Nonetheless, the magnificence of some of these wines has brought benefits, directly and indirectly, to the entire community: disillusioned buyers have returned, and international attention has been refocussed on the high quality of which Châteauneuf is capable.

White Châteauneuf is also more abundant now, with many more estates offering a bottling, albeit in small quantity, to augment their range. In 1978, 19,420 cases of white wine were made, compared with 980,000 cases of red. By 1993 the figures were 78,500 and 1,100,000 cases respectively. The overall quality has also improved dramatically, away from the heavy, low-acid, flabby wines of the 1970s and 1980s to crisper, fresher styles vinified more in stainless steel with less wood ageing and earlier bottling. The best of these merit a few years' keeping, but most are best drunk young, with some well-sauced fish or a robust poultry dish. Notwithstanding, white Châteauneuf remains an acquired taste to which, even with diligent persistence, many seasoned palates have failed to attune.

STYLES

Soil, site, yield, vintage, vinification, maturation and vine-age all impact on the quality of Châteauneuf as well as the all-important individual grape mix. Many *vignerons* are good grape-growers but poor winemakers, so disaster is more likely to occur in the cellar than in the vineyard. Nonetheless, persistent overcropping has much to answer for.

Châteauneuf is sufficiently large and well-known to attract the high-volume market and thus the *négociants*. Some are responsible firms who value the appellation's long-term reputation and believe in the producer retaining a sensible margin of profit; others, whose resale market depends entirely on price, do not, and use their muscle to bargain the supplier down to a point at which he must cut corners to make any profit. The consumer is then left with miserable wine, wondering what all the hype is about. A commercial buyer who bargains down to rock-bottom price does neither his customer nor the *vigneron* any favours.

The most reliable *négociant* is Jaboulet (qv), whose Châteauneuf (labelled either as "Les Cedres" or "La Grappe des Papes") is invariably excellent. The major outside proprietor is Chapoutier (qv) who own the 30ha of old vines at the Domaine de la Bernardine from which they produce a standard bottling (La Bernardine) and a superior *cuvée*, Barbe-Rac. The quality of both is steadily improving.

Some estates openly make their wines for early drinking, while others vinify part of their crop traditionally and part by carbonic maceration, then blend these two fractions to combine the accessible fruit flavours with a touch of structure. These styles are perfectly valid and of sound quality, though many would argue that they have little to do with "real" Châteauneuf, which they see as coming from long vatting and consequently high extraction.

Even for thorough-going traditionalists, maturation periods are tending to shorten, from 24-30 months to around 12-18. This is partly driven by commercial considerations – the sooner the wine is bottled the sooner the cash comes in – and partly by the desire not to destroy fruit by over-exposure to wood. In any case, Grenache oxidises much more readily than Syrah or Mourvèdre, and loses colour rapidly, so the tendency is to mature Grenache in larger volume and the others in small wood. Many estates are still exploring the possibilities offered by new oak, and the usual wide variety of maturation regimes can be found across the appellation.

At its best, red Châteauneuf is a warm, mouthfilling and satisfying wine, with a distinctly southerly feel and, often, hints of Provençale pine and spice. Grenache provides depth and richness which is properly balanced by the earthy tannins of Mourvèdre and the elegance and structure of Syrah. Old vines add a dimension of opulence, concentration and complexity. Its high Grenache content often makes young Châteauneuf very attractive; however, the best have built-in longevity, and usually need a decade or more to really blossom.

Old Châteauneuf can be sumptuous – complex, spicy and distinctly gamey, retaining much of its original warmth and ampleur. Some of the special *cuvées* have been spectacular and promise a splendid evolution. Others, from estates who have latched onto this money-spinning idea and now turn out a superior bottling in almost every vintage (very little merited such status in 1991, for example), are less credible. Some have even turned the idea on its head, putting everything into the top label in poor vintages on the grounds that, once created, this is what their buyers want – every year!

It is still common practice, for understandable commercial reasons, to spread bottling of the regular *cuvées* of each vintage over several months. This effectively means that there are as many wines as there are bottlings as differences between fillings are far from cosmetic. Most *vignerons* admit that the later bottlings are generally best, as the longer – up to a point – the wine remains in wood, the rounder its tannins and the greater its complexity. Reviews and tasting notes should therefore be read with this in mind.

One circumstantial factor which has a marked impact on quality is the lack of old cellars in Châteauneuf; new cellars often have high temperature fluctuations (up to 20 centigrade degrees in a single day), which makes for poor storage and rapid oxidation, especially for wines in small casks.

As with many other great French appellations, Châteauneuf-du-Pape is quietly passing into the hands of a younger, more flexible and street-wise generation, motivated by quality. This has led to greater openness and self-criticism, unheard of a generation ago, and to the realisation that tradition, while important, needs refining and developing to meet a modern, international market. Collectively, the commune has done much to shrug off its image of inconsistency and mediocrity, although there is still far too much appalling "Châteauneuf-du-Pape" coming onto the market from *négociants* and cooperatives driven entirely by short-term commercialism. For the cradle of *appellation contrôlée*, Châteauneuf's unwillingness to tighten quality control is a particular disgrace and

Vinescape near Cairanne looking towards the Dentelles de Montmirail. The lines of conifers act as windbreaks against the Mistral.

can do nothing but harm. The revitalisation of several important estates and some of the most attractive price:quality ratios in France provide an ideal opportunity to put matters right, once and for all. Those who love Châteauneuf will watch with interest.

VINTAGES

1978: A relatively abundant vintage of very fine, classic, wines. A late, cold spring, followed by wonderful weather from July onwards, led to a text-book harvest of fully ripe, well-balanced grapes. The wines started out with excellent concentration and structure and have developed superbly, retaining their intensity and grip. Most are now ready to drink, though monumental Rayas and a big, earthy Beaucastel will still benefit from further time in bottle.

1979: Also a fine vintage – much better in general than that in the Northern Rhône, except perhaps for Hermitage. 10% more wine made than in 1978. The wines are starting to fade, although a few – Rayas in particular – remain full and vigorous. At best, they are very good, if lacking the sheer opulence and verve of the 1978s. As might be expected, those *cuvées* with a higher proportion of Syrah and Mourvèdre have fared better.

1980: A late vintage, even larger than 1979, saved by a fine *fin de saison* after a cold spring and consequently delayed flowering. The wines have shed an early raw edge to develop medium-weight charm and are now fully mature and should be drunk. Beaucastel was particularly successful.

1981: A very good vintage, in general, of wines which started out somewhat awkward and angular and have steadily gained in character and charm. The crop was 5% less than 1978. In style, the wines are quite firm, with sound, ripe fruit underneath the acids and tannins. The star of the vintage is undoubtedly Beaucastel, which is developing a superb, complex array of spicy, tarry, gamey perfumes and flavours. Rayas and Mont Redon have also tasted well recently.

1982: A sound, average quality vintage. Intense heat – as in Bordeaux and elsewhere in Southern France – produced a large crop of very ripe grapes. Unfortunately it also reduced acidities to dangerously low levels and caused widespread problems controlling fermentation temperatures. The net result is a raft of wines which are rather loose-knit, over-balanced in alcohol, and, in some cases, distinctly jammy, although there are occasional surprises – for example Beaucastel, which is

still most attractive. In general: drink now.

1983: A patchy vintage, spoiled by a cold spell during the flowering which caused widespread *coulure* in the Grenache. Rain both before and during the harvest didn't help – those who picked early made the best of it. The smallest crop (79,252hl) since 1975 (62,660hl). The best wines are quite pleasant, but many are leaden-footed and four-square. Most should be consumed soon.

1984: An indifferent growing season, marked by lack of heat and sunshine, *coulure* in the Grenache, and an uneven harvest. A perforce-reduced Grenache crop unbalanced many wines, which now lack generosity. Jacques Reynaud waited until November to pick, and turned his grapes into an excellent wine. Otherwise the wines are unexciting.

1985: Originally touted by the local Syndicat as "the vintage of the century to celebrate the end of the 20th century", 1985 has developed attractively, with plenty of richness and flavour but is definitely not "in the image of 1945 and 1961". The latter part of the growing season was very hot, punctuated only by a heavy rainstorm in August, which saved the vines from drought. The crop was the largest yet recorded (113,000hl). Not dissimilar in development to the Côte d'Or 1985s, the wines have evolved rapidly and are now approaching their best. The top *cuvées* – including Rayas, Fortia, Beaucastel, Vieux Télégraphe – are seductively stylish and have the structure for further evolution. Otherwise, drink over the next few years to get the most out of this vintage.

1986: A difficult, uneven vintage, due to long summer drought, a heavy rainstorm on 24 August and a very unsettled opening fortnight of September. The crop was large (104,727hl), but the top growers exercised a rigorous *triage* to ensure only healthy grapes went into the vats. The wines vary from the good (occasionally very good – for example Bonneau's Celestins) to the mediocre. Many are unbalanced by raw astringency, while others simply lack depth and grip. Altogether something of a gambler's vintage, with the odds heavily weighted against the player!

1987: Winter snow (which is unusual for Châteauneuf), a miserable, wet spring and delayed flowering gave 1987 an unpromising start. Once again, Grenache suffered from *coulure*. The only compensation was a hot, dry August, which allowed the vegetation to catch up. Fog and rain during harvest added their own problems. At the start of harvest, on 21 September, permitted yields were officially reduced from 35 to 32hl/ha, to encourage growers to discard unripe fruit. The wines are generally light, often nervy and green and have developed into pleasant, straightforward drinking. A few are better – notably Beaucastel.

1988: Excellent growing conditions – mild spring, even flowering and a hot, almost searing, summer punctuated by two useful rainfalls – 20 July and 20 August, allowing the grapes to proceed to full maturity. Although the vines did not suffer unduly from drought, the wines reflect the season's weather in firm, tannic structures and deep colours. In most cases the aromas have been slow to evolve, and it is likely to be several years before the best are really *à point*. Top estates all made very good wines – with some fine *cuvées speciales* to be had. Rayas, Henri Bonneau's Celestins, La Gardine, Vieux Télégraphe and Mont-Olivet showed particularly well in recent tastings.

1989: In common with the Côte d'Or and Bordeaux, the wines of this vintage were characterised by an intense concentration of very lush, almost over-ripe fruit. A warm, damp spring started the vegetative cycle off early, and April rainfall provided enough water reserves to allow the vines to survive a hot, rainless, summer. Vintaging started early, on 5 September – the grapes were ripe, so their was nothing to be gained by waiting. The wines were delicious young and have remained so –

packed to bursting with richness and warmth, backed by abundant, soft tannins (were it not for these, low acidities would be a cause for concern). From many superlative wines, Beaucastel's Hommage à Jacques Perrin, Château Rayas, Henri Bonneau's Réserve des Celestins and André Brunel's Les Cailloux Cuvée Centenaire stand out as *hors classé*. There are also some noteworthy whites, including the Perrin's Roussanne Vieilles Vignes and the regular Beaucastel Blanc, and the Vieilles Vignes from La Gardine.

1990: Another five-star vintage, marked by somewhat firmer structures and more obvious power than 1989 but with less of the heady, fleshy opulence of that vintage. The summer was hot, with a couple of valuable bouts of rain on 14th and 30th August. Picking started on 10 September and the crop was large (105,848hl) and virtually perfect in health and maturity. Some *cuvées* were so rich that they fermented up to 16.5% alcohol. In general, the wines are more typical of Châteauneuf than the 1989, with remarkable balance and concentration which will see them well into the 21st century. While the standard *cuvées* from the top estates are magnificent, the *cuvées speciales* are truly stupendous – outsized wines, massively extracted, designed to last for decades. The wines of Domaine de Marcoux, Beaucastel, Rayas, La Gardine, Les Cailloux, Clos des Papes, Henri Bonneau, Domaine du Pegau, Monpertuis, La Nerthe, La Janasse, Clos du Mont Olivet, Domaine des Relanges and Vieux Donjon are particularly impressive. Among the whites, La Nerthe's Clos de Beauvenir, Rayas, both *cuvées* of Beaucastel, La Gardine and Vieux Télégraphe excel.

1991: A mild, damp April and May retarded flowering to the end of June; a hot spell followed, broken by an incredible downpour on 31 July which washed away boulders, soil and even vines (at Château Cabrières). The vintage began on 20th September, yielding a smallish crop (82,053hl). Uneven maturity, in particular with Grenache, demanded the most scrupulous triage. This left yields averaging 20–25hl/ha – less at some estates. The quality varied between good and submediocre, with some downright poor offerings and some well-structured wines with the capacity to develop. This is a vintage in which careful selection is needed, but it is by no means the write-off that many commentators christened it, without in some cases, bothering to taste.

1992: A mild spring was followed by a wet May and June, which set back the vegetative cycle. The flowering was extended over almost three weeks, which presaged uneven ripeness, though there

was minimal *coulure*. Harvest started on 10 September for the early-ripening varieties, and was interrupted by a severe storm on 22 September. The quality of the vintage is uneven, with the whites notably more successful than the reds. However, the reds are, in most cases, reasonably well-constituted, with midweight of fruit, good acidity and fair intensity of flavour. The best have interest and length and the constitution to last for five years or so. In general, a vintage for early drinking.

1993: Despite a late bud-burst, an otherwise excellent, even, growing season produced a large crop (107,030hl) of well-ripened grapes. Summer temperatures were 4–5 centigrade degrees above normal, which helped the vegetation to catch up, while spring reserves of water allowed the vines to ripen normally during six weeks without rain. The vintage started in the second week of September for the white varieties and the Syrah, later for the Grenache. Rain during the latter period of harvesting obliged growers to sort their grapes carefully. The whites show considerable promise, with plenty of fat and yet good acidities and elegance. The best reds are well-constituted, harmonious wines, without being blockbusters and seem set for a good future. Not a five-star vintage perhaps, but one which will develop well over the medium term.

1994: The climatic conditions were ideal – an early spring, with enough rainfall to top-up depleted aquifers, and a long, hot summer punctuated by three brief spells of rain. The vintage was early – 29 August to 10 September. Unfortunately hail arrived on 1 September, and rain fell during the middle of the month. The crop is small, and the quality of this vintage seems likely to be no better than "ordinary".

AC CHÂTEAUNEUF DU PAPE

Created	15 May 1935
Area (max)	n/a
Area under vine 1994	3,244ha
Base yield	35hl/ha
Minimum alcohol	12.5% (the highest minimum in France)
Growers	225 individual producers; 80 co-op members

CHATEAU DE BEAUCASTEL

It is a curious fact that, despite being leaders in pressing for and indeed formulating the AC laws, Châteauneuf remains one of the major appellations of France where neither properties nor land have ever been classified. Were this to be undertaken today, one certain result – apart from the outbreak of civil war among the commune's *vignerons* – would be the appearance of Château de Beaucastel in the top league. This estate is one of the finest and most consistent in France.

The family behind this remarkable success is the Perrins. Hardly *parvenus,* since it was in 1549 that "Noble Pierre de Beaucastel" of that family bought "a barn with its plot of land... at Coudoulet". After a succession of owners (including Elie Dussaud, companion of Ferdinand de Lesseps who constructed the Suez Canal), the property returned to Perrin hands when it passed to a scientist, Pierre Perrin, in the early part of the 20th century. His son Jacques took over until 1978 when the mantle passed to his talented sons, François and Jean-Pierre.

There are no short-cuts to quality here, just impressive, meticulous, attention to detail. Anything industrial is eschewed and there are no deliberate economies of scale; they treat what is in fact a 25,000 cases-plus annual production as if it were a 100-barrel outfit. Sitting in his unpretentious office next to the front door, François Perrin contrasts their approach with a caricature Californian winemaker waiting for his computer to warn him that the next racking is due.

Their 130-ha estate, in the *quartier* Coudoulet in the extreme north-eastern corner of the appellation, is rare in having all 13 permitted varieties planted. Only 100ha are in Châteauneuf, the remainder being Côtes du Rhone on the eastern side of the autoroute. Only 70ha of Châteauneuf are currently under vine, the other land lying fallow and awaiting planting – which occurs at the rate of one hectare per year.

Time, and success, have led to other ventures. La Vieille Ferme is Jean-Pierre's excellent Côtes de Ventoux; Coudoulet de Beaucastel is top-class red and white Côtes du Rhône, vinified and bottled at Beaucastel (the white, first released in 1991, is a delicious mix of 30% each of Viognier, Marsanne, Bourboulenc, with a 10% dab of Clairette for acidity). Le Grand Prébois is a Côtes du Rhône estate – and

François Perrin.

François' home – planted principally to Grenache (not for long, one suspects). Finally, there is "our small vineyard" – 50ha – at Tablas Creek (qv), Paso Robles, California, acquired by the brothers in 1990, in partnership with their US agent and old friend Robert Haas and some smaller private investors.

At Beaucastel, there is nothing "*a priori*". Each decision is taken on its merits, and with the benefit of the Perrins' considerable experience and the help of Claude Gouan, their number two since 1980. The viticultural regime is organic, in the belief that quality potential can only be realised if the internal make-up of the soil is maintained. Chemical fertilisers and sprays destabilize this – you cure the malady at the expense of the organism's long-term wellbeing – so it is essential to maintain the global equilibrium. This is enlightened homeopathy in preference to ever stronger drug therapy – dealing with the fundamental cause rather than just treating symptoms. François argues forcefully that whereas many *vignerons* regard soil merely as a growing medium, they should properly think of it as a balance of nutrients which exerts a powerful effect on wine quality. In Jacques Perrin's time, "*la culture naturelle*" was considered as akin to madness; now it is widespread.

The Perrins have worked hard to ensure the optimal adaptation of *cépage* to *terroir*, although they are "still researching". An interesting feature of planting policy is the systematic replacement of individual red vines with white varieties to add freshness to the blend. Globally, the red *encépagement* consists of 30% each of Grenache and Mouvèdre, 10% Syrah, 7% Counoise, 5% Cinsaut, with the rest a mix of all the remaining permitted varieties.

Much of the character of the estate comes from an atypically high percentage of Mourvèdre, increased by Jacques Perrin from 10% to 20% with cuttings from Domaine Tempier in Bandol. "It's our Pinot Noir", comments François.

When Jacques Perrin planted the Mourvèdre as a mainstay of his estate, it was thoroughly unfashionable. However, this was no whim: the soils in this sector are high in clay – ideal for a *cépage* which needs its feet in water (almost!) and its head in the air. Now that the Mourvèdre has reached 30%, the brothers are turning their attention to Counoise; a late-ripener like Mourvèdre, but less easy to grow than Grenache.

In pursuit of equilibrium without excess, the vines at Beaucastel luxuriate in a three-yearly dose of sheep-droppings, matured for a year with grape stalks. 400 tons of this fragrant, nutritious compound appears at the château as a sort of organic pyramid.

Beaucastel's vinification is relatively straightforward, apart from one peculiarity: the destemmed grapes are heated to 80°C for 1–1.5 minutes before being cooled back to 20°C. The evolution of, and rationale behind, the procedure are worth examining. In 1909 the Perrins' great grandfather, a scientist, noticed that it was traditional in Burgundy to heat at least part of the must; although sulphur was then used in candle form to disinfect casks, its action on yeasts to delay fermentation wasn't appreciated until comparatively recently. It was subsequently found moreover that unheated must oxidised more readily than heated must. Heating has the following broad effects: liberating colour and aroma compounds; destroying bacteria and enzymes which promote early oxidation, and breaking long-chain molecules to liberate valuable nitrogen for yeast nutrition. Indirect consequences are a highly desirable long, slow fermentation and a greatly reduced sulphur requirement during *élevage*. Heating must is emphatically not equivalent to pasteurizing the finished wine, which stunts its growth. However, this *quartier* is known for giving hard wines; so perhaps heating also helps to extract suppleness.

Following heating, a long *cuvaison* and malolactic in *cuve*, the final *assemblage* is made in February or March of the new year. Until then the different grape varieties are kept apart, as is the press wine, in order for each to express to the fullest extent its individuality and *terroir*. This also gives François and Jean-Pierre the widest possible palette of "colours" from which to blend. "We don't look for a house style; we want to make the best wine for the year". Any remaining wine is often used in the Coudoulet de Beaucastel Côtes du Rhone; the revenue is no less than selling it off as generic Châteauneuf.

Then, after 8–18 months or so in the Château's large oak *foudres* with periodic racking depending on its evolution, the wine is egg-white fined and bottled; eliminating filtration gives greater depth of flavour and a more complex aroma spectrum. Beaucastel reds tend to suffer badly from bottling, which often shows as a distinctive animal odour. Although this dissipates with time, the Perrins try to keep each vintage in their cellars as long as possible before release. Neatly stacked galleries house an impressive one million bottles – four vintages. Given time, the wines age magnificently, developing an elegant, almost lacy character, which is most attractive.

In 1989, François and Jean-Pierre realised a long-cherished ambition with the release of a special *cuvée* in memory of their father, who died in 1978. Jacques Perrin was respected throughout Châteauneuf, not least by his sons. "*Un grand homme*", remarked one *vigneron*, a simple but mighty compliment. Even his sons were in awe of him: Jean-Pierre started his hugely successful La Vieille Ferme partly to prove to his father that he was capable of succeeding independently.

Jacques had pioneered "*culture naturelle*", planted Mourvèdre and Counoise when they were thoroughly unfashionable and instilled in his sons the precept that to make fine wine you must, above all, have first-class grapes.

"In California, the problem is that they still haven't learnt this necessitates adapting variety to *terroir*," François adds, more in pity than derision. Tablas Creek (qv) will no doubt make the point more directly.

The 1989 vintage produced the raw material for just such a *cuvée* – fine, concentrated Mourvèdre, in particular. The blend was made: 60% Mourvèdre; 20% Grenache; 10% Syrah and 10% Counoise and both this and the 1990 "Hommage" immediately became collectors' items.

If Mourvèdre is Beaucastel's red speciality, then Roussanne has become its white hallmark. François is enthusiastic about this variety, which many winemakers distrust in the belief that it is

Drift boulders (galets roulés) surrounding ancient Châteauneuf vines.

difficult to cultivate and is unduly susceptible to oxidation. "We find Roussanne to be very good here", says François, admitting its difficulties – in particular, it suffers from a sensitivity to *oidium* and wind.

Apart from contributing significantly to the excellent standard white Châteauneuf (80% Roussanne; 15% Grenache Blanc plus 5% "*petits cépages*" – ie Bourboulenc, Clairette & Picpoul), the Roussanne appears alone as a Vieilles Vignes. This *cuvée*, developed over several years of trials and first released in 1986, consists of some 600 cases from 4ha of 65-year-old vines, vinified 50% in year-old casks and 50% in stainless-steel, with or without malolactic, as nature dictates. In the June following the vintage, the lots are casein- or bentonite-fined, then assembled, plate-filtered and bottled. The standard white sees only 20% of wood, with 5–6% of this new oak, and has a similar *élevage*.

The Perrins are becoming interested in Viognier. In 1990 they made a trial Coudoulet Blanc (not released) from 30% each of Viognier, Marsanne and Bourboulenc plus 10% of Clairette for acidity. This mix was repeated in subsequent vintages.

François and Jean-Pierre are modest people. Both exude *joie de vivre* and take justifiable pride in their considerable achievements. Although you are more likely to find François at Beaucastel and Jean-Pierre at La Vieille Ferme, they share the work and responsibility jointly for all their enterprises and try to avoid specializing. François "adores" both vineyards and cellars, and gives the impression of someone who knows every centimetre of his land. They have worked hard for their success. The fulsome praise they invariably receive is richlydeserved.

VARIETY	VINEYARD	AREA
MOURVEDRE	BEAUCASTEL	30.00
GRENACHE	BEAUCASTEL	30.00
SYRAH	BEAUCASTEL	10.00
COUNOISE	BEAUCASTEL	7.00
CINSAUT	BEAUCASTEL	5.00
OTHER REDS	BEAUCASTEL	N/A
ROUSSANNE	BEAUCASTEL	10.00
GRENACHE BLANC	BEAUCASTEL	2.00
OTHER WHITES	BEAUCASTEL	N/A
	TOTAL (hectares):	94.00

DOMAINE DE BEAURENARD

This is a stylish 39-ha estate: if not absolutely at the top, then very near it. The triumvirate of Paul Coulon (a tall, courteous man in his early 60s), and his sons Daniel and Frédéric is assisted by Madame Coulon – a charming and elegant lady who clearly makes her contribution to the important decisions: no cipher, she.

Beaurenard's headquarters is a small cluster of mostly modern buildings on the outskirts of Châteauneuf, advertised by a sign glued to the wall inviting you to: "*Faites confiance à la Tradition*". On one side of an oblong courtyard is a neat office, on the other a small shop and tasting-room open seven days a week, behind which is the *cuverie*.

Within, an impressive battery of 24 temperature-controlled stainless steel vats, installed in 1988 by Paul, who would probably have continued with the old enamelled casks had he not seen his sons' evident interest in taking over and raising the quality of the domaine's wines. The new system has meant that, instead of putting alternate layers of crushed and whole bunches into the vats, the entire de-stemmed crop is vatted straight from the crusher.

The estate traces its roots back to an act of 1695, citing the plot of "Bois Renard" from which it takes its name. It is divided into some 25 separate parcels, including an enviable 9.1ha of 60- to 80-year-old vines, situated mainly in the north-western *quartiers* of Beaurenard, Pradel and Cabrières. There are also 45ha of Côtes du Rhône at Rasteau and Séguret.

The soils are mainly well-drained clay-limestone overlaid by a thinnish layer of *galets*. This, together with the high proportion of old vines, gives good natural drought resistance: essential in years which have many days of "great heat" – ie, over 30°C. The Coulons regard their old vines – average age 40-plus – as key elements in determining the quality and balance of their wines.

Theirs is not an organic regime. However, treatments are limited to need, aided by a new straddle-tractor which has enabled them to spray with less frequency and greater precision. At harvest, a team of regular pickers ensure that only sound, ripe fruit reaches the *cuverie*. Thereafter, vinification is relatively traditional – all but one trial *cuve* being destemmed and lightly crushed – a *cuvaison* of 15–28 days, plenty of *remontage*, and temperature-controlled to a maximum

Paul Coulon and his wife.

of 32°C. One curiosity here is that while the varieties are not vinified separately, each variety is added to a *cuvée* of Grenache – so one has Syrah/Grenache, Mourvèdre/Grenache etc.

The malolactic normally follows primary fermentation without delay, and then the wine passes into large casks (20% into small 225L barrels) for 9–12 months' ageing before fining and bottling. The barrels are generally reserved for wines which have more natural tannin and structure.

The avowed aim here is to produce wine with that marketable juxtaposition of youthful appeal and good ageing potential. Somehow they seem to manage it. Part of the secret is undoubtedly the insistence on only vinifying sound, ripe fruit and using a sensible length of vatting to extract enough fruit and aromatics to balance the tannins and acids. The good dollop of warm, southerly alcohol that this Mediterranean climate regularly provides adds a rich mouth-feel and partially masks any disagreeable tannic edges.

According to Mme Coulon, Grandfather Coulon – still going strong – was meticulous about recording details of

annual weather and vinification: "he wrote everything down in notebooks". The tradition has stuck, so much so that great leather-bound ledgers are made up, each year, containing detailed weather patterns, as well as vinification statistics and harvesting information for each plot and vat – an invaluable resource. A series of foliar and soil analyses has been undertaken to enable fine-tuning of soil nutrients. The Coulons are convinced that an harmonious soil equilibrium is the necessary precursor of a balanced wine and, moreover, that these precision adjustments show in the finished wines.

Tasting a range of wines one is struck by the domaine's consistency. Careful fruit selection and distinctly un-greedy yields (30hl/ha as a 10-year average against a permitted maximum of 35hl/ha) makes for satisfying results in even the naturally less opulent vintages. 1991 and 1992, in particular, are both softening into wines which, whilst lacking something in depth and length, will give pleasurable drinking over the medium term.

In the greater years, the results are very fine. 1990 here is a magnificent success – a huge mouthful of complex, super-ripe fruit and fine tannins, beautifully balanced by acids and alcohol. Closed at present, it has all the structural elements of a 10-year plus bottle and a long life thereafter.

In 1990 the Coulons, like many other of the commune's *vignerons*, made a *Cuvée Spéciale*, Bois Renard. This comes from specially-selected parcels of old-vine Grenache and Mourvèdre which are given 28 days of *cuvaison*. The wine spends more than a year half in small and in half in large wood (20% of the former being new Allier oak), with racking every three months. It receives a fresh egg-white fining, but no filtration. The result needs a decade, at least, to mature into a thoroughly rewarding bottle.

The Coulons are a confident, enthusiastic family, determined to excel. Nothing ostentatious, just conscientiously crafted wines with only the occasional blip; a dependable domaine.

VARIETY	VINEYARD	DETAILS	AREA
GRENACHE (85%), MOURVEDRE (10%), OTHER REDS (5%)	BEAURENARD	Original family vignoble; average vine-age 80 yrs	4.50
GRENACHE (90%), OTHER REDS (10%)	CABRIERES	Average vine-age 60 yrs	4.60
GRENACHE (70%), SYRAH (10%), MOURVEDRE (10%), CINSAUT (10%)	VARIOUS SITES	Average vine-age 34 yrs	20.00
		TOTAL (hectares):	29.10

HENRI BONNEAU

As a winemaker, Henri Bonneau is at the top of the tree. As a person – small, balding, rotund – he is initially more difficult to evaluate. Given to volatile outbursts on everything from the appellation rules to the decline of society, his coruscating wit is directed unerringly at people or views he considers absurd. Politically and morally, he is well to the right of centre. He clearly relishes his moderate international renown and plays well the part expected of him. Scrape off the theatrical veneer, however, and you find a compassionate, sensitive man, with a mischievous sense of humour driven by an engaging cynicism.

Success has definitely not led to material excess. The Bonneau HQ is a modest terraced house opposite the church, a steep 200-metre climb from the parochial fountain. The barest of furnishings – at least in that part to which visitors are admitted – comprise a table, a few upright chairs, a crushed armchair, and an old-fashioned solid fuel stove.

These comforts are supplemented by a more elegant adjoining dining-room, testimony to Henri's love of food and utter disdain for poor-quality provisions. With Gérard Chave, and a few like-minded friends, he partakes regularly of "*les joyeuses*" – beef or lamb testicles – "much better flavour than sweetbreads", which are obtained by the pail full from a local slaughterhouse.

There have been Bonneaus in Châteauneuf since Napoleon – Henri being the 12th generation. His estate runs to 6ha, 5.25 of which are in La Crau north of La Nerthe, and 0.75ha on stonier soil near Courthézon. From this latter comes his Cuvée Marie Beurrier, named after an aunt of his wife's from Charolles in the Loire. An altogether richer wine is sold as Réserve des Célestins and is, without doubt, one of the finest of all Châteauneufs. The *encépagement* is 80-90% Grenache – Henri particularly dislikes Syrah, although there is some on his land – a very little Mourvèdre, some Counoise, Vaccarèse and a smidgeon of Cinsaut and Clairette. Old vines are not encouraged – the ideal age for him being 30 years – and he is positively explosive in dismissing the recent outbreak of "*cuvée vieilles vignes*" in the commune: "if you are shown some old vines, you have no means of knowing whether they belong to this person or that; the important thing is to get each plant to produce the best it can". Personally, he claims to grub up vines after 50 years.

On the subject of his own yields, Henri professes ignorance – "I've no idea" – although one suspects, given the quality, that they are not excessive. All in all, his politics and general outlook on matters viticultural are much in line with Jacques Reynaud at Château Rayas. Apparently, they are friends.

The Bonneau vinification – "I am not a technician" – is straightforward: light crushing with an antique crusher and some three weeks' *cuvaison* if the grapes are healthy, with plenty of pumping-over during the first few days. The press wine is generally added back forthwith: "I must really doubt the quality of my *vin de presse* not to put it back".

An *élevage* of some 30 months, in either very old *foudres* or in equally venerable *pièces* "depending on the space", precedes fining and then bottling two months later after *assemblage* in 11-hl *cuves*. Bonneau never filters his wines and, moreover, insists that bottle and wine are at the same temperature for bottling to avoid an unnecessary shock. He distrusts contract bottlers, and therefore undertakes this job himself.

Whether it is a matter of buying meat or buying wine, Henri is cynical about the paying public: "the trouble with the customer is that he wants something for nothing; I pay 60 francs for a fine chicken; I don't expect to get one for 30 francs – the producer must make a fair profit". Warming to his theme, he adds: "anyone who buys a Châteauneuf for 20 francs is a fool – you can't produce it and make a profit at that price". Yes, you get what you pay for – but *chez* Henri, rather more!

The cellars comprise a maze of small galleries with earth floors beneath the house. Barrels of several different sizes are huddled into obscure corners – "we try not to move them around" – and reflect the idiosyncrasy of their master.

The genial assistant, Franc, works round this jumble, topping up here and chalking up there, going after ladders, replacement bungs and pipettes as required. Here sumptuous wine from an unmarked bottle, there black, impenetrable liquid from a galvanised watering-can. It doesn't matter – the product is invariably fine.

Henri's hard work – now with his son Marcel – is evident in all his wines. A very severe *triage* at vintage ("I'd prefer not to say how much I *tri*-ed in 1991") – results in a range of exemplary Châteauneufs; some inevitably lighter in style than others, but none lacking depth or interest.

The Cuvée Marie Beurrier – a selection made either at vinification or later – is the lightest of Henri's offerings, a shade more austere than the rest perhaps. The Célestins, however, starts life as a dark, brooding, monster – intensely concentrated black fruit, supported by a massive structure of ripe, even, tannins.

What marks all Henri's wines – even in more challenging years such as 1991 and 1992, where the tendency to either dilution on the one hand or over-extraction on the other is evident elsewhere in the appellation – is a superbly tuned balance of constituents. Here is essence of Châteauneuf of remarkable consistency and class.

APPELLATION	VARIETY	DETAILS	AREA
CHATEAUNEUF	GRENACHE (mainly)	Quartier La Crau, north of La Nerthe	5.25
CHATEAUNEUF	GRENACHE (mainly)	North-east of Courthézon	0.75
		TOTAL (hectares):	6.00

LES CAILLOUX

André Brunel, a skilled and conscientious *vigneron* now in his youthful fifties, joined his father in 1971; since that date, he has turned Les Cailloux into a top-class domaine. A commercial training helped, but for the rest – brought up as he was among vines and in the cellar – he learned by osmosis. The Brunels have been in Châteauneuf since the 18th century, but not then as *vignerons*. André's father, Lucien, inherited vines from his father and started to sell wines as Les Cailloux – named after the *galets roulés* in the *quartier* Mont Redon, where the family own land. However, their 21ha (19 are red, two are white) are fragmented, making Les Cailloux, as so many other Châteauneufs, effectively a brand.

Every decision is carefully reasoned. Old vines are of prime importance, especially Grenache; so dead vines are replaced individually rather than by wholesale grubbing up. In the case of Grenache the replacements are Mourvèdre. André has several reasons for this heterodox policy. The first is practical: Syrah and Cinsaut ripen earlier than Mourvèdre or Grenache. Second, Mourvèdre does well if planted in the middle of the vineyard, among other varieties. Third, André doesn't know the characteristics of Counoise well enough to plant it among Grenache. Fourth, Mourvèdre is good producer and brings valuable structure to the *assemblage*. Fifth, Mourvèdre's tannin and structure adds an essential anti-oxidant element, which the readily oxidizable Grenache lacks. Finally, Mourvèdre doesn't take away from the typicity of Grenache, as Syrah tends to.

Mourvèdre plantings have now doubled from 10% to 20%, with Grenache at 65% and Syrah at 10%, plus 5% "*divers*". The Roussanne is similarly being increased in the 800 cases of the domaine's white Châteauneuf, at the expense of the over-productive Grenache Blanc.

The wine style has changed here since the late 1980s. Lucien neither de-stemmed nor crushed, which together helped diminish the astringency and aggressiveness which André dislikes. However, the wines only lasted 10–15 years. Working for three years with Jean-Luc Colombo (qv) led André to introduce de-stemming and to undertake a longer *cuvaison*, which in his view increases a wine's life span. Reducing de-stemming from 100% to 70–80% allows an even longer *cuvaison*, which now stands at around four weeks. The Grenache is matured in *foudres*, and the Syrah in new and old *pièces*: both for two years.

André is a leading light in Les Reflets – a group of six independent producers who share cellars, bottling and packing facilities. As with Prestige et Tradition, the aim is common marketing while retaining producer identity. It works well.

His wines reflect his own preferences: the whites, vinified with neither wood nor malolactic, are fresh and tightly structured, with broad fat flavours and plenty of *puissance*. However it is the reds which really show the quality of this

André Brunel.

house. The standard *cuvée* is usually deep in colour, with aromas tending towards plums, cherries, *fruits noirs,* with secondary leather and animal scents. There is often a hint of liquorice. This wine is invariably attractive, with long, complex flavours – sometimes spicy, sometimes earthy or minerally in character. If there is a hallmark, it is silkiness and texture – a vinification which smooths out rough edges to give the wines a seductive mouthfeel after a few years in bottle.

In 1989, the Cuvée Centenaire was introduced to mark the centenary of a

plot of vines. Five hundred cases were produced in both 1989 and 1990, but none in 1991, '92 or '93.

Both are spectacular wines of impressive depth and power, with no sacrifice in finesse, and with remarkable length and complexity. As with the regular *cuvée*, the 1989 has more *mache* and muscle – more obvious virility, while the 1990 has a firm, silky elegance. It is difficult to tell which will turn out the finer, but neither their quality nor longevity are in doubt. These are bottles to buy and treasure from one of Châteauneuf's greatest

VARIETY	APPELLATION	AREA
GRENACHE	CHATEAUNEUF	12.35
MOURVEDRE	CHATEAUNEUF	3.80
SYRAH	CHATEAUNEUF	1.90
OTHER RED VARIETIES	CHATEAUNEUF	0.95
GRENACHE BLANC	CHATEAUNEUF	0.60
ROUSSANNE	CHATEAUNEUF	0.80
CLAIRETTE	CHATEAUNEUF	0.40
BOURBOULENC	CHATEAUNEUF	0.20
	TOTAL (hectares):	21.00

CLOS DES PAPES

A stone plaque affixed to the Clos des Papes, beside the ruined château, records the Avrils as the First Consuls and Treasurers of Châteauneuf-du-Pape from 1756 to 1790. In 1902 Paul Avril's grandfather registered Clos des Papes as a trademark for all of his wines. Today, this excellent estate is run by Paul – a sprightly, tall, distinguished man in his sixties – and his equally tall son Vincent,

with help from Paul's wife with PR and administration. Their HQ is a set of unremarkable buildings on the main road out of the village, with vines on three sides. The Avrils are *très sympa*, and also shrewd judges of quality.

A map on the office wall shows their 32ha to be very fragmented. The principal plots lie to the north and south of the village, including the Clos des Papes.

Those in the west are on sandier soils, ideal for whites, and there are further parcels in La Crau, in the Courthézon sector. They tend to pick the southerly vines first, having a horror of unripe tannins and a desire for grape rather than wood tannin. In any case these vines mature some 10 days earlier than those in the north of the appellation. Yields matter, and are controlled in part by short pruning, severe de-budding and a green-pruning in early August. The Avrils are suspicious of clones, describing them as "dangerous", and seem undecided whether they are to be trusted. They do now use clonal material, albeit selected with consummate care.

In contrast to many southern Rhône estates, both whites and reds are fine wines. The former, from Avril vineyards in the westerly sector of the appellation, are some of the best to be found: complex and attractive, characterful, but with *fraîcheur* and without the flabby side of much white Châteauneuf. The vineyard mix is 10–15% Grenache; 30% Clairette; 20% each of Roussanne, Picpoul and Bourboulenc. A long fermentation – 15–21 days – at a highish temperature (18-21°C) extracts as much matter and richness as possible, while the Clairette, Picpoul and Bourboulenc provide valuable counter-balancing acidity. Young vintages tend to open-textured flavours and a fine spiciness, with attractive floral and *fruits secs* aromas. They also generally age well, developing, as do many good white Châteauneufs, characteristics reminiscent of mature Meursault – nuts, honey and an attractive breadth, yet fine and complex.

There is but a single red *cuvée* of Clos des Papes – no *cuvée prestige* here: "we don't have two classes of client", explains Vincent. Anyway, extracting an exceptional part of the crop invariably impoverishes the rest. The mix is 65% Grenache, 20% Mourvèdre, 10% Syrah plus 5% of Vaccarèse, Muscardin and Counoise. *Cuvaison* is long; *élevage* in 43–65hl *foudres* and, since 1988, no filtration.

The domaine produces around 12,000 cases of white and 100,000 cases of red Châteauneuf. The Avrils export some 60% of their production to over 18 countries, the remainder going mainly to top

Paul and Vincent Avril.

restaurants and individual clients.

As befits the respected head of an old Châteauneuf domaine, Paul plays an important part in the appellation's governance and in its festivities. In deep purple robes, he can be seen presiding over the commune's convivial Confrérie, the Echansonnerie des Papes, at the *Intronisation* of new members. He also

enjoys playing golf at nearby Avignon, but claims his golfing skills fall far short his abilities as a winemaker. Quite rightly, the domaine comes first – and the results justify the priority.

VARIETY	APPELLATION	DETAILS	AREA
GRENACHE	CHATEAUNEUF	Average vine age, 35 yrs	18.60
MOURVEDRE	CHATEAUNEUF	Average vine age, 35 yrs	6.20
SYRAH	CHATEAUNEUF	Average vine age, 35 yrs	3.00
VACCARESE, MUSCARDIN, COUNOISE	CHATEAUNEUF	Average vine age, 35 yrs	1.20
WHITE VARIETIES	CHATEAUNEUF	Average vine age, 35 yrs	3.00
		TOTAL (hectares):	32.00

CLOS MONT OLIVET

Some Châteauneuf domaines court publicity less than others. One of the more reticent is Clos Mont Olivet, an estate of 24ha run by the affable Sabon brothers. Jean-Claude is the senior, a bluff, yet quiet, down-to-earth man; and Pierre, even quieter – with their third brother, Bernard, responsible for their viticultural branch-line at Bollène, where there are 8ha of Côtes du Rhône and 200 apricot trees, the produce of which they simply leave to rot on the bough.

These are charming, gentle people, shy of journalists and critics, but makers of fine wine – as understated as themselves, but with considerable depth and class. Grandfather built up the

estate and father Joseph is still going strong at 85, chatting away amiably in the family kitchen while awaiting his lunch. An old-fashioned air pervades the office: not a whiff of labour-saving electronics, just Jean-Claude's wife working six hours a day.

The mainstay of this Châteauneuf is 15ha of vines over 80 years old, mostly Grenache; in addition, 5.5ha of 25-year-old plants, including a hectare each of Mourvèdre and Syrah, plus 0.5ha of Vaccarèse. One and a half hectares of white grapes, principally Clairette and Bourboulenc, and 3ha of younger plantings complete the *vignoble*.

These 25ha are scattered and

fragmented. From the smallest plot (21 ares) to the largest (3ha) they cover three main *quartiers* of the appellation: the young vines in the northerly Pied de Baud *quartier* lie on a clay-rich plateau of *galets roulés*; in the easterly *quartier* Montalivet are the oldest vines, on steepish clay-limestone slopes. Between these, in the southerly *quartier* Les Gallimardes, are vines on poor, very stony, well-drained gravels. The Clos itself is both a registered brand and a specific vineyard – 8ha of old vines, north of La Solitude and south of Nalys, all "*en coteaux*", facing west and thus attracting maximum evening sunshine. Mechanisation finally arrived in 1972, when the Sabons retired their last horse.

A deliberate late harvest – which entails occasional acidification – is essential to the Sabons' desire for low yields (the five-year average is 30hl/ha): "we must play poker with the weather", is how Jean-Claude sees the matter. He also confesses to talking to his vines – each has its character which must be respected.

As one might expect, vinification is uncompromisingly traditional – no de-stemming ("a tradition of the house", Jean-Claude explains), gentle crushing with grandfather Serafin Sabon's 1904 crusher, a traditional 2–3 weeks' *cuvaison* with press-wine, expressed by an ancient hydraulic press, added back. A dab of early-ripening Syrah goes into each *cuve*.

Elevage lasts for an extraordinary 2–8 years. This stems in part from lack of space underneath the house for bottle-stock; instead the brothers keep their wines in large red-edged *foudres* or a small population of old *pièces*. This entails several different bottlings of the "same" wine – the final bottling of 1984 was in June 1993 – after nearly 10 years in wood. They recently relaxed their policy of no new wood for their long-standing UK importer, for whom one solitary chalked new cask stands witness, but disliked the result. The wines are bottled by the Cave des Reflets, a cooperative venture of which the domaine is a member.

The results reflect the brothers' determination that "our wines must please our clients", although they are equally clear that they are aiming at *vins de garde*. Clos Mont Olivet are invariably characterised by a dark, but brilliant, ruby/garnet tone and by elegance of flavour and nose. Never blockbusters, as one finds elsewhere in Châteauneuf, the Sabon wines exude silky, ripe, concentrated fruit and round, approachable tannins.

There is no separate Clos *cuvée*, but in 1989 the brothers introduced the Cuvée Papet (grandfather), from centenarian vines, in part from the Clos. The 1989 produced 6,500 bottles and the 1990 8,000 bottles. These wines share the

Pierre, Joseph and Jean-Claude Sabon.

elegance of the "regular" release, but have an added dimension of richness and structure. Neither should be touched before 2010.

To anyone who doesn't know the Sabons, their life as summarised by Jean-Claude might seem unduly dull – "we never have holidays, we only know work", and "we don't go out much". In fact, they are abundantly cheerful, fulfilled people content to dedicate themselves to their wine. Tasting in the cramped cellar, beneath the modest family house on the Roquemaure road, is a marathon designed to show off their wines, young and old, where opinions are sought and listened to, memories evoked and pleasure shared.

VARIETY	APPELLATION	DETAILS	AREA
GRENACHE	CHATEAUNEUF	80+ yrs average vine age; includes some mixed plantings	15.00
GRENACHE + MOURVEDRE + SYRAH	CHATEAUNEUF	25+ yrs average vine age; includes 1 ha. each of Mourvèdre and Syrah and 0.5 ha. Vaccarèse	5.50
WHITE GRAPES	CHATEAUNEUF	1 ha. 15–20 yr old Clairette (40%), Bourboulenc (40%), Grenache Blanc (15%) and Roussanne (5%)	1.00
CLAIRETTE	CHATEAUNEUF	50+ yr old vines.	0.50
VARIOUS GRAPES	CHATEAUNEUF	2 yr old vines – 30 ares Syrah, 10 ares Grenache Blanc; 70 ares Grenache Rouge	1.10
ROUSSANNE	CHATEAUNEUF	4 yr old vines	0.20
GRENACHE (ROUGE)	CHATEAUNEUF	8 yr old vines	0.70
	COTES DU RHONE	Bollène	8.00
		TOTAL (hectares):	32.00

FONT DE MICHELLE

Jean and Michel are the third generation of Gonnets at Font de Michelle. Their father, Etienne, fought heroically to re-assemble the estate's current 30ha from 170 small plots, helped by his brother-in-law, Henri Brunier of Vieux Télégraphe, who also taught Jean Gonnet his winemaking skills.

The domaine's name derives from "The Fontaine de Michelle", a hidden spring in a hollow among the vines, and the site is recorded as being vineyard in the 17th century – although Roman artefacts indicate a much earlier occupation.

The Gonnets are serious men producing good wine, both red and white. Although there are patches of centenarian vines on their estate, half are around 40 years old, and the rest 20–30.

The vines, in the *quartier* St-Louis, are mostly on south-southeast-facing *coteaux* and on well-drained, but not drought prone, clay-limestone soils overlaid with *galets roulés* (Alpine quartzite is a feature of this sector of Châteauneuf).

The style the Gonnets aim for is best described as modified classical, with plenty of richness and concentration – yet a slant away from the traditional heavily-structured style towards greater elegance. Both red and white vinifications have their idiosyncrasies. The white, 10% of total production, is extracted from direct pressing of 50% Grenache Blanc, 25% Clairette, 20% Bourboulenc and 5% Roussanne (increasing to 10%). The Gonnets regard Clairette as a "super-grape" – aromatic, floral and distinguished, qualities often evident in their white wine. The peculiarity is that, having blocked the malolactic, they don't sterile-filter before the early, December, bottling. This gives a risk of later re-fermentation, since malic acid is unstable. The wine is not acidified and, despite the Bourboulenc and Clairette, sometimes tends to flabbiness. Perhaps the brothers should consider either acidifying or partial early harvesting, and rack the percentage of Roussanne up to 20–25 if they can. This would add structure and richness and put the wine into a different class. Nonetheless, Gonnet whites are fresh and attractive – more in finesse rather than fat – and generally among the upper echelon of white Châteauneuf.

The reds are equally well made, with the peculiarity that the 10% Syrah is given a semi-carbonic maceration – "my personal method", as Jean calls it – by putting lightly crushed grapes into carbon dioxide-saturated vats. This increases colour and aroma extraction, but without

the overtly fruity "Côté Beaujolais". This Syrah passes part of its maturation in ten new Allier casks – at present an experiment. The wines are assembled early in the new year, after malolactic, and then transferred to 50-year-old, 80-hl brewery casks for 8–10 months, and finally bottled after a total of 15–18 months with either fining or filtration – rarely both.

In 1988, the brothers added the Cuvée Etienne Gonnet to their regular offering. Unusually, this is not a special selection of old vines or particularly fine lots, but simply one-quarter of the regular production which is set aside. A quarter of this is *élevé* in second- and third-year small casks, the rest being kept in *cuves* until bottling. This wine is only released in better vintages, but the 1992 left one wondering whether it was of sufficient quality to merit the status of a special *cuvée*.

Jean and Michel Gonnet characterize

Châteauneuf as "rich, concentrated, with elegance, finesse and distinction". In general, their wines reflect this, particularly in respect of elegance and finesse. Don't expect big, dense Châteauneufs here; rather, mid-weight wines with complex aromas and finely-tuned balances. Tannins are the key to ensuring that the subtleties come through even while the wines are relatively young, but also present to a sufficient extent to guarantee reasonable longevity. The Etienne Gonnet *cuvée* is denser, richer and more complex than the standard wine, yet retains the house's overall style.

This is a fine domaine making carefully crafted wines.

VARIETY	APPELLATION	DETAILS	AREA
GRENACHE, SYRAH, MOURVEDRE, CINSAUT	CHATEAUNEUF	South-east slopes; 35 yrs average vine-age.	26.50
GRENACHE BLANC, CLAIRETTE, BOURBOULENC, ROUSSANNE	CHATEAUNEUF	20 yrs average vine-age.	3.00
		TOTAL (hectares):	29.50

CHATEAU FORTIA

Château Fortia holds an important place in the history and heart of Châteauneuf-du-Pape. It was from here, in the 1920s, that Baron Pierre Le Roy de Boiseaumarie set the wheels in motion that were to result in the establishment of the system of Appellation Contrôlée in France. Tired of cheap southern Mediterranean imitations of his commune's wines and powerless to prevent them, he was instrumental in formulating rules designed to protect him, his fellow growers and the public from what he regarded as fraud. This was to be achieved by delimiting the area of production and controlling planting and vinification, thereby guaranteeing the consumer both authenticity and typicity.

Le Roys still run Fortia. Pierre's son Henri took over in 1967 and Henri's younger son Bruno in 1994. Henri lives in the château, a rather decayed 19th-century neo-gothic edifice, surrounded by his 27ha of vines. The property is fronted by a small park with a lake, and an invaluable fresh water source next to the cellar door. Although the vines are in one slab, the soils vary. On the northern side the land is very sandy, imparting finesse to white grapes, while the southern flank

is earlier-ripening heavier clay-limestone, with an overlay of *galets roulés* – which gives structure to the reds.

Bruno is a hearty, friendly man, well aware of the work needed to restore both château and wine to their full pre-eminence, after years of comparative neglect. Matters were exacerbated by the recent death of Baron Henri's 94-year-old mother who could not be persuaded to arrange things so as to avoid massive death duties. Lack of resources seem as much human as financial. "I am general factotum here", Bruno laments, "*caviste*, gardener, maintenance man, salesman and accountant". All this as well as looking after his wife's 150-ha Blanquette de Limoux estate, 300km away, in his spare time. He seems remarkably cheerful in the face of such a daunting struggle.

In the cellars, parts of which date back

to the 14th-century Papal era, Bruno explains that nearby château La Nerthe was a German observation post during the last war, attracting considerable aerial fire from the Allies. Baron Henri was on his bicycle en route to Sorgues one afternoon when he spotted aircraft overhead; recognising them as British, he cycled on, reassured. However, while British bombers flew low, and were consequently fairly accurate, the US pilots preferred the security of height, thus scattering their payloads around. Fortia was hit and a section of 18th-century cellars damaged.

Bruno does not entirely struggle alone. He has a splendid ally in the slender yet formidable person of Tante Yvette, Henri's sister. This remarkable old lady has a memory like glue, especially for the estate's wines and their lore. She reckons that there aren't enough old vines now to make wine like it used to be, remembering vividly when they pulled up

VARIETY	APPELLATION	DETAILS	AREA
GRENACHE	CHATEAUNEUF		20.00
SYRAH	CHATEAUNEUF	Trained en cordon.	3.75
MOURVEDRE	CHATEAUNEUF		1.25
CLAIRETTE, GRENACHE BLANC AND ROUSSANNE	CHATEAUNEUF	Mixed plantings	2.00
		TOTAL (hectares):	27.00

a plot of 1948 Grenache riddled with *court-noué*, just outside her window: "I woke up one morning and it was gone".

The 1980s saw a distinct dip in wine quality at Fortia – shorter *cuvaison* perhaps, or just too long in wood and unnecessary filtration. *Cuvaison* is now 20–22 days – "it used to be a month", chimes in laser-sharp Tante Yvette – and *élevage* is around three years, whereas it used to be two. For some time now, the red Fortia has been filtered – "it gives me a fright to think of not filtering, and in any case the EEC laws oblige us to filter" (they don't), Bruno argues, unconvincingly. Tante Yvette's unfailing memory offers: "the wines had much more stuffing in them, years ago". She's right.

Without much help from the rest of the family – his elder brother, who will inherit the title, teaches handicapped children and his older sister is a married pharmacist with children – Bruno is working hard to pull the estate together and seems to be rowing in the right direction. His Montpellier oenology training helps, though his pharmaceutical qualification is of less obvious benefit.

The wines, while not in the top class, are improving. There is still inconsistency: for example the 1990 was marred by a distinctly herbaceous note on the nose and attendant *goût de rafle* on the palate, while the 1989 was a shade hollow.

It is to be hoped that Bruno Le Roy's efforts will pay off. This is potentially a fine estate and he needs all the encouragement he can get.

CHATEAU DE LA GARDINE

Château de la Gardine is a relatively modern building surmounted by an exceedingly ugly tall square tower, atop a small hill on the Roquemaure road just outside Châteauneuf.

Here, surrounded by some 54ha of vines, the Brunels turn out consistently fine Châteauneuf. Patrick, a middle-aged man with greying hair and a half-serious, half-smiling manner, and his brother Maxime, preside over the estate and appear to have made great strides up the quality ladder in recent years. Bottles from the 1970s and early 1980s were distinctly patchy.

The chief improvements have been in the quality of the raw material. In the vineyard, lower yields, helped by a late green-pruning, have clearly paid off. The frequency of spray treatments has also been reduced: "we have 50% less now", Patrick comments.

Since 1985 the Syrah crop is harvested in two separate pickings: the earlier half is fermented with some early plots of Grenache, while the later half accompanies the later Grenache; there is also a *cuve* of Grenache and Mourvèdre. A battery of ten new *cuves*, installed in 1989, have automatic punching-down and a submerged cap, giving more complete aromatic extraction. This is helped by a high fermentation termperature of 34°C and the crop is 100% de-stemmed. The Brunels have worked out that if they put the Syrah and Mourvèdre into the top of each *cuve*, they will receive more *pigeage* than the Grenache below. So "the *pigeage* finishes the crushing", which is why their Syrah and Mourvèdre are crushed more lightly to start with.

All this produces as complete and as fine a tannin extraction as possible. They have been working with Alain Brumont at Château Montus in Madiran to study aroma and tannin extraction. "We want skin tannin, not stalk tannin, and the aromas of *petit fruits rouges*, which remain in the wine for a long time". Their researches indicate that a short *cuvaison* extracts both good and bad tannins, while a long maceration period maximises extraction of noble tannin. Although there is a strong tannin leach in the first two days or so, the Brunels feel that 21–27 days is needed for a wine to clear itself of hard, aggressive, green tannin. "Most *vignerons* have a tendency to stop fermentation before maximum tannin extraction"- probably because they ferment at too low a temperature.

After this long immersion and malolactic, the Gardine reds are fined and earth-filtered. "The wine has got everything out during vatting – the idea of nourishing reds on their lees is rubbish, so we clean them up first". The Châteauneuf *élevage* lasts from 12–14 months in old casks followed by six months in *cuve*, with only 30% of the wine passing through barrels and the rest remaining in *cuve* until bottling. Before this, the wines are re-assembled from casks and *cuves*, egg-white fined and given a second Kieselguhr filtration. Interestingly, large wood is only used here for Côtes du Rhône-Villages. Wine from 4- to 10-year-vines and less promising *cuves* are sold as Deux La Gardine – the Brunels' punning second label.

In some years – not necessarily the greatest vintages – the domaine turns out a Cuvée des Generations Gaston-Philippe (Gaston is the brothers' father, Philippe their great grandfather). So far this has appeared in 1980, '85, '86, '89 and 1990. This gets the luxury treatment of 70% cask ageing, mostly in new wood, for 24–26 months. Each vintage, the wines from the parts of the *vignoble* "which please us most" – including the second Syrah

Soil preparation in progress on the plateau of Château de la Gardine.

picking – are put aside and *élevé* as potential "Generations" material, and followed through until Patrick and Maxime decide whether the quality is sufficiently high to justify a separate bottling. In 1988, for example, it was only at final tasting, when the wine had been kept apart for some considerable time, that they decided to blend it all back into the regular La Gardine *cuvée*.

Since 1980, La Gardine has also made white Châteauneuf, which since 1987 has been wholly or partly barrel-aged. There are now two white releases: the classic, a third of which sees wood (30% new) for fermentation and three months or so thereafter; and the Vieilles Vignes which is both fermented and *élevé* in new wood for up to 12 months. This latter has up to 60% Roussanne, which gives it noticeably more fat, glycerol and richness, and a good dab of Bourboulenc for acidity; with *bâtonnage* to add further depth. While the standard *cuvée* is sound, well-made wine – often starting off rather green and nervous and needing a few years' bottle age to round out and develop – the Vieilles Vignes is a much more serious offering, which in the best vintages (eg 1990) deserves several years keeping.

The Brunels are clearly traditionalists, preferring both reds and whites which improve with age. Not only this, they also bend well towards "*la tradition*" in their

preferred wine style, with an open admiration for the old-fashioned wood-aged Meursaults of Bernard Michelot, and for reds which have plenty of structure and extract, and are invariably hallmarked by a nerve of dry tannin despite complete de-stemming.

While the Cuvée Tradition is good – although you should ideally wait, even in weaker vintages, for that green nerve to soften out and integrate – the Cuvée des Generations is the pick of this cellar. Invariably substantial, big-framed items, though not necessarily heavyweights, they exude the essence of traditional Châteauneuf. Their style is individual and may not be to everyone's taste: they can start life (certainly in the 1989 and 1990 examples) with a touch of burly rusticity and the Gardine green streak, yet they do

not lack for ripe fruit and backbone.

The Brunels enjoy what they do and love experimenting. Stabs at pellicular maceration, cooling and lees contact or new wood with their whites keep them happy. If there is a general fault (they would call it a stylistic preference), it lies in a mild tannic imbalance and a lack of middle-palate flesh. Shorter *cuvaisons* and earlier bottling would add that touch of plump ripeness to moderate the green nerve, and would give the wines a bit more youthful appeal without compromising the Brunels' style.

VARIETY	APPELLATION	DETAILS	AREA
GRENACHE	CHATEAUNEUF	35 yrs average vine-age	32.40
SYRAH	CHATEAUNEUF	25 yrs average vine-age	8.10
MOURVEDRE	CHATEAUNEUF	15 yrs average vine-age	5.40
MUSCARDIN	CHATEAUNEUF	18 yrs average vine-age	1.10
BOURBOULENC, CLAIRETTE, ROUSSANNE, GRENACHE BLANC	CHATEAUNEUF	18 yrs average vine-age	7.00
GRENACHE NOIR + SYRAH + DIVERS	COTES DU RHONE VILLAGES	Vines at Rasteau and Roaix; 70% Grenache Noir, 20% Syrah, 10% others; 35 yrs av vine-age	8.00
GRENACHE NOIR + SYRAH	COTES DU RHONE	Vines at Buisson	7.00
		TOTAL (hectares):	69.00

DOMAINE DE LA JANASSE

One occasionally encounters winemakers who one realises, from the first sniff of their wine, are clearly destined for the top. Such is Christophe Sabon – a *sympa* and articulate man in his thirties who took over vinification at Domaine de la Janasse from his father, Aimé, in 1991. Before its first vintage in 1973, the estate had sold entirely to co-ops; now 10ha of Châteauneuf with an average vine age of 50-plus and good slabs of 80- to 100-year-old plants, are thoughtfully tended to produce low yields for Christophe to transform into superb wine. There are also 20ha of Côtes du Rhône, 5ha of *vin de pays* and 8ha of *vin de table*.

The Châteauneuf vines cover 15 parcels on widely varied soils: stones on the Vieux Télégraphe plateau, sand at La Crau in the north near Courthézon and a clay-sand-loam in the Beaucastel sector. The Côtes du Rhône is largely in the *quartiers* Coudoulet and Fontanel, including the *lieu-dit* which provides the grapes and the name for their splendid 100% Grenache *cuvée* Les

Garrigues, made from 65-year-old vines. By the mid 1980s, Aimé was convinced that lower yields were a key to better wines, so much green pruning is caried out to keep crops down to their 20–35hl/ha yield bracket.

Christophe's training in Beaune, with work-experience in Mâcon, Crozes-Hermitage and Brouilly, has left him with an experimental streak which he is indulging to the full while working out what really contributes to fine

Châteauneuf. Current *essais* include a Vendange Tardive white with some Roussanne, planting some Counoise and Viognier – both varieties he likes – experimenting with *bâtonnage* with his whites and trying out a few new and old casks in the cellar.

Evidence of Aimé and Christophe's interest in international quality – often a concomitant of fine winemaking – can be found in the small private cellar underneath the house where well-stocked bins of Bordeaux, California, Alsace and Sauternes attest an eclectic taste and a refreshing non-parochialism. Sitting on a

VARIETY	APPELLATION	DETAILS	AREA
GRENACHE BLANC	CHATEAUNEUF		0.30
CLAIRETTE	CHATEAUNEUF		0.30
ROUSSANNE	CHATEAUNEUF		0.40
GRENACHE NOIR	CHATEAUNEUF	Planted 1912–15, 1935, 1960; average age 50	8.00
SYRAH + MOURVEDRE	CHATEAUNEUF	Average age 50	1.00
MOURVEDRE	COTES DU RHONE	Young vines	4.00
GRENACHE	COTES DU RHONE		11.80
CARIGNAN	COTES DU RHONE	Old vines	2.10
SYRAH + CINSAUT	COTES DU RHONE		2.10
		TOTAL (hectares):	30.00

wooden Coulée de Serrant box, Christophe expounds his philosophy.

For whites, which account for 10% of Sabon production, the aim is to add a touch of oak and fat from 40% of Roussanne kept for 6–7 months in new and older small wood, as well as picking both this and the Clairette (30%) well ripened, for roundness and power. Early-harvested Grenache Blanc (30%) contributes acidity. The stainless-steel and *barrique* components are assembled in March, and bottled a month later after sterile filtration. The result is typically fat, round wine, with plenty of class and excellent ageing potential.

However, good as these are it is the reds which are Janasse's flagship. These range from 5,000 bottles of a fine, firm, Côtes du Rhône Grenache, a second Côtes du Rhône made entirely from old Carignan vines, a third from 75% Grenache, 15% old Carignan and 10% Syrah and Mourvèdre, to a trio of excellent Châteauneufs.

Until 1993 there was no red de-stemming – "we are not equipped", is the rather feeble excuse. Now Christophe is in control the matter is under review; he doesn't want inflexible total de-stemming, but considers that Syrah and Carignan need some *eraflage* since their wood and berries don't ripen simultaneously. *Cuvaison* is long – currently 18–25 days – and rising to a desired 30–35 days. Most of the Châteauneufs have 9–18 months in *foudre* then from 0–12 months in *cuve*. Christophe is adamant that Grenache in

Aimé Sabon examining an old Grenache vine.

small wood loses fruit and oxidizes rapidly; Syrah however is well adapted to such *élevage*, so there is always some kept in cask.

The Châteauneufs are highly individual. The basic wine (15,000 bottles annually) is a blend of 80% Grenache, 10–15% Syrah and the rest "*divers*" from a selection of *terroirs*. The Cuvée Chaupin (8,000 bottles) comes from a specific parcel of Grenache planted in 1912. The Vieilles Vignes (6,000 bottles) from 90% Grenache, 10% "divers", from over 80-year-old vines on a clay-limestone soil: this is 10% cask-aged.

Christophe, having done the experiment, prefers a light filtration to none at all. The wines are contract-bottled – which may fill some with horror, but which doesn't seem to diminish the quality of the finished article.

The Sabon's reds above all exude class. Even in the humbler appellations, the wines are interesting, with plenty of concentrated fruit – without, of course, the depth and complexity of their more exalted brethren. The Les Garrigues is beautifully fashioned, and the Châteauneufs have all the character, structure and power one would expect. They begin life tightly opaque, opening out to reveal supple, complex fruit supported by finely-judged tannins. Nothing light here; but equally not just sheer size at the expense of elegance.

In 1993, 6,000 bottles of a Cuvée Speciale were produced for the twentieth anniversary of the domaine's new cellar. This, from 85% Grenache plus 15% Syrah, is something of a monster – with big, spicy extracty flavours – weighing in at 14.4° alcohol. This density can partly be accounted for by the foot *pigeage* to which Christophe subjected the fruit, and by 25-plus days of *cuvaison*. All the elements here of a great wine – when it finally matures.

There is no doubt of Aimé and Christophe's determination and ability to get to the top. La Janasse is definitely a domaine to follow.

DOMAINE DE MARCOUX

The pre-eminence of Châteauneuf's great established domaines is being strongly challenged by a coterie of young, determined, and no less traditionally-minded winemakers. Among these is Philippe Armenier, a tall, distinguished, grey-haired man, with strong brown eyes and a piercing direct gaze, and his Domaine de Marcoux.

The Armeniers are no parvenus in Châteauneuf – "if you look through the records books of the Archbishops of Avignon, owners of the castle at Châteauneuf-du-Pape since 1344, you will find in every year the name of Armenier mentioned as possessor of vines".

Philippe is a passionate and articulate advocate of bio-dynamic viticulture (sometimes to the point of proselytizing) having, at the instigation of his astrologically-minded wife, succumbed to a book on astrology which struck a strong cord. After visiting Frick in Alsace

and Madame Bize-Leroy in Burgundy, he put one third of his 24ha to bio-dynamic culture in 1990. Now the entire estate is run on these lines. "We seem to have established a harmony in vines; we let cosmic forces work in soil and plant". Lest you forget, all the domaine's labels and cartons carry the legend "*domaine en bio-dynamie*".

Bio-dynamics, he says, gives vineyards one degree advance in potential alcohol – that is, not one degree more, but an advance maturity of grapes by one degree "so we can harvest earlier". Also, because plants are more in balance with themselves and their environment, any heat or light they receive is more effective, giving better photosynthesis. Philippe reports meeting a restaurateur who couldn't make *gratin dauphinois* with bio-dynamic potatoes because they contained too much sugar!

He believes that astral forces bring the various different varieties in a mixed planting into synchrony by retarding the precocious and advancing the late-ripeners so that they mature evenly. "A parcel has an identity beyond the individuals composing it". Many of the domaine's individuals are old – 4ha are centenarians which provide much of the raw material of the exceptional Cuvée Vieilles Vignes. This comes from three separate parcels totalling 4.5ha, with an average age of 95. There are 2.5ha on sandy ground at La Crau, 1ha on west-facing sandy soil behind the château and a further hectare on *galets roulés* in a southern *quartier* of the appellation.

Armenier's wines are superb – even difficult vintages such as 1991, 1992 and 1993 have real depth and complexity without rough edges. *Elevage* of 18–26 months – one-fifth in *pièces* from a bio-dynamic *vigneron* in Pouilly Fumé and four-fifths in cement *cuves* (Philippe cut up ten 50-hl *foudres* in 1994) follows fermentation at 30-32°C. Curiously, better years have shorter *cuvaisons* – 1990 took 13 days, 1991 20-24 days and 1992 and '93 both 29 days ("one lunar cycle"!).

Cellar manipulations are, as far as possible, performed on the astrologically appropriate days: "*jours de fruit*". "If you act during the right moment of the lunar cycle, you conserve aromas into the bottle; if the aroma is in the coffee shop, it isn't in the bag of coffee". Bio-dynamics also gives more protein in the wine, and thus better natural clarification.

As an interesting guide, Philippe performed some glycerol analysis on various wines of his own and his friends. The glycerol scale runs from 4 (*vin de table*) to 25 (Sauternes) and is a broad measure of a wine's richness. Philippe's 1992 Vieilles Vignes scored 19; all his friends' *cuvées prestiges* were around 14.5. QED!

Philippe's styles are carefully thought through: complex, aromatic whites with

VARIETY	VINEYARD	DETAILS	AREA
GRENACHE	LES ESQUEIRONS	1 ha 90+; 1 ha planted 1950; 0.45 ha planted 1988	2.45
GRENACHE	COSTE FROIDE	Planted 1980	0.51
GRENACHE	LES GALIMARDES	Planted 1935, 1960, 1981 & 1989	2.00
GRENACHE	LES CHARBONNIERES	90+ yrs old	2.33
SYRAH	LES PLAGNES	Planted 1973	0.46
GRENACHE, MOURVEDRE, CINSAUT, SYRAH	BEAURENARD	Planted 1950, 1965, 1970	7.32
GRENACHE	LA BIGOTE	Planted 1947	0.41
GRENACHE	LES PLAGNES	Planted 1970	0.29
GRENACHE + MOURVEDRE	LES BAS SERRES	Planted 1910–1970	1.78
GRENACHE	BEAURENARD	Planted 1945	0.70
COUNOISE, MUSCARDIN, VACCARESE, TERRET NOIR			5.75
		TOTAL (hectares):	24.00

fat and balance; reds with enormous finesse, extract and concentration. In vintages such as 1990 the quality of both is outstanding. Whether or not one accepts the astrological baggage, this is indisputably first-division stuff.

DOMAINE DE MONPERTUIS

Monpertuis is a 20ha amalgam of three domaines – Domaine de la Croze, Clos de la Cerise and Domaine de Monpertuis – dispersed by inheritance until being progressively reunited between 1982 (Cerise) and 1992 (Croze).

These lie principally to the north (*quartier* Cabrieres), west (*quartier* La Croze) and east (*quartiers* La Crau, Monpertuis and La Font du Pape) of the village, and comprise some 33 different plots: "very inconvenient for working, but good for quality" admits Paul Jeune, a tall, deliberate man in his forties, who runs this top-class domaine.

He offers three Châteauneufs. Cuvée Classique, from what he calls "young" vines – from 20 to 60 years old – is 70% Grenache; 15% Mourvèdre; 10% Syrah and 5% "other *cépages*". Cuvée Tradition, made from 60- to 110-year-old vines "and only in the best years", is 90% Grenache and the rest "*divers*". A white Châteauneuf comes from 40% Clairette, 20% Bourboulenc, 30% Grenache Blanc and 10% young Roussanne.

There is no compromise on quality: no de-stemming, long *cuvaison* (three weeks for the Classique, four to six weeks for the Tradition) and an *élevage* of 11–13 months in three- to five-year-old casks for the former, and 18–24 months in large *foudres* for the Tradition.

Paul confesses to being a fining freak, using only the lightest effective dose, and to a desire to eliminate filtration altogether; at present a plate filtration precedes bottling for the

Classique, but is eschewed for the Tradition.

The wines here are consistently excellent. A *vin de garde* white has fat and structure: its 40% Clairette is equal parts of Clairette Blanche and Clairette Rose, a rare grape whose peculiarity is to add a vein of tannin which hardens the wine initially but increases its ageing potential. The Bourboulenc adds acidity and the Grenache Blanc fat and depth, while the young Roussanne enhances aromatic development.

Paul argues that each variety needs separate vinification, and is dissatisfied with the usual practice of mixing varieties at fermentation. The Roussanne and Bourboulenc need lower temperatures, so are vinified at 16–17°C, which gives them a very strong aromatic component.

By contrast, the Clairettes and Grenache are vinified at 18–19°C and 20–22°C respectively. Paul finds that lower temperatures gives "bizarre aromas of exotic fruits – bananas, mangoes etc."

The reds are a fine pair – tending strongly towards a wilder, less disciplined animal, leather and mushroom character. Never simple, invariably challenging and interesting, they start life on an austere note, which needs bottle-age to soften.

The Tradition – started in 1988 at the request of UK and US customers – is remarkable indeed. There are between 3,000 and 20,000 bottles of dense, powerful, extracty wine, with aromas of over-ripe morello cherries and earthy, mineral, tarry, gamey flavours (1990), or more *sauvage*, fleshy notes, but in similar vein and with a better fruit-tannin balance (1989). Delicacy is not the theme here – rather structure and intense, ripe old-vine fruit. The principal sources of these grapes are Monpertuis, la Crau and the Clos de la Cerise, just behind the domaine's modern HQ, near the parochial low-cost housing in the Bois de la Ville part of the village.

If such comparisons are useful, the style is nearer to Henri Bonneau than to Jacques Reynaud – although Paul Jeune wouldn't object to either, as he admires both. This is a top-notch estate which will undoubtedly attract attention in the years to come.

WINE	APPELLATION	DETAILS	AREA
CHATEAUNEUF-DU-PAPE, CUVEE TRADITION	CHATEAUNEUF	90% Grenache, 10% "divers"; average vine-age 60–110 yrs.	6.00
CHATEAUNEUF-DU-PAPE, CUVEE CLASSIQUE	CHATEAUNEUF	70% Grenache. 15% Mourvèdre, 10% Syrah, 5% "divers, incl all 13 cépages; average vine-age, 20–60 yrs.	12.00
CHATEAUNEUF-DU-PAPE, MONPERTUIS BLANC	CHATEAUNEUF	40% Clairettes, 30% Grenache Blanc, 20% Bourboulenc, 10% Roussanne; average vine-age 15–40 yrs	2.00
		TOTAL (hectares):	20.00

CHATEAU DE MONT REDON

Vines were already growing at "Mourredon", which then belonged to the Episcopal estate, in 1334. The modern history of the domaine dates from 1923, when it was inherited by Henri Plantin. Then there were just 2ha of vines, in 12 separate plots near the village. He set about clearing woodland and reconstituted the estate, making it much as it is today. Plantin was the great-grandfather of Jean and François Abeille and of their cousin, Didier Fabre, and it is these three who are now responsible for the property.

Mont-Redon is a fine domaine, sitting atop a plateau to the north-west of the village. One hundred of its 163ha are under vine, on land which includes all three main Châteauneuf soil types: limestone slopes to the west, which give fruit and aroma to the white wines; sand, ideal for developing aromatics in Cinsaut, Mourvèdre and Grenache; and a layer of heavy *galets* on the plateau, planted to Grenache and Syrah.

A great deal of work is devoted to plant maturity. To equalize ripening, they prune the precocious Syrah later and the tardy Mourvèdre and Grenache earlier. The aim is to ferment all three together: this, they believe, develops more complex aromas. They also plant the later-ripening varieties in known early-ripening plots, and vice versa.

"By this we gain eight days' earlier maturity", explains Jean Abeille, a knowledgeable and urbane man. In wet years, such as 1992 and 1993, this expedient ripened the fruit before the rain and thus saved the crop. Abeille observes also that pollination is more successful in a mixed planting of vines than with a single variety. He has a firm conviction that aromatic potential is linked to the organic constitution of the soil. Winemaking here is an evolving logic. Mont-Redon is the largest producer of

white Châteauneuf, and the quality is excellent. The Grenache Blanc and Roussanne, both early ripeners, are picked first and vinified apart; then come the Clairette and Picpoul and finally the higher-acid Bourboulenc. "Many *vignerons* harvest all at once, so the late varieties aren't ripe, or the early ones are over-ripe".

Cool vinification at only 15-16°C extracts maximum aromatics and minimises the release of carbon dioxide, which would simply allow aromas to escape into the atmosphere. "We want our aromas in the bottle, not in the cellar". Bottling takes place after four to five months, after sterile filtration to conserve aroma and fruit. Acidity fixes perfume, so to conserve acidity the malolactic is blocked with sulphur dioxide.

The results are impressive: well-balanced wines, with aromas of wheatmeal and hay when young, transforming into Meursault-like nuts and butter after a decade or so in bottle. A 1983 enjoyed over lunch was magnificently rich without being out of balance with alcohol.

The reds are fashioned from a November pre-assemblage into three individual *cuvées*, all vinified with 90% de-stemming to maximize skin tannin extraction, part *auto-pigeantes* ("we don't turn these like cement-mixers", Jean explains, "they extract too much harsh tannin"), and 9–11 days' *cuvaison*. One *cuvée*, the most structured, is a blend during fermentation of 12% Mourvèdre, 15–20% Syrah and 70% Grenache, and is matured in casks, a proportion of which are renewed annually. The second is a

blend of 20% Syrah and 80% Grenache, which only sees two- to four-year-old casks. For each *cuve*, half stays in cask for eight months before a similar period in stainless steel and half has the reverse regime. The third, most aromatic, *cuve* comprises 75% Grenache, 6–7% Counoise, Muscardine and Vaccarèse, 5–6% Syrah and 10–15% Cinsaut. It spends 9–14 months in *foudres*. After 18–24 months the three elements are blended and left for three months to marry. An egg-white fining and a "*terre rose*" earth filtration – the most delicate, "if we do it at all" – completes the *élevage*. Tasting the three fractions from the 1993 vintage provides a striking demonstration of the effect of *cépage* mix and *élevage*. While all were fine, the blend was superior to its parts both in aromatics and flavour complexity.

The domaine has attracted criticism for not producing a *Cuvée Prestige*. Jean Abeille's defence is that extracting the cream from the crop, even in a good vintage, inevitably impoverishes what remains. He sees it the other way round: put the best wine into Mont-Redon and sell anything unsuitable for the château label in bulk, as generic Châteauneuf. This seems a perfectly reasonable policy.

Mont-Redon reds are generally not heavyweights in the grand manner, rather wines accentuating finesse and elegance. This is not to say that they don't age well; on the contrary, age brings out a splendid array of secondary aromas, which for many is what Châteauneuf is all about. While the younger wines invariably typify their vintages, it is the older wines which show what this property is capable of. In general, the reds would undoubtedly benefit from a shade more depth than they have at present.

VARIETIES	ESTATE	DETAILS	AREA
RED AND WHITE VARITIES	MONT-REDON	Average vine age, 45+ years	100.00
RED AND WHITE VARIETIES	DOMAINE DES SABLONS	Bought in 1981, near Roquemaure	20.00
		TOTAL (hectares):	120.00

CHATEAU LA NERTHE

La Nerthe is Châteauneuf's most substantial and elegant property. Although the present château was not built until 1760, the estate's existence is documented back to November 25, 1560. For nearly 300 years it belonged to the Piedmontese Tulle de Villefranche family, during which time its wine acquired a reputation for excellence. By the 1980s, however, the estate had declined perilously, until its rescue in 1985 by the French coffee family, Ricard.

Ricard installed Alain Dugas, a career accountant from Paris, as manager with *carte blanche* to restore the château, vineyards and cellars. He found the château dilapidated, vineyards in need of replanting and drainage, and the cellars full of old *foudres*, many coated in tartrate crystals and containing wine contaminated by spoilage bacteria. Châteauneuf's "Château Margaux" is now immaculate, and the historic cellar – with

its rows of back-lit casks and metal bins bearing the names of a litany of France's starred restaurants – well worth visiting.

Alain, a short, be-spectacled man in his fifties, took a sabbatical under the tutelage of Gabriel Meffre at La Courançonne where he learnt to make wine – "and to repair machinery". This helps, not only at La Nerthe, but with his own excellent Domaine de la Renjarde near Mondragon. Dugas, together with cellar-master Philippe Capelier (a winemaker by training and "*passioné du vin*"), Max Farjon in the vineyards, and the ubiquitous Noel Rabot as consulting oenologist, constitute the team dedicated to restoring Château La Nerthe to its former pre-eminence.

In the estate's magnificent 90-ha vineyard – a rare single block round the château – micro-vinification trials were made to find those clones and varieties best adapted to the soil. The property sits on a slope: at the top is a mix of sand and fine clay, well adapted to white varieties; around the château the soil is red-brown clay and *galets*; below is found a predominance of *galets roulés*. Many of the existing Grenache vines were degenerate and needed grubbing up – Grenache is especially susceptible to *court-noué*. The new regime also planted seven hectares of Mourvèdre to balance the *encépagement*. Vineyard policy is now organic, with trials of bio-dynamic methods under way.

Alain Dugas considers that Châteauneufs are often unbalanced by failure to harvest each variety at full ripeness. His research indicates that both white and red grapes deliver their maximum potential within a four-day window. Now 15–20 days of harvest ensures that each *cépage* is picked at optimum maturity, thus maximizing potential extract. The main challenge is to arrange contemporaneous maturity for Grenache, Syrah and Mourvèdre so that these can be vinified together for added complexity. Naturally, Syrah ripens first, followed by Grenache and finally Mourvèdre. However, by pruning the Mourvèdre severely in November, they gain a week's maturity.

This work continues in the cellar, which is designed to ensure that handling actually extracts this potential. There are usually three different "lots", reflecting the ripening cycle: Syrah and Grenache; Mourvèdre and Grenache; and Grenache, Mourvèdre and Syrah. The bunches are totally de-stemmed, then given three weeks' *cuvaison* with hydraulic *pigeage* for the Grenache and Mourvèdre. This process, abandoned by many domaines as too much hard work, adds massively to extraction, in Alain's opinion. Some *cuves* have up to 5% whole bunches.

Vinification is adapted to *terroir* and takes account of vine age, yield and the known characteristics of each plot, with natural yeasts which are considered essential to retaining typicity. Maximum fermentation temperature varies between 32 and 36°C. At 36° results are "spectacular", although Alain admits "we're on a knife edge here".

Pigeage renders the press-wine too tannic for use, so it goes to make the estate's *rapé*. Thereafter the wines pass

The cellar courtyard at Château la Nerthe.

into the magnificently restored 17th-century subterranean stone vats for malolactic fermentation.

Elevage depends on the lot concerned: the most tannic Mourvèdre and Grenache and Syrah and Grenache lots go into equal proportions of new, second- and third-year Allier oak casks – on view in the back-lit cellar. Less-extracted Grenache and the press wine are kept in *foudres*. The standard Châteauneuf blend, made up from a series of pre-*assemblages* during the first year, consists of equal fractions of *foudre*, *barrique* and *cuve* wine. Bottling, in one go, occurs after 18 months.

In 1986, Alain Dugas released the first of the splendid Cuvée des Cadettes, made principally from a 5ha plot of Grenache and Mourvèdre (60:40 plus a touch of Syrah), planted by La Nerthe's former owner Commander Ducos in 1900. This wine spends a year in new wood – 4–6 months longer than the cask fraction of the standard *cuvée* – and then gets a few months' more total maturation. The

Mourvèdre, in particular, needs cask-ageing to round out its firm tannins. All the reds are fined and polish-filtered before bottling.

The range is generally excellent and becoming more consistent as the team fine-tune harvesting, vinification and *élevage*. The whites in particular should not be overlooked. The mix here is equal parts of Grenache Blanc, Clairette, Roussanne and Bourboulenc, with the Bourboulenc and Grenache vinified together and the Clairette and Roussanne separately. The very good white *cuvée prestige* – Clos de Beauvenir – is 60% Roussanne plus 40% Clairette from 40-year-old vines fermented in Allier and Nevers oak, plus some second-wine barrels from the Château de Meursault. All the whites are "malolactic blocked", and bottled in the spring following the vintage. Although they have plenty of fruit and elegance in youth, Alain Dugas' white vinification is deliberately designed to produce *vins de garde*. The Clos de Beauvenir has the structure and *puissance* to develop well over a decade or more in vintages such as 1990.

La Nerthe is an estate in renaissance. Alain Dugas is doing a fine job in restoring its reputation, and the wines have improved dramatically. If there is a note of concern it is the sneaking feeling that the need to keep wholesale prices low to maintain sales for the sizeable production (200–250,000 bottles of red, 10,000 of Cadettes and 20–30,000 of white), is perhaps compromising concentration. This must be no more than a quibble with a fine domaine.

VARIETY	VINEYARD	DETAILS	AREA
GRENACHE	LA NERTHE		47.00
MOURVEDRE	LA NERTHE		12.00
SYRAH	LA NERTHE		12.00
CINSAUT	LA NERTHE		4.00
DIVERSE OTHER RED VARIETIES	LA NERTHE		6.00
CLAIRETTE	LA NERTHE	Some 40+ yr old vines	2.25
GRENACHE BLANC	LA NERTHE		2.25
ROUSSANNE	LA NERTHE		2.25
BOURBOULENC	LA NERTHE		2.25
		TOTAL (hectares):	90.00

DOMAINE DU PEGAU

Domaine du Pegau is a traditional estate, run with enthusiastic flair by Laurence Feraud and her father Paul, while Madame Feraud ("I'm not very technical") looks after the administration. Laurence prefers working in the cellars and Paul likes being among the vines, so the combination is ideal.

Their 13ha (12 of 30- to 60-year-old Grenache, Syrah and Mourvèdre with touches of field-planted Cinsaut, Counoise and Vaccarèse, plus a hectare of whites) – are widely scattered. Laurence has 2.5ha en fermage from her father plus another 1.5ha of badly-trained vines of her own. "I don't know what to do with these", she laments, surveying the gnarled stumps with evident pride.

Clay-limestone – 50% overlaid by galets –and chalk predominate, mainly on well-exposed hillsides. For Laurence "the secret lies in the soils" and in matching vine to terroir. Interestingly, they are planting Syrah on wires round vineyard borders since this gives better maturity than planting it among Grenache.

The finest Feraud vines are a mixed 1902 planting, opposite La Gardine; the rows, originally set by horses, are splendidly irregular with sprouts of Mourvèdre droit, towering above the stumpy Grenache.

Laurence admires her father, and the feeling is clearly mutual. In 1987, when it was proposed she join him, the cuverie was some way from the cellars. Laurence refused to commute and demanded new cellars; these, along with a new house, were built in 1989. Under her aegis, annual production has risen from 8,000 to 60,000 bottles, and the wines have received international acclaim.

In the new cellar, tradition rules – no de-stemming, 10-15 days' cuvaison then 2-6 years in foudres (the latter in 1979 and 1981) and neither fining nor filtration. The domaine's hardware shares the same epoch as its soul. A fine old continuous table-wine press, technically illegal in Châteauneuf, which Laurence reckons extracts more colour and aroma than modern ones, provides better oxidation-buffering and more and cleaner lees, is kept company by a skeletal piece of motorised Meccano which passes for a tractor.

The "fearfully noisy" bottling machine is no better. Due to its age and infirmity there are several goes at la mise. "We do 20,000 in three days; that's all I can take; my head's like THAT", Laurence explains, admitting that 3–6 months between first and last bottlings affects the taste.

There is, however, nothing skeletal or antiquated about the Feraud's Châteauneufs. The whites, vinified part in stainless steel and part in new wood, then élevés in new and old casks, are rich and substantial, with fat, solid structures and good ageing potential – somewhat individual, but nonetheless fine. The 1990 and 1993 stand out, while the 1991 and 1992, although fine, were less compelling. The reds are invariably dense, often opaque black-cherry, with complex aromas and well-structured mouthfilling flavours.

Paul Feraud – a charming, open man – cares for nature and tends his vines accordingly. Laurence is a confident winemaker, hesitating only when recalling the overnight fame brought by an American journalist who lauded her 1990 red. The wine sold swiftly, but then came the less highly-praised 1991 and they were stuck with unsold stock. According to Laurence, this journalist has never visited them. Those who have the power to make or break estates should at least have the courtesy to visit each property they evaluate. They would find Domaine du Pegau in thoroughly competent hands.

VARIETY	APPELLATION	DETAILS	AREA
GRENACHE, SYRAH, MOURVEDRE	CHATEAUNEUF	30–60 year old vines; rupestris du Lot rootstock	12.00
GRENACHE, CLAIRETTE, ROUSSANNE	CHATEAUNEUF	15 yr old vines; rupestris du Lot rootstock	1.00
		TOTAL (hectares):	13.00

CHATEAU RAYAS

It is difficult to assess objectively an estate which has been such an influential part of one's wine life for so long. Although its owner Jacques Reynaud may seem eccentric, often brusquely unwelcoming (if you are fortunate enough to be received at all), and his cellars distinctly scruffy, deeper acquaintance shows that such superficialities are misleading.

What matters is that his wines are supreme, outstripping almost everything else in Châteauneuf, vintage after vintage. That is the reality.

Inevitably, Jacques' dislike of journalists, and his mischievous reluctance to dispel myths, has reduced accurate information on the estate to a trickle, spawning much nonsense, with Reynaud and Rayas often severely and unjustifiably criticised. It is time to put the record straight.

The château, together with some 23ha of land, were bought and planted by Jacques Reynaud's grandfather, a notaire from Apt, in the 1890s. Between then and the 1920s, when Jacques' father Louis took over, the estate shrunk by 11ha to its present size. In 1945, Louis acquired Château de Fonsalette (qv) a fine Côtes du Rhône property at Largarde-Paréol. On Louis' death in 1978, Jacques, who had already worked with him for many years, took over.

Both Rayas and its second Châteauneuf label, Pignan, are lieux-dits, the former lying south and east across a small valley from the château towards Courthézon, the latter fringing the chai to the south and west towards Châteauneuf.

Whilst most Châteauneuf estates are signposted, Rayas prefers anonymity. "People feel that they have achieved something when they finally find us", remarks Jacques, who is well aware of the respect in which his estate is held, not least among Châteauneuf's vignerons themselves, and sees no point in expenditure on signposts which would undoubtedly augment the flow of visitors.

To find Rayas, you have to take courage in both hands and branch left up an unmade track circling Château Vaudieu, off the Courthézon road. A gentle incline leads to a solitary sign stuck into the vineyard directing you the final 100m to the cellars, a functional, square building faced in pebble-dash, with yellow metal window-frames. Below, a mellow copse of trees surrounds an uncultivated meadow – filled with flowers in spring – and in the distance the A7 autoroute streams impatient tourists to and from their beaches, and juggernauts from Marseilles across France to northern Europe.

Rayas' 13ha are planted exclusively with Grenache of some 35 years average age. By no means old vines – "the soil is poor here, so the vines die quickly", explains Jacques. "We replace them up to 20 years old, then they are left". Rather contrarily, he is planning to plant some Muscardin, a less usual variety at Châteauneuf, because "everyone has Mourvèdre". In any case, "I don't like

Jacques Reynaud. Note the sandy soil and the mixture of young and very old vines.

Mourvèdre, it has no finesse and needs a south-facing slope". So Muscardin it is.

Rayas and its owner deliberately run counter to Châteauneuf's conventional wisdom. There are no *galets roulés* on the property; some say that grandpère Reynaud removed them all by hand when he planted his vines – an unlikely, though not wholly improbable, story. In Jacques' view *"terre fin = vin fin"* so stones are a negative influence rather than the benefit most believe. Walking over a famous nearby vineyard some years ago, Jacques recalls noticing the soil cracking under his feet. "This won't give fine wine" he concluded. By contrast – "come and look, here you feel as though you are walking on a carpet"; indeed, a fine topsoil of friable, siliceous earth leaves you sinking into the ground. Underneath is a permeable layer of *molasse*, then clay: soil which needs regular water. "We could water – but we don't have any water here", Jacques chuckles. So the vines are left to get on with it.

Unlike many of the commune's better vineyards, Rayas faces mainly north – giving, in Jacques' view, longer, more even ripening, and avoiding the baking to which south-facing vines are often exposed. This, together with yields of around 15–20hl/hl (which most growers in the commune would regard as suicidally low) and nothing but Grenache (which is widely believe incapable, on its own, of producing either fine or long-lived wine), completes Rayas' somewhat eccentric view of the foundations of quality.

Here, and at Fonsalette, Jacques Reynaud follows his father's dictum: "never exceed 11 casks to the hectare". So the stubby old vines are pruned short and subjected to a green-pruning each July. The harvest tends to be late here – in 1974, for example, Reynaud was still picking away in early November, when most growers had given up. The result: a remarkable wine of great complexity and substance.

Jacques' philosophy is encapsulated in the deceptively simple principle: "what matters is to make good wine". In practice, this maxim effectively translates as "if doing X or Y improves the wine, *tant pis* for the rules". Thus there may be a dab or two of Chardonnay in the white wine, or a spoonful of Fonsalette Syrah in the red, but so what? Equally, if a spot of super-concentrated 1974 will add structure and depth to the 1973, why not?

He harbours a legendary distaste for control and officialdom, inherited from his father, who habitually labelled his wine *"1er Grand Cru"* – which meant nothing at all, beyond his unshakeable belief in its quality. Jacques is far from enamoured of those whose unfortunate job it is to police the appellation's rules ("one is not entirely in agreement with *'les officiels'*" he comments), nor of the very notion of control itself ("Appellation Contrôlée is a guarantee of mediocrity"). Fortunately, *"les officiels"*, leave him alone, by and large, probably knowing full well that it would be unwise to tangle with one of the world's greatest winemakers. In any case, any attempt at intervention would probably result in everything being labelled as Côtes du Rhône and sold at double the price.

Red vinification is, as one might expect, traditional. No mucking around with new wood or stainless steel, just long *cuvaison* of first-class raw material. The appellation rules require at least 5% of each year's crop to be discarded; Jacques Reynaud, however, doesn't hold with this: "If the grapes are good, why throw them away?". Indeed, why? He doesn't – they go into the vats with the rest. Unlike most Châteauneuf estates, the Grenache is picked first – "it gives most alcohol", is the explanation – followed by the Fonsalette Syrah and Cinsaut.

Both red and white Rayas are invariably high in alcohol – certainly not bottle-per-head stuff. Whereas most oenologists tell you that pH is more important than alcohol "we think the reverse". So the aim is to arrive at 15–16°.

How this is attained is more a question of art than science. Where most *vignerons* exercise rigorous control over fermentation temperatures, Jacques is non-committal – "I've never checked – it does what it wants". Suggesting that he might limit vat temperature elicits a shrug and "to what – poof – I have nothing to use". In fact, at 30°C, juice is drawn off and cooled by transfer. The red press-wine is invariably added back: "my press-wine is good", Jacques declares firmly. In fact Rayas was the first Châteauneuf estate to have a pneumatic press – Dr Dufays of Nalys wanted this distinction, but Louis Reynaud beat him to it. A modern Willmes now does the work.

The most cursory of glances round the cellars should convince even the least technically-minded that Rayas is not at the cutting edge of vinification technology. The small dusty entrance lobby, reached through an outside door with two opaque glass panes, where orders are assembled for collection, is also home to an antique red "one-shot" corking machine, with a small seat and a large handle. On a shelf reside some old, empty rum bottles, the remains of a bottle

VARIETY	VINEYARD	DETAILS	AREA
GRENACHE NOIR	RAYAS/PIGNAN	Average vine-age 25–35 yrs	11.00
GRENACHE BLANC	RAYAS	Average vine-age 25–35 yrs	1.00
CLAIRETTE	RAYAS	Average vine-age 25–35 yrs	1.00
		TOTAL (hectares):	13.00

of Sassicaia, and various implements. Tasting glasses are dispersed according to condition: those with feet hang from hooks, whilst those without stand inverted on a square of kitchen-paper.

Off this reception area – which is as far as many get – are three doors: one leads into a long bottle cellar, and the other two into the cask space, where a long-time resident population of greying casks and *foudres* of various formats recline at a variety of irrational angles. A flight of dangerously worn wooden stairs leads to a first-floor lobby, which in turn leads to a surprisingly modern office, complete with a secretary typing away in front of a computer screen, a couple of desks and a metal filing cabinet.

A second door screens tank rooms, for bulk storage and *assemblage*. The wooden slatted floor is punctured by round holes bunged with rag, allowing wine to be pumped around from tanks to casks or to the small bottling machine below. Old, unlabelled bottles, various tools and bits of flat-packed cartons litter the sides of these rooms and, if the network of cobwebs is anything to judge by, spiders thrive in the alcoholic haze. But these oddities matter little; quality is controlled by what ends up in the glass, not by laboratories or technicians.

Rayas reds and whites are matured entirely in large wood – "in casks, it's the end", says Jacques Reynaud. Half the red crop is bottled at the domaine after one year – by the second spring after the vintage. The rest remains a further year – "so we have something if the harvest isn't good", explains Jacques, hinting that a better vintage may be used to bolster a weaker successor – "it's forbidden, but *tant pis*". Another broadside at the rules: "once you start *reglementation*, then it just mushrooms".

A system of barely decipherable chalk marks on each *foudre* signals the nature and eventual destination of its contents. These unintelligible scrawls are in code – "to confuse *les officiels*". In lesser years, no Rayas is released, the wine being sold as Pignan, the domaine's second Châteauneuf label. It used to be Clos Pignan, but along with Louis' "*1er Grand Cru*", "Clos" was reluctantly suppressed to conform with the rules. In thoroughly dismal vintages – such as 1965 – the wine is sold in bulk to *négociants*, who buy it for the right to have the appellation; "this is the negative side of the system", Jacques remarks, "if 1965 is entitled to be called Châteauneuf...".

Louis Reynaud produced a variety of curiosities – among them a sweet

Françoise Reynaud waging war on protruding corks.

Châteauneuf. The last vintage of this delicacy was 1955. "It was a mine of sulphur" insisted Jacques, which on the evidence of a bottle shared with Jacques and his sister Françoise in 1994, was certainly true – although not sufficiently overpowering to mar the wine underneath. There was also a remarkable "*marc liquoreux*", which was confected by adding concentrated must to distilled *marc*. The 1945, Louis' final version of this, was extraordinarily concentrated and powerful, though darkened and mellowed by ageing in glass *bonbon*, gaining an explosive nose of room-filling opulence.

Jacques is far from immune from customer feedback. Criticism of his whites for being too oxidative has led him to experiment with earlier bottling. Up to the 1992 vintage, *élevage* lasted around 10 months. From 1993, until he changes his mind, bottling will take place four months earlier – in the spring following the harvest. "If customers like it, we'll continue". In that year, for the first time, the malolactic was blocked, by filtration. There wasn't anything wrong with the old-style whites – memories are still fresh of a 1957 Rayas *blanc* of great depth and power, with a splendidly concentrated nose of acacia, nuts and gently decaying butter – but they were a distinctly acquired taste. Fonsalette *blanc* was often similar in style.

The red Rayas is superb wine, and in great vintages truly remarkable. Its sheer density and concentration, in which low yields and old vines play an important part, leave all but a handful of the rest standing. Even the Pignan surpasses most other Châteauneufs. There is a rumour that Jacques Reynaud puts his best wine into the second label on the grounds that those who could afford Rayas could probably not tell the difference, while those who bought Pignan were more likely to appreciate it. The idea has Reynaud-ish appeal, but it is not true.

Jacques Reynaud's reputation for eccentricity may not be entirely without foundation. However, beneath what appears to many as brusque detachment, or sometimes vacant incomprehension, lies an impish sense of humour and deep feeling. His terseness hides a sharp analytical perceptiveness and a profound dislike of stupidity, which is less easily concealed – hardly surprising from a man who studied Greek and philosophy and can talk knowledgeably on many esoteric subjects. He admits to a love of good food ("je suis gourmand") and especially of chocolate.

He wisely stands aloof from the politics of Châteauneuf, and is regarded with considerable respect by other *vignerons*. The knowledge that you have the best engenders self-confidence and eliminates the need for competitive success. You won't find him, or his wines, at shows or up for medals – that's for the rest. With a Côtes du Rhône which generally out-distances most Châteauneufs, and Châteauneufs which invariably do, a measure of personal pride is entirely justifiable.

DOMAINE DES RELAGNES

Henri Boiron and his estate do not spring to most connoisseurs' minds when contemplating Châteauneuf. However, he and his forebears have been producing wine from their 15ha since 1905, and there is no reason to doubt that it was ever less fine than it is now. Henri is the fourth generation off Boirons here, although the estate's origins go back to the 14th century, when the Popes, attracted by its sunny situation in the heart of Châteauneuf, used Les Relagnes as a rose garden. Still a *lieu-dit*, it is now vineyard and has long since ceded its name to this domaine.

According to Henri, a warm and kindly man in his fifties, his 12ha of Châteauneuf (the other three are Côtes du Rhône), are distributed through all four points of the compass. The vines are planted on predominantly stony or sandy soils, and average 60 years of age- "without exaggeration", he adds lest you might think him guilty of the usual embellishment. The normal work to keep yields at levels commensurate with quality is augmented by a particularly severe *trie* during the harvest: "we often drop far more than the 5% required", claims Henri, noting that "we like to harvest quickly and well" – no easy undertaking.

The cellars and *cuverie* are a mix of modern, old and functional. A few old casks are ranged along the middle of the cellar under the house, surveyed by a row of large, oval, red-edged *foudres*. Here Relagnes reds spend up to three years before bottling, since Henri believes that this ripens the wine and that its character and extract require long maturation before bottling: "I still have some 1992 in *foudres*" (in 1994) – "even wines need a bit of rest, a bit of a holiday".

Boiron's red come from a 15–18 day *cuvaison* at up to 33°C, so there is plenty of colour and extract for the *foudres* to amortise. The wood only contributes indirectly, by opening up the wine and starting its long, slow aroma and flavour evolution.

A light filtration precedes bottling, although Henri admits that filtration removes goodness. He would probably prefer to bottle unfiltered, but seems reluctant – possibly fearing problems later on. He should perhaps concentrate on reducing the number of separate bottlings – currently five – of each vintage: "we would like to do one *mise*, but it is too expensive". Fining was abandoned some time ago after *cuves* lost colour as a result. This was obviously not a technical decision – just the feeling that fining denatured the wine.

There is only one *cuvée* here, which, judging by tastings of several recent vintages, is becoming ever finer. About a quarter of the crop ("I select the less good *cuves*") is sold each year to *négociants*, the rest being bottled and sold by the domaine.

Henri has been joined by his son-in-law Olivier – you don't simply marry the daughter in these small estates, the job goes with the bride. Together they make a good team – experience and enthusiasm. His second son-in-law apparently drew the short straw, and runs a fast-food outlet nearby: "The estate isn't large enough to support three families", Henri explains.

In 1994, at the annual "Fête de St-Marc" competition held by the *vignerons* of Châteauneuf to find the best red and white wines from the previous and third vintages, the 1990 Domaine de Relagnes red took first prize. Tasting a range of vintages confirms that the high quality here is no flash in the pan. Whatever the predominant style of the vintage, old-vine fruit features as a contributor to Relagnes depth and richness. Do not look for massive, heavily tannic wines; rather enjoy depth and intensity with the balance achieved by sheer concentration and power of fully ripe fruit, together with good acidities and well-judged, though not overwhelming, tannins.

The fact of several bottlings means that tasting notes should be read with caution. Tasting two bottlings of the 1989 vintage highlights differences that are more than cosmetic. A more recent bottling showed volatility at the limit of acceptability, while an earlier *mise* had an altogether fresher, cleaner nose, plums rather than meat-extract and more precise, focused flavours, with complex palate-aromas of *fruits rouges* and violets – undoubtedly finer.

While such variations make buying frustrating – you must taste first – this is something which only requires cash to put right, and must not be seen as a fundamental design fault. Henri and Olivier are clearly fully capable of making first-class wine and older vintages demonstrate a continuity of quality; nothing should detract from this fact. It is to be hoped that the achievement of the 1990 will be consolidated and built upon at this fine estate.

VARIETY	APPELLATION	DETAILS	AREA
GRENACHE	CHATEAUNEUF-DU-PAPE	60 yr average age	9.60
SYRAH	CHATEAUNEUF-DU-PAPE	60 yr average age	0.70
MOURVEDRE	CHATEAUNEUF-DU-PAPE	60 yr average age	1.40
CINSAUT	CHATEAUNEUF-DU-PAPE	60 yr average age	0.30
VARIOUS	COTES DU RHONE/VIN DU PAYS		3.00
		TOTAL (hectares):	15.00

LA VIEILLE JULIENNE

This is a domaine that is both old and new: old-established, dating from 1905, and newly resurrected in 1990. The young, lean, dark-haired and highly articulate Jean-Paul Daumen took over from his father in 1990 and has already made impressive strides towards the top class. Tasting round Châteauneuf convinced him beyond doubt of the shortcomings of earlier wines: a tendency to rusticity, undue muscle and a lack of finesse – all due, at least in part, to the total lack of investment in the property in the 1980s. Now things have changed and there are improvements, fuelled by Jean-Paul's announcement that his career lay elsewhere – in business management.

It is clear that things are on the move here: a new ageing cellar, capable of holding a complete harvest, is *en projet*. Instead of leaving most of the stems in the vats, there is now almost 100% de-stemming – this is probably the single most important change Jean-Paul has introduced. In fact, he started by de-stemming the Mourvèdre only – now everything goes through the *égrappoir*. Furthermore, a single bottling has now replaced Daumen *père*'s practice of bottling each crop as orders, or more likely cash, dictated. This ensures that wine quality determines the timing of the *mise*, and prevents wine being left to dry out in wood, as it tended to in the past.

More recently, Jean-Paul tried shifting maturation to 50% *cuve* and 50% *foudres*, but found that this produced shorter-lived wines – since the *cuve* element conserved the fruit, but at the expense of structure. Now *élevage* is entirely in oak *foudres*, for 12-18 months, which gives the wines fat whilst retaining the fruit. However, he admits that his ideal would be one-third each of small casks, *foudres* and *cuves* and to that end is trying out some new barrels.

A seminal decision is whether to vinify each variety separately and then blend, or to ferment the *cépages* together. At present, the Syrah and Mourvèdre are vinified separately, the latter with a dab of Grenache. Syrah ripens a week or 10 days earlier than Grenache and to vinify them together would mean either over-ripeness for the one or under-ripeness for the other.

Jean-Paul would like to try and even out the maturity of the different varieties – pruning might help here – since he believes that a mixed-variety vinification gives more harmonious flavour and aroma integration.

A rigorous selection policy has been introduced: in 1991, no wine was sold as Vieille Julienne; in 1992 only 150hl out of a total of 400hl. Moreover, if filtration is used the wine is not released as Vieille Julienne, but sold under the domaine's

VARIETY	APPELLATION	DETAILS	AREA
GRENACHE NOIR	CHATEAUNEUF	55 yr old vines	7.30
COUNOISE	CHATEAUNEUF	30 yr old vines	0.80
SYRAH	CHATEAUNEUF	25 yr old vines	1.00
MOURVEDRE	CHATEAUNEUF	20 yr old vines	0.80
CINSAUT	CHATEAUNEUF	50 yr old vines	0.20
GRENACHE NOIR	COTES DU RHONE	65 yr old vines	10.50
MOURVEDRE	COTES DU RHONE	30 yr old vines	0.80
CINSAUT	COTES DU RHONE	15 yr old vines	1.00
SYRAH	COTES DU RHONE	30 yr old vines	0.50
GRENACHE BLANC, BOURBOULENC, CLAIRETTE	CHATEAUNEUF		0.50
GRENACHE BLANC, BOURBOULENC, CLAIRETTE	COTES DU RHONE		1.00
		TOTAL (hectares):	24.40

second label, Grangette des Grès, for sale through the more commercial distribution chain – hypermarkets, etc. A third level of quality is sold off in bulk to *négociants*. In 1993, 250hl went to Vieille Julienne, 100hl into Grangette and 100hl to the *négoce*. There are also red and white Côtes du Rhônes and a red *vin de pays*.

Would that more estates worked on these lines. At a time when development capital is badly needed, this stringent policy leaves one in no doubt of Jean-Paul Daumen's determination to produce top quality.

There is no reason whatsoever why this estate should not flourish. The vineyard mix is excellent – a single 8-ha slab *en coteaux* in the *quartier* des Grès,

with the remaining 3ha in a dozen patches, some 2km away towards Courthézon. With an average vine-age of 50, and 40% of plantings between 70–80 years old, the ingredients for top quality are certainly there, although early releases would have benefited from a bit more concentration.

The property centres around a large group of buildings halfway between the Roman city of Orange and Châteauneuf itself. It includes a nearby farm, Julienne, which now produces excellent goat's cheese. The estate was established, before the Revolution, by a Monsieur Julienne. Were he to return today, *le vieux* would undoubtedly be encouraged by what the new generation is doing.

LE VIEUX DONJON

This 13-ha domaine was created in 1979 with the marriage of Marie-José and Lucien Michel. As the children of *viticulteurs*, both brought vineyards to the union – she, 9ha near Courthézon, he, 4ha nearer Châteauneuf, from parents who combined wine and cask-making with wine transport,

Lucien's father had registered "Vieux Donjon" as a brand and sold wine under that name from 1966. There is no dungeon, young or old: the name was inspired by Lucien *père*'s view of the ruined castle from the family home on the west side of the village. Marie-José is a charming and slightly-built blonde with a ready sense of humour and two children – a girl of twelve years, and a son of five.

The Michel *vignoble* is divided into eight different parcels, including 10ha of vines over 80 years old – mainly on the Pied Long plateau opposite Mont-Redon

and Cabrières. Here, heavy *galets roulés* soils need specially powerful tractor engines to plough and are ruinously destructive of hoes.

In 1988 they planted a hectare of white varieties on th Cabrières plateau – a third each of Roussanne, Clairette and Grenache Blanc. This is what Marie-José describes as "our cooler land", and it is harvested first. These vines produced their first commercial harvest of 5,000 bottles in 1993.

Vineyard treatments are kept to a minimum, using only Bordeaux mixture and sulphur. They are horrified at people

in Châteauneuf "who spray regularly every Monday". Harvesting is late, and very careful: each Michel picker has two separate buckets – one for good bunches, the other for sub-standard ones.

They have employed the same, now retired, people from nearby Sorgue at harvest for years; "they are lovely, they lunch in the garden and sing – we all burst laughing. We even have some old clients from Paris who come to pick just to laugh". The younger brigade can't keep pace with two of the old ladies – one of them aged 80, the other 89.

The style of wine is unashamedly

VARIETY	VINEYARD	DETAILS	AREA
GRENACHE	LE PIED LONG	80 yr old vines	4.70
SYRAH	LE PIED LONG	7 yr old vines	0.45
MOURVEDRE	LE PIED LONG	7 yr old vines	0.50
GRENACHE	PIED DE BAUD	80 yr old vines	1.67
GRENACHE	BOIS DE BOURSAN	40 yr old vines	0.63
GRENACHE	LE MOURRE DE GAUD	80 yr old vines	1.57
GRENACHE	CHAMPIGNE	30 yr old vines	1.00
SYRAH	CABRIERES	5 yr old vines	0.67
ROUSSANNE, CLAIRETTE & GRENACHE BLANC	CABRIERES	5 yr old vines	1.00
		TOTAL (hectares):	12.19

"*traditionnelle*" – *vins de garde* with plenty of backbone and muscle to them. However, these are no clumsy blockbusters, but wines with real definition and elegance underneath powerful exteriors. Old vines and late harvesting contribute much to overall concentration and to the invariably low yields – 30hl/ha in 1990; 20hl/ha in 1991 and 26hl/ha in 1992.

As one might expect from *la tradition*, there is no de-stemming here – just light crushing and a touch of whole bunches in the vats (especially in less rich years). "We prefer our Châteauneuf with plenty of structure – none of this light wine"; they also prefer grape-skin tannin to new oak, so the wine is matured in *foudres*.

Since most of the plantings are old and therefore mixed, it is impractical to consider vinifying each grape variety separately; so everything is mixed in the vats, as it is picked. Anyway, Lucien considers that the wine achieves a much greater harmony and aromatic development if "everything's cooked together". Although Marie-José is a cellular biologist by training ("which is no use at all here") and although Lucien went through technical college, "which is very useful", the couple enlist the help of an oenologist – Monsieur Paulin – to make their wines.

A longish *cuvaison* leads to 18–30 months in *foudres*. Evaluation is complicated by the fact of several bottlings of each vintage – often extending over a year. Cost, especially in view of a recently-built cellar, seems to preclude a single *mise*. Lucien and Marie-José Michel clearly don't believe that this significantly changes the wine. However, a single bottling, at a time determined entirely by the wine's evolution, would be distinctly preferable and would certainly make assessment easier.

These are well-constituted wines with great depth and extract, which manage to retain finesse. This is relatively rare in an appellation where size and clumsiness abound and one frequently looks in vain for subtlety. Not here, where there is real quality and charm which, even in lesser vintages like 1991, needs long cellaring to come to fruition. The white, from their hectare of young vines, is fresh and promising: for early drinking.

Sales of Le Vieux Donjon are not a problem for Marie-José and Lucien Michel. One can taste why.

DOMAINE DU VIEUX TELEGRAPHE

Vieux Télégraphe is one of the few large Châteauneuf estates with its vineyards in virtually one block. Here, on the Plateau des Craux, in the south-east corner of the appellation adjoining Bédarrides, lie 70ha of vines. The estate was built up principally by Jules Brunier during the early part of the 20th century and further extended by his son Henri after World War II.

Since 1988, Henri's sons Daniel and Frédéric have been in charge – capable and thoughtful men, determined to improve on the standards set by their father. In 1986 they bought the somewhat run-down, 30-ha Chateauneuf Domaine de la Roquette, which they are busy re-establishing.

Vieux Télégraphe's *encépagement* is 70% Grenache, 15% Syrah and 15% Mourvèdre, with a touch of Cinsaut, largely planted on 15cm of *galets roulés* – some of the stoniest soil in the appellation – on top of 1.2 metres of cultivatable soil. Beneath this lies impenetrable red clay – an excellent water reservoir protecting the vines from drought. The gently-sloping plateau is exposed north-south at an elevation of 120 metres – the same as that of the château at Châteauneuf. It was on this hill in 1792 that Claude Chappe, the inventor of the optical telegraph, erected one of his relay towers. The original tower is long gone, but the name "Vieux Télégraphe" remains.

Even this nearly disappeared altogether, when Jules' brother – a person of normally exemplary financial acumen – in an aberrant moment, ceded the name "Vieux Télégraphe" to Louis Reynaud of Château Rayas. It was young Henri who

Daniel Brunier – quality control at Vieux Télégraphe.

convinced his uncle of his folly, persuaded him to rescind the contract and reconciled the brothers, who by then had fallen out.

The domaine's guiding principle is that you have no business making wine from sub-standard grapes. Fortunately, the plateau soils ripen grapes a week in advance of the rest of the sector, enabling the Bruniers to harvest early – with a severe *trie* to maximise concentration. In years of significant late-September rain, such as 1993, this early ripening is an important advantage.

Vine age – the average is 40 years old, with a third 60–65 years old – also plays a role in determining quality, lowering yields and increasing concentration. "It's better", argues Daniel, "to have 30hl/ha regularly than 50hl/ha from young vines which need green-pruning and 25hl/ha from old vines. Never forget, we are in the South of France – vines suffer far less from drought than elsewhere".

The *cuverie*, for processing these carefully-selected grapes, is a model of considered practicality. Refitted at vast expense in 1979, it is cut into the hillside behind the roaring Autoroute du Soleil, a mere 14 metres away. The vertical drop allows grapes to flow by gravity into a battery of vats arranged on either side. The press travels from vat to vat on its private railway track, recently extended outside to dump the residue, so that the juice is not contaminated by grape-flies.

Only the young vines, and sometimes the Mourvèdre and part of the Syrah crop, are de-stemmed; never the old Grenache. Given even ripeness, the varieties are fermented together.

Vieux Télégraphe red is a selection of the best wine, a process which starts at vintage and may not be finalised until a year later. "We are in no hurry". The Bruniers are determined that Vieux Télégraphe will always reach a certain quality standard, and equally that they need 200,000 bottles of it each year to meet demand. A juggling act indeed. They are vehemently against the "*cuvée spéciale*" trend – "Vieux Télégraphe is our *cuvée spéciale*" – preferring to turn the concept on its head with a second label. This, Vieux Mas des Papes, takes its name from Daniel's house, a 1920s construction among the family vines. As with everything Châteauneuf, from barrels to stones, the marketing opportunity of a Papal association, however tenuous, is not to be lost.

There is no new wood here; the wines generally spend a year in neutral *cuves*, followed by 8–9 months in old wooden *foudres*, with periodic rackings to conserve fruit and to eliminate any *gout de reduit*. The aim is for suppleness in youth – "we don't like austere young wines" – and enough structure for longish ageing. This is a fine line to draw – but they generally manage it.

To retain brand image, Vieux Télégraphe (but not Vieux Mas) is kept out of "*les grandes surfaces*" – the huge supermarkets, which in France now sell everything from Yquem and Lafite to *vin de table*. There is plenty to sell – red production runs at some 25,000 cases of which around 18,000 are Vieux Télégraphe. There are also some 1,200 cases of a worthy Télégraphe white, produced from a mix of 30% Grenache Blanc, 40% Clairette; 15% each Bourboulenc and Roussanne – 85% of the latter being vinified in 2- to 3-year-old *barriques*. Bottling for the whites takes place in the spring following the vintage. The white wine is rarely floral in character, but has a distinctive strong, earthy, mineral aspect. In 1993 the Bruniers planted two additional hectares using all the permitted white varieties – no "*vin de cépage*" here! This will probably end up as Vieux Mas blanc.

The quality of Vieux Télégraphe has improved considerably from the frequently over-alcoholic, burly wines of the Seventies and early Eighties. Although varying in density, structure and flavour with the vintages – sometimes spice and liquorice, sometimes the softer summer red-fruits (raspberry tones in the 1993 Grenache, for example), Vieux Télégraphe is generally seductive and fleshy, with finesse and concentrated ripe fruit. Sometimes the search for both youthful appeal and durability may give the taster the feeling that neither is really achieved; however this, in the main, is a fine estate – not the home of blockbuster *vins de garde*, but rather a stable of classy thoroughbreds.

VARIETY	APPELLATION	DETAILS	AREA
GRENACHE	CHATEAUNEUF	Average vine age: 45	49.00
SYRAH	CHATEAUNEUF	Average vine age: 25	7.00
MOURVEDRE	CHATEAUNEUF	Average vine age: 25	7.00
CINSAUT	CHATEAUNEUF	Average vine age: 30	3.00
GRENACHE BLANC, CLAIRETTE, ROUSSANNE, BOURBOULENC	CHATEAUNEUF	Average vine age: 20	6
		TOTAL (hectares):	72.00

La Brouette; state-of-the-art incinerator for vine prunings.

GIGONDAS & VACQUEYRAS

Beneath the jagged Montmirail escarpment lies a band of some of the most attractive wine villages in France: Sablet, Cairanne, Séguret, Rasteau, Gigondas, Vacqueyras and Beaumes-de-Venise. Set off by a backdrop of *garrigue* and soft, tree-clad hillsides, their vineyards cover the plains and intermediate slopes and reach high into the hills.

Before the memorably destructive frosts of 1929 and 1956, olive trees dominated the landscape. Their livelihood largely obliterated by these disasters, farmers turned to the vine for income, mixing viticulture with olive- and fruit-growing. Between 1966 and the early 1980s wine production surged, Gigondas plantings alone exploding from 400 to 1,200ha. Most of the appellation land is now planted, although growers continue to clear some of the more inhospitable corners below the spiky Dentelles de Montmirail.

From the 19th century, Gigondas' reputation for the "warmth" of its wines led to a strong demand from Burgundy *négociants* for Gigondas in bulk for blending. From Chambertin to Corton, cutting with Châteauneuf or Gigondas was commonplace, less favoured *crus* getting cheaper, gut-scorching North African instead.

However, by 1949 a few enlightened growers, notably Amadieu, Roux and Edmond Chauvet, realising that Gigondas had abundant merit of its own, were already domaine-bottling.

Gigondas, which was granted full AC status in 1971, has a population of 700, of whom 650 are essentially dependent on wine. Of 205 listed growers, 80 make and bottle their own wine, accounting for 70% of the production, and 125 produce the remaining 30% through cooperatives.

Vacqueyras, which was only recently promoted to AC (in 1990 and retrospectively for the 1988 and 1989 vintages), has 539ha under vine (1994), of an authorised maximum of 1,690, owned by 160 growers – of whom only 27 make and bottle their own wine. Here *négociants* and cooperativess account for 68% of all bottle sales.

The Gigondas AC rules permit only red, or rosé from *saignée,* whereas Vacqueyras growers can make white wine as well.

Geologically, Gigondas and Vacqueyras are broadly similar, their vineyards lying in a band across three principal soil types at altitudes from 100 to 400m. On the plains the soil is a mix of stones and alluvial deposits with significant clay content; on the lower slopes there is sandy *molasse,* while the later-ripening higher terraces have *molasse* with a high scree-limestone

and yellow clay content on *marne* rock. Towards Sarrians in the south the soils become stonier, while nearer Sablet to the north there are outcrops of blue and red clay. These generalities hide a wide diversity: the lower slopes tending to have richer, redder soils, often on a bedrock of an impermeable, impacted sand known locally as *safre*, while in the high vineyards soils are poorer.

Growers attribute much of the finesse and elegance of their wines to the relatively light sandy soils, which both retain heat and help the vine resist drought, whereas the richer *terre rouge* of the plains brings body, warmth and richness. Ripening down here is usually two to three weeks ahead of the Dentelles terraces.

Convinced of the importance of Grenache to the typicity of their wine, Gigondas growers persuaded the authorities to raise the maximum proportion of this grape, from 1986, from 65% to 80%. The aim is to reduce plantings of Cinsaut, a grape which produces large quantities of thin wine, and to increase the proportions of Syrah and Mourvèdre.

These latter, together or separately, must now make up 15% of a grower's plantings; however, since the rules apply to the vineyard and not to the contents of the vats, proportions vary widely in finished wines. Theoretically, the rules permit a Gigondas from 100% Syrah, though you are unlikely to find one.

This increase in the permitted proportion of Grenache is controversial, since many believe that better structures derive from a higher proportion of "improver" grapes, such as Syrah and Mourvèdre, than the rules currently allow. Traditionalists point out that the reputation of Gigondas was built on a mildly-oxidised Grenache-based style – and, fine as other blends may be, they are not what Gigondas is about. However, many of the growers value such "improvers" – Mourvèdre in particular, for its anti-oxidant properties which balance the all-too-easily oxidizing Grenache.

More controversy has erupted over some growers' use of new barrels rather than larger old casks for maturation. Jean-Pierre Cartier, the first of the few, recalls his *confrères'* derision – "it isn't Gigondas you are making", they told him. "That annoyed me", he added. "In any case, they'll all be at it soon, but I'll have several years' start!".

Indeed, several domaines are dipping their toes in the water, notably Font Sane (qv) and Daniel Brusset at Cairanne. The debate is sterile: typical Gigondas

indeed comes from a high-Grenache blend, matured in large, old wood; fine, if not finer, wine comes from a higher proportion of Syrah and Mourvèdre, partly matured in small wood. Which style triumphs can only be determined by the market.

Apart from the estates profiled here, much excellent Gigondas and Vacqueyras is sold by the large merchant houses. Jaboulet produce fine versions of both, and Guigal a sound, though occasionally disappointing, Gigondas.

Styles vary from more elegant, lighter wines – exemplified by the Chapalains' Domaine de Longue Toque – through the sturdier offerings of Les Pallières and Michel Faraud's Domaine de Cayron, to the heavier-framed wines of Grapillon d'Or, Jean-Pierre Cartier's Les Goubert and Clos des Cazaux.

The range is broad, but the best share a mouthfilling, southerly *ampleur* which is abundantly satisfying.

Gigondas is an attractive, compact little village. Visit it for the views over the Ouvèze plain, westwards towards Châteauneuf, or to taste samples poured from screw-topped quarter bottles in the well-stocked Caveau des Vignerons – or better still to lunch on the vine-shaded terrace at Les Florets, where the tranquillity of the surrounding hills will enhance the senses and sharpen the appetite for eating outdoors in the warm afternoon sunshine.

AC GIGONDAS

Created	6 January 1971
Area (max)	n/a
Area under vine 1994	1,127
Base yield	35hl/ha
Minimum alcohol	12.5% (R); 12% (RO)
Growers	205

AC VACQUEYRAS

Created	9 August 1990
Area (max)	1,690ha
Area under vine 1994	539ha
Base yield	35hl/ha
Minimum alcohol	12.5% (R); 12% (W/RO)
Growers	160

DOMAINE DE CAYRON

Michel Faraud – an enthusiastic, hyper-active man in his 40s – runs this excellent domaine in the middle of Gigondas village. "I have only one product," he explains, "Gigondas". No *cuvée prestige* here, no Côtes du Rhône, nothing but a line of finely-crafted Gigondas. It was his father who decided to plant vines after many of the family's olive trees were lost in the catastrophic frosts of 1956.

The domaine's vines are scattered in small plots all over the appellation. However, it is those high up at 500m, near the Col du Cayron, which produce the finest wine and from which the estate takes its name. Here are both Grenache and Cinsaut – the latter "magnificent – but very small yields", which are invariably the last of the domaine's vines to ripen.

The global *encépagement* is roughly 70% Grenache, 15% Syrah and 15% Cinsaut with an average age of 40. *Les officiels* turned up one day recently and told Michel that he needed to add some Mourvèdre to his holdings to conform with AC rules – which clearly annoyed him, since he makes one of the finest wines in the appellation. "I don't like Mourvèdre, so I'm going to plant a bit, but on poor land", he smiles. Clearly the authorities will have a Pyrrhic victory on their hands.

Faraud *père*, who still lives in the old house, on top of the cellars, only started selling in bottle in the early 1950s – often without labels. His wines found favour and a stream of regular clients developed. Michel learned to make wine with his father and is determined not to bend to any modern technological ways or to change their style. "I always watched '*le père*', and still do things in the same way. We won't adapt to the client, its my wine, not theirs", he explains, irritated by importers telling him to put some wine in new wood or to make a *cuvée prestige*.

The cellars beneath *le père* are a mixture of old and new. Vinification and maturation are carried out in a series of underground concrete vats and large oak *foudres* in the original cellars – cramped, possibly, but they work. Temperature control is difficult because the *cuves* are below floor level, cemented into the hillside, so it simply doesn't happen.

The winemaking is straightforward with around 15 days *cuvaison* "to extract colour and matter; people who leave it eight or nine days get nothing in their wine". Syrah is fermented separately – if there isn't enough to fill the *cuve*, some Cinsaut is added. The press wine is added back and the various lots are assembled, sometime after malolactic, and then given 12-24 months in large *foudres*. This interval is determined as much by the moment at which each *foudre* is bottled off as by any quality considerations.

Michel tends to bottle 20hl at a time – "so the wine remains as long in wood as possible", he explains, although one suspects it is as much a matter of cost (bottles, corks etc) and of space than anything else. Perhaps with the new bottle cellar things will change and there will be fewer bottlings of each vintage. Inevitably, Michel admits that the first and last bottlings differ in taste and aroma – "you should buy at the end, the wine is much better". In April 1994, there was still some 1991 in wood.

Michel is a voluble man: slightly defensive perhaps, but passionate about his work and his quest for quality. He has no cause for anxiety: his 40–55,000 bottles of Gigondas are among the best to be had. Whatever the vintage – even the difficult 1992 and 1991 – he manages to achieve a richness and silkiness which make for a very seductive mouthful. His old vines add a dimension of "*fond*" which adds weight to the palate and increases complexity.

His family all pitch in to help, including his wife. They have three daughters, the eldest an accountant, the middle one with a viticultural and oenological qualification and a 15-year-old who helps out in the vineyards in her school holidays. This is a fine small family estate, whose wines are well worth searching out.

VARIETY	APPELLATION	DETAILS	AREA
GRENACHE	GIGONDAS	40 yrs average vine-age	9.80
SYRAH	GIGONDAS	40 yrs average vine-age	2.10
CINSAULT	GIGONDAS	40 yrs average vine-age	2.10
		TOTAL (hectares):	14.00

DOMAINE CLOS DES CAZAUX

Otherwise known as Domaine Archimbaud-Vache – from a maternal Archimbaud and a paternal Vache – this estate has been going for five generations. The estate is now run with panache, and fruitful innovation, by a partnership between parents and son. The older generation, Monsieur and Madame Vache, started making wine on their own account in 1980. A decade later, they were joined by their son, Jean-Michel, fresh from two disillusioning years at Montpellier: "I learned nothing about vinification and only a little about marketing; I came back and learnt how to make wine like my father – he knows ten times more than any oenologist".

Armed with this healthy distrust of the schoolmen, and an inquisitive turn of mind, this clear-headed young man is stamping his personality on the Clos des Cazaux. The focus of the enterprise is an attractive home-cum-office-cum-cellar-shop-cum-vinification facility with a magnificent view over the Dentelles de Montmirail. Surrounding this is a 20ha plot of Vacqueyras, including the Clos des Cazaux – vines over 80 years old on a slope immediately behind the house. They also own 20ha of vines in the mountains of Gigondas. They have recently built a large cellar-*cuverie*, dug into the adjoining hillside – a somewhat incongruous adjunct to their 19th-century house; functionality before aesthetics.

The overriding philosophy is to tailor their methods as far as is practicable to the individual vine, site and soil: "it's like adapting to the person you are meeting". Two generations of detailed and exacting work have gone into efforts to isolate different soil types in both appellations.

In Vacqueyras they have a broadly clay-limestone mix giving onto *safre* – a white/yellow highly permeable sand, which does not help in drought years such as 1989.

In Gigondas, the soils are a compound of broken limestone scree and blue clay with some ferruginous clay-limestone. The vines are relatively young – "*vieilles*

APPELLATION	DETAILS	AREA
GIGONDAS	Mountain vineyards	20.00
VACQUEYRAS	One block; includes plot of 80+ yr-old Grenache and 30–40 yr-old Syrah	20.00
	TOTAL (hectares):	40.00

vignes" here means 30 years old – so varieties are grown and harvested in separate parcels. As Vacqueyras grapes mature some two weeks before Gigondas, this allows more selective picking and fermenting.

Adapting vine to site is also well-studied: Mourvèdre is planted on south-facing slopes for better sun exposure, yet yields only average 18hl/ha; Syrah is deliberately sited on north parts of slopes where soils are cooler and ripening longer and more even. "Grenache is everywhere else", laughs Jean-Michel.

In the cellar "we intervene as little as possible", yet "sure, we put some of our personality in the wines". There is no de-stemming – "it would shock the berries" – and no crushing beyond that which occurs naturally; the must is cooled to 20°C as a pre-fermentive maceration to extract glycerol and to release aroma precursors – "for this the *cuve* must be stable".

Alcoholic fermentation lasts four to six days, giving a total *cuvaison* of 15 days for Grenache, and half this for Syrah, whose fermentation vigour is akin to spontaneous combustion: "Syrah here is not a ferment – it's a bomb", explains Jean-Michel. The press wine, extracted by a 1950s Vaslin, is added back and by the end of the winter, the Vaches have an idea of what the final *assemblage* for each wine will look like. Further corrections may follow, with extra Syrah or Mourvèdre being added as the *cuves* evolve.

A severe green pruning means that even a weaker vintage such as 1991 has the natural constitution to withstand at least two years' *élevage*, which, because the Vaches dislike wood ("I hate oak – I like the wine for the wine"), happens entirely in *cuve*. Half of the 1991 crop was left in the vineyards, 60% of the 1992. After so long in vat, there is no need to fine and filter.

This commitment to quality is reflected in the wines. Apart from a softish, fresh, greengagey white Vacqueyras and a Côtes du Rhône rosé, the domaine has four individual red *cuvées*.

There is a Reserve Vacqueyras, from equal parts younger Grenache and Syrah vines, destined principally for the restaurant market; spicy and not without character, a wine for two to three years' ageing. Next comes the Vacqueyras Cuvée St-Roch – 65% Grenache, 30% Syrah, 15% Cinsaut – to which vines over 50 years old contribute structure and concentration.

The Vacqueyras Cuvée Spéciale des Templiers comes entirely from 30- to 40-year-old Syrah vines, the original cuttings for which came from the Chaves at Mauves (qv). This tends to present as a deep limpid red-purple in youth, with plenty of aroma; the 1990 – "the best Templiers we have ever made" – is a remarkably fine wine. The sole Gigondas representative, called La Tour Sarrazine, is a top-notch example.

This is a fine, confident domaine which richly deserves the success that it evidently enjoys.

DOMAINE ROGER COMBE

There have been Combes in the region ever since Etienne Combe arrived at Montmirail and bought land in 1634. The present incumbent, Roger, a wiry, rather shy man, his wife, forthcoming and capable, and their daughter, Marie-Thérèse, own 30ha in Gigondas and Vacqueyras inherited from both sides of the family. These are sold as L'Oustau Fauquet (Gigondas) and La Fourmone (Vacqueyras and Côtes du Rhône).

Madame Combe presides over matters financial with every impression of iron rigour, while Roger and Marie-Thérèse confine themselves to the cellar.

Roger is utterly traditional, from his grape mix (70-80% Grenache, 15% Syrah and 5% Mourvèdre), through fermentation (no de-stemming, 8-15 days' *cuvaison* in old cement *cuves*) to *élevage* (one year in *cuve*, then another in *foudres*) to bottling (in 50-hl lots, as and when needed). Sales are largely to passing trade and restaurants, with a mite of export thrown in.

Roger and Marie-Thérèse make good wines – a trio of evocatively-named Vacqueyras: the Poet's Treasure, a light wine for early drinking; the Cellar Master's Selection, a more robust, deeper wine meriting a few years in bottle; and (from the excellent 1990) Les Ceps d'Or, a prestige *cuvée* from old Grenache vines – some of them centenarians.

There are a pair of Gigondas: l'Oustau Fauquet, the standard *cuvée*, containing all three grape varieties, and Cuvée Cigaloun – an 85% Grenache and 15% Mourvèdre *assemblage* from selected parcels, mainly of old vines.

There are also a red and white Côtes du Rhône and a couple of red *vins de table*, for which locals appear armed with plastic flagons which are filled directly from the vat via a pump. A weighing machine stands ready to settle any disputes about measure from cunning customers who turn up with non-standard receptacles, presumably hoping that Roger won't notice. A forlorn hope: he's been at it since 1964.

The wines are very good, in the early-drinking mould, with plenty of warm, ripe, mouthfilling fruit and reasonable complexity; not perhaps up to Michel Faraud or Archimbaud Vache, but attractive and reliable. The two *cuvées prestiges* – Ceps d'Or and Cigaloun – which only appear in the best vintages, provide the real interest. They offer much more density, a tighter frame and greater length. Not for keeping 20 years, but well worth forgetting about for ten.

Roger seems set to hand over to his dark-haired, lively daughter, although he probably realises that traditionalists never entirely retire. When that time comes, Marie-Thérèse would do well to review the "no-destemming" policy: stems bring nothing of value, and add a hint of grassy bitterness. This, and perhaps the merest hint of new wood for the top *cuvées*, would surely put the Combe wines into the first division.

APPELLATION	VARIETY	DETAILS	AREA
GIGONDAS	GRENACHE	Qtr LE PETIT MONTMIRAIL; oldest vines c 50 yrs	8.00
GIGONDAS	MOURVEDRE	Qtr LE PETIT MONTMIRAIL	1.50
GIGONDAS	SYRAH	Qtr LE PETIT MONTMIRAIL	0.50
VACQUEYRAS	GRENACHE	Qtr LE PARC (around 1 ha of centenarian vines)	16.00
VACQUEYRAS	SYRAH	Qtr LE PARC	3.00
VACQUEYRAS	MOURVEDRE	Qtr LE PARC	1.00
		TOTAL (hectares):	30.00

DOMAINE DE FONT-SANE

It is unusual to find a woman making the wine in this part of France, but Véronique Cunty, married to a local forester, doesn't appear to find this exceptional. Her father, Georges Peysson, helps her with their 10ha of Gigondas, 4ha of Côtes du Rhône and Côtes de Ventoux, from which they make an excellent range.

"Font-Sane" is named either after a *quartier* or after the Fontaine-Saine, a local water source.

The cream of this cellar are the two Gigondas – a good, firm, standard bottling, from a mix which reflects the domaine's *encépagement*: 70–80% Grenache, 20–25% Syrah plus a touch of Mourvèdre and Cinsaut, and the special Cuvée Fûtée which was first introduced in 1986.

The Fûtée represents a selection from their 30 different plots at Gigondas, comprising 60–65% Grenache and 35–40% Syrah – the precise proportions depending on the vintage. The wine is only released in good years (1986, '88, '89, '90 and 1991 so far; 1993 under discussion at time of writing), and is limited to 3,800–4,000 bottles. There is no de-stemming, 8–12 days' *cuvaison*, fermentation at a relatively high 33–34°C and an *élevage* of 12 months in *cuve* and a further 8–12 months in new and second-year Vosges and Nevers casks.

The Gigondas vines are on two different *terroirs*: 4ha lie at the foot of the Dentelles, on clay-limestone soils facing north and south – in fact much in the *lieu-dit* Font-Sane – while 6ha lie on the sandier, stonier soils of the flatter, lower-lying land below the village.

The vines average 30–40 years of age, with a few *ares* being replanted each year. There is a two- to three-week difference in ripening of the Dentelles hectares and the plains land – the latter ripens earlier, so harvesting is an extended matter. However, the plantings are a field mix, so apart from the odd patch of Syrah, there is no question of separate vinification for each *cépage*. Yields average 28–30hl/ha; Madame Cunty says that they never get to the appellation maximum of 35hl/ha.

The Cuvée Fûtée, in particular, is most attractive and well worth its price. The impact of the small wood was still evident on the palate of the 1990, and indeed in 1994 dominated it; in general, wood, grape and stalk tannins all contribute to a masculine wine.

There is a new generation emerging at Font-Sane today – two children and a clutch of carefully crafted wines. Véronique Cunty and her father are a fine, conscientious team.

VARIETY	APPELLATION	AREA
GRENACHE	GIGONDAS	7.00
SYRAH	GIGONDAS	2.00
CINSAULT + MOURVEDRE	GIGONDAS	1.00
VARIOUS REDS	GIGONDAS	4.00
	TOTAL (hectares):	14.00

DOMAINE LA GARRIGUE

This estate, like many throughout the Rhône Valley, is a family enterprise. If you arrive at the right moment, you are likely to find several generations of hospitable Bernards in the small office attached to the cellars. Here is *père* Albert Bernard, a large jowled man with a sun-spotted visage, squeezed uncomfortably into a chair that is far too small for his frame, knees tucked under an equally inadequate desk, shuffling around various bits of correspondence in a dogged, desultory fashion. At a table alongside one daughter is typing, while *la mère* Bernard appears from another door to see what's going on. Here is Pierre Bernard, one of two sons who has taken over day-to-day running of the domaine – a smart, precise man, with an eye for quality. In comes his brother, in goloshes and overalls, fresh from the vineyards – the work must go on despite the rain and the gusting mistral. Finally another daughter appears in the overcrowded office with her two children – her son with an arm in plaster (he broke it playing, but doesn't look the sort to be deterred by such a minor inconvenience). The family is complete: the wheels are turning.

The Bernards have 70ha in all, 45 owned outright and 25 *en fermage* of which "far too little" are in Gigondas. Twenty years ago they reconstructed many of their vineyards, to reduce the proportion of Grenache in conformity with the AC rules, which require a minimum of 25% of other varieties. The domaine's heart is in Vacqueyras — where, along a seemingly interminable track, punctuated by just enough encouraging signposts, it is headquartered. They like old vines – the average age here is over 40, with some over 60. The soils are "a bit of everything", but mainly clay-limestone with some smaller *galets*.

A variety of wines are produced, including a plump, old-fashioned, oxidative-style white Vacqueyras, a substantial Vacqueyras rosé and a fine Côtes du Rhône, Cuvée Romaine: a Grenache/Syrah blend, the proportions vary from 75:25 to 50:50 depending on the vintage. In less good vintages, they may declassify part of the Vacqueyras crop into Côtes du Rhône.

Despite a short *cuvaison* of non-destemmed grapes the wines are true *vins de garde* – just what the Bernards want. A minimum of two years in *cuve* for all the reds, even the Côtes du Rhône, is followed by bottling without either fining or filtration: "we bought a filter for the whites because we have to bottle this before the end of the year; otherwise we wouldn't filter this either".

The best wines in this cellar are the red Vacqueyras and Gigondas, of which there is more of the former. The Cuvée Romaine (first released in 1982) is partnered by a Vacqueyras prestige bottling, Cuvée Vignoble, which arrived in 1984. This has slightly less Grenache than the standard Vacqueyras and a good, strengthening dollop (25%) of Syrah. The Bernards have just taken on another property, with some Grenache Blanc planted which will add character to their white Vacqueyras, which has hitherto contained only Clairette.

The wines in this burgeoning range are useful for the family's excellent restaurant, Les Florets, in the hills above Gigondas, which is managed by Pierre. The Bernards of La Garrigue are a fine source of the region's wines.

APPELLATION	VARIETY	DETAILS	AREA
GIGONDAS	75% Grenache; 15% Syrah; 10% Cinsault + others	Mainly 45–60 year-old vines	3.00
VACQUEYRAS	75% Grenache; 15% Syrah; 5% Cinsault; 5% Mourvedre	Grenache 45–60 year-old vines, rest c.25	58.00
VCC	(Vin de consommation courant)	(Vines at Ouveze)	9.00
		TOTAL (hectares):	70.00

DOMAINE LES GOUBERT

Jean-Pierre Cartier is proud that he was the first Gigondas *vigneron* to use new wood as a matter of policy. As the present successor in a lineage which stretches back father to son to 1636, he probably felt an obligation to add something personal to his heritage. The family house – also 1636 – was the first to be built outside the walls of Gigondas (at that time a fortified village), and lies in the *quartier* Goubert, which gives the estate its name.

As succession law in France dictates, Jean-Pierre and his sister shared the family inheritance of 6ha of vines. Fortunately, his slim, dark-haired wife Mireille, brought with her 1.5ha of Sablet, and several subsequent additions have brought the domaine up to its present 21ha. These are scattered across four appellations: Gigondas, Beaumes de Venise (red), Sablet (red and white) and Côtes du Rhône (red and white). The Cartier vines are consequently somewhat fragmented – 40 different plots in all.

The white Côtes du Rhône is especially interesting, being 100% Viognier. The AC rules do not permit a Côtes du Rhône-Villages from a single *cépage*, so the wine is sold as plain Côtes du Rhône. Jean-Pierre admits to a passion for Condrieu, of which he is making a more than passable imitation. For the 1992 vintage, half the Viognier was vinified in *cuve*, half in cask. In 1993, vinification started off in *cuve* then, once fermentation had started the must was transferred to casks – seven new, five older. He tried a touch of *bâtonnage* in 1993 and professes himself pleased with the outcome: "yes, it gives more fat and finesse", so presumably this will continue. Twelve *pièces,* neatly stacked together in Jean-Pierre's cramped cellar, are all there is – 330 cases.

Tasting this Viognier from a variety of wood origins, it is clear how much oak can change the face of this distinctive, yet delicate grape. New Allier oak gave a more floral, *pain grillé* tone to the nose, and left a dry, hardish edge on the palate; whereas the Tronçais emphasised the grape's hallmark dried-fruit aromas and imparted a defined spicy element to the palate. The second-year cask gave both the nose and the palate of the Tronçais, but added a finer balance of acidity which better upheld the delicacy one always seeks in a Viognier as a foil for its natural power. A fine result – and, at 55 francs including tax per bottle at the farm gate, something to worry the men of Condrieu.

The soils which nurture Jean-Pierre's Gigondas are varied: sand round the house, red gravels in the lower part of *quartier* Les Pesquiers, and clay-limestone and stones in the higher, southeast-facing mountain vineyards. An order of picking has been determined to reflect each *terroir's* individuality. The rules don't permit machine harvesting, but neither do they specifically exclude it. Although he currently picks by hand, Jean-Pierre avers that he would rather have a good harvesting machine which he drove personally, than a team of incompetent pickers.

Lack of vat space in the cellar means that vinification of the Côtes du Rhône has to be shortened to accommodate later, more senior, arrivals. In rainy vintages, which need rapid harvesting, the problem is exacerbated. Perhaps he

Vineyards from the roof-tops of Séguret.

should stop buying vineyards and turn his cash-hose on the *cuverie*!

There is no compromise, however, on the vinification of the Sablet, Beaumes de Venise and Gigondas reds. Here Jean-Pierre knows exactly what he is after: long *cuvaisons* – at up to 31 days among the longest in the appellation – and temperatures rising to 32°C to maximise extraction. "I have no cooling apparatus", he confesses, "I just draw off the juice and store it in stainless steel overnight to cool and then put it back" – simple, and presumably effective. The type and length of *élevage* depends on the wine.

Everything except the special Gigondas Cuvée Florence is kept in concrete vats to clear space for the new vintage – the Côtes du Rhônes for 11 months, the regular Gigondas for 23 months (for the same reason, one year on).

Cuvée Florence appeared, together with Jean-Pierre's eponymous bright-eyed, red-headed daughter, in 1985. As she pits her wits against some French grammar, her 1993 is reposing in a

APPELLATION	VARIETY	DETAILS	AREA
GIGONDAS	62% Grenache noir, 25% Syrah, 9% Mourvedre, 3% Cinsault, 1% Clairette	Vine-age, 4–50 yrs	8.70
COTES DU RHONE VILLAGES, BEAUMES DE VENISE	65% Grenache noir, 26% Syrah, 9% Cinsault	Vine-age, 4–50 yrs	3.51
COTES DU RHONE VILLAGES, SABLET (Rouge)	65% Grenache noir, 13% Syrah, 13% Mourvedre, 9% Cinsault	Vine-age, 4–50 yrs	2.88
COTES DU RHONE VILLAGES, SABLET (Blanc)	58% Clairette, 25% Roussanne, 17% Bourboulenc	Vine-age, 4–50 yrs	1.38
COTES DU RHONE (Rouge)	84% Grenache noir, 16% Carignan	Vine-age, 4–50 yrs	3.59
COTES DU RHONE (Blanc)	100% Viognier	Vine-age, 4–50 yrs	1.05
		TOTAL (hectares):	21.11

mixture of Vosges, Nevers and Tronçais casks in the cellar below her desk – 56 in all, a quarter renewed annually.

After 9–18 months, the wine is fined with albumin, lightly filtered and bottled. Jean-Pierre would like to suppress the filtration but, he moans, "the market won't take it". He should try!

In style, the Cartier wines are substantial items. "I want to make *vin de garde* –

wines with matter, above all; you notice you've drunk something. I often think it would be simpler to make supple, easy-drinking wines, but it's no good – I can't work like that".

Florence rules the roost downstairs, as she probably does upstairs – a wine of great care and quality. She has some fine drinking to look forward to when she's finished her studying.

DOMAINE DE LA GRAPILLON D'OR

The mild-mannered, Dustin-Hoffman-lookalike Bernard Chauvet makes top-class Gigondas from 15ha of vines scattered over some 18 different plots. These vineyards encompass most of the appellation's varied soil-types: sand on the slopes; richer ground around the domaine itself and "poor and dry" *terre rouge* on the flatter land.

As for grape varieties, he has 80% Grenache (the maximum allowed by the AC rules), a touch of Cinsaut and 15% Syrah trained *en cordon*. He could have planted Mourvèdre, but preferred Syrah instead. Although the estate dates back to 1893 – they were the first in Gigondas to be awarded a Gold Medal in that very year – the varieties are planted separately, and not field-mixed, as was the prevailing tradition. As to age, "there is everything between 10 and 80", Bernard shrugs – "but the average is about 40".

Bernard and his wife live just below the village. In the *cuverie* beneath their house, Bernard consistently turns out splendidly deep, succulent wine – big, with plenty of concentrated ripe fruit, and long, warm, southerly flavours.

There are no secrets, not even especially low yields – "25–35hl/ha – it doesn't make any difference which, provided the grapes are healthy". There is only one *cuvée* – no prestige bottling or named wines here. Bernard's view is that

having more than one wine in the same appellation "is too difficult for the clientele". Plainly he has little confidence in the intelligence of his mainly French customers – or perhaps it's too difficult for Bernard!

Vinification is entirely classical – no quirks or tricks. No de-stemming, light crushing and 12–15 days *cuvaison*. Bernard believes that most extraction occurs during the first few days, so there is no point in prolonging this unduly. "We have no problem with colour", he says – the wines are fine evidence. There is only one pressing, in an old vertical screw-press, the wine from which is systematically added back.

Since 1990 Syrah and Grenache have been mixed during primary fermentation: this apparently gives better perfumes and "avoids lots of problems". The wines are assembled some six months later, since the malolactics may occur any time between fermentation and the following March. Then come 12 months of maturation in *foudres* followed by a year

in cement *cuves* and bottling with neither fining nor filtration; in all, two and a half years from vat to bottle.

When asked to explain how he manages to get so much richness and extract into his wine, Bernard suggests phlegmatically that the "low yields" might have something to do with it, but "I don't know exactly, it might be the long *cuvaison*… or possibly the *remontage*".

Tasting a range of the domaine's Gigondas, in their neat little *salle de reception* with the tiered glass case in the corner housing Bernard's collection of old corkscrews, the quality of the wines comes shining through. Delving into a dark recess in the back of the cellar, Bernard emerges with a bottle of 1985 – a maturing wine of great warmth and complexity.

Finally a 1981 appears – "we keep 50 bottles of each vintage", Bernard explains. These bottles are a fitting testament to the skill of this rather charming and laid-back *vigneron*. You won't get much finer Gigondas than this.

VARIETY	APPELLATION	DETAILS	AREA
GRENACHE	GIGONDAS	10–80 yr old vines	12.00
SYRAH	GIGONDAS	10–80 yr old vines	2.25
MOURVEDRE	GIGONDAS	10–80 yr old vines	0.75
VARIOUS RED VARIETIES	VACQUEYRAS	All wine sold in bulk	9.00
		TOTAL (hectares):	24.00

LES PALLIERES

When Rhône wine dynasties are discussed, it is invariably the 500-year unbroken succession of Chaves at Mauves which catches the imagination. Yet, the Roux family have been farming Les Pallières, in the hills between Gigondas and Les Sablets, from father to son since 1400. The present custodian, Pierre, a gentle, rather careworn and stooping man in his late sixties, well remembers his grandfather Hilarion (all Roux male children have this name somewhere) who died in 1933, and his grandmother, who gave the small family chapel that stands beside the family home to the parish of Gigondas. He was followed in turn by his son Joseph Hilarion, who sired three sons – Christian, who died in 1986, Maxim, a lawyer in Avignon who comes to help out occasionally, and Pierre. There are no direct heirs, all the brothers being bachelors; but "we'll find some cousins", Pierre muses, contemplating wistfully the succession to this fine estate.

In Grandfather's day, viticulture vied with olive and apricot production. However exceptionally harsh winters in 1929 and 1956 destroyed even these hardy trees throughout Vaucluse, and few of the 3,000 Roux *oliviers* survived. The family expanded their winemaking, increasing their vineyard to its current 25ha. This, all in one magnificent slab round Pierre's old house, consists of field-mixed plantings of roughly 65% Grenache, 17% Syrah, 15% Mourvèdre plus 3% of Cinsaut and "*divers*"; over half are 40- to 60-year-old vines. Joseph was in fact the first to plant Syrah in the appellation: when the commune was elevated from Côtes du Rhône to Côtes du Rhône-Villages, the rules required a greater proportion of *cépages ameliorateurs*, hence more Syrah and Mourvèdre.

The soils on this vineyard, set at 180 metres' altitude, are mountain in origin, chiefly clay-limestone rather than the gravelly *molasse* of the plains below, and highly water retentive; so the vines don't suffer in years of drought. Pierre reckons that the vine-roots penetrate two to three metres down. A well on the property provides crystal-clear drinking water – "from the mountains", Pierre remarks.

This is not an estate for cutting-edge technology; rather expect reliable, thoroughly well-made wines, with all the warmth and welcome of Pierre himself. He started working with Christian and their father in 1948 "when we left the regiment", so has nearly half a century of experience to tap. The Roux were, with

Pierre Roux.

the Chauvets and the Amadieus, pioneers of selling in bottle in 1949 and it was Joseph Hilarion who founded the Syndicat des Vignerons in Gigondas in 1931. Along with estate bottling went the continuing policy of only selling what is ready to drink. So the many visitors to the cellar door in 1994 would find the 1989 on offer, with the 1990 destined to come on stream in late 1995. Pierre tries to plan things so that when poor weather forces them to miss a vintage as happened in 1992 and 1987 there is enough stock to cover the deficiency.

Vinification is as unchanged as one imagines the neat *cuverie* to be, with its rows of red-edged, carefully polished *foudres* standing ready to be filled, or emptied. No destemming and 15–20 days' *cuvaison* help leach out maximum colour and tannin; "we vinify for *vins de garde*", adds Pierre, in case you might think they had gone mad and started making rosé for the picnic market. Maximum fermentation temperature is 35°C, and the first pressing is blended back before an *élevage* exclusively in *foudres* for at least 18–24 months. A single annual racking,

light fining and a plate filtration precede bottling, of which there may be up to five for any given vintage.

There is only one wine at Les Pallières, a Gigondas of fine quality. Usually sturdy, long-lived, warm and ripe, it strongly evokes the warm, wooded, Provençale hillsides from which it comes. Memorable bottles have been the 1981 and a superbly fine 1978, still going strong with no signs of premature senescence from a magnum in 1993. There seemed to be a drop in quality in the mid-late 1980s – Christian's death and Pierre's subsequent illness probably contributed to this – but the estate is now back on form. Current releases justify Pierre Roux's position in the top-rank of Gigondas *vignerons*.

VARIETY	APPELLATION	AREA
GRENACHE	GIGONDAS	16.25
SYRAH	GIGONDAS	4.25
MOURVEDRE	GIGONDAS	3.75
CINSAULT	GIGONDAS	0.50
DIVERSE REDS	GIGONDAS	0.25
	TOTAL (hectares):	25.00

DOMAINE LES PALLEROUDIAS

Edmond Burle is a middle-aged, cheerful, solid man, with quiffs of greying hair, who makes fine wine despite a series of misfortunes which would have buckled a less domitable spirit.

Some years ago he fell off his roof, severely damaging his spine. As a result, his wife and son went off – leaving him to run the estate and make his wine alone, helped only by a single vineyard labourer. This man returned home to Morocco for a holiday, after 23 years with Edmond, and decided to stay. To compound Edmond's problems, he was operated on for detached retinas the day after the 1993 harvest. A mischievous sense of humour has kept him going through all this and, even if the wines weren't fine, one would admire the unquenchable spirit of this man.

Fortunately, Edmond knows what he's doing, and consistently turns out rich, complex, well-balanced wines from his 17ha. Fortunately he's found another vineyard worker now to look after his 6ha of *vin de table*, 5ha of Côtes du Rhône, 4ha of Vacqueyras and 2ha of Gigondas. These are scattered round the domaine's epicentre, a cluster of buildings in the hamlet of La Beaumette, a couple of kilometres outside Gigondas.

Here, amidst a glorious jumble which to the casual visitor might appear more like a second-hand farm-machinery and bottle recycling business, Edmond crafts his wares. Most of his land is planted to Grenache – "90% at least", is the considered estimate – and the vines are "at least 60 to 70 years old". Despite this, they work hard to give Edmond his permitted maximum 35hl/ha in Gigondas. There is nothing iconoclastic in the winemaking, which is followed by an *élevage* of six months in *foudres*, then 12 months in *cuve*.

Casting a glance round the cellar, one

Edmond Burle alongside his spraying machine, turquoise from the Bordeaux mixture.

is driven to wondering how anything ever emerges from the muddle. Chaos may be organised, but it is still chaos. If finding a chair is a major challenge, then getting at a *foudre* seems a veritable assault course for this eminently likeable, but handicapped, man. Unfortunately, Edmond has to sell some of his wine in bulk, not having enough time to bottle it personally. Nonetheless, the 8,000 bottles

of Gigondas and 10,000 of Vacqueyras which manage to navigate their way out deserve consideration. Conversation is interrupted to search for the telephone; the caller a Japanese client anxious about the fate of his 100 cases of Côtes du Rhône. Unfortunately, the labelling machine has developed an apparently incurable fault, so the bottles get dressed by hand, when Edmond has time.

"Vacqueyras – Gigondas, there's no real difference", according to Edmond, referring to the appellations' entirety, rather than to his own versions of them. These are as individual as he is – big, rich mouthfillers with plenty of tannin and ripe fruit; fleshy, fine wines for mid- to long-term keeping. His Côtes du Rhône white, a somewhat old-fashioned nutty wine, is the only blot on this landscape, to which vista has recently been added a respectable Vin de Pays made from Cabernet Sauvignon and Merlot. One peculiarity of the Domaine is its pricing policy, whereby everyone pays the same, whether you buy one bottle or six thousand.

It is to be hoped that someone will come along to help Edmond with the increasingly difficult work, so that there will be a few more bottles for everyone to enjoy.

VARIETY	APPELLATION	AREA
COTES DU RHONE	MAINLY GRENACHE	5.00
VIN DE TABLE	MAINLY GRENACHE	6.00
VACQUEYRAS	MAINLY GRENACHE	4.00
GIGONDAS	MAINLY GRENACHE	2.00
VIN DE PAYS	CABERNET SAUVIGNON & MERLOT	n/a
	TOTAL (hectares):	17.00

DOMAINE RASPAIL-AY

Dominique Ay is a stocky and pugnacious man who makes one of Gigondas' best wines from 18ha of middle-aged vines, most of which are planted round his house in the Colombiers *quartier* of the village.

Here, a carefully husbanded mix of 70% Grenache, 15% Syrah, 8% Mourvèdre plus patches of Cinsaut and Clairette (this for his excellent Gigondas rosé) on gently-sloping clay/limestone soils yields first-class fruit for Ay to work on.

Sitting somewhat uneasily in his office chair – he clearly prefers to be in the

cellars or outside – Ay explains that his over-riding policy is "to let nature do as much as possible". Translated into practical terms, this means the smallest doses of fertilisers and minimal

VARIETY	APPELLATION	DETAILS	AREA
GRENACHE	GIGONDAS	35–50 yr old vines	9.00
SYRAH	GIGONDAS	35–50 yr old vines	2.00
MOURVEDRE	GIGONDAS	35–50 yr old vines	1.00
· CINSAULT & CLAIRETTE	GIGONDAS	35–50 yr old vines	1.00
SYRAH, MOURVEDRE, GRENACHE	GIGONDAS	Mixed plantings; 40–50 yr old vines	5.00
		TOTAL (hectares):	18.00

treatments, and once the crop has been harvested, a long maceration for maximum extraction. Quality here is seen as coming from the harvest, and from allowing enough time both at fermentation and during *élevage* for nature to take its course.

There is enough vat space for a normal harvest of about 50,000 bottles, so, unlike many local *vignerons*, he doesn't need to artificially shorten *cuvaison* to make room for the next load of grapes. In addition, the Raspail-Ay harvest lasts some three weeks ("we want perfect maturity"), so by the time the final lot of Mourvèdre arrives, the early Grenache and Syrah have finished fermenting, been de-*cuved* and pressed.

Nothing fancy or experimental in this vinification – 100% de-stemming and 15 days' vatting at up to 32-33°C, 18 months in *foudres* with a total *élevage* of 24-30 months. There is no fining (unless there is a particular problem to correct) and rarely a filtration ("80% of my wines aren't filtered"). Four to five times a year a contract bottler appears and bottles

The elegant Château de Raspail-Ay; not to be confused with the eponymous Domaine.

12,000 bottles or so of the current release.

The wines are indubitably good. The "house style" is for plenty of *charpente* – which occasionally over-balances the structure at the expense of fruit. Nonetheless, this is a five-star domaine.

DOMAINE SAINT GAYAN

Compared with the Roux across the Sablet road at Les Pallières, the Meffres, who only arrived here in 1600, are *parvenus* in Gigondas. This property, St-Gayan – which gives its name both to the family home and to the cadastral *quartier* – has been built up over four centuries into one of the commune's finest estates.

Its direction is currently in the hands of Jean-Pierre Meffre and his wife Martine, his affable father Roger having retired – officially – in 1993. However, Roger's 54 years' experience are there to draw on, an asset which Jean-Pierre doubtless appreciates. Unlike his father, who was taken away from the Lycée Viticole in Avignon when the bombing began in 1942, Jean-Pierre has trained formally, particularly in management. "I can teach him my job, but not about commerce", Roger comments. So provided the product remains fine, financial affairs should also prosper.

They have 33ha: 16ha in Gigondas, the rest in Côtes du Rhône and Villages except for 75 ares of Châteauneuf-du-Pape next to the Beaucastel estate at Courthézon, which produces 3,000 bottles. The Meffre vines are on average 50 years old, with patches of 100-year-old plants, put in just after the phylloxera, and their Gigondas is virtually a single block on gentle slopes around the family home. The soils here are poor and very thin, mainly clay-limestone with an overlay of flat stony scree from the Dentelles giving on to either friable tufa or, in vineyards nearest the house, on to *safre*, an impermeable hard sand.

The domaine's wines are marked by great depth of extract. This comes in part from old vines, but also from a minimum of 20 days' vatting at a highish temperature to further augment extraction. Each variety is fermented separately – Syrah first, then Grenache and finally the late-ripening Mourvèdre – and then its first-pressing press wine added back (the second pressing goes to make a gutsy *vin de table*). The wines spend two years in *cuve*, then year in 18-35hl *foudres* and 6hl *demi-muids*.

These three years before bottling are essential, according to Roger, for the final quality of the wine: "you must have the patience to wait; the wines change a lot – they gradually refine, even in *cuve*". The mix of grapes also plays its part: in the St-Gayan Gigondas there is 80% Grenache, 15% Syrah and 5% Mourvèdre plus some "*divers*" which happen to be planted among the rest. An ideal recipe, in Roger's opinion, provided that the vines are old and their yields low. Almost embarrassed at their 31-34hl/ha average, below the permitted 35hl/ha, Roger explains that it would be even lower were it not for their young vines which, despite severe de-budding and green pruning, have an irrepressible vigour.

Tasting a range of wines in the warm spring sunlight, watched by the family dog (busy, when it is not idly lapping up water from an outsized stone trough in the front courtyard, chasing minor rodents in the hedge next to the tasting room), the Meffre's no-compromise philosophy comes shining through. As Roger reminds himself, he has 40 vintages of his Gigondas in the cellar, recalling especially the 1978 with its exquisite and complex fragrance of fruit, *sous-bois* and spice and remarkable depth – a wine of both exemplary length and persistence and a joy to drink.

VARIETY	APPELLATION	DETAILS	AREA
GRENACHE	GIGONDAS	Average vine-age 50 yrs	12.80
SYRAH	GIGONDAS	Average vine-age 50 yrs	2.40
MOURVEDRE	GIGONDAS	Average vine-age 50 yrs	0.80
VARIOUS REDS	CHATEAUNEUF	Quartier Courthézon	0.75
VARIOUS REDS	COTES DU RHONE + VILLAGES		17.00
		TOTAL (hectares):	33.75

DOMAINE DE SANTA DUC

As with many domaines throughout the southern Rhône, this fine small estate owes its present status to the younger generation. Here, until 1985, the entire produce of its ten Gigondas hectares sold to *négociants*.

In that year Edmond Gras, now as much retired as any *vigneron* ever is, handed over to his son Yves, a tall handsome, blond man in his early thirties. Yves immediately decided to bottle the 1982 vintage, still in wood in the cellars, and has never looked back.

Today, 95% of his trade is export. "It's simple to explain – I couldn't wait to build up an individual clientele, so I started to export – they just kept turning up". Favourable comment from an American journalist (yet to visit the domaine) led to an outbreak of orders. Edmond is thoroughly proud of what has been achieved, and both he and Yves enjoy the personal contact that this international trade has entrained.

The estate takes its name from the Provençale "Canta Duc"- a song-bird; also a *quartier* in Gigondas, on the north side towards Sablet. The Gras have vines here, in well-drained but poor limestone soil known locally as "*calcaire garrigues*", which particularly suffers in very dry years and tends to impart a degree of rusticity to its wines. Although the estate's land is very fragmented ("this is very interesting", comments Yves, "it adds complexity and equilibrium to our wines"), 70% is concentrated in the *quartier* Les Hautes Garrigues, which surrounds the cellars on flatter ground below the village. Here the soil is predominantly clay, which balances well with the limestone of Santa Duc.

Interestingly, the *encépagement* includes a high proportion of Mourvèdre, which Yves believes contributes significantly to the quality of his wines and which, moreover, he prefers to Syrah. "I adore Mourvèdre".

For him, as for many top *vignerons*, winemaking begins in the vineyard. Yves argues that to make a fine wine from Grenache, it must be super-ripe – 13 to 13.5% alcohol minimum for "Grand Gigondas". This mean low yields, de-vigorating young vines by removing bunches in July, and defoliating in plots which hold humidity to avoid rot. It also entails a late harvest. "People harvest too early, for security". It also exacts a severe selection of the ripest grapes so Yves spends the harvest in the vineyards sorting; "It's me who *tries*; I don't trust anyone else". While "all grapes look

Detail of a lintel in Châteauneuf-du-Pape.

lovely in the cellar", it is the subtle differences which really matter to the *vigneron*.

Details of how each vintage should be handled are carefully thought through. A peculiarity, which Yves stoutly defends, is that after the bunches (still with their stems) are lightly crushed, they are given a large dose of sulphur dioxide, so as to delay the onset of fermentation by several days. This extracts colour, in particular, and stems the otherwise rapid onset of fermentation, allowing a 15–20 day maceration. It also avoids the onset of malolactic fermentation while the new wine is still on its solids, which could lead to acetic spoilage.

The crop is usually processed in three different lots: early-ripening plots of Syrah and Grenache, a *cuvée* of pure Grenache and finally the late-ripening Grenache and Mourvèdre. For Yves, assembling in the vats is less problematic than trying to do it later when the wines have become individuals, with their own distinctive personalities.

In exceptional years (1989, '90 & '93) there is a special Gigondas Cuvée Prestige des Hautes Garrigues – a selection of late-harvested older vines from this *lieu-dit*. The usual proportions

are 30% Mourvèdre and 70% Grenache. Of this, 30% spends 8–12 months in new Allier and Vosges oak, while the rest remains in *cuve* to conserve the specially ripe fruit which this *terroir* yields – in 1990 it reached 15.5° alcohol. These fractions are blended together before bottling. The standard-issue Gigondas – from 1994 one-third older casks and two-thirds *cuves* – is kept for two to three years before bottling, with a maximum of 12 months in wood.

The wines are not fined but simply polish-filtered. Although Yves would like a single bottling of each vintage (he managed it in 1990) he usually has to be content with at least two.

The wines are excellent, if individual in style. Do not come here for soft, fleshy wines; rather expect structure, muscle and robust, firm flavours which need several years in which to integrate and express themselves.

"Don't look for finesse with us", Yves confesses. "I make wines which I like – and I like muscle."

Given this context, the Cuvée Tradition leans more towards suppleness, but even this has its attendant envelope of tannin which masks the fruit underneath.

The Hautes Garrigue is several dimensions away in depth and structure. The 1990, in particular, is "*un monstre*", to the structure and density of which Mourvèdre clearly contributes, as it does in ripe vintages such as this and 1993 when its tannins tend to resemble those of new wood in character and flavour. "Our 1990s did much for our reputation", remarks Yves. If this and the difficult vintages which followed it are any indication, that reputation is well earned.

APPELLATION	VARIETY	DETAILS	AREA
COTES DU RHONE ROUGE	GRENACHE (80%), MOURVEDRE(15%), SYRAH (5%), or CLAIRETTE (3%)	Vineyards in Vacqueyras, Roaix and Séguret	5.60
GIGONDAS	GRENACHE (75%), MOURVEDRE (15%), SYRAH (10%)		10.00
GIGONDAS, LES HAUTES GARRIGUES	GRENACHE (70%), MOURVEDRE (30%)	Selection of old vines from terroir of Les Hautes Garrigues	3.50
		TOTAL (hectares):	19.00

LIRAC

Situated overlooking a large bend in the Rhône, Lirac marks an unwritten dividing line between Provence and the Languedoc. Here, from a variety of soils, ranging from ferruginous red clay through limestone (either as broken topsoils or as compacted base rock) to the *galets roulés* of Châteauneuf, with a high sand content in the sub-soils, are produced red, white and rosé wines.

The Lirac appellation spreads over some 1,000ha, although less than half are under vine, and four communes: Lirac itself, St- Laurent-des-Arbres, St-Geniès-de-Comolas and Roquemaure. Its centre comprises a vast terrace of tertiary rocks, mainly glacial deposits from the retreating Rhône, rising to an altitude of 100m. Surrounding this is a large sandy plain, bounded to the north and east by an area of limestone ridges clearly visible to anyone passing through.

The area comes with 2,000 years of viticultural history: the first vines are recorded in the era of Roman control. In the 17th and 18th centuries, Lirac basked under royal patronage.

There is the usual mix of permitted grape varieties: for reds and roses, Grenache (40% minimum in vineyard), Cinsaut, Mourvèdre and Syrah (these last two must account for a minimum of 25% of plantings), plus a maximum of 10% at harvest of Carignan. For whites, the primary grapes are Clairette, Bourboulenc and Grenache Blanc, with a maximum of 60% of any one variety. The secondary varieties, none of which may individually exceed 25% of plantings or together constitute more than 30% of the ensemble, are Ugni Blanc, Picpoul, Marsanne, Roussanne and Viognier. The minimum alcohol degree for the AC is 11.5 for white and rose and 12 for red – well below that of Châteauneuf.

Tavel and Lirac are closely associated, many domaines whose principal output is in one commune offering wine from the other to complete their range. After the war – Lirac received its AC in 1947 – it was the rosés which drove the appellation. Now, with major export markets producing an indigenous equivalent and the decline in rosé's popularity, growers are wisely concentrating on producing better, more balanced and interesting white wines – an endeavour which appears to be succeeding.

Apart from sound caves coperatives at Roquemaure and St-Laurent, there are some 18 independent producers, all but one located "sur place", in one of the com-

Lirac – rosé and red.

munes or in Tavel. Curiously, only the Château de Segriès is in Lirac itself.

The village of Lirac is pleasant, though unremarkable. It has that air of being in a state of permanent somnolence, its repose interrupted only by the occasional passing visitor, or heavy lorry arriving to collect some wine.

As with Tavel, vines have been grown here for centuries, exported through the convenient Rhône port of Roquemaure. Cask-branding, which was introduced in 1737 by a Royal Decree grouping many of the wine-making areas of the Gard under the global "La Côte du Rhone", afforded some protection to these local wines, and further gave a measure of advantage to growers shipping to Britain and elsewhere in northern Europe.

Lirac of all colours continued to be exported largely in bulk until the late 1960s. An influx of Algerian ex-colonists who bought and cleared hitherto uncultivated land generated a welcome post-war revival in the commune's fortunes and estate bottling followed in the 1970s and 1980s.

As for the *encépagement*, recent years have seen an increase in Mourvèdre in the red Lirac blend at many of the best estates. To perform well, this grape, which suffers badly in dry years, needs moisture-reten-

tive soils and low yields. When it gets these, which is not always the case, it adds depth and structure to the Grenache. Many growers, however, prefer the earlier-ripening Syrah as their "stiffener".

Lirac produces the best reds and whites in the Gard. In good vintages they well repay keeping – the whites for two to four years and the reds a shade longer. From top-class domaines these wines have interest and quality and invariably represent excellent value for money.

AC LIRAC

Created	14 October 1947
Area (max)	1,000ha
Area under vine 1994	413ha
Base yield	42hl/ha
Minimum alcohol	11.5% (W, RO); 12% (R)
Growers	18

CHATEAUX ST-ROCH & CANTEGRIL-VERDA

This is one of Lirac's best and, perhaps more significantly, most consistent domaines. The Verdas, who have owned the property since 1955, came from Châteauneuf – "we couldn't grow there", explained Jean-Jacques, a dark, dapper man in his forties. At that time Lirac was unknown, and because the local Roquemaurins didn't really want vines, preferring to plant the best land to fruit and vegetables, domaines were often small. Antoine Verda acquired 3.5ha of vines with his château, and then added 30ha of smaller parcels around the estate. He is now retired, having handed over to his sons Jean-Jacques, an oenologist who superintends cellars and vinification, and André who oversees the vineyards. "Father oversees everything", though. "Everywhere there is the eye of the proprietor".

They still have 1.1ha of Châteauneuf – "in six separate parcels, one of which is only six rows wide". This yields a few thousand bottles; nothing in comparison to that of the 30,000 cases from their 40 St-Roch hectares and 20 at Domaine Cantegril, near Roquemaure.

The red *encépagement* consists of 55% Grenache and 15% each of Cinsaut, Syrah and Mourvèdre. The white is 40% Bourboulenc plus 30% each of Clairette and Grenache Blanc. Extensive replanting in the 1960s and 1970s mean that there is now a good proportion of mature vines.

St-Roch soils are a mixture of gravel, sandy clay and flat limestone stones, on south-facing, sheltered slopes; at Cantegril clay-sand is overlaid with *galets roulés*. The *cépages* are planted separately, the Syrah vines alone being trained on wires.

Jean-Jacques' winemaking is careful and the results classy. Neither white nor rosé see any wood – old or new – but are simply fined in December and sterile-filtered before an early spring bottling. They share a style, with plenty of acidity from an unusual predominance of Bourboulenc – which needs to be slightly under-ripe otherwise this lively contribution is lost – and a sappy clean Clairette centre, enriched in 1992 by a short *macération pelliculaire*.

The Verdas are experimenters. In particular they have been trying out *pièces* from a friend in St-Emilion with each red varietal. They have concluded, somewhat surprisingly, that second-year oak gives nothing positive either to Syrah or to Mourvèdre, but seems promising for Grenache. At present, they consider 15% of small wood a sensible maximum which Lirac can tolerate without altering its typicity. The larger

Vines flourishing in seemingly inhospitable rocky terrain near Tavel.

proportion spends a year in *cuve*, six months in *foudres,* then a further six months in *cuve* before bottling.

Here again trials have convinced the Verdas that near-sterile filtration is preferable to fining. The former is a physical process, whereas the latter is a physico-chemical operation which brings subtle ionisation and adsorption changes to a wine, which go well beyond the intended effect of clarification.

In better vintages, 10% of the estate's red crop goes into a special old-vine bottling – the Cuvée Ancien Vigurie: the Vigurie Haut, (La Cévenne) and the Vigurie Bas (Rouquemaure). There is also a white Ancien Vigurie, but this is simply a late release of the standard bottling after four to five years' bottle-age.

These are excellent examples of what Lirac is capable of: finely-crafted wines with plenty of flesh and depth. For the reds, 80% de-stemming eliminates unwanted herbaceousness, while a 15-day *cuvaison* extracts and fixes fine tannins, ensuring good ageing without any hints of bitterness. The different varieties remain separate until after malolactic, when they are tasted and evaluated before final *assemblage.*

These wines are well worth buying and keeping, especially in naturally riper, more structured vintages. They are not blockbuster, high-alcohol Châteauneufs, rather mid-weight in style with, after a few years in bottle, attractive soft aromas of blackberry, quince and *sous-bois,* and enough glycerol and *gras* to balance tannins, acids and fruit.

The Verdas have developed their estate with care, and their wines reflect their skill.

VARIETY	APPELLATION	DETAILS	AREA
VARIOUS RED VARIETIES	CHATEAUNEUF-DU-PAPE	6 separate plots	1.10
GRENACHE NOIR	LIRAC	ST-ROCH	20.00
SYRAH	LIRAC	ST-ROCH	4.00
CINSAULT	LIRAC	ST-ROCH	5.00
MOURVEDRE	LIRAC	ST-ROCH	4.00
GRENACHE BLANC	LIRAC	ST-ROCH	2.00
BOURBOULENC	LIRAC	ST-ROCH	3.00
CLAIRETTE	LIRAC	ST-ROCH	2.00
GRENACHE NOIR	LIRAC	CANTEGRIL	12.00
SYRAH	LIRAC	CANTEGRIL	3.00
CINSAULT	LIRAC	CANTEGRIL	2.00
MOURVEDRE	LIRAC	CANTEGRIL	2.00
CLAIRETTE	LIRAC	CANTEGRIL	1.20
		TOTAL (hectares):	61.30

CHATEAU DE SEGRIES

Apart from being one of the trio of independent Lirac domaines dating from before the arrival of Algerian ex-colonists (the others are the Château de Clary and the Domaine du Château St-Roch), the Château de Segriès has two other notable features: first, it is the only substantial Lirac producer in Lirac itself; second, it has largely fallen down. There are no signs to show the way; if you manage to find the right track, and have the courage to follow it for a kilometer or so, you come upon a small wooded park enclosing a collection of grey-stoned buildings in various stages of decay. How much more has to fall down before the right to use the "château" designation is lost is unclear.

These ruins are the property of the Comte de Régis, whose family inherited it in 1804. The present Comte, François, a spare, jaunty man of uncertain age, has retreated to a couple of rooms in an adjoining outbuilding which, for the present, remains standing. An economist by training, he took over from his father, for 60 years one of Lirac's most respected winemakers and generally credited with the creation of the Lirac appellation. Comte François' preference for a rather unkempt and gypsyish style of life, and a somewhat eccentric persona, hides a man of charm and quality, who is dedicated to making the finest wine he can – an objective he seems to achieve virtually single-handed.

At the start of the 20th century, the *vignoble* shared the estate with cereal crops, olive trees and some cattle. There are now 20ha of vines, in one plot, surrounding the "château" – 9 of Grenache, 2.5 of Cinsault, 3 of Syrah, 1.8 of "other" red varieties and some white plantings, chiefly Clairette and Ugni Blanc, with a touch of Bourboulenc and Picpoul, which adds finesse. The vines average a respectable 30 years old.

The red varieties are on a predominantly clay-limestone soil oriented mainly north-south, the whites occupying the sandier parts of the *vignoble,* exposed to the east. The fact that the vines occupy the floor of a small depression provides some protection from drought, while the surrounding hillsides throw back their stored heat at night to help ripening.

"For financial reasons" Comte François only makes Lirac – in all three colours: about 5,500 cases of red, 1,600 cases of

Comte François Régis.

rosé and 400 cases of white. His father applied for the AC Tavel for part of his estate when *vignerons* were originally offered the choice, but this was refused, probably because to have agreed would have effectively created an enclave of Tavel in Lirac. The Comte still has 5,000 stylish Tavel labels which were printed in advance of the decision.

As Comte François hops from one concrete vat to another, drawing off samples, in the rather untidy ex-cowshed which serves as the *cuverie* and bottling hall, it becomes clear how good his wines are. A fine, sappy white from 60% Clairette and 20% each of Ugni and Bourboulenc – with a touch of Picpoul mixed in – shares the stable with a gutsy red, rather more robust than one usually finds in Lirac, made from 60% Grenache and 15% each of Cinsaut and Syrah. The Segriès rosé is a well-structured, grippy *saignée de cuve* wine, weighing in at around 14% alcohol. It is compounded from Grenache, Syrah and Cinsault to which 2–3% of Carignan is added.

Vinification is under the supervision of a local oenologist, Bruno Sabatier. Although the wines are good, an earlier bottling would help preserve some of the excellent fruit which is evident in the vats – currently the reds are *élevés* for 12–24 months. This is too long – these are not Hermitages or Châteauneufs.

Nonetheless, this is a good estate, in an under-appreciated appellation. That the château is quietly crumbling around the cellars seems to make no noticeable difference to the quality of its wines.

VARIETY	APPELLATION	DETAILS	AREA
GRENACHE	LIRAC	35+ years average vine-age	9.00
CINSAULT	LIRAC	25+ years average vine-age	2.50
SYRAH	LIRAC	25+ years average vine-age	3.00
CAIRGNAN	LIRAC	40+ years average vine-age	1.80
CLAIRETTE	LIRAC	40+ years average vine-age	1.75
UGNI BLANC	LIRAC	40+ years average vine-age	1.75
		TOTAL (hectares):	19.80

TAVEL

There are only two communes of significance on the Rhone's "*secteur meridionale*" right bank – Tavel and Lirac.

Above all, these are the home of the rosé: prettily coloured – "a light blush on the skin of a peach" (Mayberry), highish in acidity and distinctively dry. Anyone determined to eschew rosé wines as a matter of policy, might just find Tavel or Lirac a convincing counter-argument.

The role of the rosé is to supplement a white-wine deficiency in this warm, southerly climate, and as such they replace them, if not admirably then conscientiously, in much of the local gastronomy. They also provide a refreshing alternative to the invariably high alcohols of their red, Grenache-based brethren, especially welcome in the heat of summer when clean, chilled flavours are called for.

Historically, both the communes came under the authority of the Bishops of Avignon, and strict rules were implemented to regulate the shipment of wine through the nearby port of Roquemaure. Two centuries before *appellation contrôlée*, cask branding was introduced to identify wines whose transit was permitted; Châteauneuf – 10km away – was excluded.

According to legend (entirely unsubstantiated) Tavel received Royal approbation as far back as the 13th century when King Philippe le Bel, travelling through Tavel, remarked as he downed a measure: "there is no good wine except for Tavel". Exports grew and alongside them prosperity, helped no doubt by the apparent natural resilience of the wine, much of which was shipped in cask; where off-dry wines would have started re-fermenting, Tavel remained stable.

In the decades preceding phylloxera, the vignoble grew to some 730ha. However, replanting after the infestation on flatter, more workable, but less good quality land, reduced the area under vine. Despite Tavel's inexplicable popularity in the USA, by the 1960s its vineyards had shrunk to 200ha.

Geological maps show the soils of Tavel to be very varied – plenty of limestone, some chalk, clay and sand, but generally poorish soils which give good natural acidities, often retained in the wines by stopping the malolactic fermentation. The climate tends to be as uncompromising as much of the landscape.

Here the gentler slopes of Vaucluse have given way to limestone outcrops more or less covered in scrub and dotted with any trees capable of withstanding the hot, drying, powerful Mistral. Tavel itself is

Vincent de Bez.

a small, unremarkable little place, with a restaurant or two devoted to showing off the local wines.

The principal grapes are Grenache and Cinsaut – with a secondary armoury of Bourboulenc, Clairette, Carignan and Picpoul plus Calitor, which has largely vanished. Mourvèdre and Syrah which were added to the list in 1969.

There are two basic methods of making rosé: *pressurage direct*, where red grapes are pressed immediately after harvest, sometimes preceded by a light crush. The resulting juice, lightly stained from the red skins, is then vinified as white wine.

The other system involves a *saignée de cuve* , where juice is bled off vats of more or less crushed red berries. The depth of colour is determined by the period of maceration before *saignée* – generally 12-30 hours. The residual juice is left to macerate and then made into red wine. The colour and style of the rosé depends heavily on the source of the juice from which it is fermented.

In addition to direct-press and vat bleeding, a darker-coloured juice is obtained from pressing the *marc* after *saignée*. This may be added back, before fermentation, to juice from either basic method to adjust colour. There is no question here of mixing red and white wines – the standard method for low-quality, bulk rosés.

The Tavel AC extends over two communes – Tavel itself and Roquemaure – and only permits rosé. Nonetheless, styles of wine vary from soft, gluggable rather

neutral wines, through the light, mouth-puckeringly acidic brigade – fresh and lively for hot-weather use – to more structured, denser, meatier mouthfuls with a noticeable shaft of tannin and more positive personalities. These latter need a few months to integrate and gain something from this bottle-age.

However, differences tend to be less striking between the rosés than between whites and reds, and Tavels are not wines for serious analysis. They are ideal as refreshing draughts to accompany strongly flavoured charcuterie, salads and fish dishes – even minor game, if its hot and there's nothing more substantial in the cupboard.

The small "Caveau Saint Vincent" in Tavel's Grande Rue stocks samples from most of the appellations 24 growers. Tasting through the range provides an overview of styles and quality. Many Tavels lack definition and depth – far too pappy and flabby. The best, most consistent wines come from the grand Château d'Acqueria and the Méjan family.

One of the finest estates – the Domaine de la Genestière, for years apparently effectively run by the workers and the secretary, has recently been sold to Monsieur Garçin, the local *pepinièriste*. Its ex-owner, Madame André Bernard, retains the house. It will be interesting to see whether the quality of this hitherto fine domaine is maintained. The Mabys at La Forcadière also make sound wine. Over half Tavel's total production comes from the *cave cooperative*, founded in 1973.

If the situation calls for an undemanding refreshing wine, with a touch of structure and guts, then Tavel might just fill the bill.

AC TAVEL

Created	15 May 1936
Area (max)	n/a
Area under vine 1994	947ha
Base yield	48hl/ha
Minimum alcohol	11% (max. 13.5%)
Growers	24

CHATEAU D'AQUERIA

Though not large by French standards, the Château d'Aqueria is one of the most architecturally striking properties in the Gard. An imposing set of entrance gates and a fine carriage sweep lead up to a mainly 18th-century, two-storey building, raised above its extensive cellars, with a front door flanked on either side by stone steps. From its principal rooms, one has splendid, far-reaching views of the surrounding countryside.

The offices, reception room and vinification plant are tacked sympathetically on one side of the house, across an elongated gravelled courtyard. These are the province of Vincent de Bez, grandson of Jean Olivier who was responsible for buying and restoring the domaine in the 1920s. Jean's son-in-law Paul de Bez took over in the 1950s, when Jean retired (he died in 1974), and Vincent has been at the helm since 1984.

Aqueria rests on a gentle slope above a plateau covered with *galets roulés* similar to, but smaller than, those of Châteauneuf. These give on to 40cm of red clay, underneath which is a deep layer of sand, then hard limestone. This bed-rock limestone is useful in retaining water, which is then fed back to the vines by capillary action; so drought stress is not a significant problem here as it is elsewhere. This predominantly sandy soil also contributes to wine quality, imparting finesse, in contrast to heavier clays which tend to produce more weight. In fact, before being renamed in the 18th century, Aqueira was known as the "Puy Sablonneux" ("the sandy outcrop").

Vincent, a slender, dark-haired rather wiry man with a ready smile, works with his oenologist brother, Bruno, making the estate's Tavel and Liracs. At present, they have 64ha under vine – 48 Tavel, 14 red Lirac (12 acquired in 1994) and two white Lirac. In fact the vineyard is in a single block, through which the border dividing Lirac from Tavel passes. The average vine age is about 30 years, although Vincent admits there are patches of much older vines in their Lirac territory. He also confesses to an inexact knowledge of what vines they have: "I'm waiting for permission to study these to find out what's planted here, and where".

The principal problem in the Aqueria vineyards is wind. The Mistral howls across this plain, drying and destroying plants which are not carefully tied – especially in the growing season. The

The Caveau St-Vincent – Tavel's tasting cellar.

Mourvèdre is particularly susceptible to wind, which defoliates the vines leaving them no means of photosynthesis. Its drying action also reduces humidity – so the wretched Mourvèdre suffers doubly if it is not planted in sheltered, south-facing sites. "It's fine for Bandol", explains Vincent, "they're next to the sea, and hotter than Tavel".

The wines here are some of the best from either appellation. The Tavel is vinified at 18–21°C for 6–8 days in stainless steel, from a mixture of juices – 70% from a *saignée totale de la cuve* following 12–36 hours' maceration, and 30% of pre-fermentation press juice. It is a relatively substantial wine with a lightish cherry-soda colour and a good, fat mouthful of ripe fruit. The typical blend is 50% Grenache, 20% Clairette, 10% Mourvèdre, 15% Cinsaut and 5% Bourboulenc.

Vincent is convinced that vinifying the individual varieties separately enables him to fine-tune the balance of his Tavel. Each brings its contribution to the blend – Grenache for fruit and *ampleur*, Cinsaut for finesse and length, Clairette and Bourboulenc for their characteristic perfumes of flowers and fruits and the Mourvèdre for its colour, structure, and its aromas of *fruits rouges;* all of which add up to longevity for the wine. Interestingly, Vincent is not a protagonist of Syrah in

VARIETY	APPELLATION	AREA
GRENACHE NOIR	TAVEL	24.00
CINSAULT	TAVEL	6.20
MOURVEDRE	TAVEL	4.80
CLAIRETTE	TAVEL	9.60
BOURBOULENC	TAVEL	2.40
GRENACHE NOIR	LIRAC	6.30
CINSAULT	LIRAC	1.40
MOURVEDRE	LIRAC	4.90
SYRAH	LIRAC	1.40
GRENACHE BLANC	LIRAC	0.90
BOURBOULENC	LIRAC	0.70
CLAIRETTE	LIRAC	0.20
ROUSSANNE	LIRAC	0.20
	TOTAL (hectares):	63.00

Tavel – "this is not traditional for the Southern Rhone; anyway, it gives a very violet colour which is not good for rosé and is difficult to handle. It has a good taste, but the colour doesn't go". Poor old Syrah!

Aqueria's Liracs are equally good, and distinctly more serious. Vincent says that they make the only white Lirac to contain Roussanne, which he believes adds valuable aroma and structure. "To make good wine, we need several *cépages,* for both acidity and structure. Before planting, I tasted every white Lirac and concluded that I needed at least three varieties for maximum complexity". For the white, the mix is 45% Grenache Blanc (for aroma, structure and fat), 35%

Bourboulenc (for acidity) and 10% each of Clairette and Roussanne. They try to harvest all these varieties simultaneously, which is not easy, given the different ripening cycles. If the Grenache ripens first, it is picked before the rest. No wood is used for this wine, just a fermentation at 18°C, no malolactic, and bottling in February following the vintage.

Its red stable-mate, vinified from non-destemmed grapes for 15 days at 30° C, is also excellent. The mix is more or less standard – 45% Grenache, 10% Cinsaut, 35% Mourvèdre and 10% Syrah (permitted here precisely for those qualities which Vincent dislikes in his rosé). He is not a believer in small casks for *élevage*: "I don't agree with these; I've done trials

and that's enough. It's a fashion that will pass. Many producers are coming back from casks to *foudres* now: 20% *barriques* will do, not 100%". Not surprisingly, he matures his red Lirac in *foudres* for 6-8 months after 10 months in *cuve*, unlike for instance the Mabys who mature their Lirac in 100% small wood, some new.

Aqueria's label bears a marked resemblance to that of Château Rayas. According to Vincent, Jean Olivier and old Louis Reynaud were close friends; when he asked Jacques Reynaud for the history of the label's similarity, the reply came: "I don't know who stole from whom". Perhaps Paul and Vincent de Bez have a sneaking admiration for that not-so-distant estate.

DOMAINE MEJAN-TAULIER

Domaine Méjan-Taulier is a good-quality, medium-sized, family estate, run by André Méjan, a tall handsome man with a sonorous bass voice, and his son-in-law, Michel Popek. They are principally producers of rosé, with 36 of their 43ha in Tavel. They have 2.46ha of Lirac, planted to Grenache, Cinsault, Syrah & Mourvèdre, and 4.70ha of Grenache, Carignan, Cinsaut, Syrah and Mourvèdre in Côtes du Rhône.

The Tavel *encépagement* consists of 50-60% Grenache, 5% Syrah; the rest being Cinsaut, Clairettes (Blanc and Rose), Bourboulenc and Carignan. The vinification is a mixture of *saignée* and *pressurage-directe*, with no de-stalking and berries kept intact as long as possible. Blocking the malolactic with sulphur at first racking ensures, according to André Méjan, a slower evolution of the wine. They try not to acidify, considering that their rosés have sufficient natural acidity. The cost of bottling means that the operation is carried out in several separate batches, with the first some 6–8 months after fermentation.

Tasting a single vintage of Tavel, both from *cuve* and in bottle, suggests that the unbottled stock is much richer and fuller, with a shade deeper colour and without the dominating acidity of its bottled stable-mate. This indicates a possible addition of citric acid at bottling, rather than using tartaric acid much earlier at fermentation, which produces a more harmonious result.

The house's red Liracs are by and large excellent – soft and fleshy with round, well-judged tannins and good length; in some vintages, almost Pinot Noir-like in consistency and flavour. The reds are given 3–4 years' *élevage* in

André Méjan.

stainless-steel after an 8–10 day *cuvaison* of un-destemmed grapes. Once again, this is bottled in several goes: "we sell less of this so we bottle it when we need it", explains André. Their practice of both Kieselguhr filtration after malolactic and sterile filtration before bottling seems excessive: the wines have sufficient acidity and tannins to allow a much less harsh pre-bottling regime, which would put that bit more flesh back into the

wines that is needed to make all the difference. André and Michel are doing a good job; with a little fine-tuning their results could be top class.

VARIETY	APPELLATION	DETAILS	AREA
GRENACHE NOIR, CINSAULT, SYRAH, CARIGNAN, BOURBOULENC, CLAIRETTES	TAVEL	20 yr average age	36.03
GRENACHE, CINSAULT, MOURVEDRE, SYRAH	LIRAC	15 yr average age	2.46
GRENACHE, CARIGNAN, CINSAULT, SYRAH, MOURVEDRE	COTES DU RHONE	20 yr average age	4.70
		TOTAL (hectares):	43.19

COTES DU RHONE

Although Côtes du Rhône is among the humblest of the Rhône's seventeen appellations, it is the one with which many drinkers are most familiar. It is also the wine with which the volume Rhône-style blends of the New World most readily invite comparison.

Geographically, the appellation extends over six principal *départements* – Ardèche, Drôme, Gard, Loire, Rhône and Vaucluse – a swathe 100km north-south and 50km east-west at its widest. This includes parts of the northern Rhône, where the steep topography leaves little space for plain Côtes du Rhône which, in this sector, is largely replaced by the "workhorse" appellation of St-Joseph. Nonetheless, some of the best-known *cuvées* emanate from Septentrionale cellars – in particular, Guigal's red and white, and Paul Jaboulet's "Parallèle 45".

The Côtes du Rhône vineyard area now covers 44,735ha and its superior designation, Côtes du Rhône-Villages, 3,662. Together they produce some 27 million cases of wine annually from maximum permitted yields of 50hl/ha and 42 respectively, which may be increased by 3-5hl/ha in naturally prolific vintages. This supplement does not apply to Villages, where any excess must be sold as cheaper *vin de table* – a strong incentive to keep within limits.

The principal appellations connected to Côtes du Rhône have evolved in something of a messy fashion, reflecting, as one might expect in France, commercial and political interests as well as the desire to make things more predictable for the consumer. The entire *appellation contrôlée* system started in 1929, with Baron le Roy at Château Fortia, Henri Plantin at Mont-Redon – both in Châteauneuf – plus the Comte de Regis in Lirac, who all sold Côtes du Rhône.

The original aims of Baron Le Roy's *appellation contrôlée* rules were to protect products from imitation by guaranteeing both typicity and authenticity. As vinification techniques changed, enabling producers to control the style of wine they made, typicity (if such ever existed) became blurred. The advent of carbonic maceration, resulting in attractive, fruity wines for early drinking, eliminated virtually all contribution of *terroir*. Nowadays, apart from a handful of exceptional *cuvées* (from growers profiled here), the most consumers can generally expect from an appellation as extensive as Côtes du Rhône is a wine made from certain specified grape varieties, conforming to certain technical norms and free from obvious defects.

The generic Côtes du Rhône appellation

A cobbled street in the picturesque wine village of Séguret.

was created in 1937. In 1953 the notion of a higher tier of Côtes du Rhône was struck, when four communes – Gigondas, Cairanne, Chusclan and Laudun – considered as consistently producing wine of higher quality than the rest, though not meriting full individual AC status, were promoted to Côtes du Rhône plus village name.

It was not until 1966 that the full Côtes du Rhône-Villages appellation was finally established. This superior designation requires reduced yields, more of the better grape varieties and a higher degree of fruit ripeness. By 1992 Gigondas and Vacqueyras had achieved full, individual, AC status, and the Villages category had exploded – 16 communes entitled to add their name to the Côtes du Rhône-Villages, with no less than a further 54 entitled to the appellation Côtes du Rhône-Villages, without any village name. One can argue either that this reflects genuine improvements in viticulture and vinification, or that the status of AC has been diluted for commercial ends.

The much older region of Bordeaux views Côtes du Rhône's abundant, reasonably priced wines as a threat to its lesser appellations, and once sought to restrict its output to around one million cases. Now production exceeds 25 times that level and has been extended from 120 to 163 communes. "Local" appellations (eg Gigondas and Vacqueyras) have also increased in number, against the wishes of the authorities, who rightly believe that if the best villages are accorded individual appellation status, less of quality would remain for straight Côtes du Rhône.

A raft of 24 grapes – 14 designated "principal" varieties and 10 "accessory" – are authorised for Côtes du Rhône, fewer (five red and four white) for Villages appellations. The staple red grape is Grenache Noir, for white Clairette and Grenache Blanc. Growers are encouraged to plant better varieties (*cépages ameliorateurs*) such as Syrah, Mourvèdre, Roussanne and Marsanne, and many have done so. The thin, acidic Ugni Blanc is in decline as are the Grenache Blanc (which oxidises easily) and the generally weedy Carignan.

The southern Rhône is a vast network of small villages and producers who are often more adept at growing grapes than at turning them into wine. Many simply don't want the trouble or risk of vinification and sell their fruit to one of 64 local cooperatives, while others vinify their grapes and then sell the wine to one of the score of major *négociants* – large firms who buy wine in bulk, from a variety of sources to make up their own blends.

Négociants and co-ops dominate the price-driven, lower end of the spectrum, churning out volumes of more or less palatable wine, generally sound but light in character, leading consumers to believe – with some justification – that Côtes du Rhône is wine for easy, everyday drinking without need of bottle-age. Some firms also offer superior *cuvées*, often cask-aged wines and well above average in quality, at reasonable prices.

Beyond this voluminous, thirst-quenching output are a tiny caucus of highly-skilled wine-makers who are prepared to reduce yields to levels most growers would consider commercially unviable, and to increase the proportion of noble varieties in their vineyards, in the quest for quality. These growers, with neither the acreage nor the appetite for bulk vinification, strive to produce, from *terroir* not designated for great wine, something with longevity and complexity. They relish the thrill of the vintage and enjoy the challenge of experimenting with vinifications and grape mixes until they have achieved something fine. For many of these estates, Côtes du Rhône is just one of several wines produced; for others, their principal appellation. In either case, the wine receives as much care and thought as a grand Bordeaux or Burgundy. It is here that the real interest in the Côtes du Rhône lies.

Unfortunately, many otherwise sophisticated drinkers fail to appreciate that it is possible to have *vin serieux* even at this humble level, and write off the appellation wholesale. For others, social pressures

Vineyards interspersed with lavender fields in the Southern Rhone.

prevent them from offering Côtes du Rhône, however fine, probably because their guests might consider them cheapskate. So the true aficionado can decant his bottle of mature Fonsalette (qv) or Coudoulet (Beaucastel qv) safe in the knowledge that the guesses will be cast far and wide at greater appellations before its identity is revealed.

Two main keys to success are noble varieties and low yields. The finest reds, for example, contain a high proportion of Syrah or Mourvèdre, while many whites owe their quality to Marsanne, Roussanne or even the precious and delicate Viognier. Yields are reduced by careful site-selection, strict pruning, low-vigour rootstock and by using a good percentage of old-vine fruit.

Top-class Côtes du Rhône winemakers don't skimp in the cellar either. Virtually all the best wines spend some time in cask, often new oak. In contrast, a few optimistic alchemists, seeing what they regard as miracles wrought from new wood, try this as an improver for badly constituted wine. The experiment inevitably fails, although it may take the grower a while to realise that peppering an inferior joint with garlic won't turn it into a fine dish.

In deciding which domaines to include here, style played a significant part. Great (red) wines are generally *vins de garde* and Côtes du Rhône is no exception. Some highly-regarded estates make wines in a lighter, more supple vein, which does not age well. Attractive as these may be, they are never great.

The size of the Côtes region makes it impossible to include every estate of merit. In addition to those profiled here, many others take special pride in the quality of their Côtes du Rhône: the Perrins of Château de Beaucastel (qv) produce three excellent examples – Coudoulet de Beaucastel, from land adjoining their Châteauneuf vineyards, and La Vieille Ferme and Grand Prébois from separate properties. Gérard Meffre at Château de Courançonne at Violès has a highly-regarded cask-aged Villages from old vines at Séguret, and Daniel and Laurent Brusset produce several good wines, in particular their Cuvée des Templiers, Vendange Chabrille Rouge and Vendange Clavelle Viognier, from vineyards around Cairanne. Marc Français-Monnier at the Château de St-Estève at Uchaux is capable of fine bottles, although careful selection is needed. Several Châteauneuf, Gigondas and Vacqueyras domaines also offer good Côtes du Rhône or Villages. In short, there is a wealth of choice which only tasting and personal preference can narrow.

VINTAGES

Côtes du Rhône (and Villages) vintages vary in intrinsic quality. In such a vast area, generalisations are pointless, as the potential of any given wine depends on the location of the vineyards involved. In the main, vintages follow those of Châteauneuf and Gigondas.

AC COTES DU RHONE

Created	19 November 1937
Area (max)	n/a
Area under vine 1994	44,735ha
Base yield	50hl/ha
Minimum alcohol	11%

AC COTES DU RHONE-VILLAGES

Created	2 November 1966
Area (max)	n/a
Area under vine 1994	3,662ha
Base yield	42hl/ha
Minimum alcohol	12% (white and rosé); 12.5% (red)

CHATEAU DE FONSALETTE

As well as making the finest Châteauneuf at Château Rayas (qv), Jacques Reynaud also produces the finest, most concentrated and complex of Côtes du Rhones from his estate, Château de Fonsalette, at Lagarde-Paréol. The wines are made at Rayas, and are in all major respects vinified in the same manner, so that detail will not be duplicated here.

The 130-ha Fonsalette estate was bought by Louis Reynaud at the end of the Second World War, in 1945. There were patches of vines, mainly Grenache, on the property, but he wanted to extend the vineyard, so he started planting – as the Armistice was being signed.

In spite of an outbreak of maintenance in the mid-1980s, when one tower was cleaned and restored, the château itself has fallen into rather a seedy state with windows boarded up and tiles missing from the roof. Beneath the depredations it is a noble building, albeit an amalgam of architectural styles and periods.

The main, south, facade – the finest of several – is pre-Revolutionary, dating from 1750; but there is also a dreadful Gothic 1890s cake-castle, which spoils the original elevation. The only inhabitants of the château are Jacques' estate workers, who are understandably not particularly motivated to maintain it properly.

An extensive park surrounds the château on three sides, the fourth being the vineyard. This is a quiet spot, disturbed by no more than the occasional passage of traffic. There is also a magnificent stand of olive trees opposite one (unmarked) entrance, which Jacques Reynaud planted himself and of which he is very proud. "I make my own olive oil from these", he explains, beaming.

There are now 11ha of Côtes du Rhône vineyard – a mix of Grenache, Syrah and Cinsaut for red and Grenache Blanc, Clairette, Chardonnay and Marsanne for white. Jacques Reynaud reckons that Roussanne is better than Marsanne, but is fragile, susceptible to *oïdium* and needing a fine autumn to ripen properly. He tried an experimental plot of Pinot Noir, vinified on its own but

the results didn't satisfy him, so it has been grubbed up. Burgundian friends, however, were impressed and told him "if all Burgundies were like that....".

Fonsalette produces four wines: a white, a *cuvée* of pure Syrah, a red from 50% Grenache, 35% Cinsaut and 15% Syrah, and a red "La Pialade" – in effect a lesser Fonsalette. Yields average 20-25hl/ha (11 barrels per hectare).

The white had a tendency to the old-fashioned oxidative style, which comes from a long period in old wood. This changed in 1993 when, under pressure from his customers, Jacques Reynaud acceded to an earlier, spring, bottling for his whites. This is a signal improvement.

The reds are generally remarkable wines; immense, densely packed with fruit and sustained by ripe yet firm tannins. Their structure means that they need years to unpack – which sadly they rarely get, as most consumers regard Côtes du Rhône as a wine for early drinking. In 1994, the 1978 Fonsalette red was still a comparative youngster. These are no ordinary Côtes du Rhônes, but wines which confidently outshine most Châteauneufs and are unquestionably among the finest in the entire Rhône Valley.

The gem of the Fonsalette collection is the *cuvée* of pure Syrah. This is not, as many seem to think a selection of the finest *cuves*, but rather a bottling of whatever Syrah remains after the standard Fonsalette has been assembled. What left-overs! As dense as most Hermitages, although a touch rustic in comparison, Jacques Reynaud attributes the excellence

of his Syrah in part to the fact that the vines are exposed due north – which, being cooler, gives a long, even, ripening season. He adds that the variety was only planted at all because a professor from the faculty at Montpellier told his father that it would do well at Fonsalette.

In fact, there are two distinct Syrahs at Fonsalette. Syrah I, as Jacques Reynaud dubs it, comes from vines planted on heavier gravel and clay soils, while Syrah II issues from lighter soils containing less clay. Blending the two produces wine of elegance and depth, with all the elements necessary for long ageing, to which low yields add their unmistakable mark.

Wine snobs tend to ignore Fonsalette because of its simple appellation; in their ignorance they thereby lose the opportunity to taste remarkable wine. Fonsalette stands as a monument to what is achievable with low yields and careful viticulture, even in as humble an appellation as Côtes du Rhône. As Jacques Reynaud comments: "Fonsalette is not jealous of Rayas". Indeed, it has no reason to be.

VARIETY	VINEYARD	DETAILS	AREA
GRENACHE NOIR	FONSALETTE	Vines planted 1945–1960	5.00
CINSAULT	FONSALETTE	Vines planted 1945–1960	2.00
SYRAH	FONSALETTE	Vines planted 1945–1960	3.50
GRENACHE BLANC	FONSALETTE	Vines planted 1945–1960	0.75
CLAIRETTE	FONSALETTE	Vines planted 1945–1960	0.25
MARSANNE	FONSALETTE	Vines planted 1945–1960	0.20
CHARDONNAY	FONSALETTE	Vines planted 1945–1960	0.33
		TOTAL (hectares):	12.03

DOMAINE GRAMENON

This is one of the finest of all Côtes du Rhône estates. Its relative obscurity can be explained by the fact that Philippe Laurent only began domaine-bottling in 1991, having previously sold all his excellent fruit to Guigal

and Jaboulet, among others, since he bought his 15ha of vines in 1979.

Philippe, a large, jovial and strongly individual character with a firm eye for quality, is the eldest of eight children of a *vigneron* in Valréas. Among his vines

are 2ha of 100-year-old plants ("Ceps Centenaires"), which he rescued from their owner – who had unfortunately already grubbed up three similar hectares. These are mostly *gobelet*-trained Grenache: a cocktail of clones and mutants, producing bunches large and small, long and short and yielding a mere 16-23hl/ha. The rest of the 21.5ha currently in production are Grenache, Syrah, Viognier and Clairette. Most of the younger plantings are Philippe's own grafts from a *sélection massale*.

Farming and vinification are, as far as practicable, non-chemical – "I like drinking wines which don't give you a headache". So, just Bordeaux mixture when necessary to deal with mildew, and flowers of sulphur for the more frequent *oïdium*.

Soils vary from the relatively water-retentive stony ground below Philippe's pink-washed house, to sandier ground on the plains. Here, the vines do best when the season is dry.

One peculiarity is that summer leaf pruning is never performed during the phase of a full moon, since for some obscure reason a second generation of grapes – *verjus* – is the result. If this hedge-trimming is needed it is left as late as possible, although Philippe would like to abandon the operation altogether.

There are eight different *cuvées* on offer: Clairette and Viognier (varietally labelled, which is technically illegal), a direct-press rosé, and five reds: a young-vine Grenache (30-year-old vines!), a pure Syrah from 10- to 17-year-old plants and three special *cuvées* – Laurentides, mainly Grenache from over 50- year-old vines with up to 10% of Syrah added; Ceps Centenaires, from century-old Grenache vinified traditionally and, confusingly, a Ceps Centenaires from 30 days' carbonic maceration to extract maximum fruit and fine tannins.

In 1992, a fourth special *cuvée* was made, in homage to a young chef friend of Philippe's who had recently died. The grapes selected for this reached 18° potential alcohol and, after a month's cold maceration, the wine finally finished up at 16.5°.

Philippe's line on vinification is that "my idea is to adapt to the grape, not the grape to me". In weaker vintages, he tends to de-stem more (10-90% is the bracket) and work with the fruit alone. Until 1994, everything was vinified at Laurent *père's* cellar in Valréas. Now, a large *cuverie* and cellar built behind his house has brought everything under one roof.

Vinification and *élevage* differ for each *cuvée*: the Laurentides is vinified traditionally – more or less destemming, 15-20 days' *cuvaison* with *remontage* and the press-wine blended back, or not, on tasting – and spends 8-12 months in old *pièces*. The Ceps Centenaires Traditionelle is also traditionally made, but sees no wood because, Philippe reasons, "wood adds

Philippe Laurent with one of his "Ceps Centenaires".

more structure to a wine which is already structured". Instead, it has up to 24 months (for great vintages, such as 1990) in *cuve*, with one or two rackings each year. The Ceps Centenaires maceration *cuvée* is matured either in *demi-muids* or old casks (1991) while the standard wines are *élevés* entirely in *demi-muids*.

The whole winemaking process is designed to be as natural as possible. Indigenous yeasts, no sulphur dioxide apart from a touch at bottling and positively no pumps – *remontage* is achieved by draining off the juice and hoisting it by lift so as to return it to the vat by gravity: "each time you pass wine through a pump, you derange the yeasts". Of course, there is generally neither fining nor filtration, although the whites may be plate-filtered in difficult vintages such as 1993.

The white grapes are direct-pressed, without sulphur and fermented slowly in *inox* (stainless steel) at the distinctly low temperature of 12°C – "the yeasts which work at under 12° are only good". Half to two-thirds of the Viognier, but none of the Clairette, spends time in cask. Both Clairette and Viognier are varietally labelled which the absurd Appellation

rules technically forbids. Philippe heartily dislikes "*les officiels*" and recalls one year when two men in white coats appeared in the vineyard to control the health of the grapes being harvested. They asked what was being picked: "Viognier", came the reply. "It's 14.5° potential alcohol; you should have harvested it earlier – its unsaleable". "But you've never made a wine", Philippe retorted, "and I know who'll buy it".

Gramenon Côtes du Rhônes – especially the special *cuvées* – far transcend their official classification. These are wines of extraordinary depth and power, with all the concentration that Philippe can coax out of his old vines. The whites are distinctly southerly in character, but fine and attractive nonetheless. It would be a disingenuous taster who preferred a lesser Châteauneuf to a "Ceps Centenaires". Gramenon is a remarkable domaine.

APPELLATION	VARIETY	DETAILS	AREA
COTES DU RHONE	GRENACHE	"Ceps Centenaires" – 100+ yrs old	2.00
COTES DU RHONE	GRENACHE	50+ yr old vines	14.00
COTES DU RHONE	SYRAH		3.00
COTES DU RHONE	VIOGNIER	Sandy soils; some clay-limestone. Vin de pays	2.00
COTES DU RHONE	CLAIRETTE	Vin de pays	1.00
		TOTAL (hectares):	22.00

CHATEAU DU GRAND MOULAS

A relatively young domaine, the Château du Grand Moulas is run with splendidly disorganised flair by Marc Ryckwaert, whose father bought it in 1957 when the family arrived from Algeria. As an experienced *vigneron*, he would have liked to buy vineyards, but these were too expensive, so he bought fruit trees. Even now, Marc's brother, Yves, exploits 65ha of pears, apricots and apples as well as looking after the domaine's sales.

From 1972 they started to clear part of the estate for planting – difficult hillsides but "magnificent land" – and, at 270m above sea level, some of the highest vineyards in Vaucluse apart from the Dentelles de Montmirail. Here, the land is covered with large, flat stones – "like nougat" – which store up humidity and heat. Planting rights, which are not automatically granted, came slowly, but now Marc has 29ha: 18 of Grenache, nine Syrah and two of Clairette, Marsanne, Roussanne and Grenache Blanc.

The domaine's headquarters are the Château du Grand Moulas, near Mornas, a village at the foot of a dramatic limestone cliff 10 km to the north of Orange. The *cuverie* and cellars are housed in a set of dilapidated outbuildings annexed to the Château, announcing themselves as dating from 1824. Above, from a glorious muddle of an office littered with bottles, filing boxes and an assortment of unrelated objects, the jovial Marc administers his domaine.

Four wines are offered: a red Côtes du Rhône, a red and white Villages and, since

The old still at Grand Moulas.

1989, the Prestige "Cuvée de l'Ecu". In style, the wines reflect Marc's personality – open, approachable, with suppleness and finesse replacing sheer size and muscle.

The pick of the cellar, the 95-100% Syrah Cuvée de l'Ecu, is released in most vintages, but the quantity varies according

to the quality of the year. Neither crushing nor destemming precede a *cuvaison* of three to four days at 34°C. Even in this short time, Marc argues, everything necessary for a fine wine is extracted. After some nine months in *cuve* and an almost sterile filtration, the wine is bottled on site, reflecting "monumental problems with contract bottlers". Marc has strong views on the suitability of wood for *élevage*: "I don't think either Châteauneuf or Côtes du Rhône should be kept in wood – *foudres* perhaps! Wood hides the aromas of grapes, which I adore; so wood annoys me".

The wines are on the lighter side of what many would regard as fine Côtes du Rhône: soft, quite plummy mouthfuls, with enough tannin to sustain the fruit and fair power, but the accent definitely on elegance. Marc's personal taste is for young wines – but he was prepared to admit that his 1978 Grand Moulas, their first vintage, was a fine bottle. Some may feel that these are not substantial enough; that's a matter of taste. But the quality of Marc's distribution suggests that his wines have a dedicated following of clients who find his wines fine.

VARIETY	APPELLATION	AREA
GRENACHE	COTES DU RHONE + VILLAGES	18.00
SYRAH	COTES DU RHONE + VILLAGES	9.00
CLAIRETTE, MARSANNE, ROUSSANNE + GRENACHE BLANC	COTES DU RHONE-VILLAGES	2.00
	TOTAL (hectares):	29.00

DOMAINE DE L'ORATOIRE ST-MARTIN

According to their family tree, the Alary family have been in or near Cairanne for ten generations. Frédéric, who runs their 25ha estate with his brother François and his father Bernard, says that his great-grandfather devoted most of his time to silk worms and "*garance*", the root from which the red dye was made for the French Army's trousers in World War One. This made the soldiers somewhat conspicuous, and the red dye market consequently collapsed. So the Alarys turned to wine.

Their output is 80% red and 20% white, in both Côtes du Rhône and Villages. In fact, all their vineyards are entitled to be Cairanne, Côtes du Rhône-Villages, but they like to sell the produce of younger vines with the lesser appellation. Three-quarters of the vines are in the steepest sector of

Cairanne, the *quartier* St-Martin, where mechanical working is only possible with a caterpillar tractor. The soils are clay-limestone, mixed with stones and sand.

The red *encépagement* is 60% Grenache, 15% Mourvèdre and 20% Syrah. "We like Syrah and Mourvèdre, especially for ageing – although this is a bit anti-commercial because the Mourvèdre is very closed to begin with", explains Frédéric. The whites come from 30% each of Marsanne, Roussanne and Clairette, with 10% of Viognier. From these, two *cuvées* are produced. A fresh, attractive Côtes du Rhône has 70% Clairette and 30% Marsanne, plus a touch of Roussanne for *rondeur* and weight. This is overshadowed by the Cuvée Cairanne Haut-Coustias, a pure Marsanne, fermented and matured in a mixture of old and new casks, with

bâtonnage. This has noticeably more fat and substance than the straight Côtes du Rhône. The overall proportions of Marsanne and Clairette are diminishing as new plantings of Roussanne and Viognier come on stream.

Frédéric sees a good future for their whites, which account for one-fifth of production. The team are still toying with different grape blends until they find what they like. "We tasted much in the Northern Rhône and found that Roussanne there gives a lot of richness; also, we adore Hermitage and went to see Chave. We descended into the cellar at 10am and emerged at 1pm". Clearly, people of sound instincts.... They are also experimenting with a wood-aged Cairanne Viognier from young vines producing just 15hl/ha, although in general Frédéric prefers

Viognier as part of a blend in the South". The 1992 version is heavily marked by its sojourn in oak, but a decent varietal concentration is discernible underneath.

The most interesting of the domaine's several red *cuvées* is the Cairanne Haut Coustias assembled from 50% Mourvèdre, 30% Syrah and 20% Grenache. The high Mourvèdre and Syrah give a more deeply-coloured wine than either the Grenache-based Cuvée Prestige or the livelier, fruitier Réserve des Seigneurs.

The Alarys regard the Seigneurs as an experimental wine, to enable them to try out different casks and varietal mixes. Only 4,000 bottles are produced in any vintage. On the palate, the Haut Coustais

is characterised by strong mineral, earthy flavours which need time to integrate and evolve.

The domaine's red flagship is undoubtedly the Cuvée Prestige, a 60:40 Grenache-Mourvèdre blend from vines planted in 1905, yielding around 25hl/ha. This usually consists just of the press wine, which the Alarys consider more concentrated, tannic and powerful; it is *élevé* in *cuve* (in contrast to the Haut Coustais which is given 12 months in casks and 600-litre *demi-muids*).

The Alarys' carefully worked, steep-sloping vineyards are providing some *vins serieux*. They have planted 500 Muscat à Petits Grains vines after tasting

VARIETY	APPELLATION	AREA
GRENACHE NOIR	CAIRANNE	12.00
MOURVEDRE	CAIRANNE	3.00
SYRAH	CAIRANNE	4.00
CINSAULT	CAIRANNE	1.00
MARSANNE	CAIRANNE	1.50
CLAIRETTE	CAIRANNE	1.50
ROUSSANNE	CAIRANNE	1.50
VIOGNIER	CAIRANNE	0.50
	TOTAL (hectares):	25.00

Aimé Guibert's white Daumas Gassac (qv), which will be added to some Viognier when it matures. One can only admire the enthusiasm...and wait!

DOMAINE RABASSE CHARAVIN

There are only a handful of top-class female winemakers in the Rhône, probably because here you have to be able to do everything: vineyard workers apart, employees are a distinct luxury. Corinne Couturier is one of this elite. Short, with close-cropped hair, she exudes a dynamism and enthusiasm for her domaine and its wines, still fresh after nearly 25 years. Her fief consists of 68ha spread between family holdings in Cairanne and Rasteau (28ha) and 40ha *en fermage* from her father, Abel Rabasse-Charavin, who retired in 1990.

From him, Corinne learned her skills, giving up a job as a secretary in a clinic to replace him in 1984. She had started working with him in 1971, and is "traditional" to the extent of copying his methods. However, she has her own natural feel for what makes fine wine and delights in playing a hunch. In 1992, she began trials with *pigeage*: "you can only find out what's happening in a *cuve* by getting into it – you feel where it's hot and cold. I've looked at automatic *pigeage* but it has no charm". Corinne visibly grimaces. "It's tough at first, the cap is hard and cold; but after two to three days, *pigeage is* a pleasure. You know, women are better at this than boys – some of my *stagiares* couldn't take it, so I got rid of them"!

From her homely, rather jumbled office cum cellar/shop, Corinne, and the apparently ceaseless stream of family and other visitors, have a fine prospect over the vineyards which slope away toward the Cairanne-Rasteau road. She has definite views about what makes her sort of wine – her grandfather educated her palate: "I prefer low yields, although in many vintages we don't get back what we put in for work". Her guiding philosophy is that "one must respect the year, because wine is a natural product".

This doesn't mean that she won't spray, only that such treatments are carefully planned and kept to a minimum.

Corinne offers a variety of *cuvées*, from a *vin de table* through red and white Côtes du Rhônes, red Cairanne and Rasteaus, a 100% Syrah *vin de pays* and a *vin de pays rosé*, to a red Villages and the latest release, a Côtes du Rhône *rouge*, Cuvée Laure-Olivier (85:15 Grenache and Cinsault). At the top of her range stands a red Cairanne, Cuvée d'Estevenas. The wines are remarkably good. Even the simple *vin de pays* have intense dark colours, open pepper-and-spice Syrah aromas, and plenty of ripe, stylish, succulent fruit. In naturally leaner years, such as 1991, a severe selection ensures that only ripe fruit is fermented, so that the result is balanced and attractive.

The Estevenas is particularly good – coming 80% from a specific plot of 80-to100-year-old Grenache vines and 25% of 25- to 30-year-old Syrah located at the top of a south-facing clay-limestone slope. These vines yield an average of 30hl/ha against a permitted maximum of 42. Corinne prefers to keep each variety separate until after malolactic "because the wines change dramatically up to then", so any earlier attempt at *assemblage* might be flawed. Equally "lots of things happen at malolactic – a lovely wine can be awful after, and vice versa". There follows 18 months in *foudres*: "these round out wines,

especially in tougher vintages". At the prompting of a foreign customer the wines are bottled without filtration. "I found that the filtered wine aged too quickly and lost fruit" – so since 1985, no filtration!

The Estevenas has considerable power and presence; first-division Côtes du Rhône, packed with intense old-vine fruit, highly structured and immensely stylish. Not a wine for drinking young (although its finely-honed balance doesn't make that an unpleasant experience), but meriting a decade of cellaring in vintages such as 1990.

Corinne professes a lack of enthusiasm for white wine – so she confines her activities here to 20hl of Côtes du Rhône white, from 50:50 Bourboulenc and Clairette. Reds interest her more: in particular Mourvèdre, which she considers is particularly suited to Rasteau's soils and southerly aspect and accentuates the rustic nature of the commune's *terroir*. So her own Rasteau has 40% of Mourvèdre mixed in with 60% of 40- to 70-year-old Grenache, giving a big, slow-developing, earthy wine, with strong flavours of liquorice and baked prunes and, indeed, a minerally, rustic undertone which is thoroughly attractive. A wine to keep 5-8 years in the 1990 version, and then to drink with game or red meat.

This, then, is a reliable, conscientious domaine, where details count and nothing is left to chance. Corinne Couturier demonstrates what can be done with noble grapes, low yields and thoughtful winemaking from relatively humble appellations.

APPELLATION	DETAILS	AREA
COTES DU RHONE-VILLAGES (CAIRANNE)		14.00
COTES DU RHONE-VILLAGES (RASTEAU)		8.00
COTES DU RHONE-VILLAGES (VIOLES)		25.00
VIN DE TABLE, VIN DE PAYS (VIOLES)		18.00
	TOTAL (hectares):	65.00

DOMAINE MARCEL RICHAUD

Even in relatively humble appellations such as Côtes du Rhône-Villages, *terroir* matters. A forceful exponent of this view is Marcel Richaud, a 40-year-old *vigneron* for whom choice of *terroir* – together with low yields, high vine age and a considered mix of noble varieties – is fundamental. Since starting out independently in 1974, having rejected the cooperative route at the age of 15 while still at school, Marcel's domaine has continued to grow in stature.

The beginning was simple enough: a 20-year-old with neither qualifications nor cash, but imbued with the idea of independence. A few hectares were taken *en viagère* – a system which guarantees the owner rent for life, then the vines pass to the hirer – and an aunt's cellar borrowed for vinification. So old and decrepit were the *foudres* that paper had to be stuffed into the crevices to stop the wine running out. His first vintage, 1974, was an execrable one, so Marcel only bottled a little "for pride", and sold the remainder in bulk. His friends and neighbours laughed at him: "*le petit Richaud* is making wine!"

Now there is less derision and more vineyards – 40ha in Cairanne, some *en fermage* from the aunt, some *en viagère*, and 15 owned outright. Vines under 10 years old go into *vin de table* and *vin de pays* de Vaucluse; for the rest, there are a red Côtes du Rhône, Cairanne Villages red and white, and, to top things off, the Cuvée l'Ebrescade – a Cairanne from 80% Grenache vines planted around 1900, plus some Syrah and Mourvèdre. There is also Madame Richaud – a quicksilver dynamo, who rushes around keeping the domaine on the rails.

Terroir is fundamental to Marcel's thinking. As he explains, soils in Cairanne

Marcel Richaud.

are diverse, each giving an individual expression to its grapes: clay-limestone for structure and matter, sand for elegance, and *grès argileux* for harmony, finesse, elegance and substance. He

endeavours to select the best soils for each appellation and vinifies each *terroir* and plot separately, to have the greatest diversity from which to make each *assemblage*.

Vinifications are kept simple. Marcel dislikes wood, so everything is matured in *cuve*. All the pressings are incorporated into the Côtes du Rhône *assemblage* and bottling generally takes place after a year – around the new vintage. *Négociants* tried to convert him to new oak: "you'll sell thousands of cases through us, if you'll let us re-structure all your blends". Wisely, he refused – there weren't thousands of cases to sell, whatever the *élevage*.

At every level the wines are interesting. In particular, l'Ebrescade, 6-8,000 bottles from high, steep vineyards near Cairanne's southern boundary, towards Rasteau – "un *terroir* fabuleux" as Marcel describes it.

This wine started out in 1987 as 100% Grenache; it didn't age well, so Syrah and Mourvèdre were added, from younger vines grown on similar *terroir*. The result is excellent – a wine of depth and richness, often spicy, which merits several years' cellaring. Altogether this is a first-class domaine.

WINE	VARIETIES	DETAILS	AREA
CAIRANNE ROUGE	GRENACHE, SYRAH, MOURVEDRE	30 yrs average vine-age. Grenache Qtr. des Combes; Syrah & Mourvedre, Qtr. Chantal	15.00
COTES DU RHONE ROUGE	GRENACHE, SYRAH	20 yrs average age; Qtrs. Garrigues (red clay and small boulders), Beraude & Travers (mainly sandy, with compacted sand beneath)	20.00
CAIRANNE BLANC	ROUSSANNE, MARSANNE, GRENACHE BLANC, CLAIRETTE & VIOGNIER	15 yrs average vine age	2.00
CAIRANNE ROUGE, CUVEE L'EBRESCADE	GRENACHE, SYRAH, MOURVEDRE	Grenache planted c 1900, remainder younger; Qtr. l'Ebrescade, 200 metres altitude, south facing; soils: clay-limestone, with surface scree	3.00
		TOTAL (hectares):	40.00

DOMAINE DE LA SOUMADE

Rasteau is an elongated village sitting on top of a vine-clad hillside, some 20km north-east of Orange. It is best known locally for its *vins doux naturels* – Grenache-based fortified sweet wines of a distinctly acquired taste which, although consumed *en apéritif* in the region, are rarely seen elsewhere. Decline in this market has led Rasteau's growers to concentrate their skills in producing Côtes du Rhône and -Villages, leaving a handful to continue making *vins doux naturels*.

One continuing the tradition is André Romero – a short, spare *homme du*

terroir, with greying hair and protruding grey eyes. An apparently taciturn appearance hides a genuine love of wine and a mischievous sense of humour – an individual who follows his own instincts and is decidedly not a technocrat! André presides over 26ha of Côtes du Rhône and Côtes du Rhône-Villages in the commune; with 60% Grenache, 20% Syrah and 10% each of Mourvèdre and "divers".

His wines and vinification fit his mien – sturdy, a touch rough, supple underneath their tannic envelopes and

needing time to open out and communicate. The vinification is designed to maximise extraction, with automatic *pigeage* (in a commune where *remontage* is the norm), 15–25 days *cuvaison* and a maximum fermentation temperature of 33°C. A good dollop of press-wine is added to reinforce the structure, then the wines spend a year in *cuve* and a further year in *foudre*. A light plate filtration precedes bottling by André and his young son. The grapes used to be vatted with their stems, but this extracted too much tannin even for André: "we have a clientele for burly wines", he interjects. Now the bunches are 60% de-stemmed.

André doesn't like white wine, so doesn't bother to make any. What he really admires are the great Bordeaux. Since that city is only four hours away by car, he disappears from time to time to indulge his fancy. Perhaps it was from the Bordelais that he gleaned the idea of de-stemming. In homage to the greater *vignoble* he has planted 2ha with Cabernet Sauvignon and a dab of Merlot "to try". These are 100% de-stemmed and produce a pleasant Vin de Pays de la Principauté d'Orange – André's minor Mouton!

The serious business starts with the Côtes du Rhône-Villages Rasteau – a lightish wine, in Romero terms, but perfectly pleasant drinking in its first few years. However, it is with two *Cuvées Spéciales* that the Romero skill really starts to show. The Cuvée Prestige is a Côtes du Rhône-Villages from a selection of *terroirs* and vines averaging 40 years of age. The *assemblage* is broadly in the global proportions indicated above, with the different varieties mixed in at fermentation. In general, this wine has a deep colour, rather leathery overtones on the nose and real Romero density and extract; a bit rustic perhaps, but very good all the same.

"Le top-wine" in this stable is André's wonderfully-named Cuvée Confiance. "Everyone else has Vieilles Vignes", he muses, "so I chose Confiance to be different". Whether the confidence involved is that his customers should have in him, or whether the reverse, is not made explicit. Either way, it is not misplaced. The wine is a 14° Côtes du Rhône Villages Rasteau, from 20% of 40-year-old Syrah vines and 80% of 93-year-old Grenache vines, fermented together and then given two and a half years *élevage* – a year in *cuve* followed by one

Vines sprouting from winter dormancy between Rasteau and Gigondas.

and a half years in *demi-muids*. The Confiance only appears in great vintages. If the 1990 and 1993 are any indication, the wine is a veritable monster, dense black, painfully slow to evolve on either the nose or palate, and with an extraordinary concentration of almost port-like ripe fruit. Like port, a wine to lock away for 15 years and, at 55 francs including tax at the cellar door, a snip!

André's lively young son is about to go to viticultural school; one wonders

whether, given his father's entirely self-taught skills, this is an entirely wise move; he might return filled up with all manner of technological ideas. On the other hand, perhaps André is secretly hoping to pick up some ideas on how to make a First Growth out of his Cabernet Sauvignon.

VARIETY	APPELLATION	DETAILS	AREA
GRENACHE	COTES DU RHONE + VILLAGES	Vine age: 4-93, average 30 yrs	15.60
SYRAH	COTES DU RHONE + VILLAGES	Vine age: 4-93, average 30 yrs	5.20
MOURVEDRE	COTES DU RHONE + VILLAGES	Vine age: 4-93, average 30 yrs	2.60
"DIVERS" (RED)	COTES DU RHONE + VILLAGES	Vine age: 4-93, average 30 yrs	2.60
		TOTAL (hectares):	26.00

DOMAINE DE ST-ANNE

This is an interesting domaine, created from very little by the Steinmaier family who came from Chalon-sur-Saône in Burgundy. They liked the area so much that in 1965 they bought some buildings and 13ha of land, including some rather degenerate vines, in the hamlet of Les Celettes, 3km up from St-Gervais among pine- and broom-clad hills. A further 10ha and the 16th-, 17th- and 19th-century buildings which now form the nucleus of the domaine, were added in 1973 with further additions in 1976. Walls were ripped out to link the various galleries

which now form the bottle cellar, and a new *cuverie* was added in 1979. Finally, further enlargements were made in 1986 and 1989 to enable them to stock 150,000 bottles and a full year's harvest in *cuve*.

The Steinmaiers produce several *cuvées* of Côtes du Rhône-Villages: the Cuvée Notre Dame des Celettes (from old-vine Grenache from the best plots plus a touch of Syrah and Mourvèdre), the St-Gervais from 50-60% Mourvèdre with 20% each of Syrah and Grenache, and a Côtes du Rhône made from 100% Syrah aged in a mix of new Vosges and

older casks. While these are all sound – sometimes excellent – his real interest lies in the Côtes du Rhône made entirely from Viognier, a grape' at which the Steinmaiers have come to excel.

Why plant Viognier here – on limestone soils, far better adapted to red than white vines? Jean and Alain's parents apparently liked drinking Viognier and thought that they would try an experimental 1.5ha planting for fun. It performed so well that they decided to add a further 1.8ha despite the fact that vine is notoriously unsuited to limestone ground.

Here, however, at 180-220 metres' elevation, facing south-south-west towards the distant Cevennes, it seems to thrive, especially if pruned *en gobelet.* Unlike Condrieu, where a cane pruning is favoured, the Viognier St-Anne thus trained both produces more evenly and is markedly less susceptible to wood infections. The domaine still has some Viognier trained *en cordon de Royat,* but is gradually reverting back to the old-fashioned *gobelet.*

The topsoils here, on slopes with little to retain them, suffer badly from erosion, so the Steinmaiers have re-structured the vineyards into terraces and sown rye-grass to combat the problem. However, this tends to hold summer humidity as well, which can result in less vine vegetation.

Looking on the positive side, Alain comments that less vegetation also means less rot, so on balance he is content.

The Steinmaiers have also been working hard with their nurseryman since they discovered that some of their Viognier plants had different leaf and grape characteristics and also gave a much more neutral tasting wine. Further research revealed that these vines were

not true Viognier – and, moreover, that many thousands of this aberrant strain had been sold to *vignerons* over the last decade or so. There is now a field-selection programme at St-Anne to bring their vineyards up to scratch.

The St-Anne Viognier – which is sold simply as Côtes du Rhône – is a medium-weight example of the genre: clean, quite fresh, with dried fruit aromas. It generally manages a fair weight of fruit, a good nerve of backbone acidity and attractive complexity on the palate. This reflects a careful vinification at 18-20° C, blocked

malolactic and an early-ish bottling, in May following the vintage. It doesn't have the concentration of a Condrieu, but equally doesn't have the price. Perhaps a marginally earlier *mise* would conserve more of the fruit aromas and flavour, but this is not to deny the quality of what Alain and Jean Steinmaier have achieved.

WINE	VARIETIES	DETAILS	AREA
COTES DU RHONE VILLAGES	MARSANNE, ROUSSANNE, CLAIRETTE, BOURBOULENC	Average vine-age 13	2.50
COTES DU RHONE	VIOGNIER	Average vine-age 11	3.30
COTES DU RHONE VILLAGES	GRENACHE, SYRAH, MOURVEDRE	Average vine-age 16	15.00
COTES DU RHONE VILLAGES, CUVEE NOTRE DAME DES CELLETTES	GRENACHE, SYRAH, MOURVEDRE	Average vine-age 30	4.00
COTES DU RHONE VILLAGES, ST. GERVAIS	MOURVEDRE, GRENACHE, SYRAH	Average vine-age 30	2.00
COTES DU RHONE	SYRAH	Average vine-age 30	2.00
		TOTAL (hectares):	28.80

DOMAINE DES TOURS

Between the small towns of Sarrians and Jonquières, in a sprawling cluster of buildings at the top of a knoll, is the Domaine des Tours – some 38ha of vines surrounding a modest 16th-century château whose tower gives the estate its name. The land is divided between *vin de table,* *vin de pays* de Vaucluse, Vacqueyras and Côtes du Rhône. The *vin de pays* is sold as Domaine des Tours, the other appellations as Château des Tours.

The owner is Bernard Reynaud, one of Louis Reynaud's five children and the elder brother of Jacques Reynaud of Château Rayas in Châteauneuf (qv). Having worked for some years with Jacques, he knows well the winemaker's art and with his son Emmanuel – a dark, handsome and reflective man in his 30s – is quietly turning out some excellent wines, albeit in a less illustrious appellation than his brother.

"I am very traditional", explains Emmanuel from his littered desk in the *cuverie.* However, tradition costs money, so while he would like to keep his Vacqueyras and Côtes du Rhône a little longer than the present 6-8 months in *foudres,* this will have to wait until the impressive new line of stainless-steel tanks has been paid for.

About 8-10% of the output is white *vin de pays* and Côtes du Rhône. The former has 70% Clairette plus some Grenache

Blanc, while the latter comes from around 80% of Grenache Blanc with some Roussanne and Clairette added. The Côtes du Rhône is an attractive, rich wine, with a mildly oxidative, rather old-fashioned flavour, yet good acidity and length and no rough edges.

The reds are the mainstay of this domaine. At the moment the Reynauds only bottle the produce from five of their 15ha of Vacqueyras, the bulk being sold for some reason as Côtes du Rhône to the local *négoce.* What there is is excellent, with a house style which emphasises finesse above structure and has an attractive dimension of complexity. Even at the *vin de pays* level the wines have depth and interest, helped no doubt by a high percentage of old vines.

The precise composition of the Vacqueyras blend at Domaine des Tours depends in part on the success of the Grenache, which forms 90% of the Vacqueyras plantings. Grenache is notoriously susceptible to *coulure,* which

drops flowers and thus reduces crop size. If the quality and concentration are good, the *cuvée* is entirely late-harvested Grenache, otherwise 5-10% Syrah is added.

Emmanuel vinifies separate *cuvées* according to the type of *terroir* involved. "Everything from more powerful *terre fort* to finer *terre léger* – wines as different as night and day", he adds. After 12-16 months *élevage* there is a light plate filtration "just like Uncle Jacques", and then bottling on the small Rayas machine, which Emmannuel dismantles and collects for the purpose.

He and his father also follow Uncle Jacques in another important respect, yields: the maximum permitted *vin du pays rendement* is 80hl/ha – they restrict it to 55. There is similar lack of excess in the other appellations. These self-imposed limits show through in the natural concentration and equilibrium of the wines.

Emmanuel Reynaud likes tasting and admires the wines of Uncle Jacques' Rayas, which in due course he will take over. He is making a fine job of his apprenticeship for this important promotion.

APPELLATION	DETAILS	AREA
VIN DE TABLE	10-60 yr old vines	9.50
VIN DE PAYS DE VAUCLUSE	10-60 yr old vines	9.50
COTES DU RHONE	10-60 yr old vines	5.00
VACQUEYRAS	10-60 yr old vines	15.00
	TOTAL (hectares):	38.00

SOUTHERN FRANCE

Spanning the vast area between France's Italian and Spanish borders, "the Midi" is best known for volumes of pleasant "ordinaire". Now, inspired by the great wines of the Rhône, a band of pioneering vignerons are re-drawing the quality map of Southern France and demonstrating what can be done with noble grapes, care and skill. Their efforts are attracting legions of buyers, eager to tap the affordable riches of Europe's most exciting wine region.

*Vineyards sloping down towards the sea
south of Banyuls.*

SOUTHERN FRANCE

As complex as it is extended, this area stretches from the wealthy resorts bordering Italy to the less glitzy seaside town of Banyuls-sur-Mer, a few kilometres from the Spanish border. Vines have been cultivated right across the region for centuries and in the case of the Rhône delta, from Roman times.

Apart from a few notable pockets of viticulture – Bandol, Banyuls and Cassis in particular – the coastal strip is relatively vine-free. A short distance into the hinterland, however, the landscape changes to *garrigue*, characterised by grey-white limestone escarpments covered with pine and scented scrub interspersed with carpets of low bush-trained (*gobelet*) vines. Much of this is still old-fashioned, picture-book France; small, quiet villages with a couple of cafés, a *boulangerie*, the essential general store crammed with everything from vegetables to bicycle oil and a neat *mairie* flying the Tricouleur to remind citizens of their ultimate allegiance. This is the world of Manon des Sources and Jean de Floret – ostensibly peaceful, atmospheric and wonderfully individual.

Until quite recently, the region acted as bulk producer for the Frenchman's everyday litre – three or four stars embossed on the glass bottle (non-returnable plastic nowadays) to indicate increasing alcoholic strength. The 1960s brought an influx of Algerians to the Midi, who benefited from automatic French nationality. Their influence, and the widespread blending of local produce with firmer, stronger Algerian or Moroccan wine, helped to beef up intrinsically poor quality and kept the region going. With the 1980s came cheap Italian imports, falling prices and the European wine lake. The European Community then stepped in to subsidise distillation of unwanted wine into industrial alcohol and to finance a programme of replacing poor-quality vines with better stock.

Improvement has finally arrived, driven mainly by a market which is increasingly turning towards quality. The "traditional" high-yielding or high-alcohol grapes – Aramon, Cinsaut, Alicante Bouschet, Grenache, Terret Bourret etc. for reds and rosés, Ugni Blanc, Bourboulenc, Clairette, Picpoul and Maccabeo for the whites – are, with positive encouragement from "*les officiels*", being supplemented with "improvers" known as *cépages ameliorateurs*: Syrah, Mourvèdre, Cabernet Sauvignon and Merlot for reds and Chenin Blanc, Sauvignon Blanc and Chardonnay for whites.

Rhône varieties appear patchily across this landscape. While Mourvèdre is concentrated in Bandol, where it gives its most classical expression, Syrah is appearing more often in Provence and, since the 1960s, has been an increasing part of such appellations as Faugères, Corbières, St-Chinian and of the better generic Languedocs. Many top growers are now accepting the reduced yields and distinctive character Syrah brings, in order to improve quality.

Among the general upgrading of grapes, there is a band of Rhône-struck *vignerons* who have concentrated on Syrah and Mourvèdre with striking results. Some growers are also testing the water with the white Rhône varieties (Viognier, Marsanne and Roussanne) to see what can be achieved in selected, often cooler, sites of the Languedoc. "*Les officiels*" seem less certain of their attitude to these varieties.

The dreadful Aramon has largely disappeared, but the Carignan lives on as one of the most widely planted varieties in the Languedoc-Roussillon. Its high, regular yield and disease resistance are attractive to many less quality-conscious growers. A few, with plantings of very old vines, manage to coax excellent wine from it, but these are rare.

TRENDS

Southern France covers some nearly 200,000ha of vines – 20,000 in Provence, 180,000 in the Languedoc-Roussillon. These annually produce some four million hectolitres (44 million cases) of wine. The Languedoc-Roussillon alone accounts for 35% of France's total vineyard area, and boasts an annual output which exceeds that of Australia or the United States. Only 10% is *appellation contrôlée*; 30% is *vin de pays* and the rest *vin de table*.

From the 1970s, there has been a progressive upgrading of lesser Southern France appellations to full *appellation contrôlée* status – a move not always matched by a commensurate hike in quality. Collioure was elevated in 1971, Côtes de Provence and Côtes du Roussillon in 1977, Faugères and St-Chinian in 1982, Minervois in 1984, and Corbières and Coteaux d'Aix in 1985.

These changes were accompanied by a cash injection to re-equip inefficient cooperatives, of which the Corbières, Roussillon and Minervois alone boast nearly 600. This increase in technical and marketing expertise is largely responsible for the region's regeneration, though the future for a huge volume of often sound but neutral wine, in the

The medieval city of Carcassone on the western fringe of the Midi.

for a huge volume of often sound but neutral wine, in the face of international competition, is by no means secure.

Among quality-minded growers, there is an air of excitement. Buyers with a nose for a bargain are starting to explore the region to provision markets who increasingly accept that it is the grower, not the appellation which ultimately matters. As in Tuscany, much of the best wine comes, not as AC but as *vin de pays* or even *vin de table*, reflecting the fact that many of the appellations are still stuck with a "traditional" choice of varieties and don't (yet) allow pure varietals or blends which emphasise new or unusual grapes. This often creates tension between those who seek to improve overall quality within the existing AC framework – by, for example, reducing yields and tinkering with the permitted grape mix to favour *ameliorateurs* – and those with no allegiance to any appellation who want deregulation and the freedom to create the best they can. Younger vignerons openly talk of *vin de cépage* and *vin de terroir*; it is this attitude which is rejuvenating *vin de pays* and will ultimately marginalise appellations bogged down in sterile arguments over rules

and regulations. The authorities continue to pronounce on what should be planted and where from their office desks, and remain obdurately reluctant to acknowledge that fine wine can be made from non-traditional varieties. To convince them that something else might conceivably work forces growers such as Pierre and Catherine Roque at Domaine de Clovallon (qv) to produce their excellent Pinot Noir first, in some secrecy, and only then to argue with the hide-bound "*officiels*" about a credible designation (in this case, Vin de Pays d'Oc).

Fortunately, not all ACs are irretrievably stuck in the historical mud; Jean-Michel Piccinini in La Livinière, for example, is trying to establish a superior designation of "cru" to cover four communes within the Minervois appellation, on the basis of stricter yield and varietal criteria; this is a model scheme which will undoubtedly improve quality and deserves support.

The climate of the region is Mediterranean and its geology is based on limestone. However, these generalisations hide a multitude of local variations which make the difference between *ordinaire* and something better. For example, there is little in common between Pic St-Loup, Bandol and Collioure, and Faugères is significantly warmer than Bédarieux, just a few kilometres away. So *terroirs* and micro-climates really matter.

Traditionally, the best plantings were on well-exposed hillsides; as demand for mass-produced wine soared, vines rapidly spread to more productive but less propitious plains. Genuinely fine land is scarce, so the younger generation, many of whom start out without the benefit of mature, well-sited vineyards, have to scour the countryside for the right place to plant Syrah or Mourvèdre or whatever it is they want to grow.

This is a warm part of Europe, so ripening is rarely a problem. Rainfall, rather than sunshine, is usually the critical determinant of a season's quality and, while vintages matter, year-on-year variability is less pronounced than one finds further north. With conditions usually right for making "sound" wine, there is rarely talk of great vintages.

Viticulture is relatively straightforward, with little need for numerous pest or disease treatments and a low incidence of rot. The usual bush-training (*gobelet*) still dominates the landscape, although many domaines are experimenting with different forms of canopy-management to improve fruit quality – more bunches and greater ripeness. This is especially useful in parts of the Languedoc where the late season's warm sunny days are punctuated by cool nights, which prolong maturation. Top estates use little fertiliser and work to keep yields low and to harvest before sugar levels are too high and the grapes over-ripe.

Cellar practice has seen major changes over the last generation. Those who make their own wine know how to handle fruit and have the equipment to refine vinification where necessary. Fermentations are in cleaner vessels, with temperature control if things threaten to overheat. A proportion of whole bunches may be included in the red vats to soften and enrich the wines, while some growers are trying *macération pelliculaire* with their whites to add fat and depth.

In many cellars, small casks (225 litres) are replacing old *foudres* for maturation and new oak is becoming an important regular addition to the vigneron's armoury. Fortunately, there is much greater awareness of the need to bottle wine while it still has some fruit left, rather than leaving it to desiccate until an order comes along to justify the bother (and expense) of bottling. The estates profiled here have little in common with the "traditional" cellars one still finds clinging onto outdated dogma and haphazard, old-fashioned methods.

PROVENCE

Best known for its refreshing rosé, this large swathe of easterly France extends from the Bouches-du-Rhône, through the Var to just west of Fréjus. There are only four appellations of significance – Bellet, Bandol, Cassis and Palette – all relatively small, especially Palette which extends to just over 22ha and covers two principal estates, Château de Crémat and Château Simone (qv). The rest is divided between five ACs, of which Côtes de Provence is of greatest interest. From the mid-1970s, a few estates, owned by pioneering, quality-aware growers, started to plant Syrah, Mourvèdre and Cabernet Sauvignon, with considerable publicity and success. These domaines – Richeaume (qv), de Trévallon (qv) and Château Vignelaure – have now been joined by the likes of La Courtade (qv) as outposts of independence and experiment and others will doubtless follow.

Geologically the region is diverse and complex. limestone is predominant, with patches of shale and volcanic rock. Bandol (qv) is mainly limestone and silica, with outcrops of Triassic gypsum; Bellet, which produces unusual reds and rosés, is on steep limestone scree soils, while Cassis shares the same broad geology as Bandol. Palette is on mainly north-facing limestone, dominated by the impressive Mont St-Victoire. Topography and micro-climate plays an important role in the quality of many sites, although the sun is perhaps the main unifying factor.

As elsewhere in the region, quality depends upon the grape mix. Wines with more Mourvèdre and Syrah tend to be firmer and longer-lived – the former imparting something of the character of Bandol, the latter combining the finesse of the northern Rhône with the richness and Provençale flavours of the south.

LANGUEDOC-ROUSSILLON

This has been a wine-growing region since well before the Roman occupation, which was instrumental in developing viticulture, using the port of Narbonne, the Rhône Valley and the Via Domitia as export channels. The fall of the Roman empire, Saracen invasions and other vicissitudes halted expansion, but by the early 19th century things were back on course. Devastating mildew and phylloxera in the late 19th century were followed by a prolonged slump. Production then increased and, in line with the rest of Southern France, is now slowly being transformed from quantity to quality, reflecting the demands of modern consumers. From east to west the region encompasses Hérault,

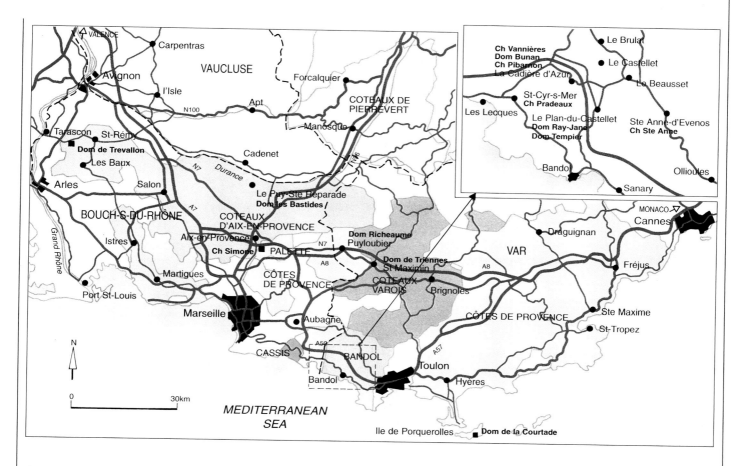

the Minervois, Corbières, the Roussillonnais and Banyuls/Collioure. The geological map of the region shows a bewildering complexity of sedimentary, metamorphic and volcanic rocks from several different time-periods and highlights the fundamental importance of *terroir*.

Languedoc

The region covers three departments: the Aude, the Gard and Hérault. The main appellations of interest here are Faugères, north of Béziers (1,400ha) and St-Chinian, to its north-west, almost in the Minervois (2,000ha). Both make red and rosé, but it is the former which is capable of generating most excitement. These are based on Carignan – maximum 40% for Faugères, 50% for St-Chinian – with a minimum 20% together or separately of Syrah and Mourvèdre for the former, 10% for the latter. The balance consists of Grenache Noir and Lladoner Pelut, a variety which has much similarity to the Grenache but experts have stopped short of declaring identical. As well as the estates profiled here, the Faugères from Bernard and Claudie Vidal's Château de la Liquière at Cabrerolles (especially the red Cuvée Cistus) are capable of excelling, if somewhat hit-and-miss. The catch-all appellation, which seems to be trapping some interesting fish, is Coteaux du Languedoc.

Minervois

This is a smallish area, covering 18,000ha and 61 communes in the departments of Aude and Hérault, which was upgraded from VDQS to AC in 1984. The interest lies mainly in reds, which have a mandatory 30% minimum of Syrah, Mourvèdre, Grenache Noir and Lladoner Pelut, with a minimum 10% of the first two varieties. The other 60% comes from Cinsaut, Picpoul Noir, Terret Noir, Aspiran Noir and Carignan. Grapes mixes vary widely across the region, as do soils and micro-climates – cooler in the hills and very hot on sheltered plains. There are some fine, individual estates here – Château Hélène (qv) and Clos Centeilles (qv) in particular.

Corbières

Also a small region, 14,000ha spanning 87 communes of the Aude *département*, bordered to the north by the Minervois, to the south by the Roussillonnais and to the east by the Mediterranean. It is split into seven principal sub-regions, reflecting different soils, climates and wine characteristics. Quality viticulture is mostly on hillsides in Les Corbières Centrales, centred round the town of Lézignan-Corbières; wines here tend to have more depth and structure, although there are pockets of excellence elsewhere. Fitou, which produces Carignan/Grenache based reds from 2,000ha, used to be part of Corbières, but has had its own appellation since 1948.

Roussillon

Another vast area, producing 3% of all French wine from *vin du pays* and *appellation contrôlée* land in the southern sector of the Department of Pyrénées-Orientales. The appellations of Côtes du Roussillon and Côtes du Roussillon Villages account for 5,400ha and yield over 32 million litres of table wine. One-third of this comes from the 1,400ha (25 communes) of Côtes du Roussillon-Villages, where yields are 45hl/ha rather than the 50 hl/ha for the more basic Côtes du Roussillon. The Villages designation is restricted to red wine only, where Carignan is capped at 70% with a minimum of Syrah and Mourvèdre of 10% each; Cinsaut, Grenache and Lladoner Pelut make up the balance.

The real interest here lies in the reds from the 1,900-ha Collioure appellation, which covers the same ground as Banyuls, famous for its magnificent, age-worthy, sweet red Vin Doux Naturel. Here, on a variety of soils and some vertiginously steep slopes fronting the Mediterranean, a minimum of 60% Grenache is buttressed by a minimum 25% of Mourvèdre and/or Syrah, the balance being Carignan and Cinsaut. This is a potentially most exciting appellation, to which top Banyuls domaines are devoting greater attention as demand for *vin doux naturel* plummets.

PRESENT AND FUTURE

Southern France's recent history has been dominated by the emergence of a handful of high-quality estates, determined to buck the bulk-wine image. The late 1970s saw the creation of Eloi Durrbach's Domaine de Trévallon (qv) and Aimé Guibert's Mas de Daumas Gassac (qv) both of which pioneered the search for quality and set standards which others have sought to emulate.

These showed what could be achieved, given good land and low yields from carefully selected varieties and, in breaking the mould, provided a strong spur to other would-be iconoclasts. Others, such as Australian Bill Hardy's Domaine des Baumes at Béziers and Robert Skalli's Fortant de France are showing that volume and interesting quality are far from incompatible; Skalli's Viognier in particular is excellent and modestly priced, ideal as a starter for anyone wanting to see what all the Condrieu fuss is about.

The best of this new wave is profiled in the pages which follow, though in a period of such rapid evolution there will inevitably be omissions. Some are breaking new ground, while others are producing top quality within the existing *appellation controlée* or *vin de table* framework. The achievements of both deserved to be recognized.

Some not profiled here are worth individual mention: Les Chemins du Bessac, the Domaine la Tour Boisée, the Leferrers at Domaine du Grand Cres in the Corbières, who produce an excellent Corbières from 55% Grenache, 30% Cinsaut and 15% Syrah – the latter could well stand alone. The 50-year-old Belgian journalist Guido Jansegers, at Château Mansenoble, whose *vin de pays* and Réserve Corbières, are made from 60% Syrah, 25% old-vine Grenache and 50% Mourvèdre, vinified traditionally with long *cuvaison* and plenty of *pigeage*. All these are well worth seeking out.

The region is slowly regenerating and the wine industry is attracting outside investment. The low quality, high volume image still remains but the international profile of some of the important "boutique" estates is gradually transforming this. These trends are likely to continue, especially as older growers cede responsibility to a younger, more forward-looking generation.

The debate over *cépages améliorateurs*, which many see as changing the fundamental character of traditional wines, will doubtless rumble on. Meanwhile, newer domaines will continue to develop wines from noble varieties.

For these, and other pioneering estates, *vin de pays* is the last refuge of liberty, and any official moves to restrict this flexibility would be criminal stupidity. For the astute buyer and the adventurous consumer, this is an area well worth mining. There are today more exciting discoveries to be made in Southern France than anywhere else in Europe.

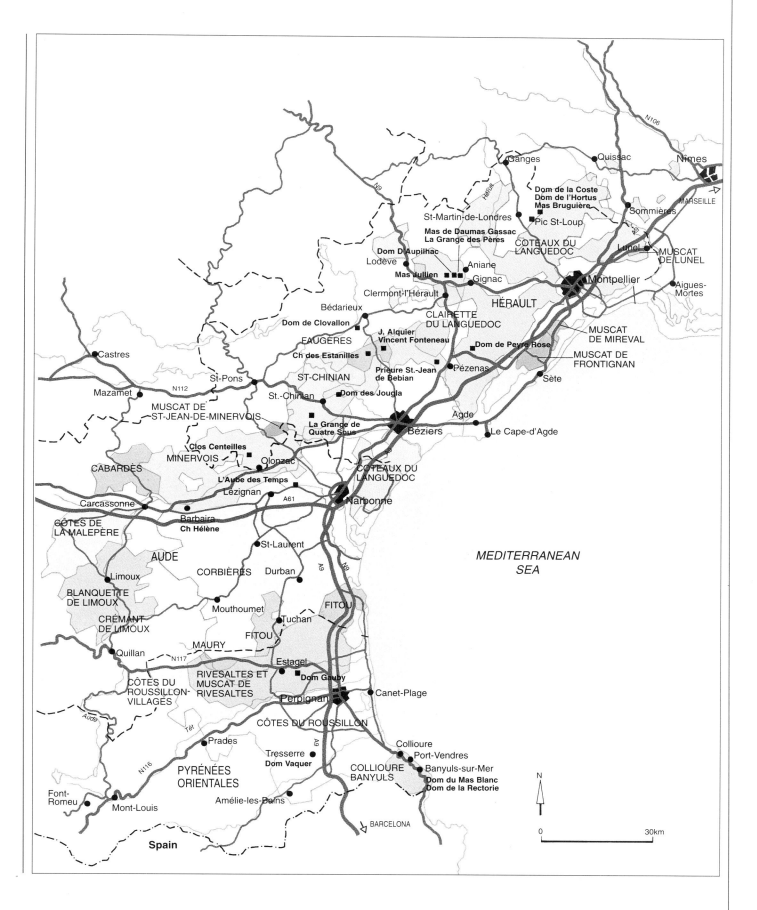

Nîmes

MARSEILLE

Quissac

Ganges

**Dom de la Coste
Dom de l'Hortus
Mas Bruguière**

St-Martin-de-Londres

Sommières

Pic St-Loup

**Mas de Daumas Gassac
La Grange des Pères**

CÔTEAUX DU
LANGUEDOC

Lunel

MUSCAT
DE LUNEL

Dom D'Aupilhac

Lodève

Aniane

Aigues-
Mortes

Mas Jullien

Gignac

Montpellier

Clermont-l'Hérault

HÉRAULT

Bédarieux

CLAIRETTE
DU LANGUEDOC

MUSCAT
DE MIREVAL

Dom de Clovallon

FAUGÈRES

**J. Alquier
Vincent Fonteneau**

Dom de Peyre Rose

Ch des Estanilles

MUSCAT DE
FRONTIGNAN

Castres

ST-CHINIAN

**Prieuré St.-Jean
de Bebian**

Pézenas

Sète

Mazamet

St-Pons

St.-Chinian

Dom des Jougla

Agde

N112

MUSCAT DE
ST-JEAN-DE-MINERVOIS

**La Grange de
Quatre Sous**

Béziers

Le Cape-d'Agde

Clos Centeilles

MINERVOIS

Qlonzac

COTEAUX DU
LANGUEDOC

CABARDÈS

L'Aube des Temps

Carcassonne

Lézignan

A61

Narbonne

MEDITERRANEAN
SEA

CÔTES DE
LA MALEPÈRE

Barbaira

Ch Hélène

AUDE

St-Laurent

CORBIÈRES

Durban

Limoux

BLANQUETTE
DE LIMOUX

Mouthoumet

FITOU

CRÉMANT
DE LIMOUX

Tuchan

MAURY

FITOU

Quillan

N117

Estagel

RIVESALTES ET
MUSCAT DE
RIVESALTES

Dom Gauby

CÔTES DU
ROUSSILLON-
VILLAGES

Perpignan

Canet-Plage

CÔTES DU ROUSSILLON

Aude

Têt

A9

Prades

Collioure

Tresserre

Port-Vendres

Font-
Romeu

N116

PYRÉNÉES
ORIENTALES

Dom Vaquer

COLLIOURE
BANYULS

Banyuls-sur-Mer

**Dom du Mas Blanc
Dom de la Rectorie**

Mont-Louis

Amélie-les-Bains

N

BARCELONA

Spain

0   30km

DOMAINE GILBERT ALQUIER & FILS

Physically and spiritually, Domaine Alquier is at the heart of Faugères. In the centre of this attractive little village in the hills above Bédarieux, Jean-Michel and Frédéric Alquier produce some of the densest and most concentrated wine of Faugères, a 1,700-ha appellation which is, apart from Fitou, the smallest in the Languedoc-Roussillon region.

The domaine, created in the 1870s by great-grandfather Alquier, originally consisted of 5ha. Its wines provisioned the bars and cafés of Paris through his son Desiré, who went to live there, bored by rural Faugères. When his son Gilbert returned from the war in 1948, he found a deal of low-grade Carignan and Aramon grapes, but neither water nor electricity. Knowing how well Syrah and Grenache sold in Paris, he set about planting both. Together with Mourvèdre and some old Carignan left for sentiment, these constitute the domaine's present 30ha. The Syrah contributes spice, perfume and a good structure, the Grenache "warmth", the Mourvèdre a fine earthy spiciness and muscle, qualities which also characterise the 60- to 80-year-old Carignan vines – although these are giving way to Mourvèdre as time passes.

Soils are poor, and entirely schist with 20cm of topsoil – mostly hand-crushed in the 1960s, as Jean-Michel painfully remembers from his school holidays. Underneath, 50cm of larger slabs give onto solid rock. The vineyards are on south/south-east slopes of varyingly vertiginous gradients yielding an average of 30–35hl/ha against a permitted 50–55hl/ha. There are three *cuvees* of Faugères. The generic blend – 30% each

of Grenache, Syrah and Carignan, plus 10% of Mourvèdre – produces 50,000 bottles. It is vinified in *cuve* and bottled early to retain fruit for more or less immediate consumption.

The Maison Jaune is altogether more structured. 35,000 bottles contain 20-year-old Syrah (50%) plus Grenache and a good dab of Mourvèdre, and 30% spends 13 months in new Vosges oak. It is released 2–3 years after the vintage, but will keep and develop well over 5–10 years, depending on the year.

Finally, in 1990 – a year after Gilbert sadly died aged 63 and Jean-Michel and his brother took over – came Les Bastides: an *assemblage* of wine from older vines, selected from 5ha of scattered plots of Syrah (70%), Grenache (20%) and Mourvèdre (10%), and kept for 14 months or so in up to 80% new wood. Minimum fining and filtration is the rule for all the Alquier Faugères .

The wines, invariably at the top of this appellation which boasts three cooperatives and 22 independent producers, have attracted much acclaim. Jean-Michel recounts with evident relish the experience of a Paris *courtier* who returned home to the remains of a sample of 1990 Les Bastides, tasted with no great

appreciation four days earlier. His wife insisted on their finishing it. Aeration had changed an ugly duckling into a majestic swan and within a week Les Bastides was on the lists of several starred Paris restaurants. Jean-Michel himself admits to misjudging the vintage and to scurrying round persuading owners to exchange their 1990 for something younger.

Great-grandfather Alquier's Faugères won a *Diplome* in Paris in 1894; a century on, the Alquier Syrah is a wine of which he would have been justifiably proud.

Jean-Michel and Frédéric are building on solid foundations, although with obvious frustration at the disadvantage of having an appellation which is too often lumped together with the mass of dull, dilute Midi.

Promoting the individuality of their wines is a constant struggle against ignorance. "People think of this area as poor wine; they don't even want to taste it". However, the message is beginning to percolate through – even to some journalists who don't appear to understand that youthful austerity is often the price of longevity. This is a first-class estate and only a snob would prefer an inferior Côte-Rôtie to the remarkable Bastides at around a third of the price.

VARIETY	APPELLATION	DETAILS	AREA
SYRAH	FAUGERES	Planted 1960 and 1988; average vine age 20; training both Cordon and extended Gobelet on wire	12.00
GRENACHE	FAUGERES	Average age 40	7.50
MOURVEDRE	FAUGERES	Average age 12	6.00
CARIGNAN	FAUGERES	60–80 yrs old	4.50
		TOTAL (hectares):	30.00

L'AUBE DES TEMPS

In a region where individuality is rife, typicity elusive, and where the best *vignerons* are generally unconcerned whether their wines appear as AC or *vin de table*, this estate must rank among the more unusual.

The main focus of L'Aube des Temps is on late-harvested white wines, of various degrees of sweetness, from a splendid range of grapes. There are Viognier, Marsanne, Chardonnay, Sémillon, Sauvignon Blanc, and Petit and Gros Manseng, while they are experimenting with patches of Riesling, Muscadelle and Gewürztraminer, Romorantin and the Jura's Savignin. In the pipeline are Furmint (of Hungary's

Tokay), Roussanne and Chenin Blanc.

Soon after buying this estate in 1986, Michel Pech and his father Guy realised that they had something special – a *micro-terroir* at the confluence of two rivers – the Aude and the Orbieu – on sedimented, sandy, alluvium soils, ideally

adapted to *vendange tardive*, with late-season humidity to concentrate the sugars, acids and aromas of bunches left on the vine. In fact, conditions approaching those of Sauternes.

One or two *passages* through the vines ensure that the grapes are picked at optimum maturity – sometimes botrytized, though this is not the express aim. Fermentations use natural yeasts and

VARIETY	VINEYARD	DETAILS	AREA
VIOGNIER	L'AUBE DES TEMPS	2–5 yr old vines; séléction massale from Condrieu	3.00
MARSANNE	L'AUBE DES TEMPS	12 yr old vines	0.20
CHARDONNAY	L'AUBE DES TEMPS	3–10 yr old vines	3.00
SAUVIGNON BLANC	L'AUBE DES TEMPS	6 yr old vines	1.00
SEMILLON	L'AUBE DES TEMPS	5 yr old vines	1.00
		TOTAL (hectares):	8.20

are made in cask. Remarkably the process is over in 4–5 days – something which attracted the attention of experts from Bordeaux, who at first refused to believe that a yeast existed which could munch up such sugar-rich musts so quickly. They took samples back to the laboratory, satisfied themselves of the phenomenon, and have now managed to culture the yeast-strain responsible.

If this discovery doesn't bring renown to the Pechs, their wines will do the job

instead: Michel Pech has capped the production at 5,000 bottles in any given vintage from all varieties.

Once the yeasts have done their work, the wines remain for a year in cask – two-thirds in new wood, one-third in second-year oak – then a year in *cuve* and finally a year in bottle before release. Michel's aim is to give the wines just a seasoning of oak – no more.

These are extraordinary wines – unusual and deliciously sippable – sold,

so far, at ludicrously reasonable prices; a situation which will undoubtedly change once the word gets round. Some of the wines lack the nerve of acidity for long keeping – perhaps because Michel doesn't deliberately block the malolactic – something which needs working on.

The slender, blue, antique-tinged Renana Breganza bottle and its label are equally original. L'Aube des Temps is a remarkable estate – another in the Midi collection.

D'AUPILHAC

This promising Languedoc estate has been re-formed and expanded from a few hectares of ancient Carignan, by the young Sylvain Fadat. His bristling black hair and gesturing, indelibly grape-blackened hands animate a friendly, confident personality, determined to make the best from resources available.

Sylvain operates his 1990s domaine from a 1620s family house – abandoned for 20 years – in Montpeyroux's rue de Plo, fronted by a magnificently be-knockered, if rather battered, double door. Inside, solid stone walls insulate a maze of small rooms and cellars – all being gradually restored – backed by a long rectangular *cuverie* with its prospect of distant vine-clad limestone hills.

Apart from an excellent, firm rosé (half *pressurage directe* and half *saignée* from each red *cuve*) and 4,000 bottles of sound white from equal parts of Grenache Blanc and Ugni Blanc, the interest here lies in two excellent reds. There are 32,000 bottles of AC Coteaux de Languedoc (roughly 25% each Syrah, Carignan and Mourvèdre, 15% Grenache and 10% Cinsaut), and 8–12,000 of a delicious, concentrated Vin du Pays de Mont Beaudile, from over 50-year-old Carignan vines on mainly deep soils of decomposed oyster-fossil and limestone.

Sylvain's first vintage was 1989. Only Carignan was available then, and most of his wine went to the co-op at three francs a litre. However, the little he bottled for passing summer tourists attracted the attention of David Pugh, an expatriate Englishman, for his Les Mimosas restaurant in nearby St-Guiraud, and thence of London wine-merchants Liz and Mike Berry. The sales which followed effectively saved the domaine.

Sylvain kept the Carignan, adding Syrah, Grenache, Mourvèdre and Cinsaut. The whole range finally came on stream in 1993. Each *cépage* is vinified separately – a month of vatting with plenty of *pigeage*, followed by 15–18 months'

Sylvain Fadat.

maturation in *cuve*. *Assemblage* is delayed until after malolactic, so each wine is in a finished a state as possible before blending, and the results rarely fined and never filtered: "*vin filtré = bon; vin non-filtré = super bon!*"

The Coteaux du Languedoc is intense, concentrated stuff, needing several years to express itself. As for the Carignan, it is the best counter-argument to "*les officiels*" who constantly claim that the grape is ignoble and best grubbed up or re-grafted. Sylvain's version, from low-yielding, old vines, is a treat: late harvested with all the sweetness of well-ripened fruit and the general tenor of a

fine Zinfandel (someone gave him a couple of bottles of Ridge (qv) for him to compare). He is clear about what's needed to make fine Carignan: "you must cut off a lot of grapes – I mean a lot – two-thirds or more". It is a prolific variety which is easily over-crops, producing thin, acidic wines. But not here. This splendid Vin du Pays is not a wine for snobs. A glass or two of Aupilhac Carignan would perfectly complement a rich game stew, topped off with a fine port jelly.

Sylvain's guiding principles are succinct: don't be inflexible and don't listen to oenologists. This man will go far.

VARIETY	VINEYARD	DETAILS	AREA
CARIGNAN	AUPILHAC	50+ average vine age	3.00
SYRAH	AUPILHAC + MONTPEYROUX	8 yrs average age	2.50
GRENACHE	AUPILHAC	Part 25+, part 5 yrs	2.50
MOURVEDRE	AUPILHAC	5–7 yrs average age	3.00
CINSAUT	AUPILHAC	0.5 ha 50+ yrs; 1 ha 10 yrs	1.50
GRENACHE BLANC	AUPILHAC	Young vines	0.50
UGNI BLANC	AUPILHAC	Young vines	0.50
	AUPILHAC	Unplanted	1.00
		TOTAL (hectares):	14.50

BANDOL

Somewhat over half way between Marseilles and Toulon lies the small seaside resort of Bandol. Once a major port, it now doubles as a fishing village and holiday centre as well as giving its name to one of Provence's most individual and exciting wines.

History has it that viticulture was established here around 600 BC by the Phocaean founders of Marseille, making it some of the oldest currently-producing vineyard land in the world. By 125 BC the Romans had taken over and, according to archaeological evidence (principally, large quantities of Roman jars), developed a thriving wine export trade. By the 18th century, Bandol's reputation was such that Louis XV was reported to have drunk "carefully prepared" wine from the Le Rouve district of Le Beausset at court at Versailles, and the consumption of Bandol continued to increase throughout his reign.

Phylloxera devastated the vineyards between 1870–72, after which recovery was slow, growers preferring high-yielding varieties to the Mourvèdre which, by tradition, formed the backbone of the red wine. Between 1880 and 1914 Mourvèdre was virtually forgotten here.

In 1941 Bandol was granted the AC, allowing production of red and rosé (minimum 50% of Mourvèdre, the rest Grenache and Cinsaut) and white from Clairette and Ugni Blanc. Only designated slopes – not the valley floor – are zoned AC, from all or part of eight communes extending in a rough semi-circle from St-Cyr in the west to Ollioules in the east, with Bandol itself and Sanary as southern outposts. The heart of the *vignoble* is in the communes of La Cadière-d'Azur and Le Plan-du-Castellet, where most of the top domaines are to be found.

THE VINEYARD

The area under vine has grown from 900ha in 1986 to 1,250 in 1994. However, there is strong temptation for growers, particularly those who can't make ends meet, to sell land for housing. This urbanisation is vigorously resisted by those who do not wish to see Bandol diminish, but money talks, and local authorities with a wider economy to consider are bending with the wind and re-zoning vineyards for development. The area is becoming hideously over-built: in one village, Le Beausset, the population has risen tenfold in the last 20 years, a trend which at present shows no signs of abating.

A bucket of marc *awaiting distillation in the log-fired still at Domaines Bunan.*

Bandol is Mourvèdre territory *par excellence* and, since 1988, the AC rules have stipulated a minimum of 50% of this grape. Although this stricture applies to planted vines, conscientious producers follow this through to the finished wine. The proportion is frequently higher, with many estates now offering *cuvées* containing 100% Mourvèdre.

The *vignoble* area covers a large semicircular south-facing amphitheatre, surrounded by *garrigue* and protected to the north by hills. The maritime micro-climate is of prime importance, with long, hot summers that are tempered by the drying, cooling Mistral, yet have enough air-borne humidity to avoid the drought this variety so dislikes. Growing conditions are ideal. There are on average more than 3,000 hours of sunshine. Most of the 650mm of rain falls during the autumn and winter – little or none during the summer. Sanitising winds greatly reduce oïdium and mildew (visiting Burgundians contemplating the 20th treatment for their vines are flabbergasted to find that only one or two are needed here).

The soils are almost entirely clay/limestone, mixed with differing proportions of sand, stones and calcium carbonate derived from the erosion and decomposition of the surrounding hills. The best sites are on the higher outcrops of 250 million-year-old Triassic soils (eg Château de Pibarnon and Mas de la Rouvière); beneath are less good cretaceous soils, and beneath these, coal. The vineyards rise to around 400 metres and are either on cleared slopes or steep terraces (*restanques*). Training is either *en gobelet* or *en cordon de Royat* and the base yield is 40hl/ha – a level good growers rarely reach, let alone surpass, even in prolific vintages. To qualify for *appellation contrôlée*, the vines must be at least eight years old – elsewhere in France the minimum is four.

CLIMATE

It would be illusory to think that vintages don't vary in this southerly Mediterranean climate. Some – for example 1982, 1985, 1988, 1990 – are distinctly more successful than others, such as 1983, 1984, 1986 and 1987 – although time sometimes transforms apparently ugly ducklings into graceful swans.

Severe drought, to which Mourvèdre is particularly sensitive, and rainfall just before or during harvest (which dilutes the berries and spreads rot in grapes that are not fully ripe), are critical determinants of quality. *Coulure* – particularly for Grenache, less for Mourvèdre – disrupts flower-set and thus reduces quantity, a less serious matter.

GRAPES

Although the rules specify a minimum of 50% Mourvèdre for both red and rosé, many estates are now producing one or more red *cuvées* with a much higher percentage – 100% in some instances – while rosés generally contain less (unofficially, of course). Even with the mandatory minimum of 18 months in wood before it can be presented for *agrément*, young Bandol can be austere to the point of brutality. While Grenache adds alcohol and flesh and Cinsaut acidity, which combine to blunt any raw edges, Mourvèdre's natural anti-oxidant properties make it a slow developer, inscrutable and unforthcoming until softened by a few years in bottle.

Time brings a striking change – earthy, often leathery, tarry flavours giving way to those of *fruits noirs*, spice and liquorice, always accompanied by an earthy edge: the Mourvèdre signature. In fine vintages, those with sufficient patience to wait are well recompensed. A mature Bandol is the equal of a great Médoc – with which, tasted blind, it is frequently confused.

With some 50 independent producers and three cooperatives, it is not surprising that quality and styles vary. However among the eight top domaines standards are uniformly high. Unfortunately, the move towards lower yields and better quality has split the growers, many of whom see larger volumes as more income – understandable in the short term but a hopeless foundation for a secure future.

On top of this, internecine strife has resulted in two separate producers' Syndicats – one run from Le Beausset, the other from St-Cyr – making cohesive marketing even more difficult.

STYLES

Despite these divisive local politics, there is much excellent wine to be had, and at attractive prices. Styles range from the uncompromisingly traditional nil or partially de-stemmed wines of Ray-Jane, Vannières and others, to the more readily tractable styles of Tempier, Bunan and the like.

Blends encompass everything from 50–100% Mourvèdre, while some growers use new wood, others not and there is the usual *gamme* of long and short *cuvaisons* with more or less *pigeage* or *remontage* to contend with.

The main general winemaking fault seems to be over-extraction, which, with the naturally tannic, ungenerous Mourvèdre, results in unbalanced wines lacking in centre. This is something that is readily correctable, but older growers appear to regard an element of palate punishment as part of Bandol's personality.

The current trend of releasing prestige blends in good vintages has produced some magnificent wines; however, once his market is created, the temptation for the grower to offer a premium product (at, of course, a premium price) every year has often proved irresistible. Hiving off the best lots, especially in lesser vintages, inevitably detracts from the "regular" blend.

Domaine Tempier produces yardstick Bandol; elsewhere, with varying degrees of reliability, you have to pick and choose. The following, all excellent sources, merit special mention as first-class: Bunan, Ray-Jane, Château de Pibarnon and Château Pradeaux.

Unfortunately, the wider wine world has largely ignored Bandol, which has yet to receive the recognition it entirely merits. The wines are in reasonable supply, and are relatively inexpensive compared with – for example – the Syrahs of the northern Rhône, so this neglect is doubly inexplicable.

AC BANDOL

Created	1941
Area (max)	1,365ha
Area under vine 1994	1,128ha
Base yield	40hl/ha
Minimum alcohol	12%
Growers	50 (+ 3 co-ops)

Rambling Bandol vines and pointed cypress trees – a quintessential Provençale landscape.

DOMAINES BUNAN

At the top of an interminably long winding road above La Cadière d'Azur is Les Moulin des Costes, the headquarters of Domaines Bunan. This 18-ha estate was bought by Paul and Pierre Bunan in 1961, when they were forced to leave their native Algeria. Paul's son, Laurent, has since joined the team, after studies in Beaune and the Napa Valley. Now there are two other estates in the Bunan portfolio: the 21-ha Château and Mas de la Rouvière, acquired in 1968 and the 25-ha Domaine de Belouve, which they run *en fermage* for its owner.

The three domaines are kept apart, although vinification is centralised at Moulin des Costes. The Moulin des Costes Bandol is a mix of 70% Mourvèdre and 30% Grenache – the Bunans consider that the absence of Cinsaut is the key to the character of this wine; the Mas de la Rouvière has 55% Mourvèdre, 20% each of Grenache and Cinsaut and 5% of Syrah. For both, the fruit is de-stemmed, yeasted and vatted in *inox* for 15–21 days.

The wine then spends 18 months in *foudres* before a light Kieselguhr, and, sometimes a plate, filtration. The aim is to preserve fruit aromas and flavours and to increase extraction. The Belouve *cuvée* has 50% Mourvèdre and 25% each of Grenache and Cinsaut.

In exceptional vintages – to date 1982, 1985, 1988, 1989, 1991 and 1993 – a special *cuvée* is released under the Château de la Rouvière label. This comes from a 6-ha plot of over 50-year-old Mourvèdre vines on south-facing terraces at la Rouvière, adjoining the Peyraud's Tourtine vineyard. This spends 24 months in *foudres*, with a short spell in 225-litre Bordeaux casks, 5–10% of which are new to add a seasoning of vanilla and richness. Yields for the main crop average 32–33hl/ha, those for the Château *cuvée* turn 30hl/ha.

As well as their red Bandols, the Bunans produce whites from Clairette and Ugni Blanc and some Bourboulenc and Sauvignon Blanc; direct-press rosés from Mourvèdre, Cinsaut (Rouvière) and Grenache added (Costes and Belouve). A great deal of work has gone into refining the whites in recent years and the results are encouraging. There are also single-variety *vins du pays* from Mourvèdre and Cabernet Sauvignon, and VDP mixes in red, white and rosé from Mont-Caume as well as a range of Côtes de Provence. A small rather chaotic office handles exports to 20 countries.

The wines are good – especially the Château de la Rouvière, which well merits cellaring – and the family warm-hearted and charming.

VARIETY	APPELLATION	DETAILS	AREA
MOURVEDRE	BANDOL	Various ages; spread over 3 estates	23.91
GRENACHE	BANDOL	Various ages; spread over 3 estates	11.80
CINSAUT	BANDOL	Various ages; spread over 3 estates	16.48
CARIGNAN	VIN DU PAYS	Various ages	1.90
SYRAH	BANDOL	Various ages; Mas de la Rouviere only	2.30
SAUVIGNON BLANC		Moulin des Costes	1.00
UGNI BLANC	BANDOL	Various ages; spread over 3 estates	3.50
BOURBOULENC	BANDOL	Rouviere only	1.00
CLAIRETTE	BANDOL	Various ages; spread over 3 estates	3.70
VARIOUS	BANDOL		2.41
		TOTAL (hectares):	68.00

Domaines Bunan's collection of grape varieties, each marked with a green sign.

CHATEAU DE PIBARNON

The Château de Pibarnon sits at the end of a long, sinuous road, on top of the wooded Télégraphe hill, once a station on the old Toulon-Paris optical telegraph relay. To the north stand the pinnacles of la Cadière d'Azur and le Castellet; to the south are Bandol, St-Cyr and the Mediterranean. In 1977 the Château was bought and restored by Comte Henri de St-Victor and his wife, who gave up a successful business elsewhere to indulge a passion. They now run the estate with their son. The house is a fine Provençale *bastide* dating from the 13th century.

The site is exceptional, with a broad semicircular amphitheatre of terraced vines stretching downwards from this 300-metre summit. A patchwork of woods and pine-clad *garrigues* combine to provide a special micro-climate above the mists of the valley below. The topsoils here are Triassic in origin, stony and rich in fossils and sandy in places, with younger soils beneath. The high lime-stone content contributes tight structure and fine tannins to the grapes grown on it, while *gobelet* training and trellissing on a single wire helps to aerate and expose the bunches, thereby gaining two weeks' maturity. A green pruning in July reduces the charge per vine to five bunches, giving average yields of 35–40hl/ha.

This is a predominantly Mourvèdre estate, with 90–95% of this grape in the Pibarnon Rouge. Vinifications follow a modified traditional pattern, with 30–50% de-stemming, three weeks of *cuvaison* and plenty of *pigeage* to extract colour, flavour and matter. After 18 months or so in wood, the lots are re-assembled and fined. Only one red Bandol is produced: 100,000 bottles on average. This is a *vin de garde* which needs 5–10 years to really show its paces. Vines of less than 10 years of age contribute to a Mourvèdre and Cinsaut *rosé de saignée*. There is also a white Pibarnon Bandol from Clairette, Bourboulenc, Marsanne, Roussanne with a touch of Petit Manseng. This is a fine, stylish estate.

VARIETY	APPELLATION	AREA
MOURVEDRE	BANDOL	40.00
GRENACHE	BANDOL	2.50
WHITE VARIETIES	BANDOL	5.50
	TOTAL (hectares):	48.00

CHATEAU PRADEAUX

The Château Pradeaux came into the Portalis family in 1752, inherited by Jean-Marie Portalis, one of Napoleon's ministers. During the 1940s, the Comtesse Arlette Portalis restored the estate and kept it running throughout the war. Her nephew (and adopted son) Cyrille and his wife Magali took over management of estate in 1983.

Approached by a long tree-lined drive and surrounded by a flat vine-covered plain, the building is a long, low structure, with the cellars tacked onto the back; something of a haphazard jumble.

The property, at St-Cyr-sur-Mer, covers 26ha of which 18 are planted as Bandol. The *encépagement* is mainly Mourvèdre, with some Grenache for the red wine and Cinsaut to accompany Mourvèdre for the rosé. No chemical treatments are used – just sulphur to combat oïdium and copper sulphate against mildew. Soils are mainly limestone, reddish in places and rocky.

The grapes are hand-picked and vatted, lightly crushed and are not de-stemmed. After a shortish fermentation lasting eight to ten days, the pulp is pressed. Press and free-run wines are kept apart until after malolactic, when they are blended together for three to five years of maturation in wood. This long *élevage*, designed to refine the wine's tannins and aromas, is felt necessary because of the high proportion (95%) of Mourvèdre, which is notoriously slow to evolve. Bottling is preceded by an egg-white fining, but no filtration.

The wine can be good. However, it is not consistent. If Cyrille gets things right, this should be a top-flight domaine.

VARIETY	APPELLATION	AREA (ha)
MOURVEDRE	BANDOL	16.00
GRENACHE	BANDOL	1.00
CINSAUT	BANDOL	1.00
	TOTAL:	18.00

DOMAINE RAY-JANE

This estate belongs to Raymond Constant and his wife Jeanne. Raymond is a splendid, mildly eccentric individual who, with his son, Alain, look after 14ha of vines A craggy, grey-haired, animated man, with large ears and prominent glasses, he claims to trace his family back to the 2nd century BC and declares that they were *vignerons* from 1288.

He is a self-confessed workaholic, with some project or other always on hand. Since taking over from his father in 1968, he has personally built the family home and cellars in the village of Le Plan du Castellet and changed the estate's name from Constant to Ray-Jane. His first bottling was in 1980.

He has also found time to indulge his other passion – collecting wine artefacts, of which he now has 8,000, of high quality, many dating from Roman times. The walls of the public sales area are festooned with some of the smaller exhibits, while the rest are either packed securely away or displayed in a small underground museum. The collection is still growing.

His knowledge and fame in this field have spread, and offers of stock pour in from far and wide. Ray frequently disappears for a few days, returning with another van-load of booty. He reckons that this is the largest collection of its kind in the world.

VARIETY	APPELLATION	DETAILS	AREA
MOURVEDRE	BANDOL	Average age 80+; ⅓ are 100+	11.20
GRENACHE	BANDOL	Average age 80+	1.40
CINSAUT	BANDOL	Average age 80+	1.40
		TOTAL (hectares):	14.00

The Constants make remarkably good Bandols. These are uncompromisingly traditional in style, reflecting Ray's philosophy of "making wine to my own taste". The vineyards, mainly *en coteaux* and all on Triassic soils, rather than the rocky limestones of the lower slopes, are maintained on a biological culture basis and hoed by hand. Many of the vines are centenarians and yields are low (32hl/ha average). Each variety is vinified separately, complete with stems because "stalks add a bit of tannin", Ray explains, adding "most *vignerons* de-stem, that's because they sell their wines young". The process is unhurried: 15–20 days' *cuvaison* followed by 2 years in *foudre*. The blend is assembled after malolactic, with only the first pressings added back,

the rest going for distillation. They avoid fining and filtration by "racking thoroughly before bottling".

The Constants' Bandols are best tackled after several years in bottle – although they manage a flash of rather austere charm earlier on.

Ray's marketing strategy is equally idiosyncratic, but clearly effective, with most of the wine going to a loyal clientele of French doctors and *la grande restauration*. "I've never given a centime to publicity", he explains, "they come to me. I sell it all myself". Occasionally he is wrong-footed, as when he received an order from the prestigious Paris restaurant Lucas Carton: "they telephoned and asked for 48 bottles of my 1985; I thought it was a hoax, so wished them 'Good day' and

hung up; they had to confirm by fax!"

His medical trade is not, however, reciprocal: "I don't take medicines; I go to the doctor, buy what he prescribes, read the counter-indications on the packet and then throw them in the bin". For him, Mourvèdre is the best medicine – "it works just like a detergent". Like their maker, these wines are very long keepers – "they don't budge". With his impish twinkle, rude good health, and restless energy, Ray Constant is an excellent ambassador for their prophylactic medicinal qualities.

CHATEAU SAINTE ANNE

There have been Dutheil de la Rochères in the 16th-century Château Sainte Anne for five generations. The present Marquis, François, took over in the 1960s and started bottling his wine. Until 1988 there was a single red Bandol "Tradition" under the Château label – a blend of 50–60% Mourvèdre, 30% Cinsaut and 5–10% Grenache. In 1989 a "Vin de Collection" was introduced: 5–10,000 bottles from 98% Mourvèdre and 2% Grenache.

The Marquis and his wife are a delightful couple who have worked tirelessly for their domaine. She, a Breton by birth and and an agricultural scientist by training, is dark-haired and vivacious, with an undisguised passion for wine. He is broad, with vine-scarred arms, which attest to days spent tending the vineyards.

The estate has 25ha of terraced vines, some on sandy soils near Le Beausset and Sainte Anne itself, from which come a white, the two reds plus a rosé, for which

there is a particularly strong local demand. Bandol accounts for 85% of production, of which 65% is red. The remainder is Côtes de Provence. As a matter of policy, the Dutheils keep back a proportion of the red Bandol in each vintage to be able to offer some older stocks – there are usually a couple on offer in their tasting-room.

Red vinifications here are somewhat unusual in using no sulphur until just before bottling. The wines are kept in old 50-hl *foudres* (no new wood) for 18–24 months, then fined and filtered. The

Collection wine is bottled unfiltered. The Tradition has several bottlings, the Collection just one.

The wines tend towards finesse rather than richness and age well. Their style perhaps reflects relatively short *cuvaisons* of 8–10 days and the policy of leaving some stems in the vats which, in some vintages, comes through as a touch of astringency, although ripe Mourvèdre stems tend to be hard rather than green. On balance this is a good domaine: taste before you buy.

VARIETY	APPELLATION	DETAILS	AREA
MOURVEDRE	BANDOL	Clay-limestone soils, some sand in subsoil. Terraces.	13.75
CINSAUT	BANDOL	Clay-limestone soils, some sand in subsoil. Terraces.	5.00
GRENACHE	BANDOL	Clay-limestone soils, some sand in subsoil. Terraces.	3.75
UGNI BLAND + CLAIRETTE	BANDOL	Clay-limestone soils, some sand in subsoil. Terraces.	2.50
		TOTAL (hectares):	25.00

DOMAINE TEMPIER

Domaine Tempier is at the heart of Bandol. Not only does it make some of the appellation's finest wine, but its proprietor, Lucien Peyraud, was instrumental in saving Bandol from lapsing into mediocrity after the 1939–45 war, by persuading reluctant growers to persevere with Mourvèdre rather than court overproductive, and then more lucrative, varieties. Half a century later, he continues to be revered as the "father of the appellation".

The domaine has been in the Tempier family since 1834; however, it wasn't until

1940, when Lucien Peyraud married Lucie ('Lulu') Tempier that today's estate was created. The Mourvèdre grape fascinated Lucien, and provided the inspiration which led him to encourage others towards lower yields and better quality – a policy of whose dividends a misguided few are, unfortunately, still unconvinced.

The domaine, now run by Lucien's sons, Jean-Marie and François, consists of several sites, covering nearly 30ha, planted 55% Mourvèdre, 23% Cinsaut, 20% Grenache plus a touch of Syrah and Carignan and some Clairette, Marsanne

and Ugni Blanc which are not accepted in the Bandol AC so are sold as (an excellent, barrel fermented) *vin de table*.

The vines are old here – some septuagenarians, the average 35. Jean-Marie and François' tenure has seen the elaboration of a number of special cuvées, from individual sites – remarkable wines, paradoxically almost atypical in their richness and concentration. Until 1967 only one red wine was produced, the Cuvée Classique; in 1968 came the Cuvée Spéciale, from 70–85% of 25-year-old Mourvèdre from le Plan du Castellet, Migoua and Tourtine plus 40 year old Grenache from Migoua; a year later, at the behest of an insistent importer,

Migoua and Tourtine themselves were created as wines from these individual sites; their success was immediate. Trials in 1984 with a 96% Mourvèdre *cuvée*, from a parcel of 40-year-old vines within La Tourtine, resulted in the first release in 1987 of the Cuvée Cabassaou, which is now 100% Mourvèdre.

These are classy wines – beautifully poised thoroughbreds. As befits most great wines, especially any containing a high proportion of Mourvèdre, they need keeping – up to ten years for the lesser vintages, double or more for the great ones. The sites play an important role in the qualities of each wine. Migoua, a 6.5ha vineyard at 180–270 metres' altitude (the domaine's highest) in Le Beausset is planted 55% Mourvèdre, the rest Cinsaut (25%) and Grenache (20%) – with a touch of Syrah, which doesn't thrive here. The exposition, all *en coteaux*, is two-thirds south, the other third split equally between east and west. The vineyard was bought in 1941, and its vines now average 30. The grape mix and the clay-limestone soils give a wine of some elegance, rarely a blockbuster, open and accessible, with notes of *fruits rouges* and *fruits noirs* and a long, spicy, finish.

In contrast, La Tourtine (bought 1951), produces a more masculine wine, with greater power and concentration than Migoua, more richness of fruit and characteristically, baked, earthy flavours. A magnificent swathe of entirely south-facing hillside, clearly visible from the domaine's *cuverie*, Tourtine covers 7ha, mainly terraced, overlooking the commune of Castellet. The *encépagement* is 55% Mourvèdre, 30% Grenache and 15% Cinsaut; the vines average 30. Some tasters find Migoua more tannic than Tourtine, others the reverse.

The Cuvée Cabassaou ("escarpment") comes from a single hectare of 45-year-old Mourvèdre vines on the lower, steeper, sector of La Tourtine. The wine, matured in 15 hl *foudres* for a more rapid evolution, is the darkest, most impenetrable of all. A covering of fine, ripe, tannins corsets a dense, highly concentrated layer of super-ripe fruit; superimposed on this majestic frame are flavours of spice, *fruits confits*, baked earth and, surprisingly since there is no new or small wood involved, vanilla. For great vintages, such as 1990, it is a cardinal sin to draw a cork before 15 years have elapsed – and then only with permission of a qualified authority. The reality probably is that little sees its tenth birthday.

The soils are generally clay-limestone in type, with differing amounts of hill-scree material depending on site, which

Jean-Marie Peyraud.

varies in particle size from predominantly stony to predominantly sandy. Tourtine and Migoua are both stony which together with the combination of clay and limestone gives power, tannin, concentration and savour to their wines. Whilst Tourtine's soils are relatively homogeneous, Migoua's varies considerably from one part of the vineyard to another – visibily changing in colour within as little as a few metres.

In Bandol's warm, dry, micro-climate mildew and oidium are rare, so little spraying is needed; François neither fertilises nor uses chemical products – just sulphur and Bordeaux mixture; artificial substances "deform" the soils – both in structure and micro-flora, with inevitable consequences for wine-quality. The vines, trained *en gobelet* – "it's tradition here" – are pruned only during the fourteen days of the waning moon. Justifying this apparently curious policy, Jean-Marie explains that after ten years, new-moon prunings have long since rotted, whereas those cut during the waning cycle are still

intact and moreover, are excellent for grilling meat.

The domaine produces around 120,000 bottles, including 40,000 of direct-press rosé with a touch of skin contact, from young vine Mourvèdre, Cinsaut and Grenache – a very attractive and elegant wine with a firm, but not too firm, structure: "If this gets too masculine, we might as well make red wine – why waste the grapes?", Jean-Marie explains. As for the reds, there are 45,000 of Cuvée Tempier Rouge, 12,000 each of Cuvée Spéciale and Tourtine, 6–8,000 of Migoua and just 4,000 of Cabassaou.

Harvesting usually comes between 20 September and 10 October, although recent years have seen it start as early as 1 September (1994). A green-pruning to lighten the load on each vine reduces vine stress in dry years; it also advances maturity by 10 days – a significant advantage as rain often arrives at the end of September.

Vines less than 11 years old are vinified as rosé, never red. The rest are de-stemmed – "noble tannins are only found in skins and pips" – and vinified in *inox* for 8–21 days, depending on the cuvée and the vintage; the Cabassaou has longest time on skins, the Tempier Rouge the shortest.

By tradition, the different grape varieties are assembled at fermentation "in the proportions we like", because they have found that this gives greater harmony, character and authenticity than separate vinification and blending later. "The whole is more than the sum of its parts; the young marriage is best. To assemble finished wine – this is the province of the *négoce* – not logical", remarks Jean-Marie. All the wines spend up to 30 months maturing in *foudres* of varying sizes – giving a long, slow, gentle evolution. The 1971 Cuvée Spéciale was left for 60 months – an exceptional wine from an exceptional vintage.

Since 1982, Tempier reds have been neither fined nor filtered. Apart from the Migoua and Cabassaou, which are bottled at one go, the higher-volume reds are bottled in line with sales (only on a waning moon: the wine ages better).

VINEYARD	LOCATION	DETAILS	AREA
LA TOURTINE (of which		Mourvèdre, Grenache, Cinsaut plus	
CABASSAOU is 1 hectare)	LE CASTELLET	small area of Syrah; 28–30 hl/ha	7.00
MIGOUA	LE BEAUSSET-VIEUX	Mourvèdre, Cinsaut, Grenache plus small area of	
		Syrah; 180–270 amsl. 30 hl/ha; 30+ average age	6.50
	LE PLAN DU CASTELLET	Mourvèdre, Grenacne, Cinsaut plus	
		1 ha of 60 yr old Carignan; several parcels	9.00
LE PETIT MOULIN	LE PLAN DU CASTELLET	Mourvèdre, Grenache, Cinsaut	6.00
		TOTAL (hectares):	28.50

According to Jean-Marie, differences between first and last bottling of any given wine (maximum three months) are slight. Mourvèdre is renowned for its powerful anti-oxidant properties, so ageing in bottle is likely to have a much more profound effect than any small difference in maturation period.

A Tempier Bandol·from a great vintage is as fine and harmonious an expression of the *terroir* and of Mourvèdre as one is likely to find. Years in bottle – arguably only outstripped in ageing potential by a top port vintage – bring out elegance and complexities which are barely discernible in the young wine.

Tempier influence extends beyond wine circles. Lulu Peyraud's genius in the kitchen has brought chefs and writers across continents to research the delights and enjoy the abundance of her Provençale table. She exudes *joie de vivre* and takes pride in the domaine, modestly acknowledging her own contribution to the success of this remarkable and welcoming family. A steady stream of visitors from abroad, eager to discover the secrets of the unusual Mourvèdre grape, attests to the domaine's reputation far beyond Bandol and cuttings from here grow in vineyards across the world.

The Peyrauds and their fine domaine inspire the esteem generally reserved for a Bordeaux First Growth.

CHATEAU VANNIERES

Château Vannières is a substantial property, situated between the villages of la Cadière d'Azur and St Cyr-sur-mer. It was built in the 19th century by a Scotsman named Scott, over 16th-century cellars, the property having been then gifted by the Abbey of St-Victor to Sieur de Lombard, the seigneur of Castellet. Its 33ha of vines adjoin the château and, rare in Bandol, are in one large block.

The estate is run by Eric Boisseaux, now in his 40s, whose maternal grandmother bought it in 1957, when Côte de Provence red fetched more than Bandol The Boisseaux family were Burgundy *négociants* in Dijon, but sold that business in 1989 to concentrate on Château Vannières. Eric's father died in a road accident in 1968, and he took over in 1981.

The vineyard is planted to Mourvèdre, Grenache and Cinsaut, from which come 70-80,000 bottles of Bandol rouge and two Bandol rosés – a standard cuvée and 3,000 bottles of Vieilles Vignes, from the first pressing only. The land is partly flat but mostly *en coteaux,* with soils which include stony clay-limestones and a good slab of sandier plain.

Eric makes the wines himself. He trained with Max Leglise in Beaune, at Macon and at Nuits St Georges, where he spent time with Gouges (Michel Gouge's wife is his aunt). However, most of his craft was learned on the spot, in Bandol.

Vannières' Bandol is more elegant and approachable than most. This is partly accounted for by the mix of soils, but is mainly due to having only 60% of Mourvèdre. The balancing Grenache softens out the young wine, and gives it flesh and richness without adding undue tannins. The grapes are mixed at fermentation, which lasts up to three weeks.

Since 1992, there has been partial de-stemming (20–30%), though Eric does not want to abandon the Vannières tradition of not removing the stalks. He places great emphasis on *pigeage*, by foot; both to avoid any stalky greenness and also to extract the maximum of flavour and matter: "You must really get under the *marc* , not just walk on it". Depending on the vintage, more or less press-wine is added, then the wine is matured for 30 months in *foudres* before fining and a light Kieselguhr filtration "for the clientèle", and then bottling.

Some have criticised Vannières for over-production – "a bit industrial". However, on present showing, the wines are very good indeed. Their deliberately lighter style makes them eminently approachable young, but they really need several years' bottle-age to show their full qualities. Eric Boisseaux refers to this as "the patience of Vannières" and, following the family tradition, keeps back a proportion of each vintage for later release. In 1995 he was offering wines from 1990 to 1973. The "impatient" side of him has a mad fascination for motor-racing, in which sport he still takes an avid interest.

A bush-trained vine in early autumn.

DOMAINE LES BASTIDES

Jean Salen left the local co-operative to create his own "cave" in 1976, since when he has built up his estate on the outskirts of Le Puy, a few miles north of Aix-en-Provence, from one hectare to thirty. He grows a mix of traditional varieties based upon Grenache, Cabernet Sauvignon and Cinsaut, with some 15% of white *cépages*.

The high proportion of Cabernet Sauvignon reflects Jean's dislike of Syrah: "it doesn't excite me much – a bit vinous". Despite the fact that the vineyards are exposed due north, they are able to harvest Cabernet reliably at 14% potential alcohol, and relatively early. "In Provence the best vineyards face north, so we harvest quite late, usually at the beginning of October. This gives a cool start to fermentation and allows us to macerate for longer."

A visitor here soon gets the sense of a close-knit family working together for quality. Jean, a bluff, greying man with an open, friendly honesty, shares all major decisions with his wife and daughter Carole – fresh from Beaune's Lycée Viticole. Here, not one palate but "*le gout familiale*", which includes two other daughters, prevails.

And "*le gout*" that the Salen family prefers is for concentrated wines, supple yet capable of reasonable ageing. The pick of the bunch here is the red Cuvée Spéciale – a blend of 50% Cabernet, 45% Grenache and 5% Mourvèdre, a selection firstly from the best vineyard plots, refined from the best cuvées, made around malolactic. Each variety is vinified separately and matured for 18–24 months in *foudres*. It only appears in good vintages – hence no 1987 or 1994. There is also a rather pedestrian white, from Ugni, Sauvignon, Rolle and Clairette, and an uncontroversial rosé.

In fact 1994 was a vintage which Jean would prefer to forget. That July, hail – so localised that vineyards on the other side of the escarpment remained unaffected – destroyed virtually all his crop, leaving the family with just a little wine to sell *en négoce*. This meant a financially crippling 100,000-bottle deficit.

Fortunately, they managed to make a tiny quantity of their speciality, *vin cuit*, a Provençale tradition which Jean revived some years ago. Sold without a vintage, this wine is made by first heating the newly-pressed juice to concentrate it, then fermenting it in the normal way. No alcohol is added; the yeasts just stop working at around 14% alcohol – leaving a deliciously perfumed, red-tawny wine with some 100–150 grammes per litre residual sugar. In a normal year 2,000 bottles are produced – and highly sought-after. A most intriguing rarity.

In spirit, this is a conservative estate, happy to use modern technology where necessary, but not to make light, fashionable wines. Les Bastides is a bastion of tradition.

VARIETY	APPELLATION	DETAILS	AREA
GRENACHE	COTEAUX D'AIX EN PROVENCE	Some 30+ yr old vines here	12.00
CABERNET SAUVIGNON	COTEAUX D'AIX EN PROVENCE	Average age 16 yrs	7.50
CINSAUT	COTEAUX D'AIX EN PROVENCE	Average age 16 yrs	3.00
CARIGNAN	COTEAUX D'AIX EN PROVENCE	Some 30+ yr old vines here	1.30
MOURVEDRE	COTEAUX D'AIX EN PROVENCE	Average age 16 yrs	1.20
UGN, ROLLE, SAUVIGNON BLANC, CLAIRETTE	COTEAUX D'AIX EN PROVENCE	Average age 16 yrs	5.00
		TOTAL (hectares):	30.00

MAS BRUGUIERE

This estate has been in the Bruguière family since the French Revolution at the end of the 18th century. Guilhem Bruguière took over in 1974 as the sixth generation of *vignerons*, in unbroken succession from father to son. He and his wife Isabelle look after nine hectares of vines, planted near their home, in the scenic country between Valflaunès and St-Martin-de-Londres.

The soils are deep clay-limestone, well-drained but poor in nutrients, consisting mainly of stony, scree material from the Pic St-Loup and l'Hortus. This is excellent land for cultivating the Grenache and Syrah which constitute the lion's share of the estate, with half a hectare each of Mourvèdre and Roussanne in addition.

The Bruguières produce five wines, all AC Coteaux du Languedoc, Cru Pic St-Loup. The sole white is a pure Roussanne and the rosé is a *saignée* from their Grenache (60%) and Syrah vats (40%). The most basic red, Vinam de Cacadiz, (12,000 bottles), is also a 60:40 Grenache: Syrah mix. It comes from young vine fruit, half of which is vinified by *macération carbonique* and is designed to drink within six months, but has the structure to age for four to five years. The the name derives from a 12th-century vineyard which belonged to the parish of Valflaunès.

Next comes the Cuvée Tradition, around 10,000 bottles of a more structured wine from slightly older Grenache and Syrah vines (50:50). This is vinified traditionally with 12–15 days vatting and bottled after six months in *cuve*. Finally there are 10,000 bottles of a true *vin de garde*, the Cuvée Elevé en Fûts de Chêne, from 60% Syrah and 20% each of Grenache and Mourvèdre, vatted for 18–20 days and matured for nine months in small wood.

The Syrah and around half the Grenache are harvested by machine, the remainder by hand. The crop is scrupulously sorted for unripe or damaged grapes – where necessary, on a hand-sorting conveyor. Each parcel of vines is vinified separately in a cellar which works as much as possible by gravity, to avoid unnecessary pumping and abrasion. The Bruguière press is a vertical champagne model, simple and gentle. The oak-aged cuvée has some new oak – 40% in 1992 and 1994, 30% in 1993.

The wines have established a growing reputation in the region; the oak-aged *cuvée* is particularly impressive. A fine estate.

VARIETY		DETAILS	AREA
GRENACHE	AC	Planted 1975; 1.5 ha. trained en gobelet; 3 ha. en cordon de Royat on 3-wire trellis	4.50
SYRAH	AC	Planted 1980; trained on 5-wire trellis en cordon de Royat	3.50
MOURVEDRE	AC	Planted 1985; trained en gobelet	0.50
ROUSSANNE	AC	Planted 1991; first crop 1994; trained on 5-wire trellis en cordon de Royat	0.50
		TOTAL (hectares):	9.00

CLOS CENTEILLES

Patricia Boyer and her husband, Daniel Domergue, bought this property in 1990, from under the noses of English bidders. It is now one of the finest wine-estates in the Minervois. The hillside site was an ancient fair-ground where, by annual tradition, the folk from the hinterland came to meet those of the Lower-Languedoc. Nearby is the imposing mainly 11th-century Church of Nôtre Dame de Centeilles. The surrounding countryside is pure Van Gogh, with tall, tight cypresses dominating a landscape of scrub interspersed with vineyards.

Technical expertise is not wanting: Daniel teaches viticulture at nearby Beziers and Patricia is a trained wine-maker. Wanting to cut her winemaking teeth away from his influence, she spent a couple of years elsewhere, perfecting her skills. An element of dissent keeps them on their mettle, with sufficient common ground to avoid an explosion. Where quality is concerned they are in total accord: only the best will do.

The heart of the domaine is the dry-stone-walled Clos de Centeilles, 13ha planted to old Carignan, Syrah, Grenache, Mourvèdre (on Lyre trellis). Without the Carignan, these provide the Tête de Cuvée, 10,000 bottles of Clos de Centeilles.

Next comes the Campagne de Centeilles – from 80–90% Cinsaut macerated for 6 weeks, plus some Syrah.

The Capitelle de Centeilles, named after the dry-stone shepherd's hut in the vineyards, is made from 100% Cinsaut macerated for two months in one of two splendid open Hungarian oak *cuves*, pot-bellied receptacles which stand, immobilised, and covered in plastic sheeting, in the middle of the *cuverie*. On their inadequately short, spindly iron legs, they look rather like a pair of comfortably caparisoned French dames with their bath-caps on.

There is also the Petit Clos de Centeilles – a Syrah/Grenache blend, which first appeared in 1991 (bottled 1994).

A trio of unusual *cuvées* complete the range: the Guigniers (cherry trees) de Centeilles, made from Pinot Noir vinified *à la Bourguignonne*, which Daniel insists was a traditional *cépage* here; then Carignanissime, from 60 to 70-year-old Carignan vinified by carbonic maceration. Finally comes the *blanc liquoreux*, a late-harvest Grenache Blanc left on the vine until it reaches around 21% potential alcohol. So sugar-rich is this juice that they have to yeast the *cuve* to get it to ferment. This wine, which is not recognised on the current appellation decree, recreates the lapsed tradition of Vin Noble de Minervois. "We wanted to be the first, not to scoop anyone else, but to keep this appellation and thus a further form of freedom".

Both Daniel and Patricia vehemently despise the Carignan – "we think its a poor *cépage*, too rustic; you can extract some finesse from it, but it isn't really fine or elegant". Having thus denounced the wretched grape Patricia adds, to drive home the point: "it's a pariah for us – our little cripple". The only way to deal with what they see as its principle characteristics – tannin and bitterness – is "to refine the tannins by carbonic

Misty autumnal evening in the Minervois.

maceration". The results are inspirational – enough to convince the most scathing of critics.

In the cellar, technology is definitely not king. The pot-bellied Dames share the *cuverie* with an ancient belt-driven must-pump, a pair of antique horizontal Vaslin presses and a remarkable contrivance, also belt-driven, which whirrs into action for bottling.

Their spreading reputation brought visits from curious neighbouring *vignerons*, to discover the Domergue secret – anxiously expecting to find shining stainless-steel and the latest modern gadgets. Some, convinced that these museum pieces were only there for show, resorted to looking beneath the *cuves* for the real articles which they surmised had been craftily hidden away.

This excellent range is linked by a

VARIETY	VINEYARD	DETAILS	AREA
GRENACHE	CLOS CENTEILLES	(Approximate area)	2.00
SYRAH	CLOS CENTEILLES	(Approximate area)	4.00
CINSAUT	CLOS CENTEILLES	(Approximate area)	4.00
CARIGNAN	CLOS CENTEILLES	(Approximate area)	3.00
MOURVÈDRE, SYRAH, GRENACHE, CINSAUT, CARIGNAN, PINOT NOIR + OTHER REDS	At TRAUSSE – 10 kms from Centeilles	(Approximate area)	4.00
		TOTAL (hectares):	17.00

common thread: finesse. The wines are rarely dense, their tannins invariably soft, their flavours supple yet firm leaving an impression of depth and elegance.

There is no mystery: low yields (25–27hl/ha for the Clos), deliberately late harvest – "as roasted as possible" for the reds – and long *cuvaisons* (3–6 weeks), with plenty of *pigeage*; thereafter, 12–14

months in *cuve*, except for the Clos which is part matured in old wood. The Domergues are self-confessed "fining maniacs", but don't generally filter: "we don't own a filter, so filtration's a real rigmarole; we have to borrow one and they're all different", Patricia explains. In short, a first-class domaine.

DOMAINE DE CLOVALLON

In mountainous, thickly wooded country, beneath a great limestone bluff just outside Bedarieux, nestles Catherine and Pierre Roque's 30 hectare domaine de Clovallon. He, an *ingenieur agronome* and she, an architect, took over 12ha from Pierre's father in 1989, and are quietly creating a top-class domaine. They "feel" as well as think their wines – adding a touch of art to a sound technique.

Their objective is to plant noble varieties in well-adapted soils and to vinify the produce to extract the maximum of varietal and *terroir* typicity, using new or newish wood without over-oaking. The old Carignan they inherited never ripened well, so they grafted over to Chardonnay, and planted selected clones of Viognier, Syrah, Muscat à Petit Grains and Pinot Noir. The most recent acquisition is some Petit Manseng, from Jurançon cuttings (taken by torchlight because the vineyard owner was concerned that his colleagues might discover that their "local" variety was being allowed out of its base appellation).

A hectare of Viognier was planted in 1988, in part from material provided by Georges Vernay ("*un homme remarkable*"), on Dolomitic limestone with a sub-soil of *grès rouge*. Since the first vintage in 1991, yields have averaged 25hl/ha; this Catherine regards as especially important: "some people produce 100hl/ha and sell the wine at high prices, but this is not good for quality; Viognier needs low yields". After 24 hours' *macération pelliculaire*, fermentation for all but a small part of the

crop continues in cask – mostly lightly charred Vosges, but with a touch of light or mid-charred Allier – with regular *bâtonnage* to add autolytic lees richness. Six months later, the *cuvée* is assembled, fish-fined and bottled with the lightest of plate filtrations.

The results are excellent – wines with depth and tight, balanced structures; although the first couple of vintages would perhaps have benefited from half a degree or so more alcohol for better equilibrium. Catherine is determined to avoid the "grapefruit and exotic fruit" style redolent of low-temperature, technical vinifications, looking more for the flowers and apricots of Condrieu – a wine they both love. Their Viognier has already convinced many top French critics – one initially disparaging sommelier performed a notable *volte-face* and proclaimed the wines worthy of his exalted list. As these vines mature, the wine will undoubtedly gain in concentration and richness.

1994 marked the debut of Clovallon Syrah, from a hectare of Northern Rhône clones planted in 1992 on a patch of schist. Although the ultimate goal is a *Septentrionale* Syrah, vinification is presently somewhat experimental: no de-stemming, a five-day pre-fermentive cold maceration, some – but not excessive – *pigeage*, followed (probably!) by 9–12

months in one-year-old Viognier casks. Bottling is confided to a travelling bottler, who is apparently daunted by the Roque's demand for bottling unfiltered. He'll learn, and soon all his customers will want things done that way.

Life is conducted at quite a pace *chez les Roques*, who have three young children. Pierre retains a thriving winemaking consultancy from his Narbonne HQ – Le Palais du Vin, a complex which includes a restaurant, offices and a wine shop – while the dynamic, petite Catherine looks after the domaine adding the occasional burst of architecting to keep her hand in. "We vinify by fax and telephone", she remarks. Meanwhile two sets of in-laws help mind the children while Pierre's parents take quiet pride in the domaine's burgeoning reputation and the startling changes which they – and many of the Roque's neighbours – regarded as "*la folie*", way back in 1989.

This is altogether a splendid estate. Apart from the Syrah and the Viognier, there are excellent Chardonnay and Pinot Noir, a Petit Manseng on the way, and a Vendange Tardive from a cocktail of white varieties left to over-ripen on the vine – a single cask, not for sale! A domaine to watch as much for what is to come as for what has already been achieved.

VARIETY	APPELLATION	DETAILS	AREA
SYRAH	VIN DU PAYS D'OC	Planted 1989 and 1992; North facing slope, schist	1.00
VIOGNIER	VIN DU PAYS D'OC	Planted 1989; dolomitic soils	1.00
		TOTAL (hectares):	2.00

DOMAINE DE LA COSTE

Luc and Elizabeth Moynier have 27ha, surrounding an arid, stony plateau on the edge of the Cévennes.

Here, on old episcopal land, are five red grape varieties producing five different wines – a rosé *de saignée* and four reds: first, a straightforward Cuvée Tradition red; then Cuvée Prestige from Mourvèdre and Grenache; Cuvée Selectionnée (pure Syrah); and Cuvée Merlette (pure Mourvèdre).

Luc Moynier – a solid, fast-talking man, with heavily-accented, sometimes barely comprehensible speech and a military-style handlebar moustache, has nursed a particular affection for Mourvèdre since visiting Bandol some years ago.

The grape does well on this scree-covered terrain, which provides sufficient humidity for the roots during the hot summer months to prevent water stress and consequent cessation of growth, to which Mourvèdre is especially susceptible. There is also usually enough sea breeze – which it adores.

Each variety is vinified separately – "fractional vinification" – with 30 *cuves* each containing a different wine: free-run wine, first pressings, second pressings, all kept apart until later. "I like to work the fruit and the *terroir*", so there is no oak ageing – just 12–18 months in *cuve* before bottling.

Designed for relatively early drinking, the wines emphasise elegance and fruit with enough, but never too much, tannin. Yields of 30–40hl/ha provide the raw material for a balanced concentration of fruit, and three to four weeks of vatting extract the maximum from the grapes. A good domaine which, with a little more effort, is likely be top class.

VARIETY	APPELLATION	DETAILS	AREA
SYRAH	COTEAUX DU LANGUEDOC	Planted 1975 and later	7.00
MOURVEDRE	COTEAUX DU LANGUEDOC	Planted 1975 and later	5.00
GRENACHE	COTEAUX DU LANGUEDOC	Planted 1972	7.00
CINSAUT	COTEAUX DU LANGUEDOC	Planted 1972	4.00
CARIGNAN	COTEAUX DU LANGUEDOC	Planted 1975 and later	4.00
		TOTAL (hectares):	27.00

DOMAINE DE LA COURTADE

On the wooded Ile de Porquerolles, west of Toulon, Paris architect Henri Vidal decided to establish a wine estate. In this stunning island setting, much of it now protected land, the 30-million-franc project started in 1983. It involved the clearing of 35ha of trees, the construction of cellars and a principal residence, and then the selection of suitable grape varieties for planting.

The vineyards and winemaking were entrusted to the 24-year-old Richard Auther, oenologist son of a small Alsatian winemaking family. Since then, this ebullient Randall Grahm look-alike has established an impressive reputation for La Courtade on the basis of low yields and noble varieties – policies which attracted derision from old local *vignerons* that has now turned to respect.

Porquerolles – named "the mushroom isle" because its dense woodlands and high humidity encourage many rare species of fungi – is pitted by four substantial plains, and it is on the central and largest of these that the Domaine La Courtade lies. Porquerolles is also the sunniest place in France (c 3,000 hours), and home to 700 different species of fig.

An insular micro-climate gives high atmospheric humidity, so drought is rarely a problem. Sea breezes temper extremes of heat and lengthen the growing season. The compact soils are sedimented quaternary in origin, part of a band of impermeable, friable schist which reappears at Fréjus on the mainland, and are unusual in both retaining moisture and allowing vine roots to penetrate deep in search of water.

The red varieties are dominated by the Mourvèdre (90%), difficult to cultivate but providing a powerful frame. This gives typical Provençale fragrances of resiny pine and *garrigue,* while Grenache (7%) adds a feminine element and Syrah (3%) a note of seasoning. The white is based on 90% Rolle and 10% Sémillon. The La Courtade label is reserved for a red and white *tête de cuvée,* while lighter, "more technological" versions in all three tints are labelled l'Alycastre.

In Richard's view wine quality has two mutually exclusive geological foundations: fault-lines – as in Alsace, Burgundy or the *Septentrionale* Rhône – which account for localised sites of excellence; or, bands of relatively homogeneous soil – as in Bordeaux or the *Meridionale* Rhône – where drainage seems to be the determining factor. Beyond this, he staunchly defends tradition – although here he had to create it first – explaining: "you don't come to Porquerolles to eat *choucrôute*, you come for *bouillabaisse*".

All the vines are trained *en cordon de Royat,* on the basis of work done by Hugelin in Alsace 25 years ago (dismissed at the time by most of his fellow *vignerons* as nonsense) that demonstrated that some parts of the vine's spur provide better fruit composition, in terms of skin:juice ratios, than others.

The red varieties are mainly de-stemmed and vinified separately for around four weeks to refine tannins and aromas. During its 12–18 months in cask (Allier and Tronçais, 25% new oak) the wine remains on its fine lees – contact which Richard regards as valuable for richness and aromatic complexity, as much in reds as in whites. La Courtade is egg-white fined, but only l'Alycastre *cuvées* filtered. The first releases, of the 1987 and 1988 vintages, were in 1990.

Henri Vidal and his wife, who owns one of Brussel's largest fashion stores, visit the estate from time to time and bring friends to enjoy the peaceful setting of its elegant, modern homestead. But credit for La Courtade's success is properly Richard Auther's: his dedication and passion are boundless. The wines are already excellent – remarkable, in fact, given the youth of their vines. As these mature, expect some stunners.

VARIETY	APPELLATION	DETAILS	AREA
MOURVEDRE	COTES DE PROVENCE	7 years average vine age; 1.5 ha. planted 1983	16.00
GRENACHE	COTES DE PROVENCE	1 ha planted 1983; goes principally into l'Alycastre Rosé	2.00
SYRAH	COTES DE PROVENCE		0.75
SEMILLON	COTES DE PROVENCE		4.00
ROLLE	COTES DE PROVENCE	1.5 ha planted 1983	12.00
		TOTAL (hectares):	34.75

MAS DE DAUMAS GASSAC

The story is well known: in 1970, Aimé Guibert, manufacturer of leather gloves, buys a farmhouse (*mas*) near Aniane; a visitor, Henri Enjalbert, professor of geography at Bordeaux University, tells him: "Aimé, you have a unique *terroir* for making fine wine"; trees felled, scrub cleared, vines planted – wine magnificent; writers ecstatic, hyperbole everywhere: "The Lafite of the Languedoc", "One of the best wines in the whole of France, "A major Grand Cru", and so on.

Of course, the reality is more complex than this; in particular, the vision and dedication of Guibert, now in his 70s; a wiry, animated, volanic man, bubbling with passion and a boyish urge to experiment. A drive round the property stimulates a non-stop commentary of fact and philosophy – as though seeing his twenty-year old vines for the first time. Stop! to see what excited Enjalbert: a cut in the *garrigue* below a clump of trees; 20 cms of organic matter, then a deep layer (20 metres in fact) of virtually inert, brick-red, sandy soil – pulverised glacial dust interspersed with smallish stones. A soil poor in organic matter, but rich in minerals – notably iron, copper and gold.

Fundamental to the quality of Daumas Gassac, the soil's importance is threefold: its depth forces the vine's rooting system to penetrate in search of nourishment – a valuable drought protection; its permeability means that it retains almost no humidity even after the most violent rainfall; and its organic poverty stresses the vine to the limit, creating exceptional aromatics in the wine.

However, this extraordinary *terroir* is more than its soil. At 500 metres, the Haute Vallée du Gassac benefits from a nocturnal current of cold air, funnelled from the surrounding foothills. This refreshes the vineyards, amortising high summer temperatures. The choice of north-facing slopes augments the effect, giving a long growing season and a generally late harvest. The effect is dramatic: when nearby Montpellier is broiling at 35°C, Daumas Gassac is relaxing at nearer 15°C.

Aimé and Véronique Guibert.

The Rhône connection here is Daumas Gassac Blanc, an *assemblage* of Viognier – planted from a *sélection massale* from Georges Vernay's' (qv) centenarian vines – Petit Manseng (from the Jurançon) and Chardonnay; three hectares of each.

In Aimé Guibert's opinion, on Daumas Gassac's individual soils – white limestone, with red glacial dust and a layer of well-drained gravel – Viognier is entirely different to that produced on Condrieu's schists, which contain little active lime. In contrast, these highly active lime soils demand careful rootstock selection and give wine which fares far better as part of a blend than as a straight varietal.

The varieties are co-fermented in small *inox cuves*, by indigenous yeasts, after eight days pre-fermentive maceration at 10°C. At around 10–15 grammes of residual sugar, the temperature peaks at 23–25°C: "This is the secret", Aimé Guibert confides – here the individual precursor aromatic chains of the three varieties rupture, recombining to give new "aromas of synergy", which are not present in the originals.

At 6–7 grammes of sugar, the wine passes into wood – one-third new – for 15–21 days. After this caress of oak, it is racked back into *inox*, where it remains on fine lees until the following February; it is then cartridge-filtered and bottled. Guibert is philosophical about the value of wood: "it's like marriage, sometimes sad, sometimes *l'amour*; all kinds of oak work in the Côte d'Or, but not here". He likens the encounter between his wine and wood to that between a Princess and a rough peasant: "it's a formidable battle, shock and resistance at the start; then, after 15–21 days, *claque*, she gives in". This is the moment to separate them – poor fellow!

Whatever the science, Daumas Gassac Blanc has a remarkable aromatic and flavour complexity invariably marked by Viognier. This is not the apricots and candied fruit of Condrieu, but a fuller, softer, more obvious and opulent, rather spicy, Viognier, which is most seductive. As for the future, there are 200 Marsanne and 200 Roussanne vines coming into production. A second Daumas Gassac Blanc in the making?

VARIETY	APPELLATION	DETAILS	AREA
VIOGNIER	VIN DE PAYS DE L'HERAULT	Planted c. 1975	3.00
CHARDONNAY	VIN DE PAYS DE L'HERAULT	Planted c. 1975	3.00
PETIT MANSENG	VIN DE PAYS DE L'HERAULT	Planted c. 1975	3.00
MARSANNE, ROUSSANNE, MUSCAT A PETITS GRAINS, BOURBOULENC	VIN DE PAYS DE L'HERAULT	Some recent plantings	N/A
		TOTAL: (white varieties only, hectares)	9.00

CHATEAU DES ESTANILLES

A visit to Michel Louison is one of the Languedoc's more entertaining experiences. The "Château" comes as something of a shock – a rather disordered courtyard surrounded by what appear to be converted farm buildings; on one side, the sales office and tasting room, on the other the Louison's home – a large sitting-room-cum-kitchen-cum-office, with a great chimney at one end.

Madame Louison's training as a midwife has failed to bring any hospital regimentation to her paper work: letters, papers, work-in, work-out, work in abeyance (by far the lion's share) repose stacked haphazardly on any surface capable of bearing them, while she argues the toss over the telephone, at maximum volume, with some distant official desirous of receiving – finally demanding to receive – some declaration or other which is a mere few months adrift of its date.

Over the head of Michel – whose flying grey hair gives him the appearance of a youthful Albert Einstein – all this washes with the air of dreary familiarity. His concern is winemaking; the officials are just an interference.

A stream of philosophy and personal experience is delivered in soft, but firm, tones. After 12 years near Geneva as an electrician, he moved here in 1975, since when 14ha have almost doubled to 25. "We planted what we wanted; there was nothing here; that's our advantage."

The three *cuvées* of red are among the finest Faugères to be had (alongside those of Jean-Michel Alquier).

Tradition, from Mourvèdre, Grenache, Cinsaut and Carignan, is vinified in *cuve*; Prestige, half Syrah, half Mourvèdre, Grenache and Cinsaut, is *élevé* for 13 months in cask, 30% of it new; and the pure Syrah is a selection of the best lots, matured 40% in new wood.

There is also an excellent white, from Marsanne and Roussanne vinified in new Allier oak, blended with Roussanne and touches of other curiosities Michel would prefer not to discuss, and *élevé sur lie* until April. If the authorities allowed it, Michel believes that the Jurançon's Petit

VARIETY	APPELLATION	DETAILS	AREA
SYRAH	FAUGERES	1/5/8/16 yr plantings	6.00
GRENACHE	FAUGERES	30 yrs average vine age	5.00
MOURVEDRE	FAUGERES	17 yrs average vine age	5.00
CINSAUT	FAUGERES	20 yrs average vine age	3.00
CARIGNAN	FAUGERES	35–40 yrs average vine age	2.50
WHITE VARIETIES	VIN DU PAYS	Roussanne, Viognier, Muscat + others; top-grafted in 1991 onto 20 yr old roots	1.50
MARSANNE		8 yrs average vine age	1.00
		TOTAL (hectares):	24.00

Manseng might be the key to white wine here, both for its aromatic qualities and for its acidity, which is particularly lacking in Faugères musts, though not in the soils.

Despite the fact that Syrah performs wonderfully in these schistous vineyards, producing wines of depth and character, local rules do not permit production of pure varietals. This difficulty doesn't worry Michel – it's the wine that counts, not the rules.

Unless you specifically decline, he will put you into his ancient 4x4 Toyota and take you up the steep Clos du Fou to show you the view, and to admire his Syrah on its slatey schist and to give you a fright into the bargain.

"It's done over 100,000 kms", says Michel proudly, taking one hand off the wheel to point to the mileometer, as you spin round a muddy corner and on up the vertiginous gradient. The view from

the top is indeed worth it and the ride memorable, but decidedly ill-advised after heavy meals.

Michel does not have the undivided respect of all his fellow winemakers, although many openly admire his wines. Apparently unconcerned, he clearly enjoys experimenting: a cask here of wine made from the dreadful Servan table grape, harvested in January: "do I call it 1992 or 1993?", Michel muses, genuinely puzzled. It hardly matters, the wine is sublime and the 50-year-old vines have since been grubbed up.

There is also a good rosé from 20-year-old Cinsaut as well as a trial cask of Mourvèdre rosé, vinified in new wood and kept on lees for a year. Michel's instincts may be traditional – but he can't suppress his creative impulses.

This is a fine, reliable, domaine – whatever the whims of its proprietor, or the idiosyncrasies of its bureaucracy.

VINCENT FONTENEAU

Vincent Fonteneau, tall, articulate and hazel-green eyed, is a self-confessed "*passioné du Syrah*", which now comprises one-fifth of his 23ha. Now in his early 30s, he took over from his mother, who sent her grapes to the Faugères co-op, in 1990.

The domaine operates from Vincent and his wife's house and cellars in the lovely hilltop village of Roquessels, approached by a precipitous drive; the views are magnificent.

Although the bulk of Vincent's 60,000-bottle production goes into a sound, if unexciting, red Faugères (made from a 60:30:10 Syrah:Grenache:Cinsaut mix), and a direct press rosé (from 50:20:30 Mourvèdre:Grenache:Cinsaut), the heart, and interest, of this cellar undoubtedly lies in the 2–3000 bottles of Syrah *pur*, sold under the name of the parental home – Le Moulin Couderc.

Vincent has tasted widely around the Rhône, preferring Septentrionale Syrah to Meridionale Grenache. In his view, Syrah

is well-suited to his temperament and to his schistous soils. Apart from being "the most aromatic of varieties", its "reliable performance and high disease resistance" make it "the most agreeable with which to work".

Yields run at 35–40hl/ha, from high-trained vines – some 25–30% below the permitted maximum yield. After 20–26 days' *cuvaison* at 20–25°C, the pulp is pressed in a splendid 1920s Coq vertical press, and the press-wine is then added back. The wine then spends 11 months in cask – of which some third is new Allier oak.

That the Faugère appellation does not allow 100% Syrah does not deter Vincent, who expresses the entirely sound belief that "the decree is not important; great wine is". He adds, with equal justification: "there's too much wine – you have to make the best, you must be the first".

Preliminary results are encouraging. Vincent exudes conscientiousness and this, coupled with the open-mindedness of all great *vignerons*, should stand him in good stead.... Faugère's newest *vigneron* and rising star is steadily building a reputation in the region.

VARIETY	APPELLATION	DETAILS	AREA
GRENACHE	FAUGERES	15–20 yrs average age	6.90
CARIGNAN	FAUGERES	40 yrs average age	6.90
SYRAH	FAUGERES	10–15 yrs averageage	4.60
CINSAUT	FAUGERES	30 yrs average age	2.30
MOURVEDRE	FAUGERES	7 yrs average age	2.30
		TOTAL (hectares):	23.00

DOMAINE GAUBY

For the enquiring visitor to the Midi, there are many fine discoveries to be made among its smaller domaines. One such is Domaine Gauby – a 40-hectare estate created by the hospitable young Gérard and Ghislaine Gauby in 1985 from rented and owned vines in and around Calce. The *encépagement* includes some old, traditional mixed plantings in both red and white grapes, as well as a rare hectare of ancient Carignan Blanc.

Gérard has planted his vines at 5,000 per hectare (3,000 is the minimum required for the Cotes du Roussillon appellation), which increases inter-vine competition for nutrients and moisture and encourages the development of a deep rooting system. This promotes resistance to drought stress and reduces the yield per vine – all of which, in the long term, increases concentration and flavour complexity.

Gérard's wide tasting experience has given him a feel for balance and quality – even at the base level of Côtes du Roussillon the wines have depth and interest. His policy of low yields (30hl/ha average) and late harvesting occasionally results in alcohols above the appellation's 13% permitted maximum. In 1994, for example, one batch of Grenache Blanc reached 14%, while another of Grenache Noir soared to 16%. Gérard had no option but to declassify both wines into *vin de table* – despite the fact that these levels arose from nothing more than naturally ripe grapes. One wonders at the mentality of those who make the rules.

In the cellar, minimum interference is the guiding principle. The prestige reds are vinified either in open *cuves*, with traditional *pigeage or* in closed *cuves* with *delestage* – a species of *remontage* which amounts to a *pigeage*; then 12–18 months in new or older wood depending on the wine.

This well-crafted range encompasses three reds and five whites. At the top, an excellent Viognier vinified in new wood, a white *vieilles vignes* from 80-year-old Carignan Blanc, Grenache Blanc and Maccabeo vinified part in new and part in older casks, and an old-vine red blend of Carignan Noir, Syrah, Mourvèdre and Grenache Noir, from vineyards on the limestone soils of Calce.

Only 40% of Gauby grapes are vinified at the domaine; the rest go the the local co-operative to provide cash. Gérard intends to increase the "home" fraction as finances permit. At present, he is happy to experiment with styles and vinifications, producing such delicious oddities as a flowery, dry Muscat from 50:50 Alexandrine and Petit Grains Muscats, which is cold-stabilised and bottled early "for cash-flow", and a majestic late-harvest white, which in 1991 was made from Grenache Gris and Blanc and Maccabeo picked in December (yield 7hl/ha).

Unfortunately, much of the 1994 *vendange tardive* crop went to the local bird population – a mere 2hl/ha reaching the *cuverie*. However, this reached 15% alcohol with nine grammes per litre of residual sugar – an event which caused Gérard to spend an hour on the telephone with Macon *vendange tardive* guru Jean Thévenet, finding out just how best to vinify this precious juice.

Although still in its formative stages, this is clearly a high-quality domaine. Once Gérard has settled on his preferred styles and vinification, Gauby is a name which will surely figure among the top echelons of the Roussillonnais.

VARIETY	APPELLATION	DETAILS	AREA
GRENACHE NOIR	COTES DU ROUSSILLON	30+ yrs old	6.00
GRENACHE BLANC	COTES DU ROUSSILLON	10+ yrs; vinified both as Doux and as Sec	10.00
MOURVEDRE	COTES DU ROUSSILLON	10 yrs	1.50
SYRAH	COTES DU ROUSSILLON	Bud-wood ex Chave; 15 yrs	4.00
CABERNET SAUVIGNON	COTES DU ROUSSILLON		1.00
VIOGNIER	VIN DE TABLE	8 yrs	1.00
CARIGNAN ROUGE	COTES DU ROUSSILLON	80–100 years old	8.00
CARIGNAN BLANC	COTES DU ROUSSILLON		1.00
	COTES DU ROUSSILLON	Mixed plantings incl. many of the above varieties plus Grenache Gris	
		TOTAL (hectares):	32.50

DOMAINE LA GRANGE DES PERES

In material terms, Laurent Vaille started with "zero, zero", since his family's land was unsuitable for vines. He did, however, have top-class work experience: a viticulture-oenology qualification, then a brief spell with Aimé Guibert who passed him to Eloi Durrbach, who in turn posted him on to Gérard Chave – three peerless mentors.

Not only does he tap the combined expertise of this trio, he also has Guibert's *égrappoir*, Durrbach's old press and Chave's discarded bottle-filler. All this has consolidated into one of the Midi's most promising young winemakers.

The domaine adjoins the road leading to Mas de Daumas Gassac, just outside Aniane. In times past, the quiet house which stands, surrounded by farmland, beside a small stream would probably have been a *dependance* of a local Priory.

Finding suitable vineyard land presented Laurent with a much greater challenge than collecting together his hardware. A year of searching yielded some "*terroir merveilleux*" – 7.3ha of *garrigue* which needed bulldozers and explosives to clear and plant.

Others considered the ground that he acquired to be too poor to bother with – hard limestone, sandy in parts – mainly glacial scree, overlaid with *galets roulés*; "mon petit Châteauneuf", remarks Laurent, adding "the same soil as Daumas Gassac, but more stones".

For his chosen varieties, he went back to Gérard Chave for Syrah, Marsanne and Roussanne, to Eloi Durrbach for Cabernet Sauvignon, to the Perrins at Beaucastel for Counoise and to François Jobard in Meursault for Chardonnay. Networking indeed! As to exposure, Laurent Vaille followed some unconventional advice of Jacques Reynaud's: plant everything facing north, except Mourvèdre which needs to face south.

The first usable fruit arrived in 1992, and its wine was bottled in late 1994. Young vines, green-pruning, leaving three to four bunches per vine, kept yields low and concentration high. The Mourvèdre performed especially well: "I never harvested it at less than 14% potential alcohol", which is unusual in this dry, comparatively cool climate, with vines at 250 metres' altitude.

In the cellars that were excavated by Laurent and his father beneath their ecclesiastically-fronted *cuverie*, rows of casks (ex- Burgundy's Coche-Dury and Jo

Roty) contain the remarkable fruits of Laurent's first vintages. Nothing is complicated – "all the wines I like are vinified simply"; so, de-stemming, plenty of foot *pigeage*, four to five week's vatting for everything but the Syrah, which has six, and 18–24 months in cask, with racking as the wine's evolution dictates. Neither fining nor filtration risk removing what has taken such care to put in.

The first white wine vintage came in 1995, and comprised 80% Roussanne plus 10% each of Marsanne and Chardonnay. The juice was fermented in cask: "very

VARIETY	APPELLATION	DETAILS	AREA
SYRAH	VIN DE PAYS D'OC	Planted 1988 & 1991	1.50
MOURVEDRE	VIN DE PAYS D'OC	Planted 1988 & 1990	2.70
ROUSSANNE	VIN DE PAYS D'OC	Planted 1991	0.80
MARSANNE	VIN DE PAYS D'OC	Planted 1992	0.40
CHARDONNAY	VIN DE PAYS D'OC	Planted 1993	0.40
CABERNET SAUVIGNON	VIN DE PAYS D'OC	Planted 1989	1.50
		TOTAL (hectares):	7.30

simple vinification, like Lafon, Coche-Dury and Chave".

Laurent Vaille's *vins de tables* will set

standards of which his mentors will undoubtedly be proud. La Grange is clearly destined for five-star status.

CHATEAU HELENE

Marie-Hélène Gau, a slim, 50-year-old mother of two, copes virtually single-handed with 42ha at Château Hélène. Since taking over in 1977, she has driven the tractor, vinified the wines, handled sales and tackled the administration – enough on its own, the way things are arranged in France. "A woman in a man's world", the Mayor of Barbaira told her when she presented her first *déclaration de récolte* at the *mairie* in 1984, adding, "you'll ruin yourself". She didn't, and the domaine goes from strength to strength.

The "Château" is a large, late 19th-century *maison de maître* sandwiched uncomfortably between the busy Carcassonne-Narbonne railway line and the even busier Carcassonne-Narbonne road. The place is somewhat run-down – but, as so often, the state of the cellars is an unreliable guide to its wines.

Since Marie-Hélène works all 12 months of the year, she has painted the old cement *cuves* puce, pink and green, adding a touch of feminine brightnesss. Otherwise, the 19th century reigns.

The bulk of the production is *vin de*

pays – red, white and rosé – presented in frivolously stencilled bottles – including a fresh *nouveau* which appears in October, a month before Beaujolais.

The AC Minervois range starts with simpler red, rosé and white *cuvées* – all called "Penelope" – the white from a mix of Roussanne, Maccabeo, Chardonnay and Sauvignon blanc. The *vins serieux* here are a pair of Minervois reds: 30,000 bottles of Cuvée Ulysse – from 50% Syrah and 25% each of Grenache Noir and

Carignan, and 6,000 bottles of Cuvée Hélène de Troyes, a selection from the best and oldest vines, 80% Syrah and 20% Grenache. Both are vinified traditionally, *cépage* by *cépage*, in *cuve*, the *assemblage* being after malolactic. They spend a year in wood – Ulysse half new and half second-year oak, Hélène de Troyes entirely new wood.

This is an excellent domaine. Marie-Hélène is adamant that quality, at every level, is the only way forward. Her 22-year-old daughter will soon join her – someone to share the decisions, the work and the rewards.

VARIETY	APPELLATION	DETAILS	AREA
CARIGNAN	MINERVOIS	Average vine age 55+ yrs	7.00
SYRAH	MINERVOIS	Planted 1978 & 1994	7.00
GRENACHE (Noir)	MINERVOIS	2 plantings – 6 ha 35 yrs & 2 ha 5 yrs	8.00
GRENACHE (Gris)	MINERVOIS	For rosé – will be grubbed up soon	6.00
GRENACHE (Blanc)	MINERVOIS	Average vine age 35 yrs	2.00
ROUSSANNE	MINERVOIS	Planted 1989	1.50
MACCABEO	MINERVOIS	Planted 1986	1.00
CHADONNAY	VIN DU PAYS	N/A	N/A
SAUVIGNON BLANC	VIN DU PAYS	N/A	N/A
VARIOUS (Red & White)	VIN DU PAYS		10.00
		TOTAL (hectares):	42.50

DOMAINE DE L'HORTUS

Wedged in the narrow plane between the dramatic peak of Pic St-Loup and the sheer limestone cliffs of Hortus are the Mas Bruguière and the Domaine l'Hortus. Since starting out in 1981, Jean Orliac has cleared and planted some 25ha on a mixture of *fermage* and purchased land, and rented a further seven. He and his wife, Marie-Thérèse, have also built a modern, Scandinavian-style wood-cladded house to which, in 1994 was added a *cuverie*.

The siting of each variety has been thoughtfully planned; the Mourvèdre, demanding a southerly exposition, is

perfectly at home situated on the "very Mediterranean" slopes of Hortus, on moderately deep stony limestone soils – much of it scree from the cliffs above. Opposite, beneath the Pic St-Loup, reside the Syrah and Grenache, on rather deeper ground, while the Viognier and Chardonnay are both consigned to the relatively fertile plain. Despite the lack of either granite or schist, Jean reckons that the conditions for his Syrah mirror those of the northern Rhône.

This is hard graft – one full-timer to help Jean with 33ha, plus whatever time Marie-Thérèse can spare from her

teaching job, with the rest of the family pitching in during school holidays.

Labour is expensive in France, where social costs are high and a worker's hours are limited to 39 per week – a socialist measure designed to create jobs which has signally backfired. When your top selling price is around 30–35 francs, including 18.6% tax, and the wholesale price considerably less, even half a worker can make the difference between profit and loss.

The usual quality factors pertain: low yields, longish *cuvaisons* with a rigorous selection for the top wine, the Grande Cuvée – a Mourvèdre-plus-Syrah mix from the oldest and most favourably sited vines, with a good spoonful of pressings superadded. White wine was a late-comer; a promising first essay was fermenting in new, rather heavily charred casks, in October 1994.

At present the Grande Cuvée is a barrel selection from lots matured in both new and older casks. This remains in wood for 15–18 months before bottling. However, "nothing is excluded", which effectively means that the composition and *élevage* of the various *cuvées* is not fixed in stone.

Indeed, Jean enjoys experimenting. He has already tried various forms and lengths of *élevage*, different degrees of de-stemming, various proportions of new and older wood, filtration or not, and a bewildering variety of grape mixes.

The current range comprises: the Grande Cuvée (60% Mourvèdre, 40%

VARIETY	VINEYARD	DETAILS	AREA
MOURVEDRE	SECTEUR HORTUS	Planted 1981/2	8.00
SYRAH	SECTEUR PIC ST. LOUP	Planted 1981/2	8.00
GRENACHE	SECTEUR PIC ST. LOUP	Planted 1981/2	7.00
VIOGNIER	PLAIN	Planted or top-grafted c 1988/9	1.50
CHARDONNAY	PLAIN	Planted or top-grafted c 1988/9	1.50
		UNPLANTED	7.00
		TOTAL (hectares):	33.00

Syrah in 1992), a second-class Grande Cuvée from the casks which remain (80% Mourvèdre, 20% Grenache in 1990), a Cuvée Classique (50% Syrah, 20% Mourvèdre, 30% Grenache in 1992) and a *rosé de saignée* (Grenache, Syrah, Mourvèdre).

There is much promise here. However, the wines need working on to balance wood and fruit elements; at present, the fruit in the Grande Cuvée is stifled by oak, an imbalance which bottle-ageing is unlikely to correct. Nonetheless, with only a handful of vintages under his belt, (1990 was the first) any definitive assessment would be premature. All the ingredients are here for star quality – let's wait and see.

DOMAINE DES JOUGLA

Alain and Josceline Jougla's researches have traced their roots in the quiet, attractive village of Prades-sur-Vernasobres, back to the Troubadour times of 1596. To reinforce this history Napoleon, who may or may not have harboured a Jougla in his retinue, presides, in full mounted cry, over the family sideboard in their cosy corner house at the top of the village.

Recent history has seen Alain Jougla's 28ha (1975) compound to some 35 (1994), with plantings of Viognier, Grenache Blanc and Syrah in particular, mainly on schistous land which he bought and cleared.

St-Chinian straddles areas of limestone and schist geology: "you can put one foot on limestone and the other on schist", Alain explains. At present, however, only red and rosé are accorded the St-Chinian appellation, although the authorities have recently allowed *vignerons* to plant Viognier, experimentally, and are looking into the suitability of Rolle, Chenin Blanc and Muscat à Petits Grains. Grenache Blanc, Roussanne and Marsanne are allowed for the "lesser" appellation Coteaux du Languedoc.

When the authorities finally decide on permitted white varieties, Alain intends to be ready for them, although he admits to having less expertise in white vinification than in red.

At present, the domaine's battle-engines consist of a direct-press Syrah rosé and three *cuvées* of St-Chinian – the Classique, from Carignan, Grenache,

Alain Jougla.

Syrah, Cinsaut and Mourvèdre (all the permitted red *cépages* for the AC); the Tradition, from Mourvèdre, Grenache and a blob of Syrah and, since 1986, the Cuvée Signée, which is a Syrah/Grenache blend, often with a good dollop of rich pressings, matured in Allier *pièces*, one-third of them new oak.

The wines are deliciously supple and relatively forward, with the fruit always evident. Low yields are an essential part of Alain's thinking, as are longish *cuvaisons* (11–15 days), incorporating a widely-used Languedocienne version of *pigeage* which consists of completely draining each *cuve* and then pumping the juice forcefully back over the solids. *Elevage* for all three wines lasts around two years – the first being in large oak *foudres*, the second in cask for the Cuvée Signée, in *cuve* for the others.

You would be lucky to find more reliable or better St-Chinian than these, especially the Signée which must be among the best value to be found anywhere – inside or outside France.

There is also the pleasure of dealing with a warm, close-knit and friendly family. Alain and Josceline's daughter, Laurence, is studying oenology at Carcassonne and their son, Alexandre, accountancy at St-Pons. When the time comes, the next generation will be ready to continue the tradition, while Napoleon will doubtless continue his relentless rout of the family sideboard.

VARIETY	APPELLATION	DETAILS	AREA
SYRAH	ST-CHINIAN	Planted 1980/86/90/94	6.81
MOURVEDRE	ST-CHINIAN	Planted 1983/85/90/92	4.80
GRENACHE	ST-CHINIAN	Planted 1960/84/90/92	7.10
CARIGNAN	ST-CHINIAN	Planted 1889 (1.04 ha), 1952/57/62	8.26
CINSAUT	ST-CHINIAN	Planted 1966/68/78	5.03
VIOGNIER	COTEAUX DU LANGUEDOC	Planted 1994	1.00
GRENACHE BLANC	COTEAUX DU LANGUEDOC	Planted 1990 (0.5 ha), 1994 (1.0 ha.)	1.50
BOURBOULENC	COTEAUX DU LANGUEDOC	Planted 1989	0.50
		TOTAL (hectares):	35.00

MAS JULLIEN

Olivier Jullien is one of the Midi's strongest influences. He left the family fold to go solo in 1985 and now, in his early 30s, is well established as top-quality both locally and further afield. Tall, dark, with slim, angular features, he readily bends the visitor's ear with his philosophy, which at times borders on proselytising.

From winemakers who are thinkers, hard fact is rare coin. Olivier is no exception. Generalities pour forth: "I make wine because I like to drink it"; "It's *terroir* that counts – the grape mix will give the equilibrium; some *cépages* have more acidity than others – Carignan and Mourvèdre, for example, so never blend them together. In my wine, these provide acidity, Syrah structure and *parfum*, Grenache gives *esprit* and Cinsaut finesse and fruit". And so on. His one-track passion has already cost Olivier his marriage, leaving him solo in another capacity, living alone in the rather soulless house, which his father helped him build, amid the vines.

What can be stated is that the domaine consists of 15ha – 12ha red, 3ha white, from which come four reds, three whites and a rosé – part *saignée*, part direct press. Olivier likes to start each vintage with neither preconceptions nor recipes, so no notes are kept of each year's blends: "every year is the first – but experience isn't lost". Should a lapse of official control ever permit, he would sell wine unlabelled, so people would taste what was in their glass rather than so many francs per bottle or what was on the label.

In the regulatory authorities and local wine politics, Olivier sees interminable strife: "It's a constant struggle here, people are either fighting the INAO (appellation authority) or the local Syndicat; someone's for this or contra that." He tries to avoid these distractions and leave politics to others, though this ideal is probably unattained. The battle he cannot avoid is the problem created by an excess of customers and a paucity of stock. After an apparently amicable tasting, a prominent local restaurateur's cordiality cracks on being told that there is no stock to spare. Olivier has apparently not telephoned her – why he should is not immediately apparent – and is only marginally susceptible to desperate flattery: "My list will not be credible without your wine". A few cases are promised and calm restored.

The aim is to extract and preserve whatever grape and *terroir* give. Some,

The philosopher – Olivier Jullien.

such as the limestones of Jonquières, emphasise fruit, so vinifications are adapted accordingly. Others, such as the Syrah and Grenache on schist at nearby Cabrières, are more complex and powerful, so from these come the more structured *vins d'élevage*.

Nothing stands still: experiments with carbonic maceration, 6- to 30-day *cuvaisons*, new and old wood, more or less de-stemming, have been made and digested. For all his own eloquence, Olivier appears to disdain theorising: "Words, words, everywhere words; I need my proof".

The white trio consists of Les Vignes Oubliées – "an ideological and demonstrative wine" – from one-third each of old-vine Terret Bourret, Carignan and Grenache Blanc vinified in cask; Sélection: a blend of 50% Grenache for the spirit, 25% of Viognier for aroma, and 25% Chenin for equilibrium; finally, the magnificent Clairette Beaudille, harvested in 1994 in early October with 200

grammes per litre of sugar: this is a wine that is sold only to favoured customers.

The reds start with Les Etats d'Ame (states of the soul) " – fruit, pleasure, sometimes exuberance… in this wine of liberty". The first release, 1990, was pure Syrah – against the Languedoc tradition of *assemblage*. Then, Les Cailloutis, from Grenache, Syrah, Mourvèdre, Cinsaut with, or without, a dab of Carignan, grown on the stony limestones of Jonquières. This, designed to express fruit rather than *terroir*, is for relatively early drinking, though it has the structure to evolve well over a few years. Next, Les Depierre, a firmly structured wine principally from Syrah planted on Cabrières schist, with some Jonquières Grenache, Cinsaut and Carignan.

Although many prefer Les Etats or Les Cailloutis for their more obvious fruit and approachability, to the Depierre's taughter structure, ("the French don't like tannin") this is undoubtedly the finer wine and the one to keep.

Finally comes a *cuvée* of 100% Cinsaut, l'Oeillade; this is the old Languedoc name for Cinsaut (*clin d'oeil*, wink or glimpse).

Tasting with Olivier, philosophising is never far away; random *pensées* pour forth: "Wine must be digestible, that's most important", adding *à propos* of nothing very much, "50% of Mas Jullien is spat out". Remarking that "quality is the only valid education" he thanks God, in passing, that he's forgotten everything he learned at school. In his universe the priority "is not to exclude".

For this talented young *vigneron* "wine is an equilibrium between what you say and what you feel". For a moment, the authority of the wines rubs off on his somewhat less secure credo.

VARIETY	VINEYARD	DETAILS	AREA
GRENACHE	JONQUIERES & CABRIERES	10–30 yrs vine age	3.00
SYRAH	CABRIERES	Schists; 20 yrs average vine age	3.00
MOURVEDRE	JONQUIERES	10–30 yrs vine age	1.20
CINSAUT	JONQUIERES	10–30 yrs vine age	3.00
CARIGNAN	JONQUIERES	30+ yrs vine age	1.80
GRENACHE BLANC		Some very old vines	1.50
VIOGNIER			0.75
CHENIN BLANC			0.75
CARIGNAN BLANC		Some very old vines	N/A
TERRET BOURRET		Some very old vines	N/A
		TOTAL (hectares):	15.00

DOMAINE DU MAS BLANC

Renowned for its remarkable range of Banyuls – medium-dry to sweet fortified wines based on the Grenache Noir grape – Dr. André Parcé's Mas Blanc also produces a quartet of benchmark dry, red Collioures from a mix of Mourvèdre, Syrah and Counoise.

Jean-Michel Parcé and his father have been developing their Collioures for twenty years, almost since the AC's creation in 1968; painstakingly searching out the best sites, and those varieties best adapted to them. At that time, with sweet Banyuls selling well, "we were the only ones making dry table wines; people took us for madmen". Time has confirmed their sanity.

Covering the same area as the Banyuls AC, Collioure's 1,800ha span four communes: Collioure itself, Port-Vendres, Banyuls-sur-Mer and Cerbère. Parcé's studies identified three distinct *terroirs*: the Piemonts, at the base of hills, on deeper, richer ground – less rocky and more fertile; Coteaux, with 15–20cms of topsoil giving onto more or less friable rock, some highly ferruginous, imparting finesse to its wines; and finally schistous gravels, close to river beds. Six hectares were planted, some on each type of *terroir*, from which Jean-Michel produces his four wines.

The Collioure *générique*, the base level wine, comes from a mix of around 60% Syrah, 30% Mourvèdre and 10% Counoise from all three sectors. Above this are three individual *crus*, each corresponding to its named *lieu-dit*.

These are: Cospron Levants, a 1.68-ha Piemont vineyard on deep, schistous clay soil; the blend is 55% Mourvèdre, 35% Syrah, plus 10% Counoise for finesse.

The relatively young Clos du Moulin is 1.44ha of gravelly river bed, planted 75% Mourvèdre and 25% Counoise; no Syrah here, it would over-produce.

Finally there is Les Junquets, nearly a hectare of hilltop site, exposed to all points of the compass, hot, powerful schistous *terroir*, ideal for Syrah. Gérard Chave suggested that they used a little white to lighten things; so, with the 90% Syrah, 5% each of Marsanne and Roussanne are planted.

The three *crus* only appear in top vintages; defined by Jean-Michel as years which permit him to vinify with whole berries – not *macération carbonique*, but when de-stemming leaves the berries intact. The more difficult the vintage the nearer the *cuvaison* approaches to three weeks, to increase extraction. Only the free-run wine is used (the pressings going into the *cuvée générique*), giving a cleaner wine to put into wood for a years' maturation. The generic blend remains in *inox* for 9–10 months.

Short pruning and, where necessary, summer crop-thinning, keep yields at around 25hl/ha, increasing concentration. However, these are not massive, blockbusting mouthfuls, rather wines of tender, ripe fruit with noble tannins and considerable finesse.

Each Cru has its own personality within this family resemblance – the Cospron having greatest elegance, the Clos du Moulin most structure, with Les Junquets somewhere in between the two.

According to Jean-Michel, the lighter wines go well with Mediterranean fish – cooked, of course, in good olive oil.

Collioure merits a wider public. The Parcé versions are capable of ageing in bottle for many years, especially in good vintages such as 1991, and are worth exploring both for their quality and for their intrinsic interest. Not forgetting, of course, the Mas Blanc Banyuls – among the best to be had, especially the remarkable Solera and the Rimage.

VINEYARD	APPELLATION	DETAILS	AREA
COSPRON LEVANTS	COLLIOURE	Planted in late 1960s; 55% Mourvèdre , 35% Syrah; 10% Counoise; average yield 18 hl/ha.	1.68
CLOS DU MOULIN	COLLIOURE	Planted 1983; 75% Mourvèdre, 25% Counoise; average yield 21 hl/ha.	1.80
LES JUNQUETS	COLLIOURE	Planted 1982; 90% Syrah + 5% each Marsanne & Roussanne; average yield 25 hl/ha.	0.99
VARIOIUS SITES	COLLIOURE	60% Mourvèdre, 30% Syrah, 10% Counoise; average vine age 30 yrs; average yield 21 hl/ha.	2.31
		TOTAL (hectares):	6.78

Autumn vineleaf.

DOMAINE DE PEYRE ROSE

In the 1980s, Marlene Soria and her husband gave up selling seaside apartments on the Camargue and training the French sailing team respectively, and devoted their slender financial resources to the creation of a wine estate from a holiday cottage with neither electricity nor running water, which they had enjoyed for ten summers.

A decade later (1994), cash is still tight, but there are 22ha of vines, planted on hand-cleared *garrigue*. Electricity for the house and the poorly-insulated, non air-conditioned *cuverie*-cum-cellar where the dynamic, dark-haired, Marlene crafts her wine, is supplied by a generator with an incessant hum reminiscent of a blue-bottle trapped in a toilet-roll.

Apart from a sound white, from 2ha of Roussanne, Rolle and a little (5%) of Viognier, the domaine's mainstays are a trio of reds. Cuvée Rafael is a blend of Grenach/Syrah/Mourvèdre, named after the couple's adopted Thai son: this is the lightest. In a different class are the Cuvées Clos des Cistes and Leone – corresponding to two individual vineyard sites – the former a 7-ha block planted 85% Syrah and 15% Grenache, the latter 5ha, planted 90% Syrah and 10% Mourvèdre. Cuvée Rafael is an *assemblage* of whatever remains and various other plantings.

The regime is *culture biologique*.

"these *garrigues* are virgin territory for viticulture"; so just sulphur and Bordeaux mixture are used, with a helping of compost to increase yields from their current miserly 15hl/ha to 25. Attractive as the countryside may be to the tourist, nature is far from generous in these uncompromising limestone soils.

With such low yields, 25 days of maceration, only 50% de-stemming, *faux pigeage* and all the press-wine added back, it is hardly surprising that the wines are loaded with tannin. Unfortunately this imparts an aggressive edge and, moreover, tends to stifle the fruit underneath. However, this masculinity hasn't staunched sales which have improved dramatically since the first vintage, 1989, which went mostly to the local *négoce*. In 1990 "they tried to screw me down on price so I kept the wine"; a decision rewarded by two stars in Guide Hachette and more sales. Marlene's 1991s brought American interest, and Paris

critics were "over the moon". "Now the trouble is that I have too little wine; 1993 was less than 15hl/ha, 1994 rather more". Things are looking up; there is talk of more insulation, even air-conditioning, and experiments are under way with new casks in a variety of sizes.

Good as the wines are, they have a fundamental tannin imbalance, with austere flavours which no amount of bottle-ageing will correct. All the ingredients are there to make superb wine but a radical re-thinking is required to achieve this. Most importantly, yields must increase – a rare recommendation! – and there should be more de-stemming and shorter *cuvaisons*. These measures, taken together with earlier harvesting, fine-tuning of *pigeage* and perhaps rather less press-wine would undoubtedly result in a better equilibrium. Earlier bottling would also help preserve fruit – some 1988 Rafael was still in *cuve* in October 1994 – a pity. Marlene seems aware of the problem and anxious to put it right. Given these caveats, Peyre Rose has the makings of a superb domaine.

VARIETY	APPELLATION	DETAILS	AREA
SYRAH	VIN DU PAYS D'OC	Planted 1984	14.00
GRENACHE	VIN DU PAYS D'OC	Planted 1984 and later	4.00
MOURVEDRE	VIN DU PAYS D'OC	Planted 1987	2.00
ROUSSANNE	VIN DU PAYS D'OC	Planted 1989/90	1.00
ROLLE	VIN DU PAYS D'OC	Planted 1991	1.20
		TOTAL (hectares):	22.20

LA PRIEURE ST-JEAN DE BEBIAN

In May 1994 this estate was bought by French wine journalist Chantale Lecouty and her historian husband Jean-Claude le Brun, so considered appraisal must wait. What can be said, however, is that Le Prieuré, under its ex-proprietor, the somewhat eccentric 48-year-old Alain Roux, made one of the finest wines of the entire Midi.

This is an uncompromisingly firm-framed giant, from a mixture principally of Grenache, Syrah, Mourvèdre (cuttings from Rayas, Chave and Tempier respectively) and Cinsaut, needing 6–12 hours' aeration to bring it to life. One needs only to taste a Roux wine to recognise its inspiration in the wines of Château Rayas (qv).

The new owners come from a tough, competitive, Paris business mould. Selling their magazine group, which included the Revue de Vin de France, gave them the means to buy Le Prieuré and to embark on the restoration of its buildings –

including the 12th-century Priory itself, reputedly the oldest Romanesque building in the Languedoc.

For the wine, however, major restoration is not part of their plans; they intend to follow Roux's tradition: "if we can do as well as Alain, with his cement *cuves*, we'll be content". At present they have little to sell – the purchase included part of the 1991 vintage in bottle, no 1992 (none was made), and the 1993 in *cuve*.

It took some fancy footwork to prepare themselves for the 1994 vintage – less than five months after taking charge. Additional old cement *cuves* were found and installed, together with a shining Demoisy *tapis de triage*, a new crusher-stemmer, and a pneumatic press ("to avoid another 1992"). The vines needed identifying and logging, as many were planted *en foule* and the only record was in Alain Roux's head; so an ampelographer and a surveyor were instructed and set to work.

The geology of the gently undulating hills between St-Jean de Bebian and Nizas is complex. As well as patches of pure limestone, it includes veins of black basalt, good for Syrah, and some clay-limestone, good for Grenache, which is also planted on more sandy clays overlaid with hard marbled limestone boulders.

The broad guidelines are well-established: in the vineyards, treatments will be limited to Bordeaux mixture and sulphur and harvesting will be later rather than sooner. In the cellar, *cuvaison* will last for 15–21 days and follows the Roux practice of putting successive layers of different varieties into each *cuve*. Fermentations will run up to 33°C, using natural yeasts, with *pigeage* and *remontage* to maximise extraction. As to *élevage*, "we are both against wood – absolutely", Chantale and Jean-Claude chorus, so the wines will be matured in *cuve*. One suspects that their sense of curiosity, coupled with the familiar fact that most of the world's great wines are matured in oak, will at least tempt them to an experiment.

Chantale and her husband's fierce determination to succeed is tempered with some apprehension that they, formerly France's toughest wine critics, will now themselves come under the microscope. There have already been mutterings of "*vin des jounalistes!*", and mild derision.

However, unblinkered realism and excellent resources should enable them to achieve their goals. Alain Roux helped them pick their first vintage and gave advice on vinification, and they have also retained the domaine's long-time consultant oenologist, François Serres, (who has also been consultant at Château

VARIETY	APPELLATION	DETAILS	AREA
SYRAH	COTEAUX DU LANGUEDOC	Sélection massale, ex Chave, Hermitage, av vine age, 25	6.00
GRENACHE	COTEAUX DU LANGUEDOC	Sélection massale, ex Ch. Rayas, Châteauneuf du Pape, average vine age, 25; incl. 2 ha. of 1920 vines	7.00
MOURVEDRE	COTEAUX DU LANGUEDOC	Sélection massale, ex Tempier, Bandol; average vine age, 25	4.60
CINSAUT	COTEAUX DU LANGUEDOC	Average vine age, 25	4.00
Diverse cépages	COTEAUX DU LANGUEDOC	Average vine age, 25	1.40
Unplanted	COTEAUX DU LANGUEDOC		2.00
		TOTAL (hectares):	25.00

Rayas for decades). The potential is definitely there; it remains to be seen whether or not they realise it. They believe that "if Parker awards 92/100 to Bebian, it's proof you can make great wine in the Languedoc". The argument may be a non-sequitur, but believing it will probably act as a powerful spur.

DOMAINE DES QUATRE SOUS

In the wild *garrigues*, beneath the hilltop village of Assignan, at the junction of two pilgrim routes, Swiss Ernst Wirz and his attractive, slim wife, Hildegard Horat, have established their eight-hectare domaine. Using his architecture and design skills, they rescued the buildings they bought in 1974 from 60 years of neglect, to make their home above a small *cuverie* and cellar, overlooking a gently undulating landscape of vines and brush. As a habitation, the site dates back to the Knights Templar of the Middle Ages and beyond – Visigoth remains have been unearthed nearby.

Much has changed since their first effort with Carignan, Aramon and Cinsaut in 1983, destined for home consumption. With advice from experts in Bordeaux and elsewhere, they opted for a mix of Bordeaux and Rhône varieties, with some Chardonnay bought in from a neighbour. Lyre trellising is used to increase foliar exposure and ripeness – this brought much local derision, along the "what are you planting – Kiwi fruit?" lines.

Although 80% of their vineyards are within the St-Chinian appellation boundary, their chosen planting density of only 3,300 vines per hectare limits the designation to Vin du Pays d'Oc – the St-Chinian appellatin rules require a minimum of 4,000.

There are presently three red wines, one white and a *rosé de saignée de Cinsaut* to choose from. The top *cuvées* are: Le Jeu du Mail – a blend of around 60% Viognier and 40% Chardonnay (c.1500 bottles) – and the red Les Serrottes: 65% Syrah and 35% Malbec (around 5,000 bottles).

The Marsanne vines will come into

Ernst Wirz and Hildegarde Horat.

production in 1996 and there are 200 Muscat à Petits Grains – both destined for the Jeu du Mail *cuvée*, so the present mix is provisional. The base-line red is a blend of Syrah, Grenache and Mourvèdre – this last ripening without difficulty here on its high trellis.

The wines are carefully thought out and skillfully crafted. Ernst and Hildegard chose their *encépagement* after tasting and, in particular, because they liked Malbec, Syrah, Viognier and Chardonnay. They use only natural yeast – tasting wines made with indigenous and bought yeasts, and advice from the kindly M. Dupuy of Château de Fieuzal in the Graves, convinced them of a difference. The Chardonnay is fermented in old

VARIETY	APPELLATION	DETAILS	AREA
SYRAH	VIN DE PAYS D'OC	Planted 1987; Lyre training	1.05
SYRAH	VIN DE PAYS D'OC	Planted 1994/5; Lyre training	1.00
MALBEC	VIN DE PAYS D'OC	Planted 1988; Lyre training	1.19
VIOGNIER	VIN DE PAYS D'OC	Planted 1991; Lyre training	0.70
MARSANNE	VIN DE PAYS D'OC	Planted 1992; Lyre training	0.64
CHARDONNAY	VIN DE PAYS D'OC	Planted 1987; Lyre training	0.66
GRENACHE	VIN DE PAYS D'OC	Planted 1985; Lyre training	0.18
MOURVEDRE	VIN DE PAYS D'OC	Planted 1985; Lyre training	0.36
CINSAUT	VIN DE PAYS D'OC	Planted 1974; part Lyre training	1.50
CABERNET FRANC	VIN DE PAYS D'OC	Planted 1990; Lyre training	0.36
CABERNET SAUVIGNON	VIN DE PAYS D'OC	Planted 1989; Lyre training	0.50
		TOTAL (hectares):	8.14

casks, the Viognier (since 1992) in *inox* – both at 18–20°C. The wines are *bâtonnéed* and bottled without malolactic – so requiring a sterile filtration – in May, in time for their summer clientele, with deliberately late *assemblage* for maximum fine-tuning of the blend.

The Jeu du Mail is attractive, with plenty of fat and good acidity – not always easy in this hot, high-sugar,

climate. The cask-fermented Viognier in the 1992 gave a noticeably richer and more harmonious feel than the *inox*-fermented Viognier of 1993; this retrograde change will hopefully soon be reversed. The addition of Marsanne and Muscat will undoubtedly add further complexity.

The Serrottes, reflecting its 25–30 days *cuvaison*, is characterised by plenty of

ripe, dryish tannins and is designed as a *vin de garde*. Maturation for a year in 225-litre or, increasingly, larger old wood has some softening effect, but in lighter vintages, such as 1992, produces a distinct tannin imbalance which definitely needs further adjustment. Ernst and Hildegard have all the resources in place for top-class ranking – a touch more fine-tuning will do it.

DOMAINE DE LA RECTORIE

Twenty years ago, Collioure was a rarity; now, in the wake of diminishing fortified wine consumption, most Banyuls estates produce one or more table wines. Marc and Thierry Parcé's Domaine de la Rectorie is no exception, offering an attractive, fat rosé and three reds. There was a white in 1993 and 1994, but this has been temporarily suspended.

Their first bottling was 1984, eight years after taking over seven hectares of vines from their grandfather, Léon Parcé – a second generation cousin of Dr André Parcé (Mas Blanc, qv). The Domaine now covers 30ha, 50–60% planted to Grenache Noir, and produces four *cuvées* of excellent, traditional Banyuls in addition to the Collioures. The vines average more than 40 years of age – a marvellous resource, from which the brothers extract the maximum.

Unusually, there is no catch-all generic Collioure, just three vineyard-designated *cuvées*. First, Coume Pascole, one and a half hectares of "very old, very good" *terroir* near Banyuls itself; the decomposed schistous soils, with some red clay, are not deep, but resist drought well. Its *encépagement* is 60% Grenache Noir and 40% Syrah, giving much the lightest wine of the trio, characterised by finesse rather than structure.

The two-hectare Seris, situated in the Seris valley, towards Banyuls' southern outpost Cerbère, has deeper soils and high humidity. With 40% of late ripening Carignan (the rest is Grenache Noir), harvest is always late, bringing a risk of equinoctial rain. The wine has more muscle than Coume Pascole and a firmer structure which to some appears as rusticity. Good wine which merits keeping, nonetheless.

Despite an identical grape mix, Les Hautes Vignes is different again. An altitude of 3–400 metres – one of the highest in the appellation – and an east-south-east exposure, mean an even later harvest than Seris. This cool micro-climate preserves wine acidity and freshness, but at the expense of *gras* and richness,

Thierry and Marc Parcé.

especially in marginal vintages.

Marc and Thierry recognise that the quality of the crop takes precedence over winemaking skills – "the cave is not there to save poor grapes". In this region where even severely pruned old vines need constant vigilance to ensure that grape-acids don't plummet before harvest intervenes, the overall heat of the vineyards makes acidity rather than alcoholic degree their principal concern. In 1994, for example, after a scorchingly hot summer, with no useful rain from mid-March to mid-September, they started analysing grape samples in mid-July and decided to harvest a month later, well before the official *ban de vendanges*.

The wines are made parcel by parcel and designed for keeping, with 10–18 months in cask, around one-third of them

new. Each *cuvée* is put together after malolactic and bottled fined, but generally unfiltered. "Our wines are *vins de garde*, not *vins de bouche*; the aromas come later". Do not expect much on the nose for a Rectorie's first few years.

Thierry and Marc learned their skills *in situ*, not in any high-tech Lycée or University oenology faculty. "We have no *a prioris* for our Collioure, the important thing is to have equilibrium", Marc explains. These Collioures, hallmarked above all by finesse, are among the best in this under-rated appellation. Léon Parcé's love of Banyuls and his worthy tradition remains in fine hands.

VARIETY	APPELLATION	DETAILS	AREA
COUME PASCOLE	COLLIOURE	40% 15 yr old Syrah, 60% 60+ yr old Grenache Noir	1.50
SERIS	COLLIOURE	60% Grenache Noir, 40% Carignan	2.00
LES HAUTES VIGNES	COLLIOURE	60% Grenache Noir, 40% Carignan	2.00
		TOTAL (Collioure vineyards only, hectares):	5.50

DOMAINE RICHEAUME

Created by a German expatriate, Henning Hoesch, and his French-Swiss wife in 1972, Richeaume has developed with quiet confidence over the intervening years. The original farm, an attractive pink-wash Provençale *mas* with 2ha of Grenache vines, has now become 25ha, producing four AC Coteaux d'Aix en Provence reds, a rosé and a white. The vines are mainly on south-facing terraces, on the slopes of the Massif de Cenge, with a striking backdrop of the Mont St-Victoire.

The estate is "*culture biologique*", in the belief that this preserves the natural equilibrium; maybe, but this ideology begs the question of whether nature is beyond improvement in the first place, and also whether the natural equilibrium is the best adapted to any given grape variety. Fertilisers are confined to organic material grown on the farm, composted with *fumeurs* from the estate's own flock of sheep. The tall, slender Hoesch, explains that this brings out "la force de la terre", whatever that signifies.

His rather austere mien conceals a historian's intellect, a cellist's sensitivity and a passion for quality. No cutting corners here or lack of care in the distinctly *art-nouveau* cellars tacked on to the back of the house. Modern sculptures adorn the terrace and an artificial water catchment provides a layer of insulation for a pair of Bordelais-style barrel cellars, where the Syrah remains for 12 months, the Cabernet for six months longer, in wood (a quarter of it new).

Everything is de-stemmed, and *cuvaisons* last three weeks – an important element in Henning Hoesch's desire to "work the body of the wine – it's dry extract" during this phase, leaving aromatic development to come with cask ageing. Frequent rackings and small-volume *élevage* produce wines that seldom require filtration, and only the lightest of finings.

The Syrah – which is released as a 100% varietal – also appears in Richeaume's latest *cuvée*, blended with Cabernet Sauvignon. Apart from a Grenache *rosé de saignée*, there is a Cuvée Tradition, a second wine, blended from Grenache and Cabernet, in no pre-determined proportions, with a dollop of press-wine superadded. One year the Cabernet dominates, another the Grenache.

Grown here, Syrah has markedly more sunshine and markedly less water than in the northern Rhône; this *terroir* expresses a plumper, less peppery and spicy side of its character. The oak adds an attractive touch of cedary smokiness, leaving a well-defined wine, often with a dry final mouthfeel, that needs a few years to develop most appealing secondary aromas.

This is one of Provence's best estates. Henning Hoesch's quietly understated passion for his *metier*, and for his music, remain undiminished, and in these respects, the wines reflect the man.

VARIETY	VINEYARD	DETAILS	AREA
SYRAH	RICHEAUME	18 yrs average vine age	4.00
GRENACHE	RICHEAUME	Average age 40; most destined for rosé; rented vines	10.00
CINSAUT	RICHEAUME	Most destined for rosé	0.50
CABERNET SAUVIGNON	RICHEAUME	Average age 18	6.00
CLAIRETTE + ROLLE	RICHEAUME	Clairette, average age 40; rented vines; Rolle young vines, owned	5.00
		TOTAL (hectares):	25.50

CHATEAU SIMONE

The tiny Palette appellation has just 22.5ha currently in production, of which Château Simone has 17 and Château Crémat the other 5.5.

Simone is an unusual *vignoble*, situated within the suburbs of Aix-en-Provence and producing red, white and rosé from a mix of grapes many of which, such as the red Castels and Manosquin, have ceased to be planted, but are enshrined in the 1948 appellation decree to preserve the tradition.

The château, an elegant and finely-proportioned building that dates mainly from the 16th century with later Napoleonic additions, is approached by a long winding track. From its magnificent terrace, dominated by two enormous sculpted yews, clearly visible beyond the domaine's vineyards are the rugged limestone ravines of Cézanne's beloved Mont St-Victoire.

The Rougier family have been at Château Simone for six generations. René Rougier, who now runs the property, together with his wife and son, is a bluff and friendly man. Although he went to Beaune and Montpellier, he ascribes his skills more to tutelage from his father than from these formal studies.

The long-established vineyard is a traditional mixed planting, rather than modern varietal blocks, dominated by Grenache for the red and rosé and Clairette for the white. The vines are trained *en gobelet*, with a supporting stake, and planted on mainly scree soils deriving from the limestone which characterises this part of Provence. Their roots go deep, giving a good degree of drought protection.

The surrounding forests give an individual micro-climate which is key to understanding this estate. Their influence regulates both temperature and moisture, and perhaps account for the balsamic, resiny note that some tasters find in the wine. In some vintages they promote a touch of noble rot to enrich the white wine. Unusually, the entire *vignoble* faces north, giving late ripening and more oblique than perpendicular sun exposure, and this brings elegance and finesse to the wines. To safeguard this important

APPELLATION	VINEYARD	DETAILS	AREA
GRENACHE	CHATEAU SIMONE	Incl. some 1891 plantings; average age 60++	5.00
MOURVEDRE	CHATEAU SIMONE	Average age 60+	2.50
CINSAUT	CHATEAU SIMONE	Average age 60+	0.50
SYRAH	CHATEAU SIMONE	Average age 60+	0.30
CABERNET SAUVIGNON	CHATEAU SIMONE	Average age 60+	0.30
OTHER RED VARIETIES	CHATEAU SIMONE	Average age 60+; mixed planting	0.40
CLAIRETTE	CHATEAU SIMONE	Incl. some 1891 plantings; average age 60++	6.40
GRENACHE BLANC	CHATEAU SIMONE	Average age 60+	0.80
UGNI BLANC	CHATEAU SIMONE	Average age 60+	0.40
MUSCAT BLANC	CHATEAU SIMONE	Average age 60+	0.40
		TOTAL (hectares):	17.00

environment, René Rougier has carefully established an elaborate fire-fighting system which involves everyone living and working on the estate.

All three wines are distinctly individual and rarely obviously varietal. The red, which is often mistaken for top-quality Bordeaux in blind tasting, contains a miniscule dab of Cabernet Sauvignon but no Merlot; and the white could easily be taken for a middle-aged Hermitage or a youngish *vin jaune*. Much of their characteristic depth and balance comes from a high proportion of very old vines; the oldest block dates from 1891 (with no vines missing) and the average age is more than 60. Dead or diseased vines are replaced by *sélection massale*, with grafts made up on the estate.

Vinifications are described by René Rougier as "grande classique". The whites (around one-third of production) issue from 80% Clairette, 10% Grenache blanc, and 3–4% each of Ugni and Muscat blanc, fermented in small *foudres* and left *sur lie* without *bâtonnage* until bottling late the following spring. The château's cold, subterranean cellars are not conducive to malolactic fermentation, which needs heat, so it isn't encouraged – this preserves valuable acidity.

René Rougier and his wife.

The excellent Simone rosé comes one-third from a "relatively long" *saignée de cuve* and two-thirds from *pressurage directe*, kept apart until the following spring and bottled in late June. This is a rosé that is generally deep in colour, with the structure more of a red than a white; a complete, quite rich wine which merits a few years' bottle-age.

The red (50% of their production), comes from a 15-day *cuvaison* of 90–95% de-stemmed Grenache, with Mourvèdre, Cinsaut and small quantities of ten other *cépages,* including 3–4% each of Syrah and Cabernet. These are vinified together and matured in large Hungarian oak of a variety of sizes; a year, and four rackings, later the rich press wine, also kept in wood, is assembled and the results put into standard casks – mostly two- three- and four-year-old, to marry for a further 12 months. By tradition, new wood is not part of the regime. The wine is fined and bottled, without further manipulation, between mid-August and mid-September of the third year. Simone Rouge is an enigma, an individual which fits into no obvious type or style. A *vin de garde*, but like Lebanon's Château Musar, entirely *sui generis* .

After 20 years at the helm, René Rougier is phlegmatic: "the typicity of Château Simone is that it is atypical". An apt summary indeed.

The view of Mont St-Victoire dominates Palette's vineyards.

DOMAINE DE TREVALLON

Trevallon is one of the best, and best-known, wines of Provence. Since its inception in 1973, its founder-owner Eloi Durrbach has established himself as one of the Midi's leading winemakers on this property which his parents – a tapestry-maker and a sculptor – bought as a holiday home in 1960.

Georges Brunet, then at Château Vignelaure, helped select the first vines – Cabernet Sauvignon (from Vignelaure) and Syrah (from Château Rayas); sadly, Mourvèdre and Grenache wouldn't ripen on this north-facing edge of the Alpilles. Now there are 20ha – including 4ha of white varieties.

The red Trevallon generally, though not invariably, contains more Cabernet than Syrah, while the white, which is currently 50:50 Marsanne:Roussanne (budded from Beaucastel's old vines), is still experimental – "j'hésite un peu". There are "a few rows" of Viognier – Eloi dislikes the variety but his vivacious dark-haired wife, whom he met while he was doing a *stage* in Fleurie – her home village, wanted some.

Since the inaugural vintage, 1977, a style has developed for the reds – firm yet supple wines, with plenty of ripe fruit; very attractive young, but which age transforms into something infinitely more complex and interesting. In early life, Syrah seems to dominate the blend, the Cabernet lying dormant until later.

Low yields (25–30hl/ha), no chemicals, *Guyot simple* pruning to four to five buds, and thin, stony, limestone soils, produce thick skins, rich in tannin, colour and flavour, which need two to three weeks of *cuvaison*; hard, ripe stems are also included. Fermentations are conducted on *laissez-faire* natural principles; so only the indigenous yeasts are used and temperatures are allowed to reach 35°C,

Eloi Durrbach.

even 40°C before the yeasts give up – temperatures which would terrify many winemakers. Eloi is perfectly relaxed: "the blocked *cuves* are often the best". Each variety is vinified separately, and only assembled after a minimum of 18 months in 3,000-litre *foudres* – corresponding to each plot of vines.

Conventional wisdom has it that Syrah is best matured in cask, Grenache in *foudre*. However, Eloi finds that his Syrah does well in *foudre;* it needs one more racking than the Cabernet, and is generally less alcoholic and animal in character than a Hermitage – more supple and less structured perhaps – but none the worse for that. The Cabernet provides

complementary qualities – tannin in particular, but without the herbaceous streak often found in Bordeaux.

The Bordelais and the AC authorities both, in their own way, cause problems. The former clearly dislike the competition of top-class, good value Cabernet from Provence, which Bordelais *sommeliers* and other influential customers seem to find hard to accept. The authorities have recently shifted the AC Coteaux d'Aix goal-posts: pre-1985, 60% Cabernet was the maximum allowed in the vineyard; since 1985 only 40% is permitted and there are proposals to reduce this to 20%. *Les officiels* suggested to Eloi that he could always rent additional vineyards, appropriately planted, to comply. His admirably robust response was to tell them that he would meet this threat by selling his wine as *vin de table* – by-passing the AC rules altogether. Fortunately, Trevallon sells itself – but Eloi is passionately concerned for the future of the area, and is now trying to create a new AC: Les Baux.

Whatever the difficulties, Eloi Durrbach has the air of a thoroughly contented man. He follows his own rules and is dismissive of technologically-driven methods, especially the over-use of sulphur in white winemaking and the reliance on consultant oenologists: "no-one knows Chave's or Clape's oenologist" (they don't have one).

Nothing is hurried here – the white wine is clearly still at the rehearsal stage and will take a few more years before it is performance-ready. Meanwhile, claret snobs will continue to avoid the Midi, leaving Trevallon's delights to those more concerned with quality than with fashion.

VARIETY	APPELLATION	DETAILS	AREA
SYRAH	COTEAUX D'AIX EN PROVENCE	Planted c 1974	7.20
CABERNET SAUVIGNON	COTEAUX D'AIX EN PROVENCE	Planted c 1974	8.80
MARSANNE	COTEAUX D'AIX EN PROVENCE	Some 1994 plantings	2.00
ROUSSANNE	COTEAUX D'AIX EN PROVENCE	Some 1994 plantings	2.00
		TOTAL (hectares):	20.00

DOMAINE DE TRIENNES

Winemakers appear to relish challenges. Here, at 450 metres, in a coolish, rather wet micro-climate of the Var, north-east of Marseilles and due east of Aix-en-Provence, two of Burgundy's finest *vignerons* are pitting their collective skills against a block of 44ha of Syrah, Viognier, Carignan, Cinsaut, Chardonnay, Cabernet Sauvignon and Merlot – plus one of Pinot Noir (which doesn't perform

well in these heavy clay/limestone soils).

Aubert de Villaine, co-owner of Domaine de la Romanée-Conti, Jacques Seysses, founder of Domaine Dujac in Morey-Saint-Denis, and a mutual friend, Michel Macaux, teamed up to buy this run-down estate in May 1990. By September, they had thrown out all the old *cuves*, built and equipped a new *cuverie* and underground cellar for 900

casks, and were just about ready for the harvest, which then consisted largely of Carignan.

Jacques has landed the job of looking after the Domaine helped by Dujac's viticulturalist, Christophe Morin, who is charged with producing top-quality fruit. The Seysses viticultural philosophy that "quality begins in the vineyard" reigns here also, so Triennes vines are tended as ecologically as possible – minimum necessary treatments, no insecticides, with grass seeded in alternate rows to limit herbicide use and soil erosion. To establish a sensible *encépagement* quickly, a team of skilled Mexicans was flown over from California to graft noble scions on to existing Carignan roots.

The project's aim is to bring the rigour and experience of Burgundy to an area largely bereft of both – spiced, no doubt, by the challenge of working with an unfamiliar range of grapes. The results so far, are attractive, both in price and quality, and include an explosively delicious Viognier, *élevé* for a year in second year casks with a couple of hours' pre-fermentive *macération pelliculaire*; a 50:50 Syrah:Cabernet *cuvée*, Les Aureliens – Monts Aurelien and Sainte Baume flank the domaine – and a 100% varietal Syrah.

Both red and white grapes are machine-harvested, for maximum speed and ripeness. Perforce de-stemmed, the red berries are part-fermented in roto-tanks and part traditionally, in open *cuves*, with some 11 days' *cuvaison*. On Alain Graillot's (qv) advice, the Syrah is well aerated to avoid developing a disagreeable, reduced character and matured in cask rather than large oak *foudres*. Syrah and Cabernet are assembled after fermentation but before malolactic, which Jacques has concluded gives the best results. There is no filtration, but a light egg-white fining may precede bottling, after a year in one- to fouu-year-old ex-Dujac casks.

Early releases were aimed at a market wanting suppleness rather than tannic *vins de garde*, though these may well come later. Triennes is a good source of interesting and impeccably made wines. The future will undoubtedly bring exciting developments – standing still is not an option here.

VARIETY	VINEYARD	DETAILS	AREA
SYRAH	TRIENNES	20-yr-old roots – surgreffé	8.50
CABERNET SAUVIGNON	TRIENNES	20-yr-old roots – surgreffé	11.50
MERLOT	TRIENNES	20-yr-old roots – surgreffé	6.50
CHARDONNAY	TRIENNES	20-yr-old roots – surgreffé	4.50
VIOGNIER	TRIENNES	20-yr-old roots – surgreffé	7.00
PINOT NOIR	TRIENNES	20-yr-old roots – surgreffé	1.00
CARIGNAN	TRIENNES	Original roots	5.00
CINSAUT	TRIENNES	Rosè "Gris de Triennes"; 2–3 hours skin contact, then saignée	5.00
		TOTAL (hectares):	45.50

DOMAINE VAQUER

The broad, beaming and voluble Fernand Vaquer is a man of firm resolve and strong opinion which he is not averse to voicing at length; an individualist who turns out interesting wine from his 30ha estate His Dijon-trained son Bernard joined him in 1983 while his daughter, Marie-José, contributes her name to the Domaine's sweet Rivesaltes, which makes up 80% of the Vaquer production.

The enterprise has several unusual features: first, the table wines are sold as Vin de Pays Catalan; Fernard could have the appellation Côtes du Roussillon but considers that his wines merit the superior Villages designation – to which, because his land lies on the wrong side of the river Tet, they are not entitled.

He therefore just labels them "Vaquer Rouge" and "Vaquer Blanc de Blancs" – encouraging his clientele to buy Vaquer first, the appellation second. To reinforce the brand, visitors to the domaine at Tresserre are guided by signs which simply proclaim "Vaquer".

A second notable feature is that there are two vinifications for the red wine – his and Bernard's. While both come from a base of Carignan and Grenache Noir, Fernand's wine has around 80% of old-vine Carignan, giving deeper, firmer structure, helped by up to five weeks' *cuvaison* and around two years' *élevage;* definitely a *vin de garde*. Bernard's, in contrast, has some 50% of Carignan and is vinified to bring out fruit, with 14 days vatting and just six months of maturation; wines for drinking within their first few

Fernand Vaquer.

years. Since 1990, Bernard has been in sole charge of vinifications; yet there is still Cuvée Fernand and Cuvée Bernard – two different wines from essentially the same raw material. In the small *caveau*, there are boxes carefully labelled "Fernand Vaquer" and "wine from my son Bernard", respectively.

A further unusual trait here is that when the raw material isn't up to Fernand and Bernard's standards, the wines are sold off in bulk; thus, you won't find any 1987, 1989, 1992 or 1993 white, nor 1987, 1992 or 1993 in red. The slogan is: "when it's not good, it's not Vaquer".

The Vaquers are also unusual in only selling wines when they regard them as mature. So, in late 1994, 1988, 1986 and 1985 were available in red, as were 1990 through to 1985, and an excellent 1979 in white. Release of the 1990 "Fernand" red was being considered.

Extracting precise information from Fernand is a demanding task – he seems convinced that vinification details need the status of a closely-guarded family recipe: tell, and you let your competitors in on the secret. He clearly dislikes uncomprehending officialdom, but has great respect for anyone who understands and shares his passion. He needs no reassurance; his wines are well above his self-imposed *vin de pays* designation.

APPELLATION	VINEYARD	DETAILS	AREA
GRENACHE NOIR	TRESSERRE		6.00
CARIGNAN	TRESSERRE	Some old vines here	6.00
SYRAH	TRESSERRE		1.00
CINSAUT	TRESSERRE		1.00
MACCABEO	TRESSERRE	Sole variety used for whites; also contributes to Rivesaltes	6.00
SEVERAL VARIETIES FOR RIVESALTES	TRESSERRE		10.00
		TOTAL (hectares):	30.00

CALIFORNIA

A quarter of a century after the "Rhône Rangers" started to make waves on the Californian wine scene, the Rhône following is gathering momentum. Across the State, outposts of excellence are manned by dedicated, often idiosyncratic, devotees, and every vintage brings a greater range and ever-improving quality.

A newly created vineyard at Tablas Creek – a promising Franco-American partnership.

CALIFORNIA

Although better known as a source of high-priced designer Chardonnays, Merlots and Cabernets, California is smouldering with growers fired by Syrah, Petite Sirah, Grenache, Mourvèdre and Viognier. The Rhône tendency, seeded in the late 1970s by a nucleus of fanatics – the "Rhône Rangers" – has mushroomed in the intervening years, sweeping up converted producers and amateurs alike. This shows every sign of broadening and strengthening as people tire of the staples and realise how exciting wines from these under-appreciated grapes can be. It only takes one sip of a great Syrah to realise what you are missing.

HISTORY

Rhône varietals came to California in the 1880s – encouraged by the desire to improve on the widely planted Mission grape, although their names did not all appear on wine labels until later. Carignan was recorded in 1883, Mataro (Mourvèdre) in the 1890s, Petite Sirah (at Geyserville) and Grenache in the 1880s. These were mainly Spanish imports; the French Syrah did not arrive until later. By 1884, Marsanne, Roussanne, Clairette Blanche and Cinsaut were also being cultivated throughout the state.

During Prohibition, which curtailed planting as well as winemaking, vast acreages of noble grapes were uprooted. Fortunately, enough of these original plantings survived though to the recent Rhône resurgence, when producers came to realise the value this resource of very old vines represented. Although Grenache and Mourvèdre fared better, by 1969 the total acreage of Syrah had shrunk to four.

A varietal wine boom in the 1980s was followed by recession in the early 1990s. This coincided with a second substantial uprooting – this time of large areas of mature vineyard planted on the degenerate AxR rootstock, which succumbed to a form of phylloxera (Biotype B). This combination of financial pressure and disease gave growers an opportunity to rethink their strategy: whether to concentrate on premium or bulk wine, to plant noble or basic varieties – and to reconsider their planting policies, instead of repeating the folly of the post-war boom by spraying vines indiscriminately around hillsides and valleys, hoping for the best. The scope for regeneration, with a diverse spectrum of interesting varieties, sensibly sited and planted in suitable soils, must not be frittered away. However, many estates will probably baulk at the complex problems involved in making this choice and simply replant with the same old mix of trendy varieties.

There has been an important change in the established practice of paying grape-growers by crude measures of ripeness – the more sugar, the more cash. Winemakers now talk noticeably more of finesse than of size, and with more sophisticated measures of grape maturity and a better idea of how the various components relate to wine qualities, they can be more specific with their growers and pay accordingly. The search for quality has also persuaded many to reduce yields, severing the traditional link between crop-size and price.

THE REGION

Viticultural California is vast, with 140,000 acres under vine. It spreads from Mendocino, well north of San Francisco, to Temecula, well south of Los Angeles, inland to cooler Eldorado and through the scorching Central Valley which runs south from Sacramento to Bakersfield. Here, a great diversity of climates, expositions and soils turns one region into many, each with its individual characteristics.

GRAPE VARIETIES

Rhône grapes appear patchily along this broad strip. There are only a few pockets in the Napa Valley – this valuable land being consecrated to fashionable Chardonnay and Cabernet – otherwise small clusters and isolated sporadic outbreaks here, there and everywhere, from Placerville, well on the way to Lake Tahoe, to coastal Monterey. This scattering has no systematic bearing on quality, as producers can buy grapes from wherever they choose – but production and planting are often separated by hundreds of miles.

Recent years have seen an explosion in Syrah and Viognier planting, although the acreage of Grenache has declined (see table below). For example, one nurseryman reported selling enough Viognier bud-wood in one year to plant 150 acres – roughly the area of Condrieu, its principal home. An element of fashion is clearly involved, as growers search for the latest money-making fad. Unfortunately, Viognier is distinctly capricious, needing far more skill than Chardonnay or Sauvignon; so only those with a genuine feel for it are likely to succeed. Elsewhere, the enterprising Denis Horton has planted some in Virginia and there are productive Viognier vineyards in Utah and Colorado.

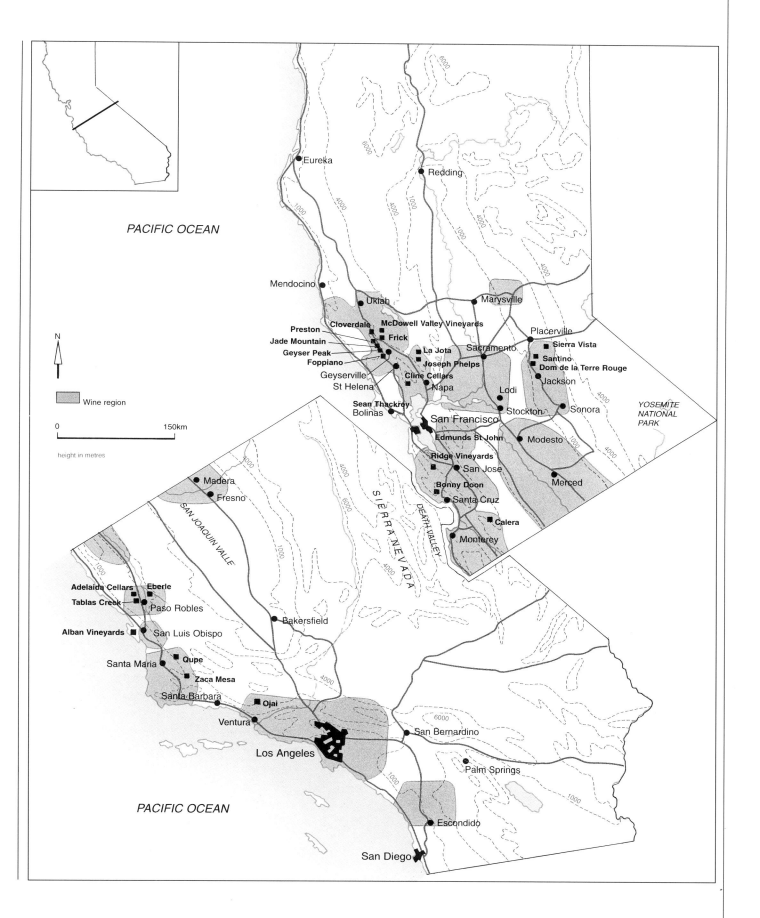

PACIFIC OCEAN

Eureka

Redding

6000

4000

1000

Mendocino

Ukiah

Marysville

Preston
Cloverdale
Jade Mountain
Geyser Peak
Foppiano
Geyserville
St Helena

McDowell Valley Vineyards
Frick
La Jota
Joseph Phelps
Cline Cellars
Napa

Placerville
Sierra Vista
Santino
Dom de la Terre Rouge
Jackson

Sacramento

Lodi

Stockton

Sonora

N

Wine region

0   150km

height in metres

Sean Thackrey
Bolinas

San Francisco

Edmunds St John

Ridge Vineyards

San Jose

Bonny Doon
Santa Cruz

Calera

Monterey

Modesto

Merced

YOSEMITE
NATIONAL
PARK

Madera

Fresno

SAN JOAQUIN VALLEY

S I E R R A   N E V A D A

DEATH VALLEY

Adelaida Cellars
Eberle
Tablas Creek
Paso Robles

Alban Vineyards
San Luis Obispo

Bakersfield

Santa Maria
Qupe

Zaca Mesa

Santa Barbara
Ojai

Ventura

San Bernardino

Los Angeles

Palm Springs

PACIFIC OCEAN

Escondido

San Diego

Unusual experiments are not confined to Viognier; for example Los Angeles attorney Lawrence Stickney has indulged his Rhône interest with just over an acre of Syrah, Grenache and Mourvèdre planted on granitic soils in a residential area of the San Rafael Hills of western Pasadena. This is hot country (region IV), and the vines need severe crop-thinning to rein in their vigour. The first crop (1993) was a respectable two tons, and although the Syrah and Mourvèdre seem to be performing well, the Grenache is reported as "disappointingly thin".

The widely-planted Petite Sirah causes rather different problems. The real nature of the grape is contentious; conventional wisdom identifies it with the Durif, a weak variety once grown extensively in the Midi. For a long time, no real distinction was made between Syrah, Petite Sirah, Serine and Durif – all were called Syrah. This continued into the 1960s, with burgeoning plantings of Durif/Petite Sirah, referred to by growers as Syrah, in the belief that what they had was the genuine northern Rhône grape. Recent attempts at identification have been hampered by doubts over the authenticity of the Durif reference sample held by UC Davis.

Whatever the facts, a small but vociferous lobby considers that "Petite" is not a noble grape and should not be treated as such or be permitted in Syrah show classes (Barbara MacCready of Sierra Vista (qv) is an articulate exponent of this view). However, in hands such as those of Paul Draper at Ridge (qv) or Warren Winiarski at Stag's Leap, Petite Sirah is undeniably capable of making superb wine. Tasted blind, it often mirrors the real Syrah, making the whole controversy somewhat sterile. Unfortunately potentially good "Petite" is often spoiled by too long in wood, excess dry tannins (probably due to too much new US oak) or an unattractive nerve of green stemminess, all faults that can easily be avoided. Like Syrah, Petite ages well.

Since 1982, California has been progressively divided into American Viticultural Areas (AVAs), somewhat akin to France's appellations. These, the smallest recognised areas of wine origin in the USA – states and counties are others – are designed to reflect distinguishing features of geography, climate, topography and geology. However, many regard AVAs as an irrelevance, realising that the grower has far more impact on wine's identity than any artificially-contrived demarcations. Moreover, bitter wrangling over boundaries has resulted in AVAs overlapping and illogical fragmentation, eroding what little respect the idea may have once enjoyed.

SOILS AND TERROIR

Earthquakes have shaped California and subsequent erosion formed its varied soils. The San Andreas Fault, where the North American Plate meets the Pacific Plate, crosses the region – and the North American is on the move north-west, albeit sluggishly. Topsoils are often limestone-based, formed from ancient marine debris of retreating oceans, and occasionally of volcanic origin, although sandstone and shales also abound. Subsoils are equally diverse and complex, varying in both depth and character from slopes to plains. Traditionally, vine plantings were on more easily worked, and more fertile, alluvial valley floors. Now sloping sites are preferred for many varieties, especially Syrah, for their drainage, sun exposure and relative coolness. Unfortunately local rules, driven largely by ecological and environmental considerations, discourage hillside plantings, while property developers value vineyards more highly as housing land. The net effect is a reduction in land available for viticulture, often in the best sites; a trend likely to worsen as urbanization pressure increases.

Arguments about AVAs parallel a fierce debate about *terroir* – the French concept linking wine quality to an amalgam of interacting influences which make one site differ from another, which underpins the *appellation contrôlée* system. The concept is by no means universally accepted in California; some regard it as of prime importance, others dismiss it as irrelevant, believing (wrongly) that yeasts, clones, malolactic strains, racking regimes – in short, everything else – are responsible for a wine's character and flavour. Those who do understand *terroir* have made great strides in matching variety with site, enabling them to extract the maximum expression of the land through the fruit grown there, without relying on artifices of vinification or viticulture to create a style. *Terroir*, especially among Rhône-style producers, is finally being taken seriously.

Whatever one's beliefs, it is doubtful whether individual *terroirs* can be definitively identified by making wine from specific sites over a short period (it took the French several centuries). Also, as the crop of any given vineyard may be widely distributed, the grape residue is not returned to the original vines and the micro-flora thus not sustained, making talk of *terroir* in its full sense, problematic.

What matters more at present is refining fruit quality. In California, where most grapes ripen too quickly, often to the detriment of quality, site selection is particularly important; for instance, it is likely that much of the Viognier planted in the explosion of recent years is on unsuitable sites. With powerful varieties such as Syrah and Mourvèdre, top-class results are only achievable where full ripeness is

Early morning in the Napa – burning phylloxera-stricken vines.

balanced with elegance; this means growing in the coolest possible area where the variety will ripen regularly.

The long-established practice of buying-in grapes and blending the results even for top-quality wines, has inevitably reduced the emphasis on site-specificity so prevalent in European viticulture. While micro-climates may matter to Californian producers seeking a balance in their wines, they are at present of marginal relevance to consumers.

CLIMATE

California has one of the widest range of climates of any wine-growing region, from the hot, arid, Central Valley to the cooler, foggy, coastal belt. The most widely-used index of climate, developed by Winkler and Amerine, defines regions by their heat summation – a measure of the amount of heat available to the vine during the April-October growing season. Region 1 has less than 2,500°F, Region V 4,001-4,500°F. Since this computes heat average, not its distribution, it only provides a crude indication of growing conditions – eg Syrah won't ripen regularly in region 1 and region V will probably cook any finesse out of Marsanne.

Summation also ignores important cooling marine influences and highly-localised temperature inversions which play a significant role in ripening. Neither do such aggregates take account of day-night variations which are important in some areas – eg McDowell Valley or the Sierra Foothills – where cool night-time air helps even out ripening. As James Halliday points out (Halliday, 1993), it blurs the picture by averaging maximum and minimum, when what matters is the moving average which measures what goes on between the extremes.

Accepting the view that a vine performs best in a marginal climate – that is at the lower limit of regular ripening – developing cooler sites with suitable soils has become a passion for many growers in pursuit of quality. But, once again, what really matters to the vine is the distribution of heat rather than its bare average, making some of the coolest sites unsuitable for ripening the varieties planted on them.

Excess rainfall, so important in Europe, especially at harvest time when a sudden storm can ruin the crop, is not critical in California, where drought is the main risk. What rain there is arrives mostly in winter, only one-fifth during the growing season. In most areas, this necessitates irrigation to keep photosynthesis going; conscientious growers keep watering to a minimum, by measured drips rather than by blanket spraying; those who over-irrigate end up with large volumes of dilute juice.

In short, while individual site and climate play a significant part in successful wine-production in California, generalisations of the sort one might usefully make about a smaller region such as Bordeaux are of little relevance in understanding this vast, complex, wine-growing area.

VARIETAL ACREAGE IN CALIFORNIA

	Grenache	Syrah	Viognier
1993	12,688	741	164
1992	12,912	532	138
1991	13,088	413	79
1990	13,644	344	50
1989	13,156	192	<50
1988	13,286	139	<50
1986	14,669	119	<50
1983	17,911	98	<50
1980	17,560	81	<50

VITICULTURE

Rhône-variety growers in California have been frustrated by a lack of sufficient authentic, virus-free material. Some have resorted to smuggling in cuttings to avoid lengthy quarantine rules, while others simply soldier on in the hope that what they have is proper Syrah or true Viognier. The Perrin's nursery of Châteauneuf varieties at Tablas Creek (qv) will provide a significant boost to planting programmes and to clonal development.

In the vineyards, many are experimenting with different systems of trellising and canopy management to achieve ideal ripeness. Some are trying alternative pruning methods to balance yield and quality, rather than over-cropping and then having to put things right in the cellar. Most top estates now use the minimum of chemicals and fertilizers, to preserve the micro-flora and fauna, and are conscious of the need to give the vine a healthy, dynamic balance of nutrients.

Too many producers still overcrop – a worldwide problem. It is not simply that low yields make for great wine, but that any given site can only ripen an optimum number of bunches; so reducing yield on an inappropriate site may just produce over-ripe grapes, because of that site's characteristics. What is needed are low-vigour rootstocks and low-vigour soils with low pH and no fertilizing, unless the vine

is thoroughly decrepit. Vertical trellising and minimal irrigation then combine with a rigorous summer pruning programme to thin crops and expose bunches to the sun. Unfortunately, producers who buy in fruit from other growers on short-term contracts have little say in farming, yields or harvest. They just have to make the best of what they get.

THE RULES

US labelling laws require that a named varietal wine contains at least 75% of that variety; if the vineyard is named, then 95% of the grapes must come from that vineyard; if it is also estate-bottled then the requirement is 100%. So a vineyard-designated Syrah could have 75% Syrah and 25% Cabernet Sauvignon (not stated on the label). The narrower the area, the higher the proportion of a named variety – eg a Napa County Syrah must have 75% minimum of Syrah; for Napa Valley this rises to 85%. At present there are no restrictions on yields – although there are suggestions that these might be introduced for AVAs. Set at low levels, these would do much to raise overall quality.

By not restricting certain sites to specified varieties, these rules allow producers considerable flexibility – of which surprisingly few take advantage – a pity, given a market saturated with the better-known varieties. By contrast, in France a *vigneron* cannot legally put Chardonnay into Condrieu or Cabernet into Côte-Rôtie, however much he may consider it beneficial. Yet in California, where winemakers are only limited by their imagination, adventurous blends are rare, as if growers were governed by some self-imposed allegiance to the traditional laws of affinity. There is no *a priori* reason why Syrah/Zinfandel, or Viognier/Chardonnay should not succeed, and there seems enough experimental zeal out there to risk a cask or two.

MARKETING

American drinking habits tend to be influenced by fashionable trends and "gurus" – something skilfully exploited throughout the 1970s and 1980s by winery marketing departments who steered newly-sophisticated drinkers towards single varietals (eg Chardonnay and Cabernet Sauvignon). This has proved a problem for Rhône-style producers who believed that Syrah, Grenache and the rest are generally more complex and interesting as part of a blend. To many consumers, who don't realise that much of the world's greatest wine is blended (eg most champagne and claret) blending suggests adulteration or impurity. Another fall-out from over-successful marketing is that people stick doggedly to "safe" varietals and are unwilling to explore. One can imagine, in image-conscious America, a host's reluctance to serve "Petite" Sirah for fear of criticism: "What's this – Petite? Cheapskate!". Fortunately for the Rhône fraternity, there are enough people willing to experiment and find a pleasant surprise in unknown blends.

Varietal loyalty backfired in the early 1990s, when recession and over-production of fashionable Chardonnay and Cabernet led to fierce price-cutting; consumers bought on price, damaging the higher-quality estates. A third wine – a Syrah or Zinfandel, perhaps – might have given them an element of insurance. The AxR rootstock debacle provides the survivors with a golden opportunity to put this right.

Compared to France, where wine is made from a multitude of different grapes, California seems absurdly restricted: you make a Chardonnay and a Cabernet, then a barrel-select Chardonnay and a Reserve Cabernet, add a Merlot and a Pinot Noir, if you can manage it, then Zinfandel, red and white – that's diversity. There are welcome signs of change, with some larger operations – Mondavi in particular – actively looking at Syrah and Grenache. Their prestige and volume would inevitably lead to much greater market awareness of Rhône varietals.

WINEMAKING TRENDS

Until the late 1980s, whatever you made, guts and power (usually alcohol) would ensure sales, even though for many the second glass proved too much. Now the trend towards less alcohol has produced a desire for finesse and delicacy – without of course losing sight of varietal character. Thus the birth of "fruit-driven" wines with "lifted flavours".

In the vineyard, precision picking has helped retain fruit and reduced over-ripeness. In the cellar, techniques have been refined to preserve aroma and flavour and winemakers are better managers of acidity and tannins, the potential nemesis of white and red wines respectively. Natural acidity is now preferred to adding tartaric, or worse, gum-puckering citric acid, neither of which integrate well, and the idea that alchemy would somehow turn a massively over-extracted, dry-tannic Syrah or Cabernet into a Hermitage or a Château Latour is fortunately far less widespread.

The quality of oak and cooperage has improved beyond recognition in the last few years in California, where American oak appeared to make much coarser wine than French (the reverse of a 1900 Bordeaux experiment where four first-growths were tasted from six different oaks – French came last!). This is hardly surprising, given that the barrels used were those churned out in thousands per day for the Bourbon industry, where raw, green flavours from rapid kiln-drying didn't matter much. Today, US wood is properly seasoned – air-dried for two years or more – and made by French coopers *à la française*. Fortunately for the consumer, winemakers are using this better-quality oak with far greater knowledge and subtlety and the old California perception of fine wine as a fruit tart, liberally sprinkled with oak chippings, is well on the way out.

What is not declining is the pervasive influence of the universities – especially UC Davis. These oenology departments turn out techno-bright winemakers with great theoretical credentials but little individual feel for quality – chemists rather than connoisseurs. Taught to make clinically clean wines, they take the merest hint of impurity as a fault and go at it fiercely. In the case of *Brettanomyces* (a yeast which imparts a barnyardy smell) or *volatile acidity*, for example, their technical mentality cannot deal with the fact that, at low controlled levels of concentration, these can add complexity to a wine. Wines must indeed be clear and stable, but over-zealous cleaning-up can remove much of the nuance which makes them interesting. These people would probably dismiss the entire Rhône Valley as a sump of impurity; true, possibly, but the wines are wonderful.

Many Rhône Rangers make it their business to taste widely, and to visit the Rhône Valley wherever possible – eager to glean every detail and to make contact with local growers. The styles and methods of the top Rhône domaines are studied and discussed, not necessarily with a view to copying, although this obviously happens, but rather to get a feel for each variety and how to handle it. Perceptions vary widely among California's producers, especially with newer varieties such as Viognier, where there is still much feeling the way. Enlightened growers may know what good Condrieu tastes like, but remain unsure how to vinify their grapes to produce a similar result. Many are simply confused.

———

This review of some of the changes and influences of the last decade shows that drinkers, collectors, winemakers and grape-growers are all taking a much keener interest in the potential of these great varieties, while estates are mastering them and developing their own styles. As the individual profiles show, there is some remarkable wine being made by the trail-blazers, while others seem certain to follow suit. For Rhône aficionados, the American revolution has just begun.

ADELAIDA CELLARS

This is a new estate, but one whose founder, John Munch, gives every hope of high quality. The first commercial vintage – 1995 – from 11 acres of Syrah, was preceded by small quantities of wine from his own vines, sold under his Swiss wife's Le Cuvier label.

John Munch is an affable, thoughtful man, who arrived in the wine milieu via a circuitous route. He spent five years with a Geneva investment company, attended law-school in San Francisco which turned into a degree in medieval English poetry: a somewhat limiting qualification which led to a spell in house-building.

Then, through his wife's connections, a Swiss capitalist asked him to find suitable vineyard land; these researches somehow left him – one thing leading, as it does, to another – as assistant winemaker at Estrella River. The Swiss venture, a sparkling wine company, failed, and this left John with the newly-formed Adelaida Cellars, but itinerant.

In 1990 wine enthusiast Don van Steenwyk, an industrialist dealing in navigational and drilling equipment, offered him land on his Paso Robles ranch. This deal made Van Steenwyk a partner in Adelaida, in return for vineyard land and a cellar-door and winery facility on the property.

John Munch is a firm believer in *terroir*, a viewpoint reinforced by differences observed in Chardonnay from different plots in his vineyard. He also considers that while drip-feeding may produce fruit which well expresses its

John Munch.

varietal character, it is only dry-farming which brings out differences in *terroir*.

His own Syrah came from Estrella bud-wood, but is planted in very different soils. Even within 11 acres, there are noticeable micro-climates which produce systematic wine differences. In general,

the Templeton Gap area is Region II – low Region III in heat summation (2,800–3,200 degree days) compared with Estrella's mid to high Region II.

At the lower end of the range, the coastal influence has a significant impact; at the higher, the climate is more continental – described by John as "savannah". Whatever it was, it attracted the Polish pianist Paderewski, who owned vines on an adjacent 6,000-acre property.

The Adelaida wines are interesting and carefully put together. One notable peculiarity of the vinification is that the free-run wine is run off and the pomace (grape residue) pressed at 8–12 Brix – well before all the sugar has been converted. This, a proceeding more usual in Australia, gives that dimension of middle-palate richness which wines that are fermented to complete dryness sometimes lack.

John Munch was instrumental in helping the Perrins of Beaucastel (qv) search for their Californian land, and it is likely that the first Tablas Creek wines will be made at Adelaida. However, he will be concentrating his efforts on his own enterprise where – if the Le Cuvier wines are reliable harbingers – there is an excellent addition to the canon of Californian Syrah on the way.

VARIETY	VINEYARD	DETAILS	AREA
SYRAH	VAN STEENWYK RANCH	Estrella River bud-wood; planted 1990	11.00
		TOTAL (acres):	11.00

ALBAN VINEYARDS

In 1983 some Fresno State University friends gathered to celebrate John Alban's birthday. One of the bottles brought for the occasion was a Condrieu. The lush, opulent wine so mesmerized John that he couldn't sleep that night. Next morning he rushed to the library to discover more only to find, after a day's search, that everything relevant could be read in 30 seconds. Oenology at Davis and extensive visiting in the Rhône, Beaujolais and Burgundy failed to quench the passion. In 1986, John returned to California with "an obsession, a vision and 12 US Viognier cuttings".

Fifty years of Northern Rhône climate records and extensive soil data convinced him that San Luis Obispo was ideally suited to Rhône varieties (no doubt he'd have imported tons of French soil, if he

had considered it necessary). Climate is the most important factor; then soils which have the right physical structure, without an excess of organic material or nitrogen, or "any quirky mineral composition". For Viognier and Syrah this meant conditions which restricted natural vigour. Here, soils are shallow and "tight" with virtually no summer rainfall. The vineyards have drips, used as little as possible as the aim is to dry-farm the reds and to limit irrigation on the whites. An elaborate eight-wire vertical trellis, an intensive shoot-positioning programme and leaf-thinning help maximize fruit ripeness and quality.

In 1989, he bought a 250-acre Edna Valley ranch, and embarked upon the painstaking task of propagating his 12 Viognier cuttings into the 60,000 he

needed. At that time there was no nursery wood to draw on, so John persuaded growers throughout the county to let him graft "test blocks" onto existing roots of varieties which weren't in demand.

Between 1987 and 1993 he established 30 acres of Viognier, 15 of Roussanne, 12 of Syrah, 4 of Grenache and 3 each of Mourvèdre and Counoise – 67 acres exclusively devoted to Rhône varieties. Wine followed "in enormous quantity": the first crush, in 1989, produced 40 bottles; the 1990, 12 cases. In 1991, 407 cases of Viognier were accompanied by a solitary case of Roussanne (the original planting was determined by what John reckoned he could personally consume in 12 months), followed in 1992 by 336 and 80 cases respectively.

John, a thin, lively man with a corrugated, open face, is convinced of the future of Viognier and Roussanne in San Luis Obispo. He sees Roussanne today where he saw Viognier ten years ago – unquestionably one of the finest white grapes. "The results were astonishing. I immediately started planting all I could find". At present only John Alban and Randall Grahm are growing Roussanne in California, although others (notably the Perrins at Tablas Creek) are dipping their toes in the water.

Vinification for Viognier is designed to preserve the grape's natural perfume and opulence: "we have so much of ourselves invested in the fruit; we are not interested in seasoning it with vinification techniques". One-third is made in 500-litre puncheons, which adds structure; the remainder in *inox*, to preserve aromas. Several trial blends later, the final *cuvée* is made up during the following spring and bottled (with filtration if malolactic has not taken place) in June.

John recognizes the individuality of Viogniers that are vinified differently – for example Guigal's Condrieu, made with indigenous yeasts, skin contact, *bâtonnage* and some new oak – none of which he uses. John's wine reflects his feeling that the majesty of Viognier lies in the "truly exceptional" combination of an "incredible perfume" with structure, length and depth. In 1993 a Central Coast Viognier, made partly from bought fruit, was added to the estate bottling. Later releases seem to have crystallized a fine style, and are distinctly more impressive than earlier efforts.

Roussanne behaves completely differently to Viognier, tending to soak up oxygen "like a sponge" and benefit from it. So it is fermented entirely in puncheons to favour this oxygenation. John finds the grape paradoxical: "it defies all wine chemistry laws (I don't think they're that important anyway), in particular the one that states that lower-pH (ie high-acid) wines live longer". Historically, Roussanne is one of the longest-lived whites yet it has one of the highest pHs. John discussed this paradox with Gérard Chave who told him that, in his experience, Marsanne and Roussanne tended to low acidity and, moreover, that the greatest vintages often correlated with the highest pHs.

To the taster, Roussanne and Viognier are "day and night" – the former honey, mineral and nuts: all richness; the latter perfumed and exotic. The Roussanne is bottled at about the same time as the Viognier.

The Mourvèdre has yet to produce satisfactory quality, so none is released. The estate Syrah and Grenache, however, do well – even though many considered John misguided to plant them in a cool region which would only reduce colour

and accentuate vegetal characters. While most Californian Syrah is of the very ripe, plummy, black-pepper style, a cooler site gives a more perfumed, floral and gamey character – cherries rather than plums, northern rather than southern Rhône – and better natural acidity.

A long, slow whole-bunch fermentation, with a gentle foot crushing, is used to kill off heavy tannins and reduce acids. This is not carbonic maceration, but rather a slow extraction: for example, colour only deepens significantly after some 12 days' vatting, not earlier. Eighteen months in large wood puncheons – no small casks, to avoid oak pick-up – with racking only if the wine's reductive state demands it, precedes bottling with neither fining (unless tannins need refining) nor filtration. Grenache vinification differs

from that of Syrah only in that the pulp is pressed sooner for better tannin balance.

The success of his wines came as some surprise to John, who imagined himself having to cultivate esoteric retailers and develop a cult following. In fact, he was overwhelmed by the interest and level of consumer knowledge – "15 years ahead of where I would have guessed".

Impressed by the great diversity of wine made in France, he sees California as unimaginatively restricted – although there are welcome signs of major players taking a serious interest in Rhône and Italian varietals.

Fortunately, John Alban combines knowledge and passion for his beloved Rhône varietals with sufficient acreage to demonstrate that quality and volume are not incompatible.

VARIETY	VINEYARD	DETAILS	AREA
VIOGNIER	ESTATE VINEYARD	planted 1987–93 mostly on 5BB rootstock	30.00
ROUSSANNE	ESTATE VINEYARD	planted 1988–1993 on 5BB rootstock	15.00
SYRAH	ESTATE VINEYARD	planted 1990-91–93 on 5BB rootstock	12.00
GRENACHE	ESTATE VINEYARD	planted 1990	1.00
GRENACHE	Co-farmed vineyard in N. part of S. Luis Obispo	Field grafted 1990-1	3.00
MOURVEDRE	Co-farmed vineyard in N. part of S. Luis Obispo	Field grafted 1990-1	3.00
COUNOISE	Co-farmed vineyard in N. part of S. Luis Obispo	Field grafted 1990-1	3.00
		TOTAL (acres):	67.00

Not a mobile telephone box but an equally important mobile convenience in isolated vineyards.

BONNY DOON VINEYARD

Comment on Bonny Doon invariably focuses on the eccentricities, zany newsletters and highly individual style of its founder, owner and chief publicist, Randall Grahm. Dubbed "Mr Rhônely-heart", Randall led the 1970s band known then, as now, as Rhône Rangers. A man whose uncompromising vision is of a California free of Cabernet and Chardonnay

His exhibitionism is balanced by a vein of highly articulate, creative intelligence. Although the wealth of his Beverley Hills family provided a useful financial cushion, Randall has not squandered his opportunities. However, his addiction to experimentation – which critics stigmatize as an exaggerated need for novelty – has given Bonny Doon a somewhat jerky evolution: Bordeaux and Burgundy gave way to the current Rhône period in the mid-1980s. Now the crush is on Italian varietals – sold under the Ca'del Solo label, although the Rhône passion remains seemingly undimmed.

It all began in 1975, when Randall – enthralled by Burgundy ("the greatest, most sensuous, fabulous wine") and determined to make the greatest Pinot Noir in the world – left his post as "a permanent arts major" to plant land bought by his parents in the hamlet of Bonny Doon in the Santa Cruz Mountains. Despite a distinctly un-Burgundian lack of limestone (he tried to import some), in went 28 acres of Pinot Noir, Chardonnay, and "if you'll pardon the expression", Cabernet.

By the mid 1980s, it became clear that these were not successful – so vines were ripped up or field-grafted to Marsanne, Roussanne, Syrah and Viognier. In 1990 came a further upheaval, as 10 acres of Chardonnay were grafted to Roussanne. Recently, the estate bought a 10.5-acre vineyard in Monterey County, planted with Cinsaut, Viognier, and other Rhône and Italian varieties.

Randall, a skilled winemaker, is his own most severe critic. Inclined to distrust *terroir* – especially in the historically short-term context of Californian viticulture – he is unimpressed by the overall quality of Californian wines: "we have an inflated view of our products". For him, the region's undoubted successes are the Mourvèdre-based wines from the "exceptional grapes" of Oakley: Cline, Edmunds St John and Sean Thackrey. "Great grapes

Mr Rhonely-Heart: Randall Grahm.

make winemakers seem cleverer than we are". The advantage of California's long growing season is balanced by the disadvantage of less interesting soils, so character can only be extracted by suitably adapted winemaking.

As with most top winemakers, fruit quality is paramount. The expense of growing his own grapes, with the labour-intensive methods his standards demand, has led Randall to source more of his fruit from outside suppliers.

Wherever possible, he tries to establish long-term contracts which allow him control of soil nutrition, husbandry and harvest date; but demand for some premium varieties often makes this difficult. Convincing growers inextricably wedded to quantity to lower yields and farm for quality can be a struggle. Now "every spare nickel of this estate is going to vineyard contracts" – although Randall admits that little top-notch fruit remains undiscovered.

Bonny Doon's Rhône range is varied and interesting. Whites are represented by a Viognier, a Marsanne/Roussanne blend (80:20 roughly) sold as Le Sophiste, and a seductive Beaumes de Venise-style Muscat Canelli, Vin de Glacier.

The Viognier – one "exquisite" barrel of it in 1992 – comes from a vineyard described by Randall as "a disaster": a mix of clones, many degenerate, prone to yellowjackets, infected with Pierce's disease (dead-arm) and susceptible to sunburn. Its future is in doubt.

The Sophiste blend of mainly estate fruit, matured in 3- to 4-year-old French oak, was first produced in 1989. As Roussanne ripens before Marsanne, they are fermented separately and assembled later. Randall calls these two grapes "the

ugly ducklings of the wine world".

The seven Bonny Doon reds include four varietals: a Mourvèdre, from Fred Cline's more than 80-year-old Oakley vines, is named Old Telegram after Vieux Télégraphe in Châteauneuf-du-Pape (qv) and labelled with a Morse-code telegram. A Grenache, from vineyards in Greenfield and Gilroy (California's garlic capital), is sold as "Clos de Gilroy – cuvée tremblant de terre, Le Gil des Rois, Le Roi des Gils" – harmless, meaningless, mimicry.

Syrah, with 10% of Viognier and Marsanne added, comes both from estate vines and from Bien Nacido in Santa Maria who also supply Au Bon Climat and Qupe (qv); and finally a Cinsaut from Dry Creek Vineyard – both for once sold as such, without embellishment. There is also a delicious, fresh, rosé: Vin Gris de Cigare, from Grenache, Mourvèdre, with additions of Cinsaut, Pinots Noir and Meunier; a wine described by Grahm both as "a surrender to the pink" and "the thinking person's pink wine – an almost Nietzschean purity of that alpine cherry top-note".

The blends are put together on a cascade system, from what remains after selection of the single-grape lots. First (in every sense), and the most interesting, is Le Cigare Volant, a broadly Châteauneuf blend of Grenache, Mourvèdre and Syrah. Since its launch in 1984, Cinsaut has found its way into the mix and Randall is now "trying to get some Counoise, from a fellow in Paso Robles". What matters is not the exact composition, but the consistency of the intensity and the concentration. The name recalls the supplemental decree issued by the zealous burgers of Châteauneuf in 1954 forbidding any flying machine or "flying cigar" to land on their territory, under penalty of being "taken off to the pound" – a measure which has proved to be remarkably effective.

In 1992 came Le Gaucher – an imaginative blend of Mourvèdre and Barbera. Randall regards these as having a natural affinity – "the Barbera is the sharply-pitched tenor, while the Mourvèdre sings basso, proffering jive and funk embellishment" (whatever that may be).

Finally, there is Big House Red, a blend of Mourvèdre, Grenache and Barbera, sold under the Ca'del Solo label – reflecting the fact that the grapes for this range are grown near California's maximum-security Soledad prison.

The blends are put together soon after malolactic fermentation and kept in tank for six months – "to enable the parts to get to know themselves". Experience has clearly made Randall more confident in his ability to fine-tune each mix, and reinforced his belief that early blending brings greater microbial and chemical stability, and promotes general harmony.

The overall scheme allows for a long, cool fermentation with a high proportion of whole berries, and importantly, more often than not, for a *saignée de cuve* (bleeding juice from a vat to gain concentration). Randall regards this operation as essential and regularly removes up to two-thirds of the unfermented juice (100 gallons from 165 total per ton). He also uses a yeast culture, finding that indigenous yeasts produce more ethyl acetate and malodorous hydrogen sulphide. When his financial position is more solid, he plans to experiment more with wild yeast fermentations. In 1993, he tried using dry-ice to cool the must and found that the mechanical turbulence created by its sublimation seemed to enhance colour extraction. The wine is left on its skins "until it starts to stink", to leach out those colour pigments which are more alcohol-soluble.

Randall is less and less enamoured of new wood, a maximum of 12–15% being his ideal. He also dislikes fining: "we do fining trials each year, and each year we decide we don't like fining". Only the Clos de Gilroy is filtered – since it is bottled young, for early drinking, in the November following the vintage.

Randall's marketing flair and the publicity his words and wines have generated have brought him many knowledgeable clients. With 65,000 cases to sell a year, from up to 30 products from two wineries (one at Bonny Doon, the other in Santa Cruz) marketing matters. One might perhaps speculate that bizarre names and labels reflect the serious thought that unusual varietals and blends need more than bland, factual presentation. Today, 75% goes to US wholesalers, 15% is exported and the remainder sold through mail-order, accompanied by the exotically worded newsletters, and to the faithful who flock to the rustic tasting-room which fronts the Bonny Doon winery. He clearly has a mischievous sense of humour, if one can believe stories about groups being ushered silently through rows of vines on the grounds that that particular variety is especially sensitive to noise.

Styles range from the eminently gluggable Clos de Gilroy to the single-varietal *vins de garde*. The estate's internationally best-known wines, Le Cigare Volante and the Old Telegram, vary markedly in quality from vintage to vintage – more so, perhaps, than the intrinsic quality of the vintages might lead one to expect.

In general they are good and, at best, well worth buying and keeping. Randall's zeal for experimentation, however, and his reluctance to discontinue any line, has led to a vast range of wines and fruit spirits. It is now essential to consolidate and concentrate on a limited number of top-quality products. Randall Grahm is capable of making first-class wine, and many who have followed his fortunes will pray that the future is not jeopardized by yet more impulse expansion.

VARIETY	VINEYARD	DETAILS	AREA
VIOGNIER	BONNY DOON ESTATE	Planted 1985/6	5.00
MARSANNE	BONNY DOON ESTATE	Planted 1985/6	4.00
ROUSSANNE	BONNY DOON ESTATE	Planted 85 – grafted over 1990/1	13.00
SYRAH	BONNY DOON ESTATE	Planted 1985/6	6.00
CINSAUT	MONTEREY COUNTY	Planted 1989	10.50
		TOTAL (acres):	38.50

CALERA WINE COMPANY

To Josh Jensen, Calera's founder, is credited the story of carrying a bottle of diagnostic sulphuric acid when searching for limestone soil upon which to plant his beloved Burgundian varieties. Even before Calera's establishment in 1975 Josh, inspired by visits to Condrieu and Château Grillet (qv) in 1969 and 1970, paid U C Davis – the oenology department of the University of California – to start a programme importing Viognier from France.

However, the early vines died, so bud-wood was procured from New York State's Geneva Research Station in 1983 and two acres planted at Calera in 1985; a further three acres from the new material were added in 1989. The first vintage, 1987, produced a mere four and a half cases.

The winery, named after a splendid 1890's *calera* (brick-kiln) on the property, is spectacularly sited on an exposed bluff at 1,200 feet in the Gavilan Mountains of California's Central Coast, some 25 miles inland from the Pacific Ocean above the

Calera's unobtrusive sign propped up against a lightning-damaged tree.

small town of Hollister. The fermenters stand outside in a line, overlooking distant Mount Diabolo, uncomfortably close to the San Andreas fault line, which runs though a lake on the estate and causes Hollister to tremble constantly. The vineyards are several miles further south, in the San Benito AVA.

Together with Phelps, Jensen is the high priest of Viognier in California. Although many regard it as "the Heartbreak Grape" (the title of Jensen's book on Pinot Noir in California, of which he is also a leading exponent) the variety does well here, at 2,200 feet on the warm slopes of Mt Harlan.

It is planted in decomposed granite soils with three-foot-deep sandy loams, mixed with limestone. The bugbear of most Condrieu growers, uneven berry set, is rare; even at low yields (two tons per acre here, although this appears to be increasing steadily) the bunches are evenly spread.

The Viognier is a sprawling vine, so it is cordon-pruned on a double vertical wire trellis. Perhaps an even taller, quadrilateral trellis would increase yields without compromising fruit ripening.

The soils are disc-ploughed, so a minimal drip irrigation is used to ensure adequate water. This combination of soil and climate stresses the vine strongly, which Jensen considers to be important for wine quality. The wine is made by Josh Jensen and Sara Steiner, who arrived in 1991. Having no experience of either Pinot Noir or Viognier, she was a "*tabula rasa*" for Jensen – the ideal apprentice.

Between them, they manage well. The aim is to push the flamboyance of the Viognier to the maximum, so grapes are harvested very ripe – 24.5 to 25 Brix (14-14.5 alcohol).

Thereafter, the policy is "minimum interference", with 80% fermented in ten-year-old French oak and 20% in *inox*, which is transferred to cask as soon as primary fermentation is over. The stainless steel fraction imparts esters and enhances fruit intensity, but

as the grape naturally gives flavours of new wood and nuts, new oak is deemed unnecessary.

Indigenous yeasts are used to mediate a two- to three-week fermentation at around 72°F; this is followed by malolactic fermentation. Six months later, the wine is bentonite-fined (for protein stability), lightly filtered, and then bottled. Throughout, there is minimum manipulation – and that, as far as possible, by gravity.

Calera's Viognier is everything Josh

Jensen and Sara Steiner strive for: rich, exotic and opulent. Even though it arrives in bottle at around 14.5% alcohol, there is no sense of alcoholic rawness, and the seductive, dried-apricot character of the grape is well preserved.

However, this is a very individual expression of Viognier which needs time in bottle to develop depth and interest. If you need a red, then Calera's Pinot Noir is well into the top class of what California is capable. Altogether, first-class winemaking.

VARIETY	VINEYARD	DETAILS	AREA
VIOGNIER	MT. HARLAN	Planted 1985	2.00
VIOGNIER	MT. HARLAN	Planted 1989	3.00
		TOTAL (acres):	5.00

CHRISTOPHER CREEK

John Mitchell, an expatriate Englishman, was chief North American executive of British sugar giant Tate & Lyle – until an English estate agent found the Russian River Valley Sotoyome winery. Mitchell "made an offer there and then.

"We arrived on 26 July 1988 and picked the grapes in August", he recalls – a veritable baptism of fire.

The domaine, atop a hillside commanding magnificent views in all directions, consists of ten acres planted around the winery, producing 2,500 cases or so of Chardonnay, Syrah and Petite Sirah, most of which filters out through a tasting room and US distribution channels. Unfortunately, the vines are on AxR roots and, although no phylloxera has yet appeared, the Mitchells are taking no chances, re-planting an acre a year – "we prefer to do it on our time plan than on mother nature's".

John Mitchell's defensive, taciturn manner hides a clear, logical mind, and a passion for quality. His wife, Susan, whom he met in the 1970s when they were both living in San Francisco's Bay area, is charming, warm and open. She shares his love of wine, especially Rhône varietals, and provides valuable support. According to Susan, they named the creek below the winery after their son, Christopher – they both have adult children by previous marriages – and the wine after the creek.

Their aim is to make top-quality premium wine in order "to make enough money so that we can continue to make top-quality premium wine". John keeps

Susan Mitchell, and behind her, a colourful string of wine awards.

his business hand in with a consultancy which "allows us not to worry about whether we can buy the groceries".

They need have little worry on the quality score; the wines are excellent and a tribute to the partnership between John and his consultant winemaker, Paul Brasset from White Oak. In the vineyard, trials with double canopy, moving to a

quadrilateral Geneva Double Curtain and thence to Lyre training have increased yields from 2.5 to 5 tons per acre. In the cellar, trials with whole bunch maceration have been discontinued because of the vegetal quality this imparted. Now, the fruit is de-stemmed and crushed, then fermented for four to five days using Prise de Mousse yeast. They toyed with extending maceration, but decided in 1993 to press out at about 3% residual sugar. This was also the first vintage in which the various vineyard plots were vinified separately.

There used to be two Rhônish reds – a "Russian River Valley Syrah" and a Petite Sirah; then in 1992 a Rhône blend (75% Cinsaut and 25% Petite Sirah) was added.

The straight Syrah has 30% new French oak for its 12 months' *élevage*, while the Petite spends another 6–12 months in wood – 20–25% of it new US wood, the rest new French oak – in a bid to transmute early, coarse tannins into something finer and rounder.

John and Susan Mitchell take justifiable pride in what, as novitiates, they have achieved since 1988. Susan positively glows as she talks about their wines and her belief in the "world-beating quality" of Petite Sirah, reinforced after tasting a 1976 Stag's Leap. She laments that this grape is frequently demeaned as a "kick-up-the-backside Pizza wine". Not here, at any rate – this estate has nobler uses for its quality fruit.

VARIETY	VINEYARD	DETAILS	AREA
PETITE SIRAH	ESTATE	planted 1982	3.50
SYRAH	ESTATE	planted 1982; 1 acre replanted 1994	5.00
		TOTAL (acres):	8.50

CLINE CELLARS

In 1982, Fred Cline bought the Firpo Winery in Oakley (50 miles east of San Francisco), with his $12,000 share of the sale of Jacuzzi (his maternal grandfather was Valeriano Jacuzzi, inventor of the eponymous whirlpool), and began to make wine from what is now 400 acres of vines from his own and friends' land.

He soon realized that a Davis oenology degree did not guarantee winemaking genius, and persuaded his younger brother, Matt, who was fresh from Davis and Conn Creek, to join him part-time as winemaker in 1986.

In 1989, Fred and his wife Nancy bought 350 acres in the Carneros district of Sonoma and moved the centre of operations there in 1991.

Early years were difficult; Fred had no money apart from a small loan from his father who had no interest in wine: "I can't pay you back", he eventually explained, so Cline Senior was made a partner instead.

Impoverishment necessitated creativity, so the office/tasting room was an old trailer and the winery was an uninsulated wooden barn which, in hot vintages, led to cooked wine. By 1988 Fred's debt had soared and the family's enthusiasm had plummeted: when a credit card company called to collect its due, Nancy begged Fred to consider another job; and when he petitioned his father for a loan to pay off $18,000 the response was "why not bankruptcy?"

However, in 1988 the business was pulled back from the brink when a high-profile journalist asked for samples and gave the wines a glowing review, boosting not only sales, but distribution. "At that point I didn't even have the money to bottle the wine", Fred comments. The current financial bulletin: "we now owe $3 million, so we must be successful".

Fred and Matt Cline are strongly Rhône-oriented. Fred had started by making orthodox varietals but soon realized his mistake: "what am I doing here, competing with 600 wineries all selling Sauvignon and Cabernet?" However, neither Zinfandel nor Petite Sirah were selling then, so, in 1985, he decided to break the mould and make wine from the "beautiful grapes in our own backyard".

Fred was well aware of the burgeoning Rhône Ranger movement, having supplied fruit to such luminaries

Fred Cline.

as Randall Grahm, Joseph Phelps and Sean Thackrey, and realized that his own superb raw material could be turned into fine wine, provided it was picked at the right sugar levels and not for maximum yield, as Krug, Beringer and others had demonstrated.

The Clines' Oakley vineyards are remarkable: unquestionably the largest holding of old vines in California – if not the world – with 260 acres of over 90-year-old Mourvèdre, plus 100 acres of over 85-year-old Carignan; in fact, Cline owns more than 90% of all old Mourvèdre remaining in California. (In 1935 there were 5,000 acres of Mourvèdre, now there are 350.)

Yields are pitiful – 1.75 tons/acre, compared with 5 tons/acre from the younger 40 Carneros acres. As the soils at Oakley are predominantly sandy, thus limiting the risk of phylloxera, the Mourvèdre and Carignan vines are all on their own roots – even the newer plantings. These splendid vineyards continue to supply fruit for many top-grade independent winemakers.

As for other Rhône varieties, Fred is optimistic. Although Carneros is a marginal climate for Syrah, planting on hillsides with drip irrigation gives it the best chance of ripening. Soils are mainly rock and basalt. These are still young vines – 1990 was the debut of Cline Syrah – but there is considerable potential if an excellent, though lightish, 1991 is anything to judge by. Their nine acres of

Viognier are also very young, and it will be interesting to see what the Clines make of that fruit. Now, total production runs at around 25,000 cases, compared with 14,000 in 1987.

The Oakley climate is peculiar. Firstly, it is dry: Carneros averages 15–20 inches of rain annually, Oakley nine inches. Secondly, although technically a high Region III on the Davis scale of heat summation, it has a cool sector – a 5- by 7-mile corridor bordering the river – resulting from a gentle breeze: "the residue of Carneros' howling gale", which preserves acidity otherwise vulnerable to the intense summer heat.

Apart from the single-*cépage* wines – Syrah, Viognier, a splendid intense, spicy, chocolaty, old-vine Carignan and a pair of Mourvèdres (a regular *cuvée* and a fine, deep, firm Reserve offering, only produced in better vintages) – there is a trio of blended *cuvées*.

These are: Angel Rosé, a cocktail of Mourvèdre, Carignan, Zinfandel and Syrah, described as having "aromas of fresh strawberries, cherries and herbs"… yum! Then the Côtes d'Oakley, intended to mimic Côtes du Rhône. According to the Clines the 1991 mix was 53% Carignan; 28% Mourvèdre; 13% Zinfandel and 8% Alicante Bouschet (ie 102%: they are clearly giving their all, and more), with some 50% of whole bunches, 8–10 days' vatting and 6–18 months in old casks contributing to its soft, quaffable character. The time the wine spends maturing depends on demand – "if we need it quicker, we get them out quicker", Fred explains.

More serious is the Oakley Cuvée, a big yet soft wine from 48% Mourvèdre, 27% Carignan, 20% Zinfandel and 5% Alicante. For this there is no whole-berry fermentation, and the wine is aged for 16–20 months in 10–15% new American oak. The results are excellent – wines which merit a few years' keeping for the high proportion of Mourvèdre to soften and open out.

There is more. In 1994 the Clines released their first vintage of Marsanne from Carneros plantings, followed in 1995 by a Roussanne from four acres, also in Carneros. This latter variety was troublesome: "*Someone* wouldn't give me the cuttings; I had to blackmail Randall (Grahm) in order to get them".

LOCATION	VARIETY	AGE	AREA
CARNEROS (Region I)	VIOGNIER	Planted 1991	4.00
OAKLEY (High region III)	VIOGNIER	Planted 1989/90	5.00
OAKLEY	SYRAH	Planted 1988/89	15.00
CARNEROS	SYRAH	Planted 1991	18.00
OAKLEY	MOURVEDRE	260 are 90+	280.00
CARNEROS	MARSANNE	Planted 1991	4.00
OAKLEY	CARIGNAN	85 yrs. ++	100.00
CARNEROS	ROUSSANNE	Planted 1992	4.00
		TOTAL (acres):	430.00

The move to the 1850s' farmhouse in Arnold Drive, Sonoma, has spawned a shop, converted from the front room, selling not only the firm's wines, but delightful curiosities such as Rhône Ranger Mustard and Mourvèdre Hot Fudge. This estate has grown up, since grandfather Jacuzzi sold grapes to the home winemakers of the East Coast – probably from his old vines. Fred and Matt Cline deserve their success; their lawyer father is probably content to have shares now, rather than the return of his $18,000 dollar stake.

EBERLE WINERY

Gary Eberle was studying for a Doctorate in Fermentation Science at Davis in the early 1970s, when his interest in Syrah was sparked by the Australian winemaker Brian Crozer.

A large, jovial character, Eberle was founder-winemaker at Estrella River (now Meridian, and owned by Nestlé) where, by 1977 he had planted 40 acres of Syrah propagated from material which he cut cut personally from UC Davis' vineyard. In developing these pioneering plantings, he was instrumental bringing Syrah into California.

Although his wine won many medals, it was unsaleable, so Gary started selling grapes to Randall Grahm and Bob Lindquist, then bud-wood, which was more profitable than the wine. He claims still to have scars on his knees from begging people to try the 1979 Syrah.

In 1982, he started his own operation, next door to Estrella in Paso Robles. Lacking confidence in Syrah, he planted Cabernet and Chardonnay instead. It wasn't until 1991, perhaps stung by a reprimand from Randall Grahm that "you got everyone interested in Syrah and Viognier and then stopped producing it", that Gary Eberle released his own Syrah, from fruit that he bought from Estrella.

Now his 41 acres of vines include four of Syrah, planted on sites that he selected with the aid of soil-maps, with a further four acres each of Syrah and Viognier arriving from a nearby contract grower. Eberle's Syrah production now amounts to some 2,000 cases.

The neat, wood-clad, Eberle winery stands on a hill, surrounded by vines and mountains. Inside, the walls and shelves of Gary's office attest to his varied interests – skiing, gastronomy, education, rafting and tasting.

It would be difficult to imagine this man making a thin, light wine; his personality and preferences (Cabernet Sauvignon, Zinfandel and Syrah) scream substance – testimony backed by his declared boredom with Pinot Noir – presumably because of its relative lightness. This helps explain his love of Viognier – "I've never enjoyed white wine as much as Viognier, especially its peachy character; it reminds me of one of my mother's favourite desserts: tree-stone canned peaches".

Fruit from Gary's cordon-trained, spur-pruned Syrah vines ripen "wonderfully well" on the gravelly, sandy loams of the Santa Lucia mountains (low Region II in heat summation), yielding "top-quality" at 5.5–5.6 tons per acre. Then, the absence of waterways in Napa and Sonoma – natural habitats for virus-transmitting insects – keeps them pest- and virus-free. In winter, overhead sprinklers use the latent heat of ice to protect buds from frost.

Time spent with Chapoutier (qv) and in Corsica in 1977 and 1979, formed his style of wine. He learned in particular that poor soils were essential: something between the extremes of 20 feet of loam and a concrete parking-lot. He is forthright in his views of the calibre of many of his colleagues: "there is lots of bullshit in this industry; so many wines are called "wonderful" which have volatile acidity, brettanomyces – spoiled wine; what we regard as good wine is often what we have learned to taste as good". For Gary, the art of winemaking doesn't include using spoilage organisms to add depth and complexity.

On a more fundamental plane, he observes that some grape varieties are bound to fail because people simply can't pronounce them: to "watch an American trying to order Gewürztraminer or Viognier" is a powerful indictment of some varietal labelling.

Gary Eberle is something of an enigma – a lad from a poor background, passing through Penn State on a football scholarship, a master's degree in Zoology then cellular genetics and fermentation science. Yet, for all his physical solidity, he has a ballerina's feel for balance and finesse in wine.

Some have noted variability in Eberle wines. Perhaps Gary is tiring a little these days – "after 20 years, I feel like an old man in this industry" – and needs to concentrate on a small, consummately-crafted range. Meanwhile the Syrah is an excellent example of its genre – and well worth buying.

VARIETY	VINEYARD	DETAILS	AREA
SYRAH	ESTATE	Planted 1992	4.00
SYRAH		Contract grower; planted 1990	4.00
VIOGNIER		Contract grower; planted 1990	4.00
		TOTAL (acres):	12.00

EDMUNDS ST JOHN

Steve Edmunds began his career as a wine retailer in Marin County, in the days when varietal labelling was rare and anything white came as "Chablis", anything red as "Burgundy".

Although he cut his teeth on genuine Burgundy and Bordeaux, he developed a strong passion for the Rhône, inspired by a 1959 Château Rayas and nutured with wines from the 1970s from Robert Mayberry.

So, in 1985, he and his wife Cornelia started what is usually called a "warehouse winery" (ie a production facility with no vines). It was based in a nondescript, functional building in a suburb of Berkeley, identified only by "Emeryville 4059" over the door, in a road that dead-ends in a construction site.

He sourced Grenache from Spring Mountain, and Syrah from Paso Robles, easily enough – but it took him months of searching to find Mataro (Mourvèdre) of acceptable quality. His enquiries were generally met with "what do you want do to with that?" The search ended with Rich and Chester Brandlin, traditional farmers with 55-year-old Carignan and Mataro vines on Mount Veeder (and even older tractors and picking boxes). Unfortunately, they had ripped out 4.5 further acres the year before, as Mataro was thoroughly unfashionable then.

Steve is a freckled, intense man, imbued by a quest for quality. In 1990 a seminal visit to the Rhône Valley, tasting 1988s in cask at Clape, Beaucastel, Chave and others, changed his own winemaking and provided a continuing point of reference. In particular, he noticed that a low oxidative winemaking regime gave fresher, better wines.

His own system for reds is to layer whole bunches and de-stemmed fruit in open vats – this gives a "delicacy, a brightness, a prettiness to the wine" – and then ferment the lot at 25–30°C, punching down but not pumping over. He dislikes the widespread practice of filtering to clean wines up before putting them into cask – a convenience maybe, but one which eliminates the valuable contribution from solids during ageing. His own method is to leave the wine on its lees for six months or so – "this has a profound impact on the mouthfeel and integrates the wine".

Steve and Cornelia produce five principal Rhône-grape wines: a gorgeous yardstick Viognier (250 cases), from Knight's Valley (an AVA within Sonoma County, created in November 1983); Les Côtes Sauvages (400 cases) – a blend in 1992 of 39% Grenache, 31% Mourvèdre, 25% Syrah and 5% Carignan; 300–350 cases each of two Syrahs – one from Durell's Sonoma vineyards, the other "Grand Heritage" from Mansfield and Durell fruit, and 300 cases of La Rose Sauvage – from Grenache with a touch of Viognier. Any remaining Syrah, Mourvèdre and Grenache goes into a "New World red".

The qualities imparted by each vineyard contribute to the complexity and style of the final blends. El Dorado and Durell granite gives the Syrah depth, backbone and elegance, whereas the same grapes, planted on heavier clay and rock soil in other Durell vineyards, has more breadth and richness.

These are fine wines – carefully thought out by a man who clearly loves his raw material and takes delight in creating something special from it (his skill at blending has distinct flashes of Gérard Chave).

In 1989, despite warnings about "what an ordeal it would be", Steve had a go at Pinot Noir; his verdict: "a piece of cake". He has now planted his own small parcel of Syrah, Mourvèdre, Grenache and Cinsaut, high in El Dorado county.

The Edmunds St John wines come complete with stylish labels offering an encomium extolling the virtues of wine and friendship, often derived from ancient mythology. This is a top-class estate – producing one of California's finest Viogniers and, incidentally, remarkably good Zinfandel.

VARIETY	VINEYARD	DETAILS
SYRAH	SONOMA / CARNEROS	Durell's vineyard, planted 1980 & 1990
SYRAH	EL DORADO	Mansfield vineyard; planted 1981/2
SYRAH	KNIGHT'S VALLEY (Sonoma)	Noble vineyard; planted 1989.
VIOGNIER	KNIGHT'S VALLEY (Sonoma)	Noble vineyard; planted 1989
MOURVEDRE	KNIGHT'S VALLEY (Sonoma)	Noble vineyard; planted 1989
MOURVEDRE & CARIGNAN	MOUNT VEEDER	Brandlin Vineyard; planted 1940s
GRENACHE	UKIAH VALLEY (Mendocino)	Pallini vineyard; planted 1940s

FIELD STONE WINERY

Field Stone was founded by Wallace Johnson, who bought a 500-acre cattle ranch in the eastern sector of Sonoma's Alexander Valley in 1956, with a fortune made from inventing aluminium scaffolding and the upright grape harvesting machine.

Plantings were finished by 1972, and a further 150 acres added in the early 1960s on an adjoining ranch. Johnson especially liked German and Alsatian wines and his harvester was designed to pick such high-sugar varietals. The winery was excavated from the hillside in 1977, its rough-hewn entrance facade crafted from field-stones selected during the work; hence the estate name.

Johnson died from a massive stroke while driving home in 1979, aged 66 – the way he wanted to go, but 30 years too early. Charge of Field Stone passed to his daughter, Katrina and son-in-law, John Staten, an ordained Presbyterian minister and theology professor – author of "The Conscience and Reality of God" and "Wine and Christianity".

A series of consulting winemakers, including the late André Tchelistcheff, passed through. Now John, with three short Davis courses under his belt and an avowed weakness in biochemistry, makes the wines in conjunction with Michael Duffy – ex-Trefethen and Balverne. His sales manager, Roger Holt, is also an ordained minister (Protestant) whose duties apparently include blessing the harvest. In 1991, John and Katrina's son, Ben, joined the team as general manager.

In 1986 the estate was split, the original 600 Redwood acres going to Johnson's sister, brother and mother, and Field Stone with its 50 acres, picturesque winery and redwood-panelled tasting-room, to John and Katrina.

Apart from 100 cases of excellent Viognier, the Rhône-varietal heart of the domaine is a remarkable Petite Sirah, issuing from ten acres of vines planted in 1894 – an old-style mixed planting, including 10% of Zinfandel and a touch of ancient Carignan; gaps are filled with Syrah and Mourvèdre. These vines are infected, as are many others of similar age, by a pre-Prohibition virus, which is fortunately not degenerative but which tints leaves red, affecting photosynthesis and vine-vigour, though not fruit-quality.

Soils here are fairly deep rock and clay, with a high iron content; tap-roots on the old Petite Sirah delve down as deep as ten feet. In this relatively temperate inland climate, with neither morning fog nor frost problems and no significant bunch-rot to worry about, the vines are dry-farmed.

The Viognier is a mix of four clones – La Jota, Ritchie Creek, Bonny Doon and a Phelps old Condrieu clone imported in 1977; these differ significantly in berry-size and flavour (even as grapes), which adds complexity to the final wine. The fruit is harvested very ripe, cask-fermented and bottled by the following June with "as much malolactic as we can induce"

Viognier and the old Petite Sirah are head-pruned while new plantings of Petite are trained on an open trellis. John Staten reckons that "Petite" grown here has an unique flavour; if it needs anything, it needs aromatic improvement, so some Viognier and Mourvèdre may be added.

He also considers that the yeast strain impacts strongly on both aroma and flavour: "different yeasts give different and distinct flavours", so before vatting a carefully selected strain is added. In the

Smudge-pots provide frost protection.

Côte-Rôtie tradition, there is "a modest field blending" of Viognier, which kills off the "undesirably harsh, grainy tannins that are often associated with this variety". In addition, 28 days of post-fermentive maceration help round out tannins.

The Field Stone Viognier is the less successful of the two varietals – sometimes seeming well over-oaked, although in fact it sees no new wood. The Petite Sirah is much better, and generally thoroughly seductive – high acids, balanced in youth by round, soft tannins with masses of black, succulent fruit to keep it alive for ages. Indubitably one of California's best "Petites".

VARIETY	VINEYARD	DETAILS	AREA
VIOGNIER	HOME RANCH	1 acre planted 1989, 1 acre budded 1989	2.00
VIOGNIER	HOME RANCH	Planted 1994	5.00
PETITE SIRAH	HOME RANCH	Planted 1894	10.00
		TOTAL (acres):	17.00

FOPPIANO VINEYARDS

Lou Foppiano (born 1911) is a charming, lively man whose looks belie his age. In 1930, in the wake of Prohibition, he took over the winery his grandfather bought in 1896. Although Reserve-quality Cabernet and Chardonnay are the flagships of this 200 acre estate, it is by its excellent Petite Sirah that many of its ABC (Anything But Chardonnay/Cabernet) customers know it.

Lou gleaned most of his considerable knowledge from "old-timers", but constantly strives for improvements – travelling to Europe if he feels there is something to be learned. He continues to be actively involved in the winery and has a fine instinct for what will work. For example, there is no A×R rootstock on the property – Lou disliked it and ripped it up – now it's all SO4.

The establishment is a curious amalgam of old-fashioned and modern. The general manager, Jim Faber, works out of an old Pacific Northwestern railway coach, beached on a set of rails next to the winery approached by a well-season pair of sleepers; unbearably hot in summer, uncomfortably draughty in

Lou Foppiano.

winter. The firm's offices nearby have a distinctly ancient air, redolent of those Prohibition days when sales of prunes kept the estate going. Now it's wine once more, but wine vinified in traditional style. There are two qualities of Petite – a standard *cuvée*, which is generally packed with ripe fruit and is structured to be cellared, showing no concessions to early drinking – and a Reserve release, which is a selection of the best lots.

The fruit is mostly estate-grown, although they buy from growers in Sonoma and Napa and receive grapes from Lou's daughter-in-law's five acres. The Reserve is not necessarily based on estate fruit; the 1991s came mainly from 65-year-old Napa vines. Lou believes that the market will support a premium product, provided it is top-notch.

For both *cuvées*, the crop is crushed and de-stemmed, yeasted and fermented to dryness in *inox*, then matured in two to three-year-old Chardonnay casks.

The wood is American, both because Lou and his winemaker, Bill Regan, consider that this has improved significantly over the last decade and also because at \$130 each compared to \$600 for the French version, there is a substantial saving on their 1,000-cask

VARIETY	VINEYARD	DETAILS	AREA
PETITE SIRAH	HOME RANCH	Planted 1991	5.60
PETITE SIRAH	HOME RANCH	Planted 1986	3.60
PETITE SIRAH	HOME RANCH	Planted 1972	5.25
PETITE SIRAH	HOME RANCH	Planted 1940	5.30
		TOTAL (acres):	19.75

requirement. The wine is unfined, and is only coarsely plate-filtered.

Lou Foppiano has a shrewd feel for his market. In his experience "people are tired of Cabernet and Chardonnay and come into our tasting room looking for Petite Sirah". His careful approach is underpinned by the pithy observation that "if people come here and buy a bottle of bum Petite Sirah, they believe the whole winery is lousy".

He also regards the Californian AVA with much misgiving: "there are too many of them. Here we are in Russian River

Valley; 200 yards away, you're somewhere else" In fact, his own vines are largely on bench land – a small, gravelly plateau – above the river valley.

These wines are made to be aged. In style, they are distinctly old-fashioned; sometimes overbalanced by dry tannins but, by and large, little the worse for that. Do not expect bright, modern, "lifted flavours" (whatever those may be) here; rather rich, spicy, almost sweet, wines of depth and substance. They age splendidly Buy, and then wait a decade!

FRICK WINERY

Bill Frick started winemaking in 1976 in the mountain hamlet of Bonny Doon, Santa Cruz; his office, the hollowed stump of an old redwood tree, his winery a corrugated gas station. The wines (especially Napa Gamay, which blind-tasted as Pinot Noir) prospered, and after transferring to Santa Cruz itself, dream became reality when the Fricks moved to Dry Creek Valley in Geyserville in 1985: "a little piece of Eden".

The winery and vineyards are hidden in the hills dividing Dry Creek and Alexander Valleys. The vines give way to steep woods of pine, oak, madrone and manzanita trees – a wild country, roamed by deer, coyote, wild pig and turkey, porcupine and mountain lion.

Here, on bench land at 400ft elevation (Region III), are five acres of Syrah and two of Viognier intended to blend with it, as Bill was attracted by its complexity. The vineyards are some 200ft above and two miles from the paradoxically flowing Dry Creek, on steep, well-drained south- and west-facing hillsides.

The micro-climate is characterised by an evening temperature inversion layer that reduces daytime heat by 40 Farenheit degrees. Locally, dramatic variations occur – one gully dropping 10-15 degrees within 50 vertical feet.

The geology is a complex, ancient sedimentary mix – a rough Dry Creek conglomerate of rocks, gravel-limestone, sandstone and clay, with patches of redder iron-bearing ground. The Syrah is on these redder, rockier hillsides – the

Viognier on the lighter, "blonde" land.

Bored with standard grapes, Bill asked local ranchers for unusual varieties. They found two acres of old Dry Creek "Mataro", which turned out to be Cinsaut (Black Malvasia); these Bill vinifies as both red and dry rosé. Three acres of 40-year-old Petite Sirah also turned up, heavily virussed, ripening slowly, and with difficulty: "If we get 23 Brix, that is very ripe". Their own Syrah and Viognier are drip-irrigated, the Petite and Cinsaut vineyards dry-farmed.

1985–1988 were "turmoil" as they tried to get planting permits – "lost years" as Bill describes them. Wine production in earnest began in 1988, and has now reached 1,200 cases. Winemaking is relatively straightforward: the Viognier is very lightly pressed and fermented in *inox* to preserve its naturally nutty, woody character which oak would mask, then bottled 11 months later without lees stirring or malolactic, but with sterile filtration. The "very sloppy and juicy" Viognier skins are not wasted, but put into the red wine vats – a brilliant stroke of lateral thinking, which undoubtedly

adds elegance. Syrah bunches are de-stemmed and lightly crushed, giving a high proportion of whole berries in the fermenters. After 10–15 days' *cuvaison* the pomace is basket-pressed – "the harder the better", to extract flavour. The reds are matured half in air-dried new US oak and half in neutral French oak ("as old as I can get"), two years for Syrah and Petite, 18 months for the Cinsaut.

With their striking exploding ink-blot label designed by Bill's wife and business partner, Judith Gannon, a talented painter, his wines have done him credit on the medal circuit and among his clientele. The Viognier and Syrah came on stream in 1995 and will doubtless add to an already fine reputation.

Like so many people of genuine quality, Bill Frick is undemonstrative and self-effacing. His charm hides a seriousness of purpose and a fine feel for style which show through in his wines. Food and cooking are his relaxations, though here there's less of a conception-consumption interval than with his wines. This is a splendid small estate which is establishing a solid reputation.

VARIETY	VINEYARD	DETAILS	AREA
SYRAH	GARIBALDI & LINDSEY VINEYARDS	Planted 1989; yields so far 2.5–3 tons per acre; drip-irrigated	4.00
VIOGNIER	GANNON VINEYARD (Judith Frick's maiden name is Gannon)	Planted 1989; yields so far 3 tons per acre; drip-irrigated	1.00
PETITE SIRAH		30+ yr old vines; 3 tons/acre; dry-farmed; fruit purchased from owner	3.00
CINSAUT		30+ yr old; dry-farmed; fruit purchased from owner	2.00
		TOTAL (acres):	10.00

GEYSER PEAK

Geyser Peak, in Sonoma's Alexander Valley, is emerging from the vicissitudes of two recent changes of ownership following 109 years of relative obscurity.

In 1989 the owner, Tony Trione, who had acquired the estate in 1982, sold a half-share to the Australian firm Penfolds, in a deal under which they provided the winemaker. Thus Daryl Groom, who had been in effective charge of making Grange Hermitage, under John Duval, arrived in California. In 1991, Penfold's owners, the Adelaide Steamship Co, failed, and the new owners, Elders, sold its interest in Geyser Peak back to the Triones. They wanted Groom back in return, but he remained in California, with responsibilities he clearly relishes.

Daryl Groom's winemaking skill – especially with Syrah, of which he is master – has revitalized Geyser Peak. In 1989/90, when there were only 180 acres of Syrah in production in California, he planted 23 acres – some field-planted, the rest grafted onto young root-stock (AxR-1 and St George) – giving Geyser Peak the largest planting in Sonoma.

The soils here are deep and loamy – typical valley floor land – and the climate relatively warm (Region III, Davis scale). Temperature average lies somewhere between the warmer Cloverdale, to the north, and the slightly cooler Healdsburg to the south: enough to ripen Syrah fully and regularly, without over-ripeness. For some reason, Syrah grows even more vigorously here than in Australia. Daryl Groom trellises his plants on a Geneva Double Curtain, which produces "better colour and richer fruit".

Vinification follows the Penfold's practice of taking the young wine off its solids after five days or so, while some sugar remains, and finishing fermentation in *inox*. This fleshes out the wine's middle palate and accentuates the "berryish" aspect of the grape.

It contrasts strongly with the more usual Californian method of fermenting to dryness and then leaving the wine on skins for extended maceration. The press-wine is kept apart, as the aim is for a richer, less tannic style – something individual and Californian, rather than an "Australian" look-alike.

The first vintage (1991) spent 14 months in a mixture of new French and US oak and second-year wood (12 casks in all!); future vintages will have more French oak which gives a "sweeter" style. Just before bottling, 10% of Malbec is added; Daryl worked with this variety in Australia and found it added softness. The wine is Kieselguhr filtered, but not fined.

Although he considers some of his wines excellent, Daryl is not entirely satisfied. The rootstocks are too vigorous for Shiraz and the site selection "needs to be more marginal".

He is also working on reducing bunch size and tightness to improve fruit quality. The newest plantings (1995) were on low-vigour roots, on less fertile ground and on hillsides.

Notwithstanding Daryl's misgivings, by October 1993, the excellent 1991 had made four show appearances and picked up four gold medals. Clearly, another five-star estate in the making.

VARIETY	VINEYARD	DETAILS	AREA
SYRAH	Middle ALEXANDER VALLEY (Hoffman Ranch)	Opposite the winery; rootstock (AXR-1/St. George) 1989, field-grafted 1990; Geneva Double Curtain trellis; gravelly loams and loams.	11.80
SYRAH	Northern ALEXANDER VALLEY (Cloverdale Ranch)	Warmer, hotter region; planted 1990; Geneva DC trellis; sandy and gravelly loams	11.42
		TOTAL (acres):	23.22

GRANITE SPRINGS

In 1979, Les and Lynne Russell left "a dream house" in the Bay area to follow another more elusive dream – that of making their own wine. They found a site, 2,400 feet up in Amador County and set to work; 1982 was their first vintage.

The Granite Springs winery is a functional, no-frills building, with a pleasant, trophy-lined tasting room nearby for visitors. It is presided over by Elaine, a Mrs Sparsit of a person from the Napa, who challenges judgement with the smallest tasting measures imaginable for visitors arriving to buy the estate's award-winning wines. This no doubt stimulates sales to those eager for a more complete tasting experience.

While Cabernet, Zinfandel and Sauvignon Blanc form the backbone of production, the Russells are keen on Syrah and Petite Sirah, which thrive here in seven to eight feet of decomposed, sandy granite. So little Petite Sirah is planted in the Amador region that Les reckons that he has to buy 90% of what there is in order to maintain his 500-case production. The wine is triumphantly successful – regularly walking away with the gold medals in state and county fairs. In two years, the 1991 vintage had pocketed four.

That many consider the "Petite" as a second-rate, non-Rhône variety is of no concern to Les, although he admits that neighbours like John MacCready "are all burned up when my Petite wins best of (Rhône) class".

As for real Syrah, Les is a novice, having just grafted two acres with bud-wood supplied by John onto rather vigorous 1980 Sauvignon roots, dry-farmed to limit yields. These produced 400 gallons in 1992, double in 1993. "I'm not really familiar with Syrah", Les confides, " so I don't know what I'm tasting for" at harvest-time. "We just look at the numbers, acids, sugars, etc".

De-stemming and a gentle crushing – "it's not beat up at all" – precedes fermentation in tank with pumping over or punching down. A French red wine yeast is used – since 1993 a new inoculum which just needed sprinkling over the juice and stirring – "you used to have little phials – it was such an ordeal to get that thing going". Seven to ten days vatting, with temperatures peaking in the low 90s, are followed by a gentle membrane pressing. After malolactic the wine is racked off gross lees into cask.

In 1993, eight new French oak barrels appeared – "there goes my new Mercedes", sighs Lynne, contentedly accepting that the wine should come first. Only the Syrah sees French wood, the Petite faring better in US oak – although Les is not sure whether even Syrah needs brand new oak; "perhaps we'll use it for

VARIETY	VINEYARD	DETAILS	AREA
SHIRAZ	GRANITE SPRINGS	Grafted in 1991 onto 1980 Sauvignon Blanc roots	2.00
PETITE SIRAH	GRANITE SPRINGS	15 yr old vines; fruit bought in.	5.00
PETITE SIRAH	PLACERVILLE	9 yr old vines; fruit bought in	5.00
		TOTAL (acres):	12.00

the Chardonnay first, then convert it to red", he muses. Racking from new casks to old provides them with a useful control over oak uptake.

Since 1985 the Petite has been vinified in closed fermenters at 65–70°F – this gives much softer tannins and brings out the fruit. During fermentation, 5% of Chenin Blanc is added (they have no Viognier!) which "brightens it up", according to Lynne, without affecting its body or colour. Then, after 18–20 months in cask, the red wines are tight-polish filtered and bottled.

Les and Lynne should be proud of what they have achieved. Their Petite has almost a cult following now, and little of the 500 or so cases is exported. The wine has depth and plenty of extract, without the burden of heavy, aggressive tannins. The dream is becoming reality.

JADE MOUNTAIN

The Napa Valley's Western Mountain vineyards fall into two groups – Mount Veeder, west of Napa itself, and the Spring Mountain wineries, clustered round St Helena. Jade Mountain, founded as a commercial venture in the 1960s by Jim Paras and the owner of Jade Mountain Ranch, a Dr Cartwright, is in the former. Today, Paras owns the Ranch, and the wine is made at White Rock, off the Silverado Trail, by the talented Douglas Danielak, a large, affable man who arrived with his wife Mary in 1989, through the intermediary of a barrel broker.

Mary runs the eclectic wine section of the stylish Oakville Grocery store, and shares Douglas' passion for wine. Having picked his first vintage at 105°F, Douglas told Paras that this wasn't Rhine Riesling and Sauvignon Blanc territory, and that his soils and micro-climate were more suited to Mediterranean varieties. The response was a couple of bottles of 1961 Côte-Rôtie and Hermitage: "You mean, just like these?".

The die was cast, and soon Jade's 1964 Cloverdale vines were budded to Syrah and Marsanne. After walking "every vineyard in the Napa", a new site was found 1,800 feet up on Mount Veeder, where a sunny, cool sub-climate increases the subtlety of flavour components, and soils of well-drained decomposed shale mirrored that of their best Cloverdale Syrah site. This parcel was already established with Bordeaux varieties, which were contributing the Reserve wines for Hess Collection and others: they ripped them up!

Time spent in Burgundy with a *courtier*, Becky Wasserman, "tasting everything" engendered a strong preference for elegance over brute size – a relatively rare sentiment in California – and gave Douglas a taste for Syrah.

"We have enough punishing wines here already", he explains, adding that the problem Americans have in taking Rhône wines seriously is that they are simply "too delicious".

Doug Danielak.

Jade's Rhônish bottlings exude charm. There are straight Syrah (900 cases; first vintage 1990), Mourvèdre, Viognier and Marsanne, plus 5–600 cases of each of two blends: Le Provençale (50–70% Mourvèdre, 10–30% Syrah, 10–20% Grenache), and Les Jumeaux (50–55% Mourvèdre, 10% or less Syrah, and 40% or less of Bordeaux varieties Cabernet Sauvignon, Merlot, Malbec and Petit Verdot). In 1993 there was another Syrah-based blend – Côtes du Soleil – from fruit effectively "declassified" to improve the straight varietal releases.

The Mourvèdre, of which there are 200–1,000 cases, first appeared in 1988. Douglas considers Oakley (Antioch) the only serious source for this, and wonders at colleagues who manage to extract so much aggressive tannin into their Mourvèdre. Jade's version is a big wine, yet with a fine, velvet texture and a soft middle palate. In 1992 a pilot barrel of Viognier appeared, followed in 1993 by one of Marsanne.

Douglas sees a honeypot of opportunity available to the skilful blender, and clearly enjoys putting together his own two mixes. His method, while laudable, is highly idiosyncratic: he buys in top-class Gigondas, Châteauneuf and Côtes du Rhône as comparators and then blends; if his own wine doesn't come out on top, he simply starts again. For Le Provençale, he keeps a particular, memorable wine in view: Michel Faraud's 1985 Domaine du Cayron (qv Gigondas) – "racy and delicious, delicious, delicious!" He is determined not to mimic the French wines which he knows and admires; yet he won't try his hand at Pinot Noir or Chardonnay until he is sure that they will be as fine as true burgundies. The dividing line between having an ideal, but yet not imitating, is invisibly fine....

Vinification is a matter of infinite care and rigour carried out in a series of splendid galleries, hewn out of a tree-clad hillside, which are the White Rock winery (where Douglas Danielak is also the winemaker). Running between growers and Becky's customers in the Côte d'Or instilled the difference between "the Lafarges of this world and your average *négociant*": that "two per cent extra – you're not off skiing in Switzerland when you should be doing the racking, you're there racking".

The reds are encouraged to achieve maximum heat early, to extract colour – even if this risks stuck fermentation. The

Syrah is aged for 16–20 months in up to 40% new French oak, the Mourvèdre for a couple of months less, with only 10–15% new wood; the blends spend 12–14 months in cask, 20% or so of them new oak.

Because of its high proportion of Grenache, Le Provençale is filtered to remove bitterness; the Syrah is generally unfiltered; for the rest, treatment depends on taste, which is how it should be.

The Viognier is vinified to extract and retain finesse, and to preserve its acidity and mineral qualities without deliberately inducing any autolytic characters. These Douglas considers detract from the perfume which largely identifies this magnificent grape. This means fermentation in four-year-old casks,

VARIETY	VINEYARD	DETAILS	AREA
SYRAH	CLOVERDALE (SONOMA)	27 yr old vines	6.00
MARSANNE	CLOVERDALE (SONOMA)	27 yr old vines	0.12
SYRAH	MOUNT VEEDER	Planted 1991	12.00
VIOGNIER	MOUNT VEEDER	Planted 1992	4.00
GRENACHE	MOUNT VEEDER		
MOURVEDRE	MOUNT VEEDER		
COUNOISE	MOUNT VEEDER		
CINSAUT	MOUNT VEEDER	Total of 4 varieties	4.00
MOURVEDRE	OAKLEY (ANTIOCH)	70+ yr old vines	4.20
		TOTAL (acres):	30.32

neither *bâtonnage* nor malolactic, and then an early bottling.

This is a fine domaine, in exemplary hands. If Douglas Danielak needed a confidence booster it came recently when Chalone took on the marketing of Jade Mountain wines in the US. Let's hope there's some left for the rest of the world.

JOSEPH PHELPS

In 1973, Joseph Phelps, a Colorado construction engineer and lifelong wine collector, was busy building the Souverain winery when he saw the 650-acre Conley cattle ranch. He bought it, and released his first wines that same year. One year later, a house and winery had been built and the first Phelps Syrah released. His love of the Rhône is seen in the fact that of his 135 acres now under vine, half are Rhône varieties: Syrah, Viognier, Grenache and Mourvèdre.

In Jo's view, the Rhône style is the natural partner for California's grilled, smoky food. Syrah became a major focus for Phelps in the late 1970s and early 1980s and, although the original vines were replaced, 1989 saw the inauguration of the Vin de Mistral programme for Rhône varietals and blends. At present this comprises 2,500 cases of Grenache Rosé, 4,000 cases of Le Mistral – a flexible blend of some 40% each of Grenache and Mourvèdre, with 10% Syrah and 5% each of Carignan and Cinsaut – 1,500 cases of Viognier and 500 of Syrah. As the vines mature, this output will increase.

Phelps is a remarkable man – he pilots his own aircraft, runs his construction firm, owns several high-quality grocery shops, and guides the estate's planting and blending. He has established a talented team round him: Craig Williams, the senior winemaker, a bespectacled, fast-talking, mid-40s Davis graduate whose softly-spoken manner hides succint, firmly-held convictions has 22 years service. His chemist and biologist colleague Gary Brookman, a slim, outgoing individual with a dry sense of humour who oversees day-to-day winemaking, has seen 15 Phelps vintages;

Gary Brookman beside a glass-ended cask containing fermenting white wine.

VARIETY	VINEYARD	DETAILS	AREA
VIOGNIER	HOME RANCH	6–7 yr vines; 3 acres on AxR1	21.00
VIOGNIER	YOUNTVILLE	Planted 1990; soils as for Syrah	2.50
VIOGNIER	CARNEROS	Planted 1989; soils as for Syrah	1.00
VIOGNIER	HOME RANCH	Planted 1993	7.50
SYRAH	YOUNTVILLE	Planted 1990; clay-like soils, not much rock;	5.00
SYRAH	HOME RANCH	Planted 1978; heavy clay/volcanic soil on sandstone base	5.00
SYRAH	STAGS LEAP	Planted 1986; rich, deep, loamy soil	1.00
SYRAH	CARNEROS	Planted 1989; heavy clay soil	1.00
MOURVEDRE	HOME RANCH	Young scion T-budded onto 1974 roots; also fruit bought from Cline (qv)	16.00
GRENACHE	MONTEREY	Fruit bought from Cline	
GRENACHE	HOME RANCH		6.00
CARIGNAN + CINSAUT		Fruit bought	
MARSANNE	HOME RANCH	Planted/budded 1993; first crop 1995	1.78
ROUSSANNE	HOME RANCH	Planted/budded 1993; first crop 1995	2.56
		TOTAL (acres):	70.34

Bush-trained vines seen from Phelps terrace.

he joined after spells in Australia's Southern Vales and with Charles Krug in the Napa. The 25 equally long-serving vineyard workers are Mexican – "all related". Many send their children to top colleges like Harvard, leading Gary to speculate that, when his own children come of age, they may well be working the land, with the Mexicans in charge.

Phelps' vineyards encompass both flats and hillsides, spread over a veritable compendium of soil types giving differing ripening dates and wine characteristics. The Viognier is all cane-pruned, while Syrahs are cordon-trained on the home ranch but cane-pruned elsewhere. The latter's natural tendency to heavy tannins is mitigated by allowing the grapes to ripen fully; however, since tannins tend to lock-on to pips and are not always easily released, careful vinification is essential.

Although their Syrah has long been one of Califoria's best, Phelps experimented during the early 1990s to develop a vinification which would give "the fruit quality which we have been seeking for years". Their conclusion was to ferment with up to 30% of whole clusters, alternating layers of crushed and whole-berry fruit. The proportion of whole clusters depends on fruit and stem

ripeness. Up to two and a half weeks' vatting is preceded by "a major colour extraction phase" of 24 hours' cold maceration with a fair dose of sulphur to delay the onset of fermentation. Natural yeasts are discouraged as they tend to stop working when two grammes per litre of sugar still remain, which bacteria will readily convert into volatile acidity.

Each block of Syrah is vinified separately and blended after malolactic, so that the team know what remains for the Mistral *assemblage*. The reds spend 18 months in 2– to 3-year-old French oak, with four rackings in the first year and one or two in the second. Bottling is preceded by a light egg-white fining – to precipitate colloids, not to reduce tannins – and a polishing plate-filtration.

These are stylish, fleshy wines, especially the Syrah, which is deliberately not released until three years following the vintage to allow it to soften, an important marketing feature, especially for their restaurant clients.

The Viognier was originally destined to be co-fermented with Syrah, to add a fruit dimension to a wine from the older, flat plots. However, by the time there was enough, the hillside Syrah was producing, and the extra fruit was not needed. By

1989, the Viognier had reached sufficient volume – 15 cases! – to go solo.

There has obviously been much in-house discussion about how to vinify the capricious Viognier and the arguments are not yet over. The main problem is balancing structure with finesse – where even the mildest excess of alcohol will destroy the grape's fragile aromas. At present, fermentation starts in *inox*; some 60% is finished in 3- to 4-year French oak, with *bâtonnage*, the rest having a brief spell in wood once fermentation is complete. To preserve valuable acidity, only part of the crop is seeded for malolactic fermentation. The two fractions are blended in January following the vintage, and bottled a month or so later.

A Phelps Viognier is invariably an attractive, finely-tuned example of the variety, although occasionally upset by a shade too much alcohol. Despite Marcel Guigal's reported view that the Phelps soil is even better for Viognier than that of Condrieu itself, this wine is not a Condrieu look-alike, but has its own personality, with a strongly varietal nose and warmth and ripeness on the palate.

Despite its size, quality is never compromised here. Joseph Phelps is undoubtedly a first-division estate.

LA JOTA

This is an important, though not large, domaine, noted for Viognier and owned and run with idiosyncratic flare by the muscular, craggy Bill Smith and his wife Joan. The "J" ranch (pronounced La Hota) sits at the end of a long, winding road at 1,800 feet in the Howell Mountain AVA; it has had vines and a splendid stone winery on it since 1898.

It was bought by the Smiths in 1974, principally as a tax haven. Early plantings were Zinfandel, Cabernets Sauvignon and Franc and Merlot; the first commercial wine was made in 1982. The area is classified mid-to high Region II on the Davis heat summation scale, and the soils are brownish red volcanic ash (tufa).

Things changed when Bill tasted 1970 Château Grillet and decided that he "really liked that wine". He tried to get some bud-wood; UC Davis' supply was virused so he turned to Cornell University – not an obvious source – who had virus-free stock on hand.

He propagated the wood and in 1983 T-budded over three acres of ten-year-old Zinfandel vineyard. This ground has a deep volcanic ash tufa-derived topsoil – Vouvrayish in type; a coincidence given Bill's love of Loire wines in general (he collects them, Coulée de Serrant and Savennières in particular). He tried Chenin Blanc, but the results were disappointing.

Viognier is notoriously difficult to vinify successfully. To shorten the odds, Bill visited the Rhône and talked to Guigal, Vernay, Multier, Faury, Pichon, Dezormeaux, and to Canet at Château Grillet. He returned thoroughly confused, with the impression of no real consensus. Should one use or not use new wood, suppress or encourage the malolactic? In default of any common fundamentals, he set about developing his own rules.

Initial trials with old wood were followed in 1988 by vinification in

What? No unleaded Syrah? What a gas!

10–20% of new wood. Now, the "regular" Viognier has one-third each of new, second-year and third-year French oak, with yeast inoculation for the alcoholic fermentation.

Although Bill considers that malolactic and *bâtonnage* mask the Viognier's opulent peach and apricot aromas (the facet he particularly seeks to retain), he readily admits to both – although malolactic is not systematic. Fortunately, he admires many different Viognier styles, so nothing is final. One senses a distinct touch of the schoolboy experimenter underneath the serious facade.

By 1993, there were enough grapes "so I could really play with the juice" – 12 tons of grapes from the three acres – "not more clusters, but larger ones". "Playing" meant drying some of the crop for a week on cement to concentrate the juice.

This process Bill enigmatically refers to as "late harvest, for want of a better name", although the bunches were picked earlier than the rest to retain acidity. The wine was entirely fermented in new wood, left on its lees and *bâtonné* for four months without malolactic, then racked in January/February back to cask and finally bottled in late April or May. In fact the "vendange tardive" experiments started in 1988, when eight cases were produced "for fun, as a give-away", from the second crop, which was left to ripen on the vine.

In 1992, having so far failed "to make a decent dry (Marsanne) wine – it doesn't easily ripen fully at this altitude" – Bill decided to try a sweet late-harvest Marsanne, by cutting the bunches and then hanging them back on the vine to concentrate. He liked the results so much that this will no doubt become an annual ritual. Fortunately there are only 80 of these troublesome Marsanne vines, so the problem is not overwhelming. As a yardstick, Bill has acquired a bottle of Chave's Hermitage Vin de Paille, standing by in case he needs to refresh his memory as to the genuine article.

Other experiments in 1993 included fermenting one white batch in *inox* with natural yeasts and then blocking the malolactic, while another involved a *cuvée* assembled from wine vinified in new second- and third-year wood, using indigenous yeasts, inoculating for the malolactic, and plenty of *bâtonnage*.

Bill Smith is a good winemaker, with an engaging personality and great *joie de vivre*. He interests himself in what goes on elsewhere and keeps informed – you are more likely to find a *stagière* from St-Emilion pumping out a vat than someone from California. Not content with the vine, he is trying to persuade endive to grow in tubs in the cellar – and no doubt there are other such essays scattered in corners round the estate.

VARIETY	VINEYARD	DETAILS	AREA
VIOGNIER	HOME RANCH	Budded onto Zinfandel roots c. 1984	3.00

MCDOWELL VALLEY VINEYARDS

McDowell Valley is one of California's major Rhône-varietal producers, both in quantity (103.4 acres) and quality. The Valley, in south-eastern Mendocino County, has its own AVA and was named after Paxton McDowell, who arrived during the gold rush to farm.

This inland river valley, protected from the Pacific Ocean by two ridges, has been vineyard since 1892. The climate is

Region III, Mediterranean in character with warm days and cool nights.

Recently, the estate has been restructured to take account of "recessionary conditions, alcohol taxes, increased competition, a glut of wine on the market, financial institutions' reluctance to extend credit, the costs of replanting due to phylloxera, and the neo-Prohibitionist movement". In 1993

the winery, but not the vineyards, was sold to Associated Vintage group, a wine services company.

Henceforth, McDowell wines will continue to be made there – but not under the hand of their articulate, talented, Rhône-passionate winemaker, John Buechsenstein, who left after guiding their seminal Rhône programme since 1985. A new desginer-label has spearheaded a marketing plan which emphasizes the firm's four Rhône varietal wines: an inexpensive Bistro Syrah, a

Grenache Rosé, a Viognier and a Syrah, 80% coming from Mendocino vines planted in 1919/20.

The first McDowell Syrah was made in 1979. However no-one, including the then owners, Karen and Richard Keehn, knew that it was in fact Syrah, so it was co-fermented with Petite Sirah. Authorities such as the eminent French ampelographer Pierre Galet and Kevin Hamel (of Preston) have failed to identify positively the origin of the estate's Syrah. So it is still referred to as the McDowell clone. In 1985, when "John B" arrived, the Syrah was "just another grape". However, having spent two years living with Syrah at Phelps and with knowledge gleaned from visits to most of the major Rhône producers, he "learned to tame the

VARIETY	VINEYARD	DETAILS	AREA
SYRAH	McDOWELL VINEYARDS	Vines planted 1919–20	26.00
SYRAH	LAKEVIEW VINEYARDS	Planted 1990; bilateral cordon; organic farming	35.00
SYRAH	McDOWELL VINEYARDS	Planted 1951; head-trained; gobelet pruned	7.00
SYRAH	McDOWELL VINEYARDS	Planted 1983; bilateral cordon	3.00
MOURVEDRE	McDOWELL VINEYARDS	T-budded 1990 onto 10 yr old roots	1.00
MOURVEDRE	LAKEVIEW VINEYARDS	Planted 1990; bilateral cordon; organic farming	10.00
GRENACHE	McDOWELL VINEYARDS	Planted 1950	14.00
CINSAUT	McDOWELL VINEYARDS	T-budded 1990 onto 10 yr old roots	0.10
VIOGNIER	McDOWELL VINEYARDS	T-budded 1990 onto 10 yr old roots	0.30
VIOGNIER	LAKEVIEW VINEYARDS	Planted 1990; bilateral cordon; organic farming	7.00
		TOTAL (acres):	103.40

beast", in particular to balance tannins.

It is to be hoped that the progress already made with Rhône varieties will be continued. This estate has the potential for making top-class wine, and should put every effort into getting there.

THE OJAI VINEYARD

Adam Tolmach trained in viticulture and oenology at UC Davis – where he claims he didn't learn "a damn thing" – then worked at the Duc de Magenta's estate in Burgundy and at Beaulieu Vineyards in the Napa. In 1981 he met Jim Clenenden and Bob Lindquist and went to join the team at Au Bon Climat. While there, he planted 2.5 acres of Estrella River Syrah at Ojai, an estate bought by his grandfather in the 1930s. Through Jim, he met Helen Hardenberg, a fresh-water ecologist, whom he married in 1985.

By 1987 things had become so busy at Au Bon Climat that Helen was running Ojai ("Oh-hi") single-handed, turning out Syrah, Sauvignon Blanc and Semillon. In 1991, Adam retired from ABC to devote himself full-time to Ojai, indulging his passion for Burgundy by adding Pinot Noir and Chardonnay from purchased grapes, to his quiver.

Ojai is an interesting estate. Although in Region II/III, its proximity to the ocean (8.5 miles) means that summer heat is tempered by cooling afternoon and evening breezes, bringing long, even ripening. This is important for Syrah, which thrives here on vigorous, clay-rich soils. In common with much of Santa Barbara and San Luis Obispo, the

Tolmachs have taken the calculated risk of planting vines on their own roots and the estate is organically farmed. The Syrah's natural vine-vigour, augmented by rich soil, requires severe pruning to reduce yields. There is no crop-thinning, but the vines are trellis-trained, systematically defoliated to expose the bunches and drip-irrigated.

With a total annual production of only 3,500 cases, the Tolmachs do most of the work themselves, to cut costs. The winery, built in 1984, has recently been extended and now consists of several small buildings, variously described as "garage" or "barn", "so the fire department doesn't get involved". Unusually, there are no cellar-door sales, the wines being distributed through local merchants and export.

The estate's 460 or so cases of Syrah are made on broadly "non-interventionist" principles which, Adam argues, best preserves the unique characteristics of a vineyard site. The fruit, 75% de-stemmed, is cold-macerated for four days, fermented for ten days and then

macerated on skins for a further 10-14 days to soften out the tannins. There are no rules on racking or élevage – treatment tends to depend upon taste, and bottling on a mixture of taste and expediency; if, for example, casks are needed, some wine may be racked back into tank. The 1991 spent only 12 months in cask, the average is nearer to 18 months .

To avoid the risk of brettanomyces, the cellar is kept cool. Adam's experience of old Rhônes – the extent of which is clear from a line of empty bottles adorning the mantelpiece in the house above the winery – has convinced him that most of those wines are completely decorated by "brett", which Helen colourfully describes as "that funky Rhône style".

There is nothing "funky" about the Ojai Syrah, which is usually a mid-weight wine, not massively structured but with soft, distinctly Rhônish, spice and pepper aromas and a long, complete raft of flavours. It can be stunning; it can however, be disappointing – for example a lean, pinched 1991 tasted in London in April 1994. On balance, Ojai deserves the benefit of any doubt. The Tolmachs are clearly dedicated to making the best, and seem to be succeeding.

VARIETY	VINEYARD	DETAILS	AREA
SYRAH	OJAI RANCH	Planted 1981	2.50

PRESTON VINEYARDS

Originally planted mostly with prunes, pears, walnuts and grass for hay, this 125-acre estate in Sonoma's Dry Creek Valley was developed as a vineyard by Lou Preston in 1973. Now in his mid-50s, Preston studied at Davis, which inspired

a search for suitable varieties for his land. As the climate is hottish, between warm Region II and a cool III, vines were mainly planted on hillsides; something rare in the Napa where planting permits for slopes are difficult to come by, both to protect

the skyline and to prevent soil erosion.

In 1989 winemaker Kevin Hamel arrived via Davis, Cockburn and Santino. Both he and his Chinese psychologist wife (an excellent cook with an excellent palate) have visited the Rhône, tasting and contemplating French winemaking and viticulture. The soils at Preston vary from sandy gravels (suitable for Petite

Syrah) to much richer ground. Increasing interest in true Syrah, from Andy Cutter of Duxoup and others in the 1970s, meant that supplies of plant-material became more readily available, from Phelps among others, so both varieties were planted side by side.

Continuous evaluation of the suitability and performance of each vine-type attests to the importance attached here to *terroir*. For example, a patch of sandy soil considered unsuitable for its Cabernet was replanted with Barbera. The best wines come from slightly raised terraces, with Syrah on selected lower land, near the river bed. The estate also has well-sited Grenache, and Viognier on sandy loams. Kevin is constantly on the look-out for port varieties, after his stay in the Douro. Bob Lindquist's Marsanne converted him to this grape, so he promptly grafted over two acres, largely on clay-gravel near the river – not perhaps an ideal site for a grape susceptible to mildew and botrytis.

Not surprisingly, the Rhône emphasis at Preston is firmly entrenched. Current releases include Viognier (600–800 cases), Marsanne (400–500 cases), Syrah (1,000 cases) and a blend – originally "Faux-Castel", which was tactfully changed to "Faux" in 1992 (3,000–4,000 cases) – of varying proportions of Syrah, Carignan, Mourvèdre, Petite Sirah and Grenache, with a shot of Cinsaut in 1993, and 15% of Zinfandel in 1991. There is also an attractive Beaumes de Venise mimic called Muscat Brulé.

Viognier and Marsanne are relatively new to Preston, so Kevin prefers to look at the fruit, rather than being influenced by traditional winemaking lore. Aroma is his chief concern with Viognier, so part is vinified in old cask, part in *inox*. Marsanne's ageing capability interests him, but he stresses the need for wine which is attractive young, it being too much to expect the average consumer to wait for even half a decade, so only part is fermented and aged in older wood. Neither white has malolactic nor *bâtonnage*; the Viognier is bottled in March, the Marsanne 4-6 weeks later, both with sterile filtration.

The pure Syrah *cuvée* is a selection of the best lots, and is the only Preston Rhône wine to see any new wood, and even then, only a seasoning (Kevin was afraid that he had overdone things with 25% of new oak in 1990 and 1991). He found a heavy influence of new oak *chez* René Rostaing in Ampuis, but believes that this would not suit his own

fruit. A bin of whole bunches is added to the each redwood or *inox* fermenter; otherwise, everything is de-stemmed. The wine is bottled, unfined and unfiltered, after spending between 16 and 18 months in cask.

In character, Preston Syrah has pronounced smoky, meaty, earthy elements with an attractive berryish component. Full-bodied, quite spicy, warm and Provençale in flavour, it is structured to age but without unpleasant raw tannins. In short, more southern than northern Rhône.

Preston's emphasis on Rhône varieties has strengthened with the grafting of vines that used to make up their popular Estate Red and White blends, and a deliberate shift from Zinfandel and Sauvignon Blanc. The importance Kevin Hamel and Lou Preston attach to *terroir*, and their determination to fine-tune vine:soil adaptation, signal clearly their unswerving commitment to quality at this excellent estate.

VARIETY	VINEYARD	DETAILS	AREA
VIOGNIER	HOME RANCH	Grafted in 1990; sandy-loam soils	5.00
SYRAH	HOME RANCH	Planted 1977 & 1989	10.50
PETITE SYRAH	HOME RANCH	Planted 1925 & 1979	4.50
CARIGNAN	HOME RANCH	Planted 1925	3.50
MOURVEDRE	HOME RANCH	Planted 1989/90	4.00
GRENACHE	HOME RANCH	Grafted 1991	4.00
CINSAUT	HOME RANCH	Planted 1991	2.50
MARSANNE	HOME RANCH	Grafted 1990	2.00
		TOTAL (acres):	36.00

QUPE

In 1982 Bob Lindquist, a bespectacled, friendly bear of a man, started Qupe (the Chumash Indian word for California Poppy, the state flower) having graduated from tour guide to winemaker at Zaca Mesa. There, eclectic tasting and the influence of Berkeley wine merchant Kermit Lynch inspired a profound love of the Rhône. Qupe is now among the finest "Rhône" estates in California.

Its headquarters are at Bien Nacido in the Santa Maria Valley – an AVA since 1981. Here cool Pacific air and morning sea-fog moderate temperatures – heat summation is Region I bordering Region II – and low rainfall (12–15 inches per annum) necessitates drip irrigation. This temperate climate gives an exceptionally long growing season, producing some of the best Syrah in California.

When Lindquist crushed his first Syrah in 1982 at Zaca Mesa, from Estrella River fruit, there were only three other estates

Bob Lindquist.

vinifying this grape – Phelps, McDowell and Estrella itself. The wine didn't sell, but Bob persevered. Two moves on, the

domaine now seems settled in a large shed at Santa Maria, adjoining the Bien Nacido ranch, shared – Heaven know's how – with Frank Ostini's The Hitching Post, Jim Clenenden's Au Bon Climat (Jim was assistant winemaker at Zaca Mesa), and Bob and Jim's joint venture, Vita Nova. To the original Syrah have been added Marsanne, Viognier and Mourvèdre plus a standard and Reserve Chardonnay. There is also a Central Coast Syrah, blended from several sources for early drinking, and a more serious *vin de garde*, Los Olivos, a blend of 60% Syrah and 40% Mourvèdre. The most recent offering is an unusual but delicious Bien Nacido *cuvée*, consisting of half-and-half Chardonnay and Viognier, which was made "on a whim" in 1992, but fared so well that it is now a regular fixture. Inspired by Aimé Guibert's Mas de Daumas Gassac Blanc, this wine combines the Viognier's distinctive perfume with the structure of the Chardonnay – a good example of the benefits of freedom from constraining

Outside Qupe's winery.

appellation-style rules (*see* Introduction, page 10, and page 190).

The Viognier and Marsanne follow broadly similar vinifications: whole cluster press, cooling, 24–48 hours' settling then fermentation in 3- to 5-year-old French casks – "old enough to be neutral, young enough to be fresh". In Bob's view neither grape benefits from lees contact, especially Marsanne, which shows a "canned corn" aspect and reduces easily to hydrogen sulphide, hence the longish settling. Yeast inoculations are used because the indigenous yeasts are "so wild and varied" that they can't be relied upon to finish fermentation. The wines remain in cask until February when they are fined, filtered and bottled. The only material difference is that the Marsanne is settled for 48 hours because the minimum lees are wanted and given more sulphur dioxide to prevent premature reduction.

The Syrah is fermented with 33–55% whole clusters, the rest de-stemmed, in open fermenters with twice-daily punching down, preceded by 24–48 hours cold maceration, with the vat covered, to extract colour. Once fermentation is over, the vats are blanketed with carbon dioxide gas and

covered for further extraction. The whole process lasts 12–16 days. *Elevage* lasts 18 months in cask: 20–25% new French oak, the rest older. Two months before bottling, the Bien Nacido is racked into tank and put on egg-white fining for 24-48 hours then returned to cask. According to Bob Lindquist, this "softens and sweetens up" the wine. The Mourvèdre, apart from being totally de-stemmed, has much the same treatment.

Two visits to the Rhône have engendered a respect for the wines of Chave, Guigal and the Perrins, and a dislike for the barnyardy style of many older Rhônes. This is largely attributable to *brettanomyces* and preventable by filtration, low pH and sensible use of sulphur dioxide – all measures which Bob takes care to implement.

The characteristics of the Los Olivos and Bien Nacido *terroirs* filter through to the wines. In general, the geological character of the Santa Barbara region stems from the alluvial deposits left by retreating waters following its historical immersion. Los Olivos soils are mainly gravel, clay and sand, with a clay hard-pan base three feet or so down, which produces quite broad, rich wines, whereas the Bien Nacido profile shows more gravel and less sand and clay, giving more complexity and finesse.

This is an area which promises well for Rhône varieties – although the quantities produced remain small. Bob Lindquist's influence is such that we will undoubtedly hear much more of Bien Nacido and the Santa Maria Valley in years to come.

VARIETY	VINEYARD	DETAILS	AREA
SYRAH	BIEN NACIDO	Planted early 1970s; grafted 1986.	14.00
VIOGNIER	LOS OLIVOS	Planted early 1970s; grafted 1986.	1.50
MARSANNE	LOS OLIVOS	Planted early 1970s; grafted 1986.	4.00
MOURVEDRE	LOS OLIVOS	Planted early 1970s; grafted 1986.	1.50
SYRAH	LOS OLIVOS	Planted early 1970s; grafted 1986.	2.50
		TOTAL (acres):	23.50

RIDGE VINEYARDS

Ridge is one of California's most impressive estates, producing wines of a depth and concentration that come from supreme dedication allied to supreme skill. Its architect is Paul Draper, a man who, like many of the world's great winemakers, exudes intellect and cares passionately about detail.

His winery, built into the mountain-side at 2,600ft, sits atop the Monte Bello ridge, in the Santa Cruz mountains above Cupertino. Here, among some of the property's original vineyards, are made some of California's most exciting Zinfandels, Cabernets, Mataros, Petites Sirahs and Chardonnays.

The history of the estate hardly presages its fame. In 1959, four Stanford research engineers bought the 2,300ft William Short vineyard as an investment and weekend retreat; one, David Bennion, made ten gallons of Cabernet that year – and then in 1962, produced one of the legendary California Cabernets of the 1960s.

In 1961, Ridge Vineyards was established. Disused terraces were gradually reclaimed and shares sold to finance a winery. In 1969, Paul Draper, a Stanford philosophy graduate, joined the venture, fresh from setting up a winery in Chile's coastal range. Improvements to the winery occupied the 1970s, with the focus shifting to the vineyards during the 1980s. Under his aegis, the estate has earned, and enhanced, its reputaton.

By 1986, many of the original partners and 150 smaller shareholders wanted to sell. After several tentative approaches from foreign-owned multi-nationals, the Japanese proprietor of a substantial pharmaceutical company, and keen Bordeaux collector, expressed a serious interest. He visited Ridge on 14 December and closed the deal on 31 December – unthinkable speed for a Japanese corporation. This take-over increased financial stability, allowing Paul Draper to focus unhindered on quality and the "rare luxury" of buying prime vineyard sites.

During the mid-1970s, he had begun to see "what we had as a heritage; not just old vines, but a field-mix of varieties which had a logic" – the notion of a vineyard's "essence" – a concept which Paul Draper respects and follows. Because, historically, Syrah did not reach California until comparatively recently, it was Zinfandel which substituted as the backbone grape of local "Rhône" blends.

Racking at Ridge.

Tasting old wines convinced him that the 19th-century field-blends – eg Zinfandel with Carignan – gave more complexity and completeness than either straight variety. He is aghast that the Tuscans, for example, have introduced Cabernet Sauvignon to their blends: "What in God's name are they doing with this grape? If I had a thousand years of a great grape – Sangiovese – I'd be perfecting it and showing what could be done with it". The refinement and elaboration of tradition plays a seminal role in the Draper philosophy.

From this *point de départ* the winemaking evolved, recognizing that each vineyard has its individuality, on which the vintage has an important bearing, and that wine should be crafted to express this character through the varietal mix. Thus each variety is vinified separately to maximize the final choice, rather than making an early *assemblage*.

This "caretaker" philosophy casts the winemaker as midwife, helping each vineyard and vintage to full expression; it diametrically opposes many Californian winemakers, who rely on technology to impose a personal style; retaining the site-specific flavours of quality ingredients rather than submerging them in another expression – the dish.

This approach demands the most flavourful, intense grapes and minimal intrusion with the "natural process", to extract maximum richness into the wine. For Paul Draper this means rigorous site selection, rather than just adapting vine to soil; in the quest for perfect sites he has worked with over 30 different individual Zinfandel vineyards alone, to arrive at two favoured sources. What he seeks is an "excitement" in the wine which he finds – for example – in York Creek, but not in Howell Mountain.

Of the current 30,000–40,000 case production 40% is Cabernet and Merlot and 40% Zinfandel, for which Ridge is renowned. There are around 2,000 cases each of Petite Sirah and Mataro (Mourvèdre), and a Geyserville Red Rhône, containing 60%-plus Zinfandel and 18% each of Mataro and Petite Sirah.

At present, Rhône varieties come from York Creek, Geyserville and Lytton Springs, with some Mataro, Petite Sirah and Carignan from a near-centenarian mixed planting on the Pagani Ranch in Sonoma Valley and more Mataro from Cline's Evangelo vineyard in Oakley – altogether a remarkable litany of ancient vines (mainly Region I heat summation) producing fruit of extraordinary intensity.

The areas differ: Geyserville, owned by the Trentadues, is up against the foothills, on a 5% south-facing slope of gravelly loam angled towards the river bed; warm days with frequent evening breezes give a long, even growing season, bringing 15-year-old Petite Sirah and 111-year-old Carignan to perfect ripeness.

In contrast, Lytton Springs – as the crow flies no more than a mile and a half from Geyserville – is benchland with low, rolling hills separating the gravelly river flood-plain from the Dry Creek Valley. A vineyard with different soils (gravelly clay predominates, with gravelly loam on hillsides), exposure (south-easterly) and drainage properties.

York Creek, source of Ridge's magnificent Petite Sirah, is on steep gravelly loam slopes at 1,250–1,800 feet on Spring Mountain; the elevation, cool mountain climate and 25- to 70-year-old vines combine to produce fruit of spectacular intensity with a characteristic liveliness – not acidity, but a brightness of fruit and spice. More of Paul's "excitement" here – something magnetic in flavour and balance tempting you to taste and re-taste. Petite Syrah may not be a true Rhône variety, but such an expression as this would fool all but the most honed of blind tasters into believing it the genuine article.

The Evangelo vineyard's Mataro vines are planted in the sandy soils of an ancient river bed, on slight undulations of varied exposure. The location, classed

Region III in heat terms, benefits from hot days and warm nights, frequently interspersed with delta fog and breezes – ideal for Mataro. Yields are 1.5–2 tons/acre.

Turning this remarkable raw material into wine demands constant vigilance. This begins at harvest where, in Paul Draper's experience, a few extra days ripening bring a striking change in flavour. One plot of Lytton Springs Mataro – analytically very ripe at 23.5 Brix – had no flavour; three days later, at 24 Brix, the difference was dramatic and the character of the vineyard had appeared – a contrast to Château de Beaucastel (qv), for example, where full maturity for Mourvèdre is rare. So, ripeness and flavour drive the harvest.

Apart from the Petite Sirah and Mataro, the crop is de-stemmed, although some tanks include a proportion of whole clusters. Exceptionally low yields means high, readily extractable tannins, making tannin management, and the goal of more complex tannins, a major concern.

Paul has found that with these two grapes, 30–40% of whole berries (they control-count them!) contribute suppleness and roundness to the wine and enhance fruit character. Including skins and whole berries also buffers pip-tannin extraction as alcohol increases. Contrary to conventional widsom, his research has demonstrated that grape-skins hold relatively little tannin compared with pips and stems.

"Minimal intervention" means that, unless a problem is envisaged or the vineyard is too young to have developed a mature micro-flora, natural yeasts are used. Paul dislikes artificial yeasts – especially those which are not wine yeasts, but industrial products whose scavenging vigour changes the fermentation sequence and thus the character of the wine. His indigenous yeasts have no problem in fermenting to dryness, so why interfere?

Each variety has its preferred vinification, which is adapted to suit each vintage. Mataro has both a floating cap – for vats containing fully-crushed fruit – and a submerged cap for those with one-third whole clusters; Petite Sirah is pumped over and vatted at the low end of the 10–14 days average; Grenache has a submerged cap, no whole clusters and is kept apart for two years. The *inox* vats are warmed up to around 70°F to get the yeasts going and the juice fermented up to an ideal 78–85°F.

For the naturally tannic Petite Sirah and Mataro, the first and second press-wines are held apart, tasted on the spot, and then blended back or not; for Carignan and Grenache, pressings are not held separately but are blended back immediately.

As soon after malolactic as possible, in November or December, the blends are put together. The wines then pass to casks of which 25–30% are new air-dried US oak; increasing this to a third began to mask the fruit with wood, so they pulled back. Provided the lees are clean, no attempt is made to remove them: "we put 'dirty' wine into barrel; this gives better esters and an added autolytic quality".

A month or so later the wine is racked, by hand and eye, "right down to the lees"; and then every three months during the first year. At each racking, the lots of each wine are re-assembled in tank to eliminate cask variation. During their second year, the wines are sealed with plastic bungs and racked four-monthly.

The moment of bottling is decided entirely on taste – in general after 18–23 months' *élevage*. There is no filtration and whether or not a wine is fined (only fresh egg-whites are used) depends both on its evolution and on the results of trial finings. Paul recalls shipping some 1967 Mouton-Rothschild in cask and bottled it unfined; it was better than the fined, château-bottled version. QED?

The origin and quantity of oak have been considered in detail by Paul, who has concluded that after 25 years of using US oak, with excellent results, there is no reason to change. "It's fine if it's properly managed". He cites the results of trials in Bordeaux in 1900, with two barrels of each of four first growths in six different oaks: Riga wood from the Baltic triumphed, followed by Stetten (German Baltic), then the Lubeck, the US white oak (*quercus alba*, probably from Ohio) and the Bosnian oak. Wood from the centre of France came last!

Paul Draper's philosophy is rooted in the belief that "one, if not the most crucial, criterion of a red wine's greatness is its ability to age – to develop in quality over time, and to achieve exceptional complexity". Such, however, is the balance and youthful appeal of even the toughest Ridge Mataro or Petite Sirah, that the temptation to drink them young is often irresistible.

For those with the self-discipline to wait, the reward is a magnificent spectrum of secondary aromas and flavours which more than justify the patience. These consistently remarkable wines are the products of an unashamedly empirical tradition which favours complex tannins, concentrated flavours and an inherently cohesive balance – the very elements upon which longevity and final quality depend.

VARIETY	VINEYARD	DETAILS	AREA
CARIGNAN	GEYSERVILLE, WHITTEN RANCH (32 year lease + right of first refusal on sale)	Planted 1883; 3 separate blocks plus 1 mixed block containing 25% CA; ranch owned by Trentadues	8.00
PETITE SIRAH	GEYSERVILLE (32 year lease + right of first refusal on sale)	2 acres planted 1883, 5 acres planted 1960s.	7.00
MOURVEDRE	GEYSERVILLE	1 acre 1880–90; 2 acres 1990; Ridge owned.	3.00
PETITE SIRAH	YORK CREEK	25–70 yr old vines; owner, Fritz Maytag; first vintage 1971.	22.50
GRENACHE	LYTTON SPRINGS	2 plots: Lytton Estate and Norton Ranch; planted 1880	5.00
PETITE SIRAH	LYTTON SPRINGS	Ridge owned; planted 1880;	5.00
CARIGNAN	LYTTON SPRINGS	Planted 1880; Ridge owned; these are mixed in all three Lytton Springs blocks.	5.00
PETITE SIRAH	LYTTON SPRINGS	Planted 1986; Ridge owned; planted on the old style – i.e. head-trained "en gobelet"	2.00
MOURVEDRE	SONOMA VALLEY (Pagani Ranch)	Half planted 1880s, half 1900; 3 year trial lease. First Ridge vintage 1991.	3.00
PETITE SIRAH	SONOMA VALLEY (Pagani Ranch)	Planted 1890s - totally mixed in with other varieties	4.00
CARIGNAN	SONOMA VALLEY (Pagani Ranch)	Planted 1890s – totally mixed in with other varieties	2.00
ALICANTE BOUSCHET	SONOMA VALLEY (Pagani Ranch)	Planted 1890s.	4.00
MOURVEDRE	OAKLEY (Cline)	Leased; planted 1890s.	10.00
		TOTAL (acres):	80.50

ROSENBLUM CELLARS

Kent Rosenblum started by making five gallons of Riesling in the family basement in 1973; the following year production leapt to 15 gallons, with 25 of Zinfandel added to flesh out the range. The neighbours objected; so Kent, a Groucho-moustached man in his 40s, his wife Kathy and her brother, borrowed $15,000 which bought them some dairy tanks for fermentation, a manual crusher, a basket press and some casks.

They rented premises for $120 a month for the 1978 vintage – Zinfandel, Chardonnay, Petite Syrah and Cabernet Sauvignon.

In 1982 the operation moved to Emeryville – but, despite medals and runaway sales, Kent and Kathy found themselves with insufficient cash to buy more grapes. In 1987 they moved again, to their present base: one end of a large, rectangular warehouse in Alameda, near Oakland.

One section houses the current crush and first-year wine, the other, the second-year stock and an elongated office festooned with the accolades that they've won, with an open tasting bar next door.

By autumn 1993, the range had grown to some 20 different wines, including Black Muscat, Pinot Noir, Merlot and "port". The Rosenblum flagships are undoubtedly the Zinfandels, which are some of California's best. Their sole Rhône representative is a Petite Syrah, made from the grapes of three different dry-farmed vineyards: 60 acres near Calistoga and two more west of St Helena, ranging in vine-age from 60 to 90-plus and cropping at 2–2.5 tons/acre.

The grapes are deliberately vinified to produce soft tannins – without extracting the massive colour or structure that might be expected from such ancient vines; wines showing lighter tones which emphasize elegance – "lovely young, for game dishes in the winter round the fireplace, when the fog comes". These qualities (not the fog) are delivered by means of a long maceration to develop softer long-chain tannins instead of the harsher, short-chain variety which appear during the earlier phase of fermentation. The final wine contains a dollop of Zinfandel, Carignan or Cabernet Sauvignon (the rules allow up to 25% in a varietal-designated wine).

Kent leads a double life – running a successful veterinary practice in Alameda in addition to the winery, whose daily work is delegated to a general and an office manager. He skis and dives for the delicious abalone in his spare time. Quality control is Kathy's reponsibility – "she only drinks red wine – the bigger, the better", he explains. These wines are good, if somewhat individual, and in a lighter, silkier style.

VARIETY	VINEYARD	DETAILS	AREA
PETITE SYRAH	PALLISADES (CALISTOGA)	60+ year old vines	40.00
PETITE SYRAH	KENEFICK (CALISTOGA)	80–85 year old vines	20.00
PETITE SYRAH	ST. GEORGE/CAKEBREAD	90+ year old vines	2.00
		TOTAL (acres):	62.00

SANTINO

Santino, at the heart of the pastoral Shenandoah valley, in Amador County, was founded in 1979 by Joseph Schweitzer, a third-generation Alsatian maltster from San Francisco, his daughter Nancy and her husband, Matt Santino.

Although Schweitzer owns the winery, the driving force behind its success has been its talented winemaker, Scott Harvey. The son of a teacher, he was sent to Bad Durkheim in Germany in 1972 as an exchange student and, after a harvest in Amador in 1974, went back to Neustadt in the Rheinpfalz to compress a two-year degree into one before returning to Amador to build Santino.

Scott Harvey is a clear-headed and logical man, with an experimental turn of mind. Dedicated to Amador County, he believes it capable of producing top-class wines – especially from Mourvèdre, Barbera, Zinfandel and Syrah – but stresses the importance of choosing the right vine for the particular soil type and climate – a matter that has not generally received sufficient attention.

The climate here is warmer than in neighbouring Fiddletown; somewhere between high Region III and Region IV in heat summation. Hot convected air rises from the Sacramento Valley during the day, while at night colder air from the Sierra funnels in beneath this warm layer. This "hot day – cool night" regime creates a high solids:liquid ratio, shrivelling the red berries which need precise picking and careful handling to avoid jamminess in the wine.

Syrah, Barbera and Zinfandel do particularly well here especially when planted on the granitic, sandy loams of the Sierra foothills. Scott makes yardstick examples of each, plus a cuvée of Zinfandel from ten acres of magnificent 120-year-old vines (the Grandfather vineyard) near the winery, which he recently bought for himself. On the completion of the deal, the banker involved enquired when he intended to grub up all those old vines and plant nice new ones.

Other notable Santino wines include a late-harvest Zinfandel and Riesling, a Muscat Canelli, varietals from Barbera and Orange Muscat, a Zinfandel/Syrah blend and a "Vintage Port", based on traditional port varieties – the result of Kevin Hamel's arrival in 1987 fresh from a spell at Cockburn in Oporto. Rhône varieties are represented by a Viognier, a Syrah and Satyricon: a blend of Grenache, Mourvèdre, Syrah, Carignan and Cinsaut.

The Viognier first appeared in 1992, from contracted vineyards cropped at three tons per acre. The following year Scott tried some skin contact, by inverting the press and crushing through the drain-holes; fermentation started in stainless-steel and finished in new and older French oak with *bâtonnage;* thereafter, six months in cask and filtration before bottling.

Satyricon takes it name from a novel by Petronius extolling the virtues of eating and drinking, and from Fellini's film: "I used to drop acid and watch this film", Scott admits, which may partly account for the wine's risqué label, showing a muscular, tanned, Satyr and an eager blonde clearly on the verge of ecstasy; "I wanted a label that says Yes!" He managed to obtain approval only by submitting a rather blurred fax copy to the omnipotent BATF. The wine is supple and user-friendly, with plenty of character; but it lacks the depth and complexity of the Syrah cuvée, which is better focused and altogether more serious.

Schweitzer has decided to sell Santino, so Scott Harvey has founded his own company, Renwood, to cope with that eventuality. His aim is to buy as much "First Growth" vineyard – old plots of Syrah and Zinfandel – as he can for his three children. It surprises him how slow others have been to latch on, as opportunities become ever scarcer.

Beneath his 1860s gold-rush house, a

magnificent private cellar reflects Scott's eclectic wine interests – Germany, Tuscany and Piedmont share racks with the Rhône and old Bordeaux. He restores old cars, hikes, fishes and skis – trading wine for lift tickets. Here is a contented *vigneron* with the air of someone who has worked out what he wants from life and is well on the way to achieving it.

VARIETY	VINEYARD	DETAILS	AREA
GRENACHE	LOMIS, PLACER, (Sierra foothills)	80+ yr old vines; 2 tons/acre	3.00
GRENACHE	FIDDLETOWN	5 yr old vines	2.00
SYRAH	AMADOR (several sources)	10 yr old vines	10.00
MOURVEDRE	FIDDLETOWN	5 yr old vines; 3 tons/acre	5.00
CINSAUT	FIDDLETOWN	5 yr old vines; 3 tons/acre	1.00
VIOGNIER	SHENANDOAH	Planted 1989	6.00
		TOTAL (acres):	27.00

SEAN THACKREY

Among the strongly individual (some might say acceptably eccentric) winemakers which form California's Rhône brigade, Sean Thackrey is one of the more remarkable. A shock-haired San Francisco art dealer, with an infectuously manic laugh and considerable charm, he operates a warehouse winery from his quiet, book-lined house on the peninsula at Bolinas, north of Los Angeles.

The unconventional layout comprises a diverse cluster of outbuildings – sheds, lean-tos etc – at the back of the house, interspersed with a variety of winemaking paraphernalia. Most of the equipment, including the press, wooden vats and sundry piles of blackened casks are left out in the open. Pipes trail everywhere and blue tarpaulins cover vats and barrels while a horizontal fermenter luxuriates cocooned in an electric blanket. All of which gives the place the appearance of a cosy, second-hand clearance yard – a far cry from the pristine high-tech of most Californian wineries. No matter: the wines are wonderful.

Sean disclaims any connection with the Rhône Ranger movement – "I'm a native Californian, just interested in old vines". He is distinctly not interested in Cabernet Sauvignon, which he believes has too limited a range of expression, and doesn't want to become a "pious imitator" of Latour, or of anything else.

Sean owns no land, but buys in fruit wherever he finds something of acceptable quality, which means old vines and almost uneconomically low yields. This makes sourcing difficult: "I try to find vineyards (and wine) which accord with my philosophy", which, Sean cryptically states, is to "make the wine from the inside out" – in other words, vinifying fruit without any preconception of the end product.

Not owning vines also means living at the behest of your grape-growers. In 1986 Sean found two tons of "fine old Syrah"

Winemaker and art-dealer, Sean Thackrey.

behind Mustard's restaurant in Oakville: "these grapes worked perfectly with my style of winemaking" and the wine sold well. Then, in 1991, a wealthy Napa winery owner who was an admirer of Sean's wines sought out the vineyard's owner and bought it, thus depriving Sean of his fruit. Universal boredom with Cabernet and Chardonnay at the upper-middle level – the staples of many Napa wineries – has fuelled a desperate search for other varieties, making those relying on gentleman's agreements for fruit particularly vulnerable.

Apart from being a specialist dealer in 19th-century European photography, posters and art, Sean has a strong interest in astrology which inspires his wines. So far there are five:

– Sirius, a Petite Sirah from the four-acre 1890 Marston vineyard on Spring Mountain, yielding 0.5 tons/acre; "nectar of the Gods", says Sean. However, he had to take some Grenache, a variety he dislikes, to get the Petite Sirah;

– Orion, a Syrah formerly from the Mustard vineyard but, since 1993, sourced from McDowell Valley Vineyards;

– Taurus, a Mourvèdre from the 1905 five-acre Rossi vineyard at St Helena. This used to come from Cline in Oakley, but

"getting the fruit picked right" became problematical – another difficulty for anyone buying grapes – leading Sean to look elsewhere.

– A Viognier, as yet unnamed, first made "for fun" in 1993 from McDowell fruit, enough for one cask. Sean had contracted for two tons, but only received 600 pounds;

– Finally, Pleiades, a relatively supple blend which Sean colourfully describes as "the chef's special for the year – whatever intrigues me from what is around; if nothing interests me, I don't issue it".

These wines are beautifully crafted, showing an instinctive feel for extracting the individual qualities from each lot of fruit. As one might expect, there are no rules or recipes, decisions are simply made on the fly. Sean compares himself to a master chef: "give me a bit of salmon, then I'll tell you how to cook it".

Critics make much of the apparently jumbled cellar arrangements – but, once explained, these are both logical and functional. "'If it ain't busted, don't fix it'", Sean argues; a perfectly reasonable viewpoint, especially given the quality of his wines.

However, vinifying in the open air has its drawbacks: one year, seven tons of fruit in small bins grew mould overnight, so Sean co-opted a crew of ten with scissors to cut it out. On another occasion, an incomplete tarpaulin cover led to the must being covered with a curious striped yellow blanket; Sean scraped off the wasps and carried on.

The broad guidelines of the red vinification consist of crushing and more or less de-stemming, 60 grammes per ton of metabisulphite to kill spoilage lacto-bacteria, then cold maceration "for as long as it takes", followed by yeasting and fermentation without cooling (ie at up to 95°F).

The press wine, extracted by an old, lopsided vertical press which reposes drunkenly on three out of the required four iron wheels, is kept separate to retain its "lovely aromas", which are lost if it is blended back. Sean's dislike of fining restricts it to the more tannic press wine; fresh egg-whites are used, the yolks going to the local raccoon population.

The wines remain in cask, with the minimum manipulation, for 18–48 months. Decisions on which barrels will contribute to the blend of any one varietal are taken over a year or so. A couple of trial samples are bottled and tasted, and the process is then repeated once or twice more before the final *assemblage* is arrived at.

New oak is used judiciously – "as a spice"; in Sean's view it easily becomes intrusive, particularly for Grenache which he feels is ruined by oak. With more new wood than he needs, there is room for experimentation.

This is one of those estates where an idiosyncratic appearance belies its class. You know from the first sniff that there is excitement here and that quality, not security, is master. These are magnificent, highly individual wines from which every theory-soaked winemaker and rule-bound official should taste, and learn.

SIERRA VISTA

High in the Sierra foothills, between Lake Tahoe and Sacramento in El Dorado County, lies Sierra Vista. Although only nine of their 43 acres are planted with Rhône varieties, John and Barbara MacCready are committed to them and are convinced that El Dorado (an evocation of the gold rush era, when more wine was produced here than in any other part of California) is the place to produce them.

Despite the loaded shotgun standing in a corner of the living room, this is a homely, friendly family. Their attractive wooden house, deep in the woods, has stunning views of the distant Sierra (which adorn their labels). While the enterprise grew John, an electrical engineer by training, continued to teach while Barbara, a forceful woman, a trained statistician and computer expert, "pruned, planted, trained vines and even moved irrigation lines", in addition to her activities as "book-keeper, marketing manager, retail sales room manager and part-time crush crew".

She recalls that at first the Mexican labourers, reluctant to take orders from a woman, did the exact opposite of what she asked. Frustrated, she resorted to reversing the orders to ensure that the work was done satisfactorily. John soon became full-time, describing his role as "winemaker, vineyard manager, tractor driver, delivery boy, fork-lift operator and design and maintenance engineer".

Research confirmed their belief that they had similar growing conditions to the Rhône – "from Côte-Rôtie to Châteauneuf-du-Pape"; this continues to influence their strategy. From their first vintage – 1,200 cases made from bought grapes in 1977 – to the current 12,000 cases, much of it from their own vines, vineyards and skills have developed and adapted. Next, Marsanne and Roussanne plantings are planned to follow an experimental acre of Viognier, as cuttings become available.

Although the terrain varies from steep hillsides to ridge tops, with soils ranging from "sandy decomposed granite to very rocky red volcanic ash with clay, loam and sand", all Sierra Vista vines are at high altitude (2,400–2,900 feet). Foliage management is therefore essential to maximize leaf and bunch exposure, and to control vine vigour in relatively deep soils. Trials have been made with T-trellis (unsuitable), quadrilaterals and, more recently, with Geneva Double Curtain and vertical shoot positioning.

Rootstock selection and increased plant density to reduce the number of Syrah bunches per vine, are also used to limit excess vigour; however, for the present, they are stuck with UC Davis' original 12ft row spacing and vines which are all on their own roots.

The Macreadys attribute much of the finesse in their wines to "air drainage", whereby hot daytime air is regularly replaced by cooler nightime air. Leaving the house late, a sharp drop in ambient temperature is evident as the road falls away, past the winery. The soft tannins produced by this long, even ripening leads John to remark that "our vineyard has a velvet glove on it".

There are several Rhône-style *cuvées*: a straight Syrah, matured hitherto in old French oak, with a touch of new wood under consideration (a Reserve Syrah was released in 1989, from bunches hand-selected by John before the picking team was let loose); Fleur de Montagne is a Grenache, Cinsaut and Mourvèdre blend, with an additional shot of Cabernet and Zinfandel "for a touch of California" (there's also a Reserve version).

Viognier, from grafting on ten-year-old vines, appeared in 1992, fermented in old French oak with lees stirring "whenever I get round to it", and malolactic or not "depending on the taste". John is concerned to keep the "delicate floral qualities" of the grape yet to add structure without the wood dominating. The 1992, tasted in 1993, was a fine, rich, yet subtle expression of the variety. John is contemplating adding a dab of Viognier to his Syrah; the Rhône is clearly never far away from this excellent range.

VARIETY	VINEYARD	DETAILS	AREA
SYRAH	SIERRA VISTA ESTATE	13 yr vines on volcanic ash.	3.00
SYRAH	HERBERT VINEYARD ESTATE	6 yr vines on decomposed granite.	2.00
GRENACHE	REEVES VINEYARD	5 yr vines on volcanic ash	3.00
VIOGNIER	SIERRA VISTA ESTATE	5 yr vines on volcanic ash	1.00
CINSAUT	REEVES VINEYARD	5 yr vines on volcanic ash	0.25
		TOTAL (acres):	9.25

TABLAS CREEK VINEYARD

It is unusual to discuss an estate which has yet to produce any wine. However the setting up of Tablas Creek, dedicated largely to Rhône varieties, by François and Jean-Pierre Perrin of Château de Beaucastel (qv) is a development which will have forcible impact on the progress of these grapes in the United States.

A joint venture by the Perrins and their long-time US agent and friend, Robert Haas, had been under discussion since 1971. They were convinced that California, having more in common with the Rhône than with Bordeaux or Burgundy, was eminently suitable for Châteauneuf varieties in particular and were surprised at the lack of plantings.

By 1987, all parties were ready to begin the project in earnest, and started searching for land which mirrored the climate (plus some cooling ocean influence) and the high pH soil-type of Beaucastel. The quest, which took them as far north as El Dorado and Nevada, and south to Santa Barbara, was long and frustrating, since basic limestone soils are rare in California. Finally, when (says John Munch, who was helping them), François and Jean-Pierre were about to throw in the towel, they heard from

Randall Grahm of a 120-acre vineyard at Tablas Creek, just west of Paso Robles, which matched the specification. Here, at an elevation of 1,300 feet, the soils are predominantly shallow rocky limestone (pH 7.9–8.4) and the climate, though warmer than Beaucastel, is moderated by cool evening Pacific air. The deal was struck in 1990, with Robert Haas and the Perrins each holding 35% of the equity and various friends the remaining 30%.

The next hurdle was to establish a nursery for propagating plants for the vineyard. The Perrins wanted to use Beaucastel bud-wood, enabling them to isolate the influence of *terroir* from that of clone or rootstock. UC Davis refused to accept Beaucastel cuttings, which were finally sent to the Geneva Research Station in New York for virus indexing. These were cleared in 1993 and taken to Tablas' new high-tech greenhouses for · propagation. In 1993 ten acres were planted from US material; thereafter the French grafts were used. The goal is 20

acres planted by 1996, with the first commercial wine around the year 2,000 (not until 65% of the blend is from the French vines). Selling authentic, virus-free, Rhône grafts commercially – for which there is a high demand – will help finance the enterprise. The eventual aim is 90 acres of vines to feed a new gravity-flow winery, and 15 acres of nursery.

As at Beaucastel, farming is organic – cultivation and disc-ploughing between rows and hand-hoeing between the vines, eschewing chemical fertilizers, systemic herbicides and pesticides.

The aims of this joint-venture are specific: i) to prove that world-class wine can be made in California from Rhône varieties (hardly contentious, one would have thought); ii) to demonstrate that blends work – both that the whole transcends any of its constituents and also that non-varietal wines can achieve acceptability in a market besotted by varietals (more difficult); iii) to promote Rhône wines as "great wines"; and iv) to

use the Perrins' expertise and methods to make fine Californian red and white wine – but emphatically not Californian Châteauneuf. Francois Perrin is convinced that these aims are achievable – "we have a reputation in the US which is not too bad", he explains, with uncharacteristic Gallic understatement.

The fledgling nursery is being run by Dick Hoenisch, with help from John Munch whose Adelaida Cellars (qv) are almost next door to Tablas. For the US's Rhône brigade, the arrival of the Perrins at Paso Robles is an event of seminal importance. It will be fascinating to see what emerges – not only the taste of the newly-christened "Castel Tablas" wines, but also how this enterprise influences growers elsewhere, many busy replanting their phylloxera-ridden vineyards.

Security has been well taken care of: any unscrupulous Rhône-gnomes hoping to help themselves to cuttings beware – there is a cougar living wild at Tablas, who is unlikely to be vegetarian.

DOMAINE DE LA TERRE ROUGE

Bill Eastin was one of the original Rhône Rangers. In 1978 he left a job in wine production elsewhere and established the Solano Cellars in Albany, a thriving wine shop and bistro, to sell "artisan" California wine. When expansion into retailing European wine led Bill to visit the Rhône; he was hooked. In 1994, Solano was sold and the Domaine de la Terre Rouge opened in Plymouth, in Amador's Shenandoah Valley.

In 1983 Bill bought a summer home in Fiddletown, also in Amador County, and soon realized that, although the wines from these Sierra Foothills were good – even bordering on world-class – "the stakes could be raised" to add the finesse which he often found lacking. Both the soils (a mixture of stone and schistous decomposed granite) and the warm Mediterranean climate were ideal.

Inspired by Rhône varieties, he sought out old plantings to buy fruit for his first wine: a blend of 1985 and 1986, released in 1986 to much praise. In time he persuaded growers ingrained, thanks to payment by tonnage, to over-production, to reduce yields to around two or three tons per acre (28 hl/ha).

He also managed to get one Fiddletown farmer to graft eight acres of Sauvignon Blanc to Syrah, two clones of Grenache, Mourvèdre and Cinsaut. This vineyard is now on a ten-year lease and farmed to Bill's specifications – which means severe pruning, no irrigation and a

green pruning which is carried out just after *veraison*.

Ripeness and pH are major factors in deciding when to pick – but a wine's balance, in Bill's view, comes primarily from not over-cropping – "the main problem of Rhône varietal growers". Grenache, especially, needs ripeness for flavour and colour, so it is picked at 25–25.5 Brix, a degree or so above the rest, and fermented in *inox*, rather than in the large picking bins which he uses for Syrah; stainless steel gets hotter and so extracts more.

Winemaking is flexible – more or less crushed fruit, more or fewer stems, perhaps a cold maceration unsulphured (eg the 1993 Grenache) and selected or indigenous yeasts, depending on the variety and quality of raw material. Machine contact is minimized by hand-shovelling the pulp from the fermenting bins and fork-lifting it into the press. The goal is that elusive balance which allows early consumption but does not stunt growth. Bill is critical of excessive tannins in Amador wines, which stifle finesse. His

method is to work more on extraction at the start of fermentation, rather than in alcoholic solution later on.

Burgundy has greatly influenced Bill's wine philosophy; although the local climate is not right for Pinot Noir, the aromatic complexity, mouthfeel, texture, middle-palate and length found in fine Burgundy are qualities which clearly exercise his thinking.

To maximize complexity, each variety is vinified separately, in small batch lots and fine lees are retained in cask for ageing. Fermentations are carefully managed, with punching-down preferred to pumping over. The press wine is blended back before the wine goes to cask – no new wood: rather 60 gallon François Frères' French oak casks from Pinot producers in Oregon. Bill cites Michel Lafarge in Volnay for his policy of a long malolactic fermentation – something of a risk, but "if you can stretch the malolactic out till April or May, it contributes to complexity".

In the late summer the blend is composed for the 750–1,200 cases of the domaine's flagship *cuvée*, Terre Rouge, before returning to cask until the following spring when it is bottled

VARIETY	VINEYARD	DETAILS	AREA
GRENACHE	PLACER COUNTY	Tattersfield vineyard; 60+ yrs. old	4
SYRAH	AMADOR COUNTY	De Stephano vineyard; 15 yrs old	5.00
SYRAH, GRENACHE, CINSAUT, MOURVEDRE	AMADOR, FIDDLETOWN	Oleta vineyard; 25 yrs. old	8.00
		TOTAL (acres):	17.00

unfined and unfiltered. First released in 1985, Terre Rouge consists of varying proportions of Grenache, Mourvèdre, Syrah and Cinsaut – with care to ensure that Syrah doesn't dominate. Bill recognizes a problem with consumers conditioned through the 1960s to believe that single varietals are better than blends: "now the problem is to educate people that what matters is the taste". For

those who baulk at the thought of a blend, there are 100–250 cases of Amador County Syrah, from 15-year-old vines, as well as a splendid "Provençale-style" Vin Gris Rosé, from 80-year-old Zinfandel vines. Plantings of Viognier, Marsanne and Roussanne are *en projet*.

Bill's wife, Jane, is a chef, which accounts in part for his emphasis on finesse. His wines are not fashioned in

the blockbuster mould, but in a lighter style which evoke a more elegant Châteauneuf or the Côte d'Or. However, a characteristic lightness of tone does not exclude a good concentration of fruit or abundant finesse. Meanwhile, Solano Cellars provides a retail outlet for the estate's wines – and, incidentally, an excellent local source of top-class, domaine-bottled Burgundy.

ZACA MESA

Zaca Mesa is a 1,500-acre estate in Santa Barbara's Santa Ynez Valley, a selected 215 of which are planted with a variety of grapes, including 18 acres of Syrah. It was established in 1972 by a property developer, John Cushman, who bought the land with some associates. He now owns it outright and, with his other partners, has added a further 630 acres of vines at the Sierra Madre Ranch in the Santa Maria Valley.

The home ranch has a mid-Region II heat summation; Sierra Madre, high Region I to low Region II. The Santa Barbara vines, in particular, benefit from a transverse mountain range running east/west (the usual orientation is north/south), which creates a natural corridor down which cool afternoon and evening breezes reach the vineyards. This is considered to add balance and to enhance varietal characteristics.

Zaca Mesa has seen a series of talented young "maverick" winemakers – including Bob Lindquist and Jim Clenenden – pass through on their way to building their own estates and reputations. In February 1993 Dan Gehrs, who founded and managed Congress Springs Vineyards, became the latest incumbent.

Apart from Syrah, Zaca Mesa's Rhône contributions include a Viognier and a Roussanne (the first appearance of both was 1993), a Syrah/Viognier blend, a Grenache and "Cuvée Z" – a blend of Grenache, Mourvèdre and Syrah.

Dan Gehr's arrival has triggered considerable change – partly to combat a noticeable stemminess in earlier vintages which caused them to add 10% Musque Chardonnay to the 1991 Syrah *cuvée*. In particular, he has replaced the old French de-stemmer/crusher with a new Amos de-stemmer and Kiesel pump.

Yields have been reduced, with severe pruning – down to a single bud per spur for Syrah, Mourvèdre and Grenache – plus further green pruning, where necessary. In the cellar, wines from these varieties will be aged only in 5- to 10-year

Helicopter drawing water from Zaca Mesa's Chapel Dam to fight bush-fires.

French oak casks that have been broken in with Chardonnay.

The heart of Zaca Mesa's expanding Rhône programme are the Chapel and Misty Ridge vineyards (Misty Ridge contains the oldest plot of Syrah in Santa Barbara – planted in 1982 from Estrella River bud-wood). In the middle of the Chapel vineyard is a large reservoir – which is regularly used as a water-source by the helicopters that fight the area's frequent bush-fires.

Jeff Maiken, Zaca Mesa's hard-working managing director, is determined to take

the estate into the first division. On past performance, the wines are good, but no better. However, early samples of Dan Gehr's first vintage, 1993, suggest a significant improvement which will be monitored with interest.

It will also be fascinating to follow the results of an invitation which has been extended by the estate to each of three of its former winemakers: to come and make a single wine from Zaca Mesa plots they have selected – with *carte blanche* in vineyard and cellar. This is undoubtedly a property to watch.

VARIETY	VINEYARD	AREA
SYRAH	CHAPEL VINEYARD	4.06
SYRAH	MISTY RIDGE VINEYARD	13.88
GRENACHE	CHAPEL VINEYARD	5.00
MOURVEDRE	CHAPEL VINEYARD	3.00
VIOGNIER	CHAPEL VINEYARD	2.04
ROUSSANNE	CHAPEL VINEYARD	1.10
CINSAUT	CHAPEL VINEYARD	0.05
	TOTAL (acres):	29.13

AUSTRALIA

Known internationally for their well-priced, attractive reds and whites, Australia's winemakers are increasingly discovering that, treated as a noble grape, Shiraz is capable of great things. Now, across the continent, a nucleus of Rhône aficianados are producing some world-class wines. Small quantities meant that very little was exported, but this is changing as the impetus grows.

Vines and Salvation Jane – an attractive if irksome weed
– in the Barossa Valley.

AUSTRALIA

There are many excellent overviews of the development and present condition of Australian viticulture and winemaking (Halliday, 1991; Johnson, 1994; Combe and Dry, ed 1992). This brief introduction is not designed to supplement them, but to highlight trends and factors that particularly concern Shiraz (the local name for Syrah), Australia's great premium red grape, and to a lesser extent, Grenache and Mataro (Mourvèdre). These trends must themselves be set against Australia's own background as a winemaking nation for two centuries, but not – until the late 1960s – to any significant extent a wine-drinking nation.

Since the 1860s, Shiraz has been the workhorse of the Australian wine industry and, at around 15,350 acres, remains its most extensively-planted variety. It established the reputation of the Barossa and Hunter Valleys and of Coonawarra, and is now doing great things for Victoria and the Lower Great Southern region of Western Australia.

Until comparatively recently however, its natural vigour and propensity for high yields cast Shiraz as an invaluable component of satisfying, but rarely inspiring, blends. Even this humble role was threatened when Pinot Noir and Cabernet Sauvignon became fashionable in the 1970s and 1980s and a government-sponsored vine-pull scheme in 1986 saw much Shiraz uprooted, especially old

— WARNING. —
EMPLOYEES ARE WARNED AGAINST ENTERING ANY TANK OR VAT WITHOUT FIRST TAKING PROPER PRECAUTIONS AGAINST FOUL AIR AND GAS. PRECAUTIONS ARE AS FOLLOWS, A LIGHTED CANDLE MUST BE LOWERED TO BOTTOM OF TANK OR PLACED IN VAT. A LIGHTED CANDLE MUST BE CARRIED BY YOU ON ENTERING ANY TANK OR VAT, IF THE CANDLE REFUSES TO BURN, YOU ARE FORBIDDEN TO ENTER OR STAY IN THE SAID CONTAINERS.   BY ORDER BESTS WINES PTY LTD.

You have been warned!

plantings, in mixed blocks, whose low yields were then seen as a commercial liability rather than a resource of superlative quality. During that period, many growers left the industry altogether.

Shiraz' proven track-record in blends reinforced its claim to be noticed – Penfolds and Bests produced excellent Shiraz-Mataro bottlings in the 1960s (Best's version labelled Shiraz-Esparte), but these gave way to Cabernet-based wines and Shiraz sank low. One Barossa winemaker recalls using carbon to strip Shiraz of colour for an acceptable sparkling wine base. It also suffered from the "poor cousin" effect: irrespective of maturity, Shiraz was harvested after "better" grapes had been picked, only vinified when the winemaker had time to spare, got the second-best wood and less general attention.

Not surprisingly, consumers and winemakers alike regarded it as incapable of anything other than *ordinaire*. It took until the mid-1970s before people at last began to appreciate its true potential – and indeed to realise that careful siting and sympathetic handling are needed to extract Shiraz' latent riches.

SHIRAZ REAPPRAISED

Fortunately, many of the well-known estates – including Penfolds, Wynns, Lindemans, Brown Bros, McWilliams, Bests, Tyrells, Wendouree and Seppelts – maintained a continuing commitment to Shiraz. Old vintages from legendary winemakers such as Max Schubert, Colin Preece and Maurice O'Shea are a remarkable testament to the quality of Shiraz being produced during these doldrum years. The derision at early vintages of Penfold's Grange Hermitage (qv) further illustrates the low esteem in which Shiraz was held in the 1950s and 1960s, even among sophisticated consumers.

With the massive increase in worldwide demand for Australian wine in the 1980s, brought about by improved quality and a favourable exchange rate, came replanting. Nurseries, lacking sufficient virus-free Cabernet stock, found that Shiraz was available. Red wine sales boomed, having overtaken white in 1974, and remained ahead into the 1990s. Though far less well-known as a variety than Cabernet, Shiraz started to be appreciated again, both solo and as the dominant partner in blends. This renaissance is attributable to several factors: first, the Australian home

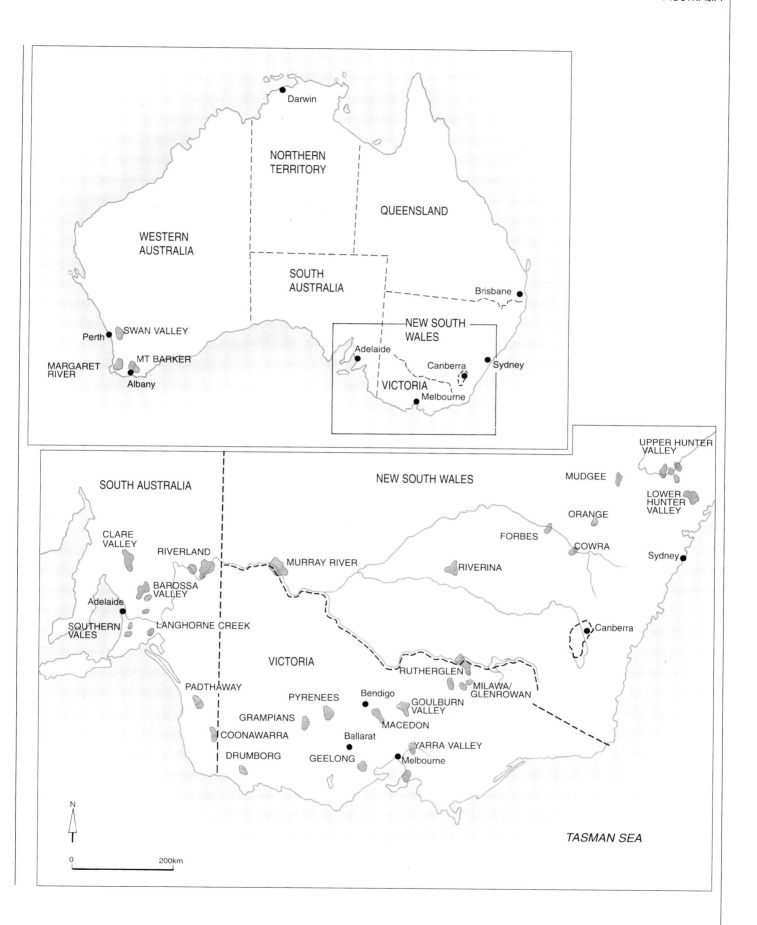

market had matured over the last generation, and with the desire for better quality came the realisation that, given patience, a tough, sometimes brutal, young Shiraz will often turn into something infinitely more agreeable. This encouraged winemakers to shift their focus from early-drinking styles towards *vins de garde* – and this is Shiraz' real strength.

Second, fickle fashion (mainly Press-driven) changed direction. In the early 1980s, Australian commentators were criticising many Shiraz as "too big" and lacking in elegance. Now, these same people are saying "we're scared because, in the quest for elegance, Australian wines are losing their richness and the stamp of longevity which made them great". In such an unpredictable climate, producers are wise to ignore the critics altogether; bending to vacillating critical whim is a sure route to extinction.

Third, and most important, the emergence of small wineries throughout the country, owned by people entirely dedicated to quality and with the comparative international wine knowledge and tasting experience to match, created a base of superb Shiraz-making, reflecting regional identities – a magnificent resource which continues to increase and evolve. Many of these estates are profiled in the pages which follow.

Two essentially Australian Shiraz styles which have enjoyed different fortunes in the last 20 years are Sparkling Shiraz, which is experiencing a small, but deserved, boom and Shiraz- (and Cabernet-) based "Vintage Port", which, with most other fortified wines, is sadly in decline. Both merit serious, unprejudiced attention.

Other Rhône varieties have (rather surprisingly) fared less well in modern Australia. Viognier appears in small patches – notably in Victoria's Goulburn Valley at Mitchelton and Château Tahbilk, where plantings will come on stream in the next few years; at Heggies in South Australia and Elgee Park in the Mornington Peninsula.

Marsanne is virtually confined to Victoria – at Goulburn and Yerinberg, where it performs well. Mataro also appears sporadically (around 1,580 acres now), adding structure to blends, with conspicuous success at Wendouree in the Clare Valley – a striking contrast to its place as the fourth most important Australian red wine grape in the 1980s.

The Grenache has suffered a similar fall from grace since peaking at 17,500 acres in the early 1970s, then second only in importance to Shiraz. It still retains a significant presence (4,830 acres) but is generally seen as making weak, poorly-coloured wine and it is now mainly confined

to South Australia, where it is either vinified as rosé or blended away with Shiraz. Both of these red varieties remain in decline, though some adventurous estates are ·testing the water with the whites.

The late 1980s and 1990s have been exciting times for the rehabilitated Shiraz. Varietal bottlings have appeared as premium wines from many estates, as viticulturalists and winemakers learn how best to grow and vinify it. Exposure to Rhône wines, in both directions, has also speeded up progress with Shiraz: winemakers are travelling more and more to visit the Rhône's great vineyards and producers; meanwhile importers are bringing top-class Rhônes to Australian consumers who then become interested in indigenous Shiraz.

However, the wine industry has been slow to shake off its perception of Shiraz as an under-Aus $10 wine making it economically difficult for quality producers to sell low-yield products at Aus$20 or $30 – rather as if a Côte-Rôtie grower was stuck with Côtes du Rhône pricing. This boomerangs on the wines, since at artifically low prices estates do not have the resources for new wood (Aus $900 per cask for French oak) or long maturation. Fortunately, in these respects, things are steadily improving.

REGIONS AND STYLES

Putting Shiraz into the premium quality (and price) bracket has revived interest in regional styles. In the Hunter Valley the traditional earthy, rich, heavily-extracted and leathery Shiraz, exemplified by Tyrell's, Lindeman's classic releases and McWilliams, which needs long ageing to come into its own, is fine in its own way – although hitherto little more than a niche market curiosity. The style has been adapted and refined, by such as Iain Riggs at Brokenwood, into something of international top quality. This has sparked a concomitant debate on the use of new and old wood, and how best to vinify to allow the fruit to express itself.

In the Barossa Valley, a wave of fine younger wine-makers has given the established berryish, briary, black fruit style a thorough shaking, re-defining quality and re-focusing some larger firms on the Valley's Shiraz potential, from which they had temporarily strayed in search of modish "cool-climate" flavours.

In the Clare Valley, new and long-established wineries have contributed to a growing reputation, with magnificent offerings from Tim Adams, Jim Barry and Wendouree – another region of considerable promise, with scope for

Dusk over the Clare Valley.

expansion. Here the wines have great depth and intensity of pure fruit, and the natural structure for longevity.

In Coonawarra, whose Shiraz stagnated in the doldrums during the 1970s, it took the five-star 1986 vintage to put it back on the map. Fierce arguments about where true Coonawarra begins and ends – the black soil versus Terra Rossa battle – have not dimmed enthusiasm, and a succession of fine wines has kept its profile high. Richness and elegance typify Coonawarra Shiraz, and make the best comparable to anything else Australia can produce. There are also promising results from the comparatively new area of Padthaway, where Penfolds, Lindemans and Seppelts jointly own 350 acres of Shiraz.

McLaren Vale, south-east of Adelaide, is also an important Shiraz-producing region. However, much of the fruit is bought by outside winemakers, who use its firm, silky qualities as an useful addition to blends, and relatively little of real class is bottled at source. Exceptions are Woodstock, Ingoldby, Ryecroft (owned by Rosemount), with occasional flashes of excellence from Chester Osborn at d'Arenberg, although the record is somewhat patchy. He makes a Shiraz/Grenache blend –

labelled "d'Arry's Original Burgundy" – and a splendidly intense, peppery, spicy "Ironstone Pressings" from about half Grenache and one-quarter each Shiraz and Cabernet Sauvignon, from 80- to 100-year-old vines. Mark Lloyd at Coriole is making increasingly impressive wine, especially the Lloyd Reserve Shiraz, from 1920s vines; his 1990 is particularly fine.

Geoff Merrill at Mount Hurtle produces a South Australian Shiraz, a Mount Hurtle Shiraz (these include some 12% of Cabernet Sauvignon) and a McLaren Vale Grenache at his attractive, gravity-fed winery at Reynella, near Adelaide. The style is soft, open and fruity; pleasant enough, but often lacking real concentration. Recent vintages, especially the 1991 Mount Hurtle Shiraz, seem to be improving. However, Geoff's Italian winemaking activities seem to be distracting him from his home base, and the wines, while invariably sound, are rarely top-quality. His flamboyance makes him a media favourite; meanwhile underneath all the extroversion there is a genuine, modest man, who admits that his Shiraz needs further work.

In Victoria, considerable progress has been made across the state – especially in the Pyrenees, at Heathcote and in

Cover crops are often sown between the vine rows as here, sprinkled with spring flowers, at Bannockburn.

the Yarra Valley — where newly-established wineries combined with thoughtful winemaking have produced some spectacular results. However an over-zealous quest for a cool, peppery Shiraz, wrongly seen as being typically Rhône, has resulted in many an awkward, hollow wine, lacking in flesh and balance. Hopefully this exaggerated style is on the way out. At Great Western, a tradition of quality Shiraz continues, with excellent wines being made from low-yielding, dry-farmed old vines.

Western Australia's Shiraz industry is in its infancy — especially in the Margaret River and Lower Great Southern, around Frankland River and Mount Barker. The main problem here seems to be geographical remoteness, which puts the region somewhat out of the mainstream of Australian wine culture. However, there are patches of excellence and a strong desire to excel. Styles are varied and still evolving.

Most Australian Shiraz appears as part of a blend — commonly with Cabernet Sauvignon — the dominant partner being indicated by the first-named grape (ie Cabernet-Shiraz or Shiraz-Cabernet). However the re-emergence of regional identities has put the widespread traditional practice of blending components from different regions somewhat into the shade, especially at the top level. Firms whose reputation has been built on this tradition

continue to blend, with conspicuous success, especially at lower price levels where consistency of style is what markets value most. Penfolds is the supreme example of this philosophy at all quality levels, and its Grange remains Australia's finest Shiraz. However, its supremacy is under threat from some of the estates profiled here. Smaller, newer wineries often prefer to promote their individuality to a market clearly interested in regional identity, especially when coupled with estate bottling and a vineyard designation. This trend is likely to continue as consumer awareness of regional styles increases.

RESEARCH AND RESULTS

On another front, a continuing and impressive effort at Adelaide's Wine Research Institute and elsewhere, has produced much worthwhile material to help the quality-conscious *vigneron*. In the vineyard, the development of better clonal material has reduced virus diseases and improved consistency of yields. In the 1970s, when clones were introduced, high yield was the main selection criterion. Now, wine quality is a primordial factor. Recent research has established that differences in wines from different Shiraz clones are negligible (in sharp contrast to Pinot Noir). The successful Penfolds' clone and the Barossa "Clone 12" are still the most strongly favoured. These improvements, together with more sophisticated site-selection, have meant better all-round quality.

A decade ago, tradition was almost the sole determinant of planting configuration. Now, inspired by the controversial viticulturalist Dr Richard Smart, growers are thinking and talking much more of "canopy management" and "shoot positioning", as means to increasing yields and quality. Smart — a genial but forceful New Zealander — believes that it is perfectly possible to crop ten tonnes per acre and still make top quality wine — anathema to those brought up to believe in an inverse relationship between yield and quality.

He advocates two "golden rules" of viticulture: a good, open, vertical canopy, with 15 shoots per metre (fewer and sunlight is wasted; more and the bunches are too shaded); secondly, pruning vines in winter to 30 buds per kilo of prunings (this is based on an inverse correlation between vine vigour and wood produced). Given the right clone in the right environment, viticulture, in Smart's view, is essentially about reconciling vine vigour, vegetation and fruit production; for this, the critical considerations are canopy management, correct pruning and water stress. However, once a balance has been achieved yields can be increased significantly without compromising quality.

A general trend, which rapidly became a fashion in some states, led growers to cool-climate viticulture in the belief that a longer, cooler growing season made for greater wine complexity. With Shiraz, the hope was that this would somehow reproduce conditions in the Rhône – that perhaps, for once, the much-misused Australian "Hermitage" label would not be a misnomer! The reality was that problems of ripening Shiraz in exaggeratedly cool sites far outweighed any benefits; the theory was flawed. Although the results were cocooned in much deflecting talk of "flavour profile", "good attack" and "fine finish" – sure signs of trouble – the reality was that many of these wines were hopelessly unbalanced, with over-emphatic peppery aromas and an excess of green tannins, invariably achieved at the expense of middle-palate richness and concentration. Neither extremes of heat or coolness are conducive to balanced ripening, the *sine qua non* of top-quality winemaking.

In the cellar, a far better understanding of the mechanisms of traditional practices has allowed winemakers to adapt their vinifications to a desired style and to the character of the vintage. Improved viticulture, in particular the decrease in irresponsible irrigation and over-cropping, is producing grapes with better solid:liquid balances and greater natural acidities. This allows conscientious winemakers to do away with many artificial adjustments and manipulations. In particular, the widespread acidification of Shiraz (sometimes genuinely necessary in hotter regions) has been drastically cut. Many estates harboured unduly exaggerated fears that low acidities would reduce a wine's lifespan and cause premature disintegration. The 1947, 1959 and 1982 red bordeaux – all low-acid vintages – convincingly exposed the fragility of that argument.

There has also been much discussion about the characteristics different dried yeasts impart to wine, and the value of using them rather than the grape's natural yeast population. The main benefit of yeast inoculation is to ensure both a rapid start and a complete finish to fermentation. However, many believe that using what is effectively a monoculture deprives the resulting wine of complexity; others strongly disagree. The debate continues.

One interesting piece of recent research, which has caused an audible buzz in Shiraz circles, has identified glucosyl-glucoses, a group of chemical compounds which are present as flavour precursors in the grapes at harvest and are later released during fermentation. Their concentration is being considered as an index of quality potential. "G-Gs", are apparently specific to Shiraz grapes – Pinot Noir, for example, has its own family of compounds which fulfil a similar role.

A great deal of progress has also been made on refining wood maturation. Several years ago, winemakers found that a much richer, more complete flavour resulted from finishing fermentation in new American oak. This is still a widely practised technique, which accounts for the distinctive, almost sweet, berryish feel of many Australian Shiraz wines – although some estates prefer the more obvious delicacy of the frighteningly expensive French oak.

There is also a greater awarness of the need to bottle Shiraz early, while some fruit remains, rather than leaving it in cask for years to dessicate. The "leathery" quality of much old Australian "Burgundy" (Shiraz), was often attributable to excessive cask-ageing. Improvement in several spheres is the consequence of winemakers travelling outside Australia. However, there are dangers in the belief that you can transplant methods from one milieu to another without risk. For example, throwing open the cellar doors in Burgundy to clarify wine after fermentation is fine at 3°C; it is inadvisable in the Barossa when the temperature is more likely to be 15°C.

Part of Henschke's Hill of Grace vineyard and the church of Gnadenberg.

"I've had enough of this vine-stress; I'm getting out". Magnificent 1870s Shiraz vines at Bests Great Western.

RULES AND REGULATIONS

A disruptive threat to the peace and prosperity of the Australian wine industry came with its agreement, for the benefit of European Community bureaucrats, to define its vineyard area in terms of zones, regions and sub-regions. So far applications have been filed for several hundred individual "Geographical Indications", and the aim is to complete the task within a few years.

Many believe that, once established, these would become immutable, effectively prohibiting further expansion. In a country where so much territory remains to be explored and evaluated, this would be nothing short of a disaster. Such delimitation might also curb the practice of buying and blending grapes and wine from several regions – an invaluable freedom, enjoyed by neither the French nor Italians, for example, who remain cemented to the maps etched for them by centuries of tradition.

Though there is at present no thought of adding any of the viti-, or vini-, cultural controls implicit in the French *appellation contrôlée* system, if the EU's track record of interfering is any guide, pressure to incorporate these further elements is likely before too long. The burgeoning, insidious tentacles of Brussels should be resisted, tooth and nail.

European skirmishes apart, the main difficulty faced by winemakers – not only in Australia – is that of striking a balance between the knowledge that most wines will be drunk young and the desire to make something magnificent which is capable of ageing. Fortunately, in Shiraz they have a grape which, given sympathetic handling, is capable of performing well at both ends of that elongated spectrum. Unfortunately, there are signs that the runaway success and booming exports of recent years have occasionally lead to compromise on quality – a misguided stragegy in the long term.

Shiraz has had a difficult passage in Australia. It is now, belatedly, recognised as a first-class grape and has attracted a sufficiently strong band of disciples, among both consumers and producers, to secure its future prosperity. If, collectively, Australia has maltreated Shiraz, it was in abandoning it as a premium variety. Thankfully Shiraz is supremely forgiving, and that is now history.

BAROSSA & CLARE VALLEYS

The Barossa Valley lies some 50km north-east of Adelaide and is widely regarded as Australia's most important wine region. In one sense, as home to around half all the country's wine *production* and to some of its major firms (Penfolds, Seppelt, Orlando, Wolf Blass, Peter Lehmann, Krondorf, Yalumba, Tollana and Saltram), it is. However, as a wine-*growing* region, it is not large, accounting for only around 10% of the national grape crush. The balance comes from bought-in fruit.

The area was established in 1837 by Colonel William Light, the then surveyor-general, who named it after a part of southern Spain of which the Barossa hills reminded him. Although the original land-owners were Scottish and English – Angaston, for example, is named after George Fife Angas from Newcastle, England – the predominant founding influence was Lutheran.

A private immigration programme, organised by Angas with quasi-Germanic thoroughness, brought a large influx of settlers to the region from Bavaria, Silesia and Poland between 1838 and 1842. These, mainly persecuted dissidents, destined to provide a labour force, were housed in village communities, carefully planned and laid out in advance. Some of the townships grew and prospered, others withered. One can see a good example of the latter at Gomersal, on the western edge of the region, with the remains of a Lutheran school and the plethora of German headstones in the churchyard.

The German cultural aura still pervades the Barossa, in its exemplary parochial tidiness, law-abiding citizenry with German names, German bakeries and food shops, a flourishing Lutheran church and an abiding Germanic architecture.

The first plantings were between 1847 and the 1880s, largely in response to the decline of vineyards in the eastern states. The region's prosperity was significantly enhanced by the Federation of 1900, which lifted trade barriers between the Australian states and allowed wine to be shipped country-wide. The pattern of wine production evolved in a somewhat unusual fashion. Historically, the settlers became grape-growers and sold their produce to others to turn into wine. This remains the case, with many enterprises, both large and small, buying in all, or most, of their fruit requirements.

Before the late 1980s, this system presented no problems, since there was an over-supply of grapes, allowing producers to pick and choose their sources.

Palm tree, vines and the small Lutheran church of Gnadenfrei in the Barossa Valley.

Now, as demand has increased, quality fruit is scarce and the shortage has put the grape-growers firmly in control – a situation with which many winemakers feel distinctly uncomfortable. Some, such as Penfolds, have always argued that vineyard ownership is essential for control and, in pursuit of that policy, have built up substantial vineyard holdings.

Until comparatively recently, the large exporting firms effectively dominated the Barossa wine industry with, it is sometimes alleged, little respect for the area itself. This reflected their perception of the region's principal red grapes – Shiraz, Grenache and Mataro - as ordinary blending varieties of little nobility. As a result, the decade 1979-1989 saw total Barossa vineyard acreage shrink from 8,400 to 5,400. In particular, the area suffered unduly from the government-sponsored vine-pull scheme of 1986, which saw 1,537 acres grubbed up, mainly of then uneconomic, low-yielding old vines. Sadly, Shiraz was the main victim.

During the 1980s, the quality mantle passed to a number of new domaines - such as Melton, St Hallett and Rockford - which took over and re-established the Barossa's reputation. Their hunger for premium, preferably old-vine, Rhône-varietal fruit, for which they were prepared to pay top prices, resuscitated a flagging grape-growing community. In the late 1980s the large companies, having deserted the area

in search of fashionable "cool" climates, returned to the Barossa for much of their fruit – realising that "cool" was not always beautiful. They needed consistent high quality and more grapes, especially Barossa's speciality, Shiraz. Most large firms now own vineyards, and many also act as major grape producers.

The Barossa still continues the strong tradition of vineyard owners, many descendants of original immigrants, selling grapes to wineries. With unprecedented demand, especially for old-vine Shiraz, growers face a dilemma: top-class wine can only be produced from restricted yields and, even at current prices for premium fruit, this is uneconomic. If supply is to be at least maintained, grape prices will have to increase substantially. To make economic sense, some have estimated that this would add around 50% to the retail price of a bottle of premium Shiraz, at which level it might well be priced out of its well-established markets. Resolving this conundrum will not be easy.

The Barossa is an attractive area – ideal for wine-minded visitors who flock in to tour and taste from Adelaide and beyond. The towns of Nuriootpa, Tanunda and Lyndoch punctuate its main axis. Its 38 wineries fall into three groups: those which are unashamedly geared to the tourist market (such as the splendid Château Yaldara), taking pressure off less visitor-oriented establishments; the small, very serious "boutique" enterprises, who rely on direct sales for an important part of their cash-flow; and thirdly the larger operators, who have processing facilities in the region, but receive fruit from a variety of places. The area is also home to Roseworthy College, known throughout Australia for the excellence of its training of viticulturists and winemakers.

The Valley, up to 5 miles wide, extends for 25-30 miles oriented roughly north-south, at altitudes of 180-290 metres. It is bounded to the west by gentle slopes and to the east by the steeper Barossa Hills which rise up to 600m. Here the mean temperature during the growing season is two centigrade degrees lower than that of the valley floor. Outside this delimited corridor, the land becomes grazing pasture and is good for hay-growing. The remains of old olive plantations are still evident, with scattered trees growing wild.

The climate, once considered too warm for quality viticulture because of a torridly hot February and March, follows a pattern of cool, wet, springs and a dry growing season. This produces vine

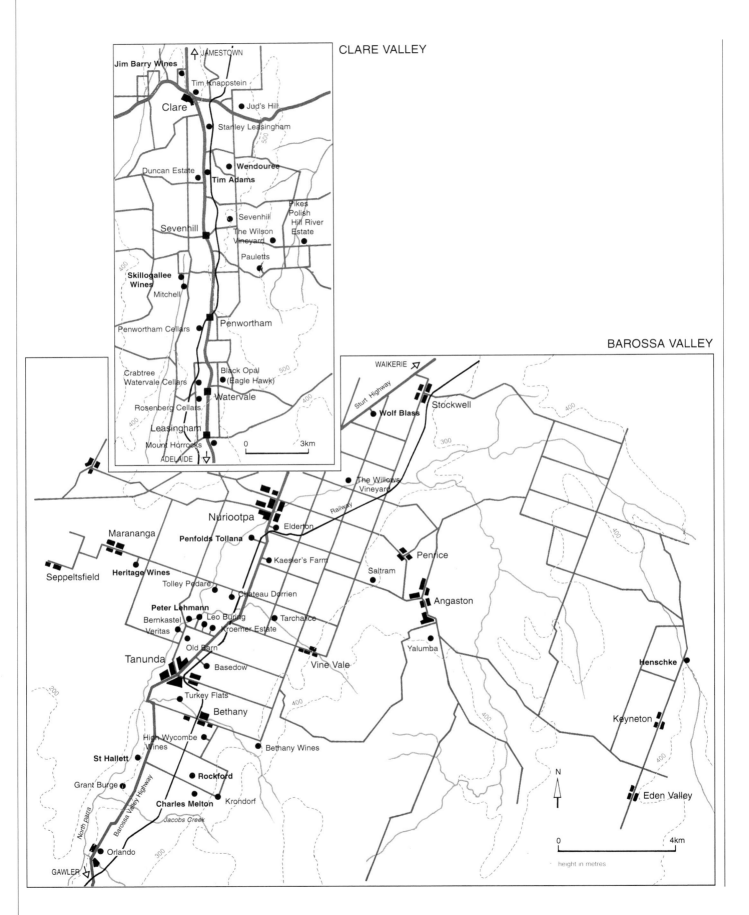

CLARE VALLEY

JAMESTOWN

Jim Barry Wines

Tim Knappstein

Clare

Jud's Hill

Stanley Leasingham

Duncan Estate

Wendouree

Tim Adams

Sevenhill

Pikes
Polish
Hill River
Estate

The Wilson
Vineyard

Pauletts

**Skillogalee
Wines**

Mitchell

Penwortham Cellars

Penwortham

Crabtree
Watervale Cellars

Black Opal
(Eagle Hawk)

Watervale

Rosenberg Cellars

Leasingham

Mount Horrocks

ADELAIDE

0   3km

BAROSSA VALLEY

WAIKERIE

Sturt Highway

Stockwell

Wolf Blass

The Willows
Vineyard

Railway

Nuriootpa

Elderton

Marananga

Penfolds Tollana

Kaesler's Farm

Penrice

Saltram

Seppeltsfield

Heritage Wines

Tolley Pedare

Chateau Dorrien

Angaston

Peter Lehmann

Leo Buring

Tarchalice

Yalumba

Bernkastel
Veritas

Kroemer Estate

Old Barn

Henschke

Tanunda

Basedow

Vine Vale

Turkey Flats

Keyneton

Bethany

High Wycombe
Wines

Bethany Wines

St Hallett

Rockford

Grant Burge

Eden Valley

Charles Melton

Krondorf

Jacobs Creek

North para

Barossa Valley Highway

N

Orlando

GAWLER

0   4km

height in metres

226

stress, which is countered, in part, by severe pruning. The moderate, mainly winter rainfall increases from north to south, as one nears the sea. The eastern edge of the Valley is drier than the rest, producing much of the top-quality, low-yielding, dry-farmed fruit. There has been significant development on this side of the Barossa, towards the Eden Valley ranges, where the long, cool growing season of the high hills imparts elegance to Shiraz.

Soils are complex and very diverse throughout the region, varying widely in physical and chemical composition. There are four main areas. At Vine Vale, which lies just east of Tanunda, soils are mainly deep, sandy and water-retentive. At Stonewell, Greenock and Marananga, to the west of Nuriootpa and Tanunda, the ground is mainly ironstone, with very limited underground water (what there is tends to be saline and therefore unusable), giving powerful, heavily-structured wines - fine for Shiraz, but useless for Riesling.

Light Pass, to the east of Nuriootpa, has richer, loamy soils which give higher yields than elsewhere. Kalimna, just west of Nuriootpa - the source of at least part of the fruit for Penfold's Grange *cuvée* - has soils which are shallow and sandy, often over clay, giving strong, vigorous wines. Elsewhere, there are grey-brown soils and patches of *terra rossa*.

The wide diversity of soil-types and micro-climates mean that the same grape grown in different parts of the Valley can produce markedly different wines. This gives winemakers a spectrum of qualities to work with in assembling their blends. The best Shiraz tends to be dry-farmed, although irrigation is permitted (up to the equivalent of four inches or 100 mm of rain) to stop serious vine-stress. The average usage is around 50-70mm.

In the hands of top estates, both Shiraz, and to a lesser extent Grenache, produce excellent, age-worthy wines. Two distinct styles of Barossa Shiraz have evolved. Traditional, old-fashioned, big-framed wines, rich in alcohol and fruit, come from fully-if not over-ripe grapes; these were generally matured for two to three years in old wood, and kept for a similar period in bottle prior to release.

The "modern" style emphasises elegance, without compromising on complexity, with somewhat shorter vinification and maturation, with the use of new wood becoming prevalent. Many follow Penfold's preference (for Grange) for American oak, which imparts a sweet, berryish flavour, especially if fermentation is finished in cask rather than in inert vats.

Exports of Barossa Shiraz have rocketed over the past decade, especially to

Rainbow over Seppelt's vineyards.

the UK, helped by favourable prices and a weak Australian dollar. A growing connoisseur market has been established and the names of the finest estates, and the personalities of some of their idiosyncratic owners, are increasingly well-known. The problems of grape supply and a strengthening currency could easily reverse these trends.

At present, the best Shiraz *cuvées* are underpriced in comparison with French and Californian equivalents.

CLARE VALLEY

To the north-west of the Barossa is the Clare Valley, some 108km from metropolitan Adelaide. This narrow, 30km-long strip of land, centred on the towns of Clare, Sevenhill, Leasingham and Auburn (from north to south), has developed since the mid 1970s into a premium wine-producing region. After losing 883 acres in the government-sponsored vine-pull in the 1980s, there now 4,500 acres under vine, making it roughly a quarter the size of Barossa. These include 787 acres of Shiraz and 320 acres of Grenache.

The region is hilly, with many vineyards at between 450 and 500m, and has a climate broadly similar to the cooler, more elevated parts of the Barossa. Although heat summation, at around 1,774, is nominally higher than Barossa's 1,715, the best wines exhibit a finesse

which seems to belie the theoretically greater warmth. Riesling performs particularly well in the Valley, which produces some of the finest Australian examples of this variety. The main hillside soil types are red and, to a lesser extent, yellow, duplex soils, with good water retention.

The area has some 23 wineries, of various sizes, including some of Australia's top Shiraz estates - Tim Adams, Jim Barry and Wendouree. Small production, perhaps, but of the very highest quality.

Apart from the estates profiled here, there are other excellent sources in the region. Notable *cuvées* include Leasingham's Domaine Shiraz, the E & E Black Pepper Shiraz from Colin Glaetzer at the growers' cooperative Barossa Valley Estates, the Heysen Vineyard Shiraz from Rolf Binder's Veritas winery, the Meshach *cuvée*, made by Grant Burge from 70-year-old vines and the Clarendon Hills Shiraz and Grenache.

Hardy's Eileen Hardy Shiraz also deserves mention. Hardys are an old firm, now part of the BRL Hardy conglomerate, producing a vast range of wines from vineyards in South and Western Australia. The Eileen Hardy bottling is the pick of the crop from Hardy's Padthaway, McLaren Vale and Clare vineyards, matured in new French and American oak for 14 months; the 1990 is particularly fine.

TIM ADAMS WINES

Tim Adams began his wine career in 1975, as a cellarhand at the Stanley Wine Company in Clare. In 1976 he became a laboratory assistant and a year later embarked on a correspondence course which led to a BSc in Wine Science. He was appointed winemaker in 1982.

In 1986 he left Stanley and formed a partnership with a local cooper, Bill Wray, to make small oak casks and wine. This prospered and the range diversified. In 1987 the partnership was dissolved, leaving Tim and his wife, Pam, in full control of the renamed "Tim Adams Wines".

A year later, they bought an existing winery site in the Clare Valley, known as Robertson's Wines, and opened the door for sales in January 1988. Annual production now runs at around 14,000 cases, with sales scattered throughout Australia and an increasing export demand.

The "Rhône" range consists of Tim Adams Shiraz, an "Aberfeldy" Shiraz and "The Fergus" – a Grenache-based wine. The enterprise owns no vines, but buys in all its fruit requirements from a group of 13 local growers. Tim Adams sees this arrangement as an advantage, allowing him to source grapes from the diverse sub-regions within the Clare district.

The winemaking here is consistently impressive – the wines have both depth and character, derived in part from a high proportion of very old vines. The Aberfeldy Shiraz comes from a vineyard planted by the Birks family in 1904 and owned by Wendouree until 1976, from where Adams has been buying the grapes since 1985.

The soil here is deep loam-limestone, varying in depth from 20cm to 2m. The vines are over 90 years old and yield a pitiful 1.25–1.75 tonnes per acre.

The fruit is harvested in March, or even April, very ripe at around 13.5–14 Baumé, and fermented for a week. The wine is then left for up to a month to macerate on its solids.

Maturation lasts 22–23 months – 18 months in old American oak followed by 4–5 in new American oak. The wine is both fined and filtered before bottling. In style the wine is avowedly "old-fashioned Aussie Shiraz", with great concentration and complexity, and it needs plenty of time to develop in bottle.

"The Fergus" is named after the owner of the Mahbrook vineyard from which it comes – Fergus (and Vyvian) Mahon. The Grenache component is harvested very late in April, having been left on the vine until it has reached around 14.5 Baumé. It is crushed onto the fermented, drained skins of Cabernet Sauvignon, Cabernet Franc and Shiraz, where it remains for some five weeks – a week's fermentation with the tanks left open, and four further weeks of maceration with the tanks closed. The pulp is then basket-pressed and the press wine incorporated, before nine months' maturation in old US oak casks. The first "Fergus" was from the 1993 vintage, and it proved a considerable success.

The Tim Adams Shiraz is 100% varietal from two local vineyards: Sheoaks, at Leasingham 13km south of Clare and the Spring Farm Valley Estate 3km south-east of Clare. The fruit is fermented to dryness and has all its pressings re-incorporated. Maturation is in oak and lasts a year.

This is an excellent trio of wines – especially the Aberfedly – putting Tim Adams Wines in the top echelons of Australia's Rhône set.

JIM BARRY WINES

Peter and Mark Barry are a self-deprecating pair who seem almost embarrassed by the fine quality they are producing. They give an impression of insouciance and disinterest, which is completely destroyed by the very first sip of their wine. Mark will tell you in one breath that he is not serious about winemaking, admitting in the next that he spends 24 hours a day, seven days a week, at the winery.

Their father, Jim Barry, was one of Roseworthy's earliest graduates, who subsequently arrived in Clare to work as winemaker at the local cooperative. He built up the well-reputed firm of Taylors in the 1960s, and established his own enterprise in north Clare in 1974, bringing the first drip irrigation system to Australia *en passant*. Mark and Peter, both in their late 30s, now run the company, having bought Jim a stud farm in the early 1990s, to indulge his passion for thoroughbreds – "we don't see him now".

They have exploited to the full the areas of the valley where a cooler, more temperate climate is ideally suited to white grapes, producing a fine range of Chardonnay, Sémillon and a magnificent Rhine Riesling from the old Leo Buring Florita vineyard. But it is through the monumental Armagh Shiraz that the Barrys have made their mark. This giant, first released in 1985, has become one of Australia's legendary Shiraz – selling for up to Aus$1,200 a bottle in fashionable restaurants.

The fruit for this wine comes from eight acres of vines planted in 1968 in the Armagh district of Clare – Mark well remembers cursing his father, who made him plant and water the young vines in his school holidays. During the 1970s and early 1980s, their fruit went into Barry's "Sentimental Bloke" port blend – "low yields, high sugars and concentration – perfect port material", according to Peter. Now these vines are largely dry-farmed, though in drought years, such as 1992, a drip-water system is used to provide 32 litres of supplemental water per vine, "otherwise they would close down".

In the poor, sandy, low-fertility soils of the Armagh vineyard, yields are around 1–2 tonnes/acre, with vines pruned to 1–3 canes each, depending on position and soil depth. The aim is to pick small berries, just beginning to shrivel, but short of jammy portiness. "You can almost tell at harvest", Peter explains, "the juice is black on crushing – not the normal green". Ideally, there will have been more than ten days with the thermometer at over 40°C to produce the flavour and concentration for the Armagh – "we really like the heat".

The Barry's confidence in Clare Valley Shiraz has resulted in 10,000 more vines being planted in the Armagh district in 1993. In 1992, a McCrae Wood Shiraz appeared – blended mainly from Hutte

VARIETY	VINEYARD	DETAILS	AREA
SHIRAZ	ARMAGH VINEYARD	Planted 1968; 1–2 tonnes/acre ; shallow top-soils 6"–24" deep onto rock	8.00
SHIRAZ	ARMAGH DISTRICT	Planted 1993	16.00
SHIRAZ	HUTTE RIVER	Planted mid 1970s, bought 1989; yields 3–4 tonnes/acre; drip-irrigated when necessary.	8.00
SHIRAZ	ARMAGH - THE FLAT	Planted 1964/5	1.00
		TOTAL (acres):	33.00

River and the Flat – with 10% Malbec added but no new wood for maturation. Conceived perhaps as a junior Armagh, this is more affordable and designed for earlier – though still not precipitously early – drinking.

Although the brothers work closely together, it is Mark who bears the main responsibility of vinification. The grapes are picked at around 13.5 Baumé, and 80–85% de-stemmed. After 14–15 days' fermentation, the wine is either run off, or left on skins under a gas blanket for 2–3 weeks longer to maximize extraction. The pressings from a gentle 30-minute tank press which "extracts every bit of juice from the skins we possibly can" are added back and the wine "cleaned up" with six weekly rackings, before passing

into heavy-toast, US oak casks coopered in Australia which have been "broken in" with Cabernet Sauvignon. Since 1990, Peter and Mark have bought and seasoned their own cask-wood, having discovered that the coopers only seasoned the wood for 18 months. After assembling the various lots and carrying out a final racking, the wine returns to cask for a further 6–8 months. It is then egg-white fined – to correct any tannin imbalance and palate "furriness" – and taken to Adelaide for bottling, where it is plate-filtered.

The Armagh is impressive stuff – a big wine with long, concentrated, extracted flavours – which demands time in bottle to develop its full potential. These opulent, complex, flavours provide a

common denominator onto which vintage differences are grafted. The style is not compromised for Show purposes, where judges tend to frown on over-extracted wines. The 1990 Armagh received no awards – not even a bronze medal at one show – and then scooped three Trophies at Perth in 1993. There is understandable cynicism in the air.

Mark is far from the mono-conversation winemaker: "I'm not really serious about wine; we don't talk wine all the time. I have friends who are doctors, bricklayers, truck-drivers – we talk about other things. We aren't serious shits – we get fun out of our wine. Many people who meet us after tasting Armagh say 'no, not you… it can't be'". It is, and none the worse for that!

C A HENSCHKE & COMPANY

It is unlikely that there are any Syrah vines in France as old as the 20 acres of "grandfathers" of the Hill of Grace. Planted in the 1860s, facing the contemporaneous Gnadenberg Church near Keyneton in the Barossa Ranges, this is one of the Southern Hemisphere's finest named vineyards. Nichlaus Stanitzky, a Polish bee-keeper and farmer, planted it from material brought to Australia from Europe by early German settlers. It came into the Henschke family when second-generation Paul married one of Stanitzky's daughters.

The original Henschke, Johann Christian, arrived in South Australia from Silesia in 1841; he settled at Krondorf and bought land at Keyneton on which he planted vines to make wine for family use. Farming was the main pursuit until the early 20th century, when winemaking expanded to meet increased demand, especially for fortified wine. However, it was under Johann's grandson Cyril's stewardship in the 1950s that the estate established its reputation for high-quality red and white table wines.

In 1979 Stephen Henschke, the fifth generation, took charge. A thoughtful man, now in his mid-40s, his skills were acquired from two years' study at the Geisenheim Institute in the Rheingau, a vintage at Domaine Dujac in Burgundy, and practical experience at various wineries in Australia. He is a trained botanist, as is his dark-haired wife Pru, whom he met whilst they were both at Adelaide University. Two young children do not hinder her from taking an active role in selecting and propagating material for the estate's planting programme

Stephen returned from Germany determined to re-invent the world of

white wine, which caused some altercations with his father; he used to visit the cellar at night to "do things which father wouldn't approve of". However, tradition supervened, and he is now firmly devoted to consolidating and improving his inheritance.

Henschke's produce a baker's dozen of wines, all but four of which are white. Of this quartet, one is an excellent Cabernet Sauvignon, named in tribute to Cyril Henschke; and the other three are based on Shiraz. The 10,000 cases of Keyneton Estate are a blend of Eden Valley Shiraz, Cabernet and Malbec, from 20 acres of the estate's 1968 plantings and some 30 acres of vineyards belonging to other growers.

Of the two pure Shirazes, the 5,000–10,000 cases of Mount Edelstone – the word means "gem-stone" – come from 40 acres of Shiraz vines (with a few Bastardo admixed) planted by Ronald Angas in the 1920s, at 400 metres altitude on an east-facing "small hill" near Keyneton. On these principally red podzolic, deep sandy loams, the vines are dry-farmed and yield just under four tonnes per acre. The first Mount Edelstone "claret" was released in 1952 and the wine became an instant success on the Show circuit.

The pinnacle of Henschke's Shiraz achievement is their Hill of Grace. In reality, this vineyard is not much of a hill – rather a flattish, horseshoe-shaped valley, set among gently undulating scenery, with rich alluvial soils and a broadly westerly aspect. It divides, notionally, into four separate blocks which are picked and vinified separately: Church Block, House Block, Windmill Block and Post-Office Block. About 0.5%

of the vines are Cabernet Sauvignon and Mataro, probably early replacements for plants which died. The exact origin of the bud-wood is unknown, though Stephen Henschke speculates that it came either direct from Hamburg, with the first settlers, or else from ships stopping over in South Africa, on voyages round the Cape. With its wealth of pre-phylloxera vine material, the Hill of Grace is something of a living viticultural museum.

The fruit is hand-harvested: Mount Edelstone over three weeks in April at 12.5–13 Baumé, the Hill of Grace at 12 Baumé onwards, at the end of March or in early April. The aim is to produce wines with "rich, silky, mature berry flavours" (not least because "people who pay a lot for a bottle want plenty of flavour"). Trials at Mount Edelstone with Scott-Henry trellising and a hanging-cane configuration, designed under the aegis of consultant viticulturalist Dick Smart, to try and increase yields without compromising quality, have complicated harvesting and yielded mixed results. The hanging-cane has not proved successful, but Scott-Henry seems promising. In 1983 Mount Edelstone yielded one tonne per acre; in the excellent 1990 vintage, four tonnes per acre. Stephen Henschke estimates the optimal crop, balancing quality and commercial viability, at 2–2.5 tonnes per acre.

Stephen and Pru believe that winemaking technique has advanced as far as it can, and that future improvements will come from more precise viticulture. One signal mistake, which Stephen admits, with obvious regret, was the grubbing up of a planting of 55-year-old Grenache in the early 1980s.

Vinification has been fine-tuned to maximize the desired "rich, silky, mature berry flavours". Stephen found that old wines tended to lack fruit and to have cooked flavours from too-hot fermentations. He tried reducing temperatures to as low as 20°C, but "that was too far"; now the range is 20–25°C, which retains aromatics and flavours without extracting hard tannins and bitterness. Half the wine finishes its fermentation in new wood, the rest in underground tanks, where it remains until the following November. The tank fraction is then racked to casks already broken-in with that year's Chardonnay and Semillon.

As Stephen describes it, in 1979 the cellar was "a museum full of old oak hogsheads and puncheons"; so he embarked on a ten-year programme to reduce the average barrel age from ten years to one. An integral part of this involved spending time with coopers to improve wood quality: US oak seemed too green and resiny for fine Shiraz. He tried, and rejected, French casks, dismantled, shipped then re-assembled in Australia: " a real circus". Now they buy their own French and US timber which is coopered in Australia when they judge it to be properly seasoned.

Since the 1986 vintage, the Hill of Grace has been matured half in new oak, half in the first-year white-wine casks; while the Mount Edelstone has 50% new and 50% one-year-old wood. The new oak used is predominantly American, with 10–15% of French wood for Hill of Grace, and 15–20% French wood for Mount Edelstone.

Steve Henschke.

Stephen is clear about the effects of various maturation media: tanks preserve fruit, but produce simple flavours; 10- to 20-year-old barrels give less colour and flavour; new casks intensify colour, bouquet and flavour. All Henschke reds spend 12–18 months in cask. The need to fine is reduced by limiting maceration to avoid extraction of hard tannins or bitterness. There is, however, a light, polishing filtration before bottling. Selection of the lots for each label is made just before bottling. Casks which are not considered fit for Hill of Grace or Mount Edelstone are declassified, as it were, into Keyneton Estate. After bottling, the wines remain in the splendid old cellars for up to three years before release.

Henschke wines are priced at the top end of the market. Whether demand has led price, price demand or fame both is debatable; in any event, the wines are still far from being over-priced, and have a strong following among Australian connoisseurs and restaurants.

Exports are a recent phenomenon – only since 1985, for instance, have Henschke wines found their way to Britain. When you can sell all you produce on the home market, there is little incentive to bother with export.

The Hill of Grace and Mount Edelstone represent the continuing achievement of five generations. Stephen and Pru are worthy custodians of a fine family tradition.

VARIETY	VINEYARD	DETAILS	AREA
SHIRAZ	HILL OF GRACE	Planted 1860s; own roots	20.00
SHIRAZ	MOUNT EDELSTONE	Planted 1920s	40.00
SHIRAZ	EDEN VALLEY	Planted 1968	20.00
SHIRAZ	Other growers	Average vine age: 40+ years	30.00
		TOTAL (acres):	110.00

HERITAGE WINES

Heritage is another mid-1980s Barossa creation. Its founder, Steve Hoff, started as a trainee at Yalumba, going on to study at Roseworthy College before returning to the Valley to work at Saltram. In 1984 he made his first Heritage wine from rented facilities in the Clare Valley, and two years later established his own "cellar-door", in a pleasant small property on the western edge of the Barossa. This is home for him, his gynaecologist wife Chris, and their new baby. For the visitor, there is a flower-decked terrace looking over vineyards towards Kaiserstuhl, Stonewell and Tanunda.

Around one-third of his fruit – he has no vines – comes from the cool Clare Valley: Riesling, Chardonnay, Sauvignon Blanc, Cabernets Sauvignon and Franc. From 1988–1990 the Shiraz was entirely sourced from Clare; now it is 100% Barossa fruit. There are two Shiraz bottlings: 500–800 cases of a standard release from grapes grown in the Kalimna vineyard, and 500 cases of "Rossco's Shiraz" from 2.5 acres of 50-year-old, organically farmed vines at Greenock, owned by a Mr Rossco.

This is a one-man band, as Steve, a large, jovial mid-30s character, dislikes employing people – except on the cellar-door to give him an occasional free weekend. He admits that finding suitable raw material is a particular problem, even if you are prepared to pay a hefty premium for low-yielding, old-vine fruit.

The economic reality is that a grower can expect no more than 10% more cash per tonne for reducing his yields than a neighbour producing double the crop – hardly a financial incentive to concentrate on quality.

Heritage sells some 4,000 cases each year, 30% of which goes through the cellar-door and 40% distributed elsewhere in Australia. The remainder is exported or sold by direct mail. Although earlier vintages of the standard Shiraz have been patchy, Steve is clearly capable of making excellent wine – particularly notable are the 1991 and 1992 Rossco's. This is a serious source of Shiraz, and one well worth watching.

VARIETY	VINEYARD	DETAILS	AREA
SHIRAZ	GREENOCK	50 yr old vines; owner Mr Rossco	2.50
SHIRAZ	KALIMNA	50/60 yr old vines	3.20
SHIRAZ	KALIMNA	45 yr old vines; 3 tonnes produced; owner E Schulz	
		TOTAL (acres):	5.50

PETER LEHMANN WINES

In contrast to most of the large Barossa wine-producers, Peter Lehmann Wines own no vines, but buy in their fruit requirements from around 200 large and small growers with whom they work. It was the plight of these people that brought the present enterprise into being. They faced ruin when liquor-giant Seagrams bought out Saltrams in 1979 and immediately told its chief winemaker, Peter Lehmann, to cancel the majority of grape contracts, Although the growers' "gentleman's agreements" had no legal force, they represented years of accumulated mutual trust which Lehmann, the son of a Lutheran pastor, was not prepared to betray. He resigned from Saltram and, with friendly outside funding, set up the business which now bears his name. Fifteen years and several changes of corporate involvement later, the firm was floated as a public company in August 1993, with many Barossan winegrowers, winery staff and local people as shareholders. "A quintessential Barossa wine company".

Peter Lehmann offers three principal Shiraz-based wines: a Barossa Valley Shiraz, a premium "Stonewell" Shiraz and a "Vintage Port". The Barossa blend is a soft, mid-weight, medium-priced wine, with plenty of fruit and some attractive complexity. It is not made to a standard style, but reflects its vintage and has the structure to evolve well over a decade or so. The Stonewell *cuvée* is altogether richer and more complex – a dark, substantial wine with powerful, concentrated fruit, needing several years

to give of its best. Unlike the Barossa blend it contains no Eden Valley fruit, but is sourced from local growers in Stonewell, Greenock, Marananga and Kalimna.

A quartet of winemakers preside in the cellars – Lehmann himself, Andrew Wigan, Peter Scholz and Leonie Bain – presumably in the belief that a team will produce the highest common factor rather than the lowest common denominator. There is considered to be enough tannin from the fruit, long maceration, pressings and new wood to eliminate the need for stems; so all fruit destined for dry reds is de-stemmed before being transferred to stainless steel. The process is a modified carbonic maceration, in that the fermenters are closed. Temperatures range from 25–32°C. The higher level is to flesh out the middle palate. The lower used to be even cooler, but although this gave elegance, it was generally at the expense of concentration. Half-way through, the juice is run off into new wood to finish fermenting and then pumped back onto its skins: this integrates any raw oak character and integrates wood and fruit. A two-week extended maceration follows to extract more, and softer, tannin. Both these processes were introduced in 1989, a vintage which marked a distinct improvement in the Stonewell Shiraz.

As far as is practicable, each batch is kept separate, with its own press-wine incorporated, until the end of the vintage, when the blends are assembled. The selection for the Stonewell bottling is

made after malolactic, when the young wine is centrifuged to remove dead yeast cells which might clog up the pores of casks, and to prepare a special bottling for the 'One Year Old' class on the Show circuit (Medals mean orders!).

After 23–30 months in wood – 100% new American oak for the Stonewell Shiraz for its "sweet, forward" flavours – the wine is cartridge-filtered and bottled. Fining is only performed to adjust tannins, as it is seen as "ripping colour and flavour out"; clarity is not normally a problem as the wine has already been centrigfuged and spent a fair amount of time in cask, both of which help to deposit unsightly fliers and flocculants.

These are good, sometimes excellent, wines. The Stonewell bottling, in particular, is a fine example of Barossa Shiraz which is well worth buying and cellaring. In recent vintages, however, the wine has been strongly dominated by its soujourn in new wood. Perhaps 100% of new US oak is really too rich for the underlying fruit.

The "Vintage Port" is truly remarkable. Not perhaps a style which would find immediate acceptance among palates nurtured on the Portuguese version, but a thoroughly seductive wine with no shortage of stuffing or personality. Greater attention to fruit selection since 1987 has resulted in a more complete, established style. The name may be a trifle unfortunate, but the wine more than merits a place in the cellar of any wine-lover with a genuinely open mind. Together with the offerings of Wendouree and McWilliams, these "Ports" are among the finest of their genre in Australia.

CHARLES MELTON WINES

In common with others who leave secure jobs to risk going it alone, Charlie (né Graeme) Melton is, above all, his own man. He lives in a converted church, near Rockfords on the Krondorf Road, with his ex-nurse wife Virginia, from Clare, their two children and the family Dalmatian, Wedgwood – they told friends who gave them cash as a wedding present that they'd buy Wedgwood with it – they did.

Charlie is thoroughly contented – he is, as he terms it, "a lifestyle person" – a man of humour and bonhomie, who makes wine as he likes it and has no ambition to expand beyond his personal control. He has spent 20 years in the Valley, starting at Krondorf in 1973, then transferring to Saltrams when Dalgety bought the firm shortly afterwards. From

there he moved, with most of Saltram's technical team, to Peter Lehman when Seagrams took over, and chose to skip an entire crush as a dramatic method of reducing stock.

His original plan was to make only botrytised wine. Fortunately he came to his senses and, in 1984, tempted by a huge glut of unsold grapes, made a couple of batches of red wine using Lehman's facilities. In 1986, Charles Melton Wines was created – along with Rob O'Callaghan's Rockford and the Schrapels at Bethany, the first of the small Barossa operations. Unlike Rockford,

Charlie owns vines – 4.5 acres of 1948 bush-trained Grenache, which are supplemented with fruit bought from independent growers.

A respected Sydney authority, John Stanford, had told Charlie that his Grenache were some of the finest in South Australia. Unfortunately, it was also thoroughly unfashionable – "you could come out, blow your trumpet and proclaim 'Grenache Dry Red' and everyone would fall over laughing – you'd go broke". As Châteauneuf-du-Pape was the only place where the variety was taken seriously, Charlie decided to market the wine as a Châteauneuf-style blend. This he called "Nine Popes" – which is what his limited command of French –

VARIETY	VINEYARD	DETAILS	AREA
SHIRAZ	KRONDORF	Planted 1948; bush-trained; dry-farmed	4.50

"you'd do me an honour to call it basic" – made of "Châteauneuf-du-Pape". Recalling only seven Popes at Avignon before the Papacy returned to Rome, he decided to put the record straight on an explanatory back-label: "by the way, there were only seven of them – trust the Frogs!"

With the first, 1988, vintage, Nine Popes took off and remains the flagship of the house; as the blackboard in the cellar-door perpetually proclaims, it is generally "Sold Out" – a status shared by an excellent Sparkling Shiraz, particularly at Christmas. It has never been a straight Grenache but a blend – typically, it is 60% Grenache, 30% Shiraz and 10% Mourvèdre.

In years when Grenache yields are reduced – such as 1993 when it was attacked by downy mildew – the proportions may change (40% Grenache; 25% Shiraz; 25% Mourvèdre). Fortunately, in that year Charlie found a "bloody wonderful" source of Mourvèdre, which provided some compensation.

A short walk from the family house are a neat winery and an attractive "cellar-door" with a small tasting-room sandwiched in between. Should he ever be tempted to cut corners in the cellar, a large notice above the winery door, reminds: "The Quality, Stupid, the Quality".

His own quality perspective is rooted in his experience of old Australian reds – wines which rewarded patient cellaring and matured magnificently. He wants to enjoy his own wines in 25 years' time, but disdains the fashionable over-use of new oak as a means of adding structure – opulent wood aromas may seduce judges on the Show circuit, but oak should be no more than seasoning: "how many great Rhônes have seen new oak?", he muses.

Another of Charlie's "*bêtes noires*" is drip irrigation: "whatever scientific papers or Dr Richard Smart say, if you drip, you always lose quality" he proclaims – adding, by way of reinforcement: "how many irrigated vines are there in Burgundy?". In pursuance of this policy, all his own Rhône-variety fruit is dry-farmed. It is also hand-picked, as machine-picked fruit will suffer more than from the inevitable delays between harvesting and crush, an important consideration for a small winery. The "bloody wonderful" Mourvèdre comes from 50- to 60-year-old vines, the Shiraz from vines planted in 1970 and 1897, and the non-estate Grenache from 10 acres of 50-year-old vines.

Vinification has evolved to retain maximum fruit character. "The majority of drinkers don't smell wine, so mouthfeel, fruit and richness on the palate are very important". To this end, from the moment of crushing everything is blanketed with carbon dioxide gas – using dry ice conveniently obtained from Krondorf, next door – and fermentation is decidedly cool (15–18°C).

Charlie encourages extended lees contact, whereby each cask gets "a good dose of gross lees". This enhances glycerol, reduces the risk of oxidation and thus the need for sulphur, and retains the important fruit character. This system developed because, lacking a filter and without the space to rack, he was forced to leave the wine on its lees. New oak – in reality, old US and French casks from Stephen Henschke, shaved back to the wood – is limited to 20%.

Each variety is kept separate until a comprehensive cask tasting decides the material for the 1,200–2,000 cases of Nine Popes, the 500–1,000 of Shiraz, and the Sparkling Shiraz. These are the most important decisions Charlie has to make: "we can't afford to slip – we have a reputation there to maintain", he explains, adding cheerily that the near-cult following for Nine Popes means that "there are probably 1,000 Aussies out there ready to chop us off at the knees the moment we make a mistake".

Fortunately, his lower limbs are still in place, and with quality if anything improving, seem set to remain so.

PENFOLDS WINE GROUP

Penfolds is a leviathan of the Australian wine industry, with annual production nearing two million cases covering all styles and price levels. The main constituent companies of this mighty group (Southcorp Wines) are Penfolds itself, based in the Barossa, Wynns in Coonawarra, Seppelts in Great Western and Lindemans, which has significant facilities in the Barossa, at Karadoc in Victoria, in the Hunter Valley and at Rouge Homme in Coonawarra. In the Shiraz range, the inevitable focusses of attention are the Magill Estate – from Dr Penfold's original vineyard – and the world-famous Grange Hermitage.

Penfold's philosophy is founded on a firm belief in style and consistency. Each wine has its preferred style and, while vintage variations occur, and indeed matter, especially at the top level, they take second place to maintaining stylistic identity. This market-oriented principle directs the entire operation from fruit-production to labelling.

Penfolds came to life in 1844, when Dr Christopher Rawson Penfold returned from medical studies in London (Dr Lindeman was a fellow student at Guy's Hospital), and planted vines at Magill in South Australia. The enterprise blossomed over the years, with the emphasis firmly on keeping quality closely related to achievable price.

Today, with combined vineyard acreage running into thousands, there are plenty of sources from which to select the fruit, and later the wine, which will go into each label. Apart from the Magill Estate which comes from one specific vineyard, Penfold-group wines are products of a continuous, narrowing screening process, based on a wide diversity of fruit sources. Selection begins in the field, where vineyard managers identify and grade blocks by quality, and continues into the cellar where each lot is further graded. Any which have "Grange potential" are transferred to new US casks to finish their primary fermentation and subjected thereafter to constant evaluation in the tasting room. The process is precise, and complex. One is invited to discount the idea that there is one large pot from which winemakers select progressively to meet their needs for each *cuvée*. While this may be so in general, it is difficult not to believe that the top wines are privileged with the pick of the crop, particularly for Grange – where fruit may come from Padthaway, Coonawarra, the Barossa, the Southern Vales, or even the Hunter: perfectly sensible if higher quality is the result.

Magill and Grange may have Shiraz in common, but they are entirely different in style. Magill deliberately exemplifies the elegance of which Shiraz is capable, in contrast to its heavyweight, super-rich, highly extracted and a degree or so more alcoholic stable-mate. The 12.5 acres of Magill fruit are hand-picked at lowish fruit maturity and correspondingly higher acidity and fermented relatively cool for around seven days, with no extended maceration. Maturation lasts around 15 months, in mostly new 50:50 US and French casks.

Grange-graded fruit is 95% machine-picked, de-stemmed and put into *inox*. Fermentation is started warm, to increase extraction, and is followed by five to seven days' further maceration. At 1–2 Baumé, the wine is run off into new, high- to-medium-charred US casks where yeasts convert the remaining sugars; this is a long-used Penfolds process which produces fine complexity and excellent fruit and wood integration.

During its 18 months in wood, the wine is racked three times; after the first of these, just after malolactic, the final blend for that year's Grange is assembled (it contains a variable proportion of Cabernet Sauvignon – up to 13%), with a view to giving the constituents as long as possible to integrate in cask. At that stage, the wine is also centrifuged.

The hallmark element of volatile acidity – which is particularly striking in older Granges – comes from a deliberately oxidative maturation, with cask bungs kept upright, rather than on an anaerobic quarter-turn. Neither Grange nor Magill are fined, but both are coarse-filtered before bottling.

The spiritual heart of Penfolds is Grange Cottage, a small, decaying building surrounded by the Magill Estate vineyard in an Adelaide suburb – reduced by creeping urbanization from 100 acres to its present 12.5. The Cottage is undergoing restoration, as is the newer tasting room and reception complex. In the adjoining winery are the original open wax-lined concrete vats in which the first Grange Hermitages were made in the early 1950s; these are now used for the Magill Estate Shiraz.

The story of Grange, now the undisputed "First Growth" of the Southern Hemisphere, has an element of excitement which adds to the triumph of the wine. In 1949, Max Schubert, Penfold's chief winemaker, was sent to Europe to study port and sherry production; he returned with a desire to produce an Australian red table wine capable of lasting 20 years and comparable with great Bordeaux.

Shiraz being more plentiful than Cabernet Sauvignon, he used this for the experimental five hogsheads made, but not released, in 1951; a 1952 was followed by a 100% Cabernet in 1953.

Their reception was disastrous. Tastings by Penfolds directors and other notables confirmed that the wine was little liked and, with stock piling up, the order was given in 1957 to cease Grange production altogether.

Max Schubert later recalled some of the critics' assessments: "A concoction of wild fruits and sundry berries with crushed ants predominating", from a respected wine man; "a very good dry port, which no-one in their right mind will buy – let alone drink", from another. A young doctor though he could use it as an anaesthetic on his girlfriend, and one

Ancient and modern: casks dwarfed by enormous blending vats at Penfold's Barossa Valley winery.

"very smart person" wanted to buy it as an aphrodisiac on the grounds that it was like bull's blood and would raise his blood count to twice the norm when the occasion demanded.

Schubert, with the connivance of his cellar staff, defied instructions and continued to make Grange undercover – without the benefit, however, of new casks. By 1960, earlier vintages had softened and started to receive some praise. Penfold's Board re-tasted and instructed him to start making Grange again, "with ample funds for the

VARIETY	VINEYARD	DETAILS	AREA
SHIRAZ	MAGILL ESTATE	Planted 1951 & 1967; Morphett Vale cuttings from John Duval's family; original budwood probably from Busby collection. Soils: deep, rich, red loam, clay underneath.	12.50
MATARO	KALIMNA	Oldest planting: 1964	34.35
SHIRAZ	KALIMNA	Planted 1948 & 1967; single cordon training; some machine pruning; manual harvest. Soils: sand and duplex sand over clay; some limestone.	213.85
SHIRAZ	KOONUNGA HILL	Red brown soils – clay-loam and limestone. Oldest planting: 1973	52.92
SHIRAZ	CLARE ESTATE	Oldest planting: 1981	30.48
SHIRAZ	TOLLANA ROESLERS VINEYARD, EDEN VALLEY	Oldest planting: 1978	9.20
SHIRAZ	TOLLANA WOODBURY VINEYARD, EDEN VALLEY	Oldest planting: 1971	104.70
SHIRAZ	SEAVIEW	Oldest planting: 1967	95.56
GRENACHE	SEAVIEW	Oldest planting: 1967	9.27
GRENACHCE	MARKARANKA (Southcorp Wines vineyard)	Oldest planting: 1969	7.85
SHIRAZ	MARKARANKA (Southcorp Wines vineyard)	Oldest planting: 1969	73.30
SHIRAZ	QUALCO (Southcorp Wines vineyard)	Oldest planting: 1968	140.72
GRENACHE	QUALCO (Southcorp Wines vineyard)	Oldest planting: 1967	190.57
SHIRAZ	HUNGERFOLD HILL VINEYARD (Hunter Valley)	Oldest planting: 1969	15.02
SHIRAZ	TULLOCH GLEN ELGIN VINEYARD (Hunter Valley)	Oldest planting: 1900	20.92
SHIRAZ	COONAWARRA	Oldest planting: 1965	94.50
SHIRAZ	KATNOOK VINEYARD (Southcorp wines)	Oldest planting: 1968	85.85
SHIRAZ	TERRA ROSSA VINEYARD (Southcorp wines)	Oldest planting: 1969	59.02
SHIRAZ	PADTHAWAY VINEYARD	Oldest planting: 1969	149.78
		TOTAL (acres):	1400.36

purpose". Grange Hermitage has never looked back.

Early Grange fruit came entirely from Magill and the Southern Vales; Kalimna fruit was not introduced into the blend until the 1960s. Now, although Penfolds are rather coy about admitting it, the wine is made from the most suitable fruit, wherever it may come from – even the Hunter or Padthaway.

Grange represents the summit of Penfold's skill and art, upon which their own reputation and that of their chief winemaker ultimately rests – however much he may protest "team effort". Grange has also become entrenched in Australia's heritage, if the outcry following Penfold's sale of part of the Magill vineyard – the sole source for many years of Grange fruit – to a housing developer is any indication. The fact that the vines lost were white varieties used only for sherry production was irrelevant!

Today, each release receives the same media coverage as might be accorded a new Krug, Mouton or Romanée-Conti, and Grange has become an international collectable. Old vintages are virtually unobtainable – except occasionally at auction where they usually fetch more than Bordeaux First Growths of comparable age.

Max Schubert, who died in 1994, was succeeded by Don Ditter in 1975. Don relinquished this prestigious mantle after the fine 1986 vintage to John Duval – a youthful, modest man – who bears his responsibilities with considerable equanimity.

The quest for improved quality pervades every level of Penfold's operations. In the vineyard, trials are in progress to determine what particular vine-stress factors produce Grange style fruit; is water or nitrogen deficiency the key, or is foliage exposure or bud concentration more important?

The work is based on the observation that the best vineyards always perform well, regardless of vintage, and the belief that the Grange style is a "combination of subtle stresses". The ability to identify and manipulate these would, the argument runs, go a long way to improving overall quality. Underneath the experimentation, viticulturalist Rob Gibson phlegmatically argues that "one of the most important things in handling Shiraz in the vineyard is controlled neglect".

Elsewhere, with an eye to their Aus$7 million annual cask budget, a research programme has been established to monitor the effect of wood provenance and treatment on wine quality. Not just to adapt maturation to overall quality, but to

Traditional cooperage at Penfolds.

refine the amount and type of wood to individual styles. Each cask is coded, enabling wine quality to be correlated with cooperage.

The Penfolds Shiraz range (those from other Southcorp companies are discussed elsewhere) is stylistically varied, each wine designed for a particular market. Apart from Grange and Magill (and a plethora of discontinued wines designated by an incomprehensible system of bin numbers), the current range consists of:

– St Henri, a blend of Kalimna and other Barossa fruit with small quantities from Clare and Coonawarra and sometimes a touch of Cabernet Sauvignon. This wine resulted from an experimental *cuvée* made in 1956 by John Devoran, who trod the grapes in open hogsheads. It was first released in 1957, bearing the label "Auldara St Henri Claret", modelled on a 19th-century label found in a loft, which design is still in use. Its vinification continues Devoran's pattern, including maturation in old 2,000-litre casks to avoid any wood contribution. In style, it is marked by an earthy, leathery character which emphasizes elegance rather than size; however it ages superbly.

– Kalimna Bin 28 is a lighter Shiraz from predominantly Barossa fruit, with additions from Magill, Clare Valley, Coonawarra and the Southern Vales.

– Bin 128 represents Coonawarra. Matured since 1980 in one-fifth new oak and two-fifths two-year-old wood, adjudged the optimal mix for a more elegant cool-climate style.

– Koonunga Hill is a Shiraz-based wine for early drinking, with 15–20% of Cabernet Sauvignon, sourced from a

variety of regions including Riverland. Even this is matured entirely in two- to five- year-old casks.

The month-long process of classifying a vintage of Penfold Shiraz starts in the June following the vintage. During the first two weeks, the "B" team – "pretty sensible people" – taste blind and grade each lot according to quality. During the final two weeks the seven-strong "A" team of John Duval and the group's other senior winemakers grade each sample individually before combining to make a final classification. Once the fate of each lot has been decided, blends are made up and tasted against up to five previous vintages of the relevant wine, to ensure stylistic continuity.

To avoid quantity becoming a decisive factor, the volumes available of each wine are not disclosed to the tasters. So classifying an individual sample as unsuitable for Grange might be rejecting ten casks or a hundred.

At the top level, the Grange style is highly individual – imitated perhaps but not surpassed. To many sophisticated palates, especially Europeans, fashioned on Northern Rhône Syrahs, it is overpowering, too extracted and concentrated, with an unacceptably high volatility. To others, these qualities are its very charms.

The Magill Estate is not – as some have sought to tag it – a junior Grange, but a Shiraz of another style and structure; altogether more elegant and less muscular; as different from Grange as Gainsborough from Rubens. Grange has also nothing in common with Jaboulet's Hermitage La Chapelle in fruit quality, mouthfeel, ageing, vinification... there is virtually no point of contact, except the grape variety – and there are even doubts on that identity. Also, Grange sometimes contains a dab of Cabernet "as a balancing factor"; there is none in La Chapelle.

Penfold's awesome size should not lead anyone to suppose that their products are commensurately industrial. This is as finely and as concientiously crafted a range of Shiraz wines as may be found in any "boutique" winery. The fact that there are 5,000-10,000 cases of Grange is a triumph of standards, not of standardization.

RBJ

This fledgling enterprise produces 150 cases of Theologicum, a 50:50 Mourvèdre-Grenache blend inspired by the Côtes du Rhône styles of Guigal and Jaboulet. Its founders Chris Ringland (Rockford's assistant winemaker), Rolf Binder and Russell Johnston buy in all their fruit. The Mourvèdre comes from 60- to 80-year-old bush vines, grown by Rolf Binder on the valley floor and by Elmor Roehr at Ebeneza at the northern end of the Barossa Valley. The Grenache, also grown by Roehr at Koonunga Hill, is almost as old. All the vines are dry-farmed, yielding only 1–2 tonnes/acre.

The wine, first released in 1991, is made at Rockfords in a distinctly *artisinale* fashion by Chris Ringland. It is fermented in open tanks at 20–25°C for 5–6 days, with the pressings and free-run wine matured separately in 3- to 4-year-old French and American oak hogsheads. This deliberately gives the wine the chance to develop Grenache perfume and Mourvèdre spiciness without the masking effect of new wood. The wine is racked, not fined, and bottled unfiltered.

The half and half mix is arbitary and may change. Chris feels that the Mourvèdre provides tannin structure and a spicy cinnamon-gingerbread lift over dense, plummy fruit, while the Grenache contributes sweet black cherry aromas, flavour-balancing acid and soft tannins. The volume may be small, but the quality is remarkably fine. This is a splendid venture, ably proving that you don't need a large investment to produce interesting quality. Definitely a label to watch.

ROCKFORDS

Both branches of Robert ("Rocky") O'Callaghan's family were grape-growers, so the inevitable happened. In 1971, after training at Seppelts in Rutherglen, he bought four acres of land in Krondorf at the southern end of the Barossa Valley, with the idea of recapturing the tradition of the 1890s, using locally-bought grapes and traditional winemaking methods. He and his wife Pam, opened their "cellar door" in 1984, using the name "Rockford" – an incomplete anagram of "Krondorf".

Rocky is now one of the most respected and high-profile of the Valley's winemakers – he has been president of the Barossa Growers' Association since 1993 and clearly enjoys wine politics. A capable, down-to-earth man, he pursues his goals with skill and determination. His pursuit of tradition, and reliance on antique winemaking equipment, have made a good and oft-repeated story, but without his feel for quality there would have been little more to it than that. It is the excellence of his wines which has made his enduring reputation.

The range includes traditional Barossa varieties – Semillon, Grenache, Mataro, Riesling and Shiraz, which is represented by 4,000 cases of Basket-Press Shiraz and 500 cases of sparkling "Black Shiraz"; there are also 1,500 cases of Dry Country Grenache. The fruit comes from 30 selected growers, whose vines range in age from 15 to 120 years, the average around 80. The different micro-climates of the Barossa, and a close relationship with his growers, enables Rocky to plan the harvest over a six-week period, so that each batch of grapes can be given unhurried and separate vinification. As harvest nears, he spends a great deal of time in the vineyard ensuring that each lot is picked at optimum ripeness.

The winery, to which a new cellar has recently been added, houses a collection of equipment assembled from others'

Colourful Rocky O'Callaghan.

throw-outs, including a 19th century Bagshawe stemmer-crusher and a manually operated basket-press. The Bagshawed fruit, much of it in whole bunches, is fermented in an open, wax-lined slate vat, rescued from the Quelltaler winery; should the temperature rise above 25°C, a sophisticated cooling system whirrs into action: a couple of old milk-vats, bought at a clearance sale, through which the juice is pumped.

Since old vines tend to give massive colour, the time on skins is only 5-6 days. At 1–2 Baumé the wine is run off and the pulp pressed in the basket press. It takes half a day to process five tonnes – the work of a few minutes for a modern press. For Rocky "there's something about being up to your ankles in grape juice each year which is so important". Each press fraction and the free-run wine are then transferred to cask. After 12 months, a pre-blend is assembled; this is then returned to cask for a further year before the definitive blend is put together. The wine is lightly bentonite and egg-white fined – to clarify and "pull the blend together", respectively – then coarse filtered "to stop rocks going through", and finally bottled. The bottles are kept for a further year before release: "it costs money ... that's all!"

Rocky O'Callaghan's wines are as individual as their creator. The emphasis on traditional methods is no fad, but the practical manifestation of a strong belief in their contribution to quality. The clientele for his fine Basket Press Shiraz has spread well beyond Australia and, but for shortage of stock, the sparkling Black Shiraz would undoubtedly follow suit. This is a special delight – combining the weight and depth of premium fruit with the bubbly lift of carbon dioxide; not a frivolous mouthful of fruity froth, but a serious wine of real class and substance.

ST HALLETT

Before 1988, it was likely that anyone who had heard of St Hallett lived in South Australia and regarded it as a producer of "port". The Lindner family who owned the estate were principally farmers – the ground floor of the existing cellar is an old killing pen – but in 1988 they decided to extend the shareholding and brought in Stuart Blackwell (ex-Stellenbosch and Zimbabwe) as winemaker, and Bob McLean (ex-Orlando and Petaluma) for his marketing skills.

Between them, Stuart – a dedicated and skilled winemaker – and Bob – a large, dedicated and skilled gastronome, known far and wide as "Sir Lunchalot" – have transformed a small, sleepy winery into one of the Barossa's quality estates.

The vehicle for this resurgence has been the "Old Block" Shiraz. Originally the produce of 3–5 acres of old vines in two "blocks" belonging to St Hallett and their neighbours, it is now a blend sourced from 28 growers in the Barossa and Eden Valleys whose vines are between 70–130 years old. The original Old Block was due to be grubbed up in 1980, but that year produced such superb wine that it was reprieved as the plough was moving in. The 1980 became the first "Old Block".

All the fruit is dry-farmed, and yields range from 0.5 to 4.5 tonnes/acre. Harvesting is delayed until the berries start to become "baggy" – the cooler Eden Valley ripening a month or so later than the Barossa. Their growers are encouraged to support the Old Block concept by severe pruning – by hand – and, where possible, hand harvesting. In reality, much of the fruit is machine harvested so that it is ready for processing as vat space becomes available.

The fruit is picked at 12.8–14.5 Baumé and vinified in 3- and 6-tonne batches. The goal is a wine with typical Barossa structure, tannin and weight and positive fruit flavours. To this end, half the crop is fermented to dryness for tannin extraction, and half run off at 4–5 Baumé to capture the fruit component.

Maturation is adapted to the source and character of each batch of fruit. Most of the Old Block material sees "new wood" – which here means American oak casks already broken in with Chardonnay – for part of the first year. What Stuart Blackwell wants is the soft, creamy vanillin fraction, rather than obvious new-oak elements.

When the time comes to start "pre-blending", there are some 50–60 different lots to work with – from such euphonic sources as Koch, Pech, Fechner and "Lowdown Grunt" ("stuffing material"). After 3–6 months, those batches which are known to be compatible – e.g. "Valley floor", "loamy" and "iron-country" fractions, are amalgamated. Wine from new growers and from plots which have undergone major changes are kept separate for as long as possible for further evaluation.

At each blending, pressings are used, as necessary, to build up weight. Thereafter, all Old Block material is left to harmonize for 24–32 months in old casks and 500-litre puncheons before light egg-white fining and coarse filtration. Surprisingly, the wine is contract bottled.

The highlight of Stuart Blackwell's year comes with the *assemblage*, when he and his assistant Peter Gambetta taste the various components at their disposal and decide which, and how much, will go into Old Block.

They start with some established principles: the foundation comes from Barossa floor wines, which are smoky, chocolatey and moderately robust. Elegance and subtlety, characterized by pepper, spice and eucalypt, are contributed by Eden Valley components. The "punch" is mainly derived from Greenock, at the north-western edge of the Barossa Valley.

Once the final blend has been compounded, the wine is put into tank for a couple of months to harmonize: "my heart is hanging on", Stuart admits, "the wine changes so often".

Old Block is generally less monumental than the high average vine-age of its raw material might lead one to expect. It is not designed as an old-style, raw tannin, gum-coating, blockbuster, rather a wine of finesse, concentration and length.

In some vintages – mainly earlier ones such as 1984 and 1986 – it would have benefited from more structure, a few days more vatting perhaps, or another dollop of pressings; but it has evolved since Stuart's 1984 debut into a reliable, complex and thoroughly satisfying wine. St Hallett is new-wave Barossa, *par excellence*.

SKILLOGALEE

This 150-acre estate dates back to the 1840s when a Cornish miner, John Trestrail – a deeply religious man who abjured drink and still managed to father 17 children – established a mixed farm on the western side of what is now the Sevenhill sub-region of the Clare Valley. Viticulture arrived in 1969, when Spencer George (father of Stephen George, winemaker at Wendouree) bought the property and planted 50 acres of vines. Twenty years later, he sold out to David and Diana Palmer, who had first tasted Skillogalee wines in Canberra, where David was a management consultant and Diana ran her own catering company.

The Palmers are a talented couple, with a shared love of food and entertaining – even as students in Scotland they would drive 50 miles to try out a restaurant. In 1987, Diana retrained as a chef; her skills now attract high praise for the estate's excellent restaurant, set in an attractive old stone cottage surrounded by vines.

Lack of investment in the property since 1980 left the soils impoverished, a problem exacerbated by compaction from heavy machinery. They are now being carefully restored, with herbicides replacing mechanical cultivation, and an autumn cover-crop introduced to retain moisture. The aim is to improve general soil-structure without doing anything brutal which might compromise quality. Fortunately, there was no winery to worry about, since the winemaking had been contracted out locally. Although David would clearly like to build his own winery, since 1989 winemaking has been entrusted to Stephen John at nearby Eaglehawk (late Quelltaler), a more economically viable option.

The 14 acres of Shiraz are planted at around 475m on steepish, east-facing slopes, in a curious kitchen-garden fashion with odd rows of this and that appearing haphazardly at the edge of blocks. The hope is that a decoy of juicy Grenache, for example, helps keep the birds off the otherwise irresistible Muscat behind. The low-trellised vines follow hillside contours, but aspect and altitude mean harvesting some 2–3 weeks later than elsewhere in the Clare Valley.

The Skillogalee style tends towards solid, full-bodied wines with relatively soft tannins and good depth of fruit. What sets them apart from everything else in

VARIETY	VINEYARD	DETAILS	AREA
SHIRAZ	ESTATE	Planted 1969–70	14.00
		TOTAL (acres):	14.00

En route to Skillogalee.

Clare is a strong eucalyptus character, which David attributes to the rare red stringy bark gums which deposit aromatic eucalyptol on the vines. The Palmers are determined that the winemaking should emphasize the character of their *terroir* rather than bear the imprint of some high-profile winemaker. Recent releases have shown a significant, and consistent,

improvement on the pre-Palmer vintages, which tended to evolved in the rich, gamey, mould. The younger wines have greater depth and purity of fruit and markedly better tannin balances. However, the questionable practice of shaving the insides of the casks after three vintages, to expose new wood, imparts a harsh green nerve to the wine.

Although this may make economic sense, it is not a quality improver and, with yields averaging 1.5 tonnes/acre, arguably unnecessary. In any case, each week of David's continuing management consultancy is "worth several French oak casks", so they shouldn't need to resuscitate the old ones. Nonetheless, this is an estate to watch.

A P BIRK'S WENDOUREE CELLARS

This is one of the most remarkable and consistently fine estates. Largely unknown, even in Australia, it is a model of understatement – no publicity, nothing as vulgar as advertising: just a range of extraordinary wines, most sold locally.

The property – one kilometre up a drive which seems like ten – was bought largely as a hobby by Alfred Percy Birks in the late 19th century. He named it Wendouree ("the place of many waters") because the water is excellent.

Birks started planting in 1896, and by the time he had finished there were 40 acres of Cabernet, Shiraz and Malbec. In 1915 Alfred's son, Roly, took over as winemaker, retiring after 60 vintages in 1974. Unfortunately, difficulties in the early 1970s forced him to sell the property to a couple of operators

involved in petroleum who used it as collateral for other ventures. When they went bankrupt, Wendouree was sold at auction to property developers who promptly stripped the cellar of wines and put up the vineyards for sale.

In October 1974 Wendouree fell into the most unlikely hands of Tony and Lita Brady, through the intervention of Lita's fruit-growing father whose interest stemmed largely from a desire to occupy his son-in-law. Their combined talents were hardly ideal for the job: Tony's wine knowledge was virtually non-existent – "I didn't even know that 'grape' had an 'e' in it" – and Lita was an ex-London dress-designer. Their first winemaker, Chris Sullivan, left to start up in the earth-moving business, although Roly Birks continued to influence winemaking until

1982 when he could no longer drive.

Tony then turned for advice to Stephen George, a Roseworthy graduate, who had left his parents' estate at nearby Skillogalee, to set up Ashton Hills vineyard in the Adelaide hills. Meanwhile Lita, courageously for someone with no scientific background, went off to Wagga to study wine-science. So the present winemaking team is a rather diverse triumvirate: Tony "the arms and legs", Lita "the brains", and Stephen "the palate". It works splendidly.

Over a quarter of a century, the Brady's stewardship has restored Birk's to its former glory. Total yield from their 25.1 acres has been cut from 250 tonnes to an average 42.8 tonnes (1981–1992) and instead of selling most of the wine in bulk (Roly Birk only bottled 500 gallons), or using it as a base for sparkling Shiraz, almost everything is now estate- bottled. Some 2,000 gallons, from higher production blocks, are sold to Stephen George for his Galah label to avoid any speculation that Wendouree might be lightening its style – perish the thought! Fortunately, Max, Lita's father, is more concerned with producing top quality, and less with a return on his investment. If economics had driven policy, things would undoubtedly have been different – irrigation, high yields etc. He is justifiably proud of what has been achieved.

A delightful natural reticence characterizes Tony Brady's approach to the market – fanning the flames of desire with the bellows of indifference, perhaps. It is effective and a refreshing contrast to the hype one finds elsewhere, invariably orchestrated by an expensive marketing department.

These are no-compromise, massively concentrated and firmly structured wines, needing considerable time to unpack. They are also thoroughly traditional in style and reflect the Brady's belief that the land, rather than the winemaker, is paramount – a philosophy of the Old World rather than of the New. Tony sees his role as the custodian of a tradition – "we must do right by the grapes".

This privileged fruit come from a breathtaking roster of old vines, planted on a variety of soils. Wendouree's youngest Shiraz vine dates from 1919, many from 1893 and 1896 and there is half an acre of 1920 Mataro for the excellent Shiraz-Mataro blend. The "cleanest vineyard in Clare" is dry-farmed with most of the vines on trellises, with canopies spread for exposure and aeration which, even with old vines, makes for a healthy environment. "Why don't we water?", jokes Tony Brady cynically: "because it increases production which simply gives you the means of paying for the watering system you put in in the first place". The main farming problem is a soil-nitrogen deficiency which can lead to undesirably high sulphides in the musts; something which he is loath to rectify, since adding nitrogen would only increase vine-vigour. The surrounding scrub provides a natural predator protection – they have only needed to spray against the light-brown apple moth once in 20 years, and even locusts have passed by indifferent.

Harvesting is critical to quality. High sugars lead to high alcohol and this to wines which age poorly. Elaborate analyses, all carefully recorded in great, hand-written ledgers, are undertaken to bring picking as close as possible to the ideal 13.5 Baumé, total acidity of 9 and

pH of 3.25. In Roly Birk's day, the system was to pick at 14.5 Baumé and then dilute the must to the desired level. This colourful practice stopped in 1975 – Tony Brady's first vintage. It took rather more time – seven years of apprenticeship – before Roly Birk was prepared to confide to him his vinification secrets.

In the cellar, the luxury of not having to cut corners means that the pursuit of quality is unencumbered. The very small berries give a high skin-tannin-to-juice ratio, which eliminates the need for additional stem-tannins, so the crop is fully de-stemmed. After crushing and yeasting, it is fermented in open fermenters, at 25–30°C, with hand *pigeage* 5–6 times each day. If hydrogen sulphide levels rise unduly, di-ammonium phosphate is added at 7–8 Baumé and encouraged to work with the help of a fish-tank aerator; otherwise, the wine is run off into cask at 2–3 Baumé.

Until it was discontinued in 1989, Wendouree's rarest and most sought-after wine was the "Pressings", issued with a blood-red label. Now the press-wine is blended back – unless the vintage is unduly hot, when it is held apart until the sugar has finished fermenting to keep tannins under control. Wendouree's *élevage* has seen a phased evolution: there were the large 100-year-old wooden casks, but these became decrepit and had to be destroyed; then came the 100% US oak period; now the mix is roughly half French, half US casks, of which a third of each are new and the rest a year old. The "bigger" the vintage, the more new wood is used. The Shiraz-Mataro has less new wood, being matured mainly in older US oak.

In November following the vintage, the triumvirate start to assess each lot, to select the 1,000 gallons (500–600 cases) for the Shiraz *cuvée*. The fruit destined for the 250-plus cases of Shiraz-Mataro is blended at fermentation; there are no fixed proportions but the Mataro usually comprises 10–25%; in 1991 it accounted for 50%, because some Shiraz was blended with a batch of "very very concentrated" Malbec; the mix was 80:20

Shiraz:Malbec, and the wine "a freak".

The need to fine is rare and filtration has been progressively reduced to a level below which Tony Brady would be "very superstitious" to go. Bottling, a matter of particular concern, is effected by a low-tech 400-dollar two-head filler at the prodigious rate of 500 gallons (3,000 bottles) a day.

The range of wines is remarkable. The Shiraz-Mataro is the least substantial, although still a rich, concentrated wine, showing some of the Mourvèdre's characteristic earthiness. The Shiraz is a dense, massively concentrated wine, with all the depth and natural richness one would expect from low-yielding old vines. Its finely-tuned structure and balance give it great longevity. World-class wine, which could hold its own in any company.

Apart from these and the Cabernet Sauvignon, there used to be a superb, magisterial "Vintage Port", made from 100% Shiraz fortified up to 19% alcohol. The first vintage was 1975, the last, sadly, 1986 – the effect of a dwindling market for fortified wine. Since 1983, there have been 500–700 litres of a delicious Muscat d'Alexandria, fortified to 15.9%. Clare's climatic indices – heat summation, average sunshine hours, mean daily temperature etc – are virtually identical to those of Orange (France), which is only 10km from Beaume de Venise, giving the wines a certain similarity of style though not of specific qualities. The wine started off as a Rhine Riesling, which was fortified "as a joke"; it won a gold medal!

Tony and Lita Brady have nurtured their estate with immense flair and success. Learning from scratch must have been daunting; but the tall, handsome, silver-haired Tony Brady is above all, a man of intellect, and not to be crushed by something as tractable as winemaking. He is imbued with tradition, though not bogged down in it, and takes an informed interest in any research or innovation which might help improve the quality of his wines. Wendouree is without question one of Australia's most impressive estates.

VARIETY	VINEYARD	DETAILS	AREA
SHIRAZ	Central block	Bush-trained vines, planted 1893; shale yield c 0.75 tonnes/acre.	1.70
SHIRAZ	Central block	Trellised vines, planted 1893; shale and red loam; yield c 3 tonnes/acre.	0.60
SHIRAZ	Central block	Trellised vines, planted 1893; sandy loam; yield c 3.3 tonnes/acre.	0.60
SHIRAZ	Central block	Trellised vines, planted 1896; red clay loam; yield 4 tonnes/acre.	0.40
SHIRAZ	Western block	Trellised vines, planted 1911; black alluvial soils; yield c 2.2 tonnes/acre.	2.10
SHIRAZ	Eastern block	Trellised vines, planted 1919; red loam over limestone; 2 blocks:	
		yields 1.9–2.3 tonnes/acre.	5.50
MATARO		Bush-trained vines, planted 1920; red loam over limestone; yield c 2 tonnes/acre.	0.50
		TOTAL (acres):	11.40

WOLF BLASS WINES

For many, both inside and outside Australia, Wolf Blass is identified with the flamboyant, publicity-loving figure of its eponymous founder. With his trademark multi-coloured bow ties, and extrovert personality, the short, dapper Wolf Blass is still regarded as a pioneer of independent, quality winemaking. Invited by Kaiserstuhl, he returned to Nuriootpa in 1960 from Europe, where he studied oenology in Germany, champagne making in Reims and cellar management at Averys of Bristol in England. At Kaiserstuhl he was responsible for developing their sparkling wine range – making, *inter alia*, "Pineapple Pearl", a sort of vinous German hand-grenade. He then spent some years as an independent consultant – in modern parlance, a "flying winemaker" – working freelance helping smaller wineries to improve their products. After a spell as manager and winemaker at Tolleys, he set up on his own in 1973. Having won the prestigious Jimmy Watson Trophy in 1974, he engaged John Glaetzer as his chief winemaker – a fruitful, enduring partnership which remains solid.

The business grew, going public in 1984, and continued to expand with acquisitions and amalgamations. In 1991 it was taken over by Mildara Wines. This group – annual turnover in excess of Aus$110 million – also owns, or controls Yellowglen, Tim Knappstein, Krondorf, Mildara, Tisdall, Quelltaler (Eaglehawk, Black Opal) and Yarra Ridge. For Wolf Blass, a long way from his early days as a $2.50 an hour jobbing winemaker!

Shiraz is a small but important part of Wolf Blass' output. Although a contributor to several blends – including the Yellow Label, a popular, inexpensive wine which "was not allowed to run out", it didn't appear solo until the 1975 vintage, as "Classic Shiraz", which remains its chief manifestation.

Some 40% of the fruit comes from 120 acres of owned vineyards in Clare, Eden and Barossa Valleys, 40% from 160 contracted acres in Clare and Eden Valleys, McLaren Vale and Langhorne Creek – from the start a favourite source for Wolf Blass. The remaining 20% "we pick up on the swings and roundabouts". Most of this is mechanically harvested and crushed as close to the vineyard as possible. With the need for over 19 separate crushing locations, John Glaetzer cannot justify spending Aus$10 million on

John Glaetzer: it pays to advertise.

their own facilities, when other people will process the fruit for Aus$120 a tonne – a saving of half on their crushing overheads. In addition, someone else has the problem of looking after the hardware: "I hate maintenance people – they always cause problems!"

In contrast to the ebullient Wolf Blass, John Glaetzer is a modest, self-effacing man, despite the innumerable accolades his wines have won. He enjoys sailing, and angling for marlin and river-fish; he once tried mountain climbing in Switzerland, an experience he has no wish to repeat: "the only thing that saved me was a pub at the the bottom".

The 6,000 or so cases of Classic Shiraz are compounded from wines made from fruit grown in several different regions – each with its own fingerprint and contribution to the final blend. The Barossa produces rich, tannic, alcoholic (more than 13%) wines; McLaren Vale has chocolate overtones and Eden Valley Shiraz is rich and plummy. Whatever the individual qualities of the constituents, John Glaetzer is firm in the belief that blending is only sensible when the whole transcends its individual components. His winemaking philosophy revolves round the idea of fruit-driven Shiraz, "big, full,

rich and soft wines, which last", but with "positively no maceration character"; they should also have oak which does not dominate the fruit: "no wood, no good".

The winemaking is relatively uncontroversial, except perhaps for de-stalking just 10% of the crop, and for only using casks which have the lightest of "toast". Otherwise, each batch is vinified separately, run off into wood at 4–5 Baumé and, as soon as the last gram of sugar has fermented, racked off its lees. John Glaetzer regards this as important and was horrified to find that in California, winemakers often macerate the new wine on skins for up to a month. However, he also admitted to being impressed by some of the wines he tasted there – "that scares me".

At second racking, after malolactic, comes the selection for the Classic Shiraz. The main criterion is intensity of flavour; lots that fail to meet the specification are destined for the worthy Yellow Label or some other blend. The Classic material is then blended together in 4,000-litre lots, by style, lightly fined, and sulphur adjusted. "Then I get very serious", John continues. Six months after the vintage, samples from each of the 35 individual lots are tasted blind and a pre-selection made. In February, just before the next harvest, the final blend is assembled and then returned to cask. "I couldn't care less about sales figures – I just put together the best wine".

After 24–30 months in wood, the wine is transferred to the Australian Bottling Company's premises at Mildura – an early Wolf Blass acquisition – where it is finely filtered and bottled. John Glaetzer admits that even then, he could envisage three totally different wines from what has emerged from cask. He's a blending addict, blissfully content playing about with a bench-full of samples, mixing and titrating to balance and enhance their various characteristics. The wines more than reward his skill and patience.

VARIETY	VINEYARD	DETAILS	AREA
SHIRAZ	CLARE	35 yr old vines	40.00
SHIRAZ	EDEN VALLEY	10 yr old vines	50.00
SHIRAZ	BAROSSA VALLLEY	25 yr old vines	30.00
SHIRAZ	CLARE VALLEY	35 yr old vines; under contract	40.00
SHIRAZ	EDEN VALLEY	35 yr old vines; under contract	30.00
SHIRAZ	MCLAREN VALE	20 yr old vines; under contract	50.00
SHIRAZ	LANGHORNE CREEK	25 yr old vines; under contract	40.00
		TOTAL (acres):	280.00

COONAWARRA

In the growth of Australian viticulture, Coonawarra was a decidedly late developer. It was discovered and planted by John Riddoch, an MP, and his brother in the 1860s, who had come to Australia from Scotland during the gold rush. The settlement was planned as a fruit-growing colony, and named Coonawarra after its prolific honeysuckle (the word is aboriginal for the plant). The brothers owned 860 square miles, and had the laudable habit of setting up anyone who served them well with a "block" of land. Although grapes formed part of the original enterprise, it was not until the 1890s that Coonawarra's potential for viticulture began to be exploited seriously. Now, with 8,500 acres under vine, the region is fully developed as a premium source of both grapes and wine, especially for Shiraz, Cabernet Sauvignon, Rhine Riesling and Chardonnay.

Coonawarra's location – some 80km from the coast, mid-way between Adelaide and Melbourne but on the way to neither – gives a feeling of cultural isolation. Unless you drive the 500-odd km from either city, the main point of entry is the small airstrip at Mount Gambier, where a sign politely requests the last arriving pilot of an evening to "please switch off the runway lights". There is also a desolate railway platform, whose general decay suggests the infrequent passage of trains.

The area is a narrow strip of land, 15km north-south and 1.5km wide, with a 4km bulge in the middle. It is bounded to the south by the small town of Penola, where Riddoch set up his fruit enterprise, and peters out some 25km south of Naracoorte.

Viticultural development was spasmodic: by 1900 there were 1,000 acres, principally Shiraz and Cabernet Sauvignon, but the great Depression and two world wars shrank this to 200 by 1945, and these mainly produced grapes for distillation. A vine-pull in the 1920s, instituted when grapes were being fed to the pigs because yields were too low to make distillation pay, also contributed to the decline – more as symptom than as cause. Fortunately, Coonawarra didn't lose any vines in the nationwide vine-pull of 1986.

In 1952, the visitor would have found two working wineries – Wynns and Redmans. During the 1960s, large wine firms came to realise the importance of this tract of special *terra rossa* soil and bought heavily into the area. Now, much of Coonawarra is owned by outside interests like Lindemans, Mildara, Penfolds, Seppelts, Rosemount and Petaluma all having significant holdings. The largest individual proprietor is Wynns, now part of the giant Penfolds group, with 1,800 acres; although indirectly and directly Penfolds now own around 45% of Coonawarra's land.

This is excellent Shiraz territory. Indeed, the grape was the mainstay of the area until the 1970s, when it began to cede primacy to Cabernet Sauvignon. Coonawarra Shiraz is characterised by great intensity of fruit, marked elegance and round tannins, with none of the "big", leathery, high-tannin qualities of the Hunter; nor the pepperiness of Macedon or the Victorian Pyrenees, or the obvious berryishness of the Barossa. If such generalisations have value, Coonawarra wines are eminently approachable young but have the ability to age gracefully. Common adjectives are raspberry, mulberry and blackberry, with notes of violets and tar. In the mid-1980s, some growers tried lightening up their wines, but most have reverted to the original style. Unfortunately, as elsewhere in Australia, Shiraz seems to have the aura of a poor cousin, which is a pity. In Coonawarra, when Shiraz is good, it is very good.

It was either Riddoch's genius, or historical accident, which found an area with a unique soil profile and a mild, Mediterranean climate. Coonawarra's proximity to the ocean moderates temperatures with cool, almost cold, nights (critical for balanced ripening) and high relative humidity. The growing season is characterised by a virtual absence of rain, heat summation averaging 1,432 and a mean January temperature of 19.4°C. However, this benign picture hides some peculiarities: the vintage months of March and April can be very wet, resulting in bunch rot problems; there is a risk of heatwaves in January and February and spring frosts are a risk from September to as late as early December. In essence, this climate will ripen grapes, with correct yields and a good flavour profile, in nine years out of ten.

The terrain is flat, with a maximum elevation of 60m, making it ideal for mechanization from pruning to harvesting. This topography has led Penfolds and others to use their vineyards for research projects into canopy management and fruit ripening. Wynns, for example, have found that the 8ft difference in height between the top and bottom of a ridge make a significant difference to grape maturity, with the top ripening two weeks earlier than the lower section, 1km away. Elsewhere, soil depth determines the severity of pruning – deeper soils giving greater vigour and thus greater need to restrict growth. Climate and topography make vintages important and the wines prone to inconsistency; a problem to some extent overcome by careful site selection.

An important, distinctive factor is the *terra rossa* soil for which Coonawarra is famous. Technically it is "non-cracking, sub-plastic clays"; in appearance, weathered limestone stained red by mineral and organic matter. These red soils form a narrow strip, 16km long and between 200m and 1.5km wide. They overlay ancient coral-based limestone, formed millions of years ago by the receding coastline, which varies from a few centimetres to a metre below the surface. The soil's excellent drainage properties, with the permanent water-table 2-4m down, also contributes to Coonawarra's viticultural phenomenon.

However, dissent has broken out between those who believe that the designation "Coonawarra" should be restricted to wine produced from *terra rossa* soils, and those who would include wine from the less propitious "black" soils, which fringe the region. A small number of farmers, hoping to cash in on Coonawarra's name, have bought and planted on non-*terra rossa* soils.

The argument is based on the claim that the sedimentary (not, as often described, volcanic) black soils are more water-retentive and produce altogether lighter wine than *terra rossa*. Detractors also point to black soils being much deeper and generally sited on lower sectors of the vineyard, which makes achieving full ripeness more difficult. However, there are some transition areas, often of greyish soil, where vines seem to perform even better than on *terra rossa*, so the case is not quite as clear as many claim. *Terra rossa* supporters contend that its very shallowness (only 6-24in depth), makes for quality, not least because this restrains vigour, especially during summer, partially stressing the vine. Moreover, they say, the quality of the fruit depends on the drainage of the soils, and the red soils happen to be better drained.

Despite the vigorous arguments, and general agreement among Coonawarra's growers that *terra rossa* produces better ripeness and taste qualities, attempts to establish a precise, official, delimitation of the area (for the purposes of a bilateral agreement with the European Community) have run into trouble. The main difficulty is to prove, to everyone's satisfaction, that the distinctive Coonawarra flavour is not present in brown and black soils outside the *terra rossa* band. Those who produce wine there counter-attack that it is better to

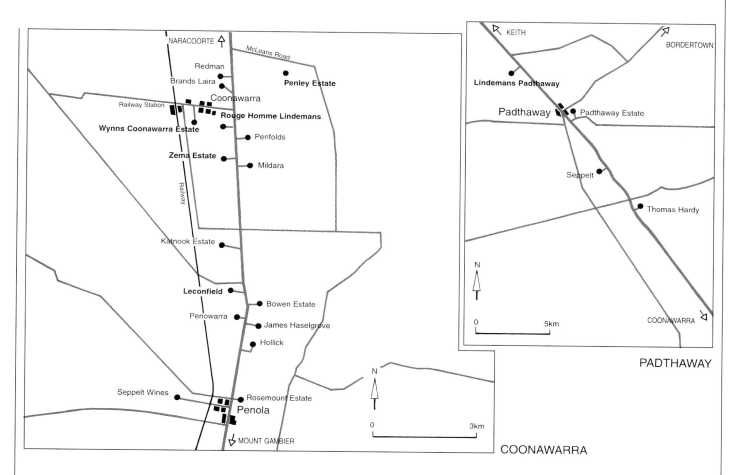

PADTHAWAY

COONAWARRA

crop 2 tonnes/acre on black soils, than 7 tonnes/acre on *terra rossa*. Although true, this is tangential and insufficient to establish their claim. What is clear is that *terra rossa* seems to give an extra dimension of depth and intensity to Coonawarra reds, which is why it is so precious. As one winemaker put it: "I don't know anyone who is growing grapes in deep soils and making fine wine in a really good Coonawarra style". In short, fine Shiraz here depends on a lack of soil.

Though the *terra rossa*-black soils contest rumbles on, a rough delimitation has finally been established. The argument is now likely to switch to the quality differences between north and south. The feeling that northern Coonawarra produces better wine than the south is not easily verifiable, although there is a noticeable difference in taste qualities – southern reds having a more berryish/cinnamon character. Those who stir this particular pot point out that, in the south, soils are generally deeper (undesirable vine-vigour) and the water-table higher. Also that more cloud cover and more ocean breeze reduce warmth and thus retard maturity. Mount Gambier is on average two centigrade degrees cooler than Naracoorte, and northern growers pick some two weeks before

their southern colleagues. However, since the region expanded from north to south, the latter has a younger average vine-age, which undoubtedly contributes to any perceived quality difference.

Planting here needs particular care. The cool climate demands well-exposed leaves and bunches to get the maximum sun: this means rows running north-south. Unfortunately, this cuts across the prevailing westerly wind, so the canopy tends to get bent and damaged. Enlightened growers now devote much work to positioning shoots, pruning and foliage exposure, using foliage control to direct the vine's energy away from leaves and wood and into the berries. Heavier soils retain moisture, which tends to result in the reverse, so careful site selection also helps. Folklore in Coonawarra has it that the vine's roots penetrate the watertable, often 15ft down. "Bullshit", says one forthright winemaker, "if you pull up a vine, the roots only go down a foot or two".

Viticulture here is perhaps best understood in terms of its limiting factors: water availability limits suitable land to within 200 square miles of Penola; conversely, much of the area is ruled out as too water-retentive, becoming waterlogged after rain. Finally there are trees covering potentially good land, but you can't just knock them down.

Fine Shiraz is produced by a number of estates, large and small, which are profiled here. Styles vary, from the deliberate elegance of Lindeman's Limestone Ridge to the deep, tight fruit of Wynns. In addition, Bowen Estate, established by Doug and Joy Bowen in the late 1970s, releases an excellent wine made from 20 acres of Shiraz, 14 planted in 1973 and a further six grafted onto 18-year-old roots in 1993/4. In style the wine is a huge, ripe statement of the grape: deep in colour, high in alcohol (14.2% for the 1991) and densely packed with intense fruit flavours; in good vintages, a rewarding prospect after a decade of cellaring.

The quality of Coonawarra Shiraz means demand, in particular for fruit, for which there is a strong market from both in and outside the area where it is often used to add finesse to a blend. While sales are booming, market awarness of Coonawarra as a premium wine region is less buoyant. Wranglings about soil have distracted growers' attention from the need to consolidate their fragile consumer image, which would only be damaged by any further confusing sub-division. However fierce the internal political divisions, marketing unity is essential if the region is to capitalize on its undoubted asset: quality.

LECONFIELD

In 1837, Richard Hamilton founded Hamilton Ewell, South Australia's first vineyard and winery. Leconfield is the heritage of that foundation, established in Coonawarra in 1974 by the 76-year-old Sydney Hamilton. In 1981 his grandson, Richard, a practising plastic surgeon, acquired the business to add to his other wine interest at Willunga, just south of the township of McLaren Vale, continuing an unbroken family succession.

Since 1990, management and winemaking have been the charge of Ralph Fowler, ex-Tyrrells, -Hungerford Hill and -Cassegrain. The Coonawarra vineyard and headquarters are at the southern, cooler, end of the *terra rossa* belt, 5km north of Penola. Here are planted Chardonnay, Riesling, a traditional Bordeaux mixture and four acres of Shiraz. The estate's finest Shiraz comes, however, not from Coonawarra, but from 23.5 acres at Willunga, including six acres of centenarian vines planted on an elevated site with open, free-draining, gravelly soils.

Ralph Fowler and Richard Hamilton work closely together on general policy and styles, on which they appear to agree. In any event, the results of this collaboration are impressive enough, if gold show medals are admissable evidence. Ralph has a wide tasting experience and is clearly *passioné du vin.* He is also a rose-grower, an enthusiasm which brought 500 rose-bushes to Leconfield in 1993.

The range includes two Shiraz: one from 1975 Coonawarra vines and the other from the centenarian McLaren Vale vineyards; there is also a "Côtes du Rhône" style Grenache-Shiraz blend – "Burton's Vineyard" – from the original bush-trained vines of Burton Hamilton, Richard's father, in McLaren Vale. The blend varies from 75:25 Grenache:Shiraz to 50:50. Before the first release in 1991,

Ralph Fowler.

the Grenache fruit was sold to Yalumba for transformation into "port".

Ralph Fowler is a traditionally minded non-interventionist, making wines as "a statement of fruit" – rather than seeking to stamp his own personality on each *cuvée*: "we have a good micro-flora and don't need to interfere". This requires low yields and careful vineyard husbandry to fully ripen both grapes and stems, whose presence in the vats helps create a bottle-ageworthy wine. The Shiraz *cuvées* are made with virtually no sulphur dioxide, natural yeasts and 20–30 days' *cuvaison* to extract softer, finer, tannins. There is a

natural "lag phase" of maceration before the start of fermentation – presumably to leach out highly-coloured anthocyanins – and temperature is only controlled if levels rise above 30°C. A Willmes bladder press nudges out the press-wine, which is immediately incorporated with the free-run – although the distinction is not one endorsed by Ralph: "pressings is not a word we use in this winery". This is, as much as it ever can be, "hands-off" winemaking.

Whilst the Coonawarra Shiraz may have a touch of new oak "to lift the character of the wine a little", the McLaren Vale has none. Both wines spend 18 months in old-oak Cabernet Sauvignon hogsheads, before light egg-white fining, to take the edge off the tannins and touch up the colour, coarse plate filtration and bottling. As with most Shiraz producers, acidification is needed to stabilize the wine. Ralph recognizes the importance of this operation, but confesses to "an emotional problem" if he has to adjust by more than 1.5 grams per litre. Fortunately the natural balance of old vine fruit helps keep his emotions on a fairly even keel.

Leconfield produces fine – and, in the case of the McLaren Vale bottling, sometimes very fine – Shiraz. These are wines which don't compromise on quality, and which can be bought with every confidence.

VARIETY	VINEYARD	DETAILS	AREA
SHIRAZ	COONAWARRA	Planted 1975, dry-farmed, cane pruned	4.00
SHIRAZ	McLAREN VALE	100+ yr old vines	6.00
SHIRAZ	McLAREN VALE	40 yr old vines	15.00
GRENACHE	McLAREN VALE	60–80 yr old bush-trained vines	2.50
		TOTAL (acres):	27.50

LINDEMAN

Lindeman's started in the 1850s, following the arrival of Dr Henry John Lindeman, a surgeon, from England in August 1840. Despite the setback of a cellar fire, started by an arsonist, in 1851, which destroyed 4,000 gallons of wine and its attendant cooperage, the business flourished. In 1912 the firm bought the famous Ben Ean vineyard at Pokolbin, and in 1914 James Busby's 1825 Kirton Vineyard, both in the Hunter Valley. Further acquisitions

followed including Château Leonay, the ex-Leo Buring base at Tanunda in the Barossa, the Florita vineyard in the Clare Valley and Rouge Homme in Coonawarra. Lindeman's presence in the Hunter Valley, Victoria and South Australia, and the consistently high quality of its wines, make it a powerful force in the Australian wine industry. Its old releases, especially the Hunter Valley Semillons (sometimes labelled "Chablis") and Shiraz (sometimes labelled "Burgundy") are some of Australia's finest mature wines. A programme of holding back stock for

later sale means that these wines can be found, with diligent searching.

Now another tentacle of the mighty Penfolds group, Rouge Homme, has become the spearhead for Lindeman's Coonawarra and Padthaway interests since being absorbed by that Leviathan in 1965. The reticular nature of this enormous business means that some wines appear under the Lindeman label, others as Rouge Homme. However, the various marketing brands do not obliterate the strenuous efforts made to maintain regional and varietal identity.

Shiraz appears under both of these designations as Shiraz-Cabernet blends: as Rouge Homme in a more modest price bracket (Aus$10 retail in 1995) and as the premium single-vineyard Lindeman's Limestone Ridge. In emphasizing fruit and elegance, the Rouge Homme wines are markedly, and expressly, different from the full, ripe berry style of their stablemate Wynns. The group seems actively responsive to the public palate, having decided that lighter, fruitier wines would have a strong appeal to new consumers, whereas Wynns continue with their house style uninfluenced by fashion.

At the viticultural level, integration is complete. The group's 3,115 Coonawarra acres are planned and managed by a single team, headed by Max Arney, in conjunction with group viticulturalists Rob Gibson and Martin Pfeiffer and noted international consultant Dr Richard Smart. Their continuing research programme to increase fruit quality is both detailed and impressive. The objective is not just analytical ripeness, but maximizing those taste and aroma qualities regarded as typical of Coonawarra. Important changes have encompassed canopy management, to control the natural vigour of deeper sections of *terra rossa* soils, and the use of cover crops to provide competition for moisture and nutrients, thus stressing the vine and forcing its roots to dig deeper for nourishment. An elaborate system of aspersion protects the vines from frost, as does higher training, each extra foot increasing warmth by 0.7°C.

Yields lie at the heart of wine quality, so vineyard regimes are tailored to the style of wine being produced. Minimal pruning – a grand-sounding species of *laissez-faire* which produces more bunches but smaller, more concentrated berries – has increased crop levels by 10%. This change in berry composition in turn gives higher skin:juice ratios and thus more extract and flavour. Results also show that minimally-pruned vines usually, though by no means invariably, give better wines than those traditionally pruned, which, to some extent overturns conventional wisdom that yield and wine-quality are inversely related.

The vineyard team does not operate in isolation: their work is increasingly integrated with what goes on in the cellar and *vice versa*. The overriding principle is that "the footsteps of the farmer must show in the bottle". Max and his colleagues clearly have a strong empathy with the vines in their care. So powerful is the influence that Max's son Toby could identify vine-maladies at the age of 12; walking through a diseased vineyard one day he was heard to comment

Greg Clayfield and Coonawarra's famous terra rossa *soil.*

accurately, if not entirely eloquently: "shit Dad, these grapes are stuffed".

For elegance, the grapes are harvested at around 12.5 Baumé – half a degree less than Wynns – although no-one is in any doubt that it is the older, dry-farmed vines which contribute most to concentration. The fruit destined for Limestone Ridge is picked in four separate lots, giving a potential production of 17–20,000 cases, although only 10–12,000 are actually made. The Limestone Ridge vineyard ripens from east to west, as a function of vine age; the eastern sector is on the Coonawarra Ridge, with thinner topsoil, whereas the western sector has deeper soil which benefits from minimal pruning.

The "elegance" theme passes to the cellars and into the experienced hands of Lindeman's chief winemaker Greg Clayfield – a jovial, no-nonsense character – and Rouge Homme's Paul Gordon. The aim is to retain maximum fruit and varietal character, emphasizing more berryishness than fashionable peppery tones, while respecting vintage variations. In general, Coonawarra Shiraz has neither the density nor the weight of wines from

either the Barossa or the Hunter.

Cool fermentation, with only 4–5 days of skin contact, helps retain fruit and enhances fleshy, berry characters; the wine is run off at 3–4 Baumé and fermentation finished in new casks as this is found to give better oak integration. The less expensive Rouge Homme blend has a mixture of new and second year US and French wood.

All the Limestone Ridge passes through the ultra-modern Roto tanks, which are used as well as traditional open fermenters.

The blending of Cabernet with the Shiraz occurs some two weeks after the vintage – ie post-malolactic – by which time the winemakers have a good idea of the quality of each lot. The classical recipe for Coonawarra "Claret" was 90% Shiraz and 10% Cabernet; now the more usual mix is 80:20, although the proportion of Cabernet varies widely, from 6% in the 1976 Limestone Ridge to 40% in 1989. The wines spend 18–24 months in wood with earth and plate filtration before bottling.

The Limestone Ridge typifies the development of Lindeman's Coonawarra

VARIETY	VINEYARD	DETAILS	AREA
SHIRAZ	BROKE VINEYARD (Broke, Hunter Valley)	Oldest planting: 1974	50.00
SHIRAZ	HUNTER RIVER VINEYARD (Pokolbin)	Oldest planting: 1969	31.75
SHIRAZ	STEVEN VINEYARD (Pokolbin)	Oldest planting: 1968	22.25
SHIRAZ	ROUGE HOMME, COONAWARRA	Oldest planting: 1967	110.00
		TOTAL (acres):	214.00

style. Constrained ultimately by the raw material – the fruit – this aims for wines which are approachable young, though with the structure and balance to age attractively. In the face of some excellent older vintages, made without cultured yeasts and very little new or small wood, one might reasonably ask whether change has meant improvement. Greg Clayfield would probably answer that

greater understanding of the factors influencing wine and the mechanisms involved lead to better average quality and less dramatic vintage variation. He admits that the turning point did not come until 1984 when "we had ultimate confidence in the methods – in particular the use of 100% new wood".

The results are by and large excellent, although the insistence on elegance

sometimes results in hollow wines which lack real flesh and conviction. As with the Wynns' cheaper Hermitage blend, the Rouge Homme Shiraz-Cabernet typifies the Australian ability to produce unsurpassable value. Both these wines age well, and are bargains in good vintages such as 1991, 1990, 1986 and 1985. In great vintages such as 1976, the Limestone Ridge can be exceptional.

PENLEY ESTATE

Kym Tolley could hardly escape the Australian wine industry, being the son of two of its most respected dynasties – his father is a Tolley, his mother a Penfold-Hyland. In his words, he "fell into it". After 17 years at Penfolds, he left in 1988, bought 166 acres in Coonawarra and founded "Pen-ley" estate, borrowing three letters from each parent on the way.

The site was "green", requiring surveying, cropping, fencing, ploughing, levelling and planting, as well as the drilling of boreholes to supply an extensive anti-frost aspersion system. The original *encépagement* included 21 acres of Shiraz planted on lightish sandy-loams for better ripeness; 20 more were added in 1994. To maintain cash-flow, a proportion of the estate's fruit is sold under a long-term contract.

Kym, an angular-jawed man in his early 40s, understands Shiraz and is confident of its potential in Coonawarra's cool climate – "provided you get it as ripe as possible". What he seeks is its richer, berryish character rather than the strong pepper mode of Macedon and elsewhere. However, Coonawarra wines are rarely "big", so to fill out the middle palate Kym tried blending. Among his first releases – vinified, from bought fruit, at Ian Hollick's winery nearby – was a Shiraz-Cabernet (60:40), 30% sourced from Barossa and McLaren Vale. In 1990 a few hundred cases of straight Coonawarra Hyland Shiraz appeared, followed by more in 1991 and 1992. Now both wines are regularly offered. Although Coonawarra's mainstay until the 1970s, Shiraz is difficult

Kym Tolley in his essentially Aussie "Drizabone" coat and bush-hat.

to master here. Critical factors appear to be soil and siting, yield and training. Kym

recalls attempts at Penfold's Kalimna estate in the late 1970s to increase Shiraz yields from one to four tonnes/acre as "a disaster". Because Shiraz is a naturally "floppy" grape, producing prolific vegetation, canopy management and restrictive pruning are essential to control yields. Penfold's Grange comes in at 1-1.5 tonnes /acre, which must be at lesson for those seriously intent upon quality.

After six years of intense planning, Penley is well-established in both domestic and international markets – as much for Cabernet Sauvignon and Chardonnay as for Shiraz. A new winery and "cellar-door" sales outlet have brought the operation under one roof and provided the opportunity to fine-tune style and vinification.

Despite its splendid designer presentation, and a steady improvement in quality over recent vintages, Hyland Shiraz is not yet in the top flight. At present, Kym runs the business from his Adelaide office, making only occasional visits to his winery. He clearly knows what top-class Shiraz is all about, but will need to spend much more time in Coonawarra in future if he is really determined to challenge the best.

VARIETY	VINEYARD	DETAILS	AREA
SHIRAZ	PENLEY ESTATE	Planted 1989; vertical shoot training; spacing 2.75x1.75m, 2025 vines/acre.	20.00
SHIRAZ	PENLEY ESTATE	Planted 1990; vertical shoot training; close planting trial: 2x1.5, 3000 vines/acre.	1.00
SHIRAZ	PENLEY ESTATE	Planted 1994	20.00
		TOTAL (acres):	41.00

WYNNS

Wynns is now part of the omnipotent Penfolds Group (qv). As with Lindemanns, Rouge Homme and Penfolds itself, its public image is that of a separate estate. In reality, there is a strong degree of integration, especially in technical matters, such as vineyard management

and classification of wine; so Wynns fruit may well end up in a Penfolds or Lindemanns bottle, but this marketing sleight of hand should not detract from the overall quality of the brand.

The firm came into being in 1951, when the Wynn family bought the John Riddoch Estate, at a time when the elegance and fruit character of Coonawarra dry reds were widely

recognized as adding value to a blend. David Wynn, son of the founder, always regarded the region as the Bordeaux of the Southern Hemisphere – something of a misnomer, since "clarets" of the 1950s were nearer 90% Shiraz, and contained only 10% Cabernet Sauvignon.

The original Riddoch estate was 280 acres of which 180 were planted. Expansion during the red table wine boom of the 1960s and 1970s took the acreage up to 600, all on *terra rossa*. The 1980s saw a strong experimental phase with clones, training and rootstocks; by the time Penfolds took Wynns over in 1985, there were 2,000 acres under vine.

Wynns offer two 100% Shiraz releases: an estate wine and a premium grade, "Michael's Selection" which, after a "one-off" appearance in 1955, was re-incarnated in the 1990 vintage.

Prior to that, David Wynn wouldn't countenance a premium Shiraz and blocked the idea. However, when a wine was proposed as a memorial to his son Michael, who died prematurely in the early 1950s, he gave it his blessing. The result is an excellent wine which is designed for bottle-ageing. The 1955 release amounted to 500 gallons, the 1990 to several thousand cases.

The Penfold Group selection process entails all Wynn's Shiraz grapes being treated in the expectation that they will become part of the Grange blend. This means harvesting fruit at pre-determined ripeness, expressed in terms of sugar, acids and flavour profile. To ensure balance, elegance and structure this deliberately covers the spectrum from 11.5-14.5 Baumé. Pruning and picking are mechanical operations here: "we haven't got Mexico to the south of us, nor a heap

VARIETY	VINEYARD	DETAILS	AREA
SHIRAZ	COONAWARRA	Oldest planting: 1925	406.65

of South African Kaffirs we can employ", is how Wynn's winemaker Peter Douglas justifies the policy.

The selection for "Michael" starts in the vineyard and continues until about one-third of the way through fermentation, when the quality potential and fate of each batch is decided. Until recently, Wynns Shiraz has been a mixture of traditional fermentation and carbonic maceration. Now, all the fruit destined for the Michael Selection, is put through a rotary fermenter, to speed up extraction, before the wine is run off at 2–3 Baumé to finish fermentation in new US oak. After malolactic, the wine is centrifuged, assembled in tank, and returned to the same casks. Only around half of what is originally identified as potential "Michael" material in fact finds its way into this prestige *cuvée*.

The casks are then turned *bande de côté* which is believed to maintain and conserve fruit character. In contrast, Penfolds use an upright bung which, in Peter Douglas' view, results in a distinctly leathery character — helped, no doubt, by the warmer temperatures of

Nuriootpa, where Penfold's Barossa wines are matured.

After 18 months' maturation, the definitive "Michael" selection is made. The wine is Kieselguhr-filtered, but not fined because tannins tend to be low – a result of mechanical harvesting, which automatically discards the stems, and Coonawarra's naturally supple character.

It is then shipped in bulk to Nuriootpa where it is further plate-filtered on the bottling line. Wynns would prefer not to filter at all, but are concerned about maintaining cleanliness and avoiding re-fermentation – a pity but, given the volumes involved, perhaps understandable.

"Michael" is only made in outstanding vintages, and once the *cuvée* has been chosen the "left-overs" are fought for by the group's army of winemakers, eager to get the best for their own blends. So the wine may end up as a component of St Henri or Bin 389. These selection complexities, and Penfold's inter-group contortions, should not detract from the quality image of Wynn's stand-alone Shirazes.

ZEMA ESTATE

This is a splendid small family estate, the heart of which is 20 acres of prime Coonawarra *terra rossa*. This land was already planted to Shiraz when the Demetri and Francesca Zema bought it in 1982. They had intended to stay in the area for a couple of years before returning to their native Calabria, but changed their plans when the chance arrived to realize a long-held an ambition to own some Coonawarra *terra rossa*. Cabernet was planted in 1984 and a further 60 acres at Cluny added in 1988, of which 20 have been planted with a Bordeaux mix and some Nebbiolo. Now, with their sons Nick and Matt, and winemaker Ken Ward – one of the Wynns team – the Zema's roots are firmly established in Coonawarra.

The Shiraz plot, bordering the main road through Coonawarra, is dry-farmed to limit vigour, hand-pruned and, seemingly without detriment to quality, machine-harvested. Yields are deliberately kept around 2.5 tonnes/acre to intensify the peppery Shiraz fruit.

The crop is harvested at 12.5–13 Baumé and pot-fermented for seven days

at below 25°C. After settling in stainless steel tanks, the first two pressings are blended back, the third separated and evaluated after six months for possible incorporation. The wine spends 12–18 months in old casks with 15–20% new wood. Before bottling, sulphur, acidity and pH are all adjusted.

The Zema Shiraz is a wine of consummate class. The style has consciously changed from the big-framed, high tannin and high acid wines of earlier vintages to the more traditional Coonawarra of the early 1970s – still substantial, but with less tannin. Nick Zema attributes much of the improvement to the changeover from their old basket-press to a gentler Vaslin. In exceptional vintages the Shiraz is released as "International Show Reserve".

These are not, however, designer wines for the Show circuit, although they regularly bring in medals. The fact that these tend to be bronze and silver, rather than gold, is perhaps more a reflection of judges' criticisms of the absence of any obvious new oak than any inherent lack

of quality. Such restrictive standards belittle the Show system. This doesn't deter the customers, who eagerly snap up the 1,500–2,000 cases of Zema Shiraz in two or three months, both in person from the cellar door and at restaurants and bottle shops in Melbourne.

Nick, a rather laid-back, swarthy man, a thorough-going Aussie with a passion for cricket, disapproves of this system, which seems to generate too many orders and a shortage of stock. They tried buying in some Shiraz to remedy the deficiency, but couldn't get the quality they wanted.

This estate may be a small, an enclave surrounded by the enormous acreages of Lindemanns, Wynns and Katnook. No matter, the product is outstanding: some of the richest, most satisfying Shiraz to be found in this Shiraz-dominated district.

VARIETY	VINEYARD	DETAILS	AREA
SHIRAZ	ZEMA ESTATE	30 yr old, hand-pruned, dry-farmed	9.00

HUNTER VALLEY

The vineyards of the Hunter Valley extend north-west from the town of Cessnock, 100 miles north of Sydney. The region is divided into two sub-regions – Upper and Lower Hunter – the former centered on Muswellbrook and Denman, the latter on the small town of Pokolbin.

The Upper Hunter, with only nine principal wineries and just 190 acres of Shiraz, is the less important of the two areas; its principal quality exponent is Rosemount Estate (qv). In contrast, the Lower Hunter has 49 wineries, densely concentrated within a narrow band north of Cessnock, and 1,125 acres of Shiraz. As the principal red grape and with a long tradition of varietal production, it was widely known as Hermitage until European leglislation, accepted by Australia for export markets in a bilateral agreement, made the name illegal. Hunter Shiraz has developed as a distinctive Australian style – as has the Hunter's other signature wine, Semillon.

Surprisingly for such a hot region, planting in the Hunter started early, in 1830. The first vineyards were established on the river flats, where in highly fertile soils, vines produced prolific vegetation and huge crops. Unfortunately, mildew was rife and growers soon retreated to the poorer soils of Pokolbin, where humidity and rainfall were less marked.

In the decades that followed, expansion was slow, and was reversed by the Depression of the 1890s and notable outbreaks of downy mildew, hail and drought between 1925 and 1927. An almost explosive planting boom between 1965 and 1979, mostly in the Upper Hunter, was soon reversed as uneconomic vineyards were grubbed up in the 1970s and the vine-pull of 1986. Now there are 7,050 acres of vineyard, 4,700 in the Lower Hunter, concentrated south of the river, and 2,350 in the Upper Hunter.

The region's climate is sub-tropical, with a growing season marked by heat (heat summation 2,075), high humidity and summer cloud. The annual rainfall is high and evaporation low, reducing the risk of heat-stress. The prevailing winds are westerly: cold during the winter, searingly hot in summer. Pests and diseases thrive in the humidity, especially the destructive light brown apple moth, the rust mite, downy mildew and botrytis, necessitating frequent spraying; there is also risk of bunch-rot at flowering. There is great variation in rainfall from year to year, so drought can be a problem, not only stressing the vine, but promulgating powdery mildew. There are often rain storms just before the harvest, which tends to be short, with fermentations starting immediately if the weather is hot, so growers prefer to inoculate with a yeast culture to have an uniform vinification. All this makes for significant vintage variations.

Phylloxera is also a potentially important problem. It is endemic in Sydney gardens, leading growers to speculate that "hobby farmers", or even visitors, might bring it to the Hunter on shoes or machinery. Many estates now plant on resistant root-stocks for protection.

Choosing the right soils and site is particularly important here for Shiraz (and indeed, for Semillon). Traditionally, the best soils – deep red loams over clay – went to red grapes and the poorest – sandy loams and sandy clays – to Semillon. The Pokolbin area has a very mixed geology: the finest Shiraz sites are on deep red clay loams, often volcanic, (duplex soils) which are found in narrow strips on some hillsides (eg at Lake's Folly and McWilliams). Elswhere, they graduate through to patches of real plasticene clay. The river flats are too alluvial for decent viticulture, and in other places (eg McWilliams' Loveday Semillon vineyard) the soils are so poor that even the rabbits are said to carry lunch boxes.

Most winemakers agree that great Hunter Shiraz is made in the vineyard. The preferred fruit comes from dry-farmed, low-yielding, struggling old vines, which produce wine with brilliant structure and intensity. As elsewhere, decisions about fruit selection, cask selection, the length and type of wood maturation, and whether or not to add back the press-wine, all play a part in creating a wine's personality.

The Hunter Shiraz is the last remaining deliberately "old-fashioned" expression of the grape in Australia. The style still has credibility, especially in Australia, where it is highly prized. So ingrained is the shiraz character that it always seems to assert its dominance – especially as the wines age. There seems to be some hidden alchemy which, with age, turns Hunter Pinot Noir and Cabernet Sauvignon into Shiraz, even though these qualities are not apparent in the young wines. Old vintages (see tasting notes) from Lindemans, McWilliams and Rothbury, attest to Shiraz's excellence and its ability to age.

In essence, the Hunter style consists of heavy, defined fruit, with a hallmark touch of earthiness. While wines may develop some finesse, this is not a region known for delicacy – rather more for extract and power. The Hunter "earthiness" is attributable to chemicals known as mercaptans, themselves mainly hydrogen sulphide derivatives, and can vary between a subtle, garlicky, leathery quality, and full-blown "sweaty saddles". While many devotees like to see some of this traditional mercaptan character in aged Hunter Shiraz, it is thoroughly disliked by judges on the important Show circuit, where estates rely upon success for publicity. Even the slightest hint means instant rejection. Judges' emphasis on purity, and their insistence on wines of almost clinical sterility, is felt by many to be slowly obliterating regional identities. If so, this is a pity, especially with wines destined for international markets, where such individuality is taken as a mark of character rather than as an analytical fault.

In recent years, vinifications have moved towards cooler fermentations, greater reliance on selected yeasts, and the use of heading boards to submerge the cap of solids during fermentation, rather than hand punching which many felt led to over-extraction. Today, maturation is more likely to be in small casks, with a proportion of new wood, than in large oak hogsheads. These improvements produce better-balanced wines, without compromising their essential Hunter character.

The pattern of production has changed over the last half-century, from small, family-owned enterprises to much larger, more commercial operations. In the Lower Hunter, Lindemans, McWilliams, Rothbury Estate and Tyrrells dominate the high-volume quality Shiraz market, while the driving force in the Upper Hunter is Rosemount Estate. Among smaller establishments, the superb quality produced by Iain Riggs at Brokenwood stands out.

The Hunter is a paradise for wine-loving visitors, who are well catered for with the winery restaurants and hotels. Families drive up from Sydney for a day or a weekend to taste and buy wine and enjoy the attractive countryside. Those who select well return with treasures of Shiraz and Semillon, knowing that, given patience, they will have something magnificent to look forward to.

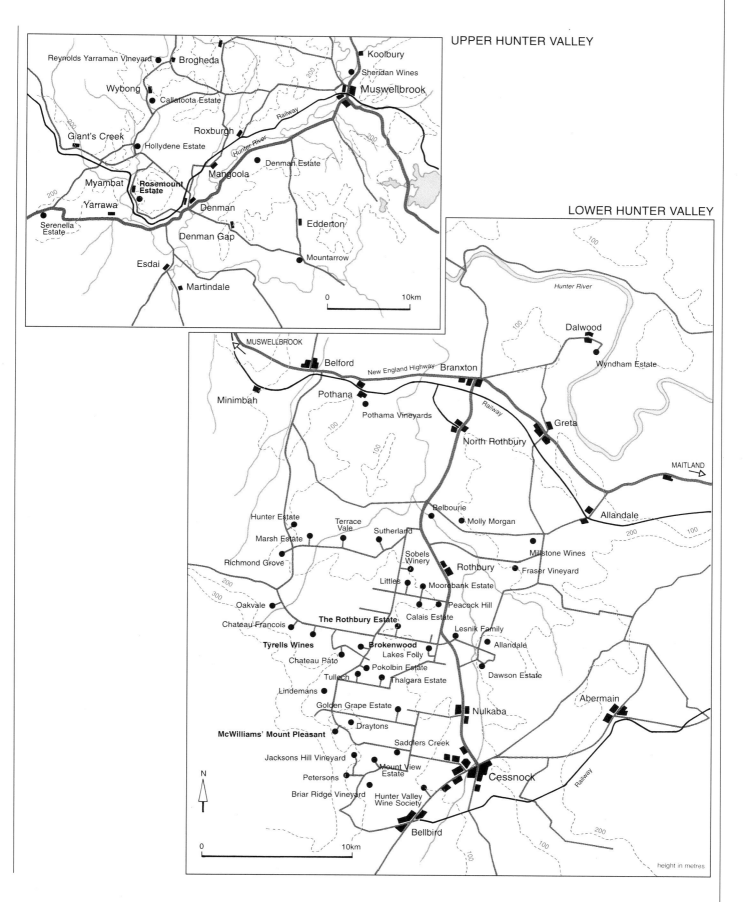

UPPER HUNTER VALLEY

Reynolds Yarraman Vineyard
Brogheda
Koolbury
Sheridan Wines
Wybong
Muswellbrook
Callatoota Estate
Railway
Roxburgh
Giant's Creek
Hunter River
Hollydene Estate
Denman Estate
Mangoola
Myambat
Rosemount Estate
Yarrawa
Denman
Serenella Estate
Denman Gap
Edderton
Esdai
Mountarrow
Martindale

0   10km

LOWER HUNTER VALLEY

Hunter River
Dalwood
MUSWELLBROOK
Belford
New England Highway
Branxton
Wyndham Estate
Minimbah
Pothana
Railway
Greta
Pothama Vineyards
North Rothbury
MAITLAND
Hunter Estate
Belbourie
Molly Morgan
Allandale
Terrace Vale
Marsh Estate
Sutherland
Millstone Wines
Richmond Grove
Sobels Winery
Rothbury
Fraser Vineyard
Littles
Moorebank Estate
Oakvale
Peacock Hill
Chateau Francois
The Rothbury Estate
Calais Estate
Lesnik Family
Tyrells Wines
Brokenwood
Allandale
Chateau Pato
Lakes Folly
Tulloch
Pokolbin Estate
Dawson Estate
Lindemans
Thalgara Estate
Abermain
Golden Grape Estate
McWilliams' Mount Pleasant
Draytons
Nulkaba
Jacksons Hill Vineyard
Saddlers Creek
Mount View Estate
Petersons
Cessnock
Briar Ridge Vineyard
Hunter Valley Wine Society
N
Railway
Bellbird
0   10km
height in metres

BROKENWOOD

Brokenwood, at the centre of the Pokolbin district of the Lower Hunter, was born in October 1970 when three Sydney solicitors, among them James Halliday, bought a ten-acre block of scrub flanked by the wine estates of Lindemans and Hungerford Hill. The first vintage, 1973, was made from Shiraz and Cabernet grapes transported to nearby Rothbury in the back of Len Evans' Bentley. Steady growth and a capital injection from six new partners allowed the purchase, in 1978, of the nearby Graveyard Vineyard – a superb site beneath the Brokenback hills on land marked as the Polkobin cemetery in the 1882 town plans.

A crucial change came when Iain Riggs, ex-Roseworthy College, Bleasdale's in Langhorne Creek and Haselmere in McLaren Vale, was appointed winemaker and managing director to oversee the construction of a new air-conditioned winery. Prior to 1983, Brokenwood was essentially a "boutique" affair, producing only reds at a time when, as now, the normal ratio was 60:40 white:red. James Halliday left in 1983 to set up his own estate, and the operation is now owned by a consortium of shareholders.

Brokenwood make two Shiraz: since 1993, a wine from McLaren Vale fruit, fermented there and trucked down to the Hunter and, from 1984, the exceptional single-vineyard "Graveyard" Hunter Shiraz, made mainly from 12 acres of vines planted on their own roots in 1968 by Hungerford Hill. Between 1990 and 1993, a further eight acres were added, this time on selected rootstocks both to avoid phylloxera and to combat the effects of low pH soils, which tend to stifle growth after 20 years. These wines have had considerable impact on the image and quality of Hunter Shiraz.

Given low yields, Iain Riggs sees striking similarities between Hunter and McLaren Shiraz. So while his 1968 Hunter vines struggle on shallow, low-fertility soils, in a vineyard of very mixed geology, yielding a miserly half-tonne per acre, he is busy sourcing McLaren Vale fruit from traditionally-planted, low-yielding plots. Very ripe grapes, low yields and small-volume fermentations contribute significantly to the extracty nature of Brokenwood Shiraz.

In 1986 Iain deliberately changed tack. He switched from the overtly leathery, classic Hunter profile, the product of early picking and bottling, vigorous tannin extraction from four weeks' vatting and vinification with inherited, distinctly primitive equipment, to an altogether

Iain Riggs.

sweeter, richer and more balanced style.

This change is due mainly to later harvesting, shorter *cuvaison* to finish fermentation in cask, and the use of new American oak. The Graveyard has a distinct touch of Grange about it. Iain discounts the widespread myth that the longer the wine is on skins, the softer the tannins. This may indeed happen, but it won't correct a heavy tannin imbalance from over-vatting in the first place.

The 600 cases of Graveyard Shiraz represent a rigorous, continuous selection from the various Graveyard lots. Vatting lasts a mere five days with extract deriving from low yields, small fermenters (two-tonne – six-cask – batches) and the alcohol developed from ripe grapes. The bunches are destemmed, crushed and inseminated with yeast, then vinified with pumping over at 18–24°C. The wine is run off at 3 Baumé then, with press-wine (from a gentle Willmes bladder press) added back, put into 100% new US oak casks. Eight months later, each lot is assessed to decide whether it can support further new oak, or will continue in older wood. After some 15 months in total in cask, the wine is egg-white fined, filtered "through silk stockings" and bottled.

The proportion of McLaren to Hunter Shiraz in the standard blend depends on

the qualities of the vintage in each area; the mix varies from 100% McLaren in 1993, through 78% in 1992 when it "rained like hell" in the Hunter, to 25% in the great 1991 Hunter vintage. This only gets 25–30% of new wood – "if it's lucky" – but exemplifies the house style, though to a lesser degree than the Graveyard.

Although the Graveyard designation did not appear until 1984, the first Shiraz from 100% Graveyard fruit was in fact made in 1980 and labelled "Hermitage". There was no Graveyard in the disastrous 1992 vintage, and precious little in 1993 when the vineyard, struggling to recover from 1992 and 18 months of drought, only cropped 2.5 tonnes from 12 acres.

In common with most great winemakers, Iain Riggs leaves little to chance – everything is done for a reason, nothing from sheer habit. He also tastes widely – especially Bordeaux, where he notices that a good balance in a wine will be apparent early on. His own wines are exemplary: the style now honed to accentuate balance and depth, facets revealed by long ageing, particularly for the Graveyard. Apart from the Shiraz *cuvées*, there is Chardonnay from the Hunter, Pinot Noir from the Yarra Valley and a gorgeous, barrel-fermented, Hunter Valley Semillon. This is a top-class estate.

VARIETY	VINEYARD	DETAILS	AREA
SHIRAZ	GRAVEYARD VINEYARD	3 blocks, planted 1968, on own roots	12.00
SHIRAZ	GRAVEYARD VINEYARD	Planted 1990–93; 2 blocks, on root-stock;	8.00
SHIRAZ	POKOLBIN	Planted 1970	10.00
		TOTAL (acres):	30.00

MCWILLIAMS WINES

McWilliams is the largest family-owned wine company in Australia. Since 1877, five generations have built and nurtured the business which, until the late 1960s, was mainly known for its ports and sherries and for the legendary wines of Maurice O'Shea.

O'Shea was a genius in his time – one of Australia's most gifted and revered winemakers, and half a century ahead of his contemporaries. His mother being French (his father was English) he finished his education in France, before returning to Australia in the 1920s and becoming a partner with McWilliams in 1930. Many of his great wines from the 1930s, 1940s and 1950s are still magnificent, and command staggering prices at wine auctions. His talent lay in his ability to recognize greatness in wine very early on, and in his knack of blending from various vineyards and regions to create a whole that was greater than the sum of its parts. His intimate understanding of vineyards and grapes was backed by a formidable palate. The present generation, Doug McWilliams with chief winemaker Phillip Ryan, strive to continue that tradition.

The firm has grown considerably, now owning half Brand's Laira in Coonawarra and Barwang vineyard in New South Wales. Although Shiraz is produced at all three facilities, the top *cuvées* come from shy-bearing old vines in the Lower Hunter. Maurice O'Shea used to name his "Hermitages" after particular friends – so Charles, Philip and Richard confusingly appeared. Now there are three regular Hunter *cuvées*: Philip, a 40,000-case blend designed for a few years' ageing; 3,000 cases from the Rosehill vineyard – in fact it produces rather more than is offered, production being deliberately restricted to maintain it as a premium product – and 1,000-1,500 cases blended from the Old Paddock and Old Hill vineyards. These two vineyards were originally planted in 1880, with vines from Tain l'Hermitage imported by Charles King, an Oxfordshire man who arrived in Australia in 1844.

The firm's top wine – 500 cases of the Maurice O'Shea selection – is simply the best wine in the cellar, irrespective of grape variety: the inaugural release, in 1987, was the OP/OH Hermitage. This has caused some company controversy. Phillip Ryan maintains that the wine should come from the Hunter, where O'Shea's finest wines were crafted; against him are "forces which think that O'Shea should be the best wine in the stable". Whatever their origin, future

Phillip Ryan.

selections will apparently be made at the grape stage rather than, as hitherto, wine.

The company aim with Brand's Laira and Barwang is to cover the entire Shiraz. spectrum. Barwang, on rich, red soils at 2,000 feet in the Hilltops area on the south-west slopes of the Great Dividing Range, exemplifies the cooler, more elegant, soft berry fruit style for young drinking. Brand's Laira – Bill and Jim Brand own the other half, and manage the property – is both the name of a vineyard and also that of the ship which bought the original grape cuttings to Australia. As well as a straight Coonawarra Shiraz, the firm produce a small amount of "Original Vineyard" Shiraz from the original 1896 plantings. In the Hunter, McWilliams also work with eight outside growers, including Phillip Ryan's own splendid 140-acre vineyard, adjoining his hilltop home.

A commendable McWilliams policy is that of holding back wines to age – in 1994, for example, they were listing wines from 1977, 1985 and 1987, as well as the

120 other wines on their roster. Apart from sales through their Mount Pleasant cellar shop, old releases are carefully targeted at "safe houses" – retailers who look after the wines. There is now an annual September release of these treasures.

Phillip Ryan's palate was trained on old vintages and the philosophy that wine should be aged – especially Hunter Shiraz and Semillon. When he started in McWilliams' Sydney laboratory in 1965, the chief chemist would bring out an old bottle every day: "we'd drink these – usually O'Shea wines – with a cheese sandwich". In those days there was no qualified winemaker, so the laboratory effectively controlled the entire production. His personal mission statement is that he is "not trying to make 'knock-'em-down-drag-'em-out reds, but elegant and above all enjoyable wines". His own ideas have also to dovetail with company policy, which favours wines with fruit, flavour and softness but without huge tannic structure and aggressiveness.

Grapes are picked in small lots, with each vineyard, grower and block being monitored separately. The main criterion is taste: "such lovely sweet, ripe flavour which is Shiraz as it ripens; we never need lunch during the harvest". Phillip is able to tell the origin of each batch at the crusher and if the wine has promise: "if it's crimson 'we've got it'; also it should smell of raspberry, not pepper". The crop is dusted with sulphur – "tiger powder: it makes you feel good" – and given a dose of di-ammonium phosphate to feed the yeasts. Chilling the yeasted crush gives a long, slow start to fermentation. After seven days' or so vatting, including a couple of days on skins after fermentation, the Rosehill and OP/OH wines are run off at 1 Baumé and the pressings re-incorporated. Then into 50:50 new and older oak, all American, for 15 months – each lot still separate, though each batch is equalized at racking. From malolactic on, the casks are given a quarter turn – *bande de côté* – so there is no headspace under the bung: this eliminates the need for topping up.

With harvest around March, the precise work of blending the hitherto

VARIETY	VINEYARD	DETAILS	AREA
SHIRAZ	OLD PADDOCK, LOWER HUNTER	Planted 1880 & 1920 – own roots and some root-stock; 2 tonnes/acre	13.00
SHIRAZ	OLD HILL, LOWER HUNTER	Planted c. 1880; mainly own roots; 2 tonnes/ acre	10.20
SHIRAZ	ROSEHILL, LOWER HUNTER	2–25 yr old vines on own roots; 2–3 tonnes/ acre	73.00
SHIRAZ	BARWANG, HANWOOD NSW	Original vineyard ; 25 yrs old; own roots	3.50
SHIRAZ	BARWANG, HANWOOD, NSW	New vineyard – 3–4 yrs old; on own roots	45.00
SHIRAZ	BRANDS LAIRA, COONAWARRA	Original vineyard, 100 yrs old	4.00
SHIRAZ	BRANDS LAIRA, COONAWARRA	Laira vineyard, 5–47 yrs old - own roots	20.00
		TOTAL (acres):	168.70

separate lots starts in August of the second year; so Old Paddock is mixed with Old Hill and the various Rosehill lots, tasted to select the *cuvée*, then blended together. These wines, the company's two best Shiraz, invariably have more new oak than the rest. Phillip Ryan wishes he could buy more, but there is an oak budget: "we face this every year", he explains. "Each of the four wineries wants oak, but we are constrained by what the marketing department can charge for the wines". This seems to be a slightly sore point.

A curious feature of company policy is that, once blended, cold-stabilized and earth-filtered, wines are sent up to Sydney for bottling. "Shifting wine around terrifies me", admits Phillip. Given the risks, with no possible gains, why are the high-quality, smaller volumes not bottled on site, at Mount Pleasant?

Trials to eliminate unnecesssary filtration have proved inconclusive. Phillip Ryan would like to abolish the present pad filtration, but concedes that this could give problems with wines which are cellared for several years before release. There seems to be a need for a clearly defined company policy on what level of risk with filtration, sulphur etc they are prepared to accept.

The McWilliams range is formidable – including, apart from classic Hunter Semillon and Shiraz, a stunning line-up of fortified wines, with which they control 25–30% of the Australian fortified market.

These include a magnificent sweet Verdelho from a 1928 solera: rich, deep and complex; an equally lovely 1979 tawny "port", from two-thirds Shiraz and one-third Cabernet, fortified with 1963 pot-still Show brandy; and a phenomenally concentrated old Liqueur Muscat from 1960/1962 soleras – a nose of candied orange and a delicate, yet supremely rich raisiny flavour, from Black Muscat grapes. It is a great pity that these market-conquering wines aren't exported. Surely not "company policy" on the march again?

ROSEMOUNT ESTATE

Rosemount is a story of business success, built firmly on the rare combination of quality, value and volume. The company was founded by Bob Oatley, a successful coffee and cocoa merchant in New Guinea, who chanced upon the site that was to become the nucleus of the estate, near Denman in the upper Hunter, in 1969. A German settler, Karl Brecht, planted vines here in 1864, but after his death in 1900, the land reverted to pasture until Oatley arrived.

The few original vineyard acres have now grown to 600, with sites in McLaren Vale, Langhorne Creek, Orange and Coonawarra as well as the home base. Rosemount is particularly known for its Chardonnays, especially its Show Reserve, and top-class releases from the invididual Roxburgh and Orange vineyards.

Winemaking is in the hands of the talented Philip Shaw, who joined Rosemount from Lindemans in 1982 "a week before the vintage". His principal interests were then Chardonnay and Pinot Noir, and although Rosemount had sold a varietal Shiraz since 1974 (labelled "Hermitage" till 1978), it was not until the late '80s that he became "motivated" by the grape. Philip admits that some of his most memorable wine experiences have been old Hunter Shiraz, including the remarkable 1958 Lindemans – "still fresh as a daisy" – and the extraordinary 1965 Bin 3110.

Shiraz is now a central focus of the Rosemount range. As well as Flame Tree Shiraz and Peppertree Shiraz-Cabernet, marketed under the Ryecroft label, there are three Rosemount Shiraz releases: a soft, lightish Shiraz-Cabernet for early drinking; an estate Shiraz, sourced

Rosemount's vineyards in the upper Hunter valley, viewed from the estate's terrace.

principally from Hunter, Mudgee and McLaren Vale fruit, and the Show Reserve Syrah (*sic*), first released in 1989, from dry-farmed, head-trained and hand-picked 100-year-old McLaren Vale vines. From the 1992 vintage, this was re-christened "Balmoral" Syrah after the Oatley family home, built in 1852.

Selection for each starts at harvest, refined by accumulated experience of the characteristics of each vineyard. Some are picked early, contributing a green-pepperiness to the blend, others left until later for the firm, soft tannins of their mature fruit. Younger vines are machine-harvested. To further fine-tune each blend, individual vineyard and picking lots remain separate for as long as practicable.

Wine styles reflect the predominance of McLaren Vale fruit, which imparts depth, warmth and richness and adds flesh and approachabilty to typically soft tannins. McLaren climate and soils vary dramatically, from very cool to very warm, and from sand (at Blewitt Springs) through *terra rossa* and high-yielding,

VARIETY	VINEYARD	DETAILS	AREA
SHIRAZ	HUNTER ESTATE	Mix of early 60s Penfold plantings and late 60s additions; own roots, minimal irrigation	50.00
SHIRAZ	MCLAREN VALE	Half 15–20 years old; 40% younger; 10% up to 100 yrs old. 85% owned by others; Rosemount have 65 acres	450.00
SHIRAZ	LANGHORNE CREEK	Planted 1992/3;	200.00
SHIRAZ	ORANGE VINEYARD, NSW	Planted 1990; own roots.	10.00
		TOTAL (acres):	710.00

heavy clays to lighter podzolic clays on hillsides. The best Shiraz is from sandy-red loams in the cooler foothills.

The Hunter, in contrast, contributes more defined fruit, tighter and firmer in structure. The Orange vineyard, planted in 1990 on Mount Canobolas, near Orange in New South Wales, gave its first crop in 1993, producing Shiraz of outstanding depth of colour and striking elegance. This has the quality to stand on its own and, it is to be hoped, will not be blended away.

Shiraz vinification has evolved round the desire to build big wines with a firm backbone. This means two weeks on skins at 28–30°C to extract softer tannins and more defined fruit components. Natural yeasts are encouraged to play their part, although supplemented with a "low-level inoculum". The Balmoral fruit is part-fermented in rototanks at up to 30°C, and part in standard fermenters. Both fractions finish their fermentations in new American casks. This furthers the aim of incorporating the maximum new oak without it showing, and gives a more harmonious oak integration. The two lesser blends generally see 5–10% of new oak while the rest is matured in older casks; lots destined for Balmoral spend 18-24 months in 100% new American oak.

Philip Shaw clearly loves playing with the different qualities of Shiraz at his command. Grading of the lots is an unhurried, continuous process; in November of each year the final blend is assembled for the Show Reserve Syrah. The wines are egg-white fined after a year, and returned to cask. Provided there are no clarity and stability problems, filtration is avoided; although a secondary fermentation on some Cabernet Sauvignon has caused a rethink.

All four Rosemount Shiraz are immensely stylish – not built for half a century of cellaring, but wines which will blossom over a decade or so, especially the Show Reserve/Balmoral bottlings.

Rosemount is very much a family business, with Bob Oatley's sons Ian and Sandy actively involved. A tightly-knit, well-motivated team is spear-headed by managing director Chris Hancock, a man with considerable personal charm and a strong feel for the market. While the need for profitability is kept firmly in view, the means are there to back innovation and improvements. You won't get the most exciting bottle of Shiraz in the world here, but you will never be disappointed.

ROTHBURY WINES LTD

Rothbury Wines is the umbrella company for 875 acres of vines and four wineries in two countries: The Rothbury Estate (Lower Hunter Valley), Baileys of Glenrowan (North-East Victoria), St Huberts (Yarra) and Vinitech (Marlborough, New Zealand). The architect and resident managing director of this business is the dynamic, irrepressible Len Evans – the *eminence grise* of the modern Australian wine scene.

Shiraz production centres on Rothbury, where there are both Estate and Reserve versions. There's also a sound, reasonably priced, though somewhat dry and austere offering from Baileys, whose resources include seven acres of 40- to 90-year-old vines. Until Rhône Syrahs began to gain international recognition the mid-1980s, Hunter Shiraz sales "floundered like a stuffed duck" and were confined to a clique market.

Len Evans' exposure to tasting, both in his travels promoting the cause of wine and as an Australian Show judge, has

Storm light over Rothbury.

shaped the style of wine made at Rothbury. Great wines have balance and structure from youth, and it is the development of this structure and mouthfeel which principally concern him in vinifying Shiraz. In particular the excellent Reserve Shiraz, from hand-picked, dry-farmed vines, mainly planted at Rothbury in 1968, is designed to exemplify these qualities. The blocks intended for Reserve material are picked at maximum flavour, not at some pre-determined Baumé and pH, because sugar content is an unreliable guide to flavour.

Thereafter vinification proceeds under the skilled hand of winemaker Keith Tullock, with Len Evans presumably never far away. The guiding philosophy is that the vineyard makes the wine, so the winemaker's job is to extract rather than change this essential Hunter character.

The fruit is de-stalked, yeasted and passed to open fermenters, deliberately wide-necked to maximize contact between cap and juice. Vatting lasts 7–8 days, with the temperature rising to

VARIETY	VINEYARD	DETAILS	AREA
SHIRAZ	ROTHBURY ESTATE (Lower Hunter)	Vines planted 1968	19.12
SHIRAZ	DENMAN ESTATE (Upper Hunter)	Productive vines 20 yrs old; 11 acres pl 1991	18.35
SHIRAZ	BROKENBACK (Lower Hunter)	22 yr old vines	22.82
SHIRAZ	AUGUSTINE (Mudgee)	Grafted 1969	3.01
SHIRAZ	BAILEYS (Glenrowan, Victoria)	3–5 yr old vines	36.06
SHIRAZ	BAILEYS (Glenrowan, Victoria)	42 yr old vines	4.94
SHIRAZ	BAILEYS (Glenrowan, Victoria)	90 yr old vines	2.22
		TOTAL (acres):	106.52

24–28°C. It is maintained at whatever level it reaches, because Keith considers that any change is likely to provoke undesirable volatile acidity and hydrogen-sulphide. Then to new French and American wood for six months, before egg-white fining in cask, and racking.

The Reserve Shiraz is a selection of the best lots from designated blocks. With large volumes to work with, there is a great deal of tasting to establish the ideal balance of fruit and tannin. In the cellar, this is achieved by proportional blending, including carefully titrated additions of separately matured

pressings. Traditionally, Hunter Shiraz had little or no new oak; however Rothbury has a new-wood programme to enhance the regional character of its Shiraz. After 18 months in wood, the Reserve Shiraz is racked into stainless steel where any final fining or acid adjustments are made.

The wine is very good and, in vintages such as 1983 and '91, excellent. As Len Evans, alluding to the Hunter's volcanic, oxidized-basalt crowns which nurture the finest Shiraz, puts it: "the old buggers knew where to go 100 years ago". The young buggers aren't doing too badly either!

TYRRELLS

Tyrrells is one of Australia's oldest wine-producers. It was started by "Uncle Dan" Tyrell in the late 1870s, who planted the Shiraz vines which still contribute to the excellent "VAT 9" blend. Now his grandson, Murray Tyrrell, a lively, forceful man in his late 70s, runs the firm, with Andrew Thomas making the wine.

Murray Tyrrell is an eminently practical man, with one eye firmly focused on the market. His reasonably-priced "Long Flat Red" and "White" have been conspicuous successes as have the "VAT"-designated wines. He believes strongly in Shiraz's future as a premium varietal, in his view the only serious competition coming from Western Australian Cabernet Sauvignon, as plantings attain maturity.

This faith is demonstrated in five Shiraz-based wines. VAT 55 is a blend of Hunter, Coonawarra or McLaren Vale Shiraz and Merlot, aged predominantly in new or second-year small wood. VAT 8 is a mix of Hunter Shiraz and Coonawarra Cabernet Sauvignon, with a higher proportion of new wood. These two contain at least 60% of Shiraz and are expressly oak-dominated for market appeal. In contrast, Tyrrell's top three *cuvées* are vinified to accentuate Hunter and Shiraz typicities. VAT 5, from Hunter vines, although lightish in tannin is firm in style with solid, powerful fruit. VAT 11 is fuller-flavoured, exemplifying the "old Hunter pongy" leather-and-meat style.

Top of the range is VAT 9, a splendidly

concentrated Shiraz from hand-harvested estate fruit – including Uncle Dan's 116-year-old vines. To preserve its typicity, and avoid submerging the fruit in oak, this is mainly matured in large, old wood, with 5–30% going into new Vosges, Tronçais, Nevers or American oak depending on the power and structure of the vintage. The wine is both quintessentially Hunter and quintessentially Shiraz.

Tasting ancient Hunter Shiraz, it was clear to Murray Tyrrell that any regional identity the wines shared had more to do with dirty, meaty, earthiness than anything else; characteristics derived from sources other than fruit, and ones which modern technologists would stigmatize as "off". In recent years, Tyrrells have striven to eliminate these, deliberately shifting to cleaner fruit-driven aromas and flavours.

Achieving this without compromising the essential Hunter-ness involved adapting winemaking to minimize the impact of spoilage organisms which thrive in the low-acid milieu of this hot region. The main casualties were the Tyrrell-selected natural yeasts, now replaced by pure cultures. Tailoring yeast strain to nitrogen demand also helped by producing cleaner, faster and

more reliable fermentations. Since 1992, a centrifuge has been increasingly used to clean up smaller batches of wine before maturation (for example, most of the 1993 VAT 9 was centrifuged) and racking frequency has also been increased to reduce malodorous hydrogen sulphide.

Tyrrell's own 150 acres of vineyards of various vine-ages around their Pokolbin winery, all except two of which are on their own roots. Unfortunately the longicorn beetle larva, which eats through the vine-trunk and blocks its arteries, has penetrated one block, reducing yields from three to one tonne per acre.

The geology is very varied, even within a small block: from limestone to deep, heavy clays and well-drained red soils which are excellent for vines. No irrigation is used, but Robyn, the estate's viticulturalist, uses canopy management to improve bunch exposure.

The wines have benefited markedly from these improvements. Recent vintages have been noticeably less cluttered with farmyardy overtones, and the fruit is purer and more compelling. Afficiandos of the old style may lament the change, but this is more than just a passing fashion.

VARIETY	VINEYARD	DETAILS	AREA
SHIRAZ	POKOLBIN	1879 vines; v. healthy, yielding 3 tonnes/acre. On own roots.	7.00
SHIRAZ	POKOLBIN	Vines circa 40 yrs old; infested with longicorn beetle, reducing yields to 1 tonne/acre. On own roots.	100.00
SHIRAZ	POKOLBIN	Vines less than 40 yrs old; all but 2 acres on own roots.	40.00
		TOTAL (acres):	147.00

VICTORIA

Victoria is a large state and home to a wealth of wine styles. Its vineyards cover a disparate range of terrains and micro-climates, from coastal Geelong, through the cool Victorian Pyrenees and Macedon ranges, the lush Yarra Valley and Heathcote, to Great Western and the hot, inland Rutherglen on the New South Wales border. In such a diverse area, generalisations have little validity.

Viticulture began here in the Yarra Valley in 1838, two years after the first settlement of Melbourne. The discovery of gold in 1851 led to a massive influx of capital, with viticulture spreading throughout the centre and the north-east. By the Great Melbourne Exhibition of 1873, some 2,000 vineyards had been established and Victorian wine was winning prizes in London, Paris and Vienna. The boom continued until the devastating phylloxera arrived in Geelong and Bendigo in the last decades of the 19th century. Thereafter, farmers found dairying more profitable (and predictable) than viticulture, and much vineyard land succumbed to the cow. The emphasis shifted to fortified wines (especially sherries) and brandies, a trend that lasted for many years and still lives on in the great, and unique, Rutherglen liqueur Muscats and Tokays.

Renaissance did not come until over half a century later, in the 1950s and 1960s, since when progress, led by a small band of pioneers setting up new enterprises throughout the state or else revitalising established ones, has been nothing short of remarkable. In 1900 there were 31,000 acres under vine in Victoria, producing 11,700,000 litres of wine; in 1960 this was 45,250 acres producing 13,700,000 litres; by 1989, the area planted had increased to 50,000 acres and production had rocketed to 70,000,000 litres.

Despite a relatively small acreage (around 1,250 in 1994), Shiraz plays an important part in Victorian viticulture and is well-suited to much of its *terroir*, especially the cooler climate regions of Central Victoria. In addition to its role in blends, it has made a considerable impact as a single varietal, in a variety of styles, in areas as different as Macedon, Goulburn, the Pyrenees and Glenrowan.

BENDIGO

Although it only has 115 acres of Shiraz in production, this is an exciting region. The main focus of interest is in the sub-region of Heathcote, 30km from Bendigo itself where wines from Jasper Hill (qv) and Mount Ida have shown what can be achieved with low yields and skilled winemaking. Phylloxera and a bank crash in 1893 led to the virtual cessation of viticulture until it was revived in 1969 by Stuart Anderson who planted at Balgownie.

The area, some 150km from Melbourne, has 17 producing wineries and several climatically distinct sub-regions. Heathcote, with heat summation of 1,590 (and mean January temperature of 21.8°C) is warm enough to make irrigation essential on most vineyard sites. The wines are full, with plenty of depth and tannins, but have great underlying finesse. Heathcote might well become the Victorian equivalent of California's premium block – the Rutherford Bench.

MACEDON

With only a dozen or so wineries, this is distinctly a "boutique" region. However its size belies its importance. It starts at the town of Sunbury, some 30km north-west of Melbourne, and stretches for 50km northwards to Kyneton.

Although the Sunbury area has a long winemaking tradition, viticulture in the remaining sub-regions only began in the early 1970s and now extends to 250 acres. Chief interest lies in the cool-climate sites, where wineries such as Craiglee (qv) near Sunbury and Knights (qv), at Baynton, in the Mount Macedon sub-region, have striven to vinify Shiraz in a "lifted pepper" mode, to emulate the great wines of the Northern Rhône, as they see them. This approach is certainly different and has met with some success.

While the soils – mainly granitic loams – bear some resemblance in type to parts of the Rhône, the climate does not. Around Mount Macedon, both heat summation (1,030) and mean January temperature (17.2°C) are low, making ripening marginal and harvesting very late (April to mid-May for Shiraz), particularly in vineyards at higher altitude . Strong, damaging winds are a serious problem which, together with water-stress, reduce yields.

This "new-wave" Shiraz has established a different style and won acclaim. The "peppery" effect, however, is often achieved at the expense of mid-palate concentration, and many of the wines (even from theoretically fine vintages, such as 1990) are hollow with, more often than not, an unattractive green streak. Critics suggest that these qualities come from over-watering, watering at the wrong time in the growing cycle and poor canopy manage-ment. Certainly, many wines are unbalanced and notably lack power and extract. Either the fashion will wither, or else growers will refine it into a more complete style. At present, novelty seems to have overtaken sound judgement.

GREAT WESTERN

This area, 220km north-west of Melbourne, lies between Stawell and Ararat, on the western edge of the Great Dividing Range. Viticulture has a long, proud history here, dating back to the gold-rush days of the 1860s, when Seppelts started digging out "drives" (long cellar passages) into the subterranean seams of granite. The district, properly known as the Grampians, of which Great Western is a sub-region, has continuing associations with sparkling wine (especially sparkling Shiraz, which it pioneered; cf separate chapter, page 264), but is also a fine source of table wine in general. Shiraz, which forms about one-fifth of total vine acreage (150 of 750), is undoubtedly Great Western's finest varietal. There are nine principal wine producers including the old-established 19th-century firms of Bests (qv) and Seppelts (qv) which have been joined by younger foundations, such as Mount Langi Ghiran (qv) where Trevor Mast crafts some of Victoria's most interesting Shiraz.

Great Western itself is between 280 and 360m above sea level. It has a warm, dry, continental climate (heat summation 1,400), with very cool nights, and a low enough summer rainfall (207mm) to necessitate irrigation. This pattern produces a long growing season and lowish yields; the compensation is a striking intensity of flavour and wines with excellent structure and ageing potential.

PYRENEES

Although a relatively new vineyard area, the Pyrenees has rapidly established a reputation as a source of premium Shiraz. It lies 55km north-east of Great Western, near to Avoca and Moonambel. This is wild, isolated country, dotted with gum trees and ringed by the gently undulating Pyrenees. In general, the climate is similar, though marginally warmer and wetter, to that of Great Western, although elevation and individual site characteristics play an important role in wine quality. Winemaking started around Moonambel in 1848, all but died out by the turn of the 20th century and then restarted again in the early

Sinuous vine-rows at Taltarni.

1960s with the establishment by Remy Martin of Chateau Remy to make brandy from Trebbiano grapes. The Shiraz crown is firmly in the grasp of Taltarni (qv) with Mount Avoca and Dalwhinnie (notable successes in 1988 and 1991, but distinctly patchy otherwise) on its heels.

GEELONG

Geelong, on the coast, 70km south-west of Melbourne, was originally one of Victoria's most important winemaking centres but was destroyed by phylloxera which first appeared in Australia (in fact near Geelong itself) in 1875. Replanting was started in 1966 by Nini and Daryl Sefton at Idyll Vineyard. Now, there are 150 vineyard acres in all, of which Shiraz accounts for 35. Of the region's 12 active wineries, Bannockburn (qv) makes the best varietal Shiraz, followed by good, if somewhat uneven, offerings from Otto Zambelli at Zambelli Estate, while Daryl Sefton produces an invariably attractive Cabernet-Shiraz blend. The region is gently undulating and the climate cool and dry, giving low yields and wines of concentration and vigour.

GOULBURN VALLEY

This section of the Goulburn River winds north to south between Murchison and Seymour – some 50km as the crow flies. On its banks, virtually next door to one another, are Mitchelton (qv) and Chateau Tahbilk (qv): both, in their way, Rhône pioneers. Tahbilk, an extraordinary property, established by public subscription in 1860, and still boasting an enviable acreage of old vines, has continued to produce wine since its foundation, and indeed was the only active winery in the area from the early 1900s to 1955.

Mitchelton is altogether newer, both in foundation (1969) and outlook. It also produces both Marsanne and Shiraz, though in a very different style from Tahbilk, with new oak an important element. Both unite in seeing the Goulburn Valley as ideal for these Rhône varieties, with a warm enough climate – heat summation 1,680 – to achieve regular ripening, but not hot enough to burn out finesse and complexity. Irrigation is essential to ensure continuing photosynthesis.

Soils tend to be alluvial near to the river, but there are areas of gravel where the water-course has receded. Some parts have sandy soils which, being phylloxera resistant, ensured the survival of Tahbilk's 1860 Shiraz and Marsanne vines.

At present there are 11 wineries, widely scattered throughout the region, exploiting 1,400 acres. This is undoubtedly set to expand.

NORTH-EASTERN VICTORIA

This area covers Rutherglen and Corowa on the New South Wales border and the vineyards around the Ovens and King rivers, centred on Glenrowan, some 40km further south. Best known for its fine liqueur Tokays and Muscat, this is not a premium Shiraz region, although it has 325 acres (from a total of 2,000) in production. The area is mainly flat, with an elevation of around 150m in places, though it rises to over 500m in the foothills of the Great Dividing Range. Some growers are experimenting with higher, cooler sites with some success (eg Brown Bros at Whitlands). The wines are big, firmly-structured and meaty, with a somewhat burly, uncompromising feel about them: one, Bailey's Bundarra Shiraz, attracted the description "a three-course meal and a good cigar". They merit bottle-ageing, and generally benefit from the experience, softening out somewhat and adding finesse.

There is no doubt that much progress has been made with Shiraz throughout Victoria. With further refinement in the pipeline, the future seems exciting and the prospects excellent.

YARRA VALLEY

VICTORIA

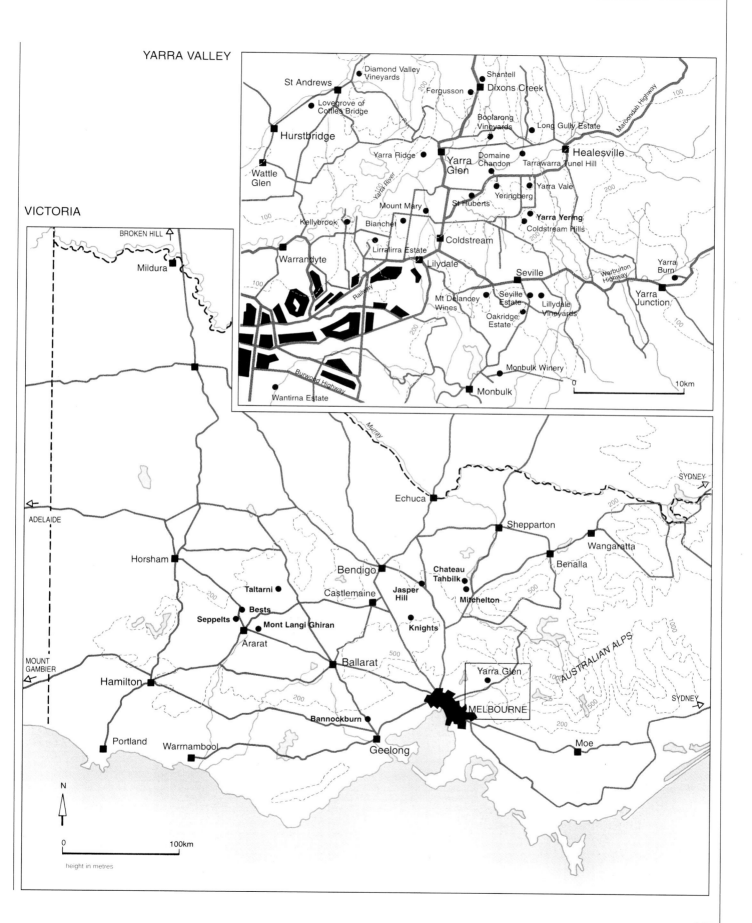

N

0   100km

height in metres

0   10km

BANNOCKBURN

Bannockburn was established by an "avid wine consumer and hobbyist", Stuart Hooper, in 1974 with the aim of "reviving the spirit of this excellent (Geelong) wine district", which had somewhat fallen into decline since phylloxera attacked in 1875.

During the following four years, 50 acres were planted with seven varieties – including Shiraz, which Hooper adores – on sites selected for their volcanic red-loam over limestone soil composition. A young Roseworthy graduate, Gary Farr, was recruited to take charge of the winemaking. In 25 years this has become one of Victoria's leading estates, specializing in Pinot Noir, Shiraz and Chardonnay.

Regular visits to Jacques Seysses at Domaine Dujac in Morey-St-Denis in Burgundy's Côte d'Or to help with the vintage led Gary Farr to rethink his winemaking. His approach now leans less on technology and more towards feel, to extract greater complexity from his cool-climate fruit. This has paid dividends with Shiraz, as well as with the Burgundian varieties of which he is a master.

The seven acres of Shiraz are in two main blocks. The original "Range Road" block, with vines planted on the conventional Australian configuration of 11ft row spacing/6ft vine spacing, has quite heavy loam, high clay, moderately fertile soils. The 1989 "Winery" block, which dates from 1989, is planted 8ft/4ft, using a vertical trellis and has more propitious friable sandy loam and gravel soils over a 2–4ft clay base. Shiraz is usually the last red grape to be picked, from mid-April onwards. This deliberate ripeness and yields of 2–2.5 tonnes/acre provide ideal raw material for firm, dense, long-lasting wine.

Unlike his mentor Jacques Seysses, who vinifies bunches whole, simply because he can't find a way of removing stalks without incurring undesirable juice oxidation, Gary Farr partially de-stems. Thereafter, vinification closely follows the Dujac pattern – open fermenters, three daily foot-*pigeages* and long, slow *cuvaison.*

As with his Pinot, the grapes are cooled and then left for a few days to start fermenting naturally. Total maceration lasts some 18 days, with temperatures peaking at 30°C. Then the pressings are extracted and added back before the new wine is transferred to 225-litre *pièces* for two years' ageing.

Until 1991, Bannockburn Shiraz had around 25% of new oak. However Gary has now reduced this to less than 5%, preferring to use three-year-old Pinot Noir casks which allow the true essence of Shiraz to come through, rather than overtly oak characters. A few new barrels allow him to monitor the performance of each vintage in new wood. The wine is racked six times and egg-white fined, but not filtered.

Gary Farr's Shiraz is consistently good – fine and deep in colour, surprisingly without noticeable loss from including stalks (which are notorious colour-absorbers), with excellent depth and balance. In style it is strongly reminiscent of the northern Rhône – so perhaps *terroir* is as much in the cellar as in the vineyard. The Côte d'Or is a strong influence at Bannockburn.

During Gary's absences in France his wife Robyn looks after the estate, while care of the cellar is confided to the capable and seasoned hands of Harold Moyle, who takes an almost proprietorial pride in its contents. Those other Victoria winemakers chasing the elusive northern Rhône Grail might well take note of Gary Farr's successful approach.

VARIETY	VINEYARD	DETAILS	AREA
SHIRAZ	RANGE ROAD BLOCK	Planted 1974, on own roots; 11ft/6 ft spacing.	4.00
SHIRAZ	WINERY BLOCK	Grafted 1989; 8ft/4 ft spacing.	3.00
		TOTAL (acres):	7.00

BEST'S (GREAT WESTERN)

Best's convoluted history began in 1839, when David Best, "a cabinet maker and wood turner", arrived in Melbourne from England, via Tasmania, where he established a successful building business. In 1857 he sold up and moved with his two sons to Great Western, to set up a slaughter-house.

In 1866, inspired by the success of friends, they planted a vineyard on the Concongella Creek, opposite their abbatoir, between Stawell and Ararat. David's grandson Charles took over, but his heart was not in the business and in 1920 he sold Concongella to Frederick Thomson, owner of the St Andrew's vineyard at Rhymney Reef, on the western spur of the Great Dividing Range.

In 1928, the depression forced the sale of Rhymney, and a year later the bank forced the Thomsons off Great Western. The family regrouped at "Misery Farm" on Lake Boga, where Frederick Thomson recreated the St Andrew's vineyard.

Meanwhile, deprived of Thomson enthusiasm, Concongella went into decline and was eventually offered back to the family.

In August 1930, the Thomsons returned to Great Western. Today, Viv Thomson and his family – the fourth and fifth generations – are the custodians of this most traditional of domaines.

Viv's aimiable friendliness hides a wealth of experience and a ferocious dedication to quality. The wine industry was, however, far from his first choice of career – he wanted to run a sheep station. "If you drank wine in the 1960s, you had a problem". Things changed dramatically when he met Christine (now his wife and, in his words, "She Who Must Be Obeyed"). "She looked pretty expensive, so I had to get a job".

Best's portfolio includes the major classic varieties. However, it is with sparkling wines and Great Western Shiraz that they have built their reputation for quality. Shiraz comes from 16 acres – including two (just 15 rows) of Henry Best's 1866 vines and blocks planted to mark the birth of two sons – Bart (1966) and Marcus (1970). Another son, Ben (1964) manages the vineyards, and the winemaker is Simon Clayfield, ex-Hungerford Hill – with Viv himself never far away.

This is excellent Shiraz country: fine, sandy-clay loam soils overlaying deep,

VARIETY	VINEYARD	DETAILS	AREA
SHIRAZ	"HENRY'S", CONCONGELLA, GREAT WESTERN	Planted 1866; 8 rows/acre	2.00
SHIRAZ	"BARTS", CONCONGELLA, GREAT WESTERN	Planted 1966	6.00
SHIRAZ	"MARCUS", CONCONGELLA, GREAT WESTERN	Planted 1970	2.00
SHIRAZ	CONCONGELLA, GREAT WESTERN	Planted 1992 and 1994	6.00
		TOTAL (acres):	16.00

water-retentive clay. The top-soils are poorly structured and "knocked around readily by cultivation" – so tillage is minimal to avoid compaction, and a cover-crop is used to promote soil-cohesion.

In this low-rainfall, continental climate, site and exposure (especially altitude) play a critical role in fruit ripening. At Best's, picking is determined by the condition of the fruit, assessed on a daily basis: if the vines look healthy the bunches are left; if leaves are dropping, the fruit is cut. All but Henry's old vines are drip-irrigated and harvested mechanically

The Thomsons' firm belief that a wine's style is made by the *terroir*, and that ultimately all the winemaker can do is to convert the potential of the grape, has led to vinifying plot by plot, to correlate wine quality with site characteristics. They have found, in particular, that stressed vines, on poor soil, give a strong pepper character not present in wine from an adjacent, more fertile, block.

The "pepperiness" found in Best's Shiraz is less pronounced than that in the wines of Trevor Mast (who was Best's winemaker from 1975–88), Dominique

Viv Thomson – backed by a puncheon.

Portet or the Macedon men. Viv Thomson's wine is above all soft and smooth, well-structured and eminently age-worthy – "guaranteed a ten-year life". The aim is not maximum extraction – this is not an area conducive to heroic, heart-

stopping brews – but a slow evolution in large wood to promote roundness and balance. In any case, ripe fruit produces a high level of natural alcohol, which will itself leach out extract.

Tradition has not blocked evolution in these splendid old tin-roofed cellars. In the early 1970s, open fermenters gave way to closed tanks, and a deliberate proportion of new wood (15–20% 460-litre US oak puncheons) replaced ancient 2,500-litre casks; the old manual basket-press was retired and a Willmes plate-press installed.

Such innovations have, to some extent, altered the style of the wine. Before 1980, the feel was firmly of mainstream "old-style" Shiraz; from 1981–1987 much greater elegance was detectable; from 1988 (the vintage following Simon Clayfield's arrival), the wine has an extra dimension of depth, giving a feeling of greater completeness and complexity.

But there are no poor wines in this remarkable range. With several members of the Thomson family so actively involved, the future of Bests seems well assured.

COBAW RIDGE

Cobaw Ridge was established by Alan and Nelly Cooper, two ex-nurses who had long had the dream of owning a winery. With an enthusiasm fired from hitch-hiking through the vineyards of Europe, they searched and in 1985 found a site at an altitude of 610 metres near Kyneton, the coolest district of the Macedon region. There they designed and built a pole-frame, mud-brick house

and winery, and planted their land to Cabernet Sauvigon, Cabernet Franc, Merlot, Chardonnay and Shiraz.

At this altitude the growing season is long and slow, with harvesting normally taking place in mid to late May. Provided the grapes ripen, these are ideal for producing clean, elegant Shiraz.

However, when the grapes are not fully ripe there is a strong temptation to mask any deficiencies with new wood. Alan and Nelly Cooper resist this, preferring to extract the maximum from

the fruit by a longish cool fermentation, supplemented with hand *pigeage*, and a month of post-fermentive maceration on skins. The wine then goes into wood, 50–60% of it new American oak.

The first vintages at Cobaw Ridge show considerable promise and flair – especially as these are wines from a couple of albeit dedicated relative novices. The wines have the depth and structure to evolve well, with no lack of ripe fruit and concentration. This estate is definitely one to watch.

CRAIGLEE

Pat Carmody is in charge here, producing around 2,500 cases of wine; of these,1,200 are Shiraz, from five acres planted in 1976, with a further 1.6 acres that were added in 1993.

This vineyard was first established by the Hon S H Johnson in the 19th century; early origins which are apparent to the visitor from the contemporary tasting room and the splendid underground cellars, reached via a vertiginous descent through a trap door.

The property is in the Sunbury district – one of six sub-regions of Macedon – about 20km north-east of Melbourne's

main airport. The climate is relatively cool, with low average rainfall (750–800mm), most of which falls during the winter. Summer irrigation is therefore essential.

The main enemy is wind – sometimes severe – which causes a variety of problems, including disrupting flowering and drying out the grapes.

The Craiglee Shiraz has received considerable acclaim – especially the 1990 vintage – for its lifted, peppery

character, which many commentators identify with the northern Rhône. However, tasting several vintages it is clear that these qualities have been achieved at the expense of middle-palate flesh and noble tannins. The wines appear to be out of balance and incomplete – not a case of lack of care, or blatant over-cropping, though Pat admits that the fruit is often "on the edge of being ripe"; however, something is clearly amiss. Vinification gives a clue as

VARIETY	VINEYARD	DETAILS	AREA
SHIRAZ	CRAIGLEE	Planted 1976	5.00
SHIRAZ	CRAIGLEE	Planted 1993	1.60
		TOTAL (acres):	6.60

to where the problem might lie. The fruit is de-stemmed and fermented in *inox*, remaining on its solids for 7-8 days, with pumping over. The wine remains in stainless steel until the malolactic is complete, when it is lightly filtered and transferred to US and French casks: here is stays for 12–14 months before bottling.

In this orthodox, uncontroversial process, it is the marginal grape ripeness and short vatting time which stand out as likely causes of hollowness. The former is often the result of over-irrigation, though yields at 3–4 tonnes/acre are hardly excessive and reducing them would probably necessitate a significant – and risky – price rise. The most likely culprit is the short vatting; just over a week is barely long enough to extract sufficient matter and depth, especially from marginally ripe fruit, to balance what must perforce be somewhat harsh tannins.

The search for the prized northern Rhône finesse has led to many unbalanced wines, especially in cooler climate areas where there is more chance of finding the Grail: it would be pointless to embark on such a quest in the heat of the Hunter Valley.

Pat Carmody is a dedicated and capable winemaker, producing good wine with care and skill. That it is different, and new, may enthuse some to exaggerated claims. Tasting his wines blind, on more than one occasion, produced a consistent impression of hollowness and disequilibrium. The skeleton is there, but it needs more flesh.

JASPER HILL VINEYARD

This 45-acre estate produces two of Australia's most complex and finely-crafted wines. Their creator, Ron Laughton – a slim, articulate man with a dry wit – is a determined solo player with clearly-defined goals and the skills to achieve them.

Success as a food scientist found him at 30 managing 3,000 employees and 13 dairies – but unsettled: "there had to be more to life that what I was doing". Following his engineer father who "had a mid-life crisis before mid-life crises were invented" and promptly took up farming, Ron left industry and embarked upon his own mid-life crisis in the mid-1970s, buying a property outside Heathcote, north-east of Melbourne. This is a quiet, straggling village, so elongated that one might easily suppose its present form to have been the result of a violent municipal tug-of-war at some earlier period.

Jasper Hill had established vines, but no house; so Ron and his wife Elva – a milliner by trade – lived in a caravan for 12 months, tending the land and building a house and cellars. Today's visitor, arriving by a track from the main road, finds a splendid two-storey brick cellar block, neat with casks and wooden stairs leading to a storage loft.

A little further on, at the top of the hill, is the family house, attractively furnished with antique tapestry and rough-hewn Indian-slate flagstones. Its broad terrace commands magnificent views through almost 360 degrees, with the eight acres of Emily's Paddock Shiraz sloping away northwards towards the Great Dividing Range. A kilometre or so to the east lie the 37 acres of Georgia's Paddock, of which all but seven acres (which are Riesling) are Shiraz.

Ron is a firm believer in Shiraz's potential for nobility and in its particular synergy with Australia. This, together with an unconcealed disdain for an epidemic

Tasting at Jasper Hill.

of smaller wineries all busily trying to out-Bordeaux Bordeaux, prompted "a knee-jerk reaction against Cabernet and Pinot". Given his avowed intention to produce "the greatest Shiraz in Australia", the choice of site was no accident. In Jasper Hill he saw an ideal conjunction of soil, aspect and climate: adequate warmth and light to ripen Shiraz, yet cool enough to impart elegance.

The inland north-facing slopes of the Range provide the climate, and the foothills the requisite coolness. The soils are unique: a Cambrian bedrock, 500–600 million years old, pulverized by fault action into red earth between 600mm (Emily's Paddock) and 3–4 metres (Georgia's Paddock) deep, giving on to a complex geology of "tin, copper, everything imaginable", dominated by red clay. Such soil depth allowed fulfilment of one further condition: no irrigation, which, in Ron's view, diminishes quality.

Luck also played its part. The existing vines (Emily) turned out to be Shiraz, planted by the previous owner, the local bulldozer driver, as a source of home winemaking fruit. The remaining planting (Georgia) – on own roots – was carried out in 1975–1976 using the single "Penfolds" clone. In 1993 three acres of Nebbiolo were added using four different

VARIETY	VINEYARD	DETAILS	AREA
SHIRAZ	EMILY'S PADDOCK	On own roots	3.00
SHIRAZ	GEORGIA'S PADDOCK	25 acres planted 1975/6; 5 acres 1988 after bush fires; own roots	30.00
		TOTAL (acres):	33.00

clones; a belated acknowledgement, perhaps, of Ron's ancestry: his grandfather, Antonio, came to Australia from Italy during the gold rush.

Although the two vineyards share similar geology, Emily has drier *terroir* and a steeper, sunnier aspect which ripens grapes two weeks before Georgia and gives a more austere, earthy, tannic wine. Georgia, despite one and a half hours' less morning sunlight than Emily, gives a wine which tends to be sweeter, with more open berry and spice flavours.

Ron sees yield as the key to balanced fruit: exceed four tonnes per acre and quality diminishes; so production is maintained at around two tonnes per acre for Georgia, half that for Emily – barely commercial, but what concentration! Though only Bordeaux mixture and sulphur are used on the vines, Ron dislikes being labelled "organic", an epithet he reserves for "bearded people who wear woolly sweaters and operate by lunar phases". Fortunately, his vines don't seem to attract the worst pest – the destructive light-brown apple moth; if they did, he is pragmatist enough to

"spray the bastards!"

From the Laughtons' first vintage in 1982, production has never exceeded 3,000 cases – 400 of Emily, 1,500–2,000 of Georgia and 600–700 of Riesling. Beyond that, Ron reckons "life becomes too difficult" – they might have to employ someone. The winemaking is "simple, simple – I do it all; if it starts with grapes which have superb balance, the wine virtually makes itself". Not entirely – though once the fruit has been de-stemmed, yeasted and put into 1,000-gallon vats, nature is left, as far as possible, to its own devices. Maceration, with the juice being pumped over, lasts 7–14 days to extract nobler tannins; a week or so later, with press-wine added, the wines are racked off their gross lees and transferred to cask.

Both wines spend 12–14 months 20-25% in wood – Georgia's ripe, sweet, red-berryish fruit responding more to American oak; Emily's tougher profile being confided to Nevers. Both wines are bottled with a light plate filtration. In short a "minimal intervention" vinification, because "each time you

interfere you change and degrade the flavours".

Ron Laughton is a family man, thoughtful and laconic, taking a quiet, unboastful pride in what he has achieved. He is respected and popular among fellow *vignerons* – a fact touchingly demonstrated in 1987 when bush fires destroyed nearly all his crop. With no wine to sell, the estate's very survival was at risk. Learning of the tragedy, his friends and neighbours spontaneously offered him some of their own Shiraz crop; these he made into "Friends' Shiraz". This act has left an indelible mark and clearly strengthened Ron's devotion to winemaking and to its milieu.

Georgia and Emily are magnificent, seductive creations with all the depth and refinement of great wine. They mirror their namesakes: Georgia the more instantly communicative of the pair – the Mouline, the Côte Blonde; Emily, the more reserved, tightly-knit, personality – the Landonne, the Côte Brune. Guigal would be proud of these wines. In Australia's already luminescent firmament, Laughton is among the brightest of stars.

KNIGHTS

This estate emerged from the decline of Great Western's sheep industry, in which Gordon Knight worked as a wool-classer. In 1971, observing what could be achieved with wine in a cool climate, he left and set himself up at Granite Hills, with an initial planting of 24 acres of Shiraz, Cabernet Sauvignon and Riesling. With replanting and the loss of an eight-acre block to drought and locusts, there are currently 23 acres under vine, including 4.5 of Shiraz.

Wine was not a regular feature of Knightly comestibles; Gordon's son, Lew, recalls his Scottish Presbyterian grandparents confining "liquor" to the brief appearance of a bottle of sweet sherry at Christmas which, once dispensed, was promptly locked away for another year. Notwithstanding, Lew is now in charge of winemaking and has worked hard with his father to enhance the reputation of their estate.

The winery adjoins the family house, an old-fashioned, homely place set amid gently rolling countryside, on a plateau some 1,800 feet up in the Macedon Hills. Here, on the cool north slopes of the Great Dividing Range, Shiraz is planted on its own roots, on east- and north-facing slopes, in well-drained, granitic, sandy soil overlaying clay. They started dry-farming, but soon discovered that the

roots tended to proliferate in the top 12 inches, avoiding the high-acid subsoils. The solution was drip-irrigation and mulching, which stabilized root systems, increased resistance to moisture stress and, incidentally, improved wine flavour.

At this altitude, the growing season is long and ripeness irregular. Wind is a particular problem, with "horrific" cold southerlies blowing during spring and early summer. Another is excess vine-vigour and abundant foliage – especially on lower north-westerly slopes. To control this, Lew and Gordon Knight experimented with various canopy configurations, finally settling for an eight-cane Scott-Henry trellis. They also discovered that spur-pruning halved yields – even with double the normal number of buds. So Shiraz is now cane-pruned to yield 4–5 tonnes/acre.

The wine combines the peppery, spicy Macedon character with firm fruit and expressly avoids the lean hollowness of much cool-climate Shiraz. Lew attributes their style principally to fruit quality and oak maturation rather than to primary vinification. However, while these may well contribute, the value of limiting skin-contact to 7–8 days to avoid over-extraction, racking the new wine off solids before dryness to reduce green

tannins and flesh out the middle palate, and discarding unduly harsh pressings, must also be acknowledged. Up to two years' maturation in 30–50% of new US oak adds breadth and sweetness, and thereby Australian market appeal. Curiously, the "US" oak they contentedly used for years turned out in fact to be German. The wine is racked twice "for flavour development", egg-white fined if it is bitter, then both earth- and plate-filtered before bottling.

Knight's Shiraz is well-made, solidly upper-middle quality – approachable young but benefiting greatly from up to a decade of bottle-age for fine vintages such as 1981. However, an overriding desire to add elegance and avoid excessively "berryish" flavours has led to a lack of real extraction. Warmer fermentation, a few days longer on skins – especially pre-fermentation – and marginally lower yields, would probably solve the problem, without compromising on the desired style. They could also usefully eliminate one filtration. Shiraz apart, Lew and Gordon Knight also make a splendid Rhine Riesling, which could take on the best of Alsace after 15 years in bottle.

VARIETY	VINEYARD	DETAILS	AREA
SHIRAZ	KNIGHTS ESTATE	Planted 1971/2 on own roots	4.50

MITCHELTON

Mitchelton was the creation of Colin Preece, one of Australia's greatest winemakers, who was commissioned in 1967 to select a site capable of producing top-quality table wine and that was scenically attractive enough for a predicted tourist boom. The project was completed in 1974, but soon went into receivership. Preece died in 1979, and the following year the owners sold out to the Valmorbida family – northern Italian emigrés who had established a food, wine and newspaper empire in Victoria and New South Wales.

The constant in all this change was Preece's apprentice-winemaker, Don Lewis, a man with a reputation for shyness (an epithet frequently attributed to anyone who thinks before speaking) under whose hand Mitchelton's wines have established a solid reputation for quality. He remains at the helm, a respected figure in the Australian wine industry.

From a product range of 60 wines, Mitchelton is unusual for being Australia's second-largest producer of Marsanne, of which they have 56 acres. The original 1974 plantings were selected by Preece and Ross Shelmerdine (Mitchelton's then owner) from Château Tahbilk – the largest producer. As proprietors of a substantial proportion of the world's Marsanne acreage, it is not surprising that they see a bright future for this rare variety in the Goulburn Valley – in particular as an alternative to Chardonnay. A naturally prolific grape, Marsanne needs careful farming but, given sensible yields, is capable of producing powerful, well-flavoured wine which ages well and accompanies rich food to perfection.

An intensive viticultural programme taking in soil, plant material selection, canopy management, pruning, pest control, irrigation and harvesting has recently been established under the skilled Mitchelton viticulturalist, Michelle Gandell. The aim is to improve yields and fruit quality. An important local influence is the Goulburn river, which borders the property on three sides, increasing humidity and lowering mean January (summer) temperature by one centigrade degree, which helps prolong fruit ripening.

Fortunately, Marsanne is relatively grower-friendly: it crops well, has good disease resistance, ripens mid-season and harvests early. At Mitchelton it is mechanically (spur) pruned and harvested by machine. Yields vary from three tonnes/acre for vines on their own roots to six tonnes for newer plantings on rootstock.

The flagship Mitchelton Marsanne, vinified *à la* Chardonnay to emphasize its keeping qualities, has recently been joined by the Thomas Mitchell Marsanne – an altogether brighter and fresher rendition of the grape, designed for early drinking.

This shrewd marketing overcomes two obstacles: first, that Marsanne is largely unknown – a situation unlikely to change as long as the only wine available was a relatively expensive premium product, and second that, even among sophisticated drinkers, the strong, straw-like, flavours of aged Marsanne are a distinctly acquired taste.

Mitchelton's Reserve Marsanne comes from the best vineyard blocks. One-fifth of the crop is given skin-contact before fermentation, which is started in *inox* and finished in cask, over four weeks. Thereafter, the wine spends 11 months, from harvest in March until the following January, on its yeast-lees, in cask (30% new French and US oak) to add further fat and complexity, followed by two years in bottle before release. The Reserve bottling is yardstick stuff – ripe, complex and stylish – a wine which is only seen at its best after several years in bottle. As with traditionally-made white Hermitage, Marsanne's *locus classicus*, it is infanticide to drink young, attractive as it may be.

Shiraz is represented by a Thomas Mitchell bottling (15,000 cases) and a Reserve blend – released since 1980 under the Print Label designation – adorned with the winning entry from Mitchelton's annual artists' print competition. The 2,000 cases of this latter come from old-vine fruit – some estate-grown, some bought-in. It is vinified in tank until after malolactic, then matured for 18–20 months in wood – 50% new French oak, the rest old wood (500-litre puncheons, 300-litre hogsheads and 225-litre *barriques*) – and bottled without filtration. It is an upper-middle example of Shiraz: invariably good, sometimes fine, which seems to be improving as Don Lewis fine-tunes it. In style, it has a more southern than northern Rhône feel, and, as with the Marsanne, needs time to develop complexity.

In 1994 Mitchelton released two new Rhône blends under the Mitchelton III label: the white, a cocktail of 80% Marsanne (half cask-fermented and kept on lees for nine months), plus 5% each of cool *inox*-fermented Viognier and white Grenache; the red from 90% Shiraz and 5% each of Mourvèdre and Grenache bottled after 17 months in year-old hogsheads (70% US, 30% French).

These excellent, moderately-priced blends show Don Lewis' readiness to innovate and the estate's firm belief in the potential for Rhône varietals in the Goulburn Valley.

VARIETY	VINEYARD	DETAILS	AREA
SHIRAZ	MITCHELTON VINEYARD	Planted 1973; ungrafted	33.60
SHIRAZ	MITCHELTON VINEYARD	Planted '93/4; grafted (SO4 etc)	15.00
MARSANNE	MITCHELTON VINEYARD	Planted 1973; ungrafted	14.80
MARSANNE	MITCHELTON VINEYARD	Planted 1987; grafted	11.40
MARSANNE	MITCHELTON VINEYARD	Planted '93/4; grafted	15.00
VIOGNIER/GRENACHE BLAN/ ROUSSANNE	MITCHELTON VINEYARD & others	Grafted '93/4	6.00
		TOTAL (acres):	95.80

MOUNT LANGI GHIRAN

In the Great Western District, some 20km as the crow flies (or more accurately perhaps the yellow-tailed black cockatoo, from which the estate takes its name) from Ararat, lies Mount Langi Ghiran, a relative newcomer to the region. In 15 years, under the skilled hands of Trevor Mast, it has become one of Australia's most respected estates and a source of top-class Shiraz.

Trevor's apprenticeship consisted of a four-year course at Geisenheim in Germany, followed by a spell as a micro-biologist at Stellenbosch in South Africa.

He returned to Australia to take responsibility for processing small volumes of Show wines at Seppelts, where he came into contact with Langi Shiraz, a wine which was highly prized even then.

In 1980, at the behest of the owners – the Fratin brothers, concrete merchants who had built the estate's underground cellars – Trevor became Mount Langi's winemaker. When the Fratins signalled their intention to sell in 1987, approaches came from China, France and Hong Kong. Fortunately for Trevor, who hoped to stay and therefore hoped for someone local, salvation came from a local financier, backed by a group of airline pilots who liked Langi's wine. The future now seems secure, with a further 120 acres of vines in the pipeline.

This cool-climate region, technically known as the Grampians, is renowned for its sparkling wines – Seppelts and Best's are here – and for Shiraz (often labelled "Hermitage"), which thrives on minerally rich, organically poor soils.

Mount Langi, on the region's eastern edge bordering the Granite Hills, has vines that enjoy the foothills' mixture of decomposed sandy-granite and sedimentary soils and the limestone/quartz on friable well-drained clay of the flat ridges – ideal for Shiraz.

The climate is relatively harsh, with winds often disrupting flowering. Although at the margin, it falls in line with what Trevor's comparative analysis of his own wine with Chave and Chapoutier Hermitages highlighted as the principal quality factors: a long growing-season and fully ripe grapes, with good acidity and pH – both the latter essential for colour extraction and stability. In this low-fertility environment, the normally vigorous Shiraz is less productive, so the rule is minimal pruning, and debudding only on the rare occasions where an excess is indicated.

Trevor has acquired something of a "green" reputation. This he discounts, although admitting to a preference for minimum intervention – and to experimenting with bio-dynamics, with mixed results. His overriding philosophy is that what matters is the contents of the bottle, an outlook backed by clear-headed business realism: if spraying is needed to save the crop, then spray!

Harvesting is principally determined by flavour. Machines enable Trevor to pick cool fruit, without delay, as the skins start to soften. He dismisses criticisms of the brutality of mechanical harvesters: if the rods are properly regulated and the driver competent, they don't pose problems.

The de-stemmed fruit, crushed but unsulphured, is macerated for a week before fermentation. At below 10°C there is no enzymatic oxidation, only chemical oxidation "which doesn't worry me". The benefit is "phenomenal colour extraction, without undue tannins".

Yeasts are added and fermentation starts – a deliberately gentle temperature-curve to avoid harsh tannic extraction from heat, excess alcohol and unnecessary skin abrasion.

The pulp is basket-pressed – more a squeeze at 0.8 atmospheres – "it's much faster: half a tonne takes five minutes – in a bladder press six tonnes takes two hours; pressings are the secret for me". After 6–7 months in *inox*, to keep the wine fresh, it is racked into wood, 35–40% of which is new oak, American with a seasoning of French. A year later it is bottled, unfined but coarse-filtered. The quality of the pressings and careful winemaking mean that the wine is usually protein- and tartrate-stable, without excess tannins, eliminating the need for fining and undue use of sulphur.

The results of Trevor Mast's feel for Shiraz are consistently excellent, well-structured wines with positive, complex aromas – often green-, black- or white-pepper-based – and good depth. He avoids the winemaking crevasse, into which some growers in the region fall headlong, of sacrificing middle-palate flavour for the "lifted pepper" character which many misguidedly see as quintessentially northern Rhône.

Sustained by a fine balance of fruit, tannins, acids and alcohol, Mount Langi Shiraz generally ages well over 5–10 years, although, in less ripe vintages (such as 1984) it can lack flesh and develop a lean, pinched character. Fortunately, this is rare.

Trevor Mast's skilled stewardship has brought Mount Langi Ghiran into the first division of Victorian, if not Australian, Shiraz.

VARIETY	VINEYARD	DETAILS	AREA
SHIRAZ	MOUNT LANGI GHIRAN	Planted 1969, own roots; Great Western Shiraz clone	16.00
SHIRAZ	MOUNT LANGI GHIRAN	Planted 1986, own roots; Great Western Shiraz clone	2.00
SHIRAZ	MOUNT LANGI GHIRAN	Planted 1989; NSW 23 clone	6.00
SHIRAZ	MOUNT LANGI GHIRAN	Planted 1989; clonal trial mix	1.50
SHIRAZ	MOUNT LANGI GHIRAN	Planted 1992; Great Western Shiraz clone	16.00
SHIRAZ	MOUNT LANGI GHIRAN	Planted 1993; NSW 23 clone	2.00
SHIRAZ	MOUNT LANGI GHIRAN	Planted 1994; NSW 23 clone	55.00
		TOTAL (acres):	98.50

B SEPPELT & SONS

Seppelts was established in 1850 by Joseph Seppelt, a Silesian settler, near Manaranga at the western extremity of the Barossa Valley. Over the four succeeding generations the operation expanded – marked physically by the appearance of striking avenues of tall palms, a massive winery and a hilltop mausoleum, and spiritually by renaming the place Seppeltsfield. In 1918 the firm acquired the Great Western estate near Ararat in Victoria, established in 1866 by Joseph Best, who employed local gold miners to excavate the extensive underground cellars (or "drives"), and famous for its distilled and sparkling products as well as table wines. Vigorous expansion took place during the 1940s under the management of Colin Preece, one of Australia's legendary winemakers, who joined the company in 1923. His era saw the Great Western vineyard acreage rise from 260 in 1941 to over 600 in 1961.

In 1984, following the pattern of late 20th-century business agglomeration, Seppelts was bought by S A Brewing Holdings and, while both the Barossa and Great Western operations remain, the name "Seppelt" is now simply a brand for premium wines. The policy of quality, happily undiminished, has passed into the experienced hands of Ian McKenzie, senior winemaker since 1983, Ian Shepherd, Mike Kluczko and Leigh Clarnette.

Seppelts release two Shiraz – both made at Great Western: 1,000 cases of "Show Sparkling Burgundy" and 2,000 of still, Great Western "Hermitage"; (to comply with the dictats of EC bureaucracy, "Burgundy" and "Hermitage" become "Shiraz" in their passage from Southern to Northern Hemispheres). The raw material for both comes from 61.5 acres planted in two phases during the 1960s, including the St Peter's vineyard – named after the earliest planting in the area, by French emigrés Jean Trouette and Emile Blampied, in 1863.

The vines are low-yielding (2–4 tonnes per acre), on sandy, well-drained soils. They are spur-pruned by hand to two buds without any fashionable canopy manipulation or hedging, but drip-irrigated. The fruit is machine-picked at maximum ripeness (13.5 Baumé is ideal) with blocks intended for sparkling wine being left longer than those destined for still "Hermitage". As such ripeness levels are only achieved at the expense of natural acidity, tartaric acid is added at fermentation to restore the balance.

The young wine remains in *inox* until each lot has been classified as still or sparkling. The still batches then spend 12–15 months in 225-litre Allier, Vosges and Tronçais casks – 70% "nearly new, just broken-in with the previous season's Chardonnay fermentation". After six months on three-quarter bung, the malolactic-in-wood fraction is blended with the malolactic-in-*inox* fraction. The wines are polish-filtered and, if necessary to adjust tannins, egg-white fined, then bottled and returned to the cellars to be released when they are considered ready.

The wine to be "champenized" is put into large old wood, for 12–15 months with 3–4 oxidative rackings to prematurely age and soften it. Before being subjected to the standard champagne process, some 4% of old reserve wine is added for depth and complexity. After just under eight years in bottle on its yeasts for the *prise de mousse*, it is hand-disgorged and topped up with 28–30 grammes/litre of a mixture of liquid sugar and old reserve wines.

Both wines are excellent. The Great Western Shiraz is designed as a big, rich, *vin de garde*, with the structure to age but not too obtrusive a frame to preclude earlier consumption. Older vintages are distinctly austere, redolent of the traditional, long maceration, heavily pressed, over-extracted style, fashioned perhaps for consumers whose taste-buds were so shot-up with apéritif spirits that only a uncompromising palate-hammer

Seppelt's "champagne" cellars – where sparkling Shiraz is matured.

would make an impression. Recent vintages, however, show a marked nod towards suppleness, for a more sophisticated market, increasingly interested in fruit and nuance. Despite its size, Seppelts clearly remains in the forefront of quality. (The Show Sparkling Burgundy is discussed on page 264).

VARIETY	VINEYARD	DETAILS	AREA
SHIRAZ	ST. PETERS VINEYARD, GREAT WESTERN	Planted early 1960s	20.00
SHIRAZ	IMPERIAL VINEYARD, GREAT WESTERN	Planted late 1960s	22.50
SHIRAZ	MCKENZIE'S VINEYARD, GREAT WESTERN	Planted 1989	19.00
SHIRAZ	PADTHAWAY	Oldest planting: 1964	93.75
SHIRAZ	PARTALUNGA VINEYARD, EDEN VALLEY	Oldest planting: 1989	10.00
SHIRAZ	SEPPELTSFIELD VINEYARD	Oldest planting: 1974	4.52
GRENACHE	SEPPELTSFIELD VINEYARD	Oldest planting: 1960	173.88
		TOTAL (acres):	343.65

CHATEAU TAHBILK

Château Tahbilk is Victoria's oldest winery. Established in 1860 by Andrew Sinclair and R H Horne on 3,025 acres of Goulburn river flats. and funded by public subscription, it has become over the years a national monument – part of the heritage of the early Australian wine industry. Similar investment provided the means to plant an 80-acre vineyard and to excavate the 90-metre long "new cellars" – cool, underground passages built of stone quarried on the property to house the estate's 35,000-case production. Its name translates as "the place of many waterholes", reflecting its situation among the backwaters of the nearby river.

Political and economic vicissitudes in the first two decades of the 20th century saw the property decline. In 1925, at the lowest point of its fortunes, it was bought by an English MP, Reginald Purbrick. Succeeding generations of Purbricks have restored the estate and secured its reputation. In 1931, Reginald's barrister son Eric took charge; he was joined in 1955 by his son John, whose son Alister became manager and winemaker in 1978.

The vineyard now extends to 318 acres, with over a dozen red and white grape varieties planted, all of which are hand-picked. An extensive range of wines includes an excellent, robust, Shiraz and more recently Viognier and Roussanne. However, it is for Marsanne that Tahbilk is especially known. It is no exaggeration to claim that, outside the Rhône Valley and Hermitage, the story of Marsanne coincides with that of its establishment and development in the Goulburn Valley, and at Tahbilk in particular.

The variety was introduced to Australia by Hubert de Castella who founded St Hubert's vineyard near Yering in the Yarra Valley during the 1860s. Its "White Hermitage" was apparently regularly served at Government House. At the end of that decade, cuttings from the vineyard found their way to Château Tahbilk and although none of those plantings survived, the estate still produces Marsanne from vines established in 1927. Although there may be the odd patch on the Hermitage hill of similar age, it would be churlish to contest Tahbilk's claim that their Marsanne is the oldest in the world.

The Shiraz also includes a venerable 1.6 acre patch of 1860 pre-phylloxera vines, planted on their own roots. Here the claim to be the oldest is more secure, since there is nothing of remotely similar age to be found in the Rhône Valley. Since 1979, the wine from this old block has been released separately, using an original label design.

Tahbilk's Marsanne shows the quality of which that unsung variety is capable. Although attractive, lemony and rather peachy in youth, it is with age that it really comes into its own, developing complexity and interest as it deepens in colour to a golden mahogany. Young vintages seem to suffer unduly from a vein of raw, green acidity. After a decade or more in bottle, the wines have shed their zingy, youthful, exuberance and transformed into something altogether richer, with characteristic notes of straw and honeysuckle. To a growing band of disciples, they epitomize a satisfying alternative: the thinking man's Chardonnay. Tahbilk is in fine hands.

VARIETY	VINEYARD	DETAILS	AREA
SHIRAZ	COMI	Planted 1937; single wire; heavy loam; 4.5 tonnes/acre	3.89
SHIRAZ	"1860"	Planted 1860; single wire; sand; 1.6 t/acre	1.60
SHIRAZ	McLOUGHLAN'S	Planted 1930s; single wire; heavy loam to sand; 4.95 t/acre	11.28
SHIRAZ	SHED	Planted 1958; single wire; heavy loam to sand; 5.29 t/acre	2.93
SHIRAZ	HOWARDS	Planted 1959; single wire; loam; 6.50 t/acre	2.63
SHIRAZ	BRYANT	Planted 1966; T-trellis; loam to sand; 5.25 t/acre	12.23
		TOTAL SHIRAZ:	34.56
MARSANNE	MADILLS	Planted 1927; single wire; loam to sand; 3.65 t/acre	16.64
MARSANNE	McLOUGHLAN'S	Planted 1930s; single wire; heavy loam to sand; 4.01 t/acre	17.09
MARSANNE	CELLAR	Planted 1983; single wire; loam; 5.50 t/acre	4.01
MARSANNE	GUGGERS	Planted 1988; arched cane; alluvial; 6.40 t/acre	26.53
MARSANNE	FOTHERGILL	Planted 1987; arched cane; sand; 6.33 t/acre	3.00
MARSANNE	OLD TREBB	Planted 1930s; arched cane; loam; 4.47 t/acre	6.71
MARSANNE	HOWARD'S	Planted 1958; single wire; loam; 5.85 t/acre	3.51
		TOTAL MARSANNE (acres)	77.49
ROUSSANNE	HOWARD'S	Planted 1990; arched cane; loam; first crop 1993	3.29
VIOGNIER	HOWARD'S	Planted 1990; arched cane; loam; first crop 1993	2.66
		GRAND TOTAL (acres):	118.00

TALTARNI VINEYARDS

Taltarni is one of five estates round the small town of Moonambel in the Avoca-Pyrenees region of western Victoria. Before the depression of the late 1920s, this was a premium wine area, but this, and the 1940s wool boom, eroded the industry to the point of extinction. A renaissance in the 1960s, accelerating a decade later, re-established quality wine

Taltarni was founded in 1972 on the base of an existing small vineyard by an American businessman, John Goelet, who already owned Clos du Val in the Napa Valley. David Hohnen, of Cape Mentelle (qv), was hired to develop the vineyards and, in 1976, Dominique Portet, brother of Clos du Val winemaker Bernard and son of an ex-*régisseur* of Château Lafite, was asked to spearhead further expansion that included more vineyards and a state-of-the-art winery "so efficient that it can be operated by just four men". Taltarni now has 225 acres of vines.

This is a remote oasis, set in a wide, sheltered semi-circle of foothills amid wild bush country, spattered with gum and eucalyptus trees. Although the vines grow up to 450 metres' altitude, the surrounding hills provide shelter from hot, drying, summer north winds; but this is arid land, hot and dry, demanding irrigation to achieve a proper balance between grape solids and liquids. The soils are generally poor – a thin, alluvial upper layer, giving onto clay – producing the low yields essential for quality. These inimical conditions are ideal for the Syrah – it thrives on stress, clay and these mainly red, iron-bearing soils (for which

Taltarni is the Aboriginal name).

Dominique expounds his clear-sighted philosophy in a delightful, crushed, French accent. His studies at Montpellier University imbued a feeling for Shiraz as well as insights as to what makes for quality. Looking at the Northern Rhône, he saw the importance of sun exposure – "the best wines are produced on the top of hills" – and of producing *vins de garde*. Until 1985, his Shiraz had a distinctly Bordelais character; thereafter the style changed, due in part to much later harvesting – "almost overripe" – and finishing fermentation in cask at lowish temperatures.

The global aims of "body, varietal character and consistency" are concise and generally met. Tasting before picking is crucial – Dominique goes round on his motor-bike sampling grapes: "one for my mouth, one into a bag for analysis". The flavours he wants are based on capsicum and pepper, with a richness that envelopes the mouth. They used to hand-pick, until 1971 when severe bush-fires broke out in the middle of the harvest. Unfortunately, all but one of the pickers were in the local fire-brigade (everyone is here); they stopped harvesting forthwith and disappeared to fight the fires, leaving one old woman who could barely lift a

bucket of grapes. The vines are now machine-harvested.

Each block is vinified separately. After six months Dominique and assistant Greg Gallagher, at Taltarni since 1979, make up a pre-blend from the lots, which until then are kept in large, old wood. The wine is then moved to 225-litre casks – of which 30% are new Allier oak, the rest second-, third- and fourth-year wood. Dominique finds that American oak gives more accessible flavours, but is not good for *vins de garde*. After 18 months in cask, the wines are egg-white fined, cold stabilized, filtered and bottled – in all, 22–26 months' maturation for 2,500 cases of estate Shiraz.

Taltarni is fortunate in having an extensive range of vintages, back to Portet's first, 1977. The wines follow the vintages, which vary significantly here. In general, they evince the spicy, minerally character found elsewhere in the Pyrenees. Until 1984, the wines exemplified the traditional Australian "leather and spice" style; these evolved well, but lacked elegance. From 1985-88, difficulties in getting the fruit to ripen as they wanted signalled a transition between the Australian and the present, distinctly Rhône style – a change which incidentally brought out more varietal character – without any noticeable sacrifice in structure or balance. Taltarni is now benchmark Pyrenean Shiraz.

VARIETY	VINEYARD	DETAILS	AREA
SHIRAZ	TALTARNI	Planted 1973; original, ungrafted vines	12.00
SHIRAZ	TALTARNI	Planted 1991	2.00
SHIRAZ	TALTARNI	Planted 1992	6.00
		TOTAL (acres):	21.00

THE TRADITION OF SPARKLING BURGUNDY

Sparkling "Burgundy" is a curious, but noble, tradition which, together with the great Victoria liqueur Muscats, comprise Australia's truly indigenous wine styles. It continues to be produced and is attracting a growing following.

The idea was born in 1893 by Hans Irvine, who made a sparkling red wine from fruit grown at his Great Western vineyards. By the time Seppelts acquired Great Western in 1918, the wine's reputation was firmly established, with markets as far afield as Calcutta and London. The 1893 *cuvée*, priced at 62 shillings a dozen (just 13 shillings less than Bollinger) won a Gold Medal at Bordeaux in 1895 and was "particularly recommended for invalids".

In those days, as well as Shiraz, Pinots Noir and Meunier were used (Irvine's winemaker, Charles Pierlot, was French); only later did it become a full-blooded Shiraz. Undoubtedly the quality of the base-wines and ideal maturation in Great Western's cool, underground "drives", dug by gold-miners, contributed much to the excellence of the end-product.

The tradition continued during Colin Preece's reign as winemaker at Seppelts in the 1940s. Then, according to contemporary blending books, the raw material was almost entirely Great Western Hermitage. By the 1950s, components were being added from other Seppelt vineyards – Malbec from Great Western, Shiraz and Cabernet from Rutherglen, and some dry red from Château Tanunda in South Australia. The 1960s saw more experimenting, with the 1963 containing some Malbec pressings, and the 1964 a 50:50 blend from two Great Western Shiraz vineyards.

The 1972 was the last of the old Show Sparkling Burgundies, the majority of the blend being Grenache and Mataro (Mourvèdre) from Tanunda. Production then ceased, but the realization that a great Australian tradition had been allowed to slip led to a resumption in 1982. Now there are two releases: a standard Sparkling Shiraz and a Show Reserve – generally an older vintage which has spent longer on lees before disgorging.

Vinification at Seppelts has changed little since the 19th century – 15 months in large wood for the base wine, with plenty of aerated rackings to prematurely age it, then up to an extraordinary eight years' secondary fermentation on the yeasts to induce the sparkle and refine the flavours. The results have standard champagne pressure and 14% alcohol. Because of this luxuriously extended period on lees, the Show Reserve is 8–10 years old on release.

A broadly similar process, with rather less ageing, is used by the increasing number of smaller estates (mainly in Barossa) now making sparkling Shiraz. Excellent examples from growers such as Rocky O'Callaghan and Charles Melton feature at the top of their ranges. Demand invariably exceeds supply, despite a premium price.

As yet, sales for these unusual wines are mainly confined to Australia, where sparkling Shiraz fits well into a gastronomy which requires something fine, yet red, to accompany substantial meals in hot weather. To most other markets, the concept of a sparkling red wine of any sort is anathema. Who would waste time and tie up money and valuable wine to produce such a curiosity? Imagine asking Gérard Jaboulet to put aside a third of his La Chapelle each year and then make it sparkle. That such a style of wine might be complex, ageworthy and utterly delicious is beyond the comprehension of most, even in sophisticated wine circles.

The wines noted here were tasted during the autumn of 1993 – those asterisked at Seppelts, Great Western; the others at a dinner built round a remarkable range of old vintages in Melbourne. The wines were in impeccable condition and most had stood well the test of time. Each reflected the underlying style of its vintage, revealing, beneath an uplifting sparkle, the fine quality of the base wine.

Sparkling Shiraz is more than a curiosity; it is a tradition that deserves to be preserved and continued and merits wider, more informed attention.

SHOW SPARKLING BURGUNDIES

*1987 Deep black; eucalypt, vegetal character of base wine showing through; soft, quite big, ripe gentle wine; will it benefit from further lees ageing? A classic Show Sparkling Burgundy.

*1986 Deep black,cherry; full, tarry nose; soft, long, complex, velvety wine. Magnificent depth and richness. Five stars.

1985 Deep gassy morello cherry; vanilla and creamy new wood dominate an exuberant cassis and mushroom nose; big, ripe, fruity wine, balanced by some sweetness and good acidity. Excellent.

*1984 Similar to 1986 – marginally lighter; dumb, slightly mushroomy nose; soft, rather light and evanescent. Not a patch on the 1986 or 1987.

1982 Good colour; heady, gassy, nose – vanillin; good full, ripe wine, with moderately concentrated sweet berry fruit.

1972 Fine, limpid, deep-plum; nose is complex – spice and tar with a strong

secondary, mushroomy, component; a substantial, meaty, multi-layered wine; complex, deep.

1967 Limpid garnet, right to tarry edge; nose initially unforthcoming, opened out to methol and resin aromas; lovely, sweet, very ripe wine, with good depth of extract; long, with flavours of lavender and spice.

1965 Immense, dense, black cherry; merest hint of ageing; a massive wine – rich, almost over-ripe, fruit, gentle mousse, long, complete. Best of the lot.

1964 Big, extracty, dark appearance; strong, smoky, tarry nose; plenty of fizz left, ripe, sweet fruit with a tarry, mildly singed undertone. A remarkably well preserved wine.

1963 (2/3 Rutherglen base) Deep garnet, tarry edge; full, forward, figgy nose; firmish, ripe wine which has matured into a delicate old age. Attractive, with plenty of life still in it.

1961 Deep plum, brick edge; heavyish, extracty, tarry wine, with firm muscle and depth. Stylish despite its rather burly exterior.

1957 (Disgorged 1982/83) Mid-back-cherry, touch of brick at meniscus – incredible consistency and depth for its age; positive, ripe, vegetal nose, strongly fungal and mushrooms; lively, not aggressive, fizz. Good, full, mushroomy flavour. Well rounded, good length. Much richer than 1954. A delight.

1954 (Disgorged 1982/3) Mid-garnet, tawny edge, good red centre; fizz all but gone; mature, celery and marmite aromas; lively dissolved prickle on tongue, soft, gentle, rounded wine; complete. No obvious varietal character; long finish. A lighter wine, distinctive and attractive.

1946 (Disgorged c. 1979) Deep red, tawny edge, with plenty of fine-beaded sparkle; very attractive yeasty, toasty, creamy, caramelly nose – with a touch of mushroom and an old amontillada, PX component; lovely, open flavours – though a bit four-square and evanescent.

1944 (Disgorged c. 1979) Mid red, with slender stream of bubbles visible; tawny edge; strong, vegetal-based secondary nose, with elements of mushroom, meat extract, tar and singed rubber. On palate, quite lively, with delicate fruit. Still drinkable, but lacks flesh and richness of 1957. Just about holding up.

YARRA VALLEY

The Yarra Valley located 35km north-east of Melbourne, near the town of Lilydale, boasts an excellent viticultural pedigree. The first vines were planted in 1838, two years after the foundation of Melbourne, and the first wine made in 1845. The area was settled largely by Swiss immigrants, fleeing persecution and poverty, whose European connections helped source French vine cuttings – especially for Cabernet, which continues to succeed here. The region flourished spectacularly through the latter quarter of the 19th century and the early decades of the 20th, until 1921, when declining demand in favour of fortified wine, and impoverished growing conditions (in particular, poor soil fertility and higher incidence of spring frosts, resulting from heavy timber clearance), saw the vineyards all but disappear. During this period, the de Pury's cellar book at Yeringberg repeatedly records "no one will buy our wine".

Despite the historic fame of its wines, the Yarra remained in the doldrums until the late 1960s. A brief renaissance was followed by a decade of stability. Then in the 1980s the place veritably took off, thanks in part to the establishment of Domaine Chandon, Moët & Chandon's Australian sparkling wine base. Now, some 30 wineries, varying in size from few-acre "boutiques" to multi-million-dollar operations, produce excellent Pinot Noir, Chardonnay and Cabernet Sauvignon.

The Yarra's topography is varied, with altitudes ranging from 160 to 1,300ft, and many vineyards planted on steepish hillsides. The climate is relatively cool: its heat summation is 1,489 with mean January temperature of 19.4°C. This is marginal, but generally enough to ripen Shiraz – especially on north-facing slopes.

While there is enough rainfall during the growing season (404mm) to avoid serious drought, a high relative humidity means more fungal disease, especially on lower-lying ground, where there is also an added frost risk. The growers' greatest bugbear is wind, which disrupts flowering and frustrates ripening.

Soils are mainly red duplex, by and large well-drained, and organically of low fertility. The harvest here is late – starting around mid-March for table wines and often continuing until early May.

With so little Shiraz planted, it is difficult to talk of a style. What is clear is that, in great vintages, such as 1986, 1988 and 1990, with fully ripe grapes and sensible yields, the natural resources exist to make impressive wines with the potential for many years' development in bottle. Dr Bailey Carrodus at Yarra Yering (qv) continues to demonstrate this potential with unswerving flair.

The Yarra's future is uncertain, as urban pressures from nearby Melbourne increase. Some have predicted an explosive vineyard expansion – which is not beyond credibility, as the area's potential continues to attract outside interest. Given continued municipal vigilance and no major changes of zoning, there are grounds for optimism that the property developers will not nibble away by stealth at the good vineyard land that remains. Although it has less than 75 acres of Shiraz – from a total vineyard acreage of 1,250 – the Yarra Valley is undoubtedly among Australia's finest areas for this variety.

Threatening weather – the vigneron's nightmare.

YARRA YERING

This domaine is the creation of Dr Bailey Carrodus, a New Zealand-born botanist who came to wine in the early 1950s via Roseworthy Agricultural College and Magdalen College, Oxford, where he took his Doctorate. Tasting European wines left him with a "European palate" – and a profound disappointment with Australian wine, which seemed to him to lack the flavour-complexity and completeness so often found in great French wines. In particular, he recalls being ashamed by an Australian wine that he served to T S R Boase, a devoted wine-lover and the then President of Magdalen.

The riposte "why don't you go and do better", and his decision to abandon an academic career, took him back to Australia where he started searching for a vineyard to keep him through to retirement. The quest for a site combining suitable soils and drainage with a northerly, frost-free, aspect encompassed Geelong, Sunbury and the Yarra Valley.

His botanical expertise enabled him to assess the suitability of soils by looking at the species of wild wayside plants at each site. In the end, however, science gave way to gut feeling with the purchase of 30 acres in the Yarra Valley.

Here are now planted 12 acres of Shiraz, patches of Marsanne and Viognier, Pinot Noir and Chardonnay. An early mistake, to which Bailey Carrodus readily admits, was the grubbing up of some Mourvèdre – which he considers to be a fabulous grape – after a long run of disastrously unripe vintages in the 1970s.

The soil profile shows a loamy topsoil, with a deep silt layer underneath, broken up by gravel – all the result of erosion from the hillsides above. The ground sets "like concrete" in the summer, becoming sticky and difficult to work after rain. Winter oats are sowed between the rows to help minimize further erosion.

Vineyard management is guided by the dictum that "you can't do better than your fruit". The main problem on these rich soils is to limit natural vigour in order to maintain concentration and balance in the grapes. So the vines are dry-farmed and the ground worked to cut unwanted lateral roots, which proliferate near the surface, discouraging the development of a more desirable deeper rooting system. At 850 vines per acre – 250 more than that already established on the property – plant density is low, in contrast to the high levels found on the relatively impoverished soils of Bordeaux and Burgundy, where 12,000 vines per acre is not unusual. The bunches per vine is

Dr Bailey Carrodus.

further limited by restricting the number of buds to 40, with Shiraz trained double-*guyot*, along a single wire.

The precise moment of harvest – to within a few hours – is principally determined by taste, with grape analysis firmly in second place. The bugbear of most warm-climate estates, low acidity, is rarely a problem at Yarra Yering. Unlike most Australian Shiraz vinification, the must is not acidified, a fact eager cellar-product salesmen are reluctant to accept.

The bunches are de-stemmed, put into metre-cube open fermenters and yeasted. A proportion of stems is added to each vat ever since Bailey Carrodus discovered that stalks left overnight exuded an almondy, spicy, savoury component he liked. The tannin in stems also helps to fix the colour.

Properly ripe fruit allows a short *cuvaison* – nearer five than ten days – avoiding any pre- or post-fermentive maceration. "If the French could get the fruit ripeness we do, they wouldn't need to bother with extended maceration", Bailey comments, adding, somewhat mischievously "however, they make better wine with extended maceration than they would without it". The must temperature is high, rising to 34°C, with hand-punching of the cap.

The *vin de goutte* is run off, still fizzing, into casks so that its gas protects the pulp from oxidation in the basket-press. The press-wine is kept apart until after malolactic, tasted and generally

added back.

Shiraz spends just short of 24 months in oak, of which 30% is new – the remainder being second-year Pinot Noir casks. The wood is all French Allier and Tronçais, since Bailey Carrodus's blind tastings led to the characteristically forthright conclusion that "American oak is a disaster – aggressive, vanillin-dominated...its impact is too obvious". The wines are fined with gelatine ("you can't tell the difference from egg-white and it's easier to use") to adjust tannins and bottled unfiltered.

To many, the wiry, short-bearded Bailey Carrodus appears as an austere, uncompromising academic. While a rigorous intellectual discipline has indeed coloured his approach, this impression is incomplete. Beneath the surface is a personality of great warmth and charm, whose serious conversation occasionally cracks into uproarious laughter.

His love of wine is deep – not pretentious chatter, but profound understanding. In particular, he is an ardent fan of fine Burgundy and Côte-Rôtie, which he describes as "marvellous, enchanting stuff"; and he is fascinated by the ability of French *vignerons* to weave layers of charm into their wines – "Australia is a bit short on charm, isn't it?" He admits to being bedevilled by a reputation as an "odd-ball", and to the entirely sound habit of not suffering fools gladly. He is a man who listens to those he respects, but is not easily influenced.

His wines are among Australia's best – concentrated, long-lived and elegant. Apart from a fine Chardonnay and a remarkable Pinot Noir, Carrodus produces two Shiraz: the Underhill and the No 2 (which is co-fermented with small amounts of Viognier and Marsanne). Both are presented in Bordeaux bottles, dressed with un-illustrated, businesslike, black and white labels. This is fine winemaking, by any standards.

VARIETY	VINEYARD	DETAILS	AREA
SHIRAZ	UNDERHILL	Planted 1972/3 (own roots)	10.00
SHIRAZ	YARRA YERING	Planted 1969 (own roots)	2.00
MARSANNE + VIOGNIER	YARRA YERING	Own roots	0.10
		TOTAL (acres):	12.10a

WESTERN AUSTRALIA

Viticulture began here in 1829, when vines were planted at Guildford in the Swan Valley – predating South Australia (by seven years) and Victoria (by five). Despite efforts elsewhere in this large state, the focus remained fixed on the Swan until the 1960s, when plantings in Margaret River and Lower Great Southern increased dramatically. Although total acreage has fallen by a quarter in recent years, this conceals a shifting pattern, with expansion in quality wine outside the Swan Valley.

This huge region divides into five main sub-regions: Swan Valley, Perth Hills (under 80 acres, only 2.5 of them Shiraz), South-West Coastal Plain, Margaret River and the Lower Great Southern. They share the moderating influence of the Indian Ocean, which amortises extremes of heat, evening out the growing season and thereby contributing finesse.

Shiraz is widely, though not extensively, planted throughout the region and is well adapted to its climate. Although most Shiraz is in the Lower Great Southern, it is attracting interest in Margaret River and the South-West Coastal Plain, with "Hermitage" from such as David Hohnen at Cape Mentelle showing what can be done with care and thought.

LOWER GREAT SOUTHERN

This vast region – roughly 170 x 120km – takes in the sub-regions of Albany, Frankland River, Mount Barker and Pemberton-Manjimup. Soils are similar throughout, mainly more-or-less sandy loams on water-retentive clay. The climate depends on proximity to the coast. Inland areas, such as Frankland River, are markedly hotter than those such as Albany, where ocean influences reduce mean daily and seasonal temperature ranges without sacrificing overall heat summation (c 1,500 degree days at Mount Barker). Mount Barker seems to break all the climatic rules, with a very short time at peak temperature (five days at above 35°C on average, with a norm nearer 25–28°C) and cloud cover usually arriving in mid-afternoon, blocking the sun and causing the temperature to plummet. Apart from the estates profiled here, sound Shiraz is also made by Alkoomi, Goundrey and Jingalla.

MARGARET RIVER

Vines came to Margaret River after a 1965 academic paper drew similarities between its soils and climate and those of Bordeaux. In 1966 Dr Kevin Cullen founded

Cullens at Willyabrup, followed a year later by Dr Tom Cullity at Vasse Felix. This is a relatively cool, Mediterranean-type climate, marked by a very small seasonal range: less than 8°C separate highest from lowest mean monthly temperatures, making true winter dormancy rare. With vineyards round the town of Margaret River itself and also to the north-west of Cowaramup, often less than 5km from the ocean, the onshore breezes matter as much to *vignerons* as to the legions of surfers. The soils are mainly well-drained and sandy, with varying proportions of loam and clay. Rainfall is 50% higher than that of Lower Great Southern, but only 17% of this falls during the growing season. Heat summation averages 1,700. Given suitable *terroir*, Shiraz performs well, giving wines of subtlety and depth. Apart from Cape Mentelle, the other main player is Vasse Felix (now owned by the Holmes-à-Court family) where Clive Otto is making increasingly interesting Shiraz from 37 acres. The wine is deliberately made in the "elegant style" – generally quite spicy and intense – but lacks the depth and concentration for top-class rating; it is possible to square this circle, as David Hohnen annually demonstrates.

SOUTH-WEST COASTAL PLAIN

This vast region is a narrow strip, never more than 4km wide and some 270km long, from 40km north of Perth southwards to the Ludlow Tuart forest, near Busselton, where it shades into Margaret River. The Indian Ocean gives a mild climate with cool, wet winters and dry, hottish summers. Afternoon sea breezes blow during the growing season, giving relatively cool nights and helping the development of flavour, complexity and character. Heat summation is around 1,750. The distinctive fertile, sandy "tuart" topsoil is also a potent influence. It sits on a well-drained limestone base soil and, together with the summer heat, makes drip irrigation a virtual necessity.

Apart from Paul Conti, who set up here in 1948, pioneering the production of Premium Shiraz from his 1958 Mariginiup vineyard 26km north of Perth, most development took place in the 1970s and 1980s. Even so, there are fewer than ten estates. Sound, if generally unexciting, Shiraz are produced by Peel Estate at Baldivis, and by Rob Bowen at Capel Vale.

Capel Vale is clearly capable of quality, if an excellent 1980 and 1981 made by the owner Peter Pratten are fair testimony. The

mid-1980s vintages, however, were distinctly patchy. However, things are looking up, with notable successes in 1988 and 1989, good 1990 and 1991s and a very promising 1992. This estate needs a period of stability: Rob Bowen knows the Rhône and admires its wines; he has empathy with Shiraz and understands its ways.

SWAN VALLEY

Viticulture came to the Swan Valley in 1830, with English settlers. At the turn of the 20th century, Dalmatian migrants brought an upsurge in winemaking. Nowadays, there are some 330ha under vine – with 75ha of Grenache and 43ha of Shiraz.

The region, with its sub-regions of Upper, Middle and West Swan, Herne Hill and Guildford, starts at the town of Guildford, a few miles north-east of Perth. Vines are grown on the flat, low-lying valleys of the Canning and Swan rivers (average height 30m above sea level). This is hot, dry country (latitude 32° south) with heat summation of 2,340, high summer temperatures and low summer rainfall, making irrigation essential. However, the land's porosity allows vine roots to dig deep into underground water reservoirs, providing some buffer against drought. The biggest threats for growers are torrential pre-harvest rainstorms. In general, soils are deep, well-drained and alluvial: not perhaps ideal for viticulture. They vary widely, from sandy loams, through clays to duplexes which tend to waterlog after heavy winter rains.

Soils and climate combine to produce high sugars and low acidities, which makes it surprising that the region gained fame for white wines, but more credible that it also became known for fortifieds. The potential for Shiraz as a quality variety has been exploited by Houghton (the first commercial vineyard in Western Australia) and by Evans and Tate (qv), whose Gnangara Shiraz manages to combine some finesse with the natural richness from the region's very ripe grapes. Swan Valley is unlikely to expand its Rhônish activities significantly while there is still scope for exploration in the cooler regions of Margaret River, Lower Great Southern and the South-West Coastal Plain.

Western Australia's *terroirs* breeds a comparable diversity of wine styles. If there is a common factor, it is finesse, but often achieved at the expense of substance. Many wines tasted (see page 300ff) lacked centre and were, frankly, one-dimensional – reflecting incomplete fruit ripeness, rather than of flawed vinification.

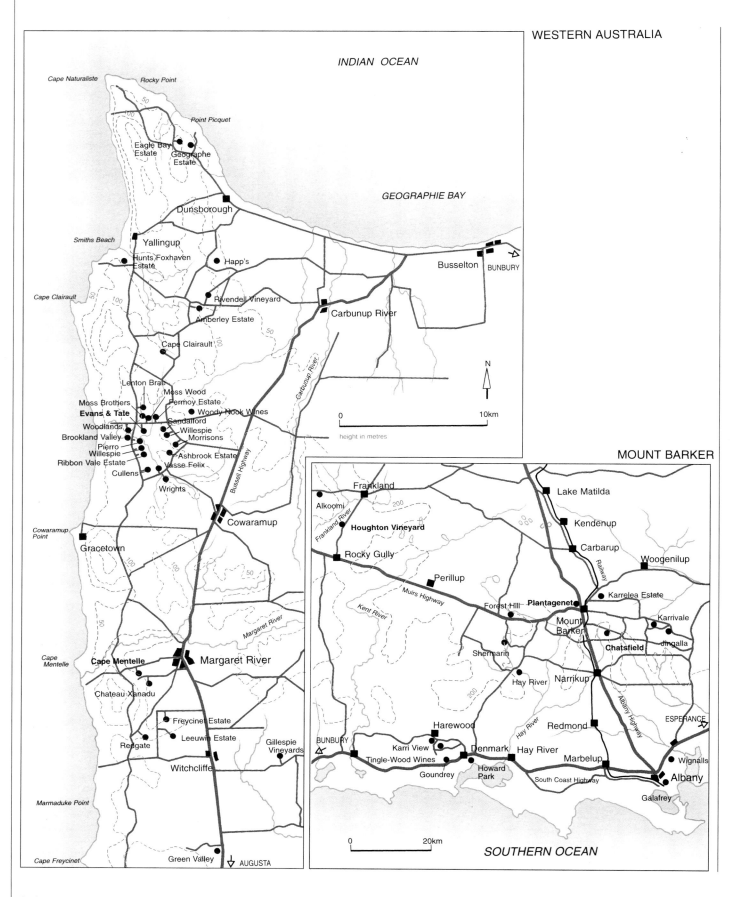

WESTERN AUSTRALIA

INDIAN OCEAN

Cape Naturaliste   *Rocky Point*

Point Picquet

Eagle Bay
Estate
Geographe
Estate

GEOGRAPHIE BAY

Dunsborough

Smiths Beach   Yallingup

Hunts Foxhaven
Estate   Happ's

Busselton   BUNBURY

Cape Clairault

Rivendell Vineyard

Amberley Estate

Carbunup River

Cape Clairault

N

Lenton Brae
Moss Wood
Fermoy Estate
Moss Brothers   Woody Nook Wines
Evans & Tate
Sandalford
Woodlands   Willespie
Brookland Valley   Morrisons
Pierro
Willespie   Ashbrook Estate
Ribbon Vale Estate   Vasse Felix
Cullens
Wrights

0   10km

height in metres

Cowaramup

*Cowaramup
Point*

Gracetown

MOUNT BARKER

Frankland   Lake Matilda

Alkoomi
Houghton Vineyard   Kendenup

Rocky Gully   Carbarup

Woogenilup

Perillup

Margaret River

Muirs Highway

Kent River
Forest Hill   **Plantagenet**   Karrelea Estate

*Cape
Mentelle*   **Cape Mentelle**   Margaret River

Mount
Barker   Karrivale

Jingalla
Chatsfield
Shermarin

Chateau Xanadu

Hay River   Narrikup

Freycinet Estate

Leeuwin Estate

Gillespie
Vineyards   ESPERANCE

Redgate
Harewood   Redmond
Karri View   *Hay River*
Denmark   Hay River   Marbelup

Witchcliffe   BUNBURY
Tingle-Wood Wines   Wignalls
Goundrey   Howard   South Coast Highway   Albany
Park

Marmaduke Point   Galafrey

SOUTHERN OCEAN

0   20km

Cape Freycinet   Green Valley   AUGUSTA

CAPE MENTELLE

Cape Mentelle, and its innovative and energetic founder David Hohnen, are best known as producers of varieties other than those of the Rhône – Cabernet Sauvignon, Semillon, Sauvignon Blanc, Chardonnay and sparkling Pelorus – and for their New Zealand sister-operation, Cloudy Bay. It is less known that David also makes a fine "Hermitage", a Mataro and a Grenache rosé – with Marsanne, Roussanne and Viognier in the pipeline.

The soils and climate are distinctive. The climate is categorized as "west coast Mediterranean", with heat summation similar to Bordeaux, much less rainfall but notably high humidity; the absence of extremes is ensured both by the maritime location, with the added softening influence of the Leeuwin current. Heavy winter rain washes out salinity and replenishes the aquafer. Cape Mentelle itself lies a few kilometres from the Indian Ocean, bounded to the east by an ancient granitic spine which runs from Cape Naturaliste south to Cape Leeuwin. The slow decomposition of this ridge has formed the soils of Mentelle's vineyards.

The profile is complex: surface gravels with iron-rich clay; below, white clay and granite bedrock. Into this clay, vine roots tap over two metres while feeding closer to the surface in the nutrition zone. Most of the best vineyards are in these granite soils of the Leeuwin-Naturaliste Ridge.

On such *terroir* Shiraz is capable of excellence. However, it tends to ripen quickly, often going from elegant pepperiness to plum-jam in just a few days. Although machines help harvest here, generally in the first fortnight of March, 40% of the Shiraz is hand-picked – for whole berries, which enhance pepperiness and contribute softer tannins

David Hohnen.

than the astringent stem-derived variety.

The Cape Mentelle "Hermitage" is a substantial wine – the product of a short, warm fermentation with vigorous pumping-over with a fire-hose to extract every gramme of matter from the cap. David Hohnen is forthright in condemning those who advocate cold fermentation to retain freshness and fruit: "bullshit, as far as I'm concerned". He

also believes in "feral ferments" – wild yeasts rather than the clinical predictability of cultures.

The wine starts off in *inox*, then goes into "big timber" (5,000 and 10,000 litre vats) for malolactic and finally spends just under two years in wood. David is experimenting with new oak. At present, one-third of the wine, especially any which is unduly "reduced", finds its way into smaller wood: four- to eight-year-old Cabernet Sauvignon casks. "We are still feeling our way with this". Selective fining (to fine-tune any overt astringency), then earth- and pad-filtrations, precede bottling. About 15% of Grenache is added to flesh out the middle palate.

The "Hermitage" has characteristic aromas and flavours of green peppercorns with some plumminess, blackberry and a touch of aniseed; slightly leaner than the Barossa style, but with a firm chewy tannin backbone, youthful sweetness and good length. It tends to start life with a rather mawkish astringency, which disappears with ageing. Yields of 3–5 tonnes/acre give a good balancing concentration without the tannins of, say, La Chapelle. David Hohnen recognizes that for top quality, yields should be halved and would dearly like to make a real blockbuster – perhaps one day.... By then, with luck, we will have had the chance to taste the Marsanne, Roussanne and Viognier.

VARIETY	VINEYARD	DETAILS	AREA
SHIRAZ	CAPE MENTELLE	Planted 1971	5.00
SHIRAZ	CAPE MENTELLE	Planted 1988	5.00
MARSANNE	CAPE MENTELLE	Planted 1994	2.00
ROUSANNE	CAPE MENTELLE	Planted 1994	2.00
VIOGNIER	CAPE MENTELLE	Planted 1994	2.00
GRENACHE	KIRUP (50 kms east of Margaret River)	Planted 1986/7	3.00
GRENACHE	KIRUP (50 kms east of Margaret River)	40+ yrs old; head-pruned	1.00
GRENACHE	KIRUP (50 kms east of Margaret River)	Planted 1992	4.00
MATARO	KIRUP (50 kms east of Margaret River)	Planted 1992	2.00
		TOTAL (acres):	26.00

CHATSFIELD

This estate was established in 1976 by Ken and Joyce Lynch, with an initial five acres of Riesling and Traminer. Since then the vineyard has tripled in size, with the addition of Cabernet Franc, Chardonnay and, increasingly, Shiraz (see the table).

The Lynchs regard this climate, with its cool summers and high annual rainfall (750–900mm) as favourable territory for developing an elegant style of Shiraz. The westerly shadows of the Porongorup Ranges provide a cooling influence,

which combines with the clay/gravel soils to contribute the typical elegance which, in the Lynchs' view, characterises their wines.

Contracting-out the winemaking (until 1994 to Goundrey, now to Plantagenet) leaves them free to concentrate on producing the best possible fruit. Vinification in stainless steel is followed

by 12–16 months' maturation, mostly in one- to two-year-old oak (80% of it French, 20% American), with an increasing proportion of new wood.

Since the first estate Shiraz release in 1988, the wine has received several awards and the future seems promising.

VARIETY	VINEYARD	DETAILS	AREA
SHIRAZ	ESTATE	Planted 1985	2.50
SHIRAZ	ESTATE	Planted 1995	10.00
		TOTAL (acres):	12.50

EVANS & TATE

This estate originated in 1971, as a partnership between the Evans and Tate families, with the planting of a small vineyard, Côte de Boulanger, on Baker's Hill. Two years later they bought the ten-acre Gnangara vineyard and winery at Henley Brook in the Swan Valley, 25km north-east of Perth. A further important acquisition followed in 1974: the Redbrook Estate, 65 acres in the Margaret River, 250 kms south-west of Perth. In 1993 they added a further 150 acres of unplanted land – the Lionel estate – also at Margaret River, which is destined exclusively for white varieties.

The Tates bought out the Evanses in 1983. Frank Tate, son of the owners Toni and John Tate, joined his parents in 1987 and became managing director in 1992. In 1993, Brian Fletcher, a Shiraz specialist

from his days at Seppelts and one of Australia's most respected winemakers, was recruited. Shiraz is grown both at Gnangara and at Redbrook. In 1989 they started converting all their vineyards to a Scott-Henry trellis, which is now the esate's preferred system.

There are two Shiraz-based wines, both designed for medium-term cellaring. The Gnangara Shiraz contains around 20% Cabernet Sauvignon. This wine, conceived as a "world-class dry red from Western Australia", has been hugely successful on the home market since the 1974 vintage first appeared in 1976. It is matured for 9-12 months in either US oak, or 50:50 US:French. Until 1993, the Cabernet came mainly from the Redbrook

vineyard, which was felt to lighten the blend; now there is more Perth Hills Cabernet in the mix, to add "further richness and depth to the wine". The Margaret River Hermitage, in contrast, is 100% Shiraz from Redbrook, made to reflect the belief that the region was capable of producing Shiraz "in classic northern Rhône style", with varietal character and "the fresh, peppery lift".

The grapes are picked at around 12.8 Baumé, fermented entirely in roto-tanks at 20–25°C, with 20% being run off to finish fermentation in new oak. Maturation is also in French and US oak for some 12 months. The first release was the 1979.

VARIETY	VINEYARD	DETAILS	AREA
SHIRAZ	GNANGARA VINEYARD (Swan Valley)	Planted 1969; Scott-Henry trellis	3.00
SHIRAZ	REDBROOK VINEYARD (Margaret River)	Planted 1975; Scott-Henry trellis	2.29
		TOTAL (acres):	5.29

HOUGHTON WINES

Based in the Middle Swan, Houghton's Rhône-variety plantings consist of 35 acres of Shiraz in the Frankland River area of Western Australia. Soils here are described as dark brown, gravel-based over a clay subsoil. The climate is cold, with temperatures averaging 21°C during March and April, but descending to around 6°C at night while the machines are harvesting. To encourage maximum fruit ripeness in these conditions, the vines are trained on a mixture of vertical and "T" trellises.

This historic estate is the earliest to be established in Western Australia, having

been originally planted between 1830 and 1836, when it became the property of a syndicate including Lt-Col Richmond Houghton. Now part of the powerful BRL Hardy conglomerate, Houghton produces two Shiraz bottlings: Wildflower Ridge and a premium "Gold Reserve" of which there is never more than 1,000 cases. The winemaker, since 1987, has been Paul Lapsley, Hong Kong-born, who spent his youth in New South Wales where his parents' love of food and wine seeded his interest.

He vinifies both Shirazes to emphasize fruit flavours and to this end uses wood

with special care – a talent perhaps refined during a spell working with Maurice Chapuis in Aloxe-Corton. The Gold Reserve spends 14–16 months in a mixture of new and one-year-old Allier, Bourgogne and Vosges oak, but the Wildflower Ridge only sees wood for 12 months, and then only old American oak.

The Gold Reserve was first released in 1992, a decade after the first Wildflower Ridge, and will only be made in very good vintages (there was none in 1993). It comes from the estate's best blocks of Shiraz and made in small fermenters at a cool 22°C; fermentation is finished in cask and, according to Paul Lapsley, the intention throughout is to minimize handling, fining and filtration.

PLANTAGENET WINES

Plantagenet was started in 1968 by Tony Smith, with plantings of Shiraz and Cabernet Sauvignon. The first vintage appeared in 1974 and the following year Plantagenet commissioned the first winery in the Great Southern region of Western Australia, in the township of Mount Barker.

There are currently 10.5 acres of Shiraz planted on two separate sites. Bouverie vineyard faces north-west and has soils of medium gravelly loams over "fractured" clay. The Wyjup vineyard has similar soils to Bouverie, but faces south.

Both vineyards are in the Denbarker area, 25km inland from the Southern Ocean, at 300 metres above sea level.

Winter and spring are cool and wet, while summer is moderately warm, with an average daytime temperature of 24°C. To gain ripeness, the vines are vertically trellissed, with one-third of the Wyjup on a Scott-Henry system. Yields average three tonnnes per acre.

Plantagenet makes a single-varietal Shiraz, released only in years when Tony Smith and winemaker Gavin Berry, consider that it meets the house standard.

It is fermented in stainless steel, using a Meursault yeast, at up to 28°C with twice-daily pumping-over. There follows a 14-day maceration "to allow some of the harder tannins to break down". The press-wine is incorporated before maturation in French (Allier) oak – one-quarter of which is new. Here it stays for 15–18 months, then it is bottled and kept a further two years before release.

VARIETY	VINEYARD	DETAILS	AREA
SHIRAZ	BOUVERIE VINEYARD	2.5 acres planted 1968; 2 acres planted 1990	4.50
SHIRAZ	WYJUP VINEYARD	Planted 1974	6.00
		TOTAL (acres):	10.50

SOUTH AFRICA

In the Cape, mountains, oceans and stunning architecture fuse into one of the world's most beautiful wine regions.
Driven by a nucleus of impassioned growers, Rhône grapes are playing an increasingly important part in quality South African wine production. Some superb Shiraz have already demonstrated what is achievable and those styles are attracting growing international interest.

A Cape Dutch farmhouse and its vineyards dwarfed by the towering Hottentot Hollands.

SOUTH AFRICA

Winemaking in South Africa dates back to the arrival in the Cape in 1652 of Jan van Riebeeck, an envoy of the Dutch East India Company and later Governor, whose diary entry for February 2, 1659 records: "Today, praise be to the Lord, wine was made for the first time from Cape grapes". However, it was under his successor, Simon van der Stel (after whom Stellenbosch was named) that viticulture really flourished, with notable improvement in the quality of both fruit and wine-making, particularly around Stellenbosch and Constantia.

Further progress came at the end of the 17th century from refugee French Huguenots, who brought their knowledge of French winemaking methods to Stellenbosch, Paarl and Franschhoek (French corner), where they principally settled. In the late 18th century and 19th centuries, the dessert wines of Constantia were famed throughout Europe – lauded by Dumas, Baudelaire, Jane Austen, Longfellow, Louis Philippe of France, Bismarck and Frederick of Prussia. Napoleon Bonaparte is said to have requested a glass of Constantia on his deathbed.

By 1795 the Cape was under British occupation, and with the end of the Napoleonic wars came the restoration of trading with France. The removal of protective tariffs brought a flood of French wine imports, causing hardship to Cape wine-growers, whose exports were inadequate to compensate for the losses. The latter decades of the 18th century also brought phylloxera and "Shiraz disease" (similar to corky bark) which compounded the misery.

Re-grafting onto phylloxera-resistant rootstocks regenerated the vineyards, but over-planting and persistent overproduction made wine uneconomic. By 1918 the Cape was producing 56 million litres – much of it unsaleable – from 87 billion vines. The quality of South African wines steadily declined, and attempts to put some order into the industry failed dismally.

In 1924 the Government stepped in, establishing the KWV – an unusual form of cooperative to which 95% of growers belonged, and in which were vested powers to limit production and set minimum prices. Merchants were persuaded to buy only from KWV members, so prices gradually rose and stability was restored. This held through the depression years of the early 1930s. In 1935, an American, Charles Winshaw – a vivid personality and erstwhile acquaintance of Buffalo Bill – founded the Stellenbosch Farmers' Winery (qv) as a producing wholesaler, concentrating on the then popular fortified wines.

The KWV and SFW remain major influences in the South African wine industry, although their role and usefulness is increasingly under debate. The KWV is not profiled in detail here since, as its marketing director, Jannie Retief and winemaker Kosie Muller candidly admit, it is not a major player in the Shiraz league. However, it does produce a sound, well-made Shiraz and the variety clearly interests Kosie, who would like to give it more emphasis within KWV in future. The organisation contributes to the South African wine industry in many ways, not least with its impressive plant improvement and certification programme.

VINEYARDS

The Cape is stunningly beautiful. Its principal grape-growing areas are relatively circumscribed, with the Atlantic and Indian oceans to the west and south respectively, meeting at the Cape of Good Hope. Against a dramatic backdrop of mountains, the vines occupy the plains and foothills, ripened by a warm, sunny and thoroughly congenial climate, which becomes progressively hotter the further one strays from maritime influence.

The estates vary in size and grandeur; many are headquartered in magnificent old Dutch Colonial buildings, others in more modern surroundings. Most encourage visitors and do much to welcome them, and owners and winemakers seem to enjoy the personal contact this brings. As in California and Australia, several estates offer other amenities, including lunches – cold platters in summer, hot, substantial food in winter – to accompany their wines, and many have restaurants, some excellent.

Administratively, the Cape vineyards are subdivided into five Regions, comprising ten Districts and 35 Wards. Apart from a handful of outposts in the hot Swartland and Robertson districts, production of quality Rhône varieties is confined to Stellenbosch, Paarl and Franschhoek. In practice this means Shiraz. Although Cinsaut (originally called Hermitage here) is the second most widely planted red variety in the Cape (4.8% of the 101,654ha in 1993) – Cabernet Sauvignon just pips it at 5% – it mainly functions as a blending wine and is rarely bottled as a varietal; when it is, the results are not particularly impressive. Grenache and Mourvèdre used to be widely planted, especially

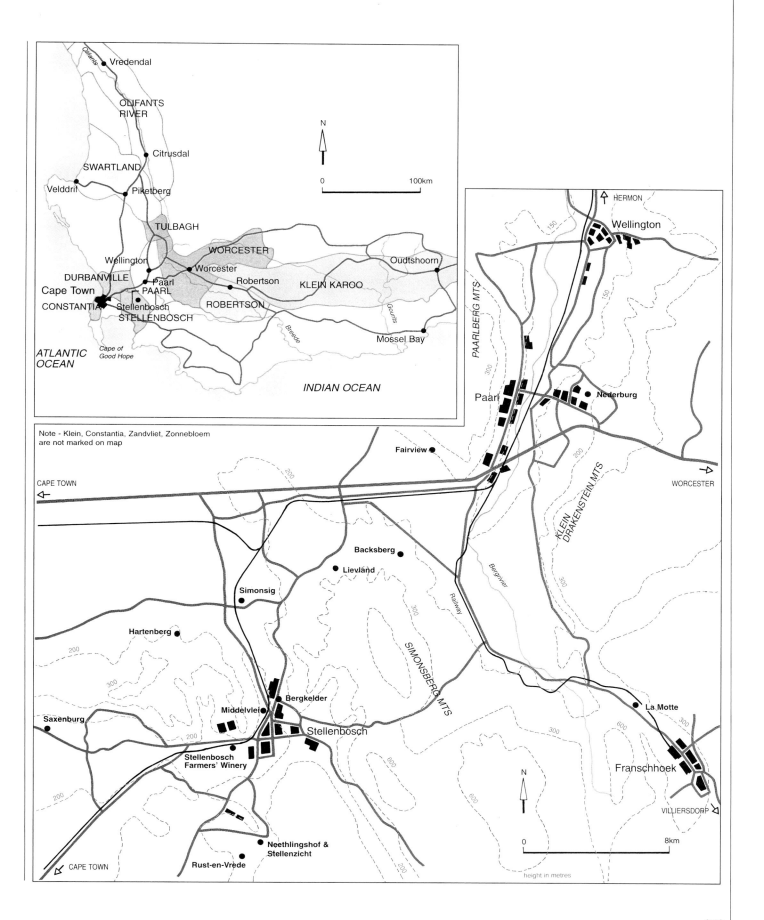

Vredendal

OLIFANTS
RIVER

Citrusdal

SWARTLAND

Velddrif   Piketberg

N

0   100km

TULBAGH

Wellington   WORCESTER

DURBANVILLE   Worcester   Oudtshoorn

Cape Town   Paarl   Robertson   KLEIN KAROO
PAARL
CONSTANTIA   Stellenbosch
STELLENBOSCH   ROBERTSON

ATLANTIC   Cape of
OCEAN   Good Hope

INDIAN OCEAN

Note - Klein, Constantia, Zandvliet, Zonnebloem
are not marked on map

HERMON

150   Wellington

PAARLBERG MTS

300

CAPE TOWN

Paarl   Nederburg

200   WORCESTER

200

Fairview

KLEIN DRAKENSTEIN MTS

Backsberg

Lievland   300

Simonsig

Bergrivier

Railway

Hartenberg

SIMONSBERG MTS

300

Bergkelder

Middelvlei   300

Saxenburg   600   La Motte

200   Stellenbosch

Stellenbosch
Farmers' Winery   600   300   600

Franschhoek

N

VILLIERSDORP

200

CAPE TOWN   Neethlingshof &
Stellenzicht

Rust-en-Vrede   0   8km

height in metres

273

around Paarl, but acreages have shrunk and there is no significant production from these varieties. Experimental patches of Viognier have recently appeared.

As in Australia and California, the Shiraz has inspired a small caucus of winemakers to challenge the supremacy of Cabernet Sauvignon in the quality arena. Fired by the great Syrahs of the Northern Rhône, these pioneers are working hard to identify the most favourable sites and to refine its cultivation and vinification, and have made great strides in developing its considerable potential in the Cape. Both climate and soils are well suited to Shiraz and there is no reason why it should not produce top-class wine, given sensible yields and sympathetic handling.

SHIRAZ HISTORY

Serious Cape Shiraz production is very recent. The vine was not among those planted by van Riebeeck, although there is speculation that van der Stel received some cuttings in a shipment from Europe. During the late 1890s de Waal, the then manager at Groot Constantia, was reputed to have imported some Shiraz cuttings collected during a visit to Australia. The earliest mention of Shiraz as a cultivar was in the 1935 wine show, where a class devoted to sweet Shiraz attracted 13 entries and another listed three dry Shiraz reds. Until quite recently, it tended to be vinified sweet (or fortified) – "very disappointing, being sweet, sticky, jammy and port-like" (Paul Benate, 1992) – or ended up as an improver for "Bordeaux" or "Burgundy" blends. These are now outlawed, which has led to the increasing use of varietal labelling.

The first so-labelled Shiraz was Bellingham's 1957 made by Bernard Podlashuk, "the father of Shiraz in South Africa". A Groot Constantia appeared in 1963, followed two years later by an offering from the Klawer cooperative in Oliphant's River. Thereafter the trickle became a steady stream. By 1968 there were ten Shiraz on the market; a decade later this had doubled. Now, the solo Shiraz of 1957 has blossomed into some 52 individual releases.

In the late 1960s, producers were encouraged to pay more attention to Shiraz as a quality cultivar. This advice unfortunately coincided with an oversupply of red wine, and plantings decreased from 480,012 vines in 1962 to 388,693 in 1971. During the '70s better prices reversed this, and plantings rose to some 2.01 million vines. Shiraz now accounts for 0.9% of total Cape acreage, a figure which has increased modestly from 0.7% over the last decade.

These plantings are concentrated in Stellenbosch (61.3%) and Paarl (24.1%). This has always been the case, with no new viticultural areas being developed for Shiraz, but rather re-planting of the variety in existing vineyards.

The development of Shiraz in the Cape is bound up with viticultural and winemaking considerations. Understanding its evolution here requires an explanation of climate, soils and changing ideas on style and vinification.

STYLES

Until quite recently, South African Shiraz was best described by the splendid Afrikaans word "dikvoet" – translated literally as "thick foot"; this accurately evokes the heavy, porty, high-alcohol wines made from late-picked, over-ripe grapes. These dramatic sledgehammers were made in the old Cabernet Sauvignon mould, big and tannic with plenty of rich press-wine to add structure. Now this sort of liquid central-heating is out of favour in the modern, international market place, which seeks clean, varietal flavours, with less alcohol and more elegant fruit.

This change presents growers who are striving to adapt with one of their two main problems: establishing a style. Some fall into the trap of over-emphasising pepperiness, which they see as the distinguishing character of the Northern Rhône. Fortunately, the weakness of the Rand has kept the cost of new French casks prohibitively high which has reined-in the usual tendency to over-oak. With improving economics giving more financial flexibility, the use of new wood with Shiraz is now a matter of continuing debate among winemakers.

Historic neglect has undoubtedly contributed to Shiraz's present difficulties. These started in the vineyard, providing the grower with his second main problem: finding suitable plant material. A current KWV list shows 31 Chardonnay clones, 22 Cabernet Sauvignon, even ten of Muscat d'Alexandrie, but just four of Shiraz, only one of which is of French origin.

The broader problem, however, is not any inherent weakness in Shiraz but the strength of Cabernet Sauvignon. Its high market profile made it the wine-maker's favourite; so if there was new wood, Cabernet got it first, leaving Shiraz the oldest, most decrepit casks. Vinification of Shiraz was of secondary importance and often clumsy; the vines tended to be over-cropped (and only harvested after Cabernet and Chardonnay, so over-ripe). The consistently unimpressive results were hardly surprising. Also, Shiraz was planted on the poorest, worst-exposed sites, on high pH, low-acid soils, which made the chance of harvesting

Splendid flame tree with the vineyards of Robertson beyond.

decent raw material to vinify remote. These effects were compounded in the marketplace, where consumers (apart from an enlightened nucleus of closet Rhône drinkers) didn't expect Shiraz to be anything but mediocre. In short, no effort was put into it. Then, Australian imports began to show the South Africans the grape's potential, and producers, seeing its success on international markets, started to take a keen interest.

Now, the controversy over "dikvoet" or "new" style has been replaced by arguments about whether to copy Australia or whether to take on the Rhône. Others see this problem in marketing terms: to tailor the product to the market or to make the best possible wine – and hesitate between early-drinking, fruit-driven styles with quick turnover and attractive cash advantages, and more austere wines which need cellaring, but are ultimately finer and thus more likely to establish an international reputation. For many, the immediate difficulty (which seems incredible to most other wine-sophisticated countries) is getting hold of top French and Australian wines to taste; imports are rare and very expensive. Those few with an established

reputation for Shiraz discuss their more esoteric concern of developing top quality in a South African style rather than in anybody else's.

CLIMATE

South Africa is not one, but half a dozen different climates. Cape weather patterns are influenced by currents from the Altantic and Indian oceans, prevailing winds and altitude; and these often highly localised factors have a seminal influence on final wine quality. Rainfall in this south-westerly tip of the continent falls mainly in winter (April – September); during the growing season, drought seems to be the norm (especially in recent years). Irrigation is therefore allowed, but needs sparing use – abundant, lush foliage and pendulous bunches of bloated berries are not compatible with quality. Shiraz reacts poorly to drought, so the ability to irrigate is useful.

The annual mean temperature of Cape Town is 17°C, while Pretoria, 1000 miles nearer the tropics, has a mean only half a degree higher, and frequent frosts – something Cape growers don't have to worry about. Temperature inversions are less dramatic nearer the coast than in the interior where very cold winter nights with clear skies follow hot, sunny days.

Uniquely in southern Africa, the Cape has a Mediterranean climate which is ideal for viticulture. Further inland, excessive heat invariably leads to loss of aromatic finesse, low sugars and high acidity. The confluence of two great oceans produces strong winds for the *vigneron* to contend with, in the form of "berg" winds from the northern interior and the – potentially more devastating – south-easterly winds. These can gust up to gale force when they become "black south-easters", which break vines and cause considerable damage.

Mountain winds also play a part in viticulture, where higher sites tend to be more exposed and cooler. Both mountain and ocean winds moderate extremes of temperature; they also dry off the vines after rain, which helps reduce rot, and minimise pest infestation.

Adequate sunshine – and thus ripening – isn't generally a problem in the Cape, although on some north- and west-facing slopes strong late afternoon summer sunshine can burn off important aroma and flavour compounds. A more tractable problem is that, in the right conditions, sugar levels can rocket from low to unacceptably high in a couple of days. Around harvest time, growers take a weekend off at their peril; Friday evening's 22 Baumé can become 26 on Monday morning – and they wanted to pick at 23.

Another related problem is that sugars can reach ideal levels without concomitant tannin ripeness. A major fault of much South African Shiraz is unripe, harsh, even green tannin which unbalances a young wine and often remains as an herbaceous green streak to dog its old age. In Europe, undue greenness is often attributable to leaving grape-stems, which contain these unpleasant tannins in relative abundance, in the fermenting vats; in the Cape, even fully de-stemmed vats can show such a fault. Many growers are trying different leaf-canopy configurations to increase exposure to the sun, hoping thereby to avoid the problem. A further, tangential, consideration is that many farms are large, with numerous different grape varieties, and have neither the time nor labour to pick each one at optimum ripeness. This, and widespread over-cropping, means that some grapes are over-ripe, others under-ripe and very little just as it should be. Shiraz, in particular, needs special care at harvest, if you are really intent on top quality.

These considerations lead growers to favour cooler sites, often at altitude, sheltered from the fiercest heat and

Thoroughbred at Zandvliet.

with a ready supply of irrigation water; hence the numerous 'dams' – artificial ponds – found on many estates.

SOILS

While Shiraz is adaptable to a reasonably wide variety of *terroirs*, it performs best on well-drained, light, granitic or pebbly soils. Richer ground produces duller, more diffuse wines which typically lack aromatic finesse and flavour complexity. In the Cape, plantings are diverse – on hillsides, plains and river gravels – and in different soil-types. Although there is some granite, particularly around eastern Stellenbosch and near Paarl, the predominant geology is relatively structureless soils in forms known as Hutton and Clovelly. These, of red and yellow aspect respectively, are well drained and have significant clay content (20-30%) in coastal areas. River gravels dominate lower-lying land and finer, decomposed soils the higher slopes.

A particular problem is that Cape soils tend to be rich in potassium; this munches up nitrogen, which diminishes natural sugar production, and also removes tartaric acid, which lowers wine acidity and leads to premature browning (a characteristic of much old-style South African Shiraz). Growers combat this in several ways: many add lime to neutralise the potassium and thus restore a more even chemical balance; others plough up the top-soil into ridges and plant along these so that the roots don't penetrate the clay layer below where potassium is concentrated; others manage the canopy to expose more of the fruit and foliage to direct sunlight which reduces potassium build-up. The old fertiliser recipe – 3 nitrogen:1 phosphorus:5 potassium – didn't help matters, and has been generally discarded in favour of a subtler cocktail.

CLONES AND VITICULTURE

It is generally felt (not just in South Africa) that diversity of clones (the upper section of a vine-graft which determines its variety) plays an important role in the complexity of a wine. Up to now, Shiraz growers in the Cape have had a limited selection to work with, and that of indifferent quality. The principal offerings are: the KWV Allesverloren clone, first released in 1973, a vigorous grower with loose bunches which gives a marked berry character; the Argentinian clone (1971), which produces full bunches but a weak colour; the KWV Meerendaal clone (1972), another vigorous stock which gives dark coloured wine – most favoured for premium wine – and a French clone, first issued in 1981. Another French clone is on trial (eg at Hartenberg), but not yet commercially available.

Unfortunately many of these older clones are heavily infected with the fan-leaf virus – Meerendaal and Allesverloren in particular – which reddens leaves and reduces sugar production: which in turn leads to lower alcohols. New, virus-free clones are currently being developed under impressive plant-improvement programmes in which KWV, SFW and Government agencies are participating. Many growers look to these for the future of quality Shiraz, believing that they will contribute a more berryish character to the wine. However, cleaned-up clones give higher yields and larger berries, so self-discipline is needed to control vine vigour and restrain yields. Shiraz is particularly sensitive to over-cropping – above a certain level, which varies from site to site, quality plummets.

Whatever you plant, how you prune and train a vine decisively influences grape composition and thus wine quality. The amount and trellissing of the foliage – for fruit exposure, sugar production and ventilation – row orientation and spacing, the height of bunches from the ground, the control of shoot density and crop size, all play a role in ensuring the most propitious micro-climate around each individual plant. Many growers in the Cape are experimenting with alternative configurations and regimes (not only with Shiraz) and are finding that careful canopy management can lead to a significant increase in fruit quality.

VINIFICATION

Winegrowers generally accept that vinification really begins at harvest. In the Cape, the tendency was to pick Shiraz over-ripe, around 14% potential alcohol, when the berries had started to shrivel. Nowadays, there is much more tasting of grapes in the vineyard to ensure that as well as adequate sugar levels, tannins are ripe. In the early 1990s, all the talk was of pH (a measure of hydrogen ion power and thus acidity); even amateur tasters were "pH crazy": "this wine's no good, look at the pH". This lunacy has fortunately come to an end; you can't drink pH.

Anxieties about acidity led to over-acidification, since oenology students are drilled never to bottle a wine above a pH of 3.5 or 3.6; few seemed concerned with what the wine tasted like. Fortunately, a new generation of winemakers are moving away from technologically-driven, analytically-correct wines, to more natural methods; if a wine is low in acidity, the chances are its tannins will sustain it.

The use of wood is also improving. Smaller casks are replacing large, old oak *foudres,* and many estates are developing close contacts with their coopers to reinforce the message that they won't accept sub-standard green, sappy wood, and to enlist their expert help in adapting cask-selection to their individual *terroir* and wine style.

In many cellars Shiraz is no longer second-best, but now has pride of place. De-stemming is more common, and vatting times are now carefully adapted to the style of the vintage. The amount of press-wine blended back is now more likely to depend upon the structure of the free-run wine rather than on cruder economic considerations. The amount of new oak used and the length of maturation before bottling are decisions made with much greater knowledge and care than hitherto. There is also a cautious, but most welcome, change towards allowing natural rather than artificial yeasts to mediate fermentation, though many still fear that nature will not finish the job properly, leaving unfermented sugars in the wine which are susceptible to bacterial attack, leading to undesirable volatile acidity.

The results of all these improvements are striking – soundly constituted wines with strong varietal character, good concentration and clean, complex fruit, well equipped for mid to long-term bottle ageing. In international terms, prices are absurdly low; something which will undoubtedly change when buyers start to discover these riches.

TRENDS, CONTROVERSIES AND THE FUTURE

Much of the Cape's Shiraz acreage is in the hands of traditional growers, many of whom have established a reputation, and a market, for the old-fashioned style (eg Meerendaal and Allesverloren) from which they do well and which they are understandably reluctant to change.

The local market has become conditioned to the heavy alcohol, mildly jammy style of Shiraz so this is unlikely to disappear altogether in the forseeable future. However, this same market has reached virtual stagnation, so it will be to exports that growers, especially the new, younger Shiraz brigade, increasingly direct their gaze. It is this international perspective which will further refine their styles.

The South African consumer psyche is staunchly traditional – convinced that Cabernet Sauvignon is *the* variety and that the older the wine the better (there is probably a good deal of vinegar "maturing" in cellars around the country). Such a conservative market is not a fertile medium for innovation.

Increased sales have given growers the means to invest and re-equip after years of economic isolation with only local sales to rely on. There are still anti-competitive niggles, such as the exorbitant cost of bottles and packaging – a 12-bottle carton costs 25-30 Rand, twice the price of Europe – absurd for a wine selling at 15 Rand a bottle.

Internationalisation has brought the role of the authorities into sharper focus. Both the KWV and the Wine and Spirit Board (which runs the official tastings for wine certification) have been heavily criticised – the former for entrenched privilege, old-fashioned attitudes and over-burdening control, the latter for "their alarming... lack of knowledge" of international markets which stultifies progress and particularly hinders the development of new products. Change is already apparent: in 1992 production-quota restrictions were removed and in 1994 minimum price guarantees were effectively scrapped. These important measures effectively remove the cushion between producers and the free market, and propel growers (some say too quickly) towards self-reliance. There are strong arguments for letting the KWV shed much of its quasi-governmental role and become a normal cooperative, making and selling wine for its 4,900 growers members, who still need the valuable marketing and research skills it provides.

A particular thorn in the flesh of quality-minded estates are the continuing bulk wine shipments to Scandinavia and elsewhere. Incompetent bottling and, it is whispered, adulteration, mean that poor-quality wine, sometimes out of condition, appears on markets with Cape labels, which does nothing for the region's reputation. Controls exist, but are less easy to enforce once the casks have been exported. There are moves to collect bottled samples at the point of sale and refuse further export certificates to producers whose wine doesn't meet required standards; but by the time faults have been detected, the damage is done. A country genuinely interested in a quality market image should insist that all its wine is bottled at source.

In 1983, perhaps partly in reaction to growing discontents, the Cape Independent Winemakers' Guild was set up, to promote winemaking excellence among those genuinely independent of wholesalers and cooperatives. An annual barrel tasting and auction of rigorously selected young wines in Cape Town is ever popular, and the Guild itself is attracting an increasing following. Many Shiraz stars are members, including Kevin Arnold of Rust-en-Vrede and Abe Beukes of Lievland (qqv).

South Africa produces more wine that it can sell. Fortunately, this is not a problem for the Shiraz-oriented estates profiled here, for whom demand frequently outstrips supply. Solid foundations have been laid, upon which much can be built as the vines mature and winemakers accumulate experience. It should also be remembered, particularly when reading the assessments and tasting notes, that few of the wines discussed here sell for more than 30 Rand a bottle retail, and most at below 20 Rand (c £3.50, US$5.6, AUS$7.8) – a price comparable to the cheapest Côtes du Rhône; this makes the high standards even more remarkable.

THE REGIONS

The Cape divides into three main regions, each with its own distinct personality:

Stellenbosch

Stellenbosch, 41km from Cape Town, was the first area to be settled by whites and is the oldest winemaking area after the Constantia Valley. Its foundation, as a pioneer settlement, by Simon van der Stel, dates from 1679. Now an academic and farming centre, with a population of some 60,000, it is home to a University whose viticulture and oenology faculty trains many of the country's new winemakers. The town centre is most attractive, and well preserves a feel of the past. It abounds with magnificent buildings in the Cape Dutch style – which draws on elements from Huguenot France, medieval Holland and

Indonesia. A stroll along Dorp Street – the longest row of historic buildings in South Africa – and around the town square, Die Braak, flanked by the attractive Anglican Church of St Mary (1852) and the old Dutch East India Powder House (1777), evokes the grace and dignity of earlier centuries.

The town plain is surrounded by vineyards and high mountains, dominated to the south by the Helderberg and Stellenbosch ranges, to the north-west by the Bottelary hills and by the impressive Simonsberg to the north-east. To the east, the towering Jonkershoek dominates one of the area's most beautiful valleys, while further west the contours soften towards the Cape Flats. The area is home to some of the Cape's finest wine estates.

Soils vary in depth and composition, though most are classified as Hutton and Clovelly. There are some patches of granite – especially on the eastern slopes – which are ideally suited to noble red varieties, while to the west the land contains more sand. Along the river beds, soils are richer, more alluvial, and in places strongly acidic, needing heavy liming to bring them into balance for viticulture.

The climate is broadly Mediterranean, with significant local variations attributable to wind, elevation and exposure. On higher sites which are open to the cooling ocean breezes of False Bay, the growing season tends to be longer than those on the hotter, sheltered plains. Annual rainfall averages 600-800mm., and the average temperature during the growing season is around 18-19°C.

Paarl

Paarl has an althogether different feel about it than Stellenbosch. The town, first settled in 1687, is elongated – strung out along 11 kilometers of seemingly interminable Jacaranda-lined main street, flanked by the usual modern shops and commerce, without any obvious central focus. There are some fine buildings here, including KWV's superbly-restored Laborie Estate at the foot of Paarl mountain. A short distance to the north is Wellington, while to the south-east is Franschhoek and twenty minutes' drive to the south-west is Stellenbosch.

In wine-growing terms, Paarl is smaller than Stellenbosch – though, as home to the KWV and Nederburg, it has gained importance by osmosis. Most of the 25 or so estates which come under its aegis are to be found to the immediate south and west of the town, on the lower slopes of Paarl mountain. The edge of the Simonsberg range lie to the south-west, while to the south and south-east are the Franschhoek and Groot Drakenstein ranges. To the east are the Klein Drakensteins, crossed by the precipitous Du Toit's Kloof pass; nowadays, the Huguenot road tunnel makes the journey easier, if far less spectacular.

The climate reflects the fact that Paarl is further inland than Stellenbosch – some 60km. from the Atlantic Ocean. This means a lowish rainfall (650mm annual average), and higher average temperatures (19-21°C), giving a drier, hotter, more continental aspect to things. The area is classed III on the Winkler scale of heat summation; frost is not a real risk here.

Around the town, soils tend to be granitic, while along the Berg river, which runs through Paarl, there is more sand. Towards Wellington there is a predominance of shale.

Franschhoek

To the south-east of Paarl, at one end of the Drakenstein valley, lies Franschhoek. This small area was christened by the first French Huguenot settlers of 1688-90, fleeing from religious persecution in France, as Le Quartier Français. Its estates continue to reflect their origins – Chamonix, La Provence, Clos Cabrière, La Couronne etc – as do the surnames of their owners – de Villiers, Rousseau, Fourie, Roux, Vivier and so on. A magnificent memorial, flanked by an wide avenue of bush-trees at the end of the long Huguenot Road, commemorates the early Huguenot settlement and symbolises religious freedom.

Viticulturally, Franschhoek's renaissance came in the early 1980s, with new vineyard plantings and restoration of many historic estates to their former grandeur. In 1984 the growers formed the Vignerons de Franschhoek to promote their wines, and the valley.

In character and topography, the Franschhoek area is broadly similar to Paarl, though somewhat wetter. Soils and micro-climates vary widely from flatter, low-lying land to steeper hillsides. Shiraz does well here, and there are signs that this corner is capable of producing wine of considerable finesse and class.

The Cape Shiraz movement is relatively young, and the wines are not yet world-class. However, the momentum is gathering as estate-owners and winemakers see the potential of Shiraz as a premium varietal, rather than a useful blending component. The Cape now has a firm nucleus of Rhône-dedicated *vignerons*, producing wine of excellent quality, of which it has every reason to be proud.

BACKSBERG ESTATE

Sydney Back is one of the Cape's senior wine men, and his estate one of its most celebrated. 1995 saw his 55th consecutive vintage at the Klein Babylonstoren property on which he grew up, and from which he helped launch the Estate Winery concept in the early 1970s.

This attractive farm, just south of Paarl and not far from Fairview, belongs to Sydney's brother Cyril. It sits on the north-east slopes of the Simonsberg, with views across to the rounded Paarl Mountain. Approached by a long, tree-lined, pot-holed drive, it has been described as "a microcosm" of the Cape's wine industry and a magnet for tourists, "who regard a visit to Backsberg in the same light as a trip up Table Mountain".

Sydney's son, Michael – a bearded, somewhat laid-back character – now oversees the estate which, in addition to the 130ha of vines, rears pigs and poultry commercially. The wines are made by Hardy Laubser.

Sydney's guiding principle was to combine quality with value – a tradition that continues today, with two ranges that include a Shiraz: one more in the popular mould, the other a premium vesion. These have evolved here since the early 1980s.

Backsberg's six hectares of Shiraz are in a single block: "a really good piece of

Sydney Back.

ground", Michael avers, on red Hutton-type soils – strongly ferruginous, decomposed granite – at the high point of the farm. They are irrigated once a year, around Christmas – with difficulty, since the remaining water system has to be shut down to give enough pressure to get it up to the vineyard.

Since the first vintage in the mid-1970s, the style has seen three distinct phases:

early releases were fermented in closed tanks and were drawn off skins with some sugar (5-6° Brix) remaining; next, the 1980s saw the era of the roto-tank – fermentation to dryness, giving rather harder, less yielding wines. In Michael's view, these early phases were "partly fashion-driven, partly convenience-driven".

Finally, around 1990, came extended maceration with 7-12 days on skins, to achieve a wine which will age but with "the accent on drinkability" – that eluvise square circle.

Since 1992, Backsberg Shiraz has been matured in small wood for 12 months or so. The Cinderella effect operates strongly here: as Michael admits, their Cabernet gets preferential treatment, which leaves no new wood for Shiraz.

However, Hardy Laubser is changing this: the 1991 saw 10% of new French oak and the 1994 will get 100%. Prince Charming has arrived! The result is generally firm-fruited and fleshy, supple but structured, with hint of portiness in some vintages; a veritable compromise between the old and new expressions of Cape Shiraz.

Even Michael seems enthusiastic: "We should plant some more Shiraz and give it some extra TLC – tender loving care". Indeed – and while they're about it why not shave one ton per hectare off the yields and really go for quality?

VARIETY	VINEYARD	DETAILS	AREA
SHIRAZ	BACKSBERG	20+ yrs average vine age; low trellis	6.00

THE BERGKELDER

The Bergkelder is a wholly-owned subsidiary of the Distillers Corporation, and a curious amalgam of cooperative, *négociant* and estate owner. It markets both its own brands – the best-known of which is Fleur du Cap – and the wines from some 13 contracting estates. Some of these, including Uitkyk, Alto and the wine and crocodile farm, Le Bonheur, are owned by the organization itself.

For some top-quality contracting estates, such as La Motte, l'Ormarins and Zandvliet (qv), it acts simply as a marketing organization. For others – for example Allesverloren, Middelvlei – it is responsible for maturation and bottling as well as for sales. Recent years have seen several estates secede from the contract, preferring to age and sell their own wine.

Between 1981 and 1986, when there was little call for Shiraz, Bergkelder bottlings were limited; now, production

has increased to reflect the new demand.

Traditionally, Bergkelder tended to determine the style of wine – leaving the grower in no doubt as to what sold and what didn't.

While this may have been an efficient process, it was also one which often excluded innovation and left open the possibility of conflicts of interest between Bergkelder's role as estate owner and the need to deal even-handedly with its

members. In addition, it discouraged public visits to its estates, which left winemakers somewhat isolated from their customers and therefore out of touch with market trends.

Despite these criticisms, of which Bergkelder's managers are well aware, the organization has done much to enhance world appreciation of premium South African wines. In particular, its *vinotheque* scheme, which lays down stocks of its members' wines, has enabled people to taste older vintages and made these available, through an annual special

VARIETY	ESTATE	DETAILS	AREA
SHIRAZ	ALLESVERLOREN	No irrigation; trellised; average vine age 5-23 yrs	26.03
SHIRAZ	L'ORMARINS	Supplementary irrigation; trellised; average vine age 19 yrs	4.52
SHIRAZ	MIDDELVLEI	Old clones, planted 1977; Clovelly / Hutton soils	5.37
SHIRAZ	MIDDELVLEI	New clones, planted 1989; similar soils to above	8.00
SHIRAZ	UITKYK, MEERENDAAL & ALTO ESTATES		32.20
		TOTAL (hectares):	76.12

release, to traders and thus a wider public.

Apart from La Motte and Zandvliet, (qqv), Bergkelder's contenders in the premium Shiraz hurdle are Middelvlei, l'Ormarins and Allesverloren. (Recent, and indeed older, wines from Meerendaal and Uitkyk – the two other would-be serious Shiraz producers in the stable – have been disappointing, lacking in definition and substance – at best, mediocre.)

Middelvlei, an attractive farm set in a bowl almost opposite the Bergkelder Stellenbosch Cellars, is run by Jan Momberg and his sons Ben and Tinnie, both of whom have recently spent time in Californian wineries. Thirteen hectares of dry-farmed, trellissed Shiraz on deepish, Hutton soils, produce some 60,000 bottles – the best lots being selected after six months in second and third fill Nevers casks for the Middelvlei label.

Maturation and bottling are carried out by Bergkelder, which recently reduced the total time in wood from 24 to around 18–21 months, in response to customer feedback indicating excess oakiness. An over-cautious quality-control department insists on absolute stability – colour, protein and tartrate – so the wines are always cold-stabilized, albumin-fined and tightly filtered. Commercial exigencies notwithstanding, this policy should be relaxed – if the intention is to compete with premium products in the international market.

These treatments, together with yields of around 11 tons per hectare, result in wines which, whilst they often show elegance and ripe, accessible fruit, lack grip, complexity and concentration; more

in the old style than anything definably new. Fortunately, this estate has the potential for high quality and there are distinct signs of willingness to change. What is needed are lower yields, longer than the present five days on skins, and a careful touch of new wood.

Understandably, when you have been isolated from the international marketplace and developed a style which sells well enough, there is no incentive to change. However, Tinnie tastes widely, both among his immediate competitors and around the world (there is a splendid, well-stocked cellar underneath his house), and undoubtedly realizes that simple, accessible, fruity wines are not the route to quality.

Middelvlei's first Shiraz release was 1988, with Tinnie's debut in 1992. His new tasting and sales outlet is bringing welcome contact with his customers – so there is scope for some local market research, should he be in any doubt of the way forward. The signs are encouraging.

L'Ormarins, which is situated in the Franschhoek ("French Corner") area, south of Paarl, is an altogether grander establishment. It is owned by Anthonij Rupert, son of the Bergkelder's founder and brother of Hanneli Neethling, the owner of nearby La Motte. From 4.52ha of oldish Shiraz, winemaker Nico Vermeulen produces, matures and bottles a consistently fine Shiraz – a satisfying wine, supple enough to drink young but with a firm, finely-tuned structure fit for a decade of graceful ageing.

Allesverloren is different again. It lies a few kilometres from Malmesbury in the

parched, dry Swartland region, an hour and a half's drive north-west of Stellenbosch, rather less from Paarl.

It exemplifies in full measure old-fashioned Cape Shiraz – something which its owner-winemakers Danie and Fanie Malan are unlikely to change, since the formula works and keeps them well.

Keys to this rich, hot, porty style start with a harvest of over-ripe fruit – at around 13.5 Brix. This sugar-saturated fruit is de-stemmed, crushed and inoculated with a Cape yeast strain; then it is fermented in open concrete and stainless steel fermenters at the relatively low temperature of 18-20°C.

After ten days on skins, for maximum colour and tannin extraction, it is moved to the Bergkelder for maturing, where it is bottled – a process preceded, presumably, by the excoriating quality control procedures already described – some 18 months later. As with all Bergkelder's top Shiraz, the wines are not released until a further two years have elapsed – admirable, were it not for the fact that the bottle store is maintained at 10–11°C, which probably brings normal development to a grinding halt.

In its maturing and marketing of its members' wines the Bergkelder fulfills two useful functions. However, its power to reject wine offered to it gives it an undue influence on styles, making it difficult for growers to experiment and evolve from pre-established norms. As more estates opt for independence, the access it affords to the international marketplace may come to be seen as its principal advantage.

FAIRVIEW ESTATE

Not only is Charles Back a skilled and innovative winemaker, he also has a rare flair for the market and takes inordinate delight in projecting its trends and anticipating them. An inherited talent perhaps, since his father, Cyril, staged the Cape's very first wine auction in 1974 – a year before Nederburg. (Little stands still at Fairview.)

Charles is a self-confident dynamo – an entrepreneur *par excellence*. Reviewing his achievements from his no-frills office, he talks proudly of Fairview's 40% share of the Cape's luxury cheese market – Camemberts, Bries, Blues and the rest; of a remarkable wine export performance – his own arrangements were in place well before sanctions ended; and of the 1.5 million Rand it cost him to buy back 30ha of vineyards and the 1722 family homestead above the

winery: "we could put a restaurant there, with a waterfall...some wooden steps up the mountain...a top chef...wedding receptions, dinners...." The corner of his mouth curves upwards, a physiognomic mirror of some imaginary sales graph.

These are not the hair-brained schemes of someone casting round for the golden goose, but the considered

expansion of a successful business, based firmly on quality and value. Visitors flock to Fairview, with its prospects of Table Mountain and Simonsberg, to taste and buy; others come to admire the elegant, raucous peacocks which strut in front of the estate shop or to watch a few of the farm's 500 goats peering lazily out of a hole in the side of their spiral tower.

Secession from the KWV cooperative in 1978 led to an "uphill battle" until momentum returned in the late 1980s.

VARIETY	DETAILS	AREA
SHIRAZ	Mountain vineyard (100 metres altitude); 13 yrs average vine age	2.00
SHIRAZ	Sandy loam, valley floor (40 metres altitude); 16 yrs average vine age	8.75
SHIRAZ	Sandy loam, valley floor (40 metres altitude); 3 yrs average vine age	3.06
SHIRAZ	Hilltop vineyard; loam (45 metres altitude); 3 yrs average vine age	4.00
SHIRAZ	Hilltop vineyard; heavy clay soils (45 metres altitude); 13 yrs average vine age	2.25
VIOGNIER	New plantings, 2000 vines	0.40
MOURVEDRE	Planted 1995, 8000 vines	1.60
	TOTAL (hectares):	22.06

The estate now extends over 200ha, in a narrow wedge stretching 3.5kms from valley floor to the granitic foothills of Paarl Mountain. A plethora of soil-types and micro-climates provides the opportunity to try a variety of cultivars, including Pinots Noir and Gris, which the Backs don't hesitate to explore.

In the early days, Cabernet was king; now Charles is committing much to Shiraz, of which he has 20ha. Remarking on its versatility, he confesses that "If I had my life over again I would plant the whole farm with Shiraz – and use it for red (dry and sweet), white, a cracking rosé, and as a base for sparkling wine". To keep abreast of trends, he tastes widely – using the office bookshelves as a temporary repository for an eclectic range of samples sent in by his international network of scouts.

He identifies two styles of Shiraz: the Australian – overtly fruity, high alcohol, ripe tannins, high extract and well wooded; and the more elegant, less oaky "classic Rhône". "I am right in the middle – this is best for this farm". Tasting a progression of vintages shows considerable meanderings between the two extremes to arrive at the present recipe. Some vintages emphasize elegance, others exude ripe, almost berryish fruit. Standing out, a massive Guigal-like 1989 that he made after a visit to the Rhône.

In better vintages, a Reserve bottling has accompanied the standard Shiraz. Recognition that "they are virtually the same", signals an intention to stick to a single *cuvée* in future. "We've got the line and light right now, since 1990".

Underneath this casual demeanour, skill and thought are at work. Quality

The goat tower at Fairview Estate.

depends on yields of less than seven tons per hectare and picking at "exact maturity for the style" – neither under- nor over-ripe to avoid having to acidify. In case nature fails and shrivelled berries appear, the exit-route is a delicious, and popular, fortified Sweet Red – "maximum three bottles per person".

Fermentation proceeds with 20% whole clusters, and using different strains of yeast – Rhône, Beaujolais and Champagne – for different vats; pumping over at high velocity onto solids drained

of juice maximizes extraction in the 6–8 days of vatting before transfer to fourth-year casks, where the remaining 40–50 grammes per litre of sugar remaining in juice trapped in the bottom of each vat, are converted to alcohol.

Although American wood is under consideration, at present only tight-grained French oak is used: "US white oak is fine for making competition wines – it's hard to beat it in blind tastings", Charles explains, adding: "tasting Australian Shiraz is fine; to finish the bottle at dinner – that's another matter!"

A weak Rand makes French oak expensive, so a pecking order has been established to use new casks to best advantage: Chardonnay breaks them in, then Sauvignon Blanc, thereafter Sémillon the following year. Only then the reds – Cabernet first ("it needs more wood", Charles explains), then finally Shiraz.

The idea is to soften tannins, help clarification and stabilization, and to speed up maturation. The casks remain in a cold store, without racking, for 12–14 months before bottling – preceded by both sheet and membrane filtrations.

The Fairview Shiraz, as presently vinified, is excellent – among the best value to be had in the Cape; it shares the Fairview stable with a gorgeously gulpable, uncomplicated Shiraz:Gamay (80:20) and a deep-coloured, soft, peppery Shiraz:Merlot (65:35).

Two thousand Viognier vines have recently appeared near the top of Fairview's 1.5-million Rand vineyard, along with 8,000 Mourvèdre "for fun – I thought I'd have a bash".

With this engaging *vigneron*, one can be sure that the proposed "bash" will be both instructive and productive.

HARTENBERG ESTATE

Hartenberg, in the lovely Devon Valley between Paarl and Stellenbosch, traces its history back to an original land grant of 1692. However, as the present owners readily admit, its production remained "modestly undistinguished" until 1949 when a new owner, local pathologist Dr Maurice Finlayson, undertook extensive replanting. Improvements were continued by Gilbeys, under whose ownership from 1970–1986 Hartenberg came into the top league.

In 1986 Gilbeys sold out to Natal businessman Ken Mackenzie, whose daughter Tania and tall, goatee-bearded son-in-law James Browne now run the estate. In 1993 Anton Beukes, a qualified winemaker as well as a viticulturalist,

took charge of the vineyards and Carl Schulz (ex-Simonsig Estate, qv) became Hartenberg's winemaker.

There are currently 110ha under vine – 17.4 of which are Shiraz. James and Carl want to develop the variety and would like to add a small batch of Premium Shiraz to the current standard release. Carl returned from a month's study trip to the Rhône and Burgundy with a string of small, but important, measures to refine quality. Until 1986, the wine was matured solely in large oak vats; now, with styles veering towards less alcohol, more fruit and greater finesse, more small oak is used. For more than a decade Carl's predecessor, Danie Treuter, made Shiraz in the old, porty style, with alcohol levels

of 13% or more. Today this is nearer to 12–12.5% alcohol.

The vineyards are ideally suited to such a change, facing mainly east-west in a north-south oriented valley. An average rainfall of 700mm – enough for dry-farming – combines with a cool early-morning mist that develops from the wetland running down the valley floor, to lengthen and even out ripening. Soils, as Anton Beukes will readily truck you across the vineyards to demonstrate, vary from sandy, greyish, decomposed granites (Clovelly) to duplex gravel on clay – altogether yellower and less vigorous, and ideal for naturally proliferous Shiraz.

Vineyard improvements have been matched by expenditure in the cellars. A magnificent underground brick labyrinth capable of accomodating 900 225-litre casks, eight 5,000-litre vats and 200,000 bottles was constructed in 1990 and new crushers were installed in 1994.

As befits "the Home of Unhurried Wines", release of top reds is delayed until four years after the vintage. Until recently, deliberately low-key marketing kept sales at home – Durban and Johannesburg in particular. Now, with volume rising, James is eyeing export opportunities – while Carl is reflecting on the possibility of a few rows of Viognier. This is a motivated, conscientious, quality-conscious young team. The future looks promising.

VARIETY	VINEYARD	DETAILS	AREA
SHIRAZ	BLOCK 33	East-facing; 5 yrs	0.85
SHIRAZ	BLOCK 20A	East-facing; 20 yrs	0.50
SHIRAZ	BLOCK 26	West-facing; 20 yrs	4.00
SHIRAZ	BLOCK 27	West-facing; 20 yrs	1.75
SHIRAZ	BLOCK 28	East-facing; 21 yrs	1.20
SHIRAZ	BLOCK 21	East-facing; 17 yrs	2.10
SHIRAZ	BLOCK 22	East-facing; 17 yrs	1.70
SHIRAZ	BLOCKS 22,23 & 24	East-facing; planted 1995	5.30
		TOTAL (hectares):	17.40

KLEIN CONSTANTIA ESTATE

A 146-ha offshoot of Groot Constantia, South Africa's most historic estate, Klein Constantia came into being in 1823. It rather went out of it again, falling into lamentable decay before it was at last purchased by accountant Duggie Jooste in 1980.

In his care, considerable expense and thought have been devoted to its restoration. Ernst Le Roux of Nedeburg was brought in to oversee the work which included clearing hectares of wood and scrub, and extensive soil-analysis to match *terroir* to vine. A magnificent new cellar and reception complex was built, next to the estate's fine Cape Dutch mansion – now the home of Duggie's son Lowell, who shares responsbility for the estate with his father.

In 1985 Ross Gower, an ex-Nedeburg (Gunter Brozel) trainee, and winemaker at Corbyn's in New Zealand from 1980–1984, was put in charge of the cellar. Since his first vintage in 1986, the estate has gained in confidence and prestige – winning accolades for its Sauvignon Blanc, Chardonnay, Cabernet Sauvignon and "Marlbrook" (Cabernets Sauvignon and Franc blend). There is also a Shiraz (just) from 1.28ha of vines planted in 1982 at 100 metres altitude, 2.89ha having been grafted over to Sauvignon Blanc after the 1994 vintage to meet increased demand. With so little Syrah in South Africa, this seems like short-sighted folly.

Klein Constantia's situation is magnificent – a wide, green swathe of vines sloping away beneath the Constantiaberg, under the lea of Table Mountain with False Bay to the east. The soils are relatively uniform Huttons – lime-adjusted decomposed granite – on which the Shiraz vines are dry-farmed. Rainfall (mostly in winter) averages 1,600mm – nearly twice that of Stellenbosch; with a strong summer wind off the Cape flats bringing additional

Klein Constantia – with the backdrop of Table Mountain.

humidity. At maximum strength it is known locally as the "black south-easter". In springtime, the localized rain-bearing north-westerly holds sway – often of sufficient ferocity to rip the vines apart. Hardly the gentle, warm, climate of the holiday brochures.

Talented as Ross Gower clearly is, as far as Shiraz goes there has been much tinkering with style. This has see-sawed between the heavier (1986, 1987 and 1991) and the lighter (1988, 1989 and 1990) with a few (1992, 1993 and 1994) somewhere in between. The Cinderella effect has also been operating here – 500-litre second-fill casks and short, rapid,

roto-tank vinifications; in Ross' view, Shiraz will always play second fiddle to Cabernet Sauvignon.

While results may vary, the potential is undoubtedly there – if an excellent 1991 is anything to judge by. Five new US oak casks appeared in 1994, so things are looking up for Klein Constantia's beleaguered Shiraz. It would be encouraging to see longer *cuvaisons* in open fermenters, a higher proportion of smaller, newer wood, and the abandoning of filtration and cold stabilization. In the meantime, some enthusiasts should get up a petition to stop them grafting over the 4,644 Shiraz vines which remain!

VARIETY	VINEYARD	DETAILS	AREA
SHIRAZ	KLEIN CONSTANTIA	Hutton soils; planted 1983	1.28

LA MOTTE

Set beneath the towering Wemmershoek range, La Motte reeks of liberal investment and exudes elegance. Its long tasting room, hung with fine tapestries and stylishly furnished, is one of the most beautiful in the Cape. Until it was bought by the Rupert family in 1970 the estate farmed grapes, supplying fruit – as it still does at the rate of 200 tons per year – to a cooperative. In 1984 a winery was added and Jacques Borman brought in from Simonsig as winemaker. Under his control, encouraged by Rupert's opera-singer daughter, Hanneli, and her equally musical husband Paul Neethling, quality has been driven to impressive heights.

Of 99ha under vine, 31 are planted to Shiraz, in four separate blocks. Although because of its relatively cool micro-climate Franschhoek is known for is whites, soil and weather suggested that reds might also do well: especially at an altitude where harvesting is a full two weeks after Paarl and Stellenbosch. Now the two mountain blocks – 4.5ha at around 322 metres on Hutton-type clays admixed with mountain rock – provide fruit for La Motte's Shiraz. A long ripening season contributes to the finesse which characterizes this wine.

Jacques is a thoughtful winemaker who tastes as widely as possible outside the Cape. Undisguised admiration for Marcel Guigal's Côte-Rôties and Jaboulet's La Chapelle is tempered by a determination not to destroy elegance and fruit with new wood – 50% has become 15%: "that's the style I fell in love with and will stick to".

Of the five commercial Shiraz clones, he eschews those giving mint-eucalyptus tones, preferring Allesverloren and Meerendal, particularly, for their spicy-leatheriness, which he considers closer in style to northern Rhône. Shiraz's natural sensitivity to overcropping – above a certain level, quality plummets – leads to thinning from 6–8 tons/acre to 5–6.

Not entirely conventional vinifications here: the press-wine is excluded from the blend. ("We macerate for two and a half to three weeks, so there isn't much left to press"). And Jacques is courageous in increasing the use of natural yeasts and deliberately including some "dirty" lees in cask for a couple of months or so, "to add extra flavour". Part of the crop is vinified in roto-tanks and the whole encouraged to reach its peak temperature of 35°C as soon as possible to maximize extraction. The wines, however, don't show massive extraction of either pigments or structure – rather bright, mid to deep garnet, with enough (but never an excess) of round tannins. The wine is never acidified – "not a drop" – an example which others who worry unduly about analytically low acids would do well to emulate.

Since Jacques' first La Motte Shiraz in 1985, his style has gained in confidence and the wine in depth, without sacrificing elegance. The search for aromatic complexity and overall finesse continues with an ever surer tread.

VARIETY	VINEYARD	DETAILS	AREA
SHIRAZ	BLOCK 1	Mountain block; Hutton soils, 322 metres altitude; 22 yrs average age	3.73
SHIRAZ	BLOCK 2	Mountain block; Hutton soils, 322 metres altitude; 22 yrs average age	1.45
SHIRAZ	BLOCK 27	River bed; dark, alluvial, well-drained gravels; average age 24 yrs	3.30
SHIRAZ	BLOCK 28	River bed; dark alluvial well-drained gravels; average age 24 yrs	2.30
SHIRAZ		Planted 1995	4.00
		TOTAL (hectares):	11.05

Trudging home in the Franschhoek Valley.

LIEVLAND ESTATE

Administratively in Paarl, in fact nearer to Stellenbosch, Lievland occupies the large part of an elongated bowl at the foot of the Simonsberg range. Here, protected by these mountains from damaging south-east winds and by the Klapmut hills from the north-westerlies, 5.5ha of mainly dry-farmed Shiraz (out of 65ha in total) ripen slowly.

The estate's modern history dates from 1933, when it was acquired by a Latvian nobleman – Baron von Stiernhielm. Unfortunately this worthy died before leaving Latvia – of blood poisoning after being struck on the nose by a wild animal.

The Baron's wife took over and, after only one further change of ownership, Lievland came into the hands of the father of the present owner, Paul Benate, in 1973. The building of a cellar in 1981 led to estate-bottling – then, in 1987, Abraham Beukes arrived as winemaker.

Paul and Abe have a passion for Shiraz – it formed the subject of Paul's 1992 Cape Wine Master's thesis – and are eloquent in its defence as a quality variety. Naturally low yields and relatively early picking help greater concentration without risking the old-fashioned, over-ripe alcoholic portiness that characterized most Cape Shiraz of the 1970s.

A Lievland Shiraz tends to softish tannins, from up to two weeks on skins after fermentation and 12-18 months in a mixture of Nevers and US wood (75:25%). Up to 1987 acidification was normal practice – especially in very ripe years when sugar levels rose sharply at the expense of acidity; this gave the wines an irremediably hard, dry nerve which destroyed their equilibrium. Now, low

acidities are of less concern – as in the Rhône, the feeling (and the experience) is that tannins and alcohol provide ample compensation for even a major analytical acid deficiency.

The final *assemblage* represents a cask selection – anything substandard goes into the catch-all Lievlander blend. Low sulphur usage, to avoid losing colour and flavour, can bring with it high volatility – so care is taken to cut out unnecessary aeration. Thus the malolactic occurs in bulk, before a first sulphur addition, and there is no racking during maturation. New wood ranges from 20–35%, both to give the fruit a chance and also to avoid the sweet, tarry flavours from American oak – even with casks made by expert French coopers.

Although Paul's stated goal is the peppery, violet elegance of Côte-Rôtie, the Lievland *terroir*, dominated by weathered granite, imparts a hallmark note of piney resin which particularly shows on earlier vintages. Abe's hand seems to have tamed this, and since 1988 the wine has shown a noticeably better balance between finesse and structure.

Paul Benate's bonhomie conceals a thinly-disguised exasperation with the South African Wine and Spirit Board – the powers who attempt to regulate the Cape's wine industry. His diatribe against

them strongly echoes the sentiments of French growers who pillory "*les officiels*" – bureaucrats who are neither competent tasters nor winemakers, and only understand the rules they are there to enforce. In Paul's view, the entire machinery is driven by bulk producers who understand little of international wine standards and are unreceptive to innovation – making progress slow.

He cites one of his own wines, highly rated by the Cape Independent Winemakers Guild, which failed the Board's Certification test – a late-harvest wine which didn't apparently conform to their blinkered norms. "The Board only recognizes the old style of South Africa; tasting panels are appointed, not selected; they are only there because of the jobs they do – they could even be accountants". Perish the thought!

His frustration is perhaps tempered by the knowledge that his concerns are common wherever fine wine is made. Regulators rarely command the respect among professionals they consider their high office merits. Despite Paul's ire, Lievland's Shiraz is in the Cape's top flight; not far from the "all pleasure and fun" this charismatic duo regard as their goal.

VARIETY	VINEYARD	DETAILS	AREA
SHIRAZ	BLOCK 8	Grafted vines – virussed (leaf-roll); 18 yrs average age	1.06
SHIRAZ	BLOCK 9	Grafted vines – virussed (leaf-roll); 18 yrs average age	1.55
SHIRAZ	BLOCK 18	Grafted vines – virussed (leaf-roll); 18 yrs average age	0.37
SHIRAZ	BLOCK 25	Grafted virus-free vines; clones 1A + 21A; average age 4 yrs	2.54
		TOTAL (hectares):	5.52

NEDERBURG

Although part of the giant Stellenbosch Farmers' Winery, Nederburg is an independent operation producing some eight million bottles a year.

Behind the magnificent 1800 Dutch-Colonial manor house that shelters beneath the imposing Drakensburg range on the outskirts of Paarl, a modern cellar handles a bewildering array of some 50 different bottlings. These range from rosé to sparkling, and include some of the Cape's finest Riesling and late-harvest wines, given international recognition by Gunther Brozel, Nederburg's cellarmaster for 33 years until his retirement in 1989. As both grapes and wine are purchased,

in addition to the fruit from its own four farms, it fulfils more of the role of a *négociant* than that of a true estate.

Since 1974, Nederburg's overall direction has been in the hands of Ernst Le Roux, a reserved, dedicated man, qualified both as viticulturalist and oenologist. In 1989, the winemaking mantle passed to South African- and German-trained Newald Marais.

Newald seems undaunted by his responsibilities, and the need to be as skilled with late harvested grapes as with the great reds – combined talents one seldom finds in the noble appellations of France, where you either excel with reds or with whites, not both. A relaxed temperament underpins a passion for his work and an articulate grasp of its detail.

He clearly has a feeling for Shiraz, which accounts for 40.7 of his 650ha. Sadly, this "very exciting variety" has suffered from a press which invariably describes it as "stinky" – hardly a marketing plus. Although plantings in the Cape have declined over the years, it is now showing signs of a strong revival in popularity and esteem.

Nederburg's own Shiraz is never offered through the normal distribution channels, appearing only at the annual April Nedeburg Auction as a limited release of a mature vintage. The Reserve Shiraz is a principally a selection of low-yielding, mainly higher (and thus cooler) south- and southwest-facing vineyard blocks, which are specially monitored throughout the growing season.

The grapes for both wines come principally from one of Nedeburg's four farms – Groenhof, near Stellenbosch. Here, in the cooler foothills of the Simonsberg Mountains, overlooking Table Mountain, a mix of clones from Nederberg's own nursery, Ernita, are planted on a variety of soils – principally yellow Clovelly sandy clays and redder, more homogeneous Huttons. These, as elsewhere in the Cape, are granitic in origin and highly acidic, with a significant aluminium content which vine-roots dislike; so massive additions of lime are used to raise the pH before planting.

Unusually, the rows are oriented east-west, rather than the conventional north-south. This shades the bunches from direct sunlight and helps drying-out after rain, since the prevailing wind runs along, rather than across, the rows. Picking around 12.5–13.0 potential alcohol (rather than the formerly fashionable overripe 13- plus, when winemakers believed that high alcohol and tannins were essential for longevity) is designed to ensure a sensible flavour balance.

Newald Marais' principal change from Gunther Brozel's vinification has been to lengthen post-fermentive maceration from 1–2 days to 3–10, to extract soft tannins and preserve as much of the fruit as possible. Most of the wine is matured in 3–6,000 litre German oak vats – not, as is more usual for Shiraz, in 225-litre casks. However, since 1992 an increasing proportion is finding its way into small wood: "we don't at this stage want to change the style dramatically – it sells well", is how Ernst Le Roux argues the case, hinting perhaps at a future change. Newald confesses that he would like to use only small wood for the Auction Reserve Shiraz, with 50% new, and to put

the wine into oak during its vintage year; at present it spends up to a year in stainless steel before seeing any wood, large or small. The pressings – 20–30 litres from 780 litres per ton of free-run – are not incorporated.

A long maturation – the 1991 was still in tank in November 1994 – results in soft, supple, wines of lightish hue, soundly (but not massively) structured, with good fruit and some complexity. Wines appear at auction at around 7-8 years after their vintage – ready to drink.

For reasons which are not entirely clear, Nedeburg won't tolerate the smallest particle of sediment in any of its wines, so the Shiraz is generally bentonite-fined, cold-stabilized and tightly filtered – wholly cosmetic operations (except perhaps for the fining when protein instability is indicated) which merely remove substance, flavour and aroma.

Less interference and a higher proportion of small wood maturation would undoubtedly give the wines more depth and interest. Newald Marais is determined to change things – why take trouble to make a rich, interesting wine, to see it eviscerated in the name of quality control? This is especially nonsensical for a wine which will only be sold at auction to bidders who are presumably aware that red wine sediments as it matures. Nedeburg Shiraz is presently "good plus"; there is no reason why it should not be top class.

VARIETY	VINEYARD	DETAILS	AREA
SHIRAZ	WOLWEDANS (grower)	Hutton soils; old clone, dry-farmed; planted 1977	3.50
SHIRAZ	CVH (grower)	Hutton / Clovelly; old clone, supplementary irrigation; planted 1978	2.50
SHIRAZ	PARKER TRUST	Hutton soils; old clone, dry-farmed; planted 1985	1.00
SHIRAZ	PARKER TRUST	Hutton soils; old clone; dry-farmed; planted 1974/5/6	6.50
SHIRAZ	PARKER TRUST	Hutton soils; new clone; dry-farmed; planted 1992	2.50
SHIRAZ	GROENHOF (Nederburg)	Hutton soils; old clone; supplementary irrigation; planted 1976	8.50
SHIRAZ	GROENHOF (Nederburg)	Hutton soils; new clone; dry-farmed; planted 1993	4.50
SHIRAZ	LANQUEDOC (Nederburg)	Hutton soils; old clone; irrigated; planted 1975	5.00
SHIRAZ	LANQUEDOC (Nederburg)	Hutton soils; new clone; irrigated; planted 1987	0.50
SHIRAZ	PLAISIR DE MERLE (Nederburg)	Hutton soils; new clone; dry farmed; planted 1993	2.50
SHIRAZ	PLAISIR DE MERLE (Nederburg)	Hutton soils; old clone; dry-farmed; planted 1975	3.20
SHIRAZ	ERNITA (Nederburg)	Hutton soils; new clone; drip irrigated; planted 1991/2	0.50
		TOTAL (hectares):	40.70

NEETHLINGSHOF & STELLENZICHT ESTATES

These two substantial Stellenbosch estates, each with some 160ha under vine, are owned by Singapore-based German banker, Hans-Joachim Schreiber. Since acquiring Stellenzicht in 1981 and Neethlingshof in 1985, he has invested heavily in improvements at both.

Neethlingshof, approached by a spectacular tree-lined drive, is a particularly lovely estate, welcoming visitors who come to buy wine or to try its excellent restaurant. Although sharing common management and marketing, each estate has its own winemaker and is, in theory at least, autonomous.

The younger of the two winemakers is André van Rensburg, in charge at

Stellenzicht. Extrovert and ready to chat about his philosophy, he admits to a passion for Shiraz: "you either love it or loathe it; if you dislike it, leave it alone". His opposite number at Neethlingshof, Schalk van der Westhuizen, is a large, tall man, more reserved and reflective in manner, but no less perceptive. Stellenzicht released the first Shiraz in 1989, followed by Neethlingshof in 1991.

Both wines have broadly similar vinification. The main difference is that Schalk uses roto-tanks in addition to standard closed fermenters; otherwise, the regime is 7–10 days of vatting, peaking at 25–30°C, followed by 8–12 months' maturation in small wood of

which 30% is new American oak, the remainder older French. The wines pass a further two years in large casks "to make them more accessible" and are blended with up to 15% of Malbec to give more obvious fruit character.

That the two wines differ at all is mainly attributable to differences in soil, vines and micro-climate. Though, as the crow flies, the estates are a mere 6kms apart, Neethlingshof, on west-facing, warm slopes, harvests its youngish vines earlier than Stellenzicht, whose cool, higher vineyards ripen later. The latter's soils are predominantly rocky Clovelly shales which, together with slightly older vines, give tougher, more concentrated wines than lower-lying Neethlingshof. There, earlier ripening, combined with mainly Hutton clay soils, produces a somewhat lighter style of Shiraz.

However, it is clear that styles at both properties are still evolving. André, in particular, feels torn between his desire to make the finest possible Shiraz – which means a dense, high tannin *vin de garde*-and the need to satisfy a market thirsty for youthful suppleness and plenty of open, ripe Australian-style fruit.

The obvious way to square this uncomfortable circle is to develop a premium product alongside a more immediately user-friendly standard bottling. The raw material is there, both

VARIETY	VINEYARD	DETAILS	AREA
SHIRAZ	STELLENZICHT	Allesverloren clone; yields 3.5–4 t/ha.	
	(Grower: Tony Orr)	21 yrs average vine-age	5.00
SHIRAZ	STELLENZICHT	New clone; 6 yrs average vine-age	3.00
SHIRAZ	STELLENZICHT	New clone; 4 yrs average vine-age	2.75
		STELLENZICHT SUB-TOTAL:	10.75
SHIRAZ	NEETHLINGSHOF	Original clone; 8 yrs average vine-age	7.30
		TOTAL (hectares):	18.05

in terms of quality and quantity, to do so.

Here are two fine estates, two committed and skilled winemakers with excellent resources at their fingertips. Stellenzicht, with its well-prepared soils and new clonal material, is particularly well-placed. First releases from both the estates are promising, though there is clearly some fine-tuning to be done. Two potential top-class players...? We'll see!

RUST-EN-VREDE

With 30ha of vines, Rust-en Vrede ("Rest and Peace") is one of the Cape's smaller properties – dwarfed on one flank by Stellenzicht's 160ha and on the other by Alto's 100ha. The consistently high quality of its five wines – all red – make it unquestionably one of the region's finest estates.

Its short recent history devolves round ex-Springbok rugby-player, now team manager, Jannie Englebrecht. With his wife Ellen, he bought the untended and unwanted property in 1978, against strong advice that it was unlikely to produce top-quality wine. Under their care, it has been sympathetically restored and revitalized.

It is a beautiful estate, at the head of a valley in the Helderberg foothills. A cluster of traditional Cape Dutch buildings in, atypically, a straight line, comprise a small manor house, a dower house and a "historical cellar". To these, in 1984, were added a low-built tasting room, wine-library and underground bottle cellar. An oasis of calm, surrounded by trees and rose gardens.

Englebrecht's first, and fundamental, decision was that Rust-en-Vrede was to become a red-wine estate. Chenin Blanc was ripped out to concentrate on Cabernets Sauvignon and Franc, Shiraz, Merlot and Portuguese Tinta Barocca.

A second – and equally important – move was made in 1987, when Kevin Arnold was appointed winemaker. Under his stewardship, the Rust-en-Vrede wines have received national and international recognition. Jean Englebrecht, Jannie's son, has recently joined the team and looks after the vineyards.

Kevin Arnold.

Rust-en-Vrede's flagship, which culls the cream of the crop, is a non-varietal blend – dominated by Cabernet Sauvignon (60–75%) with Shiraz and/or Merlot accounting for the balance (around 40% Shiraz in the 1986, none in the 1989). The remaining wines reflect the four planted varieties – the Cabernet Franc having been replaced by Kevin with more Shiraz, a variety with which he has a clear affinity. A further wine is specially blended for the Cape Independent Winemakers' Guild September auction; the mix varies from 50:50 Cabernet:Shiraz (1989) or 50:50 Shiraz:Merlot (1990).

The vineyards face north and have a warm micro-climate, but enjoy none of the sea-breezes which regularly aerate neighbouring vines 50 vertical metres above. Kevin considers this added stress intensifies flavours and aromas, by forcing the vines to extract more from the soil into the fruit. He therefore harvests by grape taste rather than by analytical criteria, convinced that Cape winemakers have worried too much about acidity at the expense of flavour, acidifying the wines "to make the analysis look good".

In his view, a sound natural balance in this hot climate is best achieved by blending different varieties, picking some

VARIETY	VINEYARD	DETAILS	AREA
SHIRAZ	RUST-EN-VREDE 1	Original planting 1982, grafted on R99 rootstock	4.00
SHIRAZ	RUST-EN-VREDE 2	Original planting 1983, grafted on R99 rootstock	1.00
SHIRAZ	RUST-EN-VREDE 3	Planted 1989, new clone SH1 on 101–14 rootstock	2.00
		TOTAL (hectares):	7.00

slightly under-ripe to avoid artificial adjustments. "We pick on the flavour of the fruit, we don't measure". This explains why the blend is regarded as superior to the individual varietal wines, and is the basis for the long-term plan to turn Rust-en-Vrede into a "one-label winery" – as is essentially the case with most Bordeaux châteaux. This perhaps spells the demise of an excellent Shiraz – despite Kevin's conviction that this hot micro-climate favours it.

Kevin Arnold is in that class of sensitive, articulate winemakers who

mind about detail, especially where fruit quality is involved. Canopy management is helping to intensify skin colour, and efforts are being made to increase yields from less than 5 tons/ha to around 7. In the cellar, with only 3–4 days' vatting, punching down the solids is preferred to pumping over, to extract as much as possible from the grape-skins. The press-wine is added back before the wine is transferred to Bordeaux barrels for 14-15 months' maturation.

For his first vintage (1979) Jannie Englebrecht used small wood for his

wines, much of it new – both revolutionary practices then. Now, the mix is 50–60% of new wood with around 85% of Nevers oak and the rest American, but French-coopered.

Against the current trend, the Shiraz is twice egg-white fined and always semi-sterile filtered before bottling.

The quality of this estate is indisputable. It would be a pity to see a fine Shiraz disappear from the Cape's roster – there are few enough as it is – but this might (just) be a justifiable sacrifice to improve an already top-notch blend.

SAXENBURG ESTATE

The Saxenburg phenomenon is extraordinary. In 1989 it was producing unexciting *ordinaires*; two years later its 1991 Cabernet had taken the trophy for the country's most promising young wine; three years on the 1991 Shiraz beat Henschke's Hill of Grace into first place in a Sydney blind tasting. In between had come the revolution: Adrian Buhrer, a red-wine-loving Swiss wine merchant had bought the property and, at the end of 1990, Nico van der Merwe had arrived as winemaker from spells at Neethlingshof and Montpellier.

Nico is a solid, rather weather-beaten individual, who clearly likes to be in charge not just in the cellar but in the vineyard as well. A mobile phone strapped across his ample frame imparts a touch of the wild west and suggests a peripatetic, outdoor existence. "I am a winegrower, not a winemaker", is his refrain.

For him, second-best simply won't do: "I want to do something I can be proud of", he explains. To begin with, he had to adapt his winemaking to a basic cellar; now the financial wheels are turning at an acceptable rate, modest improvements are in prospect – in particular, a new cask room so that hundreds of barrels don't need moving from maturation cellar to bottling hall.

As yet Saxenburg has only young Shiraz vines, so the first releases were made from purchased grapes. Nico is uncharacteristically coy about admitting this, in case anyone might conclude that he regarded his Shiraz as in some sense secondary to the wines from estate fruit. A few minutes' conversation – and a single sniff – should convince any doubter both of Nico's passion for the variety and his skill in handling it.

Nico van der Merwe.

A young Saxenburg Shiraz is a massive, dense, tannic, concentrated giant of a wine, with underlying finesse. Two Stellenbosch vineyards, covering 4.5ha, contribute to the blend, each giving a completely different style of fruit. "Trellis" – 3.5ha of low-vigour, dry-farmed vines on a south-facing, decomposed-granite slope – imparts Rhônish pepperiness and backbone, while its counterpart, "Gobelet" – one hectare of slightly older vines on gravelly soils – tends to produce higher sugars and a smoky, fat, low acid, porty style of wine. Trellis is harvested "fresh", around mid-March, a week or so later than Gobelet which is picked when the berries start to shrivel.

These components are vinified and matured apart, without racking, until 12–15 months have passed on a quarter-

bung, in small wood – mostly old Shiraz casks. "I am curious to see how these two wines develop", Nico confesses.

The success of Australian Shiraz on world markets is clearly an inspiration for this deliberately "fat" style of wine, and the use of some 20% of new US/white oak is probably more than coincidental. However, size is tempered with finesse: "Shiraz is very feminine, it needs moderate, not high, alcohol". The synthesis of these two strikingly different, complementary ingredients works superbly.

The final blend is selected from a trio of pre-*assemblages*: a mix of the best barrels from both vineyards; one a blend of "trellis" casks, the other of "*gobelet*". This leisurely process takes a week or so, during which time Nico prefers to taste in the evening, using his German wife Petra as a touchstone: "ladies can spot a problem".

Nominally, Saxenburg releases a standard Shiraz and a Reserve quality "Private Collection". However, the first has yet to make an appearance, since 1991, 1992 and 1993 all appeared as the Reserve. Only 500–1,800 cases are made.

These wines are remarkable – the more so when one stops to consider that their full retail price is some two-fifths that of any respectable Côte-Rôtie. A demonstration, if ever one were needed, that quality and cirrhosis of the wallet are not inseparable bedfellows.

The wine world is destined to hear more of Saxenburg and its ebullient winegrower.

VARIETY	VINEYARD	DETAILS	AREA
SHIRAZ	"GOBELET" VINEYARD	Planted c 1979; Stellenbosch area	1.00
SHIRAZ	"TRELLIS" VINEYARD	Planted c 1985; Stellenbosch area	3.50
		TOTAL (hectares):	4.50

SIMONSIG ESTATE

Like many Cape estates, Simonsig began with an early land grant (1682), part of which forms the present property. During the Anglo-Boer war, it was used as a horse-breeding farm by the British Cavalry, eventually becoming a wine estate in 1942. Today it is owned by Frans Malan, a gritty, determined character by all accounts, whose sons – François (vineyards), Johan (winemaking) and Pieter (marketing) – have been at the helm since the early 1980s.

With 275ha under vine – plus substantial production of plums, pears and peaches – and 170 employees to house and care for, Simonsig is a large operation. Its heart is an attractive set of buildings, between Stellenbosch and Paarl, in what is known as the Muldersvlei bowl – a coolish area beneath the Simonsberg range that is particularly well suited to Cabernet and Shiraz.

Since Simonsig's first estate bottling in 1968, the range has expanded from three to 25 labels. Its top quality lies in its reds: Pinotage (jockeying Kanonkop for pole-position), Tiara (a Bordeaux blend), Shiraz and Cabernet Sauvignon – although these constitute only 40% of production – and an excellent *méthode champenoise* which it pioneered in the Cape in 1971.

Shiraz covers 16.2ha, split between two farms – 11ha of older vines on flattish, shallow land, the rest more recent plantings on heavier, high-clay soils. Most of the old vines are virused, which naturally limits crop levels, giving typical yields of 5–6.5 tons/ha (40–50 hl/ha). The introduction of fruit from the newer, virus-free clones will undoubtedly increase yields and, Johan believes, add a berryish element to the wine.

Johan Malan's long-term aim is to concentrate on half a dozen premium varieties. For Shiraz, a recent visit to the Rhône Valley sparked a strong preference for what he describes as the "florality" of Côte-Rôtie rather than the denser style of Hermitage. Since 1984, vinifications have lengthened, four roto-tanks have been installed to complement the standard open and vertical fermenters, the fermentation temperatures have increased from 24°C to a peak of 31°C and yields are reduced. Wood maturation has evolved from all large wood to half in small wood and half in large oak for a year, then small wood thereafter – a total maturation of 20–24 months.

The Simonsig style emphasizes elegance and softness – a longish, even vinification designed to extract glycerol and fine tannins and also to "limit the influence of the vintage". Less press-wine is incorporated now – just the wine which runs freely as the press is being filled: "if you press, it's not a nice type of tannin", Johan explains.

However, his Rhône experience has put his ideas back into the melting-pot, in particular the belief that elegance and extract are somehow incompatible: "if you see the concentration that Marcel Guigal gets into his special *cuvées*, you wouldn't believe it!" The result is cautious experimentation with new US oak, which Johan considers has a particular affinity with this grape. Thus far Simonsig Shiraz has officially seen no new wood, but things may change.

Optimum vatting time is also under review. The notion that eight days is enough to extract colour and flavour without any harsh, dry tannins – and the recognition that extended maceration by itself, without complementary wood maturation, does not produce great wine ("this is not well understood in South Africa") – has been brought into question by tasting Guigal's massive, single-vineyard Côte-Rôties, which spend several weeks on skins and three years in new wood, and seem effortlessly to combine size and finesse. More change on the way, one suspects.

Experiments apart, Simonsig Shiraz is one of the Cape's most successful wines – regularly lauded by wine clubs and chosen by South African Airways' exigent tasting panel for their first-class cabins. As currently constituted, they are not designed for long keeping, but make delicious drinking over three to eight years or so – rich, supple flavours and plenty of ripe fruit, all underpinned with enough (but not excessive) tannins to keep them going. Satisfying stuff, indeed!

VARIETY	VINEYARD	DETAILS	AREA
SHIRAZ	HOME FARM	20 yrs average vine age	11.00
SHIRAZ		Planted 1993	5.00
SHIRAZ		Planted 1994	1.20
		TOTAL (hectares):	16.20

ZANDVLIET ESTATE

An outpost of serious Shiraz lies some two hours north-east of Stellenbosch, surrounded by the cereal and livestock of the Swartland. Zandvliet made an early name with a relatively light style of wine, but things are now changing, and there is good reason to suppose that, in time, it might join the first division.

This is a substantial estate, run by Paul de Wet and his wife Kuku from their cool, elegant 1954 Cape Dutch pastiche house, filled with magnificent stinkwood and yellow-wood furniture. The farm has been in the family since 1867 – but, until 1965 when Paul's father modernized the winery and upgraded the plantings, it produced mainly base wine for brandy, sherry and fortified Muscats.

Recent years have seen some financial wobbles: diversification into dairying was not successful, and the thoroughbred horse market, upon which the Zandvliet stud's income depends, is far from stable.

Despite this, Paul seems cheerful enough – and imbued with a fierce determination to succeed. Kuku, a dark, attractive girl, certain that she will end up "on the road" selling the wine, is taking more than the usual passing interest in Zandvliet's evolution. Paul's Shiraz style has changed over the years, as the tasting notes show, with recent vintages having better depth and grip. Hitherto, the wines were marketed by the Bergkelder (qv) and "made to a recipe", which Paul clearly found frustrating. Now he and his brother Dan seem anxious to develop their own style and since 1993 have been exploring export markets through their second label, Astonvale.

The soils here are excellent – relatively rich, fertile, sandy loams next to riverbeds, and the best deep-red "Karoo" soils, highish in lime, on the lower slopes of the surrounding mountains. A low average rainfall of 230mm, most of it falling in winter, between April and

VARIETY	VINEYARD	AREA
SHIRAZ	Alluvial river-bed soils and red "Karoo" slopes; earliest grafts 1969; average vine age 20 yrs.	23.00

October, makes irrigation essential: this is supplied through a sophisticated aspersion system designed to mimic real weather patterns. Careful canopy management also helps.

During the growing season, a regular south-easterly breeze keeps evenings and nights cold, and gives a diurnal temperature difference of around 15°C – the smaller this range, the better the wine. Paul also regards late-season dew as an important quality factor: it takes out latent heat, cooling the fruit, and also concentrates the juice by evaporation.

Many of the older Shiraz vines suffer from "Shiraz sickness", a root-attacking fungus, so a replanting programme, using modern clones and rootstock, is now in place. Some of the crop – usually that on alluvial soils – is harvested early to retain acidity, while the red Karoo soils, which have greater natural acidity, are picked at around 22.5–23 Brix. Paul's laudable aim is to "avoid acidifiation at all costs". Current yields, at around 8–12 tons per hectare, are too high for top quality, but this seems likely to change.

The Zandvliet Shiraz, presently marketed by Bergkelder, represents a selection "of the best" – one particular vineyard of younger vines, on red Karoo: "these give much better quality; you can see it, just walking past: the berries are blacker".

Until 1993, all the Shiraz went into Zandvliet; now two-thirds is used for the Astonvale label. This *cuvée* is made with both punching-down and pumping over, with 12–18 months' ageing to give a relatively easy-drinking wine, which seems to suit the export market. The Zandvliet fruit, though, is only pumped over, and is given longer on skins for a richer, firmer, longer-lived wine.

Paul is hesitating between the supplications of his UK agent for a soft, fruity wine – tempting indeed for a quick boost to the cash-flow after the dairy debacle – and the longer-term aim of a top quality product, which seems to be his preferred option.

One can only comment that no estate ever made an enviable reputation from "cheap and cheerful" wine – not to mention the sinful waste of fine raw material this would be. Quality may be the longer option, but it is undoubtedly the more secure in a fickle market that is awash with sound *ordinaire*.

Current experiments with new wood and reduced filtration are perhaps clues to the final direction. Lowering yields and picking a half-degree riper would also undoubtedly add depth and complexity. Let's hope Paul doesn't lose courage and go for instant gratification!

ZONNEBLOEM

Zonnebloem is the premium brand of SFW (Stellenbosch Farmers Winery), a massive winemaking operation and a subsidiary of CWD (Cape Wines and Distillers) whose principal shareholders are the KWV, the Rembrandt Group and SA Breweries. From its vast headquarters in Stellenbosch, SFW produces a wide range of wine and spirit brands spanning all sectors of the market.

Zonnenbloem Shiraz comes from 26.2ha of Stellenbosch vines yielding six to ten tons per hectare. Many have Shiraz sickness, a fungus which attacks the vine's roots, while others are affected with leaf-roll virus, so real yields, expressed in terms of a healthy vineyard, are rather higher.

Until recently, the Zonnebloem style seemed inextricably stuck in an old-fashioned, soft, slightly over-ripe, rather neutral but perfectly acceptable mould. However, in the hands of winemaker Jan de Waal things are changing – notably, earlier picking, before the berries have started to shrivel and the use of small wood: 40% of the blend spends around 6–12 months in cask, with 30% being matured in large wood and a similar amount in stainless steel. The grapes from each source are kept separate throughout, to monitor individual performance of growers, and the final blend only composed after two years' maturation.

Older vintages of Zonnebloem Shiraz showed marked colour loss, suggesting either insufficient extraction or else an adequate extraction that did not last well. In fact, the problem was threefold: old, virused and naturally less pigmented clones; harvesting over-ripe fruit at too high a pH, which made it difficult to fix any colour which was extracted; and premature browning from an over-warm maturation store .

There have also been significant improvements in the vineyards, with more emphasis placed on careful soil preparation – deep ploughing and properly titrated doses of lime to counteract the highly acidic soils of the western Cape. Old vines are being replaced with virus-free clones, which will undoubtedly improve both quality and consistency. However, Paul Wallace, SFW's senior viticulturalist, expresses some concern than the combination of new clones on perfectly prepared soils, may enhance the Shiraz's natural vigour and lead to excessive yields. Paul is also tempted by the idea of trying some Grenache and Mourvèdre – varieties which were widely planted in the Cape in the 1950s and 1960s.

The appointment of Château Margaux's Paul Pontallier as consultant has clearly had a beneficial impact on SFW's premium range. His influence has accelerated and refined the use of small oak and steered the awkward concept of "optimum ripeness" towards something defined primarily on grape taste, rather than in purely analytical terms – a trend among top French *vignerons* which has spread to the New World.

Although Zonnebloem Shiraz has improved over the last decade, with some recent vintages – especially the 1994 – showing sounder fundamental structure and thus better ageing potential, the trend has been inconsistent and there is still some way to go to reach the top level. The wines are often too loose-knit and accessible for comfort, and lack the depth and definition expected from a premium product in an international market.

A major advance would be to cap yields at eight tons per hectare, and to lengthen the time spent on skins from the present seven days – a duration that it seems is determined more by vat capacity than by the inherent needs of the wine. Shiraz's long-term potential has yet to be fully exploited at SFW.

VARIETY	VINEYARD	DETAILS	AREA
SHIRAZ	STELLENBOSCH KLOOF	Grafted vines, 75% virus-infected; 20 yrs average vine age; c 7 tons/ha	3.20
SHIRAZ	SIMONSBERG	Grafted vine, Shiraz disease prevalent; 21 yrs average vine age; c 6 tons/ha	4.00
SHIRAZ	MULDERSVLEI	Grafted, mainly healthy vines; average vine age 16 yrs; c 10 tons/ha	4.00
SHIRAZ	BRANDWACHT	Grafted, mainly healthy vines; average vine age 16 yrs; c 10 tons/ha	6.00
SHIRAZ	DEVON VALLEY	Grafted vines, virus infected; average vine age 20 yrs; c 8 tons/ha	9.00
		TOTAL (hectares):	26.20

GRAPE VARIETIES

Grape variety is a fundamental determinant of a wine's personality. Rhône grapes provide a common thread linking a wide diversity of regions and wine styles. This section describes the characteristics (and eccentricities) of 19 of the most frequently encountered major and minor Rhône varieties.

Ripening Viognier grapes.

BOURBOULENC

Bourboulenc is one of the five grapes permitted in white Châteauneuf. Its quality depends largely on when it is harvested: early, and the wine tends to be thin and neutral; late, and it develops distinctive, sturdy, rather rustic flavours with some depth, which can add a dimension of richness to blander varieties, eg Grenache Blanc and Clairette. This gives it appeal to some in the Midi, where it was widely planted at the end of the 19th century. Apart from its existence in Châteauneuf, where it contributes freshness and acidity, there are patches (often of quite old vines) in the southern Rhône, and newer plantings in Corbières, Coteaux du Languedoc and the Minervois.

CARIGNAN

Although rarely seen on its own, Carignan (sometimes "Carignane") is probably the world's most important wine grape. It is certainly important in California where it accounts for much bulk red wine, and in Spain, where it was first isolated and where it is known as Mazuela.

It is widely planted in the Midi, where it performs well in a hot, dry, sunny climate, producing average, but rarely exceptional, wine. Its susceptibility to fungal disease does not endear it to growers in cooler, wetter, regions. Much of the *vin ordinaire* of the Languedoc-Roussillon comes from a Carignan base, now that the dreadful Aramon is in terminal decline. Carignan is a heavy cropper, which explains why many growers cling on to it. Nonetheless, the drive towards finer varieties, and its poor quality image, have seen a sharp decline in plantings and have lead growers, unable to get a reasonable price for either fruit or wine, to tear out even very old plantings. It is not a permitted variety in Châteauneuf-du-Pape, but is tolerated up to a maximum of 30% in Côtes du Rhône and 10% in Côtes du Rhône-Villages.

This decline is a great pity, because there is ample evidence to suggest that, handled properly, Carignan is capable of making excellent wine. For example, Paul Draper of Ridge Vineyards (qv) who has worked with several young Carignan vineyards, senses that the variety becomes truly great as the vines get old. He cites his 1880 vines from the Whitten Ranch in Geyserville, which contribute significantly to his Geyserville blend. Some growers describe its influence as refining a wine, in terms of fruit and structure. Even with young plants, given head-training and low yields, you can get excellent intensity, if not the complexity of old vines. It needs very careful site selection – well exposed and well drained – to have any chance of producing something out of the ordinary. Others suggest that

Carignan is best vinified by carbonic maceration, to amortise its lean, rather pinched and sometimes bitter character, or turned into rosé, in which form it has enjoyed some success. Some estates with old vines are vinifying Carignan sympathetically, and as successfully as a noble grape. In particular Sylvain Fadat, at the Domaine d'Auphilac (qv) produces a magnificent wine from 50-year-old vines – even if it is only designated *vin de pays*. It can be done!

CINSAUT

Cinsaut's origins are in southern France, in the Languedoc. Here, and throughout the southern Rhône and the Midi, plantings burgeoned in the late 1960s and 1970s, encouraged by technicians and officials who sold it to growers as an improver-grape for the lake of poor-quality red wine then being produced there from Aramon and Alicante Bouschet. Its twin qualities of high yields and high sugars ensured its acceptability, though much wine made from it is poor, mean stuff. Now, it rarely appears unblended, the usual mix being with Carignan and Grenache – where it adds fruit and freshness to their respective solidity and flesh. It also thrives in hot climates without sacrificing too much in the way of acidity. This quality makes it a valued component in many Châteauneuf blends, where it is seen as contributing dried fruit (hazelnut and almond) and floral (soft rose) aromas, and freshness. However, it has a habit of developing a "reduced" character if kept too long away from oxygen, and so needs vigilance.

In California Cinsaut also appears as a dry rosé – fresh, light and fruity, but with an element of tightness and structure which takes it above the ordinary. In South Africa, where it arrived from southern France in the late 19th century, it was known as Hermitage and crossed with Pinot Noir to become Pinotage. It is used both for table wine and in some of the better fortified "ports". One of its many synonyms is "Picardan Noir", not to be confused with the Picardan (Blanc).

CLAIRETTE BLANC/GRIS

In the southern Rhône and the Languedoc-Roussillon, of which it is a native, Clairette is to white wine what Grenache is to red – the baseline variety. It shares with red Grenache those qualities of low acidity, high alcohol, marked perfume, and a certain lack of "corsets" which make it rarely suitable alone. It has a tendency to oxidise, going flat and losing freshness, which higher-acid mixers help to combat.

Together with Grenache Blanc, Clairette forms a principal constituent of many white Châteauneufs, contributing a floral perfume and supporting elegance. In the Drôme, it

appears in the excellent, sparkling Clairette de Die *brut*, made by the champagne method. In the more aromatic Cuvée Tradition it is mixed with ½ to ¼ of Muscat à Petits Grains, and vinified by the traditional *méthode Dioise*, in which fermentation is preceded by a light filtration to remove yeast and thus delay its onset. The remaining yeasts work slowly in the winter cold and by the time the wine is bottled at New Year, enough residual sugar remains for further fermentation to produce a fresh sparkle.

Outside France, Clairette is most extensively planted in South Africa's Cape winelands (2.5% of wine-grape acreage). There, it produces wine mainly filler wine for bulk blends – and is usefully employed to tone down over-assertive varieties, such as Muscat. It also appears in Australia, almost exclusively in the Hunter Valley, where it is known as Blanquette (not the same as the Blanquette de Limoux, which is Mauzac). A less common variant, Clairette Gris, has a pink-tinged skin, but otherwise similar characteristics.

COUNOISE

Counoise, another Southern France red, was well known in the older vineyards of Châteauneuf and Tavel. Today, it is found planted patchily in the Rhône Meridionale, Provence and the Languedoc, and makes a guest appearance in Collioure. It plays a secondary role providing depth and body to blends, including Châteauneuf, where it is valued for its spicy, green-peppery, slightly musky character. It both buds and ripens late, but produces reasonable yields and has good disease resistance. Recent interest is perhaps the signal for a modest re-appraisal.

GRENACHE BLANC

Grenache Blanc shares many qualities with Grenache Noir, of which it is a variant. In particular it is susceptible to oxidation and produces full, rich wines, high in alcohol and low in acidity. It is an important part of many white Châteauneuf blends, where it particularly complements Clairette and Bourboulenc, and is a significant part of many white Côtes du Rhônes and, limited to 10%, of some Villages *cuvées*. Its intrinsic dullness has benefited from modern wine-making techniques – especially cooler fermentation, stainless steel and the ability to suppress malolactic fermentation – which manage to retain more freshness and aromatic qualities than would have been the case a decade ago.

GRENACHE NOIR

Grenache Noir is the world's second most widely planted grape variety (the white Airen is the first). Its principal sites are in its country of origin, Spain (c 250,000ha) where it is known as Garnacha and makes soft, attractive, generally middle-quality wines; and in France, where there are some 80,000ha, concentrated in the Midi and southern Rhône, where it has been widely planted since the 19th century. Australia has 19,222ha planted, 86% of which is in South Australia, making it that country's third most important variety. In California, there are just under 10,000ha, much producing bulk table wine in the hot Central Valley, but occasional patches of better, cooler-climate planting.

Grenache is capable of excellence, but this is rarely seen, either because it is over-cropped or else because it is blended away with Shiraz (in France and Australia) or with Tempranillo (in Rioja). It is the staple grape of baseline quality Côtes du Rhône and Languedoc-Roussillon blends, and also of Châteauneuf-du-Pape, Gigondas, Lirac and Tavel, where it plays a dominant, but rarely solo, role. It imakes good rosé, excelling in Tavel and also in California and in Australia.

Grenache is sturdy, thriving in hot, dry climates – even in the wind-swept Mistral belt of southern France, where it seems able to establish a sufficiently strong rooting system to survive. However, choice of a drought-resistant rootstock is critical – especially in areas such as Châteauneuf-du-Pape or the hotter parts of California, where several months of the growing season can pass without rain. It is particularly vigorous, needing severe pruning and rigorous debudding if yields are to be kept at levels remotely compatible with quality. Some growers (eg Randall Grahm in California) consider that it gives better fruit quality and more interesting aromatics on cooler sites. The best results are generally found with bush (*gobelet*) training or spur pruning, helped by Grenache's naturally upright growth habit. Late harvesting, at over 15% potential alcohol, produces much better balance and appreciably increases aroma and flavour complexity.

Grenache is not too fussy about soils, although in France it is generally considered to do best in warmer sites with low-fertility, heat-retentive soils – schists, granites and on terraces at higher altitudes.

One drawback, especially in marginal climates, is its strong tendency to abortive or only partial flowering (*coulure*), which increases the proportion of dry matter (stems etc) to fruit; it then needs careful adjustment of the level of de-stemming to adapt vinification to the amount and character of the fruit. Other problems are Grenache's susceptibility to downy mildew, (a difficulty for would-be organic growers), and its tendency to bunch-rot, a result of its compact cluster configuration. In marginal climates Grenache's late ripening means an increased risk of rainfall, and thus dilution or rot, around harvest time.

Given reasonable heat, Grenache produces good natural sugars resulting in wine which is high in alcohol and lowish in acidity. This accounts for its reputation for rather loose-textured, short-lived wine, and the need to blend in additional backbone from the likes of Mourvèdre or Syrah. While heavily Grenache-based wines are often rather soft and plummy, with a distinctly gripless feel about them, old vines and low yields (below 35hl/ha), properly vinified, will produce concentrated, naturally well-structured wine that has no need whatsoever of added "corsets". Anyone in doubt should try Château Rayas (qv), RBJ Theologicum (Barossa, qv) or Clos Mogador (Spain).

The problem is that tradition implanted Grenache in regions which required high-volume, low- to medium-quality wine, so it gained a not wholly undeserved reputation for producing it – *post hoc, ergo propter hoc!* The other side of the coin is that "Grenache" rarely appears on a label, so its reputation has not been chiselled away entirely, as would be the case with massive quantities of inferior Cabernet Sauvignon or Chardonnay. There is still hope.

In the cellar, Grenache's main problems are a tendency to herbaceousness – which is controlled by careful attention to crushing and de-stemming – and a low resistance to oxidation. To combat this, it is best stored in tank and racked, without air, as little as possible. In regions where wood maturation is traditional – eg the Southern Rhône – Grenache is generally kept in large casks to avoid premature browning and deterioration. All too often the costs of bottling prevent winemakers from bottling at the right time, and the wine remains too long in wood, to its permanent detriment. Once again, prevalent practice is responsible for a misleading reputation. However, with low yields and timely bottling, Grenache is perfectly capable of far longer beneficial development than many would give it credit for.

Grenache's high alcohol often leads to the description "heady". An impression of alcohol is undesirable and such "headiness" often accompanies a lack of fruit and structure. Aggressively astringent tannins are also a feature of many badly vinified Grenaches – often a result of harsh pressing, to extract "more tannic" press wine to try and balance out a structural deficiency, or of overheated fermentations, designed with the same end in view.

Fine tannin, however, is best extracted by prolonged maceration after fermentation, where it is leached out by alcohol, rather than by excessively hot fermentations: these give that unpleasant raw edge which is frequently noted by tasters.

In character Grenache wines vary from the light coloured, raspberry-ish quaffers, through mid-weight, predominantly red-fruit-flavoured Côtes du Rhône styles, to those fleshy, mouthfilling *vins de garde* in the manner of Château Rayas or Domaine de Gramenon (qv).

In the south of France Grenache also provides the base for remarkable *vins doux naturels* such as Banyuls and Maury.

MARSANNE

Marsanne is the mainstay grape of white Hermitage, Crozes-Hermitage, white St-Joseph and St-Péray – both still and sparkling. The AC rules also allow up to 15% of either Marsanne and/or Roussanne in red Hermitage, though this concession – a hangover from the days of mixed plantings – has fallen into disuse. Its only other significant (though in acreage terms, negligible) appearance is in Australia, in the Yarra Valley and particularly in Victoria's Goulburn Valley, where it has established something of a niche since being introduced in the late 1860s. Some of the original plantings at Château Tahbilk (qv) are still productive.

It is an unusual grape, which inspires some, yet leaves others unconvinced. Northern Rhône growers suggest you drink it during its first few years or else after a decade or more in bottle – but never in middle age, when it typically undergoes a dumb, flat phase. It tends to have a deep colour, which transforms into dark mahogany with age. Fully mature, it has an attractive, complex bouquet, often reminiscent of acacia honey and jasmine or honeysuckle; young, it is marked by a flinty tang which disappears with maturation. However, Marsanne's character is not as marked as that of Chardonnay or Sauvignon Blanc and is easily stifled by new wood. It needs lowish yields and thoughtful vinification, otherwise it becomes neutral and, frankly, boring.

In the vineyard, Marsanne is vigorous, with a natural floppiness and a consistent fruit set which makes for good cropping. In contrast to Chardonnay and Riesling it has loose clusters, but is susceptible to both mildew and botrytis. It ripens mid-season and can either be harvested early, for youthful fruitiness, or late, for longer-lasting wines which need high sugars to balance out the grape's natural structure. It is particularly sensitive to climate: too hot, and the wine becomes fat and flabby; too cool, and it becomes bland.

Marsanne has the capacity – more so, for example, than Viognier – to take on character from cellar practices, such as fermentation or ageing in new oak. However, it is unforgiving, as any imbalance destroys the overall quality. It can be vinified for ageing, but most winemakers go for something with immediate appeal, realising that it is unrealistic to expect consumers to keep Marsanne for ten years. At Mitchelton (qv) in Australia, they see Marsanne as "the red-wine drinker's white wine", because of its natural weight and richness, and produce a premium release, in the hope that people will allow it to mature.

The greatest expression of Marsanne is to be found in the Rhône, in aged white Hermitage. The best deepen over time in colour and richness and are capable of lasting several decades, emerging into a finely aromatic, rich, honeyed nuttiness. They make fine partners for robust food, especially rich fish dishes, sweetbreads and even lighter game.

Marsanne is also known as "Grosse Roussette" in Savoie, and is planted in parts of Switzerland's Valais canton, where it is called "Ermitage".

MOURVÈDRE

That Mourvèdre originated in Spain, in the eastern Pyrenees, is not in dispute; whether it came from Mataró, in Catalonia, or Murviedro, in Valencia, is. It arrived in France around the late middle ages. In California and Australia it is known as Mataro. Elsewhere, it answers to a variety of names: the Spanish call it Monastrell, others Esparte, and it has apparently no less than 30 different local names in various French provinces – for example Bordeaux, where it is known as Balthazar. In colloquial usage, in the New World, it is frequently referred to as "dog strangler", on account of its youthful, somewhat aggressive, tannins.

Its true name and origins are largely irrelevant to consumers, as its appearance on labels is rare. In France, its classic and most aristocratic expression is in the red wines of Bandol (qv), where it is generally blended with Grenache and Cinsaut. Many growers there produce excellent results with special 100% *cuvées*. Elsewhere in southern France (particularly in Châteauneuf-du-Pape), in Australia and in California, it is valued as a "stiffener" for Grenache and Cinsaut. It occasionally appears as a stand-alone varietal, with notable success in Ridge's Mataro (qv), from old vines on the Evangelo Vineyard, and Jade Mountain's Mourvèdre (qv). Fred and Matt Cline (qv) have 280 acres of Mourvèdre, of which 260 are over 90 years old (a fact not picked up by the official California census of grape acreages, which registers Mourvèdre as below its minimum recording level of 50 acres).

In Australia, Mourvèdre is considered as an inconsequential grape and is treated indifferently – generally blended away with Shiraz. If James Halliday's evaluation is conventional wisdom, this is hardly surprising: "an even more rapidly fading star than Grenache, producing wine which on its own is rather hard and graceless, but which an be useful in blends." There are exceptions, in particular Wendouree's (qv) magnificent Shiraz-Mataro, both of whose constituent grapes come from ancient, low-yielding vines.

For growers, the variety is not especially problematic, provided the golden rules are followed: the hottest sites (south-facing in the northern Hemisphere and vice versa), and shelter from the wind, which it abhors; surprisingly, it seems to do best near the sea (eg at Bandol and Collioure). It is easy to train early, then grows straight upwards, a feature exploited by some Californian estates – for example Preston (qv) – to reduce the need for leaf-thinning in warmer sites. It buds late, removing any significant risk from spring frost or *coulure*, hence the need for heat to ensure ripening. Yields are not excessive and are somewhat variable – requiring careful choice of clones and rootstocks. The Clines consider that most problems arise because people insist on planting Mourvèdre in deep soils – an error, because of its natural vigour. Higher yields are best achieved by increasing plant density, not soil fertility.

Mourvèdre is now widely used in southern France as an "improver" grape – replacing Carignan and Grenache in many places. Quality appellations, such as St-Chinian, Collioure and Faugères, stipulate a minimum Mourvèdre (or Syrah) content in their blends (10-25% depending on the AC), while others such as Fitou fix a maximum (10%). Its main value in these areas is as a structural counterbalance to the weak Grenache and Carignan.

In flavour, Mourvèdre tends to produce deeply-coloured, heavily-extracted wine: slow to develop, but definitely worth the wait. In youth, it can be frustratingly dumb, with a broad earthiness, solid extract and often quite pointed tannins, reminiscent of young St-Estèphe or Pauillac. However a good balance of alcohol gives many wines – especially those from older vines – softer tannins and thus an irresistible attraction.

Unfortunately, many critics suggest that these wines are best for early drinking. As anyone who has enjoyed a mature Mourvèdre will know, an altogether different persona emerges as it ages – a complex, fine, spicy, gingerbread character. It has even been suggested, without much supporting evidence, that Mourvèdre is a distant cousin of Zinfandel; in tannin profile, perhaps; in individual flavours, implausible.

An important property of Mourvèdre is that it remains in a reduced state for much longer than many varieties, and has to be oxygenated before it will perform. In the cellar, this means plenty of aerated racking – the Clines rack their Mourvèdre 5-6 times from barrel. For the drinker, this entails either long bottle-age – the best Bandols need 10–15 years and will improve for twice as long – or decanting at breakfast for drinking at dinner.

Mourvèdre is also something of a chameleon – put it into a Pinot Noir cask and you think you are tasting highly-extracted Pinot – *mutatis mutandis* with Syrah oak.

Clearly, Mourvèdre is far from simple. It is not a variety to put into everyone's hands (whether grower or consumer) but is indisputably capable of producing wine of great breed and complexity. It deserves far better treatment that it presently gets.

MUSCARDIN

A curious grape, believed to be a clone of Mondeuse (the Grosse Syrah of Savoie). It was clearly known in the Vaucluse, as it appeared on the original list of permitted Châteauneuf varieties. However, by the mid-1950s, it had virtually disappeared from there, and was only identified and rescued by Louis Reynaud by selection and testing from mixed plantings of old vines at Château Rayas (qv). It is still used by some Châteauneuf estates – notably Beaucastel, and Jacques Reynaud is considering reviving it at Rayas. In character, it has a distinctively floral bouquet, and gives wine which is low in colour. It is useful as a *vin d'assemblage* to add sapidity and freshness.

PETITE SIRAH

The Petite Sirah is enigmatic, in that its true identity remains uncertain – despite the fact that in California, the only place where "Petite Sirah" is grown (there are several thousand acres), it has long been believed to be identical to the French Durif, originally propagated by a Dr Durif in the 1880s.

This identity crisis probably started in the late 19th century, when grape selection was largely governed by the demand for dark-coloured, full-bodied wines. Then, it was likely that true Syrah and Petite Sirah were co-planted. In 1929, an official Californian booklet lumped together Petite Sirah, Durif, Syrah and Serine as a single variety – a confusion only unscrambled in 1941 when the writer Frank Schoonmaker stated categorically that: "this grape is not the Petite Sirah... from which the great red wine of Hermitage is made".

Thereafter, until it re-emerged in the late 1960s, the true Syrah virtually disappeared from Californian vineyards. What was imported, and extensively planted instead, was Petite Sirah, which growers called Syrah, until its true identity as Durif was discovered in 1974.

In character, "Petite", as it is referred to, gives robust, tannic wine, with a certain spicy quality. Many "true Syrah" producers regard it as an ignoble mongrel, and protest vociferously at its inclusion in Syrah Show classes. However, in sensitive hands, it can be made, if not aristocratic, then something definitely more upper-middle class than peasant. Paul Draper believes that careful tannin management during vinification is essential for success, and uses a proportion of whole clusters to give suppleness and roundness. By buffering 30–40% of the grape seeds from the extractive effects of increasing alcohol, whole clusters reduce tannins and intensify fruit elements, thereby leading to a more balanced wine.

Another way to amortise Petite's undesirably harsh, grainy tannins is to field-blend a proportion of Viognier in the Côte-Rôtie tradition. Adaptive viticulture can also improve quality, particularly Petite's susceptibility to bunch rot, from a very tight cluster formation. It used to be head-trained, but modern plantings try to space out bunches by training the vine up stakes to reduce rot and increase colour.

Meanwhile, the debate about Petite's true identity rumbles on. Some, unconvinced that it is really Durif, are trying more sophisticated tests to disprove the equation. Others believe (and hope) it is related to a pre-phylloxera Rhône Syrah. Whatever the truth, and however vocal the dissenters, the variety can make excellent wine which often is indistinguishable from true Syrah. If its quality merits distinction, it seems churlish to exclude it; if not, it will sink of its own accord.

PICARDAN

While the Picardan Noir is a synonym for Cinsaut, the Picardan is a little-known white grape which, but for its inclusion in Châteauneuf's 13 permitted varieties, would probably have disappeared altogether. Even so, there appears to be some doubt as to whether it exists at all: modern ampelographers can find no individual identifiable variety corresponding to what growers call Picardan. Plantings at Châteauneuf have been identified as the table grape Oeillade Blanche. One authority states that so-called Picardan invariably turned out to be either Clairette or, more usually, Bourboulenc. Châteauneuf, however, officially recognises Picardan's existence and attributes to its wine qualities of "finesse and softness" with an agreeable, light musky note. The phantom of the vineyard!

PICPOUL

This comes as Picpoul Noir and Gris. As Gris, it is permitted in white Châteauneuf-du-Pape and as Noir in the red, although in neither manifestation does it make more than a tangential contribution. The white variant is well-perfumed, floral in character, with finesse and relatively low tannins.

According to Robinson (1986), it pre-dated either Grenache or Carignan in the Midi, is high-yielding and is prone to powdery mildew (oïdium).

ROUSSANNE

Roussanne is even more of a closet grape than its white Hermitage partner, Marsanne (qv). Its proneness to oxidation, both during vinification and maturation, led growers to replace it with Marsanne during the 1950s and 1960s. Now, with improved, cleaner vinification techniques it is enjoying something of a revival, due in good measure to the enthusiasm of the Perrins at Château de Beaucastel, who make one of only two 100% varietal Roussannes, from old vines.

During the 1970s, the Jaboulets increased the Roussanne content of their white Hermitage from 10% to 30-35%, which added both finesse and structure; while the Chaves' percentage remains around 15%, from vines over 60 years old. In Châteauneuf, where it is one of four permitted white varieties, there has also been growing interest in the quality Roussanne can bring to blends, balancing the inherent flabbiness of Grenache Blanc and Clairette. In the northern Rhône, where it is sometimes confusingly called Roussette, plantings are quietly increasing, especially in St-Péray – there to balance Marsanne rather than Grenache. (Roussette is properly the Altesse of Savoie, so its Septentrionale synonym is a misnomer).

The other pure Roussanne bottling comes from John Alban (qv), who has 15 acres planted in San Luis Obispo, whose climate and soils he believes ideally suited to it. He and Randall Grahm of Bonny Doon (qv) are the only Californian growers to produce Roussanne (1994), although sparks of interest suggest that it may not be long before others join the band. The Perrins' experimental vineyard at Tablas Creek (qv) has some Roussanne, so authentic plant material will be available for anyone wanting to try it.

Apart from its oxidative tendencies, Roussanne is susceptible to malady, so it is better planted separately rather than mixed with, for example, Marsanne, so that any disease doesn't spread. It ripens very late, so is often picked under-ripe, with low sugars and high acidity – not by desire but from necessity.

Roussanne does best in a marginal climate, with a long growing season. Exposed to great heat, it produces high sugars which then turn to high alcohol which, above 14%, tends to dominate any finesse. Its proclivity for soaking up oxygen like a sponge seems to do it little harm. Although its wine appear unduly mature in colour, rapidly turning golden, with age it deepens further

and begins to shrug off any youthful awkwardness. John Alban vinifies his in oak puncheons, where it goes through a "dramatic" dumb phase before "coming back pristine and exuberant; this is the moment to bottle". Paradoxically, Alban also finds that Roussanne tends to combine high pH (ie low acidity) with longevity – the converse of what one would expect. Gérard Chave, whom he telephoned in the hope of an answer to the enigma, told him that for him, the finest vintages are often those with the highest pHs.

Roussanne is unlikely to make headline news, or become fashionable in the way of Viognier; yet patches of quality interest, from as far afield as Provence and the Minervois, are ensuring that it won't be totally obliterated. However, some people are clearly attracted by considerations other than an intrinsic love of the grape. One Californian grower reports being visited by a major winery owner "consumed with obtaining Roussanne cuttings and getting as much information about the variety as possible", so that he could start planting and production. It was only after two hours talking to them that he realised that they had never even tasted Roussanne. Beware blind fashion!

SYRAH

The finest Syrahs indisputably merit rank equal to any wine made from Cabernet Sauvignon or Pinot Noir. Yet, outside its northern Rhône showcase, the Syrah all but loses its magic and status, blended away by growers in the Côtes du Rhône and throughout Australia to beef up other varieties – Grenache in the one case, Cabernet Sauvignon in the other. Now a caucus – almost a fraternity – of Syrah-loving winemakers is at last establishing (albeit patchily) a long-overdue international reputation for the grape.

There seems little justification for such universal neglect. Syrah is not a difficult grape either to cultivate or to vinify. It gives good yields and is adaptable to a variety of sites and treatments. Where it is planted in marginal climates, at the limit of regular ripening (where many consider it performs best), such as in the northern Rhône, microclimate and siting are critical. This explains the fact that in France, apparently insignificant differences in climate or situation translate into systematic, identifiable differences between one appellation and another. Syrah generally likes warm, sunny, hillsides with well-drained, low-fertility soils, and although sensitive to prolonged drought, especially in poor, clay soils, relishes a certain amount of water-stress. The major, and all too common, mistake is to plant Syrah on over-fertile ground – eg a valley floor – where it delivers only mediocre quality – Côtes de Ventoux rather than Côte-Rôtie.

The greatest northern Rhône Syrahs come from well-defined soil types – essentially those on, or derived from primary rock formations. Granite is especially favoured (eg at Hermitage Les Bessards, Cornas on the *coteaux*, Crozes-Hermitage at Serves, Erome and Gervans, and a substantial part of St-Joseph, particularly around Mauves). Here Syrah produces deeply coloured wine with complex aromas of spice, pepper and violets, and magnificent, finely-structured depths of flavour. Good examples of derivative soils are Côte-Rôtie's Côte Blonde (gneiss) and Côte Brune (micaschist) where the flavour profile tends towards cassis and the tannins have a shade more elegance. Syrah also does well on alluvial terraces of the Rhône and the Isère – eg Le Méal and Les Baumes at Hermitage, at Pontain at Crozes-Hermitage and in some parts of St-Joseph.

Syrah's natural vigour produces an abundance of vegetation and shoots, which need careful canopy management and rigorous debudding to achieve an optimum balance of leaf and fruit, and to ensure adequate aeration and exposure for the ripening bunches. It also has a notoriously floppy habit which requires some form of trellis to spread out the growth. Syrah is relatively disease resistant, although it is sensitive to *chlorosis* (especially on inappropriate rootstock), grey rot and grape-worm and tight-clustered clones are prone to bunch rot.

To have any prospect of making great Syrah, low yields (less than 45hl/ha or 3 tonnes per acre) are essential; above this level quality rapidly vanishes. Achieving this entails short pruning as Syrah, when generously pruned, yields correspondingly – a sore temptation for the greedy – which results in unbalanced wine and perpetuates the image of mediocrity. It has no trouble reaching respectable sugar levels, nor of developing either colour or tannins. It buds late, reducing the spring frost risk in marginal climates, and, given enough heat and light, ripens early to mid-season. Top quality also demands precise harvesting: while full ripeness is needed to avoid aggressive tannins, waiting until the grapes are overripe generally leads to an acid deficiency and worse, thick, jammy flavours and a loss of varietal character.

While local lore, to which many Rhône *vignerons* are still strongly attached, dates the advent of Syrah to the arrival at Tain l'Hermitage in 1224 of the Knight Henri Gaspard de Sterimberg, fresh from crusading in Cyprus, its true origins are a matter of academic dispute among historians and ampelographers. There are two principal theories: one has it that Syrah came westwards from Shiraz in south-eastern Persia (Iran) and arrived in the Rhône Valley with the Phocean Greeks; the other charts its progress northwards from Egypt, with Probus' Roman legions, via Syracuse, in Sicily. However, an inconvenience for both hypotheses is the lack of any evidence that Syrah was ever cultivated in either region; the Schirazi grape of Iran's Azerbaijan region, upon which some rely, was in fact a white table grape. A third, well-researched and more plausible theory, expounded by Jacques André and Louis Levadoux in 1964, suggests that Syrah originated in the north-eastern Rhône in the ancient territory of Allobrogia, now the Dauphine, as the Vitis Allobrogica, referred to by Pliny in the first century A.D. The main ground for this claim is the high genetic variability of the Syrah in the northern Rhône, which ampelographers consider incompatible with the limited importation proposed by the other two hypotheses.

What is known, from archaeological finds, is that Syrah was well-established at Tain l'Hermitage, and presumably around Vienne, by the 13th century, where it appears to have got stuck for several centuries thereafter. Dr Guyot, writing in the mid-19th century, reports it having "barely descended the Hermitage hill" to establish itself around Tournon (a very short distance away) and at Livron, south of Valence in the Drôme. (His omission of Côte-Rôtie is understandable, as the Syrah there was known as Serine, as it still is by some growers).

Only since the 1960s has Syrah spread in France to any significant degree, from its localised northern base. Now widely cultivated throughout the Rhône Meridionale and southern France, including Châteauneuf-du-Pape, it is valued as an "improver", to add finesse and structure to looser-knit southern reds. Total French plantings now exceed 15,000ha, with significant developments in the departments of Ardèche, southern Drôme, Vaucluse, Gard, Var, Hérault and Aude.

In Australia Shiraz, as Syrah is known there, has been cultivated since arriving with the first English settlers in 1788. Further sizeable importations were made by Busby and McArthur from 1810-1830, reputedly from Tain l'Hermitage, which accounts for the widespread use of "Hermitage", a name which still clings on, although European-inspired legislation is phasing out its use. With 6,140ha in production, spanning every major wine-growing region from the Hunter Valley to Margaret River, Shiraz is Australia's most important variety, accounting for 36% of all red plantings and 9.77% of total wine-grape acreage. However, because it is so obliging, too many Australian winemakers treat it as a workhorse. At the increasing number of estates where it is cosseted, it produces fine wine. In cooler areas the style emphasises Syrah's hallmark "peppery" qualities; in warmer regions the feel is more of berryish fruit, sometimes rather jammy in character.

Syrah's arrival in South Africa, in the 1650s, predates Australia by more than a century. Despite this early start, it has never been more than a minor variety in the Cape, where it covers around 700ha – less than 0.6% of the entire vineyard area. In California, by contrast, Syrah is a *parvenu* – with only four known acres (in the Napa Valley) in 1969, which expanded to 139 acres by 1988, and positively rocketed to 741 by 1993.

However, as early as 1929, a newsletter from the federal inspection service had cited Syrah and Serine (and Durif) as a synonym for Petite Syrah (qv) and thereafter, confusion over varietal identity (see below) made it difficult to establish the true extent of older Californian Syrah plantings.

Outside these countries, Syrah plantings are relatively sparse. Argentina has around 2,500ha around Mendoza and San Rafael, and there are pockets of production in the Valais Canton of Switzerland, in Brazil and in Italy, where it was introduced from Montpellier in 1899 under the names of Bragolia and Neretto di Saluzzo, since when cultivation has spread from the Alpine regions and Gattinara to Tuscany, Val d'Aosta, Umbria and Latium.

Progress has been somewhat muddied by confusion over the true identity of the Syrah, which spread far beyond its northern Rhône focus. The turbulence started with the claim that there were in fact not one, but several distinct Syrahs, giving different qualities of wine. This emanated from Côte-Rôtie, where growers were persuaded of the existence (in Côte-Rôtie, of course) of a superior, small-berried variant – "La Petite Syrah", or Serine, in contrast to "La Grosse Syrah" (ie plain Syrah), planted elsewhere. Subsequent research has shown that, while there are indeed clones of Syrah with smaller leaves and berries scattered throughout the northern Rhône, they do not differ sufficiently to justify establishing a distinct sub-species. However, at Gigondas in the Vaucluse, a five-leaved variant was discovered in 1949, and identified as Durif.

This seemed to settle the matter, until the 1970s, when the confusion was further compounded by the University of California at Davis, who introduced a small-berried vine under the name of "Petite Sirah", which was then planted by American growers believing it to be true Syrah. In 1974, ampelographers identified it as Durif, a variety regarded in California as ignoble and which has little in common with Syrah. Now, estates seeking to find out which variety they have in their vineyard are further hampered by Davis' uncertainty over the true identity of their own Durif reference sample! A further spanner in the semantic works is that in France, genuine Syrah appears both as "Grosse" and "Petite": the former is the high-yielding, lower quality, Mondeuse of Savoie and the latter is *le vrai* Syrah of the northern Rhône.

Within the true Syrah population, a variety of clones have been developed, which undoubtedly contribute to differences in wine quality. In Australia, the (genuine) Petite Syrah is used, with small berries and tight clusters, whereas in California both berries and clusters are larger. This could be a result of either higher soil fertility or of clonal selection. In the classic appellations of the northern Rhône, top-class growers regard it as essential to have only small-berried Syrah, for good liquid:solid equilibrium in their vats. To ensure this, some, such as the Chaves, prefer to select their plant material from their own vineyards (*sélection massale*). Many still consider that much of the Syrah planted, especially in the southern Rhône, is not of comparable quality and contrast the fine Petite Syrah (Serine) and the Syrah de Gervans (Grosse Syrah) which needs very short pruning to have any chance of yielding high-quality wine.

To extract Syrah's inherent riches demands careful vinification and a feel for the grape, taking into consideration the vintage and the *terroir* upon which it was grown. This accounts for consistent regional styles which are dealt with in the appropriate section. However, some common winemaking threads are identifiable. Syrah is deeply coloured and strongly tannic, both of which require a reasonably high fermentation temperature and long vatting. These extract and fix colour, which would otherwise remain unstable and rapidly break down, and also limit the amount of harsh, unpleasant tannins. Maturation is generally best in small (225-litre) oak casks or in slightly larger barrels. Some winemakers find that frequent rackings reduce tannins, which eventually polymerise (ie the chemical chains lengthen) and soften, finally precipitating out as sediment.

New wood, used with care, can contribute to structure and flavour, and has become an increasingly common feature of *élevage*. The type and amount of oak, how it is coopered, and the length of time a wine spends in it are all matters upon which there far from universal accord. In France, many traditionalists regard oak as anathema – masking the fruit and typicity while iconoclasts such as Marcel Guigal, are content to keep their best wines in 100% new wood for 30 months or more. Where new wood is used, it is invariably French: in

contrast to the New World, where American oak is widely employed. Not only is American significantly cheaper, but growers have a genuine regard for its quality, especially if the casks are made by French coopers.

One trick, developed in Australia's Barossa Valley, is to transfer the wine to cask just before fermentation is finished; this gives a much more harmonious take-up of oakiness and imparts the distinctive berry-fruit character found in many Australian Shirazes. Nowadays, anything from 9-24 months is considered ideal for cask-ageing Shiraz before bottling.

Older *vignerons* in France were too often guilty of leaving fundamentally excellent wine for much too long in old wood, until an order came along to justify the cost of bottling. There, it gradually lost its fruit and gained an unpleasant dessicated, woody flavour which many European palates came to regard as an inescapable part of northern Rhône Syrah. Now, thankfully, enlightenment has come, and it is the wine's needs which dictate the important moment of bottling.

In bottle, great Syrah ages magnificently – developing fine, multi-faceted aromas and complex, magisterial flavours. What it finally matures into depends on its constituents and how they have been vinified. Old northern Rhônes often showed a marked "barnyardy" aspect – which was much appreciated as "traditional" in some quarters. This was not entirely a feature of the Syrah grape, but more usually attributable to a yeast organism, *brettanomyces*. Modern winemakers are trained to regard "Brett" as a fault, symptomatic of poor hygiene; however, in small quantities it is far from unpleasant and, like botrytis in dry white wines, can add a dimension of complexity which clinically clean wines lack.

Aged northern Rhône Syrah tends to a marked similarity with aged red Bordeaux. Grange – the southern Hemisphere's finest expression of Syrah – ages differently – with a characteristic element of volatility. Both are indubitably fine, and entirely valid, styles; the most persuasive and eloquent witnesses to the nobility and versatility, of this remarkable grape.

TERRET NOIR

A minor variety, on the permitted list for red Châteauneuf-du-Pape. In its "Gris" and "Blanc" forms it is more widely found than as "Noir". It is a late-budding, late-ripening, very vigorous and high-yielding variety, generally giving thinly coloured, finely perfumed wine characterised by bright acidity, especially if harvested slightly under-ripe, which can provide a valuable balance to the low-acid red varieties of the Southern Rhône and the Midi. It is also allowed in red Corbières, Costières du Gard and Nîmes,

Coteaux du Languedoc, Fitou, red Minervois and in several *vins de pays*.

UGNI BLANC

Ugni Blanc originated in Italy, where it is known as Trebbiano and still widely planted. Its principal value in France is as a provider of base wine for Cognac (where it is called St-Emilion) and Armagnac. As a source of table wine, its is most often encountered in Provence, where it is used as a blending grape – chiefly because its notoriously high acidity, even in warmer climates, needs balancing richness from the likes of Grenache, Marsanne and Roussanne. It is an important player in white Bandol and Palette, also in the Costières du Gard and Languedoc, and a *cépage accessoire* in white Côtes du Rhône and Côtes du Rhône Villages, where its participation is limited to 30% and 10% respectively. Given suitable conditions its natural vigour will give very high yields and nondescript, neutral wine. However, handled with care, it is capable of better quality than its image would suggest, producing wine with distinctively floral aromas and plenty of crisp acidity – though yields need to be low if this latter is not to dominate.

VACCARÈSE

Another minor Châteauneuf variety, not found elsewhere. It gives rather four-square, tannic wine, fresh and elegant, with noticeable florality – presumably adding something to the overall blend.

VIOGNIER

The Viognier is one of the most enigmatic and fascinating grape varieties of all. With its capricious habits and unpredictable yields, growers find it a particularly hard to tame – a fickle mistress! When a seemingly perfect flowering turns into a small, unevenly ripe crop, they become, not surprisingly, disillusioned. However, for both producers and consumers prepared to take the trouble, there are rich rewards.

It is generally reckoned in Condrieu – Viognier's *locus classicus* – that the grape arrived from Dalmatia, under the auspices of Emperor Probus in AD 281; he is what we would now term ex-Yugoslavian, rather than the more often attributed Roman. The usual story is that a galley, loaded with cargo destined for the Beaujolais, was captured on its way up the Rhône, off Condrieu, and looted by the Culs de Piaux – bandits so-called because their breeches were reinforced with leather. This unlikely event is commemorated every summer with festivities in memory of those unfortunate boatmen – what better excuse for a celebration? A more prosaic, and plausible, explanation is that the grape was imported to replant the Condrieu vineyards destroyed by Probus' predecessor Vespasian. No excuse for a party here.

If the Viognier presents problems for the grower, it is no less of an enigma for the consumer. Its hallmarks are an exotic aroma of dried or candied fruits, often pear or apricot, with flavours characterised by these fruits and a dry, peel-like edge.

It is usually high in alcohol, performing best in the 13–15% range – below which it becomes thi;, above which, flabby.

At Condrieu and Château Grillet the soils are finely-divided granite, known locally as *arzelle*. This retains heat and is considered to be an important factor in the aromatic finesse of wines from this part of the Rhône. Where the grape is planted on heavier, less propitious, soils it tends to lose much of its freshness and vitality.

In the USA where the grape is currently fashionable on growers' 'change, many recent plantings are in soils and micro-climates inherently incapable of delivering decent quality. The lack of any obvious relationship between price ($12-$30 per bottle retail in 1994) and quality in Californian Viogniers, and the appearance of far too many poorly-vinified wines, no doubt baffles consumers who probably wonder what all the hype is about. There are now a plethora of American Viogniers to choose from, mainly Californian; a far cry from the original five 1970s pioneers: Bill Smith (La Jota), Randall Grahm (Bonny Doon), Calera, Joseph Phelps and John Alban when "even the worst was the 5th best Viognier producer in the USA"!

Viognier requires the utmost care, both in cultivation and vinification. Overcrop or harvest too early, and you lose aroma and extract. Harvest too late, and you lose typicity and fruit (though in this case the result is often very attractive). Growers who make the finest Condrieus will tell you that low yields (less than 35hl/ha) are essential for real quality. Too many find this simply uneconomic and continue to overcrop – with predictably poor results.

In California, many growers report that they find Viognier very difficult viticulturally; in particular, it is subject to berry-shatter and uneven fruit-set. Just before harvest one is likely to find everything from over-ripeness to greenness, which complicates the decision about when, and how, to harvest.

At Joseph Phelps (qv), they have experimented with vertical trellising – ie forcing the cane-pruned plant upwards – and are cropping 3 tons/acre, compared with 5 tons for Napa Cabernet and Chardonnay. Some Californian growers (for example Preston, qv) report no problems with berry-shatter, while others, such as Bill Smith at La Jota, obtain a much improved fruit-set by using zinc before flowering, both as a foliar spray and to the soils.

In contrast to many other varieties, where young plants often gives very opulent, fleshy, wine which, although it doesn't keep well, is excellent drinking, Viognier rarely produces its best results before the vines are 15–20 years old. For even the most talented of growers starting from scratch, as many have done, this is a signal difficulty; there have been casualties.

In the vineyard, the grape needs loving coaxing. For some reason, it may flower successfully, but pollination may then fail, leaving the grower with a poor crop. Once established, the vines themselves are long lived – 50-70 years is not unusual – although their inherent capriciousness makes very old Viognier vineyards distinctly uneconomic.

The main vinification problem, even given ripe, healthy fruit, is to balance what at first sight appear to be complete opposites – power and elegance. Extracting, and retaining, the grape's delicate, almost exotic, aromatic qualities while preserving its underlying power is the real challenge. It is precisely this counter-balance of qualities which Viognier fanatics find so seductive. This is not quite so fragile an equilibrium as one might suppose.

The most important matter is to have properly ripe, rot-free and mildew-free fruit to work with. A rapid fermentation with the minimum of oxidation is a good next step; if you leave the grapes too long in the press, you have to add sulphur to prevent the juice browning which dampens aroma and flavour in the finished wine. Some US growers – eg John Staten at Field Stone and Bill Smith at La Jota – report problems completing malolactic fermentation, which they encourage to minimise the need for filtration which, however gentle, removes both elegance and substance.

There is much discussion among growers, both in France and the USA, about the desirability of new oak for either fermentation or subsequent maturation. The present consensus is that a judicious touch (variously estimated at 20-30%) can help, but not as an expedient to add structure to a wine that is out of balance to start with. As with Chardonnay, cask-fermentation seems to bring more harmonious results than fermenting in stainless-steel or epoxy vats and then transferring the wine into barrel for maturation. A period of months in wood after fermentation generally contributes to a slow and even evolution, though an over-extended stay robs the wine of fragrance and balance.

Gentle handling at all stages of vinification is essential to preserve the Viognier's character – the fewer pumpings, rackings, filtrations and the rest, the better. Over-filtering is especially destructive. This goes back to the harvest; morning harvesting brings in cool grapes which gives better clarification and thus the need for less fining and filtration.

There has been an explosion of interest in Viognier in the 1990s, especially in the southern Rhône, where it is being used as a component for white Côtes du Rhône, and in the Ardèche and southern France where it is sold as varietal *vin de pays*, since most ACs disallow named varietals. Georges Duboeuf (qv) have 150ha under contract in the Ardèche, twice the area of Condrieu alone. On a smaller scale, the enterprising Domaine de l'Aube des Temps (qv) produce a delicious, unusual, Vendange Tardive Viognier, sold as Vin de Pays d'Oc. In Condrieu, there is increasing concern among producers that poor, often overpriced, wine damages the reputation of the entire appellation as the sole repository of top-quality Viognier.

Tasting Viogniers from Condrieu and newer French and Californian producers shows a vast variation in style, quality and varietal typicity. In general, the nose reveals all. The main faults are dilution, usually a result of over-cropping, and over-oaking, in the false belief that new wood is a valid substitute for weak fruit. Many wines show delicacy, but lack real depth – suggesting either inappropriate *terroir* or cool, neutral, fermentation – while others are clearly over-processed, almost water-white in colour, indicative of excessively zealous Bentonite fining or harsh filtration.

The Viognier is consummately capable of producing either elation or depression – whether for the grower or for the drinker. However, it needs people who are educated in Rhône varieties, who sympathise with them and understand them in their native habitats. The risk is that ignorant growers, out to follow fashion, will flood the market with poor wine. Meanwhile, for the consumer, the search for quality remains a beguiling challenge.

TASTING NOTES

This section contains individual tasting notes on over 1,500 different wines, arranged by country, region and Estate. They are intended to give an impression of the often highly individual styles of each producer and should be read in conjunction with the appropriate profile. Notes on older vintages have been included to illustrate how aromas and flavours develop as wines mature.

Tasting at Hartenberg in the Cape's Devon Valley.

NORTHERN RHONE

COTE-ROTIE

The following 1990 & 1991 wines were tasted blind in Ampuis in May 1994:
1991 COTE-ROTIE:
E DUCLAUX Mid garnet, premature browning; unattractive, stewed nose; high toned flavours – fair fruit but lacks depth and is spoilt by excess acidity. Poor, weedy. (13/20)
J-M GERIN, *LES GRANDES PLACES* Good depth of colour; ripe cherry aromas starting to show through; warm, attractive flavours, fruit presently dominated by obvious new oak; good balance of acids and tannins; depth, length and firm structure make for a promising bottle. (15+/20)
J-M GERIN, *CHAMPIN LE SEIGNEUR* Sombre, deep plum; closed nose; spicy, ripe, stylish, wine; excellent depth of fruit and sound structure. Long and complex. Seems to have integrated the oak more fully than Les Grandes Places. Elegant and very promising. (17/20)
BERNARD BURGAUD Blackish hue, opaque, carmine rim; mildly reduced nose – otherwise ripe cherries and hint of torrefaction; rather weak fruit underneath high acid and tannic frame; lacks depth but will drink well over mid-term. (14+/20)
DE BOISSEYT-CHOL Deep red; plummy nose; stony flavour with pronounced *goût de reduit*; reasonable fruit, highish acid and dry finish. (14/20)
MARIUS CHAMBEYRON, *CUVEE MARIUS CHAMBEYRON* Transparent garnet – no great depth; lightish elegant nose, not giving much; very light, soapy flavour – flabby wine with neither grip nor depth. Disgraceful. (10-/20)
BERNARD CHAMBEYRON Lightish mid-plum; gentle, singed, smoky nose; elegance rather than stuffing here, with pleasant depth of soft, ripe fruit. Long and well-balanced, though a touch hollow. Designed for a few years' keeping. Not bad at all. (15+/20)
LOUIS DREVON Mid plum; strongly cassis nose, hint of violets; elegant wine, cachou and violets, with plenty of ripe fruit and well-judged tannins. Delicious now and will doubtless keep for a few years. (16+/20)
GAEC VERNAY *(Daniel et Rolland)* Limpid red-plum to edge; closed nose – hints of animal and very ripe fruit; despite good fruit, wine has a rustic, clumsy feel to it; flabby and lacking in grip and style. Mediocre. (13?/20)
JAMET Very deep black plum; charry, smoky aromas with floral undertones; big-framed wine, oak evident; notes of animal and burnt fruit; flashes of the elegance to come. Rather flat on palate – lacks acidity – and finishes short. Good depth of fruit. All in all, rather burly, but not without attraction. (14/20)
FRANCOIS GERARD Mid plum, carmine edge; smoky nose, not giving much; tarry flavours overlay sound, ripe fruit and harmonious tannins; some new oak adds support; finishes rather short and is on the burly side. Curiously attractive, nonetheless. (15/20)
GUY BERNARD Deep garnet; attractive, almost sweet, ripe black fruit nose; spicy, smoky flavours, underpinned by very ripe, sweet fruit; mid-weight with good depth and fine length; should develop well. Very good. (16/20)
GILLES BARGE Mid black-plum, carmine rim; complex, spicy, smoky, preserved griotte-cherry nose; high-toned spicy flavours, with leather and animal components; acidity spoils wine at present but with should integrate, given time; has *puissance* but finishes short. (14+/20)
CLUSEL-ROCH *(Standard cuvée)* Limpid, virtually opaque black, deep carmine rim; nothing more than hints of ripe fruit on nose; more expressive on palate – ripe fruit and tannins combine with new oak vanillin; a complete, complex, finely-honed wine. Classy and most attractive. (17/20)
PATRICK & CHRISTOPHE BONNEFOND Deep limpid black plum; smoky, charred nose; light, weak-kneed flavours, flabby and dilute – no saving graces whatsoever. Dismal. (??10/20)
JASMIN Deepish garnet, light edge; closed nose; elegant wine, with lightish fruit encased in a balanced, round, tannic frame; long and elegant with underlying power; seems a touch insubstantial at present; more in finesse than depth. (15+/20)
DOMAINE DE BONSERINE Blackish garnet; promising, largely unforthcoming nose; ripe, long attractive flavours – griotte cherry, ripe fruit with a touch of torrefaction; on the light side; good finish, though somewhat dry edged. (15+/20)
FREDERIC BERNARD Mid-garnet – not much depth to it; attractive, elegant, red fruit nose; good, softish flavours with dry tannins; quite fleshy, though somewhat unfocussed. Lacks substance and finishes rather short. (14/20)
ANDRE FRANCOIS Mid garnet; closed nose; reduced flavours, more frame than substance and finishes short; difficult to see it going anywhere. (13/20)
PIERRE GAILLARD Firm black cherry; closed nose, though some new wood evident; sweet, ripe wood and fruit flavours; plenty of depth and good length; a substantial wine which promises to develop well. (16/20)
DELAS, *SEIGNEUR DE MAUGIRON*
Mid plum; smoky, spicy, griotte cherry and leather nose; lightish, quite elegant bright flavours; on the lean side but has a satisfying finish. Attractive, ready. (15/20)
1990 COTE-ROTIE:
J-M GERIN, *LE CHAMPIN SEIGNEUR* Limpid deepish garnet; hints of ripe *fruits noirs* on closed nose; elegant, succulent fruit finely balanced by ripe tannins and good acidity; no signs of heat; finishes long. Not a heavy-weight but has all the elements of a fine bottle in the making. (16+/20)
HENRI GALLET Extracty deep black cherry; mildly singed, tight nose; rawish green tannin nerve threatens to spoil an otherwise good wine, with sweetish fruit and some length; liquorice and spice dominate the palate at present. Rustic yet elegant! Attractive. (15/20)
JASMIN Mid-red, brick edge; soft, cooked fruit aromas; light yet plump, broad-backed wine; has reasonable length, but lacks acidity and concentration; fine for the next few years; other bottlings might be better. (15/20)
FRANCOIS GERARD Deep black cherry; aromas of new wood and *fraises des bois*; wine combines elegance and matter with a tight frame and good length. Depth, power and plenty of quality here. Should develop well over 5+ years or so. (16+/20)
J-M GERIN, *LES GRANDES PLACES* Opaque, sombre, black cherry; fine embryonic nose of super-ripe fruit and new oak; succulent, sweet, ripe elegant fruit; bags of depth and extract here. Long, powerful and complete. Great potential. Very fine indeed. (19/20)
DE BOISSEYT-CHOL Deep blackish hue, red edge; sweet, super-ripe fruit nose – v. promising; meaty, big-framed wine, with dry tannins; structure overpowers what fruit there is; lacks real depth; rustic finish. (14/20)
PATRICK AND CHRISTOPHE BONNEFOND Opaque, deep black, red-carmine edge; curious atypical aromas of garrigues and laurel; plenty of fully ripe, sweet fruit – more Grenache than Syrah in feel; long and puissant; nonetheless, attractive in its way. (16+/20)
MARCEL GUIGAL, *LA LANDONNE* Black cherry, almost to deep brick rim; big, spicy, smoky nose, heavily larded with new oak; slight volatility; massive, extracty, concentration of very ripe, sweet fruit; exceptional length, power and complexity; dominated by wood at present. Impressive, thoroughly confident wine which will need years to unpack and then last for many more (19+/20)
GAEC VERNAY *(St-Cyr)* Bright, opaque, carmine/black; reduced nose and palate; seems to have good depth of fruit, reasonable length and well-judged tannins. Could turn out very well. (15+/20)
CLUSEL ROCH *(Standard cuvée)* Opaque black cherry; big, sweetish, new oaky nose; elegant, complex, flavours from good weight of fruit – rose petal, violet, spices; plenty of depth. Long, ripe flavours – very stylish and complete. (17/20)
DOMAINE DE BONSERINE Deepish black cherry, carmine rim; singed, caramel nose; burnt, somewhat woody, flavours, with ripe, peppery fruit underneath; hottish, meat-extract feel – burly old-style, rusticity. Quite attractive, though. (15/20)
BERNARD CHAMBEYRON Translucent, mid garnet; stony, cooked red-fruit aromas; light, rather woody and dilute; lacks depth. Poor for the vintage, but drinkable. (13/20)
MARCEL GUIGAL, *LA TURQUE* Dense, opaque, black cherry; sweet, extracty oak and super-ripe fruit aromas, touch of volatility; big-framed wine, with exemplary concentration of opulent, sexy, fruit held together by firm, yet round tannins. This has everything – length, depth, complexity, power, nascent elegance and impeccable balance. (Must be a Guigal Cru!) (19++/20)
PIERRE GAILLARD Mid-deep black; new oak dominates nose; soft, lightish wine, lacking in grip and depth; what fruit there is, is stifled by new oak; good – no better. (14/20)
MARCEL GUIGAL, *LA MOULINE* Sombre, opaque, black plum; charry, chocolaty, new wood over layers of very ripe fruit; oak dominates the palate, though there is clearly more than enough balancing fruit underneath; plenty of ripe tannin, high alcohol and a long, persistent finish complete the picture. Marvellous wine in the making. (18/20)
LOUIS DREVON Deep black; reduced nose with distinct green stalky component; flavours also reduced, seems to have fair depth but lacks centre; tannins obtrude; hot feel. Not a bad wine, but needs more flesh on the bones. (15/20)
BERNARD BURGAUD Fine, opaque black cherry, carmine rim; strong, charry new oak aromas – showing hot bramble fruit underneath (very Syrah!); big framed wine with underlying elegance; clumsy tannins and dry finish threaten to spoil the balance. Evolution might possibly soften out the rough edges; could go either way. (15??/20)
CLUSEL ROCH, *LES GRANDES PLACES* Limpid deep cherry; sweet, very ripe fruit starting to show through on nose; more so on palate, where soft, new wood tannins envelop the mouth, masking the fruit underneath; long, elegant finish. Is there enough fruit for the tannin? If so, it should develop well. (16+/20)
MARCEL GUIGAL, *BRUNE ET BLONDE* Opaque, limpid, black cherry; sweet fruit aromas; elegant, very rich wine – seems to have plenty of old-vine fruit; finesse and size beautifully judged; wine has *puissance* and excellent length. Serious stuff – very fine indeed. (18+/20)
JAMET Dense, opaque, black cherry; mildly reduced nose, hints of ripe, baked fruit underneath; long, elegant flavours – plenty of depth and finesse; some new wood adds support. Excellent wine – very promising indeed. (18+/20)

BARGE

1992 COTE-ROTIE *(Lancement, en foudre)* Deep sustained purple-cherry; closed nose; spicy, firm yet silky wine; structured for medium-term.
1992 COTE-ROTIE *(Duplessis vines, en foudre)* Deeper than above, fine colour; closed nose; much better overall profile than Lancement – good depth of ripe fruit, petter and spice flavours, with more and rounder tannins and notably more *puissance*.
1991 COTE-ROTIE *(Côte Brune; wine under Pierre Barge (father) label)* Fine deep colour; spicy, ripe fruit aromas emerging; ripe spicy, *fruits noirs* flavours lifted by good acidity. Real *fond* here – long. Very attractive.
1983 COTE-ROTIE Fine deep, still youthful colour; positive, open cinnamon, spice and *sous-bois* nose; mid-weight palate with ripe, tobacco – *fruits sauvages* flavours. Long and elegant. Very good.
1978 COTE-ROTIE Fine deep red – touch of brick; opulent entirely secondary aromas – *sous-bois* with hints of torrefaction – almost old Pinot elegance; somewhat animal on the palate, lively acidity; well-knit with flavours following aromas and great length. A distinguished, silky, wine which has aged most gracefully and is now *à point*.
1971 COTE-ROTIE Marginally deeper tone; *tuilé* rim. Very rich nose – meat extract and tobacco, with a vegetal overtone; less opulent and complex than 1978. Fine long & powerful flavours; concentrated in a berryish sort of way, shorter than the 1978. Sadly Barge *Père* gave away most of Gilles' 40 bottle stock, so there are only 6 or so left. A treat!

BURGAUD

1993 COTE-ROTIE *(in cask)* Fine deep colour; high-toned, dumb, nose; highish acids over a firm, sound structure; at present somewhat green. Promising.
1993 COTE-ROTIE *(old cask - recently racked)* More depth and colour than the above; shut, smoky nose; relatively high acids again, ripish tannins and flavours of red fruits. Seems good.
1993 COTE-ROTIE *(ex new cask)* Deeper, blacker than both the above; strong oak aromas; charry wood flavours mask the wine's acidity; better structure and more complete.
1992 COTE-ROTIE Dark, limpid red; slender aromas of red fruits; mid-weight wine, attractive flavours of raspberry and summer fruit balanced by some tannins. Attractive, sound but lightish wine for the mid-term.

CHAMPET

1993 COTE-ROTIE *(bottled for the Ampuis Wine Fair)* Mid black-cherry; highly

reduced smoke and rubber nose; good meaty wine, full of succulent ripe fruit – supple, almost sweet with delicacy. Good plus.
1993 COTE-ROTIE *(in cask)* Greater depth of colour, and more fruit (cherries) on nose; solid fruit and round tannins combine to give a rich, well-structured wine – rather more of everything than the above. Very attractive.
1992 COTE-ROTIE *(old cask)* Deep, sombre tones; attractive, cherry-stone nose; meaty wine with plenty of *puissance* and good depth of structure; a bit raw, but should round out well. Excellent length and nuance. Serious stuff for 1992.
1991 COTE-ROTIE *(old cask)* Excellent, deep colour – almost black; hints of dark cherry on largely dumb nose; tight, ripe flavours – spoilt somewhat by stalky green streak; plenty of guts underneath; long and *puissant*.
1990 COTE-ROTIE *(in old cask; last racked 11/92!)* Barely translucent black cherry; big, tarry, strongly reduced nose (needs racking); similar flavours – round, full on the palate with underlying finesse and length. A bit old-fashioned, but very attractive, nonetheless.
1990 COTE-ROTIE *(bottled May 1994)* Touch more depth and much less open than the above; round, supple wine with elegance and richness supported by carefully judged tannins. Long, complete. Excellent.
1989 COTE-ROTIE, *LA VIALLIERE (Joel Champet)* Deep colour; chocolate aromas lead to firm, rich flavours underpinned by soft tannins. Mid-length finish. Very good.
1979 COTE-ROTIE Lightish, mid-garnet; mature *sous-bois* and liquorice nose; lightish, more in finesse than substance. Holding up well but needs drinking.

CLUSEL ROCH

1993 CONDRIEU *(17 hl/ha)* Fine yellow-green colour; rich, stylish floral and *fruits confits* nose; powerful, ripe succulent flavours, hint of bitterness on finish; beautifully judged oak; most attractive.
1992 CONDRIEU *(20 hl/ha)* Bright green-gold; creamy vanillin dominates nose; quite stylish but less concentration of flavour than 1993 ("we forgot to remove excess flowers"), rather short finish. Not bad though.
1993 COTE-ROTIE *(35 hl/ha, picked in rain; Champon + Viallière)* Sound plum-carmine colour; positive pepper + spice aromas; mid-weight of fruit, reasonable depth of flavour supported by tannins; fair length; seems promising.
1993 COTE-ROTIE LES GRANDES PLACES Deeper more sustained colour; closed nose; less peppery, more stuffing and *fond* than regular *cuvée*, mid-weight; has elegance and ripish tannins. Long and succulent. Good result for this difficult vintage.
1992 COTE-ROTIE *(mix of Viallière, Grandes Places and Champon – no separate Grandes Places in 1992)* Limpid, yet vibrant black cherry; lovely opening nose – pruneaux, *fruits noirs* and blackberries; wine has good depth of fruit, and excellent balance; a touch raw at present. Will develop well over medium term.
1991 COTE-ROTIE Deep black cherry; reduced nose, seems promising underneath; presents austere exterior, but has depth, richness and elegance underneath; long, ripe wine in the making, good acidity lifts flavours of pruneaux and *fruits rouges*. Should be very good indeed after 5–8 years in bottle.
1989 COTE-ROTIE LES GRANDES PLACES *(½ btl)* Superb deep, almost opaque dark plum; fine secondary nose of *sous-bois*, torrefaction and chocolate; very ripe fruit, tightly structured wine with notes of chocolate and cocoa; rather burly, yet long with 5+ years to go to soften out fully. A good but not top 1989.

DUBOEUF

1993 VIOGNIER, *Vin de Pays de l'Ardeche* Bright mid-straw; tight, stony-peachy nose; dry, earthy, Viognier flavours, good middle palate and length. Somewhat four-square, but attractive with strongly varietal character.
1991 COTE-ROTIE *(13% alcohol)* Fine, barely translucent Victoria plum; closed, sombre nose; fleshy, mouthfilling flavours, good depth of silky fruit, virtually no tannin to shed; spicy, peppery and very satisfying. Not the structure to age, but attractive now and for next 5 years. Very good.
1990 COTE-ROTIE Sustained deep plum; elegant, if somewhat hot and burnt nose, open, forward; plush, fleshy wine, good depth, round tannins and sound acidity; ready now, drink over next 5 years. Rich and satisfying.

GENTAZ-DERVIEUX

1993 COTE-ROTIE *(cask sample)* Light strawberry; elegant peppery nose; good fleshy attack; moderate richness, plenty of mache; peppery/spicy flavours. Has structure to develop well. Long, promising.
1992 COTE-ROTIE *(cask sample)* Deep limpid translucent black cherry – fine colour; ripe concentrated *fruits noirs* nose – *griottes* and *pruneaux* with pepper overtones; a powerful, complex mouthful of pure, uncluttered fruit, overlaying considerable elegance and subtlety; a really lovely wine in the making for the medium-term; one of the best of the vintage.
1991 COTE-ROTIE *(last bottling – winter 1993)* Immense opaque black hue; smoky, ripe complex aromas of cocoa, chocolate, liquorice – a long way to develop; substantial, powerful and meaty wine; good grip, highish tannin and acidity; flavours of very ripe black fruits – blackberry in particular. Great vinosity. 7–10 years to go before this should be touched. Very fine.

GERIN

1993 COTE-ROTIE, *LE CHAMPIN SEIGNEUR* Bright mid-deep dark cherry, purple rim; closed, smoky nose; tightish frame, firm fruit; good length and completeness; promising.
1993 COTE-ROTIE, *LES GRANDES PLACES* Fine dark, yet bright, translucent tone; smoky nose, griottes cherry, largely closed; ripe, sweet fruit, underneath envelope of new wood; more fruit, length and concentration than Champin.
1992 COTE-ROTIE, *LE CHAMPIN SEIGNEUR* Red purple, carmine edge; interesting nose of warm brioche & bacon; sweet, soft plummy flavours, meaty focussed fruit, ripe, long, most attractive. Well balanced in tannin yet supple and forward. Drink over next 5 years. Excellent for vintage.
1992 COTE-ROTIE, *LES GRANDES PLACES* Marginally deeper than Le Champin; sweet tarry nose, with sappy, eucalyptus contribution from new wood; on palate both more elegance and more concentration than the above. Soft, complete wine; fine length and *fond*. Delicious now, but much more expressive in 5+ years.

GUIGAL

1992 CONDRIEU Bright yellow-green; super-ripe, almost botrytised floral/acacia aromas; some gas; ripe, powerfully structured flavours, dominated by new oak; a bit short, but otherwise very attractive.
1991 HERMITAGE BLANC Bright yellow-gold; complex aromas of lime-blossom, honey and new oak; big, firmly structured wine with dry strawish flavours; lacks flesh and charm. Will develop – but will it improve?
1991 COTES DU RHONE *(50% Grenache; 25% each Syrah & Mourvèdre)* Deep plum; earthy largely closed nose; high acid attack leads to mid-weight wine with a lean envelope; not bad, but not a patch on the 1990.
1990 COTES DU RHONE Youthful, almost opaque plum; deep, brooding earthy nose; complex, well structured wine; Syrah and Mourvèdre adding richness and grip. Needs 5–10 years to show its paces. Concentrated, excellent.
1990 GIGONDAS *(53% Grenache; 35% Mourvèdre; 12% Syrah)* Good colour; hot, dry nose; austere, very dry palate; lacks flesh and succulence; strong burnt aspect. Too long in wood; drying out.
1990 CHATEAUNEUF DU PAPE *(14.5% alc)* Deep, limpid tone, carmine rim; closed nose, *pruneaux* & *fruits noirs*; uncompromisingly big, muscular wine – mouthfilling yet with touch of bitterness; again, lacks flesh – 4+ years in wood had dessicated it.
1990 HERMITAGE ROUGE Deep, extracty, virtually black wine; just starting to open out – preserved cherries and ripe cassis; palate shows similar concentrated flavours; long, powerful. Real depth here. Very good.
1990 COTE-ROTIE BRUNE ET BLONDE *(4–5% Viognier)* Mid deep black cherry, carmine rim; lovely, elegant evolving nose – raspberry, blackcurrant, blackberry and violets; substantial wine with great finesse and fine concentration with a hint of the heat of the vintage underneath; long flavours with note of animal. Plenty of wine here. Its balance will keep it for years. Excellent.
1990 COTE-ROTIE, *LA MOULINE* Opaque, massively deep colour; dense carmine edge; nose and palate dominated by new wood; deep, super-rich flavours of griotte cherry, oak, and concentrated fruit; exemplary length with some of the Mouline elegance starting to emerge. Remarkable wine. Needs 15 years at least.
1990 COTE-ROTIE, *LA TURQUE* As deep as Mouline, but marginally brighter black; more expressive nose – black fruit conserve, some elegance; yet more depth and richness, noticeably charry; extra-ordinary concentration and great length. Splendidly impressive. Needs 15+ years.
1990 COTE-ROTIE, *LA LANDONNE* Equally dense, limpid, black cherry; fine appearance; rich, opulent nose – black cherries; tighter, more charry flavours, liquorice, blackcurrant and *pruneaux*; very, very ripe, concentrated and long. Will be wonderful; needs a generation.
1983 COTE-ROTIE, *LA MOULINE* Mid deep carmine; dark cherry edge; positive, youthful roasted nose; tight, spicy, leathery flavours – layer of new wood makes its difficult to evaluate; firm tannic backbone, yet soft underneath; reasonable length.
1983 COTE-ROTIE, *LA LANDONNE* Much greater depth of red-black; closed, slightly medicinal nose; immense power on palate, firm, tightly corseted fruit; flavours still masked by wood. Clearly very fine indeed.
1982 COTE-ROTIE, *LA MOULINE* Mid-deep; less brown than '83 Mouline; gorgeous, *rotie* nose, showing oak and elegant fruit aromas; fine ripe, sweet, fruit; immense, restrained power; incredible length and well-nigh perfect balance. Quite fabulous.
1982 COTE-ROTIE, *LA LANDONNE* Magnificent, deep, silky robe, deep brick rim; powerful, extracty, closed nose; very promising indeed; similar massive, structured ripe profile as Mouline, but still tighter; fine, round tannins. A wine of enormous depth and finesse, just waiting to explode.
1978 COTE-ROTIE, *LA MOULINE* Deep, limpid appearance, high extract; gorgeous, ripe, complex nose – mint and blackcurrant; very ripe, full and complex spectrum of flavours with incredible length. Not really Côte-Rôtie, but extra-ordinary, fine, Syrah. Majestic, magnificent wine, with years of life ahead.
1978 COTE-ROTIE, *LA LANDONNE* Still black, no signs of age; reduced, aromas, closed; mouthfilling, heavily extracted flavours; immense complexity, length driven by super-ripe fruit. A magical wine – with everything going for it. At this level of quality, words are inadequate.

JAMET

1993 COTE-ROTIE *(various lots in cask/demi-muids)* Range of colours deepening with vine age and cooperage, press wine the deepest; non-destemmed lots tended to have less nose than destemmed; new casks showed sweet oak which sustained the fruit well; overall mid-weight with reasonable depth of flavour and enough tannins for moderate ageing. Seems a promising if not over-rich.
1992 COTE-ROTIE *(30 hl/ha)* Limpid dark plum; smoky liquorice and fruits noirs aromas, reduced; good fleshy flavours, supple round tannins, good acid-alcohol balance; fair length. Quite firm. Promising for mid-term drinking.
1991 COTE-ROTIE Limpid dark cherry; similar aromas to 1992 but more intense and evolved; notes of cassis and mures starting to emerge; lively acidity sustaining firm, fresh, complex flavours.Will be most attractive in 3–8 years and has excellent ageing potential.
1987 COTE-ROTIE Fine dark colour; open secondary aromas – *sous-bois* in particular; reminiscent of old Pinot Noir; ripe stylish, fleshy wine with real depth and richness – griottes cherry and *mures*; Long, attractive wine – little signs of oxidation suggest a good balance. Excellent for vintage.
1985 COTE-ROTIE Limpid dark cherry; big up-front animal nose – distinctly *renarde* – fur and torrefaction. Over time nose evolved to *sous-bois* and *mures*. Very ripe fruit, plenty of fat and richness sustained by good acidity. Not the quality of 1991, but silky and seductive, none the less. Very good.

JASMIN

1993 COTE-ROTIE *(ex-cask)* Delicate strawberry colour; clean, lightish peppery nose, hint of herbace; lifted peppery syrah flavours with strong elements of Pinot strawberry, a bit green on the finish. Finesse rather than substance. Good, not great.
1992 COTE-ROTIE *(ex-cask)* Sustained deep strawberry; more stuffing on nose than 1993, with a note of verdure; bigger tighter wine with firmer tannins and more succulent fruit underneath. Distinctly more to it than the 1993.
1991 COTE-ROTIE *(ex-cask)* Still more colour; lifted peppery nose, touch of

green-ness; silky, puissant plavours, good depth of fruit, long, fine. Note of *rafle* bitterness on finish. Good though – to very good.

OGIER

1993 COTE-ROTIE (*rough assemblage of new, 1st & older cask samples*) Fine limpid velvet plum; spicy, peppery nose; ripe succulent mid-weight wine, plenty of mache and rondeur; a bit short; lightish.

1993 LA ROSINE, *Vin de Pays Syrah* (*new and old cask assemblage*) Open less dense on nose than above; soft, supple, juicy fruit style of Syrah; less complex, but attractive (especially at 45 francs retail TTC)

1992 COTE-ROTIE Limpid dark plum; opulent nose – albeit a touch reduced, showing ripe *fruits noirs* and liquorice; complex; quite burly mouthfeel, but ripe and stylish underneath, succulent, elegant. Good wine.

1991 COTE-ROTIE Deep, almost opaque dark garnet; very rich bud of *fruits noirs* and *griottes* cherries; long, subtle wine with complexity and excellent balance; not heavy-framed, but all in finesse.

1991 LA ROSINE, *Vin de Pays, Syrah* Marginally denser than 1991 Côte-Rôtie; fine intense smoky aromas of super-ripe fruit starting to show; silky, soft ripe fruit flavours, shorter and less well-defined than its grander brother. A fine Vin de Pays, nonetheless.

DE VALLOUIT

1993 CONDRIEU (*cask; malo in progress*) Good yellow, rather flat, peachy nose; fresh flavours somewhat flattened by malo; high acidity; elegant. Seems good.

1992 CONDRIEU (*cask*) Lightish colour; open, honeyed, atypical aromas; fat, well-structued wine with power and length. Fine.

1993 CONDRIEU (*other lot already bottled*) Limpid, light green; good peachy nose, without elegance of cask sample; still some CO_2 partially masking a wine of moderate weight in the lighter style; dry finish; well-balanced, but lacks concentration.

1992 VIOGNIER (*Côtes du Rhone, from vines in Côte Rozier, Côte-Rôtie*) More yellow than 1993 Condrieu; aromas more stony than floral; rather dry, mineral flavour. Good.

1987 VIOGNIER (*Côtes du Rhône – provenance as above*) Deep mid-yellow; lovely opulent straw and honey nose; deep, ripe wine, still a touch of gas adding freshness; flavours of cooked bread. Long and very fine. Delicious!

1993 HERMITAGE BLANC (*5% Roussanne; cask sample; no malo*) Good colour; straw, hay and wheatmeal nose – greengages; tightly corseted wine with reasonable depth of fruit and good acidity. Seems rather four-square at present. Might develop well.

1993 COTES DU RHONE (*Rouge; 60–70% GR; 10% SY; rest CINS & MO; negoce wine*) Light strawberry; soft, quaffer. Respectable, no more.

1993 VIN DU PAYS, *SYRAH* Light, but vibrant purple-carmine; reduced nose; clean, spicy, lightish wine. Excellent balance. Good – needs keeping.

1991 CROZES HERMITAGE, *CHATEAU DE LARNAGE* (*Cask sample; 1.5 ha. of 40–50 yr. old vines, en Côteau; 7–8000 bottles made*) Mid-limpid black plum; spicy nose; a bit one-dimensional at present but has depth and promise. Will benefit from several years bottle ageing. Bottled wine had fair length, but was spoiled by stemminess on nose and palate, and a dry, fleshless feel.

1991 ST-JOSEPH, *LES ANGES* (*Cask sample; 50 yr. old vines above Hospice de Tournon*) Deeper than the above; firm, stony nose – almost diesel in character; long, fine flavours underpinned by good structure. Finishes with a touch of bitterness. Needs bottling.

1989 ST-JOSEPH LES ANGES (*in bottle*) Bright, deep garnet; dry, open fungal/vegetal nose and flavour; tight structure, lacks centre and tails off. Too long in cask.

1991 COTE-ROTIE (*Cask sample, standard cuvée from 25–30 yr. old vines; incl. 5% Viognier*) Mid limpid plum; fine, attractive and elegant cassis/ raspberry nose; mid-weight wine, slightly singed flavours. Succulent and very long. Fine.

1991 COTE-ROTIE, *LES ROZIERS* (*Cask sample; 50 yr. old vines*) Similar hue to the above; completely closed nose and reduced palate. Has excellent structure and *puissance*. Needs racking!

1993 HERMITAGE, *LES GREFFIERES* (*Cask sample; 80–90 yr. old vines*) Limpid, translucent, mid plum; giving nothing on nose; silky wine – finesse rather than size here; good tannin structure. Promising.

1992 HERMITAGE, *LES GREFFIERES* (*Cask sample*) Deeper and darker than the 1993; fine spice & violets nose; good concentration of fruit and ripe tannins; silky; long. Plenty of elegance, but not a heavyweight. Very good.

1991 HERMITAGE, *LES GREFFIERES* (*Cask sample*) Even deeper; brooding coffee and chocolate nose; tight, powerful wine, long,supple with fine cohesive structure. Very promising.

1990 CORNAS, *LE MEDIEVALE* Fine deep black plum; tight, complex aromas, starting to unpack; dense-flavoured wine, with firm but not aggressive tannins, succulent fruit and real fond. Years of life ahead. Brilliant Cornas.

1974 HERMITAGE (*Cask sample*) Light, browning red; light, but still sound on nose and palate; *fané*, a bit old and leathery; fruit still holding up but wine starting to maderise. Unexpectedly together after 20 years in cask!

VIDAL FLEURY

1993 COTES DU RHONE BLANC Mid yellow-straw; clean fresh aromas, elegant Viognier contirbution; Appley, zingy flavours, fresh fruity wine with straw finish.

1992 CONDRIEU Lively light yellow-gold; cinnamon and peach aromas; good rich mouthfiller, with broad peach-kernel flavours. Long, powerful mouth-feel, dry finish. Good.

1990 COTES DU RHONE ROUGE Bright deep ruby; plummy, slightly reduced nose; mix of plummy Grenache and tarry Mourvèdre flavours. Mid-weight, well-structured. Good depth and tannins; needs 3–5 years to unpack.

1990 CROZES HERMITAGE (*6 months in foudres then in cuve*) Limpid dark red-cherry; closed, reduced nose; rather flabby, soapy on palate edge; has depth, ripe tannins and good fruit, but dried out. Short finish. Lacks focus and typicity. OK, no better.

1990 COTE-ROTIE BRUNE ET BLONDE (*100% own vines incl. 5% Viognier; 1 yr. in pieces 18 months in foudres*) Bright translucent dark garnet; close nose, hints

---

of smoky griottes cherries; Burly exterior, elegance showing underneath a big, dry frame. Has length and underlying suppleness. How will it evolve?

1990 COTE-ROTIE, *LA CHATILLONNE* (*15% Viognier*) Similar appearance to above; Viognier clearly contributes to more elegant and complex aromas; mid-weight of fruit – tannins are much more in balance here and noticeably more fondu. A distinct notch up on the B & B. Drink over medium term.

1992 MUSCAT DE BEAUMES DE VENISE (*cuvée assembled from bought in wine*) Deepish mandarin orange; seductive nose of orange and old-fashioned rose; firm, biggish version of the genre; fine quality. Most attractive.

CONDRIEU

1992 CONDRIEU, CLUSEL ROCH (*half bottle sample*) Turbid light citrus; more than a whiff of sulphur on nose, masking fruit peel aromas; dry mouthfeel and rather dirty finish. Poor sample – have had much better. (Better sample would score 17+/20)

1992 CONDRIEU, LOUIS CHEZE (*half bottle*) Bright, light gold; firm, positive, apricot nose gives onto tight, firm fruit, with sweetish centre and good length. A sturdy wine which needs time to develop. Good plus. (16/20)

1992 CONDRIEU, JEAN-YVES MULTIER (*2nd wine of Château du Rozay*) Good appearance, very little aroma; clean, fresh-tasting light flavours; austere, dry finish. Insubstantial. (12/20)

1992 CONDRIEU, VIDAL FLEURY Deepish colour; rich, open, almost *surmature* nose; fino, long, eatery-peachy flavours; good acidity. Short finish. Not bad at all. (15/20)

1992 CONDRIEU, YVES CUILLERON Light green-gold; open nose and delicate, peachy flavours; good acidity and excellent balance. Lightish, but fine, with some length. (14/20)

1992 CONDRIEU, PHILIPPE PICHON Clean colour; rather neutral nose; light, crisp peachy flavours; short, green finish; lacks substance. (13/20)

1992 CONDRIEU, COTEAU CHERY, NIERO-PINCHON Good colour; richish varietal aromas and soft, mid-weight flavour; good acidity; has depth, some power and good length. A fine 1992. (16/20)

1992 CONDRIEU, CHATEAU DU ROZAY, JEAN-YVES MULTIER Light colour, unforthcoming nose; clean and strongly varietal flavours are overlaid with some CO_2; good balance and some depth; has short finish and leanness of the vintage. Not bad, though. (15/20)

1992 CONDRIEU, COTEAUX DU CHERY, ANDRE PERRET Mid gold, positive, open, poachy nose, some CO_2, clean flavours, dry edge, good presence and some power and length. A good 1992. (16/20)

1992 CONDRIEU, GEORGES VERNAY Light colour, elegant nose; wine emphasises elegance rather than concentration. Fresh, clean, attractive. (15/20)

1992 CONDRIEU, PAUL JABOULET AINE Mid yellow; nothing much on nose; dry, rather weakish flavour, somewhat oxidative; lacks concentration and typicity. (12/20)

1992 CONDRIEU, DELAS Mid-light colour, slender nose; fresh, slight Viognier flavours, some elegance but lacks real depth. Not bad for vintage. (14/20)

1992 CONDRIEU, PIERRE GAILLARD Lightish, clean colour; open, peachy nose; fresh, attractive wine, with some power and crisp acidity; dry, mildly tannic edge; stony flavours; good but lacks flesh. (14/20)

1992 CONDRIEU, COTEAUX DU COLOMBIER, DEZORMEAUX Clean, light appearance, dry gassy nose; cardboardy flavours – poor (have had better bottles of this wine).

1992 CONDRIEU, CHAPOUTIER Deepish, yellow-green; positive, spicy nose and flavour; some depth and well balanced; good, but as with many 1992, lacks charm and *ampleur*. (14/20)

1992 CONDRIEU, GUIGAL Bright yellow-green; super-ripe, almost botrytised floral/acacia aromas; some gas; ripe, powerfully structured flavours, dominated by new oak; a bit short, but otherwise very attractive. (16+/20)

CUILLERON

1993 CONDRIEU Good fresh colour; attractive, positive, open peach and fresh apricot nose – fine and aromatic; lightish sappy flavours, good acidity, quite fat and stony; fresh, yet mouthfilling. Well-crafted, elegant.

1993 CONDRIEU, LES CHAILLETS (*old vines*) Marginally deeper than the above, evident extract; much stronger, richer, aromas dominated by oak and pear skins; tighter, more structured wine than the standard *cuvée*; powerful and full with excellent balance and length. Needs time to open out.

1993 CONDRIEU, *RECOLTE TARDIVE* Attractive deep green-yellow gold; nose dominated by botrytis; gorgeous, ripe peachy flavours, medium sweetness; fresh acidity. Delicious now but should evolve well over a year or two. Fine.

DEZORMEAUX

1992 CONDRIEU, *COTEAUX DU COLOMBIER* Bright lemon juice colour; easy fruit driven nose; fullish attractive peachy and fresh apricot flavours, good *puissance* and depth. Fair length. A bit 4-square, though good for the vintage. Drink over next 2 years.

DUMAZET

1992 CONDRIEU Bright yellow-citrus; positive peach/spice aromas; full, miildly spicy wild flavour; quite fat with depth and fair length; well balanced; good indeed for vintage which it reflects.

1991 CONDRIEU Yellow-green, bright; spicy opulent nose, hints of peach kernels and almond; (spice is a characteristic of Limony Viognier); ripe opulent wine, fleshy, succulent and puissant. A really lovely bottle – now or for the next 5 years or so.

1991 COTES DU RHONE VIOGNIER Bright green-gold; smoky open nose – fruits secs; spicy rich wine, not the sheer power of the Condrieu, but mouthfilling and long. Touch of rusticity and shortness on finish shows up its AC; but this would outpace many a Condrieu proper. Very fine, especially as a CDR. (This vineyard is just below Condrieu limits, and has similar soil).

1991 CONDRIEU, *COTE FOURNET* (*13%*) Fine yellow colour; good extract,

viscious; complex developing nose of honey, almond and *fruits confits*; biggish powerful palate; plenty of fat and almost sweet fruit; good balance of alcohol and acids; long, ripe, complete.
1990 COTES DU RHONE VIOGNIER, *VENDANGES TARDIVE 15 OCTOBER 14% alcohol* Mid yellow; attractive spicy nose; *fruits confits*; acacia; v.rich surmature flavours, Chardonnay in character except for dry edge; long, complete wine; fine; remarkable for a CDR.
1989 CONDRIEU, *COTE FOURNET* Brilliant yellow-green; secondary aromas emerging – cinnamon and clove in particular; lovely soft, puissant flavour; ripe and spicy; not a big wine, all in secondary elegance. Lost some spice in glass and changed to fruits confits and "agrumes". Very complex and complete wine.

GAILLARD

1993 ST-JOSEPH, BLANC *4 yr old vines, 9 hl/ha (rain & 3 hail storms)* Deepish light green; oak dominates nose; ripe, quite fat wine, quince flavours; good stylish wine. Excellent for this difficult vintage.
1993 VIN DE PAYS, *VIOGNIER* Lightish colour; fine, *fruits confits* nose; succulent, mouthfiller; plenty of sap and structure. Very good indeed for appellation.
1993 COTES DU RHONE, *VIOGNIER CLOS DE CUMINAILLES* Light green-straw; unforthcoming nose; rich flavours of *fruits confits* – pineapple; highish acidity; well-judged wood, noticeable both on nose and palate; needs a year or two. Very good.
1993 CONDRIEU More yellow than the above; elegant *fruits confits* nose; powerfully structured wine; spice and quince, with long ripe finish. Very rich and concentrated. Excellent, one of the best of the vintage.
1992 ST-JOSEPH, ROUGE Bright garnet; curiously oily, smoky, coal-dust nose; green *goût de rafle* spoils palate, wine is supple with plenty of guts underneath. Pity. A second bottle, made with more wood *élévage* was fleshier with less of the green edge.
1991 ST-JOSEPH, ROUGE Deep, sombre black cherry; strong liquorice element on nose; a fat, seductive wine with real *fond*; touch of rafle, happily stifled by fruit. Excellent, very rich for a St-Joseph. Fine.
1989 COTE-ROTIE Deepish translucent black cherry; Smoky, open, cerises nose; which developed a chocolate tone; Good structure, mid-weight Côte-Rôtie, supple but on the light side. Not great, but respectable and interesting.
1990 COTE-ROTIE Colour as 1989; dry green aromas – distinct touch of heat; hint of torrefaction and chocolate on nose; Dry-edged, lightish wine, high acidity. 1989 is altogether more attractive and better structured.

GRILLET

1992 CHATEAU GRILLET Mid yellow-straw; rich, honeyed nose; medium weight of fruit, with flavours of acacia honey; starting to develop finesse. Although it lacks the depth and concentration for top-class and to a certain extent reflects the vintage, the wine has *puissance* and is attractive. Good indeed.

NIERO-PINCHON

1993 CONDRIEU (quartier *Roncharde*) Mid yellow-straw; fine, ripe, pear-peel nose; round, elegant wine with fat and suppleness; finishes a bit flat, but good all the same.
1993 CONDRIEU (quartier *Chery*) Limpid yellow-straw, good extract; dumb nose and flat taste; suffering from recent bottling. Retaste.
1990 CONDRIEU *(14% alcohol)* Fine, bright, green-gold; very stylish, almondy nose; rich, powerful peely flavours, long, fat and complex, backed by well-judged acidity; has some CO_2 which adds to freshness and helps hide the alcohol. Very attractive.

PERRET

1993 CONDRIEU, *CLOS CHANSON (in cask – second wine)* Green-gold; oak aromas dominate; flashes of fruits sec and pineapple; CO_2 – wood mask real character; has *puissance* and depth. Promising.
1993 CONDRIEU, *CLOS CHANSON (older cask)* More yellow in tone; less wood & more fruit on nose, closed; CO_2 again; greater richness and fat; good acidity.
1993 CONDRIEU, *COTEAU DE CHERY (old cask)* Deepish colour, touch hazy; dumb nose, hints of *fruits sec*; big ripe, stylish wine, bags of fruit with *puissance* and *gras*. Good acidity; succulent flavours. More depth and character than the Chanson. Most promising.
1993 CONDRIEU, *COTEAU DE CHERY (50+ yr. old vines) 13.5% alc* More obvious depth and viscosity than above; more *fruits confits* than sec, but unforthcoming as yet; CO_2 again; palate shows fat and puissant, with fine depth of fruit, good length and well-judged balance. Really lovely wine in the making. Old vine lack of acidity. This will be assembled with the rest – what a pity!
1992 CONDRIEU, *CLOS CHANSON* Fine, bright green-gold; delicate, positive, open & concentrated fruit sec nose; mid-weight, quite powerful; not over-concentrated but very attractive; long dryish finish. Good for vintage. Drink over next 2–3 years.
1992 CONDRIEU, *VENDANGE TARDIVE (5 October) 13% alc.* Lively, vibrant, mid-deep yellow-green; hint of botrytis dominates nose – underneath agrumes, pineapple. Ripe releve flavours, candied peel, firm yet restrained; power rather than richness. Lean muscular wine. Taut, yet fine.
1990 CONDRIEU, *VENDANGE TARDIVE (15 October; 15.2% alc.)* Marginally greener in hue than 1992 VT; distinct botrytis on nose (grapes were chestnut coloured at harvest); aromas of *fruits confits*, but not typical Viognier in style; flavours of acacia and honey; deep, powerful wine (far more so than 1992) but lacks 1992's elegance – yet! Altogether fatter and richer. Will outpace 1992 by a long way. Needs 5 further years in bottle. Deliciously seductive.

PICHON

1993 CONDRIEU *(in epoxy resin tank; 13.1% alcohol)* Light colour with green glint; perfumed floral and dried apricot nose; good acidity and length. Elegant, but insubstantial.
1993 CONDRIEU *(first crop from young Mève vines)* Lightish colour; nose more floral than fruit-based; flavours the reverse, more fruit and depth than the above;

highish acidity gives a hard mouth-feel.
1992 CONDRIEU *(13% alcohol)* Light citrus-green, good extract; clean, youthful fermentive nose; elegant ripe-yet-unripe pear-skin flavours; mid-weight of fruit and fine palate aromas; well-made and attractive; somewhat evanescent.
1991 CONDRIEU Fine, brilliant, mid green-yellow; complex aromas of candied peel, preserved pineapple and acacia; another elegant wine, with tight acidity and a dry envelope; some power and persistence, but finishes short. A touch more concentration would make all the difference.
1990 CONDRIEU Greener in colour than 1991; curious cheesy, farmyardy nose which re-appears on the palate and has little to do with Viognier; wine is flabby, lacking definition and grip. Very poor.
1991 CONDRIEU MOELLEUX *(13.5% alcohol)* Mid yellow-green; soft quince-like nose (more Vouvray than Condrieu); attractive, fleshy flavours, medium-sweet and long; spoilt by disagreeable note of rancio and short finish. A pity.

ROZAY

1992 CONDRIEU Bright light green-tinged straw; elegant pear-skin aromas which follows through to palate – clean, fresh somewhat estery wine; with some power and fair length. Not a big wine, but correct and good for the vintage.
1992 CONDRIEU, *CHATEAU DU ROZAY* Deep lemon-juice, green-tinged; mildly fermentive aromas, with much more power and peachy depth than the above; fuller and richer on the palate; good intensity and acidity; lacks dimension of complexity but is attractive, with old vines contributing balance and depth.

VERNAY

1992 CONDRIEU *(13.5% alc.)* Mid yellow-straw; direct open peach and fruits sec nose, not young fruit/floral aroma, noticeable SO_2; balanced fat and acidity, peach-kernel flavours, moderate length, combined SO_2 on finish – 1992's needed higher sulphur. Good for the vintage.
1992 LES CHAILLEES DE L'ENFER *(13.5% alc.)* First release Bright, light citrus-green; *fruits sec* and peach kernels on nose, more sombre less lively open fruit nose of generic Condrieu; guts and *puissance* on palate, dry almondy edge. Clearly alcoholic but not without charm; bit short; needs food and 3–5 years ageing.
1991 CONDRIEU Light yellow-straw; attractive complex floral – acacia nose; fullish dryish peachy flavours – more rondeur, gras, length & structure than 1992.
1991 COTEAU DE VERNON *Mise – early 1994* Marginally deeper yellow than above; dumb, closed nose; good acidity and rich fullish palate; completeness allied to *puissance*. Long, ripe with warm finish. Needs at least 3–5 years before drinking. Seems very promising.

CROZES HERMITAGE

BELLE

1992 CROZES HERMITAGE *(Blanc)* Bright light citrus; clean peachy, fresh apricot, floral nose; tight mid-weight palate, some richness with balancing acidity; dry finish; stylish, although rather four-square. Needs 3–5 years.
1992 HERMITAGE *(Blanc) (Soils: clay and galets)* Deeper than the Crozes – more canary yellow; positive, most attractive, perfumed nose – *oranges confits*, almost Viognier in character; apricot flavours, quite broad and structured; underlying power but low acidity and short finish compromise development.
1992 CROZES HERMITAGE, *LES PIERRELLES (Rouge)* Limpid deep plum; distinctly stemmy nose; green, almost stale tobacco flavours, though without bitterness or stalkiness; underneath, good, supple, ripe fruit. No great charm at present, but has structure to age. How will it turn out? Not bad.
1992 CROZES HERMITAGE, *CUVEE LOUIS BELLE* Deeper, denser than the above; closed nose, new wood evident; most flesh, depth and power and guts than Pierrelles; clean, precise wine. Well made, but rather four-square. 4–6 years to soften out.

CHAVE

1993 CROZES HERMITAGE *(Blanc, in tank)* Slight yellow tint; soft white peach aromas; residual CO_2; touch of nuttiness; complex fruit, dry, straw-like finish. Good, but lacks grip.
1993 CROZES HERMITAGE *(Blanc, new Allier cask)* More yellow than above; nose of vanillin, lead pencils; wood dominates soft ripe fruit; again, needs more grip.
1992 CROZES HERMITAGE *(Blanc, in bottle)* Good yellow-green; very ripe, opulent aromas, surmature – strongly redolent of an Alsatian Tokay VT; earthy, supple flavours; fine; most agreeable, but atypical Crozes.
1993 CROZES HERMITAGE *(Rouge, cuve)* Light mid-strawberry; hint of stems on nose; exuberantly fruity, ripe, sweet wine – balanced and stylish; enough tannin to keep it going for several years. Seems good.
1992 CROZES HERMITAGE *(Rouge, vat)* Limpid mid-plum; singed aromas, vegetal and *pruneaux* elements; ripe, fleshy, touch of bitterness; warm feel; quite good but a bit short.
1992 CROZES HERMITAGE *(Rouge, bottle)* Bright deep plum, carmine rim; reduced, closed nose, note of asparagus; substantial, supple wine, good balance of fruit and tannin; very good; needs 4–6 years; like Bernard – a big softy.
1991 CROZES HERMITAGE *(Rouge)* Good limpid, mid-deep plum; lovely silky mineral/*pruneaux* nose; soft, concentrated, sexy wine, not big-framed, but very flatteur; excellent length and depth. Gorgeous.
1992 HERMITAGE Limpid plum, good sustained robe; reduced nose; more depth, fruit and structure than the 1992 Crozes; gutsy wine; ripish. Needs 4–7 years.

GRAILLOT

1990 CROZES- HERMITAGE BLANC Bright, fine, citrus-green; positive, open nose, plenty of nuance – floral, acacia, almonds; mid-weight with powerful honeyed almost succulent fruit; sappy. In transition from primary to secondary character. Complex and most attractive.

1993 CROZES-HERMITAGE ROUGE *(in cask)* Deep, limpid, black plum; strong aromas of spice and milled pepper; lightish, clean, well structured wine; good stuffing and some complexity. Well balanced. Should develop attractively.
1992 CROZES-HERMITAGE Deep black plum, lake rim; elegant, spicy notes, violets and black fruit aromas; earthy, minerally flavours; broad-shouldered wine with underlying finesse and grainy edge. Needs 3–5 years. Good plus.
1992 CROZES-HERMITAGE LA GUIRAUDE Denser; smoky, tarry aromas with hints of violets and *griotte* cherries; much richer and more concentrated than the above; firm, round tannins complete a balanced wine needing 5 years to open out.
1991 HERMITAGE *(2 casks only made)* Deep, limpid dark plum, carmine edge; foxy nose gave way to forest fruits; supple, silky, cherryish flavours – good length and depth; tannins starting to meld. Somewhat four-square, but a wine that should develop well.

GRIVES

1993 CROZES HERMITAGE *(ROUGE)* Light ruby; positive, bright, fresh pepper nose; straightforward primeur style of wine, soft, fruity, peppery. For early drinking.
1993 CROZES HERMITAGE, *CLOS DES GRIVES* Deeper, better colour altogether, weakish edge; closed neutral nose; prlum wine with some depth and succulence; good for the vintage.
1992 CROZES HERMITAGE *(ROUGE)* Mid plum; good open *pruneaux* nose; plummy flavour with touch of greenness; quite sturdy, verging on the rustic; a bit one-dimensional and hollow. Not quite as bad a this sounds!
1992 CROZES HERMITAGE, *CLOS DES GRIVES (30% new wood)* Bright, mid plum; nose marked by new wood, good fruit underneath; supple, attractive flavours, with excellent depth of fruit; wood presently dominates; long and *puissant*. Very good for the vintage.

PAVILLON

1992 CROZES HERMITAGE *(Blanc)* Green-tinged citrus; most unusual, yet attractive floral aromas redolent of young Riesling; firm acidity, quite fat; atypical Crozes, but delicious.
1992 CROZES HERMITAGE *(young vines)* Mid red; nose of red fruits dominated by torrefaction; high acid, very animal flavours – *renardé*. Not especially attractive. (Note: no V.V. in 1992; a dealcoholising organisms affected the entire crop).
1991 CROZES HERMITAGE, *PAVILLON (VIEILLE VIGNES)* Similar deep tones to 1990 – perhaps a shade lighter; black cherry/griottes nose, equally promising. More elegance and finesse than 1990, underpinned by dense, ripe fruit. Good acidity which needs time to integrate. Long. Fine, complete wine with real *fond*.
1990 CROZES HERMITAGE, *PAVILLON (VIEILLE VIGNES)* FIne, deep virtually opaque black sherry; deep, very promising, black fruit nose; full, silky wine, plenty of mache, good length, warm finish. Not at all rustic, or burly. Excellent.
1989 CROZES HERMITAGE VIEILLE VIGNES *(Bordeaux bottle)* Deepish limpid dark red; darm smoky, almost Cabernet Sauvignon nose; big extracty wine, succulent, plenty of stuffing; just a hint of stems; fine tannin-acid-fruit balance. Long. Very good.

ROURE

1991 CROZES HERMITAGE *(Blanc)* Yellow green; oxidising nose – nuts and honey; lovely, big, fleshy wine -supple and complete; depth and finesse, with noticeable alcohol and power. Fine now, but how will it develop?
1991 CROZES HERMITAGE *(Rouge)* Deepish black plum; ripe fruit nose, marred by touch of volatile acidity; big, extracty, fleshy wine, with excellent structure and depth; unexpressive at present, but with finely-tuned balance and complex flavours of *griotte*-cherry and *pruneaux*. The VA is the only off-note.
NV ROSE *(not sold, but made from saignée of old vines)* Deep *pelure d'oignon*; full white wine structure and flavour; plenty of fruit and depth; long, rich, good. A delicious curiosity.

HERMITAGE

CHAPOUTIER

1993 CONDRIEU Dull, citrussy green; tight dried fruit, pink grapefruit nose; big, rather burly wine with estery flavours; lacks grip and length.
1992 CONDRIEU Bright yellow green-gold; ripe, dried fruit aromas; mid-weight wine with apricot flavours and dry finish. Good plus, especially for this vintage.
1993 HERMITAGE BLANC, *CHANTE ALOUETTE (100% Marsanne)* Fine light green-gold; citrus (grape-fruit) nose; pear-skin flavour from sound, ripe, fruit; well-structured, with some wood tannin. Promising.
1991 HERMITAGE BLANC, *CHANTE ALOUETTE (33% new oak)* Fine green-yellow; complex aromas of acacia, honey and white truffle; biggish, well-balanced wine, supple yet powerful; long finish. Will make a fine bottle in 5–8 years.
1991 HERMITAGE BLANC, *CUVEE L'OREE* More yellow than green, though not particularly deep; waxy nose, with element of nail-varnish (acetone); substantial, powerful quite fleshy wine; dry edge with bright acidity which makes for overall imbalance. Good, but not great.
1993 ST-JOSEPH DESCHANTS *(Red)* Bright deep black plum, crimson rim; strong myrtille nose, with components of tar and pepper; dense, plummy wine, soft yet tight; ripe tannins and finishes with a touch of bitterness. Long. Very good.
1992 ST-JOSEPH DESCHANTS *(Red)* Mid garnet; fine pine and myrtille nose; flavours of blackberry and liquorice; long, well-made.
1991 ST-JOSEPH DESCHANTS *(Red)* Deepish colour; soft, chocolate and prune nose; supple, earthy flavours, more mineral in quality than Crozes; fair length and grip, but lacks real concentration and length, under its warm envelope.
1993 CROZES-HERMITAGE ROUGE, *LES MEYSONNIERS (50 yr. old vines, 25 hl/ha)* Limpid mid-deep plum; open, fruit driven nose of plum and liquorice; firm, concentrated Syrah with flavours of tar and black fruits; some finishing bitterness. Promising.
1993 CHATEAUNEUF DU PAPE ROUGE, *LA BERNARDINE (100% Grenache)* Dense black cherry, lightening at edge; closed, smoky aromas, hints of black fruit and *pruneaux*; big, powerful mouthful, with an austere tannic envelope masking a good depth of fruit and fine length.
1992 CHATEAUNEUF DU PAPE ROUGE, *LA BERNARDINE* Bright garnet; lightish *petits fruits rouges* nose; ripish flavours, but lacks real depth. Drink over next few years.
1991 CHATEAUNEUF DU PAPE ROUGE, *LA BERNARDINE* Lightish mid-plum; ripe, biggish, quite plummy flavours; warm and longish, with fair tannins; somewhat loose-knit.
1991 CHATEAUNEUF DU PAPE ROUGE, *BARBE-RAC* Mid-deep plum; fine, old vine Grenache nose just starting to open out; firmish, broad, fleshy wine, good depth, reasonable length and warm finish; very good for the vintage.
1993 COTE-ROTIE *(60% Brune, 40% Blonde; some field mixed Viognier)* Moderately dense colour; elegant, smoky nose with a touch of violets; flavour emphasises finesse rather than size; ripe tannins sustain sound fruit; not a blockbuster but fine with reasonable length.
1992 COTE-ROTIE Limpid mid garnet; attractive open aromas of liquorice and blackberry; supple flavours of pepper and spice; some length. Not bad.
1991 COTE-ROTIE Blackish hue, lightening rim; elegant, smoky, minerally nose beginning to show; relatively light wine, with clean fruit, some power and good length; soft tannins and acidity provide balanced support; needs 3–5 years to integrate and open out. Good plus.
1991 COTE-ROTIE, *LA MORDOREE (mainly Côte Brune fruit)* Dense black, lightish edge; finely-tuned nose of some elegance; most attractive crushed, ripe fruit quality to the palate; deep, yet subtle flavours (strong violet component here); long, attractive. Excellent.
1993 HERMITAGE ROUGE, *MONIER DE LA SIZERANNE* Excellent colour; closed nose; big, ripe, extracty black fruit flavours, with oak making a contribution to the wine's structure; distinct elements of coffee and chocolate; some fine tannins. Surprisingly full for this wet vintage.
1992 HERMITAGE ROUGE, *MONIER DE LA SIZERANNE* Sombre deep garnet; aromas of *pruneaux* and liquorice; blackberry and spice flavours, highish acidity; quite supple; good for vintage.
1991 HERMITAGE ROUGE, *MONIER DE LA SIZERANNE* More density and aromatic intensity than the 1992, liquorice and tar in particular; dense, tight masculine flavours, high acidity and a distinct note of bitterness on the finish. Altogether somewhat lacking in charm. Difficult to predict how it will evolve. Points up the folly of separating the best fruit to make a special *cuvée* in a vintage such as 1991.
1991 ERMITAGE "PAVILLON" Blackish hue, moderate density; unforthcoming nose, hinting at smokiness; big, softish flavours dominated by ripe tannins and powerful, inky fruit; long, reasonably complex wine, but lacks the depth and class of either Chave or La Chapelle.

CHAVE

1993 HERMITAGE BLANC *(Marsanne + Roussanne, in inox)* Green-gold; fleshy greengage aromas; ripe, quite fat and firm wine though somewhat short.
1993 HERMITAGE BLANC *(Roussanne, inox)* Marginally deeper than the above; attractive, classy nose; plenty of fat, honeyed fruit; less power than the mix, but greater richness. The blend should be very good; undoubtedly one of the top whites of the vintage.
1992 HERMITAGE BLANC Yellow green-gold; lovely, rich honeyed, almost surmature nose and flavour; firm, tightly structured, good length; very traditional in character.
1991 HERMITAGE BLANC Deep gold; nose of acacia honey; broad, mouthfilling flavours; lowish acidity; very long. Excellent now, but will make fine old bones.
1990 HERMITAGE BLANC *(no new oak)* Good colour; complex, tight nose; full, yet delicate on the palate with good depth and length. Excellent prospects.
1989 HERMITAGE BLANC Mid straw colour; not much on the nose; succulent, biggish wine with heaps of ripe fruit and flavours which continue right across the palate; tight and powerful; structured for the medium term (i.e. 10–15 years). Will be very attractive indeed, given time.
1988 HERMITAGE BLANC Touch more colour than the 1989; hint of straw on closed nose; powerful, stony acacia and fruit flavours encased in a tight envelope; long and persistent. Excellent, but a much longer term prospect than the 1989.
1987 HERMITAGE BLANC Yellow; fine mature nuts and honey nose; substantial flavours – very long, soft and ripe; now fully evolved and stylish. Lovely.
1986 HERMITAGE BLANC A shade deeper and more golden than the 1988; nose still very closed in, with a strongly floral components and hints of acacia and nuts; more delicate and less robust than either the 1988 or 1989; impeccable balance; has the structure for longevity, but difficult to envisage precisely what it will become. Something of an enigma.
1967 HERMITAGE BLANC Fine mid old-gold, no signs of browning; gorgeous, complex mature nuts and acacia aromas with a resiny note; harmonious, ripe flavours, complex and long; still fresh and youthful underneath a mature exterior. Superb, exciting. Great white Hermitage.
1993 HERMITAGE ROUGE *(various climats, in wood)* General impression of good colours, though not particularly dense; flavours dominated by firm, strong tannins and in the case of Rocoules and Bessards surprisingly supple fruit. The overall result seems likely to be an attractive wine for the medium term.
1992 HERMITAGE ROUGE Limpid deep velvet; aromas of *fruits noirs*, especially cherry; supple, stylish fruit with round tannins. Something of the 1982 in style.
1991 HERMITAGE ROUGE *different component climats:*

- **1991 PELEAT** Deep colour; nose of bitter chocolate, stony black fruit, preserved cherry; long, vigorous flavour, ripe fruit and round tannins.
- **1991 L'HERMITE** Firmly structured yet soft, red and black fruit flavours; excellent concentration, great finesse backed by a vein of acidity.
- **1991 LES BEAUMES** Fine, perfumed wine with soft flavours – very cherryish – far less structured than L'Hermite.
- **1991 DIOGNIERES** Mid depth of colour; reduced aromas of tar and spice; long, fine and marked by acidity; strong note of cherry.
- **1991 ROCOULES** Characterised by aromas and flavours of small red fruits (red currants etc) with violets, blackberry and liquorice. Great finesse.
- **1991 LE MEAL** *(ex new cask)* Firm, closed nose; mid-weight, fleshy flavours; more spice than fruit and strongly redolent of violets. Very different to Bessards.
- **1991 LES BESSARDS** *(ex new cask)* Dense colour; intense tar and spice nose; good ripe flesh, fine length, strong palate aromas and firm structure; well

integrated oak.

1991 LES BESSARDS *(ex old cask)* Deep, rather bright wine; long and powerful, with peachy flavours and considerable concentration.

1991 HERMITAGE ROUGE Bright, mid-deep garnet, carmine rim; sombre, smoky black fruit nose; soft, silky flavours, mid-weight with fine balance and complexity. A lovely wine which will be at its best in 10 years or so.

1990 HERMITAGE ROUGE Fine, deep, impenetrable purple; magnificent tar and spice nose (no pepper), emerging; restrained mid-heavy-weight, plenty of concentrated, very ripe fruit; very, very long, persistent and complex; flavours of cherry and coffee; surprisingly elegant and approachable, attributable to an impeccable balance. A very fine wine meriting 10–15 years at least in bottle. Magnificent.

1990 HERMITAGE ROUGE, *CUVEE CATHELIN* Limpid dark plum, carmine edge; very opulent and supremely elegant nose of concentrated fruit, bordering on the over-ripe holding out the promise of a stunning aromatic development; on the palate, pure, massively extracted and concentrated fruit; exemplary length and great finesse. A remarkable wine and a supreme expression of Syrah.

1989 HERMITAGE ROUGE A shade deeper than the ("standard") 1990; rather reduced, unforthcoming nose; an immense mouthful of very sexy, fleshy, fruit with good length and very ripe tannins. A lovely wine of great distinction; not the structure of the 1990, but magnificent none the less.

1988 HERMITAGE ROUGE Youthful deep purple; big, almost cheesy nose, tarry rather than spicy; envelope of rather austere tannins encases a good depth of fruit; rather burly at present and finishes somewhat short. Will last for years, but difficult to see a noble evolution.

1987 HERMITAGE ROUGE Altogether lighter than the 1988; open, rather vegetal nose and palate of pepper and red fruits. Good length. Very attractive now.

1985 HERMITAGE ROUGE Darkish morello cherry; hints of red fruits on a largely closed nose; first impressions of supple, ripe, fruit, firm in character with soft fully integrated tannins. Ready now but not a long stayer.

1969 HERMITAGE ROUGE Mid black cherry; fine spice and asparagus aromas; palate is hard, lacking flesh to balance attensive acidity. Considerable bottle variation likely at this age.

DELAS

1993 VIOGNIER, *VIN DE PAYS D'OC* Fruity, elegant wine with clean Viognier nose and fresh, apple and dried fruit flavours. Good for its Appellation.

1992 CONDRIEU Light yellow; ripish, open dried fruit aromas; some CO_2 lifts fruit which is also sustained by some bright acidity; wine has some natural power but lacks complexity. Not a great Condrieu, but not bad for the vintage.

1992 ST-JOSEPH BLANC *(20% fermented in new wood)* Good deepish colour; nothing much on nose; palate shows clean, supple fruit with good acidity; flavours of greengage point up Marsanne; longish, dry finish. Good.

1992 HERMITAGE BLANC *(100% new wood; 13.5% alcohol)* More yellow and extracty than the above, with green tinges; enriching touch of over-ripeness on the nose; substantial wine with peachy flavours, soft and ripe, good grip and power; needs a few years for the wood to integrate. Very good for the vintage.

1991 ST-JOSEPH ROUGE Deepish plum; aromas of *pruneaux* and red fruits; bright chocolaty flavours and touch of greeness; not bad, but lacks depth.

1990 CROZES-HERMITAGE ROUGE *(from purchased fruit)* Deep plum colour; soft baked fruit aromas and slightly cooked flavours – black olive and *pruneaux* – some steminess evident; finishes with a hint of bitterness; altogether rather flat and hot. Good, no better.

1990 CORNAS Limpid, black cherry; positive, smoky, cassis and liquorice aromas verging on the over-ripe; surprisingly soft, fleshy wine, porty in character; lacks elegance but should open out into an attractive bottle in 3–5 years; leaves the impression of a sunny, although somewhat vacant, rustic.

1990 COTE-ROTIE, *SEIGNEUR DE MAUGIRON* Limpid, dark plum; smoky plum and liquorice aromas; soft fruit upheld by firm, ripe tannins; warm and supple; a bit light and one-dimensional but has attractive elegance and should develop well.

1991 HERMITAGE, *CUVEE MARQUIS DE LA TOURETTE (12.5% alcohol)* Good deepish colour, right to rim; largely closed nose with hint of baked fruit; soft, quite earthy ripe fruit, of some depth; presently rather firm and lacking in generosity but will improve over the next 5 years. Attractive, if somewhat insubstantial.

1990 HERMITAGE, *CUVEE MARQUIS DE LA TOURETTE (13.5% alcohol)* Deep black plum, denser even than the 1990 Cornas; incipiently very elegant nose of ripe/overripe black fruits – blackberry and blackcurrant especially; soft, biggish wine, rather four-square and a touch jammy; long, warm finish. Would have benefited immeasurably from a dollop of Greffieux or Meal to add elegance to the structure. Needs at least 5 years. Good to very good.

FAURIE

1992 ST-JOSEPH BLANC *(bottled January 1994)* Bright colour; attractive, open, pear-skin nose; leaner perhaps on the palate than the Hermitage 1992, but very appealing with ripe, flavours and balancing acidity. Very good for St-Joseph and for a '92.

1991 ST-JOSEPH BLANC *(bottled January 1993)* Deeper than '92 in colour, nose and flavour; biggish, ripe wine, marked by wood which has dried it out somewhat (a pity); an earlier bottling would have made a significant difference. Not bad though.

1992 HERMITAGE BLANC Good colour, rather esterated pear-skin nose; ripe, fattish, well-constituted wine; tight, yet fresh with good sweetish fruit; flashes of honey and cinnamon; long with some finesse. Attractive for the medium term.

1991 HERMITAGE BLANC *(bottled January 1993)* Marginally deeper in colour and very much deeper and richer on the nose, than the 1992 with more power and presence on the palate; good acidity and attractive length; not a big Hermitage by any means, but finely crafted. Good plus.

1991 ST-JOSEPH ROUGE *(young vines = < 10 yrs.)* Limpid mid-garnet; meaty nose; ripish flavours and some length; attractive and perfectly sound, if light.

1991 ST-JOSEPH ROUGE *(old vines; 24 months in demi-muids)* Deeper than the young vine *cuvée* and less open on either nose and palate; clearly has much more to it in terms of both structure and concentration; plenty of mache but dominated by dry tannins and a note of greenness; good length; has had too long in wood, but should manage to re-establish itself.

1991 HERMITAGE ROUGE, *LES GREFFIEUX (20 months in* demi-muids*)* Deep, translucent plum; spicy, smoky fruit-based nose; biggish, rather burly wine, with a touch of stemminess overlaying sound, tarry fruit; somewhat in the old-fashioned, rustic mould, but should develop well.

1991 HERMITAGE ROUGE, *LE MEAL (22 months in* demi-muids*)* More density of colour and intensity of black fruit perfume than the Greffieux; chocolate and spice on the nose; more depth and inherent complexity on the palate – once again a green streak spoils the picture; dry tannins are just about at the limit of balance; has power and concentration underneath. Less protracted maturation would have made for better equilibrium. Very good, nonetheless.

JABOULET

1991 HERMITAGE LA CHAPELLE *(13.5% alcohol)* Fine, deep, youthful colour; concentrated, complex smoky fruit and cassis nose starting to develop; big, ripish flavours, with plenty of depth and extract; good length and balance. A fine, vigorous wine, whose quality attests to careful grape selection. 8–19 years from maturity. (17/20)

1990 HERMITAGE LA CHAPELLE Intense, impenetrable black plum right to edge; tight, dense nose, flashes of super-ripe fruit, no obvious new oak; massive, extracted flavours, very concentrated with excellent acidity and fine, round tannins; complete wine with depth and great length. Monumental, but superbly balanced. Expect this to develop in slow motion over the next 10–20 years. Will it challenge the 1961? A masterpiece. (19+/20)

1989 HERMITAGE LA CHAPELLE Impenetrable black cherry; huge extract; closed, reduced nose; massive berry fruit flavours, very concentrated with round tannins and high alcohol; some new wood evident, but not overdone. (18.5/20)

1988 HERMITAGE LA CHAPELLE Almost opaque, deep morello, purplish rim; hot, reduced and slightly baked aromas of pepper and red fruits; fruit still dominates the palate – excellent depth and weight; round tannins and some complexity; not a blockbuster. Fine, complete, wine with a long evolution ahead. (18/20)

1986 HERMITAGE LA CHAPELLE Opaque, redder hue than 1988; nose in transit between fruit and secondary aromas; ripe, soft fruit-cake flavours; goodish length with some tannin to lose; quite meaty in character. Altogether less richness than either 1988 or 1989; a wine for the medium term. (16/20)

1985 HERMITAGE LA CHAPELLE Lighter in hue and tone than 1986, good extract; fine, open, Hermitage nose of strawberry and cassis starting to come through; on the palate, mid-weight flavours of *sous-bois* and mushroom; long finish and good balance, but lacks the concentration of either 1989 or 1990. A Chapelle of finesse, not weight. Drink now and for next decade. (15/20)

1983 HERMITAGE LA CHAPELLE Deep, maturing garnet colour; fine, complex pebbly nose, just starting to open; strongly earthy flavours, with components of meat-extract and tar; well-balanced, warm wine, with some tannins to shed and excellent length. Although more concentrated than either 1982 or 1985, yet no heavy-weight. Almost ready – drink over next 10–15 years. (17.5/20)

1982 HERMITAGE LA CHAPELLE Maturing appearance and fully evolved, elegant nose of *sous-bois*, mushroom and truffle; half the concentration of the 1983, but fine palate aromas; some tannins to lose from a mild imbalance of tannin and fruit. A good, but not great La Chapelle (not a patch on Chave's splendid 1982). Drink now and for next 5 years or so. (15/20)

1979 HERMITAGE LA CHAPELLE Mid garnet; light, quite evanescent nose, still relatively dumb; a bit raw and green on the palate, with some sweet fruit underneath; high acidity and tannin; rather one-dimensional. In short, not bad, but lacks charm and class (possibly an unrepresentative bottle). (14/20)

1978 HERMITAGE LA CHAPELLE Dense, opaque, dark cherry, right to rim; little visual sign of ageing; very closed, yet nascently complex nose – hints of redcurrants, then cassis; immense concentration of flavour – deep, tarry and tannic; complex and complete, rounded and harmonious. A big, classic, La Chapelle – not in the class of the 1961, but very rich and satisfying. Needs another decade and seems structured for everlasting life. (18.5/20)

1976 HERMITAGE LA CHAPELLE Deep but translucent morello cherry, right to edge; touch lighter than the 1978; soft, plummy aromas, still undeveloped; lightish, stylish flavours, redolent of singed fruit-cake; tightly packed, with fruit; not the weight or class of the 1978, but a fine wine which could be drunk with pleasure now, but will improve over the next few years. (16+/20)

1972 HERMITAGE LA CHAPELLE Mid-deep hue, noticeable browning, watery mensicus; tarry, burnt nose, a bit rubbery and not very expressive; ripe, fully mature flavours of meat-extract character; good length with enough sustaining fruit; very different to the 1978, but a long, fine wine nonetheless. (18/20)

1970 HERMITAGE LA CHAPELLE Touch more depth than 1972; even less forthcoming on the nose; soft, plummy flavours; lightish angular feel, with a distinctly tannic finish. Not bad, drink now. Have tasted better bottles of this vintage. (15/20)

1969 HERMITAGE LA CHAPELLE Quite dark, with little sign of ageing beyond a hint of mahogany at the rim; fine, powerful old Syrah nose; light, somewhat dilute wine, hollow and short. Nose is by far its best asset. (15/20)

1992 CONDRIEU Mid yellow; nothing much on nose; dry, rather weakish flavour, somewhat oxidative; lacks concentration and typicity.

1991 CONDRIEU Light green-gold; very aromatic, surmature nose, though not strongly varietal; fleshy, dry-edged palate, quite fat but spoilt by a lack of grip and a, short, alcoholic finish; altogether rather one-dimensional.

1992 HERMITAGE BLANC, *CHEVALIER DE STERIMBERG (60% Marsanne, 40% Roussanne)* Bright, light gold; oxidative note on largely closed nose; lively palate, with fat and acidity; has something of the Verdelho about it; altogether a bit broad and lacking in power. Drink now and for the next 5 years.

1991 HERMITAGE BLANC, *CHEVALIER DE STERIMBERG* A much better wine; nose hints at acacia and promises attractive development; palate has power and depth, with good balancing acidity and length. Excellent future.

1971 HERMITAGE BLANC, *CHEVALIER DE STERIMBERG* Fine mid yellow-gold, no browning whatsoever; rich, still fresh aroma – hazelnuts, acacia, lanolin – very complex, without any varietal character – could be easily mistaken for mature Chardonnay, Semillon or even Chenin – very enticing none the less; equally fresh on the palate, very full and quite spicy; long, elegant finish. Really lovely.

1992 CROZES HERMITAGE, *DOMAINE DE THALABERT* Deep, almost opaque, garnet; nose of liquorice and spice; lightish for Thalabert and a bit rustic still, but has length, a supple middle palate and enough to keep it going for 3–5 years. Lacks real depth.

1991 CROZES HERMITAGE, *DOMAINE DE THALABERT* Fine, deep black plum; tight, positive blackberryish nose; good depth of ripe fruit, with underlying elegance starting to come through. Attractive, long finish. Very good.
1990 CROZES HERMITAGE, *DOMAINE DE THALABERT* Limpid, opaque dark plum; fine, smoky, tarry nose; dense, extracty, pure fruit, focussed, and inherently complex, beautifully balanced by acidity and ripe tannins. Even better than the 1983; the best Thalabert yet? 8 years or so should see it mature.
1983 CROZES HERMITAGE, *DOMAINE DE THALABERT* Opaque burnt plum; almost fully mature, smoky, nose of great elegance; mid-weight wine, with dryish edge and supple, mature centre; slightly baked aspect; highish acidity holding up vigorous flavours. Very attractive indeed. *A point*, but will keep developing for several years yet.

JEAN-MARC SORREL

1993 HERMITAGE BLANC *(cask)* Good colour; open honey and nuts nose; biggish, supple, with a well-defined nerve of acidity; fair length; more finesse than size. Promising.
1992 HERMITAGE ROUGE *(cask)* Limpid mid-garnet; firm, fleshy nose of *pruneaux* and chocolate with a touch of char; mid weight of fruit, supple tannins; finishes a trifle short.
1991 HERMITAGE, *LE VIGNON "VIEILLES VIGNES" (12.5% alcohol)* Lightish plum, weak rim; nothing on nose; softish, mid-weight palate, some elegance and depth; finishes well. Good plus.
1992 HERMITAGE BLANC, *LE VIGNOT, DB* Fine, muted yellow-straw; clean, developing nose of orange-blossom and acacia; tight, complex flavours, mid-weight, elegant; good acidity and long finish. Needs 3–5 years to show its paces.
1991 HERMITAGE ROUGE, *LE VIGNOT, VIEILLES VIGNES, DB* Mid garnet; positive, open nose; clean flavours, good depth and acidity; elegance rather than weight, with tannin to lose. Satisfying wine – attractive now and over the next 5 years.
1990 HERMITAGE ROUGE, *LE VIGNOT, VIEILLES VIGNES, DB* Fine limpid colour right to deep red edge; closed nose, clearly has bags of very ripe fruit in bud; fullish wine with well-integrated tannins, good depth of fruit and fair length; complex, classy wine in the making. Five years plus to maturity.

MARC SORREL

1992 CROZES-HERMITAGE BLANC *(cask)* Fine bright green-gold; closed nose but palate showing plenty of fat, soft, ripe fruit; highish acidity and fair length. Attractive.
1991 CROZES-HERMITAGE BLANC *(12.7% alcohol)* Bright green-gold; very stylish, strongly honeyed nose; palate adds a touch of nuttiness and straw; long finish and good acidity complete a well-judged balance. Very good.
1993 HERMITAGE BLANC *(cask)* Good colour; very promising open nose; plenty of fruit and depth; an excellent wine in the making – will surprise many critics of this vintage. Marc attributes the quality to picking before the rain.
1992 HERMITAGE BLANC *(Les Rocoules, ex inox cuve)* Deepish yellow; fine, unusual, almost *oranges confits* nose; biggish, rather burly, powerful wine with long finishing flavours of exotic fruit and citrus; has a slightly dry edge. Very good.
1991 HERMITAGE BLANC, *LES ROCOULES* Light yellow-green; nutty, honeyed, oxidative aromas; lovely, silky acacia and nut flavours with a fresh uplift – a touch old-fashioned, but none the worse for that. Again, very good.
1993 HERMITAGE ROUGE, *LE GREAL (cask)* Deep colour, open nose; good concentration of flavour and well-judged wood; touch of stemminess; a good result for this difficult vintage.
1992 HERMITAGE ROUGE Mid-deep plum; open, smoky *fruits noirs* nose, *mures* and *cassis* in particular; lightish flavours with a green, stalky edge which gives an impression of rusticity; good fruit underneath. Not bad at all.
1992 HERMITAGE ROUGE, *LE GREAL* More depth of colour and extract; fine nose of spice and black cherry leading to supple ripe flavours; good length; has acid and tannin to integrate; plenty of nuance and complexity to develop.
1991 HERMITAGE ROUGE Mid garnet, flashes of purple; spicy nose with stalky note; supplish, meaty, smoky bacon flavours; hint of stemminess but otherwise well constituted; some complexity; not great, but good to very good.
1991 HERMITAGE ROUGE, *LE GREAL* Very deep, almost black, cherry; fine nose of coffee, cocoa and chocolate emerging; tight envelope of ripe tannins encloses dryish, tarry flavours; long, chocolaty, powerful; plenty of matter here, not yet very *flatteur*, but will make a very fine bottle in 10 or so years.

ST JOSEPH

CHEZE

1993 ST-JOSEPH BLANC *(ex cuve)* Light straw, green tinge; clean sappy Marsanne nose – greengages; full, open soft fruit, good structure and grip; stylish wine, long. Very good.
1991 ST-JOSEPH BLANC *(two separate pickings for optimum maturity)* Fine bright green-gold; big broad attractive open acacia- honey nose; soft, fat, honeyed wine, broad flavours, lacks grip and freshness but not length; attractive well made wine; drink soon.
1993 CONDRIEU *(recently filtered)* Mid green-gold; broad smoky, peachy nose and flavours; fair length and ripeness; wine altogether somewhat flattened by filtration.
1992 CONDRIEU Deepish colour, green tinge; opulent seductive surmature nose; peachy flavours, but lacks power and definition; the finish, though long, is evanescent. Altogether, a bit insubstantial.
1993 ST-JOSEPH *(30 yr. old Syrah vines in cask)* Deep garnet; open *fruits rouges* nose; ripe sweetish fruit, esp dark cherry; good balance, tannins and plenty of mache; excellent prospects.
1993 ST-JOSEPH *(40 yr. old Syrah vines, in cask)* Dense black cherry – carmine rim; sombre nose, *fruits noirs* aromas; tight-framed wine, fine, ripe tannins and good acidity sustaining sweetish, ripe, tarry fruit; excellent length and real *fond* here.
1992 ST-JOSEPH, *CUVEE PRESTIGIEUX DE CAROLINE (10% new wood)* Deep red cherry; open, smoky aromas – *fraises des bois*, cocoa; sweet silky wine, concentrated, dense fruit; fine, fondu tannins – but not big-framed by any means; lovely wine for 3–5 years time.
1991 ST-JOSEPH, *CUVEE PRESTIGIEUX DE CAROLINE (30% new wood)* Mid-deep black cherry; fruit aromas still holding on (esp cassis) but giving way to *sous-bois* with animal notes appearing. Ripe, stylish above all elegant; more complex and complete than '92; silky, seductive stuff. You won't find better St-Joseph than this.
1990 ST-JOSEPH, *CUVEE PRESTIGIEUX DE CAROLINE (80% new wood)* Deep blackish garnet; open elegant nose – super-ripe fruit, especially cassis and mures, touch of cocoa; open ripe, fruit-driven flavours, flatteur, almost pure concentrated cassis; long with round, fine tannins. Suppleness dominates palate – elegant wine with structure to develop over 3–5 years. Very good indeed.
1988 ST-JOSEPH, *CUVEE PRESTIGIEUX DE CAROLINE* Opaque, dark ruby rim; closed, smoky nose – fleshy but a bit rustic. More burly tannins than '90; ripe fruit, tight envelope, plenty of stuffing. Good long wine with plenty of life ahead.
1987 ST-JOSEPH, *CUVEE PRESTIGIEUX DE CAROLINE (first vintage of this wine; 100% new wood)* Deep red cherry, still opaque; cassis aromas, vegetal tone starting to emerge; good acidity and ripe tannins with enough fruit to balance; no lack of stuffing or class here. Not the weight of the '90, but good length and completeness across palate. Warm finish. Excellent for a first go in a less than top-class vintage.

COURSODON

1993 ST-JOSEPH *(white; standard cuvée, harvested in rain)* Lightish green; hay and greengage aromas; firm, appley, greenagey fruit; complex, floral, long. Fattish, well-structured; excellent.
1993 ST-JOSEPH, *PARADIS ST-PIERRE (white, 3rd. yr. wood; no malo)* Deeper green; open fruit aromas sustained by oak; wood masks good depth of fruit, puissant, with good grip, flesh and fat. Long. Very good.
1991 ST-JOSEPH, *PARADIS ST-PIERRE (malo faite)* Lovely colour, green-yellow reflets; strong acacia honey and floral aromas; rich, liquid honey, very perfumed in mouth; tight, clean, delicious. Long, complex, just starting to open out. First class St-Joseph.
1988 ST-JOSEPH *(white, standard cuvée; malo faite)* Bright, extracty, yellow-green; strong petrol nose, honeyed underneath; petrol, lanolin, honey flavours. Mid-weight, long, good *gras*, tight-structured, grippy; very good, attractive fine wine. Needs food.
1988 ST-JOSEPH, *PARADIS ST-PIERRE (white, malo faite)* Bright yellow-gold; oak (lots of 2nd. wine wood used in this vintage) gently dominates; ripe, honeyed nose, bigger, fatter, fleshier wine; more *puissance* than standard *cuvée*; lightish finish. fruit sustained by oak. Not sure that the finesse of the standard *cuvée* doesn't give it the edge.
1980 ST-JOSEPH *(white, standard cuvée)* Deep yellow-gold-green – lovely colour; honey and honeysuckle aromas, touch of nuts; gentle, lightish wine, soft, well-knit, acidity holding it together. Finishes a bit short, and bright.
1992 ST-JOSEPH *(red, standard cuvée)* Mid ruby; strong peppery, fruit-driven nose; same flavours; a bit green, good weight. Attractive.
1991 ST-JOSEPH *(red, standard cuvée)* Deep(er) plum, limpid; slender aromas, less open than 1992; fleshy, but rather unfocussed, touch of tar; fair structure but lacks centre. More matter and structure than 1992. Going through a closed phase.
1992 ST-JOSEPH, *L'OLIVAIE* Opaque deepish plum; reduced nose; black olive flavours, somewhat reduced; good matter and weight with underlying elegance. Supple mouthful. Good to very good.
1991 ST-JOSEPH, *L'OLIVAIE* More density and deeper hue than 1992; dumb nose, showing distinct note of oak; wood and concentrated fruit dominate palate; long silky, quite rich wine; finesse length and balance; very good indeed.
1990 ST-JOSEPH, *PARADIS ST. PIERRE (20 hl/ha)* Deep opaque plum; lake-purple edge; complex smoky nose: black-olive, black fruit, chocolate, *pruneaux*, animal; big rather burly wine, but lovely complexity and depth of flavour; a touch hollow but big and chocolaty, showing the heat of the vintage. Very good indeed, though.
1986 ST-JOSEPH, *PARADIS ST-PIERRE* Mid garnet, light edge; delicate mure and cassis nose, alcoholic; light wine in this company; lacks depth – breaking up, tannic, dry. Past its best.
1985 ST-JOSEPH Mid deep garnet, tuile rim; stylish gamey nose; lightish secondary flavours; high acid and dry edge. Bright notes of spice, game and animal; lacks a little flesh; just in decline; quite attractive.
1984 ST-JOSEPH, *L'OLIVAIE (first release)* Mid-deep red garnet, touch of brown; spice and sous-bois aromas; soft in mouth, somewhat dilute and lacking in grip; more harmonious though than '85; holding up well. Good for this light vintage.
1983 ST-JOSEPH, *PARADIS ST-PIERRE (first release)* Deep garnet, tuilé edge; spicy, surprisingly youthful, closed nose; old fané flavours – with big, muscular, hard tannins; no fruit left, just the corsets and bones.

FLORENTIN

1993 ST-JOSEPH, *CLOS L'ARBELESTRIER (Blanc; demi-muid)* Mid yellow-straw; strong sappy, quince nose; big, powerful wine, lifted by CO_2; a bit sherryish, but far less so than older vintages; long finish. Good, but definitely old-style St-Joseph.
1992 ST-JOSEPH, *CLOS L'ARBELESTRIER (Blanc; demi-muid)* Bright greenish-yellow; greengage-floral nose, more open than '93; rich, fat, honeyed wine, with greengagey fruit; delicious – won't benefit at all from longer in wood. Shortish finish – but that's the vintage.
1991 ST-JOSEPH, *CLOS L'ARBELESTRIER (Blanc; still in wood)* Similar tone to '92; closed nose, starting to show fruit; on the palate, more finesse than weight; lighter, more *nerveux* than '92; longish. Good, but the 1992 is undoubtedly better.
1990 ST-JOSEPH, *CLOS L'ARBELESTRIER (Blanc; bottled January 1994)* More yellow than the above; spicier, richer aromas – almonds and nuts; strong, confident wine, with fair depth, length and firm structure. Rather in the old-fashioned nuts-and-butter mould, but not bad. Needs food.
1993 ST-JOSEPH, *CLOS L'ARBELESTRIER (Rouge; en foudre)* Mid plum; positive herbal nose; ripe, pruny flavours, with good depth and plenty of mache.
1992 ST-JOSEPH, *CLOS L'ARBELESTRIER (Rouge; en foudre)* Good youthful colour; complex aromas of black fruits, spice, liquorice; juicy, mid-weight flavours; good structure and length, though lacking in the depth for longevity.

1991 ST-JOSEPH, *CLOS L'ARBELESTRIER (Rouge; en foudre)* Deepish plum; reduced tarry, *pruneaux* nose, starting to open out; full, succulent qine, with plenty of silky, ripe fruit; beautifully balanced. Needs to be bottled immediately.
1990 ST-JOSEPH, *CLOS L'ARBELESTRIER Rouge, in bottle)* Deepish plum; aromas of liquorice and very ripe cherries; tough, burly wine with quite plump, ripe, tarry fruit encased in tannin. A trifle clumsy with neither the finesse nor the length of the 1991. Not bad though.
1989 ST-JOSEPH, *CLOS L'ARBELESTRIER (Rouge; en foudre)* Deep colour with reduced, spicy nose; liquorice and spice on the palate which opened out into a wine of depth and elegance; a bit in the Domaine's older burly mode, but has charm, nonetheless. A bottled sample – all in finesse – might easily be mistaken for a Volnay!
1988 ST-JOSEPH, *CLOS L'ARBELESTRIER (Rouge; in bottle)* Deep limpid ruby; liquorice and old leather on the nose; on the palate, plenty of fruit, with real depth and a sound structure, though not yet greatly developed. A slow evolver which will repay keeping and develop finesse.

GRIPA

1993 ST-PERAY *(recent bottling)* Clean light citrus; light, cheesy; firm sappy flavours, good and ripe; seems stylish but needs time to open out.
1993 ST-JOSEPH *(White)* Similar colour to above; more fat and richness on nose, clean, sappy, greengagey aromas with hint of flowers and peaches; still closed; CO_2 on palate, full, rich well structured wine, on the lighter side; mouthfilling with *puissance*. Excellent; needs 2–3 years.
1992 ST-PERAY Light green-citrus; a bit more colour here; open attractive nose, hints of orange confits and acacia; fatter, broader wine then the above, good grip, succulent, with earthy undertone and longish peachy finish. Very good indeed. Lovely now.
1991 ST-JOSEPH, *Berceau (white)* Fine green-yellow; hints of honey, nuts and acacia on a still closed nose; more obvious power here than any of the above; ripe, full wine; firm and fat. Delicate finish slightly marred by alcoholic burn. Very good, nonetheless. Will improve over 3 years or so.
1990 ST-JOSEPH, *Berceau (white)* Fine colour – more yellow than 1991; nose completely closed; in contrast, broader more open palate than '91, marginally bigger yet with more suppleness. Fat and stylish, with a slightly raw finish. Good to v.g. Will probably even out over 3–5 years.
1992 ST-JOSEPH *(red)* Bright mid garnet; fresh, open, raspberry/pepper nose; crisp flavours, mid weight; goodish fruit and tannins; touch of green, lacks a bit of flesh. Short. Not bad for vintage.
1992 ST-JOSEPH, *Berceau (red)* More depth – sustained deep, translucent garnet; closed nose – fruit-driven underneath; soft, rather flabby feel about it; note of *goût de rafle*; otherwise, sturdy, showing alcohol and hollow middle palate; rawish finish. Good only.
1990 ST-JOSEPH *(red)* More opaque; deep garnet, lake edge; attractive open, surmature nose of *pruneaux* and *fruits confits*. No heat showing; big, rather burly feel; good attack but doesn't follow through; light, dry tarry edge. A bit figgy. Good, but not great St J. Should integrate & improve over next 3–5 years.
1990 ST-JOSEPH, *Berceau (red)* More velvet and brilliance in tone; soutenu – carmine edge; complex surmature nose; touch of oak and noticeably more concentration on palate; less hard-edged than regular *cuvée*; tannins more fondu; firm envelope; fleshy, long wine with a hint of heat. A bit big for its own good, but attractive none the less. Very good though. Needs 4 year plus.
1988 ST-JOSEPH, *Berceau (red)* Bright, almost opaque deep garnet; closed mildly chocolate & burlat cherry nose; sturdy wine – green-edge to skeleton, tight grip with unripe tannins. Lacks charm and *fond*. Needs more flesh to age well.

GRIPPAT

1993 VIN DE TABLE *(100% Marsanne)* Clean, fresh wine with light Marsanne flavours of apple and flowers; quite full; good indeed for a Vin de Table.
1992 ST-JOSEPH BLANC Deepish straw-green; more flower and greengage than the VDT, fresh and sappy with hint of spiciness. Good, mouthfilling wine.
1991 ST-JOSEPH BLANC Bright light green; nose hinting at straw and greengage; full, spicy wine with earthy undertone, sappy edge and note of confit oranges; altogether more concentration, complexity and *puissance* than the '92.
1992 HERMITAGE BLANC *(14% alcohol)* Light green-citrus; closed nose with notes of flowers and ripe greengages; not much more on palate (yet); wine clearly has more natural power and structure than the St-Joseph; presently showing some *oranges confits*, big, tough item. Good for a 1992.
1991 HERMITAGE BLANC Good colour; unforthcoming nose; bigger and more powerful than the 1992 Hermitage; somewhat old-fashioned oxidative in style; lacks the grip and complexity for top-class, but good, though.
1992 ST-JOSEPH ROUGE *(including Hospices fruit)* Good colour and curious, oxidative nose; rather tired on the palate – dry and fleshless with a hard finish.
1991 ST-JOSEPH ROUGE Sombre mid-plum; spicy plum nose; biggish wine, with good fruit, verging on the rustic in style; some stemminess. Good, but not top-notch.
1992 HERMITAGE ROUGE Deep colour; both nose and palate dominated by charry new wood; flavours distinctly burnt (wine matured in Spanish casks of US oak bought from Chapoutier!); good fruit underneath, and length. Might come through but these casks will probably have the last word. A pity.
1991 HERMITAGE ROUGE *(12.5% alcohol)* Deep plum, purple rim; sweet nose (oak in check here) with strong clove/cinnamon component; chunky, mid-weight flavours, a touch rustic and green; rather in pieces at present but has good potential.
1991 ST-JOSEPH ROUGE, *HOSPICES DE TOURNON CUVEE* Intense, limpid, deep red, plum edge; fine, smoky aromas; charry wood flavours but concentrated fruit underneath; good length and power. This is very good. Needs 5+ years to really come alive.

PARET

1993 CONDRIEU, *LES CEPS DU NEBADON, (13% alc; spring bottling)* Mid citrus colour; rather closed but attractive peachy nose; ripe, mid-weight *gras*, peachy-floral flavours, powerful wine with good acidity and fair length. A good result for the vintage.

1992 ST-JOSEPH, *LES LARMES DU PERE (February bottling)* Good mid plum colour; spice and liquorice nose, elegant, almost floral; supple mid-weight flavour, complex and long; attractive though spoilt by a touch of greenness.
1991 ST-JOSEPH, *LES LARMES DU PERE (Final bottling)* Fine limpid, bright, deep colour; closed nose, promising elegance and depth showing through; firm yet supple wine; richer and riper than 1992; element of rusticity with stalky green nerve underneath; good concentration. 3–7 years. Good plus.
1990 ST-JOSEPH, *LES LARMES DU PERE* Deepish limpid colour; grilled, smoky nose; ripe, stylish and elegant wine underneath a big frame; minty fruit with evident nerve of greenness. Good wine, but not the depth or concentration of the 1991.

TROLLAT

1993 ST-JOSEPH *(Blanc; young vines in old pieces)* Mid-straw; open floral & greengage aromas; fleshy fruit and good acidity with spicy, quince and greengage flavours. Very good.
1993 ST-JOSEPH *(Blanc; 80 yr. old vines, en Côteaux)* Deeper, yellower, colour; similar but more concentrated nose; wine has less acidity, though greater concentration than the above; by itself, a bit flabby, needs the younger vines for balance.
1993 ST-JOSEPH *(Rouge; in demi-muid)* Bright mid-garnet; soft, evolving, smoky black cherry aromas; ripe, almost sweetish palate, soft and long. Supple, rich fruit. Delicious.
1992 ST-JOSEPH *(Rouge; 2 parts free-run : 1 part press wine)* Deep blackish hue; aromas and palate characterised by soft, succulent open fruit – complex and concentrated but with a hint of verdure. Round tannins will keep it in good balance for several years yet.
1992 ST-JOSEPH *(Rouge; in cuve, has not seen oak)* Deeper, more sombre appearance; spicier, more medicinal nose than the above; bigger, fleshier wine, but with less rondeur or suppleness.
1992 ST-JOSEPH *(Rouge; just bottled)* A shade denser than the above; reduced nose, with hints of macerated *pruneaux*; meaty, yet soft, sweetish, flavours; firm texture and sound, ripe tannins; finishes short. Attractive for the mid-term.
1992 ST-JOSEPH *(Rouge; old vines; demi-muid; filtered)* Drier tannins and firmer structure with less obvious flesh; underneath there is considerably more stuffing and depth. Not for the fruit-driven consumer, but for the true *amateur* who will keep it for 5 years+.
1992 ST-JOSEPH *(Rouge; old vines; demi-muid; unfiltered)* Touch less suppleness here and more nerve; still firmly structured with marked tannins. Deep, powerful wine with long finish.

CORNAS

ALLEMAND

1993 CORNAS, *LES CHAILLOTS (in cask; 20 hl/ha)* Fine deep colour, reduced, tarry nose; sturdy wine, with deep, succulent fruit and long finish. Dry edge. Seems good for the vintage.
1993 CORNAS, *LES CHAILLOTS (same wine as above but see note)* Opaque black cherry; closed, pitchy nose; much more old vine fruit and concentration apparent; firm, tightly structured wine, long, attractive. Only difference was that this cask not prepared with sulphur candle)
1993 CORNAS, *REYNARD* Even deeper than the above; strongly tarred nose; plenty of mache and concentration. Excellent. Unlikely to find better Cornas than this in 1993.
1993 CORNAS *(in glass bonbonne; grapes left to concentrate on vine)* Black, extracty appearance, right to rim; big, gutsy, cheesy wine; firmish, mid-weight of fruit with curiously light feel about it. The fruit has concentrated at the expense of the structure. Flat, and lacking cohesion.
1992 CORNAS, *LES CHAILLOTS (28 hl/ha)* Bright, almost opaque, dark plum, purple-carmine edge; reduced, asparagussy nose followed by distinctly vegetal flavours; plenty of fruit underneath, sound, though light in structure. Rather four-square and lacking in complexity. Not bad. Needs 3–8 years.
1992 CORNAS, *REYNARD (non-destemmed fruit)* Similar to above, touch more sombre; strong black olive nose – not much else at present; firm, concentrated fruit, surprisingly supple; Tapenade; no great complexity, but has more depth than Chaillots.
1991 CORNAS, *LES CHAILLOTS* Bright opaque black cherry, violace; light Tapenade nose; rich, complex, succulent, ripe, olive/nuts flavours; masculine exterior, feminine underneath – a bit of a transvestite really! Should develop well.
1991 CORNAS, *REYNARD (32 hl/ha)* Similar tone to above; strong green and black olive aromas (seems a marker here); big, powerful mouthfilling fruit; firm, but round tannins; dryish edge. Confident, warm, concentrated, presence and great charm. 5–10 years.
1985 CORNAS *(old vines; 20 hl/ha)* Limpid black-garnet; smoky, almost burnt cooked olive aromas; firm attack onto lightish, charry flavours, elegant notes of *sous-bois*; delicate, rather ephermal finish. A bit hollow. Drink soon.
1984 CORNAS *(old vines; 14 hl/ha)* Deep tone, less intense than the 1985 with stronger brown component; touch of aromatic gaminess starting to show; lacks flesh, especially in the middle; holding its own, though distinctly delicate.
1982 CORNAS *(TA's first vintage; 300 bottles only; 12 hl/ha)* Mid-plum, lightish rim; smoky, rubbery nose leading to sweetish, ripe, elegant flavours. Lacks complexity but is good, especially for this vintage; still evolving.

BARJAC

1993 CORNAS *(two pickings – 30 Sept. and 9 Oct. Much rot)* Light, weedy, colour; mild peppery nose; slender, soft flavours – *bonbons acidulés*; altogether very light. Sound. "What am I going to do with this?" Will put into older casks"to try and add something".
1991 CORNAS Limpid, deep, translucent garnet; open, ripe griottes cherry nose, spice and liquorice; supple mid-weight syrah fruit; distinct touch of wood support (though no new oak); tarry, cherry, liquorice notes; fine with long silky finish. Excellent – will develop well over 5–8 years.

CLAPE

1993 COTES DU RHONE Lightish carmine red; closed nose; clean, sappy wine, high acidity and some tannin. Not bad.

1993 CORNAS *(15 yr. old vines)* Deep, limpid, crimson; closed nose; quite succulent wine, with some sweetish fruit. Good.

1993 CORNAS *(35 yr. old vines)* Similar appearance; no nose; bigger, meatier flavours with firm, spicy fruit on top of brightish tannins; supple.

1993 CORNAS *(old vines, Reynard)* More depth of colour; completely shut up; more burly, structured leathery character, with a rather hard edge.

1992 CORNAS *(15 yr. old vines)* Deepish dark cherry-garnet; touch of reduction on unexpressive nose; biggish, mouthfilling wine with plenty of *mache*; dry, edgy finish.

1992 CORNAS *(35 yr. old vines)* Limpid deep hue; no nose; softish, ripe, fleshy wine, with tarry fruit; round with underlying elegance. Good.

1992 CORNAS *(old vines, Reynard)* Similar appearance to the above; hint of violets showing on nose; very succulent, fleshy, tarry fruit in a firm tannic frame; much more harmonious structure, depth and length than the either of the above.

1992 CORNAS *(final blend)* Similar colour; hint of violets; elegant, mid-weight wine, quite supple with a touch of attractive rusticity. Has depth and length and some complexity. Ready from 3–7 years, depending on taste.

1991 CORNAS Mid deep ruby; smoky griotte-cherry aromas; silky, yet firm wine with plenty of ripe, stylish fruit and natural power. Needs 5–10 years in bottle. Very good indeed.

COLOMBO

1992 CORNAS, *LES TERRES BRULEES* Soft, supple wine with plenty of ripe fruit; easy drinking, but no great complexity.

1992 CORNAS, *LES RUCHETS* Deep colour; open, somewhat macerated nose; plenty of black fruit – cherry and plum – moderate tannins, long full and powerful; new oak smothers purity; rather blurred which destroys typicity.

1991 CORNAS, *LES RUCHETS* Deeper than 1992, with more aromatic refinement and evolution; similar style to the above, more depth and good length; but lacking essential Cornas character. Attractive, with good medium term future.

JUGE

1993 CORNAS, *COTEAUX (old cask)* Light strawberry-purple; strong peppery nose with noticeable VA; delicate, peppery flavours – VA also here.

1991 CORNAS, *PIED DE COTEAUX (old cask)* Fine, dense, black cherry; positive, fresh, creme de cassis aromas; hints of wood support concentrated, fleshy wine, with well-judged, round tannins; ripe, structured with grip and length. Very attractive.

1991 CORNAS, *COTEAUX* Limpid, translucent dark garnet; opulent cassis and mure nose; fleshier and rounder than PC, with a bit more length. Promising.

1991 CORNAS, *SELECTION DES COTEAUX* Deeper in colour than the above; fuller, more complex but similar aromas; more richness and tannin on the palate; long, concentrated mouthfiller, with great underlying elegance. Very stylish. Needs 5+ years.

1990 CORNAS, *SELECTION DES COTEAUX* Limpid, dark red cherry; lovely complex aromas of very ripe fruit – cassis and mure; highish acids and rather nervy tannins here which should integrate, given time, and ensure this complete, satisfying wine a splendid future. First-rate Cornas.

LEMENICIER

1992 ST-PERAY *(Cuvée non-boiseé)* Light straw colour and firm, peachy nose; sound, sappy wine, though flabby and a bit short.

1992 ST-PERAY *(Cuvée non-boiseé)* Attractive yellowish colour; soft, creamy; oak-vanillin aromas and flavours dominate, masking varietal character; good wine though, with an after-taste of straw.

1991 CORNAS *(35 hl/ha)* Deepish dark cherry hue; smoky, griotte cherry aromas with a hint of stalkiness underneath; softish, powerful flavour, succulent fruit and fair concentration. Not (yet) the silkiness of de Barjac.

1990 CORNAS Deep, almost black, plum hue; attractive, complex *sauvage* nose, notes of mint, wild fruits, cassis and liquorice; mid-weight wine, longish finish, though hollow centre; ripe, stylish wine which will evolve over next 5 years but would benefit from more depth in middle palate.

LIONNET

1993 ST-PERAY Mid-straw; firm peachy, floral nose; clean, stylish quite fat wine; fleshy, peachy, fruit. Firm, complex well balanced. Nothing rustic here. Excellent.

1992 ST-PERAY Bright yellow, green tinges; Open, almost surmature nose, esters rather than straight fruit; hint of bonbons on palate; otherwise, fat, ripe fruit, good structure. Not perhaps the complexity of the '93, but a really lovely wine for the next 3 years or so.

1991 ST-PERAY Deepish bright yellow; opening ripe fruit and honey aromas; on palate: acacia, lime-blossom, honey. Fat, balanced wine; plenty of sustaining fruit and power; long. Lovely – *à point*.

1993 COTES DU RHONE, ROUGE Peppery, rather lifted fermentive aromas; open plummy fruity wine; sappy, a bit green. Peppery above all. Honest, fresh stuff. Not bad.

1993 CORNAS *(1 yr and older casks tasted)* Good deep red-plum; note of oak on 1 yr cask sample otherwise closed nose; fleshy, ripe wine – plenty of firm fruit; newer cask had more structure. Nothing weak here – a promising wine from an indifferent vintage.

1993 CORNAS, *DOM. DE ROCHEPERTUIS (old & new casks tasted)* Brilliant dark crimson plum; dense ripe structured fruit with oak masking varietal character. Big tight wine – notably more matter and concentration than classic *cuvée*. Needs assemblage of both fractions for balance

1992 CORNAS, *DOM. DE ROCHEPERTUIS (1 month in bottle)* Mid garnet; smoky spice, tar and *fruits noirs* nose; big, sweetish wine, good concentrated fruit, with tarry edge and touch of chocolate and torrefaction on finish. Oak supports but doesn't dominate. Dense succulent wine. A bit short, but very good for vintage.

1991 CORNAS *(standard cuvée, bottled December 1993)* Lightish garnet, carmine

edge; nose of red fruits and cinnamon beginning to emerge; voluptuous, sexy fruit; silky mouthfeel sustained by integrated ripe tannins. Peppery finish; eminently fruity wine, not the length of 1992 Rochepertuis, but more finesse at present.

1991 CORNAS, *DOM. DE ROCHEPERTUIS (bottled April 1993)* Deeper tone than 1991 – verging on opacity; closed brooding nose – hint of oak, but not *boisé*, concentrated and promising; succulent, concentrated fruit, mouthfilling, long and puissant. A bit diffuse at present – but has depth and structure for medium term ageing; needs 5 years more at least. Promising.

1990 CORNAS Blacker and denser than the above; closed nose, touches of torrefaction but little else showing; big, juicy fully ripe fruit; hint of tar and mildly burnt edge; succulent, fleshy, if a touch burly; flatteur and good length. A lorry driver rather than a ballerina.

1990 CORNAS, *DOM. DE ROCHEPERTUIS* Deep garnet, opaque, dark brick rim; closed nose, hints of very ripe black fruit – fig, *pruneaux* etc; Bags of ripe, fleshy fruit, quite gutsy yet succulent. Firm structure, with fruit and wood fighting for control. Hint of heat on long finish. Good, interesting!

1989 CORNAS, *DOM. DE ROCHEPERTUIS* Opaque, dense, mid-plum; closed smoky, pruneaux nose and soft, fleshy cooked black fruit flavours, singed at the edge. Hot, but not jammy. The 1990 is better, the 1991 better still.

MICHEL

1993 CORNAS, *COTEAUX (90% égrappé, old cask)* Bright mid-cherry; strong milled pepper nose – touch of spice; light sappy flavours; sappy, longish but with a green edge; rather weedy for a Cornas.

1993 CORNAS, *LA GEYNALE (non-égrappé)* Good mid-garnet; closed mildly spicy nose; more concentrated version of the above – bright spice & pepper; touch of green. Not bad for vintage – this is proper Cornas, compared with the above.

1992 CORNAS, *COTEAUX (en cuve)* Dense colour; closed nose; firm fleshy wine with hard edge; not much charm but just might flesh out with time. Hint of chlorophyll. Fair.

1992 CORNAS, *LA GEYNALE (en cuve)* Black plum, carmine edge; deeper than above; slender aromas of cooked cherry showing through largely closed nose; tight profile – a bit green and rustic. Firm quite fleshy. Good, but not blindingly successful.

1991 CORNAS, *PIED DE COTEAUX* Limpid black cherry, carmine rim; curiously rubbery first sniff, underneath ripe *fruits noirs*; firm mid-weight wine; green edge, longish. Lacks power and weight. Good only.

1991 CORNAS, *COTEAUX* Black plum, carmine rim; deep, brooding *fruits noirs* nose; similar flavours – rather rubbery, hot, chocolatey wine, distinct torrefactive element; burly, rustic, muscular, dry wine. No charm whatever.

1991 CORNAS, *LA GEYNALE* Fine, deep fondu black cherry colour; intense, elegant nose – cassis, griottes, *fruits noirs* – complex, still in bud; similar flavours starting to come together; only the merest hint of *rafles*. At last – the *terroir* and fruit are winning! Long, complete, fine Cornas. 10 years plus. Excellent.

VERSET

1993 CORNAS *(ex-old foudre, harvested in rain)* Limpid, velvety tone; spice and pepper dominate nose; mid-weight, a bit stemmy, with concentrated, sweetish fruit underneath. Some *puissance*. Good enough.

1992 CORNAS *(ex 600 Litre Muid)* Black, extracty appearance, deep violace-carmine rim; ripe, spicy, black fruit aromas; touch stalky but full, fleshy ripe fruit largely masks this; well-extracted wine with plenty of grip, length and interest. A sample from an earlier bottling was more forward – warm, and long, with supple *cerises confits* flavours. Delicious!

VOGE

1991 CORNAS *(young vines, 40–45 hl/ha)* Limpid black-cherry/garnet, lightish rim; ripe cherry nose – touch stemmy; supple, sappy wine, slight *goût de rafle*, good, needs 3–5 years.

1991 CORNAS, *Vieilles Vignes (38–40 hl/ha)* Deeper, limpid, dark velvet; closed nose – hint of Burlat cherries, that's all; ripe cherryish fruit, soft, quite puissant and supple; fleshy, silky feel; elegant, yet with structure for ageing. Complex, rich, very good.

1990 CORNAS *(standard cuvée)* Deep, sombre black cherry; deep, smoky, almost cooked black fruit nose – pruneaux, cherry, chocolate; fleshy, smoky flavours – notably chocolate and pruneaux again. Deep, ripe, sturdy. Very good for young vines.

1990 CORNAS, *Vieilles Vignes* Deep opaque hue; big, unforthcoming nose, slightly singed – cooked dark fruit underneath – pruneaux & chocolate; touch of surmature fruit, cerisé, very ripe; flatteur, puissant, complete. Good big old-fashioned Cornas; 1991 has much better balance.

1989 CORNAS, *Vieilles Vignes* Bright, deep black cherry; touch of oxidation on nose; biggish, fleshy ripe, supple flavours, mures especially. Elegant fruit starting to emerge; mineral note. Has plenty of guts and broad shoulders; Long, puissant, though not the sheer density of the 1990. Good plus.

1990 CORNAS, *Vieille Fontaine* Opaque, limpid black cherry, rim still purple; nose dumb – reduced, hints of ripe black fruits. Huge, superbly ripe, fleshy wine; long, puissant, very rich – real *fond* here; ripe tannins to sustain; magnificent Cornas. Needs years.

SOUTHERN RHONE

CHATEAUNEUF

DE BEAUCASTEL

1992 COUDOULET DE BEAUCASTEL (BLANC), *COTES DU RHONE* Good colour, with fresh, clean nose; plenty of wine here – balanced by good acidity; mid-weight. Pleasant and interesting.

1992 CHATEAU DE BEAUCASTEL *(BLANC)* Fine colour; very little aroma; sound, ripe fruit, good acidity; otherwise rather dumb and flat on palate. Needs a few years now to reassert itself. Good for the vintage.

1992 ROUSSANNE VIEILLES VIGNES, *CHATEAU DE BEAUCASTEL* Deepish yellow-gold; soft, peachy nose leading to well-developed flavours – principally dried apricot and nuts; rich and fat. Very fine.
1992 COUDOULET DE BEAUCASTEL, *COTES DU RHONE* Deep colour; stony nose; sound, solid wine with plenty of fruit and some complexity. Now – 5 years.
1992 CHATEAU DE BEAUCASTEL *(ROUGE)* Fine deep colour; closed nose; mid-weight wine with plenty of structure and muscle; inherently complex and *puissant* though presently a bit burly and lacking in charm.
1991 CHATEAU DE BEAUCASTEL *(ROUGE)* Mid-deep ruby; fine, complex Beaucastel nose – animal and leather; has some depth and a good balance, though not the length of a great vintage. Drink over next 5 years. Quality reflects the fact that half the grapes were eliminated before vatting; a difficult vintage.
1990 CHATEAU DE BEAUCASTEL *(ROUGE)* Deep, limpid, black cherry; reduced nose; big-framed wine, with fine structure and concentration; real depth and excellent length here. Should be at its peak around the turn of the century. Very fine.
1989 CHATEAU DE BEAUCASTEL *(ROUGE)* Similar to, but a shade lighter than the 1990; gorgeous secondary gamey aromas developing; has more finesse than the 1990 at present, feels richer and has softer tannins. Long, seductive wine. More forward than the 1990. A very fine Châteauneuf.
1990 HOMMAGE A JACQUES PERRIN Fine, deep, black cherry; earthy aromas starting to show, clearly much to come; firm, deep, very concentrated flavours reflecting its high Mourvèdre content. Beautiful balance and exemplary length. Will continue to develop over a generation. A remarkable wine.
1989 HOMMAGE A JACQUES PERRIN Another fine, deep, brooding colour, little signs of age; nose still closed, but hints at very ripe fruit and tar; big, soft, fleshy wine, with bags of ripe fruit; tannins still a touch astringent but this will change with bottle-age; perfectly poised to live for 15–20 years or more. Magnificent.

BEAURENARD

1993 DOMAINE DE BEAURENARD, *BLANC* Pale bright green; clean fresh floral and apricot nose (Clairette); some CO_2 enlivening fleshy, stylish wine with plenty of guts and well-balanced acids; reasonable finish. Promising.
1992 DOMAINE DE BEAURENARD, *BLANC* Fine pale bright citrus; more closed nose than the above, nuts, acacia; altogether bigger, gutsier wine with some fat but less nerve and elegance than the 1993. Goodish.
1990 DOMAINE DE BEAURENARD, *BLANC* Lively bright gold; secondary aromas – confit pineapple and exotic fruits; elegant, balanced wint with plenty of finesse and an enriching touch of over-ripeness. Mouthfiller which is delicious now, or will keep well over the medium term. Excellent.
1988 DOMAINE DE BEAURENARD, *BLANC* Less yellow than 1990; positive, mineral aromas with a disagreeable rubbery aspect; flavours largely oxidative, flabby and chemical; highish acids, hollow middle palate; finishes short. An oddball – and frankly disagreeable. This is unlikely to fade – Coulon's disagree.
1992 DOMAINE DE BEAURENARD, *ROUGE* Bright ruby, touch of purple; positive *fruits rouges* aroma, with spice and pepper notes; elegant, mid-weight wine, with good fruit and extract, and some complexity. Not over-tannic, but has some stemminess and lacks real grip and depth.
1991 DOMAINE DE BEAURENARD, *ROUGE* Shade lighter than 1992; burnt, spicy rather four-square nose; some real depth here in a lighter vein; good, balanced fruit; excellent result for this stormy vintage (30% of fruit discarded).
1990 DOMAINE DE BEAURENARD, *ROUGE* Deep plum, no signs of age; touch of reduction on nose, underneath full, complex, very ripe *fruits noirs*, spice, cinnamon and truffle; a rich, elegant, ripe wine, with soft tannins and fine length; concentrated spicy fruit transforming into secondary flavours. A lovely wine with a fine future. Four-star stuff.
1990 DOMAINE DE BEAURENARD, *CUVEE BOIS RENARD* Fine deep, opaque, black cherry; closed nose, black fruits and cinnamon; very concentrated with more – and slightly more aggressive – tannins than the above; notes of cocoa; long and very stylish. 10 years plus.
1989 DOMAINE DE BEAURENARD, *ROUGE* Deepish ruby, to edge of meniscus; lightish spicy nose with elements of plum, cherry, spice and *sous-bois*; truffle and *sous-bois* dominate a long, stylish palate; some excess tannins to lose. Very good.
1983 DOMAINE DE BEAURENARD, ROUGE Light ruby, browning rim; elegant *secondary* vegetal nose which follows onto palate; overall quality marred by dry tannins; needs food.

BONNEAU

1993 CHATEAUNEUF-DU-PAPE Mid plum; ripe, plummy/nose; soft, plum, spice and pepper flavours, some CO_2; good but not great; second *cuvée* more fat and harmonious.
1992 CHATEAUNEUF-DU-PAPE Limpid plum; liquorice and spicy plum aromas; fine, silky wine, with succulent fruit and ripe, well-balanced tannins. Excellent (Henri compares it to his 1984).
1990 CHATEAUNEUF-DU-PAPE, *CUVEE MARIE BEURRIER (in cask)* Fine deep colour; nose closed; palate dominated by structure – a mild excess of tannins which will need 10 years to integrate. Wine underneath seems fine.
1990 CHATEAUNEUF-DU-PAPE, *CUVEE DES CELESTINS* Dense, virtually opaque black cherry; elegant hints of very ripe, fine fruit on the nose; superby structured wine, immense richness of fruit, complete and very long. Enormous power here. Superb. Needs 10+ years to full maturity, though has the balance to be enjoyable earlier.
1989 CHATEAUNEUF-DU-PAPE, *CUVEE MARIE BEURRIER (in cask)* FIne, deep colour; completely closed nose; quite fat on the palate though more restrained and somewhat austere, without the immediacy or charm of the 1990. Will be very good, given time.
1989 CHATEAUNEUF-DU-PAPE, *CUVEE DES CELESTINS* Deep colour, almost opaque; largely closed nose; a very big-framed wine, with immense depth of fruit held together by dryish, ripe tannins. Remarkable wine, stylish and impenetrably deep. Will last a generation.

CAILLOUX

1993 LES CAILLOUX, *BLANC* Light yellow-green; clean, straightforward floral and dried apricot nose; tightly structured broad flavoured wine, with fat, power and good acidity. Will improve over 4–5 years. Excellent.
1992 LES CAILLOUX, *ROUGE* Limpid mid red; stony nose with slight stemminess; sound, softish kirsch cherry flavours with some liquorice; ready now.
1991 LES CAILLOUX, *ROUGE* Mid red with signs of browning at rim; slender, mainly vegetal nose; succulent, soft flavours with some flesh. Very good for vintage – the result of rigorous *triage* (70% of crop discarded).
1990 LES CAILLOUX, *ROGUE* Deep plum; powerful aromas of *pruneaux*, plum and cherry; finely crafted flavours with rich, succulent fruit and a powerful, firm tannic envelope; very long. Has balance to drink now, but really needs 5-10 years more. Lovely.
1989 LES CAILLOUX, *ROGUE* Marginally darker and denser than the 1990; earthier nose with animal and leather aromas; flavours also more minerally and earthy in character; the wine is more virile and complete than the 1990; Mourvèdre contributes to the wine's fine, silky texture. This is the better of these two fine vintages. Very good indeed.
1980 LES CAILLOUX, *ROUGE* Tile red, with browning rim; attractive, fully mature animal/truffle/*sous-bois* aromas; wine has a dry, tannic feel and has dried out somewhat; nonetheless, a fine glass of mature Châteauneuf.
1990 LES CAILLOUX, *CUVEE CENTENAIRE* Fine colour, dense, deep black cherry; smoky nose of super-ripe fruit, almost confit; broad, brooding flavours just beginning to open out; tight, ripe tannins underneath a layer of concentrated, fleshy fruit, firm yet silky; power, length, complexity and supreme elegance – this has them all. Magnificent. 10 years plus.
1989 LES CAILLOUX, *CUVEE CENTENAIRE* Similar to 1990 Centenaire, if anything a shade deeper; nose in the same mould as the above, perhaps a touch more expressive; on the palate, all the qualities of the 1990 but noticeably firmer and more muscular. Stunning wine.

CLOS DES PAPES

1993 CHATEAUNEUF-DU-PAPE BLANC Fine green-gold hue; seductive aromas of dried apricot and flowers; gorgeous open-textured flavours, ripe and spicy, with depth, excellent balance and above all, finesse. Delicious.
1987 CHATEAUNEUF-DU-PAPE BLANC Deeper green-gold; mature nose of nuts and honey, very Meursault in character; fresh, ripe, mature flavours, complex and very attractive. Delicious in an entirely different manner.
1993 CHATEAUNEUF-DU-PAPE ROUGE Deep black cherry; nose mainly of pepper and spice – the contribution of Mourvèdre and Syrah; biggish, supple mouthful, succulent fruit, good tannins and plenty of *mache*; fine, long finish. Lovely. 5–10 years.
1992 CHATEAUNEUF-DU-PAPE ROUGE Deep cherry/plum; reduced, closed nose; full, plummy flavours, pure fruit and fine balance; plenty of guts and good length to boot. 3–5 years. Good for vintage.
1991 CHATEAUNEUF-DU-PAPE ROUGE *(18 hl/ha.)* Bright ruby, lighter than 1992; delicate *fruits rouges* and spice nose, a ringer for young Gevrey-Chambertin; lightish wine, all in finesse rather than muscle; excellent for this difficult vintage and a testament to the Avril's "no special cuvée" policy.
1990 CHATEAUNEUF-DU-PAPE ROUGE Very dense extracted black cherry; powerful, nose with hints of super-ripe *fruits rouges* and cherries; sumptuous concentration and a long rich finish. Both big and fine – dense and elegant. Excellent.
1989 CHATEAUNEUF-DU-PAPE ROUGE Limpid deep garnet; complex minerally, *terroir* nose of spice, truffle and pepper (Mourvèdre shows); very liquoricy palate, firmly structured and still closed. Good tannins and acidity will ensure longevity. Less *flatteur* than many 1989s, but fine nonetheless. 5–10 years.
1988 CHATEAUNEUF-DU-PAPE ROUGE Deep garnet; complex nose starting to open – *fruits noirs*, truffles, *griotte* cherry, spice and *pruneaux*; tight, spicy ripe flavours; very promising. 5–10 years to go.

CLOS MONT OLIVET

1993 CHATEAUNEUF-DU-PAPE BLANC Light straw; positive, ripe, floral primeur nose; well structured fruit, fat, beautifully balanced wine. Excellent.
1993 CHATEAUNEUF-DU-PAPE ROUGE *(in* foudre*)* Lightish bright ruby; youthful peppery aromas; seems rather light on the surface, but has plenty of matter underneath. A bit four-square though. Quite promising.
1992 CHATEAUNEUF-DU-PAPE ROUGE *(in* foudre*)* Bright garnet, deeper than 1993; more *sauvage* than 1992, with touch of liquorice and some grassiness; superficially light wine, but the flavour develops in the mouth; plenty of *mache* and spice. Raw and tight at present; needs keeping. Very good for the vintage.
1991 CHATEAUNEUF-DU-PAPE ROUGE *(in bottle)* Deep brilliant garnet; dumb on nose; lightish soft wine, no rough edges; quite floral (violets) underneath. Attractive but rather one-dimensional. Might develop well.
1990 CHATEAUNEUF-DU-PAPE ROUGE *(bottled March 1993)* Bright mid-ruby garnet; ripe, concentrated aromas of *mures* and *pruneaux*; mid-weight, beautifully poised, with round tannins, great style and elegance. Not a blockbuster 1990, but has bags of class.
1989 CHATEAUNEUF-DU-PAPE ROUGE *(in bottle)* Brilliant hue, more depth than '90; fine, open, *fruits noirs* nose, soft and seductive with hint of liquorice; opulent and fleshy on the palate, with real depth, richness and spice, and very ripe tannins; has more power than the '90 at present. Fine indeed.
1988 CHATEAUNEUF-DU-PAPE ROUGE *(in bottle)* Bright mid-ruby; open, spicy and elegant *fruits noirs* aromas; quite a big wine, with soft tannins and flavours of *pruneaux*; plenty of structure and good length.
1987 CHATEAUNEUF-DU-PAPE ROUGE *(bottled June 1991)* Lighter than 1988; attractive, slender nose of *petit fruits rouges*; palate dominated by high acidity and rather dilute, four-square fruit; light and quite attractive for drinking soon.
1986 CHATEAUNEUF-DU-PAPE ROUGE *(in bottle)* Lightish garnet; aromas of *fruits noirs* and *pruneaux*; surprisingly rich and fleshy for an '86; lacks acidity but drinking well.
1985 CHATEAUNEUF-DU-PAPE ROUGE *(in bottle)* Deepest colour so far, real depth here; superb secondary aromas of *fruits noirs* and *sous-bois*; fine flavours of *sous-bois*, liquorice and violets; wine is round and complex with fine length and great elegance. Still has bags of life. Very, very good.
1984 CHATEAUNEUF-DU-PAPE ROUGE *(bottled August 1993!)* Bright mid-ruby; slender nose, not much save a hint of soft, plummy fruit; ripe, elegant

flavours, no rough edges and good balance. Fine and rich for vintage, with enough matter and tannin to hold it together.
1990 CHATEAUNEUF-DU-PAPE ROUGE, *CUVEE PAPET* Fine, brilliant deep garnet; most promising rich, fleshy nose of wild fruits with touches of *mures*, liquorice and spice; fleshy above all on the palate, with soft, mouthfilling fruit, plenty of fat and fine, round tannins – a velvet underbelly. Has great power and considerable length. Will last for 20 years or more. Very fine indeed. A privelege to taste.
1989 CHATEAUNEUF-DU-PAPE ROUGE, *CUVEE PAPET* Much the same depth and tone as the 1990 Papet; bigger nose, with more delicacy than the 1990 and notes of pine and spice; another big wine, but beautifully judged balance giving the feel of a light touch, backed by power and concentration. Very long. This seems just finer than the 1990 (Jean-Claude politely disagrees).

FONT DE MICHELLE

1993 CHATEAUNEUF-DU-PAPE BLANC *(13% alcohol)* Light straw, hint of green; floral, minerally nose with component of *fruits sec*; clean, fresh, quite fat wine, with Clairette and Grenache coming through; not a blockbuster but well made with good balance.
1992 CHATEAUNEUF-DU-PAPE ROUGE, *CUVEE ETIENNE GONNET* Deepish plum; positive, up-front fruit nose, some Syrah pepperiness and new oak evident; quite rich, complex wine, with flavours of spice, liquorice and *fruits noirs*; new wood well-integrated and not dominant. A bit short, otherwise attractive. Doesn't merit special *cuvée* status.
1990 CHATEAUNEUF-DU-PAPE, *CUVEE CLASSIQUE (14.5% alcohol)* Fine deep plum; concen trated aromas of ripe, almost confit, *fruits noirs, mures* and *pruneaux*; tightly packed super-ripe fruit with firm, round tannins and excellent length. A touch hollow, if one is nit-picking.
1985 CHATEAUNEUF-DU-PAPE, *CUVEE CLASSIQUE* Deepish garnet; fine secondary aromas of animal, *sous-bois* and truffle; similar flavours over mid-weight of fruit; round and soft; longish finish. Elegance rather than concentration rule here. Very good.

FORTIA

1993 CHATEAU FORTIA BLANC Light yellow-green; fine nose of ripe peaches and pear-skin; clean, earthy wine with good fruit. A bit heavy-footed and lacking in freshness, though.
1990 CHATEAU FORTIA ROUGE *(bottling began end of 1993)* Fine deep colour; nose completely marred by herbaceous smells; underneath, lovely supple, concentrated fruit – great richness and elegance here. This would be very good indeed, were it not for the *goût de rafle*. What a pity.
1989 CHATEAU FORTIA ROUGE Deep limpid hue; fine, stony nose showing attractive ripe fruit; mid-weight wine, quite supple and *flatteur*, with round tannins and sound fruit; has fair length, but overall balance is marred by a hollow centre and excess alcohol. Not bad though, despite these caveats.

GARDINE

1992 CHATEAU DE LA GARDINE, *BLANC (40% Grenache Blanc; 20% each Roussanne and Bourboulenc; 30% new oak)* Attractive green-gold; elegant floral/wheatmeal nose starting to show; bright, sustained flavours; oak is noticeable but not over-done; fresh acidity, but rather lean on the finish. Will improve over next 3–6 years.
1990 CHATEAU DE LA GARDINE, *VIEILLES VIGNES, BLANC (same mix as above, except 10% each Bourboulenc and Clairette; 100% new oak)* Deeper colour than 1992 from vintage and wood; nose dominated by new oak, seems rich underneath; finely structured wine with *ampleur* and power; flavours of pine and dried fruit, which opened out to laurel and acacia; needs 10 years to really show its paces. A fine bottle.
1991 CHATEAU DE LA GARDINE, *ROUGE* Deep blackish purple; still very youthful nose, with ripe, spicy fruit underneath; lightish weight for a Châteauneuf, with an excess of acidity and green tannins; finishes short. Despite all this, will make a pleasant bottle by the late 1990s.
1990 CHATEAU DE LA GARDINE, *ROUGE (30% new oak)* Deeper than the above; complex, brooding nose showing ripe fruit; mid-weight with fair fruit but dry, woody edge; not bad but lacks generosity.
1989 CHATEAU DE LA GARDINE, *ROUGE* Deeper still; fine nose of very ripe *fruits noirs* and leather; stylish, earthy flavours marginally compromised by the ever-present dry tannins which detract from the overall charm; however, wine is mouthfilling and rich with good length and has the muscle and the constitution to develop. If the tannins meld this could be very good.
1990 CUVEE DES GENERATIONS Black, even deeper than the 1989 Generations; some pepperiness, but dominant aromas are of new oak; big, powerful wine, with excellent depth of fruit and good length; not quite the size of the 1989, but has muscle and equilibrium; still the vein of dry tannin. Very good plus.
1989 CUVEE DES GENERATIONS Fine deep black colour; altogether more complex and spicier on the nose than the 1986; big, plummy, over-ripe fruit with plenty of flesh. Very harmonious, though a bit burly in character; has finesse underneath and an attractive touch of rusticity. Very good indeed, if individual.
1986 CUVEE DES GENERATIONS Fine deep plum; most attractive, open, nose of cherry, *mures* and *fruits noirs*; flavours of mulberry and kirsch cherry, with good concentration and enough fat to balance a nerve of tannins; good for the vintage, but good enough for a Prestige *cuvée*?

JANASSE

1993 DOMAINE DE LA JANASSE, *BLANC (85% matured in new or 1 year casks)* Light straw; fresh, ripe nose; crisp acidity and good fruit with Roussanne freshness showing through; suffering from recent bottling.
1984 DOMAINE DE LA JANASSE, *BLANC* Light yellow-straw; strong nuts and acacia aromas, rather rancio; suprisingly soft appley flavours, supported by vein of acidity; very little evidence of age. Attractive.
1993 DOMAINE DE LA JANASSE, *VIEILLES VIGNES (30 hl/ha)* Deep, almost opaque purple plum; muted bud of ripe *griotte* cherries on nose; fine, tight classic spice and pepper flavours with plenty of depth and grip. Promising.
1993 DOMAINE DE LA JANASSE, *CUVEE SPECIALE (85% Syrah, 15% Grenache, only 500 cases made)* Very deep colour; unforthcoming nose; massive, spicy wine with flavours of plum and cocoa. Some rough edges to iron out, but will be excellent, given time. A veritable monster. Needs a decade, at least.
1991 DOMAINE DE LA JANASSE, *ROUGE* Fine ruby red; delicate fruit-based nose; spicy mid-weight wine with fair depth and complexity. Good but not great.
1990 COTES DU RHONE, *100% CARIGNAN (first vintage)* Limpid dense black; muted, earthy nose; tight, earthy flavours, with vegetal undertones; austere; note of coffee. Very good.
1990 COTE DU RHONE, *LES GARRIGUES (first vintage)* Fine, limpid black cherry; evolving aromas of coffee, cocoa and plum; mouthfilling flavours of soft fruit; silky and thoroughly seductive. Remarkable quality for its Appellation.
1989 COTES DU RHONE, *CHASTELET (Grenache + Syrah)* Mid cherry; secondary aromas starting to emerge; softer with less stuffing than the Garrigues, but has great elegance. Fine quality.
1990 DOMAINE DE LA JANASSE, *ROUGE* Fine mid cherry; dumb nose, hinting at ripe fruit and spice; complex, fleshy wine, with real depth and class. Ripe tannins hidden under layers of silky fruit. Very good indeed.
1990 DOMAINE DE LA JANASSE, *CUVEE VIEILLES VIGNES* Dense, virtually opaque; no discernible nose; immense wine, packed with sweet, spicy fruit; flavours of coffee and cocoa, *pruneaux* and kirsch cherries; splendid length. Superb!
1989 DOMAINE DE LA JANASSE, *CUVEE CHAUPIN (100% 1912 Grenache)* Deepish plum; fine aromas of *fruits noirs* with animal overtones; lighter than the VV but still has considerable depths; firm, silky fruit supported by plenty of well-defined tannins. Very high quality.
1989 DOMAINE DE LA JANASSE, *CUVEE VIEILLES VIGNES* Bright mid-deep cherry; aromas of cinnamon, cocoa and spice; big, tarry wine, with heaps of super-ripe fruit and an envelope of ripish tannins; great style and underlying elegance. Needs 6–10 years.

DE MARCOUX

1992 DOMAINE DE MARCOUX, *BLANC* Bright green-gold; as yet slender nose, nutty and honeyed; fresh, clean flavours underpinned by crisp acidity; quite robust in style with high alcohol and a rawish finish. (The 1993, in cuve, was altogether fatter and richer, and far more promising).
1993 DOMAINE DE MARCOUX, *ROUGE* Mid deep colour; elegant, open aromas of *fruits rouges*, almost Pinot Noir in character; soft, evolved flavours supported by tannins and concentrated, ripe fruit. Promising.
1993 DOMAINE DE MARCOUX, *CUVEE VIEILLES VIGNES (in* foudre*)* More depth and density than the above; fuller and richer on the nose; palate has an earthy, minerally note with good length and round tannins; an elegant wine in the making.
1992 DOMAINE DE MARCOUX, *ROUGE (in cuve)* Mid garnet; extraordinarily Pinot-like nose, leading to fine, silky, supple firmly structured flavours. Very good.
1992 DOMAINE DE MARCOUX, *VIEILLES VIGNES (in cuve)* Deeper than the above; more animal on the nose and more mineral and substance on the palate. Complex wine with a firm, balanced structure and attractive *ampleur*.
1990 DOMAINE DE MARCOUX, *ROUGE (14% alcohol)* Deepish translucent red; closed nose; very concentrated, spicy, earthy wine, with real depth of flavour and a very long, warm finish. Very fine indeed. 5–10 years.

MONPERTUIS

1991 CHATEAUNEUF-DU-PAPE BLANC *(1st. vintage with Roussanne)* Mid green-citrus; fine nose of ripe greengages; quite a lean, green wine at present, but has the underlying fat and structure to develop well and good length and depth. Needs 5–8 years. Very good.
1990 CHATEAUNEUF-DU-PAPE BLANC *(No Roussanne)* Light yellow-gold, much more colour than 1991; fat and rich wheatmeal nose, still closed; big, mouthfilling wine with bags of *gras*, a touch a tannin and good balancing acidity. Needs 5–10 years. Strongly akin to a young Rayas Blanc.
1990 CHATEAUNEUF-DU-PAPE ROUGE, *CLASSIQUE (bottled spring 1993, yield 35 hl/ha)* Limpid mid-cherry red; attractive nose of spice, pine and kirsch cherries; palate presently dominated by a lean nerve of acid and some tannins; generous fruit underneath and plenty of power to sustain it. All the elements of a fine wine. Very good.
1990 CHATEAUNEUF-DU-PAPE ROUGE, *TRADITION (15% alc; 20 hl/ha.)* Fine colour: intense, dense, limpid black cherry; splendidly complex nose of *surmature* griotte cherries, confit; meaty tarry tannin wine, with earthy, mineral undertones; fine tannins, excellent extract, long and powerful. A touch old-fashioned, but confident and splendid nonetheless. (Some vats reached 16% natural alcohol).
1989 CHATEAUNEUF-DU-PAPE ROUGE, *TRADITION (14.6% alcohol)* Similar depth to 1990 Tradition, a shade more brilliance perhaps; highly promising nose of similar character; at present, wine appears to have more flesh and suppleness than 1990, better tannin balance and greater power. Much in the style of Henri Bonneau. Very fine indeed; remarkable quality.

MONT REDON

1993 DOMAINE DE MONT-REDON, *BLANC* Light straw; floral, wheatmeal and hay nose leads to floral flavours with good depth of ripe fruit and a finely-tuned balance; enough acidity and a long finish complete a very well made wine.
1983 DOMAINE DE MONT-REDON, *BLANC* Fine bright green-gold; fully mature aromas of nuts and butter, very Meursault in character; a touch of CO_2 lifting fine, rich flavours; still has excellent acidity and finishes long and rather lean. A fine bottle.
1992 DOMAINE DE MONT-REDON, *ROUGE* Deep garnet, purple edge; liquorice and rose-petal nose which promises fine aromatic development; on the palate, a complete wine with longish flavours and reasonable concentration.
1991 DOMAINE DE MONT-REDON, *ROUGE* Limpid mid-red; nose marked by creamy new oak; lightish flavours with constituents in balance; could do with touch more concentration.
1990 DOMAINE DE MONT-REDON, *ROUGE* Deep, sustained red; strong aromas of dark chocolate; closed on palate, but clearly has richness underneath; robustly

constituted with good round tannins and good weight of ripe fruit. Delicious.
1989 DOMAINE DE MONT-REDON, *ROUGE* Deepish black cherry, hint of brick at edge; bitter chocolate again on nose; in this context wine is big-framed, with muscle and tannins though by no means a blockbuster; fair fruit underneath and starting to develop attractive complexity. Will probably outlast the 1990.
1985 DOMAINE DE MONT-REDON, *ROUGE* Limpid mid-garnet, brick rim; mature secondary aromas of *sous-bois* developing, with soft, vegetal-based flavours; rather an organic feel to it; all in finesse. Most attractive. Drink soon.
1981 DOMAINE DE MONT-REDON, *ROUGE* More colour and less development that 1985; attractive, complex nose of truffle and *sous-bois* with notes of liquorice and *mures*; warm, fleshy wine, though a touch hollow. Attractive.
1978 DOMAINE DE MONT-REDON, *ROUGE* Even deeper than the 1981 – fine colour, holding up well; spicy, ripe aromas of *sous-bois* and *mures*; relatively light flavours with fully mature palate aromas; again, all in finesse. Very seductive. *A point.*

NERTHE

1990 LA NERTHE WHITE Mid green-gold; bright; complex attractive floral nose redolent of young Meursault; acacia, *tilleul,* nuts, plenty of *gras* and finesse; excellent balance; a fine wine.
1990 CLOS DE BEAUVENIR Bright yellow green-gold – fine colour; ripe, complex nose – subtle & attractive – finesse of a young Puligny; more concentrated version of above – fat, beautifully crafted wine, real *fond* and *gras*, finely balanced. Puissant and fine. Don't touch before 1997. A masterpiece.
1991 LA NERTHE RED Deep limpid black plum, tuile edge; strong strawberry aromas – young Pinot Noir – fine, soft, complex; richish fruit, highish acid, more finesse than weight, finishes short. Reasonably promising – GR suffered from coulure, so higher % of ripe MO. Good for the vintage.
1990 LA NERTHE RED Deep, sustained mid-plum; spicy understated nose, closed; complexity underneath. Earthiness of MO and richness of GR well combined; mid-weight, good length. Quite complex, but lacks concentration for top quality. Not great in context of 1990s. Lighter press wine incorporated, which Alain Dugas admits was a mistake.
1989 LA NERTHE RED Limpid bright mid-plum; lightly *tuilé;* spicy reduced nose; pruneaux. Reduced tarry, spicy flavours – liquorice, plums. A bit burly and lacking in finesse at present. Good acidity and touch of dry tannin. A big'un for La Nerthe. Good, none the less.
1988 LA NERTHE RED Light plum, *tuilé*; vegetal nose – early maturation – soft, peppery. Light, frankly dilute; dry, lacks grip. Not a success; rather ordinary.
1985 LA NERTHE RED *(First vinification in new cellar)* Limpid sustained mid-plum; tuile; secondary aromas – *sous-bois*, mushrooms, liquorice; mature on palate, ageing and drying out somewhat; attractive *fané* old lady.
1990 CUVEE DES CADETTES Opaque deep plum, black cherry edge; spicy v. ripe fruit aromas, new wood just noticeable. New oak dominates palate; tannins strong but ripe; plenty of good ripe fruit. Puissant. Very good but not tops.
1989 CUVEE DES CADETTES Bright deep plum; greater density than 1990. Nose starting to open – tarry, spicy, liquorice notes, needs time. Surprisingly soft, fleshy wine; very rich and attractive, spice rather than fruit dominates; excellent length. Oak needs time to integrate; wine is presently rather burly; will develop and integrate over a decade or so. Very good
1988 CUVEE DES CADETTES Mid-deep plum; brown, tuile aspect; very rich vegetal – fruit based nose, spicy. Lovely ripe, spicy flavours, notes of liquorice with plenty of depth and mache. Long. Notches above 1988 regular *cuvée.* Very attractive for medium term drinking.

PEGAU

1993 DOMAINE DU PEGAU, *BLANC (vinified in new oak)* Deepish gold; rich spicy, nutty aromas; beautifully balanced flavours, very floral in character and masses of fat, ripe fruit.
1993 DOMAINE DU PEGAU, *BLANC (matured in 2nd. yr. casks)* Slightly lighter in tone with more acidity than the above; nonetheless, plenty of structure and fat; no floral flavours here. The blend of this with the above will make a very fine wine.
1992 DOMAINE DU PEGAU, *BLANC (matured in cuve)* Good, deepish colour; rather muted nose; a big wine again and rather burly and short; rich but not really a keeper.
1991 DOMAINE DU PEGAU, *BLANC* Good colour; restrained, elegant nose; quite big, but not alcoholic, enough ripe fruit and some length. Difficult to see where this is going.
1990 DOMAINE DU PEGAU, *BLANC* Deepish yellow-gold; full honeyed nose; more richness and depth than the above, with firm, sound fruit and good length. Another very individual wine, but most attractive.
1993 DOMAINE DU PEGAU, *ROUGE (in* foudre*)* Black purple; fresh fruit and pepper nose; well-constituted and balanced, with enough matter and tannin to keep it for several years.
1992 DOMAINE DU PEGAU, *ROUGE (80% Grenache; 17% Syrah, 3% Mourvèdre and Counoise)* Dense, almost impenetrable black cherry; closed, brooding nose with layers of ripe black fruits underneath; substantial, rich wine, succulent with hints of spicy Syrah pepper and firm, ripe tannins. Nothing rustic about this. Has a fine future.
1991 DOMAINE DU PEGAU, *ROUGE* Fine blackhue; nose of ripe cherries, leading to soft, liquoricey fruit; a bit short, but good for a 1991.
1989 DOMAINE DU PEGAU, *ROUGE* Mid-deep black cherryt; aromas of nuts and ripe cherries; more *flatteur* and supple than the 1991, with ripe tannins and reasonable length; finishes a shade alcoholic, but a good wine, all round.
1985 DOMAINE DU PEGAU, *ROUGE* Lighter black; curious, sherryish nose; some secondary, rather oxidative flavours; a bit burly and cooked. Altogether rather clumsy.

RAYAS

1993 CHATEAU RAYAS, *BLANC (in tank)* Deep green-gold; posiive nose of very ripe dried fruit; a full, concentrated, powerful wine with finesse and exemplary length. Fine balance. Five-star Châteauneuf.
1992 CHATEAU RAYAS, *BLANC* Limpid green-tinged yellow-gold; fresh, fruit-based nose; ripe, stylish wine, long and complex. Will last for years. Very fine.
1991 CHATEAU RAYAS, *BLANC* Bright deep green-gold; peach aromas with hints of oxidative nuts and butter; strong powerful flavours with bags of firm, ripe fruit and finely balanced acidity. Very good indeed.
1991 CHATEAUNEUF-DU-PAPE, *PIGNAN* Deepish plum (far lighter than Fonsalette 1991 q.v.); complex nose of spicy *fruits rouges* and old roses; elegance rather than size on the palate with flavours which follow the nose. Very good indeed. 4–8 years.
1990 CHATEAUNEUF-DU-PAPE, *PIGNAN* Deep, purplish garnet; emerging vegetal, fruit aromas, a touch asparagussy, soft, mid-weight, quite sexy fruit, rich, clean, finely crafted; good acidity and tannins. 5 years plus. Excellent.
1989 CHATEAUNEUF-DU-PAPE, *PIGNAN* Mid deep garnet, right to rim; fine, open, sweet fruit nose; tarry, garrigues flavours, developing fine weight; baked, fleshy fruit; long. Very good indeed.
1988 CHATEAUNEUF-DU-PAPE, *PIGNAN* Mid deep appearance; open, soft nose; goodish baked, cooked fruit balanced by round tannins; long and powerful mouthfeel, partly from 14% alcohol. Drinking well now, but will develop further over the next 5 years. Fine quality.
1993 CHATEAU RAYAS, *ROUGE (*foudre *sample)* Deep plum; ripe, open, sweet-fruit nose; fine extracty mouthfilling wine with plenty of concentration and excellent length. Essence of Grenache.
1991 CHATEAU RAYAS, *ROUGE* Oddly, lighter than the Pignan; altogether closed on the nose; great intensity of fruit, despite its colour; robustly structured, yet complex and complete. Round and long. By far the best Châteauneuf of this vintage.
1990 CHATEAU RAYAS, *ROUGE* Deepish colour; more vibrant red than the 1989; more obviously forward and elegant than the 1989, but with greater weight underneath; very long, complex, opulent. Ultimately, the greater of this remarkable pair.
1989 CHATEAU RAYAS, *ROUGE* closed nose; on the palate, remarkable density of soft, almost velvety, old-vine fruit; substantial acidity and round tannins; very long indeed, warm finish. Needs 5 years at least. Very fine quality; essence of Grenache.
1988 CHATEAU RAYAS, *ROUGE* Opaque dark plum, right to rim; huge, expansive aromas of sweet, ripe fruit; long, complex, tight flavours – splendid depth of fruit, beautiful balance. A classic Rayas in the making. Magnificent.

RELAGNES

1991 CHATEAUNEUF-DU-PAPE Lightish, mid garnet; gentle nose of *fruits rouges*, strawberries and tomatoes; lightweight wine, with too much tannin for fruit; firm finish. Not bad for the vintage.
1990 CHATEAUNEUF DU-PAPE "ST-MARC" CUVEE *(in cuve)* Sustained, mid deep, black cherry; opulent nose of spice, liquorice and old-vine fruit; meaty wine, though not a heavyweight; good depth and fine balance. Needs 5–10 years yet; very good.
1990 CHATEAUNEUF-DU-PAPE *(recently bottled)* Shade more depth of colour than the above; less open nose and distinctly less forthcoming on palate. Tannins currently dominate here.
1989 CHATEAUNEUF-DU-PAPE *(recently bottled)* Bright mid-deep plum; ripe meat-extract and *pruneaux* aromas; some volatility (on the limit of acceptable). A pity – wine seems good underneath.
1989 CHATEAUNEUF-DU-PAPE *(older bottling)* Marginally lighter colour; cleaner, altogether fresher nose, more *pruneaux* than meat; much better flavour development with notes of violet and red fruits. Very good.
1988 CHATEAUNEUF-DU-PAPE Lightish mid-garnet; closed nose showing some *fruits rouges* and *pruneaux*; substantial, with good, deep, ripe fruit, well integrated tannins and long, warm finish. Needs a few more years. Very good.
1981 CHATEAUNEUF-DU-PAPE Fine deep colour, holding well; superb, still youthful nose of ripe prunes leading to a spectrum of flavours from old vine fruit; ripe, warm finish with a touch of dryness; plenty of depth. Excellent.

VIEILLE JULIENNE

1993 CHATEAUNEUF-DU-PAPE BLANC *(12.8% alcohol)* Light citrus; young, fermentive aromas; clean, fresh and quite fat and appley; rather lacking in substance; 0.5% more alcohol would help.
1992 CHATEAUNEUF-DU-PAPE ROUGE *(blend of ⅓ cuve and ⅔* foudre *wines; 30 hl/ha.)* Deepish red plum; aromas of fruit and pepper; good, solid, frank wine with succulent fruit and plenty of *mache*; red fruit and griotte cherry flavours. Good for the vintage.
1990 CHATEAUNEUF-DU-PAPE ROUGE Fine, deep black cherry hue; gorgeous rich plum nose with hints of pine and spice; ripe, youthful flavours with round tannins and plenty of *mache*; goodish concentration and well-judged balance. A bit more depth and substance would help. A good, but not great, 1990.
1989 CHATEAUNEUF-DU-PAPE ROUGE *(not destemmed)* Note less depth of colour than 1990; opening nose of cassis and *fruits noirs*; the fruit is stifled by green, stemmy tannins; wine is altogether more rustic than the 1990.

VIEUX DONJON

1993 CHATEAUNEUF-DU-PAPE BLANC *(bottled December 1994)* Light straw-citrus; peach nose, touch of sulphur; lightish weight, with nerve of acidity; rustic finish. Quite attractive but won't make old bones.
1991 CHATEAUNEUF-DU-PAPE ROUGE Good deepish red-plum; reduced nose, somewhat cherry-stony in character; fine, soft stony flavours, complete and quite complex; a bit short. Good for the vintage and attractive, if rather lightweight.
1990 CHATEAUNEUF-DU-PAPE ROUGE Deep, almost black, plum; closed nose showing some dense, creamy ripe fruit; altogether bigger and richer than 1991, with excellent depth and plenty of balancing ripe tannins to keep it going; succulent fruit with considerable elegance evident underneath. Needs a decade or more to unravel. Very fine.

VIEUX TELEGRAPHE

1993 VIEUX TELEGRAPHE BLANC *(bottled March 1994)* Light green-gold; peach-kernel, dried fruit and honey on the nose; ripe, stylish wine with open-texture and a vein of supporting acidity; complex and long, with an earthy, chalky aftertaste.

1992 VIEUX TELEGRAPHE ROUGE *(in cuve)* Deep, almost opaque plum; strongly animal nose (which usually reverts to fruit-based aromas after a couple of years); plenty of ripe, concentrated fruit, full, fleshy with underlying elegance; finishes a bit short, but that's the vintage. Very good for a 1992.

1991 VIEUX TELEGRAPHE ROUGE Light ruby; soft, open nose; more elegance than size; palate is dominated by red fruits; quite light, but attractive and perfectly sound.

GIGONDAS & VACQUEYRAS

CAYRON

1993 GIGONDAS *(in cuve)* Deep inky purple; reduced nose (needs racking); intense deep plum and spice flavours; a complete wine, right across the palate; real *fond* here. Excellent prospects.

1992 GIGONDAS *(in foudre)* Lighter than 1993, esterated nose; fine silky wine, more in finesse than muscle; still, has good depth and some class. Drink before the above.

1991 GIGONDAS *(in foudre)* Mid-deep sustained colour; very aromatic nose with attractive, stylish, ripe fruit; in weight, mid way between the two above, with round tannins and good long finish. Second cask had more of everything – colour, depth and power.

1990 GIGONDAS *(bottle)* Deepish mulberry; smoky, *fruits noirs* nose, just starting to open; fine, earthy, silky flavours; well-balanced and needing 5 years or so to maturity. You'd be lucky to find better Gigondas than this. Lovely.

CLOS DES CAZAUX

1992 VACQUEYRAS BLANC *(malo faite)* Light green-gold; soft greengage nose and clean, fresh fruit flavours with good acidity and some length and fat. Well made wine, nothing fancy.

1991 VACQUEYRAS, *CLOS DES CAZAUX (50:50 Grenache:Syrah; 10–20 year-old vines)* Bright garnet; open, fruit based peppery nose; quite spicy, full wine; has tannin and character but clearly designed for early drinking.

1990 VACQUEYRAS ROUGE, *CUVEE ST-ROCH (65% Grenache, 30% Syrah, 5% Cinsault)* Bright garnet; positive spicy, plummy, *fruits noirs* aromas and flavours; enough acidity and tannins, but not over-muscular; 50 year-old vines contribute to the wine's depth. Good plus.

1991 VACQUEYRAS ROUGE, *CUVEE SPECIALE DES TEMPLIERS (100% 30–40 year old Syrah)* Deep, sustained, limpid red velvet; strong liquorice, pepper and tar nose; heavy-framed wine with plenty of fruit to balance structure; strong liquorice flavour, good depth and dry tannic edge which should integrate with time.

1990 VACQUEYRAS ROUGE, *CUVEE SPECIALE DES TEMPLIERS (100% 30–40 year old Syrah)* More purple and youthful hue than 1991; attractive, singed aromas of tar, leather, cedar and spice; soft attack leading to complex layer of concentrated fruit and round tannins. Will improve over a decade. Excellent wine. A touch of new wood, would add something extra still.

1990 GIGONDAS, *LA TOUR SARRAZINE (80% Grenache, 15% Mourvèdre, 5% Syrah)* Good mid-red colour; aromas of mulberry and *fruits noirs*; warm, mouthfilling wine with peppery flavours and a sound backbone. 3–5 years. Very good, though the 1990 Templiers is arguably better.

1988 GIGONDAS, *LA TOUR SARRAZINE (mix as above)* Youthful mid-plum; nose still closed; flavours of *petits fruits rouges* with hints of *sous-bois* and mushroom. Warm, powerful wine, with tannin to lose. Needs 5 years cellaring. Good plus.

COMBE

1990 GIGONDAS, *L'OUSTAU FAUQUET (14.1° alcohol)* Fine deep colour; attractive *fruits noirs* aromas coming through – especially cassis and framboise; warm, fleshy feel to this, plenty of sound, well-ripened silky fruit; hints of tar and liquorice. More seductive than the Prestige at present. Very good.

1990 GIGONDAS, *L'OUSTAU FAUQUET, CUVEE CIGALOUN (14° alcohol)* Notch more depth and limpidity than the above; on nose and palate, wine is in same mould, but clearly has much more to come, given time; at present dumb and rather four-square; only spoiled by a nerve of green rafles. Very successful though. 3–5 years needed to open out.

1990 VACQUEUYRAS, *LES CEPS D'OR (100% old vine Grenache; 13°alcohol)* Fine deep blackish garnet; concentrated cassis – mure nose; long, warm feel; meaty, chunky wine; super-ripe fruit. Rafles evident again. Good plus, though lacks the finesse of the above. 3–5 years, possibly longer.

FONT SANE

1991 GIGONDAS, *TRADITION* Good, limpid colour; fresh quite grassy, plummy nose; greenish stalky flavour overlays sound ripe fruit; a robust wine, spoilt by stemminess.

1990 GIGONDAS TRADITION *(14% alcohol)* Dark plum, deeper than 1991; fine, aromatic nose, with notes of concentrated plummy fruit; despite some stemminess, wine has a firm foundation, attractive depth and a complex, long finish. Very good.

1989 GIGONDAS TRADITION *(14.5% alcohol)* Less colour, more brightness and transparency than the 1990; slender nose of *fruits rouges*; flavours also brighter, with more obvious acidity; wine's balance marred by a green tannic envelope.

1990 GIGONDAS, *CUVEE FUTEE (65% Grenache, 35% Syrah)* Deep plum, still purple; meaty, spicy nose, quite *sauvage* and animal in character; oak appears on palate, which it dominates, but not on nose; good fruit underneath; oak, grape and stem tannin make for a very masculine wine; finishes warm, but is a bit hollow. Promising.

1989 GIGONDAS, *CUVEE FUTEE* Much as the 1990, but more sombre appearance; secondary aromas and flavours of *sous-bois* and *fruits noirs* starting to appear; a fine, concentrated wine. Best of the lot. Needs 5–10 years yet.

DE LA GARRIGUE

1993 VACQUEYRAS ROUGE *(80:20 Grenache:Syrah; in cuve)* Deepish plum; youthful peppery nose; sound, earthy, fullish wine, enough tannin and promising intensity. Should make an attractive bottle.

1993 VACQUEYRAS ROUGE *(50:50 Syrah:Grenache; in cuve)* Dense black-purple, with more pepper and spice on the nose; greater extract and weight than the above; very promising. Will end up as Cuvée Vignoble.

1993 GIGONDAS *(in cuve)* Lighter than the above; youthful, fermentive aromas; good structure and depth of fruit. Seems promising.

1991 VACQUEYRAS Red plum, with slender nose of *petits fruits rouges*; softish flavours of strawberry, but lacks length or weight for longevity. Good for vintage.

1990 VACQUEYRAS Fine deep colour; aromatic nose changing from fruit to *sous-bois* and animal; plenty of *mache* and fruit; not perhaps the power of Châteauneuf, but something of its qualities. Needs several years yet. Excellent.

1989 VACQUEYRAS Even deeper than 1990; closed nose, slightly cheesy and tarry notes; a big wine, with more aggressive tannins and less fine balance than the above; seems younger. Will probably outlive the 1990. Very fine quality.

1988 VACQUEYRAS Limpid deep garnet; spicy, meaty nose; palate is marked by heat and high acidity and lacks real depth; has oxidative flavours which will continue to dog it.

1990 VACQUEYRAS, *CUVEE VIGNOBLE* Deep red-plum; nose of meat-extract, spice and tar; contrasting, and most attractive, flavours of red fruits and mulberries. A gorgeous wine in the making. Needs 5–10 years to evolve fully.

1990 COTES DU RHONE, *CUVEE ROMAINE* A shade more purple than the above; similar nose, but less open; infinitely softer and more supple than the 1990 Vignoble and without its heavy structure. Lovely now and over the next few years.

1985 VACQUEYRAS Mid ruby, tile-coloured rim; fine mature aromas of *sous-bois*, soft fruit and spice, which continue through to palate; wine has a long, warm finish. Most attractive. *A point.*

GOUBERT

1992 COTES DU RHONE BLANC, *VIOGNIER* Light green-gold; very ripe, *surmature*, dried apricot nose with a touch of botrytis; palate is quite full, with a dryish edge and flavours of apricots; a bit short, but this is just CDR and the vintage is 1992. 1993 is richer and better balanced.

1991 GIGONDAS Limpid mid-garnet; freshly-milled pepper and spicy fruit dominate nose; clean, well-structured palate, a bit lean in the middle, but with warm finish and enough fruit to flesh out over the next 2–3 years. Good plus.

1990 GIGONDAS *(29 days vatting)* Deep, limpid, velvet plum; positive, ripe nose of *fruits noirs*; altogether richer, fuller and warmer than the 1991; wine has round tannins, plenty of substance and a good larding of glycerol; a touch of astringency on the finish. Fine and highly promising.

1991 GIGONDAS, *CUVEE FLORENCE* Similar appearance to the above, marginally less depth; oak gently dominates the nose and the palate; wine has richness, a firm structure and fair depth. A touch of stemminess spoils the overall feel and the fruit is somewhat overpowered by the wood.

1990 GIGONDAS, *CUVEE FLORENCE* Altogether denser and more substantial; nose has a strong minty component and flavours are more extracted and robust than the 1991. Warm, long finish. A big wine, needing 5–10 years to integrate. Very fine.

1989 GIGONDAS, *CUVEE FLORENCE* In appearance, a lighter, brighter version of the 1990; nose has more oak and *fruits rouges* but less richness; palate has greater *mache*, but brighter, less concentrated flavours; a dry tannic envelope detract from the overall balance. Good wine, but overshadowed by the 1990.

GRAPILLON D'OR

1993 GIGONDAS *(in foudre)* Deep black-plum; fine, stylish aromas of very ripe fruit; multi-layered wine packed with sweet, almost *surmature* fruit; long, powerful and complex. Very, very good.

1992 GIGONDAS *(in cuve)* Dull mid-plum; lightish nose of red fruits belies palate which has succulence and good depth; will turn out well.

1985 GIGONDAS Deep red plum; showing attractive aromas of *sous-bois*; mid-weight, with depth and richness – soft, maturing flavours disguising underlying power; plenty of warm concentrated stuffing. Fine wine, reaching its peak.

1981 GIGONDAS Deep, sustained hue, right to rim which has a hint of maturity; spicy, meaty nose, with animal and leather starting to come through; understated wine, mid-weight; beginning to open out; flavours persist for 30 seconds; a tightish envelope still hides seductive, warm fruit. A fine, complete and most attractive wine.

PALLIERES

1990 LES PALLIERES, *GIGONDAS (cask sample)* Mid-deep black cherry; opening aromas of *fruits confits, noirs* and *sous-bois*; somewhat reduced, but wine has sound structure, firm, ripe fruit, well-judged tannins, depth and finesse. Excellent prospects.

1989 LES PALLIERES, *GIGONDAS* Denser than the 1990; unforthcoming nose; firm frame, well-covered with supple, fleshy fruit. Not a heavyweight but has most attractive warmth and finesse. 3–5 years away from full maturity.

1986 LES PALLIERES, *GIGONDAS* Limpid deep plum; mature aromas of *cassis* and *sous-bois*; light, rather meagre on the palate; high acidity. Pleasant, but nothing special.

PALLEROUDIAS

1993 COTES DU RHONE, *ROUGE (unfined, unfiltered)* Light black cherry; more expressive on the palate than on the nose: concentrated, succulent, *pruneaux* fruit and firm structure. Good for its Appellation.

1991 VACQUEYRAS *(CUVEE BOISEE)* Touch of browning; fine, *sous-bois* nose; excellent full flavour with subtle oak component; concentrated and fleshy with a mild woody edge which doesn't detract from overall quality. Very promising.

1993 GIGONDAS Bright mid-garnet; closed nose; substantial, mouthfilling wine with heaps of seductive ripe fruit and firm, round tannins. Will make an most attractive bottle in time.

RASPAIL-AY

1993 GIGONDAS ROSE *(50% Clairette, 45% Grenache, 5% Syrah; 13.5% alcohol)* Bright red cherry; clean, fresh nose; sappy well-balanced flavours, good acidity and a touch of tannins. Quite tightly structured – at the limit of a light red. Very good.

1993 GIGONDAS ROUGE *(in cuve; 13.5% alcohol)* Mid plum, crimson rim; reduced, smoky black fruit nose; mouthfilling, tarry, with pure, concentrated fruit and good tannin-acid balance. Very good.

1992 GIGONDAS ROUGE *(in* foudre; *13.7% alcohol)* Mid plum, light purple rim; opening nose of raspberry and liquorice; lightish wine with bright, cherryish flavours; what it lacks in depth it compensates for in elegance. Good plus.

1991 GIGONDAS ROUGE *(13.7% alcohol)* Deep, translucent black cherry; smoky nose of wood and black fruits, still closed; more open on the palate, with good fruit, but lacks any real depth and is overbalanced with dry tannins. Would have benefited from less than 30 months in wood.

1990 GIGONDAS ROUGE *(14.2% alcohol)* Fine, intense opaque black; promising nose of smoky, super-ripe fruit starting to emerge; fine, extracty, concentrated flavours, loaded with fruit; perfect balalnce of tannin and alcohol. Excellent. Five stars.

1989 GIGONDAS *(14% alcohol; nearly 36 months in wood)* Black, but less intense than the 1990; unforthcoming nose, showing merest hints of red fruits and spice; biggish, heavy-framed wine, leather and spice, with dry tannic surround; less *flatteur* and shorter finish than the 1990; still very good, though.

ST-GAYAN

1989 COTES DU RHONE, *RASTEAU (70% Grenache; 30% Mourvèdre; no wood)* Bright deep-plum; nose of warm, earthy leather (Mourvèdre) and ripe, mouthfilling flavours, with plenty of muscle. More rustic than Gigondas, but ideal for rich food.

1990 GIGONDAS Intense, limpid dark colour; fine aromas of stony griotte cherry leading to a firm, well-structured palate packed with ripe fruit; there is plenty to come over the next decade. Very good plus.

1989 GIGONDAS Brighter and less limpid than the above; virtually no nose; flavours are lifted by acidity and tannins are more obvious; wine has concentration but it raw at present. Will develop over next 5 years or so, but the 1990 is classier and better balanced.

1988 GIGONDAS Similar to 1990, though less youthful; nose undeveloped, showing ripe fruit; palate is supple, but with less extract than either 1989 or 1990; has a firm structure which will need at least a decade to soften out.

SANTA DUC

1993 GIGONDAS *(cask sample)* Fine black-crimson; bright nose with some (temporary?) green stalkiness; firm flavours with plenty of sound, concentrated fruit. Promising.

1993 GIGONDAS, *CUVEE PRESTIGE* Deeper still; reduced nose; much greater depth and more rounded tannins than the standard 1993; robust, yet fine, with some oaky flavours. Very promising.

1992 GIGONDAS *(matured in* pieces *and* foudres*)* Deep plum, with purple edge; oak showing through on nose and dominates palate; firm, attractive palate with reasonable concentration and a dry tannic envelope; good length. Attractive now, but will improve over next 3–5 years.

1991 GIGONDAS Mid ruby; supple attractive wine which needs time to open; suffering from recent bottling and has excessive astringent tannins. Not Yves' best effort.

1990 GIGONDAS Sustained, extracty, mid-deep garnet; fine, very ripe, red fruits nose; on the palate, a bit, supple, complex wine with fat, ripe fruit, good length and a warm finish. A massive, powerful monster.

1990 GIGONDAS, *LES HAUTES GARRIGUES (15.5% alcohol)* Deep black cherry, dark carmine edge; creamy, new oak nose; wood dominates the palate; densely packed fruit drives, underpinned by firm, ripe tannins. Highly impressive, but the standard *cuvée* may turn out better.

LIRAC & TAVEL

D'AQUERIA

1993 TAVEL ROSE Light cherry hue; nose has no real markers, just a hint of strawberry and some fat fruit – could be taken for a white wine; palate has distinct personality, with plenty of firm, supple fruit; a substantial rosé; one can taste the structure from Mourvèdre and Cinsault. Good stuff.

1993 LIRAC BLANC Limpid, rather dull straw; excellent positive yeasty, wheatmeal and greengage nose; similar flavours with a note of estery appleness; wine is fat and complex with well-judged acidity. Might take this for a scaled-down white Châteauneuf.

1989 LIRAC ROUGE Mid garnet; explosive, very plummy nose, with the finesse and style of Pinot Noir; lightish, round, red-fruit flavours (Pinot again), good length and some subtlety developing. Classy Lirac.

MEJAN-TAULIER

1992 TAVEL ROSE *(in bottle)* Light onion-skin rose; wheaty nose and tight, firm flavours with fresh, uncomplicated fruit and attensive malic acidity. Rather characterless.

1992 TAVEL ROSE *(in cuve)* A bit more colour and aromatic depth; altogether fuller and more flavoursome, with better balanced and less obvious jarring acidity.

1991 LIRAC ROUGE *(in cuve)* Velvet plum; aromas of *petits fruits rouges* and strawberry – very Pinot Noir; quite rich, full flavour with attractive suppleness and firm structure; shortish finish.

1990 LIRAC ROUGE *(in cuve)* Limpid garnet; open strawberry jam nose; more depth and glycerol than the 1991; also greater length and a better tannin balance. Finishes short.

1988 LIRAC ROUGE *(in bottle)* Deep, limpid garnet; still quite closed, with some spicy fresh fruit aromas coming through; fullish flavour with plenty of guts

and a tannic edge; not a heavyweight, but shows the muscle of the vintage. Could do with a touch more flesh on the frame.

ST-ROCH

1992 LIRAC BLANC, *CHATEAU ST-ROCH* Deep colour; open nose of hazelnut and wheatmeal; clean, sappy Clairette flavours with crisp acidity; rather four-square. Will round out with a few years in bottle.

1990 LIRAC BLANC, *CHATEAU ST-ROCH* Better colour, more yellow; fine, honeyed nose; quite a rich wine with good fat and enough acidity; has a touch of tannin; attractive flavours of honey and hay.

1993 LIRAC ROSE, *CHATEAU ST-ROCH* On the deeper side of cherry; soft, floral Grenache dominates nose; big, fleshy style of rosé, with grip and underlying depth; would benefit from a bit more acidity. Attractive, though.

1988 LIRAC ROUGE, *CHATEAU ST-ROCH* Sustained garnet; positive, open aromas of blackberry, blackcurrant, quince with hints of *sous-bois*; succulent, moderately powerful flavours with reasonable tannin and acids; long, warm finish. Good, though rather one-dimensional.

1989 LIRAC ROUGE, *CHATEAU ST-ROCH, CUVEE ANCIEN VIGURIE* Fine deep garnet; nose of *fruits noirs* and *sous-bois*; substantial, ripe, concentrated with glycerol and old vine fruit; a note of volatility but this is by no means unpleasant. 3–5 years still to maturity. Very good.

SEGRIES

1993 LIRAC BLANC *(13.1% alcohol; 60% Clairette, 20% each Ugni Blanc and Bourboulenc)* Green gold; attractive aromas of hay and greengage; raw-flavoured at present – wheatmeal in particular – and high acidity. Needs time.

1993 LIRAC ROSE *(14% alcohol; 50% Grenache, 25% each of Syrah and Cinsault)* Red tuilé; slender mealy nose; good structure, but dominated by high acidity, which will soften with bottle-age. Another cuve with ⅔ Grenache and ⅓ CInsault had better balance and more colour.

1993 LIRAC ROUGE *(13.1% alcohol; 50% Grenache, 25% each Syrah and CInsault)* Black; reduced nose leading to broad-framed gutsy wine, with good depth of fruit and more than enough tannin. This will need years to develop fully, but seems promising.

1988 LIRAC ROUGE Fine limpid garnet; soft, maturing aromas, still fruit-based but showing signs of developing secondary complexity; soft, well-defined flavours, quite rich and warm in character.

COTES DU RHONE

FONSALETTE

1993 CHATEAU DE FONSALETTE BLANC Fine green-gold colour; open sappy, greengagey nose; flavours of slightly under-ripe fruit, good acidity, fat and long. No hint of oxidation. Very good indeed.

1992 CHATEAU DE FONSALETTE BLANC *(in bottle)* Light green-gold; attractive aromas of fresh greengages; clean, sappy flavours, much as 1993 but more developed and a shade more concentrated. Wine has good acidity and balance.

1991 CHATEAU DE FONSALETTE BLANC *(in bottle)* Mid yellow-green; fine aromas of hazelnut, peach and acacia, with something of the slightly sherryish flavours of older vintages; still attractive, though has lost some of its freshness.

1993 CINSAULT *(20 year-old vines)* Dense black cherry; minerally, *terroir* aromas and flavours – plenty of extract; a touch rustic underneath. Will add elegance to the final blend.

1993 CINSAULT III Fine limpid deep purple Cabernet Franc colour; youthful nose of red fruits; good depth of similar flavours – nothing delicate here. Again, will contribute finesse to the blend.

1993 GRENACHE *(planted 1945/6)* Much more depth and intensity than the 1993 Rayas Grenache "côté Courthezon"; fine, expansive nose; has depth and plenty of structure.

1993 SYRAH I Incredibly intense black-crimson; completely dumb, apart from distant hints of tar and liquorice; huge mouthful of ripe fruit, plenty of tannin – dry at the edge; lacks charm at present but has considerable potential.

1993 SYRAH II Equally deep; closed nose; similar weight and structure, but flavours are earthier here – very Mourvèdre in character.

1992 SYRAH III Similar appearance to the 1993s with equally closed nose; palate is altogether different, with riper, sweeter fruit and more glycerol. Very fine.

1991 CHATEAU DE FONSALETTE ROUGE Deepish black colour and fine, complex *fruits noirs* aromas; remarkably deep, intense flavours of black fruits, heavily extracted; tannins are round and starting to integrate. Needs 5–10 years. Stunning wine.

1990 CHATEAU DE FONSALETTE ROUGE Very deep,extracty, opaque black; smoky, earthy, spicy, complex nose, only just starting to emerge; deep, almost viscous ripe mulberry fruit, usual massive structure, but has considerable elegance which will continue to develop as the wine evolves. Tops many a Châteauneuf of this great vintage. Magnificent, a masterpiece.

1989 CHATEAU DE FONSALETTE ROUGE Dense, intense, deep garnet; fine, tight, stony nose; firm wine, with strong Provençale flavours and a very long finish; seems more Syrah than Grenache dominated; a bit nervy at present, but will make a lovely bottle in 5 years or so. Excellent.

1988 CHATEAU DE FONSALETTE ROUGE Deep colour, very classy nose; fine raft of flavours based on ripe old-vine fruit; concentrated and with real heart; somewhat rustic tannins. Very good indeed. 5+ years ideally, to full maturity.

GRAMENON

1993 CLAIRETTE Light straw; open, apply, spicy aromas; some gas, otherwise broad-grained, complex, long flavours; attractive wine which needs time to integrate.

1993 VIOGNIER Fine, mid-yellow colour; open peach – apricot nose; big, very ripe, full wine with power and a fine balance between aromas and structure. Not a Condrieu perhaps, but still sublime in its own way.

1993 COTES DU RHONE *(100% Grenache, made as a ligh "vin d'ete" and bottled*

after 6 months) Lightish, fresh, undemanding wine, quite dark in flavour – plum rather than spice. A delicious quaffer for a hot day – ideal with a relaxed Provençale lunch.
1992 COTES DU RHONE, *GRENACHE (Traditional vinification; 80% destemmed)* Bright mid plum; reeks of ripe Grenache; soft, succulent fruit, plummy and a bit tarry; ripe, fleshy, wine. A touch short, otherwise fine.
1991 COTES DU RHONE, *SYRAH (80% destemmed, 14.5% alc, 40 hl/ha)* Opaque black plum, very dense; wild, strongly animal nose – fur, *renardé*, bags of fruit and soft tannins; big, but not heavy-framed; Ripe, plumptious wine. *Un vrai sauvage.*
1992 COTES DU RHONE, *CUVEE LAURENTIDES (100% Grenache, 300 hl/ha, 13.5% alc going on 14.5!)* Translucent limpid deepish plum; ripe, smoky *pruneaux* nose; fleshy, sexy fruit dominates palate; wine has power and length; not weight, but elegance here. Gorgeous – a real Rokeby Venus!
1990 COTES DU RHONE, *CEPS CENTENAIRES (Traditional cuvée, 50% destemmed)* Deep limpid plum; highly promising, brooding, smoky nose; on the palate, smoky, abundant, almost surmature tar and *pruneaux*, splendid length; tannin structure too ensure 10–15 year life. Excellent.
1992 COTES DU RHONE, *CEPS CENTENAIRES (Carbonic maceration)* Deep red, touch of brown; up-front rather burnt liquorice aromas, with the character of very ripe fruits confits; immense concentration of almost sweet fruit dominates; very long. A truly remarkable wine.
1992 COTES DU RHONE, *CEPS CENTENAIRES, CUVEE "A PASCAL S" (1 month cold maceration, took 8 months to ferment sugars; malolactic in January of second year; 16.5°)* Surprisingly light colour with no great depth; dumb nose; great richness on the palate, with noticeably high alcohol; paradoxical – light yet large wine. Not a patch on the 1992 Centenaire above.

GRAND MOULAS

1993 COTES DU RHONE, *ROUGE* Bright garnet colour and open, soft peppery nose; well-made light, gluggable Côtes du Rhône.
1993 COTES DU RHONE VILLAGES, *BLANC* Light yellow-straw; fresh, clean, greengage aromas and zingy, appley flavours (no malo); bright wine, with very high acidity.
1993 COTES DU RHONE VILLAGES, *ROUGE* Plummy, maceration-style fruit characterises nose and palage; more length than the straight CDR and a touch of tannin to lose.
1993 COTES DU RHONE VILLAGES, *CUVEE DE L'ECU* Intense, extracty black cherry; closed nose; bright, plummy wine, with good depth of ripe fruit and dryish tannins. Some raw bitterness on the finish. Altogether, a bit spiky.
1992 COTES DU RHONE VILLAGES, *CUVEE DE L'ECU* Sombre mid-deep black cherry; positive baked-fruit nose and flavours; support is somewhat raw, green, tannin; wine has plenty of *mache* and seems rather crude. Perhaps its the vintage.
1986 COTES DU RHONE, *ROUGE* Mid-garnet, brick rim; attractive aromas of mushroom and *sous-bois*; strawberry fruit is giving way to *sous-bois*; wine has length, and a fine, warm finish. Best so far. Most attractive.
1986 COTES DU RHONE VILLAGES, *ROUGE* Youthful mid-plum; fine nose of truffle, *sous-bois* and spice; plenty of fruit still here, with good grip and balance and well-developed flavours. Lovely mature wine, all in finesse.
1981 COTES DU RHONE VILLAGES, *ROUGE* Limpid mid-ruby, brick rim; smoky, spicy nose; a lightish wine, vegetal flavours; starting to dry out and showing a hint of volatility. Drink soon.
1978 COTES DU RHONE, *ROUGE* Fine, sustained, deep plum colour, holding well; fully mature fruit and *sous-bois* nose; on the palate, open, but still youthful fruit, with good grip and residual robust tannins; powerful, yet "tendre". A fine example of mature Côtes du Rhône.

ORATOIRE ST-MARTIN

1993 COTES DU RHONE BLANC Light citrus; pleasant, greengagey wine, no rough edges; will get a dollop of Viognier and Roussanne in future for added weight and roundness.
1992 COTES DU RHONE, *CAIRANNE, VIOGNIER* Bright light green-gold; nose and palate both marked by smoky new oak; the concentration of sound Viognier fruit underneath is evident but it will need a couple of years to come through. In a better vintage, there would be more obvious varietal flavour.
1992 COTES DU RHONE BLANC, *CUVEE HAUT COUSTIAS* Mid green-gold; nothing much on the nose, but a round, fat palate of ripe fruit, is supported by a seasoning of oak; this is very good.
1992 CAIRANNE, *RESERVE DES SEIGNEURS* Limpid dark cherry; promising, if curious, nose of olive oil and artichoke; more conventional flavours of soft, cherry-like fruit with a vegetal component; plenty of depth and style here. Very acceptable, especially for a 1992.
1992 CAIRANNE, *CUVEE PRESTIGE (60:40 Grenache: Mourvèdre)* Deepish garnet, with closed, but promising nose; ripe, concentrated with reasonable length and good balance; Mourvèdre earthiness apparent; some attractive complexity. Needs 3–5 years. Very good for vintage.
1990 CAIRANNE, *RESERVE DES SEIGNEURS* Limpid blackish hue; nose opening to aromas of tar and super-ripe fruit; mid-weight, with fine concentration of fruit and some tannin to lose; attractive, supple and moderately long. Needs another 3 years or so.
1990 CAIRANNE, *CUVEE PRESTIGE* Moderately deep black cherry; promising nose of concentrated, very ripe *fruits noirs*; much tighter structure than the Seigneurs, more power and depth; the Mourvèdre and old-vine contributions show in the quality. A few years more to maturity. Very good indeed.
1990 CAIRANNE, *HAUT COUSTIAS* More depth of colour and intensity than the Prestige; strong, earthy nose – olive oil and minerals; closed on the palate, but flavour clearly dictated by Mourvèdre at present; appears to be going through a flat phase, but the concentration and tannins are there to bring it through. Not quite the character of the Prestige, but fine, nonetheless.

RABASSE-CHARAVIN

1993 COTES DU RHONE, *ROUGE, CUVEE LAURE-OLIVIER (85% Grenache, 15% Cinsault)* Deep colour and positive, peppery nose; pure ripe fruit, good length and reasonable depth. Needs 2-3 years. Classic Côtes du Rhône.
1993 COTES DU RHONE VILLAGES, *CAIRANNE (75% Grenache, 15% Syrah, 10% Cinsault)* Bright red plum, aromas of *fruits rouges*, more structure and presence than the above; succulent fruit, with firm tannins; 3–5 years. Good plus.
1992 COTES DU RHONE VILLAGES Good colour and nose of spicy, summer fruits; lovely warm, sunny wine with good depth of sound fruit and some secondary aromas and flavours starting to develop. A bit short, otherwise very good for vintage.
1990 COTES DU RHONE VILLAGES, *ROUGE, RASTEAU (60% Grenache, ,40% Mourvèdre)* Fine, tight, warm wine with open aromas of *fruits noirs*, plenty of *fond* and ripish tannins; spicy, liquoricey fruit. Needs 5 years. Very good indeed.
1991 CAIRANNE, *COTES DU RHONE VILLAGES, ROUGE, CUVEE D'ESTEVENAS (80% old vine Grenache, 20% Syrah)* Good colour and attractive fruit-based aromas of *fruits noirs*, spice and liquorice; tight-packed fruit, long and warm ripe flavours; powerful wine with length and class. Very good plus.
1990 CAIRANNE, *COTES DU RHONE VILLAGES, ROUGE, CUVEE D'ESTEVENAS (80% old vine Grenache, 20% Syrah)* Deep plum; closed but complex, dense, nose; much more stuffing and character than the 1991; pure *fruits noirs*; great length and class. All the components are there, they just need time to integrate. Excellent.
1990 VIN DE PAYS, *SYRAH* Deep plum; conentrated peppery nose, very ripe fruit underneath; on the palate, plenty of fine, tight Syrah; round tannins and structured fruit with flavour of violets. Would pass off as a minor Hermitage. Needs half a decade to open out. Impressive.
1991 VIN DE PAYS, *SYRAH* Less intensity than the above, but not lacking in fruit or structure; more evolved than the 1990, with notes of leather and truffle adding to *fruits noirs* and violets. Very good indeed.

RICHAUD

1993 COTES DU RHONE *(10% Syrah)* Light plum colour with clean, peppery nose; fresh, sound attractive, succulent quaffer; commercial indeed, but well made.
1993 CAIRANNE ROUGE *(60% Grenache, 20% Syrah, 20% Mourvèdre)* Soft velvet purple; youthful, rather sauvage aromas; more depth and complexity than the CDR, with firmer tannic base and good earthy finish; flavours of spice and pepper predominate.
1993 CAIRANNE VILLAGES, *CUVEE L'EBRESCADE (en cuve: one-third each, Grenache, Mourvèdre, Syrah)* Opaque limpid black plum, carmine edge; still has young, unfocussed aromas; underneath some gas, good fleshy fruit, dominated at present by dryish tannins; seems promising.
1992 CAIRANNE VILLAGES, *CUVEE L'EBRESCADE (one-third each Grenache, Syrah, Mourvèdre)* Similar to above – touch more depth; Mourvèdre earthiness with notes of *fruits rouges* showing on largely closed nose; fine, sustained flavours, earthy (Mourvèdre) spicy (Syrah) and fleshy(Grenache); long finish. A skillful assemblage and good result for a difficult, wet, vintage.
1991 CAIRANNE VILLAGES, *CUVEE L'EBRESCADE (50% Grenache, 30% Syrah, 20% Mourvèdre)* Much denser; fine aromas of framboise and *fruits noirs* starting to emerge – elegant, almost sweet fruit; spicy, earthy flavours with slight dry tannic imbalance. Nonetheless, very elegant and very Provençale.

STE-ANNE

1992 COTES DU RHONE, *VIOGNIER* Lightish green-gold with delicate dried apricot nose; green vein of acidity dominates palate, with ripe, almost sweet fruit underneath; good typicity, but lacks body. The 1993 has more richness and depth.
1991 COTES DU RHONE VILLAGES, *ROUGE* Attractive, quite light wine, with good colour and a soft, pure fruit nose; flavours are young and peppery and the wine is generally uncomplicated. A good everyday CRDV.
1992 COTES DU RHONE VILLAGES, *CUVEE NOTRE DAME DES CELETTES* Fine deep velvet colour; more red fruits and richness to the nose than the above; on the palate, direct, peppery fruit with ripe tannins and some attractive length. Well-made, but no great depth.
1991 COTES DU RHONE VILLAGES, *ST-GERVAIS (Mourvèdre)* Altogether deeper, plummier colour; fine, expressive leathery, earthy aromas – quite *sauvage* – which follow onto the palate; wine has succulent fruit, good concentration and some length; edged with round tannins; a bit young still; needs a few years yet.
1991 COTES DU RHONE, *SYRAH* Deep blackish cherry; fine peppery nose; no wood noticeable, but Vosges oak comes through on palate to support sweet, concentrated fruit; lovely balance; will need 5 years to integrate. Excellent.

SOUMADE

1993 COTES DU RHONE VILLAGES, *RASTEAU, CUVEE CONFIANCE (in cuve; 14% alcohol)* Deep plum, crimson rim; somnolent spicy, peppery nose; big-framed muscular, earthy, minerally wine, packed tightly with old-vine fruit. Will be delicious when it finally matures. 10 years plus at least.
1991 COTES DU RHONE VILLAGES, *RASTEAU* Good deep colour and lightish,open nose; quite soft (for Romero) and vegetal in flavour; rather too much tannin for the fruit. Not a conspicuous success, but perfectly drinkeable.
1990 COTES DU RHONE VILLAGES, *RASTEAU, CUVEE PRESTIGE* Dense dark plum with a positive spicy, leathery, ripe fruit nose; on the palate, long, earthy flavours with plenty of guts inside; a bit burly at present but will develop finesse, given time. Very good.
1990 COTES DU RHONE VILLAGES, *RASTEAU, CUVEE CONFIANCE (14% alcohol; 25 hl/ha)* Fine, dense, extracty black; nothing whatsoever on the nose; huge mouthful of sweet, super-ripe fruit, heavily extracted, supported by an equal density of round tannins; great power and length; some finesse, but this will come in a decade or so. A veritable monster – magnificent!

TOURS

1992 COTES DU RHONE BLANC *(90% Grenache Blanc, 10% Clairette)* Good, deepish colour; quite a chunky, ripe, stylish wine, with an attractive touch of oxidation on the nose; has good acidity and length. An old-fashioned style but delicious notwithstanding.
1990 DOMAINE DES TOURS, *VIN DE PAYS DE VAUCLUSE* Ripe, even complex, red fruit nose; clean, ripe, peppery flavours, soft and evolved; remarkably stylish for a Vin de Pays. Ready now.
1992 CHATEAU DES TOURS, *COTES DU RHONE ROUGE* Fine, perfumed wine

with abundant, fleshy fruit. Very attractive, but could do with a bit more tannin.

1992 CHATEAU DES TOURS, *VACQUEYRAS* Silky, *fruits rouges* nose and, on the palate, more power and finesse than the CDR. Well-structured. Complete and long. Excellent winemaking.

1991 VACQUEYRAS Pretty, light, colour; closed nose, spicier than the 1992; has less substance and more *mache* than the 1992. Quite good.

1993 VACQUEYRAS *(100% Grenache, in cuve)* Aromas of pepper, liquorice and spice; good, succulent fruit underneath a firm structure. Promising.

SOUTHERN FRANCE & BANDOL

ALQUIER

1994 SYRAH *(new cask; pre malo)* Deep, opaque, vibrant black purple; strong tarry, reduced nose; big, supple wine, firm round tannins; animal, visceral and liquorice flavours predominate. Long. Excellent prospects – pity it will be blended away!

1993 FAUGERES, *LA MAISON JAUNE (in cask)* Deep, limpid, black cherry, purple-crimson undertone; open, tarry, charry nose, with hints of liquorice, cherry and violet; ripe, fat, tightly structured wine with plenty of guts (Bastides material included as none produced in '93). Excellent for the vintage. 3–5 years plus.

1992 FAUGERES, *LA MAISON JAUNE (bottled September 1994)* Deep, sombre black plum; smoky, unexpressive nose, with hint of *griottes* cherry; less depth than the 1993, although not without substance; a touch hollow, needing time to integrate. Finishes rather short.

1989 FAUGERES, *LA MAISON JAUNE* Deep garnet, right to rim; fine open nose of red and black fruits; softish, leathery-tarry-red fruit flavours; quite spicy with a touch of griottes in armagnac; seductive wine with round tannins; not a heavyweight. Drink over next 5 years or so. Delicious.

1988 FAUGERES, *LA MAISON JAUNE (35–40% Syrah)* Deepish garnet; fine aromas of sous-bois, black fruits, mushrooms and griottes cherries; softening ripe wine – tar and liquorice with hint of old tea-rose and more than a hint of cherries in alcohol. Long warm finish.

1992 FAUGERES, *LES BASTIDES* Dense, opaque black; strong smoky, gamey nose – distinctly animal in character; soft, big wine with tarry underbelly. Concentrated, fine.

1991 FAUGERES, *LES BASTIDES (80% new wood)* Touch more depth than '92 and redder rim; deep leathery nose, closed but showing some fruit underneath; starting of open out on palate; attractive soft fruit beneath a biggish, firm, frame. Ripe, tarry flavours. A touch hollow; ready from around 5 years onwards.

1990 FAUGERES, *LES BASTIDES (only 6000 bottles made; first release)* Deep black cherry, touch of lightness at rim; ripe, attractive rather burnt rubber, tar and liquorice nose; substantial, very concentrated wine; round tannins with excellent depth of fruit. Length and real *fond*. Needs 5 years more. You won't find better Faugères than this. Fine indeed.

AUBE DES TEMPS

1991 VIOGNIER *(25 hl/ha; 13.5° alcohol)* Bright yellow-gold; new oak dominates a clearly late-harvest nose, discreet yet complex – notes of white peach, cinnamon, orange peel & pear skin; dry, fullish palate, with excellent aromatic persistence and fair length; good acidity. No varietal markers. A fine, complex and most unusual expression of Viognier. Needs 2–3 years for oak to meld. Remarkable!

1992 MARSANNE Fine, bright, deep gold; rich, complex, surmature nose; dry, concentrated quite powerful flavours – sherryish, dry edge, with long, delicate finish which lingered for minutes. Varietal markers submerged in over-ripeness. Curious, but delicious.

D'AUPILHAC

1993 DOMAINE D'AUPILHAC BLANC *(13.1 alc – Ugni bland 11 alc; Grenache blanc 15 alc!)* Good mid-yellow; positive candied peel nose – reeks of late harvest, most attractive; peely character continues on palate; good backbone of acidity, fair length and plenty of fruit. Fine marriage of fat and lean. Drink within 2–3 years.

1993 DOMAINE D'AUPILHAC ROSE Deep red cherry; attractive fruit-based nose; good stony flavours, plenty of firm fruit, tightly structured, showing more than a touch of tannin. Needs 2–3 years.

1990 DOMAINE D'AUPILHAC ROSE Similar to above plus touch of brick; developed, spicier aromas; on palate – cherries predominate; gutsy with *puissance* and depth. Something of the Pinot Noir about it. A serious Rosé.

1992 DOMAINE D'AUPILHAC, *AOC Coteaux du Languedoc* Limpid deep black purple, crimson edge; closed but evinces ripe red fruits and touch of hot leather; full complete wine, ripe griottes, hint of tar and cloves, peppery, good length, tannic finish. Attractive wine, needs a few years yet. Very good.

1990 DOMAINE D'AUPILHAC CARIGNAN, *Vin de Pays* Dense, blackish cherry; started closed, but opened out into fine positive, very ripe fruits *confits noirs* aromas – almost overripe – smoky element to it; delicious big, fleshy, surmature flavours; succulent, almost sweet fruit with a touch of tar. Magnificent! Who says Carignan's no good!

BANDOL

1991 BANDOL, *CHATEAU DE PIBARNON, CB* Full, youthful, deep garnet; tight red fruit nose; warm, mouthfilling, earthy flavours, brightish acidity. Long, most attractive. Needs 5 years.

1989 BANDOL, *CHATEAU PRADEAUX, CB* Deep Victoria plum; closed nose with a hint of volatility; firm, suffusing, minerally, earthy flavour; ripe, plump fruit, dry envelope and finish; lean, austere, uncompromising Mourvèdre. Individual wine; attractive, with a good future.

BASTIDES

1990 CUVEE SPECIALE, *COTEAUX D'AIX EN PROVENCE* Deepish red plum, with nose dominated by Grenache; flavours are soft and fleshy, with open,

concentrated fruit; behind the Grenache, the Cabernet is waiting to take control – at present, firm but subdominant. A well-made, attractive wine, which needs 3–5 years in bottle.

1989 CUVEE SPECIALE, *COTEAUX D'AIX EN PROVENCE* Marginally deeper than 1990, starting to open out on the nose – Cabernet more evident here; wine has markedly more depth and matter than the above, with plenty of griottes – *fruits rouges* and liquorice suffusing the palate; a wine of substance and presence, complete and complex. 5 years plus. Excellent.

1988 CUVEE SPECIALE, *COTEAUX D'AIX EN PROVENCE* Starting to lighten a shade; Cabernet trying to take over, but Grenache holding on. Struggle continues on the palate – soft fleshy Grenache versus tight, green peppery, Cabernet. Wine has more *mache* and less obvious fruit than the 1989 – will need longer in bottle. Good to very good.

BUNAN

1993 BANDOL BLANC, *MAS DE LA ROUVIERE (Ugni, Clairette, Bourboulenc, Sauvignon Blanc + Marsanne)* Bright yellow; fresh, estery nose; crisp, moderately/fat wine, redolent of pear-drops. Clean, attractive. Pellicular maceration of the Sauvignon and Bourboulenc adds richness.

1990 BANDOL ROUGE, *MAS DE LA ROUVIERE (75% Mourvèdre; 10% Grenache, 10% Cinsault; 5% Syrah)* Translucent mid-plum; smoky, earthy nose, smells of slightly singed meat-extract; full flavour, charcoaly, burnt; wine is lightish. Good, for drinking over next 2–3 years.

1989 BANDOL ROUGE, *MAS DE LA ROUVIERE* Notch deeper than 1990; nose has curious, damp, rubbery component; wine has sound fruit, but lacks flesh. Rather neutral and disappointing.

1989 BANDOL ROUGE, *CHATEAU DE LA ROUVIERE (100% Mourvèdre, 50+ year old vines)* Deep limpid Victoria plum; rich, brooding mulberry nose; firm, structured wine, presently closed; not a heavy-weight but has finesse and depth. Complexity is there, but it needs time to develop fully.

1982 BANDOL ROUGE, *CHATEAU DE LA ROUVIERE* Mid ruby, lightening at edge; strong aroma of mulberries; soft, fully evolved flavours; more in finesse than size. Lacks concentration and is rather four-square. Not bad, but not top-class.

CLOS CENTEILLES

1991 CAMPAGNE DE CENTEILLES Translucent deep plum; closed nose; fleshy, supple, warm wine, plenty of fruit, thought a slight excess of alcohol; finesse rather than size. Attractive. Needs a couple of years yet.

1992 CARIGNANISSIME DE CENTEILLES *(100% Maceration Carbonique)* Denser and darker than the above; hints of griottes cherry on nose – nothing suggesting maceration carbonique; rich, supple very elegant wine; explosive, soft fruit flavours, well balanced; a touch short on finish. Excellent result for a lighter vintage.

1991 PETIT CLOS DE CENTEILLES *(Syrah + Grenache)* Similar hue to above; nothing much on nose or palate. Mildly redolent of pine and garrigues; round tannins. Suffering from recent bottling.

1991 CAPITELLE DE CENTEILLES *(100% Cinsault)* Limpid deepish plum; more expressive on palate than on nose – deep, concentrated, ripe tarry fruit; warm, succulent, mouthfilling wine; excellent length. Needs 3–5 years, possibly more. Very good indeed.

1992 CLOS DE CENTEILLES Translucent, deep ruby/plum; dumb – hints of milled pepper which continue on palate; plenty of stuffing, though tightly structured; ripe, well-judged tannins – hints of violets and griottes cherries with touch of Mourvèdre earthiness on finish. Great elegance and charm.

1990 CLOS DE CENTEILLES More depth and density than the 1992 – black plum; complex nose, still closed, with flashes of smoky fruits noirs and liquorice; in similar style to the 1992, but more concentration and *charpente* – griottes cherry again with touch of coffee. More power and length still. Will be delicious in 3–5 years. Excellent prospects!

1992 VENDANGE TARDIVE *(100% Grenache Blanc)* Bright yellow gold; touch of botrytis (actually c. 25%) on nose, enriching fine, powerful, yet restrained palate. Long, elegant, thoroughly delicious!

CLOVALLON

1994 SYRAH *(en cuve)* 12.4° Good violet-crimson colour; positive varietal nose; lightish, peppery flavours. Seems well structured and promising at this early stage.

1993 VIOGNIER Green-straw colour; developing, peachy/dried apricot nose – gentle rather than explosive; soft, quite fat wine, plenty of fruit, good acidity. Suffering from la mise – needs 6 months to integrate. Promising.

1992 VIOGNIER Bright, yellowish-straw; medium weight apricot nose, strongly varietal; tight, peachy wine, more in finesse than sheer power; elegant, long and well balanced. Most expressive of this trio at present.

1991 VIOGNIER *(first release of Viognier)* Deep green-straw; closed nose, hints of spice; although showing little at present, the substance and structure are there which should make for an attractive bottle when it finally emerges.

LA COSTE

1991 CUVEE PRESTIGE *(80% Mourvèdre, 20% Grenache)* Lightish red; peppery, spicy aromas and flavours – low tannins and a bit dilute (1991 was a rainy vintage). Lacks fruit and depth. Fair.

1992 CUVEE SELECTIONNEE *(100% Syrah)* Much better colour – deep garnet, barely translucent; good, ripe fruit-driven nose; equally soft, spicy fruit-based flavours, long and quite elegant; low tannins again. Attractive. Drink over next few years.

1991 CUVEE SELECTIONNEE *(100% Syrah)* Deep sombre black plum; somewhat cheesy nose; firm, tight flavours with some class; more tannins than the 1992; quite fine and elegant.

1991 CUVEE MERLETTE *(100% Mourvèdre)* Mid garnet – quite light; biggest in aroma and flavour of the three 1991s, plenty of soft, concentrated fruit, with long warm, earthy finish. Dry tannic edge. On same lines as the rest, but has more focussed personality. Good plus.

LA COURTADE

1991 LA COURTADE, *COTES DE PROVENCE (R; 12,000 bottles made)* "Annee execrable". Barely translucent dark red plum; open nose – griottes cherry and *fruits noirs*; some secondary palate aromas sustain a light wine, without much substance. Drink soon.

1990 LA COURTADE, *COTES DE PROVENCE (R; 50,000 bottles made)* Much denser and more impressive appearance; spicy nose, touch of animal, emerging; bright fruit, supple mouthfeel with balancing tannins and earthy, Mourvèdre edge; succulent, long, complex. Excellent.

1989 LA COURTADE, *COTES DE PROVENCE* Similar tone to 1990; tighter, less expressive nose – hints of spice and *pruneaux*; *fruit confits, pruneaux* again, in the mouth – fleshy wine with long, warm earthy finish. Less structured than the 1990 – more *flatteur*. Very good though. 3–5 years.

DAUMAS GASSAC

1993 MAS DE DAUMAS GASSAC BLANC Mid yellow; open, spicy, ripe nose; soft, fleshy palate, with good depth of fruit and fair acidity – stylish and puissant; long, warm finish. Slight lack of grip and freshness. Very attractive, though.

1991 MAS DE DAUMAS GASSAC BLANC *(30% Viognier, 30% Chardonnay, 30% Petit Manseng, 5% Muscat à Petits Grains, 5% Marsanne, Roussanne, Bourboulenc)* Deeper light-canary yellow; more evolved and complex nose – acacia, noix, cinnamon, cloves – a gentle, controlled oxidation; similarly oxidative flavours – especially acacia. Most attractive – long and complex; *à point*.

ESTANILLES

1993 CHATEAU DES ESTANILLES, *FAUGERES* Bright garnet; strong maceration/cloves aromas; clean, fresh flavours, good fruit; wine is complete, with a longish warm finish. Needs some time to harmonise. Attractive.

1992 CHATEAU DES ESTANILLES, *FAUGERES* More density than 1993; strong liquorice and new oak components on nose; wood also dominates palate; sound, firm, ripe fruit underneath; tight tannic envelope; good length; more matter and personality than 1993. Very attractive.

1991 CHATEAU DES ESTANILLES, *FAUGERES* Deepish limpid plum, plenty of extract; fruit-based aromas, quite singed in character; concentrated, plummy fruit on palate, with oak contributing to overall feel; longish finish. Good plus.

1992 CHATEAU DES ESTANILLES, *FAUGERES, CUVEE PRESTIGE* Brighter, less dense than the standard 1992; sombre, unforthcoming nose; wine has far more subtlety however than its sibling, with elegance and structure combined with real depth of fruit; good length. Not over-rich but more complexity and completeness than the other. Stylish and very good for the vintage.

FONTENEAU

1992 FAUGERES Lightish black cherry; tarry, plummy nose; soft, non-maceration pure fruit flavours – distinctly Mediterranean overtones of pine and garrigues. Attractive and uncomplicated for drinking over 2–3 years.

1992 LE MOULIN COUDERC *(Syrah)* Deep, limpid, black cherry; nose dominated by new oak, hiding concentrated *fruits noirs*; mid-weight palate, soft, rich, complex, with firm, but ripe tannins and good depth of fruit. Long. Very good; 5 years plus.

GAUBY

1994 MUSCAT SEC Light greenish straw; open, floral Muscat nose; clean, bone dry flavours – a delicious hot weather quaffer.

1994 VIOGNIER *(In new cask)* Slightly cloudy; explosive nose, fruit dominated by oak; very rich, powerful flavours – real depth here. Excellent prospects.

1994 VIEILLES VIGNES *(60% Grenache Blanc, 30% Maccabeo, 10% Carignan Blanc; vinified in new wood; 15% alcohol, so sold as Vin de Pays)* Light canary yellow; concentrated aromas of dried fruit; firm, concentrated wine – powerful and fleshy with some residual sugar; flavours of *fruits confits/secs*; well-balanced with a long, dryish finish. Will round out given time. Very good indeed.

1993 VIEILLES VIGNES *(1 yr in wood, none new; sold as Vin de Pays)* Less yellow, more straw than 1994; fat, Grenache Blanc aromas with greater finesse and less structure than the 1994; powerful wine with dry, tannic finish. Needs time to soften. Very good.

1991 VENDANGE TARDIVE *(Grenache Gris, Grenache Blanc, Maccabeo)* Light ochre-gold amontillado; fine aromas with distinct rancio element; very rich, sherryish and vinous. Stylish, delicious!

1993 COTES DU ROUSSILLON VILLAGES *(in cask)* Deep plum; soft, almost young Pinot nose, with flavours marked by wood; dry edge. Sound, fleshy, fruit. Needs 3–5 years to integrate.

1990 VIEILLES VIGNES *(1st release of this cuvée)* Limpid black cherry; open nose of ripe fruit; flatteur and finesse rather than structure. Needs a bit more tannin for balance. Attractive, for earlyish drinking.

GRANGE DES PERES

1993 MOURVEDRE *(2nd wine cask)* Deep translucent black cherry; open, silky, very perfumed aromas – *fruits rouges*; bright acidity, but aromatic; Long, perfumed, Excellent.

1993 SYRAH *(2nd wine cask)* Denser, blacker; again strongly Pinot, fruits rouges on nose; fine, silky, tighter fruit, with more opulence; elegant raspberry/cassis fruit underneath. Very much in finesse. Highly atypical Syrah – far more Pinot Noir in character. In Hermitage terms – Les Beaumes rather than Les Bessards! A remarkable pair – very promising indeed.

1992 LA GRANGE *(final assemblage)* Just translucent deep black cherry; complex, brooding nose, fruits rouges et noires, super-ripe; supple, silky, flavours complex and elegant; plenty of fruit balanced by good acidity and rounded tannins. Barring accidents, this will be excellent.

HELENE

1990 CORBIERES, *CUVEE ULYSSE* Deep plum; perfumed, slightly baked plum

nose; elegant in feel with deep fruit; combination of oak and grape tannins hold wine together; good concentration and finishes long. 3–5 years. Good for its appellation.

1990 CORBIERES, *CUVEE HELENE DE TROIE* Denser than Ulysse, virtually opaque; tighter and less expressive nose but clearly more concentrated; dense, very ripe fruit with ample round tannins; a deep, brooding wine which will unpack over the next 5 or more years. Finishes long with an attractive note of bitterness. Lovely!

HORTUS

1992 CUVEE CLASSIQUE *(Grenache + Mourvèdre + Syrah; 2 yrs. in cuve, no wood)* Good colour; firm, spicy nose, chocolaty; succulent, ripe fruit with good depth of flavour. Complete. Needs 3 years or so. Very good.

1992 GRANDE CUVEE Fine deep plum colour; new oak dominates, stifling fruit on both nose and palate; charry flavour suggest too high-toast levels on casks. How will it evolve? Needs a radical re-think, starting with significantly less oak.

JOUGLA

1991 ST-CHINIAN, *CLASSIQUE* Bright, translucent mid plum; open fruits noirs nose, with supple, Grenache-based flavours showing notes of coffee and tar; touch raw at the edge, otherwise attractive, base-line St-Chinian.

1991 ST-CHINIAN, *TRADITION (Semi carbonic maceration vinification)* Similar appearance but more obviously Grenache aromas; soft, silky, attractive wine, spoiled by a touch of green stemminess.

1992 ST-CHINIAN, *TRADITION* Lighter in tone, more purple in hue; still closed on nose, but showing lightish, elegant *fruits rouges* flavours and attractive palate aromas. Again, a touch of stems. Good plus.

1991 ST-CHINIAN, *CUVEE SIGNEE* Translucent, mid red-plum; hint of new wood, overlaying a fine nose of super-ripe fruit – cherry and raspberry in particular; in flavour, concentrated and openly fleshy, almost confit ripe fruit; not a blockbuster, but finely wrought with a long finish. No stemminess here. Leave for 3–5 years. Very good indeed.

1992 ST-CHINIAN, *CUVEE SIGNEE (just bottled, October 1994)* Fine deep plum; no nose yet; less substance than the 1991, more in finesse perhaps, but clearly in the same mould: ripe succulent *fruits noirs/rouges*, violets. A pity to drink now – needs 2–3 years. Lovely.

MAS BRUGUIERE

1993 MAS BRUGUIERE, *CUVEE ELEVE EN FUTS DE CHENE, AC COTEAUX DU LANGUEDOC, CRU PIC ST-LOUP* Deep, opaque plum; strong smoky, milled pepper nose; firm, positive, peppery flavours, quite stony and tarry; good concentration and depth of fruit. Not the richness of 1992, but very good. 5 years plus.

1992 MAS BRUGUIERE, *CUVEE ELEVE EN FUTS DE CHENE, AC COTEAUX DU LANGUEDOC, CRU PIC ST-LOUP* More density and extract than the 1993; no pepper here, rather a brooding, complex nose with a distinctly visceral element; creamy new wood dominates, at present, with rich, very concentrated fruit waiting to unpack; wine has an earthy aspect, with a touch of stemminess. This will be delicious in 5–10 years. Very fine quality.

MAS JULLIEN

1993 LES VIGNES OUBLIEES *(ex used Roulot and Coche-Dury casks)* Bright yellow-green; new oak dominates powerful smoky nose; softish, some flesh but spoilt by SO₂ and cardboardy finish; lacks real depth.

1993 SELECTION, *COTEAUX DU LANGUEDOC* Similar tone, shade deeper; moreopen, attractive nose to above, not especially aromatic; altogether fatter and richer and more complete than V.O. – puissant. 2–5 years more to peak. Good plus.

1993 ROSE, *COTEAUX DU LANGUEDOC* Bright, deep, red cherry; well-structured Rose, freshened with some CO₂, quite fat and puissant. A wine of depth and interest.

1993 LES ETATS D'AME *(Carignan, Cinsault, Grenache)* Limpid mid-plum; soft, Grenachy, mildly mac-carb. nose; light, fruity wine, some flesh and tannin, short finish. Frankly, dull.

1992 LES DEPIERRE *(40% Syrah, 30% Grenache, rest Cinsault and Carignan; 50:50 schist and limestone soils)* Deep, sombre, plum; strong, positive, open *fruits rouge*, slightly spicy, cherry nose; yet more complexity on palate: violets, black cherry, with succulent mid-weight fruit, long, with attractive palate aromas and ripe tannins. Drink now – 5 years. Excellent.

1992 LES CAILLOUTIS Denser and deeper hue than Depierre; tarry, smoky, open aromas – complex and fine; soft, mouthfilling wine, sustained by ripe tannins; not a heavyweight, but good depth of fruit and sound structure. 2–5 years.

1991 LES DEPIERRE Notch deeper than 1992; intense aromas of super-ripe *fruits confits*; tight, beautifully crafted wine, ripe fruit balanced by firmish tannins. Flavours of garrigues and pine; long, warm finish. 5 years plus. Silky, sexy.

1991 LES CAILLOUTIS Similar to above – carmine rim; more liquorice + spice on nose than fruit; cherry stony fruit buttressed by ripe, granular tannins; still young. 5 years ++. Most attractive.

1991 LES OEILLADES *(100% Cinsault)* Deep limpid hue, touch of brick at edge; tarry nose, with note of rubber; rich, austerely tannic wine – green edge. Has depth, flesh and tight, dry, frame; good length. Needs 5 years yet. Promising.

1991 CLAIRETTE BEAUDILLE Mid yellow; open, surmature aromas followed by soft, opulent flavours – candied fruit with hint of citrus. A lovely wine – complex and charming.

MAS BLANC

1992 COLLIOURE GENERIQUE *(includes Cru material; no Crus produced in this vintage; 60% Syrah, 30% Mourvèdre, 10% Counoise)* Limpid mid black-cherry; fruit-stony nose followed up by similar flavours; fresh, quite light, with fair concentration; elegant, but somewhat four-square; mildly bitter finish.

1989 COSPRON *(40% each Mourvèdre & Syrah, 20% Counoise)* A notch deeper than the generic; more open nose, leaning to finesse rather than concentration; more personality, griottes cherry, earthy, smoky, spicy – with a touch of grilled fruit, all overlaid with a strong note of Iodine; good acid-tannin balance. Nothing

aggressive – just ripe, elegant, complex fruit.
1991 LES JUNQUETS *(90% Syrah + 5% each Marsanne & Roussanne)* Deeper again; closed nose hinting at violets; fine, stony flavours, excellent depth and concentration; well-integrated tannins; finishes long. Distinctly more structured than Cospron or Generique. More Mediterranean than the Clos du Moulin. Needs 5–10 years. Very good.
1991 CLOS DU MOULIN *(75% Mourvèdre; 25% Counoise)* Similar to above, though less well sustained; firm, meaty aromas with strong element of *fruits noirs*, chocolate and *pruneaux*; firmer altogether than any of the above, earthy, iodine, with a more obviously tight structure; noticeably higher level of tannins. Nonetheless, elegance rather than brute force drives, to which the Counoise clearly contributes. Ends with characteristic touch of bitterness. The best of the lot; excellent.

QUATRE SOUS

1993 LE JEU DU MAIL *(Viognier vinified in cuve for first time)* Light yellow; fullish, soft, peachy nose and flavours, fair depth and length, underpinned by Chardonnay rondeur. Needs a year to round out. Good.
1992 LE JEU DU MAIL *(Viognier vinified in wood)* Mid yellow-green; rich, opulent nose, hints of hazelnuts, dried peel and cocoa; much fatter and more interesting wine than the 1992 – long, puissant, and complex. Most attractive.
1992 LES SERROTTES *(65% Syrah : 35% Malbec)* Bright dark cherry, carmine rim; strong wood-smoke aromas – very un-Syrah; firm, tight, tannic wine, goodish concentration of fruit; mid-weight compared with 1991 and 1990. An excess of tannins over fruit. Malbec dominates nose, Syrah the palate. Good, though; needs 3–5 years.
1991 LES SERROTTES *(65% Syrah : 35% Malbec)* More density than 1992 and greater aromatic concentration – Malbec still overriding Syrah. Soft, rich, fleshy wine, plenty of mouthfilling fruit. Complex, stylish. Excellent quality. Needs 3–5 years yet.
1990 LES SERROTTES *(60% Syrah : 40% Malbec)* Deeper still – starting to redden at edge; nose just opening – tar and liquorice; sturdy, full wine, with ripe tannins to shed; succulent mouthfiller – densest of the trio; big-framed, muscular wine. Excellent again. 5+ years still to go to maturity.

PEYRE ROSE

1988 RAFAEL *(mostly Grenache; in cuve)* Sound deep plum; open aromas of tar, black and confits fruits, somewhat rubbery; light, dry flavours of old Grenache; lean and pinched, lacks centre. Dry finish.
1990 RAFAEL *(Grenache, Mourvèdre, Syrah; in cuve)* Opaque black plum; firm, attractive, *fruits confits* nose; quite complex with ripe fruit but dry tannins. Needs flesh. Not at all bad though.
1990 RAFAEL *(Syrah, in bottle)* Deep black; emerging aromas of super-ripe forest fruits, still largely closed up; solid, confident wine with plenty of fruit, good length and balance. Much better than the above.
1991 LEONE *(bottled September 1993)* Impenetrable, viscous black; attractive cassis/mulberry nose, still youthful and undeveloped; silky yet firm, good concentration and length; dryish finish. Needs more flesh in the middle. Will 3–5 years improve it?
1991 CISTES *(in bottle)* Jet black, crimson edge; disagreeable, highly reduced nose; big, tight, ripe wine, excellent length, austere tannins, flavours redolent of soy sauce. Difficult to see how bottle ageing will redeem tannins. All the right ingredients, but not quite in the right proportions.
1992 LEONE *(14.5°; in cuve)* Dense black, purple; reduced tar and rubber nose which improved with aeration; massive black flavours on big, muscular frame. Concentrated very ripe fruit, great power and good length, marred by lack of centre.
1992 CISTES *(14.5°; in cuve)* Equally dense; closed nose, hints of ripe fruit; curiously light given the appearance; altogether somewhat evanescent – the grin without the cat.
1993 LEONE *(90% Syrah, 10% Mourvèdre; tasted from cuve, new and older wood)* Dense, dark appearance; plenty of sound ripe fruit, concentrated. New wood sample was more harmonious, fleshy and complete – cuve sample least so, showing greater dryness and austerity. *Assemblage* and bottling after a year would capture the fruit and amortise the tannins.
1993 CISTES *(85% Syrah; 15% Grenache; tasted from cuve, new 400 litre, and older wood)* All intense, viscous black; only the cuve sample showed much nose – subdued *fruits confits* in character. Here the 2nd year cask marginally best, the new wood least good; the wine is clearly massively extracted, with considerable depth and power. Has potential to be stupendously good. Let's see when it's in bottle

RAY-JANE

1992 BANDOL *(60% Mourvèdre, 20% Grenache, 20% Cinsault)* Deep plum; concentrated, herby nose, red fruits; soft, rather bright fruit, hint of stems, good acidity; touch of tar; has power and length; unusual and attractive if somewhat rustic. 5 years plus.
1991 BANDOL *(80% Mourvèdre)* Translucent mid-plum; sombre, rather unexpressive nose, touches of mulberry and *fruits noirs*; firm tight profile, flavours of *garrigue* and mulberry, some stemminess; reasonable concentration and good length. A wine of real character. 5 years plus.
1990 BANDOL *(80% Mourvèdre)* Shade deeper than 1991; more expressive and complex nose – *fruits noirs*; supple, rich, intense flavours, in similar style to the rest but more in finesse. Soft and very *flatteur*. 2–3 years.
1989 BANDOL *(80% Mourvèdre)* Darker than 1990; closed nose, hints of ripe fruit; fleshy, sexy, wine, *flatteur* with soft tannins; less complex than '90 and shorter. A bit uni-dimensional. Just doesn't sing.
1988 BANDOL *(80% Mourvèdre)* Mid-deep plum – still youthful; denser, more meaty nose than either 1989 or 1990; fullest so far, rich, firm, confident wine with plenty of structure, round tannins and no stemminess. Very good. 5–10 years.
1987 BANDOL *(80% Mourvèdre)* Lighter than the above; aromas of mulberry and meat-extract; light, piney, *garrigue* flavours; fresh and pleasant. Drink soon.
1986 BANDOL *(5 years in* foudre*)* Fine, limpid, deepish plum colour; still closed, with hints of concentrated fruit underneat; firm, sappy flavours, good extract and length. Long and stylish. Lovely.
1985 BANDOL *(80% Mourvèdre)* Good deep colour; complex nose in transition from fruit to *sous-bois*, animal and leather – mature Bandol starting to emerge; fine, silky, opulent flavours which fill the mouth; has power and length, and still tannins to lose. Very fine. Best of the lot!

RECTORIE

1993 ROSE, *COLLIOURE* Pretty light orange-pink; fat, Grenachy nose; soft, puissant wine, plenty of gras. Definitely not a "Rose de soif"
1991 COUME PASCOLE, *COLLIOURE* Deep, opaque, extracty black cherry; tight nose, tar rather than fruit at present; succulent, mouthfilling wine, beautifully judged, ripe, tannins; great elegance underneath, needs 5 years plus to really show its paces; a complete wine of great class. Very good indeed.
1991 SERIS, *COLLIOURE (18 months in cask)* Good deep colour, though lighter than Coume; more smoky elegance on nose but less concentration; good depth of succulent, spicy fruit, spoiled by an unyielding dry tannic edge (too long in cask). Still, wine has depth and elegance and deserves 3–5 years cellaring. Good plus.
1989 LES HAUTES VIGNES, *COLLIOURE* Lightish, translucent mid plum; secondary, distinctly animal aromas coming through, with a hint of garrigues. The lightest in flavour of the trio. Perhaps taking elegance too far – would benefit from a dollop of pressings; *à point*.

RICHEAUME

1991 SYRAH Well-sustained, deepish Victoria plum; open, quite smoky, *fruits noirs* nose with ripe, supple broad, somewhat earthy flavours; new wood contributes vanillin to a plump, longish wine, the fruit overlaid with smoky, cigar-boxy palate aromas. Tight, dryish, tannic envelope. Needs 5 years plus. Promising.
1990 SYRAH Equally deep, just opaque; secondary mushrooom and *sous-bois* aromas starting to show, with strong tar component; plenty of seductive, bright fruit, with good acidity and length; dry envelope again; in transition, losing fruit to mature flavours. Confident wine; 3–5 years to go.
1988 SYRAH Similar to 1990, shade redder at rim; yet stronger secondary aromas – most attractive nose – gamey, sous-bois, with fruits rouges just holding on; firmer tannins, yet more refined than either of the above; iron-like finish; fair length. Very good, though the 1990 has the better balance.

STE-ANNE

1990 BANDOL, *CH STE-ANNE, COLLECTION* Deep ruby; strong mulberry nose; austere, with fair fruit and hint of stems (50% destemmed); finishes warm but lacks heart. Needs time.
1989 BANDOL, *CH STE-ANNE, COLLECTION* Deeper than 1990; very closed, with flashes of mulberry and *garrigues*; soft, concentrated wine, with good length and plenty of fruit; astringency again (only 25% destemmed). Not bad at all.
1989 BANDOL, *CH STE-ANNE, TRADITION* Shade lighter than the '89 Collection; closed nose; more suppleness and *rondeur* and less tannin than the above; good fruit and length.
1985 BANDOL, *CH STE-ANNE, TRADITION (50% Mourvèdre)* Translucent mid-plum; positive aromas of mulberry, with notes of pine, *garrigues* and *fruits noirs*; fine, soft wine, gentle and not enormously concentrated; silky with a touch of vanilla on the finish. Good plus.
1982 BANDOL, *CH STE-ANNE, TRADITION (50% Mourvèdre)* Similar hue to 1985; secondary aromas starting to emerge; complex, quite fat wine, with warm, longish flavours. All in finesse. Attractive.

ST-JEAN DE BEBIAN

1989 PRIEURE ST-JEAN DE BEBIAN *(Decanted 4 hours before tasting)* Deep ruby, right to rim; closed nose, touch of spice, nothing more; gorgeous, ripe, sexy wine, packed with super-ripe tarry fruit; long warm finish. Complete winee, less muscle perhaps than the 1991, but remarkable wine in any sphere. Now – 20 years or more. Superb.
1991 PRIEURE ST-JEAN DE BEBIAN *(Decanted 4 hours before tasting)* Deeper than 1989, lovely, limpid tone, still purplish underneath. Nothing yet on nose bar a slight hint of griottes cherries; tightly structured palate, encased in dryish tannins; subdued flavours of chocolate, tar, and spice, with plenty of underlying flesh; big, muscular wine, which needs time to flesh out. Majestic. A vinous firework, waiting to explode.

SIMONE

1992 CHATEAU SIMONE BLANC Fine, vibrant, mid gold; opulent, almost Burgundian nose, explosive aromas of acacia and new oak (none used); quite *nerveux* young flavours, floral, spicy, with concentrated ripe fruit, good acidity and length. Has power and a remarkably well-defined structure which will keep it going for years. Unusual and most attractive.
1993 CHATEAU SIMONE ROSE Deepish bright cherry red; closed nose – nothing much to say yet; biggish wine with a firm structure showing tannins and ripe fruit; puissant and fair length. Somewhat four-square at present. Will undoubtedly be more interesting in 2–3 years.
1990 CHATEAU SIMONE ROUGE Limpid deep garnet-plum; fine, well sustained colour; complex nose, just starting to emerge – griotte cherry, *fruits noirs*, spice with a hint of 'saveurs balsamic'; on the palate, good acidity and well balanced round tannins, holding up a mouthfilling layer of very ripe fruit; earthiness from the Mourvèdre, with plenty of Rubensesque Grenache flesh. A powerful, complete, wine which needs at least 5 years longer maturation. Very good indeed.
1987 CHATEAU SIMONE ROUGE Lightish mid-garnet red; altogether more evolved than the 1990 – secondary aromas, *sous-bois* etc. starting to show and quite stylish, mid-weight fruit on the palate. All in finesse. Ready now.

TEMPIER

1990 TEMPIER ROUGE *(50% Mourvèdre; 30% Grenache; 10% Cinsault; 10% Carignan; from all 3* terroirs*)* Transparent mid plum; complex aromas of concentrated ripe fruit beginning to show; full, soft, ripe wine; fine balance and richness; moderate power supported by well-integrated tannins. Still closed. Needs

3–5 years at least. Delicious.
1990 CUVEE SPECIALE *(85% 20 yr. old Mourvèdre from Plan du Castellet + 15% 40 yr. old Grenache from Migoua)* Touch deeper than the above; smoky otherwise closed nose; significantly more substantial wine – in both depth and structure; spicy and earthy in tenor, with notes of cinnamon and vanilla; ends with a long, attractively tarry finish. 5–10 years plus. Very attractive.
1990 CUVEE MIGOUA *(55% Mourvèdre, 25% Cinsault, 20% Grenache)* Deeper, more sombre; concentrated aromas, complex and elegant: *fruits rouges* & *noirs*, violets, with leather and animal undertones which follow on to palate; firmly structured, powerful, warm, spicy, wine. Long dryish finish. 8–10 years minimum. Excellent quality.
1990 CUVEE CABASSAOU Darkest of all; still maintaining some purple at the edge; the merest flashes of super-concentrated, ripe fruit, on otherwise unforthcoming nose; more expressive on the palate, where flavours of vanilla, earthy spice, and densely packed ripe fruit dominate; fine, complex palate aromas, considerable depth and length. A confident, majestic wine. Impeccable balance – could all to easily be drunk now; however, a beauty will emerge given 15–20 years slumber. Sumptuous wine, stunning quality.
1990 LA TOURTINE Fine, deep colour; aromas of baked earth and leather, spicier and more masculine than Migoua; intense, warm flavours of *fruits noirs*, cinnamon, liquorice, covering a layer of ripe tannins; very long and powerful, still showing youthful austerity. Needs at least a decade. Very fine.
1982 CUVEE SPECIALE *(One third each: Migoua, Tourtine and Plain fruit)* Deep plum, only merest hint of brown at rim; fine, complex, supremely elegant *sous-bois* nose; liquorice and secondary flavours derived from very ripe fruit perfuse the palate; long, puissant and complex. Delicious. *A point*, but unseemly haste unnecessary.

TREVALLON

1993 DOMAINE DE TREVALLON BLANC *(Vinified and* élèvé *in new 400 litre casks)* Deep yellow-straw; ripe tending to over-ripe – orange-blossom, hazelnuts and acacia nose; strongly honeyed, almost sweet fruit, lowish acidity; complex, soft and fleshy.
1991 DOMAINE DE TREVALLON BLANC Brighter, more yellow; similar aromas, though less open – positive Roussanne element on nose; tighter wine, brighter, more balanced, acidity level; long. Promising.
1990 DOMAINE DE TREVALLON ROUGE *(55% Syrah, 45% Cab. Sauv.)* Deep, virtually opaque black cherry; tarry, spicy aromas starting to open – more Syrah than Cab. Sauv.; very extracty, intense flavours of remarkable depth and concentration; long and warm. An iron fist in a velvet glove. Very fine indeed.
1989 DOMAINE DE TREVALLON ROUGE Fine deep, limpid, black plum; lovely *sous-bois* and fruit nose – still closed; soft, open, attractive, complex, succulent wine; warm and long. Delicious now but would benefit from another 3–5 years in bottle.
1985 DOMAINE DE TREVALLON ROUGE Mid-deep garnet, touch of brown; open, spicy nose; no lack of fruit here, soft, very seductive; ampleur and complex aromas fill the mouth. Disarmingly sexy.
1985 DOMAINE DE TREVALLON ROUGE *(*élevé *in new casks)* Wine has all the underlying qualities of the 'standard' *cuvée* above; however, a decade on, the whole is still dominated by very evident new oak, which imparts a firmer tannic edge. Will it ever fully integrate? Very good à l'americaine, though!

TRIENNES

1993 VIOGNIER, *Vin de Pays du Var* Good colour; opulent, open nose – *fruits confits*; full flavoured, plenty of exuberant, ripe fruit, power and length. Not the same expression of Viognier as Condrieu, but a deliciously seductive wine, none-the-less.
1992 LES AURELIENS *(50:50 Syrah:Cab. Sauv.), Vin de Pays du Var* Deep blackish tone; open, forward, Cabernet-dominated wine; supple, fair length; not a blockbuster. Would benefit from a shade more tannin.
1992 SYRAH, *Vin de Pays du Var* Dense Victoria plum; more concentration and presence than the above; well-endowed with ripe, fleshy fruit. Needs a year or two to show its paces. Would support a seasoning of new oak. Attractive.

VANNIERES

1990 BANDOL, *CHATEAU VANNIERES* Deep plum; smoky fruit nose; lightish, supple wine with reasonable fruit and some ripe tannins. Elegant, goodish.
1989 BANDOL, *CHATEAU VANNIERES* More density than 1990; reduced nose, again smoky with a gummy aspect; firm structure, with good depth of fruit and fair length; a bit dry overall; flavours of pine and *garrigue*. Good, needs time.
1986 BANDOL, *CHATEAU VANNIERES* Deepish, sombre, limpid plum, light edge; strong opening nose of pint and chocolate, still reduced; lovely fleshy wine with plenty of ripe fruit and a dry iron-filings finish; good length and real depth here.
1983 BANDOL, *CHATEAU VANNIERES* Good dense plum, red rim; closed mulberry and gum nose, quite earthy, promising; concentrated fruit, which has fleshed out into a long, complex wine with an attractive, earthy edge. Remarkably youthful – still needs 5 years or so. Excellent
1971 BANDOL, *CHATEAU VANNIERES* Deep red, holding colour well; splendid very ripe mulberry nose with a hint of woodsmoke which opened out to complex aromas of *fruits noirs*; on the palate, soft, sweet, ripe fruit, with a very long, dryish finish; plenty of presence and power here; a sumptuous, elegant wine will plenty still to come. Really lovely.

VAQUER

1991 VAQUER ROUGE *(Bernard's vinification)* Mid-deep velvet; attractive fruits rouges nose, with a touch of pine; tight, succulent wine, with earthy flavours and some resiny pine; open, soft red fruit dominates; needs a few years to round out.
1988 VAQUER ROUGE *(Bernard's vinification)* Deeper red; closed nose, some *fruits rouges*; fruit-based flavours, again pine and resin come through; sound, solid attractive stuff, with a bit more tannin than the above.
1990 VAQUER ROUGE *(Fernand's vinification; 80% Carignan, 20% Grenache Noir)* Deep translucent plum; completely different aromas and flavours to either of the above: fruits confits rather than rouges, with element of chocolate; fleshy, ripe, powerful wine, well-judged tannins. Will benefit from 3–5 years more in bottle. Very good.
1986 VAQUER ROUGE *(Fernand's vinification)* Deeper still, more sombre tone; soft, opening aromas of pine and garrigues; similar flavours – supple wine, with firmer, better defined structure. Excellent now, but will keep for several years.
1985 VAQUER ROUGE *(Fernand's vinification)* Good colour; tight, concentrated aromas and flavours; has a burnt element on the palate; dry mouthfeel, finishing with a note of bitterness. Confident, masculine, wine. The 1986 is the better of this pair at present.

CALIFORNIA

VIOGNIER TASTING

The following wines were tasted blind in San Francisco in October 1993. They are noted in order of tasting.
1992 KUNDE *(Sonoma)* Mid-yellow-green; big, positive, ripe candied pineapple nose; toasty new wood evident; soft, loose-knit flavours; slight excess of alcohol; short and lacking in grip. Spoilt by the palate. (13/20)
1992 LA JOTA *(Howell Mountain)* Smoky, dried apricot nose, some well-judged oak; rich, spicy fruit flavours, concentrated, some power; harmonious, complex well-knit wine if a shade unsubtle. (16/20)
1992 SOBON ESTATE *(Shenendoah Valley)* Bright green-yellow; expansive, floral, peachy aromas with elements of grapefruit; fruit salady flavours, grapefruit again; pleasant, well-made wine, but not typical Viognier; short finish. (12/20)
1992 RITCHIE CREEK *(Napa Valley)* Light green; weak nose, some sulphur, touch of peel underneath; slender weak-kneed flavours, short and lacking in concentration. Seems unripe. (10/20)
1992 VILLA HELENA *(Napa Valley)* Dull, mid green straw; smells of fresh celery; weak, dilute, superficial flavours; lacks grip and structure. Drinkable, but without any authority. (11/20)
1992 HORTON *(Virginia)* Greenish straw; positive, classy nose of dried apricots and peel, firm and complex; flavours develop well in the mouth, with mid-weight of fruit, but wine finishes short and lacks concentration - a pity after such fine aromas. (14/20)
1992 ALBAN VINEYARDS *(Edna Valley)* Bright green-citrus; mild, floral nose, with hints of candied fruit; a bit crude and alcoholic; good fruit and flavour development but spoilt by excess alcohol; short finish; not bad, but lacks class (13/20)
1992 JADE MOUNTAIN *(Central Coast)* Green-yellow, good extract; powerful alcohol component on nose with rich, peely undertones; well-defined soft, floral, apricot flavours; close-knit wine with grip and complexity. Good length. (15/20)
1992 McDOWELL VALLEY *(Hopland)* Light citrus-green; curious, slender fruit-based nose - wishy-washy; gassy, fishy flavours; not bad, but spoiled by raw, short, finish. Lacks dimension and concentration. Dull. (12/20)
1992 EDMUND ST. JOHN *(Knight's Valley)* Mid green-citrus; smoky nose, passion-fruit and apricot with some botrytis; soft, most attractive flavours; powerful, with touch of glycerol and carefully judged oak; gorgeous ripe wine, complete, long and concentrated. Quintessential Viognier (18/20)
1992 QUPE *(Santa Barbara)* Mid green-citrus; rather burly, non-varietal nose, dominated by pear-drop esters; similar light estery flavours; pleasant wine, but not varietally correct. (13/20)
1992 CALERA *(Mount Harlan)* Shade deeper than most; opulent, complex spice and pineapple aromas, underpinned by carefully judged, mildly toasted oak; subtle and concentrated flavours - not a heavyweight but plenty of fruit and character; lacks a little grip and power and slightly marred by excess alcohol, but good quality none the less. (15/20)
1992 JOSEPH PHELPS, VIN DU MISTRAL *(Napa Valley)* Dull greenish straw; watery, cardboardy nose, some sulphur showing which masks what is underneath; sulphur also on palate which shows distinctly cardboardy flavours; rough finish. Have had much better bottles (11/20)
FIELD STONE *(Alexander Valley)* Deepish colour; new oak dominates the nose, masking fruit; firm vanillin flavours, but lacks real depth of fruit underneath; too much new oak, not enough concentration. Pleasant, though atypical (12/20)
1992 SIERRA VISTA *(Placerville, El Dorado)* Dull mid-citrus; rather broad, burnt floral nose with a strong vegetal component which doesn't entirely meld; curious, but not unattractive, earthy flavours, broad and burly in style; not bad, but lacks varietal character, grip and real depth. (14/20)
1992 R. H. PHILLIPS, *Experimental Range (Esparto, Central Valley)* Citrus with greenish cast; dumb nose muted by sulphur; weak, fruit-based nose; pleasant wine with raw edge, lacking centre; has some length. Fair (13/20)
1992 ARROWOOD *(Russian River Valley)* Light straw, green tinge; restrained floral nose, some underlying complexity; mid-weight of fruit, somewhat broad and lacking in grip and concentration. Not bad, but lacks depth and focus. (13/20)

ADELAIDA

1990 SYRAH, *LE CUVIER* Black morello cherry hue; sombre, brooding, slightly baked, *fruits noirs* nose; intense, deep flavours; lively acidity and a touch of dry tannin on the finish; highish alcohol. Excellent – but would have been even better bottled at 18 months, rather than 30.
1989 SYRAH, *LE CUVIER (only 2 barrels made)* Deep morello cherry; closed cherry-stone nose; ripe, plummy fruit – direct, not cooked – good acidity and length. Very good effort.

ALBAN

1993 VIOGNIER *(in tank and puncheon)* Clean, light colour; lush, expansive aromas starting to show, esp. on puncheon sample; firm ripe fruit on palate, excellent acidity and body (tank sample); puncheon wine was broader and richer in flavour, tighter and more voluminous in mouthfeel. Blend should have both perfume and structure. Excellent (and a distinct improvement on the 1992).
1992 ROUSSANNE Mid yellow-gold, not entirely bright; honeyed coconut-oil aromas, rich & subtle; fine, rich, almost oily quality; low acidity but otherwise well-structured. Excellent balance and good length. Real class in the making.
1992 SYRAH Black cherry hue; smoky, rather reduced nose, developing bitter chocolate; rich, exotic black pepper and liquorice flavours; high acidity, fair length.

Ripe fruit underpinned by dryish tannins. Notes of leather and violet. Far removed from usual plummy, jammy Californian style. Most attractive. Excellent.

BONNY DOON

1994 CLOS DE GILROY *(100% Grenache)* Vibrant plum-purple; open, baked-fruit Grenache aromas; soft, succulent, fresh flavours with reasonable depth of fruit. Not a long stayer, but will round out over next few years.
1992 LE SOPHISTE *(77% Roussanne; 23% Marsanne)* Light yellow; lovely, almost over-ripe acacia and nuts nose; good acidity (touch added) ripe, attractive and stylish. Good length. Fine, promising – needs 3–5 years.
1992 CLOS DE GILROY *(100% Grenache)* Light plum; strong, milled white-pepper nose; light, fresh, succulent pepper-based flavours. Delicious, soft, quaffer.
1991 LE CIGARE VOLANT *(42% Grenache; 39% Mourvèdre; 19% Syr.)* Mid-deep plum; closed quite rich, plummy nose; pepper and spice; biggish wine, still tannic, with earthy, spicy flavours underneath. Good. Needs 3–5 years.
1990 LE CIGARE VOLANT *(45% Grenache; 25% Mourvèdre; 24% Syrah; 7% Cinsault)* Deeper than the above – dark cherry, plum tones; on nose, considerably greater complexity and nascent depth – tar, plum, spice, ripe fruit. Spicy attack, full complex wine, with plenty of guts and mouthwatering ripe fruit. Altogether more complexity, completeness, depth, class and length, than the 1991. Real *fond* here. Excellent, great potential.
1991 SYRAH *(only 80 cases; 6 inches of rain before harvest)* Deep plum; touch of volatility on nose; otherwise, spicy Syrah aromas underneath; clean, new wood dominates; good deep flavours, despite some volatility also on palate; touch of under-ripeness. Not bad.
1991 OLD TELEGRAM *(100% old vine Mourvèdre)* Dark cherry, vibrant carmine rim; closed nose, tarry undertones; big, broad-framed earthy wine – plenty of ripe fruit with palate aromas of tar and violets. Good concentration and length.

CALERA

1992 VIOGNIER *(14.8% alcohol; 553 cases)* Green, yellow-gold; dried apricot aromas, quite concentrated but not overpowering; on palate, candied apricots with complex, floral-based palate-aromas.
1991 VIOGNIER *(14.8% alcohol; 308 cases)* Green-gold; similar nose to 1992, with strong note of over-ripeness – a point of unctuousness; good aromatic intensity; big, powerful, wine, with *confit* aspect, long but not as complete as 1990; flavours dominated by over-ripe fruit, excellent length. Not a typical young Viognier, but delicious, none the less.
1990 VIOGNIER *(14.5% alcohol; 235 cases)* Bright, intense, yellow-green; fine, open, dried-apricot and peel nose; soft, ripe wine, with nutty component suggestive of new wood (none is used); much the feel, finish and length of the 1991, but greater delicacy.
1989 VIOGNIER *(13.9% alcohol; 308 cases)* Vibrant green-yellow, good extract; deep, complex aromas of *confit* pineapple and peel – gorgeous nose of great finesse; soft, ripe fruit, rather rough mouth-feel, but long, complete flavours. Finish develops with *confit* fruits, lanolin, nuts and acacia. Lighter than eg. 1988, but beautiful balance and great complexity. Five stars. Bravo!
1988 VIOGNIER *(14.6% alcohol; 8 cases)* Bright, vibrant, green-gold; somewhat slender nose in overall context – touches of candied fruit, pineapple and acacia; soft, "nuts & honey" flavours – floral and acacia notes; big, long, complex flavours with warm mouthfeel; Gorgeous, complete wine, no longer young Viognier, but retaining balance, structure and interest. Delicious!
1987 VIOGNIER *(14.1% alcohol; 4½ cases only; first vintage; made in a carbuoy)* Bright, intense, extracty green-gold; positive, delicate, lanolin/peach-kernel nose, reminiscent of old Semillon; very soft, voluminous wine – peachy (fresh, not dried), with notes of liquorice and an aftertaste of grilled nuts and acacia. Excellent acidity and splendid length. Distinctive, and most attractive – though no obvious Viognier marker remains. Fine.

CHRISTOPHER CREEK

1992 PETITE SIRAH *(in cask)* Very deep colour; tarry, sturdy wine; good balance, excellent depth and length. Promising.
1991 PETITE SIRAH *(in cask)* Ripe, soft attack, though higher acidity than 1992. New oak showing through; long finish. Excellent wine in the making.
1990 PETITE SIRAH Black cherry, carmine rim; closed nose; big, dense, chewy, wine; very concentrated and round with firm, but ripe tannins; real *fond* here. Stylish, elegant wine. Excellent.
1989 PETITE SIRAH *(lost ⅓ crop to Sept. rain)* Mid-deep carmine; deeper more forward nose than 1990; lightish, rather lean wine (in overall context); still plenty of guts and good balance; cherry-stone flavours. Good for the vintage.
1988 PETITE SIRAH Mid-deep Morello, carmine rim; positive, smoky, meaty, nose, hint of liquorice; fullish flavours, good fruit and ripish tannins; long with potential for 5 more years ageing.
1992 SYRAH *(new Francois Frères Nevers oak cask)* Deep black hue; reduced nose, showing new wood, tar and liquorice; wood dominates; underneath, sweet, ripe, concentrated wine supported by soft tannins. Very long; real depth and great finesse. Very fine indeed. (A vat sample had a shade more fruit and depth)
1991 SYRAH Mid-deep cherry; reduced nose; soft, fine tannins and ripe fruit, good balancing acidity; long with real *fond.* Fine wine in the making.
1990 SYRAH *(includes 5–10% Petite Sirah)* Deep plum; fine, perfumed nose; rather angular at present, showing plenty of sound, ripe, fleshy, fruit. Not a blockbuster. Good, though.
1989 SYRAH *(includes 5–10% Petite Sirah)* Lightish plum – translucent; soft, berryish nose, plummy undertones; on the lightish side, with more elegance than substance. Attractive.
1988 SYRAH *(includes 5–10% Petite Sirah; first vintage)* Mid cherry-plum; positive *fruits noirs* nose, very perfumed; mid-weight of fruit, leanish, but redeemed by length and elegance. Stylish. Ready.

CLINE

1993 COTES D'OAKLEY *(47% Carignan, 38% Mourvèdre, 8% Syrah, 5% Zinfandel, 2% Alicante Bouschet)* Mid ruby; open, smoky nose; soft, attractive fruit and plenty of personality. Most attractive and remarkable value in its price bracket.

1992 MOURVEDRE, *"Bridge Head" (100 year-old vines)* Immense, deep extracted appearance; soft, oaky nose; firm, dense complex and complete; a superbly-crafted wine with sensational concentration from these old vines. Watch out Bandol! (A *cuvée* of different origin was equally dense, but tighter and more tarry in flavour.)
1992 MOURVEDRE *"Big Break"* Deep colour, closed nose, surprisingly light mouthfeel, with more finesse and less obvious muscle than the above.
1990 MOURVEDRE Deep carmine; soft, minty nose; substantial fruit and tight, ripe flavours; fine, round tannins and real concentration. Lovely.
1989 MOURVEDRE Deep carmine; complex, perfumed berryish aromas; very rich, extracty, mulberry and blackcurrant flavours sustained by ripe, soft tannins. Slightly hollow compared with the Reserve, but fine indeed.
1989 MOURVEDRE RESERVE Marginally deeper than the above; closed nose, hints of provençale herbs and spice; greater richness and complexity than the above; exemplary concentration and ripe tannins; real old vine fruit underneath. Bags of life; 5–10 years. Splendid!
1987 MOURVEDRE *(Vinified in open Redwood fermenter)* Deep colour; minty nose with a touch of volatility; deep, very complex ripe wine, with firm tannins and a long, warm finish. Very good indeed.

DOMAINE DE LA TERRE ROUGE

1991 TERRE ROUGE, *SYRAH* Limpid, dark plum; pepper and spice nose; soft, fine, ripe, fruit; good concentration, ripe tannins, extracty. Real length and old vine concentration (15 year old vines only). Complex wine, superb!
1991 TERRE ROUGE *(35% GR; 25% MO; 30% SY & 10% CIN) 14.5 alc.* Mid garnet – surprisingly light colour; closed nose – black cherry with touch of violets; deep, brooding ripe fruit, with bags of tannin, yet soft underbelly. Full, complete wine with long warm finish. Fine quality.
1990 TERRE ROUGE *(30% each GR, SY, MO + 10% CIN)* Good colour -mid garnet, touch of purple;closed nose – hint of dark cherry; much tighter in structure than 1989 and 1991 – firmer fruit and more grip. Elegant underneath.
1989 TERRE ROUGE *(55% GR; 20% SY; 20% MO; 5% CIN)* Light mid-cherry; Grenache-based nose – four-square; cherryish notes, reminiscent of Pinot Noir; soft, rather pulpy flavours, dominated by Grenache; good acidity and tannin, some length. Mid weight. Elegant.
1988 TERRE ROUGE *(42.5% SY; 45% GR; 12.5 MO)* Mid-garnet red, darker than 1989; nose still closed, distinct Syrah contribution evident; secondary aromas starting to displace primaries; mid-weight with fair fruit concentration; mild alcohol over-balance; interesting wine – light in style yet well-textured with good length.

EBERLE

1991 SYRAH *(Paso Robles)* Morello cherry hue, not particularly dense; soft baked plum aromas developing; substantial, plummy wine, some tannin but rather loose-knit and lacking grip; awkward at present, needs time to integrate.
1979 SYRAH *(Estrella River)* Deep limpid lake-plum; ripe, sweet complex plum and berry nose, with hints of animal and viscera; substantial, mouthfilling wine – flavours of cherry, tobacco, cedar and prunes; held together by good acidity and a touch of residual tannin. Splendid length and complexity. Fully developed, but by no means fading. Most attractive. Fine.

EDMUNDS ST JOHN

1992 LES COTES SAUVAGES *(14.3 alcohol)* Deep plum – carmine, purple edge; slightly reduced tar & prunes nose; big, round plummy, cherry-stony wine, soft, ripe and concentrated; long; stony, tarry finish; wine of great poise – needs 4–6 years.
1992 SYRAH, *GRAND HERITAGE (14.2% alcohol)* Deep, opaque, dark plum; pepper and soft fruit, northern Rhone nose; soft, peppery wine, highish acidity and strong tannins; long, full flavour; gorgeous wine with excellent balance, esp. for 14.2 alcohol; 4–6 years.
1992 SYRAH, *DURELLS VINEYARD (Sonoma + Carneros fruit)* Deep plum, carmine edge; tight, closed Syrah nose – most promising; massive mouthfeel; tightly-structured fruit, high acid and ripe, round tannins; mouthwatering. Excellent wine, with great future.

FIELD STONE

1992 VIOGNIER, *FAMILY RESERVE* Limpid mid-yellow; nose screams new wood; big, oxidative new US oak dominated flavours; fruit convincingly masked. Substantial, individual wine – might be attractive to some but has little varietal typicity.
1991 PETITE SIRAH, *FAMILY RESERVE* Mid purple-plum, closed nose; firm, rather austere flavour profile, dominated by acids and tannins; somewhat hollow underneath. Will develop over the next few years. Goodish.

FOPPIANO

1991 PETITE SIRAH, *RESERVE (1200 cases, wine matured in shaved French oak casks; from 65 year old Napa vines)* Dense black; sweet oak nose, attractive, complex aromas developing; very soft, ripe, old vine fruit; real *fond* here, though still has hard tannins. Will be excellent, in the house style, in 7–10 years.
1987 PETITE SIRAH, *RESERVE (Russian River Valley)* Deep plum, purple edge; nose of liquorice, violets, touch vegetal; sweetish fruit, with a porty feel and dry edge; complex wine underneath high tannins. Excellent. Ideally needs 5 years longer.
1991 PETITE SIRAH *(Standard release)* Limpid black cherry; closed nose; huge wine which has not begun to integrate; plenty of well-structured fruit and tannin with a nerve of green acidity which needs time to meld. 10 years at least.
1990 PETITE SIRAH *(Standard release)* Nearly black, plum, deep red edges; closed cherry-stone nose, hint of violets; good ripe fruit, with dry tannic envelope; length and quality here, but some doubt as to whether pervasive dry tannins will integrate.
1987 PETITE SIRAH *(Standard release)* Deep plum, youthful edge; sweet "spice & tar" nose, touch animal; high acid and austere tannins mask good fruit and development. This lacks harmony – a pity, since there is plenty of complex, ripe

fruit underneath.
1984 PETITE SIRAH *(Standard release)* Deep, opaque black cherry; attractive, slightly singed nose; big wine, plenty of fruit, harmonious, although still has acids and tannins to lose.
1980 PETITE SIRAH *(Standard release)* Deep black, burnt brown rim; sweet "tar & spice", mildly vegetal nose – faded elegance. Lean attack, with plenty of acidity and dryish tannins overlaying sound fruit. A rich wine, fully mature, underneath a somewhat forbidding exterior. Not unattractive, but needs food.
1976 PETITE SIRAH, *Russian River Valley (Standard release)* Mid red – commutes to edge; curious damp, eggy nose, with hint of tar; dry wine, highish acids and thick-skin tannins hiding ripe berry fruit; hollow centre. Good wine, a shade over-extracted.
1973 PETITE SIRAH, *Russian River Valley (Standard Release)* Mid-deep plum, dark brick rim; burnt chocolate nose, hot, concentrated, sweet fruit; more burly than 1969. Altogether bigger and more attensive than 1969 with heaps of strapping fruit. Dry, mature tannins, high acidity. A hot mouthful, which starts well but falls off toward the finish. Reminiscent of damp carpets. Attractive.
1969 PETITE SIRAH, *Russian River Valley (Standard release)* Bright mid-garnet, amber rim; open, sweetish caramelised-onion and spice nose; complex, attractive, dominated by high acidity and lively fruit; good depth and fair length with some underlying complexity; hints of cedar and spice. A fully mature flavoury wine, but now drying out.

FRICK

1992 PETITE SIRAH, *DRY CREEK* Deep purple; young, spicy fruit nose; full, firm, powerful wine with plenty of fruit and underlying elegance; long finish. Lovely quality which needs time to integrate and unpack. Highly promising.
1992 CINSAULT Translucent bright mid-plum – a shade less dense than the above; new wood dominates a silky, open wine; good length, fine balance. Delicious now, but will improve over next few years. Real quality here.
1980 PETITE SIRAH *(Monterey County)* Deep black cherry, right to rim; dusty, asparagus nose, attractive and distinctive; similar flavours, fruit still holding on; dry tannic edge; a gentle old lady.

GEYSER PEAK

1993 RESERVE SYRAH Limpid mid-plum; sweet fruit and new oak nose with touch of smokiness; high acidity and new wood presently dominate but there is concentrated, complex fruit underneath the mask; already showing some elegance. Will need years to open out. Very promising.
1992 RESERVE SYRAH, *ALEXANDER VALLEY* Opaque, dense plum; youthful, quite opulent, creamy, oaky nose, with notes of leather and spice; palate largely mirrors this, in dense, ripe fruit; very good weight and length. Highly promising.
1991 SYRAH, *ALEXANDER VALLEY* Deep plum; stron new oak and tar nose, some underlying complexity; big, tightly-knit, spicy wine; fair tannins and high acidity; long. Needs 3–5 years. Good wine in the making.

GRANITE SPRINGS

1992 SYRAH *(first vintage; sample from 2nd. yr. cask)* Deep vibrant cherry, purple rim; promising cherry stone and black fruit nose, some oak evident; mouthfilling, ripe soft fruit, extracty. Long, strong flavoury wine, warm & complex. Fine complete finish. Excellent.
1992 PETITE SIRAH *(2nd. year cask sample)* Dense black cherry; very perfumed, almost scented nose; flavours of violet, dark cherry & black fruits, dry tannic edge. Long, very well put together. Most promising.
1991 PETITE SIRAH Deep Morello, carmine edge; closed nose, hints of Provençale pine and spice, floral and smoky undertones; big, tannic muscular wine; dry, mouthwatering tannins balanced by concentrated fruit. Austere wine, almost Amarone in character.
1989 PETITE SIRAH Mid plum; gentle leafy nose, spice and mineral notes; mid-weight fruit and tannin; somewhat hollow and short. Mineral and plum flavours. Not quite enough fruit to balance tannins. Not bad for vintage.
1986 PETITE SIRAH Deep lake plum, youthful red edge; multi-faceted smoky, tarry, spicy, betrooty, mineral nose developing fine complexity; on the palate, rich, mouthfilling and earthy flavours from bright, ripe fruit. Most attractive, cedar and tobacco finish. Complex wine still with fine future.

JADE MOUNTAIN

1993 COTES DU SOLEIL *(37% Syr., 41% Mo., 22% Petite Sirah)* Mid-weight wine, with pure fruit flavours and good depth but shortish finish. Syrah contributes elegance, Mourvèdre earthiness.
1991 PROVENCALE *(33% Syrah; 55% Mourvèdre; 12% Grenache; dry-farmed, yields around 2 tons/acre)* Deep plum; soft plum and liquorice nose; rich mouthfilling Provençale feel; tightly structured; ripe fruit, good acidity. Despite its size, has a delicate, elegant feel, with good length and dryish tannins. Very good.
1990 SYRAH Deep black cherry; closed rather reduced nose, some fragrance coming through; big mouthfiller, with bags of very ripe, tightly-packed fruit; excellent fruit-acid balance and good length. A very fine wine.
1990 MOURVEDRE Deep, dark wine; rich earthy aromas emerging; flavours are close-knit and still youthful; Mourvèdre's earthiness presently dominates, but the wine clearly has depth and complexity; long, dryish finish. Very good.

JOSEPH PHELPS

1993 VIOGNIER *(13.8% alcohol)* FIne green-gold tone; attractive, ripe, strongly varietal aromas and flavours; already fully open; finishes dry and a touch short, but a gorgeous glass of Viognier, notwithstanding.
1992 VIOGNIER Mid-citrus; gorgeous, ripe apricot & peel nose; big, rich, mouthful, well structured with good length and acidity; warm, ripe finish, with a touch of heat. Strongly varietal. Delicious.
1992 GRENACHE ROSE Deep cherry tint, dark for a rose; attractive strawberry & white pepper nose which continues onto palate. Tightly structured wine, some tannin and good length. Very good indeed; watch out Tavel!
1991 LE MISTRAL *(39% GR; 37% MO; 10% SY; 9% CAR; 5% CINS)* Deep plum; warm, spicy nose; rich, concentrated soft fruit flavour – no lack of guts; lovely balance. Will develop well over next 3–5 years plus.
1991 SYRAH Deep morello – mighty colour; closed nose; tar & spice flavours, plenty of mache with real concentration. Excellent wine with a fine future; incidentally, much more Syrah typicity than the 1990.
1990 SYRAH *(12.5% alcohol)* Lovely vibrant crimson-cherry; hints of pepper and tar on largely closed nose – strong maceration component to aroma; soft, concentrated fruit flavours – again strong maceration note; herbal tone; firm tannins. Good – will age well in medium term.
1989 SYRAH Black cherry, though not opaque; lightish nose, evincing liquorice in particular; meaty mid-weight wine with tight tannins; much greater depth and concentration than the 1986. Excellent balance and length; still youthful and attractively berryish. A fine wine.
1986 SYRAH Denser than the 1985, though aromatically more closed; feminine nose with hints of raspberry, in transition between primary and secondary aromas; on palate, somewhat Bordeaux in style – supple, smoky, meaty flavours; good weight; attractive and still youthful.
1985 SYRAH Deep cherry, almost purple at edge; surprisingly youthful; deep soft chocolate and berry nose – somewhat Bordelais in character (there was a touch of Cabernet added!); tight grainy wine; mid-weight; mouthfilling; fully evolved secondary aromas and flavours. Good, if a trifle short.
1979 SYRAH Mature appearance, brick rim; colour still holding; superb secondary and tertiary animal & vegetal aromas with flashes of tar and spice; mature visceral, spicy flavours, distinctly vegetal; complex and long with a scintilla of tannin remaining; wine still has excellent grip. Reminiscent of an old Hermitage. *A point.* Gorgeous!

LA JOTA

1993 VIOGNIER *(Cold fermented; 14.5% alcohol)* Light yellow; delicate, peachy nose; some CO_2, full yet fine flavours, with good varietal character; mid-weight, some power, though lacking in complexity. Good length and warm finish. Attractive, if rather straightforward.
1993 VIOGNIER *(Barrel fermented; 14.5% alcohol)* Similar appearance; strong, dried peel and new oak nose; creamy vanillin dominates palate, with sound, ripe fruit underneath; finishes long. Varietal character completely masked by oak. The cold fermented wine has more varietal identity, though the cask fermented wine is better. A blend (⅓ cask: ⅔ cold) transcended either component.
1993 VIOGNIER *(Sweet)* Fine mid-yellow colour; complex, concentrated, botrytised nose leading to firm, opulent flavours. broad and peachy in character; real depth and richness here; fine balance and long, suprisingly delicate, dry finish. Moelleux rather than demi-sec. Delicious.

MCDOWELL

1993 VIOGNIER *(Mendocino; 14.3 alcohol)* Light straw; exuberant, complex, apricot & dried-fruit nose; broad, ripe complex wine; good acidity and balance; highish alcohol, but well covered with fruit. A thoughtfully crafted example.
1990 SYRAH *(Mendocino)* Magenta purple; fine, developing fruit nose; delicious ripe, soft flavours, somewhat Pinot Noir in character, without a great deal of tannin; much silkier and more seductive after two hours. Very good.
1993 GRENACHE ROSE *(Mendocino, 13.8 alcohol, with 2–3% of Syrah to adjust colour and Mourvèdre as anti-oxidant)* Light salmon red; slender, rather non-descript nose; tight, structured flavours – earthy and quite meaty; develops good length and has plenty of up-front fruit. Good, despite its heavy alcohol.

OJAI

1992 SYRAH *(in cask; ¼ Zaca Mesa fruit)* Bright medium plum, not dense; nose of liquorice, spice, cinnamon and cloves; silky cherry-stone flavours, with good fruit and acidity, and excellent balance; a ripe, complete wine, with mid-weight structure which will age well over 3–5 years.
1992 SYRAH *(Bien Nacido; new cask)* Denser tone, more purple than above; reduced nose, more tar and pepper showing; altogether bigger wine, yet soft, with ripe tannins and bright, plummy fruit; long and *puissant.* Excellent prospects
1991 SYRAH *(100% Ojai fruit)* Mid carmine, plum; soft white pepper aromas; deep, very fleshy stylish wine. Long, classy.

PRESTON

1992 VIOGNIER *(13.9% alc.)* Mid straw-citrus; broad, rather unexpressive Viognier nose and flavours; touch of CO_2; somewhat flabby and over-alcoholic; short and lacking in focus. Unlikely to develop into anything interesting.
1992 MARSANNE *(14.3% alc.)* Light yellow-citrus; closed, slightly Muscat-floral nose; broad, ripe, floral fruit; flashes of spice and peel; very rich, big wine. Good plus.
1991 VIOGNIER Citrus-gold; lovely apricot-peel nose; mid-weight dried fruit flavours – candied pineapple; mouthfilling with tight grip and good length. Marred only by slightly raw finish. Much better than '92. Very good plus.
1991 MARSANNE Fine gold-green; most attractive acacia-honey nose developing; soft, ripe, peachy fuit flavours; very concentrated with real depth; harmonious acidity with touch of supporting tannin. Excellent. A fine wine.
1992 FAUX *(37% SY; 23% GR; 23% CAR; 17% MO)* Limpid, bright red; carmine-plum; soft, up-front, plummy nose; ripe, fleshy wine, good extract, tannin to lose; longish, some complexity and reasonable concentration; a well-made wine.
1991 FAUX-CASTEL *(35% SY; 30% CAR; 15% ZIN; 14% MO; 6% PS)* Mid Morello-cherry; macerative plum & spice nose; soft, a touch jammy; mid-weight ripe fruit, some tannins but finishes short; good, not great.
1992 SYRAH Bright, black cherry; nose dominated by new, lead pencil, oak; soft, fully ripe, concentrated fruit; excellent fruit-acid-tannin balance; fair length; attractive, though not a blockbuster. 3–5 years to maturity.
1990 SYRAH Mid-deep plum, blue edge; reduced nose, tarry undertones; big wine, reduced, ripe tannins and good depth of fruit; real *fond* here with good length; 5-10 year evolution in prospect. Excellent.
1989 MUSCAT BRULE *(16.1% alc.)* Vibrant light gold; positive, delicate Muscat nose – more botrytis than marzipan; soft, glyceriney wine, with flavours reminiscent of lemon curd; fine length. Excellent wine – needs 5–10 years ideally.

QUPE

1992 BIEN NACIDO *(50:50 Viognier:Chardonnay)* Citrus-straw; rich, opulent, almost surmature nose verging on candied peel; long, ripe, soft, peachy flavours; honeyed; unusual wine – positive Viognier dominated aromas underpinned by a firm, sound structure. Unusual – and excellent. Interesting to watch its development.
1992 LOS OLIVOS *(⅔ Sy; ⅓ Mo)* Mid morello hue, weakish purple rim; direct, young Mourvèdre aromas; vegetal and stalky; big, ripe open wine, starting to show finesse; distinct southerly feel about it. Promising.
1992 SYRAH, *Bien Nacido (from new cask)* Black cherry, carmine edge; attractive, bright nose of white pepper overlaid with new oak; in the mouth, pepper, spice and violets. Plenty of length and finesse; beautifully balanced. Very Northern Rhone in style, though not a big wine. Fine indeed.
1991 SYRAH, *Bien Nacido* Deep, blackish hue, red-lake edge; intense earth+tar nose with a smoky, visceral element; solft round tannins dominate layers of super-ripe fruit. Flavours of strawberry seem to emerge, with a touch of dryness on the finish; well-crafted wine whose main feature is clean, pure, fruit. A bit short at the end; otherwise, excellent.
1983 SYRAH *(Estrella River fruit)* Limpid cherry-red, tawny edge; soft, evolved, complex, nose exuding ripe fruit with a hint of barnyardy asparagus. Voluminous, fully mature palate, with notes of strawberry and spice and secondary gamey undertones emerging. Complete, long, attractive wine, with distinct brettanomyces adding dimension.

RIDGE

1991 MATARO, *EVANGELO VINEYARD* Limpid, bright garnet; complex tarmacadam nose; broad, quite tight yet mouthfilling wine with flavours of tar, spice and meat-extract;substantial yet beautifully balanced with good length. Needs 10 years. Excellent.
1990 CARIGNAN, *WHITTEN RANCH* Limpid bright garnet; sweet, ripe mulberry nose; almost exotic red fruit and bramble flavours presently dominated by new wood; otherwise, long, ripe and complex. Drink now and over the next five years.
1990 PETITE SIRAH, *YORK CREEK* Deep black cherry; strong, smoky bacon aromas; violets and mineral flavours opening on this muscular, tarry wine; seductive, sweet underbelly, with plenty of concentrated, ripe fruit envelopped in tight, dry tannins. Real depth and class here. 5–10 years. Very fine.
1987 PETITE SIRAH, *YORK CREEK* Opaque, deep black cherry; fine, sweet, ripe fruit nose which follows through to palate; plenty of tannins, but more than balanced by density of fruit. Delicious now, will improve over next few years.
1981 PETITE SIRAH, *YORK CREEK* Limpid, deep morello cherry; ripe fruit nose, overlaid with touch of tar, spice and berries; substantial wine with balanced, tarry flavours; not over-tannic. Still youthful. A fine wine.
1978 PETITE SIRAH, *YORK CREEK* Black Victoria plum, right to edge; nose virtually closed, giving little; massive, mouthfilling wine, with strong flavours of pepper and spice and balancingly substantial tannins; very dry feel and finish; goodish length. Very attractive and still youthful.

ROSENBLUM

1991 PETITE SIRAH *(Napa Valley)* Deep morello, bright carmine edge; positive, rather baked fruit on nose, with touch of volatility; on palate, volatility and dry edge masks the fruit underneath; quite a big, spicy wine. Not bad.
1990 PETITE SIRAH *(Napa Valley)* Black, opaque; no nose; big, concentrated ripe fruit flavours and firm tannins. Promising.
1989 PETITE SIRAH *(Napa Valley)* Dark, opaque appearance; closed nose; substantial, big-framed wine, with some elegance underneath a heavy skeleton; sweet, berryish fruit marginally spoiled by excessive dry tannins. Good, though.
1986 PETITE SIRAH *(Napa Valley)* Mid garnet; soft, pulpy nose; loose-textured fruit appearing as wine softens out; sound balance and some underlying complexity, but once again an excess of tannins.
1985 PETITE SIRAH *(Napa Valley)* Mid garnet; slender, berryish nose; big tannic wine, with some gas; what fruit remains is completely overpowered by tannins. Quite attractive.

SANTINO

1990 SATYRICON Mid-plum, good colour; spicy, slightly cooked, tarry nose; soft clean palate, highish acid. Mid-weight, long, mouthfilling flavours. Lightish Châteauneuf blend; good; 3–5 years.
1991 SATYRICON Morello tone, notch deeper than 1990; soft, forward plum and bubblegum nose; ripe, mouthwatering wine; full and concentrated. Real power and excellent fruit/acid/tannin balance. Long, warm finish with attractive retro-nasal aromatic component; well-judged tannins. Excellent flavoury wine – dead-ringer for Châteauneuf.
1991 SYRAH, *Renwood* Deep cherry, Victoria plum; almost opaque, morello rim; closed nose; substantial mouthfiller; gorgeous ripe (but not over-ripe) fruit and tannins. Very long and well focussed. Fine wine in the making.

SEAN THACKREY

1992 SIRIUS *(Marston Vineyard; ¼ tons/acre)* Deep black cherry, violent carmine rim; black, charry nose, intense; very tight knit, immensely concentrated wine; superb palate-aromas; altogether remarkable intensity and depth. Will be superb. Impressive.
1992 PETITE SIRAH *(Old oak)* Deep plum/morello; big, complex, cherry-stone nose – violets; huge wine with bags of mache and ripe tannins, good acidity; cherry-stony flavours; very promising.
1992 PETITE SIRAH *(New French oak)* Deeper than above; vanillin dominates sweet fruit on nose; fine, soft mouthfilling palate, very perfumed; Hermitage with a touch of Petite Sirah astringency at finish. Superb.
1992 PETITE SIRAH *(taken from fermenter 3 weeks early)* Deeper still; ripe, stony fruit; more obvious tannins and markedly less round. Otherwise, long and very concentrated.
1992 SIRIUS PRESS WINE *(Petite Sirah from Rossi Vineyard, new French oak)* Black; reduced nose, completely closed; tarry wine of great richness and typical Petite Sirah tannic profile; sweet ripe fruit, but noticeable harshness. Would it contribute to quality of blend?
1991 SIRIUS *(Petite Sirah final blend)* Black hue; beginning to show great fragrance; cherry-stony, ripe plum and *fruits noirs* flavours emerging; immense concentration of sweet, ripe fruit; perfume and great length. Impressive and exciting.
1991 TAURUS *(Mourvèdre, ex Cline, Oakley)* Deep hue, touch of maturity showing; complex, ripe, smoky nose; reasonable depth but marred by xs alcohol, high acids and dry finish; touch hollow. Not bad. Unlikely to be released.
1991 ORION *(Syrah, experimental blend, bottled March 1994)* Usual massive dark cherry hue; *fruits noirs* nose; huge, ripe, extracty, with glycerine and *fruits noirs* flavours. Fine, silky wine in the making.
1986 ORION *(Syrah; first release)* Deep black cherry, still youthful; lovely, slightly vegetal nose; seductive flavours of ripe cherry and plum; long and complete; beautifully balanced; sweet, almost luscious fruit on middle palate; dry, gamey finish. Very, very long. Utterly delicious!

SIERRA VISTA

1992 VIOGNIER *(El Dorado)* Deepish mid-yellow; fine open dried peel and apricot nose; open-textured flavours with plenty of fruit and a hint of bitterness on the finish. Good balance. An attractive expression of Viognier.
1992 SYRAH *(cask sample)* Deep purple black; gorgeous violets and milled pepper aromas followed by mid-weight flavours with firm tannin and good acidity. Promising.
1991 SYRAH *(El Dorado)* Deep plum, carmine rim, good extract; closed nose, hints of violets; long, mouthfilling, cherry-stone, spice and tar flavours; round tannins over layer of very ripe fruit. Excellent concentration and real *fond* here. Lovely wine. 5–10 years.
1990 SYRAH *(El Dorado)* Deep red-carmine; elegant, flowery nose, still closed; florality continues onto palate of soft, berryish fruit, with gamey, vegetal undertones; tannin to lose. Very good.
1989 RESERVE SYRAH *(El Dorado; first vintage)* Limpid, deepish plum; largely closed nose, with touches of complex black fruit underneath; finely balanced wine with excellent balance of acid, tannins, alcohol and fruit. Complete, long. Needs 3–5 years yet.

AUSTRALIA

Note: The following wines were tasted in Sydney and Melbourne in November 1993. I am particularly grateful to Peter Bartter, a noted wine-lover, Gary Steele, a Melbourne wine merchant, his friends Darren Harris and Norman Tranter, and Phillip John, Senior Winemaker at Lindeman's for digging into their cellars and producing this remarkable galaxy of rarities. It should be borne in mind that with wines of this age bottle variation is considerable and that storage conditions have a significant effect on quality; other bottles may taste completely different.

1941 TINTARA, *RESERVE BIN (Tintara is a McLaren Vale vineyard, belonging to Hardy's)* Moderately intense, bright garnet; toffee and caramel nose; lightish flavour, a bit hollow and flaccid; just holding on.
1956 PENFOLDS MAGILL 'BURGUNDY', *bottled March 1958* Mid-weight garnet, tarry edge; minty nose; big, sweetish wine, complete and opening onto a long, silky, finish; flavour of coffee, with an enriching touch of volatility. Very attractive.
1951 RHINE CASTLE 'BLACK LABEL HERMITAGE' *(Made by Maurice O'Shea from Junee fruit)* Fine light garnet, holding up well; nose has a touch of volatility, with good fruit underneath; flavour is all in finesse; a bit four-square and marred by a raw finish.
1959 LINDEMANS HUNTER RIVER 'BURGUNDY' BIN 1580 *(Shiraz from the Ben Ean vineyard)* Limpid red-tawny; positive, old nose, mushrooms and cabbage, with residual sweet berry fruit; somewhat redolent of old Pinot Noir; soft, loose knit, velvet palate, *sous-bois* and tar, with a long, warm finish. Description belies the quality – still a very fine wine.
1959 LINDEMANS HUNTER RIVER 'BURGUNDY' *BIN 1590* Lovely limpid old red tawny, deeper than the Bin 1580; much more harmonious and complex aromas – tar, liquorice, clove and ginger; big, sweet, ripe wine, mid-weight now, but must have started as a veritable monster; ripe fruit easing into senesence; superbly long, warm finish and a beautiful balance. Really magnificent.
1963 ROUGE HOMME SHIRAZ *(Lindemans, Coonawarra)* Fine red plum garnet, touch of mahogany; complex, cedar and red plum aromas; still has good, plummy fruit, slightly four-square, with a long, lacy elegance; lingering, sweetish finish with a final point of dryness. Lovely silky wine.
1963 WYNNS COONAWARRA ESTATE HERMITAGE Deep, slightly browning, garnet; singed earth and tar nose leading to complex, sweet, ripe fruit; high acidity keeps it going; excellent balance of fruit, alcohol and acids; mildly porty finish. Very elegant and a quite delicate. *A point.*
1963 PENFOLDS KALIMNA CABERNET/EDEN VALLEY SHIRAZ Deep black cherry, lake rim – extraordinary depth and colour preservation for a 30 year old wine; ripe, spicy, silky fruit and tar aromas and flavours, with a strong earthy element; still retains a touch of tannin; very long indeed. Superlative.
1960 PENFOLDS SHIRAZ-MATARO, *BIN 51* Red mahogany; woody, mushroomy nose; broad, rather fleshless, flavours with high acidity; residue of deep, earthy fruit evident and wine has a long, warm finish; altogether slender and loose-knit.
1963 KAISERSTUHL SHIRAZ Deep garnet; very seductive, open, perfumed nose – floral in character (violets) with great elegance (one keeps going back to this); high-toned flavours, with good fruit and grip; long and well -reserved. Gorgeous.
1969 LEO BURING COONAWARRA SHIRAZ, *BIN 238* Fine light garnet-tawny; spicy, tarry aromas with strawberry component; sweetish flavours, a bit short and evanescent. Holding on.
1959 LINDEMANS LIMESTONE RIDGE 'CLARET' *(Coonawarra)* Deep mahogany-plum, good extract; fine mature sweet-fruit aromas; stony, ripe flavours, velvet textured with a touch of tar; a bit ephermal, but fine none the less.
1939 MOUNT PLEASANT 'LIGHT DRY RED', *HUNTER VALLEY (Made by Maurice O'Shea)* Very light old tawny; complex, old, mushroom and faded fruit aromas; surprisingly rich and concentrated for a wine nearly 60 years old; finishes long. Very rare, and remarkable.
1959 ROSEHILL HERMITAGE, *MOUNT PLEASANT (McWilliams)* Faded

mahogany tinged with red; soft, sweetish gingery nose; a gentle wine, losing its fruit, but somehow holding on. One can see the riches and elegance that it once had.
1965 OLD PADDOCK HERMITAGE *(McWilliams)* Fine, deep mahogany red; open, positive, sweet fruit nose, slightly leathery; opulent flavours, underpinned by sound, concentrated fruit and good grip; perfect balance. A wine of genuine power, with an elegant, blossoming finish. Very, very fine indeed.
1967 COLIN PREECE MEMORIAL 'BURGUNDY', *SEPPELTS ("Hermitage" (=Shiraz), Mataro, "Blue Imperial" (=Cinsaut)* Limpid velvet-garnet; gorgeous ripe *sous-bois* and cedar nose, smoky and complex; silky flavours, with the residue of very ripe fruit and still plenty of muscle; long, warm, port-like finish. A very attractive old lady.
1965 HERMITAGE, *SEPPELTS GREAT WESTERN* Mid red-tawny; gentle, soft aromas, noticeable tarriness underneath residual berryish fruit; continues onto the palate, with balances highish acidity with glycerol; sweet mouthfeel gives a long finish with tails off in a stately fashion; less muscle than the 1967 above, but has poise of a ballet dancer. Very lovely.
1952 RHINE CASTLE *(A Maurice O'Shea wine, reputedly made from old-vine Shiraz from Ch Tahbilk)* Deep cherry tone, remarkably youthful; fine rich, silky nose, gloriously complex, yet delicate; very powerful wine, great length and presence, still with heaps of concentration. Truly magnificent. Five stars plus. A privelege to drink.
1952 RHINE CASTLE, *SPECIAL BIN 28 "BURGUNDY", "VICTORIAN FULL BURGUNDY, BOTTLED 1953"* Deep colour, right to mahogany-tinged edge; big, sweet, surmature nose with a touch of pepper underneath; less opulent than the above, with a point of volatility; still majestic, rich and silky.
1952 JUNEE 'LIGHT DRY RED', *MONT PLEASANT WINES PTY. (Junee is a town in NSW)* Deep red-black; fully mature aromas, showing a touch of rot; tight wine, lacking the generosity of the other 1952s; has some ripe fruit underneath an austere frame.
1969 BAILEYS 'OLD MATURED HERMITAGE' Light garnet red, heavy extract; slender, musty nose and contrastingly big, meaty, mildly minty, flavours; very high alcohol; lacks middle palate. Rather rustic.
1965 TULLOCHS POKOLBIN DRY RED, *PRIVATE BIN (The "Private Bin" was Hector Tulloch's personal selection)* Massive deep plum with a youthful purple-carmine rim; lovely big, complex, minty nose leading to a massive mouthful of leather and tar held together by sweet fruit; long, warm finish. Exemplary old-style Hunter Shiraz. Cries out for a pungent, steaming, game pie! Magnificent.
1954 TULLOCHS PRIVATE BIN Dense black cherry; ripe tarry nose; big wine still, with ripe, fleshy fruit and a streak of pure eucalyptus in the middle; long silky finish. Not as majestic as the 1965, rather a scaled-down, more mature version. Gorgeous.
1954 MCWILLIAMS MOUNT PLEASANT HERMITAGE, *BIN 54/14* Mid-garnet, watery edge; elegant, intense, ripe fruit; highish acidity with an acetic note; starting to lose fruit now, but just holding on; fine, long finish; rather lean compared with others in this galaxy.
1953 TULLOCHS POKOLBIN DRY RED, *PRIVATE BIN* Mid-garnet, browning rim; mature yet almost berryish, black fruit aromas, with hint of volatility; liquorice and chocolate dominate fully ripe fruit; lighter than the 1954 and 1965; dry, long tawny port finish.
HOUGHTON'S 'LIQUEUR HERMITAGE' *(Non vintage; 100% Shiraz; probably from the early 1950s; given by Houghton's legendary winemaker, Jack Mann, to Gary Steele)* Deep black, viscous green rim; maderised, sweet nose, very reminiscent of PX; big, thick, treacly wine, even more PX-like than the nose; long, long bitter chocolate finish. Sensational of its type and most unusual.
1961 TYRELL'S VAT 9 Mid red-garnet; damp, eggy nose (hydrogen-sulphide); palate has some good, ripe fruit, but wine unfortunately spoiled by the nose.
1963 PENFOLDS BIN 128 'COONAWARRA CLARET' Mid plum with a watery edge; fine, opulent aromas – strawberry, raspberry and black fruits; very fragrant; rather burly flavours with raw middle palate and shortish finish. Disappointing.

BAROSSA

TIM ADAMS

1993 "THE FERGUS" *(14.5% alcohol)* Deep purple-garnet; positive, open nose dominated by eucayptus and new oak yet curiously Syrah-ish in character; similar flavours, bright, quite full with a warm, alcohol derived finish; lacks middle palate, but this may flesh out, given time. Seems somewhat clumsy at present, but has the elements to knit into something finer with bottle ageing.
1992 TIM ADAMS SHIRAZ, *CLARE VALLEY* Fine, impenetrable black plum colour; gorgeous, tight, black-fruit nose; curiously dry, yet fleshy, flavours of concentrated, fully ripe, fruit; almost floral palate aromas; very elegant. Not a blockbuster, but an atttractive, well-made wine with depth, which will develop and round out over the next few years.
1992 TIM ADAMS "ABERFELDY" SHIRAZ *(13% alcohol)* Very deep, limpid red-purple; soft, new oak dominated aromas, rich and complex; palate follows nose, with a fine concentration of silky, very ripe fruit sustained by round, softening tannins; considerable palate aromatic complexity and elegance starting to emerge. Good weight of fruit and harmonious feel about it. Very good indeed.

JIM BARRY

1992 McCRAE WOOD SHIRAZ *(cask sample)* Limpid black cherry, bright carmine rim; strong meat-extract, fruit-based nose; mid-weight and elegant; not the density of Armagh, but an attractive complete wine with a finely-tuned balance. Excellent.
1993 ARMAGH *(cask sample)* Black; residual fermentive aromas, otherwise concentrated fruit; big, reduced wine, with heavy oak char and wood dominating.
1992 ARMAGH Black purple; attractive, positive nose of creamy black cherry jam and cassis, no obvious wood; massive mouthfeel – cassis, ripe, stony cherries; huge tannic envelope. 10-year wait, at least. Monumental. Superb!
1991 ARMAGH *(on skins for 5 weeks to raise VA by 0.3 to add complexity)* Opaque, dense, black cherry; nose hints of violets, liquorice, tar, meat extract and super-ripe fruit; palate is even denser and more extracted than the 1990 – a real heavyweight. Not just size, but has underlying finesse which needs time to emerge. Oak, acids, tannins, fruit, alcohol, complexity, class – everything's there. Most impressive. Grand Vin!
1990 ARMAGH Superb colour: limpid black cherry, right to edge; impressive, but presently dormant nose; big, extracty wine – larger frame than 1989, with more tannins and greater density of fruit; long finish, with plenty of rich flavours starting to emerge. 10 years plus. Excellent.
1989 ARMAGH *(3 weeks on skins, post fermentation)* Dense black, right to deep lake rim; big, deep, ripe, brooding nose of great promise with strong cassis element to it; mid-weight as Armaghs go; with plenty of firm, gutsy fruit and acids and tannin still to meld. Long, mouthfilling wine with seductive palate aromas. 5–10 years. You could broach it now, but it would be a shame!
1988 ARMAGH *(wine on skins for only 14 days)* Mid black-cherry, soft vegetal nose – very classy *sous-bois* and asparagus nose – complex and attractive; lightish mature fruit, elegant, with distinct secondary undergrowth character; quite spicy. Would have benefited from longer extraction. The lightest of the range. Drink over next 5 or so years.
1987 ARMAGH Dense, blackish Morello cherry; very ripe, extracty, sweet, but not berryish, fruit on nose; complex, with new oak still showing; lean, high-toned spicy flavours, spice; good acids and tannins, but not quite enough depth of fruit to balance; lean finish. Complex and elegant. Fine, but lacking a little something.
1985 ARMAGH Deep plum, browning at edge; ripe plum and spice nose with touch of volatility; light flavour, still retaining fruit but with VA showing through. Rather tired wine, a bit alcoholic and clumsy. Drink up.

HENSCHKE

1991 MOUNT EDELSTONE SHIRAZ Black cherry, violacé edge; spicy, new oak aromas; big, very tarry, gingery flavours, silky, concentrated fruit; good acids and length.
1990 MOUNT EDELSTONE SHIRAZ Deep morello; even denser than 1986; positive ripe tarry nose, hint of eucalyptus; fine intense wine, bags of ripe fruit, balanced by alcohol, tannins and oak; notes of black pepper and spice. Yardstick young Shiraz, exemplary concentration. Highly promising.
1986 MOUNT EDELSTONE SHIRAZ Deep morello; brooding herb and spice nose; complex underneath; sizeable mouthfilling wine, wonderful concentration, spicy; size without being clumsy; ripe, silky fruit and rich middle palate. Great length. Stunning!
1982 MOUNT EDELSTONE SHIRAZ Mid cherry – rim turning red; closed nose, gingery fruit; ripe, long, silky flavours; fine concentration of fruit; still youthful with good grip and ripe tannins. Long. Excellent.
1978 MOUNT EDELSTONE SHIRAZ Bright mid ruby; slender, smoky gingerbread nose; complex but still rather shy; silky wine, with more obvious, rather firmer structure than the '78 Hill of Grace. Spicy, gingery fruit, with good length but lacks the sheer breed of H of G. Lovely, though.
1972 MOUNT EDELSTONE SHIRAZ Bright red-tawny – more red than tawny; positive smoky, coffee-bean aromas; flavours of spice, ginger and liquorice; tight, powerful wine; fine balance and length. Holding up beautifully.
1990 HILL OF GRACE Deep limpid black cherry; complex quite closed nose – smoky, cherry, spice and prunes; flavours of new oak and stony fruit; ripe concentrated; very long, warm finish. Big, but immense class. Very fine indeed.
1986 HILL OF GRACE Fine colour: opaque morello, carmine rim; gorgeous, youthful nose, deep, with hints of wintergreen and violets; dense, ripe fruit, new wood, soft tannins. Very concentrated, exemplary balance and great length. Not quite the depth of the 1990, but very fine none the less.
1982 HILL OF GRACE Mid-deep morello; rather closed nose – flashes of green peppercorn; herbs, plums – highly promising; tight-framed wine – ripe fruit and tannins; superb balance, remarkable concentration. Stunning wine in the making. Drink over next decade.
1978 HILL OF GRACE Mid-garnet, mahogany rim; complex nose of smoky, ginger-bread, *sous-bois* and vegetation; soft attact, glycerated mouthfeel, opulent, berryish flavours; old maybe, but in fine, vigorous form. Delicious!
1972 HILL OF GRACE Slightly sedimented red-tawny; fully mature, open nose; ripe, sweet fruit, fading but still seductively silky; not completely harmonious, but has underlying power and fine length. Drink now.
1962 HILL OF GRACE Fully mature bright red-tawny, cohesive appearance; attractive evolved toasted, smoky, leathery secondary aromas; soft, velvety wine, very long and elegant. Splendid, complex, complete wine. A delight.

HERITAGE

1990 SHIRAZ *(Clare fruit)* Medium deep colour; fine aromas of blackcurrant, spice and tar starting to emerge; lightish wine, well-balanced with flavours of plum and red fruits; rather a lean backbone, keeping it alive. Attractive. (Another bottle tasted in London was altogether richer and more complete)
1991 ROSSCO'S SHIRAZ Mid-deep garnet; rich, tarry nose, with hint of bel-pepper; opulent, elegant fruit – plum, tar and spice; good tannins; excellent length. In lighter mould, with considerable elegance and class. Would benefit from more post-fermentive maceration to flesh out middle palate.
1992 ROSSCO'S SHIRAZ Deep cherry,, carmine rim; attractive, Provençale plum, tar and spice aromas; elegant wine, with flavour complexity showing through high acidity. Ripe fruit, but not the depth to merit long ageing. Good now.

CHARLES MELTON

1992 SHIRAZ *(under finings)* Opaque, deep carmine; nascent tarry, black-fruit nose, evident oak; big, black tarry: huge extract and concentration. Will need years.
1991 SHIRAZ Couple of notches deeper than 1990; deep, black, tarry nose; similar flavours – a massive, tight wine, with firm, but not aggressive, tannins, slightly astringent. Complete, long, brooding wine. Needs half a decade at least to show its paces. Impressive.
1990 SHIRAZ Mid garnet, bright red rim; meaty nose – tar and eucalyptus with overtones of spice and leather; soft elegance; leaner in mouthfeel and more elegant at present than 1991 but nonetheless a sizeable wine; attractive black-fruit quality and fine length and definition. Lovely.
1993 NINE POPES *(cask sample)* Good deep colour; rich spice and bramble/briar-fruit nose with elegant violet tones; heaps of classy ripe fruit,

temporarily dominated by new wood; fine concentration and balance. Very promising indeed.

1992 NINE POPES Limpid black-plum, carmine rim; positive, forward plum and spice nose, some oak and touch of liquorice; firmer structure than 1991, tight with an element of greenness; otherwise big, briary character not lacking in fruit; savoury, meaty snap; excellent balance. Excellent, especially for this relatively light vintage.

1991 NINE POPES Mid-deep plum, bright carmine edge; complex fruit-dominated nose of baked plum, spice and chocolate starting to emerge; some oak; very ripe, soft, plummy, fleshy wine; great concentration of rich, spicy, fruit supported by well-judged tannins; a slightly green, bitter nerve shows on finish, but this is not attensive enought to spoil an excellent wine.

PETER LEHMANN

1993 STONEWELL SHIRAZ *(Cask sample)* Intense black-cherry, deep lake rim; Powerful, ripe sweet fruit-cake nose; similar flavours and oak dominate the palate, with a firm structure. Elegant, promising.

1991 STONEWELL SHIRAZ Deep, intense, red-black; big, very intense nose dominated by sweet oak and cinnamon; enormous depth and concentration of flavour – fruit-cake, cedar and cinnamon; significant oak flavours; long, classy wine in the making. Needs at least a decade.

1990 STONEWELL SHIRAZ Similar tone and depth to 1991 – touch of deep brick on rim; tar and spice underneath a largely closed nose; extracty, toasty, on the palate, with some oak well melded and not dominant; much more complete middle palate than 1987/88. Long and elegant. 5 years.

1989 STONEWELL SHIRAZ *(JIMMY WATSON TROPHY WINNER)* Dense black cherry, lighter than 1990/1/2, elements of tar, spice and toasty oak developing fine, elegant aromas; softish, mid-weight wine, ripe fruit overlayed with sweet, vanillin oak; long with finesse.

1988 STONEWELL SHIRAZ *(CELLAR COLLECTION)* Dense black cherry, red plum rim; dumb at present; mid-weight, with firm tannins supporting fair fruit; quite concentrated tarry, berry flavours. Not a blockbuster; short and lacks finesse.

1987 STONEWELL SHIRAZ *(CELLAR COLLECTION)* Lightest of range; opaque, quite deep colour; nose still closed; seems elegant with notes of soft fruit and spice; rather burly, gutsy wine; good depth of fruit and length, but wine is four-square and hollow.

1990 VINTAGE PORT Dense appearance. Tight, slightly woody nose; heavy-weight wine of depth and concentration. Promising. Needs 5–10 years – at least.

1989 VINTAGE PORT Black, dense as 1988, plum edge; soft, elegant, without depth and density of 1988, but has warm, ripe style and long finish. 5–10 years.

1988 VINTAGE PORT Black, to edge of rim; nothing significant showing on nose; a big wine, minty, eucalyptus undertones. Powerful, high alcohol feel. Magnificent concentration. Will be superb in about 20 years.

1987 VINTAGE PORT Black, opaque, very dense; immense big, sweet wine, soft and mouthwatering; long, fruit-cake flavours, double concentration. A marvellous combination of elegance and power. Will keep for ever.

1986 VINTAGE PORT Dense black, opaque, faded lake rim; strong mind-eucalypt nose, with touch of vegetal celery; big, sweet wine, bags of ripe, mouthwatering fruit. Complete, aromatic and long. Will make a fine bottle given time.

1985 VINTAGE PORT Denser than 1983, dark red rim; big nose – fruit-cake, raisins and tar; austere sweetness, considerable depth and good length. A lovely wine which still needs time to show its real quality.

1983 VINTAGE PORT Similar appearance to 1980, touch redder at rim; attractive, developed aromas, with a curious celery, eucalypt, vegetal component; complete, soft, long, raisiny, wine, weighty but with finely-tuned balance of fruit, sweetness and structure. Excellent.

1980 VINTAGE PORT *(BIN AD 2001!)* Opaque black, mahogany rim; open rancio, fruit nose; substantial, rather thick wine, medium sweetness, with tannins and tar underneath layers of fruit. Unusual. Attractive.

PENFOLDS

Note: I am particularly grateful to John Duval for providing samples of unreleased Granges for tasting. These (1987–1991) were tasted in Sydney with Don Ditter. Also, for the complete range of Magill Estate, tasted with John at Magill. The older Granges were tasted in London in October 1992.

1991 MAGILL ESTATE SHIRAZ Opaque black-cherry, carmine rim; forward, positive highly perfumed cocoa, chocolate, plum nose; stylish wine, big for a Magill, firmer than the 1990, but not quite its class or overall balance on present showing. Excellent potential. Will be interesting to see how these two wines develop.

1990 MAGILL ESTATE SHIRAZ Deepish black-cherry, deep red-lake rim; intense,smoky nose, rather closed; powerful, very rich intense fruit, classy and silky, rather than berryish; ripe harmonious tannins will keep this wine alive for years. Has balance and structure to become a great Magill. Sumptuous.

1989 MAGILL ESTATE SHIRAZ Deep garnet, violace, lake edge; full, reduced cherry-stone nose, tight, closed; big, almost tarry wine with good concentration and depth of fruit; a heavyweight mouthfeel with a slightly hollow centre. Not the sheer class of the 1988 or 1986. Good though.

1988 MAGILL ESTATE SHIRAZ Mid-deep garnet, browning rim; powerful chocolate/cherry-stone nose, closed but clearly has nascent complexity and style; big ripe wine, with unintegrated tannin and fruit; long, powerful, complex. This should make a fine, stylish, bottle in 3–5 years.

1987 MAGILL ESTATE SHIRAZ Mid ruby, light, browning rim; closed at first, lovely baked-plum nose developed; has elegance and delicacy, without the sheer intensity of the 1986; lean, somnolent dry tones, fair length. Elegant, but won't improve.

1986 MAGILL ESTATE SHIRAZ Deep, limpid, black-cherry; tight, full nose, of very concentrated ripe fruit; intensely perfumed, hint of secondary aromas; fleshy, concentrated, big for Magill, powerful yet with a finely-judged structure of noble tannin and acids. Lovely! Drink over next 5 years or so.

1985 MAGILL ESTATE SHIRAZ Opaque, mid Morello cherry; positive, forward, sweet fruit nose, turning to secondary aromas; soft fruit, good density, length and structure. Not a heavyweight, but attractive finesse and complexity. Drink as for 1986.

1984 MAGILL ESTATE SHIRAZ Deep garnet, mahogany rim; sweet, ripe, stylish, open chocolate – fruit nose; complex; mid-weight wine, elegant, with touch of tannins and acids evident. Earthy, leathery notes. Complete, very classy stuff; fair length. Drink over next 3 years.

1983 MAGILL ESTATE SHIRAZ *(first commercial release)* Mid plum, mahogany rim; powerful, fully mature, chocolate – vegetal nose; complex and classy – *sous-bois*, mushroom and cedar; quite lean, tight wine; drought has dried fruit resulting in wine which lacks a bit of flesh and ampleur. High acids and rather short. Needs food. Attractive in an austere way – drink over next 5 years or so.

1991 GRANGE Deep, limpid, opaque black cherry; sweet, berryish nose and palate, dominated by new oak; tightly structured wine, with considerable underlying elegance and a hallmark note of volatility. An elegant, medium term Grange. 10 years. (18+/20)

1990 GRANGE Much greater density and extracty appearance than the 1991 – deep black, with a crimson rim; very promising, brooding nose with hints of chocolate; big, ripe, mouthfilling wine; broad-framed with masses of refined tannins and good acidity balancing layers of dense fruit. Nose has best of it at present, as the palate is all in pieces. This has all the signs of becoming a great Grange. 10–20 years. (19+/20)

1989 GRANGE Opaque black lage colour; concentrated, pure blackcurrant aromas; medium weight (for Grange) sweet, tarry fruit, great delicacy and finesse; very long and most harmonious. Not in the league of either the 1990 or 1991, but a classy wine nonetheless. 5 years. (17/20)

1988 GRANGE Deep opaque, black cherry, carmine rim; unforthcoming nose; fine attack, on to ripe fruit, backed by mildly stand-off tannins and good acidity; a bit lumpy at present but has enough depth and structure to evolve well over 10 years. Again, not the richness or class of the 1990 or 1991. (16/20)

1987 GRANGE Deep garnet, mature touch of mahogany; aromas starting to come through, but going through a closed phase on the palate, which shows firm, ripe fruit. Lightish for a Grange, but still in pieces. Should evolve welll over over 5–8 years. Attractive. (17/20)

1986 GRANGE *(87% Shiraz, 13% Cabernet Sauvignon)* Deep opaque black cherry, still purple rim; powerful, sweet-fruit nose, tarry and a touch volatile; tight, aggressively tannic, biggish structure and fair density of fruit. Seems a bit hollow, surprising for this fine vintage, but should flesh out into a great Grange (15/20)

1985 GRANGE *(99% Shiraz, 1% Cabernet Sauvignon)* Shade more red than 1986, equally dense and opaque; tight budded nose, distinct pepperiness; relatively light-weight, round tannins and some elegance starting to show; peppery undertone; good length; a bit raw still; needs 5 years at least. (15/20)

1983 GRANGE *(94% Shiraz, 6% Cabernet Sauvignon)* Mid deep cherry, opaque; tight, elegant nose; quite light-weight in this context, almost approachable now but has tannins to lose; fruit submerged underneath the structure; no class yet. 5–10 years +. (16/20)

1982 GRANGE *(94% Shiraz, 6% Cabernet Sauvignon)* Deep, opaque; gorgeous ripe, sweet cassis and fruit-cake nose, inherently very complex; mid-weight, good fruit and fine balance; round tannins and considerable elegance; genuine depth under the sizeable frame. 5–10 years. Very classy (18/20)

1981 GRANGE Vast, opaque plum with a touch of maturity; oak evident on nose and palate, starting to meld; massive, extracty mouthfull, real depth here, still very tightly packed with fruit. Excellent prospects to become a great Grange. Don't touch for 5 years at least. (18/20)

1980 GRANGE *(96% Shiraz, 4% Cabernet Sauvignon)* Mid black cherry; elegant, cassis nose; lightest of recent vintages, with dry element and fair balance. Minty aspect and moderately intense fruit. Marginally disappointing. Have had better bottles of this. (14/20)

1978 GRANGE *(90% Shiraz, 10% Cabernet Sauvignon)* Fine and very dense appearance, deep mahogany edge; closed, tight, quite pleasantly volatile nose – complex and no way agressive; big, warm wine, fleshy and plummy with remarkable depth; finishes somewhat short, though has long persistence. (15/20)

1977 GRANGE Opaque black plum; hints of volatility and new wood on nose (mild corkiness on this particular bottle); big, ripe, sweet wine with strong, round tannins; warm, open-textured flavours with a complete mouthfeel and consierable length. Sound bottles should be drinking well now, but will last well for years more. (16+/20)

1976 GRANGE *(89% Shiraz, 11% Cabernet Sauvignon)* Shade more red and mahogany than the 1978, no loss of depth; not much on nose – closed and rather one-dimensional; huge wine, big-framed, highish acids, strong tannins; plenty of guts, but burly rather than fine; has a distinctly masculine charm. (17/20)

1971 GRANGE *(87% Shiraz, 13% Cabernet Sauvignon)* Superb appearance – opaque, limpid, with little sign of age; fabulous, enticing nose; complex and complete with oak still contributing; powerful, intense flavours, very complex, with great elegance and multi-dimensional palate aromas; very Syrah in character; very long. Magnificent. (19+/20)

1966 GRANGE *(88% Shiraz, 12% Cabernet Sauvignon)* Opaque, mahogany rim; deep, brooding burnt aromas, showing some secondary *sous-bois* development; plenty of fruit, acid and soft tannin left; complete, though not as complex as the 1971. Nonetheless, a long, fine, substantial wine with bags of character. (18/20)

1963 GRANGE *(100% Shiraz)* Dense, nearly opaque, with mahogany-red edge; biggish, pleasantly volatile wine, complex and quite meaty nose; spicy, herbal and tarry flavours, neither as mouthfilling or complex as the 1971 and 1966; yet long and fine, retaining a sound structure. (17+/20)

RBJ

1992 RBJ THEOLOGICUM Good deep colour, more density than 1991; excellent, complex, red-berry black-fruit nose; fine, deep fruit, ripe and deliciously complex; real *fond*; well put together. Drink over next 5–10 years. Lovely, classy wine.

1991 RBJ THEOLOGICUM Mid-weight black plum;; positive, evolving, spicy, ginger-bread nosoe; big, spicy, complete wine, real sweet fruit underneath. Not the tarry Barossa style, but softer, more open-textured wine; good grip and balance. 4–6 years. Excellent.

ROCKFORDS

1993 GRENACHE *(grower = Matschoss)* Mid, turbid red-purple; strawberry aromas – rather maceration style; soft, juicy-fruit flavours – red berries. Substantial, mouthfilling, long.

1992 DRY COUNTRY GRENACHE *(no SO_2 added)* Limpid black cherry; more aromatic depth and complexity than the above; tarry and plummy; big, firm tight wine, good concentration and length. Addition of Mourvèdre will add needed depth and backbone.
1992 MOURVEDRE PRESSINGS Dense black cherry; attractive touch of VA marks a tight, black-fruit nose; ripe, open fruit, tight, long. VA adds volume. Good base material.
1991 DRY COUNTRY GRENACHE *(+ 5% Mataro and 5% Syrah)* Deep limpid plum; big tarry, spicy nose – distinctly Provençale; elegant mid-weight, complete, with length, complexity and soft centre. Excellent carefully assembled wine, with concentration rarely found in Grenache.
N.V. DRY COUNTRY GRENACHE *(in fact 1989 & 1990)* Mid plum; closed nose, hinting at black fruits; lovely elegant, complete wine with palate aromas of violets. Fair length.
1993 SHIRAZ *(Goldspink, grower, 80 yr. old vines)* Deep limpid black cherry, carmine edge; juicy fruit nose, maceration element to it; open, soft flavours, touch of eucalyptus.
1992 SHIRAZ *(Goldspink, 1 yr. in cask)* Deep dark cherry; some oak on nose, also sweet berryish fruit with touches of tar and pepper; tight concentrated wine, excellent depth of fruit; secondary flavours developing. Gorgeous base material.
1991 BASKET PRESS SHIRAZ Mid-deep black-cherry; closed, very promising nose – flashes of ripe fruit; lovely mid-weight wine, great balance of new oak and fruit and fine length. Not a blockbuster, but has considerable finesse above all.

ST HALLETT

1991 OLD BLOCK SHIRAZ Translucent, dense, black-plum; ripe, smoky, black and red fruit, stony, berryish nose; mid-weight, long, elegant palate, fine concentration allied to complexity and finesse. Long, warm, finish. Complete wine. Very good plus. Needs 5 years yet.
1990 OLD BLOCK SHIRAZ Clear deep plum; soft, positive, creamy stone-fruit nose; complex; quite evolved flavours – bel-pepper and spice predominating; ripe, harmonious tannins. Long, complex, finish. Leaner and gentler, than 1991 and 1988. Drink now – 5 years.
1988 OLD BLOCK SHIRAZ Limpid, clear, deep colour – similar to 1986; closed nose – hints of plum and black fruits; soft attack leading to broad-framed wine with attractive spicy flavours developing. Seems a bit one-dimensional at present. Rather good. Needs 5 years more.
1986 OLD BLOCK SHIRAZ Limpid crushed velvet, right to edge; deeper than 1984; ripe, complex, opulent leather, tar and cinnamon nose with some H_2S "egginess" which dispersed with aeration, soft attack – a bit soapy – with broad, open-textured flavours developing across the palate. Powerful, long, warm feel, with bitterness on the finish. Good plus. Needs 3–5 years more.
1984 OLD BLOCK SHIRAZ *(First release from new regime)* Bright, translucent deep garnet; emerging smoky, plummy, nose; soft, mid-weight wine with tight, ripe tannins and good length. Flavours – griotte cherry and dark chocolate; berryish; noticeably burly, "old style", Shiraz. Good, though. Ready.

SKILLOGALEE

1992 SHIRAZ Mid plum, light carmine edge; closed nose, hint of eucalyptus on both nose and palate; good sweet fruit, highish tannins, attractive length. Not by any means bad. 5–10 years.
1991 SHIRAZ Good colour, marginally less dense than 1990; closed nose; solid mouthful of ripe, grippy fruit sustained by high acidity; edge of raw tannins which need time to integrate. Will develop well.
1990 SHIRAZ Bright deep garnet; closed nose, but clearly promising; plenty of direct, pure fruit, with solid tannins (a touch green again) and a long, elegant finish. Very promising embryo which should open out over the next 3–5 years or so into an enjoyable wine.
1989 SHIRAZ Dark red plum; secondary, gamey aromas emerging; lovely pure maturing Northern Rhonish wine, long, with real *fond* and good balance. Some tannin to lose. Most attractive. Drink over the next 5 years.

WENDOUREE

1991 SHIRAZ Deep brooding colour, dense purple edge; sweet ginger-pepper nose, concentrated, promising, though still closed; ripe, very concentrated fruit with high acids and tannins which dominate at present; though big-framed, the wine is in balance. Very fine. 10 years plus at least.
1990 SHIRAZ Much as 1989 – right to carmine rim; smoky cherry-stone nose; highly promising; stylish, sweet, ripe, concentrated wine; plenty of subtlety, a good grip and a fine tannin-acid balance; gorgeous wine in the making, with incipient elegance underneath a rather austere youthful mask.
1990 SHIRAZ *(from 1893 vines – block 24B – magnum)* Dense black, deep purple rim; completely closed nose; massive concentration of extracty ripe old vine fruit with a sweet base; extra-ordinary richness and length and beautiful balance. A remarkable wine, underpinned by new oak. Very fine indeed. 10–20 years.
1989 SHIRAZ Mid-deep black cherry, bright purple lake edge; soft, sweet berry fruit with a touch of meat extract beginning to show on a mainly closed nose; a mid-weight wine (in this context), with a seductive elegance starting to emerge on the palate; otherwise, a tight envelope of flavours, elegant & long; needs 5–10 years yet. Lovely!
1988 SHIRAZ Opaque black cherry, carmine edge; nose unforthcoming – hints of black pepper – seems promising; big, rather burly, with element of burnt fruit; dense, tight with mild excess of tannins. Monumental but without the elegance of 1989 or 1990 and a touch hollow. Good, but not great.
1987 SHIRAZ Big, deep black plum; rather lighter, damp, meaty, nose; still dumb; leanest so far, lacks flesh of better vintages; has complexity and length and would outshine most Shiraz; however, seems somewhat one-dimensional in this galaxy.
1983 SHIRAZ Very dense, opaque, black cherry, bright lake rim, starting to show brown; tar and singed rubber nose – not unpleasant but redolent of heat (1983 was a notably dry, hot vintage). A substantial, meaty wine, with good sweet ripe fruit underneath dry tannins. A strong eucalypt element on both nose and palate. Complex with bags of fruit and intense flavours. Excellent – but needs years still!
1979 SHIRAZ Couple of notches less dense than '78; liquorice, ginger & tar dominate largely empyreumatic nose of more elegance than power; palate characterised by elegance, length and balance, not by sheer muscle; lacks the weight and concentration of 1978, but very fine all the same.
1978 SHIRAZ Deep limpid black cherry, dark red-brown rim; most attractive coffee, tar and spice nose, slighty singed; understated and complex; immense concentration of ripe, sweet, berryish fruit; complete wine with nigh-perfect balance, fabulous depth, power and great elegance; will last for years; great class. Stunning! Sheer delight!
1986 SHIRAZ-MATARO Dark colour, not as dense as the 1976; toffee and liquorice aromas, hints of singed Mataro; mid-weight of ripe fruit; a bit "hot" although long and concentrated; earthy, dry, tannins; less middle palate depth than t he 1976, but plenty of concentration and finesse. Very good.
1976'SHIRAZ-MATARO Lovely deep limpid black-cherry; most attractive sweet, smoky nose, hints of violets and molasses; equally seductive palate: opulent, soft sweet fruit of almost Port concentration; elegant and full no-compromise mouthfiller. Superb balance. Long, complete. Sensational!
1986 VINTAGE PORT Black, purple rim; big, soft forward wine, elegant and attractive, without the sheer dimensions of the 1978. Fine poise. Needs 10 years plus.
1983 VINTAGE PORT Opaque black; neither figs nor raisins, but very ripe fruit dominates nose; more elegance than 1978 – softer, more forward; fine palate aromas, and good balance. Needs 5–10 years though it wouldn't give undue pain to drink now. Delicious!
1978 VINTAGE PORT Opaque, black; big figgy, liquoricey nose – nothing shy here; remarkably concentrated and still closed – needs a further decade in bottle really; perfect balance of alcohol, tannin, sweetness and fruit. Benchmark quality for this style of wine. Magnificent, monumental!
1976 VINTAGE PORT Deep, opaque, black-red; sweet, tarry burnt raisins & liquorice aromas; big sweet, dryish wine; deep, powerful with raw alcohol showing through; very complex. Needs 10–20 years still – but has structure for decades of evolution. The 1978 may have the edge, but this is superb wine by any standards.
1991 MUSCAT D'ALEXANDRIA *(only 600 litres produced)* Bright yellow-gold; fine, Muscatelle, almond and marzipan, nose; soft, elegant flavours; plenty of fruit balanced by freshness and alcohol. Lovely.

WOLF BLASS WINES

1992 CLASSIC SHIRAZ *(Brown Label)* Mid garnet-red; soft, plummy, spicy gently oaked wine; low acidity; supple tannins; good concentration and length.
1990 CLASSIC SHIRAZ *(Brown Label)* Dense, opaque mid-garnet; closed, mildly tarry nose; sweet, warm, spicy flavours – moderate power, greater concentration than 1992; fullish, satisfying, though somewhat lacking in grip.
1989 SHIRAZ, *PRESIDENT'S SELECTION* Opaque mid plum; positive sweet-fruit and new oak nose; soft, spicy, eucalyptus flavours, warm, well balanced with ripe tannins and good length. Will develop well over next few years.
1988 CLASSIC SHIRAZ, *"Brown label", 13.5% alcohol* Soft mid garnet; open, spicy aromas, herby with a hint of tar; palate follows nose, with good sweetish, gently oaky fruit, well-balanced with a very long, warm finish. Attractive.
1987 CLASSIC SHIRAZ *(Brown Label)* Touch more sombre than 1988; elegant, soft mouthfilling wine in Blass style – good grip, mouthfilling, spicy; more concentration and richness than 1988. Very good.
1986 CLASSIC SHIRAZ *(Brown Label)* Softer, more fleshy than 1988, less obvious power but long and very satisfying. Quite delicate and piney. Good plus.
1985 "HERMITAGE" *(Brown Label)* Mid-deep plum; still closed, quite spicy nose; firm, concentration of flavour – full, round and satisfying, long and warm. A touch hollow – otherwise excellent.
1984 "HERMITAGE" Fine, silky mid-ruby, little sign of ageing; harmonious spicy, piney nose and flavours; mid-weight wine, warm and long, very elegant and satisfying. Complete, *à point*.

COONAWARRA

LECONFIELD

1993 GRENACHE/SHIRAZ, BURTON'S VINEYARD *(55 GR : 45 SH)* Deep plum, closed herbaceous nose; big, ripe wine, stalky edge; plenty of mache and round tannins; good length. Will be very fine in time.
1992 GRENACHE/SHIRAZ, *BURTON'S VINEYARD (65 GR : 35 SH)* Deep plum; intense, positive, mulberry nose; firm, spicy, complex wine, with gorgeous ripe flavours; very long and rich. Not quite the complexity of the 1993 but fine, nonetheless.
1991 GRENACHE/SHIRAZ, *BURTON'S VINEYARD (72 GR : 28 SH)* Mid plum; lifted peppery nose with herbaceous streak; moderately concentrated wine with green, tannic edge and tar and spice flavours. A bit weak-kneed; lacks depth and complexity of later vintages.
1993 LECONFIELD COONAWARRA SHIRAZ Deep black cherry; stony, fruit-driven nose, closed up; big, ripe flavours and great length – real *fond* here. Most promising.
1992 LECONFIELD COONAWARRA SHIRAZ Limpid, mid plum, garnet edge; hint of asparagus on nose – but none of pepper; bright, green pepper flavours backed by sound ripe fruit; stalky edge; fair length. 5 years plus.
1993 SHIRAZ, *100 Year-old vines, McLAREN VALE (Tank sample)* Intense purple; huge, super-ripe wine with lashings of plum/berry fruit; complex peppery, green edge to palate. Long finish. Needs time to flesh out and integrate. Has all the ingredients for a fine wine.
1992 SHIRAZ, *100 Year-old vines, McLAREN VALE* Deepish black plum; elegant tarry, spicy nose; mid-weight (in this context), with dry finish; some elegance, though a trifle four-square.
1991 SHIRAZ, *100 Year-old vines, McLAREN VALE* Deep plum, weakish rim; opulent, complex smoky nose – cloves, tar and milled pepper; attractive, very ripe, sumptuous black-fruit, splendidly concentrated and intense – right across palate; more elegance than the 1990, but less density. Altogether a very fine, complex, complete wine.
1990 SHIRAZ, *100 Year-old vines, McLAREN VALE* Mid-deep garnet with nose

hinting at eucalyptus; big-framed wine, with plenty of fruit; good length, stalky, slightly green edge. Years of life ahead. Should develop superbly – only question is over mild stalkiness.

LINDEMAN

1993 ROUGE HOMME SHIRAZ – CABERNET Dense plum, deep carmineedge; closed nose, with some fruit and fermentive aromas; good fruit and tannins, with some elegance. Not bad.
1991 ROUGE HOMME SHIRAZ – CABERNET Limpid black morello; initially closed, opening to an attractive tar, liquorice and cinnamon nose; mid-weight, rather one-dimensional; good fruit and tannin structure; will improve over 5 years; probably more typical of this style than 1990 although that may turn out the better wine.
1990 ROUGE HOMME SHIRAZ – CABERNET Gorgeous limpid black plum, dark edge; gentle, spicy alcoholic nose, with cherry-stone fruit; big gutsy wine with firm tannins and good depth. A bit short. Needs 5 years yet.
1986 ROUGE HOMME SHIRAZ – CABERNET Mid-garnet, browning; attractive, complex, vegetal, meat-extract and tar aromas; ripe berry fruit emerging as tannin integrates. Lovely wine in the making, if no great complexity. The sort of vintage to buy young and cellar.
1985 ROUGE HOMME SHIRAZ – CABERNET Similar to 1986; ripe, sweetish secondary aromas – sous-bois and asparagus; soft, elegant berry fruit – real depth here – long, attractive complex and aromatic flavours. Delicious.
1980 ROUGE HOMME SHIRAZ – CABERNET Red mahogany; putrid, rather unattractive, vegetal nose; tarry and distinctly vegetal flavours. Whether you like this depends on individual taste; it needs food.
1993 LIMESTONE RIDGE SHIRAZ-CABERNET Deep black-cherry, violace rim; intense oak and sweet fruit nose; substantial, ripe wine, good weight of fruit; oak showing through; seems to be an embryo '91 in structure and character.
1992 LIMESTONE RIDGE SHIRAZ-CABERNET Dense limpid black-cherry; similar, though less intense nose to 1993; fine, bright flavours, supported by new wood, tannins, and a nerve of acidity. Not as full as 1988 – somewhere between '88 and '87. Needs 5 years.
1991 LIMESTONE RIDGE SHIRAZ-CABERNET Dense black-cherry; elegant, smoky dark fruit nose, new oak evident; delicate fruit, just touching berryishness; sweet oak with good tannin-acid balance; good length but lacking something in middle palate; needs 5 years or so then will keep well for another 5–10. Attractive, promising.
1990 LIMESTONE RIDGE SHIRAZ-CABERNET Mid black-cherry, morello edge; elegant and positive stony fruit aromas; big, concentrated, gutsy wine, with no lack of depth or complexity. Lovely balance and class winning through; a shade short. Very different to 1991 – more guts and muscle. Needs 5 years at least. Will be a fine, possibly great, Limestone Ridge.
1989 LIMESTONE RIDGE SHIRAZ-CABERNET Bright, not particularly dense; aromas of smoky, bitter chocolate; soft red fruits, high acidity and dry tannic corset; not bad, but lacks cohesion and elegance of 1991 and depth and concentration of 1990. Could do with a bit more alcohol and *gras*. Lighter weight LR. 3–5 years.
1988 LIMESTONE RIDGE SHIRAZ-CABERNET Medium black plum; closed tarry nose, touch of mushroom; rather burly wine, big tannins, big mouthfeel, good concentration but muscle at the expense of elegance. Has underlying complexity which needs a decade or so to break through. Plenty of flesh to balance tannins. Could be a great LR. It'll be interesting to watch its evolution.
1987 LIMESTONE RIDGE SHIRAZ-CABERNET Sombre black cherry, some gas; monothematic, lightweight vegetal nose with little complexity; mid-weight wine, dominated by vegetal flavours. Rather lean and raw on the finish, but has its own elegance. Cool vintage shows through. Not for keeping.
1986 LIMESTONE RIDGE SHIRAZ-CABERNET Medium density, garnet edge; nose still closed, suggesting spice, violets and ripe fruit; immediate, seductive, sweet, ripe fruit, mouthwatering and succulent; fine length, noble tannin, good acidity. Complete, elegant, gorgeous wine in prospect. A very fine wine, made for longevity. Without doubt, the best of the younger vintages.
1985 LIMESTONE RIDGE SHIRAZ-CABERNET *(drawn from hogshead in 1987, not checked for CO_2)* Mid-garnet, brown edge, touch of gas; slender, rather stewed, mushroomy nose; palate follows: very vegetal in character, lacking in definition and middle palate; might come round, but not showing much charm or class at present.
1980 LIMESTONE RIDGE SHIRAZ-CABERNET Quite deep red-brown; CO_2 again; strong mushroom – vegetal nose, with distinctly burnt component – crushed leaves + singed vegetation; surprisingly rich, non vegetal flavours; a fullish wine with elegance and length. Fully mature. An individual wine, which may appeal to some.
1976 LIMESTONE RIDGE SHIRAZ-CABERNET Mid deep plum, browning; strong smoky, eucalypt-wintergreen nose – very attractive. Sweet, very ripe fruit with beautifully balanced tight tannins. Complex and concentrated with long, warm, fleshy finish. Really lovely wine of class and distinction. Coonawarra at its mature best. Five stars. Perfection.
Note: all Limestone Ridges 80:20 Shiraz:Cabernet, except 1990 (59:41) and 1989 (60:40).

PENLEY

1991 SHIRAZ -CABERNET Mid black cherry, purple edge; smoky oak-fruit nose, some reduction and a hint of tar underneath; much broader, more complete wine than the straight Shiraz; has good concentration of fruit, a sound structure and nascent elegance. Cassis contribution from Cabernet shows through. Well balanced, attractive wine.
1992 HYLAND SHIRAZ Bright, translucent black-cherry, purple edge; ripe, creamy nose, though rather four-square; high-toned, herbaceous flavours; fair concentration and some elegance. Better structured than 1991 – although 1992 was the lighter year. No great depth. Not bad.
1991 HYLAND SHIRAZ Extracty, mid-deep garnet; light, herbaceous/pepper nose; relatively light wine with attractive berryish fruit allied to balanced tannin and acids; a bit loose-knit. A distinctly better effort than the 1990. Promising.
1990 HYLAND SHIRAZ Lightish garnet, watery rim; soft, quite plummy fruit aromas with touch of spice; light, pleasant flavours, with no great authority.

WYNNS

1993 MICHAEL HERMITAGE Deep purple black; sweet new wood and ripe fruit aromas; lively high acid, ripe sweet fruit; oak evident – with an orange rind, caramel sort of flavour. Excellent weight and depth. Most promising.
1992 MICHAEL HERMITAGE *(will not be released)* Intense black, carmine rim; completely dumb nose; similar in style to 1990, but lacks weight, dimension and intensity of the 1991. Not bad.
1991 MICHAEL HERMITAGE Marginally less dense than 1990; touch of brown in rim; closed nose, hints of *fruits noirs*; soft, elegant wine, great balance but not the muscle and weight of the 1990 – although may flesh out with time. Fine, complex wine, perhaps more classically Coonawarra in style than the 1990, which may outlive this, but will it be better wine.
1990 MICHAEL HERMITAGE Deep limpid black cherry; lake rim; new wood and ripe mulberry/damson nose; dense, tarry old-style feel, splendid concentration of fruit; tight; fair length; excellent length. Very promising, traditional "Hermitage". Needs to flesh out in mid palate.
1993 PADTHAWAY SHIRAZ *(1 yr. old cask; not for release, but used as component of other blends)* Deep black; strong baked plum (not stewed), intense fruit nose; soft, ripe fruit, sound, fondu tannins. Promising.
1988 PADTHAWAY SHIRAZ *(not for release – as above)* More red and apparent density than Coonawarra *cuvées*; reduced, spicy, rubbery nose; big, musuhroomy wine, plenty of stuffing; despite burliness, has finesse. Good blending material.
1992 WYNNS HERMITAGE Opaque, deep, black; strong ripe mulberry; closed but clearly intense; well made, with good fruit and high acidity, but relatively light, without the weight of 1991 or 1990. Lacks completeness. No great future.
1991 WYNNS HERMITAGE Very deep, right to rim; smoky nose of ripe mulberry and white pepper; fine seductive, ripe wine, some elegance emerging; excellent acidity and complex fruit. Great potential.
1990 WYNNS HERMITAGE Intense, almost opaque, black; ripe spice, tar and cinnamon/cloves nose; closed, a touch singed; soft mushroomy wine, plummy and rather loose-knit; hint of barnyard; no real depth, but good value at Aus$9.
1989 WYNNS HERMITAGE Mid deep garnet; meaty, beef-extract nose (second bottle showed more fruit aromas); softish wine, high acidity and dry tannins. Good wine with reasonable fat, some aromatic elegance. Sound, but unexciting.
1988 WYNNS HERMITAGE Limpid, dense mid-plum, lake edge; positive ripe soft mulberry nose; quite a big wine, fair concentration; bright acidity above underlying elegance. Has complexity, but dominant acid unbalances. A bit lean in feel, dry finish. Better than the 1989, but no more.
1987 WYNNS HERMITAGE Touch more red than 1986, lighter rim; raspberry jam nose, touch vegetal but more tarry; altogether lighter in flavour and depth than 1986; high acids and fair fruit; well-made wine, but reflecting leanness of the vintage with no great depth and raw finish.
1986 WYNNS HERMITAGE Mid garnet, brown edge; intense smoky tar & wood nose; some mulberry; mid-weight mulberry fuit, good balance and length; no great complexity. Good wine, fully mature; attractive, although rather four-square. Notably superior to 1989/8/7.

ZEMA

1992 SHIRAZ *(tank sample)* Deep red-black, purple rim; closed nose; intense cherry cream-soda flavours intense, very ripe, berry fruit. Long, elegant wine, with finely-judged tannins. Super stuff in the making.
1990 SHIRAZ Fine deep plum, blue tinge; lovely pure sweet-fruit nose; biggish, ripe plummy *fruits confits* flavours, fills the mouth; fine, complex palate aromas beginning to show; nicely judged oak. Intense wine with clean lines. Will be lovely in in 5+ years.
1984 SHIRAZ Deep, intense, black-cherry; hint of brown at rim; ripe complex tarry nose, followed by big, sweet fruit on palate. Long and very elegant. No need to search for the quality here – it's all there. Really lovely wine.
1982 SHIRAZ Deep red, brown edge; smoky, tarry nose; quite leathery on palate – very much in the muscular style, though has excellent length and considerable complexity. A shade less magnificent than the 1984 – but very fine, none the less.

HUNTER

BROKENWOOD

1993 'HERMITAGE', *McLAREN VALE* Deep purple; elegant, opulent and complex, almost gingery, nose; soft, peppery, concentrated mouthfilling wine; great length. Very promising.
1993 GRAVEYARD SHIRAZ Even deeper black-purple; closed nose with flashes of Hunter tar beginning to show; concentrated, very ripe fruit – real *fond* here – understated. Stunning wine in the making.
1991 GRAVEYARD SHIRAZ *(13.5% alc)* Deep blackish cherry;gorgeous tarry, sweet berry-fruit nose; strong leather component; very focussed and complex; on palate – equally complex, soft, ripe fruit with palate-aromas of violet; biggish, tight, frame; harmonious acidity and dry finish. Great elegance and the balance to develop well over 4–10 years. The best of the range – with 1986 a close runner-up.
1988 GRAVEYARD SHIRAZ *(13% alc)* Sombre black-morello cherry, lake rim; unforthcoming nose, which opened into positive, un-Hunter, tarry aromas; tight, closed flavours, starting to show tar and leather; a bit burly but seems to have concentration and structure for longevity. Has real depth but it something of a sleeper. Very good indeed, though difficult at present to see how it will develop.
1987 GRAVEYARD SHIRAZ Deep, limpid black cherry; smoky, silky, cherry-stone character, both on nose and palate; long, mouthfilling wine of great complexity and class. Now – 8 years. Excellent.
1986 GRAVEYARD SHIRAZ *(13% alc)* Bright, deep, red-black; restrained nose of chocolate and sweet fruit, tar and berries, beginning to open out; elegant violets and spice flavours, with hint of wintergreen at the back of the palate; concentrated, fat fruit, supported by envelope of ripe tannins. Very long. Excellent.
1983 HERMITAGE *(GRAVEYARD fruit; 14+% alc)* Deep almost opaque black-cherry, browning edge; big tough, slightly Porty nose; complex but showing heat of vintage; secondary aromas starting to emerge; dry, rather hot, alcoholic, mouthful; good, but distinctly singed fruit; reasonable balance, despite heat, and

good length; dry tannic envelope; finishes short. Needs food. Would have been better vinified in Port style, with residual sugar.
1975 HERMITAGE – CABERNET SAUVIGNON Dull, mid red-brown; musty, dusty nose developing; light, medicinal piney flavours; good length. Fading but sound. An interesting curiosity.
1968 TALLAWANTA RED HERMITAGE Deep red-brown, tawny rim; splendid no-compromise old Hunter aromas – sweet fruit and leather; more than a bit mushroomy; mature, gutsy, yardstick Hunter Shiraz – real leather and tar, dry finish. No signs of decline. Needs a haunch of venison to match its thorough-going masculinity. Big, beautiful Shiraz. Delicious, *à point*!

MCWILLIAMS

1991 BARWANG SHIRAZ Deep, virtually opaque, black-cherry; stony nose, underpinned by sweet wood; palate follows: sweet, stony fruit, rich and berryish; soft, mouthfilling wine; fair length, though a bit four-square. Definite Coonawarra and non-Hunter style. Good. 3–5 years.
1991 BRANDS LAIRA SHIRAZ Deep, limpid, translucent black-red; smoky, quite meaty, sweet, new wood nose; velvety, concentrated raspberry fruit and new oak; ripe tannins. A bit short. Promising, with elegance and structure for ageing.
1987 BRANDS LAIRA SHIRAZ Limpid clear garnet; browning edge; closed nose hinting at stony, tarry fruit; elegant wine with good concentration of fruit; longish but one-dimensional; rather neutral and evanescent; touch stewed and lactic.
1991 ROSEHILL HERMITAGE Bright, clear, crimson-garnet; closed nose;oak and ripe fruit underneath; elegant, tight, raspberry, berry fruit flavours. More size and guts than 1991 OP/OH, but less complexity.
1990 ROSEHILL HERMITAGE Bit more red than 1991; rather pappy nose, not the elegance of the 91; burly, big-framed chocolaty wine, with velvet elegance about mouthfeel; mid-weight. Fine wine in the making. 3–6 years.
1989 ROSEHILL HERMITAGE Brilliant, deepish garnet; slender, smoky nose; quite a tough wine, high in acids and tannins; but enough fruit to come through; soft elegance, masked by dry tannins. Quite attractive.
1988 ROSEHILL HERMITAGE Translucent, limpid red-garnet; aromas of earthy chocolate; secondaries starting to emerge; lovely ripe chocolaty, earthy flavours, plenty of fruit, with power and attractive elegance; beginning to flesh out well. Sumptuous wine in the making. 4–6 years.
1987 ROSEHILL HERMITAGE Limpid mid-garnet; dumn nose; reasonable flesh, with elegance right across palate; good acidity and tannin. A bit short on fruit, but is developing well and should provide good drinking for 5 years or so.
1991 PHILIP HERMITAGE Mid-light plum; soft, fermentive nose, hint of tar; attractive, plummy style, not typical Hunter; lightish mouthfeel; well made but rather slender.
1987 PHILIP HERMITAGE Browner than 1991; jammy, gingery, evolved aromas, attractive; sweet, velvety flavour, with very little backing tannin; light and polished; ready for drinking.
1993 OP/OH HERMITAGE Deepish crimson/plum; attractive, sweet, berryish fruit nose showing newe wood; big, solid, confident Shiraz, hints of pepper over plummy fruit; robust, yet round tannins, excellent length. Very good prospects.
1991 OP/OH HERMITAGE Denser, yet brighter than 1993, mid-crimson; new oak overlaying fleshy, spicy, velvety fruit; similar flavours, with a silky, delicate mouthfeel; succulent warm, berry-fruit with tannins to lose. Long and most attractive. Will develop well over 5–10 years. Excellent.
1990 OP/OH HERMITAGE Touch less colour than 1991; closed nose with good fruit underneath; bigger-framed than 1991, ripe elegant fruit with more tannic structure; a bit short. Good. 3–5 years.
1989 OP/OH HERMITAGE Deep garnet, good density of colour; very closed nose with some plummy fruit starting to show; ripe, older flavours evolving; quite tannic, tight, dry edge. Neither the complexity, concentration or balance of either the 1990 or 1991. Pleasant, sound wine; good for 3–6 years.
1988 HERMITAGE, *MAURICE O'SHEA, ANNUAL SELECTION* Fine limpid deep garnet; promising, tightly budded nose, very ripe mulberry fruit; opulent, very rich fruit going right across the palate; great elegance and silky mouthfilling flavours; long, complex finish. Finely tuned with with excellent depth and length; 5 years. Superb.
1987 HERMITAGE, *MAURICE O'SHEA, ANNUAL SELECTION* Deeper, more centre than 1988; fine, chocolaty aromas and flavours starting; lovely, big, ripe wine, raspberry and berryish – almost essence of fruit flavours; long, silky and harmonious, with more elegance and less concentration than 1988. Needs 3–5 years to reach its apogee. Very fine.
1976 OP/OH SHIRAZ Deep brick red; austere, tar and leather and starting to dry out; fully mature with complex earthy, gamey flavours; a strong, manly, wine.
1964 OLD PADDOCK HERMITAGE Deep, limpid dark cherry, little signs of its age; fine, elegant aromas, dominated by a touch of chocolate; ripe, mature earthy, gamey, leathery Hunter flavours, still with a sweet middle palate; high alcohol from a hot vintage, but delicious nonetheless.

ROSEMOUNT

1993 SHIRAZ, *ORANGE VINEYARD (Tank sample)* Deep opaque morello cherry, right to rim; positive, intense, black pepper nose; mid-weight peppery Shiraz, with soft, round tannins and good acidity; long finish, dominated at present by pepper. Wine has excellent potential, though somewhat hollow on middle palate.
1993 ESTATE SHIRAZ Closed, but showing some finesse on nose and sweetish, subtle fruit on the palate; some oak evident and fair length. Attractive now, but will improve over the next few years.
1992 ESTATE SHIRAZ Deep garnet; soft plummy maceration-style nose; similar flavours, edge of attractive ripe, peppery tannin; firmer than 1991 and 1989; rather neutral in aspect, though will develop well over next few years.
1991 ESTATE SHIRAZ Mid garnet, lake rim; closed nose, hints of ripe plum; soft fleshy fruit, tight round tannins; well-made but rather four-square and chunky; short finish; again, lacks mid-palate.
1989 ESTATE SHIRAZ Limpid velvet, mid-garnet, denser than 1988; closed nose – meaty undertones; touch of CO_2 lifting rather meaty, burly wine. Sound, but one-dimensional; lacks interest and nuance.
1988 ESTATE SHIRAZ Mid black-cherry, good extract; plum and pepper nose, touch of berryish fruit showing through; soft, intense, open, plummy fruit; tails off leaving warm, mildly tannic finish; lightish weight, fully mature with 3–5 years more useful life; not a heavy-weight, but well-crafted Shiraz.
1992 BALMORAL SYRAH Opaque, intense colour, closed nose; substantial, soft, succulent, Syrah, supported by good acidity and plenty of new oak; has real depth and considerable underlying complexity. Still an infant, but has the composition for longevity. Will make an excellent bottle in 5 years or so.
1991 SHOW RESERVE SYRAH Opaque black-cherry, bright carmine edge; reduced nose; ripe fruit and soft, cinnamon aromas; concentrated, sweet, berryish fruit; excellent length; supremely silky wine, not the depth of the 1990 Show, nor the traditional Hunter style, but all the elegance of McLaren Vale, with richness and complexity of Hunter velvet. Beautiful.
1990 SHOW RESERVE SYRAH Deep plum, opaque carmine edge; soft, ripe fruit under unforthcoming nose; big wine, lashings of fleshy old-vine fruit, with overtones of spice and tar; complete, right across palate. Really lovely, long wine; good now, but better in 5–10 years.
1989 SHOW RESERVE SYRAH Mid-plum, garnet, light red rim; evolved, elegant fruit-driven nose; palate is lightish, more elegance than size; attractive, though a bit lacking in grip and depth.

ROTHBURY

1993 SHIRAZ, *HUNTER RIVER* Deep black-cherry, crimson rim; completely closed nose; big, very plummy, spicy flavours; heaps of concentrated fruit right across the palate; assertive back tannins – a shade too strong. Promising.
1992 SHIRAZ *(not Hunter)* Deep black, carmine rim; no nose evident; soft wine, lacking in tannin to balance mid-weight fruit; more pressings would do the trick. Fair.
1991 SHIRAZ, *HUNTER VALLEY* Deep black-cherry, lake rim; closed up, reduced, nose, just starting to open; very rich, complete, long and quite soft wine; ripe fruit envelopped with hard green tannins; seems good wine in the making, but clearly in an awkward phase. Reserve judgement.
1989 SHIRAZ, *HUNTER VALLEY* Deep morello cherry, lake rim; nose going through vegetal stage (asparagus) in transition from primary to secondary aromas; mid-weight, green tannins overlaying ripe fruit; very dry, green finish; showing better at present than the 1991, but that will eventually be finer.
1987 SHIRAZ, *HUNTER VALLEY* Deep garnet, mahogany edge; lactic nose; big, mildly singed mouthfilling fruit, not a blockbuster but no lack of concentration; hints of ginger and cinnamon; dryish tannins. A bit loose-knit; ready to drink.
1983 HERMITAGE, *HUNTER RIVER (Len Evans' first vintage with deliberate use of new wood)* Excellent dense black-red, mahogany rim; secondary aromas of singed, smoky, tarry liquorice dominate nose; deep concentrated big-framed tarry wine; long, mouthfilling succulent fruit with no rough edges. Copybook evolution and a tribute to Len Evans' feel for balance. Lovely.
1993 SHIRAZ, *RESERVE (Hunter Valley)* Lovely colour – deep black cherry, crimson rim; creamy new oak and rich, smoky fruit domainate nose; very ripe sweet new wood/fruit, beautifully melded together. Deep, opulent wine with lovely structure and length. Great promise.
1991 SHIRAZ, *RESERVE (Hunter Valley)* Mid-deep cherry, carmine rim; smoky, creamy toasty sweet fruit nose; deep, concentrated wine with tight, ripe, tannin corset and soft, fleshy fruit right across palate; fine vinosity and elegance. Magnificent wine in the making, with balance and structure to last for years.
1989 SHIRAZ, *RESERVE (Hunter Valley)* Mid deep garnet; spicy plum fruit nose, not as intense as 1991 but good depth with touch of underlying greenness; attractive mid-weight tarry fruit with plummy ripeness. Fair length and dry tannic edge. Good wine, all in finesse, with potential for development over the medium term.
1979 SHIRAZ, *ROTHBURY INDIVIDUAL PADDOCK* Marginally deeper than 1975; fully evolved, old-style, somewhat jammy strawberry nose; substantial wine, with a big frame and considerable power; fair depth of ripe, sweet fruit, although lack of concentration and slightly raw finish mar balance.
1975 SHIRAZ, *ROTHBURY INDIVIDUAL PADDOCK* Good red-mahogany colour; touch of mushroom overlays berryish secondary aromas; reasonable weight of fruit although wine is on lighter side; delicate balance, with an unattractive soapy, raw edge and excess acidity. Not bad, but fading.

TYRELLS

1992 SHIRAZ, *VAT 9* Deep black cherry, carmine rim; clean tarry closed nose over ripe fruit; soft, mid-weight wine, lively acidity; loose-knit, with elegance. Doesn't have either the concentration or grip for longevity.
1991 SHIRAZ, *VAT 9* Darker and deeper in appearance than 1992; completely dumb nose; more concentration and richness than 1992 – with better balance and completeness. Fair tannins. Could develop well.
1983 SHIRAZ, *VAT 9* Deep, sound sombre garnet with brown-red rim; attractive *sous-bois* nose, open and fully mature; tarry, beefy, big-framed Shiraz; good length; with dry tannic envelope. Distinctly "old style" Hunter Shiraz; good though for this drought vintage. *A point.*

VICTORIA

BANNOCKBURN

1993 SHIRAZ Mid plum, purple; youthful smoky, peppery nose; clean, bright, peppery flavours, good weight with underlying finesse, acidity and tannins. More in finesse than the 1992. Will develop attractively over the next 5 years.
1992 SHIRAZ *(from 1989 close planted vines)* Intense, dense, black-cherry, carmine edge; strong, lifted capsicum nose; concentrated, but not over extracted wine, excellent balance and real *fond*. Lovely wine in prospect.
1991 SHIRAZ Even denser; new oak added to more complex and concentrated 1992 nose; long, concentrated, finely structured wine – at present has higher acidity than 1992; seems set to develop well over next 5+ years. Excellent.
1990 SHIRAZ Dark cherry – marginally lighter than either of the above; vegetal, spice, capsicum beneath an elegant, complex, smoky nose; on the palate, *sous-bois* and mushroom developing over a dry finish. A wine of elegance and poise.
1989 SHIRAZ Deep plum – carmine rim; milled white pepper, tar and liquorice characterise a complex nose; similar flavours, though somewhat *confit*; less weight

and general presence than any of the above. Good plus.

1988 SHIRAZ Dense black cherry; fine aromas of *fruits noirs, griottes* with strong secondary component emerging; intense, berryish flavours, long, harmonious and complex; not quite the generosity of the 1989 or 1991, but has the structure of a long stayer.

1987 SHIRAZ Mid-weight, red rim; vegetal, asparagus aromas, some *sous-bois* – a typical 1987 nose; rather lean, vegetal and dry rotty character. Not bad, but less depth and balance than the rest. In this context, uninspiring.

1986 SHIRAZ Deeper than 1987, lighter than 1988 – colour still holding well; closed nose; tannin dominates – dry edge, swamping whatever fruit is underneath; hollow and rather ungenerous at present. Fruit might win through, but seems unlikely.

BEST'S

1993 GREAT WESTERN SHIRAZ *(Henry's vines; cask sample)* Inky black-purple; very concentrated ripe-fruit nose, touch of capsicum; gread depth of flavour and concentration- ripe tannins and new wood overlaid by pepper and spice flavours; elegant and finely balanced; all the quality of a young Thalabert. Really lovely.

1992 THOMSON CENTENARY SHIRAZ *(cask sample)* Dense, black-purple; completely closed nose; big, extracty, wine with noble tannins and considerable depth; a bit short; will last for years.

1991 GREAT WESTERN SHIRAZ *(cask sample)* Mid-deep purple; positive, full, ripe-fruit nose; wine dominated by new oak; not as big as 1992 or 1993 but has notable elegance.

1990 GREAT WESTERN SHIRAZ Deep plum; minerally, capsicum and black-fruit aromas; ripe, mid-weight, mouthfilling wine, with fine balancing tannins and good acidity; real *fond*. Long and most promising.

1989 GREAT WESTERN SHIRAZ Mid black-cherry, purple undertone; as yet slender cinnamon and spice nose; soft, open-textured wine; good fruit, but essentially lacks grip; short finish. Ready now.

1988 GREAT WESTERN SHIRAZ *(Simon Clayfield's debut)* Deep plum; brooding black-fruit and liquorice nose; huge mouthfiller, bags of sweet, ripe, berryish fruit; cherry-stone flavours; real depth. Rather austere at present, but unquestionably fine wine in the making.

1987 GREAT WESTERN SHIRAZ Limpid dark red; open vegetal aromas – celery, asparagus, capsicum; high acidity and CO$_2$ prickle, lift secondary *sous-bois* flavours; has finesse, but lacks flesh and depth for futher beneficial evolution. Delicious now.

1986 GREAT WESTERN SHIRAZ Translucent mid red-black, weak rim; gentle, tarry nose, touch of bitter chocolate; quite a big-framed, tarry wine; guts balanced by tannins and acids. Needs 3–5 years yet. Very good.

1985 GREAT WESTERN SHIRAZ Deeper than 1986; aromas of black-fruits and violets showing through largely closed nose; lightish, high acidity, with unusual floral flavour component; elegant. Not bad, but lacks depth.

1984 GREAT WESTERN SHIRAZ Consistent mid-deep black-cherry; intially dumb, developed strong white pepper nose; burly, peppery flavours; good acidity with some ripe tannin. Still closed; seems promising. Needs another 3–5 years.

1983 GREAT WESTERN SHIRAZ Mid deep black-cherry, some browning; virtually no aroma evident – flashes of black fruit; tight, closed tarry palate; dry tannic finish. A bit burnt, but might soften up with time.

1982 GREAT WESTERN SHIRAZ Mid black-cherry, tawny rim; fine, complex, open, tar and spice, leather and capsicum nose; lightish, with dry aspect; a bit dilute; some elegance and secondary palate aromas; attractive. Drink over next few years.

1981 GREAT WESTERN SHIRAZ Blackish, limpid deep hue, mature rim; attractive, rich, almost porty, nose; pepper and black-fruits; palate has soft, somewhat vegetal chacacter – attractive, with good concentration and length; some complexity. Delicious – will be even better in 2–3 years.

1980 GREAT WESTERN SHIRAZ Fair dark red, weak rim showing signs of browning; no nose; biggish, burly, clumsy wine; short finish. Perfectly sound but lacks finesse.

1978 GREAT WESTERN SHIRAZ Darker hue and denser than 1980;slender, black-fruit nose; elegance and dry finish dominate palate; more concentration than the '80, but again, somewhat four-square.

1977 GREAT WESTERN SHIRAZ Deep, black-cherry, mature rim; slight, milled black pepper nose; pepper, tar and singed component on palate; firm, gutsy wine; old-fashioned feel – muscle more than brains; might soften out, but doubtful.

1976 GREAT WESTERN SHIRAZ Darkish hue, mahogany undertone; dry, port-like aromas – rubber and liquorice; distinct touch of rot on both nose and palate; otherwise, big, dry, tannic wine; iron-fisted muscle – no real charm. Quintessential old-fashioned Shiraz.

COBAW RIDGE

1993 COBAW RIDGE SHIRAZ *(2 tonnes/acre; cask sample)* Big, dense, colour; yeasty aromas, plenty of guts. Seems promising.

1992 COBAW RIDGE SHIRAZ *(3 tonnes/acre)* Deep plum, right to edge; positive, complex, sweet, smoky nose; high acid, but good concentration and flavour development underneath; new oak showing, rather minty, eucalyptus tone. A bit hollow.

1991 COBAW RIDGE SHIRAZ *(4 tonnes/acre; unfiltered)* Limpid deep plum; carmine rim; strongly minty, sweet, smoky nose, dominated at present by new oak; bigger, riper than the 1992, sweet flavours, with length and concentration; well-structured, complete wine. Long finish. Very good.

1990 COBAW RIDGE SHIRAZ *(1.5 tonnes/acre)* Deep plum; closed nose; subtle, ripe flavours, a big wine with real extract, finesse and length. Very good.

CRAIGLEE

1991 SHIRAZ Deep morello, lake rim; gas evident; tight nose, with yeasty, fermentive aromas evident overlaying chocolate and spice; slender fruit, raw acidity on the palate; lacks charm and has no real depth.

1990 SHIRAZ Dense, dark cherry, carmine rim; assertive, dominant, white pepper nose and flavour; wine is dull and lumpy and angular, with dry tannins and little generosity.

1989 SHIRAZ More red than the 1990; good aromatic development – tar and

---

sweetish black fruit; more flesh than either of the above; some new wood evident; overall impression is still of skeletal, charmlessness.

1988 SHIRAZ Dense black cherry; stone and tar nose; dull, lumpy flavours, four-square, lacking in complexity; scaffold is there, but the building behind it is unbalanced.

1987 SHIRAZ Mid plum; fine, mildly mushroomy aromas with a hint of violets; dessicated flavour profile, lacking in real depth of fruit and devoid of charm.

1986 SHIRAZ Mid plum; dusty peppery dominates the nose; has guts, tannin and acids, but little nuance or finesse.

1985 SHIRAZ Marginally deeper than the 1986 and 1987; similar aromas to the 1987; quite a substantial wine, with plenty of guts and a firm frame; no faults, but lacks elegance and grace.

1984 SHIRAZ Mid plum, watery lake edge; dry, white pepper and stone nose with finesse and complexity showing through; pepper continues onto the palate which is mid-weight with some elegance. High acidity and tannins and a hollow centre, make for a pleasant, but finally dull wine.

JASPER HILL

1992 EMILY'S PADDOCK *(14.5% alc; incl. 5% Cabernet Franc)* Deep colour, verging on black; promising, but closed, nascent black fruit nose; muscular, earthy, minerally wine, immense extract and concentration. Excellent acidity, ripe, firm tannins, considerable length and feeling of youthful complexity. Brilliant.

1992 GEORGIA'S PADDOCK *(14.4% alc.)* Deep limpid plum, carmine edge; aromas tending to tar and liquorice. Another huge, viscous, mouthfiller; exuberant black plum fruit, more forthcoming than Emily. Mighty wine, with superb balance and length. A shade less dense than Emily, but more in finesse.

1990 EMILY'S PADDOCK *(13.0% alc.)* Good, deepish, red-black plum; closed nose; massive wine – black fruits and minerals, distinct touch of earthiness; plenty of mache; dry finish. Very long and extracty. Needs time to flesh out. Excellent plus.

1990 GEORGIA'S PADDOCK *(13.5% alc.)* Mid deep plum; closed nose, hint of tar and reduction; well-defined flavours of ripe plum, and spice. Softer, with less weight than 1992, but layers of sexy fruit. Lovely.

1986 EMILY'S PADDOCK *(12.0% alc.)* Deep colour, carmine-red edge; complex, ripe, minerally nose, with leather and spice, just starting to open; long, fine flavours of ripe plum, layer upon layer of complex, tight sweet fruit. Seems more tilted towards elegance, despite its substance. Very fine indeed.

1986 GEORGIA'S PADDOCK *(12.0% alc.)* Deep, youthful, morello cherry. Nose still quite closed, though clearly complex with flashes of tobacco, coffee, spice, liquorice, bitter chocolate and vegetation; coffee and spice comes through to palate which is laden with ripe, stylish, exuberant, black fruit. Secondary aromatic flavours, with a slightly baked – not cooked – quality. This wine is sublime, with great class and length; near exemplary balance, with so much richness and depth. Marvellous!

KNIGHTS

1992 KNIGHT'S SHIRAZ Mid cherry red, violacé rim; strong youthful sweetish black pepper nose; bright vibrant fruit – ripe, concentrated; vein of green acidity; fair length and balance. Rather lean at present.

1991 KNIGHT'S SHIRAZ Deep garnet; mildly smoky, cherry-stone nose; attractive, stony flavour; good length but lacks concentration and complexity for top quality. A good Crozes rather than Hermitage. Quite promising. 2–5 years.

1989 KNIGHT'S SHIRAZ Deepish ruby, weak rim; rather jammy fruit nose; quite plump, forward, elegant and gentle with no rough edges. Good length. Not bad.

1988 KNIGHT'S SHIRAZ Mid morello cherry; closed, smoky nose – tar, spice and bel pepper; bigger frame the '89, with fair concentration and good acidity. Elegant with excellent balance. A degree more depth and concentration would put this in a different class.

1986 KNIGHT'S SHIRAZ Bright garnet – showing signs of age; strong white pepper aromas; secondary, vegetal-based palate aromas on top of elegant, cherryish fruit. A bit one-dimensional. Again, lacks real concentration and depth.

1984 KNIGHT'S SHIRAZ *(tasted San Francisco, Nov 1993)* Mid-garnet, browning edge; mature aromas – spicy, leather & sweat, with a volatile component. Reasonable richness on palate – complete, good length. Fully mature. Classic old-fashioned Aussie Shiraz. Attractive.

1981 KNIGHT'S SHIRAZ Consistent deep garnet; no signs of age; strong, attractive, smoky black pepper nose; soft, firm, super-ripe fruit, with elegance, a fine tannin balance and good length. Real concentration and complexity here. The best of the lot. They can do it!

MITCHELTON

1993 MARSANNE *(tank sample, no wood)* Clean, fresh, floral nose; softish mouthfeel with unintegrated acidity; flavours of banana and pineapple; clean, zingy, finish. Not bad.

1992 MARSANNE *(100% cask fermented with skin contact; unfiltered)* Bright mid citrus; confit pineapple nose; clean, crisp fruit; good depth and some length. Quite ripe and stylish.

1986 MARSANNE *(40 cases released in 1994; all tank fermented)* Lovely bright, old-gold; opulent, mature, lanolin, honey and acacia aromas; mid-weight wine, with attractive flavours of lime-blossom and creamy fruit; point of acidification still showing as slight unharmoniousness. All in all, a splendid mature Marsanne which will drink beautifully for many years to come.

1991 SHIRAZ Mid-cherry, light-edge; soft plummy wine, quite ripe, some tannins with open young Shiraz aromas and flavours.

1991 PRINT LABEL SHIRAZ Limpid, extracted, deep plum, carmine rim; deep tar and sweet-fruit nose; huge, mouthfilling wine, ripe tannins, powerful fruit and excellent balance. Long. Classic – with a fine future.

1990 PRINT LABEL SHIRAZ *(Jimmy Watson Trophy Winner)* Deep, limpid, black-plum, edge browning slightly; gorgeous roasted, tarry nose, great purity of fruit and developing complexity underneath; long, beautifully balanced flavours, supported by judicious tannins and harmonious acidity. Drink over next 5 years or so. Delicious.

1986 CLASSIC RELEASE SHIRAZ *(i.e. Print Label quality)* Mid red-plum, borning edge; fine, evolved spicy, almost confit, sweet fruit aromas; soft, ripe, round wine, tar and spice flavours; attractive, warm Provençale aspect; bright acidity. Fully mature. Excellent!

MOUNT LANGI GHIRAN

1993 MOUNT LANGI GHIRAN SHIRAZ *(in tank, malo finished)* Deep purple; full, sweetish cooked plum nose; big wine,plenty of mache, good depth of fruit and firm, round tannins.
1992 MOUNT LANGI GHIRAN SHIRAZ Mid deep morello; youthful fermentive, tarry fruit nose; substantial wine, closed but long and concentrated. New wood evident. Has structure and qualities to make a fine bottle.
1991 MOUNT LANGI GHIRAN SHIRAZ Dense deep plum, some purple; strong green-pepper and liquorice aromas; soft, round and complete wine; mid-weight, with ripe tannins and fair length. Not a blockbuster, but all the components to develop well with a few years in bottle.
1990 MOUNT LANGI GHIRAN SHIRAZ Good dense appearance; largely closed nose – tar and spice with ripe berryish fruit underneath; fine, supremely elegant and supple fruit flavours. Length and finesse dominate. Needs 3–5 years. Very good.
1989 MOUNT LANGI GHIRAN SHIRAZ Fine limpid deep morello cherry; white pepper and paprika nose; tight flavours – white pepper again – and firm, dry tannic corset; supple fruit underneath; needs time to throw off tannins. A bit awkward at present, but should develop attractively.
1988 MOUNT LANGI GHIRAN SHIRAZ Deep, sombre tones; cinnamon, tar and spice, otherwise largely dumb nose; cherry-stone palate aromas, with stylish, concentrated, earthy fruit. Needs 5 years or more to open out. Potentially excellent.
1987 MOUNT LANGI GHIRAN SHIRAZ Mid-deep morello, noticeable browning; black pepper, shading into capsicum/vegetal nose; attractive *sous-bois* & mushroom element; ripish, open, vegetal-based flavours, dry tannins. Rather lean, and green, needs food. Good, no better.
1986 MOUNT LANGI GHIRAN SHIRAZ Deep colour – reddening; meaty spice and tar nose, with hints of bitter chocolate and cinnamon; big, gutsy mouthful, with intense, powerful, fruit and plenty of mache; a notch more *fond* than the 1985. The best of the range. Needs another 5–8 years – no hurry. Excellent!
1985 MOUNT LANGI GHIRAN SHIRAZ Sombre, deep morello cherry, mahogany rim; strong white pepper and black fruit nose; ripe, concentrated fruit covering a nerve of green tannin; long, peppery finish. Plenty of life left. Very good indeed.
1983 MOUNT LANGI GHIRAN SHIRAZ Mid deep cherry, browing rim; dry tarry, singed rubber nose; burly wine, four-square and lacking in finesse. Burnt, dry, tannic finish. A fair reflection of a hot, dry vintage.

SEPPELT

1993 GREAT WESTERN HERMITAGE *(cask sample)* Dark purple; strong peppery nose; long, elegant, good acid-tannin balance; green-peppery fruit reminiscent of a young Thalabert.
1992 GREAT WESTERN HERMITAGE Dense appearance, strong purple component; new oak and sweet fruit dominate nose; intense black, liquorice flavours, on top of a powerful, structured base; excellent balance and good length. Promising.
1991 GREAT WESTERN HERMITAGE Fine, intense, profound, black-cherry; berry and new wood nose; voluminous, powerful wine; deep & concentrated with sweet, ripe attack and fair length. At present, the 1992 seems the more promising of these two excellent wines.
1990 GREAT WESTERN HERMITAGE Deep, limpid, black-cherry; soft, peppery, quitee macerated aromas; on the palate, a big, ripe, concentrated Thalabert-style wine; long, with most attractive fruit and plenty of depth.
1988 GREAT WESTERN HERMITAGE Complete, limpid black-cherry; nose dominated by burnt, liquorice & mint-eucalypt aromas; long, complete with strong cherry-stone flavour; high acids and soft tannins complete the picture. Needs 5 years plus.
1987 GREAT WESTERN HERMITAGE Deep plum, lake edge; sound, though old, vegetal nose of the leafy, asparagus, *sous-bois* genre; palate shows good aroma and flavour development, but reflects this under-ripe vintage; dry tannic finish. Fully mature. Not bad.
1986 GREAT WESTERN HERMITAGE Intense black-cherry, carmine rim; deep, cvoncentrated, tarry nose with hints of burnt rubber and eucalyptus – still rather closed; big-framed wine with plenty of mache; goodish fruit but overbalanced in tannin. Not bad but overall somewhat burly for real quality.
1985 GREAT WESTERN HERMITAGE Lively deep garnet, mahogany rim; attractive, fully developed smoky, eucalyptus & asparagus nose; big-framed, ripe wine, with real *fond*. Some complexity allied to good length. Altogether finer balance than 1986. Very good.
1984 GREAT WESTERN HERMITAGE Deepish black-cherry, carmine rim; smoky, white pepper with note of eucalyptus on nose; mid-weight wine, with high acidity lifting flavours; dry tannic envelope. Leaner than both '85 and '86; spoilt by high acidity.
1983 GREAT WESTERN HERMITAGE Sound, limpid mid-cherry; burnt eucalyptus nose; dry, singed wine, big-framed, but lack palate centre; rather mean and skeletal; muscle without finesse. Old-style Shiraz – one for masochists.
1972 GREAT WESTERN HERMITAGE Mid-garnet, mahogany edge; positive, tarry, and distinctly burnt, milled-coffee nose; again, a big wine, coffee-flavoured, burly yet complex and long. Curiously attractive, in an austere, idiosyncratic way. Ideal accompaniment to well-hung game or a burnt cherry tart.

TAHBILK

1993 MARSANNE, *CHATEAU TAHBILK* Light citrus-straw; youthful, peachy, oatmeal aromas; moderately rich, nutty flavour, with distinct floral component; good acidity balance and some elegance; but acidity is somewhat raw in character. Not bad.
1990 MARSANNE, *CHATEAU TAHBILK* Deepish yellow, tinge of green; hints of lanolin on unforthcoming nose; some underlying complexity; youthful flavours, more grip than the 1988 or 1986. Wine marred by cardboardy sulphur.
1988 MARSANNE, *CHATEAU TAHBILK* Mid gold; nose tending to straw; open-textured wine, attractive soft flavours and some length; powerful alcohol component. Obtrusive vein of (added?) acidity which spoils the picture.
1986 MARSANNE, *CHATEAU TAHBILK* Fine, deep, mature mid-gold; most attractive, positive, aromas of acacia honey and lanolin; open-textured wine with fragile fruit dominated by unharmonious acidity; short, evanescent finish. Nose is the best part.
1991 SHIRAZ, *CHATEAU TAHBILK* Opaque, black morello, red-purple rim; very opulent, almost porty nose; ripe, stony flavours, suggesting thick skins and long maceration, with plenty of extract and round tannins; biggish mouthfiller, with balance and some depth; not a blockbuster; has finesse waiting to express itself.
1988 SHIRAZ, *CHATEAU TAHBILK* Deep plum, dense lake-mahogany rim; sweet black cherry aromas promising later complexity; light-weight flavours, a touch vegetal and rather hollow and short. More elegance than the 1986. Good though.
1986 SHIRAZ, *CHATEAU TAHBILK* Deep limpid morello, opaque; somewhat singer, tarry, stony aromas; marginally less dense than the 1981, but a bit wine, none the less, with some sweet fruit underneath a layer of rather dry tannins; highish alcohol; a bit hollow. Attractive.
1981 SHIRAZ, *CHATEAU TAHBILK* Opaque, deep lake black, mahogany edge; tight nose, showing a feintly fungal element; substantial, tight, ripe wine, with fine concentration, plenty of muscle and dense, sweet, fruit right through to a long finish. An excellent wine, of power and presence not lacking in elegance.

TALTARNI

1991 TALTARNI SHIRAZ Fine, deep colour; brooding, black-fruit nose; pure, concentrated, ripe fruit, mid-weight, touch of new wood, excellent length. Complete wine, with real *fond* and good definition. Very fine. 5–10 years.
1990 TALTARNI SHIRAZ *(a rare instance of acidification)* Deep black-cherry, light purple edge; aromas of tar and lightly baked fruit; flavours of chocolate dominate a long, relatively light, mid-weight wine. Good balance and length. More elegance than size. Lovely.
1989 TALTARNI SHIRAZ Mid-morello, not very dense; positive, delicate, cherry-stone and tar nose; palate aromas of red-fruit and cassis; lightweight in this context, less complex than most of the others. All in finesse.
1988 TALTARNI SHIRAZ Deep black cherry, carmine edge; nose mixes chocolate and ripe, singed fruit; concentrated, ripe, sweet fruit and new oak infuse this long, complete wine. Complex, with a fine finish. A long keeper.
1987 TALTARNI SHIRAZ *(acidified)* Deep plum, still signs of purple; capsicum and pepper nose, with earthy, mineral overtones; light flavours – good balance, but lacks depth and length. Slender.
1986 TALTARNI SHIRAZ Deep, opaque appearance; mineral, capsicum and pepper nose; elegant, mid-weight palate, dryish tannins and attractive tarry flavours developing. Not over-rich, but has length and finesse.
1985 TALTARNI SHIRAZ Deep, limpid plum, right to edge; secondary aromas – tar, spice and leather, underpinned by sweet fruit; touch of VA; soft attack, developing beautifully into mouthfilling, red fruit flavours; dry tannic finish. Complex. Very good indeed..
1984 TALTARNI SHIRAZ Deep morello, touch of red in rim; seductive, open, rich and multi-faceted nose – red-fruits, *sous-bois*, spice and violets; fully developed flavours – sous-bois, vegetal. Dry tannins showing through, but more than balanced by long, ripe, sexy fruit. Superb.
1983 TALTARNI SHIRAZ Deep opaque black-cherry, no browning; deep, sleeping stony, earthy nose – chocolate and meat-extract; a big wine, ripe, complex and complete, with high acidity and dryish tannins. Developing well. Individual, but very good, nonetheless.
1982 TALTARNI SHIRAZ Deep, opaque, black-cherry, no brown; splendid, fully evolved, nose – burnt, earthy, real-leather and meat-extract; rather burly wine, lacking in finesse; bright acidity; complex underneath. Could come through, with time.
1981 TALTARNI SHIRAZ Mid-morello appearance; fine, chocolatey, sweet-fruit, nose; well-developed, old-style tarry flavours, with a dry leathery edge. Long, attractive, still retaining some sweet fruit. Needs food!
1980 TALTARNI SHIRAZ *(acidified)* Deep plum; old-style, tarry, baked fruit aromas; faded, fané, old tea-rose flavours; dry tannins; burly and jammy. Tough, skeletal.
1979 TALTARNI SHIRAZ Fine, deep black-cherry; leather, tar and cinammon nose; sizeable, old-style, mouthfiller; good balance; elegant, in the old manner. Attractive.
1978 TALTARNI SHIRAZ Limpid, deep black-cherry, touch of age at edge; lovely, complex, real-leather, chocolate and liquorice nose; big, spicy wine, complete, complex – really lovely, touch of residual dry tannins; long, sweet, finish. Superb!
1977 TALTARNI SHIRAZ Very deep black-cherry, no obvious signs of age; old, rather dusty nose – burnt leather, porty; big burly wine, huge mouthfiller; size rather than finesse but has length underneath the muscle; no-compromise, old-style Aussie Shiraz. Very good.

YARRA

YARRA YERING

1991 UNDERHILL Deep black cherry; strong mineral/asparagus element on a stony plum/cherry nose; very rich cherry-stone flavours; excellent acid and soft tannins to counter-balance fine depth of fruit. Very long and complex. Attractive and highly promising.
1990 UNDERHILL Good colour; marginally more intense than 1991 and similar in aromatic style; more intensity of flavour – dominated by rich, pure, extracty fruit. More forward than 1991 on palate but not on nose. Excellent.
1991 NO. 2 Deeper than 1991 Underhill – despite contribution of white grapes; open, floral nose with hint of asparagus; soft, beautifully extracted wine; not a blockbuster, but has great delicacy and balance.
1990 NO. 2 Mid-plum; earthy, mineral aromas; broad, earthy flavours, more obvious tannins; good, but lacks the open suppleness of 1991.
1989 NO. 2 Lighter, mid-deep plum; cherry-stone nose, with strong note of Pinot strawberry and some vegetal secondary aromas coming through; lighter in mouthfeel, quite forward – red fruits and flowers; open, soft, approachable wine.

Will continue for 5 years more, perhaps longer.
1982 NO 2 Mid-deep morello, touch of brown at rim; secondary vegetal aromas dominated by mushroom & *sous-bois*; good fruit still on palate; some animal – fur components of flavour; long and spicy; dry finish. Not a big wine, but evolving beautifully. Excellent.
1980 NO 2 *(includes 10% Mourvèdre)* Youthful, deep red-brown, mahogany edge; positive, complex, almost exotic nose – vegetal, animal, coffee, with burnt component; very rich, warm, flavours develop in mouth, ripe, soft and berryish. Immense length. A very fine wine indeed; entirely sui generis. Fascinating – not yardstick Shiraz, but superb nonetheless. Undoubtedly the best of this range – perhaps of all No. 2s.

WESTERN AUSTRALIA

1992 SHIRAZ, *CHATSFIELD, MOUNT BARKER (12.5% alcohol)* Translucent, mid-garnet; fine minty, eucaplyptus & cedar nose – distinctly medicinal, but by no means unpleasant – similar flavours overlay fair fruit; lightish wine with no real tannic support; evanescent finish. Seems to make a brief appearance then vanish altogether.
1992 EVANS & TATE, *MARGARET RIVER HERMITAGE* Bright garnet; soft, nose and flavours, dominated by wood and somewhat lean underneath. Some elegance and length; low acidity. Quite attractive, but rather insubstantial and lacking in complexity.
1992 SHIRAZ, *WILDFLOWER RIDGE, HOUGHTONS* Deep garnet, some CO_2; creamy new oak dominates nose and palate; underneath, good, bright, raspberryish-cassisy fruit; highish acidity and tannins; fair length. Light, pleasant wine with some attractive berryish character.
1992 GOLD RESERVE SHIRAZ, *HOUGHTONS* Marginally denser than the above; strong, crushed raspberry nose with a touch of oak; more depth and concentration of both aroma and flavour than the Wildflower Ridge and more centre, but finally, lacks complexity. Will develop well over next few years.
1991 SHIRAZ, *WILDFLOWER RIDGE (HOUGHTON, SWAN VALLEY)* Good colour, elegant, smoky, quite complex nose; taut spicy, mid-weight flavours, now softening out. Warm satisfying wine.
1991 PLANTAGENET, *SHIRAZ* Translucent deep garnet; smoky, red fruit nose, elegant and somewhat northern Rhonish; soft flavours, low tannins and highish alcohol, which unbalances the wine. Lacks real depth.
1990 PAUL CONTI, *"HERMITAGE"* Bright garnet; raw, alcohol-driven nose; soft, plummy fruit, but alcohol dominates and blurs the flavours; lacks centre and finishes raw. Dull and out of balance.
1991 JINGALLA, *OAK MATURED SHIRAZ (11.8% alcohol)* Bright, light ruby; elegant, maturing peppery nose; fine, delicate and quite complex flavour with soft tannins, a warm undertone and a Bordeauxish finish. Light and agreeable. Attractive now, but should improve over 3–5 years.
1989 SHIRAZ, *GOUNDREY WINDY HILL, MOUNT BARKER (12.5% alcohol)* Mid garnet; clean, elegant nose with touch of maturity; warm, rather ephermal flavour, four-square; not bad, but lack real depth.
1989 SHIRAZ, *JINGALLA (Oak matured)* Limpid, deepish garnet; positive, open, complex aromas, in transition from primary to secondary stage; spicy wine, with hint of eucalyptus, some depth, albeit a shade hollow; good, long finish; attractive, satisfying wine. Ready now.
1988 SHIRAZ, *PEEL ESTATE (13.5% alcohol)* Fine deep garnet; complex, fully mature, stony nose; ripe, silky flavours with good concentration and a notably long, warm finish; balanced, thoroughly satisfying wine which has real depth and great quality. Excellent.
1988 SHIRAZ, *CHATSFIELD* Fine, bright limpid hue, brickish edge; strong attractive aromas – cinnnamon and ripe fruit; mid-weight palate, follows nose – cedary, elegant, harmonious; complex, satisfying and fully mature. Very good plus – lacks a touch in the middle palate for more.
1987 SHIRAZ, *ALKOOMI, FRANKLAND RIVER* Deep limpid garnet, good extract; complex, maturing cherry-stone nose; ripe, fleshy wine with good fruit, only marred by a hint of raw, bitterness on an otherwise fine finish; opened up in the glass. Very attractive indeed.
1986 HERMITAGE, *PLANTAGENET, MOUNT BARKER* Fine deep colour; positive, evolved, milled-pepper nose leading to fine, mature flavours derived from ripe fruit; elegance dominates over weight; long, warm finish. Lacks centre but otherwise very attractive.
1983 "HERMITAGE", *PLANTAGENET* Fine deep plum colour; no obvious signs of age; nose and flavours of kirsch cherries in alcohol; strong, soft flavour, not in any way gamey or secondary, despite age, with virtually no tannin, but well preserved. Will stay like this for years. Curious and attractive.

CAPE MENTELLE

1978 EMERALD PARK GRENACHE ROSE A delicious curiosity – light red tawny, fruity nose with touch of gaminess; spicy, gutsy, low acidity, but high alcohol keeping it going. In splendid condition for a 15 yr. old rosé. Unsaleable when it was produced – David Hohnen's mother apparently drank most of it!
1991 HERMITAGE Deep plum; spicy, green pepper nose; ripe, mid-weight flavour, concentrated without jaminess; balanaced by dryish tannins and alcohol. Not a blockbuster but has depth and harmony. Needs 5+ years. Excellent.
1990 HERMITAGE Deepish crimson; positive black pepper nose, touch of spice; mid-weight rather loose-knit wine; has tannin and fruit but lacks real grip; dry, peppery, but not really enough fruit to balance tannins and uncharacteristically hollow. Fair.
1989 HERMITAGE Deep garnet, right to rim; elegant aromas, dominated by black pepper, starting to develop (distinctly northern Rhonish); mid-weight, lighter in feel than '88/'87 & '86, but more delicacy and finese; attractive, dry, peppery fruit, dry tannic edge; long finish. Very good.
1988 HERMITAGE Deep, limpid, black-cherry; attractive nose, dominated by cinnamon and pepper; big, gusty wine, bags of fruit; a touch burly and clumsy; what it lacks in finesse, it compensates in sweet fruit and length. Rather too much tannin for fruit. Not bad, but not the best of the bunch.
1987 HERMITAGE Deep garnet, red rim; meaty "Bovril" and black pepper nose; ripe fruit and pepper, good grip but tails off at finish. Attractive. Drink now.
1986 HERMITAGE Mid plum, brick edge; dusty nose, hints of pepper; lovely mid-weight fruit, soft tannic edge; pepper and sweet fruit; complete wine – all in finesse. Ready now.
1983 HERMITAGE Shade less dense than 1979; complex, open, spice & cloves aromas – some cedar and chocolate notes – redolent of Cabernet Sauvignon; quite substantial, soft, wine, with plenty of depth and touches of tar and earthiness; fruit still holding out well. A bit short, but delicious, nonetheless.
1979 HERMITAGE Deep black cherry, brick edge; smoky, minty nose – touch of tar and shit; big, plummy, spicy fruit, ripe soft tannins with good grip and length. A fine wine, with richness and aromatics starting to develop. Palate is surprisingly youthful, retaining sweetness and no signs of drying out.

SOUTH AFRICA

BACKSBERG

1993 BACKSBERG SHIRAZ *(tank sample; ex-cask 3 weeks)* Black; similar to 1991 but denser; big, extracty nose and big tarry, firm fruit; soft underbelly. V. promising.
1991 BACKSBERG SHIRAZ Fine deep black cherry; ripe mid-weight; hovering between old and new styles – fleshiness of old, concentration and focus of new. Good plus.
1990 BACKSBERG SHIRAZ Blacker and deeper than 1989 – lake rim; strong, rather baked, open, tarry, nose; firm, fleshy wine with good round tannins and balancing acidity (tastes acidified). 3–5 years yet to maturity. Good.
1989 BACKSBERG SHIRAZ Opaque, deep blackish plum, lake rim; strongly reduced, rubbery nose; big wine – ripe, sweetish, succulent fruit; plenty of guts, yet seductively soft. Drink now – 3 years.
1987 BACKSBERG SHIRAZ Deep plum, brick rim; old style stewed fruit and vegetal nose; soft, clean wine; lacks depth and substance; finishes short. Fading.

BERGKELDER

1989 ALLESVERLOREN SHIRAZ *(14°alc)* Deep Victoria plum; big, sweet, porty aromas which follow onto palate; a high alcohol, generous, mouthfiller. More focussed fruit than the 1982.
1987 ALLESVERLOREN SHIRAZ *(12.8° alc)* Bright garnet, lightening rim; firm, sweet, rich old-style nose; full, soft, plump wine, highish, rather clumsy, hard acidity (probably added), some tannin; short finish. Not bad, although it demonstrably lacks finesse.
1982 ALLESVERLOREN SHIRAZ *(no small wood)* Deep red plum; sweet, sweaty, leathery nose (phew! what a scorcher!) big, burly, porty fruit; dry finish. Seems to be uncontrolled Rubensesque flesh, without any corsets. Fully mature and curiously appealing.
1989 L'ORMARINS SHIRAZ Limpid, marginally deeper than the 1987; ripe mulberry fruit aromas starting to show; soft, stylish, plump fruit, good grip; not the leaner elegance of the '87, but more substantial. Good plus. Will improve.
1987 L'ORMARINS SHIRAZ Mid-garnet, more red than the 1984; positive rather herby, spicy nose – cedar and cigar boxes – with similar flavours. Long and attractive – elegance outshining substance. Just too much tannin for fruit – but this would be barely noticeable with food. Most satisfying.
1984 L'ORMARINS SHIRAZ Sound mid-garnet; ripe fruit and wood showing on still closed nose; slightly sweet, peppery fruit, dominated by oak. How will it develop?
1989 MIDDELVLEI SHIRAZ Light mid-garnet; singed note on otherwise unforthcoming nose; open-textured, fleshy, mulberry fruit, good concentration with supporting tannins; finishes short and lacks complexity; will develop over next 3–5 years, but doubtful if it will improve. Not bad, but rather one-dimensional.
1988 MIDDELVLEI SHIRAZ *(first Shiraz release)* Shade deeper than the 1989; similar aromas; sound, sweetish ripe fruit, mid-weight with distinct singed dry edge to palate; lacks complexity. Not bad though, for a first attempt.

FAIRVIEW

1993 SHIRAZ-GAMAY *(80:20; 4 days carbonic maceration, then destemmed and traditionally fermented)* Vibrant, deep, Beaujolais-purple; open, maceration-fruit nose; big, gutsy, plummy mouthful; sweet, bosomy fruit. No pretensions – just delicious!
1993 SHIRAZ-MERLOT *(65:35)* Intense red-black; soft, opening nose and gentle, perfumed flavours, sustained by plenty of sound fruit. Attractive.
1993 SHIRAZ *(13.5 alc.)* Mid-deep black plum; positive, open, smoky, mulberry nose; soft, quite plummy and peppery flavours. Not a heavy-weight. Needs a few years.
1993 RESERVE SHIRAZ *(14.0 alc.)* Dense, opaque, black – fine colour; firm, largely closed nose, oak showing through, though not aggressively; big, very rich, almost porty, berryish fruit; green, tarry edge to it. Distinct oak contribution. Very good indeed. Leave for 4 more years.
1992 SHIRAZ Dense red-plum; hints of pepper and violets on nose; fruity, elegant, peppery, with gentle tannins and good acidity. 3 years or so to peak.
1991 RESERVE SHIRAZ Opaque, deep plum; pepper spice and ginger aromas; on the palate, elegance, but not at the expense of depth; good, solid fruit, with balancing acids and tannin. Long, complete. Best so far.
1990 RESERVE SHIRAZ Similar to 89 – though a shade less dense; warm, spicy, minty, aromas – griotte cherry and eucalyptus – starting to emerge; altogether different in style to 89 – lighter, fresher, more elegant with highish acids and sharper tannins. (Picked part of crop under-ripe – to try!)
1989 RESERVE SHIRAZ Opaque black cherry, right to rim; tight, closed nose; huge, warm, mouthfilling, extracty wine; quite sweet underneath lightish acidity and round tannins. 5 years minimum. Splendid. Watch out Marcel Guigal!
1988 SHIRAZ Dense black plum; strong eucalyptus nose – attractive, though strikingly different from the rest; soft, accessible fruit – opulent, spicy, eucalyptus again – encased in a firm tannic envelope. Long, warm, finish. A bit hot and burly. Drinking well now. Will change with time, but improve?
1987 RESERVE SHIRAZ Almost opaque, dense, black plum; full, somewhat unexpressive, extracty nose; flavours deftly combine ripeness, depth and elegance; succulent fruit, with a fresh acidity; complex with some real depth; ready now but will continue to improve. Very good.

1980 SHIRAZ *(Cool fermented, with punching-down)* Red-brown, tawny rim; somewhat evanescent nose and lightish, neutral flavours; sound, without complexity or depth; dry finish. Dull.
1974 SHIRAZ *(Cyril Back's first Shiraz; bottled in 1974 for his auction)* Sombre plummy red-brown; rich, old-style porty nose, redolent of baked fruit; elegant, sweetish flavours, a touch volatile and drying out; high alcohol; holding up fairly well. Attractive, if you like the style.
1994 SWEET RED *(Over-ripe Shiraz, picked at 27 Brix and fortified to 17 alc. with 6–7 Brix of residual sugar)* Dense black-purple; sweet, port-like nose, and flavours, excellent length and surprisingly approachable. Excellent and extra-ordinary value at 12.5 Rand per 75 cl bottle.

HARTENBURG

1992 SHIRAZ *(in large wood)* Mid-deep hue; quite fleshy, reduced wine (needs racking); not bad but seems rather lean at the edge. Reserve judgement.
1991 SHIRAZ *(in tank, ready for bottling)* Fine, ripe, sweet wine; deep garnet hue, tarry, earthy flavours with note of violets and a green nerve; succulent fruit. Promising.
1990 SHIRAZ Deep, limpid, red-plum; lively, elegant green-pepper nose; mid-weight, plump, fruit, strong tarriness overlaid with new wood; dry finish. Good plus.
1989 SHIRAZ *(12.0 alc)* Even denser than the 1986; largely closed, but concentrated; touch of gas, giving onto a meaty, big-framed and muscular wine; leathery, austere profile, with enough ripe fruit underneath to age well. A bit heavy-handed at present – will be interesting to see how it develops.
1987 SHIRAZ *(13.5 alc. – there was no 1988)* Dark garnet; elegant sweetish *fruits confits* nose with usual touch of tar; prickle of CO_2 again, then bright, ripe flavours – strong, positive wine characterised by dryish fleshiness; showing its alcohol more than the 1986. A bit short, but good, nonetheless.
1986 SHIRAZ *(14.0 alc)* Deep, black-red garnet; no nose; gas again, then a big, burnt, extracty layer of flavours – for once, not tar, but strong, dry fruit; all in all, somewhat clumsy and lacking in finesse. Will it ever round out?
1985 SHIRAZ *(12.8 alc)* Shade redder than 1984; smoky, singed fruit on nose; sweet attack which tails off to a dry-edge; complex, although hot; lacks balance, finishes short, and somewhat hollow. Altogether curious for a generally light, wet, vintage.
1984 SHIRAZ *(12.6 alc)* Similar in tone to 1983, though a shade lighter; tar and liquorice dominate an attractive evolving nose, with ripe mulberry fruit underneath; soft, sweet, fleshy, thoroughly elegant, berryish fruit with a tarry back-cloth which somewhat spoils the overall picture; tight, firm in feel with a touch of stemminess.
1983 SHIRAZ Sustained, limpid deep garnet; positive, expressive, aromas – mulberry and super-ripe forest fruits; palate characterised by elegance and richness – with long, opulent, warm, mouthfilling flavours tinged with tar; fine, complete wine. Real class here!
1982 SHIRAZ More red, less brown than the1980; positive, rather meaty, burly, nose which lacks sweet elegance of 1981; similar flavours – hot, tarriness rather than tannins on a big frame; no great finesse, but wine that would go well with a game stew.
1981 SHIRAZ Similar in colour to 1980 – touch browner perhaps; open, ripe mulberry & liquorice aromas, warm and complex; very attractive, open, sweet fruit with meaty underbelly and round tannins; some power and elegance, though a shade short. Silky, quite punchy yet supple wine.
1980 SHIRAZ Fine, sustained deep garnet; nose offers sweet fruit – palate a bit spicier; succulent and quite tarry; richer and tighter than 1979. Very good result for an intrinsically weak vintage.
1979 SHIRAZ Redder and denser than 1978 with firmer, more burnt aromas; tight, succulent fruit, strong tar & spice palate aromas, good length and a dry meaty finish, compound into an attractive wine. *A point.*
1978 SHIRAZ Limpid, clean deep garnet, some browning at edge; fully mature, smoky, berryish nose; firm, soft fruit – warm, tarry in character with alcohol starting to dominate as fruit dries out. A bit four-square, though holding up reasonably well. The 1979 is more harmonious and attractive.

KLEIN CONSTANTIA

1992 KLEIN CONSTANTIA SHIRAZ *(Screw-top ¼ bottle – entire crop sold to South African Airways)* Limpid mid-plum, purple rim; soft, rather maceration-style pepper and fruit nose and flavour; peppery, high acid, lean finish. Not a patch on 1991 standard blend.
1991 KLEIN CONSTANTIA SHIRAZ *(Standard blend)* Limpid mid-garnet, carmine undertone; strong, peppery aromas; soft, elegant wine; good concentration of ripe, peppery fruit. Real quality here. Most attractive.
1991 KLEIN CONSTANTIA SHIRAZ *(CIWG auction bottling – special cask selection, unfined, unfiltered)* Intense black, carmine rim; strong mulberry – blackcurrant aromas; oak evident – not dominant on nose but stifles fruit on palate; substantial, gutsy wine. Standard bottling has far more class and much better balance, though this might well please show-minded palates.
1988 KLEIN CONSTANTIA SHIRAZ Lightish mid-ruby; smoky mulberry-tar nose; light, insubstantial wine; lacks concentration; hollow. Sound, but ordinary.
1987 KLEIN CONSTANTIA SHIRAZ Limpid, mid red-plum; positive, firm nose – with strong eucalypt element; very different to 1986; soft fruit, showing elegance and length; good acidity. Attractive mid-weight wine.
1986 KLEIN CONSTANTIA SHIRAZ Bright ruby-red; smoky aromas, with burnt, singed edge; opened to an attractive minty, spicy, liquorice complex; high acidity dominates sound, ripe fruit; fair length and some power, but finishes short.

LIEVLAND

1994 LIEVLAND SHIRAZ *(cask sample, new French oak)* Mid plum; reduced nose (needs racking); soft, pine-resin flavours, good underlying depth and power; very promising.
1993 LIEVLAND SHIRAZ *(final blend; under fining)* Mid-deep plum; curious slightly woody, smoky nose; attractive open flavours, peach kernels, dominated by oak; round tannins, excellent balance. Will this outpace the 1994?
1992 LIEVLAND SHIRAZ *(12.0% alc.)* Bright, deep plum, carmine rim; closed nose – smoky, mulberry undertones; softish fruit-driven wine with soft tannins; good length; supple and flatteur, though a bit short; attractive for medium-term.
1991 LIEVLAND SHIRAZ *(11.3% alc; 2 yrs. in old Nevers oak)* Just opaque, lightish rim; rich chocolate and mulberry aromas developing; big wine – elegant high-toned fruit – acid over-rides low alcohol. Lacks fundamental balance.
1990 LIEVLAND SHIRAZ *(11.6% alc; 15 months in cask – 30:70 US:Nevers oak – 10% new)* Deep red-plum; sweet fruit aromas – plum and oak with hints of pine and pepper; much better balance than 1991; more elegance and less structure than 1989. Well-crafted, attractive wine. 3–5 years.
1989 LIEVLAND SHIRAZ *(13 months in 100% Nevers oak – ⅓ new)* Deep, almost opaque black-cherry; sweetish, ripe nose, dominated by new wood; big, fleshy wine, long, complete, puissant; dry, tarry edge. Altogether, a full, warm wine, in the style of 1986. Needs patience for around a decade.
1988 LIEVLAND SHIRAZ Translucent, mid-deep plum; aromas of tar, cherry and damson starting to emerge; tight, resinous, tarry, leathery wine, lacks real centre. Acidification hardens the edge. Will keep, but will it improve?
1987 LIEVLAND SHIRAZ Marginally deeper than 1986; meaty nose, red-fruits plus touch of pine; soft, firmly corseted fruit, pine and resin again, with notably high acidity; fair length. Acidification shows – and spoils.
1986 LIEVLAND SHIRAZ *(Abe Beukes completed this vinification)* Darkish, well sustained garnet; fine, opening rich plum, leather and chocolate aromas – first use of US white oak undoubtedly contributes – hot, tight, tarry, leathery flavours (not jammy); a touch austere still, but may well come round, given time.
1985 LIEVLAND SHIRAZ *(made by Jaco Smit; tiny % of new oak)* Deep garnet; soft open fruit nose, touch of resin and tar; similar in style to '83, but has more depth; highish acids contribute to dry edge; still fresh and elegant.
1983 LIEVLAND SHIRAZ *(made by Janie Muller)* Mid red-plum, good centre, tawny rim; delicate pine-resin aromas; firm, succulent fruit, elegant underneath; attractive wine, from a cool vintage.

LA MOTTE

1994 LA MOTTE SHIRAZ *(Cask sample)* Big, black, beauty – strong, concentrated fruit, elegance showing even at this early stage. Distinctly promising.
1993 LA MOTTE SHIRAZ *(Cask sample)* Deep, concentrated, extracty, stony flavours with a slightly singed/tarry component; elegant. Again, promising.
1992 LA MOTTE SHIRAZ *(13.6% alc.; 14–16 months in wood; pre-bottling tank sample)* More density than 1991, just translucent; closed nose, showing black, confit fruit; a big wine,in this context with fine, sweetish, flavours; good depth and concentration, and underlying elegance; marginally marred by dry tannic edge; needs 5–10 years to peak. Excellent.
1991 LA MOTTE SHIRAZ Dark, translucent plum, hint of black; nose just starting to show singed, tarry, La Motte hallmark; gentle, elegant wine; not yet as refined as the 1990, but more 1990 than 1989 in style. Drink over next 5 years. Good plus.
1990 LA MOTTE SHIRAZ Fine, sombre, limpid darkish garnet; largely closed nose; soft, supremely elegant, silky flavours – real style here; more finesse and less muscle than 1988 or 1989. Classy stuff to enjoy over next 3–5 years.
1989 LA MOTTE SHIRAZ Bright, translucent mid-plum; smoky, liquorice aromas with La Motte singed component; elegant, almost sweet mulberry fruit; quite firm in style; powerful, long, ripe flavours with some complexity. Needs a few more years yet. Attractive.
1988 LA MOTTE SHIRAZ Bright, limpid, mid-plum; more obvious ripe fruit here than in either 1986 or 1985 (no 1987 – rain stopped play); nose starting to open, some complexity evident; firm, fleshy wine underpinned by sound, ripe tannins; red fruits dominate flavour, although the wine lacks middle palate; dry finish. Might flesh out with time.
1986 LA MOTTE SHIRAZ *(Only small wood for maturation; contains 5% Cab. Sauv.)* Deep garnet; curious, mildly putrid, vegetal/tar nose – not unattractive; fuller, tighter and more concentrated than the 1985, whilst similar in style; greater definition and focussed in structure. However, dryness of vintage shows on finish.
1985 LA MOTTE SHIRAZ *(Matured 80% large wood, 20% small wood; contains 8% Cab. Sauv.)* Bright, deep, garnet; nose dominated by burnt, smoky component; mid-weight, with dry, tarry envelope; distinctly raw edge and finishes short.

NEDERBURG

1991 PRIVATE BIN SHIRAZ, *R121 (12.0% alc)* Light red garnet (pressings still to be added); closed nose; soft, fleshy wine, clean, distinctly four-square and lacking in grip; high-toned flavours. Goodish.
1985 PRIVATE BIN SHIRAZ, *R121 (12.5% alc)* Limpid, deepish garnet, touch of browning; sweetish, slender, fruit-based nose; full, very supple, ripe wine; high acidity, low tannins; moderate concentration for this wet vintage. Attractive now.
1982 SHIRAZ *(13.0% alc)* Similar appearance to 1985; strong, positive, meat-extract nose; firmer in structure than above, though by no means a big wine; soft, elegant. Low tannins. Faded-rose flavours. Fully mature. Attractive.
1976 SHIRAZ *(12.2% alc)* Bright, red tawny; soft, concentrated pruneaux and fruits confits aromas; secondary notes of *sous-bois*; a bigger wine than usual – ripe, elegant, very stylish. Long, supple, mouthfiller. Best of the range.
1974 SHIRAZ "SUPERIOR" *(12.8% alc)* Deepish hue – pronouned brown rim; attractive pruneaux, sous-bois and *fruit confits* nose; softer than 1976 – less meaty – mature secondary flavours. Elegant, attractive. Delicious!

NEETHLINGSHOF & STELLENZICHT

1994 SHIRAZ, *NEETHLINGSHOF* Deep black plum; strong new wood and confit cherries aromas; some residual gas, otherwise, ripe firm fruit, highish alcohol, warm, clean flavours. Power and concentration. Promising.
1994 SHIRAZ, *STELLENZICHT (100% new clone fruit, 10% Cabernet Sauvignon, new US cask sample)* Opaque, viscous, black plum; nose and palate dominated by sweet fruit and new oak; plenty of power and length. Equally promising.
1993 SHIRAZ, *NEETHLINGSHOF* Dense, opaque black plum; flashes of very ripe fruit on unforthcoming nose; residual gas; lightish wine, despite its colour, with touch of new oak and stylish, high-toned flavours. Dryish finish. Very good.
1993 SHIRAZ, *STELLENZICHT (100% Shiraz, recently racked from small into large wood)* Similar hue and density to its sibling; completely closed nose; mid-weight, soft, open flavours with dry edge which large oak should round out. Lacks centre and real depth. Small oak maturation could have been shortened to advantage.

1992 SHIRAZ, *NEETHLINGSHOF (bottled June 1994)* Deepish black plum, closed nose; bigger, altogether firmer wine than the 1993 – more tar and tannins; good acidity. Marginal tannin imbalance over fruit, but a well-made wine nonetheless which will need 5 years at least to show its paces. Very good.

1992 SHIRAZ, *STELLENZICHT (old clone material; 15% Malbec)* Marginally less dense than the above; nose completely closed up; lighter, yet firmer, in character at present than the Neethlingshof, with more elegance and fleshy fruit. New wood shows. A powerful wine which should develop attractively.

1991 SHIRAZ, *STELLENZICHT (old clone)* Dense, Victoria plum; smoky lead-pencil, new oak nose; fine, rich, fleshy wine, just starting to soften out. Excellent depth and concentration. Should improve over next 4–6 years.

1990 SHIRAZ, *STELLENZICHT (old clone)* Soft, deep plum; attractive fruit-based aromas starting to show from a tight bud; soft, gently fleshy wine, with plenty of ripe fruit and good balancing acidity; touch of liquorice; fair length and a warm finish. A bit four-square though. Not bad at all.

RUST-EN-VREDE

1991 RUST-EN-VREDE SHIRAZ Carmine rim on deep garnet; nose closed; style similar to 1990, though bigger-framed, more obvious tannins and concentration; hints of coffee and sweetish fruit from US oak; long; 5–10 years. Highly promising.

1990 RUST-EN-VREDE SHIRAZ Marginally lighter than 1989; nose closed; concentrated flavours, fine depth of fruit; elegant and long. Should mature a year or two before the 1991. A fine, confident wine.

1989 RUST-EN-VREDE SHIRAZ Similar to 1988 – more dark red; hint of ripe black fruits starting to show on largely closed nose; palate more forthcoming – *fruits confits*, plum and spice – well structured with good finish. Needs at least 5 years.

1988 RUST-EN-VREDE SHIRAZ *(Kevin Arnolds first vintage)* Limpid, deep, translucent black cherry; closed nose; rather lean and evanescent; lacks real substance and tails off. A poor bottle perhaps, given the younger wines?

1987 RUST-EN-VREDE SHIRAZ *(Fermented by JE, assembled and matured by KA)* Deep black cherry, right to rim; fine, stony aromas showing with good, concentrated fruit on both nose and palate; firm, complete wine finishing warm and slightly dry.

1986 RUST-EN-VREDE SHIRAZ *(earlier of several bottlings; CIWG label)* Fine dense black-red; very ripe black fruit aromas emerging; big, firm, meat-extracty wine with plenty of ripe, gutsy fruit, with distinct finesse underneath and well-judged, round tannins. A touch high-toned and estery at the margin; long, chocolaty finish. No hurry here. Fine wine.

1985 RUST-EN-VREDE SHIRAZ Sound, deep blackish garnet; closed nose, with some estery ripe fruit showing through and a hint of tar; plummy firm attack with some sweetness at the centre; not a blockbuster but well constituted. Lacks complexity. Good for this cool, wet, vintage. Ready.

1984 RUST-EN-VREDE SHIRAZ Bright deep mid-garnet, some brown at meniscus; mulberry fruit dominates rather unexpressive nose; soft, accessible, sweetish fruit, ripe but not over concentrated; hints of chocolate/coffee. Esterated, acetone component and short finish spoil the picture.

1981 RUST-EN-VREDE SHIRAZ Marginally lighter than the 1980; firm, meaty nose; rather lifted, acetone flavours; wine lacks depth and centre; fruit drying out; finishes short. A less good result from another cool, wet year.

1980 RUST-EN-VREDE SHIRAZ Sound, deep red, little sign of ageing; firm, smoky, warm nose with acceptable note of volatility; fully mature, ripe, succulent fruit; high alcohol feel; good depth of flavour – rich, almost porty. Delicious.

1979 RUST-EN-VREDE SHIRAZ Sound mid-garnet; high-toned, ethereal nose; secondary vegetal-based aromas – not unattractive; old-style, warm, ripe, leather and spice Shiraz; dry finish; altogether rather slender, though what there is seems to be holding up well.

SAXENBURG

1994 SHIRAZ 'GOBELET' VINEYARD *(old cask)* Deep black cherry, purple rim; firm, sweet, spicy berryish nose leading to long, fat concentrated flavours, supported by firm, ripe tannins; lowish acidity. Distinctly promising.

1994 SHIRAZ 'TRELLIS' VINEYARD *(new US oak cask)* Inky black hue, strong, dense; new US oak evident on both nose and palate adding a sweet, ripe, berryish component to a powerful, long, concentrated wine. Something of a young Grange here. Very exciting.

1994 SHIRAZ 'TRELLIS' VINEYARD *(2nd fill US oak cask)* More purple, but less density; flavours emphasise fruit with less obvious larding of oak. Firm, well-structured spicy fruit; excellent potential, especially as part of a blend.

1993 SHIRAZ, PRIVATE COLLECTION *(2 months in bottle)* Fine, limpid, black cherry; sweet, berryish nose; opulent, ripe, sweet fruit – long, powerful flavours dominated at present by wood; complete wine, good finish and excellent balance. Silky, rather La Mouline-ish in character. Needs 5 years, probably longer. Will be well worth the wait.

1992 SHIRAZ, PRIVATE COLLECTION Similar in appearance to 1991, though a notch deeper; closed nose; softer, more accessible fruit with less grip than the 1991 and good length. Distinct and different profile. Will mature earlier. Very good plus.

1991 SHIRAZ, PRIVATE COLLECTION Fine deepish Victoria plum hue with red rim; splendid aromas of black fruits starting to show – sweet and mulberry-like; noticeable, but not dominant, new wood element; powerful finely-structured sweet, very ripe, fruit flavours, clean and focussed – neither baked nor jammy; some dry tannins and reasonable acidity; long finish; components far from integrated – needs at least 5 years. Highly promising.

SIMONSIG

1991 SHIRAZ Mid-deep Victoria plum; attractive smoky, stony, pruneaux and cherry nose; plump, well-balanced wine, tarry and distinctly Rhonish; elegant and light in style. A bit more extraction and depth of fruit would help. Nonetheless, a satisfying mouthful.

1987 SHIRAZ Deepish garnet; developing smoky, stony, tarry aromas; tight, tarry flavours with high acidity (acidified – a pity!); again, light in style, but with lovely silky fruit and enough tannin to hold it together; warm, dry, longish finish. Less *flatteur* than the 1991. Not bad, though.

ZANDVLIET

1994 SHIRAZ *(just in wood)* Fine black plum; closed nose; firm fruit, lowish tannins. Promising raw material which will benefit immeasurably from time in oak.

1994 SHIRAZ *(in wood since fermentation)* Youthful, more purple colour; tarry, plummy, somewhat reduced nose; high tannins overlay concentrated fruit; highish alcohol and wood contribution evident. Blend of this and the above will improve on both.

1993 SHIRAZ *(1 year in wood)* Similar to above soft, plummy fruit, with little obvious evidence of wood, except firming, supporting tannins.

1993 ASTONVALE SHIRAZ *(12% alc)* Limpid deep garnet; soft, distinctly plummy fruit aromas with similar flavours, sustained by a touch of creamy new wood. Good length. An attractive wine.

1991 ZANDVLIET SHIRAZ *(13% alc)* Similar to 1990 – good deep colour, right to rim; rather loose-knit baked fruit aromas, firmer, and more tarry on the palate, with sweetish feel; rather mushroomy underneath. Well-judged tannins. 3–5 years. Distinctly old-fashioned in style compared with the 1993 Astonvale.

1990 ZANDVLIET SHIRAZ Deep plum; positive singed, motorbike fuel nose; sweet, elegant fruit, dry edge – needs a seasoning of new wood to flesh it out. Finishes short. Quite attractive.

1989 ZANDVLIET SHIRAZ Fine deep garnet; appealing smoky, pruny nose; mid-weight, elegant wine, with sound fruit and overall structure. Dry finish. A bit more concentration and a judicious touch of new wood, would make all the difference here. Not bad, though.

1987 ZANDVLIET SHIRAZ Holding its deepish garnet colour well; tight, still closed, rather pruny nose; fine, elegant flavours; good flesh, balanced by acidity and some tannin; dry edge. Attractive, though somewhat four-square.

1986 ZANDVLIET SHIRAZ Redder than 1985, with tighter, more fruit-based nose; continues on palate – fuller with more depth and structure; good length and complete feel about it. Quite soft, plummy fruit, with drying, short, finish.

1985 ZANDVLIET SHIRAZ Mid-garnet, lightening rim showing some age; fully mature nose with noticeable vegetal component; lightish, high acid, flavours – drying out now, though clean and not disintegrating. Some length. Past its best.

ZONNEBLOEM

1994 SHIRAZ *(Tank sample; 14% alc)* Black cherry hue, some black fruit aromas; elegant, soft, low acid wine, with ripe tannins. Has underlying power, but lacks real grip or depth. Some time in small wood will help structure, but needs better fruit concentration; could do with another dollop of pressings. Has promise.

1992 ZONNEBLOEM SHIRAZ *(pre-bottling tank sample)* Deep garnet; elegant, smoky nose with seasoning of oak; soft, ripe, gentle expression of Shiraz, mid-weight in depth and quite stylish. Lacks centre and finishes somewhat short – and dry.

1991 ZONNEBLOEM SHIRAZ Just translucent deep garnet; soft, mulberry fruit showing through largely closed nose; warm, lightish wine, very soft tannins. A green edge to the finish unbalances what would otherwise be a pleasant wine.

1990 ZONNEBLOEM SHIRAZ Fine, deep garnet, some browning; closed nose; soft ripe wine with fair weight of fruit and better tannin structure than the 1991; better definition and finish but rather hollow.

1988 ZONNEBLOEM SHIRAZ Redder and denser than 1990; attractive tight, tarry aromas – still in infancy; slighty corky – but depth and richness underneath. Good acidity.

1985 ZONNEBLOEM SHIRAZ *(Incl.10–20% Cabernet Sauvignon)* Deep translucent red-tawny; big, old style, rather minty, porty nose; chocolaty, open-textured flavours, mid-weight. Fully mature – *à point*. Distinct caesura between this and the 1988.

1982 ZONNEBOEM SHIRAZ Limpid velvet – similar to the above, holding colour well; ripe fruits noirs and mulberriy nose, concentrated and attractive; good, tight concentration of fruit – some real depth here – with notes of coffee and chocolate; fully mature. Quintessential old-style Shiraz.

1980 ZONNEBLOEM SHIRAZ Deep red, tawny rim; more elegance and less concentration on nose than the above – though still, surprisingly closed; light, rather loose-knit wine, drying out and losing what fruit it had; lacks definition and centre.

1978 ZONNEBLOEM SHIRAZ Splendid concentrated deep black colour – viscous cough-syrup edge; coffee and singed fruit dominate the nose – a touch figue – attractive though! Biggish framed, dry-edged, burly wine; plenty of guts but starting to dry out; warm coffee-ish finish. Needs food – game in a Port sauce would fit perfectly.

GLOSSARY

Agrément The official approval of any French wine for its respective appellation. This is based on analysis and tasting, carried out between November and April immediately following the harvest.

Arzelle The fine topsoil, widely regarded as contributing to the uniqueness of Condrieu.

Assemblage The process of amalgamating the contents of various vats or casks to unify the wine and to make a single *cuvée* for bottling. This can take place at any time after vinification but usually occurs at racking or just before bottling. This is also the moment when the conscientious grower will weed out any substandard casks.

Auto-pigeante Automatic *pigeage* by means of compressed-air pistons or rotating *cuves*.

Baguette The vine's principal fruiting cane(s) which remain after pruning.

Ban de vendanges The official proclamation of the start of harvest in France, decided by each local INAO committee. Growers picking before this date are liable to certain vinification restrictions.

Barrique A barrel; in Bordeaux 225 litres, in Burgundy 228 litres.

Bâtonner (bâtonnage) The practice of stirring white wines to ensure even distribution of the lees throughout the liquid. It can markedly enrich a wine especially in a lean year.

Brettanomyces A species of yeast which gives red wines a strong, farmyardy smell; very common in old Rhônes. "Brett" is considered a fault in the New World, but is admired by many Rhône lovers.

Cadastre The official, detailed map of each French appellation.

Chaillées Narrow terraces in the northern Rhône.

Chaptalization The addition of sugar to fermenting must to correct a natural deficiency and thus bring the final alcohol level up to the legal minimum (in France). Introduced by Chaptal in 1801, the process is not designed to increase sweetness. The method and amount of chaptalization (in France) are subject to legal control.

Cheys Dry-stone walls in the northern Rhône.

Climat Vineyard site; the term is interchangeable with *lieu-dit*.

Col Fining; designed to clarify a wine before bottling. A wine remains *sur col* for several weeks or even months, during which times its taste qualities may be distorted.

Cordon de Royat A system of training vines by laying the main vine stem horizontally along a wire, off which several vertical fruiting canes are trained. Increasingly popular in France and elsewhere as it spaces out leaves and bunches, reducing rot.

Coulure The failure of flowers to set on the vine; often caused by adverse weather conditions or too vigorous root-stocks. Fewer flowers mean fewer bunches and thus reduced yield.

Cuvée An ambiguous term referring either to an individual vat – as in "from several *cuvées* of Meursault he selected one" – or to the bottled wine, as in: "he has a *cuvée* of Hermitage and two of St-Joseph". So a grower might blend several *cuvées* of Hermitage to form a single *cuvée* which he then bottles.

Cuverie (cuve, cuvaison) The *cuves* (fermenting or storage vats) are housed in the *cuverie*. *Cuvaison* is the process of vatting grapes or juice for fermentation.

Debourbage The process of settling wine or must to allow the heavier, less desirable lees (*bourbes*) to settle out.

Délestage See *faux-pigeage*.

Demi-muid A wooden storage vessel; their capacity varies but is usually around 600 litres.

Egrappage/éraflage Separating stems and berries (*grappes*) either by hand or by machine (*égrappoir*).

Elevage (élevé) Literally means "upbringing". The skilled process involved in caring for a wine between vinification and bottling. Racking, fining, filtration etc are all part of a wine's *élevage*. The winemaker and *éleveur* may be different people – eg where a wine is sold young, in cask; hence "*négociant-éleveur*".

En foule The system of vineyard planting common in France and elsewhere up to the end of the 19th century, whereby vines were densely planted *en masse* and simply allowed to ramble – their natural propensity.

Encépagement The mix of grapes, either in a vineyard or in a wine.

Faisandé A taste referring to the gamey ("pheasanty") taste or smell of an old red wine.

Faux pigeage Literally: false *pigeage*. A southern French technique whereby a fermenting vat is completely drained and the liquid pumped back, often forcefully, over the solids (Syn: *délestage*).

Fermage A French system of vineyard tenancy whereby the tenant farms the land and keeps the totality of the crop in return for an annual rental fixed at the cash equivalent of an agreed number of casks of that vineyard's wine. Even if there is no harvest, the rental is payable. See *métayage*.

Fichage The operation of tying up the vine canes to secure them.

Foudre A large wooden storage cask.

Fruits confits Candied fruits – pineapple especially; flavours often found in wine.

Fruits noirs Tasting term referring to black fruits: eg damson, blackberry, blackcurrant, black plum, black cherry.

Fruits rouges Tasting term referring to red fruits: eg strawberries, raspberries, loganberries, redcurrants, red cherries etc.

Fruits sauvages Wild fruits: a carpet-bag tasting term which tends to refer more to the style of fruit than to the particular variety; it connotes hedgerow smells of freshly-picked berries.

Fruits secs Dried fruits especially apricots. Smells and flavours found especially in Viognier.

Fumeurs Animal droppings used as compost.

Galets roulés Large terracotta-coloured drift-boulders found principally in the vineyards of Châteauneuf-du-Pape.

Garrigue(s) Scrub-land, often herb and pine scented, a feature of Provence and southern France.

Gibier Game.

Gobelet System of vine training, using several upright shoots from the main stem, resembling a goblet. Widely used for young and old vines and especially associated in France with the Beaujolais, southern Rhône and the Midi.

Goût de terroir A tasting term meaning "earthy". Often applied to wines where the soil gives a distinct flavour of its own.

Grand Vin Grand or Great wine. A term used for a wine which is exceptional.

Gras Fat or richness.

Guyot (simple/double) System of vine training invented by Dr Guyot in the mid 18th century, consisting of either a single or double fruiting cane trained laterally off the main vine stem.

Heat summation Regional scale developed in the USA as a measure of average heat reaching vines. It measures "degree-days" which are calculated by multiplying the number of degrees Fahrenheit over 50° by the number of days when such levels are reached. The scale varies from the coolest, Region I, with less than 2,500 degree days, through region II (2,501-3,000), Region III (3,001-3,500), Region IV (3,500-4,000) to Region V (4,000-plus).

Hermitagé Wine to which red Hermitage has been added to give it body or colour. Often used in top Bordeaux until the end of the 19th century.

INAO Institut National des Appellations d'Origine. The French governmental organisation which delimits and controls all appellations, including those for pottery and chickens as well as wine.

Inox Stainless steel.

Lieu-dit Vineyard site; interchangeable with *climat*.

Macération pelliculaire A pre-fermentive maceration of white juice with grape skins to add extract and richness.

Malolactic A bacterially-mediated fermentation which turns harsh malic (apple) acid, naturally present in wine, into softer-tasting lactic (milk) acid. It follows alcoholic fermentation.

Metayage Share-cropping. An alternative system of land rental in France to *fermage*, in which rent is paid, not in cash, but in an agreed proportion of grapes or wine (usually one-third, half, or two-thirds). The share-cropper (*metayeur*) is normally responsible for all the running costs of the vineyard, except for new plants, posts and wires. The landlord sometimes pays an agreed proportion of fertilisers, sprays etc.

Millerandage A phenomenon of flowering, when embryo bunches form but fail to develop further. These millerands reduce yields but also contain tiny amounts of sugar-rich, very concentrated juice which can add significantly to a wine's concentration.

Mise Bottling.

Must Grape juice before it has finished fermenting and thus become wine.

Négociant A person or firm who buys wine either in bulk or in bottle to sell under their own label.

Pièce A standard cask – in Burgundy 228 litres, in Bordeaux 225.

Pigeage The practice of breaking up the cap of solids which forms naturally on top of a vat of fermenting red grapes, to prevent it drying out and spoiling. Although traditionally performed by human feet, nowadays it is usually done by a mechanical piston or a hand-held plunger. *Pigeage* also mixes up solids and liquid, thus improving extraction.

PLC *Plafond limite de classement*. This is the ceiling yield for any given French appellation, expressed in hl/ha and represents a percentage increase, normally 20%, over the permitted base yield. It is supposedly only authorised in prolific years.

Pressurage directe One – the best – way of making rosé. The colour comes from skin contact whilst the red grapes are in the press.

Puncheon A large maturation cask used widely outside France. Size varies.

Quartier French term for a sector of vineyard – eg in Châteauneuf or Côte-Rôtie.

Rafles (goût de rafle) Stems. Wines tasting stemmy are said to have a *goût de rafle*.

Rapé Non-AC wine made from discarded grapes; especially in Châteauneuf-du-Pape.

Reduit Literally: "reduced" – the opposite of oxygenated. A tasting term for a more or less disagreeable smell brought about by storage in a chemically reduced state – ie in the absence of oxygen. The smell disappears with aeration. When a wine in cask becomes noticeably reduced it should be racked.

Remontage Pumping over juice from the bottom to the top of a vat during red-wine fermentation. This aerates the yeasts and gets them working. It also equalises the temperature in the vat and helps keep the cap of solids moist.

Rendement Yield. The *rendement de base* (France) is the maximum yield set for each appellation, for a normal vintage. It is expressed in hl/ha – ie x 100 litres for each hectare of vines. In prolific vintages, it may be augmented by the *PLC*.

Saigner (saignée de cuve) The practice of bleeding off juice from a vat of red grapes, especially in dilute vintages, to concentrate what remains. The later you leave it, the more extract, aroma and flavour you remove. Many growers maintain that the need to *saigner* indicates over-production in the vineyard.

Sélection massale Traditional process of selecting suitable plant material by taking wood or shoots from the best and healthiest vines direct from the vineyard. The precursor of clones, and still used by some older French *vignerons*.

Sous-bois A much-used tasting term signifying undergrowth or damp vegetation – an attractive, mushroomy, leafy smell which is frequently encountered in older red wines from the Rhône and Burgundy.

Superficie Area – ie hectares or acres – of vineyard.

Taille Pruning.

Terroir An elusive, but important, concept, encapsulating the general physical environment of a vineyard. It includes micro-climate, soil, slope, exposure, drainage etc. Its value is well-recognised in the old world, but less accepted in the new.

Trie (triage) The practice of sorting through the crop to discard any unripe, rotten or imperfect grapes. A *trie* can be done in the vineyard or by hand at the *cuverie*. It is especially necessary in years

of rot or hail damage and is a prerequisite of making top quality wine.

Vendange Harvest.

Vendange verte Literally: "green harvest" – cutting a proportion of grape bunches before the proper harvest to reduce the load on each vine. This is a controversial practice, since many believe that the vine simply compensates with larger, more dilute berries. However many top-class estates green-prune regularly.

Veraison The moment at which the berries of red grape varieties turn from green to black on the vine. Usually a month or so before harvest.

Vignoble Vineyard – in reference to an area or appellation, rather than an individual plot.

Vin de bouche Literally: "wine for the mouth" – ie a wine to be drunk young. Not for keeping.

Vin de garde Wine designed to be cellared and develop with bottle-age. Not for early drinking.

Vin de paille Straw wine. Traditional style in certain areas of France (eg Hermitage, Jura). White grapes are dried on straw and the super-concentrated juice pressed and fermented. Expensive and rare.

Vin de presse/vin de goutte The press-wine is that extracted by pressing the pulp from a red wine vat after the free-run wine (*vin de goutte*) has been decanted. It is usually harsher and more tannic, depending on the pressure used to extract it.

Vin doux naturel Literally "natural sweet wine". A category of wine made across southern France from various grapes, in particular Muscat (eg Muscat de Lunel/Rivesaltes) or Grenache (Banyuls). Production and consumption have declined in recent years. The best are excellent and age superbly.

Volatile acidity Acetic acid, vinegar. Usually caused by air getting into casks (loose bung or lax topping-up) or by bacteria attacking residual sugar. An excess indicates careless vinification or sloppy cellar hygiene. In small quantities it can enhance a wine, but in large doses becomes offensive to both nose and palate and is a fault.

ACKNOWLEDGMENTS

This book would not have been possible without the co-operation of owners and winemakers, whose kindness, generosity and enthusiasm for the project, were unfailingly fantastic. Whilst individual contributions are acknowledged below, it is appropriate here to mention some particularly special help: Firstly, my wife, Geraldine, who, apart from transforming from occasional amateur "snapper" to accomplished photographer in a few months and then taking photographs which would not shame seasoned professionals, worked tirelessly during the various trips abroad, leaving me free to concentrate on visits and writing. Later, she read the manuscript and thereby made a valuable contribution to the book's consistency and style. Her help and support have been magnificent.

There are two other people, to whom I owe an incalculable debt of gratitude. Hazel Murphy – "Miss Australia" in Britain and now Germany – planned and orchestrated my visit to Australia and arranged for accomodation whilst I was there. Not only did she contact the winegrowers, among whom she is regarded with the highest respect, but managed to persuade them to collect and despatch me from one visit to the next – often involving considerable distances. Lynne Sherriff MW, who is responsible for the UK interests of many South African estates, also provided invaluable advice and help. She planned every detail of my visit to the Cape, from making appointments with the estates I had selected, to taking charge of travel and accommodation arrangements. These countries are indeed fortunate in having such able ambassadresses.

The quality of this book owes much to the patience and expertise of Duncan Baird (of Duncan Baird Publications), Prof Tony Cobb (RCA), Carrie Segrave (editor), Nigel O'Gorman (designer) and Jonathan Harley (desktop publishing). This marvellous team took the strain out of production and their encouragement and enthusiasm enlivened the entire process. Anne Ryland (ex executive editor of Mitchell Beazley) also gave me an enormous amount of advice, help and encouragement.

I should also thank those who invited me to conduct tastings: this provided the chance to taste many older vintages which might otherwise not have come my way.

Individual acts of kindness are too numerous to mention; however, thanks are especially due to the following for their help:

AUSTRALIA
Peter Bartter, Sam Miranda and John Toohey for arranging a remarkable tasting of Australian rarities. Gary Steele, Melbourne wine merchant extraordinaire, and his friends Darren Harris and Norman Tranter, for two splendid evenings of rare wine. Chris Hancock (Hon MW) and John Glaetzer shipped samples back to the UK and Julie Perrott at the AWBC in Magill sent back huge quantities of books and paper. Stephen Shelmerdine and George Searing for arranging tastings in Victoria, and Michael Hill-Smith for allowing me to use his facilities at his Universal Wine Bar in Adelaide. Drs Paul Henschke, Patrick Williams and Peter Dry of the Australian Wine Research Institute, Urrbrae, SA were most generous with their time and expertise as was Dr Richard Smart. Tony Smith (Plantagenet Wines) kindly collected and despatched samples to the UK from several Western Australia estates. Dr James Bowie FRCS, and the staff of Warren District Hospital, Manjimup provided exemplary care following a road accident.

FRANCE
Louis-Michel Bremond (Ingenieur Oenologue), Jacques Ferlay of the Growers' Federation in Châteauneuf-du-Pape, Gilbert Fribourg (Directeur, INAO, Valence) Olivier Jacquet (Specialiste Viticole), Sophie Kupelian (Syndicat des Côtes du Rhône, Avignon), Noël Rabot (consulting oenologist), Jean-Pierre Ramel (Conseilleur en Agrométéorologie), Raymond Viot (ex-inspector, Répression des Fraudes) and Becky Wassermann (broker, Bouilland, Côte d'Or).

François Perrin, Robert Niero, Brigitte Roch, Auguste and Pierre-Marie Clape, and Gérard and Jean-Louis Chave, kindly checked map detail for their respective appellations.

SOUTH AFRICA
Dr Jannie Retief, Marketing Director of the KWV arranged accommodation in the Cape and helped enormously with travel expenses as did the South African Wine Exporters Bureau. Neil Ellis and his wife provided us with accommodation and they, and Hans and Midori Schroeder who own the Oude Nektar estate, could not have been kinder or more welcoming. Phyllis Hands, Director and Founder of the Cape Wine Academy, and John Platter also provided valuable help and advice.

UK
Gabrielle Allen (Sopexa), Clive Barda and Janet Price (photographers), Liz Berry MW and Mike Berry, Kyle Cathie, Simon Farr, Mark Lefanu (Director General, Society of Authors), Kim Hughes (Vinfruco Ltd), Pam Holt (Southcorp Wines Ltd), Alison Pearson and Christine Broadbent (of Wine from Australia) and Phil Reedman and Craig (Australian Wine Centre). Tony Keys checked the Australian maps with exemplary thoroughness. Nick Clarke MW and Robin Walters MW both arranged tastings of rare wines. I would also wish to record with gratitude a contribution from Sopexa towards travel and subsistence expenses for my visits to France.

USA
The late, much missed, Geoffrey Roberts put me in touch with Steve Burns of Wines of California who in turn arranged for Bruce Cass to orchestrate my itinerary. As well as making appointments and arranging overview tastings, Bruce's compendious knowledge was invaluable. Professors Ralph Kunkee, Andrew Waterhouse, Brian Coombe, Doug Adams and Jim Lapsley – all of UC Davis – provided fascinating insights into recent research work.